URBAN DISCIPLINARY READERS

The series contains *urban disciplinary readers* organized around social science disciplines and professorial fields: urban sociology, urban geography, urban politics, urban and regional planning, and urban design. The urban disciplinary readers include both classic writings and recent, cutting-edge contributions to the respective disciplines. They are lively, high-quality, competitively priced readers which faculty can adopt as course texts and which also appeal to a wider audience.

TOPICAL URBAN ANTHOLOGIES

The urban series includes *topical urban readers* intended both as primary and supplemental course texts and for the trade and professional market. The topical titles include readers related to sustainable urban development, global cities, cybercities, and city cultures.

INTERDISCIPLINARY ANCHOR TITLE

The City Reader, fifth edition
Richard T. LeGates and Frederic Stout (eds)

URBAN DISCIPLINARY READERS

The Urban Geography Reader
Nick Fyfe and Judith Kenny (eds)

The Urban Politics Reader
Elizabeth Strom and John Mollenkopf (eds)

The Urban and Regional Planning Reader
Eugenie Birch (ed.)

The Urban Sociology Reader, second edition
Jan Lin and Christopher Mele (eds)

The Urban Design Reader, second edition
Michael Larice and Elizabeth Macdonald (eds)

TOPICAL URBAN READERS

The City Cultures Reader, second edition
Malcolm Miles, Tim Hall with Iain Borden (eds)

The Cybercities Reader
Stephen Graham (ed.)

*The Sustainable Urban Development Reader,
second edition*
Stephen M. Wheeler and Timothy Beatley (eds)

The Global Cities Reader
Neil Brenner and Roger Keil (eds)

FORTHCOMING

Cities of the Global South Reader
Faranak Miraftab and Neema Kudva (eds)

■ ■ ■ ■ ■ ■

For further information on The Routledge Urban Reader Series please visit our website:
http://www.routledge.com/articles/featured_series_routledge_urban_reader_series/
or contact

Andrew Mould
Routledge
2 Park Square, Milton Park,
Abingdon, Oxon, OX14 4RN
England
andrew.mould@routledge.co.uk

Richard T. LeGates
Department of Urban Studies
and Planning
San Francisco State University
1600 Holloway Avenue
San Francisco, CA 94132
(510) 642-3256
dlegates@sfsu.edu

Frederic Stout
Urban Studies Program
Stanford University
Stanford, California 94305-2048
fstout@stanford.edu

Plate 1 The Avinguda Gaudi in Barcelona, Spain exemplifies the substantive concerns and collaborative nature of the urban design field. The avenue functions as a diagonal four block connector in the Eixample District between the two great bookends of Catalan Modernista architecture (Antoni Gaudi's Sagrada Familia church and the Hospital de la Santa Creu i de Sant Pau by Lluís Domènech i Montaner). Begun in the early 1900s, the semi-pedestrianized street is organized around a central median that has a single lane of restricted through-traffic to either side. A variety of urban design elements come together here to create a place of urban comfort and sociability: height controlled perimeter buildings, ground-floor retail and cafés, a variety of seating choices, regularly planted shade trees, innovative paving design, exuberant street lamps, trellis structures, bollards to control traffic movement, and seasonal adaptations. The Avinguda Gaudi is an excellent example of how streets have become the primary public realm space of cities – and illustrates the integrated nature of the urban design field for the built environment professions: architects, transportation engineers, planners, developers, city officials, and landscape architects. (Photo: M. Larice)

The Urban Design Reader

Second edition

Edited by

Michael Larice

and

Elizabeth Macdonald

Routledge
Taylor & Francis Group

LONDON AND NEW YORK

First edition published 2007
Second edition published 2013
by Routledge
2 Park Square, Milton Park, Abingdon, Oxon OX14 4RN

Simultaneously published in the USA and Canada
by Routledge
711 Third Avenue, New York, NY 10017

Routledge is an imprint of the Taylor & Francis Group, an informa business

British Library Cataloguing in Publication Data
A catalogue record for this book is available from the British Library

Library of Congress Cataloging in Publication Data
The urban design reader / [edited by] Michael Larice and Elizabeth Macdonald. –
Second edition.
   Includes bibliographical references and index.
   1. City planning.   I. Larice, Michael, 1962– editor of compilation.   II. Macdonald,
Elizabeth, 1959– editor of compilation.
   NA9040.U68 2012
   307.1′216–dc23

                                                                    2012013702

ISBN: 978-0-415-66807-1 (hbk)
ISBN: 978-0-415-66808-8 (pbk)
ISBN: 978-0-203-09423-5 (ebk)

Typeset in Amasis and Berthold Akzidenz Grotesk
by Graphicraft Limited, Hong Kong

Printed and bound by CPI Group (UK) Ltd, Croydon, CR0 4YY

To Javi (ML)

and

To Jake (EM)

Contents

Plates

Acknowledgments

We would like to thank the many people who made this book possible. We are extremely grateful for the assistance we received from many of the contributors whose works are included herein and who have inspired us in our professional and academic careers.

Series editor Richard T. LeGates has been a great source of guidance during the process of putting this volume together and getting it to publication. Routledge's *The City Reader*, edited by LeGates and Frederic Stout, and *The Sustainable Urban Development Reader*, edited by Stephen M. Wheeler and Timothy Beatley, served as instructive and inspiring models for this reader. We particularly wish to thank Andrew Mould, our editor at Routledge, who has encouraged this project from the start. Thanks as well go to Faye Leerink, our editorial assistant at Routledge, along with Zoe Kruze and Melanie Attridge, the editorial assistants who helped us with the first edition, and also to Emily Senior and James Rabson our Production Editors for the Second Edition and Steve Thompson, our Production Editor for the First Edition. In addition, we owe a large debt to the several anonymous reviewers who gave us helpful and wise comments on the book's content. We are grateful to the Routledge team for their constant advice and patience in the production of this volume.

We would like to thank the following institutions for their financial assistance in helping to produce the various editions of this book: the University of Utah, the University of California, Berkeley, and the University of Pennsylvania. We are thankful to Tony Dorcey, Director of the School of Community and Regional Planning at the University of British Columbia for his help with the first edition. This support remains invaluable. Several people helped us with technical support throughout the permissions, editing, and writing process. People we would like to thank include our permissions managers and editorial assistants John "Jack" Robinson (second edition) and Molly O'Neill Robinson (first edition), as well as our wonderful student assistants on this second edition: Liz Gray and Robin Kim, and those from the first edition: Marcela de la Peña, Bryan Sherrell, Garlen Capita, and Corinne Stewart.

Michael Larice is grateful to the many people who provided personal support in the preparation of this volume, including: his very patient partner, his family, his students and colleagues, his mentor Jake; and of course, all those that help on a daily basis – Julie Harper and the other RSL soccer cousins who provide levity and release, Monday nights at the Republican, and importantly – the café life of Salt Lake City, and in particular Coffee Garden at 9th and 9th where he found an accommodating third office. Elizabeth Macdonald would like to thank her husband, Allan Jacobs, for helpful editorial comments during the writing process and most particularly for his constant support and sense of humor. As well she is grateful to the many students over the years that she has had the pleasure to work with, who provide a constant source of inspiration.

Prologue

After the success of the first edition *Urban Design Reader*, this second edition is constructed and published to capitalize on continued interest in urban design by a growing audience: students and educators, stakeholders, and professionals – but also in response to the rapidly evolving global uncertainties in future city-making. Around the globe, the number of urban design students, educators, and professionals continues to grow with each passing year. Urban designers are increasingly being hired by municipal planning departments, private sector design firms, institutions, and governments. The growth of academic programs in the field has been remarkable; and the literature on practice, process, history, and theory has burgeoned. When it was born in the 1950s, urban design practice was dominated by academics and professionals in the traditional built environment design fields (city planning, architecture, civil engineering, landscape architecture) who labored in discussions over the conceptualization of the field and their roles in designing and developing cities, projects, and places. Since then, the discussion has been joined by a host of varied participants with a new focus on outcomes – and now at a much larger scale – and with a greater sense of urgency over an unpredictable future. Disciplinary squabbles over the terrain of the field continue, similar to the first discussions that organized the field at the first urban design conferences a half century ago. To move forward in response to the temporal challenges we face collectively, these professional differences will most likely need to dissipate and new collaborative efforts emerge if we are to address the insurmountable environmental, resource, population, and infrastructure issues of the near future. This second edition provides a series of updated readings that re-introduces the field and helps us to understand some of these staggering challenges.

Over the last decade, the field of urban design has experienced a decided upswing of attention in both the academic and popular press. In particular, overlaps between urban design and the allied fields of public health, economic development, and environmental sustainability have received considerable attention. New employment opportunities are expanding across the built environment professions, in particular for those who can collaborate in team situations. Design and planning firms increasingly search for employees who possess multiple skill sets, are technically savvy, understand design process, and communicate ideas effectively. Within the development community, employers look for colleagues that easily interface between design professionals, public officials, and community stakeholders. For the public sector, urban design is increasingly seen as strategic place-making associated with larger city goals. It is becoming an integral part of urban amenity provision for visitors and residents – and important for a growing horizontal labor market that allows workers to move according to desired lifestyle choices. However, recent concerns in preparing for a less secure and resource-constrained future are driving new interest in resilience, sustainability, and systems thinking – while at the same time continuing to address present-day livability and ensure high quality of life.

Differences exist between the content of the first and second editions. While many selections have been retained for their continued pertinence and "staying power" – other pieces have been retired. As the world of communication and information access becomes more democratized, many of the first edition selections are now easily available; especially the material on urban design elements, best practices, and design guidelines. These seemed less crucial for inclusion this time around. As such, a handful of pieces have been put aside in favor of selections that help with moving forward. New work has been included on the internationalization of the field, alternative design theories, and the evolution of practice. These new inclusions draw on recent contributions of an expanding literary field. In choosing the selections we continued to seek highly readable material drawn from a variety of perspectives. Debates that were present in the retained pieces from the first edition continue across these new selections in the second edition, and readers are cautioned that some of this writing is meant to provoke.

In editing the second edition, we remained aware of our core mandate: helping to shape the next generation of urban designers. This edition will continue to provide a comprehensive introduction to key aspects of the field: its precedents, early foundations, current challenges, and approaches to practice. Each reading is introduced by way of a short essay that summarizes significant content, the importance and context of the piece, information on the author, and supplemental readings related to topical material. Selections we retained from the first edition have been updated since the time of their initial publication. Due to space limitations we have not included every last word or work on every topic, with some selections abridged for length. In editing the readings we were also compelled to omit some of the visual material because of space considerations. References to material in other sections of the original works were also omitted, in addition to excessive footnoting, citation, and bibliographic referencing where it was less connected to key messages. At times we have inserted headings and subtitles to help frame writing that is out of context from original formats. Our primary intention in editing the selections was to give readers the essential and most important material from each original piece. For those pursuing advanced perspectives, beyond an introductory sampling, we strongly encourage you to dig deeper into the supplemental readings we reference throughout the reader.

As we selected and edited material for this new edition, three themes emerged as resonant with the trajectory of the field. These appeared between and across the six parts of the *Urban Design Reader Second Edition* – through sections on historical precedents, foundations, place-making, urban development, environmental challenge, and practice. Resonance surfaced between voices and time periods that often seemed disconnected. These three themes deal with the evolution of the field and begin to address its current terrain.

The first theme to emerge was the need to recognize the many differential urbanisms existing in the world, and the inappropriateness of a universalized *good*, *best*, or *singular* formula that can be applied to all of them. This recognition may suggest the abandonment of universal design tactics. Urban pluralism disavows standardization – generalizable prescriptions turn problematic – best practices raise questions of application – design strategies become contingent. In a 2011 article, urban design Professor of Practice Jonathan Barnett of the University of Pennsylvania described over 60 contemporary urbanisms at play in current design discourse – each of them either vying for attention or particularized response. At times these urbanisms represent physical and historical traces of specific form processes, for example, Jane Jacobs' Greenwich Village or the Las Vegas Strip described by Venturi and Scott Brown; at other times they seem like normative prescriptions, for example, Corbusian modernism or Clarence Perry's Neighborhood Unit. The selections begin to highlight how varied cultural processes impact design outcomes: for example, the impact of faith beliefs in shaping Islamic cities – or the as-of-right planning processes that result in sprawl or Post Urban dissatisfaction. In response, the rise of place-making strategies is born of the need to differentiate cities in a global marketplace of competition, combat placeless urbanism, build local value, create economic resilience, and promote a sense of place-based pride.

An evident second theme is growing: design pragmatism and urgency in response to environmental uncertainty, resource depletion, and unsustainable development patterns. We found in many of the more recent readings an underlying belief in green urbanism, resiliency promotion, and integrated systems thinking. While many agree on the potential threats in failing to address each of these, debate continues to exist from partisan quarters. More troublesome is the difficulty in transferring concern over these threats into cohesive and effective action. While cities and planners regularly address resident livability issues or quality of life goals that benefit present-day consumption over the short term; more problematic is shepherding action that addresses uncertain conditions over the longer term. Whether in the spectacular development of global Dubai or the car dependent suburbs of sunbelt America, moving toward sustainability and resilience will not be an easy task. This highlights the vast gulf that lies between agreeing on a problem and deciding how to move toward rectifying it. While flashpoint shocks to the system (such as environmental calamities or unexpected spikes in energy costs) may wake us up over the short term to the need for action, ensuring this type of focus over the long term is harder to sustain. Collective action to thwart the "death of the unknowing frog in the slowly boiling water" will require conscious, long term, and concerted action by designers, developers, governments, and citizens. We all seem to be on the bandwagon, but how will it pick up speed? How can we overcome initial inertia and get it rolling in all the many directions we must go?

Through many selections, a third and final theme resonates on the need for the disciplines to come together in collaboration. From the start of the "urban design project" at the Harvard Conference in 1956, we often note a disciplinary antipathy between the various built environment professions. Part of this has to do with the need for individual design authorship; sometimes it has to do with professional bias. This difficulty in the shared project appears again and again in value differences and priorities lacking agreement between developers, engineers, activists, architects, planners, and urbanists (whether of the "Landscape" variety or the "New"). The theme runs through the book in varying shades, until we see a new call for collaboration in the final selection by Ken Greenberg. To deal collectively with the global environmental and resource issues confronting cities – whether expressed through sea-level threat, environmental degradation, or skyrocketing energy costs – urban designers will require a better understanding of disciplinary roles and a mutually supporting clarification of design objectives. Affinities between each of the traditional design professions are more easily uncovered when agreement is reached on shared threat and when design participants raise long-term public interests over short-term private objectives.

These themes can be found throughout the structure of the book. *Part 1: Historical Precedents in Urban Design* reviews clarion moments in the design of cities from Renaissance and Islamic cities to modernist prescriptions – all of these predating the establishment of the urban design field as a project of the academy. In *Part 2: Foundations of the Field*, we assemble important early writings by academics, advocates, and practitioners from the 1960s to the 1980s, who focus on debates, methods, and theories in reaction to failed mid-century design and planning. Later works in this section retarget intellectual efforts toward principles and guidelines for improving the urban design performance of cities, streets, and open spaces. In *Part 3: Growth of a Place Agenda*, readings illustrate aspects of twentieth-century placelessness and corrective place-making strategies by urban designers and the built environment professions. Of note are selections at the end of this section that describe the existential reality of postmodern urbanism, everyday urban places, and the reality of post-urban attitudes. *Part 4: Design Issues in Urban Development* brings together a set of authors who each focus on a pressing issue related to city building. Ideas about sprawl, density, community health, public space, and developer motivations are the focus here. Selections in this part also highlight important international development trends in the Middle East and China. Rather than focusing solely on the downside of global climate and resource threats, *Part 5: Addressing Environmental Challenges* offers a series of constructive design methods for highlighting the corrective roles of ecological process, landscape, sustainability, and urban resiliency. The final section, *Part 6: Urban Design Practice Now and Tomorrow*, examines professional practice: where urban designers work, what they do, their roles, their knowledge areas, and their educational development. The section concludes with several provocative position pieces on the future of urban design practice.

As part of Routledge's Urban Reader Series, *The Urban Design Reader* reaches a broad audience of people committed to improving the function, pleasure, and survivability of cities into the future. In the introductory urban design courses we teach, one of the first lecture objectives is a frank discussion on the definitions, opportunities, and frustrations of a career in urban design. Whether one becomes a "direct designer" (who masters technical and graphic skills, communicates design ideas with aplomb, and produces design as part of a project team in the private or public sector), or an "indirect designer" (who typically works for the public sector in guiding vision exercises, public participation, regulatory frameworks, design guidelines, or oversight on behalf of the public's interest in urban design success), this hybrid field offers plentiful opportunities for those who have a deep appreciation for city-making and the creative process. The field can be humbling in its need for constant adaptation, its long timeframes, and its necessary collaborations – but these are also its strengths. It requires practitioners to be fluent in a variety of skills and disciplines – and become great communicators. It favors the curious adventurer, the creative puzzle solver, and the concerned citizen – all of whom thrive on the excitement of the urban experience. In our own personal development as designers and educators, we continue to be inspired by the literature, the debates, student discovery, and the diverse positions within the field. We come back to these readings often; they continue to surprise us with new take-aways and re-appreciations. We hope this material inspires readers to the great joys of city-making, like it has for us.

PART ONE

Historical Precedents in Urban Design

Plate 2 The Place des Vosges in Paris, France is the oldest fully designed square in the city. Constructed under Henri IV in the early seventeenth century as a royal palace in the Marais District, the square has become the prototype for the traditional European residential square. The square's design is remarkably simple: a uniform four-story arcaded perimeter wall, a fenced public realm space, a symmetrical park, an equestrian statue and bosque of lindens at the center, alleés of clipped linden trees forming a secondary enclosure, plenty of bench seating and lawn space, and fountains at each of the four corners. Today the Place des Vosges has become an important and imageable part of Paris' public realm; attracting both young and old – lunchtime visitors and weekend picnics – lovers and people watchers. (Photo: E. Macdonald)

INTRODUCTION TO PART ONE

The contemporary urban design field is commonly understood to have had its birth in the mid-1950s, spurred by wide-ranging concerns related to diminishing environmental quality, both ecological and urban, and the emergence of a number of theorists and practitioners whose voices crystalized these concerns and pointed toward more environmentally conscious and humanistic approaches to city-building than the functionalist approach espoused by modernism. The ideas and design approaches of these thinkers are explored in Part Two of this reader. But first, it is important to understand what came before, the many ideas and practices that preceded and helped shape the modern urban design field. Here, in Part One, we explore some of the most important historical precedents in urban design, particularly those that still resonate and continue to influence today's urban design theory and practice.

The world's many historic and more recent cities are rich with physical urban forms. Different eras, times, geographies, and economies have produced a variety of urban physical forms that come to us as precedents. So, too, have people from different times and places produced various theories of what makes "the good city." Present-day urban designers have access to a wealth of experience, design theory, and urban form precedents to draw upon. Some historic ideas and urban forms complement and build upon each other, while others present radical breaks with earlier ideas and ways of building cities. The history of urban form and ideas about good city form have not followed a single, steady path. New physical form ideas – grand diagonal avenues, curvilinear residential streets, garden cities, traffic-protected neighborhood enclaves, high-rise towers – come and have their impacts, then retreat or move in another direction, only to be reborn later or to disappear. For urban designers, it is important to know and understand the origins and impacts of the many different forms that make up today's cities, including their theoretical foundations, in order to understand why urban fabrics are the way they are, and to have a rich palette to draw upon when creating designs for the future.

The historic ideas and practices we explore in Part One primarily come from the mid-nineteenth to mid-twentieth centuries, although for greater context we first look at the forces that shaped early Islamic cities and the flowering of urban form ideas that arose during the Renaissance period. This is not to undervalue earlier design ideas and physical forms, but rather to present the most useful set of readings for present-day students and practitioners. The ideas and physical forms that have their roots in the modernization processes that started in the early 1800s, with what is commonly referred to as the industrial revolution, are those that most powerfully resonate with our current condition and have had the greatest impact on the form of modern cities. The social and economic changes that accompanied the industrialization of European and North American cities in the late eighteenth and early nineteenth centuries brought forth some of the worst living conditions seen before or since in the western world. Central areas of cities became densely built, overcrowded, heavily polluted, and highly unsanitary. New physical form answers as well as socio-economic reforms had to be found for those conditions, and a host of concerned people came forth with answers.

Before exploring nineteenth- and twentieth-century precedents for urban design, we start with two pieces that present and analyze urban forms and theories about design coming from earlier times. First, a reading from Edmund N. Bacon's seminal *Design of Cities*, a path-breaking book in the urban design field, connects us with design ideas and professional practices of the Renaissance. We learn about how, with the invention of perspective drawing and the rise of a humanist desire for visual order, architects took on a major new role as arrangers of urban space. Next, a relatively recent journal article by Janet

Abu-Lughod analyzes the cultural forces that shaped the form of traditional Islamic cities in the Middle East and North Africa. Although Islamic cities have long been described by western scholars as having an "organic" urban form, this reading takes a contrary view, arguing that their form derived from cultural processes that profoundly influenced resulting physical forms. It is an important work that helps debunk the myth of organic urban growth that all too often creates nostalgia for earlier ways of city-building.

We turn then to the wealth of ideas and forms that sprang from industrialization. The urban modernization process, in physical terms, can be said to have started with Baron Haussmann's reconstruction of Paris in the 1850s and 1860s. The two poetically written selections from Marshall Berman's excellent book, *All That is Solid Melts into Air*, evoke the feeling of the time and the enormous social changes wrought when the city was opened up with wide new boulevards and public spaces. The glittering café life that developed along the tree-lined boulevards stood in stark contrast to the poverty of surrounding working-class areas, and people for the first time had to contend with fast-moving city traffic. The next reading, "Public Parks and the Enlargement of Towns," is a classic writing by Frederick Law Olmsted, the father of the American Parks Movement. Written at the same time that the remodeling of Paris was going on, and taking partial inspiration from Haussmann's parks and boulevards, it extols the virtues of large picturesquely designed urban parks for bringing together diverse urban populations and providing relief from the stresses of urban life. Woven within the narrative is a vision for suburban expansion that includes separated land uses and picturesquely designed residential districts.

The reading from Camillo Sitte, two chapters taken from his book *City Planning According to Artistic Principles*, which was written at the very end of the nineteenth century, directs attention to the aesthetic deficiencies of the rectilinear street and block patterns that had come into vogue. He urges a re-appreciation of the picturesque layouts of medieval cities, particularly arguing that important public gathering spaces and public buildings were much better defined and emphasized in a picturesquely laid out urban fabric, with its twists and turns and juxtapositions of spatial sizes, than in regular and uniform grid patterns. Rather than looking back to earlier urban forms, another idea from just before the turn of the twentieth century identified large industrial cities as the root cause of modern society's ills and put forward a radically new approach to city-building. Ebenezer Howard's Garden City idea, published in a short monograph, proposed decentralizing urbanization and building regional networks of small self-contained cities set within agricultural greenbelts. While Howard's proposal was expressed only in diagrammatic form and contained within it radical ideas of social reform, it was the captivating image of melding the city with the countryside that captured people's imagination and soon transformed town planning practice. Although the theoretical Garden City idea remains inspirational to many, in real-world practice it soon morphed into the idea of picturesquely designed and leafy green suburbs. Concerns about the ills of industrial cities also spawned the American City Beautiful Movement, which flourished during the first decade of the twentieth century. Very different than Howard's visionary theoretical approach, the practically focused City Beautiful Movement was concerned with cleaning up and beautifying the public realm of existing cites. William H. Wilson's piece "Ideology and Aesthetics," taken from his book *The City Beautiful Movement*, provides a good overview of the short-lived and now somewhat maligned movement, identifying how and why it came into being and its lasting influences.

By the late 1920s, widespread ownership of automobiles had transformed many cities into places where the public realm was congested with traffic, leading to a new sense of crisis that was spawned by safety concerns and the perceived need to create areas of refuge from the vehicle onslaught. It was within this context that Clarence Perry originated the neighborhood unit concept, which proposed an altogether new way of designing cities to control traffic and keep it away from residential neighborhoods, using strategies that included street hierarchies, superblocks, and inwardly focused pod-like development. First presented within the 1929 *Regional Plan of New York and Its Environs*, Perry's idea had enormous influence on the form of future residential areas in the United States, spawning the ubiquitous suburban subdivision. Finally, two pieces from *The City of To-Morrow and Its Planning* present in Le Corbusier's own words his disparagement of pre-modern urban forms and his vision for the rationalized modern city that would become such a paramount force in urban planning and architecture throughout the twentieth century and beyond. His vision compelled the massive urban clearance and redevelopment schemes and urban highway building programs of the 1950s and 1960s, which destroyed the fabrics of so many American city centers.

"Upsurge of the Renaissance"

from *Design of Cities* (1967)

Edmund N. Bacon

Editors' Introduction

The roles and filters of urban designers in the process of city-making evolved dramatically during the Renaissance with the humanist desire for visual order, the discovery of mathematical perspective, and new conceptions of space related to time and experiential movement. Early in *Design of Cities*, Edmund Bacon notes that a fundamental shift occurred from the medieval city, which was composed intuitively, perceived simultaneously from different viewpoints, and well integrated to its environment – to a perception of the Renaissance city that was dependent on the personal filters of designers at specific geographic locations and moments in time. The rise of one-point perspective in design practice elevated the individual eyes of designers and their particular focus to new importance (typically targeted at works of art or ecclesiastical and civic buildings of the powerful). In addition to reinforcing the power of capital and elite interests, Renaissance designs based in visual order and one-point perspective emphasized harmony in building design, the linearity of streets, and faster movement through the city. As a result, designers occupied a heightened role in urban decision-making processes, either in predicating new designs or in responding to the design of others (see the section on "Principle of the Second Man" herein). Despite Bacon's suggestion that the form of a city is "determined by the multiplicity of decisions made by the people who live in it," the influence of the Renaissance designer to evoke a singular vision suggests anything but a participatory multi-stakeholder process of design. Renaissance reliance on the designer's perspective elevated the role of the design eye and created a new elite class that was able to direct the focus of others and create perceptual harmonies where none previously existed.

Bacon's intention in writing *Design of Cities* was to investigate the many decisions that influence urban form and to expose the various individual acts of will used in making the noble cities of the past. This particular reading from the book is notable not only for the specific innovations of the Renaissance, but also because it echoes debates that were occurring at the time of its publication in the mid-1960s over the role of designers and planners in making cities. Emanating from Jane Jacobs' critique of elite planners and designers in *The Death and Life of Great American Cities*, Bacon politely refutes the notion of incremental growth and the ad hoc city that was gaining popularity in the mid-1960s. He rejects the notion "that cities are a kind of grand accident, beyond the control of human will," and instead contends that designers should assume responsibility for expressing "the highest aspirations of our civilization." In addition to highlighting key theories of city design, it is of little surprise that examples throughout the book accentuate individual acts of will by well-known designers through history, including Hippodamus of Miletus, Michelangelo, Sixtus V, the Woods at Bath, Haussmann in Paris, and Le Corbusier. As a well-positioned practitioner and academic who recognized the ground-shift beginning to occur in the planning field toward more participatory design, Bacon was sensitive to the need for "democratic feedback" and participatory project review to ensure that people's needs were met. Yet at the same time, he could not deny his own professional standing as a leader in the field, his faith in government to improve society on behalf of the public interest, and the power of individual design ideas that are "necessary to create noble cities in our own day." Although public participation in design practice is increasingly valorized, the role of personal agency in creativity and design leadership is still debated.

Edmund N. Bacon (1910–2005) was a planner and educator, who studied at Cornell University and the Cranbrook Academy of Art under the renowned Finnish architect Eliel Saarinen. He worked as an architect and planner in Flint (Michigan), China, and Philadelphia, before becoming managing director of the Philadelphia Housing Authority and later executive director of the City Planning Commission from 1949 to his retirement in 1970. He taught for a time at the University of Illinois and then the University of Pennsylvania between 1950 and 1987. He focused much of his design and planning career on the City of Philadelphia, where he achieved fame in the popular press in the mid-1960s, including a cover article in *Time* and a feature in *Life* magazines. Alongside significant efforts to preserve and restore the city's historic core, his visions and projects transformed the city. While some, such as Penn's Landing, Market East, the redevelopment of Society Hill, and improvements to Independence Mall, were hailed as successes, other modernist proposals for downtown expressways and various mega-projects were met with opposition. This experience as a practitioner undoubtedly helped shape his perspective on urban history and the role of the urban designer as a pivotal participant in the larger urban development process.

Other general urban form histories include: Leonardo Benevolo, *The History of the City* (London: Scolar Press, 1980); Sir Peter Hall, *Cities in Civilization* (New York: Pantheon, 1998); Mark Girouard, *Cities and People: A Social and Architectural History* (New Haven, CT: Yale University Press, 1985); Spiro Kostoff, *The City Shaped: Urban Patterns and Meanings Through History* (Boston, MA: Little, Brown, 1991) and *The City Assembled: The Elements of Urban Form Through History* (Boston, MA: Little, Brown, 1992); A.E.J. Morris, *History of Urban Form Before the Industrial Revolution, 3rd edn* (New York: John Wiley, 1994); Lewis Mumford, *The City in History: Its Origins, Its Transformation and Its Prospects* (New York: Harcourt, Brace, Jovanovich, 1961); Steen Eiler Rasmussen, *Towns and Buildings* (Cambridge, MA: MIT Press, 1994, original 1949); Aidan Southall, *The City in Time and Space* (London: Cambridge University Press, 1998); and Paul Zucker, *Town and Square: From the Agora to the Village Green* (New York: Columbia University Press, 1959).

Important books focusing on Renaissance urbanism, architecture, and urban design include: Leonardo Benevolo, *Architecture of the Renaissance* (Boulder, CO: Westview Press, 1978); Peter Murray, *Architecture of the Italian Renaissance* (New York: Schocken, 1997); Rudolf Wittkower, *Architectural Principles in the Age of Humanism* (Chichester, UK: Academy Editions, 1998, original 1949); James S. Ackerman, *The Architecture of Michelangelo* (New York: Viking Press, 1961); Leon Battista Alberti, *The Ten Books on Architecture: The 1755 Leoni Edition* (New York: Dover, 1987); and the important text that was instrumental in shaping Renaissance architecture and urbanism, Vitruvius, *The Ten Books on Architecture* (New York: Dover, 1960).

▪ ▪ ▪ ▪ ▪ ▪

The coming of the Renaissance brought new energy, new ideas, and a new rational basis for city extension in accord with the new scale of city growth. It was in Florence that the Renaissance first found full expression.

In 1420 the building of the dome over the octagonal walls at the crossing of the cathedral of Florence, designed by the architect Brunelleschi, was far more than a brilliant achievement of building technology. It provided Florence with a psychological and visual center which became the orientation point for much of the later work.

When the Servite monks decided to lay out a new street through property they owned, from the cathedral to their church of Santissima Annunziata, probably during the second half of the thirteenth

century, they set into motion a process of orderly city extension which culminated in the great expression of the emerging ideas of the Renaissance, Piazza della Santissima Annunziata. The design of Brunelleschi for the arcade of the Foundling Hospital set a level of architectural excellence that was continued around the square by later designers, so creating a spectacular architectural termination for the much earlier plan of movement from the cathedral.

Figure 1 showing the cathedral dome illustrates the direct physical relationship to it of both the Piazza della Santissima Annunziata and the Uffizi extension from Piazza della Signoria to the Arno River. This shows the partial network of interconnecting streets and squares and the principal church buildings that suggests the beginning of a

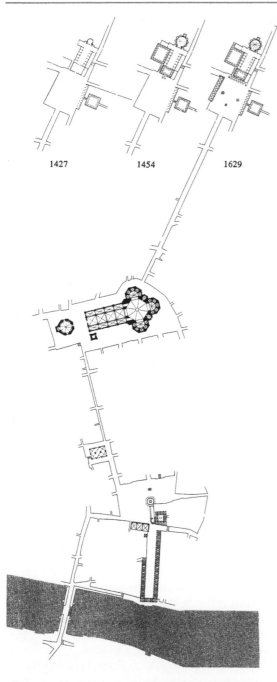

1427   1454   1629

Figure 1 Florence – showing three stages in the development of the Piazza della Santissima Annunziata at top; the Duomo and Baptistry at center; and the Piazza della Signoria, the narrow courtyard of the Uffizi Palace to the Arno River, and street connections to the Ponte Vecchio over the Arno River at the bottom. Drawing by Alois K. Strobl.

city-wide design structure on a new scale, an idea that reached full magnificence in the later development of Rome.

PRINCIPLE OF THE SECOND MAN

Any really great work has within it seminal forces capable of influencing subsequent development around it, and often in ways unconceived of by its creator. The great beauty and elegance of Brunelleschi's arcade of the Foundling Hospital found expression elsewhere in the Piazza della Santissima Annunziata, whether or not Brunelleschi intended this to be so.

The first significant change in the square, following the completion of the arcade in 1427, was the construction of a central bay of the Santissima Annunziata church. This was designed by Michelozzo in 1454 and is harmonious with Brunelleschi's work. However, the form of the square remained in doubt until 1516, when architects Antonio da Sangallo the Elder and Baccio d'Agnolo were commissioned to design the building opposite to Brunelleschi's arcade. It was the great decision of Sangallo to overcome his urge toward self-expression and follow, almost to the letter, the design of the then eighty-nine-year-old building of Brunelleschi. This design set the form of Piazza della Santissima Annunziata and established, in the Renaissance train of thought, the concept of a space created by several buildings designed in relation to one another. From this the "principle of the second man" can be formulated: it is the second man who determines whether the creation of the first man will be carried forward or destroyed.

Sangallo was well prepared for the decision he faced, having worked as a pupil of Bramante, possibly on the plan for the Vatican Cortile, which was the first great effort of the Renaissance in space-planning. Sangallo's arcade is at the left (in the map of 1629), and in the center are the fountains and the equestrian statue of Grand Duke Ferdinand I sculptured by Giambologna (placed there as a directional accent in imitation of Michelangelo's siting of Marcus Aurelius in the Campidoglio). Behind these are the architect Caccini's extensions of Michelozzo's central bay, forming the arcade of Santissima Annunziata, which was completed about 1600. Figure 1 shows three stages of the development of this piazza in relation to the design structure of Florence.

The quality of Piazza della Santissima Annunziata is largely derived from the consummate architectural expression that Brunelleschi gave the first work, the Innocenti arcade, but it is really to Sangallo that we owe the piazza in its present form. He set the course of continuity that has been followed by the designers there ever since.

IMPOSITION OF ORDER

It is impossible to enter Piazza della Signoria (at the base of the previous map) at any point without being confronted with a complete and organized design composition. The powerful impression received is largely due to the interplay of points in space defined by the sculpture with the formal façades of the medieval and Renaissance buildings behind them, a Renaissance ordering of the space of a medieval square.

If one enters by Via Calimaruzza in the northwest corner of the square, looking east, one sees a view of Bartolommeo Ammanati's massive white statue of Neptune, which is silhouetted against the shadowed north wall of the Palazzo Vecchio, and the dark equestrian figure of Cosimo I by Giambologna stands sharply outlined in the center of the sun-bathed Palazzo della Tribunale di Mercanzia. The view from the northeast shows the buildings on each side of the narrow street framing the steeply vertical composition of the Palazzo Vecchio and its tower. The equestrian figure and the figure of Neptune almost overlap, forming a plane in space, which reinforces the direction of movement of this approach to the square.

The view suddenly opens up at the entry point of the Via Vaccherercia in the southwest corner. Neptune now appears at the center of the Palazzo della Tribunale di Mercanzia's façade, and Cosimo I has moved to the center of the richly rusticated façade of the palazzo on the north side of the square. The Loggia dei Lanzi, on the south side of the square, acts as a fulcrum at the point of juncture with the Uffizi.

As one walks about the square, the variously placed sculptural groups appear to move in different directions in relation to their backgrounds and to one another, involving the onlooker in continual orientation, disorientation, and reorientation to a new set of relationships.

DESIGN IN DEPTH

One function of architecture is to create spaces to intensify the drama of living. [...] Figure 1 shows the way in which the pavilion of the Uffizi projects out into the street by the Arno, giving the effect of seizing the flow of space along the river's course, and pulling it into the Piazza della Signoria.

The principle of the recession plane and of design in depth is illustrated by ... the shaft of space contained by the Uffizi walls and framed by the arch at the end (which) links the planes together and focuses on the cathedral dome, with the result that its importance is drawn into the space of the square. [...]

One of the most remarkable aspects of the Piazza della Signoria, the plane in space established by the line of sculpture from Hercules and Cacus to the right of the Palazzo Vecchio's entrance, on to the copy of Michelangelo's David, to Ammanati's Neptune fountain, and ending in the figure of Cosimo I on horseback, starts and ends in the physical sense, but in spirit extends in each direction, exercising extraordinary influence in all parts of the square.

MICHELANGELO'S ACT OF WILL

Only by reconstructing the Capitoline Hill as it existed before Michelangelo went to work on it can we comprehend the magnitude of this artist's genius in creating the Campidoglio. This masterwork forms a link between the early Renaissance expressions of urban design in Florence and the great Baroque developments in Rome.

The drawing by J.H. Aronson, see Figure 2, based on various sketches by artists of the period, is an attempt to reconstruct the area as it existed in 1538, when Michelangelo began work. It shows the Palazzo del Senatore at the top and the Palazzo dei Conservatori at the right. [...] The formless, unplanned relationship between the medieval Palazzo del Senatore and the Palazzo dei Conservatori was complicated by mounds of earth, columns, and an obelisk. There were also the

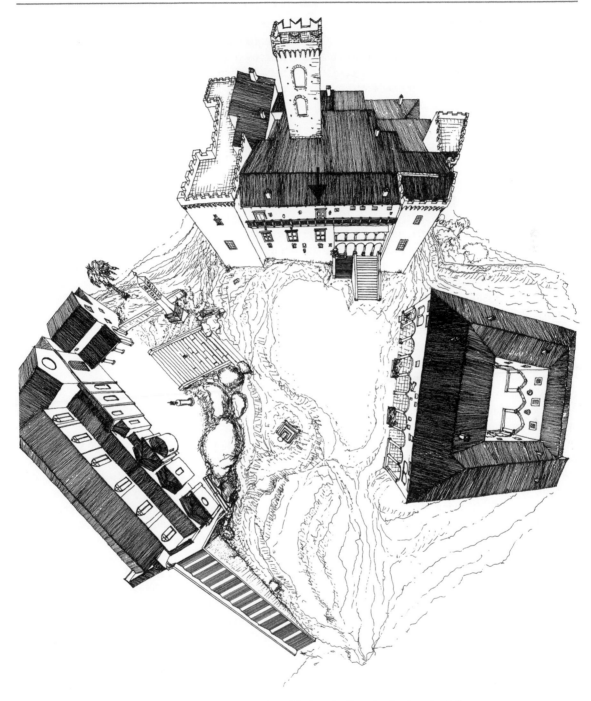

Figure 2 The Capitoline Hill before reconstruction by Michelangelo. Drawing by Joseph H. Aronson.

statues of the two Roman river gods, on each side of the entrance to the Palazzo dei Conservatori. This, then, was the physical situation with which Michelangelo was faced when he reluctantly acceded to Pope Paul III's orders to recreate the Campidoglio as the heart of Rome.

The approach Michelangelo took produced one of the great masterpieces of all time. The actual basis for the artist's design was an enormous intellectual achievement. By a single act of will he established a line of force on the axis of the Palazzo del Senatore, a line which in effect became the organizing element that pulled chaos into order.

[…]

DEVELOPMENT OF ORDER

In their discussion of the angle between the two flanking buildings of the Campidoglio, and its significance in relation to perspective as diminishing or increasing apparent distance, antiquarians sometimes seem to lose sight of the fact that this angle was determined long before Michelangelo started work. What Michelangelo did was to repeat the angle already set by the Palazzo dei Conservatori, symmetrically on the other side of the axis of the Palazzo del Senatore. Accepting this angle as a point of departure, he set about to treat the space it created. The decision he made is remarkable because it contained elements of two violently contradictory points of view.

On one hand, Michelangelo saved the basic structure of the two old palaces which he found on the site by confining his efforts to the building of new façades. On the other hand, what he did was to create a totally new effect. One might have thought a man of such drive toward order and beauty would have swept away the old buildings in order to give free rein to his own creative efforts, or, conversely, that such modesty would have led to a hodgepodge compromise. Michelangelo has proved that humility and power can coexist in the same man, that it is possible to create a great work without destroying what is already there.

On orders of the Pope, and against the advice of Michelangelo, the statue of Marcus Aurelius was moved from San Giovanni in Laterano to the Campidoglio, and Michelangelo positioned the figure and designed a base for it. The 2nd drawing by Aronson (Figure 3) shows that the first act was the setting of this figure, and by that single act the integrity of the total idea was established. Aronson's first drawing (Figure 2) shows, in the extremely disorganized front that the Palazzo del Senatore presents, the degree of imagination necessary to conceive the order that eventually would arise. […] The completion of the stairway of the Palazzo del Senatore and the positioning of the Marcus Aurelius statue establish a relationship between two architectural elements in space. Each of these is modest in extent, yet of such power that the feeling of order is already present and the drive toward the larger order is irreversibly set in motion.

Michelangelo had designed a new tower to replace the unsymmetrical medieval one, but his design was only vaguely followed when the tower was finally, in 1578, replaced by another.

A comparison (between Aronson's two drawings) reveals the admirable skill with which Michelangelo introduced a totally new scale into this space. He modulated the façade of the Palazzo del Senatore by establishing a firm line defining the basement, and above this he placed a monumental order of Corinthian pilasters. These interact effectively with the colossal two-story order of the flanking palaces which sweep from the base to the cornice in one mighty surge.

ORDER ARRIVES ON THE CAPITOL

One of the greatest attributes of the Campidoglio composition is the modulation of the land. Without the shape of the oval, and its two-dimensional star-shaped paving pattern, as well as its three-dimensional projection in the subtly designed steps that surround it, the unity and coherence of the design would not have been achieved. The paved area stands as an element in its own right, in effect creating a vertical oval shaft of space which greatly reinforces the value of the larger space defined by the three buildings. […] The product is a space which, apart from its beauty, still serves as the symbolic heart of Rome.

The Campidoglio was designed some thirty-five years after Bramante made his great plan for the Vatican Cortile, and it followed by just over twenty years Sangallo's plan for the second arcade in Piazza della Santissima Annunziata in Florence. While the Campidoglio incorporated ideas contained in each of these earlier works, it went far beyond them in the degree of integration between the architecture of the buildings, the placement of sculpture, and the modulation of the land. Furthermore, it established more powerfully than

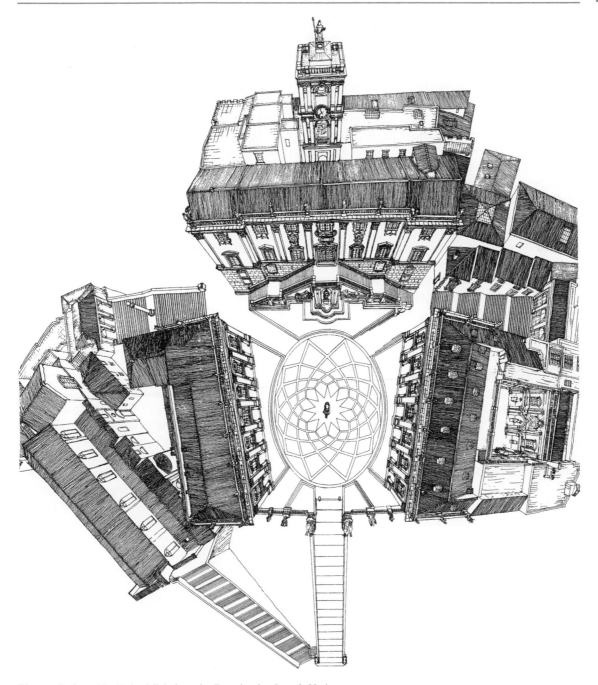

Figure 3 Campidoglio by Michelangelo. Drawing by Joseph H. Aronson.

any previous example the fact that space itself could be the subject of design. In the richness of its forms, the Campidoglio heralded the arrival of the Baroque.

[...]

STIRRINGS OF THE NEW ORDER

The first hint of the system that would lead to the new order came from the artists using the new and glittering tools of scientific perspective. We have already seen how these stemmed the intuitive flow of experience which led to the organic design of cities in the medieval period, and, how they led to positive advocacy of organized confusion.

In a drawing of Antonio Pisanello, who lived in the first half of the fifteenth century, we see the beginning of a new idea of design. [. . .] In Pisanello's drawing, he is fascinated, not with the shape of mass, but with the shape of space. He has created a tunnel of space articulated by the series of recession planes, through which his figures move in depth toward the pull of the vanishing point.

This sets into motion the idea of architectural design, not as the manipulation of mass but as articulation of experience along an axis of movement through space. It was provided by exactly the same basic scientific technology, but this was employed in a different way, which led to a liberation of the designer's thinking, and set into motion a new ordering principle in city design. Over the next two hundred years, one can observe a continuous growth and development of the seminal idea contained here, in its acceptance by designers and its application on a vast scale in actual construction on the ground.

[. . .]

INSIDE–OUTSIDE RELATIONSHIPS

Until the beginning of the seventeenth century, the energy of designers was absorbed in the problem of applying new-found Renaissance principles to the solution of the interior form of the building, and then to the façade. In the seventeenth century, after almost two hundred years of experimentation, the flow of energy was reversed. The design vitality began to spill out of the building into the streets of the city around it. The designer, having mastered the internal building problem, now cast his eye on the building's environment, and expended his extra energy in a euphoric flow of design activity to create a setting for his structure. [. . .]

The lines of energy (in Baroque design) radiate outward from a central source in a manner similar to that of Baroque design. The energies of the design expired in the depths of the city, the points of expiration themselves creating a form – as, for example, a piazza connected with a Baroque church. Out of this grew the deliberate planning of a network of lines of design energy on a city-wide basis, providing channels for the transmission of the design energy of buildings already built and at the same time creating locations calling for a new design energy in buildings yet to come.

It was the extra energy of the Baroque period, resulting from the confidence inspired by the mastery of design technique, which produced the great interaction between structure and setting. [. . .] Similar exuberance was expressed in the Roman plan of Sixtus V for a city design structure binding the points of design energy into a total system.

"The Islamic City: Historic Myths, Islamic Essence, and Contemporary Relevance"

from *International Journal of Middle East Studies* (1987)

Janet Abu-Lughod

Editors' Introduction

Pre-industrial and pre-modern cities are often used as examples of organic development – where urban form is thought to be physically determined by geography, local materials, technology, climate, and other conditions – and where populations have responded to context through craft-based creativity and local innovation in settlement patterns. Casual observers of "organic urbanism" tend to look at these places as either haphazard and unplanned – or with a wistful nostalgia and romanticism; often categorizing or over-generalizing them as idealized urban types. In accord with the work of urban historian Lewis Mumford, Janet Abu-Lughod reinforces the message that internal rationales exist to explain their urbanism, and that human culture has had a more important impact in shaping and differentiating urban form than mere physical determinism. While not discounting the role of context response, she suggests that while Arab-Islamic cities have certainly been shaped by physical determinants, socio-cultural processes better explain the variety of urbanisms across the Middle East; where Isfahan and Fez might be as different as New York and Los Angeles.

In this journal article, Janet Abu-Lughod describes the cultural forces that shaped (and continue to shape) Arab-Islamic urbanism. She is highly critical of over-generalizing and the orientalizing tendencies of western authors in describing urban form in the Middle East. In particular she sees urban form as more than a *product* to be classified, but rather as cultural *processes* that help to explain varied form. In this realization, she is able to move beyond a mere historical analysis of Islamic city form that often results in replication of the past, and begins to suggest ways for planners and designers to focus new efforts on cultural processes that are more contemporaneous. In a nuanced manner, one of her missions is also to de-mythologize the Arab-Islamic cities, often providing critique of social practice in their manifestation, including class, gender, and religious discrimination in space.

In deconstructing the processes that have impacted urban form, she focuses on three key ideas that are crucial in understanding the manifestation of Arab-Islamic cities. While acknowledging that Islam is an urban religion that requires regular gathering for prayer (either in daily or Friday mosques), the first of these ideas is the segregation of space within the city for believers and non-believers. Founded in religious law, urban Islam reinforced distinctions between classes of people based on faith, behavior, and background, if not also on differences in domestic economy. Residential segregation was often a matter of the voluntary self-sorting of households; often with the variety of believers (Christians, Jews, Moslems and other mono-theistic adherents) choosing to live together in neighborhoods – or conversely to segregate themselves according to comfort levels (much as we see ethnic neighborhoods self-sorting in the US). We can see how the distinctions between believers and non-believers continue to shape urban form today in the Arab-Islamic world – with the spaces of hotels, business, entertainment, and western lifestyle activities occupying very different urban spaces than the domestic space of local believers.

Her second hypothesis about the shaping of Arab-Islamic cities concerns gender segregation within the space of the city; for purposes of cloistering and shielding women from the unwanted gazes of men and strangers. The provision of segregated spaces for males and females (as well as children) becomes one of the most apparent and defining design principles in shaping the built environment (both in public and domestically within the house). These design devices include: meandering streets that hinder visual access, screened windows and balconies, carefully placed exterior transition spaces, and social cues to warn families of possible dangers.

Abu-Lughod's third point focuses on neighborhood function and the absence of a unifying central authority in providing either security, open spaces, or services – all of which were primarily and historically supported by district-based organizations/clans. These largely become issues of turf and territoriality and how district security is provided at the local level by residents themselves rather than depending on centralized authority. This is a point reinforced through the larger religion, where little central authority exists for universalizing and administering Islam – allowing local interpretation to suffice instead. This hypothesis suggests the difficulty of establishing centralized planning culture in those places where self-reliance has provided either a security blanket or a safety net in the past. This, of course, is changing in many progressive Middle Eastern cities, as infrastructure, service, and security provision are more efficiently delivered on a city-wide basis than a local district basis. Yet, the turf realities of a district orientation continue to challenge and vex many places today.

The way forward for Islamic cities is to focus on the processes that originally made these places, rather than any shallow recitation of form, which Abu-Lughod suggests as inauthentic, unsatisfying, colonizing, or orientalizing. At the end of this writing she puts out a call to Arabs to take up the task of planning and designing new Islamic cities – places that might avoid the historical gender, class, and religious discriminations of the past. Noting that the world is becoming more egalitarian, connected, and integrated, she urges municipal governments and city-makers to respect the beauty, cultural practices, and faith principles that continue to be admired without false urban form replications. For planners and designers, understanding the forces that shaped the Arab-Islamic city are crucial to its survival, in terms of infrastructure and housing upgrade, future sustainability, and in its assumption of new global roles. The writing by Yasser Elsheshtawy later in this edition begins to deconstruct and critique some of these global city strategies in Dubai and Abu Dhabi. For those in the West, including expatriate planners and designers (as well as political leaders), better understanding of Arab-Islamic city processes might help to establish new respect and approaches for engagement – but might also serve as an example for how to link cultural processes back home to better and more relevant urban design outcomes.

Janet Abu-Lughod is one of the pre-eminent scholars on Arab and Islamic cities. She taught at the University of Illinois, the American University in Cairo, Smith College, Northwestern, and most recently at the New School for Social Research in New York City, where she is a Professor Emerita. One of her most influential writings is *Before European Hegemony: The World System AD 1250–1350* (London and New York: Oxford University Press, 1991), where she illustrates the history of Eurasia's pre-modern world-system, which predated the current global system championed by Wallerstein, Friedmann and others. Her other key publications include: *Cairo: 1001 Years of the City Victorious* (Princeton, NJ: Princeton University Press, 1971); *Rabat, Urban Apartheid in Morocco* (Princeton, NJ: Princeton University Press, 1981); *New York, Chicago, Los Angeles: America's Global Cities* (Minneapolis: University of Minnesota Press, 1999); *From Urban Village to East Village: The Battle for New York's Lower East Side* (Oxford: Blackwell, 1994); *Changing Cities* (New York: Addison, 1991).

Other authors, such as Stefano Bianca, have written more extensively than Abu-Lughod on Arab-Islamic morphology and how urban form has reinforced both gender and district security. These include issues of over-looking, male and female space in public, the use of roofs and courtyards as family space – and importantly, the morphological relationships between the domestic unit as the cell of a neighborhood cluster (with limited street or public realm access), and how these clusters come together in a fractal/cell-like manner to form cities. Bianca also helps to deconstruct the primary physical components of some Arab-Islamic cities: courtyard house, pillared hall, souk, service building/madrassa, and caravansary. At times he forgets Abu-Lughod's message about urban form differentiation through the region; neglecting descriptions of market plazas, forts, infrastructure, and paradise gardens of other Middle Eastern / Eurasian regions. Another author of note, Besim Selim Hakim, uses the explication of Islamic religious passages to connect faith principles with urban form manifestation.

Seminal works on Middle Eastern and Islamic cities include: Nezar Alsayaad, *Cities and Caliphs: On the Genesis of Arab Muslim Urbanism* (New York: Praeger, 1981); Besim Selim Hakim, *Arabic-Islamic Cities* (New York: Columbia University Press, 1986); Hooshang Amirahmadi and Salah S. El-Shakhs (eds), *Urban Development in the Muslim World* (New Brunswick, NJ: Center for Urban Policy Research Press, 1993); Tsugitaka Sato, *Islamic Urbanism in Human History* (New York: Columbia University Press, 1996); Stefano Bianca, *Urban Form in the Arab World* (London and New York: Thames & Hudson, 2000); and Paul Wheatley, *The Places Where Men Pray Together: Cities in Islamic Lands, Seventh Through the Tenth Centuries* (Chicago: University of Chicago Press, 2001).

At the present time of a resurgence in Islamic beliefs, the question of the Islamic city has once again come to the fore. In many parts of the Arab world, and especially in Saudi Arabia and the Persian Gulf, urban planners with a newfound respect for the great achievements of the past are searching for ways to reproduce in today's cities some of the patterns of city building that have been identified as Islamic. They have been influenced, whether wittingly or not, by a body of literature produced by Western Orientalists purporting to describe the essence of the Islamic city.

THE *ISNAD* OF THE ISLAMIC CITY

In some ways, historiography takes the same form as the traditions of the Prophet. The authenticity of any proposition is judged by the *isnad* or "chain" by which it descended from the past. Certain chains are deemed more trustworthy than others. One makes reference to an earlier authority in order to substantiate a statement's authenticity or truth. The truth, therefore, is only as good as the *isnad* (chain) of its "construction."

The first part of this essay is concerned with the criteria of authority, chains of authenticity, and the construction of reality in Orientalist scholarship. Its thesis is that the idea of the Islamic city was constructed by a series of Western authorities who drew upon a small and eccentric sample of pre-modern Arab cities on the eve of Westernization (domination), but more than that, drew upon one

another in an *isnad* of authority we intend to trace here.

One of the earliest codifications of the characteristics of the Islamic city, at least the earliest generally cited in subsequent literature, was William Marçais' 1928 article, "L'Islamisme et la vie urbaine." The article introduces several themes that appear over and over again in subsequent discussions of the Islamic city.

The first is that Islam is essentially an urban religion. In support of this contention, Marçais notes that Muhammad himself was an urbanite suspicious of nomads, that the leadership cadres of the early Islamic proselytizers were members of the urban bourgeoisie of the Arabian peninsula, and that the requirement that the Friday communal prayer be solemnized at a congregational mosque made urban living necessary for the full Muslim life. Marçais uses an earlier link in the chain of Orientalism when he cites Joseph Ernest Renan, the French philologist and historian, to legitimate his view. The phrase he quotes is a simple allegation: "The mosque, like the synagogue and the church, is a thing essentially urban *(citadine)*. Islamism [sic] is a religion of cities." This quotation is particularly intriguing because it undermines the whole enterprise of defining the unique character of the Islamic city; it suggests that Islam shares with Judaism and Christianity the same quality of urbanity.

However, Marçais makes a second point as well. He notes that new cities were often founded by new powers/dynasties in Islamdom, thus acknowledging that Islamic civilization was not merely a set of religious beliefs and laws but also a functioning society that was Islamic in the sense that it organized the life of Muslims into a community not just of believers but of doers.

Finally, Marçais introduces several characteristic elements of the physical city. Citing the North African historian Ibn-Khaldun, Arab geographers, and legal doctrines, he reaches a definition of the Islamic city that he contends is quintessential: a city must have a congregational Friday mosque and it must have a market/chief bazaar nearby. Associated with the *jāmi sūq* (mosque-market) complex was a third physical feature of Islamic cities, the public bath *(hammām)*, of functional significance to prepare believers for the Friday prayer. Paraphrasing Renan, though, we might note that when the church was also the temporal power, medieval European cities were also defined by the presence of the cathedral and the marketplace in front of it. Thus far, therefore, we have only a very modestly etched idea of the Islamic city, one that poorly distinguishes it from cities in other religious/cultural contexts and one that has as yet no topography.

The ideas of William Marçais were incorporated into two articles written by Georges Marçais, namely "L'urbanisme musulman," and "La conception des villes dans l'Islam." The former, in particular, constitutes an important link in the chain of constructing the Islamic city. The 1940 discussion begins with a paradox alluded to earlier by William Marçais, namely, that despite the fact that Islam was a religion carried by nomads, it was essentially an urban religion: the mosque created the Islamic city. He notes as well the importance of baths and of markets in the making of the Muslim city.

It is Georges Marçais, however, who gives a morphology to the Islamic city. He notes the differentiation between non-residential and residential quarters and the fact that residential quarters are often specialized by ethnicity. Finally, he describes the physical organization of the city markets which he suggests are ordered in a certain hierarchy which is not completely accidental. I quote at length from this section because it is to appear again and again in subsequent works, either in quotation marks or paraphrased.

I have said that the center was occupied by the Great Mosque, the old political center, the religious and intellectual center of the city, where the courses were given to students from the various schools. Near the mosque, the religious center, we find the furnishers of sacred items, the suq of the candle sellers, the merchants of incense and other perfumes. Near the mosque, the intellectual center, we find also the bookstores, the bookbinders and, near the latter, the suq of the merchants of leather and the slipper [*babouche*]-makers which also use leather. This introduces us to the clothing industries and the commerce in cloth, which occupy so large a place in the life of Islamic cities. The essential organ is a great market, a group of markets that carry the mysterious name, Qaiçariya. The Qaiçariya . . . [is] a secure place encircled by walls where foreign merchants, above all Christians, come to display their cloth materials brought from all European countries. The Qaiçariya, placed not far from the Great Mosque, as in Fez or Marrakesh, for example, is a vital center of economic activity in the city. Beyond the commerce of textiles, of the jewellers, the makers of hats [*chechias*], we find the makers of furniture and of kitchen utensils . . . Farther out are the blacksmiths. Approaching the gates one finds places for caravans . . . then the sellers of provisions brought in from the countryside . . . In the quarters of the periphery were the dyers, the tanners, and, almost outside the city, the potters.

It is very important to note here that virtually all of the cases cited by Marçais in his article are North African. Note the specific references to *babouches* (slippers), *chechias* (tarbushes), Qaiçariya (cloth market) – Maghrib terms that are not generally used in other regions. Note also the contemporary reference to foreign (i.e., European) merchants.

These articles, then, set forth the physical characteristics of the Islamic city primarily as they were observed in North Africa. Much less attention was paid to the social organization of the city nor was any attempt made to explore the underlying causes of the particular patterns found in Islamic cities. This task was essentially left for Robert Brunschvig, in his often cited "Urbanisme medieval et droit musulman."

In this crucial piece, Brunschvig argues that it was customary law, applied by judges, that over time yielded the type of physical pattern found in the cities of Islamdom . . . In Gustave von Grunebaum's earlier book, *Medieval Islam*, there is only the briefest discussion of the role of the city in Islam. The author merely notes that "Islam, from its very outset unfolding in an urban milieu, favored city development." He further remarks that only in a city, with its Friday mosque, its markets and, possibly, its public baths, can the duties of the religion be fully performed . . . He holds with Marçais that, in contrast to Western medieval ones, Muslim towns lacked municipal organization. Also following their lead he suggests that this lack of municipal government was compensated for by the ethnically specialized quarters with their own sheikhs. Further, he accepts the views of Louis Massignon that guild-like organizations of trades knitted the social organization together, a view which has subsequently been rejected by Orientalists.

[. . .]

The fact is that most studies still focus on a single case and try to generalize rather than start with the more fundamental question: Why would one expect Islamic cities to be similar and in what ways?

Before this, however, a brief biographical note. I went to India in the late seventies, looking for (and hoping not to find) the Islamic city. To my surprise, it was easy to distinguish Muslim from Hindu urban quarters. Several cues seemed to trigger a subliminal response. First, the ratio of males to females on the street and in public places was higher in Muslim than in Hindu areas. Second, butcher shops and trades related to hides and animal products were located almost exclusively in Muslim areas. Third, it seemed that the decibel level of sounds was higher and more animated in Muslim quarters, of which the call to prayer was only one of the added elements.

These semiotics were chiefly in public space; it was harder to penetrate semiprivate and private space, except in several Hindu areas to which I had personal entree. The quarter, in the sense of a semiprivate lane or courtyard apartment house, seemed as typical of poor Hindu areas as of Muslim areas, but circumspect behavior outside the private living quarters seemed less in Hindu than in Muslim areas. One explanation for this might be differences in the rules of veiling. Hindu women veil primarily before close relatives (especially fathers-in-law) whereas Muslim women veil chiefly from outsiders. Given this, one would expect Muslims to make a greater distinction between in and out of the house. In brief, it seemed that social patterns of gender segregation and social patterns of proscribed foods were the chief religion-linked variables distinguishing Muslim from Hindu quarters in mixed cities . . . This, of course, was not a true test of the case, so I also tried to compare the urban patterns of Muslim origin cities with those of Hindu (or Vedic) origin cities. Here again it was possible to make the distinction. Cities originally occupied by Muslims or substantially expanded by them had far more convoluted street patterns than cities founded by Vedic/Hindu populations. The latter were arranged more regularly, had straight streets unencroached by structures, and achieved privacy largely through court-houses rather than alleys and dead-ends. On the basis of this, it seemed that the most probable cause of these differences might be the nature of the law of real property, rather than religion *per se*.

The next logical test was to examine the literature about Muslim cities elsewhere. With reference to Africa south of the Sahara, scholars thought there were significant differences between Islamic versus non-Islamic cities. African cities inhabited by Muslim populations were said to contain complex and narrow street systems, courtyards, and the spatial segregation of males and females.

And finally, informants suggest that cities in Muslim areas of Asia (Indonesia and China, for example) exhibit distinctive street patterns, noise levels, and a sense of Islam. By the time one comes to these cases one is sure that if there is something Islamic about cities, it must be more than simple architectural patterns and designs, since the architectural vernaculars become increasingly distant from Damascus and Fez.

What, then, can it be that is distinctive?

It is easy to say what it is not. It is not a form *per se*. The careful reader will have noted that the Orientalists' discussions of the Islamic city focus on a unique conjunction of forces that created a few cities they take to be prototypical. The forms of these cities at certain points in time are taken as ideal types and are further abstracted to obtain a final ideal that is created out of congruent forms. This, they suggest, was (is?) the Islamic city. Not only scholars but present practicing Muslims looking to build new Islamic cities have accepted this approach and are trying to find in the planning and architectural repertoire of the past the tricks and techniques that will reproduce it. However, these approaches – scholarly or practical – miss the point. Cities are the products of many forces, and the forms that evolve in response to these forces are unique to the combination of those forces. A city at one point in time is a still photograph of a complex system of building and destroying, of organizing and reorganizing, and so on. In short, the intellectual question we need to ask ourselves is: Out of what forces were the prototypical Islamic cities created?

WHAT CREATED THE "TRADITIONAL" CITY IN THE ISLAMIC WORLD?

A modest list of the forces that created the traditional Islamic city would include: a terrain/climate; a technology of production, distribution, and transportation; a system of social organization; and a legal/political system that, in Islamic places and times, could vary considerably.

It is exceedingly hard to unpack this complex bundle to determine the extent to which Islam influenced any one of them at any point in time. We must dismiss terrain entirely as being Islamic, even though the Arab region in which this genre of city building was developed had a characteristic climate/terrain as well as a historic inheritance that encouraged common solutions. We must also dismiss technology as being Islamic, for there is nothing religious about pack animals, handicraft production, small-scale market arrangements, and so forth, any more than there is something religious about terrain and climate. Once one eliminates the influence of these factors, one is left with exploring the social, political, and legal characteristics of Islam that shaped, but did not determine, the processes whereby Islamic cities were formed, transformed, and transformed again.

Let us begin with an extreme statement: namely, that the division of the Middle Eastern–North African city into a nested set of territories with clear markers and defended borders was not Islamic *per se* but was reflective of a social order that had much in common with other societies based upon the family writ large (tribalism, clans, and ethnicity). Fluctuations in the strength of the markers and the degree to which boundaries were defended, were contingent more upon the state of law and order than on shifts in religious ideology. This is a clear indication that religion was not the determining variable.

However, to say that Islam was not the only cause of urban form is not to say that it was unimportant. On the contrary, it was a crucial contributing factor in shaping cities within its realms. It contributed in several important ways.

First, it made rough juridical distinctions among population classes on the basis of their relation to the *Umma* (community of believers) and thus the state. These distinctions were available in the repertoire of territoriality and could be translated into spatial segregation under certain conditions. Furthermore, the frequent inability of the state to transcend communal organizations and the laissez-faire attitude of the state toward civil society left important functions to other units of social organization that strengthened them. Since many of these functions were vicinal ones (such as maintaining streets and utilities, guarding turf, providing lighting, and supervising and sanctioning behavior), and since many vicinal units were composed of socially related people, what we would call the neighborhood became a crucial building block of cities in the Arab world during medieval and even later times.

Second, by encouraging gender segregation, Islam created a set of architectural and spatial imperatives that had only a limited range of solutions. What Islam required was some way of dividing functions and places on the basis of gender and then of creating a visual screen between them. This structuring of space was different from what would have prevailed had freer mixing of males and females been the pattern.

Finally, one returns to the system of property laws that governed rights and obligations vis-à-vis both other property owners and the state. Such customary laws and precedents set in motion a process whereby a pattern of space was continually reproduced. Of primary importance were the pre-existing rights of individual or collective users of land and immovable property. Of secondary importance were the rights and responsibilities of proximate neighbors, followed by those of more distant ones. Then, at last, as a residual, there was *the* right of the collectivity or larger administrative unit. Under such circumstances, access to entrances took priority over major thoroughfares or the reservation of land for public purposes.

I would like here to speculate on these three themes, drawing upon evidence from both medieval and modern time periods.

TERRITORIALITY IN THE ARABO-ISLAMIC CITY

One of the most striking features of the cities of the Middle East and North Africa, certainly during medieval times but to some extent persisting feebly to this day in the older residential quarters, is its subdivision into smaller quarters whose approximate boundaries remain relatively constant over time and whose names continue to be employed as important referential terms, even when they do not appear on modern markers of street names.

In contrast, in his study of neighborhoods in Chicago, Albert Hunter found that territorial names seldom persisted for even a generation, much less a hundred years, and that there was widespread disagreement both as to the recognizability of many neighborhood designations and as to their geographic extent and borders. To some extent, the contrast between the persisting boundaries and nomenclature in Arabo-Islamic cities and the unclear and changing character of Chicago neighborhoods can be attributed to spatial design and markers.

Kevin Lynch, in his brilliant book on urban form, *The Image of the City*, tried to probe, through mental mapping, the psychology of spatial borders and spatial concepts; he concluded, interestingly enough, that some quarters and cities are more imageable than others. There is no doubt in my mind that the historic quarters of Arab cities were built to be imageable in a way that gridiron-planned Chicago was not.

The design of the Arabo-Islamic city, with its convoluted paths, was intended to subdivide space into relatively permanent quarters, but a recognition of this fact simply begs a question. Medieval European towns were equally devoid of right angles and through streets; they also were subdivided into potentially organizable subpockets. Nevertheless, they are quite different in physical pattern and were quite different in social organization from the medieval Arab city.

One must look for more than design to explain the signification of turf in the Arabo-Islamic city.

One must look for a common creator of boundaries. There may be an overarching Islamic reason for the latter. Islamic property laws about differential responsibility to neighbors and control over accessways to dwellings may have been partially responsible for the typical cellular pattern found in residential quarters of medieval Islamic cities. However, I see Islamic law as an adaptive mechanism for helping the society to achieve its goals rather than as a *deus ex machina* determining them. Therefore, we must go behind the issue of how imageable cells of residence were created and maintained to explore why they were so typically the building block of urban society. This brings us, then, to the three hypotheses I would like to advance.

TURF AND JURIDICAL CLASSES

States that make juridical distinctions among residents lay the foundation for what can evolve into a system of spatial segregation. It is a necessary but, however, not a sufficient cause of residential apartheid. That is because social distance and physical distance are not necessarily the same thing. By social distance, we mean the degree to which open egalitarian interaction is blocked or, rather, the amount of work that must be done by two parties to overcome social barriers to intimacy. By physical distance, we mean the degree to which physical contact is blocked by space or, rather, the amount of work that must be done to overcome spatial barriers to face-to-face contact. Clearly, we can all think of cases in which maximum social distance can coexist with minimal spatial segregation (master–valet, master–house slave) and, conversely, other cases where minimum social distance can be sustained over great physical distance (loved ones in other countries). Indeed, it is generally when lines of social distance become less marked that physical distance is intensified.

Medieval Islamic cities certainly did maintain the distinction between juridical classes through social distance (as evidenced by sumptuary regulations. The semiotics of clothes, body postures, and so on), but spatial distance was not always a mechanism for maintaining social distance. On occasion though, particularly during periods of tension, physical segregation was employed to intensify the social boundary markers.

ONE

For example, a juridically different category in most Middle Eastern theocracies consisted of the *dhimmis* (Christians, Jews, and Zoroastrians enjoying a special status of protection), who, where relevant, might be sub-classified by specific faith or place of origin. Always there were rules governing their behavior and regulations concerning their collective responsibilities to the state. Often there were specific restrictions on the occupations open to them. Occasionally, there were rules specifying consumption patterns (whether they could ride horses or were confined to mules and the like) and even permitted dress. For the most part, these regulations do not seem to have been viewed as oppressive. (When they became so, as, for instance, during the reign of al-Hakim in Cairo, they occasioned great comment about the sanity of the ruler, indicating how great a deviation from normal they were.)

Residential segregation, however, was not invariable and was seldom involuntary. Voluntary concentrations are noted over and over again in urban histories, either in relation to certain economic functions (Coptic quarters near ports in Cairo) or to certain political advantages (Jewish quarters near the palace of the ruler). Such concentrations facilitated the exercise of self-rule in matters of personal status and helped, in the proximity-based city of the time, to gather the density required to support common special services and institutions. These common services and institutions, in turn, created markers for quarters that indicated to outsiders who was supposed to live there and indicated to insiders that they belonged there.

But there were certain times and places where the potential for physical segregation was translated into the creation of absolute segregation by juridical status. In Moroccan cities, for example, Jews were not segregated into ghettos until the nineteenth century. The promulgation of a new government regulation was rationalized as being required for the safety of the Jewish population and it was not enforced for long.

[. . .]

GENDER SEGREGATION AND THE ARABO-ISLAMIC CITY FORM

The creation of male and female turf is perhaps the most important element of the structure of the city contributed by Islam. It is important to remember, however, that the rules of turf were not only to establish physically distinctive regions; more important, they were to establish visually distinctive or insulated regions. The object was not only to prevent physical contact but to protect visual privacy. Line-of-sight distance, rather than physical distance, was the object of urban design. Thus, Islamic law regulated the placement of windows, the heights of adjacent buildings, and the mutual responsibilities of neighbors toward one another so as to guard visual privacy. Architecture assisted this process. Not only the devices of *mashribiyya* (lattice-wood) screening but the layout of houses and even of quarters created the strangely asymmetrical reality that women could see men but men could not see women, except those in certain relationships with them. Here is Stanley Lane-Poole's description of an Egyptian upper-class house in the nineteenth century:

> [As one enters the house there] is a passage, which bends sharply after the first yard or two, and bars any view into the interior from the open door. At the end of this passage we emerge into an open court . . . Here is no sign of life; the doors are jealously closed, the windows shrouded. We shall see nothing of the domestic life of the inhabitants; for the women's apartments are carefully shut off from the court. The lower rooms, opening directly off the court are those into which a man may walk with impunity and no risk of meeting any of the women . . . [another] door opens out of the court into the staircase leading to the *harim* rooms, and here no man but the master of the house dare penetrate . . . When a man returns there, he is in the bosom of his family, and it would need a very urgent affair to induce the doorkeeper to summon him down to anyone who called to see him.

But one need not take the testimony of a foreign observer to substantiate the universality of some of the principles. In the *aqsār* (castles) of southern Morocco, one can find the same bent entrances designed to create a visual blind spot. Urban building regulations were replete with requirements that the doors of buildings occupying opposite sides of the street must not face one another, another mechanism of visual control.

ONE

Similarly, within the dwelling, the ideal was to segregate public from private space so that males could circulate without interfering with the movement and activities of females. Obviously, this was possible only, if at all, for the very wealthy, such as the household home that was described above.

A typical old house includes a wing for the men, usually on the first floor, with an access to the garden and to the ground floor balconies. In this part of the house the head of the household has his sleeping room, study, guest rooms, and sitting rooms. The second and third floors belong to the women; one is for daily living and another for receiving guests.

For the poor, no such absolute segregation was possible. Rather, signs and codes helped regulate spatial symbiosis, often by rules that governed timing.

The most obvious semiotic of sexual segregation in the Islamic city was the sign used in front of the public bath to indicate ladies' day. Subtler signs governed other divisions of time and/or space, however. Take, for example, the zone just outside the houses that share a common accessway in a dead-end quarter. These are found in most parts of the Arab world, from the Fertile Crescent to Morocco. I have elsewhere termed this space semiprivate space, a third category between public and private that is found infrequently in sex-integrated societies but is also often found in sex-segregated societies.

The fact is that the ideal of separation between the sexes is best achieved by the wealthy, who can afford to duplicate space and can afford the servant or slave girls who were never guarded from male sight or contact. Most poor women were less able to meet the ideal. For them, the family writ large permitted the doing of tasks as well as the protection from strange males because the local neighborhood was an extension of the home and therefore the family. The blind alley or dead-end court street [harah] was such a device for achieving this compromise between the exigencies of life and the directives of female seclusion. Nawal Nadim has written very sensitively on this subject in her contemporary anthropological study of life in a poor neighborhood passageway in Cairo.

A large number of activities take place in the harah passage which in other parts of Cairo, or even during different historic stages of the harah, would be restricted to the physical setting of the dwelling . . . The manner and form of familiarity with which various intimate activities are carried out in the harah passage make it evident that the alley is actually considered by both sexes to be a private domain. Members of the two sexes in the harah treat each other with familiarity similar to that existing among members of the same family. Even outside the harah, any male resident is responsible for protecting any female member of his harah. He is further responsible for what she does, and he has the right to interfere in her activities if he finds them inappropriate.

As one can see from this discussion, the family is simply written larger when it is impossible to achieve the physical and visual separation required between strangers . . .

It is clear that when densities are high and houses too small to contain the manifold activities women are supposed to do in them, the spillover space becomes appropriate as semiprivate space and co-residents who might inadvertently have visual access are appropriated into a fictive kinship relationship to neutralize danger. Dress is an important part of the semiotics of space. As Nadim notes, "clothing which is acceptable for a woman within the lodging is also acceptable in the *harah*." Nor is it only in Egypt that such adaptations take place. Elizabeth W. Fernea's descriptions of her *Street in Marrakech* indicate that when women ran next door within the enclosed portion of their street, they did not cover themselves as fully as they would have had they been going into public space. It was all in the family. Clearly, then, one of the reasons why the older pattern of city building has been maintained in many sections of Arabo-Islamic cities, even today, is that it is still well adapted to the complex demands for visual privacy for females.

I am often struck, as I wander around Arab cities, with how easy it is to tell whether I am in public space or have blundered into semiprivate space. I have often tried to identity the markers that indicate this. A sudden narrowing of the path, particularly if that narrowing has been exaggerated by the implanting of low stone posts or even a pile of bricks, is a sign of the shift, especially when the road widens again soon afterward. Even when the spatial semiotics are absent, however, the personal ones are present. There is the questioning look or the approach of someone wanting to help but clearly also wanting to know.

Institutions have been retained from earlier periods, one of which is the *nadorgi* (from *nazara*, "to sight"), who, in Nadim's Cairo *hara*, was responsible not only for overseeing proper behavior between male and female *harah* residents but also for spotting strangers. As she describes it, the:

> *nadorgi* . . . is responsible for keeping an eye on those entering the *harah* and detecting their movements. He is usually someone whose shop or house is close to the entrance to the *harah* where he remains most of the time. Besides being a source of information concerning external movement into the *harah*, the *nadorgi* can provide equally valuable insights into the internal movements of the various *harah* residents . . . Whenever illegal activities occur in the *harah*, and in most cases this is the smoking or trading of hashish, the role of the *nadorgi* becomes vital since he quickly warns of the entrance of outsiders into the *harah*. The *nadorgi* will approach the outsider under the pretense of wishing to help him find whomever he wants. This tactic serves two purposes: first, it detains the intruder and secondly, it provides the *nadorgi* with information about the outsider's destination and contact.

We shall return to this point when we investigate the other function of the neighborhood in the Arabo-Islamic city, namely, defensive space.

THE NEIGHBORHOOD AS A KEY ELEMENT IN CIVIL SOCIETY AND THE STATE

The final way in which Islam shaped the traditional Arabo-Islamic city was through neglect, ironic as that may seem. By failing to concern itself with matters of day-to-day maintenance, Islamic states often encouraged the vitality of other sub-state functional units. One of these was definitely the residential neighborhood.

The rather more rigid segregation between commercial and residential quarters in the classic Islamic city has been attributed to the need to separate private (that is, female) from public (that is, male) space. Whatever the cause, such segregation certainly did have important effects. It left to the residential areas a large measure of autonomy since many of the public functionaries (the supervisors of the marketplaces or the supervisors of public morals) operated largely in the commercial sections of the city. Neighborhoods handled many of their internal functions on a more ad hoc basis, being unable to afford more commercialized services.

A second factor that strengthened the neighborhood was its role as protector. I would like to explore the issue of turf and defended neighborhoods because I find the literature produced by Orientalists on the role of *dhu'ar* (militant), *futuwwa* (chivalrous society), and so forth, in the medieval Islamic city highly deficient in a sociological sense. I have been struck over and over again with the fact that the traditional Arabo-Islamic city was designed to maximize what Oscar Newman has termed defensible space.

In the introduction to his book, *Defensible Space: Crime Prevention Through Urban Design*, Newman writes that he is trying to find an architectural solution to the rising disorder in American cities. He claims:

> Architectural design can make evident by the physical layout that an area is the shared extension of the private realms of a group of individuals. For one group to be able to set the norms of behavior and the nature of activity possible within a particular space, it is necessary that it have clear, unquestionable control over what can occur there. Design can make it possible for both inhabitant and stranger to perceive that an area is under the undisputed influence of a particular group, that they dictate the activity taking place within it, and who its users are to be. This can be made so clearly evident that residents will not only feel confident, but that it is incumbent upon them to question the comings and goings of people to ensure the continued safety of the defined areas. Any intruder will be made to anticipate that his presence will be under question and open to challenge; so much

so that a criminal can be deterred from even contemplating entry.

Defensible space is a model for residential environments which inhibit crime by creating the physical expression of a social fabric that defends itself.

Certainly, what Newman has just described is the Arabo-Islamic semiprivate quarter *par excellence*, but is the picture as benign as he has drawn it? Yes, the neighborhood defends itself, but perhaps it is defending its criminal activities or its warfare with the rest of society. Two non-benign parallels present themselves. These are boys' gangs and the militia turf in embattled Beirut. Both offer a seamier view of the defensible space advocated by Newman.

Boys' gangs were certainly a feature of Arabo-Islamic cities in the past and continue to be present today . . . We recognize the organization of local young males for the defense of their quarter . . . We recognize the gang leader . . . and we recognize his role . . . Even the so-called codes of chivalry are to be found in boys' gangs.

Urban sociologist, Gerald Suttles, predated Newman in his conceptualization of a "defended neighborhood" which he defined as a "residential group which seals itself off through the efforts of delinquent gangs, by restrictive covenants, by sharp boundaries, or by a forbidding reputation." He goes on to specify the conditions under which defended neighborhoods become important in cities (and here he is discussing places like Chicago, not Cairo, and yet the applicability is obvious):

Granted the inability of formal procedures of social control to detect and forestall all or even most forms of urban disorder, some additional mechanisms seem necessary for the maintenance of order. Among the available mechanisms, a set of rules governing and restricting spatial movement seems a likely and highly effective means of preserving order. Such a set of rules has some fairly obvious advantages: it segregates groups that are otherwise likely to come into conflict; it restricts the range of association and decreases anonymity; it thrusts people together into a common network of social relations that overlap rather than diverge from one another.

Residents are particularly likely to intensify their defense when the order in the outside society becomes weakened.

Historically, in Arabo-Islamic cities, the neighborhood has been in dialectical process with the external society. When central power was strong and when the citywide hierarchical structure was working smoothly, agents of the central administration operated within the neighborhoods to provide information to the center and ensure conformance with central directives. This was certainly the case with the sheikh of the *hara* in Cairo at certain points, when he was essentially an informer for the police as well as for the *muhtasib* (inspector of morals). He acted, in his capacity as real estate expert, to "steer" or supervise who should have access to vacant dwelling units in the quarter. Sometimes, the neighborhood was an administrative subset of the state.

More often, however, the quarter played the opposite role, that of a defended neighborhood, particularly when chaos reigned. One reads, in the historical accounts, of civil strife/invasions/street battles and the recurring phrase, "and people closed the gates to their harat." Alternatively, to gain control over the city, conquerors always had to destroy the gates to the harat, as Napoleon's forces did when they invaded Cairo.

One has only to think of contemporary Beirut to have these phrases take on fuller meaning. During the height of disorder, virtually every block belonged to a different group or faction. Checkpoints blocked entry and exit to these defended territories. Often, barricades were constructed at the boundaries. The opposite side of defense was also evident. During the Israeli siege, neighborhood assistance was organized by block committees which allocated vacant apartments, oversaw the rationing of water use, and distributed food and medical relief as needed. One cannot resist reading back into history to evaluate some of the roles neighborhoods formerly played in the Arabo-Islamic city.

CONCLUSIONS AND A NOTE OF WARNING

In the first part of this chapter, I attempted to deconstruct Orientalist thinking about the Islamic city by showing not only that the idea itself was "created" on the basis of too few cases but, even worse, was a model of outcomes rather than one of processes. By that I mean that the goal was to generalize about a specific form of city at one long historic moment without unpacking the various causes of that particular outcome. That form was then equated with the Islamic city, regardless of whether there was anything especially Islamic about the causes.

The reason it is important to criticize this approach is that in a number of Arab countries today planners are trying to re-create Islamic cities – but by means that are terribly inappropriate because they focus on outcomes rather than processes. Such planners hope, by edict and ordinance, to preserve and to build new cities on an Islamic pattern. It should be clear by now, though, why this approach is likely to fail.

Cities are processes, not products. The three Islamic elements that set in motion the processes that give rise to Islamic cities were: a distinction between the members of the Umma and outsiders, which led to juridical and spatial distinction by neighborhoods; the segregation of the sexes, which gave rise to a particular solution to the question of spatial organization; and a legal system, which, rather than imposing general regulations over land uses of various types in various places, left to the litigation of neighborhoods the detailed adjudication of mutual rights over space and use. These three factors were Islamic *per se*.

However, in addition, the historic cities that developed in Arabo-Islamic lands in pre-modern times were deeply influenced by such non-Islamic factors as climate, terrain, technologies of construction, circulation, and production, as well as political variables, such as the relation between rulers and the ruled, the general level of inter-communal strife, and fluctuations in the degree of internal and external security. Furthermore, the nature of any Islamic city at any point in time was the result not only of the contemporaneous nature of these variables but the inherited forms that took shape under earlier and different circumstances.

It is clear, then, that one does not have the capacity to re-create Islamic cities by edict. One has only the capacity to create conditions that might set in motion processes that, in the past, generated the forms of the traditional city in the Arabo-Islamic world. It must be recognized that one cannot do that without being willing to live with the three conditions mentioned above, namely: (1) juridical distinctions between Muslims and/or citizens and outsiders; (2) segregation by gender and a virtually complete division of labor according to it; and (3) a fully decentralized and ex post facto system of land use and governmental regulation over space. In today's world, these three are considered retrogressive.

First, modern states accord basic rights and responsibilities in an egalitarian manner – at least in theory. Where distinctions are made on the basis of ascribed status, they have attracted the criticism of the world.

Second, throughout the world, there has been a trend toward increased equality between the sexes. Integration, not segregation, has been the ideal toward which many cultures are moving.

Finally, modern municipal governments stress the provision of community facilities through a centralized system and stress the establishment of laws that apply to whole classes of places and uses, that is, zoning laws, building codes, street alignments, subdivision regulations, and so on. Such regulations, as I have tried to show, are the antithesis of the assumptions and mechanisms of property law under Islamic legal approaches.

Therefore, none of the conditions still exist that would permit us to reconstruct Islamic cities by design. Only a view of the Islamic city such as that held by earlier Orientalists would allow one to even entertain such a notion.

That is not to say, however, that we could not build better cities in the contemporary Arabo-Islamic world if we paid closer attention to some of the true achievements of the past and if we learned from them. The historic Islamic city often achieved community, privacy, and beauty. It would be wise to seek these same goals, even though the old means are no longer available. Since cities are living processes rather than formalistic shells for living, they cannot be built by us. We can only encourage them to grow in the desired direction. Can we nurture neighborhoods that are supportive but not defensive? Can we foster privacy not for women alone but for households? Can we guard the rights of neighbors while still applying laws consistently? That is the task Arab city planners must set for themselves.

"The Family of Eyes" and "The Mire of the Macadam"

from *All That is Solid Melts into Air: The Experience of Modernity* (1982)

Marshall Berman

Editors' Introduction

By the mid-nineteenth century, following the industrial revolution, many cities had become extremely crowded, especially those contained by protective city walls, such as Paris and Barcelona. From 1853 through 1870, Georges Eugène Haussmann, Prefect of the Seine during the rule of Napoleon III, implemented large-scale public works in Paris that included carving wide boulevards through the dense medieval city center, laying out boulevard systems in peripheral areas to promote urban development, turning former royal hunting grounds at the edge of the city into large new public parks, and redesigning existing city parks. Drawing on Baroque axial planning ideas, the new boulevards linked important public places – train stations, public markets, civic buildings, and parks. A municipal sewer system was built under them and many thousands of trees were planted along them. The boulevards were lined with mandated six-story buildings sporting uniform empire-style façades and mansard roofs. Ground floors of these buildings held cafés and restaurants. At the time, Haussmann's work was looked upon as a model of city modernization, and the boulevards were much admired worldwide. However, particularly following the excesses and failures of the modern urban renewal projects of the 1950s and the self-reflection this engendered in the planning profession, Haussmann's Paris has been much criticized on the rightful grounds that it displaced large numbers of mostly poor people, and that it was an expression of political power meant to clear out working-class neighborhoods that were hotbeds of resistance and made it easier for Napoleon's troops to move through the city and break up political unrest.

In *All That is Solid Melts into Air: The Experience of Modernity* (New York: Simon & Schuster, 1982) Berman looks at Haussmann's Paris and the new boulevards from a different perspective. Writing at a time when the positivism associated with modernity was being highly criticized and dismissed, he dared to call attention to the expanding nature of the new urban forms Haussmann introduced into Paris. Within the chapters on Paris (other chapters discuss St. Petersburg and New York City), which use as their starting points poems written by the nineteenth-century Parisian poet and flâneur Charles Baudelaire, Berman discusses the reactions and social changes that came from people's encounters with the new boulevards. He characterizes the boulevards as the most important invention of the nineteenth century because they physically opened up the city, giving breathing room and creating spaces – the cafés, restaurants, and wide sidewalks – where new forms of urban public social life could develop, while at the same time they forced the middle and upper classes to confront the reality of urban working-class poverty because people from the dense surrounding neighborhoods spilled out onto the boulevards. The boulevards also introduced the beginnings of modern traffic into the city, because their wide and unencumbered roadways allowed private carriages to move at much faster speeds than previously possible.

As well as giving a vivid impression of the changes wrought by the new boulevards, Berman's account of Haussmann's Paris gives us insight into the complexity of the modern public realm and its physical forms, and the often neither-black-nor-white outcomes of urban design projects – there are generally both positive and negative effects associated with any urban design undertaking. One of the lessons to be taken from study of Haussmann's transformation of Paris is the power of an appointed civil servant to transform a cityscape. Latter-day civil servants who have had enormous influence on their city's built form include Robert Moses, chairman of New York City's Triborough Bridge Authority and park commissioner during the mid-twentieth century; Ed Logue, the director of Boston's redevelopment agency in the 1960s; Allan B. Jacobs, San Francisco's planning director during the late 1960s and early 1970s; and Larry Beasley, Vancouver's co-director of planning since the 1990s.

Marshall Berman is a Distinguished Professor of Political Science at the City University of New York (CUNY), where he teaches political philosophy and urbanisrn. His other writings include *The Politics of Authenticity* (New York: Athenaeum, 1970), republished by Verso (2010); *On the Town: One Hundred Years of Spectacle in Times Square* (New York: Random House, 2006); and *New York Calling: From Blackout to Bloomberg* (London: Reaktion, 2007), co-edited with Brian Berge.

Other resources on the subject of Haussmann's Paris include Nicholas Papayanis, *Planning Paris Before Haussmann* (Baltimore, MD: Johns Hopkins Press, 2004); Howard Saalman, *Haussmann: Paris Transformed* (New York: G. Braziller, 1971); and Michel Carmona, *Haussmann: His Life and Times*, translated by Patrick Camiller (Chicago, IL: I.R. Dee, 2002). A book by Haussmann's landscape architect Adolphe Alphand that contains plans and sections of Paris's new boulevards and parks has been reprinted: *Les Promenades de Paris* (Princeton, NJ: Princeton Architectural Press, 1984).

It is interesting to note that while Haussmann's classic boulevards were considered the height of modern street building in the latter half of the nineteenth century, by the 1930s they were considered outdated in the United States. These boulevards have a wide roadway in the center for fast-moving through traffic and narrow roadways on the side for slow-moving local traffic. The roadways are separated by tree-lined medians, or malls. The three-roadway configuration came to be considered dangerous by traffic engineers and they ceased to be built. However, three-roadway boulevards (or multiway boulevards, to use a recently coined term) are currently being looked to as a possible solution for handling large amounts of traffic in cities, where it is necessary to do so, without deadening the local environment. A book that documents extensive research into multiway boulevards is Allan B. Jacobs, Elizabeth Macdonald, and Yodan Rofe, *The Boulevard Book: History, Evolution, Design of Multiway Boulevards* (Boston, MA: MIT Press, 2002).

THE FAMILY OF EYES

OUR FIRST primal scene emerges in "The Eyes of the Poor." (Paris Spleen #26) This poem takes the form of a lover's complaint: the narrator is explaining to the woman he loves why he feels distant and bitter toward her. He reminds her of an experience they recently shared. It was the evening of a long and lovely day that they had spent alone together. They sat down on the terrace "in front of a new cafe that formed the corner of a new boulevard." The boulevard was "still littered with rubble," but the cafe "already displayed proudly its unfinished splendors." Its most splendid quality was a flood of new light: "The cafe was dazzling. Even the gas burned with the ardor of a debut;

with all its power it lit the blinding whiteness of the walls, the expanse of mirrors, the gold cornices and moldings." Less dazzling was the decorated interior that the gaslight lit up: a ridiculous profusion of Hebes and Ganymedes, hounds and falcons; "nymphs and goddesses bearing piles of fruits, pâtés and game on their heads," a mélange of "all history and all mythology pandering to gluttony." In other circumstances the narrator might recoil from this commercialized grossness; in love, however, he can laugh affectionately, and enjoy its vulgar appeal – our age would call it Camp.

As the lovers sit gazing happily into each other's eyes, suddenly they are confronted with other people's eyes. A poor family dressed in rags – a graybearded father, a young son, and a baby – come to a stop directly in front of them and gaze raptly at the bright new world that is just inside. "The three faces were extraordinarily serious, and those six eyes contemplated the new cafe fixedly with an equal admiration, differing only according to age." No words are spoken, but the narrator tries to read their eyes. The father's eyes seem to say, "How beautiful it is! All the gold of the poor world must have found its way onto these walls." The son's eyes seem to say, "How beautiful it is! But it is a house where only people who are not like us can go." The baby's eyes "were too fascinated to express anything but joy, stupid and profound." Their fascination carries no hostile undertones; their vision of the gulf between the two worlds is sorrowful, not militant, not resentful but resigned. In spite of this, or maybe because of it, the narrator begins to feel uneasy, "a little ashamed of our glasses and decanters, too big for our thirst." He is "touched by this family of eyes," and feels some sort of kinship with them. But when, a moment later, "I turned my eyes to look into yours, dear love, to read *my* thoughts there" (Baudelaire's italics), she says, "Those people with their great saucer eyes are unbearable! Can't you go tell the manager to get them away from here?"

This is why he hates her today, he says. He adds that the incident has made him sad as well as angry: he sees now "how hard it is for people to understand each other, how incommunicable thought is" – so the poem ends – "even between people in love."

What makes this encounter distinctively modern? What marks it off from a multitude of earlier Parisian scenes of love and class struggle? The difference lies in the urban space where our scene takes place. "Toward evening you wanted to sit down in front of a new cafe that formed the corner of a new boulevard, still piled with rubble but already displaying its unfinished splendors." The difference, in one word, is the *boulevard*: the new Parisian boulevard was the most spectacular urban innovation of the nineteenth century, and the decisive breakthrough in the modernization of the traditional city.

In the late 1850s and through the 1860s, while Baudelaire was working on *Paris Spleen*, Georges Eugène Haussmann, the Prefect of Paris and its environs, armed with the imperial mandate of Napoleon III, was blasting a vast network of boulevards through the heart of the old medieval city.[1] Napoleon and Haussmann envisioned the new roads as arteries in an urban circulatory system. These images, commonplace today, were revolutionary in the context of nineteenth-century urban life. The new boulevards would enable traffic to flow through the center of the city, and to move straight ahead from end to end – a quixotic and virtually unimaginable enterprise till then. In addition, they would clear slums and open up "breathing space" in the midst of layers of darkness and choked congestion. They would stimulate a tremendous expansion of local business at every level, and thus help to defray the immense municipal demolition, compensation and construction costs. They would pacify the masses by employing tens of thousands of them – at times as much as a quarter of the city's labor force – on long-term public works, which in turn would generate thousands more jobs in the private sector. Finally, they would create long and broad corridors in which troops and artillery could move effectively against future barricades and popular insurrections.

The boulevards were only one part of a comprehensive system of urban planning that included central markets, bridges, sewers, water supply, the Opera and other cultural palaces, a great network of parks. "Let it be said to Baron Haussmann's eternal credit" – so wrote Robert Moses, his most illustrious and notorious successor, in 1942 – "that he grasped the problem of step-by-step large-scale city modernization." The new construction wrecked hundreds of buildings, displaced uncounted thousands of people, destroyed whole neighborhoods that had lived for centuries. But it opened up the whole of the city, for the first time in its history, to all its inhabitants. Now, at last, it was possible to move not only within neighborhoods, but through them. Now, after centuries of life as a cluster of isolated cells, Paris was becoming a unified physical and human space.[2]

The Napoleon-Haussmann boulevards created new bases – economic, social, aesthetic – for bringing enormous numbers of people together. At the street level they were lined with small businesses and shops of all kinds, with every corner zoned for restaurants and terraced sidewalk cafes. These cafes, like the one where Baudelaire's lovers and his family in rags come to look, soon came to be seen all over the world as symbols of *la vie parisienne*.

Haussmann's sidewalks, like the boulevards themselves, were extravagantly wide, lined with benches, lush with trees.[3] Pedestrian islands were installed to make crossing easier, to separate local from through traffic and to open up alternate routes for promenades. Great sweeping vistas were designed, with monuments at the boulevards' ends, so that each walk led toward a dramatic climax. All these qualities helped to make the new Paris a uniquely enticing spectacle, a visual and sensual feast. Five generations of modern painters, writers and photographers (and, a little later, filmmakers), starting with the impressionists in the 1860s, would nourish themselves on the life and energy that flowed along the boulevards. By the 1880s, the Haussmann pattern was generally acclaimed as the very model of modern urbanism. As such, it was soon stamped on emerging and expanding cities in every corner of the world, from Santiago to Saigon.

What did the boulevards do to the people who came to fill them? Baudelaire shows us some of the most striking things. For lovers, like the ones in "The Eyes of the Poor," the boulevards created a new primal scene: a space where they could be private in public, intimately together without being physically alone. Moving along the boulevard, caught up in its immense and endless flux, they could feel their love more vividly than ever as the still point of a turning world. They could display their love before the boulevard's endless parade of strangers – indeed, within a generation Paris would be world-famous for this sort of amorous display – and draw different forms of joy from them all. They could weave veils of fantasy around the multitude of passers-by: who were these people, where did they come from and where were they going, what did they want, whom did they love? The more they saw of others and showed themselves to others – the more they participated in the extended "family of eyes" – the richer became their vision of themselves.

In this environment, urban realities could easily become dreamy and magical. The bright lights of street and cafe only heightened the joy; in the next generations, the coming of electricity and neon would heighten it still more. Even the most blatant vulgarities, like those café nymphs with fruits and pâtés on their heads, turned lovely in this romantic glow. Anyone who has ever been in love in a great city knows the feeling, and it is celebrated in a hundred sentimental songs. In fact, these private joys spring directly from the modernization of public urban space. Baudelaire shows us a new private and public world at the very moment when it is coming into being. From this moment on, the boulevard will be a vital boudoir in the making of modern love.

But primal scenes, for Baudelaire as later on for Freud, cannot be idyllic. They may contain idyllic material, but at the climax of the scene a repressed reality creaks through, a revelation or discovery takes place: "a new boulevard, still littered with rubble . . . displayed its unfinished splendors." Alongside the glitter, the rubble: the ruins of a dozen inner-city neighborhoods – the city's oldest, darkest, densest, most wretched and most frightening neighborhoods, home to tens of thousands of Parisians – razed to the ground. Where would all these people go? Those in charge of demolition and reconstruction did not particularly concern themselves. They were opening up vast new tracts for development on the northern and eastern fringes of the city; in the meantime, the poor would make do, somehow, as they always did. Baudelaire's family in rags step out from behind the rubble and place themselves in the center of the scene. The trouble is not that they are angry or demanding. The trouble is simply that they will not go away. They, too, want a place in the light.

This primal scene reveals some of the deepest ironies and contradictions in modern city life. The setting that makes all urban humanity a great extended "family of eyes" also brings forth the discarded stepchildren of that family. The physical and social transformations that drove the poor out of sight now bring them back directly into everyone's line of vision. Haussmann, in tearing down the old medieval slums, inadvertently broke down the self-enclosed and hermetically sealed world of traditional urban poverty. The boulevards, blasting great holes through the poorest neighborhoods, enable the poor to walk through the holes and out of their ravaged neighborhoods, to discover for the first time what the rest of their city and the rest of life is like. And as they see, they are seen: the vision, the epiphany, flows both ways. In the midst of the great spaces, under the bright lights, there is no way to look away. The glitter lights up the rubble, and illuminates the dark lives of the people at whose expense the bright lights shine.[4] Balzac had compared those old neighborhoods to the darkest jungles of Africa; for Eugène Sue they epitomized "The Mysteries of Paris." Haussmann's boulevards transform the exotic into the immediate; the misery that was once a mystery is now a fact.

The manifestation of class divisions in the modern city opens up new divisions within the modern self. How should the lovers regard the ragged people who are suddenly in their midst? At this point, modern love loses its innocence. The presence of the poor casts an inexorable shadow over the city's luminosity. The setting that magically inspired romance now works a contrary magic, and pulls the lovers out of their romantic enclosure, into wider and less idyllic networks. In this new light, their personal happiness appears as class privilege. The boulevard forces them to react politically. The man's response vibrates in the direction of the liberal left: he feels guilty about his happiness, akin to those who can see but cannot share it; he wishes, sentimentally, to make them part of his family. The woman's affinities – in this instant, at least – are with the right, the Party of Order: we have something, they want it, so we'd better "*prier le maître,*" call somebody with the power to get rid of them. Thus the distance between the lovers is not merely a gap in communication, but a radical opposition in ideology and politics. Should the barricades go up on the boulevard – as in fact they will in 1871, seven years after the poem's appearance, four years after Baudelaire's death – the lovers could well find themselves on opposite sides.

That a loving couple should find themselves split by politics is reason enough to be sad. But there may be other reasons: maybe, when he looked deeply into her eyes, he really did, as he hoped to do, "read *my* thoughts there." Maybe, even as he nobly affirms his kinship in the universal family of eyes, he shares her nasty desire to deny the poor relations, to put them out of sight and out of mind. Maybe he hates the woman he loves because her eyes have shown him a part of himself that he hates to face. Maybe the deepest split is not between the narrator and his love but within the man himself. If this is so, it shows us how the contradictions that animate the modern city street resonate in the inner life of the man on the street.

Baudelaire knows that the man's and the woman's responses, liberal sentimentality and reactionary ruthlessness, are equally futile. On one hand, there is no way to assimilate the poor into any family of the comfortable; on the other hand, there is no form of repression that can get rid of them for long – they'll always be back. Only the most radical reconstruction of modern society could even begin to heal the wounds – personal as much as social wounds – that the boulevards bring to light. And yet, too often, the radical solution seems to be dissolution: tear the boulevards down, turn off the bright lights, expel and resettle the people, kill the sources of beauty and joy that the modern city has brought into being. We can hope, as Baudelaire sometimes hoped, for a future in which the joy and beauty, like the city lights, will be shared by all. But our hope is bound to be suffused by the self-ironic sadness that permeates Baudelaire's city air.

THE MIRE OF THE MACADAM

OUR NEXT archetypal modern scene is found in the prose poem "Loss of a Halo" (Paris Spleen #46), written in 1865 but rejected by the press and not published until after Baudelaire's death. Like "The Eyes of the Poor," this poem is set on the boulevard; it presents a confrontation that the setting forces on the subject; and it ends (as its title suggests) in a loss of innocence. Here, however, the encounter is not between one person and another, or between people of different social classes, but rather between an isolated individual and social forces that are abstract yet concretely dangerous. Here, the ambience, imagery and emotional tone are puzzling and elusive; the poet seems intent on keeping his readers off balance, and he may be off balance himself. "Loss of a Halo" develops as a dialogue between a poet and an "ordinary man" who bump into each other in *un mauvais lieu*, a disreputable or sinister place, probably a brothel, to the embarrassment of both The ordinary man, who has always cherished an exalted idea of the artist, is aghast to find one here:

"What! you here, my friend? you in a place like this? you, the eater of ambrosia, the drinker of quintessences! I'm amazed!"

The poet then proceeds to explain himself:

"My friend, you know how terrified I am of horses and vehicles? Well, just now as I was crossing the boulevard in a great hurry, splashing through the mud, in the midst of a moving chaos, with death galloping at me from every side, I made a sudden move (un mouvement brusque), *and my halo slipped off my head and fell into the mire of the macadam. I was much too scared to pick it up. I thought it was less unpleasant to lose my insignia than to get my bones broken. Besides, I said to myself, every cloud has a silver lining. Now I can walk around incognito, do low things, throw myself into every kind of filth* (me livrer à la crapule), *just like ordinary mortals* (simples mortel). *So here I am, just as you see me, just like yourself!"*

The straight man plays along, a little uneasily:

"But aren't you going to advertise for your halo? or notify the police?"

No: the poet is triumphant in what we recognize as a new self-definition:

"God forbid! I like it here. You're the only one who's recognized me. Besides, dignity bores me. What's more, it's fun to think of some bad poet picking it up and brazenly putting it on. What a pleasure to make somebody happy! especially somebody you can laugh at. Think of X! Think of Z! Don't you see how funny it will be?"

It is a strange poem, and we are apt to feel like the straight man, knowing something's happening here but not knowing what it is.

One of the first mysteries here is that halo itself. What's it doing on a modern poet's head in the first place? It is there to satirize and to criticize one of Baudelaire's own most fervent beliefs: belief in the holiness of art. We can find a quasi-religious devotion to art throughout his poetry and prose. Thus, in 1855: "The artist stems only from himself. . . . He stands security only for himself. . . . He dies childless. He has been his own king, his own priest, his own God."[5] "Loss of a Halo" is about how Baudelaire's own God fails. But we must understand that this God is worshipped not only by artists but equally by many "ordinary people" who

believe that art and artists exist on a plane far above them. "Loss of a Halo" takes place at the point at which the world of art and the ordinary world converge. This is not only a spiritual point but a physical one, a point in the landscape of the modern city. It is the point where the history of modernization and the history of modernism fuse into one.

Walter Benjamin seems to have been the first to suggest the deep affinities between Baudelaire and Marx. Although Benjamin does not make this particular connection, readers familiar with Marx will notice the striking similarity of Baudelaire's central image here to one of the primary images of the *Communist Manifesto*: "The bourgeoisie has stripped off its halo every activity hitherto honored and looked up to with reverent awe. It has transformed the doctor, the lawyer, the priest, the poet, the man of science, into its paid wage-laborers."[6] For both men, one of the crucial experiences endemic to modern life, and one of the central themes for modern art and thought, is *desanctification*. Marx's theory locates this experience in a world-historical context; Baudelaire's poetry shows how it feels from inside. But the two men respond to this experience with rather different emotions. In the *Manifesto*, the drama of desanctification is terrible and tragic: Marx looks back to, and his vision embraces, heroic figures like Oedipus at Colonnus, Lear on the heath, contending against the elements, stripped and scorned but not subdued, creating a new dignity out of desolation. "Eyes of the Poor" contains its own drama of desanctification, but there the scale is intimate rather than monumental, the emotions are melancholy and romantic rather than tragic and heroic. Still, "Eyes of the Poor" and the *Manifesto* belong to the same spiritual world. "Loss of a Halo" confronts us with a very different spirit: here the drama is essentially comic, the mode of expression is ironic, and the comic irony is so successful that it masks the seriousness of the unmasking that is going on. Baudelaire's denouement, in which the hero's halo slips off his head and rolls through the mud – rather than being torn off with a violent *grand geste*, as it was for Marx (and Burke and Blake and Shakespeare) – evokes vaudeville, slapstick, the metaphysical pratfalls of Chaplin and Keaton. It points forward to a century whose heroes will come dressed as anti-heroes, and whose most solemn moments of truth will be not only described but actually experienced as clown shows, music-hall or nightclub routines-shticks. The setting plays the same sort of decisive role in Baudelaire's black comedy that it will play in Chaplin's and Keaton's later on.

"Loss of a Halo" is set on the same new boulevard as "Eyes of the Poor." But although the two poems are separated physically by only a few feet, spiritually they spring from different worlds. The gulf that separates them is the step from the sidewalk into the gutter. On the sidewalk, people of all kinds and all classes know themselves by comparing themselves to each other as they sit or walk. In the gutter, people are forced to forget what they are as they run for their lives. The new force that the boulevards have brought into being, the force that sweeps the hero's halo away and drives him into a new state of mind, is modern *traffic*.

When Haussmann's work on the boulevards began, no one understood why he wanted them so wide: from a hundred feet to a hundred yards across. It was only when the job was done that people began to see that these roads, immensely wide, straight as arrows, running on for miles, would be ideal speedways for heavy traffic. Macadam, the surface with which the boulevards were paved, was remarkably smooth, and provided perfect traction for horses' hooves. For the first time, riders and drivers in the heart of the city could whip their horses up to full speed. Improved road conditions not only speeded up previously existing traffic but – as twentieth-century highways would do on a larger scale – helped to generate a volume of new traffic far greater than anyone, apart from Haussmann and his engineers, had anticipated. Between 1850 and 1870, while the central city population (excluding newly incorporated suburbs) grew by about 25 percent, from about 1.3 million to 1.65 million, inner-city traffic seems to have tripled or quadrupled. This growth exposed a contradiction at the heart of Napoleon's and Haussmann's urbanism. As David Pinkney says in his authoritative study, *Napoleon III and the Rebuilding of Paris*, the arterial boulevards "were from the start burdened with a dual function: to carry the main stream of traffic across the city and to serve as major shopping and business streets; and as the volume of traffic increased, the two proved to be ill-compatible." The situation was especially trying and terrifying to the vast majority

of Parisians who walked. The macadam pavements, a source of special pride to the Emperor – who never walked – were dusty in the dry months of summer, and muddy in the rain and snow. Haussmann, who clashed with Napoleon over macadam (one of the few things they ever fought about), and who administratively sabotaged imperial plans to cover the whole city with it, said that this surface required Parisians "either to keep a carriage or to walk on stilts."[7] Thus the life of the boulevards, more radiant and exciting than urban life had ever been, was also more risky and frightening for the multitudes of men and women who moved on foot.

This, then, is the setting for Baudelaire's primal modern scene: "I was crossing the boulevard, in a great hurry, in the midst of a moving chaos, with death galloping at me from every side." The archetypal modern man, as we see him here, is a pedestrian thrown into the maelstrom of modern city traffic, a man alone contending against an agglomeration of mass and energy that is heavy, fast and lethal. The burgeoning street and boulevard traffic knows no spatial or temporal bounds, spills over into every urban space, imposes its tempo on everybody's time, transforms the whole modern environment into a "moving chaos." The chaos here lies not in the movers themselves – the individual walkers or drivers, each of whom may be pursuing the most efficient route for himself – but in their interaction, in the totality of their movements in a common space. This makes the boulevard a perfect symbol of capitalism's inner contradictions: rationality in each individual capitalist unit, leading to anarchic irrationality in the social system that brings all these units together.[8]

The man in the modern street, thrown into this maelstrom, is driven back on his own resources – often on resources he never knew he had – and forced to stretch them desperately in order to survive. In order to cross the moving chaos, he must attune and adapt himself to its moves, must learn to not merely keep up with it but to stay at least a step ahead. He must become adept at *soubresauts* and *mouvements brusques*, at sudden, abrupt, jagged twists and shifts – and not only with his legs and his body, but with his mind and his sensibility as well.

Baudelaire shows how modern city life forces these new moves on everyone; but he shows, too, how in doing this it also paradoxically enforces new modes of freedom. A man who knows how to move in and around and through the traffic can go anywhere, down any of the endless urban corridors where traffic itself is free to go. This mobility opens up a great wealth of new experiences and activities for the urban masses.

Moralists and people of culture will condemn these popular urban pursuits as low, vulgar, sordid, empty of social or spiritual value. But when Baudelaire's poet lets his halo go and keeps moving, he makes a great discovery. He finds to his amazement that the aura of artistic purity and sanctity is only incidental, not essential, to art, and that poetry can thrive just as well, and maybe even better, on the other side of the boulevard, in those low, "unpoetic" places like *un mauvais lieu* where this poem itself is born. One of the paradoxes of modernity, as Baudelaire sees it here, is that its poets will become more deeply and authentically poetic by becoming more like ordinary men. If he throws himself into the moving chaos of everyday life in the modern world – a life of which the new traffic is a primary symbol – he can appropriate this life for art. The "bad poet" in this world is the poet who hopes to keep his purity intact by keeping off the streets, free from the risks of traffic. Baudelaire wants works of art that will be born in the midst of the traffic, that will spring from its anarchic energy, from the incessant danger and terror of being there, from the precarious pride and exhilaration of the man who has survived so far. Thus "Loss of a Halo" turns out to be a declaration of something gained, a rededication of the poet's powers to a new kind of art. His *mouvements brusques*, those sudden leaps and swerves so crucial for everyday survival in the city streets, turn out to be sources of creative power as well. In the century to come, these moves will become paradigmatic gestures of modernist art and thought.[9]

Ironies proliferate from this primal modern scene. They unfold in Baudelaire's nuances of language. Consider a phrase like *La fange du macadam*, "the mire of the macadam." *La fange* in French is not only a literal word for mud; it is also a figurative word for mire, filth, vileness, corruption, degradation, all that is foul and loathsome. In classical oratorical and poetic diction, it is a "high" way of describing something "low." As such, it entails a whole cosmic hierarchy, a structure of norms and values not only aesthetic but metaphysical, ethical, political. *La fange* might be the nadir of the moral universe whose summit is signified by *l'auréole*. The irony here is that, so long as the poet's halo falls into "*La fange*," it can never be wholly lost, because, so long as such an image still has meaning and power – as it clearly has for Baudelaire – the old hierarchical cosmos is still present on some plane of the modern world. But it is present precariously. The meaning of macadam is as radically destructive to *La fange* as to *l'auréole*: it paves over high and low alike.

We can go deeper into the macadam: we will notice that the word isn't French. In fact, the word is derived from John McAdam of Glasgow, the eighteenth-century inventor of the modern paving surface. It may be the first word in that language that twentieth-century Frenchmen have satirically named *Franglais*: it paves the way for *le parking, le shopping, le weekend, le drugstore, le mobile-home*, and far more. This language is so vital and compelling because it is the international language of modernization. Its new words are powerful vehicles of new modes of life and motion. The words may sound dissonant and jarring, but it is as futile to resist them as to resist the momentum of modernization itself. It is true that many nations and ruling classes feel – and have reason to feel – threatened by the flow of new words and things from other shores.[10] There is a wonderful paranoid Soviet word that expresses this fear: *infiltratzya*. We should notice, however, that what nations have normally done, from Baudelaire's time to our own, is, after a wave (or at least a show) of resistance, not only to accept the new thing but to create their own word for it, in the hope of blotting out embarrassing memories of underdevelopment. (Thus the Académie Française, after refusing all through the 1960s to admit *le parking meter* to the French language, coined and quickly canonized *le parcmetre* in the 1970s.)

Baudelaire knew how to write in the purest and most elegant classical French. Here, however, with the "Loss of a Halo," he projects himself into the new, emerging language, to make art out of the dissonances and incongruities that pervade – and, paradoxically, unite – the whole modern world. "In place of the old national seclusion and self-sufficiency," the *Manifesto* says, modern bourgeois society brings us "intercourse in every direction, universal interdependence of nations. And, as in material, so in intellectual production. The spiritual creations of nations become" – note this image, paradoxical in a bourgeois world – "common property." Marx goes on: "National one-sidedness and narrow-mindedness become more and more impossible, and from the numerous local and national literatures, there arises a world literature." The mire of the macadam will turn out to be one of the foundations from which this new world literature of the twentieth century will arise.[11]

There are further ironies that arise from this primal scene. The halo that falls into the mire of the macadam is endangered but not destroyed; instead, it is carried along and incorporated into the general flow of traffic. One salient feature of the commodity economy, as Marx explains, is the endless metamorphosis of its market values. In this economy, anything goes if it pays, and no human possibility is ever wiped off the books; culture becomes an enormous warehouse in which everything is kept in stock on the chance that someday, somewhere, it might sell. Thus the halo that the modern poet lets go (or throws off) as obsolete may, by virtue of its very obsolescence, metamorphose into an icon, an object of nostalgic veneration for those who, like the "bad poets" X and Z, are trying to escape from modernity. But alas, the anti-modern artist – or thinker or politician – finds himself on the same streets, in the same mire, as the modernist one. This modern environment serves as both a physical and a spiritual lifeline – a primary source of material and energy – for both.

The difference between the modernist and the anti-modernist, so far as they are concerned, is that the modernist makes himself at home here, while the anti-modern searches the streets for a way out. So far as the traffic is concerned, however, there is no difference between them at all: both alike are hindrances and hazards to the horses and vehicles whose paths they cross, whose free movement they impede. Then, too, no matter how closely the anti-modernist may cling to his aura of spiritual purity, he is bound to lose it, more likely sooner than later, for the same reason that the modernist lost it: he will be forced to discard balance and measure and decorum and to learn the grace of brusque moves in order to survive. Once again, however opposed the modernist and the anti-modernist may think they are, in the mire of the

macadam, from the viewpoint of the endlessly moving traffic, the two are one.

Ironies beget more ironies. Baudelaire's poet hurls himself into a confrontation with the "moving chaos" of the traffic, and strives not only to survive but to assert his dignity in its midst. But his mode of action seems self-defeating, because it adds yet another unpredictable variable to an already unstable totality. The horses and their riders, the vehicles and their drivers, are trying at once to outpace each other and to avoid crashing into each other. If, in the midst of all this, they are also forced to dodge pedestrians who may at any instant dart out into the road, their movements will become even more uncertain, and hence more dangerous than ever. Thus, by contending against the moving chaos, the individual only aggravates the chaos.

But this very formulation suggests a way that might lead beyond Baudelaire's irony and out of the moving chaos itself. What if the multitudes of men and women who are terrorized by modern traffic could learn to confront it *together*? This will happen just six years after "Loss of a Halo" (and three years after Baudelaire's death), in the days of the Commune in Paris in 1871, and again in Petersburg in 1905 and 1917, in Berlin in 1918, in Barcelona in 1936, in Budapest in 1956, in Paris again in 1968, and in *dozens* of cities all over the world, from Baudelaire's time to our own – the boulevard will be abruptly transformed into the stage for a new primal modern scene. This will not be the sort of scene that Napoleon or Haussmann would like to see, but nonetheless one that their mode of urbanism will have helped to make.

As we reread the old histories, memoirs and novels, or regard the old photos or newsreels, or stir our own fugitive memories of 1968, we will see whole classes and masses move into the street together. We will be able to discern two phases in their activity. At first the people stop and overturn the vehicles in their path, and set the horses free: here they are avenging themselves on the traffic by decomposing it into its inert original elements. Next they incorporate the wreckage they have created into their rising barricades: they are recombining the isolated, inanimate elements into vital new artistic and political forms. For one luminous moment, the multitude of solitudes that make up the modern city come together in a new kind of encounter, to make a *people*. "The streets belong to the people": they seize control of the city's elemental matter and make it their own. For a little while the chaotic modernism of solitary brusque moves gives way to an ordered modernism of mass movement. The "heroism of modern life" that Baudelaire longed to see will be born from his primal scene in the street. Baudelaire does not expect this (or any other) new life to last. But it will be born again and again out of the street's inner contradictions. It may burst into life at any moment, often when it is least expected. This possibility is a vital flash of hope in the mind of the man in the mire of the macadam, in the moving chaos, on the run.

NOTES

1 My picture of the Napoleon III–Haussmann transformation of Paris has been put together from several sources: Siegfried Giedion, *Space, Time and Architecture* (1941; 5th edition, Harvard, 1966), 744–75; Robert Moses, "Haussmann," in *Architectural Forum*, July 1942, 57–66; David Pinkney, *Napoleon III and the Rebuilding of Paris* (1958; Princeton, 1972); Leonardo Benevolo, *A History of Modern Architecture* (1960, 1966; translated from the Italian by H.J. Landry, 2 volumes, MIT, 1971), I, 61–65; Françoise Choay, *The Modern City: Planning in the Nineteenth Century* (George Braziller, 1969), especially 15–26; Howard Saalman, *Haussmann: Paris Transformed* (Braziller, 1971); and Louis Chevalier, *Laboring Classes and Dangerous Classes: Paris in the First Half of the Nineteenth Century*, 1970, translated by Frank Jellinek (Howard Fertig, 1973). Haussmann's projects are skillfully placed in the context of long-term European political and social change by Anthony Vidler, "The Scenes of the Street: Transformations in Ideal and Reality, 1750–1871," in *On Streets*, edited by Stanford Anderson (MIT, 1978), 28–111. Haussmann commissioned a photographer, Charles Marville, to photograph dozens of sites slated for demolition and so preserve their memory for posterity. These photographs are preserved in the Musée Carnavalet, Paris. A marvelous selection was exhibited in New York and other American locations in 1981. The catalogue, French Institute/Alliance Française, *Charles Marville:*

Photographs of Paris, 1852–1878, contains a fine essay by Maria Morris Hamburg.

2 In *Laboring Classes and Dangerous Classes*, cited in note 1, Louis Chevalier, the venerable historian of Paris, gives a horrific, excruciatingly detailed account of the ravages to which the old central neighborhoods in the pre-Haussmann decades were subjected: demographic bombardment, which doubled the population while the erection of luxury housing and government buildings sharply reduced the overall housing stock; recurrent mass unemployment, which in a pre-welfare era led directly to starvation; dreadful epidemics of typhus and cholera, which took their greatest toll in the old *quartiers*. All this suggests why the Parisian poor, who fought so bravely on so many fronts in the nineteenth century, put up no resistance to the destruction of their neighborhoods: they may well have been willing to go, as Baudelaire said in another context, anywhere out of their world.

The little-known essay by Robert Moses, also cited in note 1, is a special treat for all those who savor the ironies of urban history. In the course of giving a lucid and balanced overview of Haussmann's accomplishments, Moses crowns himself as his successor, and implicitly bids for still more Haussmann-type authority to carry out even more gigantic projects after the war. The piece ends with an admirably incisive and trenchant critique that anticipates, with amazing precision and deadly accuracy, the criticism that would be directed a generation later against Moses himself, and that would finally help to drive Haussmann's greatest disciple from public life.

3 Haussmann's engineers invented a tree-lifting machine that enabled them to transplant thirty-year-old trees in full leaf, and thus to create shady avenues overnight, seemingly ex nihilo. Giedion, *Space, Time and Architecture*, 757–59.

4 See Engels, in his pamphlet *The Housing Question* (1872), on

the method called "Haussmann" ... I mean the practice, which has now become general, of making breaches in working-class quarters of our big cities, especially in those that are centrally situated ... The result is everywhere the same: the most scandalous alleys and lanes disappear, to the accompaniment of lavish self-glorification by the bourgeoisie on account of this tremendous success – but they appear at once somewhere else, and often in the immediate neighborhood.

Marx-Engels Selected Works, 2 volumes (Moscow, 1955), 1, 559, 606–9

5 *Art in Paris*, 1945–62, (translated and edited by Jonathan Mayne, Phaidon, 1965), 127.

6 This connection is explicated in very different terms from the ones here, by Irving Wohlfarth, "*Perte d'Auréole*: the Emergence of the Dandy," *Modern Language Notes*, 85 (1970), 530–71.

7 Pinkney, *Napoleon III*, on census figures, 151–54; on traffic counts and estimates, and conflict between Napoleon and Haussmann over macadam, 70–72; on dual function of boulevards, 214–15.

8 Street traffic was not, of course, the only mode of organized motion known to the nineteenth century. The railroad had been around on a large scale since the 1830s, and a vital presence in European literature since Dickens' *Dombey and Son* (1846–48). But the railroad ran on a fixed schedule along a prescribed route, and so, for all its demonic potentialities, became a nineteenth-century paradigm of order.

We should note that Baudelaire's experience of "moving chaos" antedates the traffic light, an innovation developed in America around 1905 and a wonderful symbol of early state attempts to regulate and rationalize the chaos of capitalism.

9 Forty years later, with the coming (or rather the naming) of the Brooklyn Dodgers, popular culture will produce its own ironic version of this modernist faith. The name expresses the way in which urban survival skills – specifically, skill at dodging traffic (they were at first called the *Trolley* Dodgers) – can transcend utility and take on new modes of meaning and value, in sport as in art. Baudelaire would have loved this symbolism, as many of his twentieth-century successors (e.e. cummings, Marianne Moore) did.

10 In the nineteenth century the main transmitter of modernization was England, in the twentieth century it has been the U.S.A. Power maps have changed, but the primacy of the English language – the least pure, the most elastic and adaptable of modern languages – is greater than ever. It might well survive the decline of the American empire.

11 On the distinctively international quality of twentieth-century modernist language and literature, see Delmore Schwartz, "T.S. Eliot as International Hero," in Howe, *Literary Modernism*, 277–85. This is also one of Edmund Wilson's central themes in *Axel's Castle* and *To the Finland Station*.

"Public Parks and the Enlargement of Towns"

American Social Science Association (1870)

Frederick Law Olmsted

Editors' Introduction

Toward the middle of the nineteenth century, at the same time that Georges Eugène Haussmann was re-constructing Paris in his role as Prefect of the Seine during the reign of Napoleon III (p. 25), the works and writings of landscape architect Frederick Law Olmsted (1822–1903) were spurring the American Parks Movement. In 1858, he and his partner Calvert Vaux entered and won the competition to design New York City's Central Park, an 843-acre open space carved out of the city's relentless gridiron. The heralded success of Central Park vaulted Olmsted, who was responsible for overseeing the park's construction and also wrote annual reports which both articulated his design ideas and documented the park's progress, into being the leading landscape architect of the day. Indeed, he is often considered the founder of the American landscape architecture profession. He went on to design Prospect Park (with Vaux) and a related series of parkways in Brooklyn as well as park systems in Boston, Buffalo, and elsewhere.

While Vaux was a trained architect who had apprenticed in Andrew Jackson Downing's highly respected landscape architecture firm, Olmsted had no formal design education or any design experience prior to de-signing Central Park, but he was a skilled empirical observer. In 1850, he undertook a six-month walking tour of England, visiting the recently built planned suburb of Birkenhead to study its large park, and roaming the countryside sketching scenery and measuring roadways and paths. In 1859, he spent three months in Europe, visiting the new public parks being built there. In England, he revisited Birkenhead Park and toured the gardens at Trentham and Blenheim Palace designed by Capability Brown. On the continent, he visited parks in a number of cities, including Brussels and Lille. He spent considerable time in Paris, looking at the new parks and boulevards being built by Haussmann, particularly studying the new boulevards around the Etoile, built to encourage and structure new residential development in the largely rural western part of the city, and took eight trips to the nearby Bois de Bologne, a former royal hunting ground at the city's western edge that was being turned into a public park. What he saw in Paris opened his eyes to the prospect of designing not only parks, but also networked park systems, and he brought this vision back to his work in America.

As well as being a designer, Olmsted was also a theorist and prolific writer. "Public Parks and the Enlarge-ment of Towns" was originally given as an address before the American Social Science Association at the Lowell Institute in Boston in 1870. In it, Olmsted articulates the rationale for the naturalistic design approach he advocated for parks and links aesthetic design to social concerns. Olmsted believed that naturalistically designed parks could play a central role in counteracting what he saw as the debilitating aspects of living in dense cities and serve as an antidote to urban life. In them, people could find relief from the stresses they encountered in the city's chaotic and crowded streets and so regain their mental and physical health. In the simplest terms, parks would improve city people's physical health by providing open spaces filled with trees, sunlight, and fresh air. In parks, city air would be "disinfected by sunlight and foliage." But Olmsted advocated that a "properly designed" naturalistic park – one with gentle landscapes – would do more. Secluded pastoral landscapes, offering views of meadows, pastures, and still waters, would be conducive to calm contemplation and so give mental recuperation to park visitors – as opposed to rugged landscapes that would bring effort to mind. Mental recuperation would give people the ability "to maintain a temperate, good-natured, and healthy state of mind" and strengthen them for productive labor in America's fast-paced, rapidly growing, and constantly transforming cities. A gently designed natural park would also educate people of the lower classes, bringing them more refined tastes and a higher moral standard, and have "a distinctly harmonizing and refining influence upon the most unfortunate and most lawless classes of the city – an influence favorable to courtesy, self-control, and temperance." The transformative power of environmental experience was central to Olmsted's philosophy and so was the idea of societal inclusion. He envisioned public parks as places where the many disparate groups in American society – newly arrived immigrants, descendants of early colonists, working people, wealthy people – could come together and, through shared aesthetic experience, develop a basis for creating community.

Aesthetic leisure is an apt description of the activities Olmsted envisioned taking place in large, naturalistically designed urban parks. He distinguished two types of recreation: exertive and receptive. Exertive recreational activities required physical or mental exertion, such as sports games or chess. Receptive recreational activities were those people engaged in without conscious effort, such as music or art. The latter was the only type of recreation Olmsted deemed appropriate for large city parks. Along with prohibiting sports from parks, he also advocated forbidding vernacular entertainments or commercial amusements of any type, which would disrupt the unified aesthetic vision Olmsted sought to achieve. The emerging popular European practice of public promenades in and near parks, in carriages and on foot, was at odds with Olmsted's park philosophy. Public pressure would push Olmsted to recognize promenading as a special type of "gregarious" receptive activity, which had a limited place in a naturalistic park but a central place in a city's park system, namely along parkways.

Olmsted worked at a time when American cities were growing very rapidly, and he advocated establishing connected park systems in advance of development as a means of structuring growth and ensuring distributed park amenities. With this advance planning way of thinking, he was the forefather of the American city planning profession. Looking to Haussmann's boulevards, but adapting them to a suburban vision of city development, Olmsted designed broad tree-lined parkways to connect urban parks.

As well as parks and parkways, Olmsted created plans for picturesquely designed suburbs. The idea was that just as parks would be an antidote to urban life, leafy suburbs would have a beneficial effect on family and community life. His 1868 plan for the Chicago suburb of Riverside, which consisted of looping and curvilinear tree-lined residential streets weaving around each other and focused on a riverside park, served as a model for later American suburban development.

After Olmsted and Vaux dissolved their partnership in 1872, they continued to collaborate on some projects, but mostly did separate work. In 1884, Olmsted created a partnership with his nephew and stepson John C. Olmsted (one and the same person; Olmsted, Sr., had married his brother's widow), Charles Eliot, and Henry Codman, both nephews of architects with whom Olmsted had worked. Later, his younger son Frederick Law Olmsted, Jr., joined the partnership. Olmsted led the firm until he retired in 1895. Codman and Eliot both died in the 1890s, but the Olmsted brothers continued the firm – known as the Olmsted Brothers – until 1950. With his associates, Olmsted, Sr., designed a number of parks and parkway systems. Perhaps most notable are the famous "emerald necklace" plan for Boston and the parkway plan for Louisville, Kentucky.

The American Parks Movement that was spawned by Olmsted's ideas and the popular success of his parks and park systems flourished in the United States throughout the late nineteenth century and many cities built parks, notably Golden Gate Park in San Francisco. Around the end of the century, following the success of the 1893 Chicago World's Columbian Exposition, the Parks Movement melded with the City Beautiful Movement, as chronicled by William H. Wilson (p. 62). Sponsored by local civic groups and led by activist women, the movement advocated improving the public realm of cities through street lighting, fountains, benches, ornamental plantings, shade trees, public art, and classically designed civic centers.

Olmsted's legacy of urban parks and park systems stands out as a positive affirmation of the benefits that can be had from long-range planning and the quality of life benefits – not to mention economic benefits – associated with urban public open spaces. Those cities with large parks and parkway systems prize them as civic jewels.

Nowadays, Olmsted's picturesque park design approach is sometimes dismissed by landscape architects because the "natural" landscape effects were artificially constructed. As well, his picturesquely designed suburbs are faulted for being the precursors to the ubiquitous modern American suburb with its disconnected street patterns. Nonetheless, Olmsted remains a major figure in the fields of city planning and landscape architecture, and his well-loved designs have stood the test of time. His vision of connected parks and parkway systems, best exemplified by Boston's "Emerald Necklace" and Chicago's linear park system, is now being rejuvenated with the Smart Growth Movement's proposals for urban greenbelts.

As a theorist and practitioner, Olmsted was concerned with issues that remain central to the present-day professions of urban planning and landscape architecture. His ideas influenced key theorists of the late 1800s and early 1900s including Ebenezer Howard (p. 53), Clarence Perry (p. 78), and Lewis Mumford. Even an idea of urbanism as fundamentally different as Le Corbusier's "tower-in-the-park" concept (p. 90) owes a debt to Olmsted in that it addresses relationships between built and natural environments.

Olmsted's address to the American Social Science Association was originally printed by the association in 1870. In 1871 it was published as "Public Parks and the Enlargement of Towns" in the *Journal of Social Science*, Volume 3: 1–36. It is reprinted with extensive editorial notes in *The Papers of Frederick Law Olmsted* (seven volumes and supplementary series), ed. Charles E. Beveridge and Carolyn F. Hoffman, Supplementary Series, Volume 1, *Writings on Public Parks, Parkways, and Park Systems* (Baltimore, MD: Johns Hopkins University Press, 1997), pp. 171–205. The multi-volume *Collected Papers of Frederick Law Olmsted* provides reprints of many of Olmsted's writings through 1882, including his personal and professional correspondence, reports prepared for professional projects, and texts of lectures. The editor's introductions to each volume together provide a detailed biography of Olmsted's life and give contextual background for his writings.

A selection of Olmsted's major writings related to city planning and landscape architecture are found in S.B. Sutton (ed.), *Civilizing American Cities: Writings on City Landscapes* by Frederick Law Olmsted (Cambridge, MA: MIT Press, 1971). Biographies of Olmsted and commentary on his work include Susan L. Klaus, *Modern Arcadia: Frederick Law Olmsted, Jr. and the Plan for Forest Hill Gardens* (Cambridge, MA: MIT Press, 2002); Witold Rybczynski, *A Clearing in the Distance: Frederick Law Olmsted and America in the Nineteenth Century* (New York: Scribner, 1999); Charles E. Beveridge, *Frederick Law Olmsted: Designing the American Landscape* (New York: Rizzoli, 1995); Cynthia Zaitzevsky, *Frederick Law Olmsted and the Boston Park System* (Cambridge: Belknap Press, 1992); Irving D. Fisher, *Frederick Law Olmsted and the City Planning Movement in the United States* (Ann Arbor, MI: UMI Research Press, 1986); Jeffrey Simpson, *Art of the Olmsted Landscape: His Works in New York City* (New York: Landmarks Preservation Commission, Arts Publisher, 1981); Elizabeth Stevenson *Park Maker: A Life of Frederick Law Olmsted* (New York: Macmillan, 1977); Laura Wood Roper, *FLO: A Biography of Frederick Law Olmsted* (Baltimore, MD: Johns Hopkins University Press, 1973); Elizabeth Barlow Rogers, *Frederick Law Olmsted's New York* (New York: Praeger, 1972); Albert Fein (ed.), *Landscape into Cityscape: Frederick Law Olmsted's Plans for a Greater New York City* (Ithaca, NY: Cornell University Press, 1967); Theodora Kimball and Frederick Law Olmsted, Jr. (eds), *Frederick Law Olmsted: Landscape Architect, 1822–1903* (New York: G.P. Putnam's Sons, 1922). Pictures of Olmsted parks by noted photographer Lee Friedlander are collected in *Photographs: Frederick Law Olmsted Landscapes* (New York: Distributed Art Publishers, 2008).

Roy Rosenzweig and Elizabeth Blackmar, *The Park and the People: A History of Central Park* (Ithaca, NY: Cornell University Press, 1992) provide an excellent in-depth social history of Central Park that spans from before the park was built through the latter half of the twentieth century. Galen Cranz, *The Politics of Park Design: A History of Urban Parks in America* (Cambridge, MA: MIT Press, 1982) gives an overview of Olmsted's design work, placing it in the context of larger concurrent social reform movements. David M. Scobey, *Empire City: The Making and Meaning of the New York City Landscape* (Philadelphia, PA: Temple University Press, 2002) identifies Olmsted as a key member of the "city-building gentry" that along with reform-minded business leaders and real-estate developers helped forge the era of metropolitan scale urbanism that arose in New York City during the second half of the nineteenth century.

We have reason to believe, then, that towns which of late have been increasing rapidly on account of their commercial advantages, are likely to be still more attractive to population in the future; that there will in consequence soon be larger towns than any the world has yet known, and that the further progress of civilization is to depend mainly upon the influences by which men's minds and characters will be affected while living in large towns.

Now, knowing that the average length of the life of mankind in towns has been much less than in the country, and that the average amount of disease and misery and of vice and crime has been much greater in towns, this would be a very dark prospect for civilization, if it were not that modern Science has beyond all question determined many of the causes of the special evils by which men are afflicted in towns, and placed means in our hands for guarding against them. It has shown, for example, that under ordinary circumstances, in the interior parts of large and closely built towns, a given quantity of air contains considerably less of the elements which we require to receive through the lungs than the air of the country or even of the outer and more open parts of a town, and that instead of them it carries into the lungs highly corrupt and irritating matters, the action of which tends strongly to vitiate all our sources of vigor – how strongly may perhaps be indicated in the shortest way by the statement that even metallic plates and statues corrode and wear away under the atmosphere influences which prevail in the midst of large towns, more rapidly than in the country.

The irritation and waste of the physical powers which result from the same cause, doubtless indirectly affect and very seriously affect the mind and the moral strength; but there is a general impression that a class of men are bred in towns whose peculiarities are not perhaps adequately accounted for in this way. We may understand these better if we consider that whenever we walk through the denser part of a town, to merely avoid collision with those we meet and pass upon the sidewalks, we have constantly to watch, to foresee and to guard against their movements. This involves a consideration of their intentions, a calculation of their strength and weakness, which is not so much for their benefit as our own. Our minds are thus brought into close dealings with other minds without any friendly flowing toward them, but rather a drawing from them. Much of the intercourse between men when engaged in the pursuits of commerce has the same tendency – a tendency to regard others in a hard if not always hardening way. Each detail of observation and of the process of thought required in this kind of intercourse or contact of minds is so slight and so common in the experience of townspeople that they are seldom conscious of it. It certainly involves some expenditure nevertheless. People from the country are even conscious of the effect on their nerves and minds of the street contact – often complaining that they feel confused by it; and if we had no relief from it at all during our waking hours, we should all be conscious of suffering from it. It is upon our opportunities of relief from it, therefore, that not only our comfort in town life, but our ability to maintain a temperate, good-natured, and healthy state of mind, depends. This is one of many ways in which it happens that men who have been brought up, as the saying is, in the streets, who have been most directly and completely affected by town influences, so generally show, along with a remarkable quickness of apprehension, a peculiarly hard sort of selfishness. Every day of their lives they have seen thousands of their fellowmen, have met them face to face, have brushed against them, and yet have had no experience of anything in common with them.

[. . .]

It is practically certain that the Boston of today is the mere nucleus of the Boston that is to be. It is practically certain that it is to extend over many miles of country now thoroughly rural in character, in parts of which farmers are now laying out roads with a view to shortening the teaming distance between their wood-lots and a railway station, being governed in their courses by old property lines, which were first run simply with reference to the equitable division of heritages, and in other parts of which, perhaps, some wild speculators are having streets staked off from plans which they have formed with a rule and pencil in a broker's office, with a view, chiefly, to the impressions they would make when seen by other speculators on a lithographed map. And by this manner of planning, unless views of duty or of interest prevail that are not yet common, if Boston continues to grow at its present rate even for but a few generations longer, and then simply holds its own until it shall be as old as the Boston in Lincolnshire now is, more men, women, and children are to be seriously affected in health and morals than are now living on this Continent.

Is this a small matter – a mere matter of taste; a sentimental speculation?

It must be within the observation of most of us that where, in the city, wheel-ways originally twenty-feet wide were with great difficulty and cost enlarged to thirty, the present width is already less nearly adequate to the present business than the former was to the former business; obstructions are more frequent, movements are slower and oftener arrested, and the liability to collision is greater. The same is true of sidewalks. Trees thus have been cut down, porches, bow-windows, and other encroachments removed, but every year the walk is less sufficient for the comfortable passing of those who wish to use it.

It is certain that as the distance from the interior to the circumference of towns shall increase with the enlargement of their population, the less sufficient relatively to the service to be performed will be any given space between buildings.

In like manner every evil to which men are specially liable when living in towns, is likely to be aggravated in the future, unless means are devised and adapted in advance to prevent it.

Let us proceed, then, to the question of means, and with a seriousness in some degree befitting a question upon our dealing with which we know the misery or happiness of many millions of our fellow-beings will depend.

We will for the present set before our minds the two sources of wear and corruption which we have seen to be remediable and therefore preventable. We may admit that commerce requires that in some parts of a town there shall be an arrangement of buildings, and a character of streets and of traffic in them which will establish conditions of corruption and of irritation, physical and mental. But commerce does not require the same conditions to be maintained in all parts of a town.

Air is disinfected by sunlight and foliage. Foliage also acts mechanically to purify the air by screening it. Opportunity and inducement to escape at frequent intervals from the confined and vitiated air of the commercial quarter, and to supply the lungs with air screened and purified by trees, and recently acted upon by sunlight, together with opportunity and inducement to escape from conditions requiring vigilance, wariness, and activity toward other men – if these could be supplied economically, our problem would be solved.

In the old days of walled towns all tradesmen lived under the roof of their shops, and their children and apprentices and servants sat together with them in the evening about the kitchen fire. But now that the dwelling is built by itself and there is greater room, the inmates have a parlor to spend their evening in; they spread carpets on the floor to gain in quiet, and hang drapery in their windows and papers on their walls to gain in seclusion and beauty. Now that our towns are built without walls, and we can have all the room that we like, is there any good reason why we should not make some similar difference between parts which are likely to be dwelt in, and those which will be required exclusively for commerce?

Would trees, for seclusion and shade and beauty, be out of place, for instance, by the side of certain of our streets? It will, perhaps, appear to you that it is hardly necessary to ask such a question, as throughout the United States trees are commonly planted at the sides of streets. Unfortunately they are seldom planted as to have fairly settled the question of the desirableness of systematically maintaining trees under these circumstances. In the first place, the streets are planned, wherever they are, essentially alike. Trees are planted in the space assigned for sidewalks, where at first, while they are saplings and the vicinity is rural or suburban, they are not much in the way, but where, as they grow larger, and the vicinity becomes urban, they take up more and more space, while space is more and more required for passage. That is not all. Thousands and tens of thousands are planted every year in a manner and under conditions as nearly certain as possible either to kill them outright, or to so lessen their vitality as to prevent their natural and beautiful development, and to cause premature decrepitude. Often, too, as their lower limbs are found inconvenient, no space having been provided for trees in laying out the street, they are deformed by butcherly amputations. If by rare good fortune they are suffered to become beautiful, they still stand subject to be condemned to death at any time, as obstructions in the highway.

What I would ask is, whether we might not with economy make special provision in some of our streets – in a twentieth or a fiftieth part, if you please, of all – for trees to remain as a permanent furniture of the city? I mean, to make a place for them in which they would have room to grow naturally and gracefully. Even if the distance between the houses should have to be made half as much again as it is required to be in our commercial streets, could not the space be afforded? Out of town space is not costly when measures to secure it are taken early. The assessments for benefit where such streets were provided for, would, in nearly all cases, defray the cost of the land required. The strips of ground required for the trees, six, twelve, twenty feet wide, would cost nothing for paving or flagging.

The change both of scene and of air which would be obtained by people engaged for the most part in the necessarily confined interior commercial parts of the town, on passing into a street of this character after the trees have become stately and graceful, would be worth a good deal. If such streets were made still broader in some parts, with spacious malls, the advantage would be increased. If each of them were given the proper capacity, and laid out with laterals and connections in suitable directions to serve as a convenient trunk line of communication between two large districts of the town or the business centre and the suburbs, a very great number of people might thus be placed every day under influences counteracting those with which we desire to contend.

These, however, would be merely very simple improvements upon arrangements which are in common use in every considerable town. Their advantages would be incidental to the general uses of streets as they are. But people are willing very often to seek recreations as well as receive it by the way. Provisions may indeed be made expressly for public recreations, with certainty that if convenient they will be resorted to.

We come then to the question: what accommodations for recreation can we provide which shall be so agreeable and so accessible as to be efficiently attractive to the great body of citizens, and which, while giving decided gratification, shall also cause those who resort to them for pleasure to subject themselves, for the time being, to conditions strongly counteractive to the special, enervating conditions of the town?

In the study of this question all forms of recreation may, in the first place, be conveniently arranged under two general heads. One will include all of which the predominating influence is to stimulate exertion of any part or parts needing it; the other, all which cause us to receive pleasure without conscious exertion. Games chiefly of mental skill, as chess, or athletic sports, as baseball, are examples of means of recreation of the first class, which may be termed that of *exertive* recreation; music and the fine arts generally of the second or *receptive* division.

Considering the first by itself, much consideration will be needed in determining what classes of exercises may be advantageously provided for. In the Bois de Boulogne there is a race-course; in the Bois de Vincennes a ground for artillery target-practice. Military parades are held in Hyde Park. A few cricket clubs are accommodated in most of the London parks, and swimming is permitted in the lakes at certain hours. In the New York Park, on the other hand, none of these exercises are provided for or permitted, except that the boys of the public schools are given the use on holidays of certain large spaces for ball playing. It is considered that the advantage to individuals which would be gained in providing for them would not compensate for the general inconvenience and expense they would cause.

I do not propose to discuss this part of the subject at present, as it is only necessary to my immediate purpose to point out that if recreations requiring large spaces to be given up to the use of a comparatively small number, are not considered essential, numerous small grounds so distributed through a large town that some one of them could be easily reached by a short walk from every house, would be more desirable than a single area of great extent, however rich in landscape attractions it might be. Especially would this be the case if the numerous local grounds were connected and supplemented by a series of trunk-roads or boulevards such as has already been suggested.

Proceeding to the consideration of receptive recreations, it is necessary to ask you to adopt and bear in mind a further subdivision, under two heads, according to the degree in which the average enjoyment is greater when a large congregation assembles for a purpose of receptive recreation, or when the number coming together is small and the circumstances are favorable to the exercise of personal friendliness.

The first I shall term *gregarious*; the second, *neighborly*. Remembering that the immediate matter in hand is a study of fitting accommodations, you will, I trust, see the practical necessity of this classification.

Purely gregarious recreation seems to be generally looked upon in New England society as childish and savage, because, I suppose, there is so little of what we call intellectual gratification in it. We are inclined to engage in it indirectly, furtively, and with complication. Yet there are certain forms of recreation, a large share of the attraction of which must, I think, lie in the gratification of the gregarious inclination, and which, with those who can afford to indulge in them, are so popular as to establish the importance of the requirement.

If I ask myself where I have experienced the most complete gratification of this instinct in public and out of doors, among trees, I find that it has been in the promenade of the Champs-Élysées. As closely following it I should name other promenades of Europe, and our own upon the New York parks. I have studiously watched the latter for several years. I have several times seen fifty thousand people participating in them; and the more I have seen of them, the more highly have I been led to estimate their value as means of counteracting the evils of town life.

Consider that the New York Park and the Brooklyn Park are the only places in those associated cities where, in this eighteen hundred and seventieth year after Christ, you will find a body of Christians coming together, and with an evident glee in the prospect of coming together, all classes largely represented, with a common purpose, not at all intellectual, competitive with none, disposing to jealousy and spiritual or intellectual pride toward none, each individual adding by his mere presence to the pleasure of all others, all helping to the greater happiness of each. You may thus often see vast numbers of persons brought closely together, poor and rich, young and old, Jew and Gentile. I have seen a hundred thousand thus congregated, and I assure you that though there have been not a few that seemed a little dazed, as if they did not quite understand it, and were, perhaps, a little ashamed of it, I have looked studiously but vainly among them for a single face completely unsympathetic with the prevailing expression of good nature and light-heartedness.

Is it doubtful that it does men good to come together in this way in pure air and under the light of heaven, or that it must have an influence directly counteractive to that of the ordinary hard, hustling working hours of town life?

You will agree with me, I am sure, that it is not, and that opportunity, convenient, attractive opportunity, for such congregation, is a very good thing to provide for, in planning the extension of a town.

[. . .]

Think that the ordinary state of things to many is at this beginning of the town. The public is reading just now a little book in which some of your streets of which you are not proud are described. Go into one of those red cross streets any fine evening next summer, and ask how it is with their residents. Oftentimes you will see half a dozen sitting together on the door-steps or, all in a row, on the curb-stones, with their feet in the gutter; driven out of doors by the closeness within; mothers among them anxiously regarding their children who are dodging about at their play, among the noisy wheels on the pavement.

Again, consider how often you see young men in knots of perhaps half a dozen in lounging attitudes rudely obstructing the sidewalks, chiefly led in their little conversation by the suggestions given to their minds by what or whom they may see passing in the street, men, women, or children, whom they do not know and for whom they have no respect or sympathy. There is nothing among them or about them which is adapted to bring into play a spark of admiration, of delicacy, manliness, or tenderness. You see them presently descend in search of physical comfort to a brilliantly lighted basement, where they find others of their sort, see, hear, smell, drink, and eat all manner of vile things.

Whether on the curb-stones or in the dram-shops, these young men are all under the influence of the same impulse which some satisfy about the tea-table with neighbors and wives and mothers and children, and all things clean and wholesome, softening, and refining.

If the great city to arise here is to be laid out little by little, and chiefly to suit the views of land-owners, acting only individually, and thinking only of how what they do is to affect the value in the next week or the next year of the few lots that each may hold at the time, the opportunities of so obeying this inclination as at the same time to give the lungs a bath of pure sunny air, to give the mind a suggestion of rest from the devouring eagerness and intellectual strife of town life, will always be few to any, to many will amount to nothing.

But is it possible to make public provision for recreation of this class, essentially domestic and secluded as it is?

It is a question which can, of course, be conclusively answered only from experience. And from experience in some slight degree I shall answer it. There is one large American town, in which it may happen that a man of any class shall say to his wife, when he is going out in the morning:

"My dear, when the children come home from school, put some bread and butter and salad in a basket, and go to the spring under the chestnut-tree where we found the Johnsons last week. I will join you there as soon as I can get away from the office. We will walk to the dairy-man's cottage and get some tea, and some fresh milk for the children, and take our supper by the brook-side"

and this shall be no joke, but the most refreshing earnest.

There will be room enough in the Brooklyn Park, when it is finished, for several thousand little family and neighborly parties to bivouac at frequent intervals through the summer, without discommoding one another, or interfering with any other purpose, to say nothing of those who can be drawn out to make a day of it, as many thousand were last year. And although the arrangements for the purpose were yet very incomplete, and but little ground was at all prepared for such use, besides these small parties, consisting of one or two families, there came also, in companies of from thirty to a hundred and fifty, somewhere near twenty thousand children with their parents, Sunday-school teachers, or other guides and friends, who spent the best part of a day under the trees and on the turf, in recreations of which the predominating element was of this neighborly receptive class. Often they would bring a fiddle, flute, and harp, or other music. Tables, seats, shade, turf, swings, cool spring-water, and a pleasing rural prospect, stretching off half a mile or more each way, unbroken by a carriage road or the slightest evidence of the vicinity of the town, were supplied them without charge and bread and milk and

ice-cream at moderate fixed charges. In all my life I have never seen such joyous collections of people. I have, in fact, more than once observed tears of gratitude in the eyes of poor women, as they watched their children thus enjoying themselves.

The whole cost of such neighborly festivals, even when they include excursions by rail from the distant parts of the town, does not exceed for each person, on an average, a quarter of a dollar; and when the arrangements are complete, I see no reason why thousands should not come every day where hundreds come now to use them; and if so, who can measure the value, generation after generation, of such provisions for recreation to the over-wrought, much-confined people of the great town that is to be?

For this purpose neither of the forms of ground we have heretofore considered are at all suitable. We want a ground to which people may easily go after their day's work is done, and where they may stroll for an hour, seeing, hearing, and feeling nothing of the bustle and jar of the streets, where they shall, in effect, find the city put far away from them. We want the greatest possible contrast with the streets and the shops and the rooms of the town which will be consistent with convenience and the preservation of good order and neatness. We want, especially, the greatest possible contrast with the restraining and confining conditions of the town, those conditions which compel us to walk circumspectly, watchfully, jealously, which compel us to look closely upon others without sympathy. Practically, what we most want is a simple, broad, open space of clean greensward, with sufficient play of surface and a sufficient number of trees about it to supply a variety of light and shade. This we want as a central feature. We want depth of wood enough about it not only for comfort in hot weather, but to completely shut out the city from our landscapes.

The word *park*, in town nomenclature, should, I think, be reserved for grounds of the character and purpose thus described.

[...]

A park fairly well managed near a large town, will surely become a new center of that town. With the determination of location, size, and boundaries should therefore be associated the duty of arranging new trunk routes of communication between it and the distant parts of the town existing and forecasted.

These may be either narrow informal elonga-tions of the park, varying say from two to five hundred feet in width, and radiating irregularly from it, or if, unfortunately, the town is already laid out in the unhappy way that New York and Brooklyn, San Francisco and Chicago, are, and, I am glad to say, Boston is not, on a plan made long years ago by a man who never saw a spring-carriage, and who had a conscientious dread of the Graces, then we must probably adopt formal Park-ways. They should be so planned and constructed as never to be noisy and seldom crowded, and so also that the straightforward movement of pleasure-car carriages need never be obstructed, unless at absolutely nec-essary crossings, by slow-going heavy vehicles used for commercial purposes. If possible, also, they should be branched or reticulated with other ways of a similar class, so that no part of the town should finally be many minutes' walk from some one of them; and they should be made interesting by a process of planting and decoration, so that in necessarily passing through them, whether in going to or from the park, or to and from business, some substantial recreative advantage may be inciden-tally gained. It is a common error to regard a park as something to be produced complete in itself, as a picture to be painted on canvas. It should rather be planned as one to be done in fresco, with con-stant consideration of exterior objects, some of them quite at a distance and even existing as yet only in the imagination of the painter.

I have thus barely indicated a few of the points from which we may perceive our duty to apply the means in our hands to ends far distant, with refer-ence to this problem of public recreations. Large operations of construction may not soon be desir-able, but I hope you will agree with me that there is little room for question, that reserves of ground for the purposes I have referred to should be fixed upon as soon as possible, before the difficulty of arranging them, which arises from private building, shall be greatly more formidable than now.

"The Meager and Unimaginative Character of Modern City Plans" and "Artistic Limitations of Modern City Planning"

from *City Planning According to Artistic Principles* (1898)

Camillo Sitte

Editors' Introduction

By the late nineteenth century, processes of modernization had speeded up and industrial mechanization of the building trades and bureaucratization of planning were taking hold. Rapid urban growth continued and people were witnessing immense changes to their cities as old areas were "modernized" and new ones were built to the modern aesthetic of straight lines and rectilinear, unornamented buildings. Within the emerging profession of city planning, an engineering approach was dominant. Public spaces were increasingly designed around the main goal of efficiently moving ever increasing amounts of carriage traffic. A faster, larger, less detailed, and less finely nuanced way of life was coming into being and was widely embraced.

Within this context, when to be modern meant looking completely to the future and ignoring the past, Viennese architect and city planner Camillo Sitte (1843–1903) argued that the past had much to offer. Coming from an arts and crafts tradition, he emerged as a strong voice for human scale in architecture, lamenting its lack in modern architecture along with the pervasive functional approach to urban design. Over a hundred years later, his laments sound familiar to our ears: the loss of public life from public spaces, bland environments, lack of detail, standardization, and excessively wide streets.

In his 1898 treatise *City Planning According to Artistic Principles*, from which these readings are taken, Sitte called for an "artistic renaissance" of city-building, arguing that a balance could be found between art and function. While giving full due to modern city planning for improving the sanitary conditions of cities, he severely criticized the profession's lack of ability to create new urban public spaces that were as good or as inviting to people as the old. He admired the picturesque qualities and human scale of pre-industrial European cities and argued for an approach to modernism that built on these traditions rather than discarded them. He advocated looking at the good public spaces of the past, determining their essential physical qualities, and applying those qualities to modern conditions. His ideas were grounded in extensive empirical observations, and he presented them using figure ground plans that analyzed and compared the spatial qualities of old and new plazas.

Sitte's ideas briefly found an audience and influenced numerous town planning ordinances throughout Europe. In the 1920s, however, modernist architects soundly renounced Sitte's theory – the architect Le Corbusier referring to Sitte's ideal of crooked streets as the pack-donkey's way. In 1965, Sitte's treatise was republished (Random House) and rediscovered by a new generation of humanistic architects and city planners. His ideas influenced the current New Urbanism movement, whose adherents look to Sitte as a seminal historic reference. His treatise was recently republished in translation under the title of *Camillo Sitte: The Birth of Modern City Planning* (Mineola, New York: Dover, 2006) by Christiane Crasemann Collins and George R. Collins.

Other writings on Sitte's ideas include Charles Bohl and Jean-François Lejeune, *Sitte, Hegemann and the Metropolis: Modern Civic Art and International Exchanges* (New York: Routledge, 2009). Two books in the same spirit as Sitte's *City Planning According to Artistic Principles* are Werner Hegemann and Elbert Peets, *American Vitruvius* (New York: B. Blom, 1972); and, much more recently, Andres Duany, Elizabeth Plater-Zyberk, and Robert Alminana, *The New Civic Art: Elements of Town Planning* (New York: Rizzoli, 2003).

THE MEAGER AND UNIMAGINATIVE CHARACTER OF MODERN CITY PLANS

How in recent times the history of the art of city building has failed to synchronize with the history of architecture and with that of the other creative arts is indeed astonishing. City planning stubbornly goes its own way, unconcerned with what transpires around it. This difference was already striking in the Renaissance and Baroque periods, but it has become even more pronounced in modern times as old styles have been revived once again. This time, of course, exactitude in imitation was taken much more seriously, the example of the Ancients being faithfully adhered to in every way possible. Actual copies of old structures were erected in monumental and costly fashion without answering any real need or practical purpose – merely out of enthusiasm for the splendor of ancient art. The Walhalla at Regensburg was created in the exact image of a Greek temple, the Loggia dei Lanzi found its imitation (the Feldherrn-Halle) at Munich, Early Christian basilicas were erected again, Greek propylaea and Gothic cathedrals were built, but what became of the plazas that belonged with them? Agora, forum, market place, acropolis – nobody remembered them.

The modern city-builder has been deprived in alarming fashion of the resources of his art. The precisely straight house-line and the cubic building-block are all that he can offer to compete with the wealth of the past. The architect is allowed millions to construct balconies, towers, gables, caryatids or anything else that his sketchbook might contain, and his sketchbook contains everything the past has ever created in any corner of the world. The town planner, on the other hand, is not given a penny for the installation of colonnades, porticoes, triumphal arches, or any other motifs that are essential to his art; not even the voids between the building blocks are put at his disposal for artistic use, because even the open air already belongs to someone else: the highway or sanitation engineer. So it has come to pass that all the good features of artistic city-building were dropped by the wayside one after the other, until nothing is left of them, not even a memory. Although we can see clearly the tremendous difference that exists between the old plazas, still charming as they are, and the monotonous modern ones, yet, despite this, we unfortunately consider it self-evident that churches and monuments must stand in the center of their plazas, that all streets must intersect at right angles and open wide all around a plaza, that the buildings need not close up about a square, and that monumental structures need not form part of such a closure. We are well aware of the effect of an old plaza, but how to produce it under modern conditions is not understood because we are no longer cognizant of the relation between cause and effect in these matters.

The theorist of modern city planning, R. Baumeister, says in his book about city expansion, '. . . the various elements which produce a pleasing architectural impression (as regards plazas) *are hardly reducible to universal rules.*' Does not this statement confirm what we have just said? Do not the results of what has been presented so far add up to precisely such general rules? – Enough rules, in fact, to compose a whole textbook on city planning, as well as a history of this art, if they are worked out in detail? A thorough study of the variations that the Baroque masters alone carried out would suffice to fill volumes. If, however, our first and thus far our only theorist in this field can express the above opinion, does this not demonstrate that we are now no longer aware of the relationship between cause and effect?

Today nobody is concerned with city planning as an art – only as a technical problem. When, as a result, the artistic effect in no way lives up to our expectations, we are left bewildered and helpless; nevertheless, in dealing with the next project it is again treated wholly from the technical point of view, as if it were the layout of a railroad in which artistic questions are not involved.

Even in modern histories of art, which discuss every insignificant thing, city planning has not been granted the humblest little spot, whereas bookbinding, pewter work, and costume design are readily allowed space next to Phidias and Michelangelo. From this it might be understood that we have lost the thread of artistic tradition in city planning, although it is not clear why. But now back to our analysis of the matter at hand.

There exist an infinite variety of derogatory opinions about modern planning. In the daily press and in professional publications they are repeated again and again. However, the most they do is to attribute the cause of bad effects to an overly pedantic straightness of line in our house fronts. Even Baumeister says, 'one rightly laments the boredom of modern streets,' and he then criticizes the 'unwieldy massive effect' of modern blocks of buildings. With regard to the siting of monuments it is only reported that several major 'monumental' catastrophes can be listed; yet no reason for the bad effects is ever given, since it is as irrevocable as natural law that every monument can only be placed in the middle of its plaza, in order that one also may have a good look at the celebrity from the rear. One of the most discerning opinions, which Baumeister mentioned, can be quoted here. It is from the Paris *Figaro* of August 23, 1874, and it says in a report about the trip of Marshal MacMahon:

Rennes does not actually feel an antipathy toward the Marshal, but the town is totally incapable of any enthusiasm. I have noticed that this is the case with all towns that are laid out along straight lines and in which the streets intersect at right angles. The straight line prevents any excitement from arising. Thus one could also observe in the year 1870 how the completely regularly designed towns could be captured by three lancers, while really old and twisted towns were ready to defend themselves to the utmost.

Straight lines and right angles are certainly characteristic of insensitive planning, but are apparently not decisive in this matter, because Baroque planning also used straight lines and right angles, achieving powerful and truly artistic effects in spite of them. In the layout of streets it is true that rectilinearity is a weakness. An undeviating boulevard, miles long, seems boring even in the most beautiful surroundings. It is unnatural, it does not adapt itself to irregular terrain, and it remains uninteresting in effect, so that, mentally fatigued, one can hardly await its termination. An ordinary street, if excessively long, has the same effect. But as the more frequent shorter streets of modern planning also produce an unfortunate effect, there must be some other cause for it. It is the same as in the plazas, namely *faulty closure of the sides of the street*. The continual breaching by wide cross streets, so that on both sides nothing is left but a row of separated blocks of buildings, is the main reason why no unified impression can be attained. This may be demonstrated most clearly by comparing old arcades with their modern imitations. Ancient arcades, nothing short of magnificent in their architectural detail, run uninterruptedly along the whole curve of a street as far as the eye can see; or they encircle a plaza enclosing it completely; or at least they run unbroken along one side of it. Their whole effect is based on continuity, for only by it can the succession of arches become a large enough unity to create an impact. The situation is completely different in modern planning. Although occasional outstanding architects have, in their enthusiasm for this magnificent old motif, succeeded in providing us with such covered walks – as, for instance, in Vienna around the Votive Church and at the new Rathaus – these hardly remind us of the ancient models, because their effect is totally different. The separate sections are larger and much more sumptuously carried out than almost any ancient predecessors. Yet the intended effect is absent. Why? Because each separate loggia is attached to its own building-block, and the cuts made by the numerous broad cross streets prevent the slightest effect of continuity. Only if the openings of these intersecting streets were spanned by a continuation of the arcade could any coherence result that might then create a grandiose impression. Lacking this, the dismembered motif is like a hoe without a handle.

For the same reason a coherent effect does not come about in our streets. A modern street is made up primarily of corner buildings. A row of isolated blocks of buildings is going to look bad under any circumstances, even if placed in a curved line.

These considerations bring us close to the crux of the matter. In modern city planning the ratio between the built-up and the open spaces is exactly reversed. Formerly the empty spaces (streets and plazas) were a unified entity of shapes calculated for their impact; today building lots are laid out as regularly-shaped closed forms, and what is left over between them become streets or plazas. Formerly all that was crooked and ugly lay hidden in the built-up areas; today in the process of laying out the various building lots all irregular wedges that are left over become plazas, since the prime rule is that '*architecturally* speaking, a street pattern should first of all provide convenient house plans. Therefore street crossings at right angles are an advantage. And it is certainly wrong to adopt irregular angles as a principle of parcelling' (Baumeister). Well, but what architect is afraid of an irregularly-shaped building lot? Indeed, that would be a man who has not advanced beyond the most elementary principles of planning. Irregular building lots are just the ones that allow, without exception, the most interesting solutions and usually the better ones; not only because they demand a more careful study of the plan and prevent mechanical, run-of-the-mill design, but because, in the interior of such a building, wedge-shaped pieces are repeatedly left over and are splendidly suited for all sorts of little extra rooms (elevators, spiral-staircases, storage rooms, toilets, etc.), a feature which we miss in regular plans. To recommend rectangular building lots for their presumed architectural advantage is completely wrong. This could only be done by those who do not understand how to lay out ground plans. Is it possible that all the attractiveness of streets and plazas could fall victim to such a trivial misconception? It would almost seem so.

Studying the ground plan of a complicated building on an irregular building lot, one finds, if it is well designed, that all halls, chambers, and other principal rooms are of excellent proportion. Here again, irregularities are concealed in the thickness of the walls or in the shape of the service rooms described above. Nobody likes a triangular room, because the sight of it is unbearable and because furniture can never be well placed in it. Yet the circle or the ellipse of a spiral staircase can be accommodated nicely in it by varying the thickness of the wall. It is quite similar to what we find in ancient city plans. The hall-like forums were of regular shape, their voids calculated for their visible effect, while all their irregularities were absorbed in the mass of surrounding structures. This was carried out down to the smallest detail, and in the end every irregularity of the site seems to dissolve away and be hidden in the thickness of the walls; it is simple and very clever. Today the exact opposite of this takes place. As illustrations, we take three plazas from the same city, Trieste: the Piazza della Caserma, the Piazza della Legna, and the Piazza della Borsa. Artistically speaking, these are not really plazas at all, but only triangularly-shaped remnants of empty space, left over in the cutting out of right-angled city blocks. When one then notices the frequency of broad, unfavorable street openings, it becomes immediately clear that it is just as impossible to position a monument on such plazas as to show a building off to advantage. Such a plaza is as unbearable as a triangular room.

Regarding this, one thing needs further discussion. A special chapter has already been devoted to proving the appropriateness of the irregularity of old plazas. One might expect it also to be applicable here. But such is not the case, for between the two kinds of irregularity there is a crucial difference: the irregularity present in (the above mentioned plazas) is obvious and immediately observable to the eye, and it becomes the more awkward, the more regular the adjoining building façades and nearby town sections are shaped; on the contrary, the other irregularities were of a kind that deceived the eye, being noticeable on the drawing board, of course, but not in actuality.

Something similar occurs in ancient structures. In the ground plans of Romanesque and Gothic churches one rarely finds the various axes at right angles to each other, since the old masters were unable to gauge this accurately enough. It does not matter in this case, because it goes unnoticed.

Similarly, there are great irregularities in the ground plans of ancient temple structures as regards the intercolumniation, etc. All this one only detects with precise measurement, not by the naked eye; it mattered little, since they were building for visual effect and not for the sake of the plan on paper. On the other hand, one has discovered almost incredible refinements in the curvatures of entablature, etc., refinements which, although they almost elude measurement, were carried out because their absence would have been noticed by the eye, and it was the eye that counted. The more comparisons we make between the old and the new methods, the more the contrast builds up, and every time the comparison turns out to the artistic disadvantage of the modern. We should keep in mind our senseless avoidance at any cost of projections and recessions in frontage lines, as well as our dread of curved streets, and the fact that, as regards height, all our houses tend to have a uniform horizontal termination. They almost always take advantage of the maximum allowable height, emphasizing the harshness of that line with a real sample-chart of ostentatious cornices. Finally we should not forget the endless rows of windows of identical size and shape, the overabundance of small pilasters and continuously repeated curlicues (mostly of ineffectually small dimension and poor industrial execution, in poured concrete, etc.), and the absence of large quiet wall surfaces, avoided even where they might result naturally since they are punctuated with blind windows.

ARTISTIC LIMITATIONS OF MODERN CITY PLANNING

Modern city planning is obliged to forgo a significant number of artistic motifs. Regardless of how painful this may be to sensitive souls, the practical artist should not let himself be guided by sentimental impulses, because no artistic (*malerisch*) planning could be a thorough or lasting success unless it complied with modern living conditions. In our public life much has irrevocably changed, depriving certain old building forms of their original purpose, and about this nothing can be done. We cannot change the fact that today public events are discussed in the daily papers, instead of, as in ancient Greece or Rome, being talked over by public readers and town criers in the baths and porticoes and on the open square. We cannot alter the fact that marketing has withdrawn more and more from the plazas, partly into inartistic commercial structures, partly to disappear completely because of direct delivery to the home. We cannot prevent the public fountains from being reduced to a merely ornamental role; the colorful, lively crowd stays away from them because modern plumbing carries the water much more conveniently directly into house and kitchen. Works of art are straying increasingly from streets and plazas into the 'art-cages' of the museums; likewise, the colorful bustle of folk festivals, of carnivals and other parades, of religious processions, of theatrical performances in the open market place, etc., disappears. The life of the common people has for centuries been steadily withdrawing from public squares, and especially so in recent times. Owing to this, a substantial part of the erstwhile significance of squares has been lost, and it becomes quite understandable why the appreciation of beautiful plaza design has decreased so markedly among the broad mass of citizenry. Life in former times was, after all, decidedly more favorable to an artistic development of city building than is our mathematically-precise modern life. Man himself has become almost a machine, and our frame of reference has shifted, not only on the whole but also in detail, since the changed conditions of our time imperiously demand many modifications.

It is above all the enormous size to which our larger cities are growing that has shattered the framework of traditional artistic forms at every point. The larger the city, the bigger and wider the plazas and streets become, and the higher and bulkier are all structures, until their dimensions, what with their numerous floors and interminable rows of windows, can hardly be organized any more in an artistically effective manner. Everything tends toward the immense, and the constant repetition of identical motifs is enough to dull our senses to such an extent that only the most powerful effects can still make any impression. As this cannot be altered, the city planner must, like the architect, invent a scale appropriate for the modern city of millions. With such an extraordinary concentration of people at one location, real estate values also increase exorbitantly, and it is not possible for an individual person or the local administration to escape the inevitable effects of this increase in value. Everywhere, as if spontaneously, lots are divided up and streets are broken through so that even in the old parts of town more and more side streets result, and something of the obnoxious building-block system surreptitiously takes over. This is a phenomenon which is naturally connected with the current value of real estate and the value of street-frontage lines; hence it cannot be eliminated by decree, least of all by aesthetic considerations. All these elements must be reckoned with as stated factors that the city planner has to take into account just as an architect must consider the strength of materials and the laws of statics – even if they impose the most disagreeable and petty limitations.

The regular parcelling of lots based on purely economic considerations has become such a factor in new plans that its effects can hardly be avoided. In spite of this one should not surrender quite so blindly to the consequences of this universal method, because it is precisely this that has led to mass slaughter of the beauties of city planning. These are the very beauties which are designated by the word 'pictorial' (*malerisch*). In a rigidly uniform arrangement where do all the picturesque street corners end up? These are a delight in old Nuremberg and anywhere else where they have still been preserved, because of the originality of their appearance: the street panoramas at the Fembohaus in Nuremberg, at the Rathaus in Heilbronn or the Brauerei of Görlitz, at the Petersenhaus in Nuremberg, and elsewhere. However, they are unfortunately diminishing in number from year to year because of constant demolition.

The high price of building lots leads to their utmost utilization, as a result of which a number of effective motifs have been abandoned in recent years. Completely building up each lot always tends to produce the characteristic cubic mass of modern times. Projections, porches, ornamental staircases, arcades, corner turrets, etc., have become for us an unthinkable luxury, even on public buildings; only high up – in the form of balconies and bay windows or on the roof – is the architect allowed to give his imagination free rein, but never below at street level where the 'building-frontage line' alone dominates. This has already become so customary that many splendid motifs, such as the monumental open staircase, no longer please us. And this whole

class of architectural elements has retreated from street and plaza into the interior of buildings, yielding to the universal trend of the time – the fear of open spaces. Yet when all the devices for achieving an effect have been discontinued how can the effect itself still be preserved? Just imagine the old city halls of Leiden or Bolsward without their splendid staircases, or the beautiful hill of the Rathaus at Heilbronn without its two corner monuments and ornamental stairway – what would still remain of their uniqueness? The artistic impact of these contrivances, so impractical according to modern standards, contributes to the adornment and embellishment of the whole town. In view of the banality now so prevalent, it would be futile to try to suggest anything similar for a new structure. Today what architect would dare to include in his design such a charming group of forms as the flight of steps, terrace, pulpit, and statue of Justice that are all combined on one street corner at the Rathaus in Görlitz? The handsome stairs, arcades, and balconies of the old city halls at Lübeck and Lemgo, of the smaller city halls at Haag (1564–1565), and at Ochsenfurth, and of so many others are, then, treasures of a past that was imbued with an enjoyment of life that has ceased for us.

As we reflect on this we become aware of the special significance of what is called 'Zeitgeist.' The whole world admires the Doge's Palace in Venice and the Capitol at Rome, yet nobody would dare propose that something comparable be constructed today. Also famous are the loggia, stairway, balconies, and gables of the Rathaus at Halberstadt, the similar combinations with staircases on the town halls of Brussels, of Deventer (1643), of Hoogstraeten, of The Hague, and the impressive portico and staircase of the Rathaus at Rothenburg o.d. Tauber. However, modern sensibilities reject such stairways, and the mere thought of slippery ice or a snow drift in the winter is enough to dispel any romantic illusions about the past. Still more besides: for us modern stay-at-homes stairs are exclusively an interior motif, and we have become so sensitive in this connection and so unaccustomed to the hubbub of streets and plazas that we cannot work when someone is watching us, we do not like to dine by an open window because somebody could look in, and the balconies of our houses usually remain empty. It is precisely *the external use of interior architectural elements* (staircases, galleries, etc.) that is a most essential ingredient in the charm of ancient and medieval designs. The striking picturesqueness of Amalfi, for example, is due mainly to its really grotesque confusion between interior and exterior motifs, so that one finds oneself at the same time inside a house and on the street, and at one spot simultaneously on the ground level and on an upper floor, depending on the interpretation one wishes to give the peculiar structural combinations. It is this which leaves the collector of vistas in a transport of delight and is what we are presented with in the stage scenery of theaters. Yet a modern section of town is never chosen for stage scenery because it would really be much too dull.

This contrasting of imaginative stage-sets and prosaic reality makes the idiosyncrasies of the picturesque, on the one hand, compare most vividly with the practical on the other. Our modern building block does not suit the theater, where artistic effectiveness is the only criterion; nevertheless, it is dubious whether in most cases we would want to translate the richly pictorial stage set into reality. Its wealth of effective motifs would certainly be desirable, and, if it were feasible, stronger architectural projections, more frequent interruptions of the building line, zig-zag and winding streets, uneven street widths, different heights of houses, flights of stairs, loggias, balconies, gables, and whatever else make up the picturesque trappings of stage architecture would in the end be no misfortune for a modern city. Yet, looking at this not just aesthetically, but as a practical builder, one knows very well that there are more obstacles to it than might be thought likely at first glance. It is utterly impossible to transpose from the ideal into reality that large class of picturesque details whose charm derives from their unfinished or ruined character. Although that which is falling apart or even dirty and which has gay touches of color or varied stone textures may look effective in a painting, in reality it appears totally different. Old castle grounds are well liked for a short visit during the warm summer months, but for permanent residence a new modern structure with its many comforts is still preferred.

It would, moreover, be quite short-sighted not to recognize the extraordinary achievements of modern city planning in contrast to that of old in the field of hygiene. In this our modern engineers, so much maligned because of their artistic blunders, have literally performed miracles and have rendered everlasting service to mankind. It is largely due to their work that the sanitary conditions of European cities have improved so remarkably – as is apparent from mortality figures which have in many cases been halved. How many individual improvements must have transpired, to the benefit of all city dwellers, for such results to emerge! This we gladly grant, but there still remains the question as to whether it is really necessary to purchase these advantages at the tremendous price of abandoning all artistic beauty in the layout of cities.

The innate conflict between the picturesque and the practical cannot be eliminated merely by talking about it; it will always be present as something intrinsic to the very nature of things. This inner struggle between the two opposing demands is not, however, characteristic of town planning alone; it is present in all the arts, even in those apparently the freest, if only as a conflict between their ideal goals and the limiting conditions of the material in which the work of art is supposed to take shape. A work of art that is not subject to these limitations can perhaps be imagined abstractly, but never realized materially. The practical artist is always faced with the necessity of embodying his ideas within the range of technical possibilities. These restraints are narrow or broad according to his technical means or depending on the various ideal aspirations and the practical, demands of a given period in time; nobody would deny this who has carefully studied the history of art.

In the field of city planning the limitations on artistry of arrangement have, to be sure, narrowed greatly in our day. Today such a masterpiece of city planning as the Acropolis of Athens is simply unthinkable. That sort of thing is for us, at the moment, an impossibility. Even if the millions were provided that such a project would entail, we would still be unable to create something of the kind, because we lack both the artistic basis for it and any universally valid philosophy of life that has sufficient vigor in the soul of the people to find physical expression in the work. Yet even if the commission be devoid of content and merely decorative – as is the case with art today – it would be frightfully difficult for our realistic man of the nineteenth century. Today's city builder must, before all, acquire the noble virtue of an utmost humility, and, what is remarkable in this case, less for economic considerations than for really basic reasons.

Assuming that in any new development the cityscape (*Stadtbild*) must be made as splendid and pictorial as possible, if only decoratively in order to glorify the locality – such a purpose cannot be accomplished with the ruler or with our geometrically-straight street lines. In order to produce the effects of the old masters, their colors as well must form part of our palette. Sundry curves, twisted streets and irregularities would have to be included artificially in the plan; an affected artlessness, a purposeful unintentionalness. But can the accidents of history over the course of centuries be invented and constructed *ex novo* in the plan? Could one, then, truly and sincerely enjoy such a fabricated ingenuousness, such a studied naturalness? Certainly not. The satisfaction of a spontaneous gaiety is denied to any cultural level in which building does not proceed at apparent random from day to day, but instead constructs its plans intellectually on the drawing board. This whole course of events, moreover, cannot be reversed, and consequently a large portion of the picturesque beauties we have mentioned will probably be irretrievably lost to use in contemporary planning. Modern living as well as modern building techniques no longer permit the faithful imitation of old townscapes, a fact which we cannot overlook

without falling prey to barren fantasies. The exemplary creations of the old masters must remain alive with us in some other way than through slavish copying; only if we can determine in what the essentials of these creations consist, and if we can apply these meaningfully to modern conditions, will it be possible to harvest a new and flourishing crop from the apparently sterile soil.

An attempt should be made regardless of obstacles. Even if numerous pictorial beauties must be renounced and extensive consideration be given to the requirements of modern construction, hygiene, and transportation, this should not discourage us to the extent that we simply abandon artistic solutions and settle for purely technical ones, as in the building of a highway or the construction of a machine. The forever edifying impress of artistic perfection cannot be dispensed with in our busy everyday life. One must keep in mind that city planning in particular must allow full and complete participation to art, because it is this type of artistic endeavor, above all, that affects formatively every day and every hour the great mass of the population, whereas the theater and concerts are available only to the wealthier classes. Administrators of public works in cities should turn their attention to this matter.

"Author's Introduction" and "The Town–Country Magnet"

from *Garden Cities of To-morrow* (1898/1902)

Ebenezer Howard

Editors' Introduction

Ebenezer Howard's Garden City vision was one of the most captivating planning and design ideas of the late nineteenth century. It spurred considerable thought about remedies for the perceived ills of industrial cities, strains of which continue to this day, and it inspired and continues to inspire the creation of new towns and "garden" suburbs in England and America and elsewhere.

A stenographer by trade, Ebenezer Howard (1850–1928) was a modest man with no formal planning or design training who became interested in cities through his own experience of difficult urban conditions. Born in London, England, into a family of shopkeepers, he emigrated to America at the age of 21 and settled in Nebraska with the intention of farming. Finding himself unsuited to farming life, he moved to Chicago where he worked as a journalist and witnessed the rebuilding of the city following the great fire. Back in England by 1876 he found work as a Parliamentary reporter and worked in this profession for the rest of his life. He became involved with political movements and was introduced to the writings of radical theorists and visionaries including social reformer Robert Owen and utopian novelist Edward Bellamy. Inspired, he began developing his own ideas for cities of the future. In 1898, he published *To-morrow: a Peaceful Path to Real Reform* (now better known under its 1902 title, *Garden Cities of To-morrow*) and set about advocating the beauty and utility of his "the Garden City idea."

Howard's idea is articulated through a series of diagrams buttressed by theoretical arguments. He begins by identifying overcrowding as the source of urban ills, and then analyzes why people are attracted to cities because of higher wages and greater social opportunities in spite of the hardships that come with city life, and why rural life is less compelling for many in spite of the beauty and fresh air available in the countryside. In his famous "Three Magnets" diagram, he juxtaposes the pros and cons of urban life under a town magnet, the pros and cons of rural life under a country magnet, and combines the pros of both under a town–country magnet. The thinking is that "town and country must be married" and "out of this joyous union will spring new hope, a new life, a new civilization." Effectively, Howard proposes that the downsides of urban and rural life can be eliminated by a joining of the two in a new urban form, the garden city.

Other diagrams, which Howard stresses are conceptual ideas rather than actual plans, show the layout of an ideal garden city for 32,000 people. A central city of 1,000 acres is surrounded by a 5,000-acre greenbelt of agricultural land. The city itself comprises several concentric rings – a central garden surrounded by a park containing important public buildings, a "Crystal Palace" ring of retail shops, a broad ring of single family homes punctuated by a "Grand Avenue" containing a generous park strip in which public schools and churches are situated, and an outer ring of "factories, warehouses, dairies, markets, coal yards, timber yards" fronting on a railway line that circles the whole town. A regional scale diagram entitled "Group of Slumless Smokeless Cities" shows how a population of 250,000 people could be accommodated on 66,000 acres within six garden cities arrayed around a somewhat larger central city, connected by concentric rings and lateral spurs of canals and railways. Along with these utopian physical arrangements comes a radical social idea: each garden city is to be largely independent, financed and managed by local citizens.

Unlike many utopian visionaries, Howard saw his ideas put into practice, although in somewhat compromised form. In England, Letchworth Garden City was built in the early 1900s and Welwyn Garden City was built after World War I. The Garden City idea quickly spread to continental Europe, America, and beyond. In the United States it inspired the creation of several New Deal Greenbelt towns and numerous garden suburbs, such as Sunnyside in Queens, and influenced Clarence Stein and Henry Wright's design for the town of Radburn, New Jersey. More recently, New Urbanism theorist and practitioner Peter Calthorpe has reconceptualized the Garden City idea in the form of suburban transit-oriented developments (TODs) linked to cities and each other with light-rail transit networks.

Garden Cities of To-morrow remains an engaging and thought provoking text and is available in a variety of formats and editions. The original edition appeared under the title *To-morrow: A Peaceful Path to Real Reform* (Sonnenschein, 1898), and an elegant new edition is now available, under the original title, edited by Peter Hall and Colin Ward (New York: Routledge, 2003). A recent reprint is available under the title *Garden Cities of To-morrow* (New York: Classic Books International, 2010.) In addition, the book was also reprinted as the second volume of Richard T. LeGates and Frederic Stout (eds), *Early Urban Planning* (nine volumes, London: Routledge/Thoemmes, 1998) and in earlier editions by Attic Books (1985), Eastbourne (1985), MIT Press (1965), and Faber and Faber (1960, 1951, and 1946).

Biographies of Ebenezer Howard include Robert Beevers, *The Garden City Utopia: A Critical Biography of Ebenezer Howard* (New York: St. Martin's, 1988) and Dugald Macfadyen, *Sir Ebenezer Howard and the Town Planning Movement* (Manchester: Manchester University Press, 1933; reprinted MIT Press, 1970). Thorough accounts of Howard and the Garden City movement may be found in Robert Fishman's *Urban Utopias in the Twentieth Century* (New York: Basic Books, 1977) and Peter Hall's *Cities of Tomorrow* (Oxford: Basil Blackwell, 1988). Analysis of Howard's ideas and the Garden City Movement from an urban form perspective may be found in Spiro Kostof's *The City Shaped: Urban Patterns and Meanings Through History* (London: Little, Brown and Company, 1991) and *The City Assembled: The Elements of Urban Form Through History*, 1992).

Additional books about Ebenezer Howard and the Garden City movement include Kermit Parsons and David Schuyler (eds), *From the Garden City to Green Cities: The Legacy of Ebenezer Howard* (Baltimore, MD: Johns Hopkins University Press, 2002); Standish Meacham, *Regaining Paradise: Englishness and the Early Garden City Movement* (Princeton, NJ: Yale University Press, 1999); Peter Geoffrey Hall and Colin Ward, *Sociable Cities: The Legacy of Ebenezer Howard* (New York: John Wiley & Sons, 1998); Stephen V. Ward (ed.), *The Garden City: Past, Present and Future* (London and New York: E & FN Spon, 1992); and Stanley Buder, *Visionaries and Planners: The Garden City Movement and the Modern Community* (Oxford: Oxford University Press, 1990).

AUTHOR'S INTRODUCTION

In these days of strong party feeling and of keenly contested social and religious issues, it might perhaps be thought difficult to find a single question having a vital bearing upon national life and well-being on which all persons, no matter of what political party, or of what shade of sociological opinion, would be found to be fully and entirely agreed . . .

[. . .]

There is, however, a question in regard to which one can scarcely find any difference of opinion . . . It is wellnigh universally agreed by men of all parties, not only in England, but all over Europe and America and our colonies, that it is deeply to be deplored that the people should continue to stream into the already over-crowded cities, and should thus further deplete the country districts.

All . . . are agreed on the pressing nature of this problem, all are bent on its solution, and though it would doubtless be quite Utopian to expect a similar agreement as to the value of any remedy that may be proposed, it is at least of immense importance that, on a subject thus universally regarded as of supreme importance, we have such a consensus of opinion at the outset. This will be the more remarkable and the more hopeful sign when it is shown, as I believe will be conclusively shown in this work, that the answer to this, one of the most pressing questions of the day, makes of comparatively easy solution many other problems which have hitherto taxed the ingenuity of the greatest thinkers and reformers of our time. Yes, the key to the problem how to restore the people to the land – that beautiful land of ours, with its canopy of sky, the air that blows upon it, the sun that warms it, the rain and dew that moisten it – the very embodiment of Divine love for man – is indeed a Master Key, for it is the key to a portal through which, even when scarce ajar, will be seen to pour a flood of light on the problems of intemperance, of excessive toil, of restless anxiety, of grinding poverty – the true limits of Governmental interference, ay, and even the relations of man to the Supreme Power.

It may perhaps be thought that the first step to be taken towards the solution of this question – how to restore the people to the land – would involve a careful consideration of the very numerous causes which have hitherto led to their aggregation in large cities. Were this the case, a very prolonged enquiry would be necessary at the outset. Fortunately, alike for writer and for reader, such an analysis is not, however, here requisite, and for a very simple reason, which may be stated thus: Whatever may have been the causes which have operated in the past, and are operating now, to draw the people into the cities, those causes may all be summed up as "attractions"; and it is obvious, therefore, that no remedy can possibly be effective which will not present to the people, or at least to considerable portions of them, greater "attractions" than our cities now possess, so that the force of the old "attractions" shall be overcome by the force of new "attractions" which are to be created. Each city may be regarded as a magnet, each person as a needle; and, so viewed, it is at once seen that nothing short of the discovery of a method for constructing magnets of yet greater power than our cities possess can be effective for redistributing

the population in a spontaneous and healthy manner.

So presented, the problem may appear at first sight to be difficult, if not impossible, of solution. "What", some may be disposed to ask, "can possibly be done to make the country more attractive to a workaday people than the town – to make wages, or at least the standard of physical comfort, higher in the country than in the town; to secure in the country equal possibilities of social intercourse, and to make the prospects of advancement for the average man or woman equal, not to say superior, to those enjoyed in our large cities?" The issue one constantly finds presented in a form very similar to that. The subject is treated continually in the public press, and in all forms of discussion, as though men, or at least working men, had not now, and never could have, any choice or alternative, but either, on the one hand, to stifle their love for human society – at least in wider relations than can be found in a straggling village – or, on the other hand, to forgo almost entirely all the keen and pure delights of the country. The question is universally considered as though it were now, and for ever must remain, quite impossible for working people to live in the country and yet be engaged in pursuits other than agricultural; as though crowded, unhealthy cities were the last word of economic science; and as if our present form of industry, in which sharp lines divide agricultural from industrial pursuits, were necessarily an enduring one. This fallacy is the very common one of ignoring altogether the possibility of alternatives other than those presented to the mind. There are in reality not only, as is so constantly assumed, two alternatives – town life and country life – but a third alternative, in which all the advantages of the most energetic and active town life, with all the beauty and delight of the country, may be secured in perfect combination; and the certainty of being able to live this life will be the magnet which will produce the effect for which we are all striving – the spontaneous movement of the people from our crowded cities to the bosom of our kindly mother earth, at once the source of life, of happiness, of wealth, and of power. The town and the country may, therefore, be regarded as two magnets, each striving to draw the people to itself – a rivalry which a new form of life, partaking of the nature of both, comes to take part in. This may be illustrated by

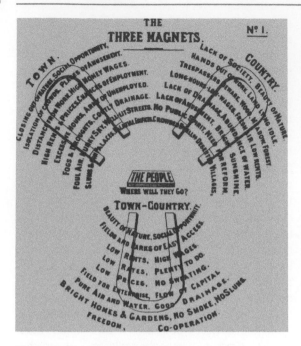

Figure 1 The Three Magnets.

a diagram (Figure 1) of "The Three Magnets", in which the chief advantages of the Town and of the Country are set forth with their corresponding drawbacks, while the advantages of the Town–Country are seen to be free from the disadvantages of either.

The Town magnet, it will be seen, offers, as compared with the Country magnet, the advantages of high wages, opportunities for employment, tempting prospects of advancement, but these are largely counterbalanced by high rents and prices. Its social opportunities and its places of amusement are very alluring, but excessive hours of toil, distance from work, and the "isolation of crowds" tend greatly to reduce the value of these good things. The well-lit streets are a great attraction, especially in winter, but the sunlight is being more and more shut out, while the air is so vitiated that the fine public buildings, like the sparrows, rapidly become covered with soot, and the very statues are in despair. Palatial edifices and fearful slums are the strange, complementary features of modern cities.

The Country magnet declares herself to be the source of all beauty and wealth; but the Town magnet mockingly reminds her that she is very dull for lack of society, and very sparing of her gifts for lack of capital. There are in the country beautiful vistas, lordly parks, violet-scented woods, fresh air, sounds of rippling water; but too often one sees those threatening words, "Trespassers will be prosecuted". Rents, if estimated by the acre, are certainly low, but such low rents are the natural fruit of low wages rather than a cause of substantial comfort; while long hours and lack of amusements forbid the bright sunshine and the pure air to gladden the hearts of the people. The one industry, agriculture, suffers frequently from excessive rainfalls; but this wondrous harvest of the clouds is seldom properly in-gathered, so that, in times of drought, there is frequently, even for drinking purposes, a most insufficient supply. Even the natural healthfulness of the country is largely lost for lack of proper drainage and other sanitary conditions, while, in parts almost deserted by the people, the few who remain are yet frequently huddled together as if in rivalry with the slums of our cities.

But neither the Town magnet nor the Country magnet represents the full plan and purpose of nature. Human society and the beauty of nature are meant to be enjoyed together. The two magnets must be made one. As man and woman by their varied gifts and faculties supplement each other, so should town and country. The town is the symbol of society – of mutual help and friendly co-operation, of fatherhood, motherhood, brotherhood, sisterhood, of wide relations between man and man – of broad, expanding sympathies – of science, art, culture, religion. And the country! The country is the symbol of God's love and care for man. All that we are and all that we have comes from it. Our bodies are formed of it; to it they return. We are fed by it, clothed by it, and by it are we warmed and sheltered. On its bosom we rest. Its beauty is the inspiration of art, of music, of poetry. Its forces propel all the wheels of industry. It is the source of all health, all wealth, all knowledge. But its fullness of joy and wisdom has not revealed itself to man. Nor can it ever, so long as this unholy, unnatural separation of society and nature endures. Town and country must be married, and out of this joyous union will spring a new hope, a new life, a new civilization. It is the purpose of this work to show how a first step can be taken in this direction by the construction of a Town–Country magnet; and I hope to convince the reader that this is practicable, here and now, and that on principles which are the very soundest, whether viewed from the ethical or the economic standpoint.

I will undertake, then, to show how in "Town–Country" equal, nay better, opportunities of social intercourse may be enjoyed than are enjoyed in any crowded city, while yet the beauties of nature may encompass and enfold each dweller therein; how higher wages are compatible with reduced rents and rates; how abundant opportunities for employment and bright prospects of advancement may be secured for all; how capital may be attracted and wealth created; how the most admirable sanitary conditions may be ensured; how beautiful homes and gardens may be seen on every hand; how the bounds of freedom may be widened, and yet all the best results of concert and co-operation gathered in by a happy people.

The construction of such a magnet, could it be effected, followed, as it would be, by the construction of many more, would certainly afford a solution of the burning question set before us by Sir John Gorst, "how to back the tide of migration of the people into the towns, and to get them back upon the land".

[. . .]

THE TOWN–COUNTRY MAGNET

The reader is asked to imagine an estate embracing an area of 6,000 acres, which is at present purely agricultural, and has been obtained by purchase in the open market at a cost of £40 an acre, or £240,000. The purchase money is supposed to have been raised on mortgage debentures, bearing interest at an average rate not exceeding 4 per cent. The estate is legally vested in the names of four gentlemen of responsible position and of undoubted probity and honour, who hold it in trust, first, as a security for the debenture-holders, and, secondly, in trust for the people of Garden City, the Town–Country magnet, which it is intended to build thereon. One essential feature of the plan is that all ground rents, which are to be based upon the annual value of the land, shall be paid to the trustees, who, after providing for interest and sinking fund, will hand the balance to the Central Council of the new municipality, to be employed by such Council in the creation and maintenance of all necessary public works – roads, schools, parks, etc. The objects of this land purchase may be stated in various ways, but it is sufficient here to say that

some of the chief objects are these: To find for our industrial population work at wages of higher purchasing power, and to secure healthier surroundings and more regular employment. To enterprising manufacturers, co-operative societies, architects, engineers, builders, and mechanicians of all kinds, as well as to many engaged in various professions, it is intended to offer a means of securing new and better employment for their capital and talents, while to the agriculturists at present on the estate as well as to those who may migrate thither, it is designed to open a new market for their produce close to their doors. Its object is, in short, to raise the standard of health and comfort of all true workers of whatever grade – the means by which these objects are to be achieved being a healthy, natural, and economic combination of town and country life, and this on land owned by the municipality.

Garden City, which is to be built near the centre of the 6,000 acres, covers an area of 1,000 acres, or a sixth part of the 6,000 acres, and might be of circular form, 1,240 yards (or nearly three-quarters of a mile) from centre to circumference. (Figure 2 is a ground plan of the whole municipal area, showing the town in the centre; and Figure 3, which represents one section or ward of the town, will be useful in following the description of the town itself – a description which is, however, merely suggestive, and will probably be much departed from. . . .)

Six magnificent boulevards – each 120 feet wide – traverse the city from centre to circumference, dividing it into six equal parts or wards. In the centre is a circular space containing about five and a half acres, laid out as a beautiful and well-watered garden; and, surrounding this garden, each standing in its own ample grounds, are the larger public buildings – town hall, principal concert and lecture hall, theatre, library, museum, picture-gallery, and hospital.

The rest of the large space encircled by the "Crystal Palace" is a public park, containing 145 acres, which includes ample recreation grounds within very easy access of all the people.

Running all round the Central Park (except where it is intersected by the boulevards) is a wide glass arcade called the "Crystal Palace", opening on to the park. This building is in wet weather one of the favourite resorts of the people, whilst the knowledge that its bright shelter is ever close at

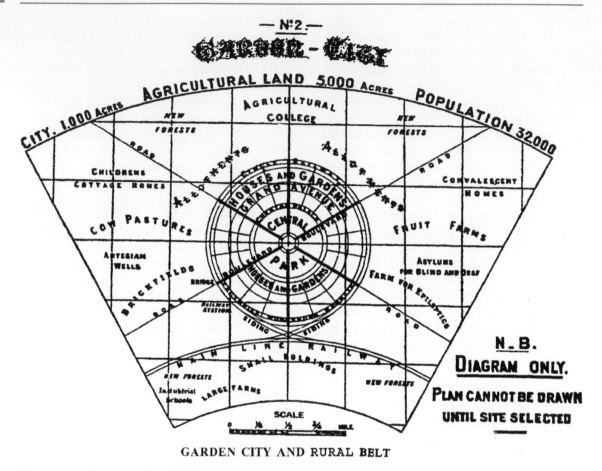

GARDEN CITY AND RURAL BELT

Figure 2 Garden City and Rural Belt.

hand tempts people into Central Park, even in the most doubtful of weathers. Here manufactured goods are exposed for sale, and here most of that class of shopping which requires the joy of deliberation and selection is done. The space enclosed by the Crystal Palace is, however, a good deal larger than is required for these purposes, and a considerable part of it is used as a Winter Garden – the whole forming a permanent exhibition of a most attractive character, whilst its circular form brings it near to every dweller in the town – the furthest removed inhabitant being within 600 yards.

Passing out of the Crystal Palace on our way to the outer ring of the town, we cross Fifth Avenue – lined, as are all the roads of the town, with trees – fronting which, and looking on to the Crystal Palace, we find a ring of very excellently built houses, each standing in its own ample grounds; and, as we continue our walk, we observe that the houses are for the most part built either in concentric rings, facing the various avenues (as the circular roads are termed), or fronting the boulevards and roads which all converge to the centre of the town. Asking the friend who accompanies us on our journey what the population of this little city may be, we are told about 30,000 in the city itself, and about 2,000 in the agricultural estate, and that there are in the town 5,000 building lots of an average size of 20 feet X 130 feet – the minimum space allotted for the purpose being 20 X 100. Noticing the very varied architecture and design which the houses and groups of houses display – some having common gardens and co-operative kitchens – we learn that general observance of street line or harmonious departure from it are the chief points as to house building, over which the municipal authorities exercise control, for, though proper sanitary arrangements are strictly enforced, the fullest

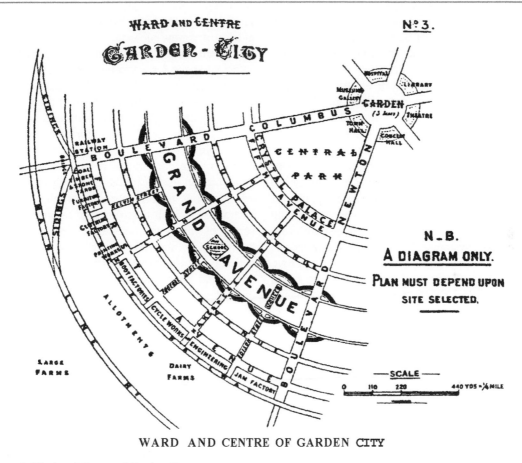

WARD AND CENTRE OF GARDEN CITY

Figure 3 Ward and Centre of Garden City.

measure of individual taste and preference is encouraged.

Walking still toward the outskirts of the town, we come upon "Grand Avenue". This avenue is fully entitled to the name it bears, for it is 420 feet wide, and, forming a belt of green upwards of three miles long, divides that part of the town which lies outside Central Park into two belts. It really constitutes an additional park of 115 acres – a park which is within 240 yards of the furthest removed inhabitant. In this splendid avenue six sites, each of four acres, are occupied by public schools and their surrounding playgrounds and gardens, while other sites are reserved for churches, of such denominations as the religious beliefs of the people may determine, to be erected and maintained out of the funds of the worshippers and their friends. We observe that the houses fronting on Grand Avenue have departed (at least in one of the wards

– that of which Figure 3 is a representation) – from the general plan of concentric rings, and, in order to ensure a longer line of frontage on Grand Avenue, are arranged in crescents – thus also to the eye yet further enlarging the already splendid width of Grand Avenue.

On the outer ring of the town are factories, ware-houses, dairies, markets, coal yards, timber yards, etc., all fronting on the circle railway, which encompasses the whole town, and which has sidings connecting it with a main line of railway which passes through the estate. This arrangement enables goods to be loaded direct into trucks from the warehouses and work shops, and so sent by railway to distant markets, or to be taken direct from the trucks into the warehouses or factories; thus not only effecting a very great saving in regard to packing and cartage, and reducing to a minimum loss from breakage, but also, by reducing the traffic on the roads of the town, lessening to a very marked extent the cost of their maintenance. The smoke fiend is kept well within bounds in Garden City; for all machinery is driven by electric energy, with the result that the cost of electricity for lighting and other purposes is greatly reduced.

The refuse of the town is utilized on the agricultural portions of the estate, which are held by various individuals in large farms, small holdings, allotments, cow pastures, etc.; the natural competition of these various methods of agriculture, tested by the willingness of occupiers to offer the highest rent to the municipality, tending to bring about the best system of husbandry, or, what is more probable, the best systems adapted for various purposes. Thus it is easily conceivable that it may prove advantageous to grow wheat in very large fields, involving united action under a capitalist farmer, or by a body of co-operators; while the cultivation of vegetables, fruits, and flowers, which requires closer and more personal care, and more of the artistic and inventive faculty, may possibly be best dealt with by individuals, or by small groups of individuals having a common belief in the efficacy and value of certain dressings, methods of culture, or artificial and natural surroundings.

This plan, or, if the reader be pleased to so term it, this absence of plan, avoids the dangers of stagnation or dead level, and, though encouraging individual initiative, permits of the fullest co-operation, while the increased rents which follow from this form of competition are common or municipal property, and by far the larger part of them are expended in permanent improvements.

While the town proper, with its population engaged in various trades, callings, and professions, and with a store or depot in each ward, offers the most natural market to the people engaged on the agricultural estate, inasmuch as to the extent to which the towns-people demand their produce they escape altogether any railway rates and charges; yet the farmers and others are not by any means limited to the town as their only market, but have the fullest right to dispose of their produce to whomsoever they please. Here, as in every feature of the experiment, it will be seen that it is not the area of rights which is contracted, but the area of choice which is enlarged.

This principle of freedom holds good with regard to manufacturers and others who have established themselves in the town. These manage their affairs in their own way, subject, of course, to the general law of the land, and subject to the provision of sufficient space for workmen and reasonable sanitary conditions. Even in regard to such matters as water, lighting, and telephonic communication – which a municipality, if efficient and honest, is certainly the best and most natural body to supply – no rigid or absolute monopoly is sought; and if any private corporation or any body of individuals proved itself capable of supplying on more advantageous terms, either the whole town or a section of it, with these or any commodities the supply of which was taken up by the corporation, this would be allowed. No really sound system of action is in more need of artificial support than is any sound system of thought. The area of municipal and corporate action is probably destined to become greatly enlarged; but, if it is to be so, it will be because the people possess faith in such

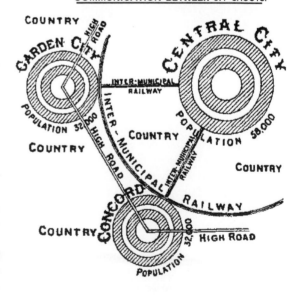

Figure 4 Correct Principle of a City's Growth.

action, and that faith can be best shown by a wide extension of the area of freedom.

Dotted about the estate are seen various charitable and philanthropic institutions. These are not under the control of the municipality, but are supported and managed by various public-spirited people who have been invited by the municipality to establish these institutions in an open healthy district, and on land let to them at a pepper-corn rent, it occurring to the authorities that they can the better afford to be thus generous, as the spending power of these institutions greatly benefits the whole community. Besides, as if those persons who migrate to the town are among its most energetic and resourceful members, it is but just and right that their more helpless brethren should be able to enjoy the benefits of an experiment which is designed for humanity at large.

"Ideology and Aesthetics"

from *The City Beautiful Movement* (1989)

William H. Wilson

Editors' Introduction

Along with Ebenezer Howard's Garden City idea, the turn of the twentieth century witnessed the rise of a short-lived but influential American social and design movement called the City Beautiful Movement. Spurred like Howard by concerns over urban ills, advocates sought to make cities better by improving their physical public realms. A joint undertaking of citizen activists and professional urban planners, the City Beautiful Movement had its heyday in America between 1900 and 1910.

The 1893 Chicago World's Columbian Exposition is generally considered to have been the birthplace of the City Beautiful Movement. A formal assemblage of white neo-classical buildings axially arranged around landscaped open spaces, it awed a vast visiting public. People came from all over the country to see the fair and were impressed. Many community leaders, architects, downtown business promoters, and just plain people went away with ideas of having something like what they had seen in their own cities.

The City Beautiful Movement was largely concerned with civic beauty, famously, but not only, with the creation of monumental civic centers designed in neo-classical architectural style. Other City Beautiful projects included grandiose schemes for citywide park, parkway, and boulevard systems, but many also focused on much smaller things including undergrounding utility wires, restricting billboards, and providing benches and water fountains in public spaces.

By the 1920s, the City Beautiful Movement started being scornfully derided by many urban planners as being merely concerned with surface aesthetics and grand effects. A new design ideology of modernism was being ushered in and along with it came a focus on city efficiency and a disdain for what was termed "ornamentation." By the 1950s and 1960s, the City Beautiful Movement was dismissed, as well, because it was deemed a design approach that focused only on the needs and desires of the well-to-do, neglecting the needs of the poor.

In *The City Beautiful Movement*, William H. Wilson offers a revisionist planning history that rehabilitates City Beautiful ideology, identifies its antecedents and lasting influences, sets the movement within its political context, and analyzes its successes as well as its limitations. He convincingly argues that the City Beautiful Movement had its antecedents in the ideas of Frederick Law Olmsted, namely Olmsted's legacy of park and parkway systems, belief in the restorative nature of natural landscapes, optimistic view that class reconciliation would take place within conducively designed public spaces, and conviction that massive urban growth was inevitable. Wilson traces the survival of City Beautiful ideals throughout the twentieth century, highlighting their continued popularity with laypeople and the re-focus on urban beauty that began in the 1970s with the preservation movement that arose partly in response to the demolition of City Beautiful buildings, such as New York's Pennsylvania Station. In addition, Wilson analyzes how the City Beautiful Movement was supported and promoted by myriad national and local civic organizations that were formed around 1900 with a focus on civic improvement, including the American Park and Outdoor Art Association (APOAA), the American League for Civic Improvement (ALCI), and the American Civic Association (ACA).

In the chapter entitled "Ideology and Aesthetics" Wilson lays out a sweeping interpretation of City Beautiful ideology, enumerating its ten key components, and analyzes how City Beautiful aesthetics linked natural beauty, naturalistic constructivism, and classicism.

William Henry Wilson was for many years Regents Professor of History at the University of North Texas. He earned his PhD (1962) in urban history at the University of Missouri. His seminal book *The City Beautiful Movement* was reprinted under the title *The City Beautiful Movement: Creating the North American Landscape* (Baltimore, MD: Johns Hopkins University Press, 1994), and was awarded the Lewis Mumford Prize of the Society for American City and Regional Planning History. Wilson's other books include *The City Beautiful Movement in Kansas City* (Columbia: University of Missouri Press, 1964); *Coming of Age: Urban America 1915–1945* (New York: Wiley, 1974); *Hamilton Park: A Planned Black Community in Dallas* (Baltimore, MD: Johns Hopkins University Press, 1998); and *Shaper of Seattle: Reginald Heber Thomson's Pacific Northwest* (Pullman: Washington State University Press, 2009).

The best analysis of Frederick Law Olmsted's contributions to the City Beautiful Movement is the chapter in Wilson's book entitled "Frederick Law Olmsted and the City Beautiful Movement." A classic work on Frederick Law Olmsted that emphasizes how his work differed from the City Beautiful Movement is David Schuyler's *The New Urban Landscape: The Redefinition of City Form in Nineteenth-Century America* (Baltimore, MD: Johns Hopkins University Press, 1986).

Two figures most associated with the City Beautiful are architect Daniel H. Burnham and planner-publicist Charles Mulford Robinson. Robinson was a chief spokesman of the City Beautiful Movement who wrote three influential books espousing its ideas: *The Improvement of Towns and Cities: Or, The Practical Basis of Civic Aesthetics* (New York and London: G.P. Putnam's Sons, 1901); *Modern Civic Art: Or, The City Made Beautiful* (New York and London: G.P. Putnam's Sons, 1903); and *City Planning, With Special Reference to the Planning of Streets and Lots* (New York and London: G.P. Putnam's Sons, 1916). Burnham directed the 1893 World's Columbian Exposition in Chicago and, with his co-author Edward Bennett, created both the 1905 Plan for San Francisco and the 1909 Plan of Chicago, which symbolized the maturation of the City Beautiful. Writings on Daniel H. Burnham and his works include Carl S. Smith's *The Plan of Chicago: Daniel Burnham and the remaking of the American City* (Chicago: University of Chicago Press, 2006); Kristen Schaffer's *Daniel H. Burnham: Visionary Architect and Planner* (New York: Rizzoli, 2003); and Charles Moore's *Daniel H. Burnham: Architect, Planner of Cities* (New York: Da Capo Press, 1968).

An early work that discusses City Beautiful ideology is Joaquin Miller's *The Building of the City Beautiful* (Trenton, NJ: A. Brandt, 1905), recently reprinted by Nabu Press (2010). More recently, a work that furthers Wilson's reappraisal of City Beautiful contributions is Robert Freestone's journal article "Reconciling Beauty and Utility in Early City Planning: The Contribution of John Nolen" (*Journal of Urban History*, March 2011, vol. 37, no. 2, 256–277), which analyses how the aesthetic aspirations of the City Beautiful Movement persisted into the subsequent City Practical Movement as beauty became wedded to utility in comprehensive planning.

In terms of naysayers, in his influential books *Culture of Cities* (New York: Harcourt, Brace Jovanovich, 1938) and *The City in History* (New York: Harcourt, Brace Jovanovich, 1961) architecture and urban planning critic William Mumford denounced the formalism of the American City Beautiful Movement, in particular its neo-classic buildings, as inappropriate for a democratic society. In *Death and Life of Great American Cities* (New York: Random House, 1961) Jane Jacobs strongly criticizes the City Beautiful Movement, which Wilson suggests is because she misunderstood the movement's purposes. More recently, Peter Hall's *Cities of Tomorrow* (London: Wiley-Blackwell, 2002) contains a lengthy chapter entitled "The City of Monuments, The City Beautiful Movement: Chicago, New Delhi, Berlin, Moscow, 1900–1945" that largely critiques, and ridicules, the City Beautiful Movement.

The City Beautiful movement worked through politics to achieve a congeries of socioenvironmental reforms related to urban design. By 1903–4 an ideology in support of the movement emerged. It was compounded from several sources, including nineteenth-century sociology, psychology, and biology, plus several planning reports. What follows is an examination of that ideology, beginning with a look at its advocates. City Beautiful advocates were mostly male and members of the urban middle class or upper middle class. They were often the owners or managers of businesses large by community standards, for example, newspaper editors, managers of manufacturing plants, or owners of sizable retail establishments. There was some representation from smaller businesses and, rarely, skilled labor. Other prominent City Beautiful supporters included professional people: attorneys, bankers, physicians, and real estate specialists and investors. These elites worked to achieve citywide, unifying planning schemes. They articulated the purposes of planning in intensive publicity campaigns conducted through boards of trade, chambers of commerce, or various ad hoc groups.

The women involved were usually from the same middle and upper classes and were often the wives of business leaders. The women were active in organizations of the municipal improvement type. They allied with the men in the same or parallel campaigns, though they tended to form separate organizations and promote more specialized causes, such as street sanitation.

Finally, there were the experts themselves, who belonged to the same class background as the City Beautiful activists, who worked well with local elites, and who sometimes participated in planning publicity.

All this is scarcely news. City Beautiful activists were similar in class, education, and general background to other reformers of the Progressive Era. The problem is, how should the motives of such people be interpreted? The usual reply is based on a sort of sociopolitical determinism. Its burden is that, as soon as we know who the reformers and their groups were, then an analysis free of old-fashioned normative categories will reveal what it was they really wanted. What they wanted turns out to be the centralization of urban functions and politics, the protection of property and property values, and the exercise of class and social control

over the (to them) dangerous urban masses. Other goals included the development of a city bureaucracy dedicated to municipal cleanliness, order, and the pursuit of legitimate business goals, and the recruitment of the experts to deal with large-scale problems of public health, transportation, and the like. Some arrangements had to be sacrificed to achieve these ends, including the relatively intimate politics of the ward based system of representation, neighborhood influence over schooling and recreation, and community-based intervention in urban politics.

There are problems with this interpretation. For one thing, the normative attitudes tossed out the front door have a way of sneaking around back. Implicit in the deterministic view is that centralization that does not allow for considerable local autonomy is wrong, that bureaucracy and expertise are antithetical to democracy, that social control is of little or no merit, and that class control is bad unless it is the working class that is asserting its privileges over those of the others. Also involved is a conviction that small-scale democracy and neighborhood control are creatable or preservable values in the era of the metropolis. The issue is not the validity of the ethical positions described, but their latent presence in the interpretation.

The determinist approach assumes that the reformers involved in a citywide activity opposed any significant concession to democracy, neighborhoods, or ideas of community. Roy Rosenzweig and Stephen Hardy have attacked determinism, arguing that working- and middle-class people were not passive but battled urban elites over questions of park design, equipment, and recreational programs, and won often enough to make the struggle worthwhile. Their observations are insightful. Most City Beautiful programs necessitated an initial democratic ratification, such as a bond issue, for implementation. Therefore, the proponents could not afford to ignore the democratic process or neighborhood or community concerns. Too many other people had to be persuaded. After a program successfully ran the democratic gauntlet, it could be removed to the realms of expertise and bureaucracy, but the experts and the bureaucrats had to produce publicly acceptable work. This need for popularly approved results remained because a park and boulevard system, a street beautification-improvement program, or a civic center was practically never complete with one bond issue. Popular approval of the next phase of land acquisition or construction depended upon citizen acceptance of what was created before. So the relationship between public and expert or citizen board was not authoritarian or undemocratic but reciprocal. Therefore, the interclass arguments over park facilities should be viewed partly as elite capitulations to the necessity of continued popular support. They might also be seen to be the neighborhood or community struggle against central control that is familiar to observers of the urban scene. On the other hand, when workers won and elites lost, the battle was decided within the durable framework created by the losers.

A third problem with the deterministic interpretation is that many vocal opponents of reform were strikingly similar to the proponents of change. They were middle- and upper-middle-class people who resembled their adversaries in occupation, age, education, social backgrounds, and group affiliation. This means that not all newspaper editors, professionals, or owners of large businesses condoned City Beautiful projects. Some belonged to the organizations that endorsed beautification programs in spite of their dissent. Endorsement of anything by a chamber of commerce meant endorsement by a majority of the group, however slender the majority. Usually a small committee of enthusiasts within the chamber carried on any campaigning or other activity resulting from the endorsement. It is possible though hardly demonstrable that those who secured group endorsements and group activism were a committed minority who swept along the indifferent majority in a burst of carefully orchestrated enthusiasm.

A determinist might make two responses to this argument. The first is that differences between pro-reform and antireform groups are discernible if one probes effectively. Thus one finds "newcomers" and "old notables" clashing at times, or entrenched downtown property interests battling rising young businessmen. The problem with this response is that the situations may be true for selected issues in one city, but not for other cities or issues. Even if a firm interpretation may be drawn along the line of group disagreements within a single city, transferring the framework to larger, smaller, or different types of cities may produce negative results.

The determinists' second reply might be that none of this makes much difference anyhow, be-cause both the proponents and opponents of City Beautiful reforms really wanted the same things from the city. That is, both factions desired centralization, the dominance of expertise, and a powerful bureaucracy. No doubt this was true at some level of abstraction, but the City Beautiful battles were too earnest and intense for them to have been over minor or incidental matters. The struggles were between people who desired a rich, full life for the residents of a beautiful city and those who saw the city in strictly utilitarian terms, who desired economical government, and who wished to leave beauty or the acquisition of it to private quests.

What may be said with certainty is that the active leadership for and against urban beautification came from roughly the same group. Both sides had access to a citywide audience, both expressed citywide concerns, and both used the press, the courts, and other devices such as pamphlets and public meetings to express their views. The fact that City Beautiful proponents came from a certain social stratum is a generalization, nothing more. Nevertheless it will serve as a basis for examining the frankly class-and-culture-oriented concerns of the City Beautiful advocates.

CITY BEAUTIFUL IDEOLOGY

First, the City Beautiful solution to urban problems – transforming the city into a beautiful, rationalized entity – was to occur within the existing social, political, and economic arrangements. City Beautiful advocates were committed to a liberal-capitalist, commercial-industrial society and to the concept of private property. They recognized society's abuses, but they posited a smooth transition to a better urban world. City Beautiful proponents were, therefore, reformist and meliorative, not radical or revolutionary. They accepted the city optimistically, rejecting a return to a rural or arcadian past.

The city was susceptible to reform because it was akin to a living organism. Thoughtful citizens could control and direct its growth somewhat as they could manipulate other organisms genetically and environmentally. McFarland wrote of an "endeavor to give us . . . in our urban habitations conditions . . . approximating those of the beautiful wild into which our forefathers came a few generations ago." Such a sweeping change could occur only if the city could be studied entire for the purpose of arranging its components in perfect symbiosis. The city had to be, as Liberty Hyde Bailey put it in 1903, "an organism." George A. Parker asserted that the city developed according to discoverable principles. "The starting point in the study of a city," he declared, "is to realize the fact that it is a living organism, whose life is not a series of accidents but conforms to the laws of growth, while undergoing constant modification in response to changing influences." If the city conformed "to biological laws," then its transformation could be understood and, possibly, directed. Guy Kirkham, a Springfield, Massachusetts, architect, suggested such a possibility when he added a Darwinian fillip. Solving architectural problems and creating a "safe" and "convenient" city would lead to a situation in which "finally the beautiful city will be evolved."

The locale for all this evolutionary progress, it should be remembered, was the city. There was little interest among the devotees of the City Beautiful in the agricultural village, the Country Life movement, industrial utopias such as Pullman, Illinois, or the Garden City concepts of Ebenezer Howard. The beautification work of John H. Patterson of the National Cash Register Company and its transforming effect on Dayton, Ohio, was of vastly greater interest than any non-urban system or scheme. The city was the arena of the future, and there the City Beautiful enthusiasts focused their aspirations.

Second, City Beautiful reformers recognized the aesthetic and functional shortcomings of cities. They sought beautiful buildings and scenes to help preserve what attractiveness remained in nineteenth-century urban settings. More, they wished to supplant the pervading ugly and unkempt atmosphere of the American city. McFarland called it "the crusade against ugliness" for good reason. Turn-of-the-century cities were ugly, and dirty too. Retail-commercial downtowns expressed their vitality by moving as they expanded, leaving behind aging buildings given over to secondhand shops, third-rate stores, light industry, or musty vacancy. Factories and business blocks vomited black, sooty smoke that lowered over Pittsburgh, Chicago, and St. Louis. The urban sections of rivers were treated as sewers, not waterscapes. Junk and rubbish littered their banks. Few cities could boast well-distributed

or well-improved parks. In gross acreage or in the improvement of one or two large landscape parks, some older American cities could compare favorably with their English or German counterparts. More often parks were poorly located, undeveloped, or uncoordinated into park and boulevard systems. In 1890 Boston and Minneapolis could be proud of their parks, but Chicago displayed just over 2,000 acres of parkland and a pitiful 799 improved acres for its more than 1 million citizens. Rochester served 133,896 inhabitants with 76 improved park acres.

Street paving of all types was often conspicuous by its absence. Boston boasted that 100 percent of its streets were paved, though 163 of its 408 street miles were only gravel covered. Boston was an exception, even for the eastern seaboard, and in cities farther west, paving conditions were much worse. In Kansas City 50 of its 267 street miles were surfaced; Dallas had paved only 5 percent of its streets. In 1903 a resident of Omaha bragged about his city's advances in street paving. Omaha, he said, embraced 350 miles of streets and alleys. Eighty-five miles were paved, and ten of those were "the remnants of what was once wooden block paving." The speaker, remember, was not criticizing. He was boasting of progress. Dirt streets – swirling dust in summer and gluey, sucking mud in spring, redolent with horse droppings – were the norm in many American cities.

The beauty sought by City Beautiful advocates was scarcely ever specifically defined, except by such supplementary nouns as proportion, harmony, symmetry, and scale. Beauty was, however, often illustrated. Well-tended flower gardens, well-done landscape parks, street furniture of straightforward but gracious design, and single or grouped monumental public buildings, all in harmonious relationships, were the basis of civic beauty. City Beautiful leaders perforce did not usually go beyond a sort of generalized Ruskinism. They knew – by intelligence, breeding, and training – what was beautiful and what was not, be it natural or man-made. They wanted enough influence to exclude "costly blunders" and "amateurish experiment" from the urban landscape. The municipal art commissions established in many cities after 1900 gave them at least advisory powers over the design of public structures. While they thus asserted a cultural dominion over the city, they were hesitant to apply it without regard for neighborhood sensibilities, the existing urban environment, or the wishes of donors and experts. Embarrassing contretemps among arbiters of public beauty, such as the furor over the statue *Bacchante* in the courtyard of the Boston Public Library, occurred rarely.

Third, those who endorsed the City Beautiful were environmentalists. When they trumpeted the meliorative power of beauty, they were stating their belief in its capacity to shape human thought and behavior. Some environmentalist statements, especially from the municipal improvement wing of the City Beautiful, seemed to echo Olmsted. E. L. Shuey of the APOAA contended that "beauty and healthfulness" were as important as they were inseparable. McFarland declared that "beauty came even before food in Eden. And while we cannot restore man to the garden, we can . . . make the city gardenlike." Civic design advocate Robinson urged preserving landscape parks, which "present the sharpest contrast to the artificiality of the city."

City Beautiful environmentalism was not, however, a linear extension of Olmsted's. The impact of Darwinism separated it from the analysis of Olmsted, a man whose fundamental ideas were formed in the first half of the nineteenth century. Endorsers of the City Beautiful were late-nineteenth- or twentieth-century people. They believed less in the Olmstedian view of beauty's restorative power and more in the shaping influence of beauty. Darwinism had compromised the old belief in man as a natural creature made in the image of God, who shared some of God's attributes and who required a beautified, naturalistic reprieve from his imprisonment in the artificial city. Man became remote from his Creator, more manipulable and malleable, a being conditioned by his environment. Therefore, the whole urban environment and the entire human experience within it were critical to the City Beautiful movement. City Beautiful advocates found secular salvation for humans in their belief in a flexible, organic city, in contrast to the intractable city of Olmsted's vision. The convictions about malleable humans and flexible cities underlay the City Beautiful insistence on a comprehensive plan, one that pervaded and unified the city and that addressed a significant number of its problems.

City Beautiful environmentalism involved social control, a subject over which a great deal of ink has been spilled. Two matters only need concern us about the City Beautiful style of social control. The first is, as Dominick Cavallo has written, that social control is an ahistorical concept. The forms and methods of social control are situational despite generalizations about their types. Considerations of social control must be specific to the intellectual and ecological setting. Paul Boyer's tour de force in urban and intellectual history (*Urban Masses and Moral Order in America, 1820–1920* [1992]) reveals how reformers focused on the problem of "moral control" of the masses from the Jacksonian era, when the city first emerged as a focus for reform effort. Boyer deftly illuminates the broad, general similarities in nonlegal, nonreligious social control, as well as some profound differences of strategy and goals.

The danger of following Boyer's comparisons and contrasts to their conclusions is in losing sight of Cavallo's point. Both the City Beautiful's rhetorical flights and its varied attack on urban problems occurred within a particular context – namely, Darwinian views of humanity and the city. They developed amid the proliferation of large, rapidly growing cities and of rapid advances in the institutionalization and municipal socialization of such staple reform concerns as the juvenile problem, poverty, crime control, utilities, and housing regulation. Therefore, the connections among the Jacksonian reformers, Olmstedians, and City Beautiful advocates are limited and specific, not continuous.

The second point about the City Beautiful's exercise in social control was that it was normative and behavioral. It was not coercive, the mechanism of the concentration camp, or utilitarian, the accommodation between the car corporation and the wage worker on the assembly line. The goal of the City Beautiful system was what Edward A. Ross, in *Social Control* (1901), termed the inculcation of "social religion," the idealized, transcendental bond among members of a community and among members of a nation or society. Ross claimed a deep emotional and instinctual basis for this civic religion, which was superior because it was an "*inward*," or internalized, control system. The problem with imputing overreaching or potentially fascistic sentiments to the City Beautiful reformers is that their system was severely self-limiting. Their rhetoric might soar, as McFarland's and Robinson's surely did, and they might occasionally overlook the individuals composing a community, but their claims for control rested upon the presumed effects of the urban environment. Effective socialization through the civic ideal was an unprovable proposition at best, tenuous or nebulous at worst. Environmental conditioning could be demonstrated in laboratory or quasi-laboratory conditions. The impact of the public environment upon such a complex organism as a human being – one subject to a succession of environments and playing a variety of social roles – was another matter entirely. The socialization of the urban dweller involved an elaborate network of circumstances and ideas, many of them beyond the reach of so exalted and transcendent a concept as the civic ideal. It would be fairer to the ideals of the City Beautiful advocates to say that they sought cultural hegemony by asserting control over the definition of beauty and the manipulation of civic symbol.

There are other difficulties with setting too much store by the rhetoric of the City Beautiful. If its language was fervent, its actions often were prosaic: a cleanup campaign, a struggle for councilmanic hearts and minds concerning a local billboard ordinance, a suit over land condemnation for a park or civic center. Perhaps the City Beautiful's very fervor was its attempt to bridge the gap between desire and actuality. City Beautiful advocates dared not ignore or override individuals or categories of individual predispositions. Ross's doubts about the permanence of specific control systems extended to civic idealism: "Civic pride and public spirit are often hot-house plants." All this suggests how mistaken it would be to view social control as a sinister side of the City Beautiful: first, because social control was only one of several objectives; second, because it was normative only; and, third, because its rhetorical excesses, typical of the Progressive Era, were not translatable into a political program.

The playground movement was more explicitly controlling and manipulative, for its goal was the socialization of youth. From early childhood to late adolescence, young people were to come under the sway of the organized playground and its director. The play movement was, like the City Beautiful, of middle-class origins, but it was focused on a particular reform, was more activist, and more militantly environmentalist. There were potential conflicts between the two movements. Park space designed for Olmsted's passive recreation and

psychic restoration was, to some play enthusiasts, mere fallow ground waiting to be converted into playgrounds. Also, an active recreation movement would compete for public funds that could otherwise go to City Beautiful projects. The conflicts were muted during the earlier years, when the playground movement had developed an ideology but had not yet jelled organizationally. Active conflict would come in 1906 with the founding of the Playground Association of America.

The playground movement was a feature of the child-saving impulse of the progressive years, but its thrust was universal. Playground advocates believed in reaching out to all children, irrespective of age and ethnic group. Team sports for the older children and adolescents taught them that what divided them was less important than what united them. Team play required the sacrifice or the tempering of individuality to a common goal. This training socialized the child, making the child receptive to the discipline of the work environment, to an efficiently organized polity, to national patriotism, and to civic idealism. A Darwinian ontogeny lay behind the inculcation of moral values, from the sandpile to team sports. Morality, in this view, was not independent and divine but environmentally conditioned. The playground movement saw itself as providing an alternative to the depraved, socially centrifugal city. The playground supplied the corrective for bad forms of recreation, including illicit drinking establishments, dance halls, and theaters of the vaudeville and burlesque types. The street gang's primitive civicism could be nurtured and its destructive appetites discouraged if only an innovative play director would inveigle it to the playground and seize its leadership.

Despite the conflicts between the City Beautiful and playground movements, what united them was more significant than their divisions. Their points of unity included social control, provided that concept is generalized to accommodate the differences, and agreement about the power of environmental influences on human nature, a nature less teleological than conditioned. Both subscribed to recreation and organized play. Urban beautifiers desired to reestablish community, a value that the playground movement sought to instill almost from the young citizen's cradle. Beautifiers and playgrounders believed in the expert and upheld efficiency. The City Beautiful advocated neighborhood playfields and was willing to concede a few acres of larger parks to playgrounds, provided the surrender did not involve the destruction of landscape values.

Fourth, the City Beautiful leadership insisted upon synthesizing beauty and utility. Olmsted and other landscape architects had long argued for the role of beauty in creating a contented workforce, attracting a superior population, and raising property values. Burnham and others advanced the venerable argument partly for Olmsted's "pocketbook" reasons, for, whatever its intellectual permutations, American society remained materialistic. The champions of the City Beautiful realized that their vocal opponents, solid middle- and upper-middle-class citizens like themselves, were content with a smoky, noisy, unkempt city so long as it got the job done: distributed goods, provided housing, and brought together employer and employee. The trick, then, was to combine the beautiful, which was beyond value, with the functional, which paid off in discernible ways.

But by the turn of the century the assertion that beauty and utility were inseparable meant something more palpable and design-related. No structure or scene could be truly beautiful without being functional as well. Jessie Good of the municipal improvement movement pinpointed the issue with an organic metaphor. "The old saying that beauty is only skin deep is deeply false," she wrote. "Beauty is as deep as the bones, the blood, the rosy flesh." The Harrisburg plan of 1901 united a report on parks and boulevards with two on mundane but essential street and sewer improvements. The city plans of Burnham and his associates concerned traffic circulation, railroad reorganization, cultural and civic centers, recreational improvements, and other functional matters. Arnold Brunner, a sensitive architect and planner in the classical mode, was so taken with the inextricable natures of beauty and utility that he coined the word "beautility" to express them. Fortunately, Brunner's neologism never gained much circulation, but it did epitomize City Beautiful functional and aesthetic aspirations.

Beauty and utility were closely related to a fifth City Beautiful ideal, efficiency. Efficiency was a Progressive Era grail, talisman, and buzzword. The presumed efficiency of some private-enterprise factories and offices could be transferred to nonpecuniary concerns including the aesthetic. To McFarland, clouds of factory smoke and soot were not only ugly or distasteful. They were visible evidence of the "waste" of fuel, a waste compounded when fly ash "spread upon houses, clothes, goods and food." McFarland loved trees, but he believed that the proper tree was an "efficient" one. The idea of the civic center was promoted in part because clustered civic buildings would ensure the efficient, economical conduct of the city's business.

Sixth, City Beautiful advocates sought expertise in the solution of urban problems. They responded to growing middle- and upper-class disgust with inept, piecemeal, patchwork efforts to stay abreast of urban needs. At the same time, experts in the youthful professional fields of architecture, landscape architecture, and engineering were available in sufficient numbers, training, experience, and eagerness to undertake municipal work.

Several desirable aspects of planning clustered around the expert. From Olmsted's time, experts had predicted headlong urban expansion, called for the acquisition of public property before continuing urbanization drove up land prices, laid out functional designs of broad scope, subordinated and integrated details, and allowed for gradual improvement within the context of a grand scheme. Without a general plan, in the words of the 1893 plan for Kansas City, "the value of selections for public purposes, their most satisfactory distribution, and the dependence of one improvement upon another, cannot be appreciated." In 1901 the Harrisburg League for Municipal Improvements conceded that "the financial condition of the city will not at present permit the carrying out of Mr. Manning's system in all its details," but urged a "substantial beginning." Two years later the Local Improvement Committee of the APOAA listed "securing the services of an expert" as of first importance to a successful improvement campaign. An expert, the committee insisted, "must be employed if the community hopes to have a beautiful entity." In *Modern Civic Art* [1904], Robinson called for a commission of experts to plan comprehensively and ensure that each year's construction fitted into the total plan. Burnham's aphorism "Make no little plans" distilled the experience of City Beautiful experts.

Lay devotees of the City Beautiful upheld expertise for two other reasons. They were comfortable with the experts who matured before the second decade of the twentieth century, partly because they shared their solid middle- and upper-class backgrounds and achievements. Expert George Kessler could work intimately with layman August Meyer, expert Warren Manning with layman J. Horace McFarland, and expert Daniel H. Burnham with layman Charles D. Norton. This relationship was an important feature of the City Beautiful movement, but it faded as younger experts, more absorbed with professionalism, strove for some distance between themselves and the laity. Further, laymen liked an expert's cachet upon their plans for promotional reasons. City Beautiful bond issue campaigns stressed the practicality of expertly drawn plans. Expert certitude could deflect doubters and detractors. An expert who spoke well or who wrote in sprightly prose could provide an excellent prop for bond issue mass meetings and rallies.

Seventh, City Beautiful ideologues were class conscious in a non-Marxian sense. They believed in individual mobility and in some class fluidity, but they accepted the reality of classes in urban America. For practical purposes they distinguished two classes split along functional lines. The upper group, composed of the owners and managers of substantial enterprises, would benefit from public improvements through a general increase in monetary values and ease of living. Through improvements the upper class would assume the obligations of class leadership. The lower group, composed of manual and nonmanual workers and their families, was oppressively citybound. Unlike the upper group, working-class people could not afford vacations, suburban residences, and surcease from the urban environment. These convictions reached back to Olmsted. New awareness of community needs, on the other hand, brought a rising emphasis on recreational facilities for the working class. These included playground parks and playgrounds within large landscape parks, public baths, baseball diamonds, picnic areas, tennis courts, and golf courses.

In preparing these palliatives City Beautiful ideologues were not impelled by fears of working-class revolt. True, Robinson warned of "the city slum," where "smoulders the fire which breaks forth in revolution," but he was practically alone in raising the issue, nor did he pursue it beyond a sentence in *Modern Civic Art*. The ability of local, state, and federal governments to contain restiveness during the depression of the nineties, returning prosperity late in the decade, the relatively dispersed charac-

ter of the country, the reformers' strong sense of community, all quieted fears of uprising. It does not follow, however, that the City Beautiful movement advanced without a sense of crisis. Environmentalism spurred the City Beautiful to forestall a demoralized and debased urban population.

The movement's fervent optimism, its eighth ideological component, also blanketed the fears of class conflict. Its evangelical confidence bubbled up from a compound containing the convictions behind the social, cultural, and ethical outlook of the middle and upper classes. Other elements in the compound included the grand, if partial, beautification achievement of preexposition Chicago and a few other American cities, the adaptable grandeur of Paris ascribed to Napoleon III and Haussmann, and the importable architectonic triumphs of Venice and Rome. The urban transformation would depend upon the dynamics of charismatic leaders who were taming scandalous politicians, immigrants, and public service corporations. Robinson's rhapsodic opening of *Modern Civic Art* was more florid than most City Beautiful declarations but it captured the spirit of them all. "The darkness rolls away, and the buildings that had been in shadow stand forth distinctly," Robinson exulted. "The tall facades glow as the sun rises; their windows shine as topaz; . . . Whatever was dingy, coarse, and ugly, is either transformed or hidden in shadow . . . There seems to be a new city for the work of a new day."

Ninth, the City Beautiful shared in what has been called the American discovery of Europe. To thoughtful Americans of the late nineteenth century, Europe was more than a nicely arranged warehouse filled with classical models. European cities seemed to be as dynamic as any in America, yet they were, by American standards, clean, well-administered, attractive, even beautiful entities whose growth and development were well controlled. Political scientist Albert Shaw in 1895 praised the pre-Haussmannic and Haussmannic ruthless destruction of medieval Paris (there were plenty of medieval structures elsewhere in France, he wrote) but was less enthusiastic about Parisian administrative and sanitary arrangements. German cities, Shaw found, were masterpieces of administration. He praised the Viennese government for forging a beautiful and practical city. Chicago, he noted, muffed a vastly greater opportunity after the

devastating 1871 fire. If the municipality had purchased the burned-out district and planned a civic
area with public buildings, parks, and boulevards,
it could have sold the leftover land for more than
enough to pay for the improvements. Since the
World's Columbian Exposition, "Chicago has had
a clear comprehension of the magnificent effects
that may be produced as the result of a large initial
plan," but, alas, too late. As Shaw dourly concluded,
"It is evident that Chicago would have been the
gainer if it could have borrowed some of Vienna's
genius for municipal administration."

In the twilight years of the City Beautiful,
Frederick C. Howe deplored the rampant individualism in American cities while he praised German
municipal ownership, taxes on the unearned increment from urban land sales, and zoning. German
cities' smooth, powerful administration, he explained, stemmed not from their great age as large
cities, for they were in that respect younger than
American and British metropolises. German success depended upon home rule and the psychology
of responsibility that home rule engendered. Howe's
paean to the German expert was an extreme
example of American infatuation with European
urbanism. Infatuations are impermanent. In 1913
McFarland revolted against an uncritical acceptance of all things German at the expense of a
realistic awareness of heavy-handed Teutonic bureaucracy. Just as some municipal reformers stood
in awe of European civic administration, so others
imbibed European civic design. They were elements
of the same awakening to those European advances
adaptable to American conditions. The parallel is complete even to the later reaction against classicism.

The tenth and culminating constituent of the
City Beautiful ideology was its enthusiastic welcome
of the city. The architects, landscape architects,
and planners of the era worked in cities and often
lived in them or their suburbs. Some rhetorical
attacks on the unnatural city persisted, but they
became rarer and more ritualistic as the twentieth
century advanced. If cities could be made beautiful and functional, then they would no longer be
running sores on the landscape. If the city became
the locus of harmony, mutual responsibility, and
interdependence between classes, mediated by
experts, then it would be a peaceful, productive place,
not a stark contrast to rural scenery. In its comprehensive view of the city and in its nonpartisan

concern for improvement, the City Beautiful par-
took of a revived civic spirit.

CITY BEAUTIFUL AESTHETICS

City Beautiful aesthetics, considered separately
from City Beautiful ideology, linked natural beauty,
naturalistic constructivism, and classicism. Reverence for natural beauty and for naturalistic constructivism, its urban counterpart, stands first in
the order of City Beautiful aesthetics. The priority
may seem misplaced, given the traditional linking
of the City Beautiful with neoclassical forms. When
we examine what City Beautiful adherents really
were thinking and doing, however, we find a reality
richer than the neoclassic. It was no accident, as
Henry Hope Reed, Jr., remarked, that the scenic
preservation and urban beautification movements
burst upon the country at the same time. There
were precedents, including the rural cemetery
movement and Downing's call for ruralized homes.
Olmsted personified the joining of rural preservation and managed conservation with the drive for
urban beauty.

As urbanization, mechanization, and commercialization roared into the twentieth century, their
levy on beauty was too great to ignore. The preservation and accentuation of natural beauty were
major motives for the Boston metropolitan park
system, Robinson's plan for Raleigh, North Carolina,
Kessler's for Dallas, and many others. City Beautiful
crusader McFarland was a landscape zealot who
fought to save Niagara Falls from continuing commercial threats, struggled unsuccessfully to preserve California's Hetch Hetchy Valley, campaigned
for a National Park Service, and became one of the
country's leading rosarians. The Olmsted brothers,
Burnham, and McKim were among those architects
and planners who traveled between intensely urban
environments for living or work and suburban,
exurban, or rural retreats. Sculptor Augustus Saint-
Gaudens ultimately betook himself to New Hampshire.
That appealing mixture of ebullience and exactitude Stanford White may once have paid a Long
Island farmer fifty dollars per tree to leave standing
a grove of potential firewood. Apocryphal or not,
the story illustrates White's love of natural beauty.
The landscape design and municipal improvement
branches of the City Beautiful praised flowers,

shrubs, and trees for their enhancing, softening qualities in city settings. Advocates from the land-scape design–municipal improvement background espoused corporate beautification, too. They urged grass plots, ground covers, flowers, and plant group-ings for the grounds of small railroad stations. They praised railroad executives and factory owners who adopted systematic beautification ideas for their properties. Such activities, they noted, often spread beyond the station or the factory gate to home improvement and heightened civic concerns.

Civic designers embraced natural beauty and naturalistic constructivism in their urban improve-ment schemes. Burnham's plans suggested boule-vards linking civic centers with waterscapes and park landscapes. They proposed new parks and park-ways to unify and extend the existing landscape-recreational facilities. Robinson's plans for Denver (1906) and Honolulu (1906) offered similar recom-mendations; so did John Nolen's designs for San Diego (1909) and Reading, Pennsylvania (1910). City Beautiful planners typically treated naturalistic parks and parkways as precious assets, not as relics to be tolerated or disfigured by the imposition of their own designs, The charge that City Beautiful plans scorned or devalued natural beauty fits nicely with models of conflict or dichotomy in city plan-ning, but the charge is simply untrue.

Granting their interest in naturalistic themes, City Beautiful designers were drawn to neoclassic architecture. To them it represented the ultimate step in the late-nineteenth-century search for an effective, expressive building style. As Carroll L.V. Meeks and others have written, nineteenth-century architects faced a new order of problems repre-sented by the office building, the railroad station, and by the need to house expanding, differentiating governments. Architects increasingly concentrated on functional solutions at the expense of bizarre eclecticism. Gothic and gaudy Mediterranean styles gave way to a severe commercial vernacular and to the Romanesque. Over time, within the Romanesque, turrets softened and shortened, roofs pitched more gently, dormers retreated and lost some excrescences, and ornament flattened into walls. For all its vogue, however, the Romanesque suffered from fatal defects. It was ecclesiastical architecture originally, difficult to adapt to the public and semipublic buildings of a secular culture without severe modifications, for which there were

no clear guides in proportion and arrangement. The genius of Richardson could impose discipline and order upon the Romanesque, as in the Allegheny County Courthouse and Jail. In weaker hands Romanesque buildings sometimes appeared ill-proportioned and fussily detailed. Their fenestration and the arrangement of horizontal and vertical elements were contradictory and confused. Even some great Romanesque buildings display features more compelling than their facades: the grace and massing of the rear of Trinity Church, the stylish severity of the Rookery's court, the powerful arch at the servant's entrance of the Glessner House, and the functional arrangement of the backs of Austin Hall and the old Kansas City Stock Exchange.

Neoclassic architecture, in contrast, offered basic conceptions of proportion and arrangement. Because of its range in time and space from classic Greek to the Beaux-Arts, it was adaptable. "It was a flexible style," Christopher Tunnard wrote, "which could make a unity of a building by combining boldness of plan with refinement of detail. It made possible the handling of entirely new building types, fre-quently of great scale, that a growing democracy required. These were the new state capitols, the railroad stations, and the public libraries, which are part of America's contributions to world architec-ture." Neoclassic architecture enjoyed other virtues besides precedent and flexibility. It was ideally suited to any building requiring easy public access to a few floors, controlled vertical movement, and a high degree of functional utility. It was, in other words, a superb envelope for buildings low in pro-portion to their length and breadth, however much their monumental domes or interior spaces sug-gested height. Tunnard's list of candidates for classic treatment could be extended to include court-houses, city halls, museums, art galleries, theaters, banks, post offices, and newspaper offices. Gothic and Romanesque details became distended and trivial on their low, broad surfaces, but classic colonnades and arches throve.

The neoclassical mode encouraged talented architects to pursue their experiments in arrange-ment and detail within the confines of a discipline. McKim, an architect whom the advocates of pictur-esque successionism dismiss as a talented copycat, did not "copy" or "derive" his buildings in any meaningful sense of those words. The Boston Public Library's multiple origins may be found in

Henri Labrouste's Bibliothèque Sainte-Geneviève in Paris, Leon Alberti's San Francesco in Rimini, Richardson's Trinity Church and his Marshall Field wholesale store, and the Roman Coliseum. Charles B. Atwood, answering the charges of plagiarism leveled at his beautiful Art Building at the Chicago fair, snapped: "The difference between me and some other architects is that I know what to take and what to leave, and I know how to combine things that come from different sources, while they do not." The designs of these and other neoclassic buildings admittedly "come from different sources," but it is a legitimate question to ask how such selection should be distinguished from the obvious borrowings and adoptions among the members of the commercial Chicago and residential Prairie schools.

The neoclassic approach encouraged skilled architects, but just as important, its discipline rescued a great many mediocre talents. So long as an architect followed precedent it was reasonably difficult for him to design a bad neoclassic building. Weak ones there were: those built without an adequate base above grade on city streets, or backed into hillsides, or covered with frivolous detail. Such errors are atypical. Devotees of the neoclassical realized that independent genius in facade design is a scarce commodity among architects. Any large city is infested with hideous buildings, failed efforts at originality, beside which a poised neoclassic structure is sweet respite for the eyes. Such contemporary failures do not settle the argument against modernism, but they do suggest that merely hurling words of dismissal such as "professional hocus-pocus" at neoclassical buildings does not end the "battle of styles."

Lastly, neoclassic architecture evoked American history and spoke to the late-nineteenth-century urban elite. Classic construction evoked the American past because it was firmly in the architectural tradition from colonial times. It flowered through the late 1840s before giving way to eclecticism. Although the Greek orders were popular, Roman modes also found favor. The differences between the classicism of the early nineteenth century and the neoclassic buildings of the American Renaissance are differences of degree, not of kind. Classic architecture symbolized the historical heritage of the United States in a way that the Gothic, Romanesque, or commercial styles never could. As James Early,

Neil Harris, and George Heard Hamilton have written, it expressed a romantic attachment to Greece and Rome and, by extension, to the Renaissance city-state. The attachment had less to do with governmental forms and more with assumed similarities of political thought and social achievement. At the dawn of the twentieth century it was still possible to believe the United States to be a republic governed in all important respects by European-descended, male-dominated elites. Despite growing suffragism women enjoyed relatively little political participation. Blacks were losing the right to significant involvement in Southern politics, and with some exceptions all racial minorities were confined to voting for whites. State houses of representatives as yet elected United States senators. State senators were chosen on a geographic, not a demographic, basis. By later standards, the federal government's role was circumscribed and remote from the citizen. It was reasonable to emphasize the greatness and the republican legacy of the United States by adapting the architecture of past republics.

Several critics have treated neoclassic architecture and naturalistic constructivism as incongruities or curious appositions. Their explanation for the reality – that in many cities the naturalistic, and often approved, lamb lies down with the neoclassical, and frequently disapproved, lion – is twofold. First, neoclassicism characterized the City Beautiful, not naturalistic constructivism. The juxtaposition of classic and naturalistic represents a sequential development: all landscape work is of pre-City Beautiful origin or inspiration, while only neoclassical buildings are in the City Beautiful mode. Second, the origins of landscape design are definitely English, while those of the classic are distinctly French and Italian. Eclectic Americans mixed the two styles uncritically.

These explanations have an appealing simplicity but they do not bear up under examination. Combining the classic and the naturalistic was not new to the City Beautiful but was a favorite device of the eighteenth and nineteenth centuries. European landscape gardening as imported to the United States was not merely Reptonian or simply picturesque but a complex heritage incorporating French and Italian survivals. Classic designs appeared in "romantic" landscapes and in "natural" English garden scenes. Olmsted, it will be recalled, learned from the English but also from Jean Alphand and

Baron Haussmann. Charles Eliot and George Kessler absorbed important Continental influences. The Paris Universal Exposition of 1889 combined axiality, formality, and naturalistic constructivism, as did its American derivative, the World's Columbian Exposition. The inspired combination of neoclassic architecture and naturalistic constructivism disturbed few contemporaries. Nor did most of them object to the later civic blendings of the two styles. The romantic appeal of neoclassical architecture and the romantic yearnings expressed in naturalistic constructivism reconciled those modes of City Beautiful design.

Indeed, the astonishment surrounding the Chicago fair's success focused as much on the celebratory aspect of the crowds in the Court of Honor as on anything else. Here was the Olmstedian ideal realized in a neoclassic setting, the friendly mingling of all classes and types of people. More than that, the crowd itself became an integral part of the spectacle, its spontaneous activity serving as counterpoint to the court's conscious artistry. The unprecedented success of the Court of Honor increased the reawakening interest in the square or city center as the focus of civic life. Urban celebrations such as New York's commemoration of Admiral Dewey fueled a taste for pageantry. Albert Kelsey's perceptive address to the Baltimore municipal art conference in 1899 related grouped public buildings to urban crowds. The buildings, he claimed, were "a perpetual exposition, drawing visitors to the city," while attracting "a desirable class of residents." The Pan-American Exposition, a financial failure remembered chiefly as the site of President McKinley's assassination, unified these conceptions of civic aspiration. The architecture of the Buffalo fair was a relatively restrained Spanish Renaissance, but the Court of Fountains was a carefully wrought, three-dimensional space of 1,400,000 square feet versus the Court of Honor's 563,000 square feet. Varied colors and colored-lighting effects heightened the sense of spectacle and pageantry, as did the careful design of the primary entrance at Buffalo. "The ensemble is full of suggestion of what may be done with open spaces in our cities," wrote Charles H. Caffin, "nor is any argument needed to prove how desirable it would be, if our great cities presented some such focal points of grandeur and human interest."

Walter Hines Page saw in the Buffalo fair the latest indications of the "gradual evolution from the severely instructive type" of exposition to "play-places, places to which we go in a holiday mood, to see instructive things of course, but especially to see beautiful spectacles." The Buffalo fair was deliberately planned to include the crowd in the ensemble. People came "in family groups, . . . every type from all grades of life," Page wrote. He caught the interplay of individual and mass, of the fairgoers simultaneously or successively assuming the role of participant and observer. "There was never such a sight under heaven as the people themselves. They gaze at the crowds . . . And they are themselves the crowning glory of the spectacle." The same year Robinson, in his *Improvement of Towns and Cities*, urged the "grouping of public buildings," based on the discussions and plans in Cleveland preceding the 1903 civic center scheme by Burnham and his associates. The Senate Park Commission's stunning designs of 1901–2 gave visual expression to the yearnings for urban pageantry, community, and beautiful civic buildings.

In the March 1902 issue of *Municipal Affairs* John DeWitt Warner drew together the historical and contemporary instances of "Civic Centers" to demonstrate how a traditional, useful, respectable idea was enjoying a renascence. Ostensibly, Warner's article was a criticism of the New York Fine Arts Federation. The federation had proposed to construct a single exhibition building to house its constituent organizations but had failed to plan a complete civic center for all the city's major public and semipublic buildings. But Warner's complaint was incidental to a historical review of the town center – the focus of civic life from the Acropolis and the Roman Forum, through modern European cities, to developments in Boston, Albany, and "current projects" in San Francisco, Chicago, and Cleveland. The Senate Park Commission plan for Washington came in for special attention. Through 1902, however, neither Warner nor anyone else had developed a theory of the civic center. Nothing existed beyond scattered mentions of European precedent, economy, civic efficiency, civic pride, and celebration. The concept of grouped public buildings was not yet fitted into the developing City Beautiful ideology.

All that changed with five publications in 1903–4: Burnham, Carrere, and Brunner's study of the group plan of Cleveland; Robinson's *Modern Civic Art*; Albert Kelsey's "The City Possible"; Charles

Zueblin's "The 'White City' and After"; and the Municipal Art Society of Hartford's *The Grouping of Public Buildings*. These works, together with previous studies, brought the rationale for the civic center to maturity.

According to these publications, the civic center would supplement, not supplant, the city's retail-commercial core. The center thereby deferred to the existing social, political, and economic arrangements. The civic center would respect the fact that most land near retail-commercial centers was too dear for much of it to be given over to parks. In other words, there was no way to bring the middle landscape to the urban core except in connection with public buildings. An administrative and cultural center would focus citizen attention and traffic near downtown, but major public buildings already were located scattershot around most downtowns. The locational problem involved finding a site compatible with commerce, yet convenient for the public. Robinson suggested a waterfront location but conceded the inconvenience in some cases and, in others, the municipality's need to use "its waterfront space for other purposes." His alternative location was on "an eminence." The elevation, if not too steep, invited buildings. Robinson, however, did not consider the convenience of collocating the civic center and the central business area. It was up to George A. Parker, writing in *Grouping of Public Buildings*, to put practicality over picturesqueness. The civic center, Parker declared, had to leave main thoroughfares free and should not "intrude upon the business center, but it should be in juxtaposition to it." The civic center, however grand, "must not interfere with" but "be subordinate" to what "our modern cities represent, commercialism and industrialism."

The civic center was intended to be a beautiful ensemble, an architectonic triumph far more breathtaking than a single building, no matter how comely, could be. Grouping public buildings around a park, square, or intersection of radial streets allowed the visual delights of perspectives, open spaces, and the contrasts between the buildings and their umbrageous settings. Robinson noted that public open space would push encroaching private structures farther away. Parker suggested that the influence of the civic center would spread outward as the city developed. Burnham invoked the need for "uniformity of style" and the "example of order,

system and reserve" given to other building operations in the city. Robinson wrote of the "stateliness," "dignity," and "scale – the adoption of a certain module to which all the buildings must strictly adhere, as they can do with no loss of individuality." Compatible buildings could achieve "beauty and harmony of repose."

Important as beauty was for itself, its role in environmental conditioning was never far from the minds of civic center advocates. The civic center's beauty would reflect in the souls of the city's inhabitants, inducing order, calm, and propriety therein. Second, the citizen's presence in the center, together with other citizens, would strengthen pride in the city and awaken a sense of community with fellow urban dwellers. Burnham pleaded for "uniform architecture" to replace the "jumble" of buildings, which "sadly disturbs our peacefulness and destroys that repose within us which is the true basis of all contentment." Zueblin's retrospective on the relationship of world's fairs to city planning recalled the day when the "full majesty" of the Chicago fair's "Court of Honor and its greatest revelation to the makers of cities" arrived – the twenty-fifth anniversary of the Chicago fire. "Then the human mass" of fairgoers "gave life to the beautiful court with its background of majestic architecture, and man's latest civic triumph had been achieved." The mass participation and the interplay of people and buildings were the great accomplishments of the White City: "There was no loss of individuality, no place for individualism. The individual was great but the collectivity was greater." Similarly, the varied color and lighting effects of the Buffalo exposition "demonstrated that there need be no loss of individuality in collective activity."

This collective activity needed some purpose beyond mere contentment. Robinson supplied the purpose – civic idealism and patriotism – wrapped in rhapsodic prose. Moving from the urban skyline, "a work of art which speaks not to the eye alone, nor to the head alone, nor to the heart alone; but unitedly, to senses, brain, and sentiment," he turned to the buildings of the civic center on their eminence. "There they would visibly dominate the town. To them the community would look up, seeing them lording over it at every turn, as, in fact, the government ought to do." Wherever located, however, a civic center would appear to be "a more majestic thing and one better worth the devotion and service of its citizens." J.G. Phelps Stokes was at least as hopeful of beauty's transforming, communal power when he wrote of the advantages of civic center groupings. "The wider the public enjoyment of the beautiful features of a city, and the larger the numbers of people who enjoy those beauties together, the wider the mutual thoughts and feelings and interests . . . and this tends to the development of a wider social morality. When we enjoy things together we for the time being feel and think together, and the more often we share the same thoughts and emotions the more unified in thought and feeling we become."

Utility, efficiency, and expertise joined beauty in civic center theory. Stokes argued that "co-operation between the departments of a city is essential if the most efficient public service is to be had; and close co-operation is more easy . . . where distances are eliminated." The "ordinary citizen" benefited from the "concentration . . . for the same reason that the department store is of great convenience to the average purchaser . . . It costs no more to group buildings," Stokes went on, "than to scatter them indiscriminately. Great economy is often involved in such grouping, particularly if all the land required for the proposed improvement can be purchased at once." Stokes's arguments echoed similar statements from Warner, Kelsey, and Robinson. Ford brought forth additional utilitarian reasons for a civic center. Proper spacing in a parklike setting would help to protect each building from fire, and their occupants from urban dust and noise. Their relatively close relationships would at the same time encourage the economy of a central heating plant. Only architects and designers could create such a complex urban artifact as a civic center. The manifold aesthetic and engineering details required it. The report on the Cleveland group plan by Burnham and his associates clinched the point in prose and graphics.

The value of a civic center extended beyond its psychic and practical benefits. Burnham urged Cleveland's civic leaders to extend the "order, system and reserve" of the center outward to a uniform style for each type of public building, to the development of the city's parks and boulevard system, and to a new "really imposing" railroad station, "a beautiful vestibule to the town" to provide "the visitor" with a "favorable" "first impression" of Cleveland. While the city would emerge

as the common artistic property of all citizens, the task of creating it fell on the cultural and political leadership, to whom Zueblin, Burnham, Robinson, and the others addressed their remarks.

Finally, the civic center took its inspiration from Europe, ancient and modern. Warner's sweeping review of the history of the civic center was perhaps the most inclusive defense of precedent. Milo R. Maltbie argued that Berlin and Paris were beautiful principally because of the arrangement, location, and surroundings of their buildings. And it was their beauty, especially Parisian beauty, that drew so many Americans away from their own cities to spend "millions" in Europe. Burnham had similar entrepreneurial and aesthetic reasons for his forceful statement in favor of the neoclassic. He reminded Clevelanders of "the lesson taught by the Court of Honor of the World's Fair of 1893," that "the highest type of beauty can only be assured by the use of one sort of architecture." Burnham and his associates recommended "that the designs of all the buildings of this group plan should be derived from the historic motives of the classic architecture of Rome." They urged uniformity of materials, scale, mass, and cornice line.

The neoclassical triumph should not be confused with the more fundamental reassertion of traditional Western aesthetics and cultural values. Robinson, in his earlier *Improvement of Towns and Cities*, had called for a public building to be "large, substantial, white, and pure . . . with detached columns and perhaps sculptured figures standing clear against the sky. So rose the Acropolis over Athens, and the opposing temples of Jupiter and Juno on the . . . Capitoline hill." By 1903 he was having second thoughts. In *Modern Civic Art* he labeled the classic "a *bourgeois* type" of architecture and wrote favorably of "the beautiful Gothic constructions of . . . Flanders." In any case, Robinson cautioned, "it would not be wise to limit the choice of architecture to a style that is alien in period and clime." Arthur A. Shurtleff's article on Harvard's college yard emphasized scale, mass, materials, and placement in relation to other buildings and to the sun's path, all part of a European tradition once acknowledged, then lost, in America. Irene Sargent's 1904 article in the *Craftsman* warned against adopting the externals of European municipal art. Sargent instead urged Americans to embrace its fundamentals: class harmony, patriotism, beauty, and civic-mindedness.

Americans did not in fact confuse the externals and the fundamentals. City Beautiful aesthetics and sociology were, like the ideal civic building, a harmonious whole.

CONCLUSION

By 1904 the advocates of the City Beautiful had forged an ideology that would serve them through the following decade. It blended earlier planning convictions, such as the psychic importance of natural beauty, with newer notions of evolution and environmentalism. It reinforced the experts' professional convictions and the leadership aspirations of the urban middle and upper-middle classes. Though incomplete and flawed, the City Beautiful ideology met one test of success. It effectively supported planning movements in cities across the United States.

ONE

"The Neighborhood Unit"

from *Regional Plan of New York and Its Environs* (1929)

Clarence Perry

Editors' Introduction

Reactions to the excesses of the nineteenth-century industrial city had long since occurred by the late 1920s, and new "scientific" and rationalized approaches to city building were well under way, most particularly public health and housing reforms. Garden suburbs, or something approximating them, were being built throughout Europe and North American cities and quickly occupied as emerging middle-class families sought escape from the congestion and perceived ills of central cities. The outlying suburbs were made possible by the rise of widespread automobile ownership, but ever increasing automobile traffic was beginning to cause urban and suburban woes. Traffic dominated the public space of streets, forced pedestrians onto sidewalks, and was perceived as dangerous for children.

Within this context, members of the New York Regional Planning Association of American (RPAA) looked to how to rationalize the burgeoning New York region and prepared a comprehensive regional plan, funded by the non-profit Russell Sage Foundation. The plan dealt with such matters as transportation, open space, housing, and commerce. Within the plan, Clarence Perry (1872–1944) articulated a distinctly American version of a garden suburb based on the concept of the self-contained neighborhood unit (Raymond Unwin and Barry Parker conceived their garden suburbs as larger wholes). The neighborhood unit was centered on an elementary school and community center, and bounded by arterial streets where apartment buildings, retail, and services were located. Ideal neighborhood size was 5,000 to 6,000 people, determined by the population necessary to yield 800 to 1,200 elementary school age children, deemed the most advantageous school size. Within the neighborhood district, through traffic was discouraged by an internally oriented curvilinear pattern of narrow streets. Parks and playgrounds were distributed throughout, connected by pedestrian paths.

Principles of the neighborhood unit concept were refined by fellow RPAA members Clarence Stein and Henry Wright in their 1928 plan for Radburn, New Jersey, which introduced superblocks, culs-de-sac, separated pedestrian and vehicle roadways, and houses oriented toward rear walkways and with garages facing the street. After World War II, planners and real estate developers seized on the neighborhood unit as a module for large-scale planned unit developments. In 1936, a much reduced version of the concept was codified by the Federal Housing Administration (FHA) into subdivision standards. These standards had and continue to have an enormous influence on the form of American suburbs. The firm of Harland Bartholomew and Associates incorporated the neighborhood unit concept as a central planning principle in many of the comprehensive plans it prepared for over 550 American cities between 1919 and 1984.

The idea of planning the city around neighborhood units remains strong today, as evidenced by both the Smart Growth Movement's and the New Urbanism Movement's focus on neighborhood design, and by the many recent city sponsored urban design plans that focus on developing urban villages, most notably those for St. Paul (Minnesota), San Diego (California), and Seattle (Washington). Although research has shown that neighborhoods are fluid rather than physically bounded, and that people's social networks and daily routines extend far beyond the immediate areas in which they live, people nonetheless identify strongly with their local neighborhood. Offering a counterpoint, Tridib Banerjee and Willam C. Baer's book *Beyond the Neighborhood Unit: Residential Environments and Public Policy* (New York: Plenum Press, 1984) challenges the applicability of the neighborhood unit concept in contemporary cities.

Perry's other writings include *Housing for the Machine Age* (New York: Russell Sage Foundation, 1939). Other writings on neighborhood theory include Kevin Lynch, "City Size and the Idea of Neighborhood," in *Theory of Good City Form* (Cambridge, MA: MIT Press, 1981); and Suzanne Keller's *The Urban Neighborhood: A Sociological Perspective* (New York: Random House, 1968). See the Editors' Introduction to Ebenezer Howard, *Garden Cities of Tomorrow*, a previous reading in this volume (p. 53), for writings on garden cities and garden suburbs.

■ ■ ■ ■ ■ ■

AUTHOR'S INTRODUCTION

What is known as a neighborhood, and what is now commonly defined as a region, have at least one characteristic in common – they possess a certain unity which is quite independent of political boundaries. The area with which the Regional Plan of New York is concerned, for instance, has no political unity, although it is possessed of other unifying characteristics of a social, economic and physical nature. Within this area there are definite political entities, such as villages, counties and cities, forming suitable divisions for sub-regional planning, and within those units there are definite local or neighborhood communities which are entirely without governmental limits and some-times overlap into two or more municipal areas. Thus, in the planning of any large metropolitan area, we find that three kinds of communities are involved:

1 The regional community, which embraces many municipal communities and is, therefore, a family of communities;
2 The village, county or city community;
3 The neighborhood community.

Only the second of these groups has any political framework, although all three have an influence upon political life and development. While the neighborhood community has no political structure, it frequently has greater unity and coherence than are found in the village or city and is, therefore, of fundamental importance to society.

[. . .]

THE NEIGHBORHOOD UNIT

The above title is the name which, to facilitate discussion, has been given to the scheme of ar-rangement for a family-life community that has evolved as the main conclusion of this study. Our investigations showed that residential communities, when they meet the universal needs of family life, have similar parts performing similar functions. In the neighborhood unit system those parts have been put together as an organic whole. The scheme is put forward as the frame-work of a model com-munity and not as a detailed plan. Its actual rea-lization in an individual real-estate development requires the embodiment and garniture which can be given to it only by the planner, the architect, and the builder.

The underlying principle of the scheme is that an urban neighborhood should be regarded both as a unit of a larger whole and as a distinct entity in itself. For government, fire and police protection, and many other services, it depends upon the municipality. Its residents, for the most part, find their occupations outside of the neighborhood. To invest in bonds, attend the opera or visit the museum, perhaps even to buy a piano, they have to resort to the "downtown" district. But there are certain other facilities, functions or aspects which are strictly local and peculiar to a well-arranged residential community. They may be classified under four heads: (1) the elementary school, (2) small parks and playgrounds, (3) local shops, and (4) residential environment. Other neighborhood institutions and services are sometimes found, but these are practically universal.

Parents have a general interest in the public school system of the city, but they feel a particular concern regarding the school attended by their children. Similarly, they have a special interest in the playgrounds where their own and their neighbors' children spend so many formative hours. In regard to small stores, the main concern of householders is that they be accessible but not next to their own doors. They should also be concentrated and provide for varied requirements.

Under the term "residential environment" is included the quality of architecture, the layout of streets, the planting along curbs and in yards, the arrangement and set-back of buildings, and the relation of shops, filling stations and other commercial institutions to dwelling places – all the elements which go into the environment of a home and constitute its external atmosphere. The "character" of the district in which a person lives tells something about him. Since he chose it, ordinarily, it is an extension of his personality. One individual can do but little to create it. It is strictly a community product.

It is with the neighborhood itself, and not its relation to the city at large, that this study is concerned. If it is to be treated as an organic entity, then it logically follows that the first step in the conversion of unimproved acreage for residential purposes will be its division into unit areas, each one of which is suitable for a single neighborhood community. The next step consists in the planning of each unit so that adequate provision is made for the efficient operation of the four main neighborhood functions. The attainment of this major objective – as well as the securing of safety to pedestrians and the laying of the structural foundation for quality in environment – depends, according to our investigations, upon the observance of the following requirements:

Neighborhood-unit principles

1 *Size.* – A residential unit development should provide housing for that population for which one elementary school is ordinarily required, its actual area depending upon population density.

2 *Boundaries.* – The unit should be bounded on all sides by arterial streets, sufficiently wide to facilitate its by-passing by all through traffic.

3 *Open Spaces.* – A system of small parks and recreation spaces, planned to meet the needs of the particular neighborhood, should be provided.

4 *Institution Sites.* – Sites for the school and other institutions having service spheres coinciding with the limits of the unit should be suitably grouped about a central point or common area.

5 *Local Shops.* – One or more shopping districts, adequate for the population to be served, should be laid out in the circumference of the unit, preferably at traffic junctions and adjacent to similar districts of adjoining neighborhoods.

6 *Internal Street System.* – The unit should be provided with a special street system, each highway being proportioned to its probable traffic load, and the street net as a whole being designed to facilitate circulation within the unit and to discourage its use by through traffic.

[For] each of these principles [. . .], it is desirable [. . .] to obtain a clearer picture of them, and for that purpose a number of plans and diagrams in which they have been applied will now be presented.

Low-cost suburban development

Character of district

[The plan shown in Figure 1] is based upon an actual tract of land in the outskirts of the Borough of Queens. The section is as yet entirely open and exhibits a gently rolling terrain, partly wooded. So far, the only roads are of the country type, but they are destined some day to be main thoroughfares. There are no business or industrial establishments in the vicinity.

Population and housing

The lot subdivision provides 822 single-family houses, 236 double houses, 36 row houses and 147 apartment suites, accommodations for a total of 1,241 families. At the rate of 4.93 persons per family, this would mean a population of 6,125 and a school enrollment of 1,021 pupils. For the whole tract the average density would be 7.75 families per gross acre [Table 1].

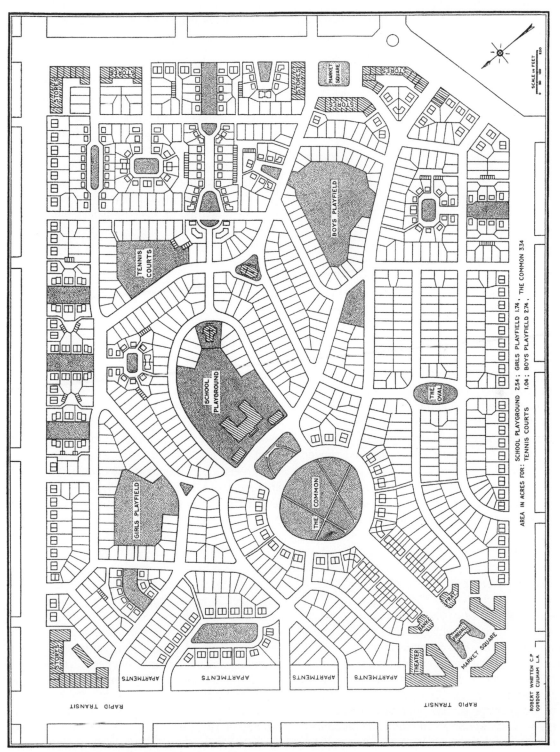

Figure 1 A subdivision for modest dwellings planned as a neighborhood unit.

Table 1 Low-cost suburban development: area relations of the plan depicted in Figure 1

Complete unit	160 acres	100 percent
Dwelling house lots	86.5	54.0
Apartment house lots	3.4	2.1
Business blocks	6.5	4.1
Market squares	1.2	0.8
School and church sites	1.6	1.0
Parks and playgrounds	13.8	8.6
Greens and circles	3.2	2.0
Streets	43.8	27.4

Open spaces

The parks, playgrounds, small greens and circles in the tract total 17 acres, or 10.6 percent of the total area. If there is included also the 1.2 acres of market squares, the total acreage of open space is 18.2 acres. The largest of these spaces is the common of 3.3 acres.

This serves both as a park and as a setting or approach to the school building. Back of the school is the main playground for the small children, of 2.54 acres, and near it is the girls' playfield of 1.74 acres. On the opposite side of the schoolyard, a little farther away, is the boys' playground of 2.7 acres. Space for tennis courts is located conveniently in another section of the district. At various other points are to be found parked ovals or small greens which give attractiveness to vistas and afford pleasing bits of landscaping for the surrounding homes.

Community center

The pivotal feature of the layout is the common, with the group of buildings, which face upon it. These consist of the schoolhouse and two lateral structures facing a small central plaza. One of these buildings might be devoted to a public library and the other to any suitable neighborhood purpose. Sites are provided for two churches, one adjoining the school playground and the other at a prominent street intersection. The school and its supporting buildings constitute a terminal vista for a parked main highway coming up from the market square.

In both design and landscape treatment the common and the central buildings constitute an interesting and significant neighborhood community center.

Shopping districts

Small shopping districts are located at each of the four corners of the development. The streets furnishing access to the stores are widened to provide for parking, and at the two more important points there are small market squares, which afford additional parking space and more opportunity for unloading space in the rear of the stores. The total area devoted to business blocks and market plazas amounts to 7.7 acres. The average business frontage per family provided by the plan is about 2.3 feet.

Street system

In carrying out the unit principle, the boundary streets have been made sufficiently wide to serve as main traffic arteries. One of the bounding streets is 160 feet wide, and the other three have widths of 120 feet. Each of these arterial highways is provided with a central roadway for through traffic and two service roadways for local traffic separated by planting strips. One-half of the area of the boundary streets is contributed by the development. This amounts to 15.3 acres, or 9.5 percent of the total area, which is a much larger contribution to general traffic facilities than is ordinarily made by the commercial subdivision, but not greater than that which is required by present-day traffic needs. The interior streets are generally 40 or 50 feet in width and are adequate for the amount of traffic, which will be developed in a neighborhood of this single-family density. By the careful design of blocks, the area devoted to streets is rather lower than is usually found in a standard gridiron subdivision. If the bounding streets were not over 50 feet wide, the percent of the total street area would be reduced from the 27.4 percent to about 22 percent. It will be observed that most of the streets opening on the boundary thoroughfares are not opposite similar openings in the adjacent developments. There are no streets which run clear through the development without being interrupted.

A neighborhood unit for an industrial section

[Figure 2] is presented as a sketch of the kind of layout which might be devised for a district in the vicinity of factories and railways [see Table 2]. Many cities possess somewhat central areas of this character, which have not been pre-empted by business or industry but which are unsuitable for high-cost housing and too valuable for a low-cost development entirely of single-family dwellings.

Economically, the only alternative use for such a section is industrial. If it were built up with factories, however, the non-residential area thereabouts would be increased and the daily travel distance of many workers would be lengthened. One of the main objectives of good city planning is therefore attained when it is made available for homes.

Along the northern boundary of the tract illustrated lie extensive railroad yards, while its southern side borders one of the city's main arteries, affording both an elevated railway and wide roadbeds for surface traffic. An elevated station is located at a point opposite the center of the southern limit, making that spot the main portal of the development.

Table 2 A neighborhood unit for an industrial section – distribution of area in Figure 2

Complete unit	101.4 acres	100 percent
Residences: houses	37.8	37.3
Residences: apartments	8.4	8.3
Parks and play spaces*	10.8	10.6
Business	5.2	5.1
Warehouses	3.2	3.2
Streets	36.0	35.5

* This aggregate of open spaces includes the sites for school and churches. When these are deducted there will still be something more than one acre per 1,000 residents. Of course, in this and the three other illustrative schemes, the provisions for open space are intended to suggest only what should be sought for in neighborhood subdivisions or developments. It is assumed in each case that elsewhere there will be provided additional land for large parks and athletic fields, bringing the combined park and recreation area of the city, as a whole, up to three acres per thousand population, or one acre for about every 300 persons. This is in conformity with the standard set forth in "Public Recreation," *Regional Survey, Vol. V*, page 132.

The functional dispositions

The above features dictated the employment of a tree-like design for the street system. Its trunk rests upon the elevated station, passes through the main business district, and terminates at the community center. Branches, covering all sections of the unit, facilitate easy access to the school, to the main street stem, and to the business district.

Along the northern border, structures suitable for light industry, garages, or warehouses have been designated. These are to serve as a buffer both for the noises and the sights of the railway yards. Next to them, separated only by a narrow service street, is a row of apartments, whose main outlooks will all be directed toward the interior of the unit and its parked open spaces.

The apartments are assigned to sites at the sides of the unit that they may serve as conspicuous visible boundaries and enable the widest possible utilization of the attractive vistas which should be provided by the interior features – the ecclesiastical architecture around the civic center and the park-like open spaces.

Housing density

The above diagram is intended to suggest mainly an arrangement of the various elements of a neighborhood and is not offered as a finished plan. The street layout is based upon a housing scheme providing for 2,000 families, of which 68 percent are allotted to houses, some semi-detached and some in rows; and 32 percent to apartments averaging 800 square feet of ground area per suite. On the basis of 4.5 persons in houses and 4.2 in suites, the total population would be around 8,800 people and there would be some 1,400 children of elementary school age, a fine enrolment for a regulation city school. The average net ground area per family amounts to 1,003.7 square feet. If the parks and play areas are included, this figure becomes 1,216 square feet.

Recreation spaces

These consist of a large schoolyard and two playgrounds suitable for the younger children, grounds

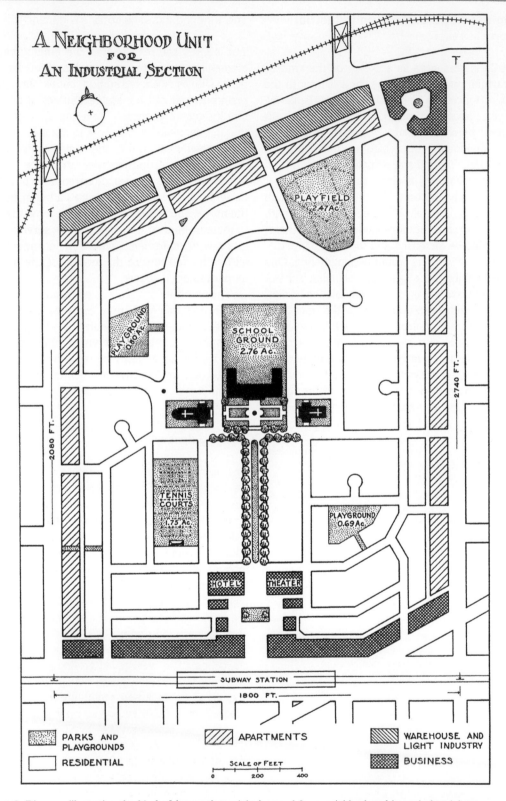

Figure 2 Diagram illustrating the kind of layout that might be used for a neighborhood in an industrial area.

accommodating nine tennis courts, and a playfield adapted either for baseball or soccer football. In distributing these spaces regard was had both to convenience and to their usefulness as open spaces and vistas for the adjacent homes. All should have planting around the edges, and most of them could be seeded, thus avoiding the barren aspect so common to city playgrounds.

Community center

The educational, religious and civic life of the community is provided for by a group of structures, centrally located and disposed so as to furnish an attractive vista for the trunk street and a pivotal point for the whole layout. A capacious school is flanked by two churches, and all face upon a small square which might be embellished with a monument, fountain, or other ornamental feature. The auditorium, gymnasium, and library of the school, as well as certain other rooms, could be used for civic, cultural and recreational activities of the neighborhood. With such an equipment and an environment possessing so much of interest and service to all the residents, a vigorous local consciousness would be bound to arise and find expression in all sorts of agreeable and useful face-to-face associations.

Shopping districts

The most important business area is, of course, around the main portal and along the southern arterial highway. For greater convenience and increased exposures a small market square has been introduced. Here would be the natural place for a motion-picture theatre, a hotel, and such services as a branch post office and a fire-engine house. Another and smaller shopping district has been placed at the northeast corner to serve the needs of the homes in that section.

Economic aspects

While this development is adapted to families of moderate means, comprehensive planning makes possible an intensive and profitable use of the land without the usual loss of a comfortable and attractive living environment. The back and side yards may be smaller, but pleasing outlooks and play spaces are still provided. They belong to all the families in common and the unit scheme preserves them for the exclusive use of the residents.

While this is primarily a housing scheme, it saves and utilizes for its own purposes that large unearned increment, in business and industrial values, which rises naturally out of the mere aggregation of so many people. The community creates that value and while it may apparently be absorbed by the management, nevertheless, some of it goes to the individual householder through the improved home and environment which a corporation, having that value in prospect, is able to offer.

The percentage of area devoted to streets (35.5) is higher than is usually required in a neighborhood unit scheme. In this case the proportion is boosted by the generous parking space provided in the market square and by the adjoining 200-foot boulevard, one-half of whose area is included in this calculation. Ordinarily the unit scheme makes possible a saving in street area that is almost, if not quite, equal to the land devoted to open spaces. The school and church sites need not be dedicated. They may simply be reserved and so marked in the advertising matter with full confidence that local community needs and sentiment will bring about their ultimate purchase by the proper bodies. If either or both of the church sites should not be taken, their very location will ensure their eventual appropriation for some public, or semi-public, use.

Apartment house unit

Population

On the basis of five-story and basement buildings and allowing 1,320 square feet per suite, this plan would accommodate 2,381 families. Counting 4.2 persons per family, the total population would number 10,000 individuals, of whom about 1,600 would probably be of elementary school age, a number which could be nicely accommodated in a modern elementary school.

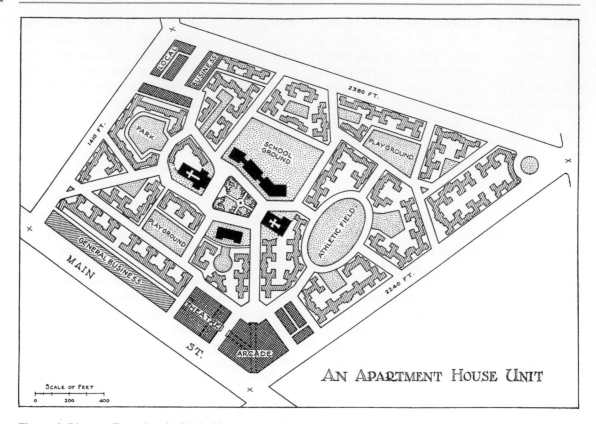

Figure 3 Diagram illustrating the kind of layout that might be used for an apartment house neighborhood.

Table 3 Apartment house unit – distribution of the area depicted in Figure 3

Complete unit	75.7 acres	100 percent
Apartment buildings	12.0	15.9
Apartment yards	21.3	28.0
Parks and playgrounds	10.4	13.8
Streets	25.3	33.4
Local business	4.9	6.5
General business	1.8	2.4

Environment

The general locality is that section where downtown business establishments and residences begin to merge. One side of the unit faces on the principal street of the city and this would be devoted to general business concerns. A theatre and a business block, penetrated by an arcade, would serve both the residents of the unit and the general public.

Street system

The unit is bounded by wide streets, while its interior system is broken up into shorter highways that give easy circulation within the unit but do not run uninterruptedly through it. In general they converge upon the community center. Their widths are varied to fit probable traffic loads and parking needs.

Open spaces

The land devoted to parks and playgrounds averages over one acre per 1,000 persons. If the space in apartment yards is also counted, this average amounts to 3.17 acres per 1,000 persons. The distribution is [shown in Table 4].

For 1,600 children the space in the school yard provides an average of 89 square feet per pupil, which is a fair allowance considering that all the pupils will seldom be in the yard at the same time. The athletic field is large enough for baseball in the

Table 4 Apartment house unit – area of open spaces depicted in Figure 3

Kind	Acres
School grounds	3.27
Athletic field	1.85
Common	0.81
Park	0.61
Playground	1.03
Playground	0.81
Circle	0.18
Small greens	1.86
Total	10.42

spring and summer, and football in the fall. By flooding it with a hose in the winter time it can be made available for skating.

On the smaller playground it will be possible, if desired, to mark off six tennis courts. The bottle-neck park is partly enclosed by a group of apartments, but it is also accessible to the residents in general.

The recreation spaces should be seeded and have planting around the edges, thus adding attractiveness to the vistas from the surrounding apartments.

Community center

Around a small common are grouped a school, two churches, and a public building. The last might be a branch public library, a museum, a "little theatre," or a fraternal building. In any case it should be devoted to a local community use.

The common may exhibit some kind of formal treatment in which a monument and perhaps a band-stand may be elements of the design. The situation is one that calls for embellishment, by means of both architecture and landscaping, and such a treatment would contribute greatly to local pride and the attractiveness of the development. The ground plan of the school indicates a type in which the auditorium, the gymnasium and the classrooms are in separate buildings, connected by corridors. This arrangement greatly facilitates the use of the school plant by the public in general and permits, at the same time, an efficient utilization of the buildings for instruction purposes.

Apartment pattern

The layout of the apartment structures follows quite closely an actual design employed by Mr. Andrew J. Thomas for a group of "garden apartments" now being constructed for Mr. John D. Rockefeller, Jr., in New York City. The suites are of four, five, six and seven rooms and, in the case of the larger ones, two bath-rooms. Light comes in three sides of a room as a rule and, in some cases, from four sides. All rooms enjoy cross-ventilation.

In the Rockefeller plan every apartment looks out upon a central garden, which is ornamented with a Japanese rookery and a foot-bridge over running water. The walks are to be lined with shrubbery and the general effect will be park-like and refreshing.

Similar treatments could be given to the various interior spaces of the unit layout. Here, however, due to the short and irregular streets and the odd positions of the buildings, the charm of a given court would be greatly extended because, in many cases, it would constitute a part of the view of not merely one, but several, apartments.

Five-block apartment house unit

Locality

The plan shown in [Figure 4] is put forward as a suggestion of the type of treatment which might be given to central residential areas of high land values destined for rebuilding because of deterioration or the sweep of a real estate movement [see Table 5]. The blocks chosen for the ground site are 200 feet wide and 670 feet long, a length which is found in several sections on Manhattan. In this

Table 5 Five-block apartment house unit: area relations depicted in Figure 4

Five blocks and four cross streets	19.07 acres
Two cross streets taken	8,000 sq. ft,
Given to boundary streets	50,800 sq. ft.
Area of set-backs	39,000 sq. ft.
Land developed	16.4 acres
Covered by buildings	6.5 acres
Coverage	40.0 percent
Three central courts	5.3 acres

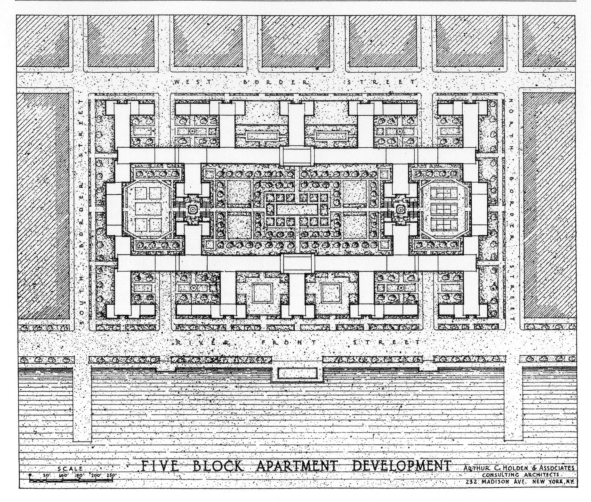

Figure 4 Diagram illustrating a five-block apartment unit that might be used to rebuild residential areas in central areas that have suffered deterioration.

plan, which borders a river, two streets are closed and two are carried through the development as covered roadways under terraced central courts.

Ground plan

The dimensions of the plot between the boundary streets are 650 feet by 1,200 feet, and the total area is approximately 16 acres. The building lines are set back from the streets 30 feet on the northern and southern boundaries. Both of the end streets, which were originally 60 feet, have been widened to 80 feet, the two 20-foot extra strips being taken out of the area of the development. The western boundary has been enlarged from 80 to 100 feet. The area given to street widening and to building

set-back amounts to 89,800 square feet, or 11,800 square feet more than the area of the two streets which were appropriated.

It will be observed that the plan of buildings encloses 53 percent of the total area devoted to open space in the form of central courts. The main central court is about the size of Gramercy Park, Manhattan, with its surrounding streets. Since this area would receive an unusual amount of sunlight, it would be susceptible to the finest sort of landscape and formal garden treatment.

Both of the end courts are on a level 20 feet higher than the central space and cover the two streets which are carried through the development. Underneath these courts are the service areas for the buildings. At one end of the central space there is room for tennis courts and, at the other, a children's playground of nearly one acre. By reason of the large open spaces and the arrangement of the buildings, the plan achieves an unusual standard as to light in that there is no habitable room that has an exposure to sunlight of less than 45 degrees. The width of all the structures is 50 feet, so that apartments of two-room depth are possible throughout the building, while the western central rib, being 130 feet from a 100-foot street, will never have its light unduly shut off by buildings on the adjacent blocks.

Accommodations

The capacity of the buildings is about 1,000 families, with suites ranging from three to fourteen rooms in size, the majority of them suitable for family occupancy. In addition there would be room for a hotel for transients, an elementary school, an auditorium, a gymnasium, a swimming pool, handball courts, locker rooms and other athletic facilities. The first floors of certain buildings on one or more sides of the unit could be devoted to shops. The auditorium could be suitable for motion pictures, lectures, little-theatre performances, public meetings, and possibly for public worship. Dances could be easily held in the gymnasium. In the basement there might be squash courts.

Height

The buildings range in height from two and three stories on the boundary streets to ten stories in the abutting ribs, fifteen stories in the main central ribs, and thirty-three stories in the two towers. Many of the roofs could be given a garden-like treatment and thus contribute to the array of delightful prospects which are offered by the scheme.

This plan, though much more compact than the three others, nevertheless observes all of the unit principles. Neither the community center nor the shopping districts are conspicuous, but they are present. Children can play, attend school, and visit stores without crossing traffic ways.

"The Pack-Donkey's Way and Man's Way" and "A Contemporary City"

from *The City of To-morrow and Its Planning* (1929)

Le Corbusier

Editors' Introduction

Swiss architect Le Corbusier (1887–1965) was a founding father of the modernism movement and an early advocate of what came to be known as the International Style in architecture. Bold, rational, concerned with efficiency, and enamored of technology, he gave voice to a new Machine Age spirit that suffused a generation of urban planners and architects and still influences designers today.

Born Charles-Edouard Jeanneret in a small Swiss town near the French border, Le Corbusier reinvented himself with his famous pseudonym after moving to Paris in his late twenties to work on theoretical architectural studies. In the 1920s, these studies advanced into designs for modernist single-family houses, which led to commissions for private homes, most notably the groundbreaking Villa Savoye. This white stucco house with ribbon windows and tubular industrial railings, which he dubbed "a house for the machine age," was lifted off the ground on pilotis (reinforced concrete stilts) that gave structural support to the building, allowing a free-floating (non-load-bearing) façade and an open floor plan on the upper floor. Many people were shocked by the spare minimalism of the design, which was completely different than traditional images of residential architecture. Le Corbusier also worked on studies for multi-family housing blocks and then moved on to studies for city districts and whole cities.

In 1922, Le Corbusier unveiled his plan for "A Contemporary City of Three Million People," which created an incredible stir. The plan consisted of a cluster of cruciform skyscrapers set in a rigid symmetrical grid pattern. The skyscrapers were to house both offices and apartments for the well-to-do. At the center was a transportation hub with buses, cars, trucks, trains, and airplanes accommodated at different levels. Smaller, zigzag apartment blocks surrounding the central skyscrapers were to house proletarian workers. Le Corbusier insisted that this utopian city was not a vision for the city of the future but rather what a city could be today. In 1925, he exhibited his *Plan Voisin*, which shockingly proposed wiping away several hundred acres of Paris's Right Bank and building sixty-story towers from the Contemporary City, set in a right-angle grid and surrounded by open park space. At the time, the scheme was criticized and scorned, but the combined ideas of clean slate urban renewal, skyscrapers in a park, and rationalized grade-separated transportation systems took hold in the minds of planners and architects alike as an appropriate solution for the perceived ills and inefficiencies of existing cities. This vision would transform the face of cities throughout the world during the twentieth century, in the form of government-sponsored public housing projects, high-end residential towers, and sprawling single-use apartment complexes.

Reprinted here are two pieces from Le Corbusier's influential book *The City of To-morrow and Its Planning*, in which he spells out his rationale and vision for a streamlined and efficient modern approach to architecture and city planning. The first piece, "The Pack-Donkey's Way and Man's Way," is a harsh criticism of traditional city structure, and a direct disparagement of Camillo Sitte's late-nineteenth-century appreciation of the picturesque qualities of medieval urban forms (p. 45). The second piece, "A Contemporary City," re-presents his utopian vision for a modern city of high rises and highways, this time shown on a vacant "tabula rasa" site.

Le Corbusier's ideas caught people's attention but did not win him many urban planning commissions. The real impact of his ideas can be seen in urban districts and cities built by others that incorporated the planning approaches and architectural designs he advocated. To Le Corbusier we owe the powerful images of high-rise residential "towers in the park" and elevated highways serving segregated traffic flows swooping through cities. In America, these ideas spurred countless central city urban renewal and urban freeway projects in the 1950s and 1960s, and similar projects at the edges of many European cities. They continue to influence city design projects throughout Asia and the developing world. The one city district Le Corbusier did have a major role in creating was the center of Chandigarh, the new capital of the Indian state of Punjab, which was started in the 1950s and was India's first planned city. The plan follows his transportation and circulation principles and is an assemblage of buildings with considerable space between them, particularly in the governmental center and the main business commercial area.

Le Corbusier was a founding member of the Congrès Internationaux d'Architecture Moderne (CIAM), whose modernist philosophy was proclaimed in its 1933 Manifesto, The Charter of Athens. Allan B. Jacobs and Donald Appleyard's "Toward an Urban Design Manifesto," *Journal of the American Planning Association* (1987), reprinted in Part Two of this volume (p. 218), takes on The Charter of Athens, rejecting its Utopian program and calling instead for an urbanism based upon social objectives for urban development and upon how people actually live and experience cities and space. Earlier, Jane Jacobs soundly refuted Le Corbusier's ideas and the modernist movement in architecture and city planning in the introduction to her book *The Life and Death of Great American Cities*, a chapter of which is also reprinted in Part Two (p. 139).

Many of Le Corbusier's most provocative writings are included in *The City of To-morrow and Its Planning* (New York: Dover, 1987) (translated by Frederich Etchells from *Urbanisme* [1929]). His other books include *Towards a New Architecture* (New York: Payson & Clarke, 1927), which has been republished numerous times including by Dover (1986); *Concerning Town Planning* (New Haven, CT: Yale University Press, 1948) (translated by Oliver Entwistle from *Propos d'Urbanisme* [1946]); *Talks with Students* (New York: Orion Press, 1961), republished under the title *Le Corbusier Talks with Students from the Schools of Architecture* (New York: Princeton Architectural Press, 1999); and *L'Urbanisme des trois etablissements humaines* (Paris: Editions de Minuit, 1959). An edited anthology of Le Corbusier's writings is *The Ideas of Le Corbusier* (New York: G. Braziller, 1981) edited by Jacques Guiton.

Discussions and criticisms of Le Corbusier's ideas and their influences can be found in M. Christine Boyer, *Le Corbusier: Homme de Lettres* (New York: Princeton Architectural Press, 2011); Nicholas Fox Weber, *Le Corbusier: A Life* (New York: Knopf, 2008); Kenneth Frampton, *Le Corbusier: World of Art* (London: Thames & Hudson, 2001); Peter Hall, *Cities of Tomorrow* (Oxford: Blackwell, 1988); Geoffrey H. Baker, *Le Corbusier, and Analysis of Form* (New York: Van Nostrand Reinhold, 1984); Robert Fishman, *Urban Utopias in the Twentieth Century* (New York: Basic Books, 1977); Henry Russell Hitchcock, *Architecture: Nineteenth and Twentieth Centuries* (Baltimore, MD: Penguin, 1967); and Siegfried Giedion, *Space, Time and Architecture: The Growth of a New Tradition* (Cambridge, MA: Harvard University Press, 1963).

For a closer look at Le Corbusier's work in Chandigarh, see Vikramaditya Prakash, *Chandigarh's Le Corbusier: The Struggle for Modernity in Postcolonial India* (Seattle, WA: University of Washington Press, 2002); and Klaus-Peter Gast and Arthur Ruegg, *Le Corbusier: Paris–Chandigarh* (Boston, MA: Birkhaüser, 2000). For background on the modernism movement, see Peter Gay, *Modernism: The Lure of Heresy* (New York: Norton, 2007); Christopher Wilk, *Modernism: Designing a New World* (London: Victoria & Albert Museum, 2006); and Richard Weston, *Modernism* (London: Phaidon, 2001).

THE PACK-DONKEY'S WAY AND MAN'S WAY

MAN walks in a straight line because he has a goal and knows where he is going; he has made up his mind to reach some particular place and he goes straight to it.

The pack-donkey meanders along, meditates a little in his scatter-brained and distracted fashion, he zigzags in order to avoid the larger stones, or to ease the climb, or to gain a little shade; he takes the line of least resistance.

But man governs his feelings by his reason; he keeps his feelings and his instincts in check, subordinating them to the aim he has in view. He rules the brute creation by his intelligence. His intelligence formulates laws which are the product of experience. His experience is born of work; man works in order that he may not perish. In order that production may be possible, a line of conduct is essential, the laws of experience must be obeyed. Man must consider the result in advance.

But the pack-donkey thinks of nothing at all, except what will save himself trouble.

The Pack-Donkey's Way is responsible for the plan of every continental city; including Paris, unfortunately.

In the areas into which little by little invading populations filtered, the covered wagon lumbered along at the mercy of bumps and hollows, of rocks or mire; a stream was an intimidating obstacle. In this way were born roads and tracks. At cross roads or along river banks the first huts were erected, the first houses and the first villages; the houses were planted along the tracks, along the Pack-Donkey's Way. The inhabitants built a fortified wall round and a town hall inside it. They legislated, they toiled, they lived, and always they respected the Pack-Donkey's Way. Five centuries later another and larger enclosure was built, and five centuries later still a third yet greater. The places where the Pack-Donkey's Way entered the town became the City Gates and the Customs officers were installed there. The village has become a great capital; Paris, Rome, and Stamboul are based upon the Pack-Donkey's Way.

The great capitals have no arteries; they have only capillaries: further growth, therefore, implies sickness or death. In order to survive, their existence has for a long time been in the hands of surgeons who operate constantly.

The Romans were great legislators, great colonizers, great administrators. When they arrived at a place, at a cross roads or at a river bank, they took a square and set out the plan of a rectilinear town, so that it should be clear and well-arranged, easy to police and to clean, a place in which you could find your way about and stroll with comfort – the working town or the pleasure town (Pompeii). The square plan was in conformity with the dignity of the Roman citizen.

But at home, in Rome itself, with their eyes turned towards the Empire, they allowed themselves to be stifled by the Pack-Donkey's Way. What an ironical situation! The wealthy, however, went far from the chaos of the town and built their great and well-planned villas, such as Hadrian's villa.

They were, with Louis XIV, the only great town-planners of the West.

In the Middle Ages, overcome by the year 1000, men accepted the leading of the pack-donkey, and long generations endured it after. Louis XIV, after trying to tidy up the Louvre (i.e. the Colonnade), became disgusted and took bold measures: he built Versailles, where both town and chateau were created in every detail in a rectilinear and well-planned fashion; the Observatoire, the Invalides and the Esplanade, the Tuileries and the Champs Elysées, rose far from the chaos, outside the town – all these were ordered and rectilinear.

The overcrowding had been exorcised. Everything else followed, in a masterly way: the Champs de Mars, l'Etoile, the avenues de Neuilly, de Vincennes, de Fontainebleau, etc., for succeeding generations to exploit.

But imperceptibly, as a result of carelessness, weakness and anarchy, and by the system of "democratic" responsibilities, the old business of overcrowding began again.

And as if that were not enough, people began to desire it; they have even created it in invoking the laws of beauty! The Pack-Donkey's Way has been made into a religion.

The movement arose in Germany as a result of a book by Camillo Sitte on town-planning, a most wilful piece of work; a glorification of the curved line and a specious demonstration of its unrivalled beauties. Proof of this was advanced by the example of all the beautiful towns of the Middle Ages; the author confounded the picturesque with the conditions vital to the existence of a city. Quite recently whole quarters have been constructed in Germany based on this *aesthetic*. (For it was purely a question of aesthetics.)

This was an appalling and paradoxical misconception in an age of motor-cars. "So much the better," said a great authority to me, one of those who direct and elaborate the plans for the extension of Paris; "motors will be completely held up!"

But a modern city lives by the straight line, inevitably; for the construction of buildings, sewers and tunnels, highways, pavements. The circulation of traffic demands the straight line; it is the proper thing for the heart of a city. The curve is ruinous, difficult and dangerous; it is a paralyzing thing.

The straight line enters into all human history, into all human aim, into every human act.

We must have the courage to view the rectilinear cities of America with admiration. If the aesthete has not so far done so, the moralist, on the contrary, may well find more food for reflection than at first appears.

The winding road is the Pack-Donkey's Way, the straight road is man's way.

The winding road is the result of happy-go-lucky heedlessness, of looseness, lack of concentration and animality.

The straight road is a reaction, an action, a positive deed, the result of self-mastery. It is sane and noble.

A city is a centre of intense life and effort.

A heedless people, or society, or town, in which effort is relaxed and is not concentrated, quickly becomes dissipated, overcome and absorbed by a nation or a society that goes to work in a positive way and controls itself.

It is in this way that cities sink to nothing and that ruling classes are overthrown.

A CONTEMPORARY CITY

The use of technical analysis and architectural synthesis enabled me to draw up my scheme for a contemporary city of three million inhabitants. The result of my work was shown in November 1922 at the Salon d' Automne in Paris. It was greeted with a sort of stupor; the shock of surprise caused rage in some quarters and enthusiasm in others. The solution I put forward was a rough one

and completely uncompromising. There were no notes to accompany the plans, and, alas! not everybody can read a plan. I should have had to be constantly on the spot in order to reply to the fundamental questions which spring from the very depths of human feelings. Such questions are of profound interest and cannot remain unanswered. When at a later date it became necessary that this book should be written, a book in which I could formulate the new principles of Town Planning, I resolutely decided *first of all* to find answers to these fundamental questions. I have used two kinds of argument: first, those essentially human ones which start from the mind or the heart or the physiology of our sensations as a basis; secondly, historical and statistical arguments. Thus I could keep in touch with what is fundamental and at the same time be master of the environment in which all this takes place.

In this way I hope I shall have been able to help my reader to take a number of steps by means of which he can reach a sure and certain position. So that when I unroll my plans I can have the happy assurance that his astonishment will no longer be stupefaction nor his fears mere panic.

A CONTEMPORARY CITY OF THREE MILLION INHABITANTS

Proceeding in the manner of the investigator in his laboratory, I have avoided all special cases, and all that may be accidental, and I have assumed an ideal site to begin with. My object was not to overcome the existing state of things, but *by constructing a theoretically water-tight formula to arrive at the fundamental principles of modern town planning*. Such fundamental principles, if they are genuine, can serve as the skeleton of any system of modern town planning; being as it were the *rules* according to which development will take place. We shall then be in a position to take a special case, no matter what: whether it be Paris, London, Berlin, New York or some small town. Then, as a result of what we have learnt, we can take control and decide in what direction the forthcoming battle is to be waged. For the desire to rebuild any great city in a modern way is to engage in a formidable battle. Can you imagine people engaging in a battle without knowing their objectives? Yet that is exactly what is happening. The authorities are compelled to do something, so they give the police white sleeves or set them on horseback, they invent sound signals and light signals, they propose to put bridges over streets or moving pavements under the streets; more garden cities are suggested, or it is decided to suppress the tramways, and so on. And these decisions are reached in a sort of frantic haste in order, as it were, to hold a wild beast at bay. That BEAST is the great city. It is infinitely more powerful than all these devices. And it is just beginning to wake. What will to-morrow bring forth to cope with it?

We must have some rule of conduct.[1]

We must have fundamental principles for modern town planning.

Site

A level site is the ideal site. In all those places where traffic becomes over-intensified the level site gives a chance of a normal solution to the problem. Where there is less traffic, differences in level matter less.

The river flows far away from the city. The river is a kind of liquid railway, a goods station and a sorting house. In a decent house the servants' stairs do not go through the drawing room – even if the maid is charming (or if the little boats delight the loiterer leaning on a bridge).

Population

This consists of the citizens proper; of suburban dwellers; and of those of a mixed kind.

(a) Citizens are of the city: those who work and live in it.
(b) Suburban dwellers are those who work in the outer industrial zone and who do not come into the city: they live in garden cities.
(c) The mixed sort are those who work in the business parts of the city but bring up their families in garden cities.

To classify these divisions (and so make possible the transmutation of these recognized types) is to attack the most important problem in town plan-

ning, for such a classification would define the areas to be allotted to these three sections and the delimitation of their boundaries. This would enable us to formulate and resolve the following problems:

1 The *City* as a business and residential centre.
2 The *Industrial City* in relation to the *Garden Cities* (i.e. the question of transport).
3 The *Garden Cities* and the *daily transport* of the workers. Our first requirement will be an organ that is compact, rapid, lively and concentrated: this is the City with its well-organized centre. Our second requirement will be another organ, supple, extensive and elastic; this is the *Garden City* on the periphery.

Lying between these two organs, we must *require the legal establishment* of that absolute necessity, a protective zone which allows of extension, *a reserved zone* of woods and fields, a fresh-air reserve.

Density of population

The more dense the population of a city is the less are the distances that have to be covered. The moral, therefore, is that we must *increase the density of the centres of our cities, where business affairs are carried on*.

Lungs

Work in our modern world becomes more intensified day by day, and its demands affect our nervous system in a way that grows more and more dangerous. Modern toil demands quiet and fresh air, not stale air.

The towns of to-day can only increase in density at the expense of the open spaces which are the lungs of a city.

We must *increase the open spaces and diminish the distances to be covered*. Therefore the centre of the city must be constructed *vertically*.

The city's residential quarters must no longer be built along "corridor-streets," full of noise and dust and deprived of light.

It is a simple matter to build urban dwellings away from the streets, without small internal courtyards and with the windows looking on to large parks; and this whether our housing schemes are of the type with "set-backs" or built on the "cellular" principle.

The street

The street of to-day is still the old bare ground which has been paved over, and under which a few tube railways have been run.

The modern street in the true sense of the word is a new type of organism, a sort of stretched-out workshop, a home for many complicated and delicate organs, such as gas, water and electric mains. It is contrary to all economy, to all security, and to all sense to bury these important service mains. They ought to be accessible throughout their length. The various storeys of this stretched-out workshop will each have their own particular functions. If this type of street, which I have called a "workshop," is to be realized, it becomes as much a matter of *construction* as are the houses with which it is customary to flank it, and the bridges which carry it over valleys and across rivers.

The modern street should be a masterpiece of civil engineering and no longer a job for navvies.

The "corridor-street" should be tolerated no longer, for it poisons the houses that border it and leads to the construction of small internal courts or "wells."

Traffic

Traffic can be classified more easily than other things.

To-day traffic is not classified – it is like dynamite flung at hazard into the street, killing pedestrians. Even so, *traffic does not fulfill its function*. This sacrifice of the pedestrian leads nowhere.

If we classify traffic we get:

(a) Heavy goods traffic.
(b) Lighter goods traffic, i.e. vans, etc., which make short journeys in all directions.
(c) Fast traffic, which covers a large section of the town.

Three kinds of roads are needed, and in superimposed storeys:

(a) Below-ground there would be the street for heavy traffic.[2] This storey of the houses would consist merely of concrete piles, and between them large open spaces which would form a sort of clearing-house where heavy goods traffic could load and unload.
(b) At the ground floor level of the buildings there would be the complicated and delicate network of the ordinary streets taking traffic in every desired direction.
(c) Running north and south, and east and west, and forming the two great axes of the city, there would be great *arterial roads for fast one-way traffic* built on immense reinforced concrete bridges 120 to 180 yards in width and approached every half-mile or so by subsidiary roads from ground level. These arterial roads could therefore be joined at any given point, so that even at the highest speeds the town can be traversed and the suburbs reached without having to negotiate any cross-roads.

The number of existing streets *should be diminished by two-thirds*. The number of crossings depends directly on the number of streets; and *cross-roads are an enemy to traffic*. The number of existing streets was fixed at a remote epoch in history. The perpetuation of the boundaries of properties has, almost without exception, preserved even the faintest tracks and footpaths of the old village and made streets of them, and sometimes even an avenue (see "The Pack-Donkey's Way and Man's Way").

The result is that we have cross-roads every fifty yards, even every twenty yards or ten yards. And this leads to the ridiculous traffic congestion we all know so well.

The distance between two bus stops or two tube stations gives us the necessary unit for the distance between streets, though this unit is conditional on the speed of vehicles and the walking capacity of pedestrians. So an average measure of about 400 yards would give the normal separation between streets, and make a standard for urban distances. My city is conceived on the gridiron system with streets every 400 yards, though occasionally these distances are subdivided to give streets every 200 yards.

This triple system of superimposed levels answers every need of motor traffic (lorries, private cars, taxis, buses) because it provides for rapid and *mobile* transit.

Traffic running on fixed rails is only justified if it is in the form of a convoy carrying an immense load; it then becomes a sort of extension of the underground system or of trains dealing with suburban traffic. *The tramway has no right to exist in the heart of the modern city.*

If the city thus consists of plots about 400 yards square, this will give us sections of about 40 acres in area, and the density of population will vary from 50,000 down to 6,000, according as the "lots" are developed for business or for residential purposes. The natural thing, therefore, would be to continue to apply our unit of distance as it exists in the Paris tubes to-day (namely, 400 yards) and to put a station in the middle of each plot.

Following the two great axes of the city, two "storeys" below the arterial roads for fast traffic, would run the tubes leading to the four furthest points of the garden city suburbs, and linking up with the metropolitan network [. . .]. At a still lower level, and again following these two main axes, would run the one-way loop systems for suburban traffic, and below these again the four great main lines serving the provinces and running north, south, east and west. These main lines would end at the Central Station, or better still might be connected up by a loop system.

The station

There is only one station. The only place for the station is in the centre of the city. It is the natural place for it, and there is no reason for putting it anywhere else. The railway station is the hub of the wheel.

The station would be an essentially subterranean building. Its roof, which would be two storeys above the natural ground level of the city, would form the aerodrome for aero-taxis. This aerodrome (linked up with the main aerodrome in the protected zone) must be in close contact with the tubes, the suburban lines, the main lines, the main arteries and the administrative services connected with all these.

THE PLAN OF THE CITY

The basic principles we must follow are these:

1 We must de-congest the centres of our cities.
2 We must augment their density.
3 We must increase the means for getting about.
4 We must increase parks and open spaces.

At the very centre we have the STATION with its landing stage for aero-taxis.

Running north and south, and east and west, we have the MAIN ARTERIES for fast traffic, forming elevated roadways 120 feet wide.

At the base of the sky-scrapers and all round them we have a great open space 2,400 yards by 1,500 yards, giving an area of 3,600,000 square yards, and occupied by gardens, parks and avenues. In these parks, at the foot of and round the sky-scrapers, would be the restaurants and cafes, the luxury shops, housed in buildings with receding terraces: here too would be the theatres, halls and so on; and here the parking places or garage shelters.

The sky-scrapers are designed purely for business purposes.

On the left we have the great public buildings, the museums, the municipal and administrative offices. Still further on the left we have the "Park" (which is available for further logical development of the heart of the city).

On the right, and traversed by one of the arms of the main arterial roads, we have the warehouses, and the industrial quarters with their goods stations.

All round the city is the *protected zone* of woods and green fields.

Further beyond are the *garden cities*, forming a wide encircling band.

Then, right in the midst of all these, we have the *Central Station*, made up of the following elements:

(a) The landing-platform; forming an aerodrome of 200,000 square yards in area.
(b) The entresol or mezzanine; at this level are the raised tracks for fast motor traffic: the only crossing being gyratory.
(c) The ground floor where are the entrance halls and booking offices for the tubes, suburban, main line and air traffic.
(d) The "basement": here are the tubes which serve the city and the main arteries.
(e) The "sub-basement": here are the suburban lines running on a one-way loop.

(f) The "sub-sub-basement": here are the main lines (going north, south, east and west).

The city

Here we have twenty-four sky-scrapers capable each of housing 10,000 to 50,000 employees; this is the business and hotel section, etc., and accounts for 400,000 to 600,000 inhabitants.

The residential blocks, of the two main types already mentioned, account for a further 600,000 inhabitants.

The garden cities give us a further 2,000,000 inhabitants, or more.

In the great central open space are the cafes, restaurants, luxury shops, halls of various kinds, a magnificent forum descending by stages down to the immense parks surrounding it, the whole arrangement providing a spectacle of order and vitality.

Density of population

(a) The sky-scraper: 1,200 inhabitants to the acre.
(b) The residential blocks with set-backs: 120 inhabitants to the acre. These are the luxury dwellings.
(c) The residential blocks on the "cellular" system, with a similar number of inhabitants.

This great density gives us our necessary shortening of distances and ensures rapid intercommunication.

Note – The average density to the acre of Paris in the heart of the town is 146, and of London 63; and of the over-crowded quarters of Paris 213, and of London 169.

Open spaces

Of the area (a), 95 percent of the ground is open (squares, restaurants, theatres).

Of the area (b), 85 percent of the ground is open (gardens, sports grounds).

Of the area (c), 48 percent of the ground is open (gardens, sports grounds).

Educational and civic centres, universities, museums of art and industry, public services, county hall

The "Jardin anglais." (The city can extend here, if necessary.)

Sports grounds: Motor racing track, Racecourse, Stadium, Swimming baths, etc.

The Protected Zone (which will be the property of the city), with its *Aerodome*, a zone in which all building would be prohibited; reserved for the growth of the city as laid down by the municipality: it would consist of woods, fields and sports grounds. The forming of a "protected zone" by continual purchase of small properties in the immediate vicinity of the city is one of the most essential and urgent tasks which a municipality can pursue. It would eventually represent a tenfold return on the capital invested.

Industrial quarters[3]
Types of buildings to be employed

For business: sky-scrapers sixty storeys high with no internal wells or courtyards.

Residential buildings with "set-backs," of six double storeys; again with no internal wells: the flats looking on either side on to immense parks.

Residential buildings on the "cellular" principle, with "hanging gardens," looking on to immense parks; again no internal wells. These are "service-flats" of the most modern kind.

GARDEN CITIES

Their aesthetic, economy, perfection and modern outlook

A simple phrase suffices to express the necessities of tomorrow: WE MUST BUILD IN THE OPEN. The lay-out must be of a purely geometrical kind, with all its many and delicate implications.

The city of to-day is a dying thing because it is not geometrical. To build in the open would be to replace our present haphazard arrangements, *which are all we have to-day*, by a *uniform* lay-out. Unless we do this *there is no salvation*.

The result of a true geometrical lay-out is *repetition*.

The result of repetition is a *standard*, the perfect form (i.e. the creation of standard types). A geometrical lay-out means that mathematics play their part. There is no first-rate human production but has geometry at its base. It is of the very essence of Architecture. To introduce uniformity into the building of the city we must *industrialize building*. Building is the one economic activity which has so far resisted industrialization.

It has thus escaped the march of progress, with the result that the cost of building is still abnormally high.

The architect, from a professional point of view, has become a twisted sort of creature. He has grown to love irregular sites, claiming that they inspire him with original ideas for getting round them. Of course he is wrong. For nowadays the only building that can be undertaken must be either for the rich or built at a loss (as, for instance, in the case of municipal housing schemes), or else by jerry-building and so robbing the inhabitant of all amenities. A motor-car which is achieved by mass production is a masterpiece of comfort, precision, balance and good taste. A house built to order (on an "interesting" site) is a masterpiece of incongruity – a monstrous thing.

If the builder's yard were reorganized on the lines of standardization and mass production we might have gangs of workmen as keen and intelligent as mechanics.

The mechanic dates back only twenty years, yet already he forms the highest caste of the working world.

The mason dates . . . from time immemorial! He bangs away with feet and hammer. He smashes up everything round him, and the plant entrusted to him falls to pieces in a few months. The spirit of the mason must be disciplined by making him part of the severe and exact machinery of the industrialized builder's yard.

The cost of building would fall in the proportion of 10 to 2.

The wages of the labourers would fall into definite categories; to each according to his merits and service rendered.

The "interesting" or erratic site absorbs every creative faculty of the architect and wears him out. What results is equally erratic: lopsided abortions;

a specialist's solution which can only please other specialists.

We must build *in the open*: both within the city and around it. Then having worked through every necessary technical stage and using absolute ECONOMY, we shall be in a position to experience the intense joys of a creative art which is based on geometry.

THE CITY AND ITS AESTHETIC

The plan of a city which is here presented is a direct consequence of purely geometric considerations.

A new unit *on a large scale* (400 yards) inspires everything. Though the gridiron arrangement of the streets every 400 yards (sometimes only 200) is uniform (with a consequent ease in finding one's way about), no two streets are in any way alike. This is where, in a magnificent contrapuntal symphony, the forces of geometry come into play.

Suppose we are entering the city by way of the Great Park. Our fast car takes the special elevated motor track between the majestic sky-scrapers: as we approach nearer there is seen the repetition against the sky of the twenty-four sky-scrapers; to our left and right on the outskirts of each particular area are the municipal and administrative buildings; and enclosing the space are the museums and university buildings.

Then suddenly we find ourselves at the feet of the first sky-scrapers. But here we have, not the meagre shaft of sunlight which so faintly illumines the dismal streets of New York, but an immensity of space. The whole city is a Park. The terraces stretch out over lawns and into groves. Low buildings of a horizontal kind lead the eye on to the foliage of the trees. Where are now the trivial *Procuracies*? Here is the CITY with its crowds living in peace and pure air, where noise is smothered under the foliage of green trees. The chaos of New York is overcome. Here, bathed in light, stands the modern city.

Our car has left the elevated track and has dropped its speed of sixty miles an hour to run gently through the residential quarters. The "setbacks" permit of vast architectural perspectives.[4] There are gardens, games and sports grounds. And sky everywhere, as far as the eye can see. The square silhouettes of the terraced roofs stand clear against the sky, bordered with the verdure of the hanging gardens. The uniformity of the units that compose the picture throw into relief the firm lines on which the far-flung masses are constructed. Their outlines softened by distance, the sky-scrapers raise immense geometrical façades all of glass, and in them is reflected the blue glory of the sky. An overwhelming sensation. Immense but radiant prisms.

And in every direction we have a varying spectacle: our "gridiron" is based on a unit of 400 yards, but it is strangely modified by architectural devices! (The "set-backs" are in counterpoint, on a unit of 600 × 400.)

The traveler in his airplane, arriving from Constantinople, or Peking it may be, suddenly sees appearing through the wavering lines of rivers and patches of forests that clear imprint which marks a city which has grown in accordance with the spirit of man: the mark of the human brain at work.

As twilight falls the glass sky-scrapers seem to flame. This is no dangerous futurism, a sort of literary dynamite flung violently at the spectator. It is a spectacle organized by an Architecture which uses plastic resources for the modulation of forms seen in light.

NOTES

1 New suggestions shower on us. Their inventors and those who believe in them have their little thrill. It is so easy for them to believe in them. But what if they are based on grave errors? How are we to distinguish between what is reasonable and an over-poetical dream? The leading newspapers accept everything with enthusiasm. One of them said, "The cities of to-morrow must be built on new virgin soil." But no, this is not true! We must go to the old cities, all our inquiries confirm it. One of our leading papers supports the suggestion made by one of our greatest and most reasonable architects, who for once gives us bad counsel in proposing to erect round about Paris a ring of sky-scrapers. The idea is romantic enough, but it cannot be defended. The sky-scrapers must be built *in the centre* and not on the periphery.

2 I say "below-ground," but *it* would be more exact to say at what we call *basement level*, for *if* my town, built on concrete piles, were realized, this "basement" would no longer be *buried* under the earth.

3 In this section I make new suggestions in regard to the industrial quarters: they have been content to exist too long in disorder, dirt and in a hand-to-mouth way. And this is absurd, for Industry, when it is on a properly ordered basis, should develop in an orderly fashion. A portion of the industrial district could be constructed of ready-made sections by using standard units for the various kinds of buildings needed. Fifty percent of the site would be reserved for this purpose. In the event of considerable growth, provision would thus be made for moving them into a different district where there was more space. Bring about "*standardization*" in the building of a works and you would have mobility instead of the crowding which results when factories become impossibly congested.

4 As before, this refers to set-backs *on plan*; buildings "à redents," i.e. with projecting salients.

PART TWO

Foundations of the Field

Plate 3 The Sculpture Garden at New York's Museum of Modern Art exhibits several urban design principles that William Whyte researched in the late 1960s and 1970s as part of New York's *Street Life Project*, which was later published in *The Social Life of Small Urban Spaces*. This environmental observation study showed how people prefer flexible seating to maximize personal comfort, the importance of food and people-watching for activating spaces, the desire for sun or shade in different climate conditions, and how gender might impact public realm choices. The *Street Life Project* contributed several new methods to urban design observation and analysis – but also debunked prevailing knowledge about pedestrian preferences, jaywalking, transport mode separation, and plaza design. (Photo: M. Larice)

INTRODUCTION TO PART TWO

Part One illustrates some of the key precedents in the history of city-making: Renaissance idealism that elevates the role of the designer, the continuing importance of culture in traditional settlement patterns, and the value of design leadership in transforming the industrial city. It ends with seminal writing that introduces modernist planning and architecture to the emerging field of "urban design" practice. Both Ebenezer Howard's and Clarence Perry's planning-oriented diagrams provide prescriptive and quantitative models for designing greenfield residential developments. Incorporating large-scale real estate development and Fordist housing production, the subsequent translation of neighborhood unit and garden city principles often resulted in far less inspiring settlements than their authors had hoped (e.g., placeless suburbs and stultifying new towns). Likewise with the work of CIAM and Le Corbusier, modernist prescriptions for remaking cities rarely resulted in socially uplifting and well-managed gardens punctuated with towers and linear apartments. From the ill-managed public housing schemes of the USA to the ego-centric masterplans for new capital cities, modern design experienced widespread criticism. Aside from a few masterworks, mid-century architecture and policy-driven planning schemes failed to build the desired city of the future.

Part Two: Foundations of the Field addresses these criticisms and how they coalesced to establish "urban design" as both a field of hopeful collaboration and an academic offering of many design and planning schools. These selections chart the first difficult years of the field – how it was shaped by the voices of critics and designers into a body of normative theory and grounded research. Part Two contains some of the most classic writing by the field's luminaries: Jane Jacobs and Kevin Lynch, Christopher Alexander and Colin Rowe, Allan Jacobs and William Whyte. As bookends to these writings, we start this part of the *Reader* with a history of the field's founding, and end it with a statement of the field's many current areas of intellectual pursuit.

The birth of "urban design" was a conscious effort by a host of international architects, planners, landscape architects, academics, and civic leaders who came together in a series of Ivy League University conferences to discuss and organize the newly emergent field. Seeking to identify a collaborative project between the various built environment professions, these conferences illustrate the difficulty of organizing a hybrid field of practitioners operating under different value systems. In the first selection, Richard Marshall chronicles the birth of urban design at the 1956 Harvard conference as both a collaborative field of practice and an academic pursuit of various disciplines. In this excerpt from *Josep Lluís Sert: The Architect of Urban Design*, Marshall provides us with a picture of a field grappling with definitional existence and how its substantive concerns might be advanced. This selection helps establish the arc of the second edition of the *Urban Design Reader* – from initial failures at inter-disciplinary collaboration, to its continued aspirations toward greater system and professional integration (as observable in later selections in Part Six by Sorkin and Greenberg).

Early foundational research and theory in the urban design field focused on how people understood the visual qualities and image of cities. Both of the next two selections are concerned with methods of perceiving and recognizing elements within existing places that might form the basis for future design action. Gordon Cullen's work in Europe focused on picturesque and emotional qualities of city design, bodily experience, and memory. In *The Concise Townscape*, Cullen relies on the pictorial aspects of cities that people recognize as they move through space, which are then subject to later recall and memory. His contributions in this writing include concepts of "serial vision" and "townscape analysis." Contemporaneous and paralleling Cullen's work in many ways, Kevin Lynch's *Image of the City* is also concerned with the visual qualities of cities, and how their image can be reinforced or made manifest. Lynch begins this writing by highlighting the importance of visual imagery in making cities legible and memorable. The methods used in Lynch's *Image of the City* were early examples of environmental psychology research that sought to understand how people's perceptions were formed by the physical structure of cities (e.g., cognitive mapping, use of survey methods, and focused interviews). The work is indicative of the growing influence that social science methods had in shaping urban design research, as well as the growing importance of public participation in urban design practice. This selection is one of the best known from the early urban design canon, and describes Lynch's famous five elements of city imageability: paths, edges, districts, nodes, and landmarks. Both of these readings focus on perceptual approaches to place and those physical qualities that are likely to influence orientation, memory, and the public image of cities (topics important to a later generation of place-making theorists).

The next four readings provide a shared and direct criticism of modern design and planning practice. Each author's dissatisfaction with modernism highlights a set of issues where rational thought fails to produce what the authors assume is good urbanism. For Jane Jacobs, her attack on modern planning is founded on the belief that contemporary attempts at city building, public housing, and highway planning created less successful places in the city than those that were produced incrementally over time. The readings taken from Jane Jacobs' book *The Death and Life of Great American Cities* outline her argument for valuing and protecting the "messy" life of neighborhood streets. Sidewalks for Jane Jacobs represent an opportunity for chance meeting, casual gathering, and social cohesion – in contrast to the sterility of modern urbanism. Christopher Alexander's article, "A City is Not a Tree," reiterates Jane Jacobs' sentiments; however, not by means of anecdotal experience, but rather through the use of mathematical set theory. Alexander argues for a city of overlapping uses, patterns, and districts (a semi-lattice) where people can find surprising juxtapositions – rather than a city of segregated uses that is designed in a more tree-like pattern that disavows integration. Alexander calls for a return to traditional city design that values things such as harmony, beauty, and soul, which he perceives as missing from modern architecture and city design.

The next two critiques are direct attacks against the establishment architecture community, arguing for more locally relevant, authentic, and communicative urban design. The selection by Robert Venturi and Denise Scott Brown ponders the design reality of the Las Vegas strip, and how it might be a more authentic representation of American culture than top-down, modern urban design thinking. With a good degree of humor, Venturi and Scott Brown suggest the everyday commercial highway might provide a better guide for designers than abstract metaphors and vocabularies (often used in modern architecture) that have little to do with place. They use the Las Vegas strip, its casinos, and parking lots as examples of American urban form that provide direct communication though their decoration, signage, and lighting. They suggest that what exists in Las Vegas merely needs to be enhanced, rather than replaced with a more elite urbanism favored by the design establishment. In writing this early essay (which was later incorporated into a larger book with co-author Steven Izenour), they acknowledge that Las Vegas is merely a vehicle to illustrate a point about communication, rather than a recommendation for urban and architectural design itself. The final critique against modern design practice comes from Colin Rowe and Fred Koetter's *Collage City*, in which they argue for an urbanism of fragmented set pieces that come together in the city as a patchwork of patterns, often colliding with each other. Rowe and Koetter analyze the city by use of figure-ground maps that enable them to see urban patterns and their interaction in space very directly. Their critique is against modernism's desire to build idealized utopias – based in large-scale diagrams within which no person can find their place. Instead they call for a city of recognizable places at the human scale that breaks cities down to a series of district experiences. These four readings provide direct critique against status quo practices in city planning and architecture. Each of them allowed urban designers to begin re-appreciating existing urban spaces in contrast to less satisfy-ing designs foisted on the public by the design establishment.

While the previous four readings provide normative arguments for re-appreciating existing cities, the next two selections show how urban design researchers began studying the public realm of cities empiric-ally and objectively. Both William Whyte and Allan Jacobs researched different physical elements of the city (plazas and streets respectively) to show how people use them and how they might be designed better. In the first of these readings – selections from *The Social Life of Small Urban Spaces* – William H. Whyte shows how people use and adapt New York City's downtown urban plazas for themselves: where they like to sit, how they adjust their chairs to grab the sun, the importance of food and drink, and the desire for human comfort. The findings from this research provided new understandings about the gendered use of space, how the amount of comfortable sitting space is the best predictor of plaza use, and im-portantly that people like being where other people are. Whyte's research methods are important in expanding our ways of observing use of the city: time lapse photography, environmental behavior methods, observation methods. The second research selection is from Allan B. Jacobs' classic book *Great Streets*, in which the most important designable qualities of streets are highlighted. Using a variety of mixed research methods (including: interviews, mapping, pedestrian counting, design drawing, and scaled comparisons), Jacobs is able to offer a list of required and suggested elements for making great streets. Both of these works have become required reading for urban designers, not just because of their topical content, but also because of the way their grounded research has resulted in new theories of the *public realm* – which has become the subject matter most naturally associated with urban design practice.

Normative theories have tended to dominate urban design practice, largely because there is little agreement on what cities should become and how they should be designed. One of the things that makes urban design such an exciting field, is that every user of the city has an opinion on what makes a "good city" – in this way, urban design can be very inclusive. At the same time, urban design becomes dominated then by unending debates over what constitutes that "good city." In the next selections we look at two of the most well-read normative statements on good urbanism. Allan B. Jacobs' and Donald Appleyard's "Toward an Urban Design Manifesto" from the *Journal of the American Planning Association* presents a ringing indictment against Garden City and modernist overreactions to the ills of the industrial city (e.g., placelessness, injustice, urban fragmentation, giantism, etc.). The article posits goals that are essential for good urban environments: livability, identity, access to joy, community life, and so on. Ideas are presented, as well, on how the fabric of a city might be structured to best achieve those goals. Kevin Lynch's book *A Theory of Good City Form* stands as the most comprehensive normative theory of good city form yet produced by the urban design field. The selection reprinted here presents Lynch's seven performance dimensions – vitality, sense, fit, access, control, efficiency, and justice – by which communities can evaluate the attributes of their own city.

The urban design field has witnessed unimaginable growth in academia from its foundation in the mid-1950s. From a small set of elite-level Ivy League conferences, urban design is now represented in academia by hundreds of programs in the USA and around the world. The spread of the field across the globe has been remarkable. We see urban design programs across the large research universities of Europe, Asia, the Middle East, Australia, and New Zealand. In terms of printed volume, researchers in the United Kingdom seem much more prolific than their American counterparts. The professional practice of urban design can be found in most design firms, and is growing in public sector planning agencies. In particular, urban design practice is flourishing in those places where centrally organized governments have both the budgets and the unencumbered freedoms to support public realm improvements (e.g., China, the UAE, many places in Europe). Over the past four decades, this growth of the field has led to many subfields within urban design. Anne Vernez Moudon's article "A Catholic Approach to Organiz-ing What Urban Designers Should Know," from the *Journal of Planning Literature*, reviews these and sets out a broad epistemology for the field (i.e. the nature and grounds of knowledge necessary to practice urban design). Focusing largely on substantive research and theory, her framework illuminates the many complex dimensions of the urban design field and its necessarily interdisciplinary nature.

"Josep Lluís Sert's Urban Design Legacy"

from *Josep Lluís Sert: The Architect of Urban Design* (2008)

Richard Marshall

Editors' Introduction

While the design of cities has existed from the earliest urbanisms, the urban design field in academia saw its birth at a series of conferences at Harvard University in the late 1950s. In this chapter from *Josep Lluís Sert: The Architect of Urban Design*, Richard Marshall charts the historical development of the urban design field and its difficult birth.

Sert was Dean of Harvard University's Graduate School of Design from 1953 to 1969. In his tenure as Dean he organized a series of conferences to discuss the formulation of the urban design field, bringing in a host of design luminaries to engage in discussions, including Lewis Mumford, Jane Jacobs, Ed Bacon, Hideo Sasaki, Charles Abrams, Victor Gruen, and the architects Richard Neutra and Garret Eckbo, among others. In organizing the conferences Sert understood urban design to be carried out by town planners who had a "complete knowledge of the means of procedure, widened by a constantly evolving world of technics." These town planners would act as coordinating facilitators of a collaborative design. Rather than urban design by a super-architect with all-knowing powers, this initial conceptualization of urban design practice was a collaborative, inter-disciplinary and multi-stakeholder undertaking. The town planner Sert has in mind would be trained in a variety of built environment professions, including both architecture and city planning.

As the first 1956 conference progressed it became clear that Sert's idealized understanding of the urban design field would not coalesce so easily. Disciplinary biases inhibited the collaboration that Sert had in mind. He suggested the design professions needed to be "re-tooled" and find "common ground" among themselves, with an expanded role for landscape architecture. However in his closing comments, Sert lamented that the planning field might not have the design skills to contribute actively to the urban design undertaking; and consequently the two fields have had difficulty coming together ever since. The field of city planning at mid-century had become much more abstract, scientifically and quantitatively oriented, and focused on policy at the expense of its physical planning origins. A series of follow-up conferences were held over the next decade to continue delineating the urban design field; with each furthering the discussion of the previous one and delving into sub-topics. Over time, little resolution was reached in broaching the planning–architecture antipathy, with planning finally leaving the GSD for the university's policy school just a few years later. By the time of the last Harvard Urban Design Conference in 1970, urban design had morphed into large-scale architecture, with a statement to this effect in 1966 by Professors Soltan and Chermayeff that "architecture and urban design are but a single profession." This definition of the field was embedded in the specific politics of Harvard, and unfortunately has contributed to lasting bias against the planning role in urban design since this time.

Harvard was not the only university engaged in academic discussions over the urban design field. A 1958 conference co-hosted by the Rockefeller Foundation and the University of Pennsylvania also took up the challenge of shaping the field. Targeted at improving the quality of human life in cities, the UPenn Conference on Urban Design Criticism was much more focused on the mid-century challenges of urban design as a multi-disciplinary undertaking. Attended by similar figures (Jane Jacobs, Kevin Lynch, Grady Clay, J.B. Jackson, Ian McHarg, and David Crane), this conference approached cities as human ecology, rather than as a mere outcome of design. Pre-dating Harvard's creation of an urban design degree program, UPenn created a joint architecture and city planning degree program in civic design under the leadership of David Crane (later renamed urban design). This program lasted until the late 1980s, when faculty departures and a loss of focus ended the program – with urban design subsequently finding a home in the city planning program (itself struggling at the time). Rather than seeing urban design as a collaborative joint pursuit in the UPenn model, Harvard established an urban design degree program in 1960–61, with courses distributed to each of the professional degree programs (including a new Department of Urban Planning and Design). The GSD model thereby treated urban design as a freely floating sub-discipline with no real home.

The programs at these schools provide two very different models for urban design education: a studio-based model where urban design is offered within various professional disciplines; and a model where urban design became associated with city planning programs primarily (where more than half of urban design programs are now hosted). Each of these models has shortcomings: the studio design model's continuing antipathy with planners inhibits collaboration; the planning model produces indirect designers with less-developed graphic and design skills (who shape the design of others through policy, regulation, and guidelines). A more hopeful third model has emerged within the past two decades, where urban design is offered as a post-professional degree program within multi-departmental Schools of Design (drawing students from a variety of academic and professional backgrounds). This model is effectively becoming a nascent fourth branch of the design professions, and begins to address the collaborative concerns that Sert voiced a half century ago.

This text is a chapter in the compilation volume *Josep Lluís Sert: The Architect of Urban Design* (New Haven, CT: Yale University Press, 2008) edited by Eric Mumford and Hashim Sarkis. Mumford is an urban design and architecture historian teaching at Washington University in St. Louis. He has become the preeminent author on the development of the urban design field from CIAM to the Harvard Conference years. His other books include: *The CIAM Discourse on Urbanism 1928–1960* (Cambridge, MA: MIT Press, 2002); *Modern Architecture in St. Louis: Washington University and Postwar American Architecture 1948–1973* (Washington University/University of Chicago Press, 2004); and *Defining Urban Design: CIAM Architects and the Formation of a Discipline 1937–1969* (New Haven, CT: Yale University Press, 2009). Hashim Sarkis is a Lebanese architect and a faculty member in Landscape Architecture and Urbanism in Muslim Societies at Harvard's GSD, where he is also the Director of the Aga Khan Program.

Richard Marshall is Director of Urban Design for Woods Bagot, a global design and planning firm. He also serves as Adjunct Professor of Architecture at University of Technology in Sydney. Prior to this he worked for EDAW/AECOM and was an Associate Professor of Urban Design and Director of the Urban Design Program at Harvard's GSD. He is a design specialist in waterfront redevelopment and has worked on projects across the globe. He has authored numerous articles and three books: *Emerging Urbanity: Global Urban Projects in the Asia-Pacific Rim* (London: Spon Press, 2003); *Waterfronts in Post-Industrial Cities* (London: Spon Press, 2001); and *Designing the American City* (Beijing: China Architecture and Building Press, 2003).

▪ ▪ ▪ ▪ ▪ ▪

The Conference laid a sound foundation for the further development of a Program in Urban Design at the Harvard Graduate School of Design. It dealt effectively with the forces that are shaping our cities today and with means of effectuating designs rather than with the problem of how to design a city. Of course, in the two days the breadth of the field could not be adequately explored nor could any one aspect be examined in depth. Dean Sert announced at the close of the Conference that a further meeting would be held in the autumn.

Report of Faculty Committee on
the Urban Design Conference

Josep Lluís Sert became dean of the Graduate School of Design in the fall of 1953. Almost immediately he set about developing a "common ground" within the school, focusing on the problems of design in the contemporary city. For Sert this common ground was a space of mediation in which architecture, landscape architecture, and planning would operate in the realm of urbanism. This initiative started as a series of courses taught by Sert and a selection of visiting professors, developed through a series of Urban Design Conferences, and led ultimately to the establishment of the urban design program at the GSD. The Urban Design Conferences brought together a collection of mid-century urban thinkers and established the emerging discourse to support new lines of academic and professional endeavor.[1]

Although there is debate as to how successfully Sert's vision was executed, his urban design legacy is evident. Not only has the program he started continued uninterrupted to this day, but urban design programs at universities around the world have direct and indirect connections to Sert and the Harvard program. A review of professional practice uncovers a tremendous scope of urban design services and specialists, many of whom are graduates of the Harvard urban design program. Yet the definition of what urban design is, or is not, has always been somewhat ambiguous. Sert's attempts to define the terms on which urban design might be founded, through an extraordinary series of conferences held at the GSD, are worthy of exploration.

Throughout his professional life Sert was preoccupied with the development of ideas and themes related to the improvement of the human environment at a variety of scales. He believed that architecture was not a hermetic pursuit but one that should engage with a wide array of issues and creative practices. His vision for the potential of urban design was instrumental to how this field of activity evolved.

THE UNITED STATES IN THE 1950s

The intellectual underpinnings of urban design can be traced to an era of tremendous change in urban situations in and around US cities. In a special edition of *Architectural Review* from December 1950 entitled "Man-Made America," one critique of the urban scene is captured well:

The American way of life is concerned fundamentally with thinking bigger, going faster, rising higher,

than the Old World; with improving on the Old World, that is to say, merely quantitatively ... far from creating a new kind of world it has merely raised to the power of "n" the potential of the old, lending to the virtues and vices of materialism a kind of giantism in which there is nothing new except the giantism, so that the new world is merely the old one drawn in caricature.[2]

In search of an emerging urban-mindedness, the editors of the *Architectural Review* asked: Where does the United States stand in this matter?

Does it wish (as other communities in the world today have shown they do) to be directly instrumental in molding its own environment, in such a way as to reflect a visual ideal – a concept of what constitutes order and propriety in the environment – or has the American community rejected a visual ideal, in favor of a laissez-faire environment – a universe of uncontrollable chaos sparsely inhabited by happy accidents?[3]

The editors at *Architectural Review* were not alone in their call for action in the urban realm. The American Institute of Architects considered inaugurating a national program to "consider the problem of relationship between buildings."[4] The time was ripe for thinking at a larger scale, and it was in this context that Sert began developing his vision for urban design at Harvard.

SERT'S EARLY THOUGHTS ON URBAN DESIGN

Evidence of an increasing concern for the plight of the city can be found in the early writings of Sert. *Can Our Cities Survive?* (1942) represents the bridge between Sert's old life in Europe and his new life in the United States. In 250 pages Sert lays out the CIAM conception of the problem with cities, breaking the city into a series of discrete categories – dwelling, recreation, work, transportation, and large scale planning – and concludes with a call for a holistic view of the city.

It is here that we find evidence of Sert's early conception of urban design. Unlike other intellectual movements that dealt with the civic aspects of urban form, notably the City Beautiful Movement,

Sert was concerned with the ordinary elements of the urban situation. He wrote that "without a re-organization of our everyday life, which depends on the proper functioning of dwellings, recreation centers, work places, and the streets and highways that are the connecting links, life in the city cannot produce benefits for the individual or for the community as a whole."[5] This interest in everyday life would set Sert's idea for urban design on a different trajectory from some of his contemporaries. Sert dissociates his intentions from the tradition of "civic design," which he regarded as being concerned only with the creation of monumental civic centers, ignoring the living conditions of people in the neighborhoods around those centers.[6]

Can Our Cities Survive? does not use the term "urban design." But it is clear that in his argument for a better articulation of a "frame" that would allow for a greater possibility of social interaction, Sert is describing his early notion of the role that urban design should play. The professional responsible for solving these urban problems, according to Sert, was the town planner, whose task was to coordinate with other specialists, sociologists, economists, hygienists, teachers, agriculturalists, and others – in the preparation of regional plans and to lead the team of specialists in the preparation of master plans. The town planner would be responsible for "determining the location of those 'organs' which are the basic elements of urban life and of establishing their layouts."[7] The term "town planner" as Sert uses it, however, refers more to a state of mind than to a professional distinction, because those that referred to themselves as town planners were for the most part trained as architects. And indeed many of the attributes associated with the town planner in *Can Our Cities Survive?* bear an uncanny resemblance to those deemed necessary for the urban designer, as they were articulated a decade later in the urban design program curriculum.

Sert stressed that his conception of a town planner required a "complete knowledge of the means of procedure, widened by a constantly evolving world of technics."[8] This certainly suggests that the role required a broader and different kind of knowledge than that of the architect. Sert was clear that he was not asserting an increased professional role for the architect. He was not arguing for the creation of a super professional, a kind of genius architect able to deal with all of the complexities of the city. Rather, he was advocating for a new attitude where the town planner would become a coordinator, a kind of urban facilitator. This remained a consistent aspect of Sert's conception of urban design and one that others would rally around. Sert's town planner would require a new and different set of skills and knowledge but should not be empowered to be the ultimate urban authority: "It should not be left to the town planner alone to determine what human needs consist of and what conditions will satisfy those needs. The complexity of the human organism and of its material and spiritual aspirations requires the assistance of . . . [others] . . . to rehabilitate existing cities or shape new ones . . . the town planner should therefore join with these specialists in a labor of collaboration."[9]

In later writings Sert would elaborate upon this notion of facilitator and collaborator.[10] He thought that it had become increasingly apparent, especially after the CIAM Frankfurt Congress of 1979, that the study of modern architectural problems led to those of city planning and that no clear line of separation could be drawn between the two. In many respects the primary concerns expressed in *Can Our Cities Survive?* shifted from singular architectural concerns to those of the entire city, and in so doing expanded the field of architectural enquiry such that "architecture and city planning were tied closer together than ever before, as many architects were faced with the problems of reconstruction and the development of new regions demanding the creation of new communities."[11] Put simply, architecture's purview was necessarily expanded by the demands of the postwar context to an understanding of the need for integration and coordination of all city planning activities to deal with the chaotic growth in cities all over the world.

Sert employs a hybrid term in an essay entitled "Centres of Community Life" that embodies much of what he aimed to accomplish in urban design. He uses "architect-planner" to describe a new kind of professional attitude that encompasses a broader kind of knowledge. The coupling of these terms is relevant in light of emerging separations between the interests of architects and those of planners, which would have tremendous consequences some decades later within the GSD. He clearly articulated what for him was the task for the architect-planner:

"The architect-planner can only help to build the frame or container within which this community life could take place. We are aware of the need for such a life, for the expression of a real civic culture which we believe is greatly hampered today by the chaotic conditions of life in our cities. Naturally, the character and conditions of such awakened civic life do not depend entirely on the existence of a favorable frame, but are tied to the political, social, and economic structure of every community."[12] These are the limitations of the architect-planner as Sert understood them. This issue recurs in much of Sert's writing and speaks to the unheroic posture that Sert saw as the domain of the urban designer, in opposition to the idea of the creative genius.

SERT AT HARVARD

In 1953 Sert was appointed professor of architecture and dean of the Graduate School of Design at Harvard University and chair of the department of architecture. The GSD'S first dean, Joseph Hudnut, and the GSD's first chairman of architecture, Walter Gropius, had both retired, leaving Sert tremendous scope in which to define a new agenda within the school. Sert embraced this opportunity.

In 1954 Sert hired Sigfried Giedion to teach and started a series of initiatives that would culminate in the formation of the urban design program in 1960. The first time the term "urban design" appeared in the GSD curriculum was in 1954–55, introduced through Giedion's *History of Urban Design* class and a course simply called *Urban Design* taught by Sert, Hideo Sasaki, and Jean-Paul Carlhian. Giedion's course dealt with the culture of cities and the development of urban design as a "natural expression" of the needs, knowledge, means, and social conditions of each period, including the structure of the community: streets, squares, open spaces, the civic core (heart of the city), pedestrians, and traffic.

Urban Design was a course of lectures and seminars that dealt with the physical expression of city planning. The course was linked to a series of collaborative problems in the urban design studio and dealt most directly with issues of measure and scale-groups of buildings, open areas, roads, and their relationships – and the effect of the different functions of the city on the design of residential sectors; parks; industrial, commercial, and business sectors; the (civic) heart of the city; and transportation networks. Giedion's history class grew to become *Space, Structure, and Urban Design* and later split into two distinct courses, one for the urban design program and the other, *Space and Structure*, for the department of architecture. The *Urban Design* course was integrated with a class called *The Human Scale* in 1960 and served as the core of the new urban design program.

After several years of developing an emerging urban design curriculum at Harvard, Sert and the GSD faculty initiated a remarkable event. The postwar situation in American architecture had rallied many people to the problem of the city. Aware of this growing momentum, Sert organized a faculty committee consisting of Professors Wells Coates, Charles Eliot, William Goodman, Huson Jackson, and Jaqueline Tyrwhitt to prepare for an urban design symposium. Harvard had a legacy of such events. Hudnut and Gropius had previously organized the *Conference on Urbanism* in March 1942 to grapple with the task of rebuilding cities. Hudnut had organized a symposium in May 1949 entitled *Debunk: A Critical Review of Accepted Planning Principles*, which Sert, as president of CIAM, attended. The other gathering of note was a symposium in March 1951 entitled *Debunk II – Metropolitan Planning*, which addressed planning in Boston. These conferences addressed, at length, planning's ability to deal with the problems of the city and involved a broad range of political, social, and economic issues. Taking this same format, the first *Urban Design Conference* was held at the GSD on April 9 and 10, 1956.

HARVARD URBAN DESIGN CONFERENCES

The aim of the first conference, as articulated by the faculty committee, was to define the essence of urban design. The intention was to gauge the broad acceptance of the emerging discourse and determine whether there was a set of readily agreeable principles around which it might cluster. The conference announcement invited participants to explore the "role of the planner, architect and landscape architect in the design and development of cities."[13] Among those in attendance were Robert Geddes, Pittsburgh Mayor David Lawrence, Edmund Bacon, Eduard Sekler, Josep Lluís Sert, Robert Little, William Muschenheim, Garrett Eckbo, Richard Neutra, Charles Eliot, Hideo Sasaki, Ladislas Segoe, Charles Abrams, Gyorgy Kepes, Lloyd Rodwin, Frederick Adams, Charles Haar, Jaqueline Tyrwhitt, Victor Gruen, Lewis Mumford, and Jane Jacobs (then an associate editor with *Architectural Forum*).

In the condensed report of the conference, edited by Tyrwhitt and published in *Progressive Architecture*, Sert spoke to the challenge that American cities were likely to face in the coming decades. "I should like to make a case for the city. We cannot deny that there is an American culture which is both civic and urban.... The younger generation in this country ... has become aware that the uncontrolled sprawl of our communities only aggravates their problems, and that the solution lies in re-shaping the city as a whole."[14]

These remarks highlight a critique of contemporary planning, which in Sert's view had lost its capacity to deal with the challenges the city presented. Sert's ambition can be seen as both expanding architecture's purview to engage more with the city and rescuing the city from the social-science positivism endemic to planning at the time. Urban design was Sert's attempt to re-engage architects in the making of city-scale propositions. After describing city planning as a "new science" concerned with careful research and analysis, he went on to say, "In late years the scientific phase has been more emphasized than the artistic one.... Urban Design is the part of city planning that deals with the physical form of the city. It is by nature three- or four-dimensional. This is the most creative phase of city planning and that in which imagination and artistic capacities can play a more important part."[15]

His opening remarks articulate another of his primary concerns – the development of a "common ground" within the professions: "Each of them [architecture, landscape architecture, road engineering, and city planning] [is] trying to establish a new set of principles and a new language of forms, but it also seems logical now that synthesis or reunion of progress in the different professions be brought together into urban design to get a total picture of our physical environment by integration of those efforts."[16]

Several key themes emerged from the conference. Based on the conference proceedings, there appears to have been equal concern for the idea of urban design from a variety of disciplinary backgrounds. Further, there seems to have been general agreement with the diagnosis that the city required a radical change and that the "professions" needed to be retooled to address these problems. Richard Neutra led a discussion panel, "Attitudes Towards Urban Design," in which he called for a renewed role for landscape architecture in the making of cities. In a similar way Sert addressed the idea that the best cities are "living organisms" that require a holistic approach. Reinforcing Sert's call for the development of common ground, the landscape architect Garrett Eckbo described what for him was the greatest issue to be addressed by the professions. He noted that the professions are "conditioned by our jobs to work within isolated fragments" and stressed the need to "work in terms of continuity of design, which does not have boundaries."[17] The participants agreed that urban design was less a discipline in its own right than a way of thinking and working that applied to all disciplines.

Another preoccupation of the conference was a discussion of "forces that are shaping cities today," which focused on the relative inability of the design professions to influence outcomes in the making of the city. Lloyd Rodwin (founder of the MIT–Harvard Joint Center for Urban Studies with Martin Meyerson and others in 1959) described the essential problem that "architects, planners and landscape architects rank among the least important of the forces." He asked who the "tastemakers in urban design" should be and "what evidence is there that these professions really do have much to contribute today to urban design? What are they doing now to justify the role they would like to have?"[18] Charles Abrams and Gyorgy Kepes, responding to Rodwin, affirmed the idea that professionals' knowledge about legal, political, and technical issues was essential to the making of cities.

Lewis Mumford and Jane Jacobs argued against the "folly of creating a physical structure at the price of destroying the intimate social structure of a community's life."[19] Here we see evidence of a degree of discord between an emerging "community" perspective and that advocating for "professional" agency in the design of cities. Hideo Sasaki, responding to Mumford and Jacobs, maintained that "since the visual aspect of a city is only that which is created, it is obvious that to a large degree the individuals mentioned [architects, planners, landscape architects] are the most responsible for the ultimate expression of the urban environment" and that there existed significant opportunities to improve the urban environment through design.[20] Sasaki was explicit about what he viewed as the chief faults in design and by implication what should be the foundation for new ways of thinking about design's agency in the city. He identified three issues that urban design should redress: eclecticism without meaning; monumentality without meaning, or lack of scale; lack of relationship with surroundings, or emphasis on the spectacular.[21]

The remainder of the conference involved a series of lectures followed by debate and a formal dinner discussion. Mayor Lawrence presented Pittsburgh as a case study; Edmund Bacon presented Philadelphia; Victor Gruen presented Fort Worth. Frederick Adams, the head of the Department of City and Regional Planning at MIT, opened the discussion of "Problems of Implementation of Urban Designs," which considered how large scale projects should be implemented. The conference was wrapped up by a general discussion titled "Is Urban Design Possible Today?"

In his closing comments Sert described an issue at the heart of his vision for urban design that would later prove to be of tremendous consequence for the urban design program and for the development of the intellectual foundation of urban design. He said that the conference indicated clear agreement between architects and landscape architects on the need for a new design role in the city. But in referring to the relationship between designers and planners, he stated, "When we come to the city planners and architects there may be a little conflict. There is a certain misgiving among architects, as someone has said here, that city planners do not know anything about the three-dimensional world we want to help shape. And the city planners think that architects know nothing about city planning. The result is when we come to the field of urban design, where both should meet and shake hands, there are many who are not prepared."

On November 26, 1956, Sert convened an *Urban Design Round Table* as a follow-up to the conference. In attendance were Bacon, Walter Bogner, Serge Chermayeff, Creighton, Eliot, Fry, Walter Gropius, Gruen, Hosburgh, Reginald Isaacs, Huson Jackson, Kepes, Lopez, Lynch, Neutra, Mario Romañach, Sasaki, Sekler, Sert, and Tyrwhitt. The purpose of the meeting was to continue the momentum that the previous spring's conference had generated. In minutes of that meeting, Sert stated, "I think there are three main points that stand out. First of all can we establish a common ground for the participation of architect and planner in urban design, or physical planning if you want to call it that, as well as a series of other professions. If this possibility does not exist, there is no hope. But if this common ground does exist then can we establish a basic program of what we want along broad lines which represent the general ideas of a whole past generation of people. . . . If we can frame this clearly we shall then have a program for action."

Sert's program of action was multifaceted. As the *Report of the Faculty Committee on the Urban Design Conference* states, the conference "laid a sound foundation for the further development of a Program in Urban Design at the Harvard Graduate School of Design."[22] In addition, it established the basis for twelve more *Urban Design Conferences* during the rest of the 1950s and through the 1960s.

The second *Urban Design Conference* (April 12 and 13, 1957) aimed to further refine the idea of urban design. The concepts agreed upon in the first conference were not discussed. In addition, the scope of the conference was reduced. It appears that Sert was concerned with the breadth of discussions at the first conference and sought greater focus and clarity in the second meeting. This reduction reflects again the growing discord between architectural and planning interests. Although economics, sociology, psychology, and other disciplines were recognized as having an impact on the contemporary form of the city, the field of urban design was intentionally reduced to the physical components only. Before the conference, the following statement was issued: "This conference is confined to a discussion of the *design section* of the planning process. This does not mean this is considered more important than other essential sections – such as the establishment of relevant data or the means of implementation – which may fall more directly in the fields of sociology, economics or government."[23]

Six statements formed the basis for discussion. The first was an affirmation for the need for re-urbanization, in opposition to suburbanization. The second was a call for the reestablishment of connections between people and nature, as well as among people. This call concerned a larger thread present in much of the conference discussions, a desire to reinforce a humanistic approach to city making in opposition to the abstraction wrought by modern planning "science." The third statement reinforced the growing dislocation between the preoccupations of planning and those of design, and further articulated the nature of the "conflict" to which Sert's closing comments at the first conference referred: "Even the best two-dimensional land-use or zoning plans cannot ensure a three-dimensional implementation that will achieve livability and beauty: therefore visual standards are as important a tool of planning."[24] Here we begin to see the emergence of a territorial claim that would separate planning from design in even more radical ways and ultimately define urban design at the GSD, based on the idea that "the essence of urban design is the inter-relation of a number of forces – visual, physical, social, economic, governmental, etc. – which all appear as causes and effects of design decisions."[25] Furthering this claim, the fourth issue was the idea that a design framework capable of coordinating between scales should be agreed on by architects, landscape architects, and city planners. Here the notion of common ground is posited, but there is also a positioning of the design professions in relation to territory controlled by planning. The fifth statement dealt with a desired separation between automobiles and pedestrians, and the sixth concerned the promotion of open space in the making of the city, reinforcing the need for thinking in terms of exterior spatial design.

DEVELOPMENT OF URBAN THINKING AT HARVARD

In April 1957 appeared the first issue of *Synthesis*, a journal published by GSD students to provide a platform for student views and work. This issue was devoted to urban design and included ten essays by students and faculty. Writers included Eckbo, Sasaki, Tyrwhitt, and Goodman. Richard Dober, working on a master's of city planning, described the current state of urban design as "the problem of the conscious, artistic design of the urban environment requiring a specialized training

for which no curriculum has yet been established."[26] He wrote that urban design was the common meeting ground for the three design professions, and as a collaborative effort it was the "most productive problem at Harvard today." Yet in his reflections, Dober freely admits the limitations of the collaborative idea at the GSD, describing "departmental introversion that too often encourages intellectual isolation." In Dober's opinion, the urban design problem was productive not in terms of its success but rather for introducing to the student a "macroscopic view of the totality to which he (she) will create and contribute a part." Dober's words highlight a struggle that was to emerge within the GSD in the 1960s – a problem that must have been recognized by Sert – of an increasing separation between the three departments.

Dober's words capture what may have been Sert's ultimate agenda with the introduction of urban design as a program within the school: "It is Harvard's recognition that if the pedagogical process itself cannot be changed, then the professional designer can be introduced to an overall view in anticipation that such an introduction, no matter how frustrating, will stimulate his imagination to ameliorating the physical paradoxes with which he must work."[27] Tyrwhitt's essay, "Definitions of Urban Design," described how shortly before Christmas 1956 the editors of *Synthesis* had written to thirty-two distinguished architects, landscape architects, planners, sociologists, economists, lawyers, and prominent citizens asking their definition of urban design; her essay summarized the responses. Ten of those replying refused to commit themselves to a definition. Four "no's" were on account of being too busy (Paul Rudolph was in this class). Three "no's" were on grounds of impossibility. Robert Moses's response was short ("I am unable to comply with your request") as was Frank Lloyd Wright's ("I am not interested"). Le Corbusier's reply attempted to define the actual form that urban design should take:

Urbanism is the most vital expression of a society. The task of urbanism is to organize the use of the land to suit the works of man, which fall into three categories: 1. the unit of agricultural production; 2. the linear industrial city; and 3. the radio-concentric city of exchange (ideas, government, commerce). Urbanism is a science with three dimensions. Height is as important to it as the horizontal expanse.

Neutra wrote: "Giving shape to a community and molding its activities is urban design. It deals with the dynamic features in space, but in time as well." Gropius offered: "Good urban design represents that consistent effort to create imaginatively the living spaces of our urban surroundings. In order to supersede today's soul-destroying robotization, the modern urban designer's exciting task is to satisfy all emotional and practical human needs by coordinating the dictates of nature, technique and economy into beautiful habitat." Giedion wrote poetically that for him, "Urban Design has to give visual form to the relationship between You and Me."

SUBSEQUENT URBAN DESIGN CONFERENCES

There was no conference in 1958; however, a series of panels met in April to prepare for the next Urban Design Conference. It was agreed that the goal of the third gathering should be to "arrive at certain principles which can guide the design of large scale residential developments of an urban character . . . both with the city complex and on the fringes of the metropolitan area."[28]

By the third conference, in April 1959, the principles of urban design seem to have been sufficiently developed so that the first case study of projects was attempted. The architectural component of the conference reinforced the separation from planning, but the diminution of landscape architecture's influence is also evident. This marks a fundamental shift from the previous two conferences and would set the tone for subsequent meetings. There was a definite attempt to deal with tangible design issues at this conference, and unlike the first two conferences, abstract notions of the "forces" shaping cities – economic, social, and political – were left off the agenda. Indeed, in his opening comments Sert spoke explicitly to this, stating that "after the second [conference] many of us realized that, though these conferences proved interesting and stimulating, it would be useless to continue discussions on general topics as we were tending to become repetitive."

Sert spoke of his frustration with the emerging urban design discourse, describing the previous conference results as a "fog of amiable generalities."[29] In his opening comments, Sert offered one of the defining aspects of urban design: "This is a conference upon Urban Design and upon a special aspect of Urban Design – the residential sector. I think I have already said enough to show that it is not a general conference upon city planning."[30] These projects were examples of how Sert imagined urban design in practice; despite the idea of urban design as "common ground," urban design was starting to carve out a territorial claim that would have consequences for the position of the program within the school. The developing rift between planning and architecture was to eventually mean that planning would leave the GSD for a new home at the Kennedy School of Government – interested more in the abstract notions of the "forces" shaping cities than in the physical design of urban situations.

At the third conference, six projects were presented: Washington Square, Philadelphia, by I. M. Pei; Mill Creek, St. Louis, by I. M. Pei; Gratiot Redevelopment (Lafayette Park), Detroit, by Mies van der Rohe and Ludwig Hilberseimer; Lake Meadows, Chicago, by Skidmore, Owings and Merrill; Don Mills, Toronto, by Macklin Hancock; and Vallingby, Stockholm, by the Stockholm Town Planning Office. Material on each project had been assembled in advance by a GSD alumnus, who then moderated a respective panel, assisted by current students. In most cases the architect of the project, the responsible developer, and the city planning director not only provided information but also took part in discussions. It is unclear why these projects were chosen above others; one can only surmise that in some way the projects represented physical manifestations of the "principles" outlined in the previous conferences. After a day of discussion, each of the six panels reported to a meeting of alumni and students, and an afternoon was spent in open discussion under the chairmanship of Robert Geddes, president of the Harvard GSD alumni association.

The six selected projects, as Geddes remarked, divided themselves fairly neatly into pairs. Vallingby and Don Mills were new towns. Lake Meadows and Gratiot were similar in terms of programs and sites. The Washington Square – Society Hill development and the Mill Creek development have similar links to their surroundings and share problems and programs. The format of the third conference proved successful and was repeated at several conferences, including the fifth one. The sixth conference changed scale and dealt with the issues of inter-city growth. The eighth conference refocused its attention on the core of the city, but by 1964 the social, political, and economic concerns outweighed any emphasis on form or aesthetics.

Overall, there was a tendency for the later conferences to become more abstract and general. The ninth and tenth conferences (1965 and 1966) addressed design education. The tenth conference again raised the issue of urban design's definition. On a panel entitled "Changing Educational Requirements in Architecture and Urban Design," there was still significant debate about exactly what urban design was. Benjamin Thomson, chair of the Department of Architecture at the GSD, described urban design as "large-scale architecture." Roger Montgomery, professor of architecture at Washington University, called it "project-scale design." GSD Professors Chermayeff and Soltan stated in a joint declaration: "Architecture and Urban Design are but a single profession. DESIGN is at the heart of these efforts." Chermayeff and Soltan precisely articulated the emerging trajectory of urban design's development. Wilhelm von Moltke, chairman of the department of urban design, in a move away from architectural definitions, stated: "Urban Design is not architecture. The function of urban design, its purpose and objective, is to give form and order to the future. As with the master plan, urban design provides a master program and master form for urban growth. It is primarily a collaborative effort involving other professions."[31]

In line with growing social and political developments in the United States, there arose a growing critique that the conferences had little to do with the reality of city life. The twelfth conference, conducted in an atmosphere of grief surrounding the assassination of Senator Robert F. Kennedy, dealt with a report of the New Communities Project, a year-long research study supported by a grant from the U.S. Department of Housing and Urban Development to investigate plans for a compact city for more than two hundred thousand people. Principal investigators for the project were Sert, William Nash, Chair of City and Regional Planning, Walter Isard, and George Pillorge.

The last of the Urban Design Conferences took place in 1970. The event was cosponsored by the GSD and the National Urban Coalition and took up the broad implications of mass-industrialized housing. This conference was strongly affected by significant changes in the GSD, as well as in American society at large. Maurice Kilbridge, a Harvard Business School professor, had replaced Sert as dean in 1969. The school was experiencing financial difficulties, and there was significant social turbulence within both the faculty and student body. An active student movement politicized the atmosphere of the conference. Discussions of the nature of urban design had given way to critiques of state and federal housing programs.

URBAN DESIGN PROGRAM AT HARVARD

Beginning in the academic year 1960–61, the GSD offered an advanced interdepartmental program in urban design, open only to selected candidates from among those who already held one of the school's first professional degrees (B. Arch., MLA, or MCP) or an equivalent qualification from another institution. The program, as it was initially developed, required a minimum of one year's study in residence and led to the degrees Master of Architecture in Urban Design, Master of Landscape Architecture in Urban Design, or Master of City Planning in Urban Design. The fact that there were three urban design degrees is in itself significant and speaks to how urban design was imagined as a floating program in which students from the three disciplines would come together in the consideration of a holistic approach to the city. Urban design was conceived as an extension of one's own disciplinary education and not as its own discipline. These separate roles were reinforced within the course of study, with each discipline engaging in different activities.[32]

Although the three departments jointly offered courses within the urban design program, continuing Sert's assertion that it be the common ground within the school, the role of landscape architects within the program was small. The Urban Design Studio of 1960 was an intensive course with problems conducted conjunctively rather than collaboratively, to give all members of the class a shared experience in the three professional aspects of the work. The fall part of the course, led by Sert, dealt with new developments or new towns. The spring session, led by von Moltke, concerned the rebuilding of large scale parts of the city. The studio used Boston as a laboratory, and the students' work addressed different parts of the city for new and redevelopment projects, with the Charles River, the Fenway, the North Shore, and Fort Point Channel among the sites of investigation. In addition, the studio included theoretical projects at the scale of some of Sert's pilot plans.

The 1962 GSD *Register* lists faculty who taught in the urban design program: Sert, Martin Meyerson, Sasaki, Soltan, Sekler, Tyrwhitt, Fumihiko Maki, François Vigier, and Shadrach Woods. These first faculty members shaped the origins of what urban design became at Harvard, and their influence informed what urban design was to become in universities throughout the United States and the rest of the world.

In its fifth year of existence at the GSD, the urban design program once again became the focus of a student publication. In an April 1965 issue of *Connection* were critical appraisals of the program by Perry Neubauer and Roy Mann. Neubauer is candid, writing: "The Urban Design Program has made considerable progress in the formulation of educational objectives and a curriculum of study; but it has not fully realized one of the concepts on which it was based: The integration of the three design disciplines of architecture, landscape architecture, and city planning. At the present time, in fact, the program seems to be setting up a fourth discipline with a definite architectural bias."[33]

ON COMMON GROUND

Although urban design was established as a field of activity rather than as a professional discipline, it quickly began to develop its own territory, both within the GSD and professionally. Neubauer's comments reflect the emergence of urban design as a "fourth discipline" at the design school. Although it was initially imagined as an extension of the core disciplines within the school, it became something quite separate. The Urban Design Conferences began as an undertaking to explore the common ground of the city. They bear testament, however, to the fragmentation of the professions and the emergence of troubled social times in the 1960s.

Once urban design arrived at Harvard, the Department of City and Regional Planning went through a tremendous crisis. Symptomatic of larger trends affecting the planning profession's view of itself, the Department increasingly moved away from a "physical" view of the city, alienating itself from the Departments of Architecture and Landscape Architecture. The divide became so wide that in 1984 the Master of City Planning degree program departed the GSD and moved to the Kennedy School of Government, although several key planning faculty members, including Vigier and William Doebele, continued to teach planning within the urban design program.

With the Master of City Planning gone from the GSD and the Department of City and Regional Planning decimated, the School established the Department of Urban Planning and Design and moved the urban design program under this new department. Urban design, the "fourth discipline," filled the void left by planning. The Department of Urban Planning and Design offered the degrees Master of Architecture in Urban Design and Master of Landscape Architecture in Urban Design.[34]

URBAN DESIGN AS A COMMON UNDERTAKING

The Urban Design Conferences (particularly the first two) were remarkable unions of interested parties engaged in the making of cities. They created the momentum that Sert and his faculty needed to establish the urban design program at Harvard. They promoted recognition of a different field of design endeavor, one that required a particular set of perspectives and skills. Sert's conferences created a place for likeminded thinkers to gather and argue about what urban design was, who would carry it out, and what role it would have within the world at large. Although an accepted understanding of the territory of urban design was never fully reached, the conferences nevertheless established a foundation for the emergence of urban design and for agreement on the need to design the future of the city.

NOTES

1 Report of Faculty Committee on the Urban Design Conference, April 24, 1956. Harvard University Archives, UAV 433.7.4, sub. IIB, Box 19.

2 "Man-Made America," *Architectural Review* 108, no. 648 (December 1950): 341.

3 Ibid., 343.

4 Edmund Bacon, "A Talk Presented to the Second Invitation Harvard Conference on Urban Design, Cambridge, Massachusetts, April 12, 1957," *Second Urban Design Conference Announcement and Program* (Cambridge, Mass.: Harvard Graduate School of Design, 1957). Special Collections, Frances Loeb Library, Harvard University Graduate School of Design (hereafter Special Collections), Rare NAC 46 Harv 1957.

5 Josep Lluís Sert, *Can Our Cities Survive? An ABC of Urban Problems, Their Analysis, Their Solutions* (Cambridge, Mass.: Harvard University Press, 1942), 229.

6 See Josep Lluís Sert, Opening Remarks to the Urban Design Conference, April 9, 1956. Special Collections, Rare NAC 46 Harv 1956.

7 Ibid.

8 Sert, *Can Our Cities Survive?* 224.

9 Ibid., 234.

10 In a later essay titled "Centers of Community Life," written as the introduction to *CIAM 8: The Heart of the City* (1952), a book Sert wrote with Jaqueline Tyrwhitt and Ernesto Rogers, he reinforced and expanded on many of the issues developed in *Can Our Cities Survive?* See *CIAM 8: The Heart of the City* (New York: Pellegrini and Cudahy, 1952).

11 *CIAM 8: The Heart of the City*, 3.

12 Ibid., 11.

13 Sert, Opening Remarks to the Urban Design Conference.

14 Sert, Report of the Faculty Committee, 98.

15 Sert, Opening Remarks to the Urban Design Conference.

16 Ibid.

17 Sert, Report of Faculty Committee, 99.

18 Ibid.

19 Ibid., 103. Also see Lewis Mumford, Letter to Sert, December 28, 1940. Special Collections.

20 Ibid., 101.

21 Ibid., 102.

22 Ibid.

23 *Second Urban Design Conference. Announcement and Program.*

24 Ibid.

25 Ibid.

26 Richard Dober, "The Collaborative Process and Urban Design at Harvard," in *Synthesis*, April 1957, p. 3.

27 Ibid.

28 *Third Urban Design Conference Program* (Cambridge, Mass.: Harvard University Graduate School of Design, [April 25, 1959]). Special Collections, Rare HT107·U712X 1959.

29 Ibid.

30 Ibid.

31 *Tenth Urban Design Conference Proceedings* (Cambridge, Mass.: Harvard University Graduate School of Design, 1966), 14. Special Collections, Rare NAC 46 Harv 1966.

32 An interview with Emeritus Professor Charles Harris at GSD, March 25, 2003. Hired by Hideo Sasaki to teach in the department of landscape architecture in 1958, Professor Harris was chair of the department of landscape architecture from 1968 to 1978.

33 Perry Neubauer, "Educating the Urban Designer," *Connection*, April 1965, p. 62.

34 The urban planning degree program was eventually reintroduced at the GSD in the mid-1990s.

"Introduction to The Concise Townscape"

from *The Concise Townscape* (1961)

Gordon Cullen

Editors' Introduction

Like Kevin Lynch (p. 125), Gordon Cullen (1914–1994) was interested in how people perceive urban environments through their sense of sight, but his emphasis was on emotional impacts rather than legibility. In his seminal book *Townscape*, later republished as *The Concise Townscape*, he defined urban design as The Art of Relationship. The goal was to manipulate groups of buildings and physical town elements so as to achieve visual impact and drama.

Cullen understood that people apprehend urban environments through kinesthetic experience as they move through them in everyday life, and felt that this fundamental body–environment relationship was a basis for design: cities should be designed from the point of view of the moving person. From this, he developed the concept of Serial Vision, which theorizes that urban scenes are experienced as a series of revelations, as current views juxtapose with emerging views. Tensions related to an observer's position in the environment – here versus there, enclosure versus exposure, constraint versus relief, etc. – could be purposefully and artfully designed for.

Cullen was also concerned with sense of place, which he theorized through the concept of This and That. He argued that to achieve a unique sense of place, individual townscape elements should be designed as part of a whole. Taking a cue from the qualities of pre-modern towns, he advocated that a sense of wholeness would be best achieved by allowing diversity within an agreed-upon common visual framework, rather than through complete visual conformity and regularity.

Within *The Concise Townscape*, Cullen illustrated his theoretical ideas with freehand ink drawings as well as photographs. Some of the most memorable drawings include a set that shows the plan of a medieval hill town with the path of a walk through it indicated, and related sketches of the sequential views seen along the path. Like Camillo Sitte before him, Cullen focused on picturesque visual effects, but he analyzed and illustrated these effects largely through perspective views rather than projected plans as Sitte had done, making his ideas perhaps more accessible.

As well as theory, Cullen laid out practical ideas for how to accomplish desired design objectives. After *Townscape*, Cullen developed a method for applying townscape ideas to urban places. The conceptual underpinning of the method involved the idea of two interlinked chains: an integrated chain of human activity, and a spatial chain of physical elements. He developed matrices of human factors and physical factors that designers could use to map a design problem. Cullen's principles for creating a unique sense of place can be derived from his proposal for the new (never built) town of Maryculter, in Scotland: fit development to the site, provide a center, provide distinctive housing areas, create distinct edges and boundaries, provide a network of recognizable landmarks, use topography and planting to create drama, and provide a series of sequential enclosures and climaxes to create a memorable unfolding sense of drama.

Cullen's ideas had an enormous influence on a generation of British urban designers, although his work has been criticized as backward-looking because of its focus on picturesque aesthetic qualities. Other resources on the kinesthetic experience of urban space are Peter Bosselmann, *Representation of Places: Reality and Realism in City Design* (Berkeley, CA: University of California Press, 1998); and Donald Appleyard, Kevin Lynch, and John R. Myer, *The View from the Road* (Cambridge, MA: MIT Press, 1965).

INTRODUCTION TO THE 1959 EDITION

There are advantages to be gained from the gathering together of people to form a town. A single family living in the country can scarcely hope to drop into a theatre, have a meal out or browse in a library, whereas the same family living in a town can enjoy these amenities. The little money that one family can afford is multiplied by thousands and so a collective amenity is made possible. A city is more than the sum of its inhabitants. It has the power to generate a surplus of amenity, which is one reason why people like to live in communities rather than in isolation.

Now turn to the visual impact which a city has on those who live in it or visit it. I wish to show that an argument parallel to the one put forward above holds good for buildings: bring people together and they create a collective surplus of enjoyment; bring buildings together and collectively they can give visual pleasure which none can give separately.

One building standing alone in the countryside is experienced as a work of architecture, but bring half a dozen buildings together and an art other than architecture is made possible. Several things begin to happen in the group which would be impossible for the isolated building. We may walk through and past the buildings, and as a corner is turned an unsuspected building is suddenly revealed. We may be surprised, even astonished (a reaction generated by the composition of the group and not by the individual building). Again, suppose that the buildings have been put together in a group so that one can get inside the group, then the space created between the buildings is seen to have a life of its own over and above the buildings which create it and one's reaction is to say 'I am inside IT' or 'I am entering IT'. Note also that in this group of half a dozen buildings there may be one which through reason of function does not conform. It may be a bank, a temple or a church amongst houses. Suppose that we are just looking at the temple by itself, it would stand in front of us and all its qualities, size, colour and intricacy, would be evident. But put the temple back amongst the small houses and immediately its size is made more real and more obvious by the comparison between the two scales. Instead of being a big temple it TOWERS. The difference in meaning between bigness and towering is the measure of the relationship.

In fact there is an *art of relationship* just as there is an art of architecture. Its purpose is to take all the elements that go to create the environment: buildings, trees, nature, water, traffic, advertisements and so on, and to weave them together in such a way that drama is released. For a city is a dramatic event in the environment. Look at the research that is put into making a city work: demographers, sociologists, engineers, traffic experts; all co-operating to form the myriad factors into a workable, viable and healthy organization. It is a tremendous human undertaking.

And yet . . . if at the end of it all the city appears dull, uninteresting and soulless, then it is not fulfilling itself. It has failed. The fire has been laid but nobody has put a match to it.

Firstly we have to rid ourselves of the thought that the excitement and drama that we seek can be born automatically out of the scientific research and solutions arrived at by the technical man (or the technical half of the brain). We naturally accept these solutions, but are not entirely bound by them. In fact we cannot be entirely bound by them because the scientific solution is based on the best that can be made of the average: of averages of human behaviour, averages of weather, factors of safety and so on. And these averages do not give an inevitable result for any particular problem. They are, so to speak, wandering facts which may synchronize or, just as likely, may conflict with each other. The upshot is that a town could take one of several patterns and still operate with success, equal success. Here then we discover a pliability in the scientific solution and it is precisely in the *manipulation of this pliability* that the art of relationship is made possible. As will be seen, the aim is not to dictate the shape of the town or environment, but is a modest one: simply to *manipulate within the tolerances.*

This means that we can get no further help from the scientific attitude and that we must therefore turn to other values and other standards.

We turn to the *faculty of sight*, for it is almost entirely through vision that the environment is apprehended. If someone knocks at your door and you open it to let him in, it sometimes happens that a gust of wind comes in too, sweeping round the room, blowing the curtains and making a great fuss. Vision is somewhat the same; we often get more than we bargained for. Glance at the clock to see the time and you see the wallpaper, the clock's carved brown mahogany frame, the fly crawling over the glass and the delicate rapier-like pointers. Cézanne might have made a painting of it. In fact, of course, vision is not only useful but it evokes our memories and experiences, those responsive emotions inside us which have the power to disturb the mind when aroused. It is this unlooked-for surplus that we are dealing with, for clearly if the environment is going to produce an emotional reaction, with or without our volition, it is up to us to try to understand the three ways in which this happens.

1. Concerning OPTICS. Let us suppose that we are walking through a town: here is a straight road off which is a courtyard, at the far side of which another street leads out and bends slightly before reaching a monument. Not very unusual. We take this path and our first view is that of the street. Upon turning into the courtyard the new view is revealed instantaneously at the point of turning, and this view remains with us whilst we walk across the courtyard. Leaving the courtyard we enter the further street. Again a new view is suddenly revealed although we are travelling at a uniform speed. Finally as the road bends the monument swings into view. The significance of all this is that although the pedestrian walks through the town at a uniform speed, the scenery of towns is often revealed in a series of jerks or revelations. This we call SERIAL VISION [Figure 1].

Examine what this means. Our original aim is to manipulate the elements of the town so that

an impact on the emotions is achieved. A long straight road has little impact because the initial view is soon digested and becomes monotonous. The human mind reacts to a contrast, to the difference between things, and when two pictures (the street and the courtyard) are in the mind at the same time, a vivid contrast is felt and the town becomes visible in a deeper sense. It comes alive through the drama of juxtaposition. Unless this happens the town will slip past us featureless and inert.

There is a further observation to be made concerning Serial Vision. Although from a scientific or commercial point of view the town may be a unity, from our optical viewpoint we have split it into two elements: the *existing view* and the *emerging view*. In the normal way this is an accidental chain of events and whatever significance may arise out of the linking of views will be fortuitous. Suppose, however, that we take over this linking as a branch of the art of relationship; then we are finding a tool with which human imagination can begin to mould the city into a coherent drama. The process of manipulation has begun to turn the blind facts into a taut emotional situation.

2. Concerning PLACE. This second point is concerned with our reactions to the position of our body in its environment. This is as simple as it appears to be. It means, for instance, that when you go into a room you utter to yourself the unspoken words 'I am outside IT, I am entering IT, I am in the middle of IT'. At this level of consciousness we are dealing with a range of experience stemming from the major impacts of exposure and enclosure (which if taken to their morbid extremes result in the symptoms of agoraphobia and claustrophobia). Place a man on the edge of a 500-ft. cliff and he will have a very lively sense of position, put him at the end of a deep cave and he will react to the fact of enclosure.

Since it is an instinctive and continuous habit of the body to relate itself to the environment, this sense of position cannot be ignored; it becomes a factor in the design of the environment (just as an additional source of light must be reckoned with by a photographer, however annoying it may be). I would go further and say that it should be exploited.

Here is an example. Suppose you are visiting one of the hill towns in the south of France. You climb laboriously up the winding road and eventually find

Figure 1 Serial Vision: to walk from one end of the plan to another, at a uniform pace, will provide a sequence of revelations which are suggested in the serial drawings, reading from left to right. Each arrow on the plan represents a drawing. The even progress of travel is illuminated by a series of sudden contrasts and so an impact is made on the eye, bringing the plan to life.

yourself in a tiny village street at the summit. You feel thirsty and go to a nearby restaurant, your drink is served to you on a veranda and as you go out to it you find to your exhilaration or horror that the veranda is cantilevered out over a thousand-foot drop. By this device of the containment (street) and the revelation (cantilever) the fact of height is dramatized and made real.

In a town we do not normally have such a dramatic situation to manipulate but the principle still holds good. There is, for instance, a typical emotional reaction to being below the general ground level and there is another resulting from being above it. There is a reaction to being hemmed in as in a tunnel and another to the wideness of the square. If, therefore, we design our towns from the point of view of the moving person (pedestrian or car-borne) it is easy to see how the whole city becomes a plastic experience, a journey through pressures and vacuums, a sequence of exposures and enclosures, of constraint and relief.

Arising out of this sense of identity or sympathy with the environment, this feeling of a person in street or square that he is in IT or entering IT or leaving IT, we discover that no sooner do we postulate a HERE than automatically we must create a THERE, for you cannot have one without the other. Some of the greatest townscape effects are created by a skilful relationship between the two, and I will name an example in India, where this introduction is being written: the approach from the Central Vista to the Rashtrapathi Bhawan,[1] in New Delhi. There is an open-ended courtyard composed of the two Secretariat buildings and, at the end, the Rashtrapathi Bhawan. All this is raised above normal ground level and the approach is by a ramp. At the top of the ramp and in front of the axis building is a tall screen of railings. This is the setting. Travelling through it from the Central Vista we see the two Secretariats in full, but the Rashtrapathi Bhawan is partially hidden by the ramp; only its upper part is visible. This effect of truncation serves to isolate and make remote. The building is withheld. We are Here and it is There. As we climb the ramp the Rashtrapathi Bhawan is gradually revealed, the mystery culminates in fulfilment as it becomes immediate to us, standing on the same floor. But at this point the railing, the wrought iron screen, is inserted; which again creates a form of Here and There by means of the screened vista. A brilliant, if painfully conceived, sequence.[2]

3. Concerning CONTENT. In this last category we turn to an examination of the fabric of towns: colour, texture, scale, style, character, personality and uniqueness. Accepting the fact that most towns are of old foundation, their fabric will show evidence of differing periods in its architectural styles and also in the various accidents of layout. Many towns do so display this mixture of styles, materials and scales.

Yet there exists at the back of our minds a feeling that could we only start again we would get rid of this hotchpotch and make all new and fine and perfect. We would create an orderly scene with straight roads and with buildings that conformed in height and style. Given a free hand that is what we might do . . . create symmetry, balance, perfection and conformity. After all, that is the popular conception of the purpose of town planning.

But what is this conformity? Let us approach it by a simile. Let us suppose a party in a private house, where are gathered together half a dozen people who are strangers to each other. The early part of the evening is passed in polite conversation on general subjects such as the weather and the current news. Cigarettes are passed and lights offered punctiliously. In fact it is all an exhibition of manners, of how one ought to behave. It is also very boring. This is conformity. However, later on the ice begins to break and out of the straightjacket of orthodox manners and conformity real human beings begin to emerge. It is found that Miss X's sharp but good-natured wit is just the right foil to Major Y's somewhat simple exuberance. And so on. It begins to be fun. Conformity gives way to the agreement to differ within a recognized tolerance of behaviour.

Conformity, from the point of view of the planner, is difficult to avoid but to avoid it deliberately, by creating artificial diversions, is surely worse than the original boredom. Here, for instance, is a programme to rehouse 5,000 people. They are all treated the same, they get the same kind of house. How *can* one differentiate? Yet if we start from a much wider point of view we will see that tropical housing differs from temperate zone housing, that buildings in a brick country differ from buildings in a stone country, that religion and social manners vary the buildings. And as the field of observation narrows, so our sensitivity to the local gods must grow sharper. There is too much insensitivity in the building of towns, too much reliance on the tank and the armoured car where the telescopic rifle is wanted.

Within a commonly accepted framework – one that produces lucidity and not anarchy – we can manipulate the nuances of scale and style, of texture and colour and of character and individuality, juxtaposing them in order to create collective benefits. In fact the environment thus resolves itself into not conformity but the interplay of This and That.

It is a matter of observation that in a successful contrast of colours not only do we experience the harmony released but, equally, the colours become more truly themselves. In a large landscape by Corot, I forget its name, a landscape of sombre greens, almost a monochrome, there is a small figure in red. It is probably the reddest thing I have ever seen.

Statistics are abstracts: when they are plucked out of the completeness of life and converted into plans and the plans into buildings they will be lifeless. The result will be a three-dimensional diagram in which people are asked to live. In trying to colonize such a wasteland, to translate it from an environment for walking stomachs into a home for human beings, the difficulty lay in finding the point of application, in finding the gateway into the castle. We discovered three gateways, that of motion, that of position and that of content. By the exercise of vision it became apparent that motion was not one simple, measurable progression useful in planning, it was in fact two things, the Existing and the Revealed view. We discovered that the human being is constantly aware of his position in the environment, that he feels the need for a sense of place and that this sense of identity is coupled with an awareness of elsewhere. Conformity killed, whereas the agreement to differ gave life. In this way the void of statistics, of the diagram city, has been split into two parts, whether they be those of Serial Vision, Here and There or This and That. All that remains is to join them together into a new pattern created by the warmth and power and vitality of human imagination so that we build the home of man.

That is the theory of the game, the background. In fact the most difficult part lies ahead, the Art of Playing. As in any other game there are recognized gambits and moves built up from experience and precedent. In the pages that follow an attempt is made to chart these moves under the three main heads as a series of cases.

INTRODUCTION TO THE 1971 EDITION

In writing an introduction to this edition of *Townscape* I find little to alter in the attitude expressed in the original introduction written ten years ago.

It has been said that a new edition of *Townscape* should rely on modern work for its examples instead of these being culled from the past. This has not been done for two reasons.

First the task of finding the sharp little needles in the vast haystack of post-war building would be quite uneconomical. This leads to the second point, why should it be so difficult? Because, in my view, the original message of *Townscape* has not been delivered effectively.

We have witnessed a superficial civic style of decoration using bollards and cobbles, we have seen traffic-free pedestrian precincts and we have noted the rise of conservation.

But none of these is germane to townscape. The sadness of the situation is that the superficials have become the currency but the spirit, the Environment Game itself, is still locked away in its little red and gilt box.

The position may indeed have deteriorated over the last ten years for reasons which are set out below.

Man meets environment: unfamiliarity, shock, ugliness and boredom according to what kind of man you are. The problem is not new but is this generation getting more than its fair share? Yes. Reason? The reason in my view is the speed of change which has disrupted the normal communication between planner and planee. The list is familiar enough: more people, more houses, more amenities, faster communications and unfamiliar building methods.

The speed of change prevents the environment organisers from settling down and learning by experience how to humanise the raw material thrown at them. In consequence the environment is illdigested. London is suffering from indigestion. The gastric juices, as represented by planners, have not been able to break down all the vast chunks of hastily swallowed stodge into emotional nutriment. We may be able to do many things our grandparents could not do but we cannot digest any faster. The process, be it in stomach or brain, is part of our human bondage. And so we have to make organisational changes in order that human scale can be brought into effective contact with the forces of development.

The first change is to popularise the art of environment on the principle that the game improves with the amount of popular emotion invested and this is the crux of the situation. The stumbling block here is that in the popular mind administrative planning is dull, technical and forbidding whilst good planning is conceived as a wide, straight street with bushy-topped trees on either side, full stop. On the contrary! The way the environment is put together is potentially one of our most exciting and wide-spread pleasure sources. It is no use complaining of ugliness without realising that the shoes that pinch are really a pair of ten-league boots.

How to explain? Example: the nearest to hand at the time of writing is Sées cathedral near Alençon. The Gothic builders were fascinated by the problem of weight, how to support the culmination of their structures, the vault, and guide its weight safely down to earth. In this building weight has been divided into two parts. The walls are supported by sturdy cylindrical columns: the vault itself, the pride of the endeavour, appears to be supported on fantastically attenuated applied columns which act almost as lightning conductors of gravity between heaven and the solid earth. The walls are held up by man, the vault is clearly held up by angels. 'I understand weight, I am strong', 'I have overcome weight, I am ethereal'. 'We both spring from the same earth together, we need each other'. Through the centuries they commune together in serenity.

As soon as the game or dialogue is understood the whole place begins to shake hands with you. It bursts all through the dull business of who did what and when and who did it first. We know who did it, it was a chap with a twinkle in his eye.

This is the Environment Game and it is going on all round us. You will see that I am not discussing absolute values such as beauty, perfection, art with a big A, or morals. I am trying to describe an environment that chats away happily, plain folk talking together. Apart from a handful of noble exceptions our world is being filled with system-built dumb blondes and a scatter of Irish confetti. Only when the dialogue commences will people stop to listen.

Until such happy day arrives when people in the street throw their caps in the air at the sight of a planner (the volume of sardonic laughter is the measure of your deprivation) as they now do for footballers and pop singers, a holding operation in two parts will be necessary.

First, streaming the environment. It is difficult to fight for a general principle, easier to protect the particular. By breaking down the environment into its constituent parts the ecologist can fight for his national parks, local authority for its green belts, antiquarians for conservation areas and so on. This is already happening.

Second, the time scaling of these streams. Change, of itself, is often resented even if it can be seen to be a change for the better. Continuity is a desirable characteristic of cities. Consequently while planning consent in a development stream might be automatic one may have to expect a built-in delay of ten or even twenty years in an important conservation area. This is not necessarily to improve the design but simply to slow down the process. This also is happening, if grudgingly, in the case of Piccadilly Circus.

But the main endeavour is for the environment makers to reach their public, not democratically but emotionally. As the great Max Miller once remarked across the footlights on a dull evening, "I know you're out there, I can hear you breathing."

NOTES

1 The President's Residence, lately Viceregal Lodge.
2 It was the cause of bitterness between Lutyens and Baker.

"The Image of the Environment" and "The City Image and Its Elements"

from *The Image of the City* (1960)

Kevin Lynch

Editors' Introduction

These two chapters by Kevin Lynch (1918–1984) from *The Image of the City* highlight his early interest and research on the legibility and visual perception of cities. *The Image of the City* is by far the best known of his writings and has had a profound influence on how designers perceive cities and urban form. His underlying idea in "The Image of the Environment" is that people understand and mentally process the form of cities through the recognition of key physical elements. By utilizing visual elements, Lynch argues that urban designers have a toolkit for making more legible and psychologically satisfying places. Not only do these elements provide organizational clues and way-finding devices for people to orient themselves in space, but also they can help in engendering emotional security and a sense of place-based ownership that comes from one's ability to recognize familiar territory. Lynch defines "imageability" as:

> that quality in a physical object which gives it a high probability of evoking a strong image in any given observer. It is that shape, color, or arrangement which facilitates the making of vividly identified, powerfully structured, highly useful mental images of the environment.

Imageability to Lynch combines both the ability of the physical object to project a strong distinctive image, as well as the ability of the observer to mentally select, process, store, organize, and endow the image with meaning. In the selection from "The City Image and Its Elements," the author identifies five key elements that provide urban imageability: paths, edges, districts, nodes, and landmarks. In the conclusion to the book, he suggests ways in which designers can process this information to provide visual plans for reinforcing the form, physical controls, and public image of cities.

The book is important not only for its findings on the visual form of cities, but also in highlighting Lynch's research methods in environmental psychology. These methods allowed researchers to "get into the heads" of research subjects to better understand how they perceived their everyday environments. His methods included cognitive mapping, in-depth oral interviews, travel maps, direct observation, field reconnaissance walks, random pedestrian interviews, aerial and ground-level photography and synthesis maps. Data from extensive use of cognitive maps (mental maps of their city that people were asked to draw from memory) was easily compiled to provide synthetic illustrations of those elements that were most recognized or remembered. The same was done with data culled from oral interviews, which was then correlated across the data pulled from the cognitive mapping. From these different methods, Lynch's research team was able to triangulate similar findings from a relatively small sample of interviewees, although he later notes the biases in these small sample sets. Although this work has not been particularly fruitful in effecting public policy on a broad scale, it has been important to urban plan-making in some specific places, such as San Francisco (California), Ciudad Guyana (Venezuela), and Brookline (Massachusetts), as well as with research on childhood experience for UNESCO. Lynch's techniques have proven particularly valuable in environmental design research, in many types of urban design plan-making, within strategic SWOT analysis (Strengths, Weaknesses, Opportunities, and Threats), in understanding public images of the city for marketing purposes, and for knowledge in place memorability.

With its publication in 1960, Lynch's contribution belongs to the first generation of works in environmental psychology and environmental behavior. This literature has burgeoned since then, including major influences on a generation of researchers such as Amos Rapoport, Clare Cooper Marcus, Oscar Newman, William H. Whyte, Kenneth Craik, and Donald Appleyard – as well as planning and design departments at several universities, MIT and UC Berkeley in particular. With regard to its lasting impacts, *The Image of the City* helped to highlight the importance of urban form-making at a time when city planners were looking to social science methods to replace what was perceived to be an underperforming physical planning tradition. And with respect to current planning interest in public participation, it was influential in consulting the substantive users and residents of the city, and bringing them back into the planning conversation at a time when decision-making and design relied primarily on expert elite knowledge. Following its publication, other authors tried to identify design methods to reinforce the "image of the city." Notable among these is work by Jack Nasar, *The Evaluative Image of the City* (New York: Sage, 1997), where the author provides methods for designing and assessing city image in practice.

Even after his death, Kevin Lynch continued to be recognized as the United States' leading urban design educator and researcher. He began his design education at Yale prior to a fellowship at Taliesin under the tutelage of Frank Lloyd Wright. He taught for many years at MIT, in addition to professional consulting work in design and planning. He wrote exhaustively, including seven books and dozens of published articles and essays. His book *The Image of the City* (Cambridge, MA: MIT Press, 1960) is considered to be the most widely read book in the history of urban design. His other books include: *The View from the Road*, co-written with Donald Appleyard and John Myer (Cambridge, MA: MIT Press, 1964); *What Time is This Place?* (Cambridge, MA: MIT Press, 1972); *Managing the Sense of a Region* (Cambridge, MA: MIT Press, 1976); *Growing Up in Cities* (Cambridge, MA: MIT Press, 1977); *Good City Form* (Cambridge, MA: MIT Press, 1981), a textbook on site-specific design, *Site Planning* (Cambridge, MA: MIT Press, 1962); and a later version co-authored with Gary Hack shortly before his death, *Site Planning, 3rd edn* (Cambridge, MA: MIT Press, 1984); plus a book published posthumously with Michael Southworth (ed.), *Wasting Away* (San Francisco, CA: Sierra Club Books, 1990).

In Tridib Banerjee and Michael Southworth's edited book of Lynch's shorter essays and articles, *City Sense and City Design: Writings and Projects of Kevin Lynch* (Cambridge, MA: MIT Press, 1990), one can find supplemental material by Lynch on environmental perception and the visual form of cities: "Environmental Perception: Research and Public Policy" (MIT Libraries' Institute Archives and Special Collections); "Reconsidering the Image of the City," in Lloyd Rodwin and Robert Hollister (eds), *Cities in Mind* (New York: Plenum, 1984); "A Process of Community Visual Survey" (MIT Libraries' Institute Archives and Special Collections); and "The Visual Shape of the Shapeless Metropolis" (MIT Libraries' Institute Archives and Special Collections).

Additional material on research and practice in environmental psychology can be found in the following: Paul A. Bell, Thomas Greene, Jeffrey Fisher, and Andrew S. Baum, *Environmental Psychology* (London: Taylor & Francis/Psychology Press, 2005); Harold M. Proshansky, William Ittleson, and Leanne Rivlin (eds), *Environmental Psychology: Man and his Physical Setting* (New York: Holt, Rinehart & Winston, 1970); Roger M. Downs and David Stea (eds), *Image and Environment: Cognitive Mapping and Spatial Behavior* (Chicago, IL: Aldine, 1973); S. Kaplan and R. Kaplan, *Cognition and Environment: Functioning in an Uncertain World* (New York: Praeger, 1982); and Robert B. Bechtel and Arza Churchman (eds), *Handbook of Environmental Psychology* (New York: John Wiley, 2002).

For literature on the relationship between environmental psychology and design, or the emerging "psychology of design" field, see the following: David Alan Kopec, *Environmental Psychology for Design, 2nd edn* (New York: Fairchild Publications, 2012); Toby Israel, *Some Place Like Home: Using Design Psychology to Create Ideal Places* (New York: Wiley Academy, 2003); Gyorgy Kepes, *Language of Vision* (Chicago, IL: P. Theobald, 1944) and *Sign, Image, Symbol* (New York: George Braziller, 1966); D. De Jonge, "Images of Urban Areas: Their Structure and Psychological Foundations," *Journal of the American Institute of Planners* (vol. 28, 1962, 266–276); and M. Gottdiener and A. Lagopoulos, *The City and the Sign: An Introduction to Urban Semiotics* (New York: Columbia University Press, 1986).

THE IMAGE OF THE ENVIRONMENT

Looking at cities can give a special pleasure, however commonplace the sight may be. Like a piece of architecture, the city is a construction in space, but one of vast scale, a thing perceived only in the course of long spans of time. City design is therefore a temporal art, but it can rarely use the controlled and limited sequences of other temporal arts like music. On different occasions and for different people, the sequences are reversed, interrupted, abandoned, cut across. It is seen in all lights and all weathers.

At every instant, there is more than the eye can see, more than the ear can hear, a setting or a view waiting to be explored. Nothing is experienced by itself, but always in relation to its surroundings, the sequences of events leading up to it, the memory of past experiences. Washington Street set in a farmer's field might look like the shopping street in the heart of Boston, and yet it would seem utterly different. Every citizen has had long associations with some part of his city, and his image is soaked in memories and meanings.

Moving elements in a city, and in particular the people and their activities, are as important as the stationary physical parts. We are not simply observers of this spectacle, but are ourselves a part of it, on the stage with the other participants. Most often, our perception of the city is not sustained, but rather partial, fragmentary, mixed with other concerns. Nearly every sense is in operation, and the image is the composite of them all.

Not only is the city an object which is perceived (and perhaps enjoyed) by millions of people of widely diverse class and character, but it is the product of many builders who are constantly modifying the structure for reasons of their own. While it may be stable in general outlines for some time, it is ever changing in detail. Only partial control can be exercised over its growth and form. There is no final result, only a continuous succession of phases. No wonder, then, that the art of shaping cities for sensuous enjoyment is an art quite separate from architecture or music or literature. It may learn a great deal from these other arts, but it cannot imitate them.

A beautiful and delightful city environment is an oddity, some would say an impossibility. Not one American city larger than a village is of consistently fine quality, although a few towns have some pleasant fragments. It is hardly surprising, then, that most Americans have little idea of what it can mean to live in such an environment. They are clear enough about the ugliness of the world they live in, and they are quite vocal about the dirt, the smoke, the heat, and the congestion, the chaos and yet the monotony of it. But they are hardly aware of the potential value of harmonious surroundings, a world which they may have briefly glimpsed only as tourists or as escaped vacationers. They can have little sense of what a setting can mean in terms of daily delight, or as a continuous anchor for their lives, or as an extension of the meaningfulness and richness of the world.

LEGIBILITY

This book will consider the visual quality of the American city by studying the mental image of that city which is held by its citizens. It will concentrate especially on one particular visual quality: the apparent clarity or "legibility" of the cityscape. By this we mean the ease with which its parts can be recognized and can be organized into a coherent pattern.

Just as this printed page, if it is legible, can be visually grasped as a related pattern of recognizable symbols, so a legible city would be one whose districts or landmarks or pathways are easily identifiable and are easily grouped into an over-all pattern.

This book will assert that legibility is crucial in the city setting, will analyze it in some detail, and will try to show how this concept might be used today in rebuilding our cities. As will quickly become apparent to the reader, this study is a preliminary exploration, a first word not a last word, an attempt to capture ideas and to suggest how they might be developed and tested. Its tone will be speculative and perhaps a little irresponsible: at once tentative and presumptuous. This first chapter will develop some of the basic ideas; later chapters will apply them to several American cities and discuss their consequences for urban design.

Although clarity or legibility is by no means the only important property of a beautiful city, it is of special importance when considering environments at the urban scale of size, time, and complexity. To understand this, we must consider not just the city as a thing in itself, but the city being perceived by its inhabitants.

Structuring and identifying the environment is a vital ability among all mobile animals. Many kinds of cues are used: the visual sensations of color, shape, motion, or polarization of light, as well as other senses such as smell, sound, touch, kinesthesia, sense of gravity, and perhaps of electric or magnetic fields. These techniques of orientation, from the polar flight of a tern to the path-finding of a limpet over the micro-topography of a rock, are described and their importance underscored in an extensive literature (Casamajor 1927; Fischer 1931; Griffin 1953; Rabaud 1927). Psychologists have also studied this ability in man, although rather sketchily or under limited laboratory conditions (Angyal 1930; Binet 1894; Brown 1932; Claparède 1943; Jaccard 1932; Ryan 1940; Sandström 1951; Trowbridge 1913; Witkin 1949). Despite a few remaining puzzles, it now seems unlikely that there is any mystic "instinct" of way-finding. Rather there is a consistent use and organization of definite sensory cues from the external environment. This organization is fundamental to the efficiency and to the very survival of free-moving life.

To become completely lost is perhaps a rather rare experience for most people in the modern city.

We are supported by the presence of others and by special way-finding devices: maps, street numbers, route signs, bus placards. But let the mishap of disorientation once occur, and the sense of anxiety and even terror that accompanies it reveals to us how closely it is linked to our sense of balance and well-being. The very word "lost" in our language means much more than simple geographical uncertainty; it carries overtones of utter disaster.

In the process of way-finding, the strategic link is the environmental image, the generalized mental picture of the exterior physical world that is held by an individual. This image is the product both of immediate sensation and of the memory of past experience, and it is used to interpret information and to guide action. The need to recognize and pattern our surroundings is so crucial, and has such long roots in the past, that this image has wide practical and emotional importance to the individual.

Obviously a clear image enables one to move about easily and quickly: to find a friend's house or a policeman or a button store. But an ordered environment can do more than this; it may serve as a broad frame of reference, an organizer of activity or belief or knowledge. On the basis of a structural understanding of Manhattan, for example, one can order a substantial quantity of facts and fancies about the nature of the world we live in. Like any good framework, such a structure gives the individual a possibility of choice and a starting-point for the acquisition of further information. A clear image of the surroundings is thus a useful basis for individual growth.

A vivid and integrated physical setting, capable of producing a sharp image, plays a social role as well. It can furnish the raw material for the symbols and collective memories of group communication. A striking landscape is the skeleton upon which many primitive races erect their socially important myths. Common memories of the "home town" were often the first and easiest point of contact between lonely soldiers during the war.

A good environmental image gives its possessor an important sense of emotional security. He can establish a harmonious relationship between himself and the outside world. This is the obverse of the fear that comes with disorientation; it means that the sweet sense of home is strongest when home is not only familiar but distinctive as well.

Indeed, a distinctive and legible environment not only offers security but also heightens the potential depth and intensity of human experience. Although life is far from impossible in the visual chaos of the modern city, the same daily action could take on new meaning if carried out in a more vivid setting. Potentially, the city is in itself the powerful symbol of a complex society. If visually well set forth, it can also have strong expressive meaning.

It may be argued against the importance of physical legibility that the human brain is marvelously adaptable, that with some experience one can learn to pick one's way through the most disordered or featureless surroundings. There are abundant examples of precise navigation over the "trackless" wastes of sea, sand, or ice, or through a tangled maze of jungle.

Yet even the sea has the sun and stars, the winds, currents, birds, and sea-colors without which unaided navigation would be impossible. The fact that only skilled professionals could navigate among the Polynesian Islands, and this only after extensive training, indicates the difficulties imposed by this particular environment. Strain and anxiety accompanied even the best-prepared expeditions.

In our own world, we might say that almost everyone can, if attentive, learn to navigate in Jersey City, but only at the cost of some effort and uncertainty. Moreover, the positive values of legible surroundings are missing: the emotional satisfaction, the framework for communication or conceptual organization, the new depths that it may bring to everyday experience. These are pleasures we lack, even if our present city environment is not so disordered as to impose an intolerable strain on those who are familiar with it.

It must be granted that there is some value in mystification, labyrinth, or surprise in the environment. Many of us enjoy the House of Mirrors, and there is a certain charm in the crooked streets of Boston. This is so, however, only under two conditions. First, there must be no danger of losing basic form or orientation, of never coming out. The surprise must occur in an over-all framework; the confusions must be small regions in a visible whole. Furthermore, the labyrinth or mystery must in itself have some form that can be explored and in time be apprehended. Complete chaos without hint of connection is never pleasurable.

But these second thoughts point to an important qualification. The observer himself should play an active role in perceiving the world and have a creative part in developing his image. He should have the power to change that image to fit changing needs. An environment which is ordered in precise and final detail may inhibit new patterns of activity. A landscape whose every rock tells a story may make difficult the creation of fresh stories. Although this may not seem to be a critical issue in our present urban chaos, yet it indicates that what we seek is not a final but an open-ended order, capable of continuous further development.

BUILDING THE IMAGE

Environmental images are the result of a two-way process between the observer and his environment. The environment suggests distinctions and relations, and the observer – with great adaptability and in the light of his own purposes – selects, organizes, and endows with meaning what he sees. The image so developed now limits and emphasizes what is seen, while the image itself is being tested against the filtered perceptual input in a constant interacting process. Thus the image of a given reality may vary significantly between different observers.

The coherence of the image may arise in several ways. There may be little in the real object that is ordered or remarkable, and yet its mental picture has gained identity and organization through long familiarity. One man may find objects easily on what seems to anyone else to be a totally disordered work table. Alternatively, an object seen for the first time may be identified and related not because it is individually familiar but because it conforms to a stereotype already constructed by the observer. An American can always spot the corner drugstore, however indistinguishable it might be to a Bushman. Again, a new object may seem to have strong structure or identity because of striking physical features which suggest or impose their own pattern. Thus the sea or a great mountain can rivet the attention of one coming from the flat plains of the interior, even if he is so young or so parochial as to have no name for these great phenomena.

As manipulators of the physical environment, city planners are primarily interested in the external agent in the interaction which produces the environmental image. Different environments resist or facilitate the process of image-making. Any given form, a fine vase or a lump of clay, will have a high or a low probability of evoking a strong image among various observers. Presumably this probability can be stated with greater and greater precision as the observers are grouped in more and more homogeneous classes of age, sex, culture, occupation, temperament, or familiarity. Each individual creates and bears his own image, but there seems to be substantial agreement among members of the same group. It is these group images, exhibiting consensus among significant numbers, that interest city planners who aspire to model an environment that will be used by many people.

Therefore this study will tend to pass over individual differences, interesting as they might be to a psychologist. The first order of business will be what might be called the "public images," the common mental pictures carried by large numbers of a city's inhabitants: areas of agreement which might be expected to appear in the interaction of a single physical reality, a common culture, and a basic physiological nature.

The systems of orientation which have been used vary widely throughout the world, changing from culture to culture, and from landscape to landscape. [. . .] The world may be organized around a set of focal points, or be broken into named regions, or be linked by remembered routes. Varied as these methods are, and inexhaustible as seem to be the potential clues which a man may pick out to differentiate his world, they cast interesting side-lights on the means that we use today to locate ourselves in our own city world. For the most part these examples seem to echo, curiously enough, the formal types of image elements into which we can conveniently divide the city image: path, landmark, edge, node, and district.

STRUCTURE AND IDENTITY

An environmental image may be analyzed into three components: identity, structure, and meaning. It is useful to abstract these for analysis, if it is remembered that in reality they always appear together. A workable image requires first the identification of an object, which implies its distinction from other things, its recognition as a separable entity. This is called identity, not in the sense of equality with something else, but with the meaning of individuality or oneness. Second, the image must include the spatial or pattern relation of the object to the observer and to other objects. Finally, this object must have some meaning for the observer, whether practical or emotional. Meaning is also a relation, but quite a different one from spatial or pattern relation.

Thus an image useful for making an exit requires the recognition of a door as a distinct entity, of its spatial relation to the observer, and its meaning as a hole for getting out. These are not truly separable. The visual recognition of a door is matted together with its meaning as a door. It is possible, however, to analyze the door in terms of its identity of form and clarity of position, considered as if they were prior to its meaning.

Such an analytic feat might be pointless in the study of a door, but not in the study of the urban environment. To begin with, the question of meaning in the city is a complicated one. Group images of meaning are less likely to be consistent at this level than are the perceptions of entity and relationship. Meaning, moreover, is not so easily influenced by physical manipulation as are these other two components. If it is our purpose to build cities for the enjoyment of vast numbers of people of widely diverse background – and cities which will also be adaptable to future purposes – we may even be wise to concentrate on the physical clarity of the image and to allow meaning to develop without our direct guidance. The image of the Manhattan skyline may stand for vitality, power, decadence, mystery, congestion, greatness, or what you will, but in each case that sharp picture crystallizes and reinforces the meaning. So various are the individual meanings of a city, even while its form may be easily communicable, that it appears possible to separate meaning from form, at least in the early stages of analysis. This study will therefore concentrate on the identity and structure of city images.

If an image is to have value for orientation in the living space, it must have several qualities. It must be sufficient, true in a pragmatic sense, allowing the individual to operate within his environment to the extent desired. The map, whether exact or not, must be good enough to get one home.

It must be sufficiently clear and well integrated to be economical of mental effort: the map must be readable. It should be safe, with a surplus of clues so that alternative actions are possible and the risk of failure is not too high. If a blinking light is the only sign for a critical turn, a power failure may cause disaster. The image should preferably be open-ended, adaptable to change, allowing the individual to continue to investigate and organize reality: there should be blank spaces where he can extend the drawing for himself. Finally, it should in some measure be communicable to other individuals. The relative importance of these criteria for a "good" image will vary with different persons in different situations; one will prize an economical and sufficient system, another an open-ended and communicable one.

IMAGEABILITY

Since the emphasis here will be on the physical environment as the independent variable, this study will look for physical qualities which relate to the attributes of identity and structure in the mental image. This leads to the definition of what might be called *imageability*: that quality in a physical object which gives it a high probability of evoking a strong image in any given observer. It is that shape, color, or arrangement which facilitates the making of vividly identified, powerfully structured, highly useful mental images of the environment. It might also be called *legibility*, or perhaps *visibility* in a heightened sense, where objects are not only able to be seen, but are presented sharply and intensely to the senses.

Half a century ago, Stern discussed this attribute of an artistic object and called it *apparency* (Stern 1914–1915). While art is not limited to this single end, he felt that one of its two basic functions was "to create images which by clarity and harmony of form fulfill the need for vividly comprehensible appearance." In his mind, this was an essential first step toward the expression of inner meaning.

A highly imageable (apparent, legible, or visible) city in this peculiar sense would seem well formed, distinct, remarkable; it would invite the eye and the ear to greater attention and participation. The sensuous grasp upon such surroundings would not merely be simplified, but also extended and deepened. Such a city would be one that could be apprehended over time as a pattern of high continuity with many distinctive parts clearly interconnected. The perceptive and familiar observer could absorb new sensuous impacts without disruption of his basic image, and each new impact would touch upon many previous elements. He would be well oriented, and he could move easily. He would be highly aware of his environment. The city of Venice might be an example of such a highly imageable environment. In the United States, one is tempted to cite parts of Manhattan, San Francisco, Boston, or perhaps the lake front of Chicago.

These are characterizations that flow from our definitions. The concept of imageability does not necessarily connote something fixed, limited, precise, unified, or regularly ordered, although it may sometimes have these qualities. Nor does it mean apparent at a glance, obvious, patent, or plain. The total environment to be patterned is highly complex, while the obvious image is soon boring, and can point to only a few features of the living world.

The imageability of city form will be the center of the study to follow. There are other basic properties in a beautiful environment: meaning or expressiveness, sensuous delight, rhythm, stimulus, choice. Our concentration on imageability does not deny their importance. Our purpose is simply to consider the need for identity and structure in our perceptual world, and to illustrate the special relevance of this quality to the particular case of the complex, shifting urban environment.

Since image development is a two-way process between observer and observed, it is possible to strengthen the image either by symbolic devices, by the retraining of the perceiver, or by reshaping one's surroundings. You can provide the viewer with a symbolic diagram of how the world fits together: a map or a set of written instructions. As long as he can fit reality to the diagram, he has a clue to the relatedness of things. You can even install a machine for giving directions, as has recently been done in New York (*New York Times* 1957). While such devices are extremely useful for providing condensed data on interconnections, they are also precarious, since orientation fails if the device is lost, and the device itself must constantly be referred and fitted to reality. [. . .] Moreover, the complete experience of interconnection, the full depth of a vivid image, is lacking.

You may also train the observer. Brown remarks that a maze through which subjects were asked to move blindfolded seemed to them at first to be one unbroken problem. On repetition, parts of the pattern, particularly the beginning and end, became familiar and assumed the character of localities. Finally, when they could tread the maze without error, the whole system seemed to have become one locality (Brown 1932). DeSilva describes the case of a boy who seemed to have "automatic" directional orientation, but proved to have been trained from infancy (by a mother who could not distinguish right from left) to respond to "the east side of the porch" or "the south end of the dresser" (deSilva 1931).

Shipton's account of the reconnaissance for the ascent of Everest offers a dramatic case of such learning. Approaching Everest from a new direction, Shipton immediately recognized the main peaks and saddles that he knew from the north side. But the Sherpa guide accompanying him, to whom both sides were long familiar, had never realized that these were the same features, and he greeted the revelation with surprise and delight (Shipton 1952).

Kilpatrick describes the process of perceptual learning forced on an observer by new stimuli that no longer fit into previous images (Kilpatrick 1954). It begins with hypothetical forms that explain the new stimuli conceptually, while the illusion of the old forms persists. The personal experience of most of us will testify to this persistence of an illusory image long after its inadequacy is conceptually realized. We stare into the jungle and see only the sunlight on the green leaves, but a warning noise tells us that an animal is hidden there. The observer then learns to interpret the scene by singling out "give-away" clues and by reweighting previous signals. The camouflaged animal may now be picked up by the reflection of his eyes. Finally by repeated experience the entire pattern of perception is changed, and the observer need no longer consciously search for give-aways, or add new data to an old framework. He has achieved an image which will operate successfully in the new situation, seeming natural and right. Quite suddenly the hidden animal appears among the leaves, "as plain as day."

In the same way, we must learn to see the hidden forms in the vast sprawl of our cities. We are not accustomed to organizing and imaging an artificial environment on such a large scale; yet our activities are pushing us toward that end.

Curt Sachs gives an example of a failure to make connections beyond a certain level (Sachs 1953). The voice and drumbeat of the North American Indian follow entirely different tempos, the two being perceived independently. Searching for a musical analogy of our own, he mentions our church services, where we do not think of coordinating the choir inside with the bells above.

In our vast metropolitan areas we do not connect the choir and the bells; like the Sherpa, we see only the sides of Everest and not the mountain. To extend and deepen our perception of the environment would be to continue a long biological and cultural development which has gone from the contact senses to the distant senses and from the distant senses to symbolic communications. Our thesis is that we are now able to develop our image of the environment by operation on the external physical shape as well as by an internal learning process. Indeed, the complexity of our environment now compels us to do so.

Primitive man was forced to improve his environmental image by adapting his perception to the given landscape. He could effect minor changes in his environment with cairns, beacons, or tree blazes, but substantial modifications for visual clarity or visual interconnection were confined to house sites or religious enclosures. Only powerful civilizations can begin to act on their total environment at a significant scale. The conscious remolding of the large-scale physical environment has been possible only recently, and so the problem of environmental imageability is a new one. Technically, we can now make completely new landscapes in a brief time, as in the Dutch polders. Here the designers are already at grips with the question of how to form the total scene so that it is easy for the human observer to identify its parts and to structure the whole (Granpré-Molière 1955).

We are rapidly building a new functional unit, the metropolitan region, but we have yet to grasp that this unit, too, should have its corresponding image. Suzanne Langer sets the problem in her capsule definition of architecture: "It is the total environment made visible" (Langer 1953).

THE CITY IMAGE AND ITS ELEMENTS

There seems to be a public image of any given city which is the overlap of many individual images.

Or perhaps there is a series of public images, each held by some significant number of citizens. Such group images are necessary if an individual is to operate successfully within his environment and to cooperate with his fellows. Each individual picture is unique, with some content that is rarely or never communicated, yet it approximates the public image, which, in different environments, is more or less compelling, more or less embracing.

This analysis limits itself to the effects of physical, perceptible objects. There are other influences on imageability, such as the social meaning of an area, its function, its history, or even its name. These will be glossed over, since the objective here is to uncover the role of form itself. It is taken for granted that in actual design form should be used to reinforce meaning, and not to negate it.

The contents of the city images so far studied, which are referable to physical forms, can conveniently be classified into five types of elements: paths, edges, districts, nodes, and landmarks. Indeed, these elements may be of more general application, since they seem to reappear in many types of environmental images. These elements may be defined as follows:

1. *Paths*. Paths are the channels along which the observer customarily, occasionally, or potentially moves. They may be streets, walkways, transit lines, canals, railroads. For many people, these are the predominant elements in their image. People observe the city while moving through it, and along these paths the other environmental elements are arranged and related.

2. *Edges*. Edges are the linear elements not used or considered as paths by the observer. They are the boundaries between two phases, linear breaks in continuity: shores, railroad cuts, edges of development, walls. They are lateral references rather than coordinate axes. Such edges may be barriers, more or less penetrable, which close one region off from another; or they may be seams, lines along which two regions are related and joined together. These edge elements, although probably not as dominant as paths, are for many people important organizing features, particularly in the role of hold-ing together generalized areas, as in the outline of a city by water or wall.

3. *Districts*. Districts are the medium-to-large sections of the city, conceived of as having two-dimensional extent, which the observer mentally enters "inside of," and which are recognizable as having some common, identifying character. Always identifiable from the inside, they are also used for exterior reference if visible from the outside. Most people structure their city to some extent in this way, with individual differences as to whether paths or districts are the dominant elements. It seems to depend not only upon the individual but also upon the given city.

4. *Nodes*. Nodes are points, the strategic spots in a city into which an observer can enter, and which are the intensive foci to and from which he is traveling. They may be primarily junctions, places of a break in transportation, a crossing or convergence of paths, moments of shift from one structure to another. Or the nodes may be simply concentrations, which gain their importance from being the condensation of some use or physical character, as a street-corner hangout or an enclosed square. Some of these concentration nodes are the focus and epitome of a district, over which their influence radiates and of which they stand as a symbol. They may be called cores. Many nodes, of course, partake of the nature of both junctions and concentrations. The concept of node is related to the concept of path, since junctions are typically the convergence of paths, events on the journey. It is similarly related to the concept of district, since cores are typically the intensive foci of districts, their polarizing center. In any event, some

nodal points are to be found in almost every image, and in certain cases they may be the dominant feature.

5. *Landmarks*. Landmarks are another type of point-reference, but in this case the observer does not enter within them, they are external. They are usually a rather simply defined physical object: building, sign, store, or mountain. Their use involves the singling out of one element from a host of possibilities. Some landmarks are distant ones, typically seen from many angles and distances, over the tops of smaller elements, and used as radial references. They may be within the city or at such a distance that for all practical purposes they symbolize a constant direction. Such are isolated towers, golden domes, great hills. Even a mobile point, like the sun, whose motion is sufficiently slow and regular, may be employed. Other landmarks are primarily local, being visible only in restricted localities and from certain approaches. These are the innumerable signs, store fronts, trees, doorknobs, and other urban detail, which fill in the image of most observers. They are frequently used clues of identity and even of structure, and seem to be increasingly relied upon as a journey becomes more and more familiar.

The image of a given physical reality may occasionally shift its type with different circumstances of viewing. Thus an expressway may be a path for the driver, and edge for the pedestrian. Or a central area may be a district when a city is organized on a medium scale, and a node when the entire metropolitan area is considered. But the categories seem to have stability for a given observer when he is operating at a given level.

None of the element types isolated above exist in isolation in the real case. Districts are structured with nodes, defined by edges, penetrated by paths, and sprinkled with landmarks. Elements regularly overlap and pierce one another. If this analysis begins with the differentiation of the data into categories, it must end with their reintegration into the whole image. Our studies have furnished much information about the visual character of the element types. This will be discussed below. Only to a lesser extent, unfortunately, did the work make revelations about the interrelations between elements, or about image levels, image qualities, or the development of the image. These latter topics will be treated at the end of this chapter.

[. . .]

ELEMENT INTERRELATIONS

These elements are simply the raw material of the environmental image at the city scale. They must be patterned together to provide a satisfying form. The preceding discussions have gone as far as groups of similar elements (nets of paths, clusters of landmarks, mosaics of regions). The next logical step is to consider the interaction of pairs of unlike elements.

Such pairs may reinforce one another, resonate so that they enhance each other's power; or they may conflict and destroy themselves. A great landmark may dwarf and throw out of scale a small region at its base. Properly located, another landmark may fix and strengthen a core; placed off center, it may only mislead, as does the John Hancock Building in relation to Boston's Copley Square. A large street, with its ambiguous character of both edge and path, may penetrate and thus expose a region to view, while at the same time disrupting it. A landmark feature may be so alien to the character of a district as to dissolve the regional continuity, or it may, on the other hand, stand in just the contrast that intensifies that continuity.

Districts in particular, which tend to be of larger size than the other elements, contain within themselves, and are thus related to, various paths, nodes, and landmarks. These other elements not only structure the region internally, they also intensify the identity of the whole by enriching and deepening its character. Beacon Hill in Boston is one example of this effect. In fact, the components of structure and identity (which are the parts of the image in which we are interested) seem to leapfrog as the observer moves up from level to level. The identity of a window may be structured into a pattern of windows, which is the cue for the identification of a building. The buildings themselves are interrelated so as to form an identifiable space, and so on.

Paths, which are dominant in many individual images, and which may be a principal resource in organization at the metropolitan scale, have intimate interrelations with other element types. Junction nodes occur automatically at major intersections and termini, and by their form should reinforce those critical moments in a journey. These nodes, in turn, are not only strengthened by the presence of landmarks (as is Copley Square) but provide a setting which almost guarantees attention for any such mark. The paths, again, are given identity and tempo not only by their own form, or by their nodal junctions, but by the regions they pass through, the edges they move along, and the landmarks distributed along their length.

All these elements operate together, in a context. It would be interesting to study the characteristics of various pairings: landmark-region, node-path, etc. Eventually, one should try to go beyond such pairings to consider total patterns.

Most observers seem to group their elements into intermediate organizations, which might be called complexes. The observer senses the complex as a whole whose parts are interdependent and are relatively fixed in relation to each other. Thus many Bostonians would be able to fit most of the major elements of the Back Bay, the Common, Beacon Hill, and the central shopping, into a single complex. This whole area, in the terms used by Brown (1932) in his experiments referred to earlier, has become one locality. For others, the size of their locality may be much smaller: the central shopping and the near edge of the Common alone, for example. Outside of this complex there are gaps of identity; the observer must run blind to the next whole, even if only momentarily. Although they are close together in physical reality, most people seem to feel

only a vague link between Boston's office and financial district and the central shopping district on Washington Street. This peculiar remoteness was also exemplified in the puzzling gap between Scollay Square and Dock Square which are only a block apart. The psychological distance between two localities may be much greater, or more difficult to surmount, than mere physical separation seems to warrant.

Our preoccupation here with parts rather than wholes is a necessary feature of an investigation in a primitive stage. After successful differentiation and understanding of parts, a study can move on to consideration of a total system. There were indications that the image may be a continuous field, the disturbance of one element in some way affecting all others. Even the recognition of an object is as much dependent on context as on the form of the object itself. One major distortion, such as a twisting of the shape of the Common, seemed to be reflected throughout the image of Boston. The disturbance of large-scale construction affected more than its immediate environs. But such field effects have hardly been studied here.

THE SHIFTING IMAGE

Rather than a single comprehensive image for the entire environment, there seemed to be sets of images, which more or less overlapped and interrelated. They were typically arranged in a series of levels, roughly by the scale of area involved, so that the observer moved as necessary from an image at street level to levels of a neighborhood, a city, or a metropolitan region.

This arrangement by levels is a necessity in a large and complex environment. Yet it imposes an extra burden of organization on the observer, especially if there is little relation between levels. If a tall building is unmistakable in the city-wide panorama yet unrecognizable from its base, then a chance has been lost to pin together the images at two different levels of organization. The State House on Beacon Hill, on the other hand, seems to pierce through several image levels. It holds a strategic place in the organization of the center.

Images may differ not only by the scale of area involved, but by viewpoint, time of day, or season. The image of Faneuil Hall as seen from the markets should be related to its image from a car on the Artery. Washington-Street-by-night should have some continuity, some element of invariance, with Washington-Street-by-day. In order to accomplish this continuity in the face of sensuous confusion, many observers drained their images of visual content, using abstractions such as "restaurant" or "second street." These will operate both day and night, driving or walking, rain or shine, albeit with some effort and loss.

The observer must also adjust his image to secular shifts in the physical reality around him. Los Angeles illustrated the practical and emotional strains induced as the image is confronted with constant physical changes. It would be important to know how to maintain continuity through these changes. Just as ties are needed between level and level of organization, so are continuities required which persist through a major change. This might be facilitated by the retention of an old tree, a path trace, or some regional character.

The sequence in which sketch maps were drawn seemed to indicate that the image develops, or grows, in different ways. This may perhaps have some relation to the way in which it first develops as an individual becomes familiar with his environment. Several types were apparent:

a. Quite frequently, images were developed along, and then outward from, familiar lines of movement. Thus a map might be drawn as branching out from a point of entrance, or beginning from some base line such as Massachusetts Avenue.
b. Other maps were begun by the construction of an enclosing outline, such as the Boston peninsula, which was then filled in toward the center.
c. Still others, particularly in Los Angeles, began by laying down a basic repeating pattern (the path gridiron) and then adding detail.
d. Somewhat fewer maps started as a set of adjacent regions, which were then detailed as to connections and interiors.
e. A few Boston examples developed from a familiar kernel, a dense familiar element on which everything was ultimately hung.

The image itself was not a precise, miniaturized model of reality, reduced in scale and consistently abstracted. As a purposive simplification, it was made by reducing, eliminating, or even adding elements to reality, by fusion and distortion, by relating and structuring the parts. It was sufficient, perhaps better, for its purpose if rearranged, distorted, "illogical." It resembled that famous cartoon of the New Yorker's view of the United States.

However distorted, there was a strong element of topological invariance with respect to reality. It was as if the map were drawn on an infinitely flexible rubber sheet; directions were twisted, distances stretched or compressed, large forms so changed from their accurate scale projection as to be at first unrecognizable. But the sequence was usually correct, the map was rarely torn and sewn back together in another order. This continuity is necessary if the image is to be of any value.

IMAGE QUALITY

Study of various individual images among the Bostonians revealed certain other distinctions between them. For example, images of an element differed between observers in terms of their relative density, i.e., the extent to which they were packed with detail. They might be relatively dense, as a picture of Newbury Street which identifies each building along its length, or relatively thin, when Newbury Street is characterized simply as a street bordered by old houses of mixed use.

Another distinction could be made between concrete, sensuously vivid images, and those which were highly abstract, generalized, and void of sensuous content. Thus the mental picture of a building might be vivid, involving its shape, color, texture, and detail, or be relatively abstract, the structure being identified as "a restaurant" or the "third building from the corner."

Vivid does not necessarily equate with dense, nor thin with abstract. An image might be both dense and abstract, as in the case of the taxicab dispatcher's knowledge of a city street, which related house numbers to uses along block after block, yet could not describe those buildings in any concrete sense.

Images could be further distinguished according to their structural quality: the manner in which their parts were arranged and interrelated. There were four stages along a continuum of increasing structural precision:

a. The various elements were free; there was no structure or interrelation between parts. We found no pure cases of this type, but several images were definitely disjointed, with vast gaps and many unrelated elements. Here rational movement was impossible without outside help, unless a systematic coverage of the entire area were to be resorted to (which meant the building up of a new structure on the spot).

b. In others, the structure became positional; the parts were roughly related in terms of their general direction and perhaps even relative distance from each other, while still remaining disconnected. One subject in particular always related herself to a few elements, without knowing definite connections between them. Movement was accomplished by searching, by moving out in the correct general direction, while weaving back and forth to cover a band and having an estimate of distance to correct overshooting.

c. Most often, perhaps, the structure was flexible; parts were connected one to the other, but in a loose and flexible manner, as if by limp or elastic ties. The sequence of events was known, but the mental map might be quite distorted, and its distortion might shift at different moments. To quote one subject: "I like to think of a few focal points and how to get from one to another, and the rest I don't bother to learn." With a flexible structure, movement was easier, since it proceeded along known paths, through known sequences. Motion between pairs of elements not habitually connected, or along other than habitual paths, might still be very confusing, however.

d. As connections multiplied, the structure tended to become rigid; parts were firmly interconnected in all dimensions; and any distortions became built in. The possessor of such a map can move much more freely, and can interconnect new points at will. As the density of the image builds up, it begins to take on the characteristics of a total field, in which interaction is possible in any direction and at any distance.

These characteristics of structure might apply in different ways at different levels. For example, two city regions may each possess rigid internal structures, and both connect at some seam or node. But this connection may fail to interlock with the internal structures, so that the connection itself is simply flexible. This effect seemed to occur for many Bostonians at Scollay Square, for example.

Total structure may also be distinguished in a still different way. For some, their images were organized rather instantaneously, as a series of wholes and parts descending from the general to the particular. This organization had the quality of a static map. Connection was made by moving up to the necessary bridging generality, and back down to the desired particular. To go from City Hospital to the Old North Church, for example, one might first consider that the hospital was in the South End and that the South End was in central Boston, then locate the North End in Boston and the church within the North End. This type of image might be called hierarchical.

For others, the image was put together in a more dynamic way, parts being interconnected by a sequence over time (even if the time was quite brief), and pictured as though seen by a motion picture camera. It was more closely related to the actual experience of moving through the city. This might be called a continuous organization, employing unrolling interconnections instead of static hierarchies.

One might infer from this that the images of greatest value are those which most closely approach a strong total field: dense, rigid, and vivid; which make use of all element types and form characteristics without narrow concentration; and which can be put together either hierarchically or continuously, as occasion demands. We may find, of course, that such an image is rare or impossible, that there are strong individual or cultural types which cannot transcend their basic abilities. In this case, an environment should be geared to the appropriate cultural type, or shaped in many ways so as to satisfy the varying demands of the individuals who inhabit it.

We are continuously engaged in the attempt to organize our surroundings, to structure and identify them. Various environments are more or less amenable to such treatment. When reshaping cities it should be possible to give them a form which facilitates these organizing efforts rather than frustrates them.

REFERENCES

Angyal, A., "Über die Raumlage vorgestellter Oerter," *Archiv für die Gesamte Psychologie*, Vol. 78, 1930, pp. 47–94.

Binet, M.A., "Reverse Illusions of Orientation," *Psychological Review*, Vol. I, No. 4, July 1894, pp. 337–350.

Brown, Warner, "Spatial Integrations in a Human Maze," *University of California Publications in Psychology*, Vol. V, No. 5, 1932, pp. 123–134.

Casamajor, Jean, "Le Mystérieux Sens de l'Espace," *Revue Scientifique*, Vol. 65, No. 18, 1927, pp. 554–565.

Claparède, Edouard, "L'Orientation Lointaine," *Nouveau Traité de Psychologie*, Tome VIII, Fasc. 3, Paris, Presses Universitaires de France, 1943.

Fischer, M.H., "Die Orientierung im Raume bei Wirbeltieren und beim Menschen," in *Handbuch der Normalen und Pathologischen Physiologie*, Berlin, J. Springer, 1931, pp. 909–1022.

Granpé-Molière, M.J., "Landscape of the N.E. Polder," translated from *Forum*, Vol. 10:1–2, 1955.

Griffin, Donald R. "Sensory Physiology and the Orientation of Animals," *American Scientist*, April 1953, pp. 209–244.

Jaccard, Pierre, *Le Sens de la direction et l'orientation lointaine chez l'homme*, Paris, Payot, 1932.

Kilpatrick, Franklin P., "Recent Experiments in Perception," *New York Academy of Science, Transaction*, No. 8, Vol. 16, June 1954, pp. 420–425.

Langer, Susanne, *Feeling and Form: A Theory of Art*, New York, Scribner, 1953.

New York Times, April 30, 1957, article of the "Directomat."

Rabaud, Etienne, *L'Orientation Lointaine et la Reconnaissance des Lieux*, Paris, Alcan, 1927.

Ryan, T.A. and M.S., "Geographical Orientation," *American Journal of Psychology*, Vol. 53, 1940, pp. 204–215.

Sachs, Curt, *Rhythm and Tempo*, New York, Norton, 1953.

Sandström, Carl Ivan, *Orientation on the Present Space*, Stockholm, Almqvist and Wiksell, 1951.

Shipton, Eric Earle, *The Mount Everest Reconnaissance Expedition*, London, Hodder & Stoughton, 1952.

deSilva, H.R., "A Case of a Boy Possessing an Automatic Directional Orientation," *Science*, Vol. 73, No. 1893, April 10, 1931, pp. 393–394.

Stern, Paul, "On the Problem of Artistic Form," *Logos*, Vol. V, 1914–15, pp. 165–172.

Trowbridge, C.C., "On Fundamental Methods of Orientation and Imaginary Maps," *Science*, Vol. 38, No. 990, Dec. 9, 1913, pp. 888–897.

Witkin, H.A., "Orientation in Space," *Research Reviews*, Office of Naval Research, December 1949.

"Author's Introduction" and "The Uses of Sidewalks: Contact"

from *The Death and Life of Great American Cities* (1961)

Jane Jacobs

Editors' Introduction

By the 1950s, the well-intentioned but misguided efforts of American city planners to create more healthful and efficient living environments was manifesting itself in large-scale urban renewal schemes and central city freeway construction projects. In 1961, Jane Jacobs' book *The Death and Life of Great American Cities* was published and immediately shocked the world of city planning. Jacobs (1916–2006) lived in Greenwich Village, where she was raising three children and engaging in neighborhood protests against local renewal projects and freeways. She wrote for the magazine *Architectural Forum*, where to her surprise and with no training she had been quickly elevated to the status of planning and urban development "expert." This experience gave her a lifelong skepticism of credentialed expertise. The book railed against abstract "drawing board" planning, and celebrated the dynamic qualities of cities and urban life.

Jacobs was fascinated by cities, how they worked and supported daily life. She learned about cities through close looking, and developed her theories through inductive analysis, generalizing from the particulars that she directly experienced. In *The Death and Life of Great American Cities*, she describes the four necessary physical conditions for dynamic urban life: multifunctional neighborhoods, short blocks and connected street systems, varied age residential areas, and a high concentration of people. These conditions help sustain a diversity of people and provide the critical mass to support urban amenities and services. To Jacobs, cities are living organisms in which streets are the "lifeblood." She describes the wealth of everyday life happening there as a "sidewalk ballet." Dense, street-oriented residential buildings mixed with small-scale local commercial shops provide "eyes on the street" that keep the city safe.

The two readings from *The Death and Life of Great American Cities* reprinted here summarize Jane Jacobs' attack on the planning establishment and present some of Jacobs' most important ideas regarding the social life of streets. In "The Uses of Sidewalks: Contact" Jacobs describes how casual interaction with others on everyday urban streets leads to social cohesion and a sense of belonging. The exquisitely articulated arguments she presents, along with the arguments presented in several other chapters on streets, began the rehabilitation of city streets as public spaces.

When *The Death and Life of Great American Cities* was published, Jacobs was disparaged by some of the most established planning professionals and academics, most particularly Lewis Mumford, on the grounds that since she had no professional training, she had no right to theorize about planning. Her methods were deemed unscientific, anecdotal, and arbitrary. But to those dismayed by the destruction of inner city neighborhoods and disaffected by the sterility of modern developments, Jacobs' celebration of the "messy" street life of vibrant cities struck home. She has inspired and continues to inspire generations of urban planners and architects, many of whom hold *The Death and Life of Great American Cities* to be the seminal book of the urban design field. Her revaluing of city streets as important public social spaces was a major influence on the later work of Allan B. Jacobs, Donald Appleyard, Peter Bosselmann, and a host of other urban design researchers and practitioners. Her ideas about the important qualities of urban streets and neighborhoods have been implemented in cities across North America and elsewhere, in the form of design guidelines that attempt to shape urban forms so as to achieve "eyes on the street," small blocks, and connected street patterns. The design guidelines prepared during the 1990s for Vancouver's False Creek North neighborhood are notable examples of this practice.

In the 1960s, Jane Jacobs moved with her family to Toronto, where she led the successful fight against the Spadina Expressway. She was a strong activist voice within Toronto and Canada until her death in 2006.

Jane Jacobs' other writings include *The Economy of Cities* (New York: Random House, 1969); *Cities and the Wealth of Nations* (New York: Random House, 1984); *Systems of Survival* (New York: Random House, 1992); *The Nature of Economies* (New York: Random House, 1998); and *Dark Age Ahead* (New York: Random House, 2004). These books place the city in larger historical and economic contexts and explore fundamental human values. A biography of her life and ideas by Max Allen is *Ideas that Matter: The Worlds of Jane Jacobs* (Owen Sound, Ont.: Ginger Press, 1997).

Works that offer perspectives on Jane Jacobs' early activism in New York City include Roberta Brandes Gratz, *The Battle for Gotham: New York in the Shadow of Robert Moses and Jane Jacobs* (New York: Nation Books, 2010) and Anthony Flint, *Wrestling with Moses: How Jane Jacobs Took on New York's Master Builder and Transformed the American City* (New York: Random House, 2009). Other books that offer insights into her life and work are Glenna Lang, *Genius of Common Sense: Jane Jacobs and the Story of The Death and Life of Great American Cities* (Boston, MA: David R. Godine, 2009) and Alice Sparberg Alexiou, *Jane Jacobs: Urban Visionary* (New Brunswick, NJ: Rutgers University Press, 2006).

AUTHOR'S INTRODUCTION

This book is an attack on current city planning and rebuilding. It is also, and mostly, an attempt to introduce new principles of city planning and rebuilding, different and even opposite from those now taught in everything from schools of architecture and planning to the Sunday supplements and women's magazines. My attack is not based on quibbles about rebuilding methods or hairsplitting about fashions in design. It is an attack, rather, on the principles and aims that have shaped modern, orthodox city planning and rebuilding.

In setting forth different principles, I shall mainly be writing about common, ordinary things: for instance, what kinds of city streets are safe and what kinds are not; why some city parks are marvelous and others are vice traps and death traps; why some slums stay slums and other slums regenerate themselves even against financial and official opposition; what makes downtowns shift their centers; what, if anything, is a city neighborhood, and what jobs, if any, neighborhoods in great cities do. In short, I shall be writing about how cities work in real life, because this is the only way to learn what

principles of planning and what practices in rebuilding can promote social and economic vitality in cities, and what practices and principles will deaden these attributes.

There is a wistful myth that if only we had enough money to spend – the figure is usually put at a hundred billion dollars – we could wipe out all our slums in ten years, reverse decay in the great, dull, gray belts that were yesterday's and day-before-yesterday's suburbs, anchor the wandering middle class and its wandering tax money, and perhaps even solve the traffic problem.

But look what we have built with the first several billions. Low-income projects that become worse centers of delinquency, vandalism and general social hopelessness than the slums they were supposed to replace. Middle-income housing projects which are truly marvels of dullness and regimentation, sealed against any buoyancy or vitality of city life. Luxury housing projects that mitigate their inanity, or try to, with a vapid vulgarity. Cultural centers that are unable to support a good bookstore. Civic centers that are avoided by everyone but bums, who have fewer choices of loitering place than others. Commercial centers that are lackluster imitations of standardized suburban chain-store shopping. Promenades that go from no place to nowhere and have no promenaders. Expressways that eviscerate great cities. This is not the rebuilding of cities. This is the sacking of cities.

Under the surface, these accomplishments prove even poorer than their poor pretenses. They seldom aid the city areas around them, as in theory they are supposed to. These amputated areas typically develop galloping gangrene. To house people in this planned fashion, price tags are fastened on the population, and each sorted-out chunk of price-tagged populace lives in growing suspicion and tension against the surrounding city. When two or more such hostile islands are juxtaposed the result is called "a balanced neighborhood". Monopolistic shopping centers and monumental cultural centers cloak, under the public relations hoohaw, the subtraction of commerce, and of culture too, from the intimate and casual life of cities.

That such wonders may be accomplished, people who get marked with the planners' hex signs are pushed about, expropriated, and uprooted much as if they were the subjects of a conquering power. Thousands upon thousands of small businesses are destroyed, and their proprietors ruined, with hardly a gesture at compensation. Whole communities are torn apart and sown to the winds, with a reaping of cynicism, resentment and despair that must be heard and seen to be believed. A group of clergymen in Chicago, appalled at the fruits of planned city rebuilding there, asked,

> Could Job have been thinking of Chicago when he wrote:
>
>> Here are men that alter their neighbor's landmark ... shoulder the poor aside, conspire to oppress the friendless.
>> Reap they the field that is none of theirs, strip they the vineyard wrongfully seized from its owner ...
>> A cry goes up from the city streets, where wounded men lie groaning ...

If so, he was also thinking of New York, Philadelphia, Boston, Washington, St. Louis, San Francisco and a number of other places. The economic rationale of current city rebuilding is a hoax. The economics of city rebuilding do not rest soundly on reasoned investment of public tax subsidies, as urban renewal theory proclaims, but also on vast, involuntary subsidies wrung out of helpless site victims. And the increased tax returns from such sites, accruing to the cities as a result of this "investment," are a mirage, a pitiful gesture against the ever increasing sums of public money needed to combat disintegration and instability that flow from the cruelly shaken-up city. The means to planned city rebuilding are as deplorable as the ends.

Meantime, all the art and science of city planning are helpless to stem decay – and the spiritlessness that precedes decay – in ever more massive swatches of cities. Nor can this decay be laid, reassuringly, to lack of opportunity to apply the arts of planning. It seems to matter little whether they are applied or not. Consider the Morningside Heights area in New York City. According to planning theory it should not be in trouble at all, for it enjoys a great abundance of parkland, campus, playground and other open spaces. It has plenty of grass. It occupies high and pleasant ground with magnificent river views. It is a famous educational center with splendid institutions – Columbia University, Union Theological Seminary, the Juilliard School of Music, and half a dozen others of eminent respectability. It is the beneficiary of good hospitals and churches. It has no industries. Its streets are zoned in the main against "incompatible uses" intruding into the preserves for solidly constructed, roomy, middle- and upper-class apartments. Yet by the early 1950's Morningside Heights was becoming a slum so swiftly, the surly kind of slum in which people fear to walk the streets, that the situation posed a crisis for the institutions. They and the planning arms of the city government got together, applied more planning theory, wiped out the most run-down part of the area and built in its stead a middle-income cooperative project complete with shopping center, and a public housing project, all interspersed with air, light, sunshine and landscaping. This was hailed as a great demonstration in city saving.

After that, Morningside Heights went downhill even faster.

Nor is this an unfair or irrelevant example. In city after city, precisely the wrong areas, in the light of planning theory, are decaying. Less noticed, but equally significant, in city after city the wrong areas, in the light of planning theory, are refusing to decay.

T
W
O

Cities are an immense laboratory of trial and error, failure and success, in city building and city design. This is the laboratory in which city planning should have been learning and forming and testing its theories. Instead the practitioners and teachers of this discipline (if such it can be called) have ignored the study of success and failure in real life, have been incurious about the reasons for unexpected success, and are guided instead by principles derived from the behavior and appearance of towns, suburbs, tuberculosis sanatoria, fairs, and imaginary dream cities – from anything but cities themselves.

If it appears that the rebuilt portions of cities and the endless new developments spreading beyond the cities are reducing city and countryside alike to a monotonous, unnourishing gruel, this is not strange. It all comes, first-, second-, third- or fourth-hand, out of the same intellectual dish of mush, a mush in which the qualities, necessities, advantages and behavior of great cities have been utterly confused with the qualities, necessities, advantages and behavior of other and more inert types of settlements.

There is nothing economically or socially inevitable about either the decay of old cities or the fresh-minted decadence of the new unurban urbanization. On the contrary, no other aspect of our economy and society has been more purposefully manipulated for a full quarter of a century to achieve precisely what we are getting. Extraordinary governmental financial incentives have been required to achieve this degree of monotony, sterility and vulgarity. Decades of preaching, writing and exhorting by experts have gone into convincing us and our legislators that mush like this must be good for us, as long as it comes bedded with grass.

Automobiles are often conveniently tagged as the villains responsible for the ills of cities and the disappointments and futilities of city planning. But the destructive effects of automobiles are much less a cause than a symptom of our incompetence at city building. Of course planners, including the highwaymen with fabulous sums of money and enormous powers at their disposal, are at a loss to make automobiles and cities compatible with one another. They do not know what to do with automobiles in cities because they do not know how to plan for workable and vital cities anyhow – with or without automobiles.

The simple needs of automobiles are more easily understood and satisfied than the complex needs of cities, and a growing number of planners and designers have come to believe that if they can only solve the problems of traffic, they will thereby have solved the major problem of cities. Cities have much more intricate economic and social concerns than automobile traffic. How can you know what to try with traffic until you know how the city itself works, and what else it needs to do with its streets? You can't.

[. . .]

THE USES OF SIDEWALKS: CONTACT

Reformers have long observed city people loitering on busy corners, hanging around in candy stores and bars and drinking soda pop on stoops, and have passed a judgment, the gist of which is: "This is deplorable! If these people had decent homes and a more private or bosky outdoor place, they wouldn't be on the street!"

This judgment represents a profound misunderstanding of cities. It makes no more sense than to drop in at a testimonial banquet in a hotel and conclude that if these people had wives who could cook, they would give their parties at home.

The point of both the testimonial banquet and the social life of city sidewalks is precisely that they are public. They bring together people who do not know each other in an intimate, private social fashion and in most cases do not care to know each other in that fashion.

Nobody can keep open house in a great city. Nobody wants to. And yet if interesting, useful and significant contacts among the people of cities are confined to acquaintanceships suitable for private life, the city becomes stultified. Cities are full of people with whom, from your viewpoint, or mine, or any other individual's, a certain degree of contact is useful or enjoyable; but you do not want them in your hair. And they do not want you in theirs either.

In speaking about city sidewalk safety, I mentioned how necessary it is that there should be, in the brains behind the eyes on the street, an almost unconscious assumption of general street support when the chips are down – when a citizen has to choose, for instance, whether he will take responsibility, or abdicate it, in combating barbarism or protecting strangers. There is a short word for this assumption of support: trust. The trust of a city street is formed over time from many, many little public sidewalk contacts. It grows out of people stopping by at the bar for a beer, getting advice from the grocer and giving advice to the newsstand man, comparing opinions with other customers at the bakery and nodding hello to the two boys drinking pop on the stoop, eying the girls while waiting to be called for dinner, admonishing the children, hearing about a job from the hardware man and borrowing a dollar from the druggist, admiring the new babies and sympathizing over the way a coat faded. Customs vary: in some neighborhoods people compare notes on their dogs; in others they compare notes on their landlords.

Most of it is ostensibly utterly trivial but the sum is not trivial at all. The sum of such casual, public contact at a local level – most of it fortuitous, most of it associated with errands, all of it metered by the person concerned and not thrust upon him by anyone – is a feeling for the public identity of people, a web of public respect and trust, and a resource in time of personal or neighborhood need. The absence of this trust is a disaster to a city street. Its cultivation cannot be institutionalized. And above all, *it implies no private commitments.*

I have seen a striking difference between presence and absence of casual public trust on two sides of the same wide street in East Harlem, composed of residents of roughly the same incomes and same races. On the old-city side, which was full of public places and the sidewalk loitering so deplored by Utopian minders of other people's leisure, the children were being kept well in hand. On the project side of the street across the way, the children, who had a fire hydrant open beside their play area, were behaving destructively, drenching the open windows of houses with water, squirting it on adults who ignorantly walked on the project side of the street, throwing it into the windows of cars as they went by. Nobody dared to stop them. These were anonymous children, and the identities behind them were an unknown. What if you scolded or stopped them? Who would back you up over there in the blind-eyed Turf? Would you get, instead, revenge? Better to keep out of it. Impersonal city streets make anonymous people, and this is not a matter of esthetic quality nor of

a mystical emotional effect in architectural scale. It is a matter of what kinds of tangible enterprises sidewalks have, and therefore of how people use the sidewalks in practical, everyday life.

The casual public sidewalk life of cities ties directly into other types of public life, of which I shall mention one as illustrative, although there is no end to their variety.

Formal types of local city organizations are frequently assumed by planners and even by some social workers to grow in direct, common-sense fashion out of announcements of meetings, the presence of meeting rooms, and the existence of problems of obvious public concern. Perhaps they grow so in suburbs and towns. They do not grow so in cities.

Formal public organizations in cities require an informal public life underlying them, mediating between them and the privacy of the people of the city. We catch a hint of what happens by contrasting, again, a city area possessing a public sidewalk life with a city area lacking it, as told about in the report of a settlement-house social researcher who was studying problems relating to public schools in a section of New York City:

Mr. W— (principal of an elementary school) was questioned on the effect of J— Houses on the school, and the uprooting of the community around the school. He felt that there had been many effects and of these most were negative. He mentioned that the project had torn out numerous institutions for socializing. The present atmosphere of the project was in no way similar to the gaiety of the streets before the project was built. He noted that in general there seemed fewer people on the streets because there were fewer places for people to gather. He also contended that before the projects were built the Parents Association had been very strong, and now there were only very few active members.

Mr. W— was wrong in one respect. There were not fewer places (or at any rate there was not less space) for people to gather in the project, if we count places deliberately planned for constructive socializing. Of course there were no bars, no candy stores, no hole-in-the-wall *bodegas*, no restaurants in the project. But the project under discussion was equipped with a model complement of meeting rooms, craft, art and game rooms, outdoor benches, malls, etc., enough to gladden the heart of even the Garden City advocates.

Why are such places dead and useless without the most determined efforts and expense to inveigle users – and then to maintain control over the users? What services do the public sidewalk and its enterprises fulfill that these planned gathering places do not? And why? How does an informal public sidewalk life bolster a more formal, organizational public life?

To understand such problems – to understand why drinking pop on the stoop differs from drinking pop in the game room, and why getting advice from the grocer or the bartender differs from getting advice from either your next-door neighbor or from an institutional lady who may be hand-in-glove with an institutional landlord – we must look into the matter of city privacy.

Privacy is precious in cities. It is indispensable. Perhaps it is precious and indispensable everywhere, but most places you cannot get it. In small settlements everyone knows your affairs. In the city everyone does not. Only those you choose to tell will know much about you. This is one of the attributes of cities that is precious to most city people, whether their incomes are high or their incomes are low, whether they are white or colored, whether they are old inhabitants or new, and it is a gift of great-city life deeply cherished and jealously guarded.

Architectural and planning literature deals with privacy in terms of windows, overlooks, sight lines. The idea is that if no one from outside can peek into where you live – behold, privacy. This is simpleminded. Window privacy is the easiest commodity in the world to get. You just pull down the shades or adjust the blinds. The privacy of keeping one's personal affairs to those selected to know them, and the privacy of having reasonable control over who shall make inroads on your time and when, are rare commodities in most of this world, however, and they have nothing to do with the orientation of windows.

Anthropologist Elena Padilla, author of *Up from Puerto Rico*, describing Puerto Rican life in a poor and squalid district of New York, tells how much people know about each other – who is to be trusted and who not, who is defiant of the law and who upholds it, who is competent and well informed and who is inept and ignorant – and how these things are known from the public life of the sidewalk and its associated enterprises. These are matters of public character. But she also tells how select are those permitted to drop into the kitchen for a cup of coffee, how strong are the ties, and how limited the number of a person's genuine confidants, those who share in a person's private life and private affairs. She tells how it is not considered dignified for everyone to know one's affairs. Nor is it considered dignified to snoop on others beyond the face presented in public. It does violence to a person's privacy and rights. In this, the people she describes are essentially the same as the people of the mixed, Americanized city street on which I live, and essentially the same as the people who live in high-income apartments or fine town houses, too.

A good city street neighborhood achieves a marvel of balance between its people's determination to have essential privacy and their simultaneous wishes for differing degrees of contact, enjoyment or help from the people around. This balance is largely made up of small, sensitively managed details, practiced and accepted so casually that they are normally taken for granted.

Perhaps I can best explain this subtle but all-important balance in terms of the stores where people leave keys for their friends, a common custom in New York. In our family, for example, when a friend wants to use our place while we are away for a weekend or everyone happens to be out during the day, or a visitor for whom we do not wish to wait up is spending the night, we tell such a friend that he can pick up the key at the delicatessen across the street. Joe Cornacchia, who keeps the delicatessen, usually has a dozen or so keys at a time for handing out like this. He has a special drawer for them.

Now why do I, and many others, select Joe as a logical custodian for keys? Because we trust him, first, to be a responsible custodian, but equally important because we know that he combines a feeling of good will with a feeling of no personal responsibility about our private affairs. Joe considers it no concern of his whom we choose to permit in our places and why.

Around on the other side of our block, people leave their keys at a Spanish grocery. On the other side of Joe's block, people leave them at the candy store. Down a block they leave them at the coffee shop, and a few hundred feet around the corner from that, in a barber shop. Around one corner from two fashionable blocks of town houses and apartments in the Upper East Side, people leave their keys in a butcher shop and a bookshop; around another corner they leave them in a cleaner's and a drug store. In unfashionable East Harlem keys are left with at least one florist, in bakeries, in luncheonettes, in Spanish and Italian groceries.

The point, wherever they are left, is not the kind of ostensible service that the enterprise offers, but the kind of proprietor it has.

A service like this cannot be formalized. Identifications . . . questions . . . insurance against mishaps. The all-essential line between public service and privacy would be transgressed by institutionalization. Nobody in his right mind would leave his key in such a place. The service must be given as a favor by someone with an unshakable understanding of the difference between a person's key and a person's private life, or it cannot be given at all.

Or consider the line drawn by Mr. Jaffe at the candy store around our corner – a line so well understood by his customers and by other storekeepers too that they can spend their whole lives in its presence and never think about it consciously. One ordinary morning last winter, Mr. Jaffe, whose formal business name is Bernie, and his wife, whose formal business name is Ann, supervised the small children crossing at the corner on the way to P.S. 41, as Bernie always does because he sees the need; lent an umbrella to one customer and a dollar to another; took custody of two keys; took in some packages for people in the next building who were away; lectured two youngsters who asked for cigarettes; gave street directions; took custody of a watch to give the repair man across the street when he opened later; gave out information on the range of rents in the neighborhood to an apartment seeker; listened to a tale of domestic difficulty and offered reassurance; told some rowdies they could not come in unless they behaved and then defined (and got) good behavior; provided an incidental forum for half a dozen conversations among customers who dropped in for oddments; set aside certain newly arrived papers and magazines for regular customers who would depend on getting them; advised a mother who came for a birthday present not to get the ship-model kit because another child going to the same birthday party was giving that; and got a back copy (this was for me) of the previous day's newspaper out of the deliverer's surplus returns when he came by.

After considering this multiplicity of extramerchandising services I asked Bernie, "Do you ever introduce your customers to each other?"

He looked startled at the idea, even dismayed. "No," he said thoughtfully.

"That would just not be advisable. Sometimes, if I know two customers who are in at the same time have an interest in common, I bring up the subject in conversation and let them carry it on from there if they want to. But oh no, I wouldn't introduce them."

When I told this to an acquaintance in a suburb, she promptly assumed that Mr. Jaffe felt that to make an introduction would be to step above his social class. Not at all. In our neighborhood, storekeepers like the Jaffes enjoy an excellent social status, that of businessmen. In income they are apt to be the peers of the general run of customers and in independence they are the superiors. Their advice, as men or women of common sense and experience, is sought and respected. They are well known as individuals, rather than unknown as class symbols. No; this is that almost unconsciously enforced, well-balanced line showing, the line between the city public world and the world of privacy.

This line can be maintained, without awkwardness to anyone, because of the great plenty of opportunities for public contact in the enterprises along the sidewalks, or on the sidewalks themselves as people move to and fro or deliberately loiter when they feel like it, and also because of the presence of many public hosts, so to speak, proprietors of meeting-places like Bernie's where one is free either to hang around or dash in and out, no strings attached.

Under this system, it is possible in a city street neighborhood to know all kinds of people without unwelcome entanglements, without boredom, necessity for excuses, explanations, fears of giving offense, embarrassments respecting impositions or commitments, and all such paraphernalia of obligations which can accompany less limited relationships. It is possible to be on excellent sidewalk terms with people who are very different from oneself, and even, as time passes, on familiar public terms with them. Such relationships can, and do, endure for many years, for decades; they could never have formed without that line, much less endured. They form precisely because they are by-the-way to people's normal public sorties.

"Togetherness" is a fittingly nauseating name for an old ideal in planning theory. This ideal is that if anything is shared among people, much should be shared. "Togetherness," apparently a spiritual resource of the new suburbs, works destructively in cities. The requirement that much shall be shared drives city people apart.

When an area of a city lacks a sidewalk life, the people of the place must enlarge their private lives if they are to have anything approaching equivalent contact with their neighbors. They must settle for some form of "togetherness," in which more is shared with one another than in the life of the sidewalks, or else they must settle for lack of contact. Inevitably the outcome is one or the other; it has to be; and either has distressing results.

In the case of the first outcome, where people do share much, they become exceedingly choosy as to who their neighbors are, or with whom they associate at all. They have to become so. A friend of mine, Penny Kostritsky, is unwittingly and unwillingly in this fix on a street in Baltimore. Her street of nothing but residences, embedded in an area of almost nothing but residences, has been experimentally equipped with a charming sidewalk park. The sidewalk has been widened and attractively paved, wheeled traffic discouraged from the narrow street roadbed, trees and flowers planted, and a piece of play sculpture is to go in. All these are splendid ideas so far as they go.

However, there are no stores. The mothers from nearby blocks who bring small children here, and come here to find some contact with others themselves, perforce go into the houses of acquaintances along the street to warm up in winter, to make telephone calls, to take their children in emergencies to the bathroom. Their hostesses offer them coffee, for there is no other place to get coffee, and naturally considerable social life of this kind has arisen around the park. Much is shared.

Mrs. Kostritsky, who lives in one of the conveniently located houses, and who has two small children, is in the thick of this narrow and accidental social life. "I have lost the advantage of living in the city," she says, "without getting the advantages of living in the suburbs." Still more distressing, when mothers of different income or color or educational background bring their children to the street park, they and their children are rudely and pointedly ostracized. They fit awkwardly into the suburbanlike sharing of private lives that has grown in default of city sidewalk life. The park lacks benches purposely; the "togetherness" people ruled them out because they might be interpreted as an invitation to people who cannot fit in.

"If only we had a couple of stores on the street," Mrs. Kostritsky laments.

"If only there were a grocery store or a drug store or a snack joint. Then the telephone calls and the warming up and the gathering could be done naturally in public, and then people would act more decent to each other because everybody would have a right to be here."

Much the same thing that happens in this sidewalk park without a city public life happens sometimes in middle-class projects and colonies, such as Chatham Village in Pittsburgh for example, a famous model of Garden City planning.

The houses here are grouped in colonies around shared interior lawns and play yards, and the whole development is equipped with other devices for close sharing, such as a residents' club which holds parties, dances, reunions, has ladies' activities like bridge and sewing parties, and holds dances and parties for the children. There is no public life here, in any city sense. There are differing degrees of extended private life.

Chatham Village's success as a "model" neighborhood where much is shared has required that the residents be similar to one another in their standards, interests and backgrounds. In the main they are middle-class professionals and their families.[1] It has also required that residents set themselves distinctly apart from the different people in the surrounding city; these are in the main also middle class, but lower middle class, and this is too different for the degree of chumminess that neighborliness in Chatham Village entails.

The inevitable insularity (and homogeneity) of Chatham Village has practical consequences. As one illustration, the junior high school serving the area has problems, as all schools do. Chatham

Village is large enough to dominate the elementary school to which its children go, and therefore to work at helping solve this school's problems. To deal with the junior high, however, Chatham Village's people must cooperate with entirely different neighborhoods. But there is no public acquaintanceship, no foundation of casual public trust, no cross-connections with the necessary people – and no practice or ease in applying the most ordinary techniques of city public life at lowly levels. Feeling helpless, as indeed they are, some Chatham Village families move away when their children reach junior high age; others contrive to send them to private high schools. Ironically, just such neighborhood islands as Chatham Village are encouraged in orthodox planning on the specific grounds that cities need the talents and stabilizing influence of the middle class. Presumably these qualities are to seep out by osmosis.

People who do not fit happily into such colonies eventually get out, and in time managements become sophisticated in knowing who among applicants will fit in. Along with basic similarities of standards, values and backgrounds, the arrangement seems to demand a formidable amount of forbearance and tact.

City residential planning that depends, for contact among neighbors, on personal sharing of this sort, and that cultivates it, often does work well socially, if rather narrowly, *for self-selected upper-middle-class people*. It solves easy problems for an easy kind of population. So far as I have been able to discover, it fails to work, however, even on its own terms, *with any other kind of population*.

The more common outcome in cities, where people are faced with the choice of sharing much or nothing, is nothing. In city areas that lack a natural and casual public life, it is common for residents to isolate themselves from each other to a fantastic degree. If mere contact with your neighbors threatens to entangle you in their private lives, or entangle them in yours, and if you cannot be so careful who your neighbors are as self-selected upper-middle-class people can be, the logical solution is absolutely to avoid friendliness or casual offers of help. Better to stay thoroughly distant. As a practical result, the ordinary public jobs – like keeping children in hand – for which people must take a little personal initiative, or those for which they must band together in limited common purposes,

go undone. The abysses this opens up can be almost unbelievable.

For example, in one New York City project which is designed – like all orthodox residential city planning – for sharing much or nothing, a remarkably outgoing woman prided herself that she had become acquainted, by making a deliberate effort, with the mothers of everyone of the ninety families in her building. She called on them. She buttonholed them at the door or in the hall. She struck up conversations if she sat beside them on a bench.

It so happened that her eight-year-old son, one day, got stuck in the elevator and was left there without help for more than two hours, although he screamed, cried and pounded. The next day the mother expressed her dismay to one of her ninety acquaintances. "Oh, was that *your* son?" said the other woman. "I didn't know whose boy he was. If I had realized he was *your* son I would have helped him."

This woman, who had not behaved in any such insanely calloused fashion on her old public street – to which she constantly returned, by the way, for public life – was afraid of a possible entanglement that might not be kept easily on a public plane.

Dozens of illustrations of this defense can be found wherever the choice is sharing much or nothing. A thorough and detailed report by Ellen Lurie, a social worker in East Harlem, on life in a low-income project there, has this to say:

It is . . . extremely important to recognize that for considerably complicated reasons, many adults either don't want to become involved in any friendship-relationships at all with their neighbors, or, if they do succumb to the need for some form of society, they strictly limit themselves to one or two friends, and no more. Over and over again, wives repeated their husband's warning:
"I'm not to get too friendly with anyone. My husband doesn't believe in it."
"People are too gossipy and they could get us in a lot of trouble."
"It's best to mind your own business."
One woman, Mrs. Abraham, always goes out the back door of the building because she doesn't want to interfere with the people standing around in the front. Another man, Mr. Colan . . . won't

let his wife make any friends in the project, because he doesn't trust the people here. They have four children, ranging from 8 years to 14, but they are not allowed downstairs alone, because the parents are afraid someone will hurt them.[2] What happens then is that all sorts of barriers to insure self-protection are being constructed by many families. To protect their children from a neighborhood they aren't sure of, they keep them upstairs in the apartment. To protect themselves, they make few, if any, friends. Some are afraid that friends will become angry or envious and make up a story to report to management, causing them great trouble. If the husband gets a bonus (which he decides not to report) and the wife buys new curtains, the visiting friends will see and might tell the management, who, in turn, investigates and issues a rent increase. Suspicion and fear of trouble often outweigh any need for neighborly advice and help. For these families the sense of privacy has already been extensively violated. The deepest secrets, all the family skeletons, are well known not only to management but often to other public agencies, such as the Welfare Department. To preserve any last remnants of privacy, they choose to avoid close relationships with others. This same phenomenon may be found to a much lesser degree in non-planned slum housing, for there too it is often necessary for other reasons to build up these forms of self-protection. But, it is surely true that this withdrawing from the society of others is much more extensive in planned housing. Even in England, this suspicion of the neighbors and the ensuing aloofness was found in studies of planned towns. Perhaps this pattern is nothing more than an elaborate group mechanism to protect and preserve inner dignity in the face of so many outside pressures to conform.

Along with nothingness, considerable "togetherness" can be found in such places, however. Mrs. Lurie reports on this type of relationship:

Often two women from two different buildings will meet in the laundry room, recognize each other; although they may never have spoken a single word to each other back on 99th Street, suddenly here they become "best friends." If one of these two already has a friend or two in her own building, the other is likely to be drawn into that circle and begins to make her friendships, not with women on her floor, but rather on her friend's floor.

These friendships do not go into an ever-widening circle. There are certain definite well-traveled paths in the project, and after a while no new people are met.

Mrs. Lurie, who works at community organization in East Harlem, with remarkable success, has looked into the history of many past attempts at project tenant organization. She has told me that "togetherness," itself, is one of the factors that make this kind of organization so difficult. "These projects are not lacking in natural leaders," she says.

They contain people with real ability, wonderful people many of them, but the typical sequence is that in the course of organization leaders have found each other, gotten all involved in each others' social lives, and have ended up talking to nobody but each other. They have not found their followers. Everything tends to degenerate into ineffective cliques, as a natural course. There is no normal public life. Just the mechanics of people learning what is going on is so difficult. It all makes the simplest social gain extra hard for these people.

Residents of unplanned city residential areas that lack neighborhood commerce and sidewalk life seem sometimes to follow the same course as residents of public projects when faced with the choice of sharing much or nothing. Thus researchers hunting the secrets of the social structure in a dull gray-area district of Detroit came to the unexpected conclusion there was no social structure.

The social structure of sidewalk life hangs partly on what can be called self-appointed public characters. A public character is anyone who is in frequent contact with a wide circle of people and who is sufficiently interested to make himself a public character. A public character need have no special talents or wisdom to fulfill his function – although he often does. He just needs to be present, and there need to be enough of his counterparts. His main qualification is that he *is* public, that he talks to lots of different people. In this way, news travels that is of sidewalk interest.

Most public sidewalk characters are steadily stationed in public places. They are storekeepers or barkeepers or the like. These are the basic public characters. All other public characters of city sidewalks depend on them – if only indirectly because of the presence of sidewalk routes to such enterprises and their proprietors.

Settlement-house workers and pastors, two more formalized kinds of public characters, typically depend on the street grapevine news systems that have their ganglia in the stores. The director of a settlement on New York's Lower East Side, as an example, makes a regular round of stores. He learns from the cleaner who does his suits about the presence of dope pushers in the neighborhood. He learns from the grocer that the Dragons are working up to something and need attention. He learns from the candy store that two girls are agitating the Sportsmen toward a rumble. One of his most important information spots is an unused breadbox on Rivington Street. That is, it is not used for bread. It stands outside a grocery and is used for sitting on and lounging beside, between the settlement house, a candy store and a pool parlor. A message spoken there for any teen-ager within many blocks will reach his ears unerringly and surprisingly quickly, and the opposite flow along the grapevine similarly brings news quickly in to the breadbox.

Blake Hobbs, the head of the Union Settlement music school in East Harlem, notes that when he gets a first student from one block of the old busy street neighborhoods, he rapidly gets at least three or four more and sometimes almost every child on the block. But when he gets a child from the nearby projects – perhaps through the public school or a playground conversation he has initiated – he almost never gets another as a direct sequence. Word does not move around where public characters and sidewalk life are lacking.

Besides the anchored public characters of the sidewalk, and the well-recognized roving public characters, there are apt to be various more specialized public characters on a city sidewalk. In a curious way, some of these help establish an identity not only for themselves but for others. Describing the everyday life of a retired tenor at such sidewalk establishments as the restaurant and the *bocce* court, a San Francisco news story notes, "It is said

of Meloni that because of his intensity, his dramatic manner and his lifelong interest in music, he transmits a feeling of vicarious importance to his many friends." Precisely.

One need not have either the artistry or the personality of such a man to become a specialized sidewalk character – but only a pertinent specialty of some sort. It is easy. I am a specialized public character of sorts along our street, owing of course to the fundamental presence of the basic, anchored public characters. The way I became one started with the fact that Greenwich Village, where I live, was waging an interminable and horrendous battle to save its main park from being bisected by a highway. During the course of battle I undertook, at the behest of a committee organizer away over on the other side of Greenwich Village, to deposit in stores on a few blocks of our street supplies of petition cards protesting the proposed roadway. Customers would sign the cards while in the stores, and from time to time I would make my pickups.[3] As a result of engaging in this messenger work, I have since become automatically the sidewalk public character on petition strategy. Before long, for instance, Mr. Fox at the liquor store was consulting me, as he wrapped up my bottle, on how we could get the city to remove a long abandoned and dangerous eyesore, a closed-up comfort station near his corner. If I would undertake to compose the petitions and find the effective way of presenting them to City Hall, he proposed, he and his partners would undertake to have them printed, circulated and picked up. Soon the stores round about had comfort station removal petitions. Our street by now has many public experts on petition tactics, including the children.

Not only do public characters spread the news and learn the news at retail, so to speak. They connect with each other and thus spread word wholesale, in effect.

A sidewalk life, so far as I can observe, arises out of no mysterious qualities or talents for it in this or that type of population. It arises only when the concrete, tangible facilities it requires are present. These happen to be the same facilities, in the same abundance and ubiquity, that are required for cultivating sidewalk safety. If they are absent, public sidewalk contacts are absent too.

The well-off have many ways of assuaging needs for which poorer people may depend much on sidewalk life – from hearing of jobs to being recognized by the headwaiter. But nevertheless, many of the rich or near-rich in cities appear to appreciate sidewalk life as much as anybody. At any rate, they pay enormous rents to move into areas with an exuberant and varied sidewalk life. They actually crowd out the middle class and the poor in lively areas like Yorkville or Greenwich Village in New York, or Telegraph Hill just off the North Beach streets of San Francisco. They capriciously desert, after only a few decades of fashion at most, the monotonous streets of "quiet residential areas" and leave them to the less fortunate. Talk to residents of Georgetown in the District of Columbia and by the second or third sentence at least you will begin to hear rhapsodies about the charming restaurants, "more good restaurants than in all the rest of the city put together," the uniqueness and friendliness of the stores, the pleasures of running into people when doing errands at the next corner – and nothing but pride over the fact that Georgetown has become a specialty shopping district for its whole metropolitan area. The city area, rich or poor or in between, harmed by an interesting sidewalk life and plentiful sidewalk contacts has yet to be found.

Efficiency of public sidewalk characters declines drastically if too much burden is put upon them. A store, for example, can reach a turnover in its contacts, or potential contacts, which is so large and so superficial that it is socially useless. An example of this can be seen at the candy and newspaper store owned by the housing cooperative of Corlears Hook on New York's Lower East Side. This planned project store replaces perhaps forty superficially similar stores which were wiped out (without compensation to their proprietors) on that project site and the adjoining sites. The place is a mill. Its clerks are so busy making change and screaming ineffectual imprecations at rowdies that they never hear anything except "I want that." This, or utter disinterest, is the usual atmosphere where shopping center planning or repressive zoning artificially contrives commercial monopolies for city neighborhoods. A store like this would fail economically if it had competition. Meantime, although monopoly insures the financial success planned for it, it fails the city socially.

Sidewalk public contact and sidewalk public safety, taken together, bear directly on our country's most serious social problem – segregation and racial discrimination.

I do not mean to imply that a city's planning and design, or its types of streets and street life, can automatically overcome segregation and discrimination. Too many other kinds of effort are also required to right these injustices.

But I do mean to say that to build and to rebuild big cities whose sidewalks are unsafe and whose people must settle for sharing much or nothing, *can* make it *much harder* for American cities to overcome discrimination no matter how much effort is expended.

Considering the amount of prejudice and fear that accompany discrimination and bolster it, overcoming residential discrimination is just that much harder if people feel unsafe on their sidewalks anyway. Overcoming residential discrimination comes hard where people have no means of keeping a civilized public life on a basically dignified public footing, and their private lives on a private footing.

To be sure, token model housing integration schemes here and there can be achieved in city areas handicapped by danger and by lack of public life – achieved by applying great effort and settling for abnormal (abnormal for cities) choosiness among new neighbors. This is an evasion of the size of the task and its urgency.

The tolerance, the room for great differences among neighbors – differences that often go far deeper than differences in color – which are possible and normal in intensely urban life, but which are so foreign to suburbs and pseudosuburbs, are possible and normal only when streets of great cities have built-in equipment allowing strangers to dwell in peace together on civilized but essentially dignified and reserved terms.

Lowly, unpurposeful and random as they may appear, sidewalk contacts are the small change from which a city's wealth of public life may grow.

Los Angeles is an extreme example of a metropolis with little public life, depending mainly instead on contacts of a more private social nature.

On one plane, for instance, an acquaintance there comments that although she has lived in the city for ten years and knows it contains Mexicans, she has never laid eyes on a Mexican or an item of Mexican culture, much less ever exchanged any words with a Mexican.

On another plane, Orson Welles has written that Hollywood is the only theatrical center in the world that has failed to develop a theatrical bistro.

And on still another plane, one of Los Angeles' most powerful businessmen comes upon a blank in public relationships which would be inconceivable in other cities of this size. This businessman, volunteering that the city is "culturally behind," as he put it, told me that he for one was at work to remedy this. He was heading a committee to raise funds for a first-rate art museum. Later in our conversation, after he had told me about the businessmen's club life of Los Angeles, a life with which he is involved as one of its leaders, I asked him how or where Hollywood people gathered in corresponding fashion. He was unable to answer this. He then added that he knew no one at all connected with the film industry, nor did he know anyone who did have such acquaintanceship. "I know that must sound strange," he reflected. "We are glad to have the film industry here, but those connected with it are just not people one would know socially."

Here again is "togetherness" or nothing. Consider this man's handicap in his attempts to get a metropolitan art museum established. He has no way of reaching with any ease, practice or trust some of his committee's potentially best prospects.

In its upper economic, political and cultural echelons, Los Angeles operates according to the same provincial premises of social insularity as the street with the sidewalk park in Baltimore or as Chatham Village in Pittsburgh. Such a metropolis lacks means for bringing together necessary ideas, necessary enthusiasms, necessary money. Los Angeles is embarked on a strange experiment: trying to run not just projects, not just gray areas, but a whole metropolis, by dint of "togetherness" or nothing. I think this is an inevitable outcome for great cities whose people lack city public life in ordinary living and working.

NOTES

1 One representative court, for example, contains as this is written four lawyers, two doctors, two engineers, a dentist, a salesman, a banker, a railroad executive, a planning executive.

2 This is very common in public projects in New York.

3 This, by the way, is an efficient device, accomplishing with a fraction of the effort what would be a mountainous task door to door. It also makes more public conversation and opinion than door-to-door visits.

"A City is Not a Tree"

from *Architectural Forum* (1965)

Christopher Alexander

Editors' Introduction

Echoing the sentiments of other critics who were discontented with the bankrupt results of twentieth-century city-making, Christopher Alexander provides both a critique of practice and a corrective way of thinking about cities. Throughout his early work (including this selection) Christopher Alexander combined his background in architecture, mathematics, and physics to suggest new ways of thinking about design and cities. In his practice and writing, he rejects conventional design processes of the mainstream built environment professions – which are perceived to be overly reductionist and lacking the complexity that allows life, beauty, and place-based harmonies to emerge. He is highly critical of the profit-driven construction and development industries, which are understood to be responsible for the tragedy of late-twentieth-century urban form and aesthetics. Like other urban critics of the time, he is interested in human desires for comfort, the spirituality of place, and other subjective values (often disregarded in the professional design studio).

In this article, Alexander suggests that a city's inherent complexity should be viewed as a multilayered lattice-work, rather than a branched and tree-like diagram that separates and fragments functions and activities. Instead of thinking about cities as reductionist formulae, he suggests we should understand cities as overlaid sets, subsets, and infinite possibilities of interaction. In many ways this writing reflects the contemporaneous critiques being offered by Jane Jacobs, Lewis Mumford, Ian McHarg, and other urbanists. He provides critiques of several designers within the text, including Garnier, Le Corbusier, Soleri, and Kahn. He condemns design theories that seek to separate rather than integrate uses within the city, including the transportation and residential segregation so loved by modernist architects, and recommended in CIAM's Charter of Athens. His insights into complex human needs suggest that overlap and messy place-based choices are more important than rationally designed, efficient, and unencumbered mono-cultures of placeless urbanism. This writing also presages later work on systems and complexity theory that would rise anew at the end of the twentieth century.

His subsequent writings develop the theme of this article more fully through prescriptions about how contemporary cities can revalidate historic traditions and fulfill human psychological and spiritual needs. His theses call for a return to self-built places without the help of design professionals. These are the vernacular processes that produced simpler, more meaningful places that people have loved for eons, and consequently provided cultural differentiation across the globe. He also calls for a more participatory design that is directed by the intuitive needs and desires of everyday life, rather than the abstract and over-intellectualized design practices influenced by scientific process, regulations, professional standards or academic theories. Just as important is Alexander's revalorization of the concept of beauty, which had long been discarded from intellectual design discourse. His built works are thoroughly participatory and vernacular in design, including well-published projects in Mexicali-Mexico, near Tokyo-Japan, San Jose-California, and West Sussex-England. For participants in Alexander's design process, the buildings provide a sense of belonging and a connection to place. For those within the establishment architecture profession, Alexander's position is disconcerting in its lack of respect for linear thinking and design-by-formula.

In the mid-1970s, Alexander and a number of writing partners began a six-volume series of texts through the Center for Environmental Structure. The most important of these is his masterwork, *A Pattern Language*, where he provides a scalar hierarchy of recommended "patterns" for designing regions, cities, districts, buildings, and interiors. It examines several dozen historical urbanisms and architectures to draw design lessons (or patterns) that can be used in contemporary design practice. Upon its publication it was embraced by lay people, city-lovers, and ecologically minded designers who shared the author's values. In like manner, it was rejected by many within the built environment professions as pedantic, overly prescriptive, anachronistic, and iconoclastic. The success of *A Pattern Language*, however, has spawned a movement of dedicated followers and numerous websites dedicated to Alexander's work.

Many of Alexander's later works are infused with religious, mystical, and spiritual allusions. His book *The Timeless Way of Building* (Oxford/New York: Oxford University Press, 1979) begins to summarize a theoretical stance developed across the arc of his career. It reads similarly to the *Tao Te Ching*. The esoteric statements of the text seem to require meditation in their vagueness. Alexander calls for a return to a timeless way of building towns, structures, and places where people can feel alive again: "There is one timeless way of building. It is thousands of years old, and the same today as it has always been." *The Timeless Way of Building* serves as a synopsis of his theories and the use of living patterns drawn from nature, everyday life, and traditional environments.

In the sixth volume, *A New Theory of Urban Design* (Oxford/New York: Oxford University Press, 1987), Alexander extends his critique of architectural practice to similar concerns in urban design, specifically the deadening nature (and often unrealizable goals) of master planned urbanism. Like modernist architecture that streamlines design to overt simplicity, so too does master planning, which often lacks the organic and incremental nature of more loved cities, such as Florence, London, or Prague.

Not surprising, these works were written at a time that also saw the rise of authors interested in vernacular traditions, everyday landscapes, and material culture studies. A few of these, such as J.B. Jackson and Paul Groth, were located at the University of California, Berkeley alongside Alexander. They were interested in describing the role and importance of working landscapes, utilitarian buildings, self-built domestic structures, and everyday places often overlooked within courses on architectural history, which typically valorize high-pedigree buildings and places. For more information on vernacular design see the following work by John Brinckerhoff Jackson: *Discovering the Vernacular Landscape* (New Haven, CT: Yale University Press, 1984) and *A Sense of Place, a Sense of Time* (New Haven, CT: Yale University Press, 1994). With an eye to re-educating Americans about hand-built traditions, Bernard Rudofsky made a career in the study of the vernacular in such works as *Architecture Without Architects: A Short Introduction to Non-Pedigreed Architecture* (Albuquerque, NM: University of New Mexico Press, 1964, 1987) and *Streets for People: A Primer for Americans* (Garden City, NY: Doubleday, 1969). See also: Paul Groth and Todd W. Bressi (eds), *Understanding Ordinary Landscapes* (New Haven, CT: Yale University Press, 1997) and Thomas Carter and Elizabeth Collins Cromley, *Invitation to Vernacular Architecture: A Guide to the Study of Ordinary Buildings and Landscapes* (University of Tennessee Press, 2005).

Christopher Alexander is an architect, builder and theorist, now living in the UK after a teaching career at Harvard, MIT, the Prince of Wales Institute of Architecture, and the University of California, Berkeley, where he spent the bulk of his academic career. He gained early notoriety with his PhD dissertation, published as *Notes on the Synthesis of Form* (Cambridge, MA: Harvard University Press, 1964), which influenced a generation of computer scientists. He continues to work through a variety of design and research centers that champion his theories. Alexander and his followers have conducted design experiments, advised city leaders, and built hundreds of buildings in the Americas, Asia, and Europe. Their design work is highly participatory and interactive, resulting in innovative building technologies and work that emerges from the ideas of their clients. His writings have been highly influential in reviving the craft of building, illuminating the value of vernacular environments, and transforming the status quo practices of architecture and town planning. Among a lifetime of awards, in 2009 he was awarded the Vincent Scully Award by the US National Building Museum.

Books in the Center for Environmental Structure Series (all published in New York by Oxford University Press) are: *The Oregon Experiment* (1975), *A Pattern Language*, written with Sara Ishikawa, Murray Silverstein et al. (1977), *The Timeless Way of Building* (1979), *The Linz Cafe* (1981), *The Production of Houses*, written with Howard Davis, Julio Martinez, and Donald Cormer (1985) and *A New Theory of Urban Design*, written with Hajo Neis, Artemis Anninou, and Ingrid King (1985).

Other important texts by Alexander include the ambitious four-volume text *The Nature of Order: An Essay on the Art of Building and the Nature of the Universe* (Berkeley, CA: Center for Environmental Structure, 2003): Volume 1, *The Phenomenon of Life*; Volume 2, *The Process of Creating Life*; Volume 3, *A Vision of a Living World*; and Volume 4, *The Luminous Ground*. Additional material on Alexander's life and work can be found in his biography by Stephen Grabow, *Christopher Alexander The Evolution of a New Paradigm in Architecture* (Boston, MA: Oriel Press, 1983); and an overview of his design work by Ingrid F. King and Toshio Nakamura, "Christopher Alexander and Contemporary Architecture" in *Architecture + Urbanism* (August, 1993). Two documentaries have been produced on Alexander's work: *Places for the Soul: The Architecture of Christopher Alexander* (1990) and *Christopher Alexander and Contemporary Architecture* (1993). The influence of Christopher Alexander's work is wide and impressive: computer science and programming, mathematics, design theory, architecture, urban design, participatory practice, vernacular design, and even computer gaming with impacts on *SimCity* and other *Sims* programs.

The tree of my title is not a green tree with leaves. It is the name of an abstract structure. I shall contrast it with another, more complex abstract structure called a semi-lattice. The city is a semi-lattice, but it is not a tree. In order to relate these abstract structures to the nature of the city, I must first make a simple distinction.

NATURAL AND ARTIFICIAL CITIES

I want to call those cities which have arisen more or less spontaneously over many, many years *natural cities*. And I shall call those cities and parts of cities, which have been deliberately created by designers and planners *artificial cities*. Siena, Liverpool, Kyoto, Manhattan are examples of natural cities. Levittown, Chandigarh, and the British New Towns are examples of artificial cities.

It is more and more widely recognized today that there is some essential ingredient missing from artificial cities. When compared with ancient cities that have acquired the patina of life, our modern attempts to create cities artificially are, from a human point of view, entirely unsuccessful.

Architects themselves admit more and more freely that they really like living in old buildings more than new ones. The non-art loving public at large, instead of being grateful to architects for what they do, regards the onset of modern buildings and modern cities everywhere as an inevitable, rather sad piece of the larger fact that the world is going to the dogs.

It is much too easy to say that these opinions represent only people's unwillingness to forget the past, and their determination to be traditional. For myself, I trust this conservatism. People are usually willing to move with the times. Their growing reluctance to accept the modern city evidently expresses a longing for some real thing, something which for the moment escapes our grasp.

The prospect that we may be turning the world into a place peopled only by little glass and concrete boxes has alarmed many architects, too. To combat the glass box future, many valiant protests and designs have been put forward, all hoping to recreate in modern form the various characteristics of the natural city which seem to give it life. But so far these designs have only remade the old. They have not been able to create the new.

"Outrage," the *Architectural Review*'s campaign against the way in which new construction and telegraph poles are wrecking the English town, based its remedies, essentially, on the idea that the spatial sequence of buildings and open spaces must be controlled if scale is to be preserved – an idea that really derives from Camillo Sitte's book about ancient squares and piazzas.

Another kind of remedy, in protest against the monotony of Levittown, tries to recapture the richness of shape found in the houses of a natural old town. Llewelyn Davies' village at Rushbrooke in England is an example – each cottage is slightly different from its neighbor, the roofs jut in and out at picturesque angles, the shapes are "interesting" and cute.

A third suggested remedy is to get high density back into the city. The idea seems to be that if the whole metropolis could only be like Grand Central Station, with lots and lots of layers and tunnels all over the place, and enough people milling around in them, maybe it would be human again. The artificial urbanity of Victor Gruen's schemes and of the LCC's scheme for Hook New Town, both betray this thought at work.

Another very brilliant critic of the deadness which is everywhere is Jane Jacobs. Her criticisms are excellent. But when you read her concrete proposals for what we should do instead, you get the idea that she wants the great modern city to be a sort of mixture between Greenwich Village and some Italian hill town, full of short blocks and people sitting in the street.

The problem these designers have tried to face is real. It is vital that we discover the property of old towns which gave them life, and get it back into our own artificial cities. But we cannot do this merely by remaking English villages, Italian piazzas and Grand Central Stations. Too many designers today seem to be yearning for the physical and plastic characteristics of the past instead of searching for the abstract ordering principle which the towns of the past happened to have, and which our modern conceptions of the city have not yet found. These designers fail to put new life into the city, because they merely imitate the appearance of the old, its concrete substance: they fail to unearth its inner nature.

What is the inner nature, the ordering principle, which distinguishes the artificial city from the natural city? You will have guessed from the first paragraph what I believe this ordering principle to be. I believe that a natural city has the organization of a semi-lattice; but that when we organize a city artificially, we organize it as a tree.

TREES AND SEMI-LATTICES

Both the tree and the semi-lattice are ways of thinking about how a large collection of many small

systems goes to make up a large and complex system. More generally, they are both names for structures of sets.

In order to define such structures, let me first define the concept of a set. A set is a collection of elements which for some reason we think of as belonging together. Since, as designers, we are concerned with the physical living city and its physical backbone, we most naturally restrict ourselves to considering sets which are collections of material elements like people, blades of grass, cars, bricks, molecules, houses, gardens, water pipes, the water molecules that run in them, etc.

When the elements of a set belong together, because they co-operate or work together somehow, we call the set of elements a system.

Here is an example. In Berkeley [California], at the corner of Hearst and Euclid, there is a drug store, and outside the drug store is a traffic light. In the entrance to the drug store there is a newsrack where the day's papers are displayed. When the light is red, people who are waiting to cross the street stand idly by the light; and since they have nothing to do, they look at the papers displayed on the newsrack which they can see from where they stand. Some of them just read the headlines; others actually buy a paper while they wait.

This effect makes the newsrack and the traffic light interdependent; the newsrack, the newspapers on it, the money going from people's pockets to the dime slot, the people who stop at the light and read the papers, traffic light, the electric impulses which make the lights change, the sidewalk which they stand on form a system – they all work together.

From the designer's point of view, the physically unchanging part of this system is of special interest. The newsrack, the traffic light, and the sidewalk between them, related as they are, form the fixed part of the system. It is the unchanging receptacle in which the changing parts of the system – people, newspapers, money, and electrical impulses – can work together. I define this fixed part as a unit of the city. It derives its coherence as a unit both from the forces which hold its own elements together, and from the dynamic coherence of the larger living system, which includes it as a fixed, invariant part.

Other examples of systems in the city are: the set of particles which go to make up a building; the set of particles which go to make up the human body; the cars on the freeway, plus the people in them, plus the freeway they are driving on; two friends on the phone, plus the telephones they hold, plus the telephone line connecting them; Telegraph Hill [San Francisco] with all its buildings, services and inhabitants; the chain of Rexall drug stores; the physical elements of San Francisco that fall under the administrative authority of City Hall; everything within the physical boundary of San Francisco, plus all the people who visit the city regularly and contribute to its development (like Bob Hope or the president of Arthur D. Little), plus all the major sources of economic welfare which supply the city with its wealth; the dog next door, plus my garbage can, plus the garbage out of my garbage can which he lives on; the San Francisco chapter of the John Birch Society.

Each one of these is a set of elements made coherent and co-operative by some sort of inner binding forces. And each one, just like the traffic light–newsrack system, has a physically fixed part which we think of as a unit of the city.

Of the many, many fixed concrete subsets of the city which are the receptacles for its systems, and can therefore be thought of as significant physical units, we usually single out a few for special consideration. In fact, I claim that whatever picture of the city someone has is defined precisely by the subsets he sees as units.

Now, a collection of subsets which goes to make up such a picture is not merely an amorphous collection. Automatically, merely because relationships are established among the subsets once the subsets are chosen, the collection has a definite structure.

To understand this structure, let us think abstractly for a moment, using numbers as symbols. Instead of talking about the real sets of millions of real particles which occur in the city, let us consider a simpler structure made of just half a dozen elements. Label these elements 1, 2, 3, 4, 5, 6. Not including the full set (1, 2, 3, 4, 5, 6), the empty set (-), and the one element sets (1), (2), (3), (4), (5), (6), there are 56 different subsets we can pick from these six elements.

Suppose we now pick out certain of these 56 sets (just as we pick out certain sets and call them units when we form our picture of the city). Let us say, for example, that we pick the following subsets: (123), (34), (45), (234), (345), (12345), (3456).

What are the possible relationships among these sets? Some sets will be entirely part of larger sets,

as (34) is part of (345) and (3456). Some of the sets will overlap, like (123) and (234). Some of the sets will be disjoint – that is, contain no elements in common, like (123) and (45).

We can see these relationships displayed in two ways (see Figure 1). In Diagram A, each set chosen to be a unit has a line drawn round it. In Diagram B, the chosen sets are arranged in order of ascending magnitude, so that whenever one set contains another, as (345) contains (34), there is a vertical path leading from one to the other. For the sake of clarity and visual economy, it is usual to draw lines only between sets which have no further sets and lines between them; thus the line between (34) and (345), and the line between (345) and (3456), make it unnecessary to draw a line between (34) and (3456).

As we see from these two representations, the choice of subsets alone endows the subsets as a whole with an overall structure. This is the structure which we are concerned with here. When the structure meets certain conditions, it is called a semi-lattice. When it meets other more restrictive conditions, it is called a tree.

The semi-lattice axiom goes like this: *A collection of sets forms a semi-lattice if and only if, when two overlapping sets belong to the collection, then the set of elements common to both also belongs to the collection.*

The structure illustrated in Diagrams A and B is a semi-lattice. It satisfies the axiom since, for instance, (234) and (345) both belong to the collection and their common part, (34), also belongs to it. (As far as the city is concerned, this axiom states merely that wherever two units overlap, the area of overlap is itself a recognizable entity and hence a unit also. In the case of the drug store example, one unit consists of the news rack, sidewalk, and traffic light. Another unit consists of the drug store itself, with its entry and the news rack. The two units overlap in the newsrack. Clearly this area of overlap is itself a recognizable unit, and so satisfies the axiom above which defines the characteristics of a semi-lattice.)

The tree axiom states: *A collection of sets forms a tree if and only if, for any two sets that belong to the collection, either one is wholly contained in the other, or else they are wholly disjoint.*

The structure illustrated in Diagrams C and D is a tree. Since this axiom excludes the possibility of overlapping sets, there is no way in which the

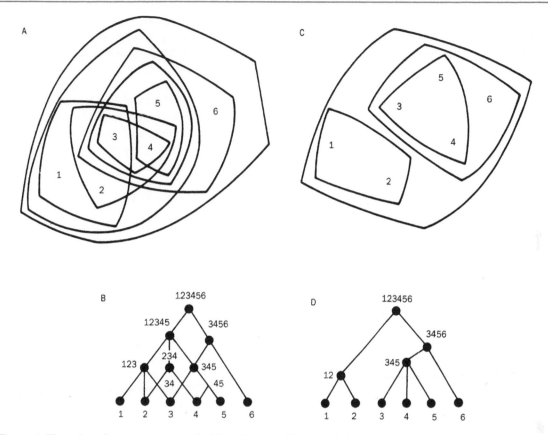

Figure 1 These four diagrams represent the idea of the semi-lattice and the tree. Diagrams A and B depict the idea of the *semi-lattice*, rich in overlap and union. Diagrams C and D depict the idea of a *tree*, with its segregated elements, no overlap and less richness.

semi-lattice axiom can be violated, so that every tree is a trivially simple semi-lattice.

However, in this paper we are not so much concerned with the fact that a tree happens to be a semi-lattice, but with the difference between trees and those more general semi-lattices which are *not* trees, because they *do* contain overlapping units. We are concerned with the difference between structures in which no overlap occurs, and those structures in which overlap does occur.

It is not merely the overlap which makes the distinction between the two important. Still more important is the fact that the semi-lattice is potentially a much more complex and subtle structure than a tree. We may see just how much more complex a semi-lattice can be than a tree in the following fact: a tree based on 20 elements can contain at most 19 further subsets of the 20, while a semi-lattice based on the same 20 elements can contain more than one million different subsets.

This enormously greater variety is an index of the great structural complexity a semi-lattice can have when compared with the structural simplicity of a tree. It is this lack of structural complexity, characteristic of trees, which is crippling our conceptions of the city.

ARTIFICIAL CITIES WHICH ARE TREES

To demonstrate, let us look at some modern conceptions of the city, each of which I shall show to be essentially a tree. It will perhaps be useful, while we look at these plans, to have a little ditty in our minds:

Big fleas have little fleas
Upon their back to bite' em;
Little fleas have lesser fleas,
And so ad infinitum.

This rhyme expresses perfectly and succinctly the structural principle of the tree.

[In the original publication, Alexander provides examples of several artificial cities and city plans designed by famous architects and planners, including: Columbia, Maryland (Community Research and Development, Inc.), Greenbelt, Maryland (Clarence Stein), the Greater London Plan (Abercrombie and Forshaw), the Tokyo Plan (Kenzo Tange), Mesa City (Paolo Soleri), Chandigarh (Le Corbusier), Brasilia (Lucio Costa), and Communitas (Paul and Percival Goodman). Alexander suggests that each of these designs represents the idea of a "tree" and that each of them is too reductionist and over-simplified in diagram and design to offer the type of vitality, overlap and sense of possibility offered by the "semi-lattice."]

[. . .]

The most beautiful example of all, I have kept until last, because it symbolizes the problem perfectly. It appears in Hilberseimer's book called *The Nature of Cities*. He describes the fact that certain Roman towns had their origin as military camps, and then shows a picture of a modern military encampment as a kind of archetypal form for the city. It is not possible to have a structure which is a clearer tree.

The symbol is apt for, of course, the organization of the army, which was created precisely in order to create discipline and rigidity. When a city is endowed with a tree structure, this is what happens to the city and its people. Hilberseimer's own scheme for the commercial area of a city is based on the army camp archetype.

Each of these structures is a tree.

The units of which an artificial city is made up are always organized to form a tree. So that we get a really clear understanding of what this means, let us define a tree again:

Whenever we have a tree structure; it means that within this structure no piece of any unit is ever connected to other units, except through the medium of that unit as a whole.

The enormity of this restriction is difficult to grasp. It is a little as though the members of a family were not free to make friends outside the family, except when the family as a whole made a friendship.

The structural simplicity of trees is like the compulsive desire for neatness and order that insists that the candlesticks on a mantelpiece be perfectly straight and perfectly symmetrical about the centre. The semi-lattice, by comparison, is the structure of a complex *fabric*; it is the structure of living things – of great paintings and symphonies.

It must be emphasized, lest the orderly mind shrink in horror from anything that is not clearly articulated and categorized in tree form, that the ideas of overlap, ambiguity, multiplicity of aspect, and the semi-lattice, are not less orderly than the rigid tree, but more so. They represent a thicker, tougher, more subtle and more complex view of structure.

Let us now look at the ways in which the natural city, when unconstrained by artificial conceptions, shows itself to be a semi-lattice.

A LIVING CITY IS AND NEEDS TO BE A SEMI-LATTICE

Each unit in each tree that I have described is the fixed, unchanging residue of some system in the living city. A house, for instance, is the physical residue of the interactions between the members of a family, their emotions and their belongings. A freeway is the residue of movement and commercial exchange. But a tree contains only very few such limits so that in a tree-like city only a few of its systems can have a physical counterpart. Thousands of important systems have no physical counterpart.

In the worst trees, the units which do appear fail to correspond to any living reality; and those real systems, whose existence actually makes the city live, have been provided with no physical receptacle.

Neither the Columbia plan nor the Stein plan, for example, corresponds to social realities. The physical layout of the plans, and the way they function, suggests a hierarchy of stronger and stronger closed social groups, ranging from the whole city down to the family, each formed by associational ties of different strength. Yet this is entirely unreal.

In a traditional society, if we ask a man to name his best friends and then ask each of these in turn to name their best friends, they will all name each other so that they form a closed group. A village is made of a number of separate closed groups of this kind.

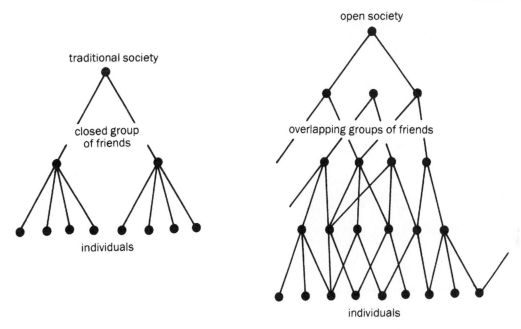

Figure 2 These two diagrams represent different versions of social structure as seen through the diagram of the *tree*, at left (which represents a traditional society); and the *semi-lattice* diagram, at right (which describes a modern, open society).

But today's social structure is utterly different. If we ask a man to name his friends and then ask them in turn to name their friends, they will all name different people, very likely unknown to the first person; these people would again name others, and so on outwards. There are virtually no closed groups of people in modern society. The reality of today's social structure is thick with overlap – the systems of friends and acquaintances form a semi-lattice, not a tree; see Figure 2.

In the natural city, even the house on a long street (not in some little cluster) is a more accurate acknowledgment of the fact that your friends live not next door, but far away, and can only be reached by bus or automobile. In this respect Manhattan has more overlap in it than Greenbelt. And though one can argue that in Greenbelt, too, friends are only minutes away by car, one must then ask: since certain groups have been emphasized by the physical limits of the physical structure, why are they socially irrelevant ones?

Another aspect of the city's social structure which a tree can never mirror properly is illustrated by Ruth Glass's redevelopment plan for Middlesborough, a city of 200,000, which she recommends be broken into 29 separate neighborhoods. After

picking her 29 neighborhoods by determining where the sharpest discontinuities of building type, income, and job type occur, she asks herself the question: "If we examine some of the social systems which actually exist for the people in such a neighborhood, do the physical units defined by these various social systems all define the same spatial neighborhood?" Her own answer to this question is "No, they do not."

Each of the social systems she examines is a nodal system. It is made of some sort of central node, plus the people who use this center. Specifically she takes elementary schools, secondary schools, youth clubs, adult clubs, post offices, greengrocers, and grocers selling sugar. Each of these centers draws its users from a certain spatial area or spatial unit. This spatial unit is the physical residue of the social system as a whole, and is therefore a unit in the terms of this paper. The units corresponding to different kinds of centers for a single neighborhood, Waterloo Road, are shown in Figure 3.

The hard outline is the boundary of the so-called neighborhood itself. The white circle stands for the youth club, and the small solid rings stand for areas where its members live. The ringed spot is the adult club, and the homes of its members form the unit

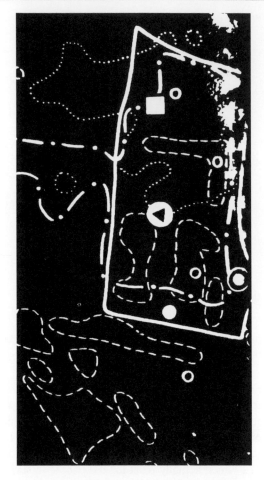

Figure 3 Mapping the system of overlapping places and boundaries of the Waterloo Road neighborhood.

marked by dashed boundaries. The white square is the post office, and the dotted line marks the unit which contains its users. The secondary school is marked by the spot with a black triangle in it. Together with its pupils, it forms the system marked by the dot-dashed line.

As you can see at once, the different units do not coincide. Yet neither are they disjoint. They overlap.

We cannot get an adequate picture of what Middlesborough is, or of what it ought to be, in terms of 29 large and conveniently integral chunks called neighborhoods. When we describe the city in terms of neighborhoods, we implicitly assume that the smaller elements within any one of these neighborhoods belong together so tightly that they only interact with elements in other neighborhoods through the medium of the neighborhood to which they themselves belong. Ruth Glass herself shows clearly that this is not the case.

The following diagrams, see Figure 4, are two pictures of the Waterloo neighborhood. For the sake of argument, I have broken it into a number of small areas. The first diagram shows how these pieces stick together in fact, and the second diagram shows how the redevelopment plan pretends they stick together.

There is nothing in the nature of the various centers, which says that their catchment areas should be the same. Their natures are different. Therefore the units they define are different. The

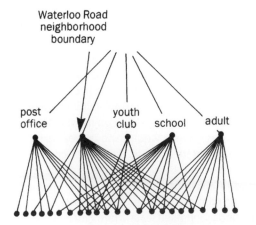
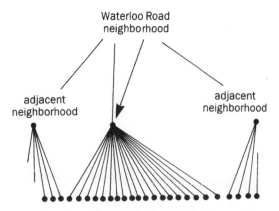

Figure 4 Two versions of the Waterloo Road neighborhood: in the diagram at the left, the neighborhood is depicted as a set of overlapping uses and boundaries (similar to the illustrated neighborhood in the map); in the diagram at the right, the neighborhood is presented as an entity that is identifiable and separated from adjacent neighborhoods.

natural city of Middlesborough was faithful to the semi-lattice structure they have. Only in the artificial tree conception of the city are their natural, proper and necessary overlaps destroyed.

The same thing happens on a smaller scale. Take the separation of pedestrians from moving vehicles, a tree concept proposed by Le Corbusier, Louis Kahn, and many others. At a very crude level of thought, this is obviously a good idea. It is danger-ous to have 60 mph cars in contact with little chil-dren toddling. But it is not always a good idea. There are times when the ecology of a situation actually demands the opposite. Imagine yourself coming out of a Fifth Avenue store: you have been shopping all afternoon; your arms are full of par-cels; you need a drink; your wife is limping. Thank God for taxis!

Yet the urban taxi can function only because pedestrians and vehicles are not strictly separated. The prowling taxi needs a fast stream of traffic so that it can cover a large area to be sure of finding a passenger. The pedestrian needs to be able to hail the taxi from any point in the pedestrian world, and to be able to get out to any part of the pedes-trian world to which he wants to go. The system which contains the taxicabs needs to overlap both the fast vehicular traffic system and the system of pedestrian circulation. In Manhattan, pedestrians and vehicles do share certain parts of the city, and the necessary overlap is guaranteed.

Another favorite concept of the CIAM theorists and others is the separation of recreation from everything else. This has crystallized in our real cities in the form of playgrounds. The playground, asphalted and fenced in, is nothing but a pictorial acknowledgment of the fact that "play" exists as an isolated concept in our minds. It has nothing to do with the life of play itself. Few self-respecting children will even play in a playground.

Play itself, the play that children practice, goes on somewhere different everyday. One day it may be indoors, another day in a friendly gas station, another day in a derelict building, another day down by the river, another day on a construction site which has been abandoned for the weekend. Each of these play activities, and the objects it requires, forms a system. It is not true that these systems exist in isolation, cut off from the other systems in the city. The different systems overlap one another, and they overlap many other systems besides. The

units, the physical places recognized as play places, must do the same.

In a natural city this is what happens. Play takes place in a thousand places – it fills the interstices of adult life. As they play, children become full of their surroundings. How can a child become filled with his surroundings in a fenced enclosure? He can't. In a semi-lattice, he can; in a tree, he can't.

A similar kind of mistake occurs in trees like those of the Goodmans' Communitas, or Soleri's Mesa City, which separate the university from the rest of the city. Again, this has actually been realized in the common American form of the isolated campus.

What is the reason for drawing a line in the city so that everything within the boundary is uni-versity, and everything outside is non-university? It is conceptually clear. But does it correspond to the realities of university life? Certainly it is not the structure which occurs in non-artificial univer-sity cities.

Take Cambridge University, for instance. At certain points, Trinity Street is physically almost indistinguishable from Trinity College. One pedes-trian crossover in the street is literally part of the college. The buildings on the street, though they contain stores and coffee shops and banks at ground level, contain undergraduates' rooms in their upper stories. In many cases the actual fabric of the street buildings melts into the fabric of the old college buildings so that one cannot be altered without the other.

There will always be many systems of activity where university life and city life overlap: pub-crawling, coffee drinking, the movies, walking from place to place. In some cases whole departments may be actively involved in the life of the city's inhabitants (the hospital-cum-medical school is an example). In Cambridge, a natural city where uni-versity and city have grown together gradually, the physical units overlap because they are the phys-ical residues of city systems and university systems which overlap, see Figure 5.

Let us look next at the hierarchy of urban cores realized in Brasilia, Chandigarh, the MARS plan for London and, most recently, in Manhattan's Lincoln Center, where various performing arts serving the population of greater New York have been gathered together to form just one core.

Does a concert hall ask to be next to an opera house? Can the two feed on one another? Will

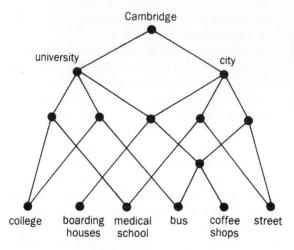

Figure 5 Semi-lattice diagram of Cambridge.

anybody ever visit them both, gluttonously, in a single evening, or even buy tickets from one after going to a concert in the other? In Vienna, London, Paris, each of the performing arts has found its own place. Each has created its own familiar section of the city. In Manhattan itself, Carnegie Hall and the Metropolitan Opera House were not built side by side. Each found its own place, and now creates its own atmosphere. The influence of each overlaps the parts of the city which have been made unique by it.

The only reason that these functions have all been brought together in the Lincoln Center is that the concept of performing art links them to one another.

But this tree and the idea of a single hierarchy of urban cores, which is its parent, do not illuminate the relations between art and city life. They are merely born of the mania every simple-minded person has for putting things with the same name into the same basket.

The total separation of work from housing, started by Tony Garnier in his industrial city, then incorporated in the 1929 Athens Charter, is now found in every artificial city and accepted everywhere where zoning is enforced. Is this a sound principle? It is easy to see how bad conditions at the beginning of the century prompted planners to try to get the dirty factories out of residential areas. But the separation misses a variety of systems which require, for their sustenance, little parts of both.

Jane Jacobs describes the growth of backyard industries in Brooklyn. A man who wants to start a small business needs space, which he is very

likely to have in his own backyard. He also needs to establish connections with larger going enterprises and with their customers. This means that the system of backyard industry needs to belong both to the residential zone and to the industrial zone – these zones need to overlap. In Brooklyn they do. In a city which is a tree, they can't.

Finally, let us examine the subdivision of the city into isolated communities. As we have seen in the Abercrombie plan for London, this is itself a tree structure. Yet the individual communities have no reality as functioning units. In London, as in any great city, almost no one manages to find work which suits him near his home. People from one community work in factories, which are in other communities.

There are, therefore, many hundreds of thousands of worker-workplace systems, each consisting of a man plus the factory he works in, which cut across the boundaries defined by Abercrombie's tree. The existence of these units, and their overlapping nature, indicates that the living systems of London form a semi-lattice. Only in the planner's mind have they become a tree.

The fact that we have so far failed to give this any physical expression has a vital consequence. As things are, whenever the worker and his workplace belong to separately administered municipalities, the community which contains the workplace collects huge taxes and has relatively little to spend it on, while the community where the worker lives, if it is mainly residential, collects only little in the way of taxes, and yet has great additional burdens on its purse in the shape of schools, hospitals, etc. Clearly, to resolve this inequity, the worker-workplace systems must be anchored in physically recognizable units of the city, which can then be taxed.

It might be argued that, even though the individual communities of a great city have no functional significance in the lives of their inhabitants, they are still the most convenient administrative units, and should, therefore, be left in their present tree organization.

However, in the political complexity of a modern city, even this is suspect.

Edward Banfield, in a recent book called *Political Influence*, gives a detailed account of the patterns of influence and control that have actually led to decisions in Chicago. He shows that although the lines of administrative and executive control have a formal structure which is a tree, these formal chains of influence and authority are entirely over-shadowed by the *ad hoc* lines of control which arise naturally as each new city problem presents itself. These *ad hoc* lines depend on who is interested in the matter, who has what at stake, and who has what favors to trade with whom.

This second structure, which is informal, working within the framework of the first, is what really controls public action. It varies from week to week, even from hour to hour, as one problem replaces another. Nobody's sphere of influence is entirely under the control of any one superior; each person is under different influences as problems change. Although the organization chart in the mayor's office is a tree, the actual control and exercise of authority is semi-lattice-like.

THE ORIGIN OF TREE-LIKE THOUGHT

The tree – though so neat and beautiful as a mental device, and though it offers such a simple and clear way of dividing a complex entity into units – does not describe correctly the actual structure of naturally occurring cities, and does not describe the structure of the cities that we need.

Now, why is it that so many designers have conceived cities as trees when the natural structure is in every case a semi-lattice? Have they done so deliberately, in the belief that a tree structure will serve the people of the city better? Or have they done it because they cannot help it, because they are trapped by a mental habit, perhaps even trapped by the way the mind works; because they cannot encompass the complexity of a semi-lattice in any convenient mental form; because the mind has an overwhelming predisposition to see trees wherever it looks and cannot escape the tree conception?

I shall try to convince you that it is for this second reason that trees are being proposed and built as cities – that it is because designers, limited as they must be by the capacity of the mind to form intuitively accessible structures, cannot achieve the complexity of the semi-lattice in a single mental act.

Let me begin with an example.

Suppose I ask you to remember the following four objects: an orange, a watermelon, a football and a tennis ball. How will you keep them in your mind, in your mind's eye? However you do it, you will do it by grouping them. Some of you will take the

two fruits together; the orange and the watermelon, and the two sports balls together, the football and the tennis ball. Those of you who tend to think in terms of physical shape may group them differently, taking the two small spheres together – the orange and the tennis ball, and the two larger and more egg-shaped objects – the watermelon and the football. Some of you will be aware of both groupings.

Either grouping taken by itself is a tree structure. The two together are a semi-lattice, see Figure 6. Now, let us try and visualize these groupings in the mind's eye. I think you will find that you cannot visualize all four sets simultaneously because they overlap. You can visualize one pair of sets and then the other; and you can alternate between the two pairs extremely fast, so fast that you may deceive yourself into thinking you can visualize them all together. But in truth, you cannot conceive all four sets at once in a single mental act.

You cannot bring the semi-lattice structure into a visualizable form for a single mental act. In a single mental act you can only visualize a tree.

This is the problem we face as designers. While we are not, perhaps, necessarily occupied with the problem of total visualization in a single mental act, the principle is still the same. The tree is accessible mentally, and easy to deal with. The semi-lattice is hard to keep before the mind's eye, and therefore hard to deal with.

It is known today that grouping and categorization are among the most primitive psychological processes. Modern psychology treats thought as a process of fitting new situations into existing slots and pigeon holes in the mind. Just as you cannot put a physical thing into more than one physical pigeon hole at once, so, by analogy, the processes of thought prevent you from putting a mental construct into more than one mental category at once. Study of the origin of these processes suggests that they stem essentially from the organism's need to reduce the complexity of its environment by establishing barriers between the different events which it encounters.

It is for this reason – because the mind's first function is to reduce the ambiguity and overlap in a confusing situation, and because, to this end, it is endowed with a basic intolerance for ambiguity – that structures like the city, which do require overlapping sets within them, are nevertheless persistently conceived as trees.

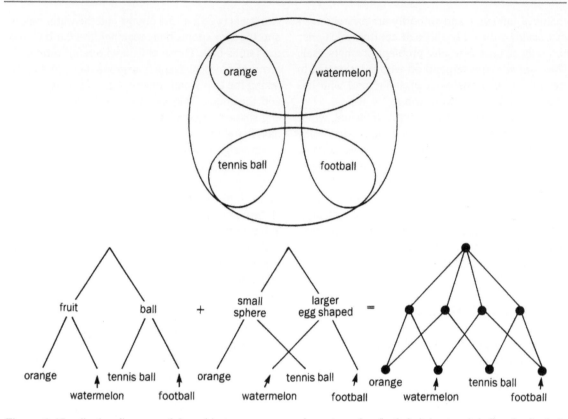

Figure 6 Visualization diagrams of four objects: an orange and a watermelon (both fruits); a tennis ball and a football (both balls). Different groupings can be seen as both *tree* and *semi-lattice* structures.

The same rigidity dogs even the perception of physical patterns. In experiments by Huggins and myself at Harvard, we showed people patterns whose internal units overlapped, and found that they almost always invented a way of seeing the pattern as a tree – even when the semi-lattice view of the patterns would have helped them perform the experimental task.

The most startling proof that people tend to conceive even physical patterns as trees is found in some experiments by Sir Frederick Bartlett. He showed people a pattern for about a quarter second, and then asked them to draw what they had seen. Many people, unable to draw what they had seen, simplified the patterns by cutting out the overlap in them . . .

These experiments suggest strongly that people have an underlying tendency, when faced by a complex organization, to reorganize it mentally in terms of non-overlapping units. The complexity of the semi-lattice is replaced by the simpler and more easily grasped tree form.

You are no doubt wondering, by now, what a city looks like which is a semi-lattice, but not a tree. I must confess that I cannot yet show you plans or sketches. It is not enough merely to make a demonstration of overlap – the overlap must be the right overlap. This is doubly important, because it is so tempting to make plans in which overlap occurs for its own sake. That is essentially what happens in the high density "life-filled" city plans of recent years. But overlap alone does not give structure. It can also give chaos. A garbage can is full of overlap. To have structure, you must have the right overlap, and this is for us almost certainly different from the old overlap which we observe in historic cities. As the relationships between functions change, so the systems which need to overlap in order to receive these relationships must also change. The recreation of old kinds of overlap will be inappropriate, and chaotic instead of structured.

The work of trying to understand just what overlap the modern city requires, and trying to put

Figure 7 Simplified structure of Simon Nicholson's painting.

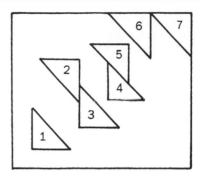

Figure 8 Diagrammatic structure of Simon Nicholson's painting.

this required overlap into physical and plastic terms, is still going on. Until the work is complete, there is no point in presenting facile sketches of ill thought out structure.

However, I can perhaps make the physical consequences of overlap more comprehensible by means of an image. The painting illustrated is a recent work by Simon Nicholson, see Figure 7. The fascination of this painting lies in the fact that although it is constructed of rather few simple

triangular elements, these elements unite in many different ways to form the larger units of the painting. If we make a complete inventory of the perceived units in the painting, see Figure 8, we find that each triangle enters into four or five completely different kinds of unit, none contained in the others, yet all overlapping in that triangle. If we number the triangles and pick out the sets of triangles which appear as strong visual units, we get the semi-lattice shown, see Figure 9.

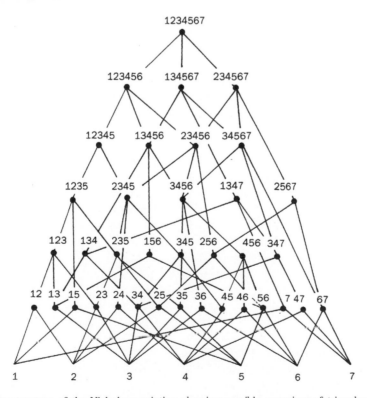

Figure 9 Semi-lattice structure of the Nicholson painting, showing possible groupings of triangles and other implied visual units.

[Triangles] 3 and 5 form a unit because they work together as a rectangle; 2 and 4 because they form a parallelogram; 5 and 6 because they are both dark and pointing the same way; 6 and 7 because one is the ghost of the other shifted sideways; 4 and 7 because they are symmetrical with one another; 4 and 6 because they form another rectangle; 4 and 5 because they form a sort of Z; 2 and 3 because they form a rather thinner kind of Z; 1 and 7 because they are at opposite corners; 1 and 2 because they are a rectangle; 3 and 4 because they point the same way, like 5 and 6, and form a sort of off-centre reflection of 5 and 6; 3 and 6 because they enclose 4 and 5; 1 and 5 because they enclose 2, 3, and 4. I have only listed the units of two triangles. The larger units are even more complex. The white is more complex still, and is not even included in the diagram, because it is harder to be sure of its elementary pieces.

The painting is significant, not so much because it has overlap in it (many paintings have overlap in them), but rather because this painting has nothing else in it except overlap. It is only the fact of the overlap, and the resulting multiplicity of aspects, which the forms present, that makes the painting fascinating. It seems almost as though the painter had made an explicit attempt to single out overlap as a vital generator of structure.

All the artificial cities I have described have the structure of a tree rather than the semi-lattice structure of the Nicholson painting. Yet it is the painting, and other images like it, which must be our vehicles for thought. And when we wish to be precise, the semi-lattice, being part of a large branch of modern mathematics, is a powerful way of exploring the structure of these images. It is the semi-lattice we must look for, not the tree.

When we think in terms of trees we are trading the humanity and richness of the living city for a conceptual simplicity which benefits only designers, planners, administrators and developers. Every time a piece of a city is torn out, and a tree made to replace the semi-lattice that was there before, the city takes a further step toward dissociation.

In any organized object, extreme compartmentalization and the dissociation of internal elements are the first signs of coming destruction. In a society, dissociation is anarchy. In a person, dissociation is the mark of schizophrenia and impending suicide. An ominous example of city-wide dissociation is the separation of retired people from the rest of urban life, caused by the growth of desert cities for the old, like Sun City, Arizona. This separation is only possible under the influence of tree-like thought.

It not only takes from the young the company of those who have lived long, but worse, it causes the same rift inside each individual life. As you yourself pass into Sun City, and into old age, your ties with your own past will be unacknowledged, lost, and therefore broken. Your youth will no longer be alive in your old age – the two will be dissociated; your own life will be cut in two.

For the human mind, the tree is the easiest vehicle for complex thoughts. But the city is not, cannot, and must not be a tree. The city is a receptacle for life. If the receptacle severs the overlap of the strands of life within it, because it is a tree, it will be like a bowl full of razor blades on edge, ready to cut up whatever is entrusted to it. In such a receptacle life will be cut to pieces. If we make cities which are trees, they will cut our life within to pieces.

"The Significance of A&P Parking Lots, or Learning from Las Vegas"

from *Learning from Las Vegas* (1972)

Robert Venturi and Denise Scott Brown

Editors' Introduction

This early version of *Learning from Las Vegas* has become a classic of postmodern design theory. The essay inflamed the design cognoscenti of the time with their assertions that the urbanism of the Vegas Strip should be valued for its richness of communication, its representation of everyday consumer values, and its example as a truly representative American urbanism (more so than the top-down minimalist urbanism and architecture that was under critical fire at that time). Written in the early 1970s, and later revised as a larger book with colleague Steven Izenour, Venturi and Scott Brown assert that the semiotic truthfulness of Las Vegas is implicitly American – its signage, decorated casinos, and entertainment-oriented design. The American urban arterial, as illustrated through the example of Las Vegas, is as notable for its lack of pedigree as it is for its consumer/vehicle functionalism. With a good degree of dry humor in considering this street phenomenon on par with traditional urbanism, Venturi and Scott Brown forced the design community to address their disconnect with the way in which the American city was being built. As part of their strategy, they suggest that the spaces of Las Vegas are comparable to both a Roman piazza (with respect to the enclosure qualities of the Strip itself), and the landscape of Versailles (with respect to the ubiquitous A&P parking lot). While their assertions often sound both ridiculous and grandiose, particularly for those who value the usual suspects of urban design worship (the well-enclosed plaza, the boulevard, the pedestrian qualities of compact villages), *Learning from Las Vegas* has become more pertinent as time has passed.

Learning from Las Vegas received both supportive and highly critical reviews. Progressives enjoyed the indictment of elite designers. High profile design was perceived to have lost its ability to communicate and find value with the general public. Modern architecture and urban design were seen as dull and monotonous, life-sucking of their cities, and far less successful as large scale sculpture. The design establishment, however, saw this as a direct attack on their very beings (which was intended); similar in spirit to Jane Jacobs' attack on the planning establishment in the introduction to *Death and Life of Great American Cities*. Diatribes against *Learning from Las Vegas* soon followed. Of note is a particularly rancorous 1971 debate with the architectural historian and theorist Kenneth Frampton, in which Denise Scott Brown defends both popular tastes as expressed in everyday places, "consumer folk culture," and the text of her article *Learning from Pop* (which predates *Learning from Las Vegas*). Frampton speaks on behalf of a more elite design sensibility, with architects (who at this time were also functioning as urban designers), having the intellectual capacity and societal role of producing projects that could both uplift the masses and restore the built environment in the face of consumer kitsch. Interestingly, Frampton is also critical of other picturesque "townscape" theorists, such as Gordon Cullen and Kevin Lynch (both in this volume). Frampton's aspirations for the design professions seem noble but overly idealized given the great amount of placelessness forming in cities around the world.

The effect of Venturi and Scott Brown's polemic on willing adherents was design that often failed to meet the tests of criticism or lasting value (many have made similar assertions with regard to New Urbanist projects). Early postmodern designers sought an architecture and urbanism that would communicate to the general public through its visual referents – which Venturi and Scott Brown describe as Ducks (buildings that are shaped as direct representations of their function) and Decorated Sheds (buildings that communicate directly through applied text and signage). And so we see in the first years of postmodern urbanism and architecture an overt desire to connect meaning to design; often with results that haven't aged well; for example, Charles Moore's Piazza d'Italia in New Orleans, the Portland, Oregon municipal building by Michael Graves, Phillip Johnson's Chippendale highboy atop the AT&T tower in New York City. These attempts at re-communicating the meaning of architecture and urbanism were later derided for their shallowness, camp and irony, disconnect from context, and lack of gravitas – which light-heartedness often evokes. A second phase of postmodern urbanism arose in response, valuing context, place-based design, critical regionalism, and more locally authentic meanings.

In their thesis, Venturi and Scott Brown acknowledge that their text shouldn't be understood as a prescription for making cities; they even imply that the architecture of the Strip might be the worst outcomes of the design professions at that time; and interestingly, the problematic of the urban arterial continues to this day as one of the great unsolved aspirations of contemporary redevelopment. Their analogies to European urbanism don't address qualitative differences between the commercial highway or parking lot and these traditional places, subsequently leaving some designers to ponder how to translate the lessons they learned in Las Vegas. Making this even more difficult, especially to those uninitiated to *archi-speak*, the text is filled with jargon and insider terminology. Yet despite the criticism and lack of direction, over time the text has evolved in meaning and become a clarion call to designers to get real in approaching development process, reducing idealistic expectations, and coming to terms with the culture of the American urban landscape – despite its low-brow character. The widespread re-appreciation of the writing reminds us of these place and context lessons. In addition to its re-appreciation, it is also recognized as having seeded many new theories that would emanate later in the century, including Rem Koolhaas' recognition of the "Generic City" as a type of Post-Urbanism, Crawford and Kaliski's "Everyday Urbanism," and much of the place-based design strategies valued by planners, designers, and the public today.

Robert Venturi and his wife/professional partner Denise Scott Brown are architects, theorists, urbanists, and educators living in Philadelphia, Pennsylvania. Their writings and theories were developed from courses, lectures, and professional work. They've had significant impact on the way designers consider everyday environments and how design intentions are communicated. Their interests in design expression deal with the semiotic nature of design communication and how both buildings and urban design projects speak to viewers both directly through text, but also symbolically through design referents. Venturi is widely known for the phrase "less is a bore," a postmodern play on Mies van der Rohe's maxim "less is more." He was awarded the Pritzker Prize in 1991 for his life contributions to the field of architecture; and together they won the Vincent J. Scully Prize in 2003 from the US National Building Museum.

Both of them taught intermittently at a number of east coast Ivy League universities, which often helped spur their written work. Venturi's text for *Complexity and Contradiction in Architecture* (New York: Museum of Modern Art, 1966) emanated from a series of lectures at the University of Pennsylvania and has now been translated into dozens of languages. Other works by Venturi include: *Iconography and Electronics upon a Generic Architecture: A View from the Drafting Room* (Cambridge, MA: MIT Press, 1998); *Mother's House* (New York: Rizzoli, 1992); and *The Architecture of Robert Venturi* (Albuquerque, NM: University of New Mexico Press, 1989). Denise Scott Brown is the author of the following: "Learning from Pop," *Casabella* (December 1971, 359–360); and *Having Words (Architecture Words 4)*, a compilation of essays on architectural writing (London: Architectural Association, 2009). Together they wrote: *A View from the Campidoglio: Selected Essays 1953–1984*, edited with Peter Arnell, Ted Bickford, and Catherine Bergart (New York: Harper & Row, 1984); and *Architecture as Signs and Systems: For a Mannerist Time* (Cambridge, MA: Harvard University Press, 2004).

Steven Izenour (1940–2001) was also an architect, urbanist, and theorist; and became a co-author on *Learning from Las Vegas*. He worked as a Principal at Venturi, Scott Brown and Associates for many years, collaborating on many writing and design projects. He taught at UPenn, Yale, and Drexel Universities. His collaboration with Venturi and Scott Brown on *Learning from Las Vegas* began in a studio at the University of Pennsylvania as a teaching assistant.

The theories, writing, and professional work of Venturi and Scott Brown are the subject of plentiful analysis, criticism, and monographs. Other supportive and critical writing on the work of Venturi, Scott Brown and Associates includes: Kester Rattenbury and Samantha Hardingham, *Robert Venturi and Denise Scott Brown: Learning from Las Vegas: SuperCrit #2* (Abingdon: Routledge, 2008); Stanislaus von Moos, *Venturi, Scott Brown and Associates: Buildings and Projects 1986–1989* (New York: Monacelli Press, 2000); David B. Brownlee, David G. Delon, and Katherine B. Hiesinger (eds), *Out of the Ordinary: Robert Venturi, Denise Scott Brown and Associates Architecture, Urbanism, Design* (Philadelphia Museum of Art, 2001); and Aron Vinegar and Michael J. Golec (eds), *Relearning from Las Vegas* (Minneapolis: University of Minnesota Press, 2008).

■ ■ ■ ■ ■ ■

Substance for a writer consists not merely of those realities he thinks he discovers; it consists even more of those realities which have been made available to him by the literature and idioms of his own day and by the images that still have vitality in the literature of the past.

Stylistically, a writer can express his feeling about this substance either by imitation, if it sits well with him, or by parody, if it doesn't.

Richard Poirier[1]

Learning from the existing landscape is a way of being revolutionary for an architect. Not the obvious way, which is to tear down Paris and begin again, as Le Corbusier suggested in the 1920s, but another way which is more tolerant: that is to question how we look at things.

The Commercial Strip, the Las Vegas Strip in particular – it is the example par excellence – challenges the architect to take a positive, non-chip-on-the-shoulder view. Architects are out of the habit of looking non-judgmentally at the environment because orthodox Modern architecture is progressive, if not revolutionary, utopian and puristic; it is dissatisfied with *existing* conditions. Modern architecture has been anything but permissive: architects have preferred to change the existing environment rather than enhance what is there.

But to gain insight from the commonplace is nothing new: fine art often follows folk art. Romantic architects of the eighteenth century discovered an existing and conventional rustic architecture. Early Modern architects appropriated an existing and conventional industrial vocabulary without much adaptation. Le Corbusier loved grain elevators and steam ships; the Bauhaus looked like a factory;

Mies [van der Rohe] refined the details of American steel factories for concrete buildings. Modern architects work through analogy, symbol, and image – although they have gone to lengths to disclaim almost all determinants of their forms except structural necessity and the program – and they derive insights, analogies, and stimulation from unexpected images. There is a perversity in the learning process: we look backward at history and tradition to go forward; we can also look downward to go upward.

Architects who can accept the lessons of primitive vernacular architecture, so easy to take in an exhibit like "Architecture Without Architects," and of industrial, vernacular architecture, so easy to adapt to an electronic and space vernacular as elaborate neo-Brutalist or neo-Constructivist megastructures, do not easily acknowledge the validity of the commercial vernacular. Creating the new for the artist may mean choosing the old or the existing. Pop artists have relearned this. Our acknowledging existing, commercial architecture at the scale of the highway is within this tradition.

Modern architecture has not so much excluded the commercial vernacular as it has tried to take it over by inventing and enforcing a vernacular of its own, improved and universal. It has rejected the combination of fine art and crude art. The Italian landscape has always harmonized the vulgar and the Vitruvian: the *contorni* around the *duomo*, the *potiere*'s laundry across the *padrone's portone*, Supercortemaggiore against the Romanesque apse. Naked children have never played in *our* fountains and I.M. Pei will never be happy on Route 66.

ARCHITECTURE AS SPACE

Architects have been bewitched by a single element of the Italian landscape: the piazza. Its traditional, pedestrian-scaled, and intricately enclosed space is easier to take than the spatial sprawl of Route 66 and Los Angeles. Architects have been brought up on Space, and enclosed space is the easiest to handle. During the last forty years, theorists of Modern architecture ([Frank Lloyd] Wright and Le Corbusier sometimes excepted) have focused on space as the essential ingredient which separates architecture from painting, sculpture, and literature. Their definitions glory in the uniqueness of the medium, and although sculpture and painting may sometimes be allowed spatial characteristics, sculptural or pictorial architecture is unacceptable. That is because space is sacred.

Purist architecture was partly a reaction against nineteenth-century eclecticism. Gothic churches, Renaissance banks, and Jacobean manors were frankly picturesque. The mixing of styles meant the mixing of media. Dressed in historical styles, buildings evoked explicit associations and Romantic allusions to the past to convey literary, ecclesiastical, national, or programmatic symbolism. Definitions of architecture as space and form at the service of program and structure were not enough. The overlapping of disciplines may have diluted the architecture, but it enriched the meaning.

Modern architects abandoned a tradition of iconology in which painting, sculpture, and graphics were combined with architecture. The delicate hieroglyphics on a bold pylon, the archetypal inscriptions on a Roman architrave, the mosaic processions in Sant' Apollinare, the ubiquitous tattoos over a Giotto chapel, the enshrined hierarchies around a Gothic portal, even the illusionistic frescoes in a Venetian villa all contain messages beyond their ornamental contribution to architectural space. The integration of the arts in Modern architecture has always been called a good thing. But one didn't paint *on* Mies. Painted panels were floated independently of the structure by means of shadow joints; sculpture was in or near but seldom on the building. Objects of art were used to reinforce architectural space at the expense of their own content. The Kolbe in the Barcelona Pavilion was a foil to the directed spaces: the message was mainly architectural. The diminutive signs in most modern buildings contained only the most necessary messages, like "Ladies," minor accents begrudgingly applied.

ARCHITECTURE AS SYMBOL

Critics and historians who documented the "decline of popular symbols" in art, supported orthodox Modern architects who shunned symbolism of form as an expression or reinforcement of content: meaning was to be communicated through the inherent, physiognomic characteristics of form. The creation of architectural form was to be a logical process, free from images of past experience, determined solely by program and structure, with an occasional assist, as Alan Colquhoun has suggested,[2] from intuition.

But some recent critics have questioned the possible level of content to be derived from abstract forms. And others have demonstrated that the functionalists despite their protestations, derived a formal vocabulary of their own, mainly from current art movements and the industrial vernacular; latter-day followers like the Archigram group have turned, while similarly protesting, to Pop Art and the space industry. Indeed, not only are we

> not free from the forms of the past, and from the availability of these forms as typological models, but . . . if we assume we are free, we have lost control over a very active sector of our imagination, and of our power to communicate with others.[3]

However, most critics have slighted a continuing iconology in popular commercial art: the persuasive heraldry which pervades our environment from the advertising pages of the *New Yorker* to the super-billboards of Houston. And their theory of the "debasement" of symbolic architecture in nineteenth-century eclecticism has blinded them to the value of the representational architecture along highways. Those who acknowledge this roadside eclecticism denigrate it because it flaunts the cliché of a decade ago as well as the style of a century ago. But why not? Time travels fast today.

The Miami-Beach Modern motel on a bleak stretch of highway in southern Delaware reminds the jaded driver of the welcome luxury of a tropical resort, persuading him, perhaps, to forgo the gracious plantation across the Virginia border called Motel Monticello. The real hotel in Miami alludes to the international stylishness of a Brazilian resort, which, in turn, derives from the International Style of middle Corbu. This evolution from the high source through the middle source to the low source took only thirty years. Today, the middle source, the neo-Eclectic architecture of the 1940s and 1950s is less interesting than its commercial adaptations. Roadside copies of Ed Stone [Edward Durrell Stone] are more interesting than the real Ed Stone.

The sign for the Motel Monticello, a silhouette of an enormous Chippendale highboy, is visible on the highway before the motel itself. This architecture of styles and signs is antispatial; it is an architecture of communication over space; communication dominates space as an element in the architecture and in the landscape. But it is for a new scale of landscape. The philosophical associations of the old eclecticism evoked subtle and complex meanings to be savored in the docile spaces of a traditional landscape. The commercial persuasion of roadside eclecticism provokes bold impact in the vast and complex setting of a new landscape of big spaces, high speeds, and complex programs. Styles and signs make connections among many elements, far apart and seen fast. The message is basely commercial, the context is basically new.

A driver thirty years ago could maintain a sense of orientation in space. At the simple crossroad a little sign with an arrow confirmed what he already knew. He knew where he was. Today the crossroad is a cloverleaf. To turn left he must turn right, a contradiction poignantly evoked in the print by Allan D'Arcangelo. But the driver has no time to ponder paradoxical subtleties within a dangerous, sinuous maze. He relies on signs to guide him – enormous signs in vast spaces at high speeds.

The dominance of signs over space at a pedestrian scale occurs in big airports. Circulation in a big railroad station required little more than a simple axial system from taxi to train, by ticket window, stores, waiting room, and platform, virtually without signs. Architects object to signs in buildings: "if the plan is clear you can see where to go." But complex programs and settings require complex combinations of media beyond the purer architectural triad of structure, form, and light at the service of space. They suggest an architecture of bold communication rather than one of subtle expression.

THE ARCHITECTURE OF PERSUASION

The cloverleaf and airport communicate with moving crowds in cars or on foot, for efficiency and safety. But words and symbols may be used in space for commercial persuasion. The Middle Eastern bazaar contains no signs, the strip is virtually all signs. In the bazaar, communication works through proximity. Along its narrow aisles buyers feel and smell the merchandise, and explicit oral persuasion is applied by the merchant. In the narrow streets of the medieval town, although signs occur, persuasion is mainly through the sight and smell of the real cakes through the doors and windows of the bakery. On Main Street, shop-window displays for pedestrians along the sidewalks, and exterior signs, perpendicular to the street for motorists, dominate the scene almost equally.

On the commercial strip the supermarket windows contain no merchandise. There may be signs announcing the day's bargains, but they are to be read by the pedestrians approaching from the parking lot. The building itself is set back from the highway and half hidden, as is most of the urban environment, by parked cars. The vast parking lot is in front, not at the rear, since it is a symbol as well as a convenience. The building is low because air conditioning demands low spaces, and merchandising techniques discourage second floors; its architecture is neutral because it can hardly be seen from the road. Both merchandise and architecture are disconnected from the road. The big sign leaps to connect the driver to the store, and down the road the cake mixes and detergents are advertised by their national manufacturers on enormous billboards inflected toward the highway. The graphic sign in space has become the architecture of this landscape. Inside, the A&P has reverted to the bazaar except that graphic packaging has replaced the oral persuasion of the merchant. At another scale, the shopping center off the highway returns in its pedestrian mall to the medieval street.

HISTORICAL TRADITION AND THE A&P

The A&P parking lot is a current phase in the evolution of vast space since Versailles. The space which divides high-speed highway and low, sparse buildings produces no enclosure and little direction. To move through a piazza is to move between high enclosing forms. To move through this landscape is to move over vast expansive texture: the mega-texture of the commercial landscape. The parking lot is the parterre of the asphalt landscape. The patterns of parking lines give direction much as the paving patterns, curbs, borders, and *tapis verts* give direction in Versailles; grids of lamp posts substitute for obelisks and rows of urns and statues, as points of identity and continuity in the vast space. But it is the highway signs through their sculptural forms or pictorial silhouettes, their particular positions in space, their inflected shapes, and their graphic meanings which identify and unify the megatexture. They make verbal and symbolic connections through space, communicating a complexity of meanings through hundreds of associations in few seconds from far away. Symbol dominates space. Architecture is not enough. Because the spatial relationships are made by symbols more than by forms, architecture in this landscape becomes symbol in space rather than form in space. Architecture defines very little: the big sign and the little building is the rule of Route 66.

The sign is more important than the architecture. This is reflected in the proprietor's budget: the sign at the front is a vulgar extravaganza, the building at the back, a modest necessity. The architecture is what's cheap. Sometimes the building *is* the sign: the restaurant in the shape of a hamburger is sculptural symbol and architectural shelter. Contradiction between outside and inside was common in architecture before the Modern Movement, particularly in urban and monumental architecture. Baroque domes were symbols as well as spatial constructions, and they were bigger in scale and higher outside than inside in order to dominate their urban setting and communicate their symbolic message. The false fronts of western stores did the same thing. They were bigger and taller than the interiors they fronted to communicate the store's importance and to enhance the quality and unity of the street. But false fronts are of the order and scale of Main Street. From the desert town on the highway in the West of today we can learn new and vivid lessons about an impure architecture of communication. The little low buildings, grey brown like the desert, separate and recede from the street which is now the highway, their false fronts disengaged and turned perpendicular to the highway as big high signs. If you take the signs away there is no place. The desert town is intensified communication along the highway.

Las Vegas is the apotheosis of the desert town. Visiting Las Vegas in the mid-1960s was like visiting Rome in the late 1940s. For young Americans in the 1940s, familiar only with the auto-scaled, gridiron city, and the antiurban theories of the previous architectural generation, the traditional urban spaces, the pedestrian scale, and the mixtures yet continuities of styles of the Italian piazzas were a significant revelation. They rediscovered the piazza. Two decades later architects are perhaps ready for similar lessons about large open space, big scale, and high speed. Las Vegas is to the Strip what Rome is to the Piazza.

There are other parallels between Rome and Las Vegas: their expansive settings in the Campagna and in the Mojave Desert, for instance, which tend to focus and clarify their images. Each city vividly superimposes elements of a supranational scale on the local fabric: churches in the religious capital, casinos and their signs in the entertainment capital. These cause violent juxtapositions of use and scale in both cities. Rome's churches, off streets and piazzas, are open to the public; the pilgrim, religious or architectural, can walk from church to church. The gambler or architect in Las Vegas can similarly take in a variety of casinos along the Strip. The casinos and lobbies of Las Vegas which are ornamental and monumental and open to the promenading public are, a few old banks and railroad stations excepted, unique in American cities. Nolli's map of the mid-eighteenth century, reveals the sensitive and complex connections between public and private space in Rome. Private building is shown in gray hatching which is carved into by the public spaces, exterior *and* interior. These spaces, open or roofed, are shown in minute detail through darker poché. Interiors of churches read like piazzas and courtyards of palaces, yet a variety of qualities and scales is articulated. Such a map for Las Vegas would reveal and clarify the public and the private at another scale, although the iconology of the signs in space would require other graphic methods.

A conventional map of Las Vegas reveals two scales of movement within the gridiron plan: that of Main Street and that of the Strip. The main street of Las Vegas is Fremont Street, and the earlier of two concentrations of casinos is located along three or four blocks of this street. The casinos here are bazaar-like in the immediacy of their clicking and tinkling gambling machines to the sidewalk. The Fremont Street casinos and hotels focus on the railroad depot at the head of the street; here the railroad and main street scales of movement connect. The bus depot is now the busier entrance to town, but the axial focus on the rail depot from Fremont Street is visual, and possibly symbolic. This contrasts with the Strip, where a second and later development of casinos extends southward to the airport, the jet-scale entrance to town.

One's first introduction to Las Vegas architecture is a replica of Eero Saarinen's TWA Terminal, which is the local airport building. Beyond this piece of architectural image, impressions are scaled to the car rented at the airport. Here is the unraveling of the famous Strip itself, which, as Route 91, connects the airport with the downtown.

SYSTEM AND ORDER ON THE STRIP

The image of the commercial strip is chaos. The order in this landscape is not obvious. The continuous highway itself and its systems for turning are absolutely consistent. The median strip accommodates the U-turns necessary to a vehicular promenade for casino-crawlers, as well as left turns onto the local street pattern which the Strip intersects. The curbing allows frequent right turns for casinos and other commercial enterprises and eases the difficult transitions from highway to parking. The street lights function superfluously along many parts of the Strip which are incidentally but abundantly lit by signs; but their consistency of form and position and their arching shapes begin to identify by day a continuous space of the highway, and the constant rhythm contrasts effectively with the uneven rhythms of the signs behind.

This counterpoint reinforces the contrast between two types of order on the Strip: the obvious visual order of street elements and the difficult visual order of buildings and signs. The zone *of* the highway is a shared order. The zone *off* the highway is an individual order. The elements of the highway are civic. The buildings and signs are private. In combination they embrace continuity *and* discontinuity, going *and* stopping, clarity *and* ambiguity, cooperation *and* competition, the community *and* rugged individualism. The system of the highway gives order to the sensitive functions of exit and entrance, as well as to the image of the Strip as a sequential whole. It also generates places for individual enterprises to grow, and controls the general direction of that growth. It allows variety and change along its sides, and accommodates the contrapuntal, competitive order of the individual enterprises.

There is an order along the sides of the highway. Varieties of activities are juxtaposed on the Strip: service stations, minor motels, and multimillion dollar casinos. Marriage chapels ("credit cards accepted") converted from bungalows with added neon-lined steeples are apt to appear anywhere toward the downtown end. Immediate proximity of related uses, as on Main Street where you walk from one store to another, is not required along the Strip since interaction is by car and highway. You *drive* from one casino to another even when they are adjacent because of the distance between them, and an intervening service station is not disagreeable.

THE ARCHITECTURE OF THE STRIP

A typical casino complex contains a building which is near enough to the highway to be seen from the road across the parked cars, yet far enough back to accommodate driveways, turnarounds, and parking. The parking in front is a token: it reassures the customer but does not obscure the building. It is prestige parking: the customer pays. The bulk of the parking, along the sides of the complex, allows direct access to the hotel, yet stays visible from the highway. Parking is never at the back. The scales of movement and space of the highway determine distances between buildings: they must be far apart to be comprehended at high speeds. Front footage on the Strip has not yet reached the value it once had on main street and parking is still an appropriate filler. Big space between buildings is characteristic of the Strip. It is significant that Fremont Street is more photogenic than the Strip. A single post card can carry a view of the Golden Horseshoe, the Mint Hotel, the Golden Nugget, and the Lucky Casino. A shot of the Strip is less spectacular; its enormous spaces must be seen as moving sequences.

The side elevation of the complex is important because it is seen by approaching traffic from a greater distance and for a longer time than the facade. The rhythmic gables on the long, low, English medieval style, half-timbered motel sides of the Aladdin Casino read emphatically across the parking space and through the signs and the giant statue of the neighboring Texaco station, and contrast with the modern Near-Eastern flavor of the casino front. Casino fronts on the Strip often inflect in shape and ornament toward the right, to welcome right-lane traffic. Modern styles use a porte-cochére which is diagonal in plan. Brazilianoid International styles use free forms. Service stations, motels, and other simpler types of buildings conform in general to this system of inflection toward the highway through the position and form of their elements. Regardless of the front, the back of the building is styleless because the whole is turned toward the front and no one sees the back.

Beyond the town, the only transition between the Strip and the Mojave Desert is a zone of rusting beer cans. Within the town the transition is as ruthlessly sudden. Casinos whose fronts relate so sensitively to the highway, turn their ill-kept backsides toward the local environment, exposing the residual forms and spaces of mechanical equipment and service areas.

Signs inflect toward the highway even more than buildings. The big sign – independent of the building and more or less sculptural or pictorial – inflects by its position, perpendicular to and at the edge of the highway, by its scale and sometimes by its shape. The sign of the Aladdin Casino seems to bow toward the highway through the inflection in its shape. It also is three-dimensional and parts of it revolve. The sign at the Dunes is more chaste: it is only two-dimensional and its back echoes its front, but it is an erection twenty-two stories high which pulsates at night. The sign for the Mint Casino on Route 91 at Fremont Street inflects towards the Casino several blocks away. Signs in Las Vegas use mixed media – then words, pictures, and

sculpture – to persuade and inform. The same sign works as polychrome sculpture in the sun and as black silhouette against the sun; at night it is a source of light. It revolves by day and moves by the play of light at night. It contains scales for close up and for distance. Las Vegas has the longest sign in the world, the Thunderbird, and the highest, the Dunes. Some signs are hardly distinguishable at a distance from the occasional highrise hotels along the Strip. The sign of the Pioneer Club on Fremont Street talks. Its cowboy, sixty feet high, says "Howdy Pardner" every thirty seconds. The big sign at the Aladdin has spawned a little sign with similar proportions to mark the entrance to the parking. "But such signs!" says Tom Wolfe. They

> soar in shapes before which the existing vocabulary of art history is helpless. I can only attempt to supply names – Boomerang Modern, Palette Curvilinear, Flash Gordon Ming-Alert Spiral, McDonald's Hamburger Parabola, Mint Casino Elliptical, Miami Beach Kidney.[4]

Buildings are also signs. At night on Fremont Street whole buildings are illuminated, but not through reflection from spotlights; they are made into sources of light by closely spaced neon tubes.

LAS VEGAS STYLES

The Las Vegas casino is a combination form. The complex program of Caesar's Palace – it is the newest – includes gambling, dining, and banqueting rooms, night clubs and auditoria, stores, and a complete hotel. It is also a combination of styles. The front colonnade is San Pietro Bernini in plan, but Yamasaki in vocabulary and scale; the blue and gold mosaic work is Early Christian, tomb of Galla Placidia. (Naturally the Baroque symmetry of its prototype precludes an inflection toward the right in this facade.) Beyond and above is a slab in Gio Ponti, Pirelli-Baroque, and beyond that, in turn, a lowrise in neo-Classical Motel Moderne. Each of these styles is integrated by a ubiquity of Ed Stone screens. The landscaping is also eclectic. Within the Piazza San Pietro is the token parking lot. Among the parked cars rise five fountains rather than the two of Carlo Maderno. Villa d'Este cypresses further punctuate the parking environment;

Gian da Bologna's *Rape of the Sabine Women*, and various statues of Venus and David, with slight anatomical exaggerations, grace the area around the porte-cochére. Almost bisecting a Venus is an Avis: a sign identifying No. 2's office on the premises.

The agglomeration of Caesar's Palace and of the Strip as a whole approach the spirit if not the style of the late Roman Forum with its eclectic accumulations. But the sign of Caesar's Palace with its Classical, plastic columns is more Etruscan in feeling than Roman. Although not so high as the Dunes sign next door or the Shell sign on the other side, its base is enriched by Roman Centurions, lacquered like Oldenburg hamburgers, who peer over the acres of cars and across their desert empire to the mountains beyond. Their statuesque escorts, carrying trays of fruit, suggest the festivities within, and are a background for the family snapshots of Middle Westerners. A massive Miesian light-box announces square, expensive entertainers like Jack Benny in 1930s-style marquis lettering appropriate for Benny, if not for the Roman architrave it almost ornaments. The light-box is not in the architrave; it is located off-center on the columns in order to inflect toward the highway.

THE INTERIOR OASIS

If the back of the casino is different from the front for the sake of visual impact in the autoscape, the inside contrasts with the outside for other reasons. The interior sequence from the front door back, progresses from gambling areas to dining, entertainment, and shopping areas to hotel. Those who park at the side and enter there can interrupt the sequence, but the circulation of the whole focuses on the gambling rooms. In a Las Vegas Hotel the registration desk is invariably behind you when you enter the lobby; before you are the gambling tables and machines. The lobby is the gambling room. The interior space and the patio, in their exaggerated separation from the environment, have the quality of an oasis.

LAS VEGAS LIGHTING

The gambling room is always very dark; the patio, always very bright. But both are enclosed: the former has no windows, the latter is open only to the sky. The combination of darkness and enclosure of the gambling room and its subspaces makes for privacy, protection, concentration, and control. The intricate maze under the low ceiling never connects with outside light or outside space. This disorients the occupant in space and time. He loses track of where he is and when it is. Time is limitless because the light of noon and midnight are exactly the same. Space is limitless because the artificial light obscures rather than defines its boundaries. Light is not used to define space. Walls and ceilings do not serve as reflective surfaces for light, but are made absorbent and dark. Space is enclosed but limitless because its edges are dark. Light sources, chandeliers, and the glowing, juke-box-like gambling machines themselves, are independent of walls and ceilings. The lighting is anti-architectural. Illuminated baldachini, more than in all Rome, hover over tables in the limitless shadowy restaurant at the Sahara Hotel.

The artificially lit, air conditioned interiors complement the glare and heat of the agoraphobic auto-scaled desert. But the interior of the motel patio behind the casino is literally the oasis in a hostile environment. Whether Organic Modern or neo-Classical Baroque, it contains the fundamental elements of the classic oasis: courts, water, greenery, intimate scale, and enclosed space. Here they are a swimming pool, palms, grass, and other horticultural importations set in a paved court surrounded by hotel suites balconied or terraced on the court side for privacy. What gives poignancy to the beach umbrellas and chaises lounges is the vivid, recent memory of the hostile cars poised in the asphalt desert beyond. The pedestrian oasis in the Las Vegas desert is the princely enclosure of the Alhambra, and it is the apotheosis of all the motel courts with swimming pools more symbolic than useful, the plain, low restaurants with exotic interiors, and the shopping malls of the American strip.

THE BIG, LOW SPACE

The casino in Las Vegas is big, low space. It is the archetype for all public interior spaces whose heights are diminished for reasons of budget and air conditioning. (The low, one-way mirrored ceilings also permit outside observation of the gambling rooms.) In the past, volume was governed by structural spans: height was relatively easy to achieve. For us, span is easy to achieve, and volume is governed by mechanical and economic limitations on height. But railroad stations, restaurants, and shopping arcades only ten feet high reflect as well a changing attitude to monumentality in our environment. In the past, big spans with their concomitant heights were an ingredient of architectural monumentality. But our monuments are not the occasional tour de force of an Astrodome, a Lincoln Center, or a subsidized airport. These merely prove that big, high spaces do not automatically make architectural monumentality. We have replaced the monumental space of Pennsylvania Station by a subway aboveground, and that of Grand Central Terminal remains mainly through its magnificent conversion to an advertising vehicle. Thus, we rarely achieve architectural monumentality when we try; our money and skill do not go into the traditional monumentality which expressed cohesion of the community through big scale, united, symbolic, architectural elements. Perhaps we should admit that our cathedrals are the chapels without the nave; that apart from theaters and ball parks the occasional communal space which is big is a space for crowds of anonymous individuals without explicit connection with each other. The big, low mazes of the dark restaurant with alcoves combine being together and yet separate as does the Las Vegas casino. The lighting in the casino achieves a new monumentality for the low space. The controlled sources of artificial and colored light within the dark enclosure, by obscuring its physical limits, expand and unify the space. You are no longer in the bounded piazza but in the twinkling lights of the city at night.

INCLUSION AND THE DIFFICULT ORDER

Henri Bergson called disorder all order we cannot see. The emerging order of the Strip is a complex order. It is not the easy, rigid order of the Urban Renewal project or the fashionable megastructure – the medieval hilltown with technological trappings. It is, on the contrary, a manifestation of an opposite direction in architectural theory: Broadacre City – a travesty of Broadacre City perhaps, but a kind of vindication of Frank Lloyd Wright's predictions

for a commercial strip within the urban sprawl is, of course, Broadacre City with a difference. Broadacre City's easy, motival order identified and unified its vast spaces and separate buildings at the scale of the omnipotent automobile. Each building, without doubt, was to be designed by the Master or by his Taliesin Fellowship, with no room for honky-tonk improvisations. An easy control would be exercised over similar elements within the universal, Usonian vocabulary to the exclusion, certainly, of commercial vulgarities. But the order of the Strip *includes*: it includes at all levels, from the mixture of seemingly incongruous advertising media plus a system of neo-Organic or neo-Wrightian restaurant motifs in Walnut Formica. It is not an order dominated by the expert and made easy for the eye. The moving eye in the moving body must work to pick out and interpret a variety of changing, juxtaposed orders, like the shifting configurations of a Victor Vasarely painting. It is the unity which "maintains, but only just maintains, a control over the clashing elements which compose it. Chaos is very near; its nearness, but its avoidance, gives . . . force."[5]

Las Vegas is analyzed here only as a phenomenon of architectural communication; its values are not questioned. Commercial advertising, gambling interests, and competitive instincts are another matter. The analysis of a drive-in church in this context would match that of a drive-in restaurant because this is a study of method not content. There is no reason, however, why the methods of commercial persuasion and the skyline of signs should not serve the purpose of civic and cultural enhancement. But this is not entirely up to the architect.

ART AND THE OLD CLICHÉ

Pop Art has shown the value of the old cliché used in a new context to achieve new meaning: to make the common uncommon. Richard Poirier has referred to the "de-creative impulse" in literature:

Eliot and Joyce display an extraordinary vulnerability . . . to the idioms, rhythms, artifacts associated with certain urban environments or situations. The multitudinous styles of Ulysses are so dominated by them that there are only intermittent sounds of Joyce in the novel and no extended passage certifiably is his as distinguished from a mimicked style.[6]

Eliot himself speaks of Joyce's doing the best he can "with the material at hand."[7] A fitting requiem for the irrelevant works of Art which are today's descendants of a once meaningful Modern architecture are Eliot's lines in *East Coker*.

> *That was a way of putting it –*
> *not very satisfactory:*
> *A periphrastic study in a worn-*
> *out poetical fashion,*
> *Leaving one still with the*
> *intolerable wrestle*
> *With words and meanings.*
> *The poetry does not matter.*[8]

NOTES

1 Richard Poirier, "T.S. Eliot and the Literature of Waste," *The New Republic* (20 May 1967): 21.

2 Alan Colquhoun, "Typology and Design Method," *Arena, Architectural Association Journal* (June 1967).

3 Ibid., 14.

4 Tom Wolfe, *The Kandy-Kolored Tangerine Flake Streamline Baby* (New York: Farrar, Straus and Giroux, 1965), 8.

5 August Heckscher, *The Public Happiness* (New York: Atheneum Publishers, 1962).

6 Poirier, "T.S. Eliot and the Literature of Waste," op. cit., 20.

7 Ibid., 21.

8 T.S. Eliot, *Four Quartets* (New York: Harcourt, Brace and Co., 1943), 13.

"Collage City"

Architectural Review (1975)

Colin Rowe and Fred Koetter

Editors' Introduction

Modernist urban design and architecture – from the work of CIAM in the early twentieth century to the proliferation of a watered-down and incoherent urbanism of the mid-century – experienced a barrage of criticism from both the high critics of design taste and the discontented general public. Infamous critiques of modern design and planning processes (see the work of Jane Jacobs, Christopher Alexander, and Edward Relph in this edition) focused on the failed utopian and heroic aspirations of designers with "messiah" delusions who utilized totalizing design strategies in attempting to control outcomes. In *Collage City*, Colin Rowe and Fred Koetter launch a direct attack on the profession of which they are a part. They disdain the "retarded nature of architectural debate," the weak science used to support project justification, and the poor state of design poetics.

While the previous selection, from *Learning from Las Vegas*, provides critique of modern urban design through the filter of everyday landscapes, *Collage City* uses the historical city as a launching point of criticism. This essay, which spawned a larger later revision, has become a classic of early postmodern critique, influencing designers and urbanists, and re-injecting the morphological lessons of the traditional city into a design era that had lost its way. The text of *Collage City* is both inspiring in message and dense in delivery. The writing is often opaque, circular and difficult to digest. In this selection we have edited the text to highlight key messages and provide easier access to its key meanings.

Rowe and his students at Cornell in the 1970s began an evolution in urban form analysis through the rediscovery of figure-ground drawings (black plans). This methodological drawing convention contrasts the architectural solids and private spaces of the city (inked black as figures) against the public realm of the city (left white as the ground of the drawing). The white spaces include most of the public realm of the city: piazzas, streets, interior courtyards, open-sky space, and landscape areas. Studying the method of Giambattista Nolli's figure-ground drawings of late-Baroque Rome (*Pianta Grande di Roma*, etched in 1748), these Cornell studios revived an analytical method that had nearly disappeared in design education and could begin to show the tissues, fabrics, and "coarseness or fineness of grain" of urban form elements. Patterns of historic form emerged from these drawings – exposing the relative size of blocks and buildings, the shaping of space, and the relationship between discrete and identifiable parts of the city. This became a favored method of design educators and urban morphologists throughout the late twentieth century, and culminated in the comparably scaled figure-ground street maps of Allan Jacobs in his book *Great Streets* (Cambridge, MA: MIT Press, 1993), which have become a widespread convention in their own right.

The title of the article, later a book, refers to how historical cities were constructed over time through a process of accretion, fragmentation, and overlay – different patterns and building sets introduced incrementally by generations of city builders. In studying the fragments of imperial, medieval, Renaissance and Baroque Rome, the ruins of Hadrian's Villa in Tivoli, and other valued historic urbanisms, Rowe and Koetter begin to construct *Collage City* as a critique of the totalizing urban design, aesthetic purity, and reductionist abstraction of modernist designers they seek to overturn. Colin Rowe was a great admirer of nineteenth-century eclecticism and competing styles. It is not surprising then that he advocates the compartmentalization of the city into a series of overlaid "collage" elements, where each has its own internal rationale, organization, and experiential validity. Rather than a single heroic gesture (illustrated, for example in Le Corbusier's *Plan Voisin* to bulldoze parts of Paris in the 1920s) they turn to methods of bricolage, collision, erasure, and addition. The city of Rowe and Koetter then, becomes a series of episodes, inviting the participation of designers and developers at a variety of smaller scales who can insert projects into the larger patchwork.

The structure of *Collage City* is presented as an unfolding argument that leads to a final prescription for how urban designers should begin approaching the city. Throughout the book, Rowe and Koetter utilize a series of philosophical references that help them to support and shape their findings, including Isaiah Berlin, Karl Popper, Levi-Strauss, and Richard Rorty. The book is organized in five chapters and begins with a critique of utopian and modernist thinking, before utilizing a series of science fiction-versus-picturesque comparisons to ask the question: "why should we be obliged to prefer a nostalgia for the future to that for the past?" Their chapter entitled "Crisis of the Object: Predicament of Texture" provides the argument that cities can be viewed as a series of contrasting objects and textures, very similar in conception to the methodological figure-ground drawings the authors use for analysis. Their final chapters propose that urban designers and architects use both collage (creation of compositions constructed with varied elements) and bricolage (creation using material found at hand) techniques for the construction of cities. *Collage City* sees the act of city-building as a series of strategic and incremental juxtapositions of smaller projects layered onto a larger whole, rather than a utopian or totalitarian project. And importantly it allows designers to reference the lessons of historical and valued urbanism rather than hopping on a non-stop treadmill of ceaseless innovation re-making the wheel.

From 1962 until his death in 1999, Colin Rowe was a Cornell professor of architecture, urbanism and urban design. He had a profound impact on the theory and history of American architecture through the latter half of the twentieth century. His first notable contribution was the speculative essay "The Mathematics of the Ideal Villa" (1947), in which he compared the mathematical rules of Palladio's villas to similar systems used by Le Corbusier in several housing projects. Rowe's rhetorical strategies and cross historical methods (influenced by the work of Camillo Sitte from nearly a century earlier) provided him with a mechanism for using tradition to assess contemporary urbanism (a model that would be used successfully in *Collage City* and reconnects urban design practice with historical origins that modernism seemed to disavow). Over the course of his career, his criticism of modern urban design and architecture provided a lasting contribution to the development of postmodern critique and the emerging urban design field. With the publication of *Collage City* (first as a journal article in 1975, and later as a book by MIT Press in 1978), Rowe influenced a generation of late-twentieth-century theorist/practitioners, including Aldo Rossi, Robert Venturi, James Stirling, Peter Eisenman, and Dan Solomon. Although not a prodigious writer, his other significant works include: *The Architecture of Good Intentions* (1994); *As I Was Saying: Recollections and Miscellaneous Essays*, three volumes (Cambridge, MA: MIT Press 1999); "The Present Urban Predicament," *The Cornell Journal of Architecture* (No. 1, 1981); "Roma Interrotta," *Architectural Design Profile* (Vol. 49, No. 3–4, 1979); and a revised publication of *The Mathematics of the Ideal Villa and Other Essays* (Cambridge, MA: MIT Press, 1976).

Fred Koetter is the co-author with Colin Rowe of *Collage City*. He was an architecture professor at Cornell, Harvard and Yale Universities; at this last school serving as dean from 1993 to 1998. He is a founding partner of Koetter, Kim and Associates – Architecture and Urban Design in Boston, Massachusetts with his partner Susie Kim. Their office focuses on urban design, corporate, educational, and civic projects. Their work is widely published and has won numerous urban design and architecture awards. He is the author of numerous essays, including "The Corporate Villa," *Design Quarterly* (No. 135, 1978) and "Notes on the In-Between," *Harvard Architecture Review* (Vol. 1, Spring 1980). *Collage City* has been cited reverentially in reviews, anthologies, and texts of design theory more times than can be counted.

Figure-ground perception has been explained in greater depth through gestalt psychology and visual analysis. For more on this consult: Barry Smith (ed.), *Foundations of Gestalt Psychology* (Munich/Vienna: Philosophia Verlag, 1988); D. Brett King and Michael Wertheimer, *Max Wertheimer and Gestalt Theory* (New Brunswick, NJ: Transaction Publishers/Rutgers, 2007); Steven Yantis (ed.), *Visual Perception* (London: Taylor

& Francis/Psychology Press, 2001); and Charles Wallschlaeger and Cynthia Busic-Snyder, *Basic Visual Concepts and Principles for Artists, Architects and Designers* (New York: McGraw-Hill, 1992).

A large body of material exists on the impacts of *Collage City* and the use of figure-ground drawings. Of particular note is architect and CNU member Dan Solomon's chapter on Black Plans and Colin Rowe's contributions in: *Global City Blues* (Washington, DC: Island Press, 2003). Others include: Wayne William Cooper, *The Figure Grounds* (Ithaca, NY: Cornell University Press, 1967); and Roger Trancik, *Finding Lost Space: Theories of Urban Design* (New York: Wiley, 1986). For examples of figure-ground analysis in urban design see the journal *Urban Morphology* published by the International Seminar on Urban Form (University of Birmingham, UK / Wiley); as well as these books: Eric Jenkins, *To Scale: One Hundred Urban Plans* (Abingdon: Routledge, 2008); Robert F. Gatje, *Great Public Squares: An Architect's Selection* (New York: W. W. Norton, 2010); and Nathan Cherry, *Grid/Street/Place: Essential Elements of Sustainable Urban Districts* (Chicago, IL: American Planning Association, 2009).

■ ■ ■ ■ ■ ■

It was not so many years ago that the Graduate School of Design at Harvard issued a brochure entitled *Crisis*. It was an opulent production, blood-red letters on a white ground, and its message was not at all oblique. There exists an environmental crisis but the Graduate School of Design possesses most of the know-how to be able to propound the solution; and, therefore, in order that it may realize its mission, give, give to the Graduate School of Design.

The strategy [of architectural crisis] of course, begins to be ancient, but it continues, apparently to be irresistible and the notion of impending and monstrous cataclysm would now seem to be ingrained in the psychology of modern architecture. Apocalyptic catastrophe, instant millennium. The threat of damnation, the hope of salvation. Irresistible change which still requires human cooperation. The new architecture and urbanism as emblems of the New Jerusalem. The corruptions of high culture. The bonfire of vanities. Self-transcendence towards a form of collectivized freedom. The architect, divested of his cultural wardrobe and fortified by the equivalent of religious experience, may now revert to the virtues of his primal condition.

This is to caricature, though not seriously to distort, a complex of sentiments which might be designated the Savonarola syndrome, sentiments often lying just beneath the threshold of consciousness; and, therefore, it should be without surprise that one observes a recent *RIBA Journal* – yet again Crisis (this time *red* letters on a *black* ground), and this time not an appeal for money but rather an incitement to public self-flagellation.

Now the notice of how the techniques of the crudest revivalism have been so much ingested by what used to be called the Modern Movement is neither to deplore crude revivalism (the ecstasy and the guilt of the latest Appalachian convert), nor is it, altogether, to deprecate modern architecture; and, certainly, it should not be understood as condemning a missionary enthusiasm or intimating that convictions of crisis are in any way illusory. It may be presumed that a crisis exists; but it must also be insisted that the peddling of crisis by the architect begins to become an objectionable platitude, that it is now one of those retarded gambits of criticism which any sense of obligation should feel obliged to avoid.

In his *Decline and Fall of the Roman Empire* Gibbon speaks of *the ancient and popular doctrine of the Millennium*:

So pleasing was this hope to the mind of believers that the New Jerusalem, the seat of this blissful kingdom, was quickly adorned with all the gayest colors of the imagination. A felicity consisting only of pure and spiritual pleasure would have appeared too refined for its inhabitants, who were still supposed to possess their human nature and senses. A Garden of Eden, with the amusements of the pastoral life was no longer suited to the advanced state of society which prevailed under the Roman Empire. A city was therefore erected of gold and precious stones, and a supernatural plenty of corn and wine was bestowed on the adjacent territory; in the free enjoyment of whose spontaneous productions, the happy and benevolent people was never to be restrained by any jealous laws of exclusive property. The assurances of such a Millennium was carefully inculcated by a succession of fathers . . . (and) . . . Though it might not be universally received, it appears to have been the reigning sentiment of the orthodox believers; and it seems so well adapted to the desires and apprehensions of mankind, that it must have contributed to a very considerable degree to the progress of the Christian faith.

That a somewhat similar constellation of hopes and beliefs, *not universally received* did contribute *to a very considerable degree* to the progress of modern architecture we now know very well. There was the vision of a city, half Garden of Eden, half New Jerusalem, a city, admittedly, which was not to be erected *of gold and precious stones*, but still a city which was to be shining, scintillating and brilliant, a city of glass and concrete, a city which would – as a triumph over the injuries of time – arise entire and pure, a city in which plenty and benevolence were for ever to prevail.

[. . .]

The rise of the natural sciences in the seventeenth century, with the ensuing prestige of Newtonian physics, was to lead in the Enlightenment to the widespread insistence that society could and should be reconstructed on analogous scientific principles. It was to lead slightly later to such a person as Henri de Saint-Simon conceiving of himself as the Newton of the political order; but, if it was thus that a more literal Utopianism now began to emerge, this was a development which now represented only one half of the situation. For, alongside the rise of science, there is also to be placed the less spectacular ebullition of the historical consciousness. It should be unnecessary to insist too much that, in the later Enlightenment, alongside science – still thought of as largely static and in terms of mechanism – there began to emerge an historical view of things which speculated about growth and change and which, consequently, was prone to think about society not so much as *mechanism* but as *organism*. For most histories of ideas and criticism will tell us something to this effect; and, probably, most of them will go on to imply that the protagonists of *mechanism* were largely French and the protagonists of *organism* largely German. These are, of course, big and deplorably crude generalizations to throw around; but, allowing for

crudeness, it is probably true to say that Auguste Comte might represent the climax of the *mechanist* world view and George Friedrich Hegel of its *organicist* corollary.

The world and society as *mechanism*, the world and society as *organism*: it is obvious that with Charles Darwin one gets something of a put-together; and, if there is no reason to suppose that Darwin would ever have been interested in the productions of either Comte or Hegel, if he might still seem to have been above all else the culturally unsophisticated English empiricist, he is still one of those persons who inadvertently fused the French and German points of view. For *Origin of Species* is, after all, a version of science as a version of history. Its inference is that geology and biology have come to collaborate with history to present an evolutionary view of things which is doubly valid – both scientific and historical.

The Darwinian performance was crucial; but far more crucial, and far more deliberate, was the equivalent performance of Karl Marx. For, whatever it was supposed to be, Marx's undertaking was no *mere* scientific enterprise. It was surely, above all else, a cultural construction. One takes French Positivism (the idea of scientific and rational politics in a more or less static world) and one confronts it with German historicism (the idea of motion, change, flux and flow proceeding in more or less ineluctable pattern); and then, out of this dialectic, one achieves something which seems to combine both the precise and the dynamic, in which the Hegelian view of an ever-expanding World Spirit becomes optimistically conflated with a professedly hardnosed fantasy – a fantasy of the World Spirit as having become matter of fact, as having become an ascertainable, measurable principle which, by enlightened preference, now operates from a recognition of *real* values.

For present purposes Darwin and Marx have been dragged on stage and subjected to rather perfunctory handling in order to illustrate the devolution of classical Utopia. Circular and finite Utopia was long a-dying. It remained beloved of the French disciples of Saint-Simon, Comte and Fourier; and it remained equally beloved of the American and English descendants of Robert Owen; but, if Marx had stigmatized all such proposals as pocket editions of Utopia, then, well before the end of the nineteenth century, there was a very different smell in the breeze; and, if Utopia had not ceased to be poetry, it had certainly become politics. The lay monasteries, the drop-out communes, the phalansteries of Owenite and Fourierist imagination had suddenly been swept away. Utopia had long long ceased to be a metaphorical city and it now ceased to be a fortified one. It became instead open, expansive and forward looking; and, with its form no longer showing any relationship to the imaginary music of the sphere, Utopia now came to present itself as an impulse or an axis of development. The surrender of circular, finite and Platonic Utopia to Utopia as extrusion one might suppose to be the meaning of Soria y Mata's proposal for a linear city of 1882; one might also suppose the same glad surrender to extrusion (this time vertical) to be also involved in the idealized Milan of Sant' Elia's fantasy; and, though it is never entirely satisfactory to attempt to make visual images speak for explicit ideas, what – with these particular images – might be suggested is their ultimate derivation from a body of thought which includes both Comte and Hegel, both Darwin and Marx.

Which is not to say that there is here anything explicitly Darwinian or Marxian: but which is to imply that, without the Darwinian and Marxian syntheses, such proposals as these would, probably, have been impossible. One notices the forward looking excelsior which both of them obtrude. They propound energy and extension. Fifty years earlier each would have been quite impossible. For both of these images advertise a situation without limits, a situation which was previously either unrecognized or unknown; and, particularly, the second, the later, the Futurist image, which can seem to celebrate the inexorable exigencies of power, may easily lend itself to interpretation as an emblem of the machine, or of the piston, now become the index of history.

And, at this stage, a turning point in argument is reached. For what to say about the generosity, the magnanimity, the largeness involved in the Futurist "protest"? Do we say that, inspired by Nietzsche and Sorel, it was a well publicized aspect of Italian aspirations towards *bella figura*? Or do we say with Igor Stravinsky that the Futurists were not the great big aeroplanes that they thought they were but, in spite of that, were a crowd of nice, noisy little Vespas. Or, following Kenneth Burke, do we observe that the Futurists made of abuse a virtue, that to the cry: *the streets are noisy*, they

replied: *we like it that way*, and to the clamour: *the drains smell*, they were apt to answer: *but we just love stink*? In any case, and if this may be part of the style of argument *à rebours* which characterized aspects of late nineteenth-century decadence, there still remains the spectacle of the futurist Utopia which is far less respectable than the Marxian one and which can only elicit the notice that Marinetti, the apostle of Futurism became Mussolini's esteemed (or tolerated) Minister of Culture.

But something like this, which is surely part of the *degringolade* of Futurism, ought to be noticed. The movement was abundantly prophetic and, perhaps, nowhere so much as in its decay. Futurism dealt with "inevitabilities" to which the emancipated, the bold and the free must, automatically, attach themselves; and it was something which, in its cult of violent action, rendered itself supremely available to authoritarian take-over. The rule of energy rather than the rule of law, the Futurist–Fascist sequence may also compel a comparison with the manner in which the Weimar Republic, abundantly a rule of love, transformed itself (by Spenglerian euthanasia?) into the Third Reich; and then this comparison may also permit the suspicion to be entertained that when active benevolence becomes the social goal it is probably time to look out. For, if the ideal society must and should be a feast of love, the suspicion might still be entertained that any existing society will be just as much structured by animosity and doubt.

And at this stage, when we are unavoidably presented with the issues of the *res publica* and the *res privata*, with our public socialist persona and our private capitalist drive, that one might revert yet again to the prophetic imagination of the 1920s and to its contemporary bureaucratic rendition, the cut-price *ville radieuse*, and, confronted with this squalid evolution, one might then proceed to ask whether this was indeed the necessary denouement, whether the prophetic imagination of 50 years ago really did conceive of itself as literal prescription? But the answer is, almost certainly, yes: Le Corbusier and others might have been constructing an ideal world, but they were also constructing a world which they believed to be imminent: and, in the process of constructing this world, whatever might have been its ideality has been reduced to platitude and, whatever might have been its poetry has been rendered as the most brutal prose.

So we are thus left with the metaphorical Utopia of the Renaissance which lent itself to no sudden and rapid degradation and the literal Utopia of the early twentieth century – post Marx, post Darwin, post Hegel, post Comte and Saint-Simon – which, almost invariably, has turned itself into its opposite. In St Louis, Pruitt-Igoe is built as the bureaucratic rendition of this Utopia; and then (and with possibly undue melodrama) Pruitt-Igoe is blown up, which is the obvious and matter-of-fact commentary upon the model bequeathed to us by the 1920s. There is the model, for all its merits heavily equipped with political and societal ambiguity: and then there is its derivative *which both inspires and deserves destruction.*

AFTER THE MILLENNIUM

The city of modern architecture which, now that it seems to have become an almost irresistible reality, has begun to invite so much criticism, has, of course, prompted two quite distinct styles of reaction which are neither of recent formulation. Perhaps in its origins, this city was a gesture to social and psychological dislocations brought about by the First World War and the Russian Revolution. One style of reaction has been to assert the inadequacy of the initial gesture. Modern architecture did not go far enough. Perhaps dislocation is a value in itself: perhaps we should have more of it: perhaps, hopefully embracing technology, we should now prepare ourselves for some kind of computerized surf ride, over and through the tides of Hegelian time, to some possibly ultimate haven of emancipation.

Such might seem to be the approximate inference of the Archigram image [an architecture that seeks to break the bonds of permanent stasis, moving across the landscape, adjusting to its temporal needs – a type of architectural and dynamic science fiction]; but we wish to parallel it with an image of which the inference is completely the reverse. As an exhibition of townscape, the Harlow town square involves a conscious attempt to placate and console. [Harlow was a mid-century British New Town, whose architecture was modern in form, but which based its urban pattern on traditional pedestrian experiences to evoke a familiar image of European, if not British, urbanism. Since the time

of this writing, it has undergone redevelopment.] The first image is ostensibly forward looking, the second deliberately nostalgic; and, if both are highly random, the randomness of the one is intended to imply all the vitality of an unprejudiced imaginary future, while the randomness of the other is intended to suggest all the casual differentiations which might have been brought about by the accidents of time. The implication of the second image is of an English market place (imaginably it could also be Scandinavian) which, though it is absolutely of the moment (the moment being c1950) is also a product of all the accumulations and vicissitudes of history.

[...]

However, an important issue, *the* important issue, remains the exclusiveness of both these images, the presumption of prophecy by the one, the assumption of nostalgia by the other. Like the two English images previously observed, the one is nearly all anticipation, the other almost all recollection; and, at this stage, it surely becomes relevant to propose the deep absurdity of this particular split which seems to be more a matter of heroic posture than of anything else.

Certainly it is a type of schism all the more gross because, on each side, there is an entirely false psychology assumed – a type of schism which scarcely helps. For, given that the fantasy of the comprehensive city of deliverance has lead to a situation which is abominable, the problem remains what to do. Reductionist Utopian models will certainly founder in the cultural relativism which, for better or worse, immerses us and it would seem only reasonable to approach such models with the greatest circumspection; the inherent debilitations of any institutionalized *status quo* ... would also seem to indicate that neither simple "give them what they want" nor unmodified townscape are equipped with sufficient conviction to provide more than partial answers; and, such being the case with reference to all of the prominent models, it becomes necessary to envisage a strategy which might, hopefully and without disaster, accommodate the ideal and which, plausibly and without devaluation, might respond to what the real might be supposed to be.

In a recent book, *The Art of Memory*, Francis Yates speaks of Gothic cathedrals as mnemonic devices. The bibles and the encyclopaedias of both the illiterate and the literate, these buildings were intended to articulate thought by assisting recollection; and, to the degree that they acted as Scholastic classroom aids, it becomes possible to refer to them as having been *theaters of memory*. And the designation is a useful one, because, if today we are only apt to think of buildings as necessarily prophetic, such an alternative mode of thinking may serve to correct our unduly prejudiced naiveté. The building as *theater of prophecy*, the building as *theater of memory* – if we are able to conceive of the building as the one, we must, also inherently be able to conceive of it as the other; and, while recognizing that without benefit of academic theory, these are both of them the ways in which we habitually interpret buildings, this memory–prophecy theater distinction might then be carried over into the urbanistic field.

Having said just so much and no more, it goes almost without saying that exponents of the city as prophecy theater will likely be thought of as radicals, while exponents of the city as memory theater will, almost certainly, be described as conservatives; but, if there might be some degree of truth in such assumption, it must also be established that block notions of this kind are not really very useful. The mass of mankind is likely to be, at any one time, both conservative and radical, to be preoccupied with the familiar and diverted by the unexpected; and, if we all of us both live in the past and hope for the future (the present being no more than an episode in time), it would seem reasonable that we should accept this condition. For, if without prophecy there can be no hope, then, without memory – there can be no communication.

Obvious, trite and sententious though this may be, it was – happily or unhappily – an aspect of the human mind which the early proponents of modern architecture were able to overlook – happily for them, unhappily for us. But, if without such distinctly perfunctory psychology "the new way of building" could never have come into being, there cannot any longer be excuse for the failure to recognize the complementary relationship which is fundamental to the processes of anticipation and retrospection. Interdependent activities we cannot perform without exercising them both; and no attempt to suppress either in the interest of the other can ever be protractedly successful. We may receive strength from the novelty of prophetic declamation;

but the degree of this potency must be strictly related to the known, the perhaps mundane and the necessarily memory-laden context from which it emerges.

The dichotomy of memory–prophecy, so important for modern architecture, might therefore be regarded as entirely illusory, as useful up to a point but academically absurd if pressed; and, if such may be allowed and, if it seems plausible that the ideal city which we carry in our minds should accommodate our known psychological constitution, it would seem to follow that the ideal city which might now be postulated should, at one and the same time, behave as both theater of prophecy and theater of memory.

CRISIS OF THE OBJECT: PREDICAMENT OF TEXTURE

We have so far attempted to specify two versions of the Utopian idea: Utopia as an, implicit, object of contemplation and Utopia as an, explicit, instrument of social change; we have then deliberately muddied this distinction by the introduction of fantasies of architecture as anticipation and architecture as retrospection; but briefly to forget these secondary issues: it would be facetious further to indulge speculation in the area of Utopian concern without first directing some attention to the evaluations of Karl Popper. For present purposes these are two essays of the late 1940s, *Utopia and Violence* and *Towards a Rational Theory of Tradition*; and it must be a matter of surprise that neither of these seems, so far, to have been cited for its possible commentary upon the architectural and urbanistic problems of today.

Popper, as might be expected, is hard on Utopia and, correspondingly, soft on tradition; but these essays should also be placed in the context of that massive criticism of simple inductivist visions of science, of all doctrines of historical determinism and of all theorems of the closed society which he has continuously conducted and which increasingly begins to appear as one of the more important twentieth century constructs. The Viennese liberal, long domiciled in England and using what appears to be a Whiggish theory of the state as the cutting edge of an attack upon Plato, Hegel and, not so incidentally, the Third Reich, it is in terms of this background that Popper must be understood as the critic of Utopia and the exponent of tradition's usefulness.

For Popper tradition is indispensable – communication rests upon tradition; tradition is related to a felt need for a structured social environment: tradition is the critical vehicle for the betterment of society; the "atmosphere" of any given society is related to tradition; and tradition is somewhat akin to myth – or, to say it in other words, specific traditions are somehow incipient theories which have the value, however imperfectly, of helping to explain society.

But such statements also require to be placed alongside the conception of science from which they derive; the conception of science as not so much the accumulation of facts but as the rigorous criticism of hypotheses. It is hypotheses which discover facts and not *vice versa*; and, seen in this way – so the argument runs – the role of traditions in society is roughly equivalent to that of hypotheses in science. That is: just as the formulation of hypotheses or theories results from the criticism of myth:

> *Similarly traditions have the important double function of not only creating a certain order or something like a social structure, but also of giving us something on which we can operate; something that we can criticize and change. (And) just as the invention of myth or theories in the field of natural science has a function – that of helping us to bring order into the events of nature – so has the creation of traditions in the field of society.*

And it is presumably for such reasons that a rational approach to tradition becomes contrasted by Popper with the rationalist attempt to transform society by the agency of abstract and Utopian propositions. These are *dangerous and pernicious*. Utopia proposes a consensus about objectives; and *It is impossible to determine ends scientifically. There is no scientific way of choosing between two ends.* This being so:

> *the problem of constructing a Utopian blue print cannot possibly be solved by science alone; since we cannot determine the ultimate ends of political actions scientifically . . . they will at least partly have the character of religious differences. And there can be no tolerance between these different Utopian*

religions. . . . The Utopianist must win over or else crush his competitors.

In other words, if Utopia proposes the achievement of abstract goods rather than the eradication of concrete evils, it is apt to be coercive since there can far more easily be a consensus about concrete evils than there can be about abstract goods; and, if Utopia introduces itself as a blueprint for the future, then it is doubly coercive since the future *cannot* be known to us. But, in addition to this, Utopia is particularly dangerous since the invention of Utopias is likely to occur in periods of rapid social change; and, when Utopian blueprints are liable to be rendered obsolete before they can be put into practice, then it is only too probable that the Utopian engineers will proceed to inhibit change – by propaganda, by suppression of dissident opinion, and if necessary, by physical force.

It is perhaps unfortunate in all this that Popper makes no distinction between Utopia as metaphor and Utopia as prescription; but, this being said, what we are here presented with (though the treatment of tradition is, perhaps, unduly sophisticated and the handling of Utopia certainly a little bitter and abrupt) is, by inference, one of the most completely devastating critiques of the twentieth-century architect and planner.

[. . .]

The maintained endorsements of Utopia are one thing, its criticism is another; but for the architect, of course, the ethical content of the good society has always been something which building was to make evident. Indeed it has, probably, always been his primary reference; for, whatever other controlling fantasies may have merged to assist him – antiquity, tradition, technology – these have invariably been conceived of as aiding and abetting, in some way, a benign or decorous social order.

[. . .]

In his famous essay Isaiah Berlin discriminates two personalities: the hedgehog and the fox. *The fox knows many things but the hedgehog knows one big thing.* This is the text which is chosen for elaboration and made to serve as a pretext for the following:

> *there exists a great chasm between those, on one side, who relate everything to a single central vision, one system less or more coherent or articulate, in*

terms of which they understand think and feel – a single, universal, organizing principle in terms of which all that they are and say has significance – and, on the other side, those who pursue many ends, often unrelated and even contradictory, connected, if at all, only in some de facto way, for some psychological or physiological cause; related by no moral or aesthetic principle; these last lead lives, perform acts, and entertain ideas which are cen-

trifugal rather than centripetal, their thought is scattered or diffused, moving on many levels, seizing upon the essence of a vast variety of experiences and objects for what they are in themselves, without, consciously or unconsciously seeking to fit them into or exclude them from anyone unchanging . . . at times fanatical, unitary inner vision. The first kind of intellectual and artistic personality belongs to the hedgehogs, the second to the foxes.

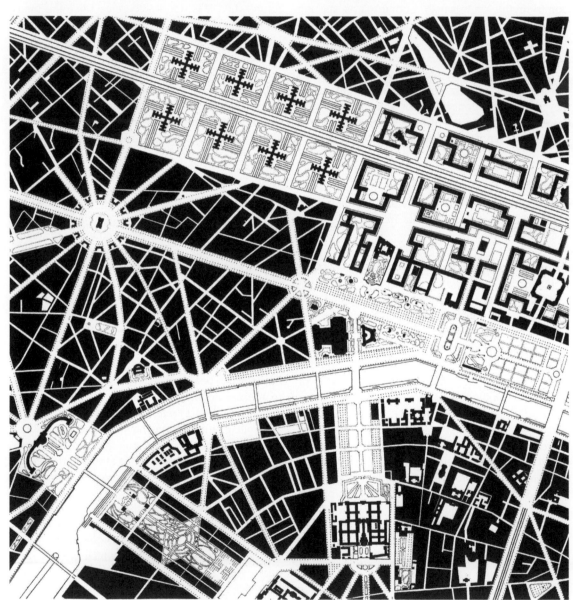

Figure 1 Figure ground drawing of Le Corbusier's Plan Voisin for Paris, 1925. The drawing clearly depicts Le Corbusier's modern insertions into the tight traditional urban fabric of Paris; (cruciform towers and linear garden apartments set in open space vs. blocks fully infilled with buildings that frame narrow streets as open space).

And the great ones of the earth divide fairly equally: Plato, Dante, Dostoevsky, Proust are, needless to say, hedgehogs; Aristotle, Shakespeare, Pushkin, Joyce are foxes. This is the rough discrimination; but, if it is the representatives of literature and philosophy who are the critical concern, the game may be played in other areas also. Picasso, a fox, Mondrian, a hedgehog, the figures begin to leap into place; and, as we turn to architecture, the answers are almost

entirely predictable. Palladio is a hedgehog, Giulio Romano, a fox; Hawksmoor, Soane, Philip Webb are probably hedgehogs, Wren, Nash, Norman Shaw almost certainly foxes; and, closer to the present day, while Wright is unequivocally a hedgehog, Lutyens is just as obviously a fox. But, to elaborate the results of, temporarily, thinking in such categories, it is as we approach the area of modern architecture that we begin to recognize the impossibility of arriving

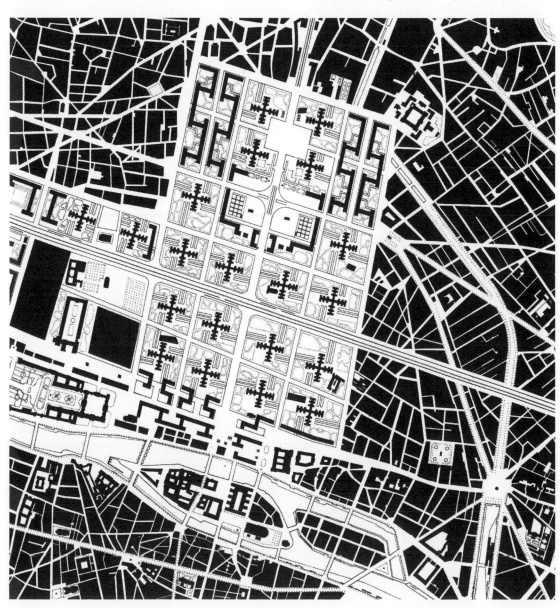

at any so symmetrical a balance. For, if Gropius, Mies, Hannes Meyer, Buckminster Fuller are clearly eminent hedgehogs, then where are the foxes whom we can enter into the same league? The preference is obviously one way. The *single, central vision* prevails. One notices a predominance of hedgehogs; but, if one might sometimes feel that fox-like propensities are surrounded with dubiety and, therefore, not to be disclosed, of course there still remains the job of assigning to Le Corbusier his own particular slot, *whether he is a monist or a pluralist, whether his vision is of one or of many, whether he is of a single substance or compounded of heterogeneous elements.*

These are questions which Berlin asks with reference to Tolstoy – questions which (he says) may not be wholly relevant; and then, very tentatively, he produces his hypothesis:

> *that Tolstoy was by nature a fox, but believed in being a hedgehog; that his gifts and achievement are one thing, and his beliefs, and consequently his interpretation of his own achievement, another; and that consequently his ideals have led him, and those whom his genius for persuasion has taken in, into a systematic misinterpretation of what he and others were doing or should be doing.*

Like so much other literary criticism shifted into a context of architectural focus, the formula seems to fit; and, if it should not be pushed too far, it can still offer partial explanation. There is Le Corbusier, the architect, with what William Jordy has called *his witty and collusive intelligence*. This is the person who sets up elaborately pretended Platonic structures only to riddle them with an equally elaborate pretence of empirical detail, the Le Corbusier of multiple asides, cerebral references and complicated *scherzi*; and then there is Le Corbusier, the urbanist, the deadpan protagonist of completely different strategies who, at a large and public scale, has the minimum of use for all the dialectical tricks and spatial involutions which, invariably, he considered the appropriate adornment of a more private situation. The public world is simple, the private world is elaborate; and, if the private world affects a concern for contingency, the would-be public personality long maintained an almost too heroic disdain for any taint of the specific.

But, if the situation of *complex house–simple city* seems strange (when one might have thought that the reverse was applicable) and, if to explain the discrepancy between Le Corbusier's architecture and his urbanism one might propose that he was, yet again, a fox assuming hedgehog disguise for the purposes of public appearance, this is to build a digression into a digression. We have noticed a relative absence of foxes at the present day; but, though this second digression may later be put to use, the whole fox–hedgehog diversion was initiated for ostensibly other purposes. It was initiated to establish Hadrian and Louis XIV as, more or less, free-acting representatives of these two psychological types who were autocratically equipped to indulge their inherent propensities; and then to ask of their products: which of these two might be felt the more exemplary for today – the accumulation of set pieces in collision or the total coordinated display? [Rowe and Koetter illustrate these two design types with the example of Hadrian's Villa (Villa Adriana) on the one hand, where its plan is comprised of a series of colliding classical architecture and landscape set pieces – which seem to have been randomly scattered within the landscape to provide surprise and unexpected relationship; versus the plan of Versailles, which exhibits a controlled axial regularity that dominates the overall layout – and is perceived here as less exciting, less adaptive, and less participatory over time from an evolutionary standpoint.]

Given the anti-Utopian polemic of Karl Popper, given the – fundamentally – anti-hedgehog innuendo of Isaiah Berlin, the bias of this argument should now be clear: it is better to think of an aggregation of small, and even contradictory, set pieces (almost like the products of different régimes) than to entertain fantasies about total and "faultless" solutions which the condition of politics can only abort. Its implication is an installation of the Villa Adriana as some sort of model presenting the demands of the ideal and the needs of the *ad hoc*; and its further implication is that some such installation begins, politically, to be necessary.

[...]

But, of course, the Villa Adriana is not simply a physical collision of set pieces. It is not merely a reproduction of Rome. For it also presents an inconography as complex as its plan. Here the reference is supposed to be Egypt, there we are supposed to be in Syria, and, elsewhere we might be in Athens; and thus, while *physically* the villa presents itself as a version of the Imperial metropolis, it further operates as an ecumenical illustration of the mix provided by the Empire and, almost as a series of momentos of Hadrian's travels . . . in Villa

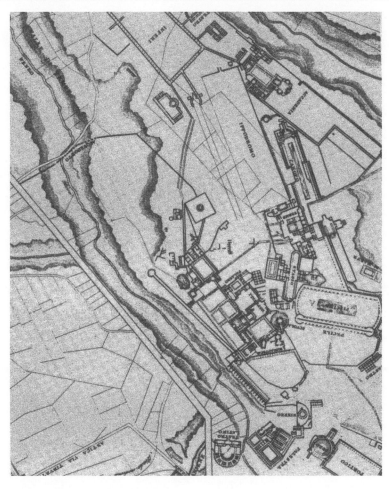

Figure 2 Plan of Hadrian's Villa, after Luigi Canina.

Adriana, we are in the presence of something like what, today, it is customary to speak of as *collage*.

COLLISION CITY AND THE POLITICS OF BRICOLAGE

The cult of crisis in the inter-war period: the before-it-is-too-late society must rid itself of outmoded sentiment, thought and technique; and if, in order to prepare for its impending deliverance, it must be ready to make *tabula rasa*, the architect as key figure in this transformation, must be ready to assume the historical lead. For the built world of human habitation and venture is the very cradle of the new order and, if he is properly to rock it, the architect must be ready to come forward as a front-line combatant in the battle for humanity. Perhaps, while claiming to be scientific, the architect had never previously operated within quite so

fantastic a psycho-political milieu; but, if this is to parenthesize, it was for such reasons – Pascal and reasons of the heart – that the city became hypothesized as no more than the result of "scientific" findings and a completely glad "human" collaboration. Such became the activist Utopian total design. Perhaps an impossible vision; and for those who, during the past 50 or 60 years (many of them must be dead) have been awaiting the establishment of this city, it must have become increasingly clear that the promise – such as it is – cannot be kept. Or so one might have thought; but, although the total design message has had a somewhat spotted career and has often elicited skepticism, it has remained, and possibly to this day, as the psychological substratum of urban theory and its practical application. Indeed it has been so little repressible that, in the last few years, a newly inspired and wholly literal version of this message has been

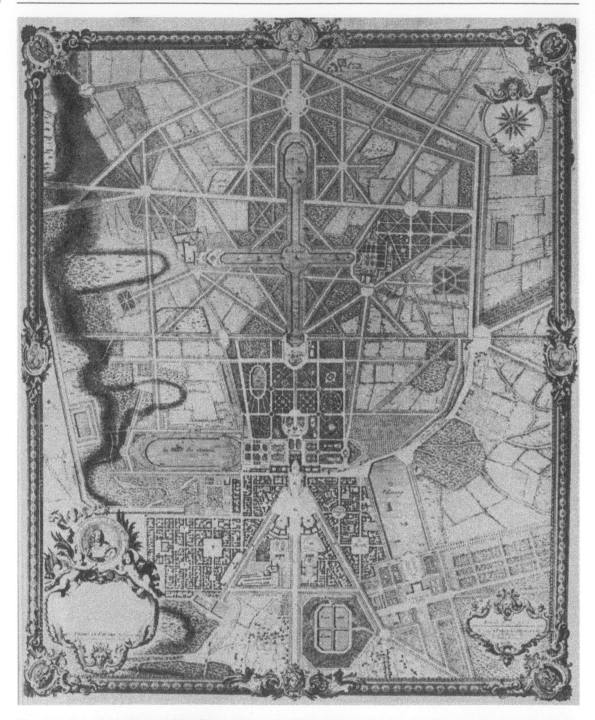

Figure 3 Plan of the Palace of Versailles and its surrounding landscape.

enabled to appear as renditions of the "systems" approach and other "methodological" finds.

We have largely introduced Karl Popper to support an anti-Utopian argument with which we do not wholly agree; but in our interpretation of the activist Utopia our indebtedness to Popper's position should surely be evident. It is a position which, particularly when stated at length as in *The Logic of Scientific Discovery* (1934) and *The Poverty of Historicism* (1957), is hard to evade; and one might have thought that the idea of modern architecture as science, as potentially part of a unified comprehensive science, ideally like physics (the best of all possible sciences) could scarcely have protracted itself to survive into a world which also included the Popperian critique of just such fantasies. But this is to misunderstand the hermetic and retarded nature of architectural debate: and, in those areas where Popperian criticism appears to be unknown and where the "science" of early modern architecture is also presumed to be painfully deficient, it goes without saying that the problem-solving methods proposed are laborious and often extended.

One has only to contemplate the scrupulousness of the operation in a text such as [Christopher Alexander's] *Notes on the Synthesis of Form* to get the picture. Obviously a "clean" process dealing with "clean" information, atomized, cleaned and then cleaned again, everything is ostensibly wholesome and hygienic; but, resulting from the inhibiting characteristics of commitment, especially physical commitment, the product seems never to be quite so prominent as the process. And something comparable might be said about the related production of stems, webs, grids and honeycombs which, in the later 1960s, became so conspicuous an industry. Both are attempts to avoid any imputation of prejudice; and if, in the first case, empirical facts are presumed to be value-free and finally ascertainable, in the second, the coordinates of a grid are awarded an equal impartiality. For, like the lines of longitude and latitude, it seems to be hoped that these will, in some way, eliminate any bias, or even responsibility, in a specification of the infilling detail.

But, if the ideally neutral observer is surely a critical fiction, if among the multiplicity of phenomena with which we are surrounded we observe what we wish to observe, if our judgments are inherently selective because the quantity of factual information is finally indigestible, and if any literal usage of a "neutral" grid labors under approximate problems, the myth of the architect as eighteenth century natural philosopher, with all his little measuring rods, balances and retorts, as both messiah and scientist, Moses and Newton (a myth which became all the more ludicrous after its annexation by the architect's less well-pedigreed cousin, the planner), must now be brought into proximity with *The Savage Mind* and with everything which *bricolage* represents.

There still exists among ourselves, says Claude Levi-Strauss, *an activity which on the technical plane gives us quite a good understanding of what a science we prefer to call "prior" rather than "primitive" could have been on the plane of speculation. This is what* is commonly called "bricolage" in French; and he then proceeds to an extended analysis of the different objectives of *bricolage* and science, of the respective roles of the "bricoleur" and the engineer:

> *In its old sense, the verb "bricoler" applied to ball games and billiards, to hunting, shooting and riding. It was however always used with reference to some extraneous movement: a ball rebounding, a dog straying or a horse swerving from its direct course to avoid an obstacle. And in our time the "bricoleur" is still someone who works with his hands and used devious means compared to those of the craftsman.*

Now there is no intention to place the entire weight of the argument which follows upon Levi-Strauss' observations. Rather the intention is to promote an identification which may, up to a point, prove useful; and, so much so, that, if one may be inclined to recognize Le Corbusier as a fox in hedgehog disguise, one may also be willing to envisage a parallel attempt at camouflage: the "bricoleur" disguised as engineer.

> *Engineers fabricate the tools of their time . . . Our engineers are healthy and virile, active and useful, balanced and happy in their work . . . our engineers produce architecture for they employ a mathematical calculation which derives from natural law.*

Such is an almost entirely representative statement of early modern architecture's most conspicuous prejudice. But then compare Levi-Strauss:

The bricoleur *is adept at performing a large number of diverse tasks; but, unlike the engineer, he does not subordinate each of them to the availability of raw materials and tools conceived and procured for the purpose of the project. His universe of instruments is closed and the rules of his game are always to make do with "whatever is at hand", that is to say with a set of tools and materials which is always finite and is also heterogeneous because what it contains bears no relation to the current project, or indeed to any particular project, but is the contingent result of all the occasions there have been to renew or enrich the stock or to maintain it with the remains of previous constructions or destructions. The set of the* bricoleur's *means cannot therefore be defined in terms of a project (which would pre-suppose besides, that, as in the case of the engineer, there were, at least in theory, as many sets of tools and materials, or "instrumental sets", as there are different kinds of projects). It is to be defined only by its potential use . . . because the elements are collected or retained on the principle that "they may always come in handy". Such elements are specialized up to a point, sufficiently for the* bricoleur *not to need the equipment and knowledge of all trades and professions, but not enough for each of them to have only one definite and determinate use. They represent a set of actual and possible relations; they are "operators", but they can be used for any operations of the same type.*

For our purposes it is unfortunate that Levi-Strauss does not lend himself to reasonable laconic quotation. For the *bricoleur*, who certainly finds a representative in "the odd job man," is also very much more than this. *It is common knowledge that the artist is both something of a scientist and of a "bricoleur"*; but, if artistic creation lies mid-way between science and *bricolage*, this is not to imply that the *bricoleur* is "backward". *It might be said that the engineer questions the universe while the "bricoleur" addresses himself to a collection of oddments left over from human endeavors*; but it must also be insisted that there is no question of primacy here. Simply, the scientist and the *bricoleur* are to be distinguished *by the inverse functions which they assign to events and structures as means and ends, the scientist creating events . . . by means of structures and the "bricoleur" creating structures by means of events.*

But we are here, now, very far from the notion of an exponential, increasingly precise "science"

(a speedboat which architecture and urbanism are to follow like highly inexpert water skiers); and, instead, we have not only a confrontation of the *bricoleur*'s "savage mind" with the "domesticated" mind of the engineer, but also a useful indication that these two modes of thought are not representatives of a progressive serial (the engineer illustrating a perfection of the *bricoleur*, etc) but are, in fact, necessarily co-existent and complementary conditions of the mind. In other words, we might be about to arrive at some approximation of Levi-Strauss *"pensee logique au niveau du sensible"*.

For, if we can divest ourselves of the deceptions of professional *amour propre* and accepted academic theory, the description of the *bricoleur* is far more a "real-life" specification of what the architect-urbanist is and does than any fantasy deriving from "methodology" and "systemics." Indeed the predicament of architecture which, because it is always, in some way or another, concerned with amelioration, with by some standard, however dimly perceived, making things better, with how things ought to be, is always hopelessly involved with value judgments and can never be scientifically resolved – least of all in terms of any simple empirical theory of "facts." And, if this is the case with reference to architecture, then, in relation to urbanism (which is not even concerned in making things stand up) the question of any scientific resolution of its problems can only become more acute. For, if the notion of a "final" solution through a definitive accumulation of all data is, evidently, an epistemological chimera, if certain aspects of information will invariably remain undiscriminated or undisclosed, and if the inventory of "facts" can never be complete because of the rates of change and obsolescence, then, here and now, it surely might be possible to assert that *the prospects of scientific city planning should, in reality, be regarded as equivalent to the prospects of scientific politics.*

For, if planning can barely be more scientific than the political society of which it forms an agency, in the case of neither politics nor planning can there be sufficient information acquired before action becomes necessary. In neither case can performance await an ideal future formulation of the problem as it may, at last, be resolved; and, if this is because the very possibility of that future where such formulation might be made depends on imperfect action now, then this is only once more to intimate the role of *bricolage* which politics so much resembles and city planning surely should.

But are the alternatives of "progressivist" total design (propelled by hedgehogs?) and "culturalist" *bricolage* (propelled by foxes?) genuinely, at the last analysis, all that we have available? We believe that they are; and we suppose that the political implications of total design are nothing short of devastating. No ongoing condition of compromise and expediency, of willfulness and arbitrariness, but a supremely irresistible combination of "science" and "destiny," such is the unacknowledged myth of the activist or historicist Utopia; and, in this complete sense, total design was, and is, make believe. For, on a mundane level, total design can only mean total control, and control not by abstractions relating to the absolute value of science or history but by governments of man; and, if the point scarcely requires emphasis, it can, still, not be too strongly asserted that total design (however much it may be loved) assumes for its implementation a level of centralized political and economic control which, given the presumption of political power as it now exists anywhere in the world, can only be considered thoroughly unacceptable.

The most tyrannical government of all, the government of nobody, the totalitarianism of technique. Hannah Ahrendt's image of a horror may also now come to mind; and, in this context, what deviousness of history and change, of the certainty of future sharp temporal caesuras, of the full tonality of societal gesture, a conception of the city as intrinsically, and even ideally, a work of *bricolage* begins to deserve serious attention. For, if total design may represent the surrender of logical empiricism to a most unempirical myth and if it may seem to envisage the future (when all will be known) as a sort of dialectic of non-debate, it is because the *bricoleur* (like the fox) can entertain no such prospects of conclusive synthesis, because, rather than with one world – infinitely extended though subjected to the same generalizations – his very activity implies a willingness and an ability to deal with a plurality of closed finite systems *(the collection of oddments left over from human endeavor)* that, for the time being at least, his behavior may offer an important model.

Indeed, if we are willing to recognize the methods of science and *bricolage* as concomitant propensities, if we are willing to recognize that they are,

both of them, modes of address to problems, if we are willing (and it may be hard) to concede equality between the "civilized" mind (with its presumptions of logical seriality) and the "savage" even be possible to suppose that the way for a truly useful future dialectic could be prepared.

A truly useful dialectic? The idea is simply the conflict of contending powers, the almost fundamental conflict of interest sharply stipulated, the legitimate suspicion about others' interests, from which the democratic process – such as it is – proceeds: and then the corollary to this idea is no more than banal: if such is the case, that is if democracy is compounded of libertarian enthusiasm and legalistic doubt, if it is inherently a collision of points of view and acceptable as such, then why not allow a theory of contending powers (all of them visible) as likely to establish a more ideally comprehensive city of the mind than any which has, as yet, been invented?

With the Villa Adriana already in mind, the proposition leads us (like Pavlov's dogs) automatically to the condition of seventeenth century Rome, to that inextricable fusion of imposition and accommodation, that highly successful and resilient traffic jam of intentions, an anthology of closed compositions and *ad hoc*: stuff in between which is simultaneously a dialectic of ideal types, plus a dialectic of ideal types with empirical context; and the consideration of seventeenth century Rome (the complete city with the assertive identity of its sub-divisions: Trastevere, Sant' Eustachio, Borgo, Campo Marzo, Campitelli . . .) leads to the equivalent interpretation of its predecessor where forum and *thermae* pieces lie around in a condition of inter-dependence, independence and multiple interpretability. And Imperial Rome is, of course, far the more dramatic statement. For, with its more abrupt collisions, more acute disjunctions, its more expansive set pieces, its more radically discriminated matrix and general lack of "sensitive" inhibition, Imperial Rome, far more than the city, of the High Baroque, illustrates something of the *bricolage* mentality at its most lavish – an obelisk from here, a column from there, a range of statues from somewhere else, even at the level of detail the mentality is fully exposed: and, in this connection, it is amusing to recollect how the influence of a whole school of historians was, at one time, strenuously dedicated to presenting the ancient Romans as

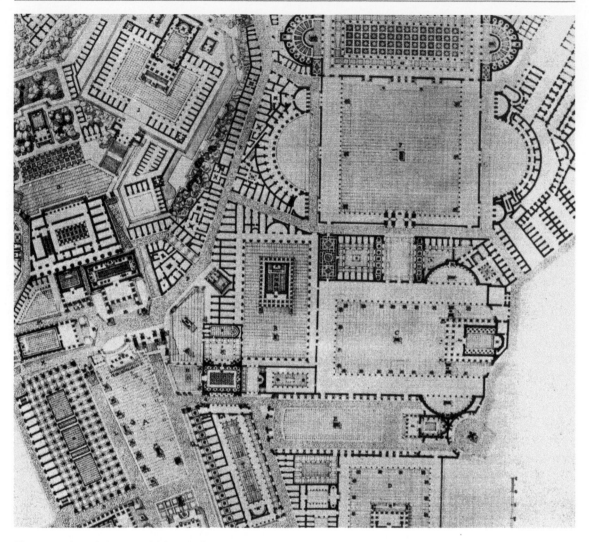

Figure 4 Plan of the Imperial Fora in Rome.

inherently nineteenth century engineers, precursors of Gustave Eiffel, who had somehow, and unfortunately, lost their way.

So Rome, whether Imperial or Papal, hard or soft, is here offered as some sort of model which might be envisaged as alternative to the disastrous urbanism of social engineering and total design. For, while it is recognized that what we have here are the products of a specific topography and two particular, though not wholly separable cultures, it is also supposed that we are in the presence of a style of argument which is not lacking in universality. That is: while the physique and the politics of Rome provide perhaps the most graphic example of *collisive fields* and *interstitial debris*, there are calmer versions.

Rome, for instance, is – if you wish to see it so – an imploded version of London: and the Rome–London model may, of course, perfectly well be expanded to provide a comparable interpretation of a Houston or a Los Angeles. But to introduce detail would be, unduly, to protract the argument: and simply to terminate: rather than any Hegelian *indestructible bond of the beautiful and the true*, rather than ideas of a permanent and future unity, we would prefer to consider the complementary possibilities of consciousness and sublimated conflict: and, if there is here urgent need for both the fox and the *bricoleur*, it is just possible that, in the face of prevailing scientism and conspicuous *laissez aller*, their activities could provide the true and constant *Survival Through Design*.

COLLAGE CITY AND THE RECONQUEST OF TIME

The tradition of modern architecture, always professing a distaste for art, has characteristically conceived of society and the city in highly conventional artistic terms – unity, continuity, system; but there is an alternative and apparently far more "art" prone method of procedure which, so far as one can see, has never felt any need for such literal alignment with "basic" principles. This alternative and predominant tradition of modernity – one thinks of such names as Picasso, Stravinsky, Eliot, Joyce – exists at a considerable remove from the ethos of modern architecture: and, because it makes of obliquity and irony a virtue, it by no means conceives itself to be equipped with a private pipe line to either the truths of science or to the patterns of history.

> *I have never made trials nor experiments, I can hardly understand the importance given the word research. Art is a lie which makes us realize the truth, at least the truth it is given us to understand. The artist must know the manner of convincing others of the truthfulness of his lies.*

With such statements as these of Picasso's one might be reminded of Coleridge's definition of a successful work of art (it might also be the definition of a successful political achievement) as that which encourages *a willing suspension of disbelief.* The Coleridgean mood may be more English, more optimistic, less drenched with Spanish irony: but the drift of thought – the product of an apprehension of reality as far from tractable – is much the same; and, of course, as soon as one begins to think of things in this way, all but the most entrenched pragmatist gradually becomes very far removed from the advertised state of mind and the happy certainties of what is sometimes described as modern architecture's "mainstream." For one now enters a territory from which the architect and the urbanist have, for the most part, excluded themselves. The vital mood is now completely trans-

formed. One is no less in the twentieth century; but the blinding self-righteousness of unitary conviction is at last placed alongside a more tragic cognition of the dazzling and the scarcely to be resolved multiformity of experience.

The two formulations of modernity which elaborate themselves may thus be more or less characterized; and, allowing for two contrasted modes of "seriousness", one may now think of Picasso's *Bicycle Seat (Bull's Head)* of 1944:

> *You remember that bull's head I exhibited recently? Out of the handlebars and the bicycle seat I made a bull's head which everybody recognized as a bull's head. Thus a metamorphosis was completed; and now I would like to see another metamorphosis take place in the opposite direction. Suppose my bull's head is thrown on the scrap heap. Perhaps some day a fellow will come along and say:* why there's something that would come in very handy for the handlebars of my bicycle . . . and so a double metamorphosis would have been achieved.

Remembrance of former function and value (bicycles and minotaurs); shifting context; an attitude which encourages the composite; an exploitation and recycling of meaning (has there ever been enough to go around?); desuetude of function with corresponding agglomeration of reference; memory; anticipation; the connectedness of memory and wit: this is a laundry list of reactions to Picasso's proposition; and, since it is a proposition evidently addressed to "people," it is in terms such as these, in terms of pleasures remembered and values desired, of a dialectic between past and future, of an impacting of iconographic content, of a temporal as well as a spatial collision, that, resuming an earlier argument, one might proceed to specify an ideal city of the mind.

With Picasso's image one asks: what is "false" and what is "true," what is "antique" and what is "of today"; and it is because of inability to make halfway adequate reply to this pleasing difficulty that one is obliged, finally, to identify the problem of composite presence (already prefigured at the Villa Adriana) in terms of *collage*. Collage and the architect's conscience, collage as technique and collage as state of mind: Levi-Strauss tells us that *the intermittent fashion for "collages", originating when craftsmanship was dying, could not . . . be anything but the* transposition of "bricolage" into the realms of contemplation; and, if the twentieth century architect has been the reverse of willing to think of himself as a *bricoleur*, it is in this context that one must also place his frigidity in relation to a major twentieth century discovery. Collage has seemed to be lacking in sincerity, to represent a corruption of moral principles, an adulteration. One thinks of Picasso's *Still Life with Chair Caning* of 1911–1912, his first collage, and begins to understand why.

In analyzing this production, Alfred Barr speaks of:

> the section of chair caning which is neither real nor painted but is actually a piece of oilcloth facsimile pasted on to the canvas and then partly painted over. Here in one picture Picasso juggles reality and abstraction in two media and at four different levels or ratios. (And) if we stop to think which is the most "real" we find ourselves moving from aesthetic to metaphysical contemplation. For what seems most real is most false and what seems most remote from everyday reality is perhaps the most real since it is at least an imitation.

And the oilcloth facsimile of chair caning, an *objet trouvé* snatched from the underworld of "low" culture and catapulted into the superworld of "high" art, might illustrate the architect's dilemma. For collage is simultaneously innocent and devious.

Indeed, among architects, only that great straddler Le Corbusier, sometimes hedgehog, sometimes fox, has displayed any sympathy towards this kind of thing. His buildings, though not his city plans, are loaded with the results of a process which might be considered more or less equivalent to that of collage. Objects and episodes are obtrusively imported and, while they retain the overtones of their source and origin, they gain also a wholly new impact from their changed context. In, for instance, the Ozenfant studio one is confronted with a mass of allusions and references which it would seem are all basically brought together by collage means.

Disparate objects held together by various means, *physical, optical, psychological*:

> the oilcloth with its sharp focused facsimile detail and its surface apparently so rough yet actually so smooth ... partly absorbed into both the painted surface and the painted forms by letting both overlap it

With very slight modifications (for oilcloth facsimile substitute fake industrial glazing, for painted surface substitute wall, etc) Alfred Barr's observations could be directly carried over into interpretation of the Ozenfant studio. And further illustrations of Le Corbusier as *collagiste* cannot be hard to find: the too obvious De Beistégui penthouse; the roofscapes – ships and mountains – of Poissy and Marseilles, random rubble at the Porte Molitor and the Pavilion Suisse; an interior from Bordeaux-Pessac; and, particularly, the Nestlé exhibition pavilion of 1928.

[...]

It is suggested that a collage approach, an approach in which objects (and attitudes) are conscripted or seduced from out of their context, is – at the present day – the only way of dealing with the ultimate problems of either or both, Utopia and tradition; and the provenance of the architectural objects introduced into the social collage need not be of great consequence. It relates to taste and conviction. The objects can be aristocratic or they can be "folkish," academic or popular. Whether they originate in Pergamum or Dahomey, in Detroit or Dubrovnik, whether their implications are of the twentieth or the fifteenth century, need be no great matter. Societies and persons assemble themselves according to their own interpretations of absolute reference and traditional value; and, up to a point, collage accommodates both hybrid display and the requirements of self-determination.

But up to a point: for if the city of collage may be more hospitable than the city of modern architecture, if it might be a means of accommodating emancipation and allowing all parts of a pluralist situation their own legitimate expression, it cannot any more than any other human institution be completely hospitable. For the ideally open city, like the ideally open society, is just as much a figment of the imagination as its opposite. The open and the closed society, either envisaged as practical possibilities, are both of them the caricatures of contrary ideals; and it is to the realm of caricature that one should choose to relegate all extreme fantasies of either emancipation or control. Thus, the bulk of Popper's arguments in favor of the emancipatory interest and the open society must surely be conceded; but, while the need for the reconstruction of an operative critical theory after its long negation by scientism, historicism, psychologism, should be evident, if we are concerned with the production of an open city for an open society, we may still be concerned with an imbalance in Popper's general position comparable to that in his critique of tradition and Utopia. This can seem to be a too exclusive focus on what, after all, are highly idealized empirical procedures; and a corresponding unwillingness to attempt any construction of positive ideal types.

[...]

Habitually Utopia, whether Platonic or Marxian, has been conceived of as *axis mundi* or as *axis istoriae*; but, if in this way it has operated like all totemic, traditionalist and uncriticized aggregations of ideas, if its existence has been poetically necessary and politically deplorable, then this is only to assert the idea that a collage technique, by accommodating a whole range of *axis mundi* (all of them vest pocket Utopias – Swiss canton, New England village, Dome of the Rock, Place Vendome, Campidoglio, etc) might be a means of permitting us the enjoyment of Utopian poetics without our being obliged to suffer the embarrassment of Utopian politics. Which is to say that, because collage is a method deriving its virtue from its irony, because it seems to be a technique for using things and simultaneously disbelieving in them, it is also a strategy which can allow Utopia to be dealt with as image, to be dealt with in *fragments* without our having to accept it *in toto*, which is further to suggest that collage could even be a strategy which, by supporting the Utopian illusion of changelessness and finality, might even fuel a reality of change, motion, action and history.

TWO

"Introduction," "The Life of Plazas," "Sitting Space," and, "Sun, Wind, Trees, and Water"

from *The Social Life of Small Urban Spaces* (1980)

William H. Whyte

Editors' Introduction

In working on an update of New York City's comprehensive plan in the late 1960s, William H. Whyte began pondering the design effectiveness of the city's plazas, playgrounds, and parks. Because of developers' growing desire for taller skyscrapers, the city had begun to grant density and height bonuses in exchange for public space amenities at the base of new buildings. Whyte applied for a grant to study plaza use, plaza form, general street life, playgrounds, and parks in New York and other cities. Along with a group of young, energetic research assistants, Whyte's Street Life Project researched the effectiveness and use of these public spaces over a multiyear period. The team developed innovative methods of observing and mapping physical activity in the public realm, including the use of time-lapse photography, film, unobtrusive observation, behavior mapping, questionnaires, personal interviews, and pedestrian path analysis.

In analyzing the data, many of the team's early hypotheses were either validated or refuted. Some of their key findings suggested the importance of seating supply and the adaptability of space for personal needs. Other findings about gender preferences, plaza size, sun exposure, and food vending were more surprising. Whyte's work was some of the first to recognize the impacts of the built environment on the behavioral differences of men and women; concluding that women were more careful in selecting preferred seat locations. Some of the broader conclusions from this work suggest that "what attracts people most, it would appear, is other people," and the necessity of well-used public spaces in facilitating greater civic engagement and community interaction – a function both of democracy and quality of life.

William Hollingsworth (Holly) Whyte (1917–1999) graduated from Princeton University, served in the Marine Corps and, in 1946, began his career at *Fortune Magazine* where he coincidentally came in contact with Jane Jacobs. Selling more than two million copies, his first literary triumph was *The Organization Man* (New York: Simon & Schuster, 1956), which chronicled the rise of corporate influence and the conformity of the middle class to corporate ideals in the mid-twentieth century. His books on urban form, public space, and design include an edited book, *The Exploding Metropolis* (New York: Doubleday, 1957); *The Last Landscape* (New York: Doubleday, 1968); and *City: Rediscovering the Center* (New York: Doubleday, 1988). A collection of Whyte's writings can be found in Albert LaFarge (ed.), *The Essential William H. Whyte* (New York: Fordham University Press, 2000).

The impacts of this book and the larger Street Life Project were numerous. In addition to the book, a short film of the same name was produced to help disseminate the results of the research to a wider audience. The Street Life Project helped the New York City Planning Commission implement new regulations and guidelines for subsequent development and design review. The observational and mapping methods of William

Whyte have been adopted by a number of built-environment researchers and his ideas were influential in the establishment of the Project for Public Spaces in New York City.

For additional reading on environmental behavior research and associated methods see: Edward T. Hall, *The Hidden Dimension* (New York: Doubleday, 1966); Robert Sommers, *Personal Space: The Behavioral Basis of Design* (Englewood Cliffs, NJ: Prentice-Hall, 1969); William H. Michelson, *Behavioural Research Methods in Environmental Design* (New York: John Wiley, 1975); Amos Rapoport, *Human Aspects of Urban Form: Towards a Man–Environment Approach to Form and Design* (Oxford: Pergamon, 1977); Marguerite and Michael Brill, *Environmental Design Research: Concepts, Methods and Values* (Washington, DC: National Endowment for the Arts, 1981); John Zeisel, *Inquiry by Design: Tools for Environment-Behavior Research* (Cambridge: Cambridge University Press, 1984) and *Inquiry by Design: Environment / Behavior / Neuro-science in Architecture, Interiors, Landscape, and Planning*, updated and revised edn (New York: W.W. Norton, 2006); Allan B. Jacobs, *Looking at Cities* (Cambridge, MA: MIT Press, 1985); and Jon Lang, *Creating Architectural Theory: The Role of the Behavioral Sciences in Environmental Design* (New York: Van Nostrand Reinhold, 1987). The Environmental Design Research Association also has several series of publications on this type of material.

INTRODUCTION

This book is about city spaces, why some work for people, and some do not, and what the practical lessons may be. It is a by-product of first-hand observation.

In 1970, I formed a small research group, The Street Life Project, and began looking at city spaces. At that time, direct observation had long been used for the study of people in far-off lands. It had not been used to any great extent in the U.S. city. There was much concern over urban crowding, but most of the research on the issue was done somewhere other than where it supposedly occurred. The most notable studies were of crowded animals, or of students and members of institutions responding to experimental situations – often valuable research, to be sure, but somewhat vicarious.

The Street Life Project began its study by looking at New York City parks and playgrounds and such informal recreation areas as city blocks. One of the first things that struck us was the *lack* of crowding in many of these areas. A few were jammed, but more were nearer empty than full, often in neighborhoods that ranked very high in density of people. Sheer space, obviously, was not of itself attracting children. Many streets were.

It is often assumed that children play in the street because they lack playground space. But many children play in the streets because they like to. One of the best play areas we came across was

a block on 101st Street in East Harlem. It had its problems, but it worked. The street itself was the play area. Adjoining stoops and fire escapes provided prime viewing across the street and were highly functional for mothers and older people. There were other factors at work, too, and, had we been more prescient, we could have saved ourselves a lot of time spent later looking at plazas. Though we did not know it then, this block had within it all the basic elements of a successful urban place.

As our studies took us nearer the center of New York, the imbalance in space use was even more apparent. Most of the crowding could be traced to a series of choke points – subway stations, in particular. In total, these spaces are only a fraction of downtown, but the number of people using them is so high, the experience so abysmal, that it colors our perception of the city around, out of all proportion to the space involved. The fact that there may be lots of empty space somewhere else little mitigates the discomfort. And there is a strong carry-over effect.

This affects researchers, too. We see what we expect to see, and have been so conditioned to see crowded spaces in center city that it is often difficult to see empty ones. But when we looked, there they were.

The amount of space, furthermore, was increasing. Since 1961, New York City has been giving incentive bonuses to builders who provided plazas.

For each square foot of plaza, builders could add 10 square feet of commercial floor space over and above the amount normally permitted by zoning. So they did – without exception. Every new office building provided a plaza or comparable space: in total, by 1972, some 20 acres of the world's most expensive open space.

We discovered that some plazas, especially at lunchtime, attracted a lot of people. One, the plaza of the Seagram Building, was the place that helped give the city the idea for the plaza bonus. Built in 1958, this austerely elegant area had not been planned as a people's plaza, but that is what it became. On a good day, there would be a hundred and fifty people sitting, sunbathing, picnicking, and schmoozing – idly gossiping, talking "nothing talk." People also liked 77 Water Street, known as "swingers' plaza" because of the young crowd that populated it.

But on most plazas, we didn't see many people. The plazas weren't used for much except walking across. In the middle of the lunch hour on a beautiful, sunny day the number of people sitting on plazas averaged four per 1,000 square feet of space – an extraordinarily low figure for so dense a center. The tightest-knit CBD (central business district) anywhere contained a surprising amount of open space that was relatively empty and unused.

If places like Seagram's and 77 Water Street could work so well, why not the others? The city was being had. For the millions of dollars of extra space it was handing out to builders, it had every right to demand much better plazas in return.

I put the question to the chairman of the City Planning Commission, Donald Elliott. As a matter of fact, I entrapped him into spending a weekend looking at time-lapse films of plaza use and nonuse. He felt that tougher zoning was in order. If we could find out why the good plazas worked and the bad ones didn't, and come up with hard guidelines, we could have the basis of a new code. Since we could expect the proposals to be strongly contested, it would be important to document the case to a fare-thee-well.

We set to work. We began studying a crosssection of spaces – in all, 16 plazas, 3 small parks, and a number of odds and ends. I will pass over the false starts, the dead ends, and the floundering arounds, save to note that there were a lot and that

the research was nowhere as tidy and sequential as it can seem in the telling. Let me also note that the findings should have been staggeringly obvious to us had we thought of them in the first place. But we didn't. Opposite propositions were often what seemed obvious. We arrived at our eventual findings by a succession of busted hypotheses.

The research continued for some three years. I like to cite the figure because it sounds impressive. But it is calendar time. For all practical purposes, at the end of six months we had completed our basic research and arrived at our recommendations. The City, alas, had other concerns on its mind, and we found that communicating the findings was to take more time than arriving at them. We logged many hours in church basements and meeting rooms giving film and slide presentations to community groups, architects, planners, businessmen, developers, and real-estate people. We continued our research; we had to keep our findings up-to-date, for now we were disciplined by adversaries. But at length the City Planning Commission incorporated our recommendations in a proposed new open-space zoning code, and in May 1975 it was adopted by the city's Board of Estimate. As a consequence, there has been a salutary improvement in the design of new spaces and the rejuvenation of old ones.

But zoning is certainly not the ideal way to achieve the better design of spaces. It ought to be done for its own sake. For economics alone, it makes sense. An enormous expenditure of design expertise, and of travertine and steel, went into the creation of the many really bum office building plazas around the country. To what end? As this manual will detail, it is far easier, simpler to create spaces that work for people than those that do not – and a tremendous difference it can make to the life of a city.

THE LIFE OF PLAZAS

We started by studying how people use plazas. We mounted time-lapse cameras overlooking the plazas and recorded daily patterns. We talked to people to find where they came from, where they worked, how frequently they used the place and what they thought of it. But, mostly, we watched people to see what they did [Figure 1].

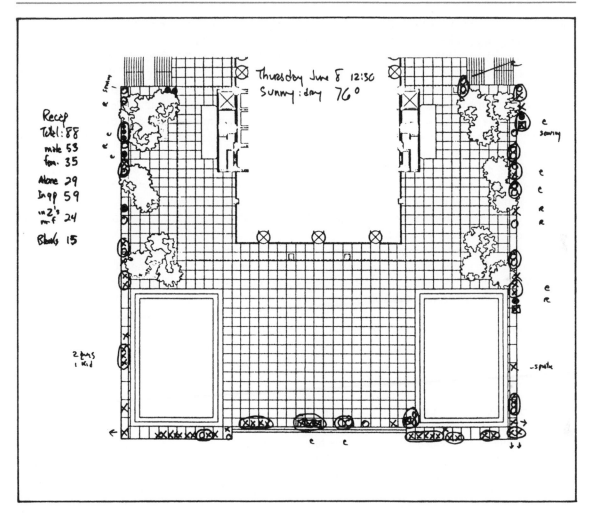

Figure 1 This is a typical sighting map. We found that one could map the location of every sitter, whether male (X), female (O), alone, or with others (XO), in about five minutes, little more time than a simple head count would take.

Most of the people who use plazas, we found, are young office workers from nearby buildings. There may be relatively few patrons from the plaza's own building; as some secretaries confide, they'd just as soon put a little distance between themselves and the boss. But commuter distances are usually short; for most plazas, the effective market radius is about three blocks. Small parks, like Paley and Greenacre in New York, tend to have more assorted patrons throughout the day – upper-income older people, people coming from a distance. But office workers still predominate, the bulk from nearby.

This uncomplicated demography underscores an elemental point about good urban spaces: supply creates demand. A good new space builds a new constituency. It stimulates people into new habits – al fresco lunches – and provides new paths to and from work, new places to pause. It does all this very quickly. In Chicago's Loop, there were no such amenities not so long ago. Now, the plaza of the First National Bank has thoroughly changed the midday way of life for thousands of people. A success like this in no way surfeits demand for spaces; it indicates how great the unrealized potential is.

The best-used plazas are sociable places, with a higher proportion of couples than you find in less-used places, more people in groups, more people meeting people, or exchanging goodbyes. At five of the most-used plazas in New York, the proportion of people in groups runs about 45 percent; in five of the least used, 32 percent. A high proportion of people in groups is an index of selectivity. When people go to a place in twos or threes or rendezvous there, it is most often because they have decided to. Nor are these sociable places less congenial to the individual. In absolute numbers, they attract more individuals than do less-used spaces. If you are alone, a lively place can be the best place to be.

The most-used places also tend to have a higher than average proportion of women. The male-female ratio of a plaza basically reflects the composition of the work force, which varies from area to area – in midtown New York it runs about 60 percent male, 40 percent female. Women are more discriminating than men as to where they will sit, more sensitive to annoyances, and women spend more time casting the various possibilities. If a plaza has a markedly lower than average proportion of women, something is wrong. Where there is a higher than average proportion of women, the plaza is probably a good one and has been chosen as such.

The rhythms of plaza life are much alike from place to place. In the morning hours, patronage will be sporadic. A hot-dog vendor setting up his cart at the corner, elderly pedestrians pausing for a rest, a delivery messenger or two, a shoeshine man, some tourists, perhaps an odd type, like a scavenger woman with shopping bags. If there is any construction work in the vicinity, hard hats will appear shortly after 11:00 A.M. with beer cans and sandwiches. Things will start to liven up. Around noon, the main clientele begins to arrive. Soon, activity will be near peak and will stay there until a little before 2:00 P.M. Some 80 percent of the total hours of use will be concentrated in these two hours. In mid and late afternoon, use is again sporadic. If there's a special event, such as a jazz concert, the flow going home will be tapped, with people staying as late as 6:00 or 6:30 P.M. Ordinarily, however, plazas go dead by 6:00 and stay that way until the next morning.

During peak hours the number of people on a plaza will vary considerably according to seasons and weather. The way people distribute themselves over the space, however, will be fairly consistent, with some sectors getting heavy use day in and day out, others much less. In our sightings we find it easy to map every person, but the patterns are regular enough that you could count the number in only one sector, then multiply by a given factor, and come within a percent or so of the total number of people at the plaza.

Off-peak use often gives the best clues to people's preferences. When a place is jammed, a person sits where he can. This may or may not be where he most wants to. After the main crowd has left, the choices can be significant. Some parts of the plaza become quite empty; others continue to be used. At Seagram's, a rear ledge under the trees is moderately, but steadily, occupied when other ledges are empty; it seems the most un-crowded of places, but on a cumulative basis it is the best-used part of Seagram's.

Men show a tendency to take the front-row seats, and, if there is a kind of gate, men will be the guardians of it. Women tend to favor places slightly secluded. If there are double-sided benches parallel to a street, the inner side will usually have a high proportion of women; the outer, of men.

Of the men up front, the most conspicuous are girl watchers. They work at it, and so demonstratively as to suggest that their chief interest may not really be the girls so much as the show of watching them. Generally, the watchers line up quite close together, in groups of three to five. If they are construction workers, they will be very demonstrative, much given to whistling, laughing, direct salutations. This is also true of most girl watchers in New York's financial area. In midtown, they are more inhibited, playing it coolly, with a good bit of sniggering and smirking, as if the girls were not measuring up. It is all machismo, however, whether uptown or downtown. Not once have we ever seen a girl watcher pick up a girl, or attempt to.

Few others will either. Plazas are not ideal places for striking up acquaintances, and even on the most sociable of them, there is not much mingling. When strangers are in proximity, the nearest thing to an exchange is what Erving Goffman has called civil inattention. If there are, say, two smashing blondes on a ledge, the men nearby will usually put on an elaborate show of disregard. Watch closely, however, and you will see them give themselves away with covert glances, involuntary primping of the hair, tugs at the earlobe.

Lovers are to be found on plazas. But not where you would expect them. When we first started interviewing, people told us we'd find lovers in the rear places (pot smokers, too). But they weren't usually there. They would be out front. The most fervent embracing we've recorded on film has usually taken place in the most visible of locations, with the couple oblivious of the crowd.

Certain locations become rendezvous points for coteries of various kinds. For a while, the south wall of Chase plaza was a gathering point for camera bugs, the kind who like to buy new lenses and talk about them. Patterns of this sort may last no more than a season – or persist for years. Some time ago, one particular spot became a gathering place for raffish younger people; since then, there have been many changeovers in personnel, but it is still a gathering place for raffish younger people.

Self-congestion

What attracts people most, it would appear, is other people. If I belabor the point, it is because many urban spaces are being designed as though the opposite were true, and that what people liked best were the places they stay away from. People often do talk along such lines; this is why their responses to questionnaires can be so misleading. How many people would say they like to sit in the middle of a crowd? Instead, they speak of getting away from it all, and use terms like "escape," "oasis," "retreat." What people *do*, however, reveals a different priority.

This was first brought home to us in a study of street conversations. When people stop to have a conversation, we wondered, how far away do they move from the main pedestrian flow? We were especially interested in finding out how much of the normally unused buffer space next to buildings would be used. So we set up time-lapse cameras overlooking several key street corners and began plotting the location of all conversations lasting a minute or longer.

People didn't move out of the main pedestrian flow. They stayed in it or moved into it, and the great bulk of the conversations were smack in the center of the flow – the 100 percent location, to use the real-estate term. The same gravitation characterized "traveling conversations" – the kind in which two men move about, alternating the roles of straight man and principal talker. There is a lot of apparent motion. But if you plot the orbits, you will find they are usually centered around the 100 percent spot.

Just why people behave like this, we have never been able to determine. It is understandable that conversations should originate within the main flow. Conversations are incident to pedestrian journeys; where there are the most people, the likelihood of a meeting or a leave-taking is highest. What is less explainable is people's inclination to remain in the main flow, blocking traffic, being jostled by it. This does not seem to be a matter of inertia but of choice – instinctive, perhaps, but by no means illogical. In the center of the crowd you have the maximum choice – to break off, to continue – much as you have in the center of a cocktail party, itself a moving conversation growing ever denser and denser.

People also sit in the mainstream. At the Seagram plaza, the main pedestrian paths are on diagonals from the building entrance to the corners of the steps. These are natural junction and transfer points and there is usually a lot of activity at them. They are also a favored place for sitting and picnicking. Sometimes there will be so many people that pedestrians have to step carefully to negotiate the steps. The pedestrians rarely complain. While some will detour around the blockage, most will thread their way through it.

Standing patterns are similar. When people stop to talk on a plaza, they usually do so in the middle of the traffic stream. They also show an inclination to station themselves near objects, such as a flagpole or a statue. They like well-defined places, such as steps, or the border of a pool. What they rarely choose is the middle of a large space.

There are a number of explanations. The preference for pillars might be ascribed to some primeval instinct: you have a full view of all comers but your rear is covered. But this doesn't explain the inclination men have for lining up at the curb. Typically, they face inwards, toward the sidewalk, with their backs exposed to the dangers of the street.

Foot movements are consistent, too. They seem to be a sort of silent language. Often, in a shmoozing group no one will be saying anything. Men stand bound in amiable silence, surveying the passing scene. Then, slowly, rhythmically, one of the men rocks up and down: first on the ball of the foot, then back on the heel. He stops. Another man starts the same movement. Sometimes there are reciprocal gestures. One man makes a half turn to the right. Then, after a rhythmic interval, another responds with a half turn to the left. Some kind of communication seems to be taking place here, but I've never broken the code.

Whatever they may mean, people's movements are one of the great spectacles of a plaza. You do not see this in architectural photographs, which typically are empty of life and are taken from a perspective few people share. It is quite misleading one. At eye level the scene comes alive with movement and color – people walking quickly, walking slowly, skipping up steps, weaving in and out on crossing patterns, accelerating and retarding to match the moves of the others. There is a beauty that is beguiling to watch, and one senses that the players are quite aware of it themselves. You see this, too, in the way they arrange themselves on steps and ledges. They often do so with a grace that they, too, must sense. With its brown-gray monochrome, Seagram's is the best of settings – especially in the rain, when an umbrella or two spots color in the right places, like Corot's red dots.

How peculiar are such patterns to New York? Our working assumption was that behavior in other cities would probably differ little, and subsequent comparisons have proved our assumption correct. The important variable is city size. As I will discuss in more detail, in smaller cities, densities tend to be lower, pedestrians move at a slower pace, and there is less of the social activity characteristic of high-traffic areas. In most other respects, pedestrian patterns are similar.

Observers in other countries have also noted the tendency to self-congestion. In his study of pedestrians in Copenhagen, architect Jan Gehl mapped bunching patterns almost identical to those observable here. Matthew Ciolek studied an Australian shopping center, with similar results. "Contrary to 'common sense' expectations," Ciolek notes, "the great majority of people were found to select their sites for social interaction right on or very close to the traffic lines intersecting the plaza. Relatively few people formed their gatherings away from the spaces used for navigation."

The strongest similarities are found among the world's largest cities. People in them tend to behave more like their counterparts in other world cities than like fellow nationals in smaller cities. Big-city people walk faster, for one thing, and they selfcongest. After we had completed our New York study, we made a brief comparison study of Tokyo and found the proclivity to stop and talk in the middle of department-store doorways, busy corners, and the like, is just as strong in that city as in New York. For all the cultural differences, sitting patterns in parks and plazas are much the same, too. Similarly, shmoozing patterns in Milan's Galleria are remarkably like those in New York's garment center. Modest conclusion: given the basic elements of a center city – such as high pedestrian volumes, and concentration and mixture of activities – people in one place tend to act much like people in another.

SITTING SPACE

In their use of plazas, New Yorkers were very consistent. Day in, day out, many of them would sit at certain plazas, few at others. On the face of it, there should not have been this variance. Most of the plazas we were studying were fairly comparable. With few exceptions, they were on major avenues and usually occupied a block front. They were close to bus stops and subway stations and had strong pedestrian flows on the sidewalks beside them. Yet when we rated plazas according to the number of people sitting on them at peak time, there was a very wide range – from 160 people at 77 Water Street to 17 at 280 Park Avenue.

How come? The first factor we studied was the sun. We thought it might well be the critical one, and our initial time-lapse studies seemed to bear this out. Subsequent studies did not. As I will note later, they showed that the sun was important, but did not explain the difference in the popularity of plazas.

Nor did aesthetics. We never thought ourselves capable of measuring such factors, but did expect our research to show the most successful plazas would tend to be the most pleasing visually. Seagram's seemed very much a case in point. Here again, the evidence proved conflicting. Not only was clean, elegant Seagram's successful; so was the fun plaza at 77 Water Street, which some architects look on as kitsch. We also noticed that the elegance and purity of a building's design seems to have little relationship to the use of the spaces around it.

The designer sees the whole building – the clean verticals, the horizontals, the way Mies turned his corners, and so on. The person sitting on the plaza may be quite unaware of such matters. He is more apt to be looking in the other direction: not up at other buildings, but at what is going on at eye level. To say this is not to slight the designer's eye or his handling of space. The area around Seagram's is a great urban place and its relationship to McKim, Mead & White's Racquet Club across the street is integral to it. My personal feeling is that a sense of enclosure contributes to the enjoyment of using the Seagram plaza. But I certainly can't prove this with figures.

Another factor we considered was shape. Urban designers believed this was extremely important and hoped our findings might support tight criteria for proportions and placement. They were particularly anxious to rule out "strip plazas" – long narrow spaces that were little more than enlarged sidewalks, and empty more often than not. Designers felt a developer shouldn't get bonuses for these strips, and to this end they wanted to rule out spaces the length of which was more than three times the width.

Our data did not support such criteria. We found that most strip plazas were, indeed, empty of people most of the time. But was the shape the cause? Some square plazas were empty, too, and several of the most heavily used places were, in fact, long narrow strips. One of the five most popular sitting places in New York is essentially an indentation in a building – and long and narrow. Our research did not prove shape unimportant or designers' instincts misguided; as with the sun, however, it did prove that other factors were more critical.

If not shape, could the *amount* of space be the key factor? Some conservationists were sure this would be it. In their view, people seek open spaces as a relief from the overcrowding they are normally subjected to, and it would follow that places affording the greatest feeling of light and space would draw the most. If we ranked plazas by the amount of space, there surely would be a positive correlation between the size of the plazas and the number of persons using them.

Once again, we found no clear relationship. Several of the smaller spaces had lots of people, several of the larger had lots of people, and several of the larger had very few people. Sheer space, it appears, does not draw people. In some circumstances, it can have the opposite effect.

What about the amount of *sittable* space? Here we begin to get close. The most popular plazas

tend to have considerably more sitting space than the less well-used ones. The relationship is rough. For one reason, the amount of sitting space does not include any qualitative factors: a foot of concrete ledge counts for as much as a foot of comfortable bench space. We considered weighting the figures on a point basis – so many points for a foot of bench with backrest, with armrests, and so on. This would have produced a nicer conformance. We gave up the idea, however, as too manipulative. Once you start working backwards this way, there's no end to it.

There was no necessity. No matter how many variables we checked, one point kept coming through. We at last saw that it was the major one:

People tend to sit most where there are places to sit.

This may not strike you as an intellectual bombshell, and, now that I look back on our study, I wonder why it was not more apparent to us from the beginning. Sitting space, to be sure, is only one of the many variables, and, without a control situation as a measure, one cannot be sure of cause and effect. But sitting space is most certainly prerequisite. The most attractive fountains, the most striking designs, cannot induce people to come and sit if there is no place to sit.

Integral sitting

Ideally, sitting should be physically comfortable – benches with backrests, well-contoured chairs. It's more important, however, that it be *socially* comfortable. This means choice: sitting up front, in back, to the side, in the sun, in the shade, in groups, off alone.

Choice should be built into the basic design. Even though benches and chairs can be added, the best course is to maximize the sittability of inherent features. This means making ledges so they are sittable, or making other flat surfaces do double duty as table tops or seats. There are almost always such opportunities. Because the elevation changes somewhat on most building sites, there are bound to be several levels of flat space. It's no more trouble to make them sittable than not to.

It takes real work to create a lousy place. Ledges have to be made high and bulky; railings put in;

surfaces canted. Money can be saved by not doing such things, and the open space is more likely to be an amenable one.

This is one of the lessons of Seagram's. Philip Johnson recounts that when Mies van der Rohe saw people sitting on the ledges, he was quite surprised. He had never dreamt they would. But the architects had valued simplicity. So there were no fussy railings, no shrubbery, no gratuitous changes in elevation, no ornamentation to clutter spaces. The steps were made easy and inviting. The place was eminently sittable, without a bench on it. The periphery includes some 600 feet of ledge and step space, which is just right for sitting, eating, and sunbathing. People use all of it.

So ledges ought to be sittable. But how should this be defined? If we wanted sittable ledges in the New York City zoning amendments we thought we would have to indicate how high or low ledges should be, how deep, and, since there were adversary proceedings ahead, be able to back up the specifications with facts.

The proceedings turned out to be adversary in a way we hadn't expected. The attack came on the grounds that the zoning was *too specific*. And it came not from builders, but from members of a local planning board. Rather than spell out the requirements in specific detail, the board argued, the zoning should deal only with broad directives – for example, make the place sittable – leaving details to be settled on a case-by-case basis.

Let me pause to deal with this argument. It is a persuasive one, especially for laymen, and, at the inevitable moment in zoning meetings when someone gets up and says, "Let's cut through all this crap and get down to basics," everyone applauds. Be done with bureaucratic nitpicking and legal gobbledygook.

But ambiguity is a worse problem. Most incentive zoning ordinances are very, very specific as to what the developer gets. The trouble is that they are mushy as to what he is to give, and mushier yet as to what will happen if later he doesn't. Vague stipulations, as many cities have learned, are unenforceable. What you do not prescribe quite explicitly, you do not get.

Lack of guidelines does not give builders and architects more freedom. It reinforces convention. That is why so few good plazas were built under the 1961 zoning resolution. There was no law

preventing builders from providing better plazas. There weren't any guidelines either. And most builders do not do anything far out of the ordinary. A few had sought special permits for amenities not countenanced by existing regulations. But the time-consuming route to obtain special permits makes the builder and architect run a gauntlet of city agencies, with innovation as likely to be punished as rewarded.

Sitting heights

One guideline we expected to establish easily was the matter of sitting heights. It seemed obvious enough that somewhere around 17 inches would probably be near the optimum. But how much higher or lower could a surface be and still be sittable? Thanks to the slope of sites, several of the most sat-upon ledges provided a range of continuously variable heights. The front ledge of Seagram's, for example, started at 7 inches at one corner, rising to 44 at the other. Here was a dandy chance, we thought, to do a definitive study. By repeated observation, we could record how many people sat at which point over the range of heights; as cumulative tallies built, preferences would become clear.

They didn't. At a given time there might be clusters of people on one part of the ledge, considerably fewer on another. But correlations didn't last. When we cumulated several months of observation, we found that people distributed themselves with remarkable evenness over the whole range of heights. We had to conclude that people will sit almost anywhere between a height of one foot and three, and this is the range specified in the new zoning. People will sit on places higher or lower, to be sure, but there are apt to be special conditions.

Another dimension is more important: the human backside. It is a dimension architects seem to have forgotten. Rarely will you find a ledge or bench deep enough to be sittable on both sides; some aren't deep enough to be sittable on one. Most frustrating are the ledges just deep enough to tempt people to sit on both sides, but too shallow to let them do so comfortably. Observe such places and you will see people making awkward adjustments. The benches at General Motors plaza are a case in point. They are 24 inches deep and normally used on only one side. On Sundays, however, a heavy influx of tourists and other people will sit on both sides of the benches. Not in comfort: they have to sit on the forward edge, erectly, and their stiff demeanor suggests a tacit truce.

Thus to another of our startling findings: ledges and spaces two backsides deep seat more people comfortably than those that are not as deep. While 30 inches will do it, 36 is better yet. The new zoning provides a good incentive. If a ledge or bench is 30 inches deep and accessible on both sides, the builder gets credit for the linear feet on each side. (The 30-inch figure is thoroughly empirical; it is derived from a ledge at 277 Park Avenue, the minimum-depth ledge we came across that was consistently used on both sides.)

For a few additional inches of depth, then, builders can double the amount of sitting space. This does not mean that double the number of people will use the space. They probably won't. But that is not the point. The benefit of the extra space is social comfort – more room for groups and individuals to sort themselves out, more choices and more perception of choices.

Steps work for the same reason. The range of space provides an infinity of possible groupings, and the excellent sight-lines make virtually all the seats great for watching the theater of the street. The new zoning ordinance does not credit steps as sitting space. It was felt that this would give builders too easy an out and that some plazas would be all steps and little else. But the step principle can be applied with good effect to ledges.

Corners are functional. You will notice that people often bunch at the far end of steps, especially when an abutting ledge provides a right angle. These areas are good for face-to-face sitting. People in groups gravitate to them.

One might, as a result, expect a conflict, for corners are also the places where pedestrian traffic is heaviest. Most people take short cuts, and pedestrian flows in plazas are usually on the diagonals between the building entrance and the corners of the steps. We see this at Seagram's. As mentioned previously, the main flow to and from the building cuts directly across the step corners, and it is precisely there that you will find the heaviest concentration of people sitting, sunbathing, and picnicking. But, for all the bustle, or because of it, the sitters seem to feel comfortable. The walkers

don't seem to mind either, and will carefully negotiate through the blockages rather than detour around them.

We find similar patterns at other places. All things being equal, you can calculate that where pedestrian flows bisect a sittable place, that is where people will most likely sit. And it is not so perverse of them. It is by choice that they do. If there is some congestion, it is an amiable one, and a testimonial to the place.

Circulation and sitting, in sum, are not antithetical but complementary. It is to encourage both that the zoning stipulates the plaza not be more than three feet above or below street level. The easier the flow between street and plaza, the more likely people are to move between the two – and to tarry and sit.

This is true of the handicapped, too. If circulation and amenities are planned with them in mind, the place is apt to function more easily for everyone. Drinking fountains that are low enough for wheelchair users are low enough for children. Pedestrian paths that are made easier for the handicapped by ramps, handrails, and steps of gentle pitch are easier for all. The new zoning makes such amenities mandatory, specifying, among other things, that all steps along the main access paths have treads at least 11 inches deep, closed risers no higher than 7.5 inches, and that ramps be provided alongside them. For the benefit of the handicapped, the zoning also requires that at least 5 percent of the seating spaces have backrests. These are not segregated for the handicapped, it should be noted. No facilities are segregated. The idea is to make all of a place usable for everyone.

Benches

Benches are artifacts the purpose of which is to punctuate architectural photographs. They're not so good for sitting. There are too few of them; they are too small; they are often isolated from other benches or from whatever action there is on the plaza. Worse yet, architects tend to repeat the same module in plaza after plaza, unaware that it didn't work very well in the first place. For example, Harrison and Abramowitz's plazas at Rockefeller Center are excellent in many respects, but the basic bench module they've stuck to is exquisitely wrong in its dimensions – 7.5 feet by 19 inches. A larger rectangle would be proportionately as good but work vastly better, as some utilitarian benches in the same area demonstrate.

The technological barriers to better bench design are not insuperable. The prime specification, that benches be generously sized, is the easiest to meet. Backrests and armrests are proved devices. The old-fashioned park bench is still one of the best liked because it provides them; of the newer designs that also do, some of the stock ones of the play- and park-equipment manufacturers are best. Architects have had a way with chairs; for some reason they seem to come a cropper with benches.

They do worst when they freeze their bench designs in concrete permanence. If some of their assumptions prove wrong – that, say, people want to sit away from the action – it will be too late to do much about it. This has been a problem with a number of pedestrian malls, where all design bets were made before the mall was opened. If some of the sitting areas go unused, there's no easy way of heeding the lesson, or, indeed, of recognizing that there is one.

Why not experiment? Some features, like ledges and steps, will be fixed, but benches and chairs don't have to be. With sturdy wooden benches or the like, some simple market research can be done to find out where and in what kind of groupings they work best. People will be very quick to let you know. We have found that by the second day the basic use patterns will be established, and these won't change very much unless the set-up is changed. And it will be clear in what direction the changes should be made.

If one looks. This is the gap. Rarely will you ever see a plan for a public space that even countenances the possibility that parts of it might not work very well: that calls for experiment and testing, and for post-construction evaluation to see what does work well and what doesn't. Existing spaces suffer a similar fate. There are few that could not be vastly improved, but rarely is an evaluation undertaken. The people responsible for the place are the least likely of all to consider it.

Chairs

Now, a wonderful invention – the movable chair. Having a back, it is comfortable; more so, if it has an armrest as well. But the big asset is movability. Chairs enlarge choice: to move into the sun, out of it, to make room for groups, move away from them. The possibility of choice is as important as the exercise of it. If you know you can move if you want to, you feel more comfortable staying put. This is why, perhaps, people so often move a chair a few inches this way and that before sitting in it, with the chair ending up about where it was in the first place. The moves are functional, however. They are a declaration of autonomy, to oneself, and rather satisfying.

Small moves say things to other people. If a newcomer chooses a chair next to a couple or a larger group, he may make some intricate moves. Again, he may not take the chair very far, but he conveys a message. Sorry about the closeness, but there's no room elsewhere, and I am going to respect your privacy, as you will mine. A reciprocal move by one of the others may follow. Watching these exercises in civility is itself one of the pleasures of a good place.

Fixed individual seats are not good. They are a design conceit. Brightly painted and artfully grouped, they can make fine decorative elements: metal loveseats, revolving stools, squares of stone, sitting stumps. But they are set pieces. That is the trouble with them. Social distance is a subtle measure, ever changing, and the distances of fixed seats do not change, which is why they are rarely quite right for anybody. Loveseats may be all right for lovers, but they're too close for acquaintances, and much too close for strangers. Loners tend to take them over, placing their feet squarely on the other seat lest someone else sit on it.

Fixed seats are awkward in open spaces because there's so much space around them. In theaters, strangers sit next to each other without qualm; the closeness is a necessity, and convention makes it quite tolerable. On plazas, the closeness is gratuitous. With so much space around, fixed-seat groupings have a manipulative cuteness to them. The designer is saying, now you sit right here and you sit there. People balk. In some instances, they wrench the seats from their moorings. Where there is a choice between fixed seats and other kinds of sitting, it is the other that people choose.

To encourage the use of movable chairs, we recommended that in the zoning amendment they be credited as 30 inches of sitting space, though most are only about 19 inches wide. The Building Department objected. It objected to the idea of movable chairs at all. The department had the responsibility of seeing that builders lived up to requirements. Suppose the chairs were stolen or broken and the builder didn't replace them? Whether the department would ever check up in any event was a moot point, but it was true that the fewer such amenities to monitor, the easier the monitoring would be.

Happily, there was a successful record at Paley and Greenacre parks to point to, and it was decisively persuasive. The chairs stayed in. They have become a standard amenity at new places, and the maintenance experience has been excellent. Managements have also been putting in chairs to liven up existing spaces, and, even without incentives, they have been adding more chairs. The most generous provider is the Metropolitan Museum of Art. Alongside its front steps, it puts out up to 200 movable chairs and it leaves them out, 24 hours a day, seven days a week. The Met figured that it might be less expensive to trust people and to buy replacements periodically rather than have guards gather the chairs in every night. That is the way it has worked out. There is little vandalism.

How much sitting space?

A key question we had to confront was how much sitting space should be required. We spent a lot of time on this – much too much, I now realize – and I'm tempted to recount our various calculations to demonstrate how conscientious we were. The truth is that almost any reasonable yardstick would work as well as ours. It's the fact of one that is important.

This said, let me tell how conscientious we were. We measured and remeasured the sitting space on most of the plazas and small parks in midtown and downtown New York. As sitting space, we included all the spaces meant for people to sit on, such as benches, and the spaces they sat on whether meant to or not, such as ledges. Although architects' plans were helpful, we did most of the measuring with a tape, on the ground, in the process stirring inordinate curiosity from passersby and guards.

Next, we related the amount of sitting space to the size of the plaza. The square feet of sitting space on the best-used plazas ran between 6 and 10 percent of the total open space. As a ballpark figure, it looked like somewhere around 10 percent would be a reasonable minimum to require of builders.

For other comparisons we turned to linear feet. This is a more precise measure of sitting space than square feet, and a more revealing one. As long as there's some clearance for one's back, the additional square inches behind one don't matter very much. It is the edges of sitting surface that do the work, and it is the edges that should be made the most of.

For a basis of comparison, we took the number of linear feet around the total site. Since the perimeter includes the building, the distance is a measure of the bulk of the project and its impact on the surrounding environment. Amenities should therefore be in some proportion to it. On the most popular plazas, there were almost as many feet of sitting space as there were perimeter feet. This suggested that, as a minimum, builders could be asked to provide that amount of sitting space.

Even on the best plazas, the architects could have done better. To get an idea of how much better, we calculated the additional space that could have been provided on various plazas rather easily, while the original plans were being made. We did not posit any changes in basic layout, nor did we take the easy way of adding a lot of benches. We concentrated on spaces that would be integral to the basic design.

In most cases, it was possible to add as much as 50 percent more sitting space, and very good space at that. The Exxon plaza, for example, has a fine pool bordered by two side ledges that you can't sit on. You can sit on the front and back ledges, but only on the sides facing away from the pool. With a few simple changes, such as broadening the ledges, sitting capacity could have been doubled, providing some of the best poolside space anywhere. All in all, these examples indicated, builders could easily furnish as many feet of sitting space as there are feet around the perimeter of the project.

The requirement finally settled on was a compromise: one linear foot of sitting space for every thirty square feet of plaza. This is reasonable, and builders have been meeting the requirement with no trouble. They could meet a stiffer one. The exact ratio is not as important, however, as the necessity of considering the matter. Once an architect has to start thinking of ways to make a place sittable, it is virtually impossible not to surpass any minimum. And other things follow. More thought must be given to probable pedestrian flows, placement of steps, trees, wind baffles, sun traps, and even wastebaskets. One felicity leads to another. Good places tend to be all of a piece – and the reason can almost always be traced to a human being.

SUN, WIND, TREES, AND WATER

Sun

The most satisfying film I've ever seen is our first time-lapse record of the sun passing across the Seagram plaza. In late morning, the plaza was in shadow. Then, shortly before noon, a narrow wedge of sunlight began moving across the plaza and, as it did, so did the sitters. Where there was sun, they sat; where there was none, they didn't. It was a perfectly splendid correlation, and I cherished it. Like the urban designers, I believed a southern exposure of critical importance. Here was abundant proof.

Then something went wrong. The correlations vanished – not only at Seagram's but at other places we were studying. The sun still moved; the people didn't. The obvious at length dawned on us: May had been followed by June. While midday temperatures hadn't risen a great deal, the extra warmth was enough to make the sun no longer the critical factor.

It was about this time that much of Paley Park's sunlight began to be cut off by an office building going up across the street. From its scaffolding we focused time-lapse cameras on the park and recorded the effect of the new building. It was surprisingly little. Although the sunlight was curtailed, people used Paley as much as they had before. Perhaps they would have used it more had the sun remained; without an identical place as control, one can never be sure. The more important point is that, unfortunate as the loss may have been, the park was able to sustain it.

What simple figures don't measure, however, is the quality of the experience, which can be much greater when there is sun. For then you have choice – of sun, or shade, or in-between. The best time

to sit beneath a tree is when there is sunlight to be shaded from. The more access to sun, the better, and, if there is a southern exposure, it should be made the most of. New York's zoning now requires that new plazas and open spaces be so oriented.

Access to the sun should be protected. One way of doing so is by acquiring air rights to low buildings across the way, so they will stay low. This can be expensive, very much so if the speculative pressures in the area are rising. For the same reason, however, purchase can prove a good investment. The rights can have a high leverage over subsequent development, and there would be the possibility of selling part of the rights for construction designed to cast minimum shadow on the open space. At present, most air-rights transactions involve purchase of unused rights over one building so that another one can be built higher than normally permissible. It would not be a bad idea to apply the principle the other way around to keep bulk lower than permissible.

On the other hand, there is a good side to our seemingly negative findings about the importance of the sun: places that have little or no sun because of a northern exposure or intervening buildings are not a lost cause. With adroit design, they can be made to seem as if they had sun.

Why not borrow sun? The same new buildings that cast shadows also reflect light in considerable amounts. Along with mirror walls, glass and stainless steel, architects have been laying on travertine with a heavy hand, and their new buildings have sent the glare index of cities soaring. But light has also been bouncing into many places that didn't receive it before. In eight years of filming, I have found that several streets have become photographically a half-stop faster. A number of open spaces that otherwise would be dark much of the time are bathed in reflected light, sometimes on the second or third bounce. Grace Plaza, for example, gets no direct sun at all but benefits most of the afternoon from light reflected by the southern exposure of the building to the north. Give travertine its due. It bounces light admirably, especially in the late afternoon, when it can give a benign glow to the streetscape.

So far such effects are wholly inadvertent. Sun studies made for big new buildings tend to be defensive in nature, so that planning boards can be shown the building won't cast an awful lot more shadow than is cast already by other buildings. Few studies try to determine the light a new building will cast, what benefits there might be from it, to whom and when.

Yet benefits of great potential value can be planned and negotiated in advance. There could be, for example, sun easements, through which, in effect, the developer of a building sells reflected light to neighbors. On an incentive basis, the program could be administered by the city's planning commission, with the developer given bonus points for the benefits reflected. The complexities, of course, might be awesome, but they are the kind of complexities that lawyers and planners involved in urban design find stimulating.

Warmth is just as important as sunlight. The days that bring out the peak crowds on plazas are not the sparkling sunny days with temperatures in the seventies, good as this weather might be for walking. It is the hot, muggy days, sunny or overcast, the kind that could be expected to make people want to stay inside and be air conditioned, when you will find the peak numbers outside. People do like warmth. In summer, they will generally sit in the sun as well as in shade; only in very hot weather – 90 degrees or more – will the sunny spots be vacant. Relative warmth is important, too. One of the peak sitting days is the first warm day in spring, even though the same temperature later would be felt too cool for sitting. Similarly, the first warm day after a stretch of cool or rainy days will be a peak day.

Cool weather can be good for sitting, too. It is then that a space open to the radiant heat of the sun's rays can make the difference between sitting comfortably and not sitting at all. People will actively seek the sun and, given the right spots, they will sit in surprising numbers in quite cold weather. The more northern the latitude, the more ardently will they do so.

Wind

What people seek are suntraps. And the absence of winds and drafts are as critical for these as sun. In this respect, small parks, especially those enclosed on three sides, function well. Physically and psychologically, they feel comfortable, and this is one of the reasons why their relative carrying capacity is so high. New York's Greenacre Park has infrared heaters, but they are used only in extremely cold weather. With sun and protection from wind, the park is quite habitable even on nippy days.

Spaces around new buildings are quite another matter. In winter, many are cold and drafty, and even in moderate weather few people will tarry in such places. The errors are of omission. Wind-tunnel tests on models of new buildings are now customary, but they are not made with people much in mind. The tests for the World Trade Center largely determined stresses in the towers, and the structural steel necessary. What the towers themselves might generate in the way of wind, and the effects on people below, apparently were not a matter of much concern.

The effects are, however, quite measurable. It is now well established that very tall, free-standing towers can generate tremendous drafts down their sides. This has in no way inhibited the construction of such towers, with the result, predictably, that some spaces are frequently uninhabitable. At one bank plaza in Seattle the gusts are sometimes so fierce that safety lines must be strung across the plaza to give people something to hang on to. Chicago has the windiest places, not because of the local wind (which isn't really so very much stronger than in other cities), but because the drafts down the sides of the giant John Hancock and Sears towers are macro in force – often so strong as to prevent people from using the plazas, even if they had reason to.

James Marston Fitch, who has done more than any other architect to badger the profession to consider environmental effects, points out that the problem is conceptual, not technical.

Adverse effects are simply ignored, and the outdoor space designed as if for some ideal climate, ever sunny and pleasantly warm. Thus [the spaces] fail in their central pretension – that of eliminating gross differences between architectural and urbanistic spaces, of extending in time the areas in which urban life could freely flow back and forth between the two.

Technically, as Fitch points out, we can greatly lengthen the effective season of outdoor spaces. By asking the right questions in sun and wind studies, by experimentation, we can find better ways to hoard the sun, to double its light, or to obscure it, or to cut down breezes in winter and induce them in summer. We can learn lessons in the semi-open niches and crannies that people often seek. Most new urban spaces are either all outdoors or all indoors; more could be done to encourage in-betweens. With the use of glass canopies or small pavilions, semi-outdoor spaces could be created that would be usable in all but the worst weather. They would be particularly appropriate in rainy cities, like Seattle and Portland.

Trees

There are all sorts of good reasons for trees, but for climatic reasons alone we should press for many more of them, big ones too, along the sidewalks and open spaces of the city. New York's new open space zoning has sharply stepped-up require-ments: developers must provide a tree for every 25 feet of sidewalk. It must be at least 3.5 inches in diameter and planted flush with the ground. In plazas, trees must be provided in proportion to the space (for a plaza of 5,000 feet, a minimum of six trees).

Trees ought to be related much more closely to sitting spaces than they usually are. Of the spaces we have studied, by far the best liked are those affording a good look at the passing scene and the pleasure of being comfortably under a tree while doing so. This provides a satisfying enclosure; people feel cuddled, protected – very much as they do under the awning of a street cafe. As always, they'll be cooler, too.

Unfortunately, guy wires and planting beds often serve to rule out any sitting; even if they don't, the fussiness of design details works to the same effect. Everything is so wired and fenced you can neither get to the tree or sit on what surrounds it. Where large planters are used, they are generally too high and their rims too narrow for comfort.

Developers should be encouraged to combine trees and sitting spaces. They should also encour-age planting trees in groves. As Paley Park has demonstrated, if trees are planted closely together, the overlapping foliage provides a combination of shade and sunlight that is very pleasing. Arbors can do the same.

Water

Water is another fine element, and designers are doing rather well with it. New plazas and parks provide water in all sorts of forms: waterfalls, water-walls, rapids, sluiceways, tranquil pools, water tunnels, meandering brooks, fountains of all kinds. In only one major respect is something lacking: access.

One of the best things about water is the look and feel of it. I have always thought that the water at Seagram's looked unusually liquid, and I think it's because you know you can splash your hand in it if you are of a mind to. People do it all the time: they stick their hands in it, their toes, and feet, and, if they splash about, some security guard does not come rushing up to say them nay.

But in many places water is only for looking at. Let a foot touch it and a guard will be there in an instant. Not allowed. Chemicals in the water. Danger of contamination. If you let people start touching water, you are told, the next thing they'll start swimming in it. Sometimes they do. The new reflecting pool at the Christian Science Headquarters in Boston is only a few feet deep, but when it first opened many people started using it for wading and even swimming. It was with some difficulty that the pool was put off limits to such activity and reclaimed for its ornamental function.

It's not right to put water before people and then keep them away from it. But this is what has been happening across the country. Pools and fountains are installed, then immediately posted with signs admonishing people not to touch. Equally egregious is the excessive zeal with which many pools are continually emptied, refilled, vacuumed, and cleaned, as though the primary function of them was their maintenance. Grand Old Buckingham Fountain in Chicago's Grant Park has been put off limits with an electrified fence.

Safety is the usual reason given for keeping people away. But there are better ways than elec-trocution to handle this problem. At the Auditorium Forecourt Fountain in Portland, Oregon, people have been climbing up and down a complex of sluiceways and falls for some six years. It looks dangerous – designer Lawrence Halprin designed it to look dangerous – and, since the day it opened, there have been no serious mishaps. This splendid fountain is an affirmation of trust in people, and it says much about the good city of Portland.

Another great thing about water is the sound of it. When people explain why they find Paley Park so quiet and restful, one thing they always mention is the waterwall. In fact, the waterwall is quite loud: the noise level is about 75 decibels close by, measurably higher than the level out on the street. Taken by itself, furthermore, the sound is not especially pleasant. I have played tapes to people and asked them what they thought it was. Usually they grimace and say a subway train, trucks on a freeway, or something just as bad. In the park, however, the sound is perceived as quite pleasant. It is white sound and masks the intermittent honks and bangs that are the most annoying aspects of street noise. It also masks conversations. Even though there are many others nearby, you can talk quite loudly to a companion – sometimes you almost have to – and enjoy a feeling of privacy. On the occasions when the waterwall is turned off, a spell is broken, and the place seems nowhere as congenial. Or as quiet.

T
W
O

"Conclusion: Great Streets and City Planning"

from *Great Streets* (1993)

Allan B. Jacobs

Editors' Introduction

In urban areas, streets occupy more land than any other public use and make up between 25 and 35 percent of all developed land. As an example, if one measures all of the public space in San Francisco including Golden Gate Park, the Presidio, Ocean Beach, and McClaren Park, and add to it all the public buildings, they don't equal land in the public rights-of-way. Streets are the public realm. They are used for necessary services, transportation, fire and police protection, access to property, and all kinds of social and economic uses. They are not stagnant but rather constantly in change, even though the changes may seem minute, such as repaving. They are owned by the public, which is responsible for them. By locating and designing streets well, one has largely designed the city. In most modern North American cities, and indeed most cities elsewhere in the world, most of the space of city streets is devoted to traffic movement. The functional aspects of streets have received much more attention than their social or community building aspects.

Taking these realities as a point of departure, Allan B. Jacobs undertook research to determine the qualities and characteristics of the world's best streets. He conducted surveys of people on the street and professionals to get their perspectives on good streets, and then observed and measured suggested streets as well as those he knew from his own experience. His book *Great Streets* documents his findings with chapters that classify types of streets, not by traffic but by design characteristics, and presents scaled plans, cross-sections, and perspective sketches of the very best as well as less good streets. *Great Streets* has quickly become a classic urban design text. It is found in the offices of professionals as well as on the desks of students. Many cities have adopted or are in process of adopting *Great Streets* programs and plans. Here, in the conclusion to *Great Streets*, Jacobs speaks eloquently of the importance of design and "magic" in creating good streets.

Other writings by Allan B. Jacobs include *Making City Planning Work* (Chicago, IL: American Society of Planning Officials, 1978), which recounts his experience as San Francisco's Planning Director in the late 1960s and early 1970s; *Looking at Cities* (Cambridge, MA: Harvard University Press, 1985), which argues that much knowledge about cities can be gained by looking closely at them and reading the clues; *The Boulevard Book: History, Evolution, Design of Multiway Boulevards*, co-authored with Elizabeth Macdonald and Yodan Rofé (Cambridge, MA: MIT Press, 2002), which documents an extensive research study on one of the street types discussed in *Great Streets*, the multiway boulevard; and *The Good City: Reflections and Imaginations* (Abingdon: Routledge, 2011).

Other seminal readings on streets and street design include Bernard Rudofsky, *Streets for People: A Primer for Americans* (Garden City, NY: Doubleday, 1969); Jane Jacobs, *Death and Life of Great American Cities* (New York: Random House, 1961); Donald Appleyard, M. Sue Gerson, and Mark Lintell, *Livable Streets* (Berkeley, CA: University of California Press, 1981); and Anne Vernez Moudon, *Public Streets for Public Use* (New York: Columbia University Press, 1991). More recent works include Michael Southworth and Eran Ben-Joseph, *Streets and the Shaping of Towns and Cities* (New York: McGraw-Hill, 1997); and Stephen Marshall, *Streets and Patterns* (London: Spon, 2005).

The twentieth century has seen the development and widespread acceptance of two major city design manifestos; that of the new town or garden city movement, and the Charter of Athens.[1] Both were in large measure responses to the building excesses and resultant foul living conditions of the nineteenth-century industrial city. Change was in order and dramatic changes were proposed. Both manifestos, reflections perhaps of not so different utopian ideals, concentrated on new building, and both ultimately eschewed streets as they had been known as central and positive to urban living. Ultimately the new town-and-garden-city-inspired communities became the models for the moderate- and low-density suburban development that emphasized central green areas rather than streets as the means of achieving face-to-face communication, and buildings well set back and, if possible, divorced from streets. The superblock idea, not inherently anti-street, became that way as it became part and parcel of both design movements.[2] Both, too, called for a separation of land uses, rather than a healthy integration, and both were to achieve their ends via massive public initiatives and centralized ownership and design of land.

The Charter of Athens could find realization on either new sites, like Chandigarh or Brasilia, or in the older central cities. In the latter, there would have to be clearance of large unhealthy urban environments in order to rebuild at a scale necessary to have an impact. Here, the rejection of streets as places for people and for the making and expression of community was even stronger, in favor of efficiency, technology, and speed, and, to give credit, of health as well, as the prime determinants of street design.[3] Building orientation to streets was seen as a fundamental wrong. The most memorable images of what those developments might look like are perspectives taken from a viewpoint high in the air with the uniform height of tall, tall buildings as the horizon line, or drawings of two people sitting at a table somehow overlooking a large, presumably public space with no one in it. This could not be said of the early garden cities, notably in communities like Welwyn Garden City, where houses did indeed face narrow streets. [. . .]

As well-intentioned and socially responsive as those manifestos were, their results, abundantly visible by the 1960s, rarely encourage or celebrate public life. They seem to be more consistent with separation and introspection – buildings and people alone, with space on all sides – than with encountering and dealing with people regularly. They have been more consistent with vehicle movement than with people movement. Fewer things that people need or want are close at hand within walking distance. They seem to have forgotten that communities are not made in automobiles, nor are people directly encountered.

Better models than these two were in order: ones not so dependent on central power and ownership and design, ones that saw incremental physical change and conservation as more desirable than massive clearance of what existed, ones that were based on not only an acceptance but also a desire for and love of urban life, of encountering people in healthy environments. They were forthcoming, not least in Jane Jacobs's book of the 1960s, *The Death and Life of Great American Cities*, that challenged the city-building practices of the times.[4] Other notable critiques and alternatives have followed.[5] Kevin Lynch's *Theory of Good City Form* set out values that a good city should strive to achieve as well as Lynch's own utopian model, with remarkably comprehensive appendixes that catalogue other theories and models.[6] In 1987, the late Donald Appleyard and I put our thoughts into writing, spurred and aided by students, in what we called "Toward a New Urban Design Manifesto."[7] Responding to social values and objectives of urban life such as comfort, identity and control, access to opportunity, imagination and joy, authenticity and meaning, community and public life, and urban self-reliance, we called, in rather general terms, for six physical qualities: livability; a minimum density; an integration of uses; buildings that defined space rather than being set in space; many rather than fewer buildings; and public streets. The present inquiry has been directed toward spelling out in greater detail what is required to achieve one of the fundamental parts of good cities; good, no, great streets.

There remains considerable tenuousness, iffiness, in the determination of what makes great streets, and that will continue. Places to walk, physical comfort, definition, qualities that engage the eyes, complementarity, and good maintenance are physical characteristics of all great streets, but far from all streets that have them are great. More is required: what I have been calling magic. In some respects, the problem, if it can be called that, starts with the multiple social purposes of streets. It is useful to review them.

Beyond functional purposes of permitting people to get from one place to another and to gain access to property, streets – most assuredly the best streets – can and should help to do other things: bring people together, help build community, cause people to act and interact, to achieve together what they might not alone. As such, streets should encourage socialization and participation of people in the community. They serve as locations of public expression. They should be physically comfortable and safe. The best streets create and leave strong, lasting, positive impressions; they catch the eyes and the imagination. They are joyful places to be, and given a chance one wants to return to them. Streets are places for activity, including relaxation. The best streets continue, are long-lived.

It may be that the purposes of streets relating to movement and access are afforded greater attention in industrial societies because they seem reasonably clear, easily objectified, measurable. Comfort is increasingly measurable, the other objectives much less so. Participation and socialization often mean different things to different people. Imagination and joy cover many concrete possibilities. Community may be realized by directly working with others or by each person doing his or her part separately. It is not always clear why people go to one street and not to another – the reasons may change, and they may have nothing to do with physical qualities. Physical qualities of streets, it has been observed, may not be the most important contributor to making community. They can help, but their direct contributions are likely to remain murky. Nonetheless, they are important; people spend time and money on making them fine settings for their activities, and it is the physical qualities that designers design.

Considerable progress has been made in establishing operative definitions of some of the qualities that make great streets. More is measurable and definable than we once thought. We continue to know more about definition, transparency, spacing (of trees, for example), human scale, and what makes new buildings fit in with others in specific environments. Much, however, remains uncertain, and so it is not easy to know when a quality has been achieved in the best way, or when, for example,

buildings are so tall as to be oppressive. In the realm of street design, it may not be all that critical to know the answers to some of these questions with precision. Understanding what the most critical factors are, and knowing what has been tried and has worked or failed in a variety of situations, may be enough. Street design, like any other creative act, always involves leapmanship, a point where it is necessary to jump from the known to something else that is desired, without knowing for sure where one will land.

There is magic on great streets, and presumably in their making. It is more than putting all of the required qualities on a street, and it is more than having a few or many of the physical, desirable things that contribute to them. Sorcery and charm, imagination and inspiration are involved, and may be the most crucial ingredients. But not without social purpose. The making of great streets is not an exercise in design for design's sake, to satisfy alone someone's concept of beauty. The magic may not be all that exciting or dramatic at the time of design. To use a nonstreet example, it seems that Thomas Jefferson was clear in his social and educational objectives for the University of Virginia: community, teachers and students living together while respecting each other's privacy, the centrality of knowledge as expressed in the library, the importance of land and gardens and of views as parts of a full life. He put them together in a straightforward, seemingly simple way, not without knowledge of physical models gained from study and experience. The result is, in the end, magic. One can imagine that the best streets were done that way, and will continue to be. Models, a knowledge of what has been done in the past, can help bring the magic into being. Jefferson used and adapted models for his university. Too often, however, models aren't referenced or used. Finding them – what they look like, their dimensions, their contexts, their relationships to each other – has been difficult. That is a major purpose of this book: to offer knowledge about the best streets so that the creativeness, the magic, may come to be for new streets.

Design counts! Great streets do not just happen. Overwhelmingly, the best streets derive from a conscious act of conception and creation of the street as a whole. The hands of decision makers, sometimes of specific designers, are visible. In cases where the initial layout and properties of the street evolved, such as at Strøget or the Ramblas, there is likely to have been a major concerted design effort at some point in time to make the street what it has become. By contrast, some fine streets have evolved to what they are without planning, the Via dei Giubbonari most notably, and there seems little in the way of program or special policy to maintain it. Similarly, compelling streets in medieval cities are plentiful, and they are all of one type. The objective of design may well have been not a great street, but rather a street that simply does its job. And there are as many or more bad streets that have been designed. But the best streets, by and large, get designed and then are cared for, continuously.

Technology, some say, makes cities as we have known them unnecessary. Advances in communication and new methods of production make it less necessary for people to live in close proximity to each other. Today's cities are leftovers from methods of production and achieving security that are no longer necessary and can disappear. There is evidence as well that many people, particularly in North America, given a choice, would not prefer cities – but rather what has become known as a suburban lifestyle or a low-density, nonurban lifestyle. Nonetheless, even assuming that they were unnecessary, cities would still be desirable for many people. We can build and live in cities because we want to, not because we have to but because they offer the prospect of a fulfilling gregarious life. Urban streets have been and can be major contributors to that kind of life.

Continually I return to an awareness of the large proportion of urban developed land that is devoted to streets and to the understanding that the purpose of streets is much more than to get from one place to another. Streets more than anything else are what make the public realm. They are the property of the public or are under direct public control. The opportunity to design them in ways that meet public objectives, including the making of community itself, is as exciting as it is challenging. If we do right by our streets we can in large measure do right by the city as a whole – and, therefore and most importantly, by its inhabitants.

The best new streets need not be the same as the old, but as models the old have much to teach. Delightful, purposeful streets and cities will surely follow.

NOTES

1 Ebenezer Howard, *Garden Cities of Tomorrow* (London: Faber and Faber, 1946; first published 1898); Le Corbusier, *The Athens Charter*, trans. Anthony Eardley (New York: Grossman, 1973; first published 1943, from a conference of 1933).

2 Clarence Stein, *Toward New Towns for America* (Liverpool: University Press of Liverpool, 1951). See particularly Sunnyside Gardens as compared to later designs, such as for Radburn, New Jersey, and Greenbelt, Maryland.

3 See, for example, the chapter on "Traffic" in *The Athens Charter*.

4 Jane Jacobs, *The Death and Life of Great American Cities* (New York: Random House, 1961).

5 For example, see Richard Sennett, *The Fall of Public Man* (New York: Alfred A. Knopf, 1974).

6 Kevin Lynch, *A Theory of Good City Form* (Cambridge: MIT Press, 1981).

7 Appleyard and Jacobs, "Toward a New Urban Design Manifesto," *Journal of the American Planning Association*, 1987.

TWO

"Toward an Urban Design Manifesto"

from *Journal of the American Planning Association* (1987)

Allan B. Jacobs and Donald Appleyard

Editors' Introduction

In the early 1980s, Allan B. Jacobs and Donald Appleyard (1928–1982), following a seminar on urban physical form in the Department of City and Regional Planning at the University of California, Berkeley that included strong criticism of the Le Corbusier-led CIAM design manifesto, were urged by their students to write a design manifesto that articulated a counter-position. They took the challenge and wrote "Toward an Urban Design Manifesto." Initially rejected for publication by the *Journal of the American Planning Association* on the grounds that it was without scholarly merit because of its experiential methodology, Jacobs was later invited to have it included in a special urban design oriented issue of the same journal.

The manifesto – informed by Jacobs' extensive professional experience, Appleyard's research on street livability, and their shared feeling that CIAM and the Garden City Movement both represented overly strong design reactions to the physical decay and social inequities of industrial cities – was a validation of cities and urban life. At the same time, it was intended as a critique of the city planning profession for its growing lack of attention to urban physical form in favor of social planning. The argument was that social, economic, and cultural factors are necessarily influenced by physical form factors, not in a deterministic way but rather in terms of possibilities and probabilities, and so to neglect the physical is to neglect an essential part of planning.

The Manifesto identifies problems for modern urban design – poor living environments, giantism and loss of control, large-scale privatization and loss of public life, centrifugal fragmentation, destruction of valued places, placelessness, injustice, and rootless professionalism – and then sets out central values for urban life. Goals that serve individuals and small social groups include authenticity and meaning, livability, identity and control, and access to opportunity, imagination, and joy. Those that serve larger social goals include community and public life, urban self-reliance, and an environment for all. From these goals, Jacobs and Appleyard theorize the essential qualities of city grain that must be present to achieve a good urban environment: livable streets and neighborhoods, a minimum residential density and intensity of use, integration of activities, buildings that define public space, and many different buildings and spaces with complex arrangements and relationships.

"Toward an Urban Design Manifesto" remains an important touchstone for present-day urban design practitioners, not least because it cautions against dehumanization, retreat into formalism, and over-dependence on standards that might or might not achieve desirable ends.

Allan B. Jacobs served as San Francisco's Planning Director from 1967 to 1975, where he and a group of talented young planners prepared a citywide urban design plan, which to this day is held to be an exemplary model of such a plan. Donald Appleyard worked as a consultant to the plan, researching the quality of life along neighborhood streets, which resulted in his well-known and highly influential street livability study. Jacobs and Appleyard became colleagues at the University of California, Berkeley, where they established an urban design concentration and collaborated until Appleyard's untimely death in 1982. Jacobs remains a professor and in the early 1990s started the Master of Urban Design program with colleagues from the architecture and landscape architecture programs.

Other writings by Appleyard include *The View from the Road*, co-authored with Kevin Lynch and John Myer (Cambridge, MA: MIT Press, 1963) and *Livable Streets*, co-authored with M. Sue Gerson and Mark Lintell (Berkeley, CA: University of California Press, 1981). Other writings by Jacobs include *Making City Planning Work* (Chicago, IL American Society of Planning Officials, 1978), which recounts his professional experience in San Francisco through a series of case studies; *Looking at Cities* (Cambridge, MA: Harvard University Press, 1985), which argues that much knowledge about cities can be gained by looking closely at them and reading the clues; *Great Streets* (Cambridge, MA: MIT Press, 1993), which identifies the qualities of the best streets and presents hand-drawn scaled plans and sections of representative examples worldwide; *The Boulevard Book: History, Evolution, Design of Multiway Boulevards*, co-authored with Elizabeth Macdonald and Yodan Rofe (Cambridge, MA: MIT Press, 2002), which reconsiders boulevards as a useful street type for modern cities; and *The Good City: Reflections and Imaginations* (Abingdon: Routledge, 2011).

Researchers and practitioners within the urban design field continue to develop normative theories of good city form. Of particular note is the public effort recently undertaken by the New Zealand Ministry for the Environment, documented in two reports, available for download from the ministry's website (http://www.mfe.govt.nz/). The Value of Urban Design surveys the urban design literature and research and identifies the economic, social, and environmental benefits of urban design. The New Zealand Urban Design Protocol, similar to Jacob's and Appleyard's Manifesto, identifies goals for urban life and essential design qualities.

We think it's time for a new urban design manifesto. Almost 50 years have passed since Le Corbusier and the International Congress of Modern Architecture (CIAM) produced the Charter of Athens, and it is more than 20 years since the first Urban Design Conference, still in the CIAM tradition, was held (at Harvard in 1957). Since then the precepts of CIAM have been attacked by sociologists, planners, Jane Jacobs, and more recently by architects themselves. But it is still a strong influence, and we will take it as our starting point. Make no mistake: the charter was, simply, a manifesto – a public declaration that spelled out the ills of industrial cities as they existed in the 1930s and laid down physical requirements necessary to establish healthy, humane, and beautiful urban environments for people. It could not help but deal with social, economic, and political phenomena, but its basic subject matter was the physical design of cities. Its authors were (mostly) socially concerned architects, determined that their art and craft be responsive to social realities as well as to improving the lot of man. It would be a mistake to write them off as simply elitist designers and physical determinists.

So the charter decried the medium-size (up to six storys) high-density buildings with high land coverage that were associated so closely with slums. Similarly, buildings that faced streets were found to be detrimental to healthy living. These seemingly limitless horizontal expansion of urban areas devoured the countryside, and suburbs were viewed as symbols of terrible waste. Solutions could be found in the demolition of unsanitary housing, the provision of green areas in every residential district, and new high-rise, high-density buildings set in open space. Housing was to be removed from its traditional relationship facing streets, and the whole circulation system was to be revised to meet the needs of emerging mechanization (the automobile). Work areas should be close to but separate from residential areas. To achieve the new city, large land holdings, preferably owned by the public, should replace multiple small parcels (so that projects could be properly designed and developed).

Now thousands of housing estates and redevelopment projects in socialist and capitalist countries the world over, whether built on previously undeveloped land or developed as replacements for old urban areas, attest to the acceptance of the charter's dictums. The design notions it embraced have become part of a world design language, not just the intellectual property of an enlightened few, even though the principles have been devalued in many developments.

Of course, the Charter of Athens has not been the only major urban philosophy of this century to influence the development of urban areas. Ebenezer Howard, too, was responding to the ills of the nineteenth-century industrial city, and the Garden City movement has been at least as powerful as the Charter of Athens. New towns policies, where they exist, are rooted in Howard's thought. But you don't have to look to new towns to see the influence of Howard, Olmsted, Wright, and Stein. The superblock notion, if nothing else, pervades large housing projects around the world, in central cities as well as suburbs. The notion of buildings in a park is as common to garden city designs as it is to charter-inspired development. Indeed, the two movements have a great deal in common: superblocks, separate paths for people and cars, interior common spaces, housing divorced from streets, and central ownership of land. The garden city-inspired communities place greater emphasis on private outdoor space. The most significant difference, at least as they have evolved, is in density and building type: the garden city people preferred to accommodate people in row houses, garden apartments, and maisonettes, while Corbusier and the CIAM designers went for high-rise buildings and, inevitably, people living in flats and at significantly higher densities.

We are less than enthralled with what either the Charter of Athens or the Garden City movement has produced in the way of urban environments. The emphasis of CIAM was on buildings and what goes on within buildings that happen to sit in space, not on the public life that takes place constantly in public spaces. The orientation is often inward. Buildings tend to be islands, big or small. They could be placed anywhere. From the outside perspective, the building, like the work of art it was intended to be, sits where it can be seen and admired in full. And because it is large it is best seen from a distance (at a scale consistent with a moving auto). Diversity, spontaneity, and surprise are absent, at least for the person on foot. On the other hand, we find little joy or magic or spirit in the charter cities. They are not urban, to us, except according to some definition one might find in a census. Most garden cities, safe and healthy and even gracious as they may be, remind us more of

suburbs than of cities. But they weren't trying to be cities. The emphasis has always been on "garden" as much as or more than on "city."

Both movements represent overly strong design reactions to the physical decay and social inequities of industrial cities. In responding so strongly, albeit understandably, to crowded, lightless, airless, "utilitiless," congested buildings and cities that housed so many people, the utopians did not inquire what was good about those places, either socially or physically. Did not those physical environments reflect (and maybe even foster) values that were likely to be meaningful to people individually and collectively, such as publicness and community? Without knowing it, maybe these strong reactions to urban ills ended up by throwing the baby out with the bathwater.

In the meantime we have had a lot of experience with city building and rebuilding. New spokespeople with new urban visions have emerged. As more CIAM-style buildings were built people became more disenchanted. Many began to look through picturesque lenses back to the old preindustrial cities. From a concentration on the city as a kind of sculpture garden, the townscape movement, led by the *Architectural Review*, emphasized "urban experience." This phenomenological view of the city was espoused by Rasmussen, Kepes, and ultimately Kevin Lynch and Jane Jacobs. It identified a whole new vocabulary of urban form – one that depended on the sights, sounds, feels, and smells of the city, its materials and textures, floor surfaces, facades, style, signs, lights, seating, trees, sun, and shade all potential amenities for the attentive observer and user. This has permanently humanized the vocabulary of urban design, and we enthusiastically subscribe to most of its tenets, though some in the townscape movement ignored the social meanings and implications of what they were doing.

The 1960s saw the birth of community design and an active concern for the social groups affected, usually negatively, by urban design. Designers were the "soft cops," and many professionals left the design field for social or planning vocations, finding the physical environment to have no redeeming social value. But at the beginning of the 1980s the mood in the design professions is conservative. There is a withdrawal from social engagement back to formalism. Supported by semiology and other abstract themes, much of architecture has become a dilettantish and narcissistic pursuit, a chic component of the high art consumer culture, increasingly remote from most people's everyday lives, finding its ultimate manifestation in the art gallery and the art book. City planning is too immersed in the administration and survival of housing, environmental, and energy programs and in responding to budget cuts and community demands to have any clear sense of direction with regard to city form.

While all these professional ideologies have been working themselves out, massive economic, technological, and social changes have taken place in our cities. The scale of capitalism has continued to increase, as has the scale of bureaucracy, and the automobile has virtually destroyed cities as they once were.

In formulating a new manifesto, we react against other phenomena than did the leaders of CIAM 50 years ago. The automobile cities of California and the Southwest present utterly different problems from those of nineteenth-century European cities, as do the CIAM-influenced housing developments around European, Latin American, and Russian cities and the rash of squatter settlements around the fast-growing cities of the Third World. What are these problems?

PROBLEMS FOR MODERN URBAN DESIGN

Poor living environments

While housing conditions in most advanced countries have improved in terms of such fundamentals as light, air, and space, the surroundings of homes are still frequently dangerous, polluted, noisy, anonymous wastelands. Travel around such cities has become more and more fatiguing and stressful.

Giantism and loss of control

The urban environment is increasingly in the hands of the large-scale developers and public agencies. The elements of the city grow inexorably in size, massive transportation systems are segregated for single travel modes, and vast districts and complexes are created that make people feel irrelevant.

People, therefore, have less sense of control over their homes, neighborhoods, and cities than when they lived in slower-growing locally based communities. Such giantism can be found as readily in the housing projects of socialist cities as in the office buildings and commercial developments of capitalist cities.

Large-scale privatization and the loss of public life

Cities, especially American cities, have become privatized, partly because of the consumer society's emphasis on the individual and the private sector, creating Galbraith's "private affluence and public squalor," but escalated greatly by the spread of the automobile. Crime in the streets is both a cause and a consequence of this trend, which has resulted in a new form of city: one of closed, defended islands with blank and windowless facades surrounded by wastelands of parking lots and fast-moving traffic. As public transit systems have declined, the number of places in American cities where people of different social groups actually meet each other has dwindled. The public environment of many American cities has become an empty desert, leaving public life dependent for its survival solely on planned formal occasions, mostly in protected internal locations.

Centrifugal fragmentation

Advanced industrial societies took work out of the home, and then out of the neighborhood, while the automobile and the growing scale of commerce have taken shopping out of the local community. Fear has led social groups to flee from each other into homogeneous social enclaves. Communities themselves have become lower in density and increasingly homogeneous. Thus the city has spread out and separated to form extensive monocultures and specialized destinations reachable often only by long journeys – a fragile and extravagant urban system dependent on cheap, available gasoline, and an effective contributor to the isolation of social groups from each other.

Destruction of valued places

The quest for profit and prestige and the relentless exploitation of places that attract the public have led to the destruction of much of our heritage, of historic places that no longer turn a profit, of natural amenities that become overused. In many cases, as in San Francisco, the very value of the place threatens its destruction as hungry tourists and entrepreneurs flock to see and profit from it.

Placelessness

Cities are becoming meaningless places beyond their citizens' grasp. We no longer know the origins of the world around us. We rarely know where the materials and products come from, who owns what, who is behind what, what was intended. We live in cities where things happen without warning and without our participation. It is an alien world for most people. It is little surprise that most withdraw from community involvement to enjoy their own private and limited worlds.

Injustice

Cities are symbols of inequality. In most cities the discrepancy between the environments of the rich and the environments of the poor is striking. In many instances the environments of the rich, by occupying and dominating the prevailing patterns of transportation and access, make the environments of the poor relatively worse. This discrepancy may be less visible in the low-density modern city, where the display of affluence is more hidden than in the old city; but the discrepancy remains.

Rootless professionalism

Finally, design professionals today are often part of the problem. In too many cases, we design for places and people we do not know and grant them very little power or acknowledgment. Too many professionals are more part of a universal professional culture than part of the local cultures for whom we produce our plans and products. We carry our "bag of tricks" around the world and bring them out wherever we land. This floating professional culture has only the most superficial conception of particular place. Rootless, it is more susceptible to changes in professional fashion and theory than to local events. There is too little inquiry, too much proposing. Quick surveys are made, instant solutions devised, and the rest of the time is spent persuading the clients. Limits on time and budgets drive us on, but so do lack of understanding and the placeless culture. Moreover, we designers are often unconscious of our own roots, which influence our preferences in hidden ways.

At the same time, the planning profession's retreat into trendism, under the positivist influence of social science, has left it virtually unable to resist the social pressures of capitalist economy and consumer sovereignty. Planners have lost their beliefs. Although we believe citizen participation is essential to urban planning, the professionals also must have a sense of what we believe is right, even though we may be vetoed.

GOALS FOR URBAN LIFE

We propose, therefore, a number of goals that we deem essential for the future of a good urban environment: livability; identity and control; access to opportunity, imagination, and joy; authenticity and meaning; open communities and public life; self-reliance; and justice.

Livability

A city should be a place where everyone can live in relative comfort. Most people want a kind of sanctuary for their living environment, a place where they can bring up children, have privacy, sleep, eat, relax, and restore themselves. This means a well-managed environment relatively devoid of nuisance, overcrowding, noise, danger, air pollution, dirt, trash, and other unwelcome intrusions.

Identity and control

People should feel that some part of the environment belongs to them, individually and collectively, some part for which they care and are ever responsible, whether they own it or not. The urban environment should be an environment that encourages people to express themselves, to become involved, to decide what they want and act on it. Like a seminar where everybody has something to contribute to communal discussion, the urban environment should encourage participation. Urbanites may not always want this. Many like the anonymity of the city, but we are not convinced that freedom of anonymity is a desirable freedom. It would be much better if people were sure enough of themselves to stand up and be counted. Environments should therefore be designed for those who use them or are affected by them, rather than for those who own them. This should reduce alienation and anonymity (even if people want them); it should increase people's sense of identity and rootedness and encourage more care and responsibility for the physical environment of cities.

Respect for the existing environment, both nature and city, is one fundamental difference we have with the CIAM movement. Urban design has too often assumed that new is better than old. But the new is justified only if it is better than what exists. Conservation encourages identity and control and, usually, a better sense of community, since old environments are more usually part of a common heritage.

Access to opportunity, imagination, and joy

People should find the city a place where they can break from traditional molds, extend their experience, meet new people, learn other viewpoints, have fun. At a functional level people should have access to alternative housing and job choices; at another level, they should find the city an enlightening cultural experience. A city should have magical places where fantasy is possible, a counter to and an escape from the mundaneness of everyday work and living. Architects and planners take cities and themselves too seriously; the result too often is deadliness and boredom, no imagination, no humor, alienating places. But people need an escape from the seriousness and meaning of the everyday. The city has always been a place of excitement; it is theater, a stage upon which citizens can display themselves and see others. It has magic, or should

have, and that depends on a certain sensuous, hedonistic mood, on signs, on night lights, on fantasy, color, and other imagery. There can be parts of the city where belief can be suspended, just as in the experience of fiction. It may be that such places have to be framed so that people know how to act. Until now such fantasy and experiment have been attempted mostly by commercial facilities, at rather low levels of quality and aspiration, seldom deeply experimental. One should not have to travel as far as the Himalayas or the South Sea Islands to stretch one's experience. Such challenges could be nearer home. There should be a place for community utopias; for historic, natural, and anthropological evocations of the modern city, for encounters with the truly exotic.

Authenticity and meaning

People should be able to understand their city (or other people's cities), its basic layout, public functions, and institutions; they should be aware of its opportunities. An authentic city is one where the origins of things and places are clear. All this means an urban environment should reveal its significant meanings; it should not be dominated only by one type of group, the powerful; neither should publicly important places be hidden. The city should symbolize the moral issues of society and educate its citizens to an awareness of them.

That does not mean everything has to be laid out as on a supermarket shelf. A city should present itself as a readable story, in an engaging and, if necessary, provocative way, for people are indifferent to the obvious, overwhelmed by complexity. A city's offerings should be revealed or they will be missed. This can affect the forms of the city, its signage, and other public information and education programs.

Livability, identity, authenticity, and opportunity are characteristics of the urban environment that should serve the individual and small social unit, but the city has to serve some higher social goals as well. It is these we especially wish to emphasize here.

Community and public life

Cities should encourage participation of their citizens in community and public life. In the face of giantism and fragmentation, public life, especially life in public places, has been seriously eroded. The neighborhood movement, by bringing thousands, probably millions of people out of their closed private lives into active participation in their local communities, has begun to counter that trend, but this movement has had its limitations. It can be purely defensive, parochial, and self-serving. A city should be more than a warring collection of interest groups, classes, and neighborhoods; it should breed a commitment to a larger whole, to tolerance, justice, law, and democracy. The structure of the city should invite and encourage public life, not only through its institutions, but directly and symbolically through its public spaces. The public environment, unlike the neighborhood, by definition should be open to all members of the community. It is where people of different kinds meet. No one should be excluded unless they threaten the balance of life.

Urban self-reliance

Increasingly cities will have to become more self-sustaining in their uses of energy and other scarce resources. "Soft energy paths" in particular not only will reduce dependence and exploitation across regions and countries but also will help re-establish a stronger sense of local and regional identity, authenticity, and meaning.

An environment for all

Good environments should be accessible to all. Every citizen is entitled to some minimal level of environmental livability and minimal levels of identity, control, and opportunity. Good urban design must be for the poor as well as the rich. Indeed, it is more needed by the poor.

We look toward a society that is truly pluralistic, one where power is more evenly distributed among social groups than it is today in virtually any country, but where the different values and cultures of interest – and place-based groups are acknowledged and negotiated in a just public arena.

These goals for the urban environment are both individual and collective, and as such they are frequently in conflict. The more a city promises for the individual, the less it seems to have a public life; the more the city is built for public entities, the less the individual seems to count. The good urban environment is one that somehow balances these goals, allowing individual and group identity while maintaining a public concern, encouraging pleasure while maintaining responsibility, remaining open to outsiders while sustaining a strong sense of localism.

AN URBAN FABRIC FOR AN URBAN LIFE

We have some ideas, at least, for how the fabric or texture of cities might be conserved or created to encourage a livable urban environment. We emphasize the structural qualities of the good urban environment – qualities we hope will be successful in creating urban experiences that are consonant with our goals.

Do not misread this. We are not describing all the qualities of a city. We are not dealing with major transportation systems, open space, the natural environment, the structure of the large-scale city, or even the structure of neighborhoods, but only the grain of the good city.

There are five physical characteristics that must be present if there is to be a positive response to the goals and values we believe are central to urban life. They must be designed, they must exist, as prerequisites of a sound urban environment. All five must be present, not just one or two. There are other physical characteristics that are important, but these five are essential: livable streets and neighborhoods; some minimum density of residential development as well as intensity of land use; an integration of activities – living, working, shopping – in some reasonable proximity to each other; a manmade environment, particularly buildings, that defines public space (as opposed to buildings that, for the most part, sit in space); and many, many separate, distinct buildings with complex arrangements and relationships (as opposed to few, large buildings).

Let us explain, keeping in mind that all five of the characteristics must be present. People, we have said, should be able to live in reasonable (though not excessive) safety, cleanliness, and security. That means livable streets and neighborhoods: with adequate sunlight, clean air, trees, vegetation, gardens, open space, pleasantly scaled and designed buildings; without offensive noise; with cleanliness and physical safety. Many of these characteristics can be designed into the physical fabric of the city.

The reader will say, "Well of course, but what does that mean?" Usually it has meant specific standards and requirements, such as sun angles, decibel levels, lane widths, and distances between buildings. Many researchers have been trying to define the qualities of a livable environment. It depends on a wide array of attributes, some structural, some quite small details. There is no single right answer. We applaud these efforts and have participated in them ourselves. Nevertheless, desires for livability and individual comfort by themselves have led to fragmentation of the city. Livability standards, whether for urban or for suburban developments, have often been excessive.

Our approach to the details of this inclusive physical characteristic would center on the words "reasonable, though not excessive . . ." Too often, for example, the requirement of adequate sunlight has resulted in buildings and people inordinately far from each other, beyond what demonstrable need for light would dictate. Safety concerns have been the justifications for ever wider streets and wide, sweeping curves rather than narrow ways and sharp corners. Buildings are removed from streets because of noise considerations when there might be other ways to deal with this concern. So although livable streets and neighborhoods are a primary requirement for any good urban fabric – whether for existing, denser cities or for new development – the quest for livable neighborhoods, if pursued obsessively, can destroy the urban qualities we seek to achieve.

A *minimum density* is needed. By density we mean the number of people (sometimes expressed in terms of housing units) living on an area of land, or the number of people using an area of land.

Cities are not farms. A city is people living and working and doing the things they do in relatively close proximity to each other.

We are impressed with the importance of density as a perceived phenomenon and therefore relative to the beholder and agree that, for many purposes, perceived density is more important than an "objective" measurement of people per unit of land. We agree, too, that physical phenomena can be manipulated so as to render perceptions of

greater or lesser density. Nevertheless, a narrow, winding street, with a lot of signs and a small enclosed open space at the end, with no people, does not make a city. Cities are more than stage sets. Some minimum number of people living and using a given area of land is required if there is to be human exchange, public life and action, diversity and community.

Density of people alone will account for the presence or absence of certain uses and services we find important to urban life. We suspect, for example, that the number and diversity of small stores and services – for instance, groceries, bars, bakeries, laundries and cleaners, coffee shops, secondhand stores, and the like – to be found in a city or area is in part a function of density. That is, that such businesses are more likely to exist, and in greater variety, in an area where people live in greater proximity to each other ("higher" density). The viability of mass transit, we know, depends partly on the density of residential areas and partly on the size and intensity of activity at commercial and service destinations. And more use of transit, in turn, reduces parking demands and permits increases in density. There must be a critical mass of people, and they must spend a lot of their time in reasonably close proximity to each other, including when they are at home, if there is to be an urban life. The goal of local control and community identity is associated with density as well. The notion of an optimum density is elusive and is easily confused with the health and livability of urban areas, with lifestyles, with housing types, with the size of area being considered (the building site or the neighborhood or the city), and with the economics of development. A density that might be best for child rearing might be less than adequate to support public transit. Most recently, energy efficiency has emerged as a concern associated with density, the notion being that conservation will demand more compact living arrangements.

Our conclusion, based largely on our experience and on the literature, is that a minimum net density (people or living units divided by the size of the building site, excluding public streets) of about 15 dwelling units (30–60 people) per acre of land is necessary to support city life. By way of illustration, that is the density produced with generous town houses (or row houses). It would permit parcel sizes up to 25 feet wide by about 115 feet deep. But other building types and lot sizes also would produce that density. Some areas could be developed with lower densities, but not very many. We don't think you get cities at 6 dwellings to the acre, let alone on half-acre lots. On the other hand, it is possible to go as high as 48 dwelling units per acre (96 to 192 people) for a very large part of the city and still provide for a spacious and gracious urban life. Much of San Francisco, for example, is developed with three-story buildings (one unit per floor) above a parking story, on parcels that measure 25 feet by 100 or 125 feet. At those densities, with that kind of housing, there can be private or shared gardens for most people, no common hallways are required, and people can have direct access to the ground. Public streets and walks adequate to handle pedestrian and vehicular traffic generated by these densities can be accommodated in rights-of-way that are 50 feet wide or less. Higher densities, for parts of the city, to suit particular needs and lifestyles, would be both possible and desirable. We are not sure what the upper limits would be but suspect that as the numbers get much higher than 200 people per net residential acre, for larger parts of the city, the concessions to less desirable living environments mount rapidly.

Beyond residential density, there must be a minimum intensity of people using an area for it to be urban, as we are defining that word. We aren't sure what the numbers are or even how best to measure this kind of intensity. We are speaking here, particularly, of the public or "meeting" areas of our city. We are confident that our lowest residential densities will provide most meeting areas with life and human exchange, but are not sure if they will generate enough activity for the most intense central districts.

There must be an *integration of activities* – living, working, and shopping as well as public, spiritual, and recreational activities – reasonably near each other.

The best urban places have some mixtures of uses. The mixture responds to the values of publicness and diversity that encourage local community identity. Excitement, spirit, sense, stimulation, and exchange are more likely when there is a mixture of activities than when there is not. There are many examples that we all know. It is the mix, not just the density of people and uses, that brings life to an area, the life of people going about a full range

of normal activities without having to get into an automobile.

We are not saying that every area of the city should have a full mix of all uses. That would be impossible. The ultimate in mixture would be for each building to have a range of uses from living, to working, to shopping, to recreation. We are not calling for a return to the medieval city. There is a lot to be said for the notion of "living sanctuaries," which consist almost wholly of housing. But we think these should be relatively small, of a few blocks, and they should be close and easily accessible (by foot) to areas where people meet to shop or work or recreate or do public business. And except for a few of the most intensely developed office blocks of a central business district or a heavy industrial area, the meeting areas should have housing within them. Stores should be mixed with offices. If we envision the urban landscape as a fabric, then it would be a salt-and-pepper fabric of many colors, each color for a separate use or a combination. Of course, some areas would be much more heavily one color than another, and some would be an even mix of colors. Some areas, if you squinted your eyes, or if you got so close as to see only a small part of the fabric, would read as one color, a red or a brown or a green. But by and large there would be few if any distinct patterns, where one color stopped and another started. It would not be patchwork quilt, or an even-colored fabric. The fabric would be mixed.

In an urban environment, *buildings* (and other objects that people place in the environment) *should be arranged in such a way as to define and even enclose public space, rather than sit in space*. It is not enough to have high densities and an integration of activities to have cities. A tall enough building with enough people living (or even working) in it, sited on a large parcel, can easily produce the densities we have talked about and can have internally mixed uses, like most "mixed use" projects. But that building and its neighbors will be unrelated objects sitting in space if they are far enough apart, and the mixed uses might be only privately available. In large measure that is what the Charter of Athens, the garden cities, and standard suburban development produce.

Buildings close to each other along a street, regardless of whether the street is straight, or curved, or angled, tend to define space if the street is not too wide in relation to the buildings. The same is true of a plaza or a square. As the spaces between buildings become larger (in relation to the size of the buildings, up to a point), the buildings tend more and more to sit in space. They become focal points for few or many people, depending on their size and activity. Except where they are monuments or centers for public activities (a stadium or meeting hall), where they represent public gathering spots, buildings in space tend to be private and inwardly oriented. People come to them and go from them in any direction. That is not so for the defined outdoor environment. Avoiding the temptation to ascribe all kinds of psychological values to defined spaces (such as intimacy, belonging, protection – values that are difficult to prove and that may differ for different people), it is enough to observe that spaces surrounded by buildings are more likely to bring people together and thereby promote public interaction. The space can be linear (like streets) or in the form of plazas of myriad shapes. Moreover, interest and interplay among uses is enhanced. To be sure, such arrangements direct people and limit their freedom – they cannot move in just any direction from any point – but presumably there are enough choices (even avenues of escape) left open, and the gain is in greater potential for sense stimulation, excitement, surprise, and focus. Over and over again we seek out and return to defined ways and spaces as symbolic of urban life emphasizing the public space more than the private building.

It is important for us to emphasize *public places* and a *public* way system. We have observed that the central value of urban life is that of publicness, of people from different groups meeting each other and of people acting in concert, albeit with debate. The most important public places must be for *pedestrians*, for no public life can take place between people in automobiles. Most public space has been taken over by the automobile, for travel or parking. We must fight to restore more for the pedestrian. Pedestrian malls are not simply to benefit the local merchants. They have an essential public value. People of different kinds meet each other directly. The level of communication may be only visual, but that itself is educational and can encourage tolerance. The revival of street activities, street vending, and street theater in American cities may be the precursor of a more flourishing public environment, if the automobile can be held back.

There also must be symbolic, public meeting places, accessible to all and publicly controlled. Further, in order to communicate, to get from place to place, to interact, to exchange ideas and goods, there must be a healthy public circulation system. It cannot be privately controlled. Public circulation systems should be seen as significant cultural settings where the city's finest products and artifacts can be displayed, as in the piazzas of medieval and renaissance cities.

Finally, *many different buildings and spaces with complex arrangements and relationships* are required. The often elusive notion of human scale is associated with this requirement – a notion that is not just an architect's concept but one that other people understand as well.

Diversity, the possibility of intimacy and confrontation with the unexpected, stimulation, are all more likely with many buildings than with few taking up the same ground areas.

For a long time we have been led to believe that large land holdings were necessary to design healthy, efficient, aesthetically pleasing urban environments. The slums of the industrial city were associated, at least in part, with all those small, overbuilt parcels. Socialist and capitalist ideologies alike called for land assembly to permit integrated, socially and economically useful developments. What the socialist countries would do via public ownership the capitalists would achieve through redevelopment and new fiscal mechanisms that rewarded large holdings. Architects of both ideological persuasions promulgated or were easily convinced of the wisdom of land assembly. It's not hard to figure out why. The results, whether by big business or big government, are more often than not inward-oriented, easily controlled or controllable, sterile, large-building projects, with fewer entrances, fewer windows, less diversity, less innovation, and less individual expression than the urban fabric that existed previously or that can be achieved with many actors and many buildings. Attempts to break up facades or otherwise to articulate separate activities in large buildings are seldom as successful as when smaller properties are developed singly.

Health, safety, and efficiency can be achieved with many smaller buildings, individually designed and developed. Reasonable public controls can see to that. And, of course, smaller buildings are a lot more likely if parcel sizes are small than if they are large. With smaller buildings and parcels, more entrances must be located on the public spaces, more windows and a finer scale of design diversity emerge. A more public, lively city is produced. It implies more, smaller groups getting pieces of the public action, taking part, having a stake. Other stipulations may be necessary to keep public frontages alive, free from the deadening effects of offices and banks, but small buildings will help this more than large ones. There need to be large buildings, too, covering large areas of land, but they will be the exception, not the rule, and should not be in the centers of public activity.

ALL THESE QUALITIES . . . AND OTHERS

A good city must have all those qualities. Density without livability could return us to the slums of the nineteenth century. Public places without small-scale, fine-grain development would give us vast, overscale cities. As an urban fabric, however, those qualities stand a good chance of meeting many of the goals we outlined. They directly attend to the issue of livability though they are aimed especially at encouraging public places and a public life. Their effects on personal and group identity are less clear, though the small-scale city is more likely to support identity than the large-scale city. Opportunity and imagination should be encouraged by a diverse and densely settled urban structure. This structure also should create a setting that is more meaningful to the individual inhabitant and small group than the giant environments now being produced. There is no guarantee that this urban structure will be a more just one than those presently existing. In supporting the small against the large, however, more justice for the powerless may be encouraged.

Still, an urban fabric of this kind cannot by itself meet all these goals. Other physical characteristics are important to the design of urban environments. Open space, to provide access to nature as well as relief from the built environment, is one. So are definitions, boundaries if you will, that give location and identity to neighborhoods (or districts) and to the city itself. There are other characteristics as well: public buildings, educational environments,

places set aside for nurturing the spirit, and more. We still have work to do.

MANY PARTICIPANTS

While we have concentrated on defining physical characteristics of a good city fabric, the process of creating it is crucial. As important as many buildings and spaces are *many participants* in the building process. It is through this involvement in the creation and management of their city that citizens are most likely to identify with it and, conversely, to enhance their own sense of identity and control.

AN ESSENTIAL BEGINNING

The five characteristics we have noted are essential to achieving the values central to urban life. They need much further definition and testing. We have to know more about what configurations create public space: about maximum densities, about how small a community can be and still be urban (some very small Swiss villages fit the bill, and everyone knows some favorite examples), about what is perceived as big and what small under different circumstances, about landscape material as a space definer, and a lot more. When we know more we will be still further along toward a new urban design manifesto.

We know that any ideal community, including the kind that can come from this manifesto, will not always be comfortable for every person. Some people don't like cities and aren't about to. Those who do will not be enthralled with all of what we propose.

Our urban vision is rooted partly in the realities of earlier, older urban places that many people, including many utopian designers, have rejected, often for good reasons. So our utopia will not satisfy all people. That's all right. We like cities. Given a choice of the kind of community we would like to live in – the sort of choice earlier city dwellers seldom had – we would choose to live in an urban, public community that embraces the goals and displays the physical characteristics we have outlined. Moreover, we think it responds to what people want and that it will promote the good urban life.

"Dimensions of Performance"
from *Good City Form* (1981)

Kevin Lynch

Editors' Introduction

Attempts to describe concepts of the "good city" through normative filters have a long history in the early practice of civic design, as well as the later-emerging field of urban design. Many of these normative theories (those theories that link human values to city form) tend toward highly prescriptive recommendations or the subjective leanings of individual authors in specific contexts. In this reading from *Good City Form*, it is Kevin Lynch's intention to go beyond personal values and describe theoretical characteristics of city form which are as general as possible and can be applied contextually to any culture. In the opening chapters of the book, Lynch (1918–1984) categorizes popular theories of the city into three branches of thought: planning or decision theory that focuses on how public decisions should be made, functional theory that describes how cities operate, and normative theory that attempts to link human values with city form and the nature of the "good city." Reaching back through the history of cities, he recognizes three distinct types of normative theory: cosmic, machine, and organic – each of which he finds either problematic or limited when applied to contemporary society. He suggests that the values inscribed within current spatial policy and design practice are either strong (and thus justifiable), or conversely wishful, weak, hidden, or neglected. Lynch relies instead on the identification of measurable value-based performance dimensions upon which a normative theory of good city form could be built. In this reading, he proposes and then applies an exhaustive list of general criteria to identify these performance dimensions (vitality, sense, fit, access, and control) and two additional meta-criteria that help contextualize the previous five (efficiency and justice). These performance dimensions are not new ideas, and Lynch provides a list of the influences and previous theories that impacted his thinking in one of the very readable appendices to the book. At the end of the text, he suggests that the appropriate use of these dimensions lies in their ability to evaluate existing places and show where improvements in urban form can be made.

Kevin Lynch's biographical profile and primary works are included in his earlier selection in this volume (see pp. 125–126). His other works on normative theory and urbanism include: "A Theory of Urban Form," written with Lloyd Rodwin, *Journal of the American Institute of Planners* (vol. 24, no. 4, pp. 201–214, 1958); "Quality in City Design," in Laurence Holland (ed.), *Who Designs America?* (Princeton, NJ: Princeton University and New York: Doubleday, 1966); "The Possible City," in *Environment and Policy* (Bloomington, IN: Indiana University Press, 1968); and "Grounds for Utopia," in Basil Honikman (ed.), *Responding to Social Change* (Stroudsburg, PA: Dowden, Hutchinson & Ross, 1975).

Other writers who discuss normative theories of urban design and the built environment can roughly be split into two groups: those who write about the concept of "theory" and those who advocate a specific theory of urbanism and urban design. Those writing on the concept of theory, include: Kate Nesbitt (ed.), "Introduction," in *Theorizing a New Agenda for Architecture: An Anthology of Architectural Theory 1965–1995* (New York: Princeton Architectural Press, 1996); several chapters in Jon Lang, *Urban Design: The American*

Experience (New York: Van Nostrand Reinhold, 1994); Anne Vernez Moudon, "A Catholic Approach to Organizing What Urban Designers Should Know," *Journal of Planning Literature* (vol. 6, no. 4, pp. 331–349, 1992); and Alexander Cuthbert (ed.), "Introduction," *Designing Cities: Critical Readings in Urban Design* (Oxford: Blackwell, 2003). Those writing on specific normative theories of urban design are a very large group. Some of the best include: D. Gosling and B. Maitland, *Concepts of Urban Design* (London: Academy Editions, 1984); Geoffrey Broadbent, *Emerging Concepts in Urban Space Design* (London: Van Nostrand Reinhold International, 1990); David Sucher, *City Comforts: How to Build an Urban Village* (City Comforts Inc., 2003); Nan Ellin, *Integral Urbanism* (London: Routledge, 2006) and *Good Urbanism* (London: Routledge, 2012); Mark L. Hinshaw, *True Urbanism: Living In and Near the Center* (Chicago: APA / Planner's Press, 2007); Christopher B. Leinberger, *The Option of Urbanism: Investing in a New American Dream* (Washington, DC: Island Press, 2009); and Jan Gehl, *Cities for People* (Washington, DC: Island Press, 2010). In addition to these, no shortage of normative theory exists on the key drivers of contemporary city planning and urban design: sustainability, livability, smart growth, compact cities, landscape urbanism, and urban villages.

In contrast to those dealing in normative ideas, a number of researchers are attempting to identify more objective metrics for quantifying the qualities that make places successful. In large part, this is a trend toward objective-based science in city and regional planning, as well as the desire to avoid the subjectivities of normative theory. A number of researcher-advocates offer methods that aggregate many different characteristics into a single "score" or "rating" that can let consumers understand the comparative differences between places. The place-rating material is well known throughout the world in its attempts to name the most livable or best cities: Susan L. Cutter, *Rating Places: A Geographer's View on Quality of Life* (Washington, DC: Association of American Geographers, 1985); David Savageau, *Places Rated Almanac*, 25th edn. (Places Rated Books LLC, 2007); and Bert Sperling and Peter Sander, *Cities Ranked and Rated*, 2nd edn. (New York: Wiley, 2007). This material is particularly useful for those thinking of relocating their primary residence or business; or conversely, those looking for a retirement location or vacation destination. Not surprisingly, the place-rating material has been championed by city marketers and boosters who want to compete globally for economic share, business relocations, tourism, and reputation. What becomes interesting in this material is the fluidity of how cities change positions in place ranking from year to year, even though not much may have changed within a city compared to the previous year. Simple methodological changes in how the rankings are calculated might adjust the relative ranking of cities, and thus we see an alternating list of places that claim they offer the highest quality of life or become the best places for retirement. For example, one year it is Geneva, the next Melbourne, followed by Vancouver. Place-rating methods are examined critically by John D. Landis and David S. Sawicki in "A Planner's Guide to the 'Places Rated Almanac'," *Journal of the American Planning Association* (vol. 54, no. 3, pp. 336–346, 1988), where the authors caution against the method, priority of weighting, and usefulness of the Places Rated method in planning practice. Others using metrics for the quantification of place quality include many focusing on walkability (http://www.walkscore.com and http://www.activelivingresearch.org); the carbon or ecological footprint (http://www.footprintnetwork.org); and the health-related quality of life (http://www.healthmeasurement.org). Academics are increasingly creating urban design metrics to bolster their research agenda, gain respect from social science-oriented colleagues, and better compete for research funding from scientific organizations. Key issues with these metrics include: the attempt to numerically quantify that which might be normatively subjective, the reduction of place complexity to a single number, the pseudo-science used in calculating the measurements, and, importantly, the lack of capacity that many cities have for ongoing measurement, interpretation, and application. Irony exists here in the lack of robustness of these more scientific methods, in comparison to the respect that Lynch's more normative approach has received.

Performance characteristics will be more general, and the easier to use, to the degree that performance can be measured solely by reference to the spatial form of the city. But we know that the quality of a place is due to the joint effect of the place and the society which occupies it. I can imagine three tactics for avoiding the necessity of taking the entire universe into account in this attempt to measure city performance. First, we can elaborate those linkages between form and purpose which exist because of certain species-wide or human settlement-wide regularities: the climatic tolerances of human beings, for example, or the importance of the small social group, or the very general function of any city as a network of access. Second, we can add to the description of the spatial form of a place those particular social institutions and mental attitudes which are directly linked to that form and repeatedly critical to its quality, as I have already done. Both of these tactics will be employed below.

Third and last, however, we must realize that it would be foolish to set performance *standards* for cities, if we mean to generalize. To assert that the ideal density is twelve families to the acre, or the ideal daytime temperature is 68°F., or that all good cities are organized into residential neighborhoods of 3,000 persons each, are statements too easily discredited. Situations and values differ. What we might hope to generalize about are performance *dimensions*, that is, certain identifiable characteristics of the performance of cities which are due primarily to their spatial qualities and which are measurable scales, along which different groups will prefer to achieve different positions. It should then be possible to analyze any city form or proposal, and to indicate its location on the dimension, whether by a number or just by "more or less." To be general, the dimensions should be important qualities for most, if not all, persons and cultures. Ideally, the dimensions should also include all the qualities which any people value in a physical place. (Of course, this last is an unbearably severe criterion.)

For example, we might consider *durability* as a performance dimension. (But we won't. This is a red herring.) Durability is the degree to which the physical elements of a city resist wear and decay and retain their ability to function over long periods. In choosing this dimension, we assume that everyone has important preferences about the durability of his city, although some want it evanescent and others would like it to last forever. Furthermore, we know how to measure the general durability of a settlement, or at least how to measure a few significant aspects of durability. A tent camp can be compared to a troglodyte settlement, and, given the values of a particular set of inhabitants, we can tell you which one of them is better, or people can make that evaluation for themselves. They can also decide how much durability they are willing to give up in return for other values. Perhaps we can show that very low or very high durabilities are bad for everyone, and so we identify an optimum range. Although the linkage of durability to basic human aims is only a chain of assumptions, we believe that the assumptions are reasonable. Correlations of durability with preference exist, and people are content to use this idea as a workable intermediate goal. Meanwhile, its connection to city form – to such concrete physical characteristics as building material, density, and roof construction – can be explicitly demonstrated.

To be a useful guide to policy, a set of performance dimensions should have the following characteristics:

1. They should be characteristics which refer primarily to the spatial form of the city, as broadly defined above, given certain very general statements about the nature of human beings and their cultures. To the extent that the value set on those characteristics varies with variations in culture, that dependence should be explicit. The dimension itself and its method of analysis should remain unchanged.
2. The characteristics should be as general as possible, while retaining their explicit connection to particular features of form.
3. It should be possible to connect these characteristics to the important goals and values of any culture, at least through a chain of reasonable assumptions.
4. The set should cover all the features of settlement form which are relevant, in some important way to those basic values.
5. These characteristics should be in the form of dimensions of performance, along which various groups in various situations will be free to choose optimum points or "satisficing" thresholds. In other words, the dimensions will be usable where values differ or are evolving.

6 Locations along these dimensions should be identifiable and measurable, at least in the sense of "more or less," using available data. They may be complex dimensions, however, so that locations on them need not be single points. Moreover, the data, while conceivably available, may for the present escape us.

7 The characteristics should be at the same level of generality.

8 If possible, they should be independent of one another. That is, setting a level of attainment along one dimension should not imply a particular setting on some other dimension. If we are unable to produce uncontaminated dimensions of this kind, we can settle for less, if the cross-connections are explicit. Testing for independence will require detailed analysis.

9 Ideally, measurements on these dimensions should be able to deal with qualities which change over time, forming an extended pattern which can be valued in the present. More likely, however, the measurements will deal with present conditions, but may include the drift of events toward the future.

There have been many previous attempts to outline a set of criteria for a "good city." The dimensions I propose below are not original inventions. Previous sets have always broken at least some of the rules above. They have at times been so general as to go far beyond settlement form and to require a complex (and usually impossible) calculation which involves culture, political economy, and many other non-formal features. Or they refer to some particular physical solution that is appropriate only in a particular situation. They may mix spatial and nonspatial features, or mix levels of generality, or mix the scale of application. Frequently, they are bound to a single culture. They do not include all the features of city form which are important to human values. They are often given as absolute standards, or they call for minimizing or maximizing, instead of being dimensions. The qualities are sometimes not measurable, or even identifiable, in any clear way. They frequently overlap each other.

The list that follows is an attempt to rework and reorder the material in a way that escapes those difficulties. The presumed generality of this list lies in certain regularities: the physical nature of the universe, the constants of human biology and culture, and some features which commonly appear in contemporary large-scale settlements, including the processes by which they are maintained and changed.

But some view of the nature of human settlements, however unclear or general is necessarily assumed in making any list. Unfortunately, it is much easier to say what a city is not: not a crystal, not an organism, not a complex machine, not even an intricate network of communications – like a computer or a nervous system – which can learn by reorganizing its own patterns of response, but whose primitive elements are forever the same. True, somewhat like the latter, the city is interconnected to an important degree by signals, rather than by place-order or mechanical linkages or organic cohesion. It is indeed something changing and developing, rather than an eternal form, or a mechanical repetition which in time wears out, or even a permanent recurrent cycling which feeds on the degradation of energy, which is the concept of ecology.

Yet the idea of ecology seems close to an explanation, since an ecosystem is a set of organisms in a habitat, where each organism is in some relation to others of its own kind, as well as to other species and the inorganic setting. This system of relations can be considered as a whole, and has certain characteristic features of fluctuation and development, of species diversity, of intercommunication, of the cycling of nutrients, and the pass-through of energy. The concept deals with very complex systems, with change, with organic and inorganic elements together, and with a profusion of actors and of forms.

Moreover, an ecosystem seems to be close to what a settlement is. Complicated things must in the end be understood in their own terms. An image will fail to stick if it is only a borrowing from some other area, although metaphorical borrowings are essential first steps in understanding.

Apt as it is, the concept of ecology has its drawbacks, for our purpose. Ecological systems are made up of "unthinking" organisms, not conscious of their fatal involvement in the system and its consequences, unable to modify it in any fundamental way. The ecosystem, if undisturbed, moves to its stable climax of maturity, where the diversity of species and the efficiency of the use of energy passing through are both at the maximum, given the fixed limits of the inorganic setting. Nutrients recycle but may gradually be lost to sinks, while energy inevitably escapes the system or becomes unavailable. Nothing is learned; no progressive developments ensue. The inner experiences of the organisms – their purposes and images – are irrelevant; only their outward behavior matters.

An evolving "learning ecology" might be a more appropriate concept for the human settlement, some of whose actors, at least, are conscious, and capable of modifying themselves and thus of changing the rules of the game. The dominant animal consciously restructures materials and switches the paths of energy flow. To the familiar ecosystem characteristics of diversity, interdependence, context, history, feedback, dynamic stability, and cyclic processing, we must add such features as values, culture, consciousness, progressive (or regressive) change, invention, the ability to learn, and the connection of inner experience and outer action. Images, values, and the creation and flow of information play an important role. Leaps, revolutions, and catastrophes can happen, new paths can be taken. Human learning and culture have destabilized the system, and perhaps, some day, other species will join the uncertainty game. The system does not inevitably move toward some fixed climax state, nor toward maximum entropy. A settlement is a valued arrangement, consciously changed and stabilized. Its elements are connected through an immense and intricate network, which can be understood only as a series of overlapping local systems, never rigidly or instantaneously linked, and yet part of a fabric without edges. Each part has a history and a context, and that history and context shift as we move from part to part. In a peculiar way, each part contains information about its local context, and thus, by extension, about the whole.

Values are implicit in that viewpoint, of course. The good city is one in which the continuity of this complex ecology is maintained while progressive change is permitted. The fundamental good is the continuous development of the individual or the small group and their culture: a process of becoming more complex, more richly connected, more competent, acquiring and realizing new powers – intellectual, emotional, social, and physical. If human life is a continued state of becoming, then its continuity is founded on growth and development (and its development on continuity: the statement is circular). If development is a process of becoming more competent and more richly connected, then an increasing sense of connection to one's environment in space and in time is one aspect of growth. So that settlement is good which enhances the continuity of a culture and the survival of its people, increases a sense of connection in time and space, and permits or spurs individual growth: development, within continuity, via openness and connection. (The bias of the teacher is now unmasked.)

These values could, of course, be applied to judging a culture as well as a place. In either case, there is an inherent tension as well as a circularity between continuity and development – between the stabilities and connections needed for coherence and the ability to change and grow. Those cultures whose organizing ideas and institutions deal successfully with that tension and circularity are presumably more desirable, in this view. Similarly, a good settlement is also an *open* one: accessible, decentralized, diverse, adaptable, and tolerant to experiment. This emphasis on dynamic openness is distinct from the insistence of environmentalists (and most utopians) on recurrence and stability. The blue ribbon goes to development, as long as it keeps within the constraints of continuity in time and space. Since an unstable ecology risks disaster as well as enrichment, flexibility is important, and also the ability to learn and adapt rapidly. Conflict, stress, and uncertainty are not excluded, nor are those very human emotions of hate and fear, which accompany stress. But love and caring would certainly be there.

Any new model of the city must integrate statements of value with statements of objective relationships. The model I have sketched is neither a developed nor an explicit one, and I retreat to my more narrow concern with normative theory. But the surviving reader will see that these general preferences – for continuity, connection, and openness – underlie all the succeeding pages, even while the theory makes an effort to see that it is applicable to any context.

Given that general view and the task of constructing a limited set of performance dimensions for the spatial form of cities, I suggest the following ones. None of them are single dimensions; all refer to a cluster of qualities. Yet each cluster has a common basis and may be measured in some common way. I simply name the dimensions at this point.

There are five basic dimensions:

1 *Vitality:* the degree to which the form of the settlement supports the vital functions, the biological requirements and capabilities of human beings – above all, how it protects the survival of the species. This is an anthropocentric criterion, although we may some day consider the way in which the environment supports the life of other species, even where that does not contribute to our own survival.

2 *Sense:* the degree to which the settlement can be clearly perceived and mentally differentiated and structured in time and space by its residents and the degree to which that mental structure connects with their values and concepts – the match between environment, our sensory and mental capabilities, and our cultural constructs.

3 *Fit:* the degree to which the form and capacity of spaces, channels, and equipment in a settlement match the pattern and quantity of actions that people customarily engage in, or want to engage in – that is, the adequacy of the behavior settings, including their adaptability to future action.

4 *Access:* the ability to reach other persons, activities, resources, services, information, or places, including the quantity and diversity of the elements which can be reached.

5 *Control:* the degree to which the use and access to spaces and activities, and their creation, repair, modification, and management are controlled by those who use, work, or reside in them.

If these five dimensions comprise all the principal dimensions of settlement quality, I must of course add two meta-criteria, which are always appended to any list of good things:

6 *Efficiency:* the cost, in terms of other valued things, of creating and maintaining the settlement, for any given level of attainment of the environmental dimensions listed above.

7 *Justice:* the way in which environmental benefits and costs are distributed among persons, according to some particular principle such as equity, need, intrinsic worth, ability to pay, effort expended, potential contribution, or power. Justice is the criterion which balances the gains among persons, while efficiency balances the gains among different values.

These meta-criteria are distinct from the five criteria that precede them. First, they are meaningless until costs and benefits have been defined by specifying the prior basic values. Second, the two meta-criteria are involved in each one of the basic dimensions, and thus they are by no means independent of them. They are repetitive subdimensions of each of the five. In each case, one asks: (1) What is the cost (in terms of anything else we choose to value) of achieving this degree of vitality, sense, fit, access, or control? and (2) Who is getting how much of it?

I propose that these five dimensions and two meta-criteria are the inclusive measures of settlement quality. Groups and persons will value different aspects of them and assign different priorities to them. But, having measured them, a particular group in a real situation would be able to judge the relative goodness of their place, and would have the clues necessary to improve or maintain that goodness. All five can be defined, identified, and applied to some degree, and this application can be improved.

Now, is this really so? Do the dimensions really meet all the criteria which were given at the beginning of this section? Do they in fact illuminate the "goodness" of a city, or are they only a verbal checklist? Can locations on these dimensions be identified and measured in a concrete way? Are they useful guidelines for research? Do they apply to varied cultures and in varied situations? Can general propositions be made about how optima vary according to variations in resource, power, or values? Can degrees of achievement on these dimensions be related to particular spatial patterns, so that the benefits of proposed solutions can be predicted? Do our preferences about places indeed vary significantly as performance changes? All that remains to be seen.

"A Catholic Approach to Organizing What Urban Designers Should Know"

from *Journal of Planning Literature* (1992)

Anne Vernez Moudon

Editors' Introduction

Urban design is a holistic and integrative field whose practitioners must have a wide range of knowledge, including how people behave in physical environments, how people perceive places, how places came to be, dimensional natures of different urban forms, and how design proposals may relate to the natural, physical, and cultural environments in which they are situated. Because relevant research findings come from many different disciplines – urban design, architecture, landscape architecture, geography, sociology, the cognitive sciences, and art, to name a few – even in an electronic age it can be difficult for designers to know where to find them.

Urban design professor Anne Vernez Moudon has been at the forefront of making sense of the knowledge base necessary to practice urban design. Here, in "A Catholic Approach to Organizing What Urban Designers Should Know," which was published in the *Journal of Planning Literature*, she sets out a classification that covers areas of substantive knowledge that can inform design practice and research, purposefully leaving out normative design theories – that is, theories about what should be done – on the grounds that designers should not rush to prescriptive solutions. The classification is "catholic" in the sense that it encompasses a broad range of research subject matters and approaches. The categories are useful to students because they let them know where in the broader framework their research interests lie, and useful to practitioners and researchers because they encourage them to broaden their research approaches and not get caught in repetitive patterns that are not as rich as they might be. Included with the reading is an extensive bibliography that provides a rich resource of research and theory pertaining to urban design-related issues.

Anne Vernez Moudon is Professor of Architecture, Landscape Architecture, and Urban Design and Planning at the University of Washington, Seattle, where she runs the Urban Forms Lab. She also serves on the National Advisory Committee for Active Living Research for the Robert Wood Johnson Foundation. Her book *Built for Change: Neighborhood Architecture in San Francisco* (Cambridge, MA: MIT Press, 1986), which presents a thorough analysis of the evolution and development of physical form of the Alamo Square neighborhood in San Francisco from the mid-nineteenth century through the 1980s, stands as an important example of the use of the typomorphological method. Her other books include the edited volumes *Public Streets for Public Use* (New York: Columbia University Press, 1991), and *Monitoring Land Supply with Geographic Information Systems*, co-authored with Michael Hubner (New York: John Wiley, 2000). She has also published several edited monographs, including *Urban Design–Reshaping our Cities* (Seattle, WA: Urban Design Program, College of Architecture and Urban Planning, University of Washington, 1995) co-edited with Wayne Attoe; and *Master-Planned Communities: Shaping Exurbs in the 1990s* (Seattle, WA: Urban Design Program, College of Architecture and Urban Planning, University of Washington, 1990).

Much of Anne Vernez Moudon's recent work has focused in the areas of typomorphological studies and relationships between built form and pedestrian behavior. Seeking to make typomorphology accessible to a North American audience, her chapter "Getting to Know the Built Landscape: Typomorphology," in Karen A. Franck and Lynda H. Schneekloth (eds), *Ordering Space: Types in Architecture and Design* (New York: Van Nostrand Reinhold, 1994) discusses the various European typomorphological schools of thought and their contributions to knowledge about built urban form. Another article, which seeks to establish typomorphological studies as an interdisciplinary research endeavor, is "Urban Morphology as an Emerging Interdisciplinary Field," *Urban Morphology* (vol. 1, pp. 3–10, 1997). Her research on urban form and pedestrian behavior has been published in numerous research reports.

Writings by others that focus on normative urban design theories and design responses, rather than substantive knowledge, include Geoffrey Broadbent, *Emerging Concepts in Public Open Space Design* (New York: Van Nostrand Reinhold, 1990) and Kevin Lynch, *Good City Form* (Cambridge, MA: MT Press, 1980).

■ ■ ■ ■ ■ ■

Urban design is familiar to both architects and urban planners. Although some continue to associate urban design with tall downtowns and large-scale architecture, most recognize it as an interdisciplinary approach to designing our built environment. Urban design seeks not to eliminate the planning and design professions but to integrate them and in so doing, to go beyond each one's charter. It extends the architect's focus on the built project. It makes urban planning policies operational by taking into account their impact on the form and meaning of the environments produced. Recently, landscape architects have also added some of their concerns to urban design. As a young enterprise at the edge of established professions, urban design must endure many punches, pushes, and pulls. But its institutional survival is essential to guarantee even a glimpse of interdisciplinary activity in planning and design.

Urban design emerged sometime in the 1960s – its exact origins have yet to be determined, coveted as they are by many different groups. The field was born out of a search for quality in urban form. This search continues to date, focused on urban environments that have both functional and aesthetic appeal to those who inhabit them. The thrust of the field has lain in practical rather than academic pursuits: urban designers worry about "what should be done" and "what will work."

By and large also, the "theories" guiding practice have remained at a paradigmatic level, based on different exemplary solutions. The history of the field is characterized by many such theories that have come and gone, the victims of the elusive complexities of practice (to mention only a few such theories: functionalism, modernism, participatory design, neo-rationalism, and pattern languages).

This article poses a different question: "what should urban designers know?" It is based on the premise that a mature, successful practice and its concomitant long-lasting theories rest on "knowing." An attempt to pull together the significant body of existing knowledge, this work starts to define an epistemology *for* urban design – to study the nature and grounds of knowledge necessary to practice urban design.

The approach taken is emphatically catholic. In the laic, generic sense of the word, "catholic" means broad in sympathies, tastes, and interests. Being catholic is not to be nonpartisan, but rather nonsectarian, tolerant of and open to different approaches. Hence the body of knowledge surveyed herein comes from various fields and disciplines allied to urban design that, together, lay the groundwork for an epistemology for urban design. Some of the research is informative in nature, seeking to describe or explain certain phenomena. Other research goes one step further into theory building. The differences between these two types of research will not be discussed specifically, however, because the nature and scope of theory in, of, or for urban design is too undefined to deal with within the confines of this article.

The article is divided into two parts. One scans a conceptual framework delineating the basic elements of a catholic approach to building an epistemology for urban design, including a range of areas of inquiry, research strategies, and research methods. The second part discusses specific areas of inquiry that add to such an epistemology. References are drawn primarily, but not exclusively, from literature available in English.

SCANNING FIELDS OF KNOWLEDGE

What are the basic sources of knowledge available to the urban designer? In this country, the work of the late Kevin Lynch (1960, 1972, 1981) and especially his studies of people's images of cities perhaps come first to mind as a source of important information. Lynch's influence in putting urban design on the intellectual map of city planning is undeniable and astonishingly broad: not only is his work well known in Europe and Japan, but it is readily used in different fields and disciplines such as planning, architecture, and geography. Recently, Christian Norberg-Schulz (1980, 1985) has grown influential as well. His classification of elements and meanings in environments has impressed both students and practitioners. William Whyte's (1980) work on downtown plazas and Appleyard's (1981) studies of livable streets are often referred to in urban design as well. But also, Grady Clay's (1973) explanations of the American city, J.B. Jackson's (1980, 1984) reconstructions of the American landscape, and Amos Rapoport's (1977, 1982, 1990) elaborate explanations of people's interactions with their environment, all come to mind as substantive studies for urban design. Further contributors include Lewis Mumford (1961), Edmund Bacon (1976), Jonathan Barnett (1986) on the Elusive City, Jay Appleton (1975, 1980) on a prospect/refuge theory, and more recently, Anne Whiston Spirn (1984) regarding the ecology of the city. Some of these works lean toward architectural design, others are more landscape architecture oriented, yet others are closer to urban planning concerns.

The list of works of importance in urban design can, and does, go on. Influences are numerous and scattered. Even if Lynch emerges as a powerful figure, his legacy is made less clear when coupled with all the other bits and pieces of research available. In truth, all research and theories are *partial*: they address some but never all of the issues faced by the designer. They also stress a particular view or philosophy of what is important in city design – for instance, Lynch's emphasis on how people see

and feel about their environment, Rapoport's focus on the use of and meanings in the built environment, Spirn's concerns for the physical health of the city, and so on. Only when considered together do this research and these theories begin to yield a more complete set of information to the designer. They can indeed be complementary, although sometimes they are also contradictory. To build up actual knowledge in urban design, one should not look for the *correct* approach or theory but should instead compile and assess all the research that adds to what the urban designer must be familiar with.

Thus the task is to map out knowledge readily available, to identify the collection of works pertaining to the central concerns of urban design, and to devise a conceptual framework organizing this collection. To help gather this collection and map its organization, several elements need to be considered and are reviewed below.

The normative-prescriptive versus substantive-descriptive dilemma

It is important to distinguish first between *normative* or *prescriptive* information (emphasizing the "what should be") and *substantive* or critically *descriptive* knowledge (emphasizing the "what is" and perhaps also the "why") (Lang 1987; Moudon 1988). Stated more concretely, *understanding* a city or a part of a city and *designing* it are two different things. Logically, one needs to understand what cities are made of, how they come about and function, what they mean to people, and so on, in order to design "good" cities. So far, research most used in urban design not only looks for explanations of the city, but it customarily moves into evaluation and recommendations for future design.[1] This is not surprising: urban design is a normative, prescriptive field, and urban designers are trained to imagine and execute schemes for the future. While research is usually associated with substantive information and with understanding specific phenomena, it is expected that research for urban design will yield information that has normative dimensions and that eventually helps design. Hence while understanding (describing) cities and designing (prescribing) them are *opposite* conceptual poles, they also represent a *continuum* (see Table 1).

Table 1 Knowledge versus action and associated terms

Understanding cities	Designing cities
Past/present	Present/future
What was, what is	What should be
Descriptive	Prescriptive
Substantive	Normative
Research, reflection, knowledge	Action, projection
Urban science, urbanism	Urban design

These distinctions, however, are usually not well articulated in the planning and design fields. For example, the Anglo-Saxon term "urban design" is coveted by Latins who have to contend with *urbanisme* or *urbanismo*, terms that are clearly more reflective, less action-oriented than "urban design." Only in Italy can one find "urban science" and "urbanism" used commonly to define the spectrum of description versus prescription, research versus design.

Closer to home, Kevin Lynch's work is a good case in point illustrating the tensions between the two conceptual poles: Lynch researched people's mental images and constructs of cities and analyzed the history, evolution, and meaning of places in order to seek better ways to design cities. However, while in *The Image of the City* (1960), substantive information is separated from prescriptive or normative advice, in *A Theory of Good City Form* (1981), the two are closely interwoven. Similarly, as Christopher Alexander and his team (Alexander *et al.* 1977) rampage through existing cities they deem "good," they collect, sort out, and discard bits and pieces that they believe will constitute patterns or elements for designing new cities. However, they are essentially not interested in describing critically existing environments per se. On the architectural side of urban design, the brothers Krier (*Rational Architecture* 1978) have peaked [sic] into a prototypical medieval town for identifying the antidote to the ills of modern design theories. Their American followers, architects and town planners Duany and Plater-Zyberk (Knack 1989), have found their norms in the late nineteenth-century American small town, which, after some study, they have then modified and spiced up with garden city and city beautiful theories to establish their own theory of design.

The attractiveness of the normative stand is obvious: it provides unmitigated guidance for designers in their everyday endeavors. Yet its limitations are serious: in the light of the wholesomeness and complexity inherent to design, all normative theories eventually run into difficulties and often fail outright. Further, it is disturbing to find that many normative theories use research to justify or substantiate a priori beliefs when, in fact, the reverse should take place, and research results should be interpreted to *develop* theories.

In order to enter the next generation of urban design theory, urban designers will need to pay more attention to the substantive side of research and to refrain from making quick prescriptive inferences from such research. They will need to separate conceptually the art of description from that of prescription and to devise clean and honest ways of evaluating existing or past situations (for opposing views on this matter, see Jarvis 1980 and Oxman 1987). This is not to say that description or substantive work is "true"; that is, free of values and interpretation. Description is just as subjective – dependent on who is doing it – as prescription. As the art of seeing, hearing, smelling, feeling, and knowing, description can only reflect the capabilities and sensitivities of the researcher (Relph 1984). But if descriptive activity is just as morally bounded as prescription, and if it tells what is right or wrong subjectively, it does nonetheless stop short of venturing into what should be done.

For the design and planning professions to mature properly, time must be taken to focus on substantive information. Some scholars have even advocated the need to describe solely without seeking explanation because they see explanation (the "why" attached to the "what") as yet another incentive not to grasp fully the object or phenomenon being described (Relph 1984). Whatever the case may be, substantive approaches will force designers and planners to engage personally in the information at hand, to interpret it, and to apply it to the specific context of their activities.

The gap between knowledge and action is not an easy one to bridge. It requires careful synthesis. As the perennial example of substantive information, the use of historical studies provides a case in point: today work in history is fashionable and touched upon by many urban designers, yet the dialectic between practice and historical knowledge remains elusive at best, and so far seemingly capricious and idiosyncratic. Careful assessment must precede jumping to practical conclusions.

For these reasons, this article focuses on substantive research and theories. A companion part to this article remains to be written which would map the scope and breadth of normative theory in urban design. Some of this work has been done by French urbanist and philosopher Françoise Choay. Choay has framed an epistemology of urban design as a normative, prescriptive field in two seminal books that, although they include Anglo-Saxon literature, are only available in French. One, *Urbanisme, utopies et réalités* (1965), is an anthology of key texts on urban design since the nineteenth century. The second, *La régle et le modèle* (1980), posits two fundamental texts defining an explicit, autonomous conceptual framework "to conceive and produce new spaces": Alberti's *De re aedificatoria* (1988), first published in 1452, which, according to Choay, proposes rules for urban design, and Thomas More's *Utopia* (1989), first published in 1516 as a model for urban design.

Others have started to assemble normative theories of urban design, notably Gosling and Maitland (1984), Jarvis (1980), and recently, Geoffrey Broadbent (1990). Broadbent's latest book paints a broad yet condensed chronological picture of "emerging *concepts* in urban *space* design" (my emphases of Broadbent's book title). It promises to encourage future critical assessment of the significance and effectiveness of normative theories of and paradigms in urban design.

Concentrations of inquiry

Substantive research and theories can first be classified by their area of concentration, according to specific views and aspects of the city on which they are focusing. Establishing different concentrations of inquiry is to accept that there are several different lenses through which the design and the making of the city can be viewed and that, in consequence, no single approach to design may suffice. As pedestrian as this realization may appear to, for instance, engineers or physicians who are used to studying their problems from many different angles, it is a challenging proposal to the urban designer accustomed to thinking about singular, "correct"

approaches. Nine concentrations of inquiry have been identified: urban history studies, picturesque studies, image studies, environment-behavior studies, place studies, material culture studies, typology-morphology studies, spacemorphology studies, and nature-ecology studies. The definition and contents of these areas constitutes the second part of this article.

Research strategies

The specific research strategies that can be used to develop knowledge are, again, several. One quickly discovers that the choice of a research strategy unveils the true philosophical basis of the research itself. The first research strategy is termed the *literary approach*: it emanates from the humanistic fields – literature and history being the most prominent ones – and it relies on literature searches, references and reviews, and archival work of all kinds, as well as personal accounts of given situations. The intent of the literary approach is to relate a story of a given set of events.

Second is the *phenomenological approach*, which projects a holistic view of the world, everything being related to everything, and whose practice depends entirely on the researcher's total experience of an event. It is similar to the artist's approach because it is both learned and intuitive, synthetic and wholesome, or eidetic (signifying that it uses specific examples of behavior, experience, and meaning to render descriptive generalizations about the world and human living [Seamon 1987, 16]). Phenomenologists describe events with all their feelings, senses, and knowledge. They usually refuse to explain the "why" of their findings because they see explanation rooted in interpretation and misinterpretation – leading quickly to abuse of information. Phenomenologists therefore oppose the third research strategy, *positivism*, which portrays the value of description in explanation.

Positivism maintains that knowledge is based on natural phenomena to be verified by empirical science. Positivism implies certainty of cause and effect. It is the tool of the sciences, which are based on the reduction of wholes and on systems of interconnected parts.

While most attempts to describe built environments have used literary or positivistic approaches, phenomenological approaches have recently flourished, according to Seamon, because of a practical crisis in the design fields, where nonholistic approaches have led to partially successful environments, and because of a philosophical crisis in the sciences due to the limitations of positivist thinking. Recently also, however, there have been attempts to reconcile positivism and phenomenology and to see them as complementary (Hardie *et al.* 1989; Seamon 1987).

Modes of inquiry

Specific modes of inquiry are identified to distinguish further between the various research strategies used. Two modes seem to prevail. One is the *historical-descriptive* mode, in which the research is based primarily on accounts of historical evidence – whether on site or via historical documents, plans, drawings, painting, archives, or analyses of the topic. The historical-descriptive mode is generally not used for theory-building purposes, but focuses on highlighting specific events and things. Literary and phenomenological research strategies usually use this mode of inquiry.

The other mode is *empirical-inductive*, where the research is set to observe a given phenomenon or to collect information on it, which is then described via an analysis of the information gathered. Through induction, the explanations of the phenomenon may be generalized upon to develop a theory. ("Empirical" means relying on experience and observation alone, often without due regard for system or theory, or capable of being verified by observation or experiment. "Empiricism" is the theory that all knowledge originates in experience or the practice of relying upon observation and experiment; it is especially used in the natural sciences.) This mode prevails in positivistic research but can be found in phenomenological work as well.

A third mode is *theoretical-deductive*, in which a theory is developed on the basis of past knowledge, which is then tested via research. Used primarily in quantitative research (Carter 1976), this mode is rarely found in the design fields, because they encompass problems that are either too complex or, as Horst Rittel has termed them, too wicked to be approached quantitatively (Rittel and Webber 1972). In such cases, this mode seems to lead to truisms (e.g., all grid plans are the result of a planned approach to making cities) or then to problems that have limited significance to the design of whole environments (e.g., economic theories related to real estate taxation, theories of land use allocation, housing choices, and so on).

Research focus: object/subject

A third screen needs to be applied to areas of inquiry, the research focus. Most research in this country focuses on the study of *people* in the environment. This *subject* orientation enlarged in the 1960s when research became seen as a necessary addition to the practice of planning and design. The primacy of subject-oriented research can be explained as a reaction to "old guard" designers' earlier focus on the physical components of the environment. Theirs was an orientation toward the *object* – a second possible research focus – which became increasingly suspicious as theories of good health, safety, and welfare relying on the need for clean, airy environments continued to bring unsatisfactory results. The ultimate blow to the object orientation of physical planners was the failure of urban renewal schemes, which proved that poverty, not environment, was the primary reason for epidemics, crime, and ethically questionable lifestyles. That good environments can do little to alleviate the basic state of poverty was a hard lesson to learn after four decades of work. From then on, research on the object qualities of the environment became unpopular, and a single focus on people in the environment prevailed with, for instance, sociologist Herbert Gans (1969) as its greatest advocate.

Later, some researchers urged concentration on the interaction between people and environments as a specific phenomenon that could explain well the nature of our environments (see Rapoport 1977; G. Moore *et al.* 1985). Today, the field of person-environment relations, or environment-behavior research, is at least present in planning and design. At the same time, it is under heavy inside and outside criticism largely for neglecting the "environment" part of the person-environment couplet. A return to the study of the object has been advocated by many, especially architects influenced by theorists like Rossi (1964, 1982), who has gone so far as to argue the autonomy of architecture as a discipline that is separate from the sciences and the arts. More modest postures favoring a return to object-oriented research, with complementary rather than primacy over subject research, have been argued as well by, for instance, geographer M.P. Conzen (1978), environmental psychologists D. Canter (1977) and J. Sime (1986) and architect L. Groat (Moudon 1987). This trend corresponds also to a rising interest in the study of vernacular environments as the physical evidence of people's long-standing interactive relationship with their surroundings. Vernacular environments thus offer attractive prospects: many are unusual physical objects, yet not the objects of a few planners and designers, but those traditions and customs that are an intrinsic part of culture. Indeed this "culturally ground object" can uncover the deep relationship between people and environments.

Research ethos: etic/emic

Finally, research needs to be screened for its ethos – this term is selected to depict the "heart" of the research. Two categories of ethos come to mind: the *etic* and *emic* ethos. Borrowed from anthropology, these terms were first popularized in design circles by Amos Rapoport (1977). They come from *phonetic* – related to the written language – and *phonemic* – related to the spoken language. The difference can be further grasped by comparing the two French terms, *la langue* and *la parole*, the first being language as a structured system of sound or signs to be studied for its internal logic, and the second, a no less structured, yet only practiced system of sounds. Applied to studies of people and culture, etic and emic relate to the nature of the source of the information gathered – etic in the case of the informant being the researcher, the person who will use the information, and emic in the case of the informant being the person observed.

Environment and behavior studies were the first to seek to bring an emic orientation to the design professions: they unearthed information about the uses of environments directly from the users, without relying on the opinion of design and planning professionals. However, the actual methods used in person-environment studies can be more or less emic. For instance, unstructured interviews, oral histories, and self-studied methods of all sorts are

straightforwardly emic. But observations of behaviors, although emic in their intent, are, in the true sense of the term, etic because they are done by professionals. Rapoport has called these research approaches "derived" etic and has opposed them to "imposed" etic approaches, which he condemns as mere fabrications of the researcher's mind.

The importance of getting emically significant information about the environment cannot be understated. Lynch's (1960) studies of people's images of cities popularized the need for an emic ethos in the information necessary to the planning and urban design professions. These studies complemented earlier works in parallel areas of anthropology and sociology: the Lynds' critical description of people's lives in *Middletown* (1929); W. Lloyd Warner's *Yankee City* (1963); Herbert Gans's controversial *The Levittowners* (1967); E.T. Hall's compilation of an environment both limited and enhanced by our physiological beings, in *The Silent Language* ([1959] 1980) and *The Hidden Dimension* (1966); and Robert Sommer's *Personal Space* (1969). All opened the door to an enormous field of yet untapped information.

AREAS OF CONCENTRATION

The concerns of urban designers and the nature of the decisions they make are necessarily wide-ranging. The interdisciplinary nature of urban design is likely to remain, and it is doubtful that the field will ever become a discipline with its own teachings separate from the established architecture, landscape, and planning professions. But if primarily architectural research (in, for instance, building science, architectural styles, or programming) and urban planning research (in employment, transportation, and housing demand) are only tangentially relevant to urban design, general socio-economic issues relating to the environment always loom near the foreground of urban design concerns. In this sense, all social science research pertaining to the environment is of interest. Similarly, all information concerning urban space and form will be useful. Yet a search for breadth must nonetheless be constrained for the sake of practicality. The literature surveyed focuses on the products of urban design or the human relationship with the built environment and related open spaces. The city, and more generally, the landscape as modified by people; its physical form and characteristics; the forces that shape it; the ways in which it is designed, produced, managed, used, and changed – all are central to a search for work that informs urban design. This essentially humanistic view of urban design justifies, at least within the confines of this article, further exclusions – to wit, literature on development and real estate finance, marketing, economic theory, and urban political theory that, unfortunately, relate only marginally at this point to the powers of urban designers.

The literature assembled according to these criteria has then been subjected to various classification exercises in an effort to identify salient areas of relevant inquiry. Thus the classification proposed emphasizes the types of questions posed by the different research, and groups the different works on the basis of the similarity of their quests rather than on the particularities of the methods used. The classification also offers a conceptual framework that is simple enough for both students and practitioners to remember and to work with over time.

Nine areas of concentration are proposed to encompass research useful to urban design. The list of areas should be seen as open-ended. Further, individual researchers can belong to one or more areas of inquiry, depending on the scope of their particular works. Some of these concentrations will be readily accepted as mainstream urban design. But some will raise eyebrows and need further discussion. The following pages review the nature and coverage of each area of concentration. Included is a tentative critique of each area's current status with respect to the level of its development and its current place in building an epistemology for urban design.

Urban history studies

The study of urban history has expanded remarkably over the past two decades to include now significant information for the practicing urban designer. This area's early dependence on art history and its traditional emphasis on "pedigreed" environments (Kostof 1986), on their formal and stylistic characteristics, is gone. Studies of places inhabited by ordinary people, explanations of why and how they inhabit them, have become the focus of an increasing number of scholarly works. Women, special needs groups, and the lower economic echelons of our social class structure are now an integral part of urban historical research. The history of the Anglo-Saxon suburb occupies an important place in historical studies today as suburbs constitute a substantial part of contemporary cities. Further, while Western influences continue to prevail, the overreliance on the European experience is waning, especially with Asian, Islamic, and other cultures embarking into internationally recognized scholarly endeavors.

Classical work on the history of urban form has come from design and planning historians, to include S.E. Rasmussen (1967), A.E.J. Morris (1972), and John Reps (1965), and from historical geographers such as Gerald Burke (1971), Frederick Hiorns (1956), Robert Dickinson (1961), Marcel Poëte (1967), and Henri Lavedan (1941). On the architectural side, there are Norma Evenson (1973, 1979), Spiro Kostof (1991), Norman Johnston (1983), Mark Girouard (1985), and Leonardo Benevolo (1980). Lewis Mumford (1961) remains a powerful critic, although his influence is diminishing with the emergence of more detailed research on various aspects of his writings. But the classical understanding of the history of the city is being enriched and also challenged by the growing explorations of ordinary landscapes, as in the works of Sam Bass Warner (1962, 1968), J.B. Jackson (1984), David Lowenthal and Marcus Binney (1981), Reyner Banham (1971), and recently, John Stilgoe (1982), Edward Relph (1987), and Michael Conzen (1980, 1990). James Vance (1977, 1990) emerges as a wide-ranging scholar of the processes shaping the physical construct of the urban environment. Considering the social history of environments also adds reality to historical forms that in the work of Bernard Rudofsky (1969), Alan Artibise and Paul-André Linteau (1984), Roy Lubove (1967), Anthony Sutcliffe (1984), Dolores Hayden (1981), and Gwendolyn Wright (1981), for instance, come alive in the descriptions of people's everyday struggles to shape their surroundings. How cities have actually been built is another subject of increasing interest – with Joseph Konvitz (1985), David Friedman (1988), and Mark Weiss (1987) standing out as promising contributors.

Work in history continues to be primarily etic and based on literary research (Dyoz 1968). However, derived etic research is beginning to dominate social history. Similarly, phenomenological approaches are increasingly taken – Relph's and J.B. Jackson's work being some of the best received by urban designers. Historians in this category can be object- or subject-oriented, or they can deal with the interaction between people and the physical environment.

The many new publications on increasingly varied subjects related to urban history exercise a growing influence on design and planning professionals. Correspondingly, a few historians are willing to venture into discussing the implications of historical experience for the present – for instance, Joseph Konvitz (1985), Robert Fishman (1977, 1987), Richard Sennett (1969), and Kenneth Jackson (1985; Jackson and Schultz 1972). Conversely, design-oriented scholars are reaching out into history in an attempt to develop theory – as for instance, Dolores Hayden (1984), Peter Rowe (1991), and Geoffrey Broadbent (1990).

The emerging richness of the field warrants further classification and analysis to help the urban designer to select the appropriate works and to uncover more than can be recognized in this article. Work in historical geography and urban preservation is worth reviewing as it includes critical inventories of urban environments. Similarly, historical guidebooks of cities, as well as contemporary guides emphasizing a city's history (Wurman 1971, 1972; Lyndon 1982) yield material that adds to historical knowledge of particular cities. Finally, journalistic criticism is an area that parallels history in its evaluative approach to existing environments and needs to be explored. While such criticism used to be limited to the isolated, yet powerful works of a few – for example, Jane Jacobs (1961), Hans Blumenfeld (1979), Ada Louise Huxtable (1970), Robert Venturi and Denise Scott Brown (Venturi et al. 1977), and recently, Joel Garreau (1991) – several publications have emerged that begin to provide a vehicle for systematic and continued critiques of implemented ideas (for instance, *Places, the Harvard Architectural Review*, and others).

Picturesque studies

Picturesque studies of the urban landscape were the foundations and the keystone of urban design

until the late 1960s. Today they keep a prominent position in both education and practice, and they offer some of the widely read introductory texts in urban design. These studies are running personal commentaries of the attributes of the physical environment. Authors identify and describe both verbally and graphically what they think are "good" environments. Such good environments are analyzed for their relevance to contemporary urban design problems.

Object-oriented, these works emphasize the visual aspect of the environment, which is seen as a stage set or a prop of human action. Gordon Cullen's *Concise Townscape* (1961) remains one of the most memorable contributions to urban design in the picturesque style. Cullen caught the fancy of both architects and planners disturbed by the technical, barren aspects of modernism. He helped them to formulate the scope of urban design as an interdisciplinary activity requiring both architectural and planning skills.

Precursors of the picturesque genre include Camillo Sitte ([1889] 1980) and Raymond Unwin (1909), both of whom have recently regained popularity in urban design. While the postwar work of Thomas Sharp (1946) on English villages has yet to be rediscovered by urban designers, Paul Spreiregen's *Urban Design: The Architecture of Towns and Cities* (1965) remains a standard introductory urban design text today. Also prominent are the writings of Edmund Bacon (1976) and Lawrence Halprin (1966, 1972).

The term "picturesque" is not widely recognized to encompass the works of Sitte, Cullen, Bacon, or Halprin. It has been used in this capacity by Panerai *et al.* (1980) in an effort to capture the emphasis on the pictorial component of the environment that characterizes works in this category. Robert Oxman (1987) used Cullen's own words and called the work "townscape analysis."

For all their popularity, however, picturesque studies are unevenly "practiced," and there have not been publications following this research and thinking mode in several years. Developments in the intellectual context of urban design have lessened the forcefulness of the original picturesque argument. First, if these studies are etic and phenomenological in nature – stands that remain in good currency in contemporary planning and design discourse – they do not espouse these philosophical beliefs in a conscious manner. Rather, they appear to assume a naïve "good-professional-knows-it-all" posture that has been rightfully questioned since the early 1970s. Simply put, they lack the literary references of more recent phenomenological writings such as Relph's or J.B. Jackson's. And they lack the theoretical and philosophical underpinnings of a Norberg-Schultz. It follows that picturesque studies do not fare well either with social science approaches in planning and design research: their unabashed etic stand is unacceptable on this score, and the idiosyncratic swinging between highly personal descriptions and specific prescriptions puts these works in an old-fashioned league.

Finally, whereas picturesque studies were innovative in their early consideration of vernacular landscapes, they have been superseded recently by the several bona fide historical works of scholars such as Thomas Schlereth (1985b), Dell Upton (Upton and Vlach 1986), John Stilgoe (1982), R.W. Brunskill (1981, 1982), Stefan Muthesius (1982), and others. Thus picturesque studies maintain a high profile for the beginning student of urban design but do not sustain well more rigorous and deep investigation.

Image studies

Image studies include a significant amount of work on how people visualize, conceptualize, and eventually understand the city. This category would not exist without Kevin Lynch's *The Image of the City* (1960), whose influence was paramount in launching subsequent research. In fact, many planners and designers see image studies as the main contribution of urban design to the design fields. The Lynchian approach is sometimes understood as continuing the picturesque tradition because of its focus on how the urban environment is perceived visually. Yet the posture of image studies is reversed from that of picturesque studies: it is the people's image of the environment that is sought out, not the professional observer's. Thus image studies are intrinsically emic and subject oriented. Lynch had been influenced by the works of E.T. Hall ([1959] 1980, 1966), Rudolph Arnheim (1954, 1966), and Gyorgy Kepes (1944, 1965, 1966). As a student, he was part of Kepes's MIT group of environmental thinkers who sought to create and understand environmental art – art in space and art as space, so to speak.

Image studies are witnesses to the growing influence of the social sciences on design since the 1960s. They focus on the physiological, psychological, and social dimensions of environments as they are used and experienced by people, and on how those aspects do or should shape design and design solutions. The importance given in these studies to the lay person's view of the surrounding environment has transformed urban design activity: not only are Lynch's five elements used (and, according to Lynch himself, abused [Lynch in Rodwin and Hollister 1984]), but questionnaires, surveys, and group meetings are now standard fare backing up the majority of complex design processes. Among the many studies looking to verify and to expand on Lynch's findings, the ones that brought systematic comparisons (and oppositions) between the professional's and the lay person's views, were his own student's, Donald Appleyard (Appleyard *et al.* 1964; Appleyard 1976). Working closely with psychologist Kenneth H. Craig, Appleyard's group at the University of California at Berkeley trained many students to research people and environments as a sound basis for urban design. Robin Moore (R. Moore 1986) and Mark Francis (Francis *et al.* 1984; Francis and Hester 1990) are products of Lynch's and Appleyard's programs and are now themselves eminent contributors in this arena. The scientific basis of their work has in effect closed the loop linking image studies and environment-behavior studies, and these researchers are now commonly associated with this latter area of concentration.

Environment-behavior studies

The study of relations between people and their surroundings is an interdisciplinary field whose history has yet to be documented fully. Stemming from work done since the turn of the century in environmental psychology and sociology, these studies have grown rapidly since the 1960s, supported by a variety of federally sponsored laws in such areas as community mental health, energy conservation, environmental protection, and programs directed at special needs populations, children, the elderly, the physically impaired, and others.

In the 1960s, the design and planning professions turned to sociology and environmental psychology as sources of valuable information in this new emic realm of research on the environment. Since then, person–environment relations has become a bona fide part of the architectural profession, covering research on how people use, like, or simply behave in given environments. The field also rapidly spread to urban design as Amos Rapoport, Kevin Lynch, and Donald Appleyard began to investigate the human dimension of neighborhoods, urban districts, and cities at large.

Environment-behavior research, as it is increasingly called today, has until recently been almost totally positivistic. Actually, its original influence on design was due to its science-based approach, which was deemed more serious, reliable, and rational than the then-traditional intuitive, often highly personal, design process. The introduction of the social sciences to planning and design was part of a broader trend of interest in multidisciplinary activity, itself the product of system-thinking developed by the military during World War II. In England, the influences of both modernism and the systems approach divided architectural schools of the postwar period into two groups: one at the Bartlett, where Llewelyn Davis was to assume a multidisciplinary approach to design, and the other at Cambridge University, with Martin and March, which was to focus on space, urban form, and land use (Hillier 1986).

In the United States in the early 1960s, the University of California at Berkeley was first to create a College of Environmental Design, thus expanding the professions of architecture and planning to the general design of environments, including industrial design. In the new curriculum at Berkeley, "user studies" (meant to collect information on people expected to use the facilities to be designed) and "design methods" involving the coordination of different interests and expertise (from the user to the investor) ranked high on the list of important courses that students were to take.

Although environment-behavior studies have recently suffered some setback at least in architecture (their development is perceived to have taken away from design – or is it Design?), they are in fact well entrenched in design thinking. People like Amos Rapoport (1977, 1982, 1990), Robert Gutman (1972), Michael Brill (Villeco and Brill 1981), Sandra

Howell (G. Moore et al. 1985), Jon Lang (1987), Karen Franck (Franck and Ahrentzen 1989), Clare Cooper Marcus (1975; Marcus and Sarkissian 1986), and Oscar Newman (1972, 1980) remain important figures in education and practice nationally. The Environmental Design Research Association (EDRA) celebrated its twentieth year with many of its members holding appointments in schools of design around the country (Hardie et al. 1989). The term "environmental design research" has been proposed to cover those studies that relate specifically to design and to eliminate the polarity and actual conflicts that the couplet environment-behavior engenders (Villeco and Brill 1981).

Influential figures contribute to the field: I. Altman (1986; Altman and Wohlwill 1976–85), D. Canter (1977), L. Festinger (1989), D. Stokols and I. Altman (1987), and J.F. Wohlwill (1981, 1985), among others. Principal authors directly related to issues of urban design include: Amos Rapoport (1977, 1982, 1990) on residential environments, city, and settlement; Donald Appleyard (1976, 1981) on city and streets; W.H. Whyte (1980) on urban open spaces and city; Jack Nasar (1988) on environmental aesthetics; Robin Moore (1986) on children and environments; Mark Francis (Francis et al. 1984) on urban open space; William Michelson (1970, 1977) on neighborhoods; Clare Cooper Marcus (1975; Marcus and Sarkissian 1986) on residential environments; both Jan Gehl (1987) and Roderick Lawrence (1987) on streets and residential environments; Oscar Newman (1972, 1980) on residential environments; and S. and R. Kaplan (1978) on open spaces. Further, if most of the studies conducted in this area relate to ordinary environments some deal with differences in values and preferences between professional designers and lay people (Cant 1977; Nasar 1988).

The broad, multidisciplinary nature of the field makes information retrieval somewhat difficult. There are many organizations sponsoring and publishing research (G. Moore et al. 1985), and many journals that have yet to provide comprehensive indexes. However the School of Architecture at the University of Wisconsin in Milwaukee, has published a handy bibliography for use by their doctoral students (G. Moore et al. 1987). Useful surveys of the field are also being produced (Altman and Wohlwill 1976–85; G. Moore et al. 1985; Stokols and Altman 1987; Zube and Moore 1987). As an interesting aside, G. Moore *et al.* (1987) include J.B. Jackson and other geographers as part of environmental design research. But in our classification, these works appear to fit best under material culture studies. If this overlap is of course proof of some of the issues related to the classification (and to classification in general), it is as evidence of rich relationships among areas of research of which only some are commonly associated with urban design.

The primarily positivistic stand of environment-behavior studies has become an area of contention and cause for criticism less from designers and planners as mentioned earlier, than from the field's own ranks. Questions are raised as to whether people's attitudes feelings, behaviors, and so on, should be pigeonholed in such categories as perception and cognition. What about the whole of people and environment relationships? What about the intangible, the spiritual? As noted earlier, these and other issues have led some to use phenomenological methods to carry out research. Further, a perceived overemphasis on the subject at the expense of the object qualities of the environment has led to dissatisfaction. In reaction, a group of researchers, scholars, and theoreticians has emerged, who are offshoots of environment-behavior studies in their concerns yet do not care to be formally related to the field. It was decided to put them in a category loosely called "place studies."

Place studies

Place studies gather many thinkers who have yet to crystallize as a bona fide group (identified but not articulated as such in G. Moore *et al.* 1985, xviii, 59–73). Since the late 1970s, several studies have set out to create knowledge and theories of place that are based on the importance of people's relations to their environment and yet do not fit properly within the environment-behavior category. First, they do not employ solely positivistic research strategies. Second, while the concern for both object and subject is central, the emphasis is on the object as an important preoccupation in design. Third, these studies look for the emotional as well as for the perceptual aspects of people–environment relations. Further, and perhaps most important, they bend toward derived etic and outright etic interpre-

tations. These studies thus appear as the black sheep of environment-behavior studies: abiding by the principles, but bending some of the basic rules.

Place studies include a great variety of research, which, because of its personal bent, is difficult to categorize further. However, one group of scholars consists of design and planning professionals; this may explain in part some of the object and etic emphases in this category. Norberg-Schulz (1980, 1985), Hester (1975, 1984), Allan Jacobs (1985), Violich (1983), Lerup (1977), Hillier and Hanson (1984), Thiel (1986), Greenbie (1981), Lynch (1972, 1981; most of his work following *The Image of the City*), and recently, Charles Moore and his collaborators (C. Moore *et al.* 1988), Seamon and Mugerauer (1989), and Francis and Hester (1990) are all representatives of this group. They share a sophisticated knowledge of the design process, the history of urban form, and the value of the cultural landscape. They show particular empathy for cross-cultural research, and they prefer to turn their attention to vernacular places. Although they also belong to this group, Higuchi (1983) and Ashihara (1983) stand out because of their close ties with picturesque and image studies.

A second group is made up of social scientists who have sought to relate closely to the object of design, as, for instance, Tuan (1974, 1977), Perin (1970, 1977), Sime (1986), Relph (1976), Appleton (1975), Jakle (1987), and Walter (1988). Grady Clay (1973) and Tony Hiss (1990), both journalists, and Mark Gottdiener (1985), a sociologist, also belong to this category. The common trait of these works is their highly individualistic character, combined with the primacy given to the sociopsychological dimension of the built environment and the modified landscape. Place studies research is especially well received in urban design circles, presumably because it incorporates many of the complex relationships that must be synthesized during the design process.

The name "place studies" has been selected to cover the range of these eclectic studies and to reflect the emphasis on the physical environment and on its sensual and emotional contents. It should be noted, however, that environment-behavior studies also claim the concept of place as central to their endeavors (as in Canter 1977; Rapoport 1982, 1990; Appleyard 1981; Lawrence 1987), thus making the line between the two areas sometimes difficult to draw.

Material culture studies

Material culture is a branch of anthropology that focuses on the study of objects as reflections and tools of cultures and societies. While the objects of study are wide-ranging, including stamps, kitchen utensils, clothes, and so on, the field has flourished into a rich and popular scholarly endeavor since utilitarian machines of all kinds have become everyday staples. Elements of the cultural landscape are increasingly part of the field. Geographers have contributed to material culture as well (see Lewis 1975, for instance). And as architects, landscape architects, and urban designers are becoming more reflective and studying systematically the material manifestations of our environment, they too are adding, even if unknowingly so in many cases, to material culture studies (Wolfe 1965).

Thomas Schlereth (1982, 1985a) has spent considerable effort to explain the scope and evolution of the material culture studies undertaken over the past eighty or ninety years. A skilled observer and critic of the physical environment (Schlereth 1985b), he has identified three stages in the development of material culture studies. He calls them the age of collecting, the age of description, and the age of analysis (Schlereth 1982). Schlereth shows how the field has increased in complexity from a simple collector's activity to a critical scholarly endeavor. Hence initial questions regarding the legitimacy of a field that includes match box collectors and car buffs are no longer posed. Further, as the methods used to present and analyze cultural artifacts grow increasingly sophisticated, material culture studies provide knowledge that parallels and indeed competes with art history: the study of shopping centers, jewelry, or pigsties no longer has to be justified as high or low art (or as any kind of art for that matter), thus enhancing the potential for gathering information about the material world. The growth of the field is particularly important since postindustrial societies continue to encumber themselves with an increasingly large plethora of objects that may have little significance in and of themselves, but surely do together and collectively.

For now, material culture studies are, for all intents and purposes, part of the field of American studies. In Europe, ethnographers and ethnologists, and to some extent, urban and ethno-archaeologists, are beginning to expand into the study of more recent cultural artifacts. But my own limited investigations have not detected the emergence of material culture studies per se there.

Schlereth includes J.B. Jackson, Grady Clay, and Robert Venturi as contributors to the study of the material environment, but Henry Glassie, a folk culture scholar, emerges as a giant of the field. Little known to environmental designers, Glassie's work includes detailed analyses of folk houses in Virginia (1968, 1975) and the thorough description of an Ulster community (1982). His meticulous research and complex methodology – a mixture of structuralism and phenomenology – serve as a model for good, significant research. Even closer to designers' interests is Upton and Vlach's (1986) work on vernacular places and Groth's (1990) on cultural landscapes. A close watch on this field will be necessary in the future.

Typology-morphology studies

This area of concentration is not well known in the United States. Sometimes associated with the Krier brothers' (*Rational Architecture* 1978) and Aldo Rossi's (1964, 1982) works, it is often reduced to an architectural design philosophy that borrows from the premodern city (Vidler 1976; Moneo 1978). In fact, typology and morphology research encompasses a long tradition of studying cities, their form, and especially the socioeconomic processes that govern their production. The Kriers and Rossi have relied on such studies. They have popularized the notion that the study of architecture leads to an understanding of society that is as valid as the understanding gained from such established disciplines as economics or sociology. However, neither the Kriers nor Rossi have explicitly introduced to the design fields the substantial data on urban form and urban form-making that have been generated by research in typology and morphology (Moudon in progress).

"Typomorphological studies" – a term coined by Italian architect Aymonino (Aymonino *et al.* 1966) – use building types to describe and explain urban form and the process of shaping the fabric of cities. Geographers working in this area have preferred to talk about urban morphology only to stress their interest in documenting the form of the city. Others, including architects, convinced that buildings and their related open spaces are the essential elements of city form, have focused on classifying them by type to explain the physical characteristics of cities. They prefer to be called typologists.

All typomorphologists approach the study of building types in a special way: they are not so much interested in the form of buildings or in their architectural style as they are in the relationship between buildings and the open spaces surrounding them. Thus they see buildings and complementary open spaces as interconnecting units of space that are usually defined by the boundaries of land ownership. These units of space are made and manipulated by their owners or users. Together, they constitute the urban fabric. Buildings and open spaces are classified by type: types represent different generations pertaining to successive building traditions, or within each generation, types reflect the different socioeconomic strata of the people for whom they were intended.

Because typomorphologists claim to explain the structure and the evolution of the city, their analyses include all building types, both monumental and ordinary. But they necessarily expend most of their efforts in the study of common residential buildings that constitute the greater part of the urban fabric. Hence typomorphological study differs from works emanating from art history, rejecting not only its focus on special building types (usually highly designed and nonutilitarian ones), but especially its typical isolation of individual buildings from the city as a whole and its treatment of buildings as timeless, unchangeable memories of a past.

Typomorphological studies are object oriented. However, the built environment is treated not as a stagnant object but as one constantly changing in the hands of people living in and using it. Indeed the term "morphogenesis" – the study of processes leading to the formation and transformation of the built environment – is preferred over "morphology" – the study of form – to define the nature of research in this area. The approach is thus rooted in history, as traces of the past are strong and inescapably ingrained in the dynamics of all urban environments. This approach to history relates direct and specifically to the design and planning profession.

In North America, Barton Myers and George Baird's studies of Toronto (Myers and Baird 1978) and my own of San Francisco (Moudon 1986) stand as examples of typomorphological studies. Geographer M.R.G. Conzen is an important figure who has used this approach for British medieval cities (Conzen 1960; Whitehand 1981). His training dates from the early part of this century in Berlin, where geographers refined a morphological approach applicable to the study of urban settlements. Geographers influenced by M.R.G. Conzen have organized an Urban Morphology Research Group (1987 to the present) at the University of Birmingham. Membership in the group is expanding rapidly in the English-speaking world and in Europe. Accordingly, the group publications include work from many parts of the world and from several disciplines (Slater 1990). In Italy, architects have debated the value and methodological issues of typomorphological studies for more than three decades. There, Gianfranco Caniggia (1983; Caniggia and Maffei 1979) stands out with the most expansive work. He was an assistant of Saverio Muratori (1959; Muratori et al. 1963), who carried out two seminal studies of Venice and Rome in the late 1950s. Lately, Paolo Maretto (1986) is emerging as an important historian in this area. In France, a multidisciplinary group of architects, urban designers, geographers, and sociologists have done such studies for some twenty years (Castex et al. 1980; Panerai et al. 1980). They are now consolidated as a research laboratory called LADRHAUS (Laboratoire de Recherche "Histoire Architecturale et Urbaine – Sociétés"), which works closely with groups in Italy, Spain, and Latin America (Moudon in progress).

Space-morphology studies

This area of concentration was formalized after World War II at Cambridge University with Leslie Martin and Lionel March as the founders of the Center for Urban Form and Land Use Studies. The focus of this research group is to uncover the fundamental characteristics of urban geometries. The underlying assumptions behind these studies include the existence of spatial elements that generate urban form – such as rooms, transportation channels, and so on – and the need for quantifying both elements and their relationships.

Christopher Alexander worked with the Cambridge Group in the early 1960s when he was a student of mathematics just beginning to take an interest in design and architecture. His *Notes on the Synthesis of Form* (1964) reflects the concerns and methods used by the group. While Alexander was quick to reject the value of this approach, others have continued in this direction. Martin and March published basic texts in this area (Martin and March 1972; March 1977). The work of Philip Steadman covers the area of architectural geometry (Steadman 1983). William Mitchell, one of Martin and March's collaborators, continues to develop computerized approaches to manipulating spatial elements (Mitchell 1990). Lionel March has in fact taken Mitchell's old position as head of the Department of Architecture at UCLA. Clearly this group reflects architects' long-standing interest in generating and manipulating form in a systematic way – with D'Arcy Thompson's ([1917] 1961) work as a common philosophical basis, and F.L. Wright's and Le Corbusier's Usonian and Citroën houses as reflections of the fascination for interrelated spatial elements.

Perhaps the most broad-ranging effort in this area is being made at the Bartlett by Bill Hillier and his group. Hillier is researching the underlying generative elements of space and looking for a so-called spatial grammar *as it relates* to social systems. He is thus linking concerns in both the social and geometrical dimensions of space. Quite complex and difficult to understand entirely, Hillier's approach is explained in *The Social Logic of Space* (Hillier and Hanson 1984). This work is of special interest, however, because it demonstrates the need to stress linkages between environmental design research and research in urban morphology. In this sense, it also belongs to place studies.

In the United States, the space-morphology area had a brief hiatus in the 1960s with the publication of *Explorations into Urban Structure* (Webber 1964). A joint University of California at Berkeley and University of Pennsylvania effort, the book summarizes interests and search in categorizing the fundamental elements of environmental space. But while the British research is carried out primarily by architects, this American work is the result of thinking by planners. Unfortunately, the U.S. work has seen little follow-up. Instead, following Webber's own contribution, which questioned the importance of physical and material space relative to its socioeconomic dimension, planners have gone on to explore the functional aspects of urban space. Thus,

in the United States, the area of urban spatial structures now deals solely with transportation, land use, and locational variables, at a scale that prohibits the consideration of objective material space (see, for instance, Bourne 1971).

Kevin Lynch and Lloyd Rodwin also tackled the analysis of spatial and morphological elements in their early research (Lynch and Rodwin 1958). But this common interest quickly forked out into Lynch's focus on image studies and Rodwin's interest in larger socioeconomic urban models.

Thus, in the 1960s, interest in space-morphology showed possible collaboration between architects and planners on the issue of spatial structures. But the end of the decade brought this to an abrupt halt with the now-obvious professional split over the relative importance of socioeconomic space and over the different scales at which issues of planning and design emerge. In the area of spatial structures today, the legacy of Christaller (Berry and Red 1961) and the Chicago School of Sociology prevails in the planning fields, while spatial grammars and computers dominate in the architectural arena.

There are independent researchers whose work may also fit this category, because it rests on the geometric characteristics of space. Passonneau and Wurman (1966; Wurman 1974) studied urban geometries and densities. Stanford Anderson's (1977) mapping of public and private uses of space and Philippe Boudon's (1971, 1991) definition of architecturology also come to mind. Anderson's interest in small-scale definition of territories is unfortunately not applied to enough different cases to permit the development of a theoretical framework for design (Anderson 1986). Boudon's claim that architectural space is not geometrical space because spatial dimensions are what define architectural space – a 10-foot square room is essentially different from a 100-foot square room, even if their geometries are similar – is challenging but little known in the United States. Searching appropriate ways to describe built space, Boudon argues that space can only be qualified as it stimulates sensory responses: objects cannot be described, but the sensations and feelings they generate can (Boudon 1971, 1991). This recognition suggests that these works could also fit in place studies.

It is worth mentioning at this point that work in spatial semiotics does not appear to fit well in any of the areas of concentrations devised here. The work is laden with controversy (can architecture be considered to produce systems of signs or languages?) and difficult to understand. Undefined intent and complex method make it tenuous to classify (Gottdiener 1986). But semiotics could belong to the area of space-morphology if it were accepted that its intent is to uncover a spatial logic in built form.

Finally, space-morphology and typology-morphology overlap in the way they seek to identify the generative structure of space. But they differ fundamentally in that typology-morphology grounds analysis and explanation of space on the history and evolution of material space, while the area of space-morphology remains essentially *a-historical*.

Nature-ecology studies

Recent research and theories have shown urban ecology to be a necessary and essential component of urban design. Light, air, and open space have always been part of the discourse of urban design, but planners and architects have tended to limit the consideration of their impact to the health, comfort, and visual qualities of environments. The role of greenery in the city has been a major concern since the latter part of the nineteenth century – as a romantic drive to bring nature into the exploding metropolis and as a necessary outlet for the recreation of growing masses of urbanites. The second half of the twentieth century has brought serious concerns about excessive energy consumption in urban environments, but most of the work done to address these concerns has dealt primarily with transportation functions and the automobile industry in particular. Some architects also responded at that time by focusing on energy-conscious buildings. Since then, however, the larger field of ecology has grown considerably, affecting many disciplines (Odum 1971). Urban ecology emerged across disciplinarian boundaries, introducing systemic methods of analyzing and planning the city (Detwyler and Marcus 1972; Douglas 1983; George and McKinley 1974; Goudie 1990; Havlick 1974). These methods consider geology, topography, climate, air pollution, water, soils, noise, vegetation, and wildlife. Inclusive approaches to understanding the city and its environs as a naturally balanced environment are now being developed (Gordon 1990; Todd and Todd 1984; Van der Ryn and Calthorpe 1986; Yaro *et al.* 1988).

Landscape architects are making substantial contributions to this field. Ian McHarg's seminal *Design with Nature* (1971) has been followed by Anne Whiston Spirn's *The Granite Garden* (1984). John Lyle's (1985) and Michael Hough's (1984) recent works also provide essential information for integrating natural processes in city design. These publications demonstrate how the movement of water and air affects pollution and health, how air pollution generated by cars can be alleviated by proper design of streets and buildings, how vegetation affects air flows, and so on. They also include elements of flora and fauna as integral inhabitants and hence determinants of cities. The effect of trees in the urban context is treated in increasing detail (Moll and Ebenreck 1989). Bridging these new concerns with traditional urban design interests, Anne Spirn is now working on the repercussions of ecological design urban aesthetics.

Although these works have yet to be brought to the center of urban design, they begin to show the relationships that exist between the more commonly considered social and psychological components of the environment and its biological dimension. The city and its inevitable cultural and ecological system is treated by Kenneth Schneider in *On the Nature of Cities* (1979). Links to urban history are made by Hughes in *Ecology in Ancient Civilizations* (1975). Finally, much of the research carried out in the natural sciences remains to be interpreted for the detailed design of the environment.

CONCLUSION

This first attempt at building an epistemology for urban design emanated from the practical need to introduce students to a large body of literature, to encourage them to focus their readings, and to help them relate these readings to actual issues and problems of the field. At this pedagogical level, the "catholic approach" has been a successful guide to students as they meander through the complexities of this literature. In return, students will probably help keep the "catholic approach" up-to-date, as new areas are likely to emerge from related fields and as influences on urban design are broadened or simply changed.

The relevance of the "catholic approach" to the large context of research and practice still awaits acceptance. Future discussions of the validity and usefulness of the nine concentrations of inquiry will, if nothing else, broaden the repertoire of references used by most practitioners. It will help them explain their personal preferences and inclinations and to identify areas of unexpected neglect. More important, however, the nine concentrations proposed map out and, hence, highlight specific focus of professional concerns. Urban historical studies offer critical assessments of various design processes and explain their resulting forms. Picturesque studies combine different interpretations of the built environment's visual attributes. Image studies explain ordinary people's visual cognition of cities. Environment-behavior studies begin to assemble the complete puzzle of interactions between people and their surroundings. Place studies bring forth the special meanings, symbols, and generally the deep emotional contents of the built environment and related open spaces. Material culture studies concentrate on the object qualities of the modified landscape and its value to society. Typology-morphology studies explain the products and procedures related to the citybuilding process. Space-morphology studies offer explanations about the functional impacts of space and its geometry. Finally, nature-ecology studies examine the relationships between the city and the natural environment. These nine areas serve to scan what is known about how cities are made, used, and understood and to focus on ways of developing this knowledge.

The future effectiveness of the field depends on its ability to digest this substantive knowledge and to use it to evaluate normative theories and practices. In the end, knowledge of urban design, as practiced and theorized, and knowledge of the city, as perceived, produced, and lived in, must become intimately related.

NOTE

1 According to Lang (1987), there is also research pertaining to the 'procedural' aspects of urban design that relates to how urban design should be practiced and that focuses on methods of practicing urban design – for example, Barnett (1974), A. Jacobs (1978), and Wolfe and Shinn (1970). Procedural research is not included in this epistemological map.

REFERENCES

Alberti, Leon Battista (1404–72). (1452) 1988. *On the art of building in ten books (De re aedificatoria)*. J. Rykwert, N. Leach, and R. Tavernor, trans. Cambridge, Ma.: MIT Press.

Alexander, Christopher. 1964. *Notes on the synthesis of form*. Cambridge, Ma.: Harvard University Press.

Alexander, Christopher, Sara Ishikawa, and Murray Silverstein. 1977. *A pattern language: Towns, buildings, construction*. New York: Oxford University Press.

Altman, Irwin. 1986. *Culture and environment*. Cambridge: Cambridge University Press.

Altman, Irwin, and Joachim F. Wohlwill, eds. 1976–85. *Human behavior and environment: Advances in theory and research*, Vols. 1–5. New York: Plenum.

Anderson, Stanford. 1986. Architectural and urban form as factors in the theory and practice of urban design. In *A propos de la morphologie urbaine*, Françoise Choay and Pierre Merlin, eds. Tome 2, *Communications*. Paris: Laboratoire "Théorie des mutations urbaines en pays développés," Université de Paris VIII, Institut d'urbanisme de l'Académie de Paris, E.N.P.C., March.

——, ed. 1977. *On streets*. Cambridge, Ma.: MIT Press.

Appleton, Jay, ed. 1980. *The aesthetics of landscape: Proceedings of Symposium, University of Hull, 17–19 September, 1976*. Didcot, Oxon: Rural Planning Services.

——. 1975. *The experience of landscape*. New York: Wiley.

Appleyard, Donald. 1981. *Livable streets*. Berkeley: University of California Press.

——. 1976. *Planning a pluralistic city: Conflicting realities in Ciudad Guayana*. Cambridge, Ma.: MIT Press.

Appleyard, Donald, Kevin Lynch, and John Myer. 1964. *The view from the road*. Cambridge, Ma.: MIT Press.

Arnheim, Rudolf. 1966. *Toward a psychology of art: Collected essays*. Berkeley: University of California Press.

——. 1954. *Art and visual perception: A psychology of the creative eye*. Berkeley: University of California Press.

Artibise, Alan F.J., and Paul-André Linteau. 1984. The evolution of urban Canada: An analysis of approaches and interpretations. In *Institute of Urban Studies*, Report 4. Winnipeg: Institute of Urban Studies, University of Winnipeg.

Ashihara, Yoshinobu. 1983. *The aesthetic townscape.* Cambridge, Ma.: MIT Press.

Aymonino, C., M. Brusatin, G. Fabbri, M. Lena, P. Loverro, S. Lucianetti, and A. Rossi. 1966. *La città di Padova, saggio di analisi urbana.* Rome: Officina edizoni.

Bacon, Edmund. 1976. *Design of cities.* New York: Penguin.

Banham, Reyner. 1971. *Los Angeles, the architecture of four ecologies.* Baltimore, Md.: Pelican.

Barnett, Jonathan. 1986. *The elusive city: Five centuries of design, ambition and ideas.* New York: Harper & Row.

——. 1974. *Urban design as public policy: Practical methods for improving cities.* New York: Architectural Record Books.

Benevolo, Leonardo. 1980. *The history of the city.* London: Scolar.

Berry, Brian J.L., and Allen Red. 1961. *Central Place Studies, a bibliography of theory and applications.* Regional Science Institute, Bibliography Series, No. 1. Philadelphia: Regional Science Institute.

Blumenfeld, Hans. 1979. *Metropolis and beyond: Selected essays by Hans Blumenfeld,* edited by Paul D. Spreiregen. New York: Wiley.

Boudon, Philippe. 1991. *De l'architecture à l'épistémologie, la question de l'échelle.* Paris: Presses Universitaires de France.

——. 1971. *Sur l'espace architectural: Essai d'épistémologie de l'architecture.* Paris: Dunod.

Bourne, Larry S., ed. 1971. *Internal structure of the city: Readings on urban form, growth and policy.* New York: Oxford University Press.

Broadbent, Geoffrey. 1990. *Emerging concepts in urban space design.* London: Van Nostrand Reinhold (International).

Brunskill, R.W. 1982. *Houses.* London: Collins.

——. 1981. *Traditional buildings of Britain: An introduction to vernacular architecture.* London: Victor Gollancz.

Burke, Gerald. 1971. *Towns in the making.* London: Edward Arnold.

Caniggia, Gianfranco. 1983. Dialettica tra tipo e tessuto nei rapporti preesistenza-attualità, formazione-mutazione, sincronia-diacronia. Extracts from *Studi e documenti di architettura* 11 (June).

Caniggia, Gianfranco, and Gian Luigi Maffei. 1979. *Composizione architettonica e tipologia edilizia, 1. Lettura dell'edilizia di base.* Venice: Marsilio Editori.

Canter, David. 1977. *The psychology of place.* London: Architectural Press.

Carter, Harold. 1976. *The study of urban geography.* New York: Wiley.

Castex, Jean, Patrick Céleste, and Philippe Panerai. 1980. *Lecture d'une ville: Versailles.* Paris: Editions du Moniteur.

Choay, Françoise. 1980. *La régle et le modèle, sur la théorie de l'architecture et de l'urbanisme.* Paris: Editions du Seuil.

——. 1965. *Urbanisme, utopies et réalités: Une antologie.* Paris: Editions du Seuil.

Clay, Grady. 1973. *Close-up: How to read the American city.* New York: Praeger.

Conzen, Michael P., ed. 1990. *The making of the American landscape.* Boston: Unwin Hyman.

——. 1980. The morphology of nineteenth-century cities in the United States. In *Urbanization in the Americas: The background in comparative perspective,* W. Borah, J. Hamoy, and G. Stelter, eds. Ottawa: National Museum of Man.

——. 1978. Analytical approaches to the urban landscape. In *Dimensions of human geography,* Research Paper 186, Karl W. Butzer, ed. Department of Geography, University of Chicago.

Conzen, M.R.G. 1960. *Alnwick, Northumberland: A study in town-plan analysis.* Publication No. 27. London: Institute of British Geographers.

Cullen, Gordon. 1961. *The concise townscape.* New York: Van Nostrand Reinhold.

Detwyler, Thomas R., and Melvin G. Marcus. 1972. *Urbanization and environment: The physical geography of the city.* Belmont, Ca.: Duxbury.

Dickinson, Robert E. 1961. *The west European city: A geographical interpretation.* London: Routledge & Kegan Paul.

Douglas, Ian. 1983. *The urban environment.* Baltimore, Md.: Edward Arnold.

Dyoz, H.J., ed. 1968. *The study of urban history.* New York: St. Martin's Press.

Evenson, Norma. 1979. *Paris: A century of change, 1878–1978.* New Haven, Ct.: Yale University Press.

——. 1973. *Two Brazilian capitals: Architecture and urbanism in Rio de Janeiro and Brasilia.* New Haven, Ct.: Yale University Press.

Festinger, Leon. 1989. *Extending psychological frontiers: Works of Leon Festinger.* New York: Russell Sage Foundation.

Fishman, Robert. 1987. *Bourgeois utopias: The rise and fall of suburbia.* New York: Basic Books.

——. 1977. *Urban utopias in the twentieth century: Ebenezer Howard, Frank Lloyd Wright, and Le Corbusier.* New York: Basic Books.

Francis, Mark, Lisa Cashdan, and Lynn Paxson. 1984. *Community open spaces: Greening neighborhoods through community action and land conservation.* Washington, D.C.: Island Press.

Francis, Mark, and Randolph Hester, eds. 1990. *The meaning of gardens: Idea, place, and action.* Cambridge, Ma.: MIT Press.

Franck, Karen A., and Sherry Ahrentzen. 1989. *New households, new housing.* New York: Van Nostrand Reinhold.

Friedman, David. 1988. *Florentine new towns: Urban design in the late middle ages.* Cambridge, Ma.: MIT Press.

Gans, Herbert J. 1969. Planning for people, not buildings, *Environment and Planning* 1, 1: 33–46.

——. 1967. *The Levittowners: Ways of life and politics in a new suburban community.* New York: Pantheon.

Garreau, Joel. 1991. *Edge city: Life on the new frontier.* New York: Doubleday.

Gehl, Jan. 1987. *Life between buildings: Using public space.* New York: Van Nostrand Reinhold.

George, Carl J., and Daniel McKinley. 1974. *Urban ecology: In search of an asphalt rose.* New York: McGraw-Hill.

Girouard, Mark. 1985. *Cities and people: A social and architectural history.* New Haven, Ct.: Yale University Press.

Glassie, Henry. 1982. *Passing the time in Baleymenone: Culture and history of an Ulster community.* Philadelphia: University of Pennsylvania Press.

——. 1975. *Folk housing in middle Virginia.* Knoxville: University of Tennessee Press.

——. 1968. *Pattern in the material folk culture of the eastern United States.* Philadelphia: University of Pennsylvania Press.

Gordon, David, ed. 1990. *Green cities.* Montreal: Black Rose.

Gosling, David, and Barry Maitland. 1984. *Concepts of urban design.* London: Academy Editions.

Gottdiener, Mark. 1986. *The city and the sign: An introduction to urban semiotics.* New York: Columbia University Press.

——. 1985. *The social production of urban space.* Austin: University of Texas Press.

Goudie, Andrew. 1990. *Human impact on the natural environment.* Cambridge, Ma.: Blackwell.

Greenbie, Barrie B. 1981. *Spaces: Dimensions of the human landscape.* New Haven, Ct.: Yale University Press.

Groth, Paul, ed. 1990. *Vision, culture, and landscape.* Working Papers for the Berkeley Symposium on Cultural Landscape Interpretations. Berkeley: Department of Landscape Architecture, University of California.

Gutman, Robert. 1972. *People and buildings.* New York: Basic Books.

Hall, E.T. [1959] 1980. *The silent language.* Westport, Ct.: Greenwood.

——. 1966. *The hidden dimension.* Garden City, N.Y.: Doubleday.

Halprin, Lawrence. 1972. *Cities.* Cambridge, Ma.: MIT Press.

——. 1966. *Freeways.* New York: Reinhold.

Hardie, Graeme, Robin Moore, and Henry Sanoff, eds. 1989. *Chang paradigms.* EDRA 20, Proceedings of Annual Conference. School of Design, North Carolina State University.

Havlick, Spencer W. 1974. *The urban organism: The city's natural sources from an environmental perspective.* New York: Macmillan.

Hayden, Dolores. 1984. *Redesigning the American dream: The future of housing, work, and family life.* New York: W.W. Norton.

——. 1981. *The grand domestic revolution: A history of feminist design for American homes, neighborhoods, and cities.* Cambridge, Ma.: MIT Press.

Hester, Randolph. 1984. *Planning neighborhood space with people.* New York: Van Nostrand Reinhold.

——. 1975. *Neighborhood space.* Stroudsburg, Pa.: Dowden, Hutchinson & Ross.

Higuchi, Tadahiko. 1983. *The visual and spatial structure of landscape.* Cambridge, Ma.: MIT Press.

Hillier, Bill. 1986. Urban morphology: The UK experience, a personal view. In *A propos de la morphologie urbaine*, Françoise Choay and Pierre Merlin, eds. Tome 2. *Communications.* Laboratoire "Théorie des mutations urbaines en pays développés," Université de Paris VIII. Paris: Institut d'urbanisme de l'Académie de Paris, E.N.P.C. March.

Hillier, Bill, and Julienne Hanson. 1984. *The social logic of space.* Cambridge: Cambridge University Press.

Hiorns, Frederick R. 1956. *Town-building in history: An outline review of conditions, influences, ideas, and methods affecting 'planned' towns through five thousand years.* London: George G. Harrap.

Hiss, Tony. 1990. *The experience of place.* New York: Knopf.

Hough, Michael. 1984. *City form and natural process: Towards a new urban vernacular.* Beckenham, Kent: Croom Helm.

Hughes, J. Donald. 1975. *Ecology in ancient civilization.* Albuquerque: University of New Mexico Press.

Huxtable, Ada Louise. 1970. *Will they ever finish Bruckner Boulevard?* New York: Macmillan.

Jackson, J.B. 1984. *Discovering the vernacular landscape.* New Haven, Ct.: Yale University Press.

——. 1980. *The necessity for ruins and other topics.* Amherst: University of Massachusetts Press.

Jackson, Kenneth. 1985. *Crabgrass frontier: The suburbanization of the United States.* New York: Oxford University Press.

Jackson, Kenneth, and Stanley Schultz, eds. 1972. *Cities in American history.* New York: Knopf.

Jacobs, Allan. 1985. *Looking at cities.* Cambridge, Ma.: Harvard University Press.

——. 1978. *Making city planning work.* Chicago: American Society of Planning Officials.

Jacobs, Jane. 1961. *The death and life of great American cities.* New York: Random House.

Jakle, John A. 1987. *The visual elements of landscape.* Amherst: University of Massachusetts Press.

Jarvis, R.K. 1980. Urban environments as visual art or as social settings? *Town Planning Review* 51, 1: 50–65.

Johnston, Norman. 1983. *Cities in the round.* Seattle: University of Washington Press.

Kaplan, Stephen, and Rachel Kaplan. 1978. *Humanscape: Environments for people.* North Scituate, Ma.: Duxbury.

Kepes, Gyorgy. 1966. *Sign, image, symbol.* New York: G. Braziller.

——. 1965. *The nature and art of motion.* New York: G. Braziller.

——. 1944. *Language of vision.* Chicago: P. Theobald.

Knack, Ruth Eckdish. 1989. Repent, ye sinners, repent. *Planning* 55, 8: 4–13.

Konvitz, Joseph. 1985. *The urban millennium: The city-building process from the early middle ages to the present.* Carbondale: Southern Illinois University Press.

Kostof, Spiro. 1991. *The city shaped: Urban patterns and meanings through history.* Boston: Bulfinch Press/ Little, Brown.

——. 1986. Cities and turfs. *Design Book Review* 10 (Fall): 9–10, 37–39.

Lang, Jon. 1987. *Creating architectural theory: The role of the behavioral sciences in environmental design.* New York: Van Nostrand Reinhold.

Lavedan, Henri. 1941. *Histoire de l'urbanisme: Renaissance et temps modernes.* Paris: Laurens.

Lawrence, Roderick. 1987. *Housing, dwellings and homes: Design theory, research and practice.* New York: Wiley.

Lerup, Lars. 1977. *Building the unfinished: Architecture and human action.* Beverly Hills, Ca.: Sage.

Lewis, Peirce F. 1975. Common houses, cultural spoor. *Landscape* 19, 2: 1–22.

Lowenthal, David, and Marcus Binney, eds. 1981. *Our past before us?* London: Temple Smith.

Lubove, Roy. 1967. The urbanization process: An approach to historical research. *Journal of the American Institute of Planners* 33: 33–39.

Lyle, John T. 1985. *Design for human ecosystem: Landscape, land use and natural resources.* New York: Van Nostrand Reinhold.

Lynch, Kevin. 1981. *A theory of good city form.* Cambridge, Ma.: MIT Press.

——. 1972. *What time is this place?* Cambridge, Ma.: MIT Press.

——. 1960. *The image of the city.* Cambridge, Ma.: MIT Press.

Lynch, Kevin, and Lloyd Rodwin. 1958. A theory of urban form. *Journal of the American Institute of Planners* 24: 201–14.

Lynd, R.S., and H.M. Lynd. 1929. *Middletown: A study in contemporary American culture.* London: Constable.

Lyndon, Donlyn. 1982. *The city observed: Boston.* New York: Random House.

McHarg, Ian. 1971. *Design with nature.* Garden City, N.Y.: Doubleday.

March, Lionel. 1977. *Architecture of form.* Cambridge, Ma.: MIT Press.

Marcus, Clare Cooper. 1975. *Easter Hill Village: Some social implications of design.* New York: Free Press.

Marcus, Clare Cooper, and Wendy Sarkissian. 1986. *Housing as if people mattered: Site design guidelines for medium-density family housing.* Berkeley: University of California Press.

Maretto, Paolo. 1986. *La casa veneziana nella storia della città, dalle origini all'ottocento.* Venice: Marsilio Editori.

Martin, Leslie, and Lionel March, eds. 1972. *Urban space and structures.* Cambridge: Cambridge University Press.

Michelson, William. 1977. *Environmental choice, human behavior, and residential satisfaction*. New York: Oxford University Press.

——. 1970. *Man and his environment*. Reading, Ma.: Addison-Wesley.

Mitchell, William J. 1990. *The logic of architecture, design, computation, and cognition*. Cambridge, Ma.: MIT Press.

Moll, Gary, and Sara Ebenreck, eds. 1989. *Shading our cities: A resource guide for urban and community forests*. Washington, D.C.: Island Press.

Moneo, Raphael. 1978. On typology. *Oppositions* 13 (Summer): 23–45.

Moore, Charles W., William J. Mitchell, and William Turnbull, Jr. 1988. *The poetics of gardens*. Cambridge, Ma.: MIT Press.

Moore, Gary T., and the Faculty of the Ph.D Program. 1987. *Resources in environment-behavior studies*. Milwaukee: School of Architecture and Urban Planning, University of Wisconsin.

Moore, Gary T., D. Paul Tuttle, and Sandra C. Howell, eds. 1985. *Environmental design research directions, process and prospects*. New York: Praeger Special Studies.

Moore, Robin. 1986. *Childhood domain: Play and place in child development*. London: Croom Helm.

More, Thomas, Sir, Saint (1478–1535). [1516] 1989. *Utopia*. New York: Cambridge University Press.

Morris, A. E. J. 1972. *History of urban form: Prehistory to Renaissance*. New York: Wiley.

Moudon, Anne Vernez. In progress. City building. Manuscript.

——. 1988. Normative/substantive and etic/emic dilemmas in design education. *Column 5 Journal of Architecture, University of Washington* (Spring): 13–15.

——. 1987. The research component of typomorphological studies. Paper presented at the AIA/ACSA Research Conference, Boston, November.

——. 1986. *Built for change: Neighborhood architecture in San Francisco*. Cambridge, Ma.: MIT Press.

Mumford, Lewis. 1961. *The city in history: Its origins, its transformations, and its prospects*. New York: Harcourt, Brace & World.

Muratori, Saverio. 1959. *Studi per una operante storia urbana di Venezia*. Rome: Instituto Poligrafico dello Stato.

Muratori, Saverio, Renato Bollati, Sergio Bollati, and Guido Marinucci. 1963. *Studi per una operante*

storia urbana di Roma*. Rome: Consiglio nazionale delle ricerche.

Muthesius, Stefan. 1982. *The English terraced house*. New Haven, Ct.: Yale University Press.

Myers, Barton, and George Baird. 1978. Vacant lottery. *Design Quarterly 108* (special issue).

Nasar, Jack L., ed. 1988. *Environmental aesthetics: Theory, research, and applications*. Cambridge: Cambridge University Press.

Newman, Oscar. 1980. *Community of interest*. Garden City, N.Y.: Anchor Press/Doubleday.

——. 1972. *Defensible space: Crime prevention through urban design*. New York: Macmillan.

Norberg-Schulz, Christian. 1985. *The concept of dwelling*. New York: Rizzoli.

——. 1980. *Genius loci: Toward a phenomenology of architecture*. London: Academic Editions.

Odum, Eugene P. 1971. *Fundamentals of ecology*. Philadelphia: W.B. Saunders.

Oxman, Robert M. 1987. *Urban design theories and methods: A study of contemporary researches*. Occasional paper. Sidney, Australia: Department of Architecture, University of Sidney.

Panerai, Philippe, Jean-Charles Depaule, Marcelle Demorgon, and Michel Veyrenche. 1980. *Eléments d'analyse urbaine*. Brussels: Editions Archives d'Architecture Moderne.

Passonneau, Joseph R., and Richard S. Wurman. 1966. *Urban atlas: 20 American cities, a communication study notating selected urban data at a scale of 1:48,000*. Cambridge, Ma.: MIT Press.

Perin, Constance. 1977. *Everything in its place: Social order and land use in America*. Princeton, N.J.: Princeton University Press.

——. 1970. *With man in mind: An interdisciplinary prospectus for environmental design*. Cambridge, Ma.: MIT Press.

Poëte, Marcel. [1929] 1967. *Introduction à l'urbanisme*. Paris: Editions Anthropos.

Rapoport, Amos. 1990. *History and precedents in environmental design*. New York: Plenum.

——. 1982. *The meaning of the built environment: A nonverbal communication approach*. Beverly Hills, Ca.: Sage.

——. 1977. *Human aspects of urban form: Towards a man-environment approach to form and design*. Oxford: Pergamon.

Rasmussen, S.E. 1967. *London: The unique city*. Cambridge, Ma.: MIT Press.

Rational architecture: The reconstruction of the European city. 1978. Bruxelles: Editions des Archives de l'Architecture Moderne.

Relph, Edward. 1987. *The modern urban landscape.* Baltimore, Md.: Johns Hopkins University Press.

——. 1984. Seeing, thinking and describing landscape. In *Environmental perception and behavior: An inventory and prospect,* T. Saarinen *et al.* eds. Research Paper No. 29. Chicago: Department of Geography, University of Chicago.

——. 1976. *Place and placelessness.* London: Pion.

Reps, John W. 1965. *The making of urban America: A history of city planning in the United States.* Princeton, N.J.: Princeton University Press.

Rittel, Horst, and Melvin M. Webber. 1972. *Dilemmas in a general theory of planning.* Working Paper No. 194. Berkeley: Institute of Urban and Regional Development, University of California.

Rodwin, Lloyd, and Robert M. Hollister, eds. 1984. *Cities of the mind.* New York: Plenum.

Rossi, Aldo. 1982. *The architecture of the city.* Cambridge, Ma.: MIT Press. [First Italian edition, 1966].

——. 1964. Aspetti della tipologia residenziale a Berlino. *Casabella* 288 (June): 10–20.

Rowe, Peter. 1991. *Making a middle landscape.* Cambridge, Ma.: MIT Press.

Rudofsky, Bernard. 1969. *Streets for people: A primer for Americans.* Garden City, N.Y.: Anchor Press/ Doubleday.

Schlereth, Thomas J., ed. 1985a. *Material culture: A research guide.* Lawrence: University of Kansas Press.

——. 1985b. *US 40: A roadscape of the American experience.* Indianapolis: Indiana Historical Society.

——. ed. 1982. *Material culture studies in America.* Nashville, Tn.: American Association for State and Local History.

Schneider, Kenneth R. 1979. *On the nature of cities: Toward enduring and creative human environments.* San Francisco: Jossey-Bass.

Seamon, David. 1987. Phenomenology and environment/behavior research. In *Advances in environment, behavior, and design,* E.H. Zube and G.T. Moore, eds. New York: Plenum.

Seamon, David, and Robert Mugerauer, eds. 1989. *Dwelling, place, and environment.* New York: Columbia University Press.

Sennett, Richard, ed. 1969. *Nineteenth-century cities: Essays in the new urban history.* New Haven, Ct.: Yale University Press.

Sharp, Thomas. 1946. *The anatomy of the village.* Harmondsworth, Middlesex: Penguin.

Sime, Jonathan D. 1986. Creating places or designing spaces? *Journal of Environmental Psychology* 6, 1: 49–63.

Sitte, Camillo. [1889] 1980. *L'art de bâtir les villes: L'urbanisme selon ses fondements artistiques.* Paris: Editions de l'Equerre.

Slater, T.R., ed. 1990. *The built form of Western cities.* London: Leicester University Press.

Sommer, Robert. 1969. *Personal space: The behavioral basis of design.* Englewood Cliffs, N.J.: Prentice-Hall.

Spirn, Anne Whiston. 1984. *The granite garden: Urban nature and human design.* New York: Basic Books.

Spreiregen, Paul. 1965. *Urban design: The architecture of towns and cities.* New York: McGraw-Hill.

Steadman, Philip. 1983. *Architectural morphology: An introduction to the geometry of building plans.* London: Pion.

Stilgoe, John R. 1982. *Common landscape of America, 1580 to 1845.* New Haven, Ct.: Yale University Press.

Stokols, D., and Irwin Altman, eds. 1987. *Handbook of environmental psychology.* New York: Wiley.

Sutcliffe, Anthony, ed. 1984. *Metropolis 1890–1940.* Chicago: University of Chicago Press.

Thiel, Philip. 1986. *Notations for an experimental envirotechture.* Seattle: College of Architecture and Urban Planning, University of Washington.

Thompson, D'Arcy W. [1917] 1961. *On growth and form.* Cambridge: Cambridge University Press.

Todd, Nancy Jack, and John Todd. 1984. *Bioshelters, ocean arks, city farming.* San Francisco: Sierra Club Books.

Tuan, Yi-Fu. 1977. *Space and place: The perspective of experience.* Minneapolis: University of Minnesota Press.

——. 1974. *Topophilia: A study of environmental perceptions, attitudes and values.* Englewood Cliffs, N.J.: Prentice-Hall.

Unwin, Raymond. 1909. *Town planning in practice: An introduction to the art of designing cities and suburbs.* New York: B. Blom.

Upton, Dell, and John Michael Vlach, eds. 1986. *Common places: Readings in American vernacular architecture.* Athens: University of Georgia Press.

Urban Morphology Research Group. 1987 to present. *Urban morphology newsletter.* Department of Geography, University of Birmingham.

Van der Ryn, Sim, and Peter Calthorpe. 1986. *Sustainable communities: A new design synthesis for cities, suburbs, and towns.* San Francisco: Sierra Club Books.

Vance, James E., Jr. 1990. *The continuing city: Urban morphology in Western civilization.* Baltimore, Md.: Johns Hopkins University Press.

——. 1977. *This scene of man: The role and structure of the city in the geography of Western civilization.* New York: Harper's.

Venturi, Robert, Denise Scott Brown, and Steven Izenour. 1977. *Learning from Las Vegas: The forgotten symbolism of architectural form.* Cambridge, Ma.: MIT Press.

Vidler, Anthony. 1976. The third typology. *Oppositions* 7: 28–32.

Villeco, Margo, and M. Brill. 1981. *Environmental design research: Concepts, methods and values.* Washington, D.C.: National Endowment for the Arts.

Violich, Francis. 1983. *An experiment in revealing the sense of place: Subjective reading of six Dalmatian towns.* Berkeley: Center for Environmental Design Research, College of Environmental Design, University of California, Berkeley.

Walter, Eugene Victor. 1988. *Placeways: A theory of the human environment.* Chapel Hill: University of North Carolina Press.

Warner, Sam Bass. 1968. *The private city: Philadelphia in three periods of its growth.* Philadelphia: University of Pennsylvania Press.

——. 1962. *Streetcar suburbs: The process of growth in Boston, 1870–1900.* Cambridge, Ma.: Harvard University Press.

Warner, W. Lloyd. 1963. *Yankee city.* New Haven, Ct.: Yale University Press.

Webber, Melvin M. 1964. *Explorations into urban structure.* Philadelphia: University of Pennsylvania Press.

Weiss, Mark Allan. 1987. *The rise of the community builders: The American building industry and urban land planning.* New York: Columbia University Press.

Whitehand, J.W.R., ed. 1981. *The urban landscape: Historic development and management, papers by M.R.G. Conzen.* Institute of British Geographers, Special Publication No. 13. New York: Academic Press.

Whyte, William H. 1988. *City: Rediscovering the center.* New York: Doubleday.

——. 1980. *The social life of small urban spaces.* Washington, D.C.: Conservation Foundation.

Wohlwill, Joachim F. 1985. *Habitats for children: The impacts of density.* Hillsdale, N.J.: Lawrence Erlbaum Associates.

——. 1981. *The physical environment and behavior: An annotated bibliography.* New York: Plenum.

Wolfe, M.R. 1965. A visual supplement to urban social studies. *Journal of the American Institute of Planners* 31, 1: 51–1.

Wolfe, M.R., and R.D. Shinn. 1970. *Urban design within the comprehensive planning process.* Seattle: University of Washington.

Wright, Gwendolyn. 1981. *Building the dream: A social history of housing in America.* New York: Pantheon.

Wurman, Richard Saul. 1974. *Cities: A Comparison of form and scale: Models of 50 significant towns.* Philadelphia: Joshua Press.

——. 1972. *Man-made Philadelphia: A guide to its physical and cultural environment.* Cambridge, Ma.: MIT Press.

——. 1971. *Making the city observable.* Minneapolis: Walker Art Center.

Yaro, Robert D., Randall G. Arendt, Harry L. Dodson, and Elizabeth A. Brabec. 1988. *Dealing with change in the Connecticut River Valley: A design manual for conservation and development.* Amherst: Center for Rural Massachusetts, University of Massachusetts.

Zube, Ervin H., and Gary T. Moore. 1987. *Advances in environment, behavior, and design.* New York: Plenum.

TWO

PART THREE

Growth of a Place Agenda

Plate 4 **The Textile Souk in the Bur Dubai District of Dubai in the United Arab Emirates** was recently renovated using traditional place characteristics associated with Gulf coast and Middle Eastern urbanism. Souks are covered market streets that allow retailers to engage pedestrians with goods sold from adjacent shops. This renovated souk (in one of Dubai's oldest districts) incorporates traditional, yet updated, urban design elements that were historically developed in response to the need for shade, light, and comfort in unbearably hot desert climates. The design of this Dubai souk helps contribute to the traditional image and expectation of visitors and tourists, which stands side-by-side with the city's larger global strategy of spectacle and superlative. The souks of Dubai are some of the most desirable and walkable places within the city – very different in inspiration than the Burj al Arab hotel or the Burj Khalifa skyscraper. The urban design principles used in this project are associated with critical regionalism, postmodern urbanism, and everyday urbanism (all of which are discussed in this part of the *Reader*). (Photo: M. Larice)

INTRODUCTION TO PART THREE

Dissatisfied with the increasing homogeneity and soullessness of mid-twentieth-century urban spaces, a number of authors began investigating issues of space and place as a means of correction. In Part Two we examined how theorists approached these issues through normatively based theories to better guide design and physical outcomes. Some of the authors in Part Three approach the same manifest problems by trying to understand the relationship of personal experience to places. Other authors at the end of Part Three fall into existential description of the difficulties in doing so. While this volume's body of literature explores the relationship between physical settings and human subjects, the focus in this part of the *Reader* is primarily on the physicality of the tangible world and our ability to design places that evoke a sense of place.

Research in place studies tends to be both empirical and phenomenological in nature, largely incorporating observational and environmental behavior methods. Researchers in this tradition utilize an eclectic array of theories in defining notions of place, but seemingly they all stem from a pervasive unhappiness with non-place-based forms and difficulties in reading modern urbanism. In many ways it is a highly reactive and critical literature, often looking backwards to traditional and everyday environments where places were better differentiated and place-based meanings were more easily understood.

This part of the *Reader* begins with a chapter from Edward Relph's book *Place and Placelessness*, where he defines and differentiates the concept of place from the placeless geographies of "endless similarity." To Relph, places are "directly experienced phenomena of the lived-world and hence are filled with meanings, real objects, and ongoing activities." In this reading he warns about the power of placelessness and its potential consumption of our place-based world. In the next selection by Christian Norberg-Schulz, "The Phenomenon of Place" introduces us to phenomenological understandings of place and the Roman concept of *genius loci*, or the guardian spirit of place. Here, the concept of place is examined through our conscious ability to connect with the physical character of geographic settings, thereby bestowing the place with identity and meaning. For Norberg-Schulz, like Martin Heidegger, place is inextricably connected to existential realities and helps us define our personal identities relative to those places we inhabit. A third reading on place studies concerns the historical loss and contemporary need for places within our communities. Ray Oldenburg's chapter from *The Great Good Place* suggests we need and utilize "third places" to supplement our home and work lives with meaningful places of leisure and informal social relations. Here the concept of place is derived through the socio-spatial opportunities allowed by cafés, bookstores, pubs, and other hangouts. It is a notion of place that turns on society's ability to provide places for people to come together freely and voluntarily to make contact and enjoy public life.

The readings presented here are theoretical in nature, rather than dealing directly with urban design or design guidance. Other theoretical authors within the place studies tradition, who are not included herein, deserve mention as well. Henri Lefebvre's classic text *The Production of Space*, translated by David Nicholson-Smith (Oxford: Blackwell, 1991), provides a critical unitary theory of space that integrates the physical space of the everyday lifeworld, the mental space of abstractions, and the relational realm of social space. In a similar critical manner to the writings above, he suggests that physical everyday places are disappearing in favor of the abstract spaces of capitalism, which are a social product subject to the mode of production. In like manner, David Harvey examines the capitalist production of space and analyzes how command over the forces of production relates to power in urban space: *Consciousness and the Urban Experience* (Baltimore, MD: Johns Hopkins Press, 1985) and *The Condition of Postmodernity* (Oxford: Blackwell, 1989). Authors looking at society's role in the provision of urban space include Mark Gottdiener, *The Social Production of Urban Space* (Austin, TX: University of Texas Press, 1985); Ali Madanipour, *Design of Urban Space: An Inquiry into a Socio-Spatial Process* (Chichester, UK: John Wiley, 1996). A much loved and widely read perspective on domestic space, spatial psychology, and daydreaming can be found in Gaston Bachelard, *The Poetics of Space* (Boston, MA: Beacon Press, reprint edition, 1994).

The desire for more meaningful places has resulted in a wide variety of approaches to place reinforcement and place-making. Designers attempting to reinsert meaning into place utilize various elements of physical character to highlight local distinctions, such as environmental imagery, natural history, craft and cultural traditions, memory, history, formal aesthetics, and beauty. While the bulk of design practice remains oriented to functional, pragmatic, and economic concerns, a number of theorists and practitioners have sought a deeper design discourse that employs local and contextually based imagery to create distinctive place identities. To defeat this sense of growing globalized placelessness, urban designers are assuming new roles to foster local sense of place; including emerging roles as storytellers, midwives, public educators, local historians, urban repair specialists, and heretics (demanding change within the field itself).

Reinforcing the importance of context, a number of authors suggest that designers should look to materiality, history, nature, and craft traditions for motivating local place reinforcement. The term Critical Regionalism was first coined by Alexander Tzonis and Liane Lefaivre in describing contemporary Greek architecture that utilized geographic context as the inspiration for modern architecture that might better approximate local landscape and cultural traditions. The theory of Critical Regionalism was further defined by the architectural historian Kenneth Frampton in his 1983 essay "Towards a Critical Regionalism: Six Points for an Architecture of Resistance." In this essay Frampton suggests contemporary designers should incorporate local place attributes in their work (topography, light, climate, materiality, tradition), rather than disavowing any sense of modern form or technology. Critically regionalist design resists universal globalism, yet continues to represent the modern zeitgeist – while also utilizing those qualities that speak to place. In some ways, these authors are describing a design movement that had already been coalescing in practice prior to the release of these essays; in the works of Alvar Aalto, Luis Barragán, Alvaro Siza, Raj Rewal, Tadao Ando, Charles Correa, and Glenn Murcutt. In his very accessible writing, Douglas Kelbaugh advocates a Critical Regionalism that reinforces place qualities through the operationalization of place character in design. He describes several physical aspects that can be used for design inspiration without reducing design to cliché, camp, or inauthenticity.

A very different approach to place is the reinforcement of historical form patterns with the use of urban design and building types that are appropriate to local contexts. While the terms morphology and typology are different in many senses, they both approach the study of form through scientifically rational goggles. Typology refers to the study of categorized form types in architecture, and increasingly in urban design and landscape architecture as well. As opposed to building type, which refers to functionality, architectural typologies refer to the form characteristics of buildings. Morphology on the other hand is the study of larger urban structures, patterns, and form issues. Some authors have taken to combining the terms into a new term, "typomorphology," which focuses on larger-scale urban form patterns. Others refer to this topical material as "tissue studies." Opposed to the image studies, environmental behavior research, and phenomenological approaches of previous authors in this *Reader*, morphologists are interested primarily in the tangible physical world of objects and less interested in subject experience or the social use of space. Many study urban form longitudinally, looking at change over time. Others look at predominant form types to help guide present-day design efforts.

The use of figure-ground drawings, square mile maps, street sections, aerial photos, and computer-generated drawings in the study and comparison of urban form patterns is so common nowadays that we often forget how new these tools actually are. The emergence of typological and morphological practice in the late 1950s provided urban designers with a research arm that was particularly suited to exploring issues of urban spatial form and the efficacy of modern urbanism. Morphology and typology gained popularity rapidly in the late 1970s with rediscovered interest in the benefits of traditional urbanism. Researchers such as Aldo Rossi, Saverio Muratori, Gianfranco Caniggia, M.R.G. Conzen, Leon and Robert Krier, and Anne Vernez Moudon created and drove the exploration of these new research interests. Researchers with the International Seminar on Urban Form and the University of Birmingham's Urban Morphology Research Group are central loci for interest in this field of inquiry.

Over the next 25 years, morphological practice would assume many forms, both as a primary research tool and a device to inform design practice. Typological practice has been particularly influential in the development of prescriptive design guidelines and urban design codes in use among the New Urbanists. In the academies, morphological methods are woven into much urban design research nowadays. In the selected chapters from Brenda Scheer's recent book *The Evolution of Urban Form: Typology for Planners and Architects*, she shows how types used in architecture and urban design are the result of the economic and cultural conditions at play in any given context, and will proliferate so long as those conditions exist. The prevalent types in use at any time drive the urban design outcomes that designers, developers, and officials grapple with on a daily basis. Within the selection, Scheer reviews various definitions of type, charts the history of typology, and explores how type is used in form-based codes for regulating urban design and development.

Readers interested in the topics of typology and morphology should refer to the following works for supplemental reading: Colin Rowe and Fred Koetter, *Collage City* (Cambridge, MA: MIT Press, 1978); Aldo Rossi, *The Architecture of the City* (Cambridge, MA: MIT Press, English translation 1982, first Italian text 1966); Robert Krier, *Urban Space* (London: Academy Editions, 1979, first German text 1975); Anthony Vidler, "The Third Typology," *Oppositions* 7 (Winter, 1976); Spiro Kostoff, *The City Shaped: Urban Patterns and Meanings Through History* (Boston, MA: Little, Brown and Bulfinch Press, 1991); Allan Jacobs, *Great Streets* (Cambridge, MA: MIT Press, 1993); Anne Vernez Moudon, "Getting to Know the Built Landscape: Typomorphology," in Karen A. Franck and Lynda H. Schneekloth (eds), *Ordering Space: Types in Architecture and Design* (New York: Van Nostrand Reinhold, 1994); and Michael Southworth and Eran Ben-Joseph, *Streets and the Shaping of Towns and Cities* (New York: McGraw-Hill, 1997).

The search for place in the final decades of the twentieth century grew into a wide variety of design movements, platforms, theories, and practices. The growing importance of place is a significant characteristic of postmodern urbanism – that much debated period / concept that continues to engender either passion, confusion, or disdain. The historical period is signified by a rejection of universal meta-narratives (including any universal modernism in design) and a growing appreciation for relativism, pluralism, and choice. Key attributes of postmodern urbanism include a desire for history, comfort, entertainment, and importantly, readable meaning. These design interests are supported both by common public desires for more meaningful places, as well as by key economic agents in contemporary society, such as real estate developers, chambers of commerce, and city marketers. Not surprisingly, the growing tourism industry benefits from places that are distinct and imageable, encouraging likely tourist destinations to reinforce their historical and place-based identities. The results have been mixed, resulting both in places that authentically incorporate a sense of place, as well as places that utilize inauthentic and shallow forms of "theming" to evoke past histories and otherness.

One of the key design movements of the postmodern period is the New Urbanism. Succinct and pointed in its declarations, the *Charter of the New Urbanism* is a manifesto that articulates an approach to regional, urban, and neighborhood design that relies on the restoration of urban centers, towns, and communities according to principles of neo-traditional urbanism. It grew from a meeting sponsored by the California Local Government Commission at the Ahwahnee Hotel at Yosemite National Park in 1991, attended by: Andres Duany and Elizabeth Plater-Zyberk, Daniel Solomon, Peter Calthorpe, Michael Corbett, Stefanos Polyzoides, and Elizabeth Moule – many of whom became founding members of the

Congress for the New Urbanism in 1993. The resulting document, the *Ahwahnee Principles* sought to guide land use planning and new community design, as well as redirect the bland suburbanism and sprawl that was becoming a focus of concern for many urbanists. Under the larger umbrella of the Smart Growth Movement, it developed a number of ideas that are now associated with the movement, including: transit-oriented development, the pedestrian pocket, traditional neighborhood design, and transect planning.

In practice, New Urbanism has become a model for suburban small town development based largely on the ideals of Main Street walkable urbanism. In a few short pages, the *Charter* provides recommendations for a variety of geographic scales, from the human-scaled building to metropolitan regional form. Early built examples of the New Urbanism took the form of upper-income, greenfield and small town developments, such as Seaside, FL, the Kentlands in Gaithersburg, MD, and Celebration, FL. The movement has been exceedingly popular with real estate developers, city planning departments, and its growing consumer base. It was granted new legitimacy when its principles were adopted by the US Department of Housing and Urban Development to guide its multi-billion dollar public housing replacement program. The New Urbanism has spread around the world, as witnessed in new towns such as Jakriborg – Sweden, Orchid Bay – Belize, and Poundbury – England. As the movement progressed New Urbanism began to be applied to higher density urban settings in cities such as Vancouver, San Francisco, and Boston.

New Urbanism has also come under criticism from a number of perspectives including a group that developed a competing document called the *Lone Mountain Compact*. Its authors are libertarian academics who oppose the land use, design, and transportation controls recommended in New Urbanist practice. These critics have become defenders of suburbanism, free market economics, and consumer freedoms in allowing people to live where they want – even if this means lower density development, traffic congestion, and unsustainable building practices. Other designers disdain the shallow and inauthentic nostalgia used in many New Urbanist community designs (see the Michael Sorkin selection later in Part Six: pp. 618–634). Despite these criticisms, the movement has become one of the leading urban design movements of the past few decades and continues to grow in popularity.

The last few readings in Part Three are critical descriptions of contemporary city-building and difficulties in place-making at the end of the twentieth century. The first of these selections summarizes the larger content of postmodern urban design practices. The selection from Nan Ellin's *Postmodern Urbanism* describes the practices of place-making and urban design in the period of the 1970s to the 1990s. She is highly critical of several aspects of postmodern design (e.g. inauthentic fictionalizing, apolitical designers, capitalist profit-seeking, design narcissism, and the growing culture of fear in society), but also acknowledges the benefits that have accrued through the reintroduction of context, local history, and urbanity, as well as the revalorization of the public realm. The book has become seminal reading on the theories and design practices of the postmodern period for urban designers.

Another selection describing our current urban milieu, is the work of Margaret Crawford in describing Everyday Urbanism. In opposition to the nostalgic and neo-traditional practices of the New Urbanism, Everyday Urbanism is less ambitious, less interested in creating idealized communities, and less design-oriented. It describes the ordinary places produced naturally by the way we live, move, shop, and play. These are the spaces of outlet malls, freeways, vacant lots, food trucks, and un-pedigreed design. Like Robert Venturi and Denise Scott Brown (see pp. 167–177), Crawford and her collaborators (John Kaliski and John Chase) are describing the contemporary vernacular, and finding both possibility and vitality in the places that higher-minded designers would just as soon replace. In this selection from *Everyday Urbanism*, Crawford provides an introduction to the concept and elaboration on the public realm of the everyday – a place where the expression of democracy might take new forms and importance.

And finally, in a very similar manner to the existential writing of *Everyday Urbanism*, Rem Koolhaas describes a post-urban world where the centrality of traditional cities loses its magnetism, in favor of the centrifugal and fragmented forces of contemporary development practices. Very much in opposition to previous readings that reinforce place-making practices, Koolhaas discusses the virtues/cautions of modern design and heterogeneous urbanism in two selections from his book *S, M, L, XL* ("Whatever Happened to Urbanism?" and "The Generic City"). Rem Koolhaas is an existential realist who suggests that the placeless and generic city is both acceptable and reflective of contemporary society. The Generic City is the fragmented place where developments crop up with little relation to a larger urban idea; where heterogeneity of urban motivation is contradicted by the homogeneity of design; where the beige and expected become the norm. What happened to urbanism for Koolhaas? We stopped being urbanists. We focused more on architectural moments rather than the totality of our cities. We became nostalgic. We didn't respond appropriately to the failures of modernism. And importantly, we failed to grow our cities according to the needs of urbanization. Although recognizing its usefulness as "modernism's little helper," Koolhaas abhors the postmodern reflex described by Ellin or advocated by the CNU. In the readings by both Crawford and Koolhaas we hear very different critical voices willing to find virtue in the places of the present, without the need to re-engineer society toward some mythical ideal outcome. Both of these selections suggest perplexing issues for urban designers; to embrace the everyday and post-urban as a reality – or to work once again toward corrective measures of a more livable and sustainable urbanism.

THREE

"Prospects for Places"

from *Place and Placelessness* (1976)

Edward Relph

Editors' Introduction

A leading early voice to identify and analyze the growing sense of placelessness that was occurring throughout the world by the latter half of the twentieth century was geographer Edward Relph. In his now classic book *Place and Placelessness*, Relph uses critical observation to make connections between the visible landscape, everyday life experiences, and the abstract social and economic processes that contribute to their transformation. Written in straightforward language and grounded in experience of actual places, Relph's ideas were easily accessible to physical planners and urban designers, providing an intellectual base on which place-making proposals could rest.

Within "Prospects for Places," Relph describes the main features of place and placelessness. He identifies meaningful experience, a sense of belonging, human scale, fit with local physical and cultural contexts, and local significance as the important qualities of place. Placelessness, on the other hand, is associated with an overriding concern for efficiency, mass culture, and anonymous, exchangeable environments. Going beyond critical description to provide useful direction for planning and urban design professionals, he suggests how authentic place-making could be achieved in modern times. Dismissing either unstructured laissez-faire chaos or rigid bureaucratic prescription, he argues instead for a self-conscious planned diversity that allows people to make their own places, rooted in local contexts and filled with local meaning.

Edward Relph teaches geography at the University of Toronto. His other writings that focus on landscape and place include *Rational Landscapes and Humanistic Geography* (Totowa, NJ: Barnes & Noble, 1981) and *The Modern Urban Landscape* (London: Croom Helm, 1987; Baltimore, MD: Johns Hopkins University Press, 1987). A more recent book *The Toronto Guide* (Toronto: Centre for Urban and Community Studies, University of Toronto, 1997) is a guide to the city for "deliberate tourists."

Other writings that deal with placelessness include: James Kuntsler, *The Geography of Nowhere: The Rise and Decline of America's Man-Made Landscape* (New York: Simon & Schuster, 1993); Joel Garreau, *Edge City: Life on the New Frontier* (New York: Doubleday, 1991); Michael Sorkin, *Variations on a Theme Park: The American City and the End of Public Space* (New York: Hill & Wang, 1992); and Sharon Zukin, *Landscapes of Power: From Detroit to Disney World* (Berkeley, CA: University of California Press, 1991). A work that deals with placelessness from the perspective of landscape architecture is Michael Hough, *Out of Place: Restoring Identity to the Regional Landscape* (New Haven, CT: Yale University Press, 1990), a selection from which is reprinted in this *Reader* (pp. 523–533).

There are at least two experienced geographies: there is a geography of places, characterised by variety and meaning, and there is a placeless geography, a labyrinth of endless similarities. The current scale of the destruction and replacement of the distinctive places of the world suggests that placeless geography is increasingly the more forceful of these, even though a considerable diversity of places persists. It is not immediately apparent whether this persistence is the remnant of an old place-making tradition and is shortly to disappear beneath a tide of uniformity, or whether there exist ongoing and developing sources of diversity that can be encouraged. In other words the prospects for geography of places are uncertain, but one possibility is the inevitable spread of placelessness, and an alternative possibility is the transcending of placelessness through the formulation and application of an approach for the design of a lived-world of significant places. [Here] . . . these possibilities are considered in the context of summaries of the main features of place and placelessness.

PLACE

Places are fusions of human and natural order and are the significant centres of our immediate experiences of the world. They are defined less by unique locations, landscape, and communities than by the focusing of experiences and intentions onto particular settings. Places are not abstractions or concepts, but are directly experienced phenomena of the lived-world and hence are full with meanings, with real objects, and with ongoing activities. They are important sources of individual and communal identity, and are often profound centres of human existence to which people have deep emotional and psychological ties. Indeed our relationships with places are just as necessary, varied, and sometimes perhaps just as unpleasant, as our relationships with other people.

Experience of place can range in scale from part of a room to an entire continent, but at all scales places are whole entities, syntheses of natural and man-made objects, activities and functions, and meanings given by intentions. Out of these components the identity of a particular place is moulded, but they do not define this identity – it is the special quality of insideness and the experience of being

inside that sets places apart in space. Insideness may relate to and be reflected in a physical form, such as the walls of a medieval town, or it may be expressed in rituals and repeated activities that maintain the peculiar properties of a place. But above all it is related to the intensity of experience of a place. Alan Gussow (1971?, p. 27) has written of this: "The catalyst that converts any physical location – any environment if you will – into a place, is the process of experiencing deeply. A place is a piece of the whole environment that has been claimed by feelings."

It is possible to distinguish several levels of experience of the insideness of places, and it is perhaps these that tell us most about the nature of the phenomenon of place. At the deepest levels there is an unselfconscious, perhaps even subconscious, association with place. It is home, where your roots are, a centre of safety and security, a field of care and concern, a point of orientation. Such insideness is individual but also intersubjective, a personal experience with which many people can sympathise; it is the essence of a sense of place. And it is perhaps presymbolic and universal insofar as it is an aspect of profound place experience anywhere, yet is not associated with the culturally defined meanings of specific places. This is, in fact, existential insideness – the unselfconscious and authentic experience of place as central to existence. The next level of experience is also authentic and unselfconscious, but it is cultural and communal rather than individual: it involves a deep and unreflective participation in the symbols of a place for what they are. It is associated particularly with the sacred experience of involvement in holy places, and with the secular experience of being known in and knowing the named and significant places of a home region. At a shallower level of insideness there is an authentic sense of place that is selfconscious, and which involves a deliberate attempt to appreciate fully the significance of places without the adoption of narrow intellectual or social conventions and fashions. This is the experience of a sensitive and open-minded outsider seeking to grasp places for what they are to those who dwell in them and for what they mean to him. It is an attitude of particular importance in terms of the possibilities it offers to contemporary and authentic place-making. In contrast is the superficial level of insideness, which involves simply being in a place without attending in any sensitive way to its qualities or significances. Though each of us must experience many of the places we visit like this, since concern with our activities takes precedence and it becomes impossible to concentrate on the place itself, when this is the only form of experience of place it denotes a real failure to 'see' or to be involved in places. For those swayed by the easy charms of mass culture or the cool attractions of technique this does seem to be the primary, perhaps the only, way of experiencing environments; and consequently they feel no care or commitment for places: they are geographically alienated.

The various levels of insideness are manifest in the creation of distinctive types of places. The deep levels of existential insideness are apparent in the unselfconscious making of places which are human in their scale and organisation, which fit both their physical and cultural contexts and hence are as varied as those contexts, and which are filled with significances for those who live in them. Authentic and selfconscious insideness offers a similar, though less completely involved, possibility for expressing man's humanity in places. In both instances "the making of places is", as Rapoport (1972, p. 3-3-10) writes, "the ordering of the world", for it differentiates the world into qualitatively distinct centres and gives a structure that both reflects and guides experiences. This is not so with incidental insideness, for such non-commitment opens the way for the development of environments ordered by conceptual principles or mass fashions rather than by patterns of direct experience. In short, uncommitted insideness is the basis for placelessness.

PLACELESSNESS

Placelessness describes both an environment without significant places and the underlying attitude, which does not acknowledge significance in places. It reaches back into the deepest levels of place, cutting roots, eroding symbols, replacing diversity with uniformity and experiential order with conceptual order. At its most profound it consists of a pervasive and perhaps irreversible alienation from places as the homes of men: "He who has no home now will not build one anymore", Rilke declared, and this was echoed by Heidegger – "Homelessness

is becoming a world fate" (both cited in Pappenheim, 1959, p. 33). At less deep levels placelessness is the adoption of the attitude described by Harvey Cox (1968, p. 424) as an "abstract geometric view of place, denuded of its human meaning", and it is manifest in landscapes that can be aptly described by Stephen Kurtz' specific account (1973, p. 23) of Howard Johnson's restaurants: "Nothing calls attention to itself; it is all remarkably unremarkable ... You have seen it, heard it, experienced it all before, and yet ... you have seen and experienced nothing ..."

As a selfconsciously adopted posture placelessness is particularly apparent in *technique*, the overriding concern with efficiency as an end in itself. In *technique* places can be treated as the interchangeable, replaceable locations of things, as indeed they are by multinational corporations, powerful central governments, and uninvolved planners. As an unselfconscious attitude placelessness is particularly associated with mass culture – the adoption of fashions and ideas about landscapes and places that are coined by a few 'experts' and disseminated to the people through the mass media. The products of these two attitudes are combined in uniform, sterile, other-directed, and kitschy places – places which have few significances and symbols, only more or less gaudy signs and things performing functions with greater or lesser efficiency. The overall result is the undermining of the importance of place for both individuals and cultures, and the casual replacement of the diverse and significant places of the world with anonymous spaces and exchangeable environments.

THE INEVITABILITY OF PLACELESSNESS?

The places that we have known belong now only to the little world of space on which we map them for our own convenience. None of them was ever more than a thin slice held between the contiguous impressions that composed our life at that time; remembrance for a particular form is but regret for a particular moment, and houses, roads, avenues, are as fugitive, alas, as the years.

Thus Marcel Proust (1970, p. 288) expressed with nostalgia the insignificance of places for modern man. No more is there the "sense of continuity with place" which Harvey Cox (1968, p. 423) believes is so necessary for people's sense of reality and so essential for their identity; the meanings of places have become as ephemeral as their physical forms. Cox judges this as "one of the most deplorable characteristics of our time", but deplore it, condemn it, criticise it as we might, there often appears to be little that can be done to prevent the diminishing of significant relations with places.

The prospect of inevitable placelessness is supported by Jacques Ellul's view of *technique*, one of the main forces behind the developing placeless geography. He writes (1964, p. 436): "The attitude of scientists, at any rate, is clear. Technique exists because it is technique. The golden age will be because it will be. Any other answer is superfluous." In other words *technique* has a drive of its own that is universal, we can no longer think in terms other than those of *technique* because it is the only language we know, and the only possibility is that placelessness will come to dominate. If we regret the disappearance of significant places this is only sentimentality and we should at least acknowledge the benefits of the new geography. As George Grant (1969, p. 138) expresses it:

It might be said that the older systems of meaning have been replaced by a new one. The enchantment of our souls by myth, philosophy or revelation has been replaced by a more immediate meaning – the building of free and equal men by the overcoming of chance.

But in what sense freedom and in what sense equality? To master chance in human and non-human nature requires the most efficient use of *technique* that is possible, and that in turn requires the perfection of science and powerful central government. Louch (1966, p. 239) has declared: "Totalitarianism is too weak a word and too inefficient an instrument to describe the perfect scientific society." Alexis de Tocqueville (1945, vol. II, p. 337) wrote: "The will of man is not shattered but softened, bent and guided – such centralised power does not destroy, but compresses, enervates, extinguishes and stupefies a people."

If Tocqueville, Grant, and Ellul are correct, and in the landscape of industrial cultures there is massive evidence to support them, then opposition to

technique and to central authorities – two of the primary sources of placelessness – seems either futile or impossible. We may protest it, deplore it, propose alternatives to it, but the fundamental basis for our experience of the landscapes we live in is increasingly becoming the attitude of placelessness.

DESIGNING A LIVED-WORLD OF PLACES

But such pessimism and fatalism are not yet justified. There may indeed come a time when placelessness is inevitable because it is the only geography we know, but so long as there are what Grant (1969, p. 139) calls "intimations of authentic deprival", then the possibility of some different way of thinking and acting must remain. David Brower (in Gussow, 1971?, p. 15) is in fact quite specific about what must be done: "The best weapon against the unending deprivation that would be the consequence of ... unending demand is a revival of man's sense of place." How this is to be achieved he does not make clear, but it is certain that loss of attachment to places and the decline of the ability to make places authentically do constitute real deprivations, and that the redevelopment of such attachments and abilities is essential if we are to create environments that do not have to be ignored or endured. Furthermore, there appears to be a possibility of doing this outside the context of *technique*, for sense of place is in its essence both prescientific and intersubjective.

The possibilities for maintaining and reviving man's sense of place do not lie in the preservation of old places – that would be museumisation; nor can they lie in a selfconscious return to the traditional ways of placemaking – that would require the regaining of a lost state of innocence. Instead, placelessness must be transcended. "That human activity should become more dispersed is inevitable", Georges Matoré (1966, p. 6) has written, "but to compensate let the occupied, lived-in space acquire more cohesion, become as rich as possible, and grow large with the experience of living." Similarly Harvey Cox (1968, p. 424) has argued that beyond the stage of homogeneous space, in which every place is interchangeable with every other place, lies a stage of human space in which "space is for man and places are understood as giving pace, variety and orientation to man". This will not come about automatically but through deliberate effort and the development of 'secularisation', an attitude which corresponds closely to selfconscious authenticity. Secularisation "dislodges ancient oppressions and overturns stultifying conventions. It turns man's social and cultural life over to him, demanding a constant expenditure of vision and competence" (Cox, 1965, p. 86). While the danger always remains of this being short-circuited by new orthodoxies that will result in placelessness, secularisation provides a very real basis for optimism about places so long as we can live up to the responsibilities it demands. Cox continues: "A secular civilisation need not be monochrome or homogeneous. But the character lent by diversity cannot be left to chance. Like everything else in the secular city variety must be planned or it does not happen."

The creating of a variety of places which give pace, orientation, and identity to man is clearly no simple task. It involves what Nairn (1965, p. 93) has called "the terrific assumption" that "each place is different, that each case must be decided on its own merits, that completely different solutions may be needed for apparently similar cases". To acknowledge this does not mean that humanist place-making must be chaotic and unstructured, but rather that its order must be derived from significant experience and not from arbitrary abstractions and concepts as represented on maps and plans. The implication is that selfconscious and authentic place-making is not something that can be done programmatically. A method like that developed by Christopher Alexander (Alexander, 1964, 1966; Alexander and Poyner, 1970), based on the decomposition of sets of environmental objects and activities into their atomic elements, and the reconstitution of these into a design solution, does have considerable value for improving current design strategies and possibly for achieving designs that fit local situations well; and approaches like Gordon Cullen's analysis (1971) of the structures of visual experience of townscape are potentially of great use in improving the quality of appearance of landscapes. But these, and almost all the other procedures of environmental design, are either too formal and too rigidly prescriptive, or they treat experience and meaning only as other variables capable of manipulation.

What is needed is not a precisely mathematical procedure that treats the environments we live in like some great machine that we do not yet quite understand, but an approach to the design of the lived-world of both everyday and exceptional experiences – an approach that is wholly self-conscious yet does seek to create wholly designed environments into which people must be fitted, an approach that is responsive to local structures of meaning and experience, to particular situations and to the variety of levels of meaning of place; an approach that takes its inspiration from the existential significance of place, the need that many people have for a profound attachment to places, and the ontological principles of dwelling and sparing identified by Heidegger (Vycinas, 1961). Such an approach cannot provide precise solutions to clearly defined problems, but, proceeding from an appreciation of the significance of place and the particular activities and local situations, it would perhaps provide a way of outlining some of the main directions and possibilities, thus allowing scope for individuals and groups to make their own places, and to give those places authenticity and significance by modifying them and by dwelling in them.

David Brower (in Gussow, 1971?, p. 15) has written that "the places we have roots in, and the flavour of their light and sound and feel when things are right in those places, are the wellsprings of our serenity". It is not possible to design rootedness nor to guarantee that things will be right in places, but it is perhaps possible to provide conditions that will allow roots and care for places to develop. To do this is no easy task, and indeed how or whether such a complex synthesis of procedure and sentiment can be achieved in designing a lived-world of places is by no means clear. But if places matter to us, if we are at all concerned about the psychological consequences and moral issues in uprooting and increasing geographical mobility and placelessness, then we must explore the possibility of developing an approach for making places selfconsciously and authentically. The only alternatives are to celebrate and participate in the glorious non-place urban society, or to accept in silence the trivialisation and careless eradication of the significant places of our lives. And, as Sinclair Gauldie (1969, p. 182) has written: "To live in an environment which has to be endured or ignored rather than enjoyed is to be diminished as a human being."

CONCLUSION

A deep human need exists for associations with significant places. If we choose to ignore that need, and to allow the forces of placelessness to continue unchallenged, then the future can only hold an environment in which places simply do not matter. If, on the other hand, we choose to respond to that need and to transcend placelessness, then the potential exists for the development of an environment in which places are for man, reflecting and enhancing the variety of human experience. Which of these two possibilities is most probable, or whether there are other possibilities, is far from certain. But one thing at least is clear whether the world we live in has a placeless geography or a geography of significant places, the responsibility for it is ours alone.

REFERENCES

Alexander, C. (1964) *Notes on the Synthesis of Form* (Cambridge, Mass: Harvard University Press).

Alexander, C. (1966) "A city is not a city" *Design* 206 47–55.

Alexander, C., and Poyner, B. (1970?) "The atoms of environmental structure" Working Paper No. 42, Centre for Planning and Development Research, University of California, Berkeley.

Cox, H. (1965) *The Secular City* (Toronto: Macmillan).

Cox, H. (1968) "The restoration of a sense of place" *Ekistics* 25 422–424.

Cullen, G. (1971) *The Concise Townscape* (London: Architectural Press).

Ellul, J. (1964) *The Technological Society* (New York: Random House).

Gauldie, S. (1969) *Architecture: The Appreciation of the Arts 1* (London: Oxford University Press).

Grant, G. (1969) *Technology and Empire* (Toronto: Anansi).

Gussow, A. (1971?) *A Sense of Place* (San Francisco: Friends of the Earth).

Kurtz, S. (1973) *Wasteland: Building the American Dream* (New York: Praeger).

Louch, A.R. (1966) *Explanation and Human Action* (Berkeley: University of California Press).

Matoré, G. (1966) "Existential space" *Landscape* 15 (3) 5–6.

Nairn, I. (1965) *The American Landscape* (New York: Random House).

Pappenheim, F. (1959) *The Alienation of Modern Man* (New York: Modern Reader Paperbacks).

Proust, M. (1970) *Swann's Way*, Part Two (London: Chatto & Windus).

Rapoport, A. (1972) "Australian aborigines and the definition of place" *Environmental Design: Research and Practice* Ed. W.J. Mitchell, Volume 1, Proceedings of the 3rd EDRA Conference, Los Angeles, pp. 3-3-1 to 3-3-14.

Tocqueville, A. de (1945) *Democracy in America* Volume II (New York: Vintage Books).

Vycinas, V. (1961) *Earth and Gods* (The Hague: Martinus Nijhoff).

THREE

"The Phenomenon of Place"

from *Architectural Association Quarterly* (1976)

Christian Norberg-Schulz

Editors' Introduction

Design theories are often derived from the larger philosophical and cultural movements where they draw their inspiration. This is certainly the case with the use of phenomenology and its application to environmental knowledge as expressed in the writings of Christian Norberg-Schulz (1926–2000). He draws on the phenomenological works of both Edmund Husserl and Martin Heidegger to develop a critique of modern architecture and urbanism and urge a return to place-based design.

Phenomenology was first delineated by Edmund Husserl in his 1906 work *The Idea of Phenomenology*. It attempted to explain how people receive sensory material about the physical world (the phenomena of objects and situations) and consciously process this material to find meaning. Norberg-Schulz adopts Husserl's need for a "return to things" within the everyday lifeworld, whereby people can readily find meaning in the physical elements that structure place-based experience. In this article, he reintroduces the reader to important concepts such as physical character, identity, space, and place, as well as the Roman concept of *genius loci*, the guardian spirit or essence of place. The work is also influenced by Martin Heidegger's short essay, "Building Dwelling Thinking," which poses existential questions relating "being" and identity to notions of place, highlighted by the author's example of place-based identity markers found in common language – "I am a New Yorker," or "I am a Roman."

"The Phenomenon of Place," along with other works by Norberg-Schulz, is a direct response to a perceived crisis in the design professions. Environmental phenomenology arose as a means of providing a more communicative method of design, whereby place-based meaning could be transmitted more clearly than the overly diagrammatic and mixed messages found in modernism. Because of its universalizing nature and non-place qualities, modern design is perceived here as the product of elite and abstract mental constructs often devoid of accessible or popular meaning. This perception is very different from the critical regionalist understanding that modernism itself can be made relevant to varied regional contexts. Within his writing, Norberg-Schulz bemoans the loss of design's communicative role. He suggests designers should make visible, differentiate, and "concretize" the physical character and essence of places. Here Norberg-Schulz parallels the efforts of other authors interested in design communication, such as Charles Jencks, Kevin Lynch, Aldo Rossi, and Robert Venturi, who address issues of semiotics, text, legibility, and imageability in design.

Norberg-Schulz's work has had various positive impacts on the design field. In many ways, environmental phenomenology provides a theoretical basis for contextualism and renewed design interests in materiality, texture, sensory experience, and the poetics of design. His writing on place, *genius loci*, identity, and physical character is part of a larger thematic literature on theories of place and space that began in academic circles in the late 1960s and continues nowadays. His advocacy of place in design is central to the growth of place-making strategies, Critical Regionalism, and the work of many designers around the world.

Christian Norberg-Schulz was a theorist and professor of architecture at the Oslo School of Architecture. He studied at Harvard, the Zurich Polytechnic and the Technical University of Trondheim, Norway. He was associated with the Norwegian CIAM group in the 1950s and was co-director of Lotus International. He was a voluminous author of architectural and design history and theory. His works include the following: *Intentions in Architecture* (Cambridge, MA: MIT Press, 1965); *Existence, Space and Architecture* (New York: Praeger, 1971); *Meaning in Western Architecture* (New York: Praeger, 1975); *Architecture, Meaning and Place* (New York: Rizzoli, 1980); *Genius Loci: Towards a Phenomenology of Architecture* (New York: Rizzoli, 1980); "Heidegger's Thinking on Architecture," in *Perspecta 20* (New Haven, CT: Yale Architectural Journal, 1983); *The Concept of Dwelling: On the Way to Figurative Architecture* (New York: Rizzoli, 1985); and *Architecture, Presence, Language and Place* (Milan: Skira, 2000).

Other key texts on environmental phenomenology and its use in design include: Gaston Bachelard, *The Poetics of Space* (Boston, MA: Beacon Press, 1994, original 1958); Martin Heidegger's essays "Building Dwelling Thinking" and ". . . Poetically Man Dwells . . . ," in *Poetry, Language, Thought*, trans. Albert Hofstadter (New York: Harper & Row, 1971); Kenneth Frampton, "On Reading Heidegger," in *Oppositions 4* (October 1974); David Seamon and Robert Mugerauer (eds), *Dwelling, Place and Environment: Towards a Phenomenology of Person and World* (New York: Columbia University Press, 1985); David Seamon (ed.), *Dwelling, Seeing, and Designing: Toward a Phenomenological Ecology* (Albany, NY: State University of New York Press, 1993); Sarah Menin (ed.), *Constructing Place: Mind and the Matter of Place-Making* (London: Routlege, 2004); and Dylan Trigg, *The Memory of Place: A Phenomenology of the Uncanny* (Athens, OH: Ohio University Press, 2012).

For a comprehensive overview of the history of space and place see: Edward S. Casey, *Getting Back into Place: Toward a Renewed Understanding of the Place-World* (Bloomington, IN: Indiana University Press, 1993) and *The Fate of Place: A Philosophical History* (Berkeley, CA: University of California Press, 1997); Yi-Fu Tuan, *Space and Place: The Perspective of Experience* (Minneapolis MN: University of Minnesota Press, 2001); Tim Cresswell, *Place: A Short Introduction* (New York: Wiley/Blackwell, 2004); and Phil Hubbard and Rob Kitchin (eds), *Key Thinkers on Space and Place*, 2nd edn. (New York: Sage Publications, 2010).

For critical perspectives on the production and use of space see: Henri Lefebvre, *The Production of Space*, trans. David Nicholson-Smith (Oxford: Blackwell, 1991); Mark Gottdiener, *The Social Production of Urban Space* (Austin, TX: University of Texas Press, 1985); Ali Madanipour, *Design of Urban Space: An Inquiry into a Socio-Spatial Process* (Chichester, UK: John Wiley, 1996); and Doreen Massey, *Space, Place and Gender* (Minneapolis, MN: University of Minnesota Press, 1994).

Our everyday life-world consists of concrete "phenomena." It consists of people, of animals, of flowers, trees and forests, of stone, earth, wood and water, of towns, streets and houses, doors, windows and furniture. And it consists of sun, moon and stars, of drifting clouds, of night and day and changing seasons. But it also comprises more intangible phenomena such as feelings. This is what is "given," this is the "content" of our existence. Thus Rilke says: "Are we perhaps *here* to say: house, bridge, fountain, gate, jug, fruit tree, window, – at best: Pillar, tower" (Rilke, 1972, Elegy XI). Everything else, such as atoms and molecules, numbers and all kinds of "data," are abstractions or tools which are constructed to serve other purposes than those of everyday life. Today it is common to mistake the tools for reality.

The concrete things which constitute our given world are interrelated in complex and perhaps contradictory ways. Some of the phenomena may for instance comprise others. The forest consists of trees, and the town is made up of houses. "Landscape" is such a comprehensive phenomenon. In general we may say that some phenomena form an "environment" to others. A concrete term for environment is *place*. It is common usage to say that acts and occurrences *take place*. In fact it is meaningless to imagine any happening without reference to a locality. Place is evidently an integral part of existence. What, then, do we mean with the word "place"? Obviously we mean something more than abstract location. We mean a totality made up of concrete things having material substance, shape, texture and colour. Together these things determine an "environmental character," which is the essence of place. In general a place is given as such a character or "atmosphere." A place is therefore a qualitative, "total" phenomenon, which we cannot reduce to any of its properties, such as spatial relationships, without losing its concrete nature out of sight.

Everyday experience moreover tells us that different actions need different environments to take place in a satisfactory way. As a consequence, towns and houses consist of a multitude of particular places. This fact is of course taken into consideration by current theory of planning and architecture, but so far the problem has been treated in a too abstract way. "Taking place" is usually understood in a quantitative, "functional" sense, with implications such as spatial distribution and dimensioning. But are not "functions" inter-human and similar everywhere? Evidently not. "Similar" functions, even the most basic ones such as sleeping and eating take place in very different ways, and demand places with different properties, in accordance with different cultural traditions and different environmental conditions. The functional approach therefore left out the place as a concrete "here" having its particular identity.

Being qualitative totalities of a complex nature, places cannot be described by means of analytic, "scientific" concepts. As a matter of principle science "abstracts" from the given to arrive at neutral, "objective" knowledge. What is lost, however, is the everyday life-world, which ought to be the real concern of man in general and planners and architects in particular.[1] Fortunately a way out of the impasse exists, that is, the method known as *phenomenology*. Phenomenology was conceived as a "return to things," as opposed to abstractions and mental constructions. So far, phenomenologists have been mainly concerned with ontology, psychology, ethics and to some extent aesthetics, and have given relatively little attention to the phenomenology of the daily environment. A few pioneer works however exist but they hardly contain any direct reference to architecture.[2] A phenomenology of architecture is therefore urgently needed.

Some of the philosophers who have approached the problem of our life-world, have used language and literature as sources of "information." Poetry in fact is able to concretize those totalities which elude science, and may therefore suggest how we

might proceed to obtain the needed understanding. One of the poems used by Heidegger to explain the nature of language, is the splendid "A Winter Evening" by Georg Trakl (Heidegger, 1971). The words of Trakl also serve our purpose very well, as they make present a total life-situation where the aspect of place is strongly felt:[3]

A Winter Evening

Window with falling snow is arrayed,
Long tolls the vesper bell,
The house is provided well,
The table is for many laid.
Wandering ones, more than a few,
Come to the door on darksome courses,
Golden blooms the tree of graces
Drawing up the earth's cool dew.
Wanderer quietly steps within;
Pain has turned the threshold to stone.
There lie, in limpid brightness shown,
Upon the table bread and wine.

We shall not repeat Heidegger's profound analysis of the poem, but rather point out a few properties which illuminate our problem. In general, Trakl uses *concrete* images which we all know from our everyday world. He talks about "snow," "window," "house," "table," "door," "tree," "threshold," "bread and wine," "darkness" and "light," and he characterizes man as a "wanderer." These images, however, also imply more general structures. First of all the poem distinguishes between an *outside* and an *inside*. The *outside* is presented in the first two lines of the first stanza, and comprises *natural* as well as *man-made* elements. Natural place is present in the falling snow which implies winter, and by the evening. The very title of the poem "places" everything in this natural context. A winter evening, however, is something more than a point in the calendar. As a concrete presence, it is experienced as a set of particular qualities, or in general as a *Stimmung* or "character," which forms a background to acts and occurrences. In the poem this character is given by the snow falling on the window, cold, soft and soundless, hiding the contours of those objects which are still recognized in the approaching darkness. The word "falling" moreover creates a sense of *space*, or rather: an implied presence of earth and sky. With a minimum of words, Trakl thus brings a total natural environment to life. But the outside also has man-made properties. This is indicated by the vesper bell, which is heard everywhere, and makes the "private" inside become part of a comprehensive, "public" totality. The vesper bell, however, is something more than a practical man-made artifact. It is a symbol, which reminds us of the common values which are at the basis of that totality. In Heidegger's words: "the tolling of the evening bell brings men, as mortals, before the divine" (Heidegger, 1971, p. 199).

The *inside* is presented in the next two verses. It is described as a house, which offers man shelter and security by being enclosed and "well provided". It has, however, a window, an opening which makes us experience the inside as a complement to the outside. As a final focus within the house we find the table, which "is for many laid". At the table men come together, it is the *centre* which more than anything else constitutes the inside. The character of the inside is hardly told, but anyhow present. It is luminous and warm, in contrast to the cold darkness outside, and its silence is pregnant with potential sound. In general the inside is a comprehensible world of *things*, where the life of "many" may take place.

In the next two stanzas the perspective is deepened. Here the *meaning* of places and things comes forth, and man is presented as a wanderer on "darksome courses." Rather than being placed safely within the house he has created for himself, he comes from the outside, from the "path of life," which also represents man's attempt at "orienting" himself in the given unknown environment. But nature also has another side: it offers the grace of growth and blossom. In the image of the "golden" tree, earth and sky are unified and become a *world*. Through man's labour this world is brought inside as bread and wine, whereby the inside is "illuminated", that is, becomes meaningful. Without the "sacred" fruits of sky and earth, the inside would remain "empty". The house and the table receive and gather, and bring the world "close". *To dwell in a house therefore means to inhabit the world.* But this dwelling is not easy; it has to be reached on dark paths, and a threshold separates the outside from the inside. Representing the "rift" between "otherness" and manifest meaning, it embodies suffering and is "turned to stone." In the threshold, thus, the *problem* of dwelling comes to the fore (Heidegger, 1971, p. 204).

Trakl's poem illuminates some essential phenomena of our life-world, and in particular the basic properties of place. First of all it tells us that every situation is local as well as general. The winter evening described is obviously a local, nordic phenomenon, but the implied notions of outside and inside are general, as are the meanings connected with this distinction. The poem hence concretizes basic properties of existence. "Concretize" here means to make the general "visible" as a concrete, local situation. In doing this the poem moves in the opposite direction of scientific thought. Whereas science departs from the "given", poetry brings us back to the concrete things, uncovering the meanings inherent in the life-world (Norberg-Schulz, 1963, chapter on "symbolization").

Furthermore Trakl's poem distinguishes between natural and man-made elements, whereby it suggests a point of departure for an "environmental phenomenology." Natural elements are evidently the primary components of the given, and places are in fact usually defined in geographical terms. We must repeat however, that "place" means something more than location. Various attempts at a description of natural places are offered by current literature on "landscape," but again we find that the usual approach is too abstract, being based on "functional" or perhaps "visual" considerations (see, for instance, Appleton, 1975). Again we must turn to philosophy for help. As a first, fundamental distinction Heidegger introduces the concepts of "earth" and "sky," and says: "Earth is the serving bearer, blossoming and fruiting, spreading out in rock and water, rising up into plant and animal . . ."

The sky is the vaulting path of the sun, the course of the changing moon, the glitter of the stars, the year's seasons, the light and dusk of day, the gloom and glow of night, the clemency and inclemency of the weather, the drifting clouds and blue depth of the ether . . .

Heidegger, 1971, p. 149

Like many fundamental insights, the distinction between earth and sky might seem trivial. Its importance however comes out when we add Heidegger's definition of "dwelling:" "the way in which you are and I am, the way in which we humans *are* on the earth, is dwelling . . ." But "on the earth" already means "under the sky" (Heidegger, 1971, pp. 147, 149). He also calls what is *between* earth and sky *the world*, and says that "the world is the house where the mortals dwell" (Heidegger, 1957, p. 13). In other words, when man is capable of dwelling the world becomes an "inside."

In general, nature forms an extended comprehensive totality, a "place," which according to local circumstances has a particular identity. This identity, or "spirit," may be described by means of the kind of concrete, "qualitative" terms Heidegger uses to characterize earth and sky, and has to take this fundamental distinction as its point of departure. In this way we might arrive at an existentially relevant understanding of *landscape*, which ought to be preserved as the main designation of natural places. Within the landscape, however, there are subordinate places, as well as natural "things" such as Trakl's "tree." In these things the meaning of the natural environment is "condensed."

The man-made parts of the environment are first of all "settlements" of different scale, from houses and farms to villages and towns, and secondly "paths" which connect these settlements, as well as various elements which transform nature into a "cultural landscape." If the settlements are organically related to their environment, it implies that they serve as *foci* where the environmental character is condensed and "explained." Thus Heidegger says:

> the single houses, the villages, the towns are works of building which within and around themselves gather the multifarious in-between. The buildings bring the earth as the inhabited landscape close to man, and at the same time place the closeness of neighbourly dwelling under the expanse of the sky.
>
> Heidegger, 1957, p. 13

The basic property of man-made places is therefore concentration and enclosure. They are "insides" in a full sense, which means that they "gather" what is known. To fulfill this function they have openings which relate to the outside. (Only an *inside* can in fact have openings). Buildings are furthermore related to their environment by resting on the ground and rising towards the sky. Finally the man-made environments comprise artifacts or "things," which may serve as internal foci, and emphasize the gathering function of the settlement. In Heidegger's

words: "the thing things world," where "thinging" is used in the original sense of "gathering," and further: "Only what conjoins itself out of world becomes a thing" (Heidegger, 1971, pp. 181–2).

Our introductory remarks give several indications about the *structure* of places. Some of these have already been worked out by phenomenologist philosophers, and offer a good point of departure for a more complete phenomenology. A first step is taken with the distinction of natural and man-made phenomena. A second step is represented by the categories of earth-sky (horizontal-vertical) and outside-inside. These categories have spatial implications, and "space" is hence re-introduced, not primarily as a mathematical concept, but as an existential dimension (Norberg-Schulz, 1971, where the concept "existential space" is used). A final and particularly important step is taken with the concept of "character." Character is determined by *how* things are, and gives our investigation a basis in the concrete phenomena of our everyday life-world. Only in this way we may fully grasp the *genius loci*, the "spirit of place" which the ancients recognized as that "opposite" man has to come to terms with, to be able to dwell.[4] The concept of *genius loci* denotes the essence of place.

THE STRUCTURE OF PLACE

Our preliminary discussion of the phenomena of place led to the conclusion that the structure of place ought to be described in terms of "landscape" and "settlement," and analyzed by means of the categories "space" and "character." Whereas "space" denotes the three-dimensional organization of the elements which make up a place, "character" denotes the general "atmosphere" which is the most comprehensive property of any place. Instead of making a distinction between space and character, it is of course possible to employ one comprehensive concept, such as "lived space."[5] For our purpose, however, it is practical to distinguish between space and character. Similar spatial organizations may possess very different characters according to the concrete treatment of the space-defining elements (the *boundary*). The history of basic spatial forms have been given ever new characterizing interpretations.[6] On the other hand it has to be pointed out that the spatial organization puts certain limits to characterization, and that the two concepts are interdependent.

"Space" is certainly no new term in architectural theory. But space can mean many things. In current literature we may distinguish between two uses: space as three-dimensional geometry, and space as perceptual field (Norberg-Schulz, 1971, pp. 12ff). None of these however are satisfactory, being abstractions from the intuitive three-dimensional totality of everyday experience, which we may call "concrete space." Concrete human actions in fact do not take place in an homogeneous isotropic space, but in a space distinguished by qualitative differences, such as "up" and "down." In architectural theory several attempts have been made to define space in concrete, qualitative terms. Giedion thus uses the distinction between "outside" and "inside" as the basis for a grand view of architectural history (Giedion, 1964). Kevin Lynch penetrates deeper into the structure of concrete space, introducing the concepts of "node," "landmark," "path," "edge," and "district" to denote those elements which form the basis for man's orientation in space (Lynch, 1960). Paolo Portoghesi finally defines space as a "system of places," implying that the concept of space has its roots in concrete situations, although spaces may be *described* by means of mathematics (Portoghesi, 1975, pp. 88ff). The latter view corresponds to Heidegger's statement that "spaces receive their being from locations and not from 'space'" (Heidegger, 1971, p. 154). The outside–inside relation, which is a primary aspect of concrete space, implies that spaces possess a varying degree of *extension* and *enclosure*. Whereas landscapes are distinguished by a varied, but basically continuous extension, settlements are enclosed entities. Settlement and landscape therefore have a *figure–ground* relationship. In general, any enclosure becomes manifest as a "figure" in relation to the extended ground of the landscape. A settlement loses its identity if this relationship is corrupted, just as much as the landscape loses its identity as comprehensive extension. In a wider context any enclosure becomes a *centre*, which may function as a "focus" for its surroundings. From the centre space extends with a varying degree of continuity (rhythm) in different directions. Evidently the main directions are horizontal and vertical, that is, the directions of earth and sky. *Centralization*, *direction* and *rhythm* are therefore other important

properties of concrete space. Finally it has to be mentioned that natural elements (such as hills) and settlements may be clustered or grouped with a varying degree of *proximity*.

All the spatial properties mentioned are of a "topological" kind, and correspond to the well-known "principles of organization" of Gestalt theory. The primary existential importance of these principles is confirmed by the researches of Piaget on the child's conception of space (Norberg-Schulz, 1971, p. 18). Geometrical modes of organization only develop later in life to serve particular purposes, and may in general be understood as a more "precise" definition of the basic topological structures. The topological enclosure thus becomes a circle, the "free" curve a straight line, and the cluster a grid. In architecture geometry is used to make a general comprehensive system manifest, such as an inferred "cosmic order."

Any enclosure is defined by a boundary: Heidegger says: "A boundary is not that at which something stops but, as the Greeks recognized, the boundary is that, from which something begins its presencing" (Heidegger, 1971, p. 154: presence is the old word for being). The boundaries of a built space are known as *floor*, *wall* and *ceiling*. The boundaries of a landscape are structurally similar, and consist of ground, horizon, and sky. This simple structural similarity is of basic importance for the relationship between natural and man-made places. The enclosing properties of a boundary are determined by its *openings*, as was poetically intuited by Trakl when using the images of window, door and threshold. In general the boundary, and in particular the wall, makes the spatial structure visible as continuous and/or discontinuous extension, direction and rhythm.

"Character" is at the same time a more general and a more concrete concept than "space." On the one hand it denotes a general comprehensive atmosphere, and on the other the concrete form and substance of the space-defining elements. Any real *presence* is intimately linked with a character (Bollnow, 1956). A phenomenology of character has to comprise a survey of manifest characters as well as an investigation of their concrete determinants. We have pointed out that different actions demand places with a different character. A dwelling has to be "protective," an office "practical," a ballroom "festive" and a church "solemn." When we visit a foreign city, we are usually struck by its particular character, which becomes an important part of the experience. Landscapes also possess character, some of which is of a particular "natural" kind. Thus we talk about "barren" and "fertile," "smiling" and "threatening" landscapes. In general we have to emphasize that *all places have character*, and that character is the basic mode in which the world is "given." To some extent the character of a place is a function of time; it changes with the seasons, the course of the day and the weather, factors which above all determine different conditions of *light*.

The character is determined by the material and formal constitution of the place. We must therefore ask: *how* is the ground on which we walk, *how* is the sky above our heads, or in general: *how* are the boundaries which define the place. How a boundary is depends upon its formal articulation, which is again related to the way it is "built." Looking at a building from this point of view, we have to consider how it rests on the ground and how it rises towards the sky. Particular attention has to be given to its lateral boundaries, or walls, which also contribute decisively to determine the character of the *urban* environment. We are indebted to Robert Venturi for having recognized this fact, after it had been considered for many years "immoral" to talk about "facades" (Venturi, 1967, p. 88). Usually the character of a "family" of buildings which constitute a place, is "condensed" in characteristic *motifs*, such as particular types of windows, doors and roofs. Such motifs may become "conventional elements," which serve to transpose a character from one place to another. In the boundary, thus, character and space come together, and we may agree with Venturi when he defines architecture as "the wall between the inside and the outside" (Venturi, 1967, p. 89).

Except for the intuitions of Venturi, the problem of character has hardly been considered in current architectural theory. As a result, theory has to a high extent lost contact with the concrete life-world. This is particularly the case with technology, which is today considered a mere means to satisfy practical demand. Character however, depends upon *how things are made*, and is therefore determined by the technical realization ("building"). Heidegger points out that the Greek word *techne* meant a creative "re-vealing" *Entbergen* of truth, and belonged to

poiesis, that is, "making" (Heidegger, 1954, p. 12). A phenomenology of place therefore has to comprise the basic modes of construction and their relationship to formal articulation. Only in this way architectural theory gets a truly concrete basis.

The structure of place becomes manifest as environmental totalities which comprise the aspects of character and space. Such places are known as "countries," "regions," "landscapes," "settlements," and "buildings." Here we return to the concrete "things" of our everyday life-world, which was our point of departure, and remember Rilke's words: "Are we perhaps *here* to say . . ." When places are classified we should therefore use terms such as "island," "promontory," "bay," "forest," "grove," or "square," "street," "courtyard," and "floor," "wall," "roof," "ceiling," "window," and "door."

Places are hence designated by *nouns*. This implies that they are considered real "things that exist," which is the original meaning of the word "substantive." Space, instead, as a system of relations, is denoted by *prepositions*. In our daily life we hardly talk about "space," but about things that are "over" or "under," "before" or "behind" each other, or we use prepositions such as "at," "in," "within," "on," "upon," "to," "from," "along," "next." All these preparations denote topological relations of the kind mentioned before. Character, finally, is denoted by *adjectives*, as was indicated above. A character is a complex totality, and a single adjective evidently cannot cover more than one aspect of this totality. Often, however, a character is so distinct that one word seems sufficient to grasp its essence. We see, thus, that the very structure of everyday language confirms our analysis of place.

Countries, regions, landscapes, settlements, buildings (and their sub-places) form a series with a gradually diminishing scale. The steps in this series may be called "environmental levels" (Norberg-Schulz, 1971, p. 27). At the "top" of the series we find the more comprehensive natural places which "contain" the man-made places on the "lower" levels. The latter have the "gathering" and "focusing" function mentioned above. In other words, man "receives" the environment and makes it focus in buildings and things. The things thereby "explain" the environment and make its character manifest. Thereby the things themselves become meaningful. That is the basic function of *detail* in our surroundings (Norberg-Schulz, 1971, p. 32). This does not imply, however, that the different levels must have the same structure. Architectural history in fact shows that this is rarely the case. Vernacular settlements usually have a topological organization, although the single houses may be *strictly* geometrical. In larger cities we often find topologically organized neighbourhoods within a general geometrical structure, etc. We shall return to the particular problems of structural correspondence later, but have to say some words about the main "step" in the scale of environmental levels: the relation between natural and man-made places.

Man-made places are related to nature in three basic ways. Firstly, man wants to make the natural structure more precise. That is, he wants to *visualize* his "understanding" of nature, "expressing" the existential foothold he has gained. To achieve this, he *builds* what he has seen. Where nature suggests a delimited space he builds an enclosure; where nature appears "centralized," he erects a *Mal* (Frey, 1949); where nature indicates a direction, he makes a path. Secondly, man has to *symbolize* his understanding of nature (including himself). Symbolization implies that an experienced meaning is "translated" into another medium. A natural character is for instance translated into a building whose properties somehow make the character manifest (Norberg-Schulz, 1963). The purpose of symbolization is to free the meaning from the immediate situation, whereby it becomes a "cultural object," which may form part of a more complex situation, or be moved to another place. Finally, man needs to *gather* the experienced meanings to create for himself an *image mundi* or *microcosmos* which concretizes his world. Gathering evidently depends on symbolization, and implies a transposition of meanings to one place, which thereby becomes an existential "centre."

Visualization, symbolization and gathering are aspects of the general processes of settling; and dwelling, in the existential sense of the word, depends on these functions. Heidegger illustrates the problem by means of the *bridge*; a "building" which visualizes, symbolizes, and gathers, and makes the environment a unified whole. Thus he says:

The bridge swings over the stream with ease and power. It does not just connect banks that are already there, the banks emerge as banks only as the bridge crosses the stream. The bridge designedly causes them to lie across from each other. One side is set off against the other by the bridge. Nor do the banks stretch along the stream as indifferent border strips of the dry land. With the banks, the bridge brings to the stream the one and the other expanse of the landscape lying behind them. It brings stream and bank and land into each other's neighbourhood. The bridge gathers the earth as landscape around the stream.

Heidegger, 1971, p. 152

Heidegger also describes *what* the bridge gathers and thereby uncovers its value as a symbol. We cannot here enter into these details, but want to emphasize that the landscape as such gets its value *through* the bridge. Before, the meaning of the landscape was "hidden," and the building of the bridge brings it out into the open.

The bridge gathers Being into a certain "location" that we may call a "place." This "place," however, did not exist as an entity before the bridge (although there were always many "sites" along the river-bank where it could arise), but comes-to-presence with and as the bridge.

Richardson, 1974, p. 585

The existential purpose of building (architecture) is therefore to make a site become a place, that is, to uncover the meanings potentially present in the given environment.

The structure of a place is not a fixed, eternal state. As a rule places change, sometimes rapidly. This does not mean, however, that the *genius loci* necessarily changes or gets lost. Later we shall show that *taking place* presupposes that the places conserve their identity during a certain stretch of time. *Stabilitas loci* is a necessary condition for human life. How then is this stability compatible with the dynamics of change? First of all we may point out that any place ought to have the "capacity" of receiving *different* "contents", naturally within certain limits.[7] A place which is only fitted for one particular purpose would soon become useless. Secondly it is evident that a place may be "interpreted" in different ways. To protect and conserve the genius loci in fact means to concretize its essence in ever new historical contexts. We might also say that the history of a place ought to be its "self-realization." What was there as possibilities at the outset, is uncovered through human action, illuminated and "kept" in works of architecture which are simultaneously "old and new" (Venturi, 1967). A place therefore comprises properties having a varying degree of invariance.

In general we may conclude that *place* is the point of departure as well as the goal of our structural investigation; at the outset place is presented as a given, spontaneously experienced totality, at the end it appears as a structured world, illuminated by the analysis of the aspects of space and character.

THE SPIRIT OF PLACE

Genius loci is a Roman concept. According to ancient Roman belief every "independent" being has its *genius*, its guardian spirit. This spirit gives life to people and places, accompanies them from birth to death, and determines their character or essence. Even the gods had their *genius*, a fact which illustrates the fundamental nature of the concept (Paulys, n.d.). The *genius* thus denotes what a thing is, or what it "wants to be," to use a word of Louis Kahn. It is not necessary in our context to go into the history of the concept of *genius* and its relationship to the *daimon* of the Greeks. It suffices to point out that ancient man experienced his environment as consisting of definite characters. In particular he recognized that it is of great existential importance to come to terms with the *genius* of the locality where his life takes place. In the past survival depended on a "good" relationship to the place in a physical as well as a psychic sense. In ancient Egypt, for instance, the country was not only cultivated in accordance with the Nile floods, but the very structure of the landscape served as a model for the lay-out of the "public" buildings which should give a man a sense of security by symbolizing an eternal environmental order (Norberg-Schulz, 1975, pp. 10ff).

During the course of history the *genius loci* has remained a living reality, although it may not have been expressively named as such. Artists and writers have found inspiration in local character and have "explained" the phenomena of everyday life as well as art, referring to landscapes and urban milieu. Thus Goethe says: "It is evident, that the eye is educated by the things it sees from childhood

on, and therefore Venetian painters must see everything clearer and with more joy than other people" (Goethe, 1786). Still in 1960 Lawrence Durrell wrote: "As you get to know Europe slowly tasting the wines, cheeses and characters of the different countries you begin to realize that the important determinant of any culture is after all – the spirit of place" (Durrell, 1969, p. 156). Modern tourism proves that the experience of different places is a major human interest, although also this value today tends to get lost. In fact modern man for a long time believed that science and technology had freed him from a direct dependence on places.[8] This belief has proved an illusion; pollution and environmental chaos have suddenly appeared as a frightening *nemesis*, and as a result the problem of place has regained its true importance.

We have used the word "dwelling" to denote the total man–place relationship. To understand more fully what this word implies, it is useful to return to the distinction between "space" and "character." When man dwells, he is simultaneously located in space and exposed to a certain environmental character. The two psychological functions involved, may be called "orientation" and "identification."[9] To gain an existential foothold man has to be able to *orientate* himself; he has to know where he is. But he also has to *identify* himself with the environment, that is, he has to know *how* he is in a certain place.

The problem of orientation has been given a considerable attention in recent theoretical literature on planning and architecture. Again we may refer to the work of Kevin Lynch, whose concepts of "node," "path," and "district" denote the basic spatial structures which are the object of man's orientation. The perceived interrelationship of these elements constitutes an "environmental image," and Lynch asserts: "A good environmental image gives its possessor an important sense of emotional security" (Lynch, 1960, p. 4). Accordingly all cultures have developed "systems of orientation," that is, spatial structures which facilitate the development of a good environmental image. "The world may be organized around a set of focal points, or be broken into named regions, or be linked by remembered routes" (Lynch, 1960, p. 7). Often these systems of orientation are based on or derived from a given natural structure. Where the system is weak, the image-making becomes difficult, and man feels "lost." "The terror of being lost comes from the necessity that a mobile organism be oriented in its surroundings" (Lynch, 1960, p. 125). To be lost is evidently the opposite of the feeling of security which distinguishes dwelling. The environmental quality which protects man against getting lost, Lynch calls "imageability," which means "that shape, colour or arrangement which facilitates the making of vividly-identified, powerfully-structured, highly useful mental images of the environment" (Lynch, 1960, p. 9). Here Lynch implies that the elements which constitute the spatial structure are concrete "things" with "character" and "meaning." He limits himself, however, to discuss the spatial function of these elements, and thus leaves us with a fragmentary understanding of dwelling.

Nevertheless, the work of Lynch constitutes an essential contribution to the theory of place. Its importance also consists in the fact that his empirical studies of concrete urban structure confirm the general "principles of organization" defined by Gestalt psychology and by the researches into child psychology of Piaget.[10]

Without reducing the importance of orientation, we have to stress that dwelling above all presupposes *identification* with the environment. Although orientation and identification are aspects of one total relationship, they have a certain independence within the totality. It is evidently possible to orientate oneself well without true identification; one gets along without feeling "at home." And it is possible to feel at home without being well acquainted with the spatial structure of the place, that is, the place is only experienced as a gratifying general character. True belonging however presupposes that both psychological functions are fully developed. In primitive societies we find that even the smallest environmental details are known and meaningful, and that they make up complex spatial structures (Rapoport, 1975). In modern society, however, attention has almost exclusively been concentrated on the "practical" function of orientation, whereas identification has been left to chance. As a result true dwelling, in a psychological sense, has been substituted by alienation. It is therefore urgently needed to arrive at a fuller understanding of the concepts of "identification" and "character."

In our context "identification" means to become "friends" with a particular environment. Nordic man has to be friends with fog, ice, and cold winds; he has to enjoy the creaking sound of snow under the feet when he walks around, he has to experience the poetical value of being immersed in fog, as Hermann Hesse did when he wrote the lines: "strange to walk in fog! Lonely is every bush and stone, no tree sees the other, everything is alone . . ."[11] The Arab, instead, has to be a friend of the infinitely extended, sandy desert, and the burning sun. This does not mean that his settlements should not protect him against the natural "forces"; a desert settlement in fact primarily aims at the exclusion of sand and sun. But it implies that the environment is experienced as *meaningful*. Bollnow says appropriately: "*Fede Stimmung ist Übereinstimmung*," that is, every character consists in a correspondence between outer and inner world, and between body and psyche (Bollnow, 1956, p. 39). For modern urban man the friendship with a natural environment is reduced to fragmentary relations. Instead he has to identify with man-made things, such as streets and houses. The German-born American architect Gerhard Kallmann once told a story which illustrates what this means. Visiting at the end of the Second World War his native Berlin after many years of absence, he wanted to see the house where he had grown up. As must be expected in Berlin, the house had disappeared, and Mr Kallmann felt somewhat lost. Then he suddenly recognized the typical pavement of the sidewalk: the floor on which he had played as a child! And he experienced a strong feeling of having returned home.

The story teaches us that the objects of identification are concrete environmental properties and that man's relationship to these is usually developed during childhood. The child grows up in green, brown or white spaces; it walks or plays on sand, earth, stone, or moss, under a cloudy or serene sky; it grasps and lifts hard and soft things; it hears noises, such as the sound of the wind moving the leaves of a particular kind of tree; and it experiences heat and cold. Thus the child gets acquainted with the environment, and develops perceptual *schemata* which determine all future experiences (Norberg-Schulz, 1963, pp. 41ff). The schemata comprise universal structures which are inter-human, as well as locally-determined and culturally-conditioned structures. Evidently every human being has to possess schemata of orientation as well as identification.

The *identity* of a person is defined in terms of the schemata developed, because they determine the "world" which is accessible. This fact is confirmed by common linguistic usage. When a person wants to tell who he is, it is in fact usual to say: "I am a New Yorker," or "I am a Roman." This means something much more concrete than to say: "I am an architect," or perhaps: "I am an optimist." We understand that human identity is to a high extent a function of places and things. Thus Heidegger says: "Wir sind die Be-Dingten" (Heidegger, 1971, p. 181).[12] It is therefore not only important that our environment has a spatial structure which facilitates orientation, but that it consists of concrete objects of identification. *Human identity presupposes the identity of place.* Identification and orientation are primary aspects of man's being-in-the-world. Whereas identification is the basis for man's sense of *belonging*, orientation is the function which enables him to be that *homo viator* which is part of his nature. It is characteristic for modern man that for a long time he gave the role as a wanderer pride of place. He wanted to be "free" and conquer the world. Today we start to realize that true freedom presupposes belonging, and that "dwelling" means belonging to a concrete place.

The word to "dwell" has several connotations which confirm and illuminate our thesis. Firstly it ought to be mentioned that "dwell" is derived from the Old Norse *dvelja*, which meant to linger or remain. Analogously, Heidegger related the German "wohnen" to "bleiben" and "sich aufhalten" (Heidegger, 1971, pp. 146ff). Furthermore he points out that the Gothic *wunian* meant to "be at peace," "to remain in peace." The German word for "peace," *Friede*, means to be free, that is, protected from harm and danger. This protection is achieved by means of an *Umfriedung* or enclosure. *Friede* is also related to *zufrieden* (content), *Freund* (friend) and the Gothic *frijön* (love). Heidegger uses these linguistic relationships to show that *dwelling means to be at peace in a protected place.* We should also mention that the German word for dwelling *Wohnung*, derives from *das Gewohnte*, which means what is known or habitual. "Habit" and "habitat" show an analogous relationship. In other words, man knows what has become accessible to him through dwelling. We here return to the *Übereinstimmung* or correspondence between man and his environment, and arrive at the very root of the problem of "gathering."

To gather means that the everyday life-world has become "gewohnt" or "habitual." But gathering is a concrete phenomenon, and thus leads us to the final connotation of "dwelling." Again it is Heidegger who has uncovered a fundamental relationship. Thus he points out that the Old English and High German word for "building," *buan*, meant to dwell, and that it is intimately related to the verb *to be.*

What then does *ich bin* mean? The old word *bauen*, to which the *bin* belongs, answers: *ich bin, du bist*, mean: I dwell, you dwell. The way in which you are and I am, the manner in which we humans *are* on earth, is *buan*, dwelling.

Heidegger, 1971, p. 147

We may conclude that dwelling means to gather the world as a concrete building or "thing," and that the archetypal act of building is the *Umfriedung* or enclosure. Trakl's poetic intuition of the inside–outside relationship thus gets its confirmation, and we understand that our concept of *concretization* denotes the essence of dwelling (Norberg-Schulz, 1963, pp. 61ff, 68).

Man dwells when he is able to concretize the world in buildings and things. As we have mentioned above, "concretization" is the function of the work of art, as opposed to the "abstraction" of science (Norberg-Schulz, 1963, pp. 168ff). Works of art concretize what remains "between" the pure objects of science. Our everyday life-world *consists of* such "intermediary" objects, and we understand that the fundamental function of art is to gather the contradictions and complexities of the life-world. Being an *imago mundi*, the work of art helps man to dwell. Hölderlin was right when he said:

Full of merit, yet poetically, man
Dwells on this earth.

This means: man's merits do not count much if he is unable to dwell *poetically*, that is, to dwell in the true sense of the word. Thus Heidegger says: "Poetry does not fly above and surmount the earth in order to escape it and hover over it. Poetry is what first brings man onto the earth, making him belong to it, and thus brings him into dwelling" (Heidegger, 1971, p. 218). Only poetry in all its forms (also as the "art of living") makes human existence meaningful, and *meaning* is the fundamental human need.

Architecture belongs to poetry, and its purpose is to help man to dwell. But architecture is a difficult art. To make practical towns and buildings is not enough. Architecture comes into being when a "total environment is made visible," to quote the definition of Susanne Langer (1953). In general, this means to concretize the *genius loci*. We have seen that this is done by means of buildings which gather the properties of the place and bring them close to man. The basic act of architecture is therefore to understand the "vocation" of the place. In this way we protect the earth and become ourselves part of a comprehensive totality. What is here advocated is not some kind of "environmental determinism." We only recognize the fact that man *is* an integral part of the environment, and that it can only lead to human alienation and environmental disruption if he forgets that. To belong to a place means to have an existential foothold, in a concrete everyday sense. When God said to Adam: "You shall be a fugitive and a wanderer on the Earth,"[13] he put man in front of his most basic problem: to cross the threshold and regain the lost place.

NOTES

1 The concept "everyday life-world" was introduced by Husserl in *The Crisis of European Sciences and Transcendental Phenomenology* (1936).

2 Heidegger, "Bauen Wohnen Denken"; Bollnow, "Mensch und Raum"; Merleau-Ponty, "Phenomenology of Perception"; Bachelard, "Poetics of Space"; also L. Kruse, *Räumliche Umwelt* (Berlin: 1974).

3 Ein Winterabend

Wenn der Schnee ans Fenster fältt,
Lang die Abendglocke läutet,
Vielen ist der Tisch bereitet
Und das Haus ist wohlbestellt.
    Mancher auf der Wanderschaft
Kommt ans Tor auf dunklen Pfaden.
Golden blüht der Baum der Gnaden
Aus der Erde kühlem Saft.
    Wanderer tritt still herein;
Schmerz versteinerte die Schwelle.
Da erglänzt in reiner Helle
Auf dem Tische Brat und Wein.

4 Heidegger points out the relationship between the words *gegen* (against, opposite) and *Gegend* (environment, locality).

5 This has been done by some writers, such as K. Graf von Dürckheim, E. Straus, and O.F. Bollnow.

6 We may compare with Alberti's distinction between "beauty" and "ornament."

7 For the concept of "capacity" see Norberg-Schulz, *Intentions* (1963).

8 See M.M. Webber, *Explorations into Urban Structure* (1963), who talks about "non-place urban realm."

9 Norberg-Schulz, *Intentions* (1963), where the concepts "cognitive orientation" and "cathetic orientation" are used.

10 For a detailed discussion, see Norberg-Schulz, *Existence* (1971).

11 Seltsam, im Nebel zu wandern! Einsam ist jeder Busch und Stein, kein Baum sieht den anderen, jeder ist allein.

12 Heidegger, "We are the be-thinged," the conditioned ones.

13 *Genesis*, chapter 4, verse 12.

REFERENCES

Appleton, J. (1975) *The Experience of Landscape*. London.

Bollnow, O.F. (1956) *Das Wesen der Stimmungen*. Frankfurt am Main.

Durrell, L. (1969) *Spirit of Place*. London.

Frey, D. (1949) *Grundlegung zu einer vergleichenden Kunstwissenschaft*. Vienna and Innsbruck.

Giedion, S. (1964) *The Eternal Present: The Beginnings of Architecture*. London.

Goethe, J.W. von (1786) *Italianische Reise*, 8, October.

Heidegger, M. (1954) Die Frage nach der Technik. In *Vorträge und Aufsätze*. Pfullingen.

Heidegger, M. (1957) *Hebel der Hausfreund*. Pfullingen.

Heidegger, M. (1971) *Poetry, Language, Thought*, ed. A. Hofstadter. New York.

Husserl, E. (1936) *The Crisis of European Sciences and Transcendental Phenomenology*. Evanston, IL.

Langer, S. (1953) *Feeling and Form: A Theory of Art*. New York.

Lynch, K. (1960) *The Image of the City*. Cambridge, MA.

Norberg-Schulz, C. (1963) *Intentions in Architecture*. Oslo and London.

Norberg-Schulz, C. (1971) *Existence, Space and Architecture*. London and New York.

Norberg-Schulz, C. (1975) *Meaning in Western Architecture*. London and New York.

Paulys (n.d.) *Realencyclopedie der Klassischen Altertumwissenschaft*, VII.

Portoghesi, P. (1975) *Le inibizioni dell'architettura moderna*. Bari, Italy.

Rapoport, A. (1975) Australian Aborigines and the definition of place. In P. Oliver (ed.), *Shelter, Sign and Symbol*. London.

Richardson, W.J. (1974) *Heidegger: Through Phenomenology to Thought*. The Hague.

Rilke, R.M. (1972) *The Duino Elegies*. New York.

Venturi, R. (1967) *Complexity and Contradiction in Architecture*. New York.

Webber, M.M. (1963) *Explorations into Urban Structure*. Philadelphia.

"The Problem of Place in America"

from *The Great Good Place* (1989)

Ray Oldenburg

Editors' Introduction

As the previous two readings show, issues of place in modern society have become important because of declines in both design quality and resulting activity levels in urban space. In this first chapter of *The Great Good Place*, Ray Oldenburg suggests urban decline is associated with historical post-war trends of suburbanization, urban renewal, increasing residential mobility, growing auto dependency, freeway expansion, and single-use zoning – all of which have contributed to the disappearance of informal gathering spaces. Newer suburban subdivisions and neighborhoods failed at providing spaces for community life for inhabitants largely due to the increasing isolation of family life and the extreme individualization championed by American society. In physical settings dependent on single-occupancy auto trips to the strip mall and the zoned illegality of neighborhood retail uses, few opportunities exist for chance meetings on sidewalks, in corner bars or at a local café within walking distance from home. In households where one's work life takes up so much time, and where television has become the primary source of nightly entertainment, it becomes no surprise that people have little time for community-oriented activities such as bowling, bocce, and billiards. In a related manner, the increasing prevalence of obesity, chronic heart disease, and high stress levels can also be attributed to unwalkable suburban form, the increase in auto dependency, and lack of places to relax and blow off steam.

In light of this systematic loss of social space, Ray Oldenburg posits that a possible solution to "the problem of place in America" might be the championing of the "third place." He defines third places as those informal public gathering spaces where people can come together on neutral ground, free of charge, to develop friendships, enjoy conversation, voluntarily interact and enjoy being part of a larger spatial community. Oldenburg suggests third places are essential ingredients to a well-functioning democracy, for developing social cohesion, endowing a sense of identity and providing psychological support outside of home (the first place) and the work setting (the second place). They are the pubs, coffee houses, general stores, bookshops, post offices, laundromats, beauty salons, community centers, bowling alleys, stadiums, and other quasi-public social spaces (including streets, sidewalks, and parks) where people can come together to enjoy each other's company and conversation. Third places might be thought of as regular local hangouts (without the negative connotation of a dive) or like the French rendezvous (without the romantic connotation). Because of their accessibility and inclusiveness, third places promote social equality and are considered social levelers, places where little distinction is made on the basis of demographic, economic, social, or cultural differences. These places tend to allow people of different backgrounds to get to know one another in settings that are socially expansive and non-threatening.

Although he focuses primarily on programmatic land use elements, urban designers can take inspiration in Oldenburg's valorization of the public realm as a locus for social life. While not addressing specific design issues, those interested in improving streets, parks, and other public meeting grounds will be forced to consider the physical elements that make these places function for active human occupation, including: streetscaping, seating, lighting, climate protection, and other amenities that help to make places comfortable and useable.

Third places were much more prevalent in earlier times, especially in the denser, urban villages of traditional pedestrian-oriented towns and cities. Historically they provided compensatory social space away from home and work. In modern American society, however, they became rare with the rise of suburbia and zoning. With renewed interest for in-town living, as well as the rise of creative class interests in place-based urban lifestyles, we are beginning to see a rebound in the number of cafés, pubs, and local-serving retail nodes in closer proximity to housing. Counter-productive to the concept of the third place, however, are recent efforts at the privatization of public space, the growing prevalence of private security and policing, and heightened surveillance activities in light of real and perceived threats of crime and terrorism. These new concerns can be witnessed in the rise of gated communities, theme parks, malls, office parks, entertainment centers, mega-projects, and new towns, places where behavior is monitored and other personal freedoms are often limited.

Ray Oldenburg is an urban sociologist and Professor Emeritus of Sociology at the University of West Florida in Pensacola, Florida. He continues to work as a consultant to cities and community-based advocacy groups around the world. He has taught at the University of Nevada, the University of Wisconsin-Stout, and the University of Minnesota. He also edited a companion piece to *The Great Good Place* titled *Celebrating the Third Place: Inspiring Stories from the "Great Good Places" at the Heart of our Communities* (New York: Marlowe/Avalon, 2001). Other articles and chapters by Oldenburg include: selections on Third Places, Bars and Pubs in the *Encyclopedia of Community*, Karen Christensen (ed.) (Great Barrington, MA: Berkshire Publishing Group, 2003); and, "The Essential Hangout," with Dennis Brissett, *Psychology Today* (April 1980).

For other books on third spaces and informal social meeting grounds see: Bernard Rudofsky, *Streets for People: A Primer for Americans* (Garden City, NY: Doubleday, 1969); Claude Fisher, *To Dwell Among Friends* (Chicago, IL: University of Chicago Press, 1982); Anne Vernez Moudon (ed.), *Public Streets for Public Use* (New York: Van Nostrand Reinhold, 1987); Jan Gehl, *Life Between Buildings: Using Public Space* (New York: Van Nostrand Reinhold, 1987); and Christian Mikunda, *Brand Lands, Hot Spots and Cool Spaces: Welcome to the Third Place and the Total Marketing Experience* (London: Kogan Page, 2004).

Other literature on the importance of public space in the making of community can be found in: Don Mitchell, *The Right to the City: Social Justice and the Fight for Public Space* (New York: Guildford Press, 2003); Setha Low, Dana Taplin, and Suzanne Scheld, *Rethinking Urban Parks: Public Space and Cultural Diversity* (Austin, TX: University of Texas Press, 2005); Anthony M. Orum and Zachary P. Neal, *Common Ground? Readings and Reflections on Public Space* (London: Routledge, 2009); Jeffrey Hou (ed.), *Insurgent Public Space: Guerilla Urbanism and the Remaking of Contemporary Cities* (London: Routledge, 2010); Magda Angeles, *In Favour of Public Space* (Barclona: Actar, 2010); and Ali Madanipour, *Whose Public Space? International Case Studies in Urban Design and Development* (London: Routledge, 2010), excerpted in this volume (see pp. 443–458).

Books on the decline of social life, public space, and increasing privatization include: David Riesman, Nathan Glazer, and Reuel Denney, *The Lonely Crowd* (New Haven, CT: Yale University Press, 1950); Vance Packard, *A Nation of Strangers* (New York: Pocket Books, 1972); Martin Pawley, *The Private Future: Causes and Consequences of Community Collapse in the West* (London: Pan, 1973); Richard Sennett, *The Fall of Public Man* (New York: Alfred A. Knopf, 1977); David Popenoe, *Public Pleasure, Private Plight* (New Brunswick, NJ: Transaction, 1984); Philip Slater, *The Pursuit of Loneliness: American Culture at the Breaking Point* (Boston, MA: Beacon Press, 20th anniversary edition, 1990); Michael Sorkin (ed.), *Variations on a Theme Park: The New American City and the End of Public Space* (New York: Noonday Press, 1992); Robert D. Putnam, *Bowling Alone: The Collapse and Revival of America Community* (New York: Simon & Schuster, 2001) and *Better Together: Restoring the American Community* (New York: Simon & Schuster, 2003); Don Mitchell, *The Right to the City: Social Justice and the Fight for Public Space* (New York: Guilford Press, 2003); and Margaret Kohn, *Brave New Neighborhoods: The Privatization of Public Space* (London: Routledge, 2005).

A number of recent American writings indicate that the nostalgia for the small town need not be construed as directed toward the town itself: it is rather a "quest for community" (as Robert Nisbet puts it) – a nostalgia for a compassable and integral living unit. The critical question is not whether the small town can be rehabilitated in the image of its earlier strength and growth – for clearly it cannot – but whether American life will be able to evolve any other integral community to replace it. This is what I call the problem of place in America, and unless it is somehow resolved, American life will become more jangled and fragmented than it is, and American personality will continue to be unquiet and unfulfilled.

MAX LERNER. *America as a Civilization*, 1957

The ensuing years have confirmed Lerner's diagnosis. The problem of place in America has not been resolved and life *has* become more jangled and fragmented. No new form of integral community has been found; the small town has yet to greet its replacement. And Americans are not a contented people.

What may have seemed like the new form of community – the automobile suburb – multiplied rapidly after World War II. Thirteen million plus returning veterans qualified for single-family dwellings requiring no down payments in the new developments. In building and equipping these millions of new private domains, American industry found a major alternative to military production and companionate marriages appeared to have found ideal nesting places. But we did not live happily ever after.

Life in the subdivision may have satisfied the combat veteran's longing for a safe, orderly, and quiet haven, but it rarely offered the sense of place and belonging that had rooted his parents and grandparents. Houses alone do not a community make, and the typical subdivision proved hostile to the emergence of any structure or space utilization beyond the uniform houses and streets that characterized it.

Like all-residential city blocks, observed one student of the American condition, the suburb is "merely a base from which the individual reaches out to the scattered components of social exis-

tence."[1] Though proclaimed as offering the best of both rural and urban life, the automobile suburb had the effect of fragmenting the individual's world. As one observer wrote: "A man works in one place, sleeps in another, shops somewhere else, finds pleasure or companionship where he can, and cares about none of these places."

The typical suburban home is easy to leave behind as its occupants move to another. What people cherish most in them can be taken along in the move. There are no sad farewells at the local taverns or the corner store because there are no local taverns or corner stores. Indeed, there is often more encouragement to leave a given subdivision than to stay in it, for neither the homes nor the neighborhoods are equipped to see families or individuals through the cycle of life. Each is designed for families of particular sizes, incomes, and ages. There is little sense of place and even less opportunity to put down roots.

Transplanted Europeans are acutely aware of the lack of a community life in our residential areas. We recently talked with an outgoing lady who had lived in many countries and was used to adapting to local ways. The problem of place in America had become her problem as well:

After four years here, I still feel more of a foreigner than in any other place in the world I have been. People here are proud to live in a 'good' area, but to us these so-called desirable areas are like prisons. There is no contact between the various households, we rarely see the neighbors and certainly do not know any of them. In Luxembourg, however, we would frequently stroll down to one of the local cafés in the evening, and there pass a very congenial few hours in the company of the local fireman, dentist, bank employee or whoever happened to be there at the time. There is no pleasure to be had in driving to a sleazy, dark bar where one keeps strictly to one's self and becomes fearful if approached by some drunk.

Sounding the same note, Kenneth Harris has commented on one of the things British people miss most in the United States. It is some reasonable approximation of the village inn or local pub; our neighborhoods do not have it. Harris comments:

The American does not walk around to the local two or three times a week with his wife or with his son, to have his pint, chat with the neighbors, and then walk home. He does not take out the dog last thing every night, and break his journey with a quick one at the Crown.[2]

The contrast in cultures is keenly felt by those who enjoy a dual residence in Europe and America. Victor Gruen and his wife have a large place in Los Angeles and a small one in Vienna. He finds that: "In Los Angeles we are hesitant to leave our sheltered home in order to visit friends or to participate in cultural or entertainment events because every such outing involves a major investment of time and nervous strain in driving long distances."[3] But, he says, the European experience is much different:

In Vienna, we are persuaded to go out often because we are within easy walking distance of two concert halls, the opera, a number of theatres, and a variety of restaurants, cafés, and shops. Seeing old friends does not have to be a prearranged affair as in Los Angeles, and more often than not, one bumps into them on the street or in a café.

The Gruens have a hundred times more residential space in America but give the impression that they don't enjoy it half as much as their little corner of Vienna.

But one needn't call upon foreign visitors to point up the shortcomings of the suburban experiment. As a setting for marriage and family life, it has given those institutions a bad name. By the 1960s, a picture had emerged of the suburban housewife as "bored, isolated, and preoccupied with material things."[4] The suburban wife without a car to escape in epitomized the experience of being alone in America.[5] Those who could afford it compensated for the loneliness, isolation, and lack of community with the "frantic scheduling syndrome" as described by a counselor in the northeastern region of the United States:

The loneliness I'm most familiar with in my job is that of wives and mothers of small children who are dumped in the suburbs and whose husbands are commuters . . . I see a lot of generalized loneliness, but I think that in well-to-do

communities they cover it up with a wealth of frantic activity. That's the reason tennis has gotten so big. They all go out and play tennis.[6]

A majority of the former stay-at-home wives are now in the labor force. As both father and mother gain some semblance of a community life via their daily escapes from the subdivision, children are even more cut off from ties with adults. Home offers less and the neighborhood offers nothing for the typical suburban adolescent. The situation in the early seventies as described by Richard Sennett is worsening:

In the past ten years, many middle-class children have tried to break out of the communities, the schools and the homes that their parents have spent so much of their own lives creating. If any one feeling can be said to run through the diverse groups and life-styles of the youth movements, it is a feeling that these middle-class communities of the parents were like pens, like cages keeping the youth from being free and alive. The source of the feeling lies in the perception that while these middle-class environments are secure and orderly regimes, people suffocate there for lack of the new, the unexpected, the diverse in their lives.[7]

The adolescent houseguest, I would suggest, is probably the best and quickest test of the vitality of a neighborhood; the visiting teenager in the subdivision soon acts like an animal in a cage. He or she paces, looks unhappy and uncomfortable, and by the second day is putting heavy pressure on the parents to leave. There is no place to which they can escape and join their own kind. There is nothing for them to do on their own. There is nothing in the surroundings but the houses of strangers and nobody on the streets. Adults make a more successful adjustment, largely because they demand less. But few at any age find vitality in the housing developments. David Riesman, an esteemed elder statesman among social scientists, once attempted to describe the import of suburbia upon most of those who live there. "There would seem," he wrote, "to be an aimlessness, a pervasive low-keyed unpleasure."[8] The word he seemed averse to using is *boring*. A teenager would not have had to struggle for the right phrasing.

Their failure to solve the problem of place in America and to provide a community life for their inhabitants has not effectively discouraged the growth of the postwar suburbs. To the contrary, there have emerged new generations of suburban development in which there is even less life outside the houses than before. Why does failure succeed? Dolores Hayden supplies part of the answer when she observes that Americans have substituted the vision of the ideal home for that of the ideal city.[9] The purchase of the even larger home on the even larger lot in the even more lifeless neighborhood is not so much a matter of joining community as retreating from it. Encouraged by a continuing decline in the civilities and amenities of the public or shared environment, people invest more hopes in their private acreage. They proceed as though a house can substitute for a community if only it is spacious enough, entertaining enough, comfortable enough, splendid enough – and suitably isolated from that common horde that politicians still refer to as our "fellow Americans."

Observers disagree about the reasons for the growing estrangement between the family and the city in American society.[10] Richard Sennett, whose research spans several generations, argues that as soon as an American family became middle class and could afford to do something about its fear of the outside world and its confusions, it drew in upon itself, and "in America, unlike France or Germany, the urban middle-class shunned public forms of social life like cafés and banquet halls."[11] Philippe Ariès, who also knows his history, counters with the argument that modern urban development has killed the essential relationships that once made a city and, as a consequence, "the role of the family over-expanded like a hypertrophied cell" trying to take up the slack.[12]

In some countries, television broadcasting is suspended one night a week so that people will not abandon the habit of getting out of their homes and maintaining contact with one another. This tactic would probably not work in America. Sennett would argue that the middle-class family, given its assessment of the public domain, would stay at home anyway. Ariès would argue that most would stay home for want of places to get together with their friends and neighbors. As Richard Goodwin declared, "there is virtually no place where neighbors can anticipate unplanned meetings – no pub or corner store or park."[13] The bright spot in this dispute is that the same set of remedies would cure both the family and the city of major ills.

Meantime, new generations are encouraged to shun a community life in favor of a highly privatized one and to set personal aggrandizement above public good. The attitudes may be learned from parents but they are also learned in each generation's experiences. The modest housing developments, those *un*-exclusive suburbs from which middle-class people graduate as they grow older and more affluent, teach their residents that future hopes for a good life are pretty much confined to one's house and yard. Community life amid tract housing is a disappointing experience. The space within the development has been equipped and staged for isolated family living and little else. The processes by which potential friends might find one another and by which friendships not suited to the home might be nurtured outside it are severely thwarted by the limited features and facilities of the modern suburb.

The housing development's lack of informal social centers or informal public gathering places puts people too much at the mercy of their closest neighbors. The small town taught us that people's best friends and favorite companions rarely lived right next door to one another. Why should it be any different in the automobile suburbs? What are the odds, given that a hundred households are within easy walking distance, that one is most likely to hit it off with the people next door? Small! Yet, the closest neighbors are the ones with whom friendships are most likely to be attempted, for how does one even find out enough about someone a block and a half away to justify an introduction?

What opportunity is there for two men who both enjoy shooting, fishing, or flying to get together and gab if their families are not compatible? Where do people entertain and enjoy one another if, for whatever reason, they are not comfortable in one another's homes? Where do people have a chance to get to know one another casually and without commitment before deciding whether to involve other family members in their relationship? Tract housing offers no such places.

Getting together with neighbors in the development entails considerable hosting efforts, and it depends upon continuing good relationships between households and their members. In the usual course of things, these relationships are easily strained or ruptured. Having been lately formed and built on little, they are not easy to mend. Worse, some of the few good friends will move and are not easily replaced. In time, the overtures toward friendship, neighborliness, and a semblance of community hardly seem worth the effort.

IN THE ABSENCE OF AN INFORMAL PUBLIC LIFE

We have noted Sennett's observation that middle-class Americans are not like their French or German counterparts. Americans do not make daily visits to sidewalk cafés or banquet halls. We do not have that third realm of satisfaction and social cohesion beyond the portals of home and work that for others is an essential element of the good life. Our comings and goings are more restricted to the home and work settings, and those two spheres have become preemptive. Multitudes shuttle back and forth between the "womb" and the "rat race" in a constricted pattern of daily life that easily generates the familiar desire to "get away from it all."

A two-stop model of daily routine is becoming fixed in our habits as the urban environment affords less opportunity for public relaxation. Our most familiar gathering centers are disappearing rapidly. The proportion of beer and spirits consumed in public places has declined from about 90 percent of the total in the late 1940s to about 30 percent today.[14] There's been a similar decline in the number of neighborhood taverns in which those beverages are sold. For those who avoid alcoholic refreshments and prefer the drugstore soda fountain across the street, the situation has gotten even worse. By the 1960s, it was clear that the soda fountain and the lunch counter no longer had a place in "the balanced drug store."[15] "In this day of heavy unionization and rising minimum wages for unskilled help, the traditional soda fountain should be thrown out," advised an expert on drugstore management. And so it has been. The new kinds of places emphasize fast service, not slow and easy relaxation.

In the absence of an informal public life, people's expectations toward work and family life have escalated beyond the capacity of those institutions to meet them. Domestic and work relationships are pressed to supply all that is wanting and much that is missing in the constricted life-styles of those without community. The resulting strain on work and family institutions is glaringly evident. In the measure of its disorganization and deterioration, the middle-class family of today resembles the low-income family of the 1960s.[16] The United States now leads the world in the rate of divorce among its population. Fatherless children comprise the fastest-growing segment of the infant population. The strains that have eroded the traditional family configuration have given rise to alternate life-styles, and though their appearance suggests the luxury of choice, none are as satisfactory as was the traditional family when embedded in a supporting community.

It is estimated that American industry loses from $50 billion to $75 billion annually due to absenteeism, company-paid medical expenses, and lost productivity.[17] Stress in the lives of the workers is a major cause of these industrial losses. Two-thirds of the visits to family physicians in the United States are prompted by stress-related problems.[18] "Our mode of life," says one medical practitioner, "is emerging as today's principal cause of illness."[19] Writes Claudia Wallis, "It is a sorry sign of the times that the three best-selling drugs in the country are an ulcer medication (Tagamet), a hypertension drug (Inderal), and a tranquilizer (Valium)."[20]

In the absence of an informal public life, Americans are denied those means of relieving stress that serve other cultures so effectively. We seem not to realize that the means of relieving stress can just as easily be built into an urban environment as those features which produce stress. To our considerable misfortune, the pleasures of the city have been largely reduced to consumerism. We don't much enjoy our cities because they're not very enjoyable. The mode of urban life that has become our principal cause of illness resembles a pressure cooker without its essential safety valve. Our urban environment is like an engine that runs hot because it was designed without a cooling system.

Unfortunately, opinion leans toward the view that the causes of stress are social but the cures are individual. It is widely assumed that high levels of stress are an unavoidable condition of modern life, that these are built into the social system, and that one must get outside the system in order to gain relief. Even our efforts at entertaining and being entertained tend toward the competitive and stressful. We come dangerously close to the notion that one "gets sick" in the world beyond one's domicile and one "gets well" by retreating from it. Thus, while Germans relax amid the rousing company of the *bier garten* or the French recuperate in their animated little bistros, Americans turn to massaging, meditating, jogging, hot-tubbing, or escape fiction. While others take full advantage of their freedom to associate, we glorify our freedom *not* to associate.

In the absence of an informal public life, living becomes more expensive. Where the means and facilities for relaxation and leisure are not publicly shared, they become the objects of private ownership and consumption. In the United States, about two-thirds of the GNP is based on personal consumption expenditures. That category, observes Goodwin, contains "the alienated substance of mankind."[21] Some four *trillion* dollars spent for individual aggrandizement represents a powerful divisive force indeed. In our society, insists one expert on the subject, leisure has been perverted into consumption.[22] An aggressive, driving force behind this perversion is advertising, which conditions "our drive to consume and to own whatever industry produces."[23]

Paragons of self-righteousness, advertisers promulgate the notion that society would languish in a state of inertia but for their efforts. "Nothing happens until somebody sells something," they love to say. That may be true enough within a strictly commercial world (and for them, what else is there?) but the development of an informal public life depends upon people finding and enjoying one another outside the cash nexus. Advertising, in its ideology and effects, is the enemy of an informal public life. It breeds alienation. It convinces people that the good life can be individually purchased. In the place of the shared camaraderie of people who see themselves as equals, the ideology of advertising substitutes competitive acquisition. It is the difference between loving people for what they are and envying them for what they own. It is no coincidence that cultures with a highly developed informal public life have a disdain for advertising.[24]

The tremendous advantage enjoyed by societies with a well-developed informal public life is that, within them, poverty carries few burdens other than that of having to live a rather Spartan existence. But there is no stigma and little deprivation of experience. There is an engaging and sustaining public life to supplement and complement home and work routines. For those on tight budgets who live in some degree of austerity, it compensates for the lack of things owned privately. For the affluent, it offers much that money can't buy.

The American middle-class life-style is an exceedingly expensive one – especially when measured against the satisfaction it yields. The paucity of collective rituals and unplanned social gatherings puts a formidable burden upon the individual to overcome the social isolation that threatens. Where there are homes without a connection to community, where houses are located in areas devoid of congenial meeting places, the enemy called boredom is ever at the gate. Much money must be spent to compensate for the sterility of the surrounding environment. Home decoration and redecoration becomes a never-ending process as people depend upon new wallpaper or furniture arrangements to add zest to their lives. Like the bored and idle rich, they look to new clothing fashions for the same purpose and buy new wardrobes well before the old ones are past service. A lively round of after-dinner conversation isn't as simple as a walk to the corner pub – one has to host the dinner.

The home entertainment industry thrives in the dearth of the informal public life among the American middle-class. Demand for all manner of electronic gadgetry to substitute vicarious watching and listening for more direct involvement is high. Little expense is spared in the installation of sound and video systems, VCRs, cable connections, or that current version of heaven on earth for the socially exiled – the satellite dish. So great is the demand for electronic entertainment that it cannot be met with quality programming. Those who create for this insatiable demand must rely on formula and imitation.

Everyone old enough to drive finds it necessary to make frequent escapes from the private compound located amid hundreds of other private compounds. To do so, each needs a car, and that car is a means of conveyance as privatized and antisocial as the neighborhoods themselves. Fords and "Chevys" now cost from ten to fifteen thousand dollars, and the additional expenses of maintaining, insuring, and fueling them constitutes major expenditures for most families. Worse, each drives his or her own car. About the only need that suburbanites can satisfy by means of an easy walk is that which impels them toward their bathroom.

In the absence of an informal public life, industry must also compensate for the missing opportunity for social relaxation. When the settings for casual socializing are not provided in the neighborhoods, people compensate in the workplace. Coffee breaks are more than mere rest periods; they are depended upon more for sociable human contact than physical relaxation. These and other "time-outs" are extended. Lunch hours often afford a sufficient amount of reveling to render the remainder of the working day ineffectual. The distinction between work-related communications and "shooting the breeze" becomes blurred. Once-clear parameters separating work from play become confused. The individual finds that neither work nor play are as satisfying as they should be.

The problem of place in America manifests itself in a sorely deficient informal public life. The structure of shared experience beyond that offered by family, job, and passive consumerism is small and dwindling. The essential group experience is being replaced by the exaggerated self-consciousness of individuals. American life-styles, for all the material acquisition and the seeking after comforts and pleasures, are plagued by boredom, loneliness, alienation, and a high price tag. America can point to many areas where she has made progress, but in the area of informal public life she has lost ground and continues to lose it.

Unlike many frontiers, that of the informal public life does not remain benign as it awaits development. It does not become easier to tame as technology evolves, as governmental bureaus and agencies multiply, or as population grows. It does not yield to the mere passage of time and a policy of letting the chips fall where they may as development proceeds in other realms of urban life. To the contrary, neglect of the informal public life can make a jungle of what had been a garden while, at the same time, diminishing the ability of people to cultivate it.

In the sustained absence of a healthy and vigorous informal public life, the citizenry may quite literally forget how to create one. A facilitating public etiquette consisting of rituals necessary to the meeting, greeting, and enjoyment of strangers

is not much in evidence in the United States. It is replaced by a set of strategies designed to avoid contact with people in public, by devices intended to preserve the individual's circle of privacy against any stranger who might violate it. Urban sophistication is deteriorating into such matters as knowing who is safe on whose "turf," learning to minimize expression and bodily contact when in public, and other survival skills required in a world devoid of the amenities. Lyn Lofland notes that the 1962 edition of Amy Vanderbilt's *New Complete Book of Etiquette* "contains not a single reference to proper behavior in the world of strangers."[25] The cosmopolitan promise of our cities is diminished. Its ecumenic spirit fades with our ever-increasing retreat into privacy.

TOWARD A SOLUTION: THE THIRD PLACE

Though none can prescribe the total solution to the problem of place in America, it is possible to describe some important elements that any solution will have to include. Certain basic requirements of an informal public life do not change, nor does a healthy society advance beyond them. To the extent that a thriving informal public life belongs to a society's past, so do the best of its days, and prospects for the future should be cause for considerable concern.

Towns and cities that afford their populations an engaging public life are easy to identify. What urban sociologists refer to as their interstitial spaces are filled with people. The streets and sidewalks, parks and squares, parkways and boulevards are being used by people sitting, standing, and walking. Prominent public space is not reserved for that well-dressed, middle-class crowd that is welcomed at today's shopping malls. The elderly and poor, the ragged and infirm, are interspersed among those looking and doing well. The full spectrum of local humanity is represented. Most of the streets are as much the domain of the pedestrian as of the motorist. The typical street can still accommodate a full-sized perambulator and still encourages a new mother's outing with her baby. Places to sit are abundant. Children play in the streets. The general scene is much as the set director for a movie would arrange it to show life in a wholesome and thriving town or city neighborhood.

Beyond the impression that a human scale has been preserved in the architecture, however, or that the cars haven't defeated the pedestrians in the battle for the streets, or that the pace of life suggests gentler and less complicated times, the picture doesn't reveal the *dynamics* needed to produce an engaging informal public life. The secret of a society at peace with itself is not revealed in the panoramic view but in examination of the average citizen's situation.

The examples set by societies that have solved the problem of place and those set by the small towns and vital neighborhoods of our past suggest that daily life, in order to be relaxed and fulfilling, must find its balance in three realms of experience. One is domestic, a second is gainful or productive, and the third is inclusively sociable, offering both the basis of community and the celebration of it. Each of these realms of human experience is built on associations and relationships appropriate to it; each has its own physically separate and distinct places; each must have its measure of autonomy from the others.

What the panoramic view of the vital city fails to reveal is that the third realm of experience is as distinct a place as home or office. The informal public life only seems amorphous and scattered; in reality, it is highly focused. It emerges and is sustained in *core settings*. Where the problem of place has been solved, a generous proliferation of core settings of informal public life is sufficient to the needs of the people.

Pierre Salinger was asked how he liked living in France and how he would compare it with life in the United States. His response was that he likes France where, he said, everyone is more relaxed. In America, there's a lot of pressure. The French, of course, have solved the problem of place. The Frenchman's daily life sits firmly on a tripod consisting of home, place of work, and another setting where friends are engaged during the midday and evening *aperitif* hours, if not earlier and later. In the United States, the middle classes particularly are attempting a balancing act on a bipod consisting of home and work. That alienation, boredom, and stress are endemic among us is not surprising. For most of us, a third of life is either deficient or absent altogether, and the other two-thirds cannot be successfully integrated into a whole.

Before the core settings of an informal public life can be restored to the urban landscape and reestablished in daily life, it will be necessary to articulate their nature and benefit. It will not suffice to describe them in a mystical or romanticized way such as might warm the hearts of those already convinced. Rather, the core settings of the informal public life must be analyzed and discussed in terms comprehensible to these rational and individualistic outlooks dominant in American thought. We must dissect, talk in terms of specific payoffs, and reduce special experiences to common labels. We must, urgently, begin to defend these Great Good Places against the unbelieving and the antagonistic and do so in terms clear to all.

The object of our focus – the core settings of the informal public life – begs for a simpler label. Common parlance offers few possibilities and none that combine brevity with objectivity and an appeal to common sense. There is the term *hangout*, but its connotation is negative and the word conjures up images of the joint or dive. Though we refer to the meeting places of the lowly as hangouts, we rarely apply the term to yacht clubs or oak-paneled bars, the "hangouts" of the "better people." We have nothing as respectable as the French *rendez-vous* to refer to a public meeting place or a setting in which friends get together away from the confines of home and work. The American language reflects the American reality – in vocabulary as in fact the core settings of an informal public life are underdeveloped.

For want of a suitable existing term, we introduce our own: the third place will hereafter be used to signify what we have called "the core settings of informal public life." The third place is a generic designation for a great variety of public places that host the regular, voluntary, informal, and happily anticipated gatherings of individuals beyond the realms of home and work. The term will serve well. It is neutral, brief, and facile. It underscores the significance of the tripod and the relative importance of its three legs. Thus, the first place is the home – the most important place of all. It is the first regular and predictable environment of the growing child and the one that will have greater effect upon his or her development. It will harbor individuals long before the workplace is interested in them and well after the world of work casts them aside. The second place is the work setting, which reduces the individual to a single, productive role. It fosters competition and motivates people to rise above their fellow creatures. But it also provides the means to a living, improves the material quality of life, and structures endless hours of time for a majority who could not structure it on their own.

Before industrialization, the first and second places were one. Industrialization separated the place of work from the place of residence, removing productive work from the home and making it remote in distance, morality, and spirit from family life. What we now call the third place existed long before this separation, and so our term is a concession to the sweeping effects of the Industrial Revolution and its division of life into private and public spheres.

The ranking of the three places corresponds with individual dependence upon them. We need a home even though we may not work, and most of us need to work more than we need to gather with our friends and neighbors. The ranking holds, also, with respect to the demands upon the individual's time. Typically, the individual spends more time at home than at work and more at work than in a third place. In importance, in claims on time and loyalty, in space allocated, and in social recognition, the ranking is appropriate. In some countries, the third place is more closely ranked with the others. In Ireland, France, or Greece, the core settings of informal public life rank a *strong* third in the lives of the people. In the United States, third places rank a weak third with perhaps the majority lacking a third place and denying that it has any real importance.

The prominence of third places varies with cultural setting and historical era. In preliterate societies, the third place was actually foremost, being the grandest structure in the village and commanding the central location. They were the men's houses, the earliest ancestors of those grand, elegant, and pretentious clubs eventually to appear along London's Pall Mall. In both Greek and Roman society, prevailing values dictated that the *agora* and the *forum* should be great, central institutions; that homes should be simple and unpretentious; that the architecture of cities should assert the worth of the public and civic individual over the private and domestic one. Few means to lure and invite citizens into public gatherings were overlooked. The forums, colosseums, theaters, and amphitheaters were grand structures, and admission to them was free.

Third places have never since been as prominent. Attempts at elegance and grand scale continued to be made but with far less impact. Many cultures evolved public baths on a grand scale. Victorian gin palaces were elegant (especially when contrasted to the squalor that surrounded them). The winter gardens and palm gardens built in some of our northern cities in the previous century included many large and imposing structures. In modern times, however, third places survive without much prominence or elegance.

Where third places remain vital in the lives of people today, it is far more because they are prolific than prominent. The geographic expansion of the cities and their growing diversity of quarters, or distinct neighborhoods, necessitated the shift. The proliferation of smaller establishments kept them at the human scale and available to all in the face of increasing urbanization.

In the newer American communities, however, third places are neither prominent nor prolific. They are largely prohibited. Upon an urban landscape increasingly hostile to and devoid of informal gathering places, one may encounter people rather pathetically trying to find some spot in which to relax and enjoy each other's company.

Sometimes three or four pickups are parked under the shade near a convenience store as their owners drink beers that may be purchased but not consumed inside. If the habit ever really catches on, laws will be passed to stop it. Along the strips, youths sometimes gather in or near their cars in the parking lots of hamburger franchises. It's the best they can manage, for they aren't allowed to loiter inside. One may encounter a group of women in a laundromat, socializing while doing laundry chores. One encounters parents who have assumed the expense of adding a room to the house or converting the garage to a recreation room so that, within neighborhoods that offer them nothing, their children might have a decent place to spend time with their friends. Sometimes too, youth will develop a special attachment to a patch of woods not yet bulldozed away in the relentless spread of the suburbs. In such a place they enjoy relief from the confining over-familiarity of their tract houses and the monotonous streets.

American planners and developers have shown a great disdain for those earlier arrangements in which there was life beyond home and work. They have condemned the neighborhood tavern and disallowed a suburban version. They have failed to provide modern counterparts of once-familiar gathering places. The gristmill or grain elevator, soda fountains, malt shops, candy stores, and cigar stores – places that did not reduce a human being to a mere customer, have not been replaced. Meantime, the planners and developers continue to add to the rows of regimented loneliness in neighborhoods so sterile as to cry out for something as modest as a central mail drop or a little coffee counter at which those in the area might discover one another.

Americans are now confronted with that condition about which the crusty old arch-conservative Edmund Burke warned us when he said the bonds of community are broken at great peril for they are not easily replaced. Indeed, we face the enormous task of making "the mess that is urban America" suitably hospitable to the requirements of gregarious, social animals.[26] Before motivation or wisdom is adequate to the task, however, we shall need to understand exactly what it is that an informal public life can contribute to both national and individual life. (Therein lies the purpose of this book.)

Successful exposition demands that some statement of a problem precede a discussion of its solution. Hence, I've begun on sour and unpleasant notes and will find it necessary to sound them again. I would have preferred it otherwise. It is the solution that intrigues and delights. It is my hope that the discussion of life in the third place will have a similar effect upon the reader, just as I hope that the reader will allow the bias that now and then prompts me to substitute Great Good Place for third place. I am confident that those readers who have a third place will not object.

NOTES

1 Goodwin, Richard N. (1974) "The American Condition," *New Yorker* (28 January 1974), 38.

2 Harris, Kenneth (1949) *Traveling Tongues*. London: John Murrary, 80.

3 Gruen, Victor (1973) *Centers for Urban Environment*. New York: Van Nostrand Reinhold, 217.

4 Slater, Philip E. (1971) "Must Marriage Cheat Today's Young Women?" *Redbook Magazine*. February 1971.

5 Gordon, Suzanne (1976) *Lonely in America*. New York: Simon & Schuster.

6 *Ibid.*, 105.

7 Sennett, Richard (1973) "The Brutality of Modern Families," in *Marriages and Families*, ed. Helena Z. Lopata. New York: D. Van Nostrand, 81.

8 Riesman, David (1957) "The Suburban Dislocation," *The Annals of the American Academy of Political and Social Science*. November 1957, 142.

9 Hayden, Dolores (1984) *Redesigning the American Dream*. New York: W.W. Norton, Chapter 2.

10 See Sennett, *op. cit.*, and Ariès, Philippe (1977) "The Family and the City." *Daedalus*. Spring 1977, 227–237 for succinct statements of the two views.

11 Sennett, *op. cit.*, 84.

12 Ariès, *op. cit.*, 227.

13 Goodwin, *op. cit.*, 38.

14 Kluge, P.F. (1982) "Closing Time," *Wall Street Journal* (27 May 1982).

15 Ferguson, Frank L. (1969) *Efficient Drug Store Management*. New York: Fairchild Publications, 202.

16 Bronfenbrenner, Urie (1979) "The American Family: An Ecological Perspective," in *The American Family: Current Perspectives*. Cambridge, Mass.: Harvard University Press, Audiovisual Division (audio cassette).

17 Wallis, Claudia (1983) "Stress: Can We Cope?" *Time* (6 June 1983).

18 *Ibid.*

19 *Ibid.*

20 *Ibid.*

21 Goodwin, Richard (1970) "The American Condition," *New Yorker* (4 February 1970), 75.

22 Kando, Thomas M. (1980) *Leisure and Popular Culture in Transition*, 2nd ed. St. Louis: C.V. Mosby.

23 *Ibid.*, 101.

24 Generally, the Mediterranean cultures.

25 Lofland, Lyn H. (1973) *A World of Strangers*. Prospect Heights, Ill.: Waveland Press, 117.

26 Sometimes the phrase employed is "the mess that is man-made America." Planners appear to use it as much as anyone else.

"Critical Regionalism: An Architecture of Place"

from *Repairing the American Metropolis: Common Place Revisited* (2002)

Douglas S. Kelbaugh

Editors' Introduction

Although we tend to think of regionalism as a twentieth-century pursuit, regional attitudes in design are recognizable characteristics of most pre-industrial place-based settlements. These urbanisms had to rely on building materials that could be sourced regionally, designs that were scaled and erected based on human physical capability, and local craftsmanship that developed in response to local conditions for construction. Prior to the industrial revolution when transport, communication, and manufacturing processes liberalized access to resources and technical innovations, we might say that most built environments were *de facto* regional. Then in the industrial period, all of this changed as materials could be transported across the globe, factory-based production could mass produce building components, and communication improvements allowed the sharing of design techniques and strategy without regard to context. A conscious turn to regional design became a strategy in the eighteenth and nineteenth centuries, and again in the late twentieth century to reinstill a sense of place and local culture that had been lost with growing industrialization, global homogenization, and the widespread use of universalizing (and often oppressive) architecture movements. Regional design approaches helped to make neo-classicism, factory-based production, and international style modernism more palatable to local tastes – as well as help to reinforce a sense of place-based pride. From Marie Antoinette's rustic milkmaid's cottage, to Barry and Pugin's Houses of Parliament – from the Craftsman aesthetics of Ruskin, to Le Corbusier's Chandigarh buildings – notions of regionalism have been used to conjure up and reinforce imagery associated with local culture, everyday life, regional craft traditions, and national identity.

Critical Regionalism in the late twentieth century was born of a similar discontent with the universalizing and globalizing nature of modern design. The term was first defined in 1981 by Alexander Tzonis and Liane Lefaivre to describe the work of several Greek architects in the mid-twentieth century who were able to combine local inspiration and regional attitudes with the prevailing modernism of the time. It was further defined in a series of ground-breaking articles by Kenneth Frampton. These and other authors suggest that Critical Regionalism is an attempt to resurrect local differentiation in design with the pragmatic realization that it will be modulated by the exigencies of the modern world, for example, the inclusion of modern technologies in form-making. It is "critical" in two senses: first, it is a critique of the universalizing intentions of international modernism, and second, it is a critique of the sentimentalizing and nostalgic practices of regional culture and local traditions in themselves. This burgeoning movement alerts us to the often placeless nature of modernism, while attempting to reinforce a contemporary and phenomenologically based authenticity – one that is more representative of places and local constraints.

In the reading included here, Douglas S. Kelbaugh suggests that Critical Regionalism might be perceived as "regionalism with an edge." His writing is an attempt to define the term in clear language and in a manner that is highly accessible to practitioners and lay readers. His "Five Points of a Critical Regionalism" imply ways in which the practice of Critical Regionalism might be guided thematically: by reinforcing place qualities, valorizing nature, highlighting local histories, and emphasizing regional craft traditions. Importantly he also suggests the importance of limits, boundaries, and constraints in design decision-making – qualities that might lead to better scaled and more responsive design solutions. While a strong advocate of critical regionalist theory, Kelbaugh also considers dissenting and critical voices in his writing – a practice seldom used by other authors on the topic.

Douglas S. Kelbaugh FAIA is Professor of Architecture and Urban Planning, and the former Dean of the University of Michigan's A. Alfred Taubman College of Architecture + Planning. He has taught at several design schools around the world. At the University of Washington, he popularized use of the modern urban design charrette. He has been partner in several design firms over the course of his career, most recently joining the Dubai-based development firm Limitless as Executive Director of Design and Planning. Other books by Kelbaugh include: *The Pedestrian Pocket Book: A New Suburban Design Strategy*, written with Peter Calthorpe (New York: Princeton Architectural Press, 1989); *Common Place: Toward Neighborhood and Regional Design* (Seattle, WA: University of Washington Press, 1997); *Repairing the American Metropolis: Common Place Revisited* (Seattle, WA: University of Washington Press, 2002); and most recently, *Writing Urbanism: A Design Reader*, edited with Kit McCullough (London: Routledge, 2008). His article *Three Urbanisms: New, Everyday and Post* (Ann Arbor, MI: University of Michigan, 2002) has become an important piece in comparing the leading design theories of late-twentieth-century urbanism.

The literature on Critical Regionalism and larger issues of contextualism are steadily growing as it becomes a dominant theme in postmodern urbanism: see Nan Ellin's discussion of Critical Regionalism in her book *Postmodern Urbanism*, revised edition (New York: Princeton Architectural Press, 1999). Works on Critical Regionalism by Kenneth Frampton include: "Towards a Critical Regionalism: Six Points for an Architecture of Resistance," in Hal Foster (ed.), *The Anti-Aesthetic: Essays in Postmodern Culture* (Port Townsend, WA: Bay Press, 1983); "Prospects for a Critical Regionalism," *Perspecta* (no. 20, 1983); *Modern Architecture: A Critical History* (New York: Thames & Hudson, 1985); and "Place-form and Cultural Identity," in John Thackara (ed.), *Design after Modernism: Beyond the Object* (New York: Thames & Hudson, 1988). For additional readings on this topic see several works by Alexander Tzonis and Liane Lefaivre, "The Grid and the Pathway: An Introduction to the Work of Dimitris and Susana Antonakakis," *Architecture in Greece* (Athens: no. 5, 1981); "Why Critical Regionalism Today?" *Architecture and Urbanism* (no. 235, May 1990); *Critical Regionalism: Architecture and Identity in a Globalized World* (Munich: Prestel, 2003); *Architecture of Regionalism in the Age of Globalization: Peaks and Valleys in the Flat World* (London: Routledge, 2011); and Alexander Tzonis, Liane Lefaivre, and Bruno Stagno (eds), *Tropical Architecture: Critical Regionalism in the Age of Globalization* (New York: John Wiley, 2001).

Other key texts on Critical Regionalism include: Thomas Schumacher, "Regional Intentions and Contemporary Architecture: A Critique," in *Center 3* (1987); Alan Colquhoun, "Regionalism and Technology," in *Modernity and the Classical Tradition* (Cambridge, MA: MIT Press, 1989); Douglas Reichert Powell, *Critical Regionalism: Connecting Politics and Culture in the American Landscape* (Chapel Hill, NC: University of North Carolina Press, 2007); and Vincent Canizaro, *Architectural Regionalism: Collected Writings on Place, Identity, Modernity and Tradition* (New York: Princeton Architectural Press, 2007).

I didn't like Europe as much as I liked Disney World. At Disney World all the countries are much closer together, and they show you just the best of each country. Europe is boring. People talk strange languages and things are dirty. Sometimes you don't see anything interesting in Europe for days, but at Disney World something different happens all the time and people are happy. It's much more fun. It's well designed.

A college graduate just back from her first trip to Europe

Regionalism is an ambiguous term. To an urban planner it means thinking bigger: planning at the scale of a region rather than at the scale of the sub-division or municipality. To an architect, regionalism means thinking smaller: resisting the forces that tend to homogenize buildings across the country and around the globe in favor of local forces. Critical Regionalism is a term coined by architects that means thinking regionally in ways that are both reactive and liberative. It guards against the mindless nostalgia and sentimentality for traditional architecture to which regionalism has been prone in the past.

This chapter is about the theory of regionalism as opposed to regional architecture. It theorizes about what kind of architecture is appropriate for regionalism in general rather than for one region in particular. It is not about the particular characteristics of the architecture of a specific metropolitan region, like Seattle, or a bioregion, like the Pacific Northwest (where, for example, the prevalence of wood, large windows and overhangs, attention to views, a soft and impure color palette, and Japanese influence are defining characteristics).

Critical Regionalism is actually more of an attitude than a theory or a set of motifs. It is an attitude that celebrates and delights in what is different about a place. What makes a local architecture local and unique is valued more than what makes it typical and universal. In that sense it is a reaction to the standardization and universality that Modernism promoted. It is also an attitude of resistance, sometimes an angry response to many of the changes made in the name of progress that are blanching geographic differences in place and culture. It is against foreign ideas and styles that are imposed rather than imported.

Architecture is in a rare position to embody and express regional differences – more so than manufactured products like cars, chairs, shoes, or even clothing. Perhaps only food is as local, although regional food products are now shipped far and wide. Because architecture is one of the few remaining items in modern life that is usually not mass-produced and mass-marketed, it can resist the commodification of culture. Because it is a site-specific and one-of-a-kind production, it can resist the banalization of place. And because it is one of the few hand-built items left in the industrialized world, it can resist standardization. Architecture can still be rooted in local climate, topography, flora, building materials, building practices, architectural types, cultures, history, and mythology.

Before exploring Critical Regionalism's general principles – ones that could be applied anywhere – it is necessary to take a relatively lengthy and admittedly subjective look at recent architectural history. First, a few words about the twentieth-century chronology of architectural history in this country might be helpful. Roughly speaking, the century started during an architecture of Neoclassical or Beaux-Arts style. In America, Neoclassicism – sometimes simply called Classicism – was given a big boost by the World's Columbian Exposition in Chicago in 1893. Beaux-Arts refers to the Parisian academy where leading architects of the era studied the axial formality and monumentality that often characterized civic architecture during the City Beautiful Movement around the turn of the last century. Modernism started as an avant-garde movement in Europe after World War I. It was brought to America in the 1930s, debuting as the International Style in a show at the Museum of Modern Art. It slowly became accepted by American corporations, institutions, and individual clients and was the prevalent architectural mode after World War II. Postmodernism emerged in the 1970s, about the time solar and environmental architecture was a movement. Deconstructivism replaced Postmodernism in the late 1980s, but has lost momentum. Critical Regionalism started to gain a following in the 1980s.

[. . .]

REGIONALISM WITH AN EDGE

If Modernism as it was once known is dead, Postmodernism finished, and Deconstructivism in decline, there is an existential dilemma for architects. On the one hand, the social and technological agenda of Modernism still seems correct. But the Modernist commitment to place, context, history, craftsmanship, and resource and energy conservation seems distinctly lacking. On the other hand, the urban agenda of Postmodernism still seems right-minded, but its Neoclassical ornament and tectonics seem pasty and superficial when attempted today. There is something spiritually as well as physically hollow about most Postmodern structures. And Deconstructivism gives in too easily to the dehumanizing and alienating forces of the millennium at hand.

On another axis altogether is a third position that breaks this existential bind and "distances itself equally from the Enlightenment Myth of Progress and from a reactionary, unrealistic impulse to return to architectonic forms of the pre-industrial past" (Frampton 1983, 17). This alternative way of looking at things is Critical Regionalism, a term popularized and given gravity by Kenneth Frampton. To further quote his seminal text, Critical Regionalism resists the contemporary practice of architecture that is "increasingly polarized between, on the one hand, a so-called 'high-tech' approach predicated exclusively upon production and, on the other, the provision of a 'compensatory facade' to cover up the harsh realities of this universal system" (ibid). This resistance to global production and consumerism seems more valid today than two decades ago.

Critical Regionalism is two-handed. On the right hand is the mark of a particular region: each region determining its own architectural fate and shaping its built environment without mimicking other places. On the left hand are characteristics common to regionalist architecture in any region in the country, perhaps the world. These regional characteristics are most easily expressed at the scale of small buildings, especially residential architecture, where designs and builders are often most sensitive to site, climate, and tradition. Large buildings, particularly high-rise and long-span structures, have design determinants that are more universal, such as gravity, wind, and, to a lesser extent, seismic loads. Climate affects large buildings less because their heating and cooling needs are driven by the internal loads of lights and people rather than ambient solar radiation and temperature. Accordingly, they are less likely to develop regional idiosyncrasies or variations.

FIVE POINTS OF A CRITICAL REGIONALISM

These five characteristics or attitudes, originally proposed in 1985, are my attempt to define Critical Regionalism:

1 Sense of place

Critical Regionalism first and foremost starts out with a love of place. This topophilia seeks to liber-ate the genius loci. It is critical of simpleminded or excessive importation of culture from other places. It honors local climate, topography, vegetation, building materials, and building practices. It prefers local authenticity to sophisticated imitation. That which makes a place unique is worth celebrating and protecting with architecture. This act of protection is also an act of resistance. Critical Regionalism says no to outside influence and hot new ideas more than it says yes. It must be picky and stubborn in this age of aggressive hype and universal civilization. It realizes that the more well-defined and highly evolved a place is, the less likely it is to be improved by random imports, experimentation, or change for change's sake. It resists the kind of cultural homogenization and commodification that makes the Puget Sound Basin like California's Bay Area, Sydney like Perth, Houston like Atlanta, and that makes one suburb like the next.

Critical Regionalism must, on the other hand, be careful not to be too sensitive or resistive to change, lest it turn into a sour cynicism or saccharin sentimentality. It also has the potential to degenerate into a scared or snobbish xenophobia. It must walk that thin line between conservation and reactionaryism. It can't afford to be bitter about lost battles for former good causes or it will risk becoming too negative about today's challenges. As Jacques Barzun ends The *Columbia History of the World*: "The building or rebuilding of states and cultures, now or at any time, is more becoming to our nature than longings and lamentations" (Barzun 1992, 1165).

Critical Regionalism is not provincialism, a myopic cousin of regionalism. Provincials don't know what they don't know. Critical Regionalists know the limits of their world, which can be cosmopolitan without being elitist. Travel can build an understanding of what is worthy of both bringing home and returning home for. Indeed, the revolution during the 1960s in air travel, which made it possible for the middle class to see the world, accelerated the awareness of regional differences. As much as they respect place, Critical Regionalists are not sentimental about it. They resist indulging in nostalgia and literally recapturing how sweet it was in the old days or old country. Critical Regionalism may at times be too self-conscious about what is worth preserving about a place, but cannot be afraid when it is necessary to be bold and visionary about the future.

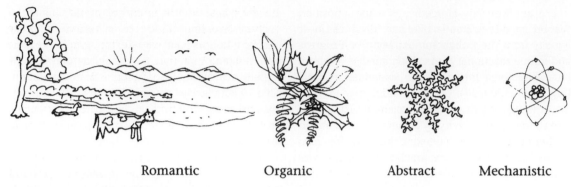

Romantic   Organic   Abstract   Mechanistic

Figure 1 Nature has been viewed and copied at different scales by different epochs. Critical Regionalists, like environmentalists, particularly admire and are inspired by nature at the organic level. Modernists preferred the abstract mechanics of atomic physics, just as Romanticists took great strength from pastoral landscapes. Deconstructivists have mimicked fractal geometry, which attempts to describe naturally occurring shapes that repeat themselves at any scale. Some contemporary architectural thinkers have been inspired by chaos theory in another attempt to copy nature.

2 Sense of nature

Human subtlety will never devise an invention more beautiful, more simple, or more direct than does Nature.

Leonardo da Vinci

Nature is a good model for design because it holds the key to vitality, beauty, and sustainability. Designers can learn from the incredible simplicity and sophistication of biological and ecological systems. Diversity, symbiosis, synergy, balance – these are profound and inspiring messages for all designers. Working together, architects, industrial designers, landscape architects, urban designers, and urban planners can fulfill an ecological role, namely to protect and preserve ecosystems, natural cycles and chains, and the symbiosis between organisms and their environment. Their role is also to reverse entropy, which is done by creating order and meaning. The most meaningful and highly evolved order is to be found in nature.

Nature has inspired designers and artists in different ways. The word "natural" has been used over the years to describe and defend varying positions, such as romantic, picturesque, and organic. Nature per se does not demand any one interpretation. In fact, all phenomena can be called natural in the final analysis.

Many positions, some opposing, can be taken from or based on nature and natural phenomena. It depends on the scale at which the artist or architect views nature. It can be called romantic at the landscape scale, humanistic at the anatomical level, organic at the vegetable level, abstract at the microscopic level, and mechanistic at the atomic level [Figure 1]. Nature seems most understandable and accessible at the scale of fauna and flora. These scales, although ruled by natural laws that can be expressed as abstract mathematical formulae and Euclidean and fractal geometries, are less abstract to the human eye. The animal and plant kingdoms are full of figural, ornate form.

Nature has provided a bottomless source of forms and images. The Romantic Age looked to nature at the scale of the bucolic landscape. The Art Nouveau period looked to nature at the vegetative scale – the palm frond and sinuous vine – much as the Victorians had admired the giant lily pads they imported into their hot-houses from distant continents. The Arts and Crafts movement had its love affair with wisteria, dripping from wooden arbors. Modernist architects and theorists have also extolled the virtues of nature, looking for underlying formal principles there rather than in history or culture. One scale at which nature seemed to inspire them was atomic physics. This sub-visual scale represents nature at its most abstract, which is not a surprising preference given the Modernist mania for abstract form. Natural forms at a visual scale, like the symmetrical snowflake or the nautilus shell that grows in a pure spiral, were also an inspiration to Modernists.

Critical Regionalists and green architects can wax enthusiastic about a water hyacinth or sea manatee, which can cleanse sewage treatment wastes of heavy metals. They might also be attracted to the fuzziness of chaos theory, which deals with natural phenomenon that are too complex to be described or even understood by linear analysis and conventional geometry. A sense of nature for them is messier, more organic, and not as visual as the precise, dry, Euclidean geometry of Modernism. While Modernism looked to physics and engineering for lessons and inspiration, regionalism looks to the life sciences and ecology, which have enjoyed great attention and breakthroughs in recent decades. Buildings and cities, like plants and animals, can be viewed as vital rather than as inert and denatured. They can be treated as organisms which are conceived, grow, flex, adapt, interact, age, die and decay – always rooted in their habitat. Site-specific design – with its sensitivity to the living environment – is fundamental to a sense of nature.

We must occasionally remind ourselves that human culture and its artifacts are young and immature compared to nature. A trip to the mountains or the forests is a sobering if pleasant reminder of nature's power. Architects who cavalierly dip into the history of architecture for pleasing and familiar forms rather than into nature for enduring patterns and types must beware: history's gene pool is smaller, its process of natural selection far briefer. A Gothic cathedral, as refined as it is, pales before the overwhelming complexity and four-dimensional order of a rain forest or salt marsh, perhaps even a cubic yard of rich topsoil. A modern metropolis might match the complexity of an ecosystem but not its order or sustainability. The history of architecture, replete as it is with impressive and wonderful achievements, is nowhere near as amazing or as sublime as nature.

3 Sense of history

No one can deny that the best buildings, gardens, and cities of the past are overwhelming in the awe and joy they can elicit. But they yield more than beauty and pleasure. They offer lasting lessons – ones that are more easily applied than the lessons of nature. History should be respectfully studied for design principles rather than used as a grab bag of forms. Time-tested architectural types are more valuable antecedents than specific historical styles,

however beautiful they may still appear. An architectural type that has stood the test of time, like the basilica or courtyard house, must be doing something right in terms of responding to climate, social and cultural needs, tradition, and economy. The best buildings from the past – whether vernacular or Architecture with a capital A – continue to set the high standard of excellence for today's designers.

Architectural history is also a deep and rich archive for designers. Whether by a vernacular farmhouse or classical temple, architects have always been inspired by the past. Historical precedents are a good point of departure when designing buildings. Their design vocabulary and syntax can be creatively transformed to express and to accommodate new technical and programmatic forces. Traditional architectural language can evolve, much as spoken language does in multilingual dialects and much as new words are coined to name new scientific and technological developments. This incremental evolution applies to both vernacular and high-style architecture. Conventional architectural language can be converted, subverted, inverted, or perverted. If it evolves too suddenly, it loses its meaning and power. Change is most successful when it is fresh but not too radical or too abrupt, so that it "rhymes" with a familiar imagery. Rhyme – likeness tempered by slight variation – is naturally pleasing to the human eye, as it is to the ear.

To paraphrase psychologist Nicholas Humphrey, aesthetic pleasure must convey some biological advantage, as nature gives away nothing for free (Humphrey 1980, 159). His thesis shines a different light on the role of history in aesthetics. If aesthetic pleasure, like sexual and appetite gratification, has played an important role in our biological survival and evolution, it is because it provokes and encourages human beings to classify the sensory world visually. Subtle variations on a shape are more visually stimulating than exact repetitions of a shape. Unstimulating patterns are inherently less interesting to the viewer and therefore less likely to be viewed attentively. Sorting out and correctly reading the sensory world were critical to survival and evolution. To put it simply: the more pleasurable the task, the greater the attention, the greater the understanding, and the greater the biological advantage. Humphrey postulates that what is both stimulating and legible is imagery that "rhymes" with other familiar images, whether across space or over time. To "rhyme," images must be neither too similar nor too dissimilar. In the former case, the human tends to lose interest too easily and in the latter case to become confused and discouraged too easily. Thus, the happy medium between these two extremes has over millions of years, Humphrey hypothesizes, come to be seen as beauty. The aesthetic pleasure it affords is functional as much as titillating. When design rhymes across time it demonstrates a sense of history, and when it rhymes across space, it reinforces a sense of place. (For further development of these and other ideas on the origins and role of aesthetic pleasure, see the writings of both Jay Appleton and Grant Hildebrand, especially the latter's latest book, *The Origins of Architectural Pleasure*.)

4 Sense of craft

The construction of buildings has become junkier. Stewart Brand, who has studied the evolution of building technology since founding *The Whole Earth Catalogue* a generation ago, agrees. "The trend in construction during this century has been toward ever lighter framing with the result that buildings look and feel increasingly like movie sets: impressive to the eye, flimsy to the touch, and incapable of aging well" (Brand 1994, 113). They are usually built with less human care and of less natural and less substantial materials. Copper has given way to aluminum, brass to brass plate, slate to asphalt, marble to plastic laminate, wood to particle board, tongue and groove siding to Texture-One-Eleven plywood, and plaster to Sheetrock. It's the last of these, gypsum drywall, which epitomizes the deterioration of quality in our buildings and the slippage from tectonic toward scenographic design. The Sheetrocking of every new house in America has brought a slow and subtle loss of precision and substantiality in construction. The ubiquitous aluminum sliding glass door has had an equally wide-scale and dumbing effect.

The loss of craft is part of a bigger economic web that is unfortunately beyond the control of the designer, or for that matter, the region. Basically, architectural craft and detail are getting relatively more expensive than manufactured items – especially products that take advantage of miniaturization and mass production. Because the construction of architecture is labor-intensive, it is doomed in the foreseeable future to fall further and further behind more mechanized and industrialized production. Unlike the performing and visual arts, which suffer economically from a similar labor intensity, there is little government subsidy for architecture. For the public's dollars, architecture also has to compete with ever-cheaper consumer items, such as televisions, cars, clothes, and travel – all of which continue to become cheaper in real dollars. Most Americans will choose, understandably, a $400 CD player over a solid-core oak door. In the meantime, Critical Regionalists keep ripping the fake plastic wood off their dash-boards and refrigerator handles.

The ongoing slippage in the quality of construction is exacerbated if not actually caused by the way contemporary real estate development is financed. Investors, developers, and builders are typically blinded by methodologies and mindsets that have become gospel at American business schools. For the past forty years, MBAs have learned "discounted cash flow" as a method to compare alternative investments. Along with "net present value" and "internal rate of return," different projected cash flows can be compared over time to select the alternative with the highest yield.

As Robert Davis, founder / developer of Seaside and former Chair of the Congress for the New Urbanism, has written, this methodology has tended to produce the short-term thinking and investing that is now pervasive in the industry (Davis & Leinberger 1999, 43–50). It is the thinking that makes Wal-Mart willing to build on the outskirts of town a new 60,000-square-foot store that has an expected life span of five years. After the local market has been primed, they build a 110,000 square-foot building a little further out and abandon the first building, whose cheap roof and mechanical system are beginning to wear out. While Wal-Mart and other bigbox discount retailers represent other interesting controversies and dilemmas, there is little disagreement about the low quality of their building construction, which is not surprising given that the building is treated more like an operating expense than an investment. Their real estate development strategy is becoming commonplace, with investors encouraging developers to build retail and office space with the cheapest available systems and materials, not to mention repeatable designs that are often gussied up with signage and entrance marquees to look different from one another and more upscale than they are. There is, of course, nothing new about architecture pretending to be more than it is, but the life expectancy and craftsmanship of buildings in the United States has never been lower, including the wood buildings thrown up in the "wild west." Real estate investment, before discounted cash flow and its short-term returns became widely accepted, used to be built to last.

5 Sense of limits

The Modern Movement, especially the International Style, saw space as abstract, neutral, and continuous. It placed objects in a universal Cartesian grid, ignoring circumstance and place. At the regional scale this grid ultimately came to spread itself evenly across the countryside. At the architectural scale, Modernists saw space as flowing freely within open interiors and between the interior and exterior in buildings that were increasingly transparent. With Postmodernism there arose a renewed interest in discrete, static space. Human-scale rooms began to replace free-flowing spaces. The notion of a room before Modernism was positive, figural, contained, often symmetrical, and enclosed by thick walls of real mass. These are the attributes of Postmodern space, although the mass is now more apparent than real. The notion of public space as finite, contained, outdoor rooms, defined by background buildings and punctuated by foreground buildings, was also revived in the 1980s.

The room as a discrete architectural element was respectable again. Also seen as positive were other aspects of finite geometry: the axis, which establishes geometric beginning and terminus; symmetry, which creates a centerline; frontality, which distinguishes front layers from back layers; and fat walls, which rely or pretend to rely more on compression than tension for structural stability. These formal devices all resulted in an architecture and urban design that looked and felt more finite, more massive, and more static.

A sense of limits is about the need for finitude for physical and temporal boundaries to frame and limit human places and activities. It is about the need for human scale in the built environment. It is also about the need for psychological boundaries – ones that make life more understandable and negotiable. As others have pointed out, spatial boundaries demarcate the beginning of the presencing of a place as much as the ending of a place and its power. Boundless architectural and urban space has less nearness, less presence. Limits are what differentiate place from raw space, whether they separate sacred from profane space or one secular space from another. The German language has the word "raum" to describe a finite place or room. The Japanese use "ma" to denote a bounded space, although it literally translates as "interval." English is less precise about place.

The appreciation of natural resources as limited was parallel and simultaneous to the renewed perception of architectural space as finite. This sense of limits is one position on which passive solar architecture, Critical Regionalism, and Postmodernism all converged in the early 1980s. Typology is another idea on which architectural and urban theory converged during that period. All these ideas are now worth reconsideration a generation later.

CRITICAL REGIONALISM CRITICIZED

There have been some negative responses to Critical Regionalism. One has been that it is inherently elitist because of the low regard in which it sometimes holds popular taste. This disdain, architects like Dan Solomon claim, is as nonconducive to the making of everyday neighborhoods and cities as is the Modernist preoccupation with individual buildings. This is a fair comment, as many of the architects (Utzon, Ando, Botta, Wolfe) cited in Kenneth Frampton's essays on Critical Regionalism are striving for a profound architecture. This aspiration is not particularly amenable to doing quiet background buildings or to sublimating the designer's ego to the court of community opinion. This is not a problem when designing isolated buildings. But, in the urban context, architectural heroics can be problematic.

The contemporary works of Tadao Ando, Toyo Ito, and many of their fellow Japanese architects are examples of strong and exquisite design. It is an architecture that places a high premium on originality and creativity and that thumbs its nose

T
H
R
E
E

at its urban context, which has lost much of its coherence since World War II. It may be an inevitable and necessary irony in a society so driven by social consensus and conformity that individual clients and architects express themselves so insistently with architectural statements. This single-minded pursuit of architectural originality and integrity is beautifully realized on remote sites. The context-be-damned attitude also produces fine individual buildings in tightly packed cities but a chaotic urban fabric. A certain urban homogeneity sets in because many buildings are close together, similarly sized, and consistently inconsistent. So a rough-cut uniformity ironically emerges from and within the egotistical variety; another kind of conformity and uniformity obtains. Nonetheless, this self-referential work, like its counterparts in Europe and America, is often more interested in finding a place in glossy international journals and the annals of architectural history than in the local neighborhood.

Another criticism has been that Critical Regionalism can be socio-politically reactionary – a step back into the brutal national and regional ethno-centrism and racism of the past. Alan Balfour, while chair of the AA School of Architecture in London, makes these observations:

> The emergence of a European economic union is coupled, in paradox, by aggressive assertions of nationalism. Consider, for example, what is already underway in those nations lately released from the grip of Russia – Hungary, Poland, and Romania – where architecture is seen as the most potent means of restoring and representing the national identity. Students are encouraged to resurrect ancient mysteries, that is, to imagine objects that may unwittingly reinforce racial and tribal differences. In spite of good intentions, the monsters may return. Critical Regionalism seemed at first a benign proposition but is now proving to have a sinister subtext. Such forms may bring with them all the wrath of unresolved injustices. Architecture must hold its place in this maelstrom of mediated reality that will increasingly try to dislocate the future. It cannot all be left to television . . . to construct the present only from the past is to condone the death of the future.
>
> Balfour 1994, 51

This statement has some truth to it. Architectural regionalism and nationalism have been invoked by fascist movements. Critical Regionalism can look darkly conservative. However, it's a question of scale. First, Critical Regionalism is not nationalism. Regions are smaller than most nation-states. The ideal region is arguably the metropolis. Secondly, Modernism, however international or liberal, wasn't able to banish "ancient mysteries" or "racial and tribal differences." It simply repackaged these questions at increasingly larger scales. It has consorted with corporate and governmental giganticism, whether capitalist or socialist, and been party to this century's trade-up from national to global commerce and world war. Multinational and supra-national corporations, international finance, continental trading groups, and universal culture can be as brutal as national and regional rivalries – only cooler and more insidious. Wars can now be very impersonal, fought at great physical distance on cool video screens with push buttons and electronic mice – without in-your-face screams and blood.

The "wrath of unresolved injustices" is less sinister and more likely to be understood and resolved at the more personal and humane scale of the city and region than at the numbing scale of the universal civilization which Modernism tends. To be sure, the bad ghosts and negative karma that haunt local, internecine conflict are hot and ugly. But visceral conflicts are less likely to be fought than war with distant enemies who are faceless abstractions and objects of manufactured hatred. Balfour is absolutely right, however, about the need for architecture to hold its place in a reality that is more and more electronically mediated. But contemporary reality is least mediated at the regional and local scale that Critical Regionalism attempts to revive. That is precisely where it hopes to establish and find an existential foothold – not against the future but against placeless internationalism.

A third critique has been that regionalism, whether good or bad, no longer makes technological or economic sense. Modern industrial production and transport make regional building practices and materials a romantic anachronism. Regionalism is wishful thinking and indulgent longing for a past that is lost forever. This argument is based on a straight-line projection of technological revolution-without-end. It fails to take into account that the march of technology and mass culture will not continue indefinitely if enough people no longer believe that it is delivering a better life. Progress may not always be measured in economic terms, at least not as we presently understand progress and economics. We need not be slavish technological drones, committed to every new breakthrough. Technology has been so spectacularly successful for so long that we've been blinded by its light and are only now fully realizing the trade-offs and total cost – whether it be in economic, social, environmental, or moral currency. Just because there is the technological know-how and the money to dress every new Asian hotel lobby and restroom in marble from Italy doesn't mean it's sensible to ship the Carrara Mountains halfway round the planet (a tectonic shift that would make geologists blush). It may appear economical with today's market pricing, but this pricing system must and will change to better reflect the costs. As prices and costs are more accurately aligned (they will never be exactly because external costs are continually being created or discovered), regionalism and localism may be not only more possible but more automatic.

Yet another criticism has been that a singular attitude to architectural design is no longer possible, given the realities of global electronic communication. Peter Eisenman, formerly a zeitgeister, argues that it is now impossible to operate with a single spirit of the times – the unitary organizing world view that animated the work of past eras:

> What characterizes the Rome of Sixtus V, Haussmann's Paris or the work of Le Corbusier ... is that their plans derived from a singular body politic. Now, ironically, at a time when the entire world can be seen as part of a single operating network, such a singular world view is no longer possible. Today, the world can be explained not by a single zeitgeist, but by two divisions. The first division is a traditional one based on land, industry and people. The other division is based on information, which links technologically and culturally sophisticated world centers ... A Berliner of today probably has more in common with a New Yorker than with a resident of another German city, so similar are Berlin and New York as cultural and information centers. When physical proximity is no longer a part of the zeitgeist of a place, the traditional notions of city and architecture are thrown into question.
>
> Eisenman 1994, 51

These are accurate and perceptive comments on contemporary circumstances. Eisenman acknowledges that places such as Serbia and Slovakia are still brought together primarily by shared characteristics, land, and language. However, places that have shifted from the mechanical to the electronic age are problematic for architecture. They must, he argues, confront the possibility of a placeless, electronic reality. It is a truism that modern telecommunications – infinitely light and almost infinitely fast electrons – are transforming our world. Computers, phone, facsimile, e-mail, internet, video, virtual reality, etc., are subversive of traditional life and culture. They will be superseded by even faster, more powerful and more convenient mediations of reality and modes of communication. But none of these developments makes traditional architecture, urbanism, and regionalism less necessary and meaningful. Indeed, it can and already has been argued that the fleeting world of electronic information increases the human appetite for real, palpable place. This is especially true in residential and neighborhood design. It's one thing for Eisenman to design a de-centered convention center in Columbus, Ohio, or a deconstructed office building in Tokyo; quite another for him to play with a residential quarter. He is mistaken to suggest that electronic media might kill the human need for the physical proximity of the traditional city. Like Marshall McLuhan's prediction in the 1960s that new electronic media would kill the book, and unlike Victor Hugo's prediction that books would supplant the cathedral, his prognostication will prove more wrong than right.

Last, Steven Moore of the University of Texas has argued that Critical Regionalism, as espoused by Frampton anyway,

> relies upon philosophical assumptions drawn from opposing camps. Critical regionalism proposes to retain its hope in technology and simultaneously wants to revalue nature and place as positive forces in history ... In other words, to construct a hypothesis that relies alternately upon opposing assumptions of critical theory and those of Martin Heidegger leads to philosophical

confusion. What is needed . . . is not more hybridization of disparate forces, but a single set of philosophical assumptions that will lead to a coherent position.

Moore 1999, 2

His position assumes that the Modernist pre-occupation with technology is completely contrary to the Postmodernist interest in place, that the two are polar opposites. Although they tend to be polarizing forces, they need not be. Technology can be related to, if not rooted in, place, especially with computerized industrial production capable of customizing individualized units. As for conflicting philosophical bases, reality is full of contradictions and antinomies. Indeed, this internal contradiction gives Critical Regionalism vitality, just as I will soon suggest that its external polarity with typology gives it other energies.

The human desire and need for the commodity, firmness, and delight, as well as the meaning that architecture can provide will not be erased by information technology. Architecture *is* information. Moreover, it embodies knowledge. Architecture is a unique and irreplaceable way of knowing the world – its own epistemology. Looking at a monitor or talking into a telephone all day makes face-to-face human interaction in well-designed buildings and outdoor spaces all the more necessary, satisfying, and worthwhile. Regional differences are relished and appreciated all the more. Authenticity and materiality command a higher, not a lower, premium in this increasingly mediated world. In the end, architecture is not words, metaphors, or paper, but buildings.

> Formidable or modest, they occupy a place, they transform a landscape, they loom in front of our eyes, they can be inhabited. They are the stage of power, commerce, worship, toil, love, life . . . This is the art that does not represent and does not signify but is.
>
> Larson 1993, 252

If a region keeps seriously at it, with enough thoughtful designing and building, something critically regionalist will emerge. This is especially true for small-scale residential and institutional construction, which is most subject to local climate and building practices as well as local tradition and tastes. Careful and critical work can develop regional integrity and character any time or any place, urban or rural. It is not a question of size or wealth or age. Charleston, Savannah, and Siena achieve their greatness despite their small size; Istanbul, Bombay, and Palermo despite their poverty; Sydney, Seattle, and Vancouver despite their newness. It is a question of cultural confidence and fortitude, as well as critical intelligence, discrimination, and sensitivity. In the end, respect for place, nature, history, craft, and limits will precipitate a Critical Regionalism. These five tenets contribute to an architecture of place – not an abstract and cerebral architecture but a real, palpable one. However, for all its power to satisfy the basic human need for particular place and for home, Critical Regionalism gives us little help in connecting to universal meaning in the built environment or in our lives. For that equally basic human need we turn to typology.

BIBLIOGRAPHY

Appleton, Jay. 1990. *The Symbolism of Habit*. Seattle, WA: University of Washington Press.

Appleton, Jay. 1996. *The Experience of Landscape*. New York: Wiley.

Balfour, Alan. 1994. 'Education – The Architectural Association,' *Journal of the Indian Institute of Architects*. October 1994.

Barzun, Jacques. 1992. *The Columbia History of the World*. New York: Harper and Row.

Brand, Stuart. 1994. *How Buildings Learn*. New York: Viking-Penguin.

Davis, Robert and Christopher Leinberger. 1999. 'Financing New Urbanism,' *Threshold 18, Design and Money*. Boston, MA: MIT Department of Architecture.

Eisenman, Peter. 1994. 'Confronting the Double Zeitgeist,' *Architecture*. October 1994.

Frampton, Kenneth. 1983. 'Critical Regionalism,' in *The Anti-Aesthetic*, Hal Foster (ed.). Port Townsend, WA: Bay Press.

Hildebrand, Grant. 1999. *The Origins of Architectural Pleasure*. Berkeley, CA: University of California Press.

Humphrey, Nicholas. 1980. 'Natural Aesthetics,' *Architecture for People*. London: Cassel.

Larson, Margali Sarfatti. 1993. *Beyond the Post Modern Façade*. Berkeley, CA: University of California Press.

Moore, Steven. 1999. 'Reproducing the Local,' *Platform*. Spring 1999.

"A Crisis in the Urban Landscape," "The Origins and Theory of Type," and "Legitimacy and Control"

from *The Evolution of Urban Form: Typology for Planners and Architects* (2010)

Brenda Case Scheer

Editors' Introduction

Earlier readings in this section discuss key concepts and issues related to place and identify the reasons why place-making has become a central concern of the urban design field. Over the last 25 years, practicing urban designers have been grappling with how to achieve a sense of place in contemporary built environments given the array of social and economic forces that seem to work against it. An approach that some designers advocate relies on the use of built form types that derive from typological and morphological study. In the physical design fields, typology is the theory and study of architectural types and, increasingly, also landscape types. Closely related, morphology is the study of urban form patterns (street and block layouts, lot divisions, buildings, and land uses) at a range of related scales (region, city, neighborhood, and site) typically over time. Some theorists have taken to combining the terms into a new term, "typomorphology," which focuses on larger scale urban form patterns. Others refer to this as "tissue studies."

Today, the use of figure-ground plans to study and compare urban form patterns is so common that it is easy to forget that the design fields only recently re-embraced this method, which had been used during the Renaissance. Beginning in the late 1970s, architects and urban designers who had become disillusioned with the Modern Movement's focus on functionalism and its abandonment of traditional building forms in favor of industrially inspired "international style" (i.e. traditionless) forms, and alarmed at the negative effects modern buildings and their placements were having on urbanism, began looking back to building forms from earlier eras for inspiration of an alternative design approach. Author-theorists working in Europe, such as Aldo Rossi, Saverio Muratori, Gianfranco Caniggia, M.R.G. Conzen, T.R. Slater, Leon and Robert Krier, and Philippe Panerai, created and drove the exploration of these new research interests, many arguing for the reconstruction of the European City. Theorist Leon Krier declared that the Modern Movement's "form follows function" dictum, which spurred the search for a new built form for every design commission, was absurd and inefficient. He argued that most spatial and architectural design problems had been previously solved, often with elegant form, and that there was no need for architects to constantly reinvent new form. He and others studied and made classifications of enduring form types, both the exceptional and the commonplace, and argued that great richness could be found in those types that had stood the test of time. In the United States, interest in typological and morphological methods was championed by Colin Rowe and Fred Koetter in their writings on *Collage City* (see Part Two pp. 178–197).

In today's urban design practice, typological and morphological approaches are used for research and to guide design practice. Typological practice has been particularly influential in the development of form-based design guidelines and form-based codes in use among adherents of the New Urbanism.

Brenda Case Scheer's recent book *The Evolution of Urban Form: Typology for Planners and Architects*, selected parts of which are reprinted here, explores the history, theory, and current use of architectural types, expressly linking theory and research with contemporary urban design and architectural practice. Like many others, Scheer laments the placelessness found in many contemporary urbanized areas, which is caused in large measure by the repetitive use of standardized architectural types, such as strip malls, tilt-up office buildings, and fast-food restaurants. However, rather than attributing blame solely to the perverse effects of ill-conceived land use regulations or cultural amnesia of better building forms, she argues that these modern types are emergent from existing cultural and economic conditions. Her goal is to give planners and designers an understanding of how types originate and evolve, so that they can help manipulate change effectively. She deals, as well, with the nuances of built form types in order to inform the development of place-appropriate form-based codes.

For readers, it may be helpful to know some definitions. *Type* is a three-dimensional template that gets used over and over in endless variations. *Archetype* is the ideal expression of a type. A *model* is a type realized as a real, individual building. It reflects the accommodation and particularization of the type to the specifics of site and context, and is also an expression of its designer, builder, and owner. A *prototype* is a standardized, mass-produced expression of a type that contains little or no individuality, a prime example being suburban tract housing. Proponents of typologically based urban design practice argue that using tried and true building types that fit existing contexts and achieve a sense of complementarity through form similarity, but which also have authentic differences because of their considered variations (i.e. nuanced models rather than standardized prototypes) can achieve sense of place.

Scheer is Dean and Professor of Architecture and City and Metropolitan Planning at the College of Architecture + Planning at the University of Utah. She has for many years practiced architecture, urban design, and real estate development through her firm Scheer and Scheer, Inc., and was formerly the director of urban design for the City of Boston. Scheer's other works related to typology include *Suburban Form: An International Perspective* (New York: Routledge, 2004), co-edited with Kiril Stanilov, which includes her piece "The Radial Street as a Timeline: A Study of the Transformation of Elastic Tissues." Her many journal articles include "The Anatomy of Sprawl," *Places: A Forum of Environmental Design* (vol. 14, no. 2, pp. 25–37, Fall 2001), "Destruction and Survival: The Story of Over-the-Rhine," *Urban Morphology* (vol. 5, no. 2, pp. 15–27, 2001), and "Edge City Morpohology: A Comparison of Commercial Centers," *Journal of the American Planning Association* (vol. 64, no. 3, pp. 298–310, Summer 1998), co-authored with Mintcho Petkov. In addition, with Karl Kropf she revised Susan Jane Fraser's English translation of Gianfranco Canniggia and Gian Luigi Maffei's *Architectural Composition and Building Typology: Interpreting Basic Building* (Firenze: Alinea, 2001). Sheer has also written extensively on issues related to design review, including *Design Review: Challenging Urban Aesthetic Control* (New York: Chapman & Hall, 1994), co-edited with Wolfgang F.E. Preiser.

For writings that speak to the use of type in a range of disciplines, in both research and theory, look to the many excellent essays in *Ordering Space: Types in Architecture and Design* (New York: Van Nostrand Reinhold, 1994), edited by Karen A. Franck and Lynda H. Schneekloth. Within this book, Anne Vernez Moudon's excellent piece "Getting to Know the Built Landscape: Typomorphology," reviews three European schools of thought on typomorphology – the Italian School, the Versailles School, and the English or Conzenean School – and analyzes their contributions to knowledge about built urban form. Moudon's book *Built for Change: Neighborhood Architecture in San Francisco* (Cambridge, MA: MIT Press, 1986) presents a thorough analysis of the evolution and development of physical form of San Francisco's Alamo Square neighborhood from the mid-nineteenth century through the 1980s, providing an excellent example of how the Conzenean method of typomorphological analysis can be used for urban design research.

Early works concerned with type that come from the architectural field are Anthony Vidler's "The Third Typology," *Oppositions* (vol. 7, Winter 1976); Aldo Rossi's highly theoretical book *The Architecture of the City*, a translation by Diane Ghirardo and Joan Ockman of *L'Architettura della Citta* (Cambridge, MA: MIT Press, 1982); Robert Krier's *Urban Space* (New York: Rizzoli, 1979, first German text 1975) and *Elements of Architecture Architectural Design Profile* (London: Architectural Design AD Publications, volume 49, 1983); and Leon Krier, *Houses, Palaces, Cities* (London: Architectural Design AD Editions, volume 54, 1984).

More recently, architect Douglas S. Kelbaugh, who is both a New Urbanist and a Critical Regionalist and recently served as Dean of the Taubman School of Architecture and Urban Planning at the University of Michigan, has written an evocative book that challenges the current state of architecture and urban design education and practice, *Repairing the American Metropolis: Common Place Revisited* (Seattle, WA: University of Washington Press, 2002). The book contains an excellent chapter called "Typology: An Architecture of Limits" that speaks of the use of typology in architecture and urban design practice, arguing that it provides an enduring, universal code of urban design that can help link the uniqueness of local place to the larger world of human culture. John Ellis' article "Explaining Residential Density Places," *Places* (vol. 15. no. 2, pp. 34–43, 2004), shows how the concept of type is useful for understanding potential residential densities associated with different building forms, and hence a method for developing urban design framework plans. Ellen Dunham-Jones and June Williamson's *Retrofitting Suburbia* (Hoboken, NJ: John Wiley & Sons, 2011) explores the use of architectural types that can be used to transform suburban areas into more urban and sustainable places. A work that theorizes the use of typomorphology in the landscape architecture field is Katherine Crew and Anne Forsyth, "LandSCAPES: A Typology of Approaches to Landscape Architecture," *Landscape Journal* (vol. 22, no. 1, pp. 37–53, 2003).

Writings on form-based codes include Daniel G. Parolek, Karen Parolek, and Paul C. Crawford's *Form-Based Codes: A Guide for Planners, Urban Designers, Municipalities, and Developers* (Hoboken, NJ: J. Wiley and Sons, 2008) and David R. Walters's *Designing Community: Charrettes, Masterplans, and Form-Based Codes* (London: Elsevier/Architectural Press, 2007).

A CRISIS IN THE URBAN LANDSCAPE

We know how to design cities. Designers can whip out attractive watercolor drawings that envision a rejuvenation of our sad urban landscape of strip malls, car dealerships, fast food kiosks, ragged garden apartments, wide parking-dominated streets, and isolated subdivisions. If the new urbanism had not already offered us clear examples of better design, we have but to walk the streets of Paris or Savannah, Georgia, or St. Petersburg, Russia, to breathe in ancient and timeless lessons from our ancestors.

So why is it that for every much-heralded 50-acre new urbanism gesture, there are literally thousands of acres of new strip malls, gas stations, apartment complexes, office parks, subdivisions, and big box stores?[1] Multiscreen theaters, convention centers, soccer stadiums, airports, and shopping malls all resist the good urbanism lessons. Observe the far edge of any city: Why do big box stores proliferate like weeds in a garden, despite the efforts of planners and designers? What is it that we don't understand that confounds our attempts to change this ubiquitous landscape?

Planners and designers have been searching for the answers for some time, with mixed results. One probable culprit is ordinary land-use regulation, which can prohibit good urbanism.[2] There is considerable merit in this idea. Twentieth-century building has evolved in unanticipated ways, such that zoning has had a very limited effect on urban form. Zoning is not oriented around a formal plan; rather, a zoning map has blocks of color that describe the perimeters of a regulated area. Land-use and zoning plans indicate none of the apparatus that might constitute an urban design: street layouts and sizes, parcel size and shape, public space, building form, and scale. A land-use plan frustrates urban density and spatial form with its metrics of setbacks and floor area ratios that are driven by the goal to limit intensity and isolate uses. Parking ratios, subdivision regulations, and separation of uses can also prevent a well-designed urban form. A predominant opinion among planners and designers is that if we could change the regulation, we would produce more compact and livable cities.

A second prominent idea is that, as a culture, we have forgotten what is good and we need to be reminded through examples.[3] If only we could show people that dense urbanism is attractive and healthy and socially interesting, they would come to demand it everywhere. If only we could all develop a shared ideal about what is livable and good, as people who lived in traditional urban environments apparently did, we would be able to build it.

Both of these answers to the question of why we don't make cities the way we should – inadequate regulation or lack of appropriate examples – make a leap of faith: The proper, that is, traditional, urban form will blossom, eventually crowding out the strip mall and big box weeds if only regulation can be aligned and better design can be demonstrated to the public. It is assumed that in order to redesign our cities and suburbs according to smart growth principles, our culture will need to produce new building types on a grand scale. For example, big box stores should be replaced by mixed use types, and low-density single-family homes by higher-density types.

In this book, I offer a different perspective, born of research in many different places over time. In any one place, most buildings conform to one or another of a limited set of building types – for instance, a strip mall is an example of a type. These types are used over and over because they align with the conditions of the culture and economy. In other words, they emerge or evolve as a complete resolution of a complex, interwoven set of problems. As long as the conditions that gave rise to the type continue to exist, the type will proliferate, with minor variations. Only when conditions change will these types evolve to respond to the new conditions, with some allowance for natural resistance to change. Changing types on a grand scale so that they emerge naturally is difficult without first creating a corresponding change in these conditions. Thus it is that big box stores, for example, continue to be far more prolific than mixed use retail types.

Managing the dynamic of typological change is an essential skill for planners. Yet most urban design ideas are based on a static understanding of the built environment, and they anticipate an end, when the plan is complete. A master plan is an imagined future environment, a blueprint or framework to get from one point of time to a day in the future. Few plans actually are completed with any fidelity, however, for a variety of reasons. A major one is the simple fact that conditions of the urban economy and culture change too profoundly and too frequently for the master plan to be relevant for a long period of time. A plan that is a singular vision, or which is very precise, may not have the flexibility to be adapted for these changes. This is a con-

founding problem for planning in general, but especially for urban design, whose pretty pictures can seem laughable 20 years down the road. Like an old science fiction movie, planners' illustrated visions of the future can seem oddly anachronistic in ways that written documents might not.

This dilemma cannot be easily solved. Design, for designers, has historically meant the creation of an object. Urban design, as practiced, assumes the creation of an object, albeit a rather large and complicated one with multiple parts built at different times. Alternatively, many urban designers now understand urban design less as the creation of a series of specific buildings and open spaces and more as a framework for change that is continuous and ever evolving.

In plotting an urban design strategy, planners can manipulate or limit the conditions that affect and change the physical environment over long periods of time. This requires an understanding of the normal dynamic forces that operate on the built landscape. Some of these forces are obvious to planners: zoning, markets, transportation, and so on. What is not well understood is the mechanism by which these forces work their magic. Why does a big box store happen, or a strip mall? How can we change these places? Often the frustrating answer is that, despite our knowledge of better ideas, we cannot change them; instead, they keep popping up. These ordinary building types are persistent, ubiquitous, and resistant to the planner's bag of tricks.

Since ordinary building types are the most visible building blocks of the urban landscape, planners must study the naturalized conditions under which they arise, flourish, and change to have any hope of transforming them or the urban landscape that contains them. By understanding types as emergent from culture, we can recognize that it is not possible to invent new types or substantially alter a type solely for the purpose of serving a different kind of urban design idea; these attempts betray a fundamental misunderstanding of how the urban environment creates and recreates itself. Instead, we must see types for what they are: natural adaptations that satisfy a specific set of conditions. It is the conditions themselves that can be manipulated, not the type.

A wholesale change in the urban environment cannot be accomplished without orchestrating this evolution. This book is about understanding how types originate and evolve, so that planners and designers can help to manipulate this change effectively with the tools at hand. Assisting and encouraging the evolution of common types is in the long run, the only way to ensure that more urban types will be successful on their own terms – that is, that good types will appear more or less spontaneously, without excessive regulation to force them to happen. Manipulation of types requires a sophisticated understanding of building types and their relationship to urban form and the conditions that drive them. Although we can imagine an ideal city, it may not be possible to build it or rebuild our urban landscape significantly unless the complicated processes of typological and urban transformation are understood.

That is not to say that altering the course of urban development is impossible in the long run. In less than a century, the urban and suburban form of the United States was dramatically reshaped by a combination of interrelated forces, including the globalization of the economy (which brought us Wal-Mart, for example); technological shifts in communication, construction, and transportation (cars, jets, electricity, TV, phones, steel, computers); the transformation of education, civil rights, and the role of women; the rise of corporations, governments; and so much more. The reason we do not build cities in the lovely traditional forms that we know from history is obvious: the patterns and types in older cities emerged from completely different cultural, technological, and economic conditions. The dramatic shifts over the past 100 years guaranteed that a new urban landscape would emerge to challenge the traditional form.

That emergent urban landscape is all around us, for better and worse. It reflects our shared values and embodies our expectations, which is why American cities are so similar everywhere. Citizens of older cities also shared similar common expectations of form, if not explicit values about how a city should be. Building types from the 18th and 19th centuries embody those expectations. In the same way, our contemporary building types, like it or not, also embody the habits, values, society, and economics that have lately evolved.

There are good reasons why designers are not satisfied with the types that emerge from cultural processes. Our shared values have serious problems and weaknesses that are worth questioning. Are Wal-Mart and strip shopping centers the best we can do? Are incessant growth and expansion necessary for quality of life? Is it worthwhile and perhaps even critical to take on the complicated task of deeply understanding the emergent types that surround us and the conditions that create them? It may even be possible to push evolutionary change to happen more quickly by manipulating the conditions under which these types thrive.

Consumer values and expectations are components of these conditions. Seen in this way, the design and construction of an idealistic new urbanism project does not represent an evolutionary shift but a form of consumer advertising that may slightly influence the slow process of typological change over time.

At present there are many exemplary urban-style projects that are featured in design media. Most of these arise from very particular situations that almost always include massive control of a single large site. These exemplary projects can be seen as leaps, not evolutions. Most exemplary projects give preference to satisfying ideals: the formal and imagistic attributes of a place predominate. As a result, they must often overcome enormous resistance to be built at all. This resistance can take the form of irate neighbors, reluctant bankers, planning regulation, dicey market studies, parking needs, and a host of other cultural and economic barriers. Because they have not emerged or evolved from the crucible of complex cultural conditions, these exemplary projects cannot be expected to proliferate naturally. Although they may be financially successful – our ultimate measure of value in this culture – they are still much riskier than "normal" development.

This book undertakes the task of unraveling the idea of building types as emergent forms that drive most urban development and transformation. By studying types and how they change over time, designers and planners can become connoisseurs of the physical environment, easily recognizing a wide variety of urban patterns and able to classify, date, and analyze the strengths and weaknesses of them.

Building *type* is an idea that actually has many related but different meanings in architecture. Typologies are classification systems, with important uses in fields as different as linguistics and biology.[4] In architecture, the most common use of the term describes a loose classification of buildings based on their primary use – library, school, airport, for example. Buildings of the same use-type have the same function but may take many different configurations. Later in this chapter, I will describe use-types and other ideas of building types, but everywhere else in this book the word *type* will be used to describe formal types. Formal types share characteristics of the same form – for instance, a big box or a row house – but may be adapted easily for many different functions, even though they may be commonly associated with one function and originally derived from that function. Form types are particularly useful because they constitute a way of analyzing and describing the space, shape, density, and many other physical configurations of the built environment. Just as the term *land use* does not give us much information about the physical configuration of a place, use-types – library, retail, and so on – do not tell us the shape or scale or configuration of buildings.

Formal types, on the other hand, can be used to describe the shape, feel, scale, and configuration of the environment but without being specific about the precise architectural character, building use, or intensity of activities. This opens up an important arena for planners and planning regulation. By describing the existing and future city according to building types and their urban configurations, planners have a tool that is oriented toward creating specific physical configurations of the city rather than – or in addition to – the economic and intensity configuration, or what is known as *land use*. Using type as a basis for physical planning also implies a certain flexibility and possibility for change – of use, character, intensity, and so on – that is missing in most regulatory systems.

In particular, planners who are creating form-based codes or aesthetic zoning are already involved in a regulatory system that relies on a sophisticated understanding and coding of types. This book is specifically intended to help planners understand the subtleties of the idea and answer confounding questions about use-type and formal types, architectural guidelines, site plans, and form-based codes, and how type is related to the urban form. In the next chapter, I also introduce a brief history of the idea of *type*, which can provide a background

to those who want to understand the development of typology and morphology (the study of urban form) as developed since the Enlightenment.

In this book, I will be demonstrating the following four theories of type, which are derived from the study of the evolution of six American cities and towns, including several suburban examples:[5]

1 Most buildings are exemplars of particular definable types. These types are not arbitrary but represent the resolution of forces impinging on the building industry and culture in general at the time they were built. Types are not autonomous, plucked from previous eras and imposed in a new place. At their origin, they participate in a culture, which means that they interact with the culture and all its conditions. A new or transformed type can be introduced successfully on a grand scale only when the conditions for its introduction are right.

2 Because types emerge and evolve rather than being wholly invented, improving the built environment implies an understanding of how the process of typological transformation occurs, especially through changing conditions such as market demand, technology, cultural values, infrastructure creation, and regulation.

3 Typological observation is an important urban analysis tool. Existing environments reveal their recent and even ancient history through a close reading of their origins, common types, and their transformation over time. Signs of transformation are particularly informative: the story told by the observable typological and morphological process adds an unusually concrete and yet subtle confirmation of the written history of a place and is an essential step in urban design.

4 Building types in and of themselves represent ideas that are carried forward in time. This signification and historical continuity imbue building types with a design value and power. Designers often deliberately impose some historic typological characteristics on a new building in order to endow it with some of the significance of a historic type. As a culture, we vaguely recognize types and have expectations about them, which can be reflected – with subtlety or with more overt quotation – by the architect.

Formal types

What is a type? A type is a class of buildings having formal characteristics in common, usually as a result of having certain global functions in common. There are several defining characteristics of a type: circulation, overall shape and scale, entrance conditions, and situation on the site. Building types are abstract. Each individual building of a given type is an exemplar of that type, a variation that contains all the elements of the abstract term but may also look quite different from any other exemplar.

Take the example of a 19th-century row house: it has multiple stories; it is relatively narrow, with party walls; and it has small punched windows and a tall stoop. . . . It is typically entered on one side of a three-part facade division, which indicates its internal circulation pattern. Stairs and corridors inside the building are along one side of the structure in a central core, with front rooms and back rooms open to light. The row house was used primarily for residences initially, with an internal configuration leaving the main family with the first, second, and third floor; the uppermost floors were used by servants; and the lower level, beside or below the stoop, could be rented out.

As with most types, this type has a common site configuration relative to its neighbors and to the street. It is arranged in rows, usually lining the street, with a rear yard of varying depth. This type appears in many places and in many styles, with some variation in stories but not in proportion, original use, or site configuration.[6]

Each variation could be considered a different type, or for some purposes, within a family of similar types. There is not a systematic or universal nomenclature or classification of types; types are sometimes named and identified within regions – for example, Boston's triple-decker – but the same type could be classified or named differently in a different region. . . . To complicate it even more, names like "row house" have no specific universal meaning.

Type is related to function but not precisely. We might consider building types to be the customary building of countless vernacular builders over time. The row-house type just described is a common one in European urban culture because it fit very well with the conditions of its time. One of these conditions was the original use of the building, but a very precise fit with function is counterproductive to the useful life of a type. Buildings of a particular type may have significantly different functions as they exist over time. In the row house, the servants no longer live on the top floor, and the family may have long been replaced by a law office and four small apartments, all with minimal damage to the building or even to its fit with the original type abstraction. This flexibility of internal configuration, urban scale, and use, which is common in some types, gave the row-house type a magnificent resilience. Over time, particular buildings may come and go, but the type itself can remain serviceable for many centuries by the means of minor transformations.

On the other hand, some types become obsolete more quickly, especially if they are tied inflexibly to a single function – for example, a blacksmith's shop. One of the most important forces of transformation is obsolescence. Types sometimes become obsolete or are regulated out of existence, a particular opportunity or concern for those who make policy.

In the United States, the flexible, attractive row house is in danger of such lethal regulation. The tall stoop of a residential row house is not accessible to people with physical disabilities. In most places, this means the row house can be built only as a single-family home, not as a place of business or multiple dwellings, which gives it its flexibility. With clever design, one can make a building that somewhat resembles the original, but not within the framework of the original type, which assumes that everyone will climb up and down. Even though historic row-house buildings continue to be popular – see Boston, San Francisco, Chicago, and Brooklyn, New York – the type, with its inherent use flexibility, cannot be reproduced in a new neighborhood.

While we enjoy and still occupy older types such as row houses, their currency today is to represent a few ideas that we would like to retain, since it is difficult for row houses to satisfy contemporary conditions. We admire the urban environment, the public facade, the street character, the density, the scale, and the materials of the row-house type. But so far, contemporary adaptations of this type generally fall far short of the desirable 19th-century urban environment. The conditions under which a type arises are a cultural package, and it is difficult or impossible to separate out one or two desired characteristics of a row house without losing the integrity of the type altogether.

On the other hand, all types evolve. The row house has not directly evolved much in recent years in the United States because it has been edging toward obsolescence for many decades, even as a single-family home. It has no parking, it has a limited garden, its tall ceilings require expensive heating, and its height and vertical arrangement of spaces have fallen out of favor for residences. It must be built as a single-ownership unit with fire-proof party walls. It is too narrow to adapt for large units that need width, light, and good circulation. To be occupied by more than one family or a business, it has to be equipped with an expensive elevator, further constraining width and light. These problems can be overcome in the Back Bay of Boston, or the Upper West Side of New York City, where property values allow these expensive adaptations, but for speculative building on a large scale, the row house of the 19th century can no longer be considered a model except as an image.

The great-grandchild of the row-house type is the town house, a similar building in that it is built side by side in rows. . . . The town house is a single-family building that may or may not have street frontage and rarely has a stoop. It may form a street wall or a courtyard with others. Its proportion and frontage are very different from the row house, because it lacks a stoop, each floor has a greatly diminished floor-to-ceiling height, and it usually has only three floors (though two floors are also common). In some forms, a garage constitutes the first floor, dramatically affecting the urban realm.

Just as important to the urban context and the public realm, the old-style row-house type was owned fee simple: it sits on its own plot of land and shares only a wall with its neighbor, not a contractual relationship. Built separately, one at a time, each row house was somewhat unique and sometimes had no architectural similarity to its neighbors except the loose characteristics of the type that they both exemplify. The owner customarily expected to extensively remodel both the outside and the inside at will, within a legal framework suited to continuous adaptability.[7]

The contemporary town house, on the other hand, is developed as part of an ensemble, a much larger project that has strong architectural similarity – scale, massing, detail, material, and landscape – and a much freer relationship to the site, parking, garden, and street. Even when owned separately, town houses are governed by private regulations, and it is difficult for an owner acting independently of the association that controls the complex to modify their own town house on the exterior or interior. . . . This means that it is not nearly as flexible in responding to changes in cultural and social conditions. This particular constraint did not exist in the older row-house type.

Other definitions of type

This section will describe other uses of the word *type* so that we can understand how they are different from the formal type. A *use-type* is very commonly associated with architectural design. In this definition, a building type is a series of buildings that have an identifiable use, such as a library or recreation center. Architects study building types to assist with programming a new building, programming being the definition of spaces and their relationship, size, and requirements. Type studies primarily focus on unusual architecture, so standard configurations – say, a simple school plan with classrooms and a center hall – tend not to be documented unless they have significant innovations. Architects are interested in innovations, so looking at the latest library helps to visualize how the functional and stylistic characteristics of libraries are changing.

[. . .]

The limitation of use-type in describing form can be illustrated by retail types. Formally, retail can function successfully in any of these types: an indoor mall, a lifestyle center, a main street, a strip mall, a freestanding store, a big box, and a drive-through. Retail uses can also be part of another dominant use, such as an airport, an office building, or a hospital. So designating a block of land as retail or commercial on a land-use or zoning plan tells us nothing about its eventual urban form. Similarly, knowing that a building is retail tells us nothing about its configuration.

Residential types commonly combine the idea of formal type and use-type. Residential types include row houses, lofts, garden apartments, courtyard houses, cottages, high-rise apartments, motels, and so on. While the characterization of use is key, all of these at least imply a certain formal arrangement, even if it is understood only vaguely.

On the other hand, there are other residential use-types that do not imply form at all: multifamily apartment, single-family house, dormitory, retirement home, monastery, shelter, or halfway house. Each of these can be designed with several different types.

Describing and showing examples of use-types helps architects to precisely program specific spaces: What are the common pieces and parts, and how do they work together? How big is a hotel dining room? Where is the kitchen in relation to it? Even more important are the technical conditions that are revealed in use-type study, such as laboratory configurations, the need for ventilation, the code requirements for exiting, and so on. These variables can be quite different and compelling in different uses. Expertise in these areas is valued and rewarded, and this is one reason why a use-type retains its power as an organizing idea for architectural practice.

Most of the time, there is no assumption of a standard formal arrangement or part in a use-type; in fact the innovative projects that appear in the architecture type study are singular and architecturally interesting buildings, not ones that demonstrate business as usual. The use-type is also inventive – that is, architects are encouraged to create new use-types through imaginative combinations of old uses or the recognition of new uses.

Architects, historians, and critics make extensive comparisons of use-types to analyze contemporary and historic modes of expression and to track and validate design trends. What does a cathedral of today look like? In a cathedral building type study, the critic might find several common themes of contemporary practice: soaring space and manipulation of light characterized by streaks and patterns, deep shadows, and dramatic highlights. She might point out that today's cathedrals demonstrate a striking sublimation of iconography or even symbolism, that they are spaces scrubbed of overt religious expression and yet somehow spiritual and contemplative. There is no science in this interpretation: the examples chosen exemplify the themes because they were specifically chosen to do so, and those that did not were left out. Over time and with editing, critics can develop use-type comparisons to define iconography that has its own life, much as historians revisit or reinterpret the past to reveal patterns.

The pervasive confusion of formal type and use-type derives from historical patterns, where these ideas were much more difficult to separate. For example, a cathedral, in certain eras and regions, came in only one or two formal types.[8] The use and the form were very specifically aligned. Many use-types – schools, office buildings, factories – originated with this congruity of form and use, only to diverge as the culture, technology, and economy diversified.

Because designers enjoy the potential for invention that is glorified in the use-type, they also are compelled from time to time to invent new types. The *innovation-type* is an imaginary building created to propose an extraordinary idea that would propel the built world in a specific direction or toward specific goals, often idealistic in nature. Myriad examples of these exist, from Boullée and Ledoux . . . to Le Corbusier's Unité d'Habitation.[9] Innovation-types are like architectural experiments, speculative and not likely to emerge through the normal processes of typological evolution. They represent an idea that would be a special leap. Projects such as these are often heralded as new types, and they are interesting in their own rights as thoughtful reactions to specific contemporary conditions or as influential models for real buildings.

An innovation-type is a building intended to be used over and over, thus singular speculations cannot be classified as innovation-types. A project that speculates on using shipping containers for housing in many places and contexts is an innovation-type. Similarly, proposals for buildings over and under interstate highways, or thin buildings that line highways and mediate between pedestrian spaces and auto zones, are innovation-types in that they represent an idea about how to treat many such places that exist all over the world. . . . These are speculative solutions that do not arise naturally, because they do not address most conditions of contemporary urban form: they satisfy only one or two conditions that are important to their inventor.

Innovation-types are rarely popularized or adopted in the way that their authors hope – as solutions – although some versions are built as examples, almost as experiments. Occasionally an innovation-type that is built will resonate very strongly and influence the evolution of similar forms.

Finally, a *prototype* is a building deliberately designed for no specific site and meant to be copied almost exactly, with minor adjustments in size and orientation to fit the conditions of different sites. Branded businesses – for example, chain motels, McDonald's, and Jiffy Lube – all use prototypes, and so do some religious organizations and shoestring-budget public agencies such as school districts, fire departments, and transit authorities. Although based in economies of repetition, the prototype has other cultural conditions attached to it, especially its branding and marketing potential. A hallmark of prototypes often is that they are very easy to read; one might almost call them "logo" buildings. People are conditioned to interpret these buildings correctly and know almost instantly what experiences can be found inside.

Even when they are vacated, they still have power: A Taco Bell prototype that has been stripped of its signage and abandoned for another use can still be easily associated with the brand. . . .

THE ORIGINS AND THEORY OF TYPE

To understand the origin of type is to understand the origin and legitimacy of architecture itself: Are types found in nature? Inspired by God? Evolved from some original primitive types? Or generated from rational principles? Even today, planners are referencing "ideal" building types as one way to judge whether a building conforms to the preferred type (making it more likely to be approved) or deviates from it (possibly leading to its rejection).

A simple system of classification is likely to have encoded the earliest buildings into "house" and "not-house." Since, formally, a house in a given culture is a simple form repeated over and over, *house type* conflates both form and use. Something that was "not-house" arose when cultures began to specialize functions: priests and rulers needed temples, palaces, and storehouses. The differing forms of the temple type and the storehouse type reflected very different ideas about their relative place in the culture, especially their place in the cosmology.

Over time, the number of types and their variety became more sophisticated. Typology as a classi-

fication was not much remarked upon before the Enlightenment, since the differences in buildings were obvious and types were somewhat standardized within a culture. Before the Renaissance, architects passed along ideas of what a temple, a palace, or a basilica type should be, primarily by imitating or elaborating on previous examples. Occasionally architects would adapt a previous type for a new use. These types were sanctified and legitimized by imitation and by their presumed sacred origin. Scandal could ensue if "proper" models were abused.[10]

Houses were even simpler forms of imitation–copies of ideas that were so generally accepted over a given geographic area that the form was repeated without really considering any substantive alternative or variation, except through a very slow evolution.[11]

According to the architectural historian Anthony Vidler, in the 18th century Enlightenment theorists began proposing that legitimacy in architecture was not the result of divine approbation and that it might be otherwise created by nature or reason. The explicit understanding and classification of building types reflected a conscious effort to provide rational explanations for existing types and provided a rational legitimacy for architectural form.

In particular, Enlightenment architects were interested in origins, as most Enlightenment thinkers were. To discover the first building and the succession of buildings that followed was to give architecture legitimacy not through God or imitation but through nature and the rational perfection of nature over time. The purpose of the search for origins was to legitimize certain formal ideas while declaring others to be degenerate. The approved ideas were known as *types*, using the word to mean abstract models.

Most of the initial rationales for origins included the imitation of nature, which the Abbé Laugiér proposed was man's first lesson in shelter. He embroidered on Vitruvius's primitive hut – a theoretical explanation for the first architecture that presumed tree trunks as uprights, with a roof of crossed branches. . . . This hut, it was thought, might have provided man with all subsequent ideas of construction: tapered columns, peaked roofs, and details of joinery. Architecture evolving – being perfected – from this system would have columns with organic-themed capitals, for example. French

Enlightenment theorist Quatremère de Quincy re-stated it this way: "One should turn one's eyes to the type of the hut in order to learn the reason for everything that may be permitted in architecture, to learn the use, intention, verisimilitude, suitability and utility of each thing."[12]

Types were at first defined as ideal models. This idea arose from the 18th-century admiration for Greek art and architecture, as opposed to the "de-generate" forms of the Baroque. Greek sculpture, for example, idealized the human body: no actual person was depicted in such an idealization, but instead the artist selected the perfect features, the perfect body, and so on.[13] Greek architecture, it was theorized, had been derived originally from the primitive hut and perfected over time through adapt-ation to human proportion, ideal climate, landscape, and freedom. The resulting architecture – for example, the Greek temple of the classical period – was seen as an ideal model for all architecture.

It was Quatremère, writing in the early 19th century, who for the first time used the word *type* in ways that are directly related to our understand-ing today.

> The word type presents less the image of thing to copy or imitate, than the idea of an element, which ought in itself to serve as a rule for the model. The model, as understood in the practice of an art, is an object that should be repeated as it is; the type, on the contrary, is an object with respect to which each artist can conceive works of art that may have no resemblance to each other. All is precise and given in the model, all is more or less vague in the type.[14]

Moving away from the historical practice of imita-tion as a legitimizing force in architecture, he de-fined building type as an ideal, abstract form of a building, not an actual example to be duplicated or closely imitated. With this distinction, Qua-tremère allowed the possibility that man (architects) could create new abstractions and forms (types), albeit he preferred that they did so within a system of ideals, which he believed could only be based on classical Greek architecture.

Quatremère was interested in Origins as well and he engaged the question, current at the time: Did ancient Greek architecture influence ancient Egyptian or the other way around?[15] Were there

rational principles that drove their similarities? What could explain their differences? His thesis laid out the proposal that there were three forms of primitive building from which all architecture derived: the cave, the tent, and the carpentered building – that is, the primitive hut. Quatremère proposed that Egyptian and Greek architecture evolved from two different primitive types: the Egyptian from caves, and the Greek from carpentry. Any similarities were explained by slight cultural contamination. Furthermore, he speculated that Chinese architecture was evolved from tents, and the details and expressions of their design could be attributed to that. This idea specifically denied the sacredness of form and detail in favor of a rational idea of primitive man and his available resources and common living practices. Quatremère also believed that only Greek architecture had been fully developed and perfected, since it arose in perfect conditions of ideal climate and local materials, mature aesthetic and philosophic appre-ciation, and relative freedom of thought. This idea later influenced those who believed that types were a resultant of specific conditions of place, history, and culture.[16]

At the same time that Quatremére was writing, J.N.L. Durand was a teacher at the École Polytech-nique, one of the first formal training grounds for architects. Durand published two important books, which illustrated ideas of type in two ways. The first was his *Parallèle*, a huge, handsome book that reproduced plans, elevations, and sections of his-toric buildings at the same scale. . . .[17] Used for generations by architecture students as a reference, it included examples from many traditions and cul-tures, not just classical. Importantly, Durand usually arranged the buildings in his *Parallèle* by functional and formal classification: churches, lodges, palaces, and so on. This reiterated the blossoming scientific idea of type: a classification system by form and function, inclusive of all important examples and without judgment as to their ideal nature.[18] By reproducing the buildings at the same scale and with the same drawing technique, Durand treated disparate examples as if they were scientific specimens.

Durand's second important contribution to the idea of type was quite different. As a teacher, he developed an ideal but rational system of archi-tecture using columns, walls, and pure geometric forms, with the goal of allowing the architect to more clearly express the function of buildings without resorting to copying unsuitable classical buildings. Durand was particularly interested in rethinking function as a way of generating new forms, and creating architecture that could vary and yet have the legitimacy of working within a rational system of rules. These rules were derived from simple parts and simple geometry combined in specific relationships.[19]

In his book *Précis*, Durand proposed that using building systems in this manner freed the architect to discard imitation and address contemporary conditions through an infinitely variable system. His system required the architect to work with symmetry and classical elements, proportions, and materials, but it allowed the specific design to vary according to the needs of the building.[20] Durand thus invented a system flexible enough to accommodate the rapidly changing contemporary programs but restrictive enough to provide a uniform architectural standard. . . .

Both Quatremére and Durand, although very different in their intentions, discarded mimesis as a legitimate force and completed the transformation of architecture from its basis in classical examples and divine inspiration to the rational justifications we know today. This rational basis for architecture would lead away from imitation and into the simple geometry that was assumed to be closer to original types, or geometric purity derived from ideal Greek form.

Durand, with his reliance on the generative qualities of geometry and rational functionalism, is considered one of the first modern architects, heralding a shift to legitimacy through rationality, a notion that persists today. Durand's system, a language of architecture, demonstrated the very powerful essence of building types: a way of designing that was neither entirely free of constraint nor overly prescribed, yet resulted in works that had automatic legitimacy.

In later generations, this generative principle gave the idea of type its power: types are abstractions that follow certain rules (that is, contain certain widely accepted characteristics) yet allow the artistic interpretation of those characteristics, to the point where, as Quatremére wrote, "each artist can conceive works of art that may have no resemblance to each other."[21]

Some ideas thus produced in the Enlightenment include that type is a product of culture, that types provide a set of rules or characteristics but allow design variety, that types confer legitimacy as long as each type reflects specific kinds of values, and that types can support a rational classification system derived from both form and function. In the next period when the idea of type gained traction again – the middle of the 20th century – these ideas were transformed slightly and greatly expanded.

Round two: type has a moment in the sun

Although the modern movement in architecture derived in part from the acceptance of typologies based on function and structure, modernists did not devote much discussion to the idea of type. Prototypes – that is, models intended for appropriation in different places – were common. For instance, Le Corbusier's Unité d'Habitation was intended to provide a model for high-rise housing blocks everywhere.[22] Repetition of industrial parts was one of the hallmarks of modernism, so modularity, modes of production, repetition, and universality of programs and forms overwhelmed subtle ideas about type, bringing modernism more in line with earlier ideas of mimesis rather than the more flexible notion of type.

Modernism's willful rejection of the extant city and desire to entirely remake the urban form led to a powerful reaction in the middle of the 20th century. Ideas of building type were revived as a way to recover and provide continuity with the fabric of old cities.[23] As these ideas progressed and changed in different intellectual settings, more or less vague ideas of typology gained great currency among architects and urban designers, peaking in the 1980s with the translation of a number of important treatises into English.[24]

The primary differences between the earliest Enlightenment ideas of type and those of the 20th century were the latter's emphasis on the city, and the role of building types in the city. In the Enlightenment, the city was not mentioned as a part of typological legitimacy or idealism, nor were the ordinary buildings of the city – the houses and shops – seen as worthy of consideration for architects. Types were recognized for public buildings, sacred buildings, and great palaces.

In the 20th century, this situation was reversed, with the ordinary fabric of the city becoming a revered model and the initiation of the "continuity of the city" ideal. Early in the century, modernists were focused on common structures such as mass housing, and these became an important arena for architects for the first time. But because modernist architects promoted high-density towers for cities, the separation of uses and transport, and the destruction of the crowded, infected old city, by mid-century the modernist project had many critics.

The Italians, in particular, mourned a crisis brought on by modern architecture's intent to destroy the historic urban fabric. They sought a design method that would act through the analysis of urban form to unite contemporary architecture with history and provide the urban continuity denied by modernism.[25]

In the 1950s, Salvatore Muratori and his disciple, Gianfranco Caniggia, helped to form the Italian school, which was a fertile group of architects who emphasized the nature of the crisis as a failure to understand or adapt to processes of change in architecture and the city. . . . Through intensive study of Rome and Florence, they uncovered a rigorous method of discovering and defining types.[26]

Caniggia saw types not as reflective of an ideal but as organic, arising and changing according to specific conditions of time and place. The city was an agglomeration of these types, both the profane and magnificent, which varied over time and space. Any given urban type, he theorized, could be traced to a simpler type, an original type, and eventually all these types could be traced to a single-room structure. A particular type could vary in several ways: if it was in the middle of the block, it would likely be different than if it was on a corner, for example. Due to their slightly different traditions, a row house in Padua would have variations from a row house in Rome, even during the same historic era. Over time, the row-house type in Rome would itself evolve to be different than in earlier eras.[27]

Although this was primarily an analytical approach, most of the Italians were clear that their intentions were to appropriate these typological ideas into design. In a similar vein, the Krier brothers, Rob and Léon, abstracted ideas of geometric types found in the historic fabric – for example, a

courtyard house – into generic forms and made suggestive transformations of these through formal manipulation. . . . The results were a catalogue of types that recalled pieces of the city and that would fit with the city but did not relate to specific functions.[28] These were not meant to be inclusive, but suggestive of a method of design, in the same vein as Durand's *Précis*.

These Europeans viewed the typological project as a method of putting a stop to excessive individuality that was disruptive to the continuity of cities. They also saw it as a method of bringing contemporary architecture into alignment with the specific and unique nature of different cultures, which naturally had developed different urban forms and types over time. This was a specific critique of modernism, which deliberately internationalized and universalized architectural expression.

The most intensive and controversial message of the typological project, however, was the idea that types convey meaning. Architects can exploit these meanings in one of two ways: by using the type to relate specifically to a historical moment, as when a temple type is appropriated for use as a bank; or by using the type as part of a subversive or critical stance, as when a form associated with a prison is appropriated as a city hall. This technique, subtle as it is in using historic forms to convey critical themes such as the abuse of power, posed a real danger of being misunderstood, especially in the translation from Europe to the United States.[29]

Critics have suggested that the typological project reached its nadir when the critical stance was overcome by simple iconographic appropriation, which led to the postmodern historic pastiche so reviled by contemporary architects. Appropriation of historic motifs without the analytical and critical understanding of type and its relationship to the city was a degenerative situation that led to architecture that simply put a historic-looking face on a building without considering its urban situation or subtleties of type.[30]

The geographers of the English school approached the problem of the city far more analytically, and their discoveries informed others working in a more architectural vein. M.R.G. Conzen did not start out from a typological approach but discovered the importance of the town plan to the definition of a type.[31] Conzen proposed that the town plan – lots, blocks, and streets – was the underlying formal constraint of all buildings. In studying the city, he looked at both the ordinary situations of these configurations and also the unusual configurations that would present themselves – for example, in the "fringe belts" at the edge of urban development.[32]

Even after Italian and American architects exhausted the typological project as an overworked architectural moment, urbanists still continue to explore morphological patterns and their relationship to building types, developing an analytic approach that now encompasses cities of great variety on all continents. That approach is reflected in this book.

Although architects can be dismissive of the architectural misadventures of the late 20th-century typological project, new urbanists such as Léon Krier and Andres Duany have significantly extended its urbanistic ideas, molding it into a populist movement that dismisses the excesses of modem architecture and the "elite" architects that work in that vein today.[33] It is due to this movement and its many supporters that ideas such as form-based codes and the legitimacy of type as a basis for judgment have become more commonplace.

[. . .]

LEGITIMACY AND CONTROL

Urban design, planning, and urban form

Accepting, for the moment, that current planning practice points in the direction of urban continuity and that sustainability goals are not incompatible with this practice, it is clear that planning controls that exploit an understanding of morphology and typology can be very successful in controlling the look and feel of a physical environment and its urban design.

By contrast, for much of the 20th century, planners operated with tools that were inadequate to address urban form; and indeed, that was not their intention. In the 18th and 19th centuries in the United States, cities and towns were invariably founded with a grid of streets. Over time, as a place grew, new town land was needed, and a new section of gridded streets was added to the first, sometimes with a slightly different orientation and a slightly different scale or block structure. . . . Therefore, at the heart of most American cities is a set of gridded districts, now often interrupted by an overlay of highways, railroads, and utility corridors.

The grids of streets created blocks, and those blocks were subdivided to be sold off at the same time the grid was created. The lots thus created were scaled to receive specific building types. A variety of building types could be accommodated because grids and lots are not always uniform. A close examination of the historic lots and blocks in some places reveals a sophisticated understanding of this idea.

In New York City, for example, the lots that face numbered streets are relatively narrow and were intended for common housing types. When lots on the same block faced the wider avenues, dimensions shifted, and larger, grander types were built. Some of these support commercial use. . . . Although much of what was built no longer exists, this contrast in scale and type persists today, with large grand buildings presiding over the avenues, while smaller buildings cluster along the streets.

Perhaps the finest example of this grid differentiation can be found in Savannah, Georgia, with its lovely parks and streets. The character and types found here vary because some streets are interrupted by parks, while others are not.[34] Alleys provide a third level of distinction. . . . Because these places were built with a common understanding of the building types, and with very real technological and material limitations, the initial development tended to be quite consistent. The lot dimensions, which were minimal to support the types, acted as a check on development, preventing intrusive and overscaled projects but also reinforcing a specific density.

This situation prevailed into the early 20th century, when zoning was first introduced. At the time these codes were developed, it was assumed that some kind of orderly tissue – a grid of streets and lots – would exist; so, for example, a 10-foot minimum setback would provide a consistent frontage and prevent a tone-deaf builder from invading the common space of the street. Design was already restricted, so to speak, by the consistent types and the lot and street dimensions.

The standard for the zoning laws of very large cities provided the legislative template for all places, no matter how inappropriate. Cities at the turn of the 20th century were overcrowded and unhealthy to a degree that is hard to imagine now except by visiting third-world countries. Responding to intense and persuasive urban issues of that age, the ideals reflected in zoning, especially in places such as Chicago and New York, addressed problems of intensive and very unhealthy overcrowding; noxious industries and their resulting smoke, toxins, and water pollution; and the lack of access to green open areas. The ideals conveyed in the zoning laws included, naturally, separation of land uses, provision of greater open space, and limits on the size and density of buildings. But since zoning's main purpose was to prevent noxious land uses, such as tanneries and other urban industries, from invading nice neighborhoods, the importance of the underlying tissue framework was never emphasized.

Since zoning emphasized land-use and intensity limitations, physical dimensional limitations were somewhat neglected, especially since zoning was promoted at the dawn of the automobile era, when urban dimensions, orderly blocks, and consistent types could be assumed. As development pushed out to the suburbs, this framework also disappeared. Without an orderly underlying tissue and consistent lot size, the few dimensional aspects of zoning, such as setbacks and floor area ratios, had no consistent physical results.

Transferring zoning ideals to small towns and suburbs never made much sense, but that transfer occurred anyway through the standardization of zoning codes throughout the country. The zoning template allowed even small towns some measure of control that had not existed, and they seized it in record numbers. The control of land use, in particular, was a very powerful tool that gave city leaders a politically attractive leverage over virtually all landowners. The politicization of zoning, and its usefulness in manipulating land values, made it an even less effective tool for formal control.

The early 20th century gave people the means and the incentive to move out of the city and into the countryside: the private automobile. The standard grid additions gave way to a wholly new kind of place development: the stand-alone subdivision, barely anchored to the old system of roads that connected towns. . . .[35] Town founding and orderly growth through the means of a layout of grids and grid additions halted completely. Urban development exploded beyond the bounds of these

limitations. A sparsely distributed set of country roads, instead of dense urban grids, provided the backbone of all urban development, which was sporadically extended into the countryside. . . . Highway builders struggled to keep up, widening the former country roads over and over to accommodate the traffic.

A new set of controls was developed to overcome another set of problems with isolated subdivisions. Subdivision regulations were devised to set construction standards and minimum sizes for new lots, and these tended to match the goals of zoning: lower density, green spaces, and an enforced consistency of use and size. These standards were also technical, including the sizing and minimum specifications for sidewalks, lighting, grading, sewers, water, and the like. Because these were isolated places, the actual layout of the lots and streets did not receive much scrutiny, nor was continuity of the urban fabric acknowledged as a concern. As subdivisions became the only system of creating new local streets and lot patterns in expanding areas, jurisdictions gave over their historic town-planning role to private interests.

As long as the primary tools to control private development were so general, the urban design of places was impossible to control. Cities allocated land to different uses, but the uses could and did take an infinite variety of forms, so the results were both unsatisfying and physically unrelated to one another. Cities also laid out approximate locations for arterial streets and highways and dictated the amount of open space, but they did not plan their own street networks or arrange open space as a complement to public space design. Open spaces were relegated to leftover land.

The manner in which zoning has been applied has also been a failure for urban continuity. An older section of a town might have a consistent tissue and common types, but these have been ignored in order to apply the ideal zoning formulas that privilege large lots, open space, and large setbacks. Thus, a nice older neighborhood in Denver – where the average size of a lot is 4,500 square feet – until recently was zoned for a minimum lot size of 8,000 square feet. The lack of association between the reality on the ground and the zoning restrictions has caused much difficulty, especially as neighborhoods change and buildings turn over within them.

By the middle of the 20th century, it became fairly clear that zoning was not sufficient to control development, preserve great places, and actually plan for attractive growth. Two related planning ideas grew from this dissatisfaction: historic preservation and design guidelines. Preservation focused on recognizing and saving places, especially individual buildings that retained their historic character. Many neighborhoods that might have been destroyed by the misguided application of zoning were saved by preservation efforts.

Design guidelines were inspired by the effectiveness of historic preservation efforts. Without much thought, jurisdictions based them on the template of historic preservation guidelines, emphasizing materials, details, styles, and sign controls. These were applied to nonhistorical neighborhoods in an attempt to control the aesthetic quality of places and manage change.[36]

Many issues arise in the application of design guidelines, whether regulatory or not. Most of these stem from the difficulty of defining "good" design and from the need to justify most regulations on some basis. Guidelines, often very arbitrary, are difficult to develop, are difficult to administer, and go against the grain of what most people feel is their right to determine how their property looks.

Perhaps the most important shortcoming is that design guidelines are often ineffective in producing a coherent urban environment, unless one already exists. Design guidelines tacitly promote the idea that the disorder and ugliness of the urban environment is a cosmetic problem, that it can be solved with sign controls, consistent styles, street trees, and a limited color palette. Without an understanding of the importance of morphology and typology in creating order, guidelines can have peculiar results. This happens when an arbitrary style is applied to a contemporary type, such as the pueblo style strip shopping center or more banal examples of contemporary types dressed up with less than authentic historic styles. . . .

Typology and codes

Much of the task of urban design is to foster a sense of order in the built environment, while still allowing growth, change, and a great diversity of activities, aesthetics, and forms. While order can be created using a variety of techniques – landscapes, vistas, axes, geometric configurations, and architectural consistency – our newly burgeoning value of urban continuity privileges a particular kind of incremental physical arrangement typified by lots, blocks, and open spaces arranged in traditional configurations.

Even this kind of order can actually be quite messy: the underlying tissue of the city grid of most big cities creates substantial orderliness, even though there is a cacophony of signs, uses, type variations, and the visual messiness of everyday comings and goings. This is a lively urban order. Having a strong tissue and similar building types creates a background datum against which a lively variety can play. . . .

In this kind of environment, the order is found as a background, mostly provided by the uniformity and consistency of the tissues and a certain overall consistency in building types. The urban types themselves work best when their architectural language is within a range of scale, variation, and richness, defined by the rhythms of openings in the facade, three-dimensional depth, and material application, rather than style.

On the other end of the spectrum is the calm, leafy green order that we associate with suburban subdivisions and office parks. The underlying tissue here is just as orderly: a pattern of similar-sized lots and streets, with a related set of building types. Instead of the cacophony of lively and visually stimulating objects layered onto a strong order, we have "soft" order – widely spaced and somewhat varied types, with a gentle but steady rhythm of house, space, house. A variety of site conditions – lawns and driveways, walls and fences, gardens and groves – provide variety and visual interest. . . .

These two environments represent two poles in the kinds of districts where attention to building types and tissues is an effective technique for controlling urban form. Their commonality is that they have an underlying street and lot pattern – static tissue – that retains a basic order and provides a strict limitation on what can be built there. For example, in a typical single-family neighborhood, the lot size and orientation restrict the size and general type of the building. Circumscribing that further are legal restrictions such as setbacks and height limits. Uniformity is gained through these, while variety comes from variations in materials, colors, landscaping, details, and, to a lesser extent, some variation of the types found in the neighborhood.

In order to reinforce a sense of order and allow for variety in static districts, it is necessary to define and preserve the critical characteristics of the tissue and the common building types. This same strategy works whether you are talking about a suburban neighborhood, a business park, or a lively urban downtown. It is possible, and sometimes desirable, to manipulate the standard controls of traditional zoning for this purpose, although certain concepts such as floor area ratio, which has no predictable formal result, must be abandoned in favor of clear delineation of maximum (not minimum) setbacks and building envelopes.

Changing traditional zoning parameters in a given jurisdiction is often easier than substituting an entirely new and untried system of controls such as a form-based code. On the other hand, zoning regulations are very strict in their application of land-use separations, which may not be desirable in a more urban environment. And zoning is a useless tool for formal control if the underlying tissue is highly varied and there is no sense of typological consistency.

Even in consistent static tissues, zoning is a tool designed to direct land use and economic and functional priorities, not form. It may not be possible or appropriate to use zoning to address the subtleties of building types. A possible alternative is aesthetic zoning, or form-based codes, a system of regulation that explicitly foregrounds the formal characteristics of a place as the critical criterion to be controlled. Form-based codes usually discard zoning altogether and replace it with a place-based regulation of formal configurations that can be built, which implies a range of density and some limitation on land use. However, land uses are more lightly regulated so that a mix of uses in a particular district can be promoted. Form-based codes recognize different neighborhood configurations and densities, and they act to preserve and enhance the relationship between each property and its surrounding physical and formal context.

Form-based codes and typology

Form-based codes are designed to preserve static neighborhoods and create new development that has specific formal layouts and goals. Such codes are specifically typological, in that they implicitly reference the types that are acceptable in a place, according to a set of ideals that usually give preference to higher-density development. Although types are referenced, they are not usually described holistically in a form-based code. Instead, they are described by regulating their pieces and parts: frontages (architectural features on the public way), setbacks, building envelopes, side yards, and so on.[37]

The code is developed and applied in different districts that correspond to different densities and appropriate types. As with zoning, there is a map, with delimited territories where different regulations apply. Within those boundaries, a form-based code will enumerate frontages, setbacks, lot sizes, building heights, parking, and land uses.[38] Building types can also be defined and restricted. In addition, there may be some regulation of the street design, with attention to sidewalks, travel lanes, and landscaping. Civic spaces can also be required and regulated as to their function, design, and location. Some form-based codes go further and regulate the building design – materials, window shapes, and so on. Form-based codes thus combine the functions of subdivision regulation, preservation, and design guidelines, and they hark back to the traditions of old-fashioned town planning.

Given this program of regulation, it is easy to see how the concepts and flexible logic of urban morphology and typology can be channeled for this purpose. As in lot-block and all other static tissues built in history, the expected and customary building types are the foundation that inspires the creation of a specific tissue pattern. A form-based code uses regulation to create or strengthen an urban tissue and to restrict types, whether by defining types or by defining a building envelope and other details. Form-based codes are a way of returning to a tradition of city building, albeit with heavy regulation instead of the limitations of expectations, culture, technology, and custom.

The underlying assumption of a form-based code is that the physical configuration of a place can be manipulated as a means to control economic function, density, social goals, and ecological priorities. Like zoning, however, and unlike traditional city formations, form-based codes have a very specific political and social agenda, so that they legitimize certain building types and disdain others. The ones that tend to be ignored or shuffled off into special zones are some of our most enduring and prosaic types: the suburban office building, strip shopping centers, gas stations, storage buildings, stadiums, big box stores, airports, and so on. These are types that do not tend to be compatible with the small-scale lot-block static tissue that is the key element of the effectiveness of form-based codes.

Using morphology and typology in form-based codes

One of the shortcomings of form-based codes as they currently are promoted is that they are not usually place specific. The SmartCode used in many places as a template specifies eight categories of place – known as transects – with very specific regulations and types appropriate for those categories. It also suggests calibrating the code to common local types, which is usually interpreted as adopting some of the unique building types or frontages found in a place.

If codes are really to be reflective of place, however, common templates must be rethought entirely. Creating a code requires that an existing place be thoroughly analyzed for its morphological history and its current typological conditions. The subtleties of the tissue formation and evolution are particularly revealing of why and how a place developed over time, and what the forces still acting on it might be. For example, it would be important to understand Salt Lake City's peculiar grid and its effects over time . . . to prepare a code that would respond to those unique and still extant conditions. Superficial analysis and application of a standard transect would miss the importance of lot size and orientation to the subsequent failures in the urban context. Opportunities to exploit the large block size and unusual alley structure would also be lost.

Form-based codes on undeveloped land require the development of an underlying tissue, which must be exactly specified by the planner or the developer. The code will not operate correctly without a plan of the tissue, which is analogous to the old grid plan layouts used by town founders everywhere.[39] Sophisticated variations within the lot configurations of the plan, especially those responding to natural conditions, street variation, and civic space, could suggest a variety of acceptable types, as they do in Savannah, Georgia.

In the historic process of town development, tissues were designed to fit the types that were common at the time of the tissue formation, not to make a statement about density, best practices, or the like. A key lesson, drawn from Salt Lake City and other places, is that creating a tissue that is misaligned with common development types can have repercussions through time. Idealism, whether it is Brigham Young's ideal low-density village or the new urbanist ideal high-density village, will only go so far in holding back the forces of urban development and transformation.

As a start for a form-based code, the acceptable types should be drawn from regional examples, with the idea that building types are regionally unique and created to address specific conditions. In some places, duplexes are common; in others, they barely exist. The theory of typology assumes that there are economic, social, and environmental conditions that shape demand for types. Designing a place for an unproven type or one that clearly is not really desired will slow down the development and cause other problems later. The tissue plan and the code developed for new areas of a region should recognize common types or encourage slight modifications to common types that already exist in that region.

Where a pattern already exists, it should be thoroughly understood, particularly the forces that have acted on it. Only then can a code be aligned with the typological transformations that have already occurred and will likely occur in the future.

A particular issue is the proposed reuse of some older types, for example, a row house. Some historic types are no longer viable due to modern building codes, technological innovations, and car culture. Their modern equivalents may not have the same character or public face.

Form-based codes – a caution

Although form-based codes are a way of creating and enforcing order, they cannot be used for certain kinds of existing tissues. As we have seen, the concepts of type, morphology, and the fit of a certain tissue to the common types are very relevant to creating a form-based code. But without a clear and relatively small-scale static tissue, a form-based code has little meaning, just as a given zoning set-back has no physical result on a five-acre site.

Therefore, form-based codes are a reasonable solution where static tissues occur, yet they have very limited applicability in regulating the elastic or campus tissues that dominate in the suburbs. . . . Where a consistent tissue does not exist or cannot be created with new development or by repair, the problem of creating order and variety is much more complex and cannot be simply guided through a hands-off application of form-based codes. . . .

Several other critiques of form-based codes can also be asserted, based on lessons that typological transformation and morphology present to us. The first is that ideology can be a problem. The Enlightenment concept of type was born in a cru-cible of ideology, defining as good those buildings that reflected the ideal types, based on their origins and their evolution from classical forms. Quickly, though, that idealism gave way to the judgment of types based on their fit with function, standardized classical parts, and structure.

The return to idealism today is troubling. Typo-logical transformations always move away from their historic origins, by branching into several different new types or by extensive modification. These types respond to exact values and conditions at first, and then become common and stubbornly persistent standards, before finally being supplanted by new types. To the extent that form-based codes recreate anachronistic places or require anachro-nistic types, they are moving against the tide of evolutionary development and have a risk of failing.

There is nothing in the technique or regulatory methods of form-based codes that requires a backward-looking agenda, however. But, just as with the initial applications of zoning law, there is a desire to codify a set of ideal formulas and principles that address perceived problems in present-day American cities. These problems are chiefly centered on auto-centric development and sprawl, and the answer seems to be higher density and a mix of uses.

In the 1920s, zoning took aim at deplorable overcrowding, pollution, and the lack of open space. Yet we are still living with the techniques of zoning, even though the problem set has completely changed. Adaptation of the zoning technique to new prob-lems has been difficult, not because the tool lacks flexibility but because of the initial idealism attached

to zoning and thoroughly encoded in it. Zoning encourages the public and their officials to view urban problems as questions of general density, land-use separation, and street hierarchies.

The technique of form-based coding is not lim-ited to solving one or two contemporary issues – it might be flexible enough to solve different kinds of problems as they arise in this century. This will be true if certain idealistic agendas are not so firmly attached to the technique and are replaced with a more pragmatic and open-ended position. A variety of goals should be offered, with examples of how coding can be applied. Form-based codes could be effective in problems of environmental degradation or landscape integration, for example, but not if the "right" answer is always higher density, pedes-trian districts, and mixed use.

The key to this kind of flexibility is to recognize urban change and transformation as central condi-tions of all active cities. In a form-based code, this will mean abandoning inflexible ideals or standard-ized formulas in favor of representing and codifying the actual place as it has been acted upon over time. Even new development occurs in the regional landscape and reflects the farm roads and fields that were its residents' first marks on the land.[40]

Successful and truly urban places change con-stantly, especially at the level that design guidelines were created to control: signs, colors, and porch details. Enacting a code that freezes current types might seem attractive to those who fear change, but it will limit the ability of types to have trans-formative effects and successful adaptations. Look-ing back at Over-the-Rhine or any 19th-century city, it is clear that a dense fabric arose on the same tissue template of smaller types. Historically, it would have been unfortunate if there had been a regulatory resistance to replacing the poor wooden structures with grand five-story buildings.

On the other hand, the emphasis on creating sound tissues in form-based codes is completely consistent with the desire for orderly change: the initial urban tissue has immense effect on the future development of the city. It may not be the only way to organize an orderly place, but it is a method that offers enormous flexibility for the future.

For this reason, form-based codes should be explicitly about guiding change, not preserving a place as a historic relic. New types will eventually evolve and replace the types put in place today.

How can the form-based codes created today allow and encourage this eventuality while still providing order? It may be possible to design form-based codes to be minimally restrictive, as opposed to the current trend that planners have in mind to regulate all things physical. A strong emphasis on carefully designed and varied tissues and public spaces is the most obvious answer, a lesson we can easily glean from a place such as Savannah, Georgia. By the same token, building types should be defined with more flexibility, and design guidelines should be very limited, in order to insure that types can evolve and respond to changing conditions and tastes.

NOTES

1 Stephen M. Wheeler, "Built Landscapes in Metropolitan Regions," *Journal of Planning Education and Research* 27 (2008): 410.

2 D. Parolek, K. Parolek, and P. Crawford, *Form-Based Codes* (Hoboken, N.J.: John Wiley & Sons, 2008). This book is intended as a guide for planners producing form-based codes.

3 Witold Rybczynski, "Architects Must Listen to the Melody," *New York Times*, September 24, 1989. Like many critics of modernism, Rybczynski here argues that contemporary disorder is due to a lack of "collective wisdom" and "architectural good manners."

4 Lindsay J. Whaley, *Introduction to Typology: The Unity and Diversity of Language* (Thousand Oaks, Calif.: Sage, 1997). This book is a summary of the linguistic idea of type.

5 Brenda Scheer, "The Anatomy of Sprawl," *Places: A Forum of Environmental Design* 14, no. 2 (Fall 2001): 25–37; "Who Made This Big Mess?" *Urban Design*, no. 93 (Winter 2005): 25–27; Brenda Scheer and Mintcho Petkov, "Edge City Morphology: A Comparison of Commercial Centers," *Journal of the American Planning Association* 64, no. 3 (Summer 1998): 298–310; and Brenda Scheer and Dan Ferdelman, "Destruction and Survival: The Story of Over-the-Rhine," *Urban Morphology* 5, no. 2 (2001): 15–27. These are research case studies of types and their urban patterns.

6 Eric Firley and Caroline Stahl, *The Urban Housing Handbook: Shaping the Fabric of Our Cities* (London: John Wiley & Sons, 2009). This book is an excellent and well-produced catalogue of high-density low-scale urban types, both traditional and contemporary.

7 Anne Vernez Moudon, *Built for Change: Neighborhood Architecture in San Francisco* (Cambridge. Mass.: MIT Press, 1986). This is a groundbreaking study of a San Francisco neighborhood.

8 Sir Nikolaus Pevsner, *A History of Building Types* (London: Thames & Hudson, 1976). This is an iconic catalogue of use-types conflated with formal types in historical examples.

9 Anthony Vidler, "The Third Typology," *Oppositions* 7 (Winter 1976): 3–4; and *The Writing of the Walls: Architectural Theory in the Late Enlightenment* (Princeton, N.J.: Princeton Architectural Press, 1987). Vidler is a major force in the historic understanding of the idea of type, especially as it was understood in the Enlightenment.

10 Anthony Vidler, *The Writing of the Walls: Architectural Theory in the Late Enlightenment* (Princeton, N.J.: Princeton Architectural Press, 1987), 126.

11 Gianfranco Caniggia and Gian Luigi Maffei, *Interpreting Basic Building: Architectural Composition and Building Typology* ([1979] Florence: Alinea Editrice, 2001), 43–45.

12 A. C. Quatremère de Quincy, "Type" [1825], introd. and trans. Anthony Vidler, *Oppositions* 8 (Spring 1977): 147–50.

13 Vidler, *The Writing of the Walls*, 125–38.

14 Quatremère de Quincy, "Type," 147–50.

15 Sylvia Lavin, *Quatremère de Quincy and the Invention of a Language of Modern Architecture* (Cambridge, Mass.: MIT Press, 1992), 42–61.

16 Ibid.

17 Jean-Nicolas-Louis Durand, *Recueil et parallèle des edifices de tout genre anciens et moderns, remarquables par leur beaute, par leur grandeur ou par leur singuIarite, et dessines sur une même echelle* (Paris: Gillé, 1799).

18 Sergio Villari, *J. N. L. Durand (1760–1834): Art and Science of Architecture* (New York; Rizzoli International, 1990), 55.

19 Antoine Picon, "From 'Poetry of Art' to Method: The Theory of Jean-Nicolas-Louis Durand," in J. N. L. Durand, *Précis of the Lectures on Architecture; With Graphic Portion of the Lectures on Architecture* ([1802] Los Angeles: Getty Research Institute, 2000).

20 Durand, *Précis of the Lectures on Architecture*.

21 Quatremère, quoted in Vidler, *Writing of the Walls*, 152.

22 David Vanderburgh, "Typology," in *Encyclopedia of 20th-Century Architecture*, vol. 3. ed. R. Stephen Sennott (London: Fitzroy Dearborn, 2003), 1,356.

23 Aldo Rossi, *Architecture of the City*, trans. Diane Ghirardo and Joan Ockman ([1966] Cambridge, Mass.: MIT Press, Oppositions Books, 1982). This is *L-architettura della citta*, the classic text that caused much excitement when it was translated into English.

24 Terence Goode, "Typological Theory in the U.S.: The Consumption of Architectural Authenticity," *Journal of Architectural Education* 46, no. 1 (1992): 2–13. Goode takes a somewhat controversial stance that links typological theory to post modern pastiche.

25 Caniggia and Maffei, *Interpreting Basic Building*, 1–40.

26 Anne Vernez Moudon, "Getting to Know the Built Landscape: Typomorphology," in *Ordering Space: Type in Architecture and Design*, ed. Karen A. Franck and Linda Schneekloth (New York: Van Nostrand Reinhold, 1994). This is the authoritative history of the three movements – Italian, English, and French – of urban morphology.

27 Caniggia and Maffei, *Interpreting Basic Building*, 70–82.

28 Rob Krier, *Urban Space* (New York: Rizzoli, 1979).

29 Goode, "Typological Theory in the U.S."

30 Ibid.

31 M. R. G. Conzen, "Alnwick, Northumberland: A Study in Town-plan Analysis," publication no. 27 (London: Institute of British Geographers, 1960).

32 M. R. G. Conzen, "The Use of Town-plans in the Study of History," in *The Study of Urban History*, ed. H. J. Dyos (New York: St. Martin's Press, 1968), 114–30.

33 Léon Krier and Diru Thadani, *The Architecture of Community* (Washington, D.C.: Island Press, 2009).

34 Stanford Anderson, "Savannah and the Issue of Precedent: City Plan as Resource," in *Settlements in the Americas: Cross-cultural Perspectives*, ed. Ralph Bennett (Cranbury, N.J.: Associated University Press, 1993), 114–37.

35 Michael Southworth and Peter Owens, "The Evolving Metropolis: Studies of Community, Neighborhood, and Street Form at the Urban Edge," *Journal of the American Planning Association* 59, no. 3 (Summer 1993): 271–87.

36 Brenda Scheer, "Invitation to Debate," in *Design Review: Challenging Aesthetic Control*, ed. Brenda Case Scheer and Wolfgang F. E. Preiser (New York: Chapman & Hall, 1994), 1–10.

37 See SmartCode, created by Duany Plater-Zyberk & Company, available as open source online at www.smartcodecentral.org/smart-filesv9_2.html.

38 D. Parolek, K. Parolek, and P. Crawford, *Form-Based Codes* (Hoboken, N.J.: John Wiley & Sons, 2008).

39 Practitioners developing form-based codes use the term regulating plan to refer to the entire map of a place that identifies areas subject to different regulations, which would be analogous to a zoning map. This is not the historic meaning of the term. Some also refer to each specific area as a transect – analogous to a zoning district – another confusing use of the term, which also has a different meaning in history.

40 Brenda Scheer, "The Anatomy of Sprawl," *Places: A Forum of Environmental Design* 14, no. 2 (Fall 2001): 25–37.

"Charter of the New Urbanism"

Congress for the New Urbanism (1996)

Editors' Introduction

The leading current movement directed toward combating urban sprawl and creating compact, walkable neighborhoods is a professionally based movement called the New Urbanism. It emerged in the 1980s as architects and urban designers sought ways to re-create what were felt to be the best physical qualities of traditional neighborhoods and small towns – connected street grids, local shopping, community parks, rear alleys, and front porches. Initially referred to as "Traditional Neighborhood Design," the movement coalesced under the rubric of the New Urbanism in 1993 and organized itself as the Congress for the New Urbanism (CNU). Several years later, the CNU issued a charter that reaffirmed the principles articulated in the 1991 Ahwahnee Principles, which had been developed by the non-profit Local Government Commission with the help of leading members of the fledgling movement, and incorporated physical form approaches that had been developed in the first New Urbanist projects, particularly at the new town of Seaside, Florida. The Charter of the New Urbanism, reprinted here, outlines twenty-seven guiding principles for architecture and urban planning that focus on physical spatial structure. The principles are organized according to three interrelated spatial scales: metropolis, city, and town; neighborhood, district, and corridor; and block, street, and building.

The New Urbanism is criticized, especially in academic circles, on numerous grounds: that its traditionally inspired built forms are anti-modern and nostalgic; that its recommendations are too prescriptive and formulaic; that its emphasis on form smacks of physical determinism; that its projects are elitist because they are not particularly affordable; and that it is contributing to urban sprawl because many projects are built on greenfield sites and are of relatively low density. Nonetheless, the movement represents a coming together of many practicing professionals who, understanding the nature of the land development and housing industry, are intent on achieving urban development that is highly livable, community building, and more socially and environmentally responsible than would otherwise be built. In some ways, New Urbanism can be likened to a movement of utopian-minded former students, shocked by the realities of the "real world" and the limitations of public urban planning, and focused upon creating something better – something they thought they might be doing when they entered the field initially. And, inherent problems and faults notwithstanding, the New Urbanism is proving popular in the marketplace.

Leading practitioners of the New Urbanism, and founding members of the CNU, are Miami-based Elizabeth Plater-Zyberk and Andres Duany, Berkeley-based Peter Calthorpe, Dan Solomon of San Francisco, and Stefanos Polyzoides and Elizabeth Moule of Los Angeles. Elizabeth Plater-Zyberk and Andres Duany designed Seaside, on the Florida panhandle. Since then they have had a hand in designing numerous other communities, including the well-known Kentlands. The firm pioneered the development of form-based codes as an alternative to traditional zoning practices, developed a New Urbanist "Lexicon," and created a New Urbanist "Transect," which organizes development guidelines along a rural to urban continuum. Their own writings and writings about their work include Andres Duany and Elizabeth Plater-Zyberk, *Towns and Town-Making Principles*, edited by Alex Krieger with William Lennertz (New York: Rizzoli, 1991); Andres Duany, Elizabeth Plater-Zyberk, and Jeff Speck, *Suburban Nation: The Rise of Sprawl and the Decline of the American* Dream (New York:

North Point Press, 2000); and Andres Duany, Jeff Speck, and Mike Lydon, *The Smart Growth Manual* (New York: McGraw Hill, 2010). Peter Calthorpe focuses on regional planning and has been a leading advocate for "transit-oriented development." His book *The Next American Metropolis* (Princeton, NJ: Princeton Architectural Press, 1993) promotes clustering new developments at stops along transit lines and presents guidelines for achieving walkable, transit-oriented neighborhoods. His firm has developed the concept into a plan for the Metropolitan Portland region, and several new communities have been built, most notably Orenco Station. Peter Calthorpe's recent book *Urbanism in the Age of Climate Change* (Washington, DC: Island Press, 2011) looks at how regionally scaled urbanism can be combined with green technology to address climate change issues. Dan Solomon and his firm have designed numerous urban infill projects in San Francisco, the Bay Area, and elsewhere. Solomon writes eloquently about the shortcomings of modern architectural practice and design education in his book *Global City Blues* (Washington, DC: Island Press, 2003). In Britain, notable proponents of the New Urbanism include Great Britain's Prince Charles, who has promoted its concepts through the Prince of Wales Institute. In Europe, the most influential advocates are architects Leon and Rob Krier, who have produced many designs for new city neighborhoods.

Writings on the New Urbanism include Ellen Dunham-Jones and June Williamson, *Retrofitting Suburbia* (Hoboken, NJ: John Wiley & Sons, 2011); Philip Langdon, *New Urbanism Best Practices Guide* (Ithaca, NY: New Urban News, 2009); Tigran Haas (ed.), *New Urbanism and Beyond: Designing Cities for the Future* (New York: Rizzoli, 2008); Douglas Faar, *Sustainable Urbanism* (Hoboken, NJ: Wiley, 2008); Jill Grant, *Planning the Good Community: New Urbanism in Theory and Practice* (New York: Routledge, 2008); Emily Talen, *New Urbanism and American Planning* (New York: Routledge, 2005); Peter Katz, *The New Urbanism: Toward an Architecture of Community* (New York: McGraw-Hill, 1994); and Todd W. Bressi (ed.), *The Seaside Institute, The Seaside Debates: A Critique of the New Urbanism* (New York: Rizzoli, 2002).

Writings on the techniques of New Urbanism include Daniel G. Parolek, Karen Parolek, and Paul C. Crawford, *Form Based Codes: A Guide for Planners, Designers, Municipalities and Developers* (Hoboken, NJ: John Wiley & Sons, 2008); and David Walters, *Designing Community: Charrettes, Masterplans and Form-Based Codes* (Oxford: Architectural Press Elsevier, 2007).

For more information on the Ahwahnee Principles, see the Local Government Commission's website (http://www.lgc.org/ahwahnee/principles.html). The Congress for the New Urbanism's website provides information about New Urbanist activities and available publications (http://www.cnu.org/).

THE CONGRESS FOR THE NEW URBANISM views disinvestment in central cities, the spread of placeless sprawl, increasing separation by race and income, environmental deterioration, loss of agricultural lands and wilderness, and the erosion of society's built heritage as one interrelated community-building challenge.

WE STAND for the restoration of existing urban centers and towns within coherent metropolitan regions, the reconfiguration of sprawling suburbs into communities of real neighborhoods and diverse districts, the conservation of natural environments, and the preservation of our built legacy.

WE RECOGNIZE that physical solutions by themselves will not solve social and economic problems, but neither can economic vitality, community stability, and environmental health be sustained without a coherent and supportive physical framework.

WE ADVOCATE the restructuring of public policy and development practices to support the following principles: neighborhoods should be diverse in use and population; communities should be designed for the pedestrian and transit as well as the car; cities and towns should be shaped by physically defined and universally accessible public spaces and community institutions; urban places should be framed by architecture and landscape design that celebrate local history, climate, ecology, and building practice.

WE REPRESENT a broad-based citizenry, composed of public and private sector leaders, community activists, and multidisciplinary professionals. We are committed to reestablishing the relationship between the art of building and the making of community, through citizen-based participatory planning and design.

WE DEDICATE ourselves to reclaiming our homes, blocks, streets, parks, neighborhoods, districts, towns, cities, regions, and environment.

We assert the following principles to guide public policy, development practice, urban planning, and design:

The region: metropolis, city, and town

1 Metropolitan regions are finite places with geographic boundaries derived from topography, watersheds, coastlines, farmlands, regional parks, and river basins. The metropolis is made of multiple centers that are cities, towns, and villages, each with its own identifiable center and edges.

2 The metropolitan region is a fundamental economic unit of the contemporary world. Governmental cooperation, public policy, physical planning, and economic strategies must reflect this new reality.

3 The metropolis has a necessary and fragile relationship to its agrarian hinterland and natural landscapes. The relationship is environmental, economic, and cultural. Farmland and nature are as important to the metropolis as the garden is to the house.

4 Development patterns should not blur or eradicate the edges of the metropolis. Infill development within existing urban areas conserves environmental resources, economic investment, and social fabric, while reclaiming marginal and abandoned areas. Metropolitan regions should develop strategies to encourage such infill development over peripheral expansion.

5 Where appropriate, new development contiguous to urban boundaries should be organized as neighborhoods and districts, and be integrated with the existing urban pattern. Noncontiguous development should be organized as towns and villages with their own urban edges, and planned for a jobs/housing balance, not as bedroom suburbs.

6 The development and redevelopment of towns and cities should respect historical patterns, precedents, and boundaries.

7 Cities and towns should bring into proximity a broad spectrum of public and private uses to support a regional economy that benefits people of all incomes. Affordable housing should be distributed throughout the region to match job opportunities and to avoid concentrations of poverty.

8 The physical organization of the region should be supported by a framework of transportation alternatives. Transit, pedestrian, and bicycle systems should maximize access and mobility throughout the region while reducing dependence upon the automobile.

9 Revenues and resources can be shared more cooperatively among the municipalities and centers within regions to avoid destructive competition for tax base and to promote rational coordination of transportation, recreation, public services, housing, and community institutions.

The neighborhood, the district, and the corridor

1 The neighborhood, the district, and the corridor are the essential elements of development and redevelopment in the metropolis. They form identifiable areas that encourage citizens to take responsibility for their maintenance and evolution.

2 Neighborhoods should be compact, pedestrian-friendly, and mixed-use. Districts generally emphasize a special single use, and should follow the principles of neighborhood design when possible. Corridors are regional connectors of neighborhoods and districts; they range from boulevards and rail lines to rivers and parkways.

3 Many activities of daily living should occur within walking distance, allowing independence to those who do not drive, especially the elderly and the young. Interconnected networks of streets should be designed to encourage walking, reduce the number and length of automobile trips and conserve energy.

4 Within neighborhoods a broad range of housing types and price levels can bring people of diverse ages, races, and incomes into daily interaction strengthening the personal and civic bonds essential to an authentic community.

5 Transit corridors, when properly planned and coordinated, can help organize metropolitan structure and revitalize urban centers. In contrast, highway corridors should not displace investment from existing centers.

6 Appropriate building densities and land uses should be within walking distance of transit stops, permitting public transit to become a viable alternative to the automobile.

7 Concentrations of civic, institutional, and commercial activity should be embedded in neighborhoods and districts, not isolated in remote, single-use complexes. Schools should be sized and located to enable children to walk or bicycle to them.

8 The economic health and harmonious evolution of neighborhoods, districts, and corridors can be improved through graphic urban design codes that serve as predictable guides for change.

9 A range of parks, from tot-lots and village greens to ballfields and community gardens, should be distributed within neighborhoods. Conservation areas and open lands should be used to define and connect different neighborhoods and districts.

The block, the street, and the building

1 A primary task of all urban architecture and landscape design is the physical definition of streets and public spaces as places of shared use.

2 Individual architectural projects should be seamlessly linked to their surroundings. This issue transcends style.

3 The revitalization of urban places depends on safety and security. The design of streets and buildings should reinforce safe environments, but not at the expense of accessibility and openness.

4 In the contemporary metropolis, development must adequately accommodate automobiles. It should do so in ways that respect the pedestrian and the form of public space.

5 Streets and squares should be safe, comfortable, and interesting to the pedestrian. Properly configured, they encourage walking and enable neighbors to know each other and protect their communities.

6 Architecture and landscape design should grow from local climate, topography, history, and building practice.

7 Civic buildings and public gathering places require important sites to reinforce community identity and the culture of democracy. They deserve distinctive form, because their role is different from that of other buildings and places that constitute the fabric of the city.

8 All buildings should provide their inhabitants with a clear sense of location, weather and time. Natural methods of heating and cooling can be more resource-efficient than mechanical systems.

9 Preservation and renewal of historic buildings, districts, and landscape affirm the continuity and evolution of urban society.

"Themes of Postmodern Urbanism"

from *Postmodern Urbanism* (1996)

Nan Ellin

Editors' Introduction

The postmodern era of the late twentieth century is a highly debated topic among academics, not just as historic periodization but also as an identifiable design movement (which many say continues today). To some chroniclers, postmodernism is the cultural expression associated with a very specific period of time beginning in the 1950s, through the turn of the century. The cultural work of this period includes a wide range of fields, including: literature, linguistics, philosophy, sociology, religion, history, music, and anthropology. Postmodern social movements and characteristics are well known: feminism, post-structuralism, pluralism, cultural relativism, and the end of paradigmatic meta-narratives. The postmodern here refers to a continuing critique of Enlightenment attitudes that challenge dominant structures of modernism, science and theology. To others, such as Frederic Jameson and David Harvey, the postmodern is synonymous with the period of late capitalism, often associated with consumer perspectives, globalization, neo-Marxism, and multinational corporate interests.

Within the built environment professions, the postmodern period is associated with both discontentment and rejection of modern design and planning practices – but also a design movement that championed improved communication of design intentions, humor-irony-camp-kitsch, and the rebirth of place-based contextualism. Some of the discontented include a list of now-famous authors and designers associated with the history of urban design, including: Jane Jacobs, Christopher Alexander, Robert Venturi and Denise Scott Brown, Colin Rowe, Edward Relph, the CNU, and Douglas Kelbaugh (all represented in this volume). With reference to the built environment professions, postmodern debates continue and become intensified, as many practitioners seek to distance themselves from comparisons and connotations to built works from the early years of the movement, including some very shallow and ill-appreciated projects, for example, the Piazza d'Italia in New Orleans, or any number of dated office buildings, museums, or libraries with thinly applied decoration. The great chronicler of this movement within the design professions is Charles Jencks in his 1977 publication, *The Language of Postmodern Architecture* (New York: Rizzoli).

In a literary tour-de-force, Nan Ellin's *Postmodern Urbanism* has become one of the more important texts describing the postmodern period. What Jencks does for postmodern architecture, Ellin does for postmodern urban design and urbanism. Describing the key elements of the postmodern reflex, as well as its European and Anglo-American branches, she provides a comprehensive synthesis of a complex history, which she manages to make highly accessible. In early chapters she reviews the various design characteristics and larger theoretical attributes of the postmodern period of the 1960s to 1990s, while in later chapters she situates postmodern urban design within the professions, provides objective critique, and looks to the future. The central chapter in which she describes the themes, critiques, and outcomes of postmodern urbanism is presented here in an abridged form, providing the key lessons from the beginning and end of the chapter.

For Ellin, "postmodern urbanism" is defined relative to the previous modernism: first, by a return to historicism and a renewed search for urbanity; second, by a new emphasis on contextualism, regionalism, site/place, pluralism, and the search for character and populism; third, by the renewed use of decoration, ornamentation, symbolism, humor, collage, and human scale (among others); and fourth, by a humble and anti-utopian apoliticism that no longer seeks ideal solutions on a large scale. Postmodern urban design is associated with characteristics of small-scale, legible and neo-traditional projects that cater to consumer tastes and involve citizen participation (to name a few of its key elements). In assessing the postmodern urban she illustrates four different critical stances from which we might peer more deeply into its reality: *Form Follows Fiction*; *Form Follows Fear*; *Form Follows Finesse*; and *Form Follows Finance*. These are summarized below. At the end of the reading she considers the positive contributions of postmodern urbanism and how it might be morphing to address more serious concerns and correct its past infatuations with nostalgia and the inauthentic.

With respect to *Form Following Fiction*, she presents postmodern urbanism's enchantment with the pre-industrial past, the use of irony, nostalgia, facadism, and the romanticizing of history; a history which rarely corresponds "to contemporary needs and tastes," such as desires for speed, efficiency, nuisance-free living and convenience. In re-creating the facades of previous eras, postmodern designers sampled from a variety of styles, materials, and histories to emphasize appearance and aesthetics, regardless of their inappropriateness with respect to context, geography, or semiotics. This first critique suggests that postmodern urbanism can all too easily devolve into kitsch, inauthenticity, and sentimentality based on the simulation of set pieces from other times.

The second critique involves the decline of the public realm, the increasing prevalence of physical controls, surveillance, and policing, and the growing privatization of public space due to *Form Following Fear*. She attributes this to the triumph of individualism in western society, the corresponding increase of single-family dwellings and gated communities, and the growing importance of the home – relative to the decline of public life. Privatization also takes a corporate face in the controlled and policed spaces of the shopping mall, theme park, office complex, and new town development. Accompanying these is the decline of public space in the city, attributable to both fear in the city (associated with perceptions of crime, the ghetto, poverty and the "other") and many cities' neglect and poor maintenance of these spaces. Here postmodern urbanism has become a language of security, which includes the privatization and control suggested above, but also the use of comfortable neo-traditional trappings.

Ellin's critique of *Form Following Finesse* is the most difficult to grasp, dealing with elite concerns for aesthetics, semiotics, and political neutrality. Postmodern urbanism is viewed here as a narcissistic undertaking of architects engaging in "archi-speak" among themselves, producing work for the sake of image and fame, and a preoccupation with aesthetics rather than solving social problems. Ellin points out the economically regressive nature of some postmodern projects (despite their use of progressive planning and design theories) that, indeed, make the city less affordable and less accessible to moderate income residents. With respect to the social critiques and idealism apparent in modernism, postmodern urbanism abandons most discussions of politics, critical social theory, or political economy.

The final critique, *Form Following Finance*, suggests that because of the apolitical stance of many designers, postmodern urbanism exacerbates existing urban inequalities and reinforces corporate capitalist agendas. Because of its populist nature, postmodern design may in fact be promoting enhanced opportunities for consumption and profit-making. The adaptive reuse of historic buildings, the rise of the festival marketplace, the growth of themed resorts, and the prevalent post-industrial redevelopment formula (cineplexes, food courts, entertainment, bookstores, stadia, malls, and museums) all suggest an increasing commercialization of urban development and the importance of market forces in the postmodern urban.

Nan Ellin is an urban theorist, Professor and Chair of the Department of City and Metropolitan Planning at the University of Utah in Salt Lake City. Having also taught at Arizona State University, she teaches urban design, urbanism, community building, and place-making. In her writing she advances ideas about sustainable urbanism and collaborative engagement with communities. Her work in Phoenix, Arizona has helped to leverage interest in reuse of the city's vast and under-utilized canal network. In addition to *Postmodern Urbanism* (New York: Princeton Architectural Press, 1999), she is the author of *Integral Urbanism* (London: Routledge,

2006); *Phoenix: 21ˢᵗ Century City*, with Edward Booth-Clibborn (London: Booth-Clibborn Editions, 2006); "The Tao of Urbanism," in Stephen Goldsmith and Lynne Elizabeth (eds), *What We See: Advancing the Investigations of Jane Jacobs* (Oakland, CA: New Village Press, 2010); and *Good Urbanism* (London: Routledge, forthcoming). She is also the editor of *Architecture of Fear* (New York: Princeton Architectural Press, 1997). She holds a PhD from Columbia University and was a Fulbright Scholar in France, where she studied European New Urbanism.

Theoretical works on the concepts, history, and critiques of postmodernism include: Jean-François Lyotard, *The Postmodern Condition* (Manchester: Manchester University Press, 1984); Frederic Jameson, *Postmodernism or the Cultural Logic of Late Capitalism* (Durham, NC: Duke University Press, 1984); David Harvey, *The Condition of Postmodernity: An Enquiry into the Origins of Cultural Change* (Oxford: Blackwell, 1989); Edward W. Soja, *Postmodern Geographies: The Reassertion of Space in Critical Social Theory* (London: Verso, 1989); Mike Featherstone, *Undoing Culture: Globalization, Postmodernism and Modernity* (London: Sage, 1995); David Lyon, *Postmodernity*, 2nd edn. (Minneapolis, MN: University of Minnesota Press, 1999); Michael J. Dear, *The Postmodern Urban Condition* (Oxford: Blackwell, 2000); Christopher Butler, *Postmodernity: A Very Short Introduction* (New York/Oxford: Oxford University Press, 2003); Jim Powell, *Postmodernism for Beginners* (Danbury, CT: For Beginners Books, 2007); and Stuart Sim (ed.) *The Routledge Companion to Postmodernism* (London: Routledge, 2011).

Classic texts on postmodern design, urbanism, and planning include: Charles Jencks, *The Language of Postmodern Architecture* (New York: Rizzoli, 1977); Robert Venturi, Denise Scott Brown, and Steven Izenour, *Learning from Las Vegas: The Forgotten Symbolism of Architectural Form* (Cambridge, MA: MIT Press, 1977); Tom Wolfe, *From Bauhaus to Our House* (New York: Farrar Strauss Giroux, 1980); Michael J. Dear, "Postmodernism and Planning," *Environment and Planning D: Society and Space* (vol. 4, pp. 367–384, 1986); Sharon Zukin, "The Postmodern Debate over Urban Form," *Theory, Culture, Society* (vol. 5, nos. 2–3, pp. 431–446, 1988); Michael J. Dear, "The Premature Demise of Postmodern Urbanism," *Cultural Anthropology* (vol. 6, no. 4, pp. 538–552, 1991); Michael Sorkin (ed.), *Variations on a Theme Park: The New American City and the End of Public Space* (New York: Noonday Press, 1992); John Urry, *Consuming Places* (London: Routledge, 1995); Mark Gottdiener, *The Theming of America: Dreams, Visions, and Commercial Spaces* (New Haven, CT: Yale University Press, 1997); Charlene Spretnak, *The Resurgence of the Real: Body, Nature and Place in a Hypermodern World* (London: Routledge, 1997); Philip Allmendinger, "Planning Practice and the Post-Modern Debate," *International Planning Studies* (vol. 3, no. 2, pp. 227–248, 1998) and *Planning in Postmodern Times* (London: Routledge / RTPI Library Series, 2001); John Hannigan, *Fantasy City: Pleasure and Profit in the Postmodern Metropolis* (London: Routledge, 1998); and David Grahame Shane, *Urban Design Since 1945: A Global Perspective* (New York: Wiley, 2011).

The reactions to modernist architecture and planning can be mapped along two axes, one indicating the formal ambitions of urban designers and the other the ways in which they perceive their role [Figure 1]. These axes meet at the point where urban designers aspire to realize their personal artistic and financial ambitions, with little or no theoretical justification entering the mix, and the axes diverge along the designers' respective theoretical paths. The formal ambition axis moves from producing good and beautiful built forms to drawing inspiration from mass culture, the social context, the site, and the past. The urban designer's role axis proceeds from the business-person and artist to the facilitator, political activist, and social engineer. Although the reactions to modernist architecture and planning might be mapped along these axes, such an exercise would ultimately reveal little since theory is often a mask or justification for personal ambitions or vice versa.

Rather than chart the rhetoric of these various approaches, then, this chapter peers beyond it, by reviewing and assessing the major themes which fall along the axes of postmodern urbanism as inscribed within the larger postmodern reflex. These overlapping themes include contextualism, historicism,

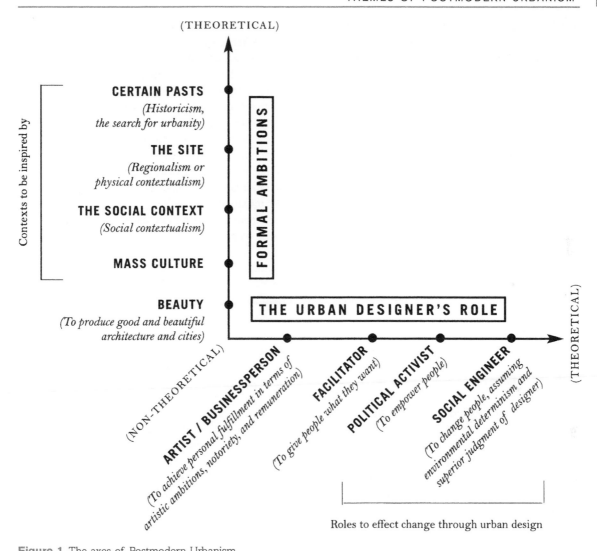

Figure 1 The axes of Postmodern Urbanism.

the search for urbanity, regionalism, antiuniversalism, pluralism, collage, self-referentiality, reflexivity, preoccupation with image/decor/scenography, superficiality, depthlessness, ephemerality, fragmentation, populism, apoliticism, commercialism, loss of faith, and irony. The critique of postmodern urbanism advanced in this chapter is organized as follows: Form Follows Fiction; Form Follows Fear; Form Follows Finesse; Form Follows Finance; and The Result. The concluding section, On Balance, presents certain correctives of postmodern urbanism as well as promising initiatives that have emerged in the 1990s.

The challenge to the modern project and the decline of the public realm to which modern urban-

ism was accomplice called for new responses from urban designers. Whereas "modernism from the 1910s to the 1960s . . . responded to the challenge of establishing social order for a mass society; postmodernism since the 1960s . . . responded to the challenge of placelessness and a need for urban community" (Ley 1987, 40). In contrast to modern urbanism's insistence upon structural honesty and functionality, postmodern urbanism sought to satisfy needs that were not merely functional and to convey meanings other than the building tectonics. In architectural theory, Ada Louise Huxtable observed, there was "a search for meaning and symbolism, a way to establish architecture's ties with human experience, a way to find and express a value system, a concern for architecture in the context of society" (Huxtable 1981a, 73–74).

As modernism's minimalist tendencies grew ever more stifling, urban designers embraced maximalism and inclusivity, as expressed in the maxims "Less is a bore" (Venturi 1966) and "More is more" (Stern in Williams 1985). The parallel shift occurring in literature is evocatively portrayed by the protagonist in John Barth's *Tidewater Tales* (1986), a writer whose increasingly minimalist style ultimately blocks his ability to write or dream until circumstances (including the birth of his first child) reignite his creative juices, this time in a maximalist form. Likewise in urban design theory, universalism and purism were gradually supplanted by pluralism and contextualism while the role of the urban designer shifted from that of inspired genius, artist, or social engineer to that of a more humble, and at times servile, facilitator.

[. . .]

THE RESULT

A principal feature of postmodern urbanism is contextualism (historical, physical, social, and mass cultural), in contrast to modern urbanism's break from the past and the site. When contextualism is achieved in urban design, it is usually appreciated (successful) unless somehow inappropriate or regarded by the users as a patronizing gesture. In most cases, however, contextualism is not achieved, because of economic and political constraints, the invention of histories, shortcomings of urban designers (who may only be paying lip service to contextualism while pursuing more personal goals), and other reasons. In short, these goals usually prove elusive owing to urban designers' ironic failure to acknowledge the larger contexts in which they build. When contextualism is not achieved, the urban design initiative is usually not appreciated (unsuccessful), except in certain instances where people believe a place is historically, physically, or socially contextual (even if it is not) or don't care because the place succeeds for other reasons such as the standard of living it offers, its prestige, and/or its location.

The contextual attempts to gain inspiration from the site, the social context, and mass culture have more in common with attempts to gain inspiration from the past than may initially appear to be the case. Indeed, they converge where urban design draws from a fictionalized and mediamassaged past or vernacular.[1] Like the historicist tendency, these others betray a sense of insecurity and/or confusion and suggest a desire for self-affirmation, self-expression, self-discovery, and "rootedness." And like historicism, these efforts also tend to be more rhetorical than real, largely because their premises contain denials and because the formulation and implementation of these agendas by elites subvert their initial claims. We might say that postmodern urban form follows fiction, finesse, fear, and finance as well as function. But then so did modern urban form.

Ultimately, despite its efforts to counter the negative aspects of modern urbanism, postmodern urbanism falls into many of the same traps. Despite its eagerness to counter the human insensitivity of modern urbanism, postmodern urbanism's preoccupation with surface treatments and irony makes it equally guilty of neglecting the human component. By denying transformations that have taken place, postmodern urbanism may even be accentuating the most criticized elements of modern urbanism such as the emphasis on formal considerations and elitism. Ingersoll has asserted:

> To project a return to a "traditional" city and with it a future of "neovillagers" may be more of a fantasy than any science-fiction vision of a society dominated by robots. If the urban process is confined to aesthetic criteria alone, the social consequences, such as the elimination of emancipatory demands from the urban program, may be as unpleasant as those wrought by the functionalist fallacies of the postwar period . . . It is as if *urbs*, the bound city form of the past, could be considered without *civitas*, the social agreement to share that lost urban promised land.
>
> (Ingersoll 1989a, 21)[2]

As Clarke has said, although its agenda suggests an antithesis, "postmodernism has a legacy from modernism it has yet to contradict" (Clarke 1989, 13). Although architects "may no longer be talking of the unadorned cube as the aesthetic model," he contends, their works are still divorced from the larger context, particularly social, in which they are situated (ibid.). Although this style may look different on the surface, it is just as fragmented as what it pretends to be criticizing, because flexible accumulation favors urban design interventions which distinguish themselves, thereby mitigating against contextualism.[3] The modernist refusal to acknowledge context, as epitomized in the reflecting glass wall (see Jameson 1984; Holston 1989; Harvey 1989, 88), might be interpreted as a refusal to acknowledge the emergent mass culture and culture of consumption.[4] But postmodern urbanism's continued denial of the conditions of a mass society, despite its efforts to acknowledge them through contextualism, merely exacerbates the problems of modern urbanism. This denial is epitomized by certain postmodernists' refusal to build any physical structure or place, only to design or theorize. Although justified as a form of resistance, this informed choice only perpetuates the conditions they oppose (Dutton 1986, 23).

ON BALANCE

While much ink has been spilled on pronouncing the banes of postmodern urbanism (along with postmodernism generally), there is also widespread sentiment that it offers a number of correctives to that which preceded it. Indeed, Relph has suggested that these reactions to modern urbanism have ushered in "a quiet revolution in how cities are made and maintained" with the result that "repressive architecture and planning by great corporate or government bureaucracies is being replaced by more sensitive and varied alternatives" (Relph 1987, 215; see Mangin 1985; Muschamp 1994b).

Although historicism can be "essentially elitist, esoteric, and distant" (Clarke and Dutton 1986, 2) and can devolve into kitsch, it can also provide a sense of security and "rootedness" when judiciously applied, as in the reconstruction of European central cities (Gleye 1983). The potentially creative component of borrowing from the past is suggested by folklorist Barbara Kirshenblatt-Gimblett, who maintains that "traditionalizing" or "restoring" (Kirshenblatt-Gimblett 1983, 208) is a universal behavior which entails a process of giving form and meaning by referring to something old while creating "new contexts, audiences, and meanings for the forms" (Kirshenblatt-Gimblett, 211).[5]

Other contextualisms have also succeeded to some extent in achieving an urbanism that is meaningful to more people (i.e. a more pluralistic urbanism). Efforts to design in a physically contextual manner have, for the most part, been an antidote to the modernist emphasis on the architectural object and disregard for the site. Its close cousin, regionalism, has also proven to be a welcome departure from the high modernist contempt for existing styles even though, like historicism, it may appear as a caricatured, mass-produced travesty of the regional context, and/or a neocolonialist undertaking (by developers, technocrats, and urban designers) to prevent the "natives" from becoming more cosmopolitan (like the earlier French colonial urban design).

Residential design in postmodern urbanism offers certain advantages over that of modernism. The Athens Charter maintained that instead of connected low-rise housing lining the streets, housing should be provided in high-rise buildings located in the center of large lots away from streets and from each other in order to maximize open green space and natural light in the homes. Secondly, it maintained that these buildings should be raised onto *pilotis* to open up views from the ground and endow large buildings with a sense of lightness. Finally, it recommended that roofs be flat to offer additional living space. Urban design theory since the 1960s reverses each of these tenets, with towers and slabs (*tours* and *barres*) giving way to houses and apartment buildings and with superblocks supplanted by city blocks (*îlôts*). These changes have been applauded for providing a more human scale, offering more personalized and personalizable living spaces, and adding visual interest to the landscape.[6]

Concerted efforts to create high-quality public spaces have also produced some welcome results. In many instances, the "return to the street" from the shopping mall has been successful in bringing vitality back to street life. Increased attention to the provision of traditional public space – parks, plazas, and squares – as well as to landscaping, has offered an antidote to the privatization and concreting of urban settings. Likewise, the effort to design "mixed-use" projects has provided an antidote to modernism's rigid and anti-urban separation of functions.

And while hyperreal environments may be criticized for being artificial, it can be argued that it is precisely that quality which people like about them. Accused of distracting people from the injustices and ugliness of their lives, of placating them, and of being places of "spectacle and surveillance" (as in Harvey's criticism of Baltimore's Inner Harbor, 1989), hyperreal environments might also be applauded for the diversion they offer, for simply providing places in which people can relax and have fun in the company of family and friends.[7] Other beneficial aspects of these environments are the vast multipliers they create in the local economy (Ley and Mills 1993). And for urban designers, themed environments remain one of the few major opportunities to give full rein to their powers of creative expression.

The critique of postmodern urbanism as enhancing settings for consumption is a double-edged sword that really boils down to a critique of consumption. While critics of mass society highlight the extent to which the market dictates our sense of identity, forces us to consume, and exacerbates social inequalities, others point out the market's potential for empowerment since we can personalize or resist that which it offers us. There is no question that people worldwide prefer abundance over scarcity, full shelves over empty ones, and that they vindicate their "right" to select from a variety of options along with their "freedom" to shop. As Ley and Mills have pointed out, "Access to goods (as basic as bread) is as much a facet of democratization as free elections and guarantees for the rights of the marginalized. [The] hardback editions for the few become the paperback editions for the many" (Ley and Mills 1993, 271). And as long as we are going to shop, why not do so in a pleasant environment?

While the preservation movement may be criticized for inventing histories (and therefore not really preserving anything) and for advancing the interests of certain elites, the valorization it bespeaks of the existing urban fabric (including industrial and commercial landscapes) represents a welcome corrective to modernism's obsession with forgetting the past and starting over on a clean slate. It also suggests a valorization of cultural traditions and of cultural differences that was largely absent from modern urbanism. Indeed, many developers would say we have gone overboard in this direction as local communities' attachment to existing forms and nostalgia for the past leads them to rally behind saving every fast-food restaurant in their neighborhood.

And while movements to "preserve" nature or wildlife may sometimes be thinly veiled attempts to preserve the intimacy of one's community as well as land values, no one would deny the importance of designing in harmony with nature. The growing sensitivity towards the environment represents a great advance in contemporary urban design theory, expressed in terms of "growth management" or "sustainable design." Such theory and practice focuses on design intervention that does not deplete any natural resources or impose hardship upon any people, and preferably enhances the environment and living conditions.[8]

Most of the more exemplary recent urban design initiatives are engaged in healing scars left by interventions of the modern era, when the building of railroads and highways was undertaken with little consideration for the surrounding communities and natural landscapes. Much of this work has to do with re-using abandoned transit corridors, designing new ones, and redesigning existing fabrics both urban and suburban, sometimes in collaboration with local communities. While sharing the emphasis on enhancing the public realm with the neotraditionalists, this tendency is not necessarily intent upon emulating past townscapes, but considers instead contemporary lifestyles and preferences and aspires to retain the valuable elements of modern urbanism and architecture.

And rather than direct its focus to the traditional center, this tendency is more often concerned with the edge between the city, suburb, and countryside; between neighborhoods; and between functional uses, as well as the more metaphorical edges between disciplines, professions, and local communities. In its more extreme versions, it even champions the elimination of the traditional center, which brings with it old social inequalities. Speaking generally (not about urban design specifically), Hal Foster describes this as a "postmodernism of resistance" or "reaction" entailing "a critique of origins, not a return to them" (Foster 1983, vii).

Rather than preserve, renovate, or create a center or a past, this urban design theory holds that we should focus attention on the edge/periphery/border with an eye towards the future. Acknowledging that most biological activity occurs in nature where different zones meet, for instance, Richard

Sennett maintains that "urban design has similarly to focus on the edge as a scene of life" (Sennett 1994, 69). Sensitive to the fragmentation of the built environment as well as among the urban design professions and between these and their constituents, then, designers have been increasingly setting themselves the task of "mending seams."[9]

In Western Europe, ironically, the concerted search for urbanity and the creation of centrality has been largely played out on urban wings rather than on center stage, as suburbs increasingly become the site for urbanization, immigration, and government subsidy for building. Consequently, many architects and planners began adapting these ideas to the building of satellite cities, industrial re-use, and the reorganization of suburban sprawl, as exemplified by the French program *Banlieues '89*, launched in 1985. Carriers of the modern torch also turned their gaze to suburbs because, as François Barre maintained,[10] "Classic urbanity loses its logic there ... but modernity finds without a doubt a great many promising departures" (in Nouvel 1980, 17). Barre asserted,

> it is on the periphery that urban development is now taking place. The notion of center itself is dissolving ... If the suburbs interest people today, it is precisely because of the wild production there which does not refer to any model but instead to a sort of superposition or collage ... It is without doubt the most faithful representation of the present time ... The suburb offers an accumulation of modesty and a slightly wild abundance ... ; this reality expresses itself more through music, film, and the city than any thing one could find in architecture.
>
> (Barre 1985, 54–55)

And the way one assesses the situation, he reminds us, depends on one's perspective, both geographical and ideological: "Things look different depending on whether you look at them from the periphery or the center" (Barre 1985, 54).

Architects of all persuasions, then, grew interested in designing on the edges of cities, including Krier (Berlin project), Rossi (1991, Berlin project), Rem Koolhaas (Euralille), and Steven Holl (1991, projects for American cities). The apotheosis of this attention to the edge and to integrating functionalist tenets with the traditional city is found in

the restructuring of the Barcelona waterfront, as overseen by the architect Oriol Bohígas.[11] With this renewed focus on the periphery, Donald Olsen suggests, the central city "may revert to its preindustrial role as a work of art, designed for ostentation rather than for use, a symbol of prestige, a center of specialized consumption, a place to indulge in luxurious vice, to spend money made elsewhere" (Olsen 1983, 266). Or, this interest in the periphery may be symptomatic of the growing irrelevance of distinctions between the city, the suburb, and the countryside and between urbanism and suburbanism as ways of life, as foreseen by Marx (1858), Arthur Schlesinger (1940), and Herbert Gans (1962).

The mending of seams has been central to a number of recent urban design initiatives in North America, as apparent, for instance, in the re-use of transit corridors. Landscape architect and urban designer Diana Balmori has proposed building a light rail system and green way on the site of an abandoned canal and rail line connecting New Haven to the center of Connecticut and the Massachusetts border, to create a corridor that unites segregated communities and enhances pedestrian ways (E. Smith 1994, 7). The Greenway Plan for Metropolitan Los Angeles similarly centers on revitalizing 400 miles of abandoned rail and infrastructure rights-of-way as well as river and flood control channels (E. Smith, 6).[12] And in Boston, where a tunnel is being substituted for the expressway which disrupted a formerly vibrant lower-middle-class neighborhood, Alex Krieger proposed restoring the urban fabric and interweaving it with open spaces in an effort to resonate with the past but also consider current and future uses (E. Smith, 7).[13]

The re-use of abandoned transit lines has been greatly assisted by the Rails-to-Trails Conservancy (RTC), a national nonprofit organization created in 1988 to assist local activists around the United States in converting abandoned railroad corridors into public "linear parks," also called rail-trails or rails-with-trails (Ryan and Winterich 1993; Ryan 1993). With a nationwide membership in 1994 of 60,000, RTC had conducted 13 assessment studies around the country and almost 1,000 miles of trails had been constructed, with others in progress. Studies of rail-trails in Baltimore, Seattle, and the East Bay of San Francisco reported that properties adjacent to the trails sold better than before the trails were built and that the trails also generate economic activity for the communities through which they pass (LAING 1994).

The design of new transportation hubs and corridors is another instance of healing scars and mending seams. A number of proposals for subway and light rail stations for the Los Angeles metropolitan area, for example, aspire to retain that which the local community values while providing that which it desires. Johnson Fain and Pereira Associates devised a plan for a Chatsworth station which includes a replica of the historic Chatsworth Station, a child-care center, and other civic and commercial services, all linked to the natural landscape by pedestrian and bicycle paths (E. Smith, 6). For a more urban site, Koning Eisenberg Architects proposed a station in Hollywood which would retain the small scale of the residential blocks while providing market stalls clustered around the station along with a larger mercado, and necessary housing (including a single-room occupancy hotel) over shops at street level, all in an effort to enhance the neighborhood identity. California-based architects Marc Angélil and Sarah Graham sought to create a center for the town of Esslingen, Switzerland by clustering shops, offices, and housing around a railroad station, all heated and cooled by an extensive system of solar energy (E. Smith, 11). And in a plan for a highway corridor for the small town of Chanhassen in Minnesota, the architect William Morrish and landscape architect Catherine Brown aspired to retain the small-town character which its inhabitants valued, preserve the natural environment, and integrate the new road into the community rather than allow it to divide and conquer the community (Muschamp, 1994a).[14]

A final emergent trend to note is the effort to go beyond shaping the physical environment, to also affect changes in public policy and in public opinion regarding the potential value of urban design. Along with DPZ and Calthorpe, Morrish and Brown are also engaged in these efforts, as demonstrated by their 1987 master plan for the public art program in Phoenix, which "used art as a bridge between the public and those who make public policy" (Muschamp 1994a) and in two more recent efforts in Minneapolis, one to create jobs while also providing a series of small neighborhood parks at the Hennipin County Works, and the other to better integrate public housing with private-sector housing (ibid.).

A number of efforts to reclaim vacant lots for use by the surrounding neighborhoods also go beyond shaping the physical environment. The landscape architect Achva Benzinberg Stein, for instance, designed the Uhuru Garden in Watts, Los Angeles, to include gardens as well as facilities for instruction in gardening and for selling what is grown. Intended primarily for use by the local residents of a public housing project, students at the local public school, and members of a local drug rehabilitation center, this garden incorporates native California vegetation as well as indigenous irrigation techniques (E. Smith, 14). Other efforts to convert vacant lots into community gardens in South Central Los Angeles have been undertaken from the grassroots by the LA HOPE Horticulture Corps and the LA Regional Food Bank Garden.

In certain regards, then, we might consider contemporary urban design theory as the mature young adulthood emerging and benefiting from the mistakes of its rebellious modern adolescence.[15] To best seize this moment, however, the urban design professions must be vigilant.

NOTES

1 Joseph Rykwert contends that history is back, but

> It is a catalogue history, devoid of narration, in which the phenomenal past is digested to a set of timeless motifs on which the designer can call to deck out his project in a garb which will produce, so it is generally thought, the right kind of denotation response in the public. While market forces, the traffic engineer and the planning administrators operate as before, their sins are now covered by a skin of ornament borrowed from the history books.
>
> (Rykwert 1988, Preface)

2 Ingersoll's chilling question brings this home:

> Is it only coincidence that the exploded housing blocks of Pruitt-Igoe, the icons that have come to symbolize the end of modernism, were blown up in 1972, the same year

that the neutron bomb was unveiled as America's ultimate weapon?

(Ingersoll 1989, 21)

3 Clarke elaborates: "Flexible accumulation has become the mobilization of image – the employment of spectacle within the urban arena. Disneyland becomes an urban strategy" (Clarke 1989, 14). Disneyland presents seductive images, he says, but these

> seem alien and fragmented. While the style is new, the fragmentation is much like that of the previous architectural epoch. It occurs because symbolic capital must distinguish itself. It must define its edges to protect itself as both symbol and investment. As such it cannot be "infill" within the urban continuum [cannot be contextual], it has to be a separate event.
>
> (ibid.)

4 The Athens Charter (1933) has been criticized for insufficiently acknowledging the cultural, historical, or topographical contexts of cities. Rather than design with regards to contemporary contingencies, this de-contextual approach posited "an imagined future . . . as the critical ground in terms of which to evaluate the present" (Holston 1989, 9). As Holston maintains, this

> teleological view of history dispenses with a consideration of intervening actors and intentions, of their diverse sources and conflicts. Rather, the only kind of agency modernism considers in the making of history is the intervention of the prince (state head) and the genius (architect-planner).
>
> (ibid.)

A fatal contradiction of the Modern movement, then, inhered in the putative desire to help usher in a more egalitarian society alongside a conviction that the architect/planner is infallible and must have unlimited power.

5 "The impossibility of perfect or complete replication," Kirshenblatt-Gimblett says, "offers opportunities for innovation, for reflection about the relationship between the proposed 'original' and the restoration, between the past and the present" (Kirshenblatt-Gimblett 1983, 212).

6 These changes have been most apparent in the many new styles of public housing (for example, Moley (1979); Querrien (1985); Maitino and Sompairac (1986); Barbe and Duclent (1986)), even though less public housing has been built during this period than the modern one. These changes have also been apparent in the effort to generate "traditional neighborhood developments" or an "urbanism of houses."

7 Ley and Mills highlight these practices, "which escape the imputed social control of spectacle" (Ley and Mills 1993, 259). Even Harvey concedes that such environments might accomplish "the construction of some limited and limiting sense of identity in the midst of a collage of imploding spatialities" (Harvey 1989, 303–304).

8 An ACSA/AIA teachers' seminar on the theme of "Sustainability and Design" was held in May 1994.

9 This attention to the edge has nothing to do with the building of "edge cities," which instead of breaking down barriers, create new ones, and which are market-driven rather than the product of considered thought and action.

10 Barre was editor of *Architecture d'Aujourd'hui* before becoming Director of the Public Development Corporation of La Villette.

11 In addition to Bohígas, the other architects of the master plan for the Barcelona waterfront, called La Nova Icària, are Josep Martorell, David Mackay and Albert Puigdomènech. See Lampugnani (1991, 114–117) and Bohígas (1991, 119–123). Michael Rotondi, Director of the Southern California Institute of Architecture, has described this interest in edges saying,

> All the things talked about now . . . regardless of the title, are really about order and disorder, trying to understand the relationship of center to periphery . . . It has to do with the redefinition of centers as a result of astronomical discoveries.
>
> (in G. White 1988, 173)

Anthony Vidler has described the "posturban sensibility" saying, "the margins have entirely invaded the center and disseminated its focus" (1992, 186).

12 This plan was developed by Johnson Fain and Pereira Associates.

13 The Boston Planning Department ultimately decided to dedicate 75 percent of this corridor as open space, rather than adhere to Krieger's proposal for more built space (E. Smith 1994, 7).

14 Morrish directs the Design Center for American Urban Landscape in Minneapolis, Minnesota (founded in 1989), which emphasizes connections among people, built form, and nature, as well as among the design professions in the tradition of Frederick Law Olmsted. Other major influences on the Center's work include J.B. Jackson's emphasis on the integration of natural and human artifacts, Kevin Lynch's cognitive mapping, Ian McHarg's ecological planning, and earlier efforts at community participation (Muschamp 1994a).

15 Ada Louise Huxtable expresses this optimism, specifically with regards to architecture: "I have a feeling that when the scores are finally in and architects have stopped beating their father-figures and smashing icons, the art of architecture will have emerged into a new and very vital period," which she describes as "the natural if somewhat stormy evolution of modernism into something of much greater range and richness" (Huxtable 1981b, 104–105). Huxtable explains: "I see it as a much broadened phase of modernism – not as the undoing of modernism. I do not like the phrase post-modernism because it implies that something has been finished and replaced" (Huxtable 1981b, 104). In similar fashion, Lesnikowski interprets our misguided efforts as preparing the ground for more substantial and worthwhile change:

Undeniably the present developments in architectural thought – whether connected with promising consolidations of classicist attitudes or with the continuation of individualistic romantic postmodern attitudes, even if they are at the present shallow and naive – represent a necessary and unavoidable step in the direction of correcting modern architecture's mistakes, and this is why they are so encouraging and important.

(Lesnikowski 1982, 318)

BIBLIOGRAPHY

Barbe, Bernard and Alain Duclent. 1986. *Le Vécu de l'architecture. La Noiserai. (H. Ciriani), Les Arcades du Lac (R. Bofill), 135 rue do l'Ourcq, Paris 19e (Levy, Maison-Haute, Coutine).* Paris: Plan Construction.

Barre, François. 1985. *Banlieue et monumentalité.* Round table discussion in Esprit.

Barth, John. 1986. *Tidewater Tales.* New York: Putnam.

Bohígas, Oriol. 1991. 'Barcelona 1992,' *The New City: Foundations.* University of Miami School of Architecture. Fall 119–123.

Clarke, Paul Walker. 1989. 'The Economic Currency of Architectural Aesthetics: Modernism and Postmodernism in the Urbanism of Capitalism,' in M. Diani and C. Ingraham (eds), *Restructuring Architectural Theory.* Evanston, IL: Northwestern University.

Clarke, Paul Walker and Thomas A. Dutton. 1986. 'Notes toward a Critical Theory of Architecture,' *The Discipline of Architecture: Inquiry Through Design.* Proceedings of the 73rd ACSA Meetings, Washington DC.

Dutton, Thomas A. 1986. 'Toward an Architectural Praxis of Cultural Production: Beyond Leon Krier,' in J. William Carswell and David Saile (eds), *Purposes in Built Form and Culture Research.* Proceedings of Conference on Built Forms and Culture Research at the University of Kansas, 21–6.

Foster, Hal (ed.). 1983. *The Anti-Aesthetic.* Seattle: Bay Press.

Gans, Herbert. 1962. *The Urban Villagers.* Glencoe: Free Press.

Gleye, Paul Henry. 1983. *The Breath of History.* PhD Dissertation UCLA.

Harvey, David. 1989. *The Condition of Postmodernity.* Oxford: Blackwell.

Holston, James. 1989. *The Modernist City: An Anthropological Critique of Brasilia.* Chicago: University of Chicago Press.

Huxtable, Ada Louise. 1981a. 'The Troubled State of Modern Architecture,' *Architectural Record.* 169 (January): 72–79.

Huxtable, Ada Louise. 1981b. 'Is Modern Architecture Dead?' *Architectural Record.* 169 (October): 100–105.

Ingersoll, Richard. 1989. 'People without Housing and Cities without People. Postmodern Urbanism: Forward into the Past,' *Design Book Review.* 17 (Winter): 21–25.

Jameson, Fredric. 1984. 'Postmodernism, or the Cultural Logic of Late Capitalism,' *New Left Review*. 146, July–August: 52–92. Revised and expanded edition of 1983.

Kirshenblatt-Gimblett, Barbara. 1983. 'The Future of Folklore Studies in America: The Urban Frontier,' *Folklore Forum*. 16(2): 175–234.

LAING (Los Angeles Independent Newspaper Group). 1994. 'Study Pinpoints New Trail Opportunities in the L.A. Area,' *Los Angeles Independent Newspaper*. November 2: A, B1, B2, C.

Lampugnani, Vittorio Magnago. 1991. 'The City of Tolerance: Notes on Present Day Urban Design,' *The New City: Foundations*. University of Miami School of Architecture. Fall: 107–118.

Lesnikowski, Wojciech G. 1982. *Rationalism and Romanticism in Architecture*. New York: McGraw-Hill.

Ley, David. 1987. 'Styles of the Times: Liberal and Neo-conservative Landscapes in Inner Vancouver, 1968–1986,' *Journal of Historical Geography*. 13(1): 40–56.

Ley, David and Caroline Mills. 1993. 'Can There be a Postmodernism of Resistance in the Urban Landscape?' in Paul L. Knox (ed.), *The Restless Urban Landscape*. New York: Prentice-Hall, 255–278.

Maitino, Hilda and Arnaud Sompairac. 1986. *Formes urbaines et habitat social. 120 réalisations expérimentales du Plan Construction et Habitat (1978–1984)*. Paris: Plan Construction.

Mangin, David. 1985. 'L'architecture urbaine dans l'impasse,' *Architecture d'Aujourd'hui*. 240 (September).

Marx, Karl. 1973 [1858]. *Gundrisse: Foundations of the Critique of Political Economy*. New York: Vintage.

Moley, C. 1979. *L'Innovation architecturale dans la production du logement social*. Paris: Plan Construction.

Muschamp, Herbert. 1994a. 'Two for the Roads: A Vision of Urban Design,' *New York Times*. February 13: H1, H33.

Muschamp, Herbert. 1994b. 'Architecture as Social Action, and Vice Versa,' *New York Times*. February 27: H40.

Nouvel, Jean (compiler). 1980. *Biennale de Paris*. Paris: Academy Editions.

Olsen, Donald J. 1983. 'The City as a Work of Art,' in Derek Fraser and Anthony Sutcliffe (eds). *The Pursuit of Urban History*. London: Edward Arnold.

Querrien, Gwendael. 1985. 'Logement social 1950–1980,' *Bulletin d'Informations Architecturales*. Supplement. 95 (May).

Relph, Edward. 1987. *The Modern Urban Landscape*. Baltimore: Johns Hopkins University.

Rossi, Aldo, Josef Paul Kleihues, and Giorgio Grassi. 1991. 'Berlin Tomorrow: Potsdamer and Leipziker Platz,' *The New City: Foundations*. Fall: 1, 124–131.

Ryan, Karen-Lee (ed.). 1993. *Trails for the Twenty-First Century*. Washington DC: Island Press.

Ryan, Karen-Lee and Julie A. Winterich (eds). 1993. *Secrets of Successful Trails*. Washington DC: Rails-to-Trails Conservancy.

Rykwert, Joseph. 1988, 1950 original. *The Idea of a Town*. Cambridge, MA: MIT Press.

Schlesinger, Arthur. 1970 [1940]. 'A Panoramic View: The City in American History,' in Paul Kramer and Frederick L. Holborn (eds), *The City in American Life*. New York: Putnam, 13–36.

Sennett, Richard. 1994. 'The Powers of the Eye,' *Urban Revisions: Current Projects for the Public Realm*. Cambridge, MA: MIT.

Smith, Elizabeth A.T. (compiler). 1994. 'Urban Revisions,' *Urban Revisions: Current Projects for the Public Realm*. Cambridge, MA: MIT 3–15.

Venturi, Robert. 1966. *Complexity and Contradiction in Architecture*. New York: Museum of Modern Art.

Vidler, Anthony. 1992. *The Architectural Uncanny*. Cambridge, MA: MIT.

White, Garrett. 1988. 'SCI-Arc,' *L.A. Style*. September: 168–174, 264.

Williams, Sarah. 1985. 'More is More,' (On Robert Stern). *Art News*. January: 11–13.

"Introduction," "Preface: The Current State of Everyday Urbanism," and "Blurring the Boundaries: Public Space and Private Life"

from *Everyday Urbanism* (2008)

Margaret Crawford

Editors' Introduction

The idea that cities are social entities that must be responsive to local concerns and daily life has been central to user-based urban design theory since the 1960s. In the 1990s, this idea coalesced into a theoretical and practical stance known as Everyday Urbanism which valorizes the spontaneous, un-pedigreed, un-self-conscious vernacular design of everyday urban settings and contends that the public and domestic life that centers on these spaces, particularly that of poorer and more marginal members of the community, is rich with complex meaning and substance. Everyday Urbanism theory cautions designers to not apply design assumptions based on high design style or elite spatial form precedents to their work in cities, especially lower-income areas. Rather, design proposals should be informed by an understanding and appreciation of everyday activities, which provide a vital link to real community issues.

Critics of Everyday Urbanism argue that it is city-making by default rather than by design, become troubled by the absence of larger design aspirations, and worry that it speaks to an erasure of professional design expertise. Defenders argue that it is pragmatic and inclusive, and that designers don't disappear from city-building but become co-authors of neighborhood transformations along with local communities.

First published in 1999 and republished in an expanded version in 2008, the book *Everyday Urbanism*, edited by John Leighton Chase, Margaret Crawford, and John Kaliski, established the basis of the field. The book's "Introduction" and "Preface," written by Margaret Crawford, lay out the intellectual underpinnings and scope of Everyday Urbanism, with the latter, written for the 2008 edition, discussing how the field has grown and changed since its inception and offering a rebuttal to criticism.

Crawford's chapter "Blurring the Boundaries: Public Space and Private Life" addresses an issue that has been of major concern for urban designers in recent years: a perceived loss of the public realm. Crawford contends that while places where people gather have become increasingly privatized and commercialized, for example, shopping malls, this does not mean that democratic public space no longer exists. Through observations of how people in Los Angeles use the sidewalks, parks, and parking lots in their communities for everyday activities that include political expression and small-scale local exchange, such as vending, she concludes that these "marginal" public spaces constitute a "new urban arena for democratic action that challenges normative definitions of how democracy works."

Additional key essays within *Everyday Urbanism* (2008) are Walter Hood's "Urban Diaries: Improvisation in West Oakland, California," John Leighton Chase's "The Space Formerly Known as Parking," John Kaliski's "The Present City and the Practice of City Design," and the book's concluding chapter "Everyday Urban Design: Toward Default Urbanism and/or Urbanism by Design" also by John Kaliski.

Margaret Crawford is Professor of Architecture at the University of California at Berkeley and was formerly Professor of Urban Design and Planning Theory at the Harvard Graduate School of Design and before that Chair of the History, Theory and Humanities program at the Southern California Institute for Architecture. Her research focuses on the evolution, use, and meanings of urban space. Crawford's other books include *Building the Workingman's Paradise* (London, New York: Verso, 1995), which chronicles the rise and fall of American company towns, and *The Car and the City: the automobile, the built environment, and daily urban life* (Ann Arbor, MI: University of Michigan Press, 1992) co-edited with Martin Wachs, which was spurred by an interest in Los Angeles urbanism. She has also written numerous book chapters and journal articles on topics as varied as immigrant spatial practices and shopping malls. One of three offerings in the "Michigan Debates on Urbanism" series, the book *Everyday Urbanism: Margaret Crawford vs. Michael Speaks* (Ann Arbor, MI: University of Michigan, A. Alfred Taubman College of Architecture, 2005) edited by Rahul Mehrotra, presents an elaboration of a series of debates about the leading competing "urbanisms" (New Urbanism, Everyday Urbanism, and Post Urbanism) which were held at the University of Michigan's Taubman College of Architecture and Urban Planning during the winter of 2004.

Other recent books that deal with Everyday Urbanism include Jeffrey Hou (ed.), *Insurgent Public Space: Guerrilla Urbanism and the Remaking of Contemporary Cities* (New York: Routledge, 2010); and Karen A. Franck and Quentin Steven (eds), *Loose Space: Possibility and Diversity in Urban Life* (London: Routledge, 2007). A study that focuses on design activism is Bryan Bell and Katie Wakeford (eds), *Expanding Architecture* (New York: Metropolis Books, 2008). Douglas Kelbaugh's article "Toward an Integrated Paradigm: Further Thoughts on the Three Urbanisms" published in *Places* in 2007 (vol. 19, no. 2, pp. 12–19) identifies Everyday Urbanism, New Urbanism and Post Urbanism as the dominant urban design paradigms and compares and contrasts them.

Books that address issues of spatial justice include Don Mitchell's *The Right to the City: Social Justice and the Fight for Public Space* (New York: Guilford Press, 2003); David Harvey's *Social Justice and the City* (Athens, GA: University of Georgia Press, 2009); and Edward Soja's *Seeking Spatial Justice* (Minneapolis, MN: University of Minnesota Press, 2010). Works of social theory that address issues of spatial production include Henry Lefebvre's *The Production of Space* (Oxford: Blackwell, 1991) translated by Donald Nicholoson-Smith; Michel de Certeau's *The Practice of Everyday Life* (Berkeley, CA: University of California Press, 1984) translated by Steen Rendall; and Edward Soja's *Postmodern Geographics: The Reassertion of Space in Critical Social Theory* (London: Verso, 1989).

INTRODUCTION

What do we mean by everyday urbanism? These two words – one ordinary, the other obscure – together identify a new position in understanding and approaching the city. Rather than urban design, urban planning, urban studies, urban theory, or other specialized terms, urbanism identifies a broad discursive arena that combines all of these disciplines as well as others into a multidimensional consideration of the city. Cities are inexhaustible and contain so many overlapping and contradictory meanings – aesthetic, intellectual, physical, social, political, economic, and experiential – that they can never be reconciled into a single understanding. Urbanism is thus inherently a contested field. The term also carries with it important echoes of the sociologist Louis Wirth's famous essay title and characterization "Urbanism as a Way of Life."[1] This formulation emphasizes the primacy of human experience as the fundamental aspect of any definition of urbanism.

"Everyday" speaks to this element of ordinary human experience and itself conveys many complicated meanings. At a common-sense level, everyday describes the lived experience shared by urban residents, the banal and ordinary routines we know all too well – commuting, working, relaxing, moving through City streets and sidewalks, shopping, buying and eating food, running errands. Even in this descriptive incarnation, the everyday city has rarely been the focus of attention for architects or urban designers, despite the fact that an amazing number of social, spatial, and aesthetic meanings can be found in the repeated activities and conditions that constitute our daily, weekly, and yearly routines. The utterly ordinary reveals a fabric of space and time defined by a complex realm of social practices – a conjuncture of accident, desire, and habit.

The concept of everyday space delineates the physical domain of everyday public activity. Existing in between such defined and physically identifiable realms as the home, the workplace, and the institution, everyday urban space is the connective tissue that binds daily lives together. Everyday space stands in contrast to the carefully planned, officially designated, and often underused public spaces that can be found in most American cities, These monumental spaces only punctuate the larger and more diffuse landscape of everyday life, which tends to be banal and repetitive, everywhere and nowhere, obvious yet invisible. Ambiguous like all in-between spaces, the everyday represents a zone of social transition and possibility with the potential for new social arrangements and forms of imagination.[2]

Between philosophy and common sense

Although the incoherence of everyday space might seem to defeat any conceptual or physical order, the concepts of everyday life as identified by Henri Lefebvre, Guy Debord, and Michel de Certeau serve as an introduction to this rich repository of urban meaning. These three French theorists, all of whom died in the last decade, were, respectively, a Marxist philosopher and sociologist, a filmmaker and would-be revolutionary, and an anthropologist and historian. Pioneers in investigating the completely ignored spheres of daily existence, their work identified the everyday as a crucial arena of modern culture and society. While acknowledging the oppression of daily life, each discovered its potential as a site of creative resistance and liberatory power. In contrast to the French theorists such as Jacques

Derrida and Michel Foucault, who dominated academic and architectural discourse over the last two decades, Lefebvre, Debord, and de Certeau insisted on the connection between theory and social practices, between thought and lived experience. Lefebvre pointed out that "when the philosopher turns back towards real life, general concepts which have been worked out by means of a highly specialized activity and abstracted from everyday life are not lost. On the contrary, they take on a new meaning for lived experience."[3] All of the authors included in this book share with these three philosophical predecessors similar assumptions about everyday life.

The belief that everyday life is important governs our work. Lefebvre was the first philosopher to insist that the apparently trivial everyday actually constitutes the basis of all social experience and the true realm of political contestation. Lefebvre described daily life as the "screen on which society projects its light and its shadow, its hollows and its planes, its power and its weakness."[4] In spite of this significance, Lefebvre warns, the everyday is difficult to decode due to its fundamental ambiguity. As the first step in analyzing this slippery concept, Lefebvre distinguished between two simultaneous realities that exist within everyday life: the *quotidian*, the timeless, humble, repetitive natural rhythms of life; and the *modern*, the always new and constantly changing habits that are shaped by technology and worldliness.[5] Lefebvre structured his analysis of everyday life around this duality, looking past potentially alienating aspects in an effort to unearth the deeply human elements that still exist within the everyday. While most urbanists influenced by Lefebvre have critiqued modernity's negative effects on the city,[6] we have tried optimistically to focus on the other side of the equation – the possibility of reclaiming elements of the quotidian that have been hidden in the nooks and crannies of the urban environment. We have discovered these qualities in overlooked, marginal places, from streets and sidewalks to vacant lots and parks, from suburbia to the inner city.

We believe that lived experience should be more important than physical form in defining the city. This perspective distinguishes us from many designers and critics who point to the visual incoherence of everyday space as exemplifying everything that is wrong with American cities. Like Lefebvre, Debord, and de Certeau, we understand urbanism to be a human and social discourse. The city is, above all, a social product, created out of the demands of everyday use and the social struggles of urban inhabitants. Design within everyday space must start with an understanding and acceptance of the life that takes place there. This goes against the grain of professional design discourse, which is based on abstract principles, whether quantitative, formal, spatial, or perceptual. Whatever the intention, professional abstractions inevitably produce spaces that have little to do with real human impulses. We agree with Raymond Ledrut's conclusion "The problem today – which has nothing 'philosophical' about it – is that of the real life 'of' the city and 'in' the city. The true issue is not to make beautiful cities or well-managed cities, it is to make a work of life. The rest is a by-product."[7]

For us, the play of difference is the primary element in the "real life" of the city. Lefebvre observed that abstract urban spaces, primarily designed to be reproduced, "negated all differences, those that come from nature and history as well as those that come from the body, ages, sexes, and ethnicities."[8] This is visible everywhere in increasingly generic yet specialized spaces that parcel daily experience into separate domains. Though difference is progressively negated in urban space, however, it nonetheless remains the most salient fact of everyday life. Its burdens and pleasures are distributed unevenly, according to class, age, race, and gender. Lefebvre focused particular attention on the victims of everyday life, especially women sentenced to endless routines of housework and shopping. Lefebvre also identified immigrants, low-level employees, and teenagers as victims of everyday life, although "never in the same way, never at the same time, never all at once."[9]

To locate these differences physically in everyday lives is to map the social geography of the city. The city of the bus rider or pedestrian does not resemble that of the automobile owner. A shopping cart means very different things to a busy mother in a supermarket and a homeless person on the sidewalk. These differences separate the lives of urban inhabitants from one another, while their overlap constitutes the primary form of social exchange in the city. The intersections between an individual or defined group and the rest of the city are everyday space – the site of multiple social and economic transactions, where multiple experiences accumulate in a single location. These places where differences collide or interact are the most potent sites for everyday urbanism.

The goal of everyday urbanism is to orchestrate what the literary theorist Mikhail Bakhtin called "dialogism." A mode of textual analysis, dialogism can easily be applied to design practices. Bakhtin defined dialogism as the characteristic epistemological mode of a world dominated by "heteroglossia" – the constant interaction between meanings, all of which can potentially influence the others. "Dialogization" occurs when a word, discourse, language, or culture becomes relativized, deprivileged, and aware of competing definitions for the same things. Undialogized language remains authoritarian or absolute.[10] To dialogize design in the city challenges the conceptual hierarchy under which most design professionals operate. Everyday life provides a good starting point for this shift because it is grounded in the commonplace rather than the canonical, the many rather than the few, and the repeated rather than the unique; and it is uniquely comprehensible to ordinary people.

Not surprisingly, since everyone is potentially an expert on everyday life, everyday life has never been of much interest to experts. Lefebvre pointed out that although experts and intellectuals are embedded in everyday life, they prefer to think of themselves as outside and elsewhere. Convinced that everyday life is trivial, they attempt to evade it. They use rhetoric and metalanguage as "permanent substitutes for experience, allowing them to ignore the mediocrity of their own condition."[11] Lefebvre also described the purpose of such distancing techniques: "Abstract culture places an almost opaque screen (if it were completely opaque the situation would be simpler) between cultivated [people] and everyday life. Abstract culture not only supplies them with words and ideas but also with an attitude which forces them to seek the 'meaning' of their lives and consciousness outside of themselves and their real relations with the world."[12]

To avoid this breach with reality, everyday urbanism demands a radical repositioning of the designer, a shifting of power from the professional expert to the ordinary person. Widespread expertise in everyday life acts as a leveling agent, eliminating the distance between professionals and users, between specialized knowledge and daily experience. The designer is immersed within contemporary society rather than superior to and outside it, and is thus forced to address the contradictions of social life from close up.

Time and space

Both Michel de Certeau and Henri Lefebvre argued that the temporal is as significant as the spatial in everyday life. De Certeau drew a distinction between two modes of operation: strategies, based on place, and tactics, based on time. Strategies represent the practices of those in power, postulating "a place that can be delimited as its own and serve as the base from which relations with an exteriority composed of targets or threats can be managed." Strategies establish a "proper" place, either spatial or institutional, such that place triumphs over time. Political, economic, and scientific rationalities are constructed on the strategic model. In contrast, a tactic is a way of operating without a proper place, and so depends on time. As a result, tactics lack the borders necessary for designation as visible totalities: "The place of a tactic belongs to the other." Tactics are the "art of the weak," incursions into the field of the powerful. Without a proper place, tactics rely on seized opportunities, on cleverly chosen moments, and on the rapidity of movements that can change the organization of a space. Tactics are a form of everyday creativity. Many of the urban activities we describe are tactical. By challenging the "proper" places of the city, this range of transitory, temporary, and ephemeral urban activities constitutes counterpractices to officially sanctioned urbanisms.

Lefebvre also identified another set of multiple temporalities composing urban life. Everyday time is located at the intersection of two contrasting but coexisting modes of repetition, the cyclical and the linear. The cyclical consists of the rhythms of nature: night and day, changing seasons, birth and death. Rational processes define linear patterns, time measured into quantifiable schedules of work and leisure with such units as timetables, fast food, coffee breaks, and prime time. Repeated across days, weeks, months, years, and lifetimes, these competing rhythms shape our lived experience. More important to Lefebvre than these predictable oscillations, however, is a third category of time,

the discontinuous and spontaneous moments that punctuate daily experience – fleeting sensations of love, play, rest, knowledge. These instants of rupture and illumination, arising from everyone's daily existence, reveal the possibilities and limitations of life.[13] They highlight the distance between what life is and what it might be. Although these moments quickly pass into oblivion, they provide the key to the powers contained in the everyday and function as starting points for social change. Guy Debord saw them as potential revolutions in individual everyday life, springboards for the realization of the possible.[14] By recognizing and building on these understandings of time, we can explore new and barely acknowledged realms of urban experience.

The politics of everyday life

Like these writers, we want to draw attention to the transformational possibilities of the everyday. Alice Kaplan and Kristen Ross have pointed out that the political is hidden within the contradictions and possibilities of lived experience.[15] The most banal and repetitive gestures of everyday life give rise to desires that cannot be satisfied there. If these desires could acquire a political language, they would make a new set of personal and collective demands on the social order. Therefore the practices of everyday urbanism should inevitably lead to social change, not via abstract political ideologies imposed from outside, but instead through specific concerns that arise from the lived experience of different individuals and groups in the city.

While acknowledging our debts to Lefebvre and Debord, the general position of writers included in this book is not identical to theirs. Both Lefebvre and Debord identified the urban environment as a unique site for contesting the alienation of modern capitalist society and believed that this alienation could be overcome, thus rendering individuals whole once again. They saw both the society they attacked and the future society they desired as totalities.[16] We instead acknowledge fragmentation and incompleteness as inevitable conditions of postmodern life. We do not seek overarching solutions. There is no universal everyday urbanism, only a multiplicity of responses to specific times and places. Our solutions are modest and small in scale – microutopias, perhaps, contained in a sidewalk, a bus bench, or a minipark. In a rare nontotalizing moment, Debord declared that "One day, we will construct cities for drifting . . . but, with light retouching, one can utilize certain zones which already exist. One can utilize certain persons who already exist."[17]

[. . .]

PREFACE: THE CURRENT STATE OF EVERYDAY URBANISM

. . . The concept [of Everyday Urbanism] originally emerged from a specific context, our own daily experience of the endlessly fascinating urban landscape of Los Angeles. Continually being re-inhabited in new ways and reinvented by its residents, the city challenged us, as design professionals and academics, to engage with it in a productive way. The liveliness of the urban life around us heightened our dissatisfaction with the limits of prevailing urban design discourse. Whether engaged in normative professional practice or avant-garde speculation, urban designers often seemed unable to appreciate the city around them and displayed little interest in the people who lived in it. Instead, they approached the city in primarily abstract and normative terms. We conceived of Everyday Urbanism as an alternative urban design concept, a new way to reconnect urban research and design with ordinary human and social meanings. Borrowing selectively from the concepts of everyday life provided by Henri Lefebvre, Michel de Certeau, and Mikhail Bakhtin, we proposed a new set of urban design values. These put urban residents and their daily experiences at the center of the enterprise, encouraged a more ethnographic mode of urban research, and emphasized specificity and material reality. Depicting and designing for an almost infinite variety of everyday lives demanded a broad range of representations, leading us to explore various genres of writing and to encourage contributors to experiment with new types of expressive drawing and hyper-realistic model making and photo collage.

. . . In retrospect, it seems clear that rather than inventing a new idea, Everyday Urbanism actually encapsulated a widespread but not yet fully articulated attitude toward urban design. It turned out that many architects, planners, and students around the world were already paying keen attention to the existing city, reading Lefebvre and de Certeau, and adjusting their design approaches accordingly. Doug Kelbaugh's recognition of Everyday Urbanism as one of the three dominant paradigms of contemporary urbanism reflects this widespread resonance.[18] By giving this collection of influences, sympathies, and interest a name, Everyday Urbanism provided a concept to which, it turned out, a surprising number of people could relate. Their responses acknowledged our aspiration to make EU an "open work," an umbrella concept that could shelter many different activities, rather than an exclusive or regulated enterprise . . . Everyday Urbanism embraces the diversity of life, in contrast to other schools of urban design that target a particular ethos and then create an approach to further this worldview. If upper case Everyday Urbanism still designates a design approach, lower case everyday urbanism has become an accepted term to positively describe ordinary urban places and activities.

[. . .]

We now understand that Everyday Urbanism functions more as an attitude or a sensibility about the city. In practice we have moved away from developing or following a body of theory to embodying an approach that can be applied to many different situations and activities. Although ideas provided by Lefebvre, de Certeau, and Bakhtin initially enabled us to engage with everyday life, once that engagement begins, responding to the demands of specific urban situations ensures that the project immediately takes on a life of its own. Rather than a singular formal product, this can result in any number of different outcomes. Radically empirical rather than normative and generalizable, Everyday Urbanism constitutes a flexible collection of ideas and practices that can be reconfigured according to particular circumstances.

Multiple and heterogeneous, Everyday Urbanism was never intended to be an over-arching approach to design. Since it does not seek to transform the world or even the built environment, Everyday Urbanism can work partially in many different situations. Unlike most urban design techniques, it can maneuver in the nooks and crannies of existing urban environments. An accretional approach, it makes small changes that accumulate to transform larger urban situations. As a practice, it is appropriate for certain circumstances but perhaps not for others. It is not intended to replace other urban design practices but to work along with, on top of, or after them. Similarly, depending on the situation, Everyday Urbanists can step in and out of professional roles if they discover other ways of accomplishing their goals. Although frustrating to critics, this shape-shifting quality provides Everyday Urbanism with a flexibility noticeably absent in other urban design approaches and is, we would argue, fundamental to operating in a world of constant changes.

Everyday Urbanists take advantage of their lack of affiliation to think about ordinary places in new ways. Although understanding existing urban situations is our starting point, the essence of Everyday Urbanism is to reinterpret and re-imagine them. Finding unforeseen possibilities in ordinary places requires invention and creativity. Thus, Everyday Urbanism needs to work both from the bottom up (in terms of subject and sympathy) and from the top down (utilizing sophisticated knowledge and techniques). In de Certeau's terms, this means being both tactical (unofficial action that is not authorized by government or any official power structure) and strategic (plans formed on a top down basis by those with power). By trying to produce "ordinary magic" out of circumstances that most designers would find unpromising, Everyday Urbanism may in fact have more visionary and transformative goals than any other form of contemporary urbanism.

Finally, our work with residents, city governments, and local organizations on real projects has pointed to another important dimension of everyday urban practice: the many aspects of urban life that are deeply embedded in the daily workings of city government and its regulation and enforcement functions. This realization challenged some of our theoretical assumptions: Lefebvre, de Certeau, and Bakhtin all depicted and dismissed the state as monolithic, reactionary, and at odds with everyday life. Our experience with local politicians, city agencies, and officials suggests a far more complex and contradictory reality. Boundaries between local governments and citizens are often blurry. Many people occupy multiple roles, moving between identities as citizen, bureaucrat, professional, or advocate. Elected politicians and city officials can be both obstructive and supportive of innovative solutions. We have also gained a new appreciation for the crucial role that middle class public opinion plays in the micro-public sphere of neighborhood and urban politics. Public meetings, the local press, vocal individuals, and organized pressure groups all come together to shape both public opinion and public action. This has led us to emphasize representation and communication as one of our key contributions to political discourse and action, giving us a stronger voice in these ongoing debates. We have also realized that even if we don't prevail, by visualizing and communicating alternatives, our visions of transforming everyday urban life can still play a powerful role in shaping municipal debates and policy initiatives. The ongoing struggles of urban politics highlight another ordinary but important temporal dimension we neglected – the slow pace and ongoing commitment necessary to realize projects in a democratic context.

[...]

BLURRING THE BOUNDARIES: PUBLIC SPACE AND PRIVATE LIFE

[...] the following investigation originated in my dissatisfaction with a critical position that emerged in architectural discourse a few years ago. Critics and historians began to see multiple versions of the theme park in the increasingly spectacular and centralized zones of leisure and consumption – gentrified shopping streets, massive shopping malls, festival marketplaces. According to Michael Sorkin, one of the primary theorists in this arena, these ersatz and privatized pieces of the city – pseudopublic places – were distinguished by consumption, surveillance, control, and endless simulation . . .

What concerned me more than the emerging theme-park sensibility as depicted in these studies was part of the book's subtitle, "The End of Public Space." This summarizes a fear repeated by many other critics, urbanists, and architects. In his essay in Sorkin's book, Mike Davis expresses alarm at the "destruction of any truly democratic urban spaces."[19] It is easy to find evidence to support this argument. Los Angeles, for example, is often cited as an extreme demonstration of the decline of public space. The few remaining slices of traditional public space (for example, Pershing Square, historically the focus of the downtown business district, which was recently redesigned by Ricardo

Legorreta) are usually deserted, while Citywalk, the simulated cityscape, shopping, and entertainment center collaged from different urban elements by MCA and Universal Studio, is always jammed with people.

The existence and popularity of these commercial public places is used to frame a pervasive narrative of loss that contrasts the current debasement of public space with golden ages and golden sites – the Greek agora, the coffeehouses of early modern Paris and London, the Italian piazza, the town square. The narrative nostalgically posits these as once vital sites of democracy where, allegedly, cohesive public discourse thrived, and inevitably culminates in the contemporary crisis of public life and public space, a crisis that puts at risk the very ideas and institutions of democracy itself.

It is hard to argue with the symptoms these writers describe, but I disagree with the conclusions they draw. This perception of loss originates in extremely narrow and normative definitions of both "public" and "space" that derive from insistence on unity, desire for fixed categories of time and space, and rigidly conceived notions of private and public. Seeking a single, all-inclusive public space, these critics mistake monumental public spaces for the totality of public space. In this respect, critics of public space closely echo the conclusions of social theorists such as Jürgen Habermas and Richard Sennett, whose descriptions of the public sphere share many of the same assumptions.[20] Habermas describes the public sphere as overwhelmed by consumerism, the media, and the state, while Sennett laments in his book's very title "the fall of public man." The word "man" highlights another key assumption of this position: an inability to conceive of identity in any but universalizing terms. Whether as universal man, citizen, consumer, or tourist, the identified subjects posit a normative condition of experience.

Not surprisingly, the political implications that follow from the overwhelmingly negative assessments of the narrative of loss are equally negative. Implicit is a form of historical determinism that suggests the impossibility of political struggle against what Mike Davis calls "inexorable forces."[21] The universal consumer becomes the universal victim, helpless and passive against the forces of capitalism, consumerism, and simulation. This tyranny is com-pounded by the lack of a clear link between public space and democracy. The two are assumed to be closely connected, but exact affinities are never specified, which makes it even more difficult to imagine political opposition to the mall or theme park.

This universalization, pessimism, and ambiguity led me to seek an alternative framework – a new way of conceptualizing public space and a new way of reading Los Angeles. This essay represents an account of my attempts to rethink our conceptions of "public," "space," and "identity." The investigation revealed to me a multiplicity of simultaneous public activities in Los Angeles that are continually redefining both "public" and "space" through lived experience. In vacant lots, sidewalks, parks, and parking lots, these activities are restructuring urban space, opening new political arenas, and producing new forms of insurgent citizenship.

Rethinking "public"

Nancy Fraser's article "Rethinking the Public Sphere" provided an important starting point for my quest.[22] Her central arguments clarify the significant theoretical and political limitations of prevailing formulations of "public." Fraser acknowledges the importance of Jürgen Habermas's characterization of the public sphere as an arena of discursive relations conceptually independent of both the state and the economy, but she questions many of his assumptions about the universal, rational, and non-contentious public arena.

Habermas links the emergence of the "liberal model of the bourgeois public sphere" in early modern Europe with the development of nation-states in which democracy was represented by collectively accepted universal rights and achieved via electoral politics. This version of the public sphere emphasizes unity and equality as ideal conditions. The public sphere is depicted as a "space of democracy" that all citizens have the right to inhabit. In this arena, social and economic inequalities are temporarily put aside in the interest of determining a common good. Matters of common interest are discussed through rational, disinterested, and virtuous public debate. Like the frequently cited ideal of Athenian democracy, however, this model is structured around significant exclusions.

In Athens, participation was theoretically open to all citizens, but in practice the majority of the population – women and slaves – were excluded; they were not "citizens." The modern bourgeois public sphere also began by excluding women and workers: women's interests were presumed to be private and therefore part of the domestic sphere, while workers' concerns were presumed to be merely economic and therefore self-interested. Middle-class and masculine modes of public speech and behavior, through the required rational deliberation and rhetoric of disinterest, were privileged and defined as universal.

Recent revisionist histories, notes Fraser, contradict this idealized account, demonstrating that nonliberal, nonbourgeois public spheres also existed, producing their own definitions and public activities in a multiplicity of arenas.[23] For example, in 19th and 20th century America, middle-class women organized themselves into a variety of exclusively female volunteer groups for the purposes of philanthropy and reform based on private ideals of domesticity and motherhood. Less affluent women found access to public life through the workplace and through associations including unions, lodges, and political organizations such as Tammany Hall. Broadening the definition of public to encompass these "counterpublics" produces a very different picture of the public sphere, one founded on contestation rather than unity and created through competing interests and violent demands as much as reasoned debate. Demonstrations, strikes, riots, and struggles over such issues as temperance and suffrage reveal a range of discursive sites characterized by multiple publics and varied struggles between contentious concerns.

In the bourgeois public sphere, citizenship is primarily defined in relation to the state, framed within clear categories of discourse, and addressed through political debate and electoral politics. This liberal notion of citizenship is based on abstract universal liberties, with democracy guaranteed by the state's electoral and juridical institutions. Fraser argues instead that democracy is a complex and contested concept that can assume a multiplicity of meanings and forms that often violate the strict lines between private and public on which the liberal bourgeois public sphere depends. In the United States, counterpublics of women, workers, and immigrants have historically defended established civil

rights but also demanded new rights based on their specific roles in the domestic or economic spheres. Always changing, these demands continually redefine democracy and redraw boundaries between private and public.

Fraser's description of multiple publics, contestation, and the redefinition of public and private can be extended to the physical realm of public space. First, these ideas suggest that no single physical environment can represent a completely inclusive space of democracy. Like Habermas's idealized bourgeois public sphere, the physical spaces often idealized by architects – the agora, the forum, the piazza – were constituted by exclusion. Where these single publics are construed as occupying an exemplary public space, the multiple counterpublics that Fraser identifies necessarily require and produce multiple sites of public expression. These spaces are partial and selective in response to the limited segments of the population they serve from among the many public roles that individuals play in urban society.

Redefining "space"

In order to locate these multiple sites of public expression, we need to redefine our understanding of "space." Just as Nancy Fraser looked beyond the officially designated public to discover the previously hidden counterpublics of women and workers, we can identify another type of space by looking beyond the culturally defined physical realms of home, workplace, and institution. I call this new construction "everyday space." Everyday space is the connective tissue that binds daily lives together, amorphous and so persuasive that it is difficult even to perceive. In spite of its ubiquity, everyday space is nearly invisible in the professional discourses of the city. Everyday space is like everyday life, the "screen on which society projects its light and its shadow, its hollows and its planes, its power and its weakness."[24]

In the vast expanses of Los Angeles, monumental, highly ordered, and carefully designed public spaces like Pershing Square or Citywalk punctuate the larger and more diffuse space of everyday life. Southern California's banal, incoherent, and repetitive landscape of roads is lined with endless strip malls, supermarkets, auto-repair facilities, fast-food outlets, and vacant lots that defeat any conceptual or physical order. According to Lefebvre, these spaces are like everyday life: "trivial, obvious but invisible, everywhere and nowhere." For most Angelenos, such spaces constitute an everyday reality of infinitely recurring commuting routes and trips to the supermarket, dry cleaner, or video store. The sites for multiple social and economic transactions, these mundane places serve as primary intersections between the individual and the city.

Created to be seen and approached from moving vehicles, this generic landscape exists to accommodate the automobile, which has produced the city's sprawling form. Connected by an expansive network of streets and freeways, Los Angeles spreads out in all directions with few differences of density or form. Experienced through the automobile, the bus, or even the shopping cart, this environment takes mobility as its defining element. Everyday life is organized by time as much as by space, structured around daily itineraries, with rhythms imposed by patterns of work and leisure, week and weekend, and the repetitious gestures of commuting and consumption.

In contrast to the fluidity of its urban fabric, the social fabric of Los Angeles is fragmented; it is not a single city but a collection of microcities defined by visible and invisible boundaries of class, race, ethnicity, and religion. This multiplicity of identities produces an intricate social landscape in which cultures consolidate and separate, reacting and interacting in complex and unpredictable ways. Spatial and cultural differences exist even within these groups. "Latino," for example, describes the now dominant ethnic group but hides the significant differences between Mexicans and Cubans, for example, or even between recent immigrants and second- or third-generation Chicanos. Mobility prevails here too. When new immigrants arrive from Central America, they tend to move into African American neighborhoods. Both African Americans and Latinos shop in Korean and Vietnamese shops. Other areas of the city, once completely white, then primarily Latino, are now mostly Asian.

These generally distinct groups came together – intensified and politicized – in the urban disturbances of 1992. According to Nancy Fraser's redefinition of the public sphere, these events can be seen as a form of public expression that produces an alternative discourse of "public" and "space." Both the direct causes of the riots and their expression of the riots were embedded in everyday life. For Rodney King, a drive on the freeway ended in a savage beating that shocked the world. The ordinary act of purchasing a bottle of juice in a convenience market after school resulted in Latasha Harlin's death. The verdicts in the Harlin and King trials unleashed a complex outpouring of public concern. Multiple and competing demands (some highly specific, others barely articulated), a spontaneous and undefined moment of public expression, exploded on the streets and sidewalks of Los Angeles. African Americans, many of whom called the uprising the "justice riots," attacked the criminal-justice system. Concepts of universally defined civil rights failed to ameliorate or condemn the visible racism of the Los Angeles Police Department and the court system, which to many constituted a denial of the fundamental rights of citizenship.

The riots dramatized economic issues: poverty, unemployment, and the difficulty of financial self-determination, all exacerbated by recession and long-term effects of deindustrialization. The disturbances also revealed the city's tangled racial dynamics: 51 percent of those arrested were Hispanic (and of that group, most were recent immigrants) while only 34 percent were African American. Immigrants were pitted against one another, and stores owned by Koreans were the focus of much of the burning and looting.

The automobile played a prominent role in the rioting, from the initial act of pulling Reginald Denny from his truck to the rapid expansion of looters who moved across the city by car. Spaces formerly devoted to the automobile – streets, parking lots, swap meets, and strip malls – were temporarily transformed into sites of protest and rage, into new zones of public expression.

Everyday public spaces

The riots underlined the potent ability of everyday spaces to become, however briefly, places where lived experience and political expression come together. This realm of public life lies outside the domain of electoral politics or professional design, representing a bottom-up rather than top-down restructuring of urban space. Unlike normative public spaces, which produce the existing ideology, these spaces help to overturn the status quo. In different areas of the city, generic spaces become specific and serve as public arenas where debates and struggles over economic participation, democracy, and the public assertion of identity take place. Without claiming to represent the totality of public space, these multiple and simultaneous activities construct and reveal an alternative logic of public space.

Woven into the patterns of everyday life, it is difficult even to discern these places as public space. Trivial and commonplace, vacant lots, sidewalks, front yards, parks, and parking lots are being claimed for new uses and meanings by the poor, the recently immigrated, the homeless, and even the middle class. These spaces exist physically somewhere in the junctures between private, commercial, and domestic. Ambiguous and unstable, they blur our established understandings of these categories in often paradoxical ways. They contain multiple and constantly shifting meanings rather than clarity of function. In the absence of a distinct identity of their own, these spaces can be shaped and redefined by the transitory activities they accommodate. Unrestricted by the dictates of built form, they become venues for the expression of new meanings through the individuals and groups who appropriate the spaces for their own purposes. Apparently empty of meaning, they acquire constantly changing meanings – social, aesthetic, political, economic – as users reorganize and reinterpret them.

Temporally, everyday spaces exist in between past and future uses, often with a no-longer-but-not-yet-their-own status, in a holding pattern of real-estate values that might one day rise. The temporary activities that take place there also follow distinct temporal patterns. Without fixed schedules, they produce their own cycles, appearing, reappearing, or disappearing within the rhythms of everyday life. Use and activity vary according to the seasons, vanishing in winter, born again in spring. They are subject to changes in the weather, days of the week, and even time of day. Since they are usually perceived in states of distraction, their meanings are not immediately evident but unfold through the repetitious acts of everyday life.

Conceptually, these spaces can be identified as what Edward Soja, following Henri Lefebvre, called the "thirdspace," a category that is neither the material space that we experience nor a representation of space."[25] Thirdspace is instead a space of representation, a space bearing the possibility of new meanings, a space activated through social action and the social imagination. Multiple public activities are currently transforming Los Angeles everyday spaces, among them the garage sale and street vending.

The garage sale

An unexpected outcome of the recession of the 1980s and the collapse of the real-estate market in Southern California was the proliferation of garage sales, even in the city's wealthiest areas. As an increasing number of people found themselves un- or underemployed, the struggle for supplemental income turned garage sales into semipermanent events, especially on the west side of Los Angeles. Cities such as Beverly Hills have passed ordinances limiting the number of garage sales per household to two per year. The front yard, an already ambiguous territory, serves as a buffer between residential privacy and the public street. Primarily an honorific space, the lawn is activated as the garage sale turns the house inside out, displaying the interior on the exterior. Presenting worn-out possessions, recently the contents of closets and drawers, for public viewing and purchase transforms the usually empty lawn into a site of representation. Unwanted furniture, knickknacks, and clothes are suddenly accessible to anyone passing by, melding the public and the extremely private. The same economic forces that caused the proliferation of garage sales also produced their mobile clientele, shoppers who drive through the city in search of sales or who discover them accidentally on the way to somewhere else.

In the Mexican American barrio East Los Angeles, with its less affluent population of homeowners and low real-estate values, commerce and domesticity have coexisted for a long time. A more permanent physical restructuring has already taken place, generated by a distinct set of social and economic needs: the front yard is marked by a fence, delineating an enclosure. The fence structures a more complex relationship between home and street. Different configurations of house, yard, and fence offer flexible spaces that can easily be adapted for commercial purposes. The fence itself becomes a display for ads or goods. Paving the lawn, a widespread practice, creates an outdoor shop. For Latino women who don't work outside the house, the garage sale has become a permanent business. Many move beyond recycling used items to buying and reselling clothes from nearby garment factories. Garages are simultaneously closets and shops, further linking the commercial and the domestic and producing a public place for neighborhood women. Men use the paved yards differently, as spaces for auto repair or car customizing. This attracts other neighborhood men, establishing a gathering place that is similarly domestic and commercial.

Street vendors

All over the city, informal vendors appropriate marginal and overlooked sites chosen for their accessibility to passing motorists and pedestrians: street corners, sidewalks, and parking lots and vacant lots that are often surrounded by chain-link fences. Through the types of goods they sell, vendors bring to these urban spaces the qualities of domestic life. Used dresses from innumerable closets form a mural of female identity. Cheap rugs cover the harshness of chain link, overlaying the fence with the soft textures and bright patterns of the interior, defining a collective urban living room and evoking a multiplicity of dwelling places, an analogue for the diversity of the city. The delicate patterning of lace, flowers, and pillows, the softness of T-shirts and stuffed animals – all invoke the intimacy of the interior rather than the no-man's-land of the street. In public places, familiar items such as tables, chairs, and tablecloths, usually seen inside the home, transform neglected and underused space into islands of human occupation. Exchange both commercial and social, including that of the messages transmitted by T-shirts and posters, takes place. The vendors' temporary use hijacks these spaces, changing their meaning. Publicly owned spaces are briefly inhabited by citizens; private spaces undergo an ephemeral decommodification. Temporarily removed from the marketplace, these spaces now represent more than potential real-estate value.

Vending is a complex and diverse economy of microcommerce, recycling, and household produc-

tion. Like the garage sale, vending supplements income rather than constituting an occupation – or, more likely, supports only the most marginal of existences. The varieties of vending visible across the city publicly articulate its multiple economic and social narratives. In neighborhoods populated by Central American immigrants, women prepare or package food or craft items in the home for sale on the sidewalk, extending the domestic economy into urban space. The social dramas of migration to Los Angeles are played out daily on the streets. The ubiquitous orange sellers, found on street dividers all over the city, are recent and undocumented arrivals who work to pay off the *coyote* who brought them across the border. Other immigrants vend for economic mobility, an alternative to sweatshop labor, that may eventually lead to a stall at a swap meet or to a small shop. Both sellers and goods can be read as local messages, attesting to the economic necessities and cultural values of a neighborhood.

Vending on public property, streets, and sidewalks is illegal in both the city and county of Los Angeles. When enough vendors congregate in a single place regularly enough, however, they can muster the political power to change the nature of urban space. Chanting "We are vendors, not criminals," Central American vendors demonstrated at the Rampart police station, demanding the right to pursue their economic activities without police harassment. Since many of the vendors are undocumented, this makes them doubly illegal. Central American vendors have organized themselves, acquired legal representation, and pressured the city to change its laws to permit limited vending. Through the defense of their livelihood, vendors are becoming a political and economic force in the city.

Democracy and public space

This brings us back to the question that started this investigation: how can public space be connected with democracy? Individual garage sales might not in themselves generate a new urban politics, but the juxtapositions, combinations, and collisions of people, places, and activities that I've described create a new condition of social fluidity that begins to break down the separate, specialized, and hierarchical structures of everyday life in Los Angeles.

Local yet also directed to anyone driving or passing by, these unexpected intersections may possess the liberatory potential that Henri Lefebvre attributes to urban life. As chance encounters multiply and proliferate, activities of everyday space may begin to dissolve some of the predictable boundaries of race and class, revealing previously hidden social possibilities that suggest how the trivial and marginal might be transformed into a kind of micropolitics.

In some specific circumstances, as I've suggested, the intersection of publics, spaces, and identities can begin to delineate a new urban arena for democratic action that challenges normative definitions of how democracy works. Specifically constituted counterpublics organized around a site or activity create what anthropologist James Holston calls "spaces of insurgent citizenship."[26] These emergent sites accompany the changes that are transforming cities such as Los Angeles. Global and local processes, migration, industrial restructuring, and other economic shifts produce social reterritorialization at all levels. Residents with new histories, cultures, and demands appear in the city and disrupt the given categories of social life and urban space. Expressed through the specific needs of everyday life, their urban experiences increasingly become the focus of their struggle to redefine the conditions belonging to society. Once mobilized, social identities become political demands, spaces and sites for political transformation, with the potential to reshape cities.

The public sites where these struggles occur serve as evidence of an emerging but not yet fully comprehensible spatial and political order. In everyday space, differences between the domestic and the economic, the private and the public, and the economic and the political are blurring. Rather than constituting the failure of public space, change, multiplicity, and contestation may in fact constitute its very nature. In Los Angeles, the materialization of these new public spaces and activities, shaped by lived experience rather than built space, raises complex political questions about the meaning of economic participation and citizenship. By recognizing these struggles as the germ of an alternative development of democracy, we can begin to frame a new discourse of public space, one no longer preoccupied with loss but instead filled with possibility.

NOTES

1 "Urbanism as a Way of Life," first published in 1938, has been extensively reprinted. See Albert J. Reiss, ed., *On Cities and Social Life* (Chicago: University of Chicago Press, 1938); and Richard Sennett, ed., *Classic Essays in the Culture of Cities* (Englewood Cliffs, N.J.: Prentice Hall, 1969). For a discussion of other meanings of urbanism, see Nan Ellin, *Postmodern Urbanism*, (New York: Basil Blackwell, 1996), 225.

2 For Victor Turner's concept of liminality, "betwixt and between," see *The Forest of Symbols* (Ithaca, N.Y.: Cornell University Press, 1967), 93–110. Also see Donald Weber on the related concept of "border," in "From Limen to Border: A Meditation on the Legacy of Victor Turner for American Cultural Studies," *American Quarterly* 47 (September 1995): 525–37.

3 Henri Lefebvre, *Critique of Everyday Life* (London: Verso, 1991), 95.

4 Ibid., 18.

5 Henri Lefebvre, *Everyday Life in the Modern World* (New York: Harper, 1971), 25.

6 See, for example, Kristen Ross, *Fast Cars and Clean Bodies* (Cambridge, Mass.: MIT Press, 1995); Edward Soja, *Postmodern Geographies* (London: Verso, 1989), and *Thirdspace: Journeys to Los Angeles and Other Real and Imagined Places* (New York: Blackwell, 1996); and Mark Gottdeiner, *The Social Production of Urban Space* (Austin: University of Texas Press, 1985).

7 Raymond Ledrut, "Speech and the Silence of the City," in *The City and the Sign: An Introduction to Urban Semiotics*, ed. Mark Gottdeiner and Alexandros Langopoulos (New York: Columbia University Press, 1986), 133.

8 Henri Lefebvre, "Space: Social Product and Use Value," in *Critical Sociology: European Perspectives*, ed. J.W. Freiberg (New York: Irvington, 1979), 289.

9 Lefebvre, *Critique of Everyday Life*, 127.

10 Mikhail Bakhtin, *The Dialogic Imagination: Four Essays*, ed. Michael Holmquist (Austin: University of Texas Press, 1981), 426–27.

11 Lefebvre, *Everyday Life in the Modern World*, 92.

12 Lefebvre, *Critique of Everyday Life*, 238.

13 Henri Lefebvre, *La Somme et le Reste*, vol. 2 (Paris: La Nef de Paris, 1959), discussed in David Harvey, "Afterword" in Henri Lefebvre,

The Production of Space (New York: Blackwell, 1991), 429.

14 Guy Debord, "Preliminary Problems in Constructing a Situation," in Ken Knabb, *Situationist International Anthology* (Berkeley: Bureau of Public Secrets, 1981), 43–45.

15 Alice Kaplan and Kristen Ross, introduction to "Everyday Life" issue of *Yale French Studies* 73 (Fall 1987): 4.

16 Further discussions of the concept of totality see Martin Jay, *Marxism and Totality: The Adventures of a Concept from Lukas to Habermas* (Berkeley: University of California Press, 1984), 276–99; and Peter Wollen, "Bitter Victory: The Art and Politics of the Situationist International," in *On the Passage of a Few People Through a Brief Moment in Time*, ed. Elizabeth Sussman (Cambridge, Mass.: MIT Press, 1989).

17 Guy Debord, "La Théorie de la dérive," in *Les Levres Nues* 9 (November 1956): 10.

18 See Doug Kelbaugh's introduction to *Everyday Urbanism: Margaret Crawford vs. Michael Speaks* in the series Michigan Debates on Urbanism (Ann Arbor: A. Alfred Taubman College of Architecture and Urban Planning, 2005).

19 Mike Davis, "Fortress Los Angeles: The Militarization of Urban Space," in Michael Sorkin, ed.,

Variations on a Theme Park: The New American City and the End of Public Space (New York: Hill and Wang, 1990), 155.

20 See Jürgen Habermas, *The Structural Transformation of the Public Sphere: An Inquiry into a Category of Bourgeois Society* (Cambridge, Mass.: MIT Press, 1989); and Richard Sennett, *The Fall of Public Man* (New York: Vintage Books, 1974).

21 Davis, "Fortress Los Angeles," 154–80.

22 Nancy Fraser, "Rethinking the Public Sphere: A Contribution to the Critique of Actually Existing Democracy," in *The Phantom Public Sphere*, ed. Bruce Robbins (Minneapolis: University of Minnesota Press, 1993).

23 Joan Landes, *Women and the Public Sphere in the Age of the French Revolution* (Ithaca, N.Y.: Cornell University Press, 1988); Mary P. Ryan, *Women in Public: Between Banners and Ballots, 1825–1880* (Baltimore: Johns Hopkins University Press, 1990).

24 Henri Lefebvre, *Critique of Everyday Life*.

25 Edward Soja, *Thirdspace: Journeys to Los Angeles and Other Real and Imagined Places* (New York: Basil Blackwell, 1996).

26 James Holston, "Spaces of Insurgent Citizenship," *Planning Theory* 13 (Summer 1996): 30–50.

"The Generic City" and "Whatever Happened to Urbanism?"

from *S, M, L, XL* (1994)

Rem Koolhaas

Editors' Introduction

For those able to muster the patience to penetrate the visual cacophony of the book *S, M, L, XL* by Rem Koolhaas, his firm the Office for Metropolitan Architecture (OMA), and Bruce Mau, there exists within its eye-popping graphics a couple of very lucid statements about contemporary cities: "The Generic City" and "Whatever Happened to Urbanism?" The book itself is a mixed-media collage of contemporary architectural images, manifestos, travelogues, works from Koolhaas' professional practice OMA, a glossary of terms that punctuates the entire work, and various critiques or essays on the state of contemporary architecture and urbanism. The book is organized in a spatially scalar way according to its title, from issues of the Small (houses, bus stops, hotels, details, and such) to the Extra Large (issues of cities, regions, urban form, mega-projects, and so on).

The two pieces presented here share Koolhaas' deft use of language that both sensationalizes and poses questions worthy of his celebrity. As with his past writing, Koolhaas provides an often humorous, unsentimentalized and existential view of the contemporary urban scene. The themes in these two pieces focus on a similar outcome – an urbanism that has lost its way. In the first, he describes the urbanism of the generic city, and in the second he provides a call to action.

In the first selection Koolhaas describes the unsatisfactory urbanism we tend to produce all too regularly and which is found increasingly at the periphery of traditional city centers. Koolhaas suggests the Generic City is a justified reflection of present-day need and society's current urban abilities. Its physical characteristics are spaces of anomie and atomism, neutral and beige with unnoticeable buildings, dominated by the automobile, signified by an increasingly tropical friendliness, where people dine at waterfronts on shrimp that tastes like nothing. From the fun he derives in describing these characteristics, one might get the impression that Koolhaas is not only an existential documentarian, but might be the Generic City's champion. He writes very similarly to the ways in which Robert Venturi and Denise Scott Brown described Las Vegas or Joel Garreau defined the Edge City. But to assume Koolhaas is satisfied with this state of conditions would be to underestimate his call for a deeper and more serious urbanism.

Koolhaas' critical stance in this work is "simply to abandon what doesn't work – what has outlived its use – to break up the blacktop of idealism with the jackhammers of realism and to accept whatever grows in its place" – in this case the dominance and propping up of the exhausted historic urban center. He argues against the straitjacket of urban identity building and the destructive centralization that is required to keep central urban areas flourishing. In its place, the importance of the periphery is put forth as the true representation of contemporary urbanism, not only as a place where modernism can flourish in the form of shopping centers, parking lots, freeways and airports, but also as "free style" spaces where architects are free to innovate without the strictures and limitations of historic contexts. Although he notes the unstoppable march of postmodern choice and style, his critique also suggests both "the death of the street" as well as "the final death of planning." For the traditional urbanist, reading Koolhaas was akin to the experiences of seeing a horror movie – causing one to flinch uncomfortably, sometimes scream, feel repulsion, and continuously look over the shoulder when leaving the theater – because one knows that danger lurks, yet hopes it was all fiction. As many commuters know from passing through the urban periphery on a daily basis – whether outside Atlanta or Paris – this is no fiction.

In the second short piece, "Whatever Happened to Urbanism?" (an addition to "The Generic City" within this second edition of this *Reader*), Koolhaas laments the loss of the "profession of urbanism." He suggests that urbanism has sabotaged itself and been ridiculed out of existence by the failed modernist project, the irrelevant use of nostalgia, and the city's devolution to a mere set of architectural elements – without any underlying connective tissue, responsive infrastructure, or collective rationale. And all of this dissatisfaction with traditional design practice, he suggests, has led to no credible alternative to the chaos of our current urban predicament. This piece provides a very direct clarion call for resuscitating urbanism, addressing the need to grow our cities in response to urbanization pressures, and supporting an urban attitude. He suggests we focus on becoming supporters of urban thinking and look to ways of growing and modifying our cities – rather than simply producing architecture. The theme of this work parallels several other critiques of status quo urban design practice provided in this *Reader*, including those by Rowe and Koetter, Michael Sorkin, and several of the environmentalists.

Remment (Rem) Lucas Koolhaas is an architect and theorist working out of multiple Offices for Metropolitan Architecture in Rotterdam, New York, Hong Kong, and Beijing. A counterpart to OMA is AMO: a research studio that pushes the boundaries of urbanism and architecture to investigate media, technology, fashion, sociology, and other temporal interests. Koolhaas gained early notoriety for his 1982 entry into the Parc de la Villette competition, ultimately placing behind winner Bernard Tschumi. A winner of the Pritzker Architecture Prize in 2000, his many projects include the masterplans for Lille and Almere; housing in Fukuoka, Japan; several Prada retail stores and catwalks; the public library in Seattle; museum projects and performance halls in Dallas, St. Petersburg-Russia, Paris, Taipei, Porto, and Seoul; and the Dutch Embassy in Berlin. Just as interesting as his built works are the number of OMA competition entries and unrealized designs across the world.

Key texts by Koolhaas include: *Delirious New York: A Retroactive Manifesto for Manhattan* (New York: Monacelli Press, 1997, original 1978); *Mutations: Harvard Project on the City*, edited with Stefano Boeri, Sanford Kwinter, Nadia Tazi, and Daniela Fabricius (Barcelona: Actar, 2001); *Colours*, written with Norman Foster and Alessandro Mendini (Basel: Birkhäuser, 2001); *Project on the City II: The Harvard Design School Guide to Shopping: Harvard Project on the City*, edited with Chuihua Judy Chung, Jeffrey Inaba, and Sze Tsung Leong (Cologne: Taschen, 2001); *Project on the City I: Great Leap Forward*, edited with Chuihua Judy Chung, Jeffrey Inaba, and Sze Tsung Leong (Cologne: Taschen, 2002); *Content* (Cologne: Taschen, 2004); a transcribed interview between Koolhaas and Hans Ulrich Obrist, *Project Japan: Metabolism Talks*, edited with Kayoko Ota and James Westcott (Cologne: Taschen, 2011); and *The Maddalena Effect: An Architectural Affair*, written with Guido Bertolaso and Stefano Boeri, and edited with Michele Brunello and Francisca Insulza (New York: Rizzoli, 2010).

A number of texts and monographs have been written on Koolhaas and his professional work at the Office for Metropolitan Architecture. The most important of these are: Heike Sinning, *More is More: OMA/Rem Koolhaas* (Tübingan: Wasmuth, 2001); Jean Attali, et al. *What is OMA? Considering Rem Koolhaas and the Office for Metropolitan Architecture* (Rotterdam: NAi, 2004); Germano Celant (ed.) *Rem Koolhaas: Unveiling the Prada Foundation* (Milan: Fondazione Prada, 2008); Roberto Gargiani, *Rem Koolhaas/OMA: Essays in Architecture* (London: Routledge, 2008); and Albena Yaneva, *Made by the Office for Metropolitan Architecture: An Ethnography of Design* (Netherlands: Uitgeverij: 2009).

Forms of contemporary urbanism are characterized often by two very different expressions, both implied by Koolhaas in this reading. The first, Everyday Urbanism, cannot be considered a design movement in any sense of the term, but rather a description of the lived realities of the un-idealized populist city. Everyday Urbanism is the non-utopian informalism of trailerparks, freeway signage, the ad-hoc use of vacant lots, community gardens, garage sales, and the vast informal settlements found in poor countries, for example. Considered a classic of the postmodern era, Robert Venturi, Denise Scott Brown, and Steven Izenour's *Learning from Las Vegas* (Cambridge, MA: MIT Press, 1977) was an early recognition of the populist themes found in Everyday Urbanism, although these authors do not allude to the term itself (see the selection by these authors in Part Two: pp. 169–177). Other authors describing Everyday Urbanism include: John Chase, John Kaliski, and Margaret Crawford (eds), *Everyday Urbanism* (New York: Monacelli Press, 1999) (excerpted in Part Three: pp. 344–357); and Rahul Mehrotra (ed.), *Everyday Urbanism: Michigan Debates on Urbanism* (Ann Arbor, MI: Taubman School, University of Michigan, 2005).

A second form of contemporary urbanism, Post Urbanism, has been directly associated with the built work of Koolhaas and OMA, as well as designers such as Zaha Hadid, Bernard Tschumi, Daniel Libeskind, Frank Gehry, Lebbeus Woods, Herzog & de Meuron, and Peter Eisenman, among others. It is physically characterized by decontextualized design, stylistic sensationalism, dependent on "shock and awe," with respect to its use of non-contextual and overpowering forms. Post Urban design tends to be free-form, avant-garde architecture that is at times abstractly geometrical, frequently relying on surface detailing of a building's skin, and in most instances, personal expressions of the designer. Key texts in Post Urban literature include: Bernard Tschumi, *Architecture and Disjunction* (Cambridge, MA: MIT Press, 1994); *The State of Architecture at the Beginning of the 21st Century*, edited with Irene Cheng (New York: Monacelli Press, 2004), and *Event Cities 1, 2 and 3* (Cambridge, MA: MIT Press, 1994, 2001, 2005); Charles Jencks, *The Architecture of the Jumping Universe – A Polemic: How Complexity Science is Changing Architecture and Culture* (London: Academy Editions, 1997); Lebbeus Woods, *Anarchitecture: Architecture is a Political Act* (Chichester, UK: John Wiley/ Architectural Monographs 22, 1992); Roy Strickland (ed.), *Post Urbanism and Reurbanism: Michigan Debates on Urbanism* (Ann Arbor, MI: Taubman School, University of Michigan, 2005); and Gyan Prakash (ed.), *Noir Urbanisms: Dystopic Images of the Modern City* (Princeton, NJ: Princeton University Press, 2010). Written before the introduction of landscape or ecological urbanism, Douglas Kelbaugh provides a very accessible review of contemporary design theories dominating the literature, including both post and everyday urbanism, in *Three Urbanisms: New, Everyday and Post* (Ann Arbor, MI: University of Michigan, 2000).

These readings are indicative of a long line of Post Urban critiques and histories that suggest the traditional monocentric city may be passing into obsolescence, often replaced by a new megapolitan or mega-region urbanism. These authors acknowledge the rise of a new poststructuralist/metropolitan/polycentric/sub-urban/non-place urban realm. Those describing this Post Urban zeitgeist include: Melvin Webber, "Order in Diversity: Community without Propinquity," in Lloyd Wingo Jr. (ed.), *Cities and Space – The Future Use of Urban Land* (Baltimore, MD: Johns Hopkins University Press, 1963); Jean Gottmann, *Megalopolis, The Urbanized Northeastern Seaboard of the United States*, 3rd edn. (Cambridge, MA: MIT Press, 1966), *The Urban Place and Non-Place Urban Realm: Explorations into Urban Structure* (Philadelphia, PA: University of Pennsylvania, 1964), and "The Post-City Age," *Daedalus* (vol. 97, no. 4, pp. 1091–1110, 1968); Francoise Choay, *L'Histoire et la Methode en Urbanisme* (Paris: Annales ESC, 1970); Kenneth Jackson, *Crabgrass Frontier: The Suburbanization of the United States* (New York: Oxford University Press, 1985); Robert Fishman, *Bourgeois Utopias: The Rise and Fall of Suburbia* (New York: Basic Books and HarperCollins, 1987) and "America's New City: Megalopolis Unbound," in *The Wilson Quarterly* (Washington, DC: Woodrow Wilson International Center for Scholars, Winter 1990, pp. 25–45); Jean Gottmann and Robert Harper (eds), *Since Megalopolis: The Urban Writings of Jean Gottmann* (Baltimore, MD: Johns Hopkins University Press, 1990); Joel Garreau, *Edge City: Life on the New Frontier* (New York: Doubleday, 1992); Jon C. Teaford, *The Metropolitan Revolution: The Rise of Post-Urban America*, The Columbia History of Urban Life (New York: Columbia University Press, 2006); Peter Hall and Kathy Pain, *The Polycentric Metropolis: Learning from Mega-City Regions in Europe* (London: Routledge, 2009); Catherine Ross (ed.), *Megaregions: Planning for Global Competitiveness* (Washington DC: Island Press, 2009); and Arthur C. Nelson and Robert E. Lang, *Megapolitan America: A New Vision for Understanding America's Metropolitan Geography* (Chicago: APA/ Planner's Press, 2011).

THE GENERIC CITY

1. Introduction

1.1 Is the contemporary city like the contemporary airport – "all the same"? Is it possible to theorize this convergence? And if so, to what ultimate configuration is it aspiring? Convergence is possible only at the price of shedding identity. That is usually seen as a loss. But at the scale at which it occurs, it *must* mean something. What are the disadvantages of identity, and conversely, what are the advantages of blankness? What if this seemingly accidental – and usually regretted – homogenization were an intentional process, a conscious movement away from difference toward similarity? What if we are witnessing a global liberation movement: "down with character!" What is left after identity is stripped? The Generic? **1.2** To the extent that identity is derived from physical substance, from the historical, from context, from the real, we somehow cannot imagine that anything contemporary – made by us – contributes to it. But the fact that human growth is exponential implies that the past will at some point become too "small" to be inhabited and shared by those alive. We ourselves exhaust it. To the extent that history finds its deposit in architecture, present human quantities will inevitably burst and deplete previous substance. Identity conceived as this form of sharing the past is a losing proposition: not only is there – in a stable model of continuous population expansion – proportionally less and less to share, but history also has an invidious half-life – as it is more abused, it becomes less significant – to the point where its diminishing handouts become insulting. This thinning is exacerbated by the constantly increasing mass of tourists, an avalanche that, in a perpetual quest for "character," grinds successful identities down to meaningless dust. **1.3** Identity is like a mousetrap in which more and more mice have to share the original bait, and which, on closer inspection, may have been empty for centuries. The stronger identity, the more it imprisons, the more it resists expansion, interpretation, renewal, contradiction. Identity becomes like a lighthouse – fixed, over determined: it can change its position or the pattern it emits only at the cost of destabilizing navigation. (Paris can only become more Parisian – it is already on its way to becoming hyper-Paris,

a polished caricature. There are exceptions: London – its only identity a lack of clear identity – is perpetually becoming even less London, more open, less static.) **1.4** Identity centralizes; it insists on an essence, a point. Its tragedy is given in simple geometric terms. As the sphere of influence expands, the area characterized by the center becomes larger and larger, hopelessly diluting both the strength and the authority of the core; inevitably the distance between center and circumference increases to the breaking point. In this perspective, the recent, belated discovery of the periphery as a zone of potential value – a kind of pre-historical condition that might finally be worthy of architectural attention – is only a disguised insistence on the priority of and dependency on the center: without center, no periphery; the interest of the first presumably compensates for the emptiness of the latter. Conceptually orphaned, the condition of the periphery is made worse by the fact that its mother is still alive, stealing the show, emphasizing its offspring's inadequacies. The last vibes emanating from the exhausted center preclude the reading of the periphery as a critical mass. Not only is the center by definition too small to perform its assigned obligations, it is also no longer the real but an overblown mirage on its way to implosion; yet its illusory presence denies the rest of the city its legitimacy. (Manhattan denigrates as "bridge-and-tunnel people" those who need infrastructural support to enter the city, and makes them pay for it.) The persistence of the present concentric obsession makes us *all* bridge-and-tunnel people, second-class citizens in our own civilization, disenfranchised by the dumb coincidence of our collective exile from the center. **1.5** In our concentric programming (author spent part of his youth in Amsterdam, city of ultimate centrality) the insistence on the center as the core of value and meaning, font of all significance, is doubly destructive – not only is the ever-increasing volume of dependencies an ultimately intolerable strain, it also means that the center has to be constantly *maintained*, i.e., modernized. As "the most important place," it paradoxically has to be, at the same time, the most old and the most new, the most fixed and the most dynamic; it undergoes the most intense and constant adaptation, which is then compromised and complicated by the fact that it has to be an unacknowledged transformation, invisible to the naked eye. (The city of

Zurich has found the most radical, expensive solution in reverting to a kind of reverse archaeology: layer after layer of new modernities – shopping centers, parking, banks, vaults, laboratories – are constructed underneath the center. The center no longer expands outward or skyward, but inward toward the center of the earth itself.) From the grafting of more or less discreet traffic arteries, bypasses, underground tunnels, the construction of ever more *tangentiales*, to the routine transformation of housing into offices, warehouses into lofts, abandoned churches into nightclubs, from the serial bankruptcies and subsequent reopenings of specific units in more and more expensive shopping precincts to the relentless conversion of utilitarian space into "public" space, pedestrianization, the creation of new parks, planting, bridging, exposing, the systematic restoring of historic mediocrity, all authenticity is relentlessly evacuated. **1.6** The Generic City is the city liberated from the captivity of center, from the straitjacket of identity. The Generic City breaks with this destructive cycle of dependency: it is nothing but a reflection of present need and present ability. It is the city without history. It is big enough for everybody. It is easy. It does not need maintenance. If it gets too small it just expands. If it gets old it just self-destructs and renews. It is equally exciting – or unexciting – everywhere. It is "superficial" – like a Hollywood studio lot, it can produce a new identity every Monday morning.

2. Statistics

2.1 The Generic City has grown dramatically over the past few decades. Not only has its size increased, its numbers have too. In the early seventies it was inhabited by an average of 2.5 million official (and ±500,000 unofficial) residents; now it hovers around the 15 million mark. **2.2** Did the Generic City start in America? Is it so profoundly unoriginal that it can only be imported? In any case, the Generic City now also exists in Asia, Europe, Australia, Africa. The definitive move away from the countryside, from agriculture, to the city is not a move to the city as we knew it: it is a move to the Generic City, the city so pervasive that it has come to the country. **2.3** Some continents, like Asia, aspire to the Generic City; others are ashamed by it. Because it tends toward the tropical – converging

around the equator – a large proportion of Generic Cities is Asian – seemingly a contradiction in terms: the over-familiar inhabited by the inscrutable. One day it will be absolutely exotic again, this discarded product of Western civilization, through the resemanticization that its very dissemination brings in its wake . . . **2.4** Sometimes an old, singular city, like Barcelona, by oversimplifying its identity, turns Generic. It becomes transparent, like a logo. The reverse never happens . . . at least not yet.

3. General

3.1 The Generic City is what is left after large sections of urban life crossed over to cyberspace. It is a place of weak and distended sensations, few and far between emotions, discreet and mysterious like a large space lit by a bed lamp. Compared to the classical city, the Generic City is *sedated*, usually perceived from a sedentary position. Instead of concentration – simultaneous presence – in the Generic City individual "moments" are spaced far apart to create a trance of almost unnoticeable aesthetic experiences: the color variations in the fluorescent lighting of an office building just before sunset, the subtleties of the slightly different whites of an illuminated sign at night. Like Japanese food, the sensations can be reconstituted and intensified in the mind, or not – they may simply be ignored. (There's a choice.) This pervasive lack of urgency and insistence acts like a potent drug; it induces a *hallucination of the normal*. **3.2** In a drastic reversal of what is supposedly the major characteristic of the city – "business" – the dominant sensation of the Generic City is an eerie calm: the calmer it is, the more it approximates the pure state. The Generic City addresses the "evils" that were ascribed to the traditional city before our love for it became unconditional. The serenity of the Generic City is achieved by the *evacuation* of the public realm, as in an emergency fire drill. The urban plane now only accommodates necessary movement, fundamentally the car; highways are a superior version of boulevards and plazas, taking more and more space; their design, seemingly aiming for automotive efficiency, is in fact surprisingly sensual, a utilitarian pretense entering the domain of *smooth* space. What is new about this locomotive public realm is that it cannot be measured in dimensions.

The same (let's say ten-mile) stretch yields a vast number of utterly different experiences: it can last five minutes or forty; it can be shared with almost nobody, or with the entire population; it can yield the absolute pleasure of pure, unadulterated speed – at which point the sensation of the Generic City may even become intense or at least acquire density – or utterly claustrophobic moments of stoppage – at which point the thinness of the Generic City is at its most noticeable. **3.3** The Generic City is fractal, an endless repetition of the same simple structural module; it is possible to reconstruct it from its smallest entity, a desktop computer, maybe even a diskette. **3.4** Golf courses are all that is left of otherness. **3.5** The Generic City has easy phone numbers, not the resistant ten-figure frontal-lobe crunchers of the traditional city but smoother versions, their middle numbers identical, for instance. **3.6** Its main attraction is its anomie.

4. Airport

4.1 Once manifestations of ultimate neutrality, airports now are among the most singular, characteristic elements of the Generic City, its strongest vehicle of differentiation. They have to be, being all the average person tends to experience of a particular city. Like a drastic perfume demonstration, photomurals, vegetation, local costumes give a first concentrated blast of the local identity (sometimes it is also the last). Far away, comfortable, exotic, polar, regional, Eastern, rustic, new, even "undiscovered": those are the emotional registers invoked. Thus conceptually charged, airports become emblematic signs imprinted on the global collective unconscious in savage manipulations of their non-aviatic attractors – tax-free shopping, spectacular spatial qualities, the frequency and reliability of their connections to other airports. In terms of its iconography/performance, the airport is a concentrate of both the hyper-local and hyper-global – hyper-global in the sense you can get goods there that are not available even in the city, hyper-local in the sense you can get things there that you get nowhere else. **4.2** The tendency in airport gestalt is toward ever-greater autonomy: sometimes they're even practically unrelated to a specific Generic City. Becoming bigger and bigger, equipped with more and more facilities unconnected to travel,

they are on the way to replacing the city. The in-transit condition is becoming universal. Together, airports contain populations of millions – plus the largest daily workforce. In the completeness of their facilities, they are like quarters of the Generic City, sometimes even its reason for being (its center?), with the added attraction of being hermetic systems from which there is no escape – except to another airport. **4.3** The date/age of the Generic City can be reconstructed from a close reading of its airport's geometry. Hexagonal plan (in unique cases penta- or heptagonal): sixties. Orthogonal plan and section: seventies. Collage City: eighties. A single curved section, endlessly extruded in a linear plan: probably nineties. (Its structure branching out like an oak tree: Germany.) **4.4** Airports come in two sizes: too big and too small. Yet their size has no influence on their performance. This suggests that the most intriguing aspect of all infrastructures is their essential elasticity. Calculated by the exact for the numbered – passengers per year – they are invaded by the countless and survive, stretched toward ultimate indeterminacy.

5. Population

5.1 The Generic City is seriously multiracial, on average 8% black, 12% white, 27% Hispanic, 37% Chinese/Asian, 6% indeterminate, 10% other. Not only multiracial, also multicultural. That's why it comes as no surprise to see temples between the slabs, dragons on the main boulevards, Buddhas in the CBD (central business district). **5.2** The Generic City is always founded by people on the move, poised to move on. This explains the insubstantiality of their foundations. Like the flakes that are suddenly formed in a clear liquid by joining two chemical substances, eventually to accumulate in an uncertain heap on the bottom, the collision or confluence of two migrations – Cuban emigres going north and Jewish retirees going south, for instance, both ultimately on their way someplace else – establishes, out of the blue, a settlement. A Generic City is born.

6. Urbanism

6.1 The great originality of the Generic City is simply to abandon what doesn't work – what has outlived its use – to break up the blacktop of idealism with the jackhammers of realism and to accept whatever grows in its place. In that sense, the Generic City accommodates both the primordial and the futuristic – in fact, only these two. The Generic City is all that remains of what used to be the city. The Generic City is the post-city being prepared on the site of the ex-city. **6.2** The Generic City is held together, not by an over-demanding public realm – progressively debased in a surprisingly long sequence in which the Roman Forum is to the Greek agora what the shopping mall is to the high street – but by the residual. In the original model of the moderns, the residual was merely green, its controlled neatness a moralistic assertion of good intentions, discouraging association, use. In the Generic City, because the crust of its civilization is so thin, and through its immanent tropicality, the vegetal is transformed into Edenic Residue, the main carrier of its identity: a hybrid of politics and landscape. At the same time refuge of the illegal, the uncontrollable, and subject of endless manipulation, it represents a simultaneous triumph of the manicured and the primeval. Its immoral lushness compensates for the Generic City's other poverties. Supremely inorganic, the organic is the Generic City's strongest myth. **6.3** The street is dead. That discovery has coincided with frantic attempts at its resuscitation. Public art is everywhere – as if two deaths make a life. Pedestrianization – intended to preserve – merely channels the flow of those doomed to destroy the object of their intended reverence with their feet. **6.4** The Generic City is on its way from horizontality to verticality. The skyscraper looks as if it will be the final, definitive typology. It has swallowed everything else. It can exist anywhere: in a rice field, or downtown – it makes no difference anymore. The towers no longer stand together; they are spaced so that they don't interact. Density in isolation is the ideal. **6.5** Housing is not a problem. It has either been completely solved or totally left to chance; in the first case it is legal, in the second "illegal"; in the first case, towers or, usually, slabs (at the most, 15 meters deep), in the second (in perfect complementarity) a crust of improvised hovels. One solution consumes the sky, the other the ground. It is strange that those with the least money inhabit the most expensive commodity – earth; those who pay, what is free air. In either case, housing proves to be surprisingly accommodating – not only does the population double every so many years, but also, with the loosening grip of the various religions, the average number of occupants per unit halves – through divorce and other family-dividing phenomena – with the same frequency that the city's population doubles; as its numbers swell, the Generic City's density is perpetually on the decrease. **6.6** All Generic Cities issue from the tabula rasa; if there was nothing, now they are there; if there was something, they have replaced it. They must, otherwise they would be historic. **6.7** The Generic Cityscape is usually an amalgam of overly ordered sections – dating from near the beginning of its development, when "the power" was still undiluted – and increasingly free arrangements everywhere else. **6.8** The Generic City is the apotheosis of the multiple-choice concept: all boxes crossed, an anthology of all the options. Usually the Generic City has been "planned," not in the usual sense of some bureaucratic organization controlling its development, but as if various echoes, spores, tropes, seeds fell on the ground randomly as in nature, took hold – exploiting the natural fertility of the terrain – and now form an ensemble: an arbitrary gene pool that sometimes produces amazing results. **6.9** The writing of the city may be indecipherable, flawed, but that does not mean that there is no writing; it may simply be that we developed a new illiteracy, a new blindness. Patient detection reveals the themes, particles, strands that can be isolated from the seeming murkiness of this Wagnerian *ur*-soup: notes left on a blackboard by a visiting genius 50 years ago, stenciled UN reports disintegrating in their Manhattan glass silo, discoveries by former colonial thinkers with a keen eye for the climate, unpredictable ricochets of design education gathering strength as a global laundering process. **6.10** The best definition of the aesthetic of the Generic City is "free style." How to describe it? Imagine an open space, a clearing in the forest, a leveled city. There are three elements: roads, buildings, and nature; they coexist in flexible relationships, seemingly without reason, in spectacular organizational diversity. Anyone of the three may dominate: sometimes the "road" is lost – to be found meandering on an incomprehensible detour; sometimes you see no building, only nature; then, equally unpredictably, you are surrounded only by building. In certain frightening spots, all three are simultaneously absent. On these "sites" (actually, what is the opposite of a site? They are like holes bored through the concept of city) public art emerges like the Loch Ness Monster, equal parts figurative and abstract, usually self-cleaning. **6.11** Specific cities still seriously debate the mistakes of architects – for instance, their proposals to create raised pedestrian networks with tentacles leading from one block to the next as a solution to congestion – but the Generic City simply enjoys the benefits of their inventions: *decks, bridges, tunnels, motorways* – a huge proliferation of the paraphernalia of connection – frequently draped with ferns and flowers as if to ward off original sin, creating a vegetal congestion more severe than a fifties science-fiction movie. **6.12** The roads are only for cars. People (pedestrians) are led on rides (as in an amusement park), on "promenades" that lift them off the ground, then subject them to a catalog of exaggerated conditions – wind, heat, steepness, cold, interior, exterior, smells, fumes – in a sequence that is a grotesque caricature of life in the historic city. **6.13** There *is* horizontality in the Generic City, but it is on the way out. It consists either of history that is not yet erased or of Tudor-like enclaves that multiply around the center as newly minted emblems of preservation. **6.14** Ironically, though itself new, the Generic City is encircled by a constellation of New Towns: New Towns are like year-rings. Somehow, New Towns age very quickly, the way a five-year-old child develops wrinkles and arthritis through the disease called progeria. **6.15** The Generic City presents the final death of planning. Why? Not because it is not planned – in fact, huge complementary universes of bureaucrats and developers funnel unimaginable flows of energy and money into its completion; for the same money, its plains can be fertilized by diamonds, its mud fields paved in gold bricks . . . But its most dangerous *and* most exhilarating discovery is that planning makes no difference whatsoever. Buildings may be placed well (a tower near a metro station) or badly (whole centers miles away from any road). They flourish/perish unpredictably. Networks become over-stretched, age, rot, become obsolescent; populations double, triple, quadruple, suddenly disappear. The surface of the city explodes, the economy accelerates, slows down, bursts, collapses. Like ancient mothers that still nourish titanic embryos, whole cities are built on colonial infrastructures of which the oppressors

took the blueprints back home. Nobody knows where, how, since when the sewers run, the exact location of the telephone lines, what the reason was for the position of the center, where monumental axes end. All it proves is that there are infinite hidden margins, colossal reservoirs of slack, a perpetual, organic process of adjustment, standards, behavior; expectations change with the biological intelligence of the most alert animal. In this apotheosis of multiple choice, it will never be possible again to reconstruct cause and effect. They work – that is all. **6.16** The Generic City's aspiration toward tropicality automatically implies the rejection of any lingering reference to the city as fortress, as citadel; it is open and accommodating like a mangrove forest.

7. Politics

7.1 The Generic City has a (sometimes distant) relationship with a more or less authoritarian regime – local or national. Usually the cronies of the "leader" – whoever that was – decided to develop a piece of "downtown" or the periphery, or even to start a new city in the middle of nowhere, and so, triggered the boom that put the city on the map. **7.2** Very often, the regime has evolved to a surprising degree of invisibility, as if, through its very permissiveness, the Generic City resists the dictatorial.

8. Sociology

8.1 It is very surprising that the triumph of the Generic City has not coincided with the triumph of sociology – a discipline whose "field" has been extended by the Generic City beyond its wildest imagination. The Generic City is sociology, happening. Each Generic City is a petri dish – or an infinitely patient blackboard on which almost any hypothesis can be "proven" and then erased, never again to reverberate in the minds of its authors or its audience. **8.2** Clearly, there is a proliferation of communities – a sociological zapping – that resists a single overriding interpretation. The Generic City is loosening every structure that made anything coalesce in the past. **8.3** While infinitely patient, the Generic City is also persistently resistant to speculation: it proves that sociology may be the worst system to capture sociology in the making. It outwits each established critique. It contributes huge amounts of evidence for and – in even more impressive quantities – against each hypothesis. In *A* tower blocks lead to suicide, in *B* to happiness ever after. In *C* they are seen as a first stepping stone toward emancipation (presumably under some kind of invisible "duress," however), in *D* simply as passé. Constructed in unimaginable numbers in *K*, they are being exploded in *L*. Creativity is inexplicably high in *E*, nonexistent in *F*. *G* is a seamless ethnic mosaic, *H* perpetually at the mercy of separatism, if not on the verge of civil war. Model *Y* will never last because of its tampering with family structure, but *Z* flourishes – a word no academic would ever apply to any activity in the Generic City – because of it. Religion is eroded in *V*, surviving in *W*, transmuted in *X*. **8.4** Strangely, nobody has thought that cumulatively the endless contradictions of these interpretations prove the richness of the Generic City; that is the one hypothesis that has been eliminated in advance.

9. Quarters

9.1 There is always a quarter called Lipservice, where a minimum of the past is preserved: usually it has an old train/tramway or double-decker bus driving through it, ringing ominous bells – domesticated versions of the Flying Dutchman's phantom vessel. Its phone booths are either red and transplanted from London, or equipped with small Chinese roofs. Lipservice – also called Afterthought, Waterfront, Too Late, 42nd Street, simply the Village, or even Underground – is an elaborate mythic operation: it celebrates the past as only the recently conceived can. It is a machine. **9.2** The Generic City had a past, once. In its drive for prominence, large sections of it somehow disappeared, first unlamented – the past apparently was surprisingly unsanitary, even dangerous – then without warning, relief turned into regret. Certain prophets – long white hair, gray socks, sandals – had always been warning that the past was necessary – a resource. Slowly, the destruction machine grinds to a halt; some random hovels on the laundered Euclidean plane are saved, restored to a splendor they never had . . . **9.3** In spite of its absence, history is the major preoccupation, even industry, of the Generic City. On the liberated grounds, around the restored hovels, still more hotels are constructed to receive additional tourists in direct proportion to the erasure of the past. Its disappearance has no influence on their numbers, or maybe it is just a last-minute rush. Tourism is now independent of destination . . . **9.4** Instead of specific memories, the associations the Generic City mobilizes are general memories, memories of memories: if not all memories at the same time, then at least an abstract, token memory, a deja vu that never ends, generic memory. **9.5** In spite of its modest physical presence (Lipservice is never more than three stories high: homage to/revenge of Jane Jacobs?) it condenses the entire past in a single complex. History returns not as farce here, but as *service*: costumed merchants (funny hats, bare midriffs, veils) voluntarily enact the conditions (slavery, tyranny, disease, poverty, colony) that their nation once went to war to abolish. Like a replicating virus, worldwide, the colonial seems the only inexhaustible source of the authentic. **9.6** 42nd Street: ostensibly the places where the past is preserved, they are actually the places where the past has changed the most, is the most distant – as if seen through the wrong end of a telescope – or even completely eliminated. **9.7** Only the memory of former excess is strong enough to charge the bland. As if they try to warm themselves at the heat of an extinguished volcano, the most popular sites (with tourists, and in the Generic City that includes everyone) are the ones once most intensely associated with sex and misconduct. Innocents invade the former haunts of pimps, prostitutes, hustlers, transvestites, and to a lesser degree, artists. Paradoxically, at the same moment that the information highway is about to deliver pornography by the truckload to their living rooms, it is as if the experience of walking on these warmed-over embers of transgression and sin makes them feel special, alive. In an age that does not generate new aura, the value of established aura skyrockets. Is walking on these ashes the nearest they will get to guilt? Existentialism diluted to the intensity of a Perrier? **9.8** Each Generic City has a waterfront, not necessarily with water – it can also be with desert, for instance – but at least an edge where it meets another condition, as if a position of near escape is the best guarantee for its enjoyment. Here tourists congregate in droves around a cluster of stalls. Hordes of "hawkers" try to sell them the "unique" aspects of the city. The unique parts of all Generic Cities together have created a universal souvenir, scientific cross between Eiffel Tower, Sacre Coeur, and Statue of Liberty: a tall building (usually between 200 and 300 meters) drowned in a small ball of water with snow or, if close to the equator, gold flakes; diaries with pockmarked leather covers; hippie sandals – even if real hippies are quickly repatriated. Tourists fondle these – nobody has ever witnessed a sale – and then sit down in exotic eateries that line the waterfront: they run the full gamut of food today: spicy: first and ultimately maybe most reliable indication of being elsewhere; patty: beef or synthetic; raw: atavistic practice that will be very popular in the third millennium. **9.9** Shrimp is the ultimate appetizer. Through the simplification of the food chain – and the vicissitudes of preparation – they taste like English muffins, i.e., nothingness.

10. Program

10.1 Offices are still there, in ever greater numbers, in fact. People say they are no longer necessary. In five to ten years we will all work at home. But then we will need bigger homes, big enough to use for meetings. Offices will have to be converted to homes. **10.2** The only activity is shopping. But why not consider shopping as temporary, provisional? It awaits better times. It is our own fault – we didn't think of anything better to do. The same spaces inundated with other programs – libraries, baths, universities – would be terrific; we would be awed by their grandeur. **10.3** Hotels are becoming the generic accommodation of the Generic City, its most common building block. That used to be the office – which at least implied a coming and a going, assumed the presence of other important accommodations elsewhere. Hotels are now containers that, in the expansion and completeness of their facilities, make almost all other buildings redundant. Even doubling as shopping malls, they are the closest we have to urban *existence*, 21st-century style. **10.4** The hotel now implies imprisonment, voluntary house arrest; there is no competing place left to go; you come and stay. Cumulatively, it describes a city of ten million all locked in their rooms, a kind of reverse animation – density imploded.

11. Architecture

11.1 Close your eyes and imagine an explosion of beige. At its epicenter splashes the color of vaginal folds (unaroused), metallic-matte aubergine, dusty pumpkin; all cars on their way to bridal whiteness ... **11.2** There are interesting and boring buildings in the Generic City, as in all cities. Both trace their ancestry back to Mies van der Rohe: the first category to his irregular Friedrichstadt tower (1921), the second to the boxes he conceived not long afterward. This sequence is important: obviously, after initial experimentation, Mies made up his mind once and for all against interest, for boredom. At best, his later buildings capture the spirit of the earlier work – sublimated, repressed? – as a more or less noticeable absence, but he never proposed "interesting" projects as possible buildings again. The Generic City proves him wrong: its more daring architects have taken up the challenge Mies abandoned, to the point where it is now hard to find a box. Ironically, this exuberant homage to the interesting Mies shows that "the" Mies was wrong. **11.3** The architecture of the Generic City is by definition beautiful. Built at incredible speed, and conceived at even more incredible pace, there is an average of 27 aborted versions for every realized – but that is not quite the term – structure. They are prepared in the 10,000 architectural offices nobody has ever heard of, each vibrant with fresh inspiration. Presumably more modest than their well-known colleagues, these offices are bonded by a collective awareness that something is wrong with architecture that can only be rectified through their efforts. The power of numbers gives them a splendid, shining arrogance. They are the ones who design without any hesitation. They assemble, from 1,001 sources, with savage precision, more riches than any genius ever could. On average, their education has cost 30,000 dollars, excluding travel and housing; 23% have been laundered at American Ivy League universities, where they have been exposed – admittedly for very short periods – to the well-paid elite of the other, "official" profession. It follows that a combined total investment of 300 billion dollars ($300,000,000,000) worth of architectural education ($30,000 [average cost] × 100 [average number of workers per office] × 100,000 [number of worldwide offices]) is working in and producing Generic Cities at any moment.

11.4 Buildings that are complex in form depend on the curtain-wall industry, on ever more effective adhesives and sealants that turn each building into a mixture of straitjacket and oxygen tent. The use of silicone – "we are stretching the facade as far as it will go" – has flattened all facades, glued glass to stone to steel to concrete in a space-age impurity. These connections give the appearance of intellectual rigor through the liberal application of a transparent spermy compound that keeps everything together by intention rather than design – a triumph of glue over the integrity of materials. Like everything else in the Generic City, its architecture is the resistant made malleable, an epidemic of yielding no longer through the application of principle but through the *systematic* application of the unprincipled. **11.5** Because the Generic City is largely Asian, its architecture is generally air-conditioned; this is where the paradox of the recent paradigm shift – the city no longer represents maximum development but borderline underdevelopment – becomes acute: the brutal means by which universal conditioning is achieved mimic inside the building the climatic conditions that once "happened" outside – sudden storms, mini-tornadoes, freezing spells in the cafeteria, heat waves, even mist; a provincialism of the mechanical, deserted by gray matter in pursuit of the electronic. Incompetence or imagination? **11.6** The irony is that in this way the Generic City is at its most subversive, its most ideological; it elevates mediocrity to a higher level; it is like Kurt Schwitter's *Merzbau* at the scale of the city: the Generic City is a *Merzcity*. **11.7** The angle of the facades is the only reliable index of architectural genius: 3 points for sloping backward, 12 points for sloping forward, 2-point penalty for setbacks (too nostalgic). **11.8** The apparently solid substance of the Generic City is misleading: 51% of its volume consists of atrium. The atrium is a diabolical device in its ability to substantiate the insubstantial. Its Roman name is an eternal guarantor of architectural class – its historic origins make the theme inexhaustible. It accommodates the cave-dweller in its relentless provision of metropolitan comfort. **11.9** The atrium is void space: voids are the essential building block of the Generic City. Paradoxically, its hollowness insures its very physicality, the pumping up of the volume the only pretext for its physical manifestation. The more complete and repetitive its interiors, the less their essential repetition is noticed. **11.10** The style choice is postmodern, *and will always remain so.* Postmodernism is the only movement that has succeeded in connecting the practice of architecture with the practice of panic. Postmodernism is not a doctrine based on a highly civilized reading of architectural history but a method, a mutation in professional architecture that produces results fast enough to keep pace with the Generic City's development. Instead of consciousness, as its original inventors may have hoped, it creates a new unconscious. It is modernization's little helper. Anyone can do it – a skyscraper based on the Chinese pagoda *and/or* a Tuscan hill town. **11.11** All resistance to Postmodernism is anti-democratic. It creates a "stealth" wrapping around architecture that makes it irresistible, like a Christmas present from a charity. **11.12** Is there a connection between the predominance of mirror in the Generic City – is it to celebrate nothingness through its multiplication or a desperate effort to capture essences on their way to evaporation? – and the "gifts" that, for centuries, were supposed to be the most popular, efficient present for savages? **11.13** Maxim Gorky speaks in relation to Coney Island of "varied boredom." He clearly intends the term as an oxymoron. Variety cannot be boring. Boredom cannot be varied. But the infinite variety of the Generic City comes close, at least, to making variety normal: banalized, in a reversal of expectation, it is repetition that has become unusual, therefore, potentially, daring, exhilarating. But that is for the 21st century.

12. Geography

12.1 The Generic City is in a warmer than usual climate; it is on its way to the south – toward the equator – away from the mess that the north made of the second millennium. It is a concept in a state of migration. Its ultimate destiny is to be tropical – better climate, more beautiful people. It is inhabited by those who do not like it elsewhere. **12.2** In the Generic City, people are not only more beautiful than their peers, they are also reputed to be more even-tempered, less anxious about work, less hostile, more pleasant – proof, in other words, that there is a connection between architecture and behavior, that the city can make better people through as yet unidentified methods. **12.3** One of the most potent characteristics of the Generic City is the stability of its weather – no seasons, outlook sunny – yet all forecasts are presented in terms of imminent change and future deterioration: clouds in Karachi. From the ethical and the religious, the issue of doom has shifted to the inescapable domain of the meteorological. Bad weather is about the only anxiety that hovers over the Generic City.

13. Identity

13.1 There is a calculated (?) redundancy in the iconography that the Generic City adopts. If it is water-facing, then water-based symbols are distributed over its entire territory. If it is a port, then ships and cranes will appear far inland. (However, showing the containers themselves would make no sense: you can't particularize the generic through the Generic.) If it is Asian, then "delicate" (sensual, inscrutable), women appear in elastic poses, suggesting (religious, sexual) submission everywhere. If it has a mountain, each brochure, menu, ticket, billboard will insist on the hill, as if nothing less than a seamless tautology will convince. Its identity is like a mantra.

14. History

14.1 Regret about history's absence is a tiresome reflex. It exposes an unspoken consensus that history's presence is desirable. But who says that is the case? A city is a plane inhabited in the most efficient way by people and processes, and in most cases, the presence of history only drags down its performance . . . **14.2** History present obstructs the pure exploitation of its theoretical value as absence. **14.3** Throughout the history of humankind – to start a paragraph the American way – cities have grown through a process of consolidation. Changes are made on the spot. Things are improved. Cultures flourish, decay, revive, disappear, are sacked, invaded, humiliated, raped, triumph, are reborn, have golden ages, fall suddenly silent – all on the same site. That is why archaeology is a profession of digging: it exposes layer after layer of civilization (i.e., city). The Generic City, like a sketch which is never elaborated, is not improved but abandoned. The idea of layering, intensification, completion are

alien to it: it has no layers. Its next layer takes place somewhere else, either next door – that can be the size of a country – or even elsewhere altogether. The archaeologue (= archaeology with more interpretation) of the 20th century needs unlimited plane tickets, not a shovel. **14.4** In its improvements, the Generic City perpetuates its own amnesia (its only link with eternity?). Its archaeology will therefore be the evidence of its progressive forgetting, the documentation of its evaporation. Its genius will be empty-handed not an emperor without clothes but an archaeologist without finds, or a site even.

15. Infrastructure

15.1 Infrastructures, which were mutually reinforcing and totalizing, are becoming more and more competitive and local; they no longer pretend to create functioning wholes but now spin off functional entities. Instead of network and organism, the new infrastructure creates enclave and impasse: no longer the grand récit but the parasitic swerve. (The city of Bangkok has approved plans for three competing airborne metro systems to get from A to B – may the strongest one win). **15.2** Infrastructure is no longer a more or less delayed response to a more or less urgent need but a strategic weapon, a prediction: Harbor X is not enlarged to serve a hinterland of frantic consumers but to kill/reduce the chances that harbor Y will survive the 21st century. On a single island, southern metropolis Z, still in its infancy, is "given" a new subway system to make established metropolis W in the north look clumsy, congested, and ancient. Life in V is smoothed to make life in U eventually unbearable.

16. Culture

16.1 Only the redundant counts. **16.2** In each time zone, there are at least three performances of *Cats*. The world is surrounded by a Saturn's ring of meowing. **16.3** The city used to be the great sexual hunting ground. The Generic City is like a dating agency: it efficiently matches supply and demand. Orgasm instead of agony: there is progress. The most obscene possibilities are announced in the cleanest typography; Helvetica has become pornographic.

17. End

17.1 Imagine a Hollywood movie about the Bible. A city somewhere in the Holy Land. Market scene: from left and right extras cloaked in colorful rags, furs, silken robes walk into the frame yelling, gesticulating, rolling their eyes, starting fights, laughing, scratching their beards, hairpieces dripping with glue, thronging toward the center of the image waving sticks, fists, overturning stalls, trampling animals . . . People shout. Selling wares? Proclaiming futures? Invoking Gods? Purses are snatched, criminals pursued (or is it helped?) by the crowds. Priests pray for calm. Children run amok in an undergrowth of legs and robes. Animals bark. Statues topple. Women shriek – threatened? Ecstatic? The churning mass becomes oceanic. Waves break. Now switch off the sound – silence, a welcome relief – and reverse the film. The now mute but still visibly agitated men and women stumble backward; the viewer no longer registers only humans but begins to note spaces between them. The center empties; the last shadows evacuate the rectangle of the picture frame, probably complaining, but fortunately we don't hear them. Silence is now reinforced by emptiness: the image shows empty stalls, some debris that was trampled underfoot. Relief . . . it's over. That is the story of the city. The city is no longer. We can leave the theater now . . .

WHATEVER HAPPENED TO URBANISM?

This century has been a losing battle with the issue of quantity.

In spite of its early promise, its frequent bravery, urbanism has been unable to invent and implement at the scale demanded by its apocalyptic demographics. In 20 years, Lagos has grown from 2 to 7 to 12 to 15 million; Istanbul has doubled from 6 to 12. China prepares for even more staggering multiplications.

How to explain the paradox that urbanism, as a profession, has disappeared at the moment when urbanization everywhere – after decades of constant acceleration – is on its way to establishing a definitive, global "triumph" of the urban condition?

Modernism's alchemistic promise – to transform quantity into quality through abstraction and repetition – has been a failure, a hoax: magic that didn't work. Its ideas, aesthetics, strategies are finished. Together, all attempts to make a new beginning have only discredited the *idea* of a new beginning. A collective shame in the wake of this fiasco has left a massive crater in our understanding of modernity and modernization.

What makes this experience disconcerting and (for architects) humiliating is the city's defiant persistence and apparent vigor, in spite of the collective failure of all agencies that act on it or try to influence it – creatively, logistically, politically.

The professionals of the city are like chess players who lose to computers. A perverse automatic pilot constantly outwits all attempts at capturing the city, exhausts all ambitions of its definition, ridicules the most passionate assertions of its present failure and future impossibility, steers it implacably further on its flight forward. Each disaster foretold is somehow absorbed under the infinite blanketing of the urban.

Even as the apotheosis of urbanization is glaringly obvious and mathematically inevitable, a chain of rearguard, escapist actions and positions postpones the final moment of reckoning for the two professions formerly most implicated in making cities – architecture and urbanism. Pervasive urbanization has modified the urban condition itself beyond recognition. "The" city no longer exists. As the concept of city is distorted and stretched beyond precedent, each insistence on its primordial condition – in terms of images, rules, fabrication – irrevocably leads via nostalgia to irrelevance.

For urbanists, the belated rediscovery of the virtues of the classical city at the moment of their definitive impossibility may have been the point of no return, fatal moment of disconnection, disqualification. They are now specialists in phantom pain: doctors discussing the medical intricacies of an amputated limb.

The transition from a former position of power to a reduced station of relative humility is hard to perform. Dissatisfaction with the contemporary city has not led to the development of a credible alternative; it has, on the contrary, inspired only more refined ways of articulating dissatisfaction. A profession persists in its fantasies, its ideology, its pretension, its illusions of involvement and control, and is therefore incapable of conceiving new modesties, partial interventions, strategic realignments, compromised positions that might influence, redirect, succeed in limited terms, regroup, begin from scratch even, but will never reestablish control.

Because the generation of May '68 – the largest generation ever, caught in the "collective narcissism of a demographic bubble" – is now finally in power, it is tempting to think that it is responsible for the demise of urbanism – the state of affairs in which cities can no longer be made – paradoxically *because* it rediscovered and reinvented the city.

Sous le pavé, la plage (under the pavement, beach): initially, May '68 launched the idea of a new beginning for the city. Since then, we have been engaged in two parallel operations: documenting our overwhelming awe for the existing city, developing philosophies, projects, prototypes for a preserved *and* reconstituted city and, at the same time, laughing the professional field of urbanism out of existence, dismantling it in our contempt for those who planned (and made huge mistakes in planning) airports, New Towns, satellite cities, highways, high-rise buildings, infrastructures, and all the other fallout from modernization. After sabotaging urbanism, we have ridiculed it to the point where entire university departments are closed, offices bankrupted, bureaucracies fired or privatized.

Our "sophistication" hides major symptoms of cowardice centered on the simple question of taking positions – maybe the most basic action in making the city. We are simultaneously dogmatic and evasive. Our amalgamated wisdom can be easily caricatured: according to Derrida we cannot be *Whole*, according to Baudrillard we cannot be *Real*, according to Virilio we cannot be *There*. "Exiled to the Virtual World": plot for a horror movie.

Our present relationship with the "crisis" of the city is deeply ambiguous: we still blame others for a situation for which both our incurable utopianism and our contempt are responsible. Through our hypocritical relationship with power – contemptuous yet covetous – we dismantled an entire discipline, cut ourselves off from the operational, and condemned whole populations to the impossibility of encoding civilizations on their territory – the subject of urbanism.

Now we are left with a world without urbanism, only architecture, ever more architecture. The neatness of architecture is its seduction; it defines, excludes, limits, separates from the "rest" – but it also consumes. It exploits and exhausts the potentials that can be generated finally only by urbanism and that only the specific imagination of urbanism can invent and renew.

The death of urbanism – our refuge in the parasitic security of architecture – creates an immanent disaster: more and more substance is grafted on starving roots.

In our more permissive moments, we have surrendered to the aesthetics of chaos – "our" chaos. But in the technical sense chaos is what happens when nothing happens, not something that can be engineered or embraced; it is something that infiltrates; it cannot be fabricated. The only legitimate relationship that architects can have with the subject of chaos is to take their rightful place in the army of those devoted to resist it, and fail.

If there is to be a "new urbanism" it will not be based on the twin fantasies of order and omnipotence; it will be the staging of uncertainty; it will no longer be concerned with the arrangement of more or less permanent objects but with the irrigation of territories with potential; it will no longer aim for stable configurations but for the creation of enabling fields that accommodate processes that refuse to be crystallized into definitive form; it will no longer be about meticulous definition, the imposition of limits, but about expanding notions, denying boundaries, not about separating and identifying entities, but about discovering unnameable hybrids; it will no longer be obsessed with the city but with the manipulation of infrastructure for endless intensifications and diversifications, shortcuts and redistributions – the reinvention of psychological space. Since the urban is now pervasive, urbanism will never again be about the "new," only about the "more" and the "modified." It will not be about the civilized, but about underdevelopment.

Since it is out of control, the urban is about to become a major vector of the imagination. Redefined, urbanism will not only, or mostly, be a profession, but a way of thinking, an ideology: to accept what exists. We were making sand castles. Now we swim in the sea that swept them away.

To survive, urbanism will have to imagine a new newness. Liberated from its atavistic duties, urbanism redefined as a way of operating on the inevitable will attack architecture, invade its trenches, drive it from its bastions, undermine its certainties, explode its limits, ridicule its preoccupations with matter and substance, destroy its traditions, smoke out its practitioners.

THREE

The seeming failure of the urban offers an exceptional opportunity, a pretext for Nietzschean frivolity. We have to imagine 1,001 other concepts of city; we have to take insane risks; we have to dare to be utterly uncritical; we have to swallow deeply and bestow forgiveness left and right. The certainty of failure has to be our laughing gas/oxygen; modernization our most potent drug. Since we are not responsible, we have to become irresponsible.

In a landscape of increasing expediency and impermanence, urbanism no longer is or has to be the most solemn of our decisions; urbanism can lighten up, become a *Gay Science-Lite* Urbanism.

What if we simply declare that there *is* no crisis – redefine our relationship with the city not as its makers but as its mere subjects, as its supporters?

More than ever, the city is all we have.

PART FOUR

Design Issues in Urban Development

Plate 5 Retail development of the One New Change Shopping Mall in the City of London is being constructed at a pace, scale, and density that addresses both developer desires for economic gain and government aspirations for economic development. While the "City" is the historic and global financial hub of London, it is being incrementally diversified with new commercial, cultural, and residential structures. This photo of the One New Change Shopping Mall (designed by Jean Nouvel and under construction in the mid-2000s) is taken from the dome of St. Paul's Cathedral adjacent to the project in the Cheapside area. Urban development in the district is coordinated by the City of London Corporation (the local government administration), and benefits from special tax laws that provide incentives for businesses locating there. Urban design and development is tightly controlled to ensure a coherent urban fabric that harmonizes with the historic structures in the area. At the same time, these new structures will provide highly imageable and modern settings for flagship stores, high end restaurants, and retailers that cater to the elite business interests of the district. (Photo: M. Larice)

INTRODUCTION TO PART FOUR

For many urban designers, the final readings in Part Three allude to contemporary development problems in city-making. The existential phenomena of postmodern urbanism, everyday urbanism, or post urbanism each present a different set of dissatisfactions and problems in approaching the future of the city. The arguments embedded within these urbanisms imply direct critiques of contemporary urban development practices. Within postmodern urbanism, the development industry is primarily concerned with the economic development realities of consumer comfort, nostalgia, place-making, private control, and popular marketing – largely at the expense of socio-economic problems facing cities. For everyday urbanism, the contemporary city is the result of incremental development processes that are less about the creation of engineered and coherent urbanism, and more about the uncoordinated patchwork of ordinary places produced by atomistic and budget conscious developers. And within post urbanism, developers treat the city as a series of separate internalized projects with little concern for holding the larger urban fabric together. Each of these urbanisms responds directly to localized issues, but may be approaching irrelevancy when addressing larger temporal urban concerns we face with respect to sustainability, climate change, public health, resource availability, the growing wealth gap, or even local livability.

It would seem natural that the built environment professions would be on the front lines in responding to the physical development concerns of cities. And indeed, many professionals are inclined toward addressing these issues (as some of the readings in Part Four suggest). However, as competition for design work increases (largely in response to tighter budget realities and growth in the total number of built environment professionals), many designers lose their more noble ambitions in the face of daily bread-winning. While each of the built environment professions maintains some measure of ethical responsibility for responding to temporal problems (as outlined in each associated professional code of ethics), the larger reality of practice suggests many designers have devolved into mere client service providers for short-term interests – with less concern for long-term implications. All of this is quite understandable when we recognize that built environment activity rides on the back of professional firm and public agency employment, weekly project staffing, contracts and budgeting, bill-paying, and each professional's domestic economy. As much as we'd like to think the urban design professions are acting in concert to solve the crushing problems of our time, these responsibilities are falling primarily to policy-makers and government officials for large-scale direction – and secondarily to those who champion these concerns (individually or organizationally) and would translate or implement the spirit of this direction.

Perceptions of urban designers, architects, and landscape architects as out-of-touch and irresponsible aesthetes (or planners as elite social scientists or growth machine advocates) are melting away as each profession reinvents itself and moves toward more responsive and pragmatic problem solving. In addition to increasing democratization and participation in city planning, planners are also responding with policies that address key environmental, social, and economic concerns. Many architects are embracing sustainable building practices. Most landscape architects recognize the role their work plays in helping to sustain resources and integrate urban and natural systems. Nowadays, many designers and activists are engaged in advocating and producing responsible designs that challenge status quo development forms and processes. Issues of sustainability, ecological responsibility, smarter growth, and livability are increasingly at the forefront of design practice. Some of these responses take the form of new design movements. Some use manifestos to declare their positions. Others appear as interest groups convening over a strong idea. What is common here is an interest in avoiding the unsustainable mistakes of previous development patterns and discovering a new way forward. While these new movements are diverse and their motives different, they often utilize similar design strategies in implementing their visions: more compact urban form, denser housing models, greener technologies, more walkable streets, more land use mixing, more human-scaled design, more user-friendly communities, greater resource conservation, advanced technologies, and fewer negative environmental externalities.

We start this part of the *Reader* with an exploration of the definitions and characteristics of sprawl. Oliver Gillham's first chapter from *The Limitless City* discusses the reasons for suburban sprawl and its impacts on metropolitan regional form. In discussing sprawl, he highlights both the formal design aspects as well as the institutional, economic, and systemic rationales for low-density urban development. The next reading, Eduardo Lozano's chapter on urban density, "Density in Communities, or the Most Important Factor in Building Urbanity," champions denser urban development and the usefulness of density in building a sense of urbanity. He explores the reasons why density is generally unpopular, and later debunks myths about higher density housing and overcrowding. Lozano's closing recommendations suggest the need to find acceptable building typologies, greater and more sensitive ways to integrate density into communities, and wider choice in environmental, social, and physical outcomes. This reading is largely associated with the Smart Growth movement that first developed in the United States but is now spreading globally.

The next two selections each target a different problem associated with contemporary development patterns. In the excerpts from Frank, Engelke, and Schmid's *Health and Community Design: The Impact of the Built Environment on Physical Activity*, the authors suggest the obesity epidemic and other chronic health conditions in the United States (and arguably elsewhere across the globe) are partly the result of urban form patterns that favor vehicular use at the expense of physical activity. They argue for a policy shift in city planning and urban design that would redirect development standards, design guidelines and transportation policy to encourage healthier living. They advocate urban design patterns that are better connected and encourage walking, biking, and the social life of the city.

Rather than focusing on public health, Ali Madanipour's selection from *Whose Public Space?: International Case Studies in Urban Design and Development* highlights the importance of the public realm of cities for maintaining socio-cultural health. He sees a danger in the increasing privatization of public space and its increasingly contested nature. To correct this trend, Madanipour calls for maximizing access to what is normally considered public space. Both of these last two selections are concerned with community health practices within urban design. Interestingly the design arguments within each of the selections (whether targeting public or social health) focus on greater connectivity, access, and a validation of public realm strategies and policies.

In Ian Bentley's chapter "Profit and Place" from his book *Urban Transformations: Power, People and Urban Design*, the author addresses contemporary urban development processes directly. Bentley sees the quality of life and the physical quality of contemporary cities declining because of profit-motivated changes in the way cities are developed. He presents his argument about declining urban quality in the form of three transformations of wealth in the process of real estate development. In the first transformation, the author discusses how wealth is converted into property through land, locations, materials, and labor. Developers are able to maximize profits from cost savings and scrimping in quality within each of these categories. A second transformation of wealth occurs through the design professions themselves, and how costs can be saved by hiring specialized designers, deskilled construction labor, globalized design practices, and more homogenous designs – all of which results in less daring, less interesting, and less place-based products. The final wealth transformation happens when developers bring their products to market – offering expected building types, short-changing the public realm, and marketing economically "safe" design. Bentley's litany of cost savings by developers is both stunning and not surprising to urban observers who've already witnessed a decline in the construction and design quality of cities over time.

Very different to Bentley's thesis on declining urban quality, the urban design of globalizing cities suggests a very different set of urban development problems. The final two selections focus on two very different urban development phenomena: the spectacular rise of Arabian Gulf coast cities, and the rapid urbanization of China's huge population. In Yasser Elsheshtawy's new writing for this volume "Urban Dualities in the Arab World," he suggests Gulf coast cities exhibit two varied implications in their global strategies: first, a sense of cultural loss as urban history is erased by new development and gentrification, and second, a growing wealth gap that converts residents into economic winners and losers. In the case studies of Dubai and Abu Dhabi, Elsheshtawy shows how two cities are approaching global competitiveness through very different strategies: Dubai based on urban spectacle, real estate and finance sector development, and a lust for superlatives; Abu Dhabi based on global culture, government largesse, and progressive urban design and planning practices. In maturing the UAE's "insta-cities" into legitimate urbanisms, a host of regional urban development and design problems surface: unsustainable energy practices, costly water desalinization, coastal ecosystem degradation, problematic labor practices, human rights issues, problems in overcoming unbearable heat in making a vibrant public realm, and the construction of livable urbanism in arid geographies. While similarities and differences exist between these two Emirati urban strategies, globalization produces greater development problems elsewhere.

The urbanization and globalization of Chinese cities presents a very different set of urban development concerns. The rapid growth of cities and internal movement of the Chinese population to urban places is being managed and coordinated with both amazing efficiency and staggering scale. The selections from Tom Campanella's book *The Concrete Dragon: China's Urban Revolution and What It Means for the World* present the scale of Chinese urbanization over the last few decades, in addition to its global ambitions in reshaping the nature of Chinese cities. The chapters presented here, "The Urbanism of Ambition" and "China Reinvents the City" illustrate the scale of this growth and evolution. Like the Emirati cases by Elsheshtawy, Campanella's Chinese urbanization presents a number of urban development issues that should be a concern to all of us. These urban development issues are challenging China directly, but also presage crises coming to the rest of the world: the growing competition for rare energy resources, global climate change vis-à-vis carbon emission and pollution issues, and the need to house exponential population growth. China's central government (like the centralized power of the UAE's royal sheikdoms) has the unfettered ability and open budgets to expedite this urbanization, but to what end?

For smaller nation-states with strong, centralized social governments (e.g., the UK, Sweden, Denmark, Germany) addressing urban development and sustainability issues has been an ongoing and incremental policy arena that's been developing over time (see the selection by Beatley on "Planning for Sustainability in European Cities" in Part Five of this *Reader*, pp. 558–568). For places with massive poverty and without the bureaucratic or economic ability to marshal desirable urban outcomes (think Lagos-Nigeria or Dhaka-Bangladesh), solving massive infrastructure, service, and housing problems becomes nearly unfathomable. And for free-market liberal democracies like the United States (where power is dispersed and decentralized) the examples of the UAE and China might be less applicable. How does a country like the USA respond to large-scale crises or coordinate long-term national urban change (either in response to resource challenges, wealth-gap concerns, or climate change for example), when attending to short-term local objectives is the norm? In comparison to China's ability and scale of national urbanization, consider the American difficulties in implementing affordable housing, local mass transit, high-speed rail, or infrastructure upgrade.

"What is Sprawl?"

from *The Limitless City: A Primer on the Urban Sprawl Debate* (2002)

Oliver Gillham

Editors' Introduction

Although typically associated with nineteenth-century industrialization, the seeds of sprawl in the United States were planted with the early institutionalization of strong individual property rights, the country's frontier spirit, and the rise of profit-driven speculative development. With the building of streetcar lines, first and second ring suburbs were built around the historic centers of towns and cities, beginning their stretch into previously peripheral areas. The massive proliferation of sprawl, however, is largely associated with late industrialization, the widespread distribution of automobiles and freeways, the rise of zoning practices that emphasized low-density development, federal tax programs that provided economic incentives to both homebuyers and builders, and an ever-increasing volume and scale of production housing by corporate developers. Post-war production of tract housing exacerbated the speed and march of sprawl in historic developments such as Levittown, and continues across many parts of the world today. Although this reading focuses primarily on the United States, indicators of sprawl can be seen from Canada to Australia, South Africa to Southeast Asia.

Oliver Gillham was a pragmatist who presents a balanced portrayal of both the benefits and detriments of low-density suburban development in his book *The Limitless City: A Primer on the Urban Sprawl Debate*. In his introductory chapter to *The Limitless City*, he defines the characteristics and causes of suburban sprawl in clear and simple language. He closes the chapter with a discussion of the metropolitan and regional effects of unimpeded, low-density suburban growth. A large portion of the book tackles the externalities of suburban development and the sprawl debates that continue to rage among academics, civic leaders, advocates, and lobbyists. While recognizing the likely survival of sprawl, he concludes the book with an eye to mitigating future negative impacts by means of policy, infrastructure, and design initiatives.

Oliver Gillham was an architect and planner based in Cambridge, Massachusetts. He worked on urban revitalization and sprawl alleviation projects around the world. He was an architecture graduate of Harvard University, and was influenced heavily in his career by his great uncle Frank Lloyd Wright. After his death in 2008 at age 59, his last book was published: *Urban Design for an Urban Century: Placemaking for People*, written with Lance Jay Brown and David Dixon (New York: Wiley, 2009).

In addition to Gillham, several other authors have made attempts at defining the characteristics of sprawl, including: Reid Ewing, "Characteristics, Causes, and Effects of Sprawl," *Environmental and Urban Issues* (vol. 20, no. 2, pp. 1–15, 1994); J. Thomas Black, "The Economics of Sprawl," *Urban Land* (vol. 53, no. 3, pp. 6–52, 1996); Kenneth A. Small, *Urban Sprawl: A Non-Diagnosis of Real Problems* (Cambridge, MA: Lincoln Institute of Land Policy, 2000); Dolores Hayden, *A Field Guide to Sprawl* (New York: W.W. Norton, 2004); Robert Burchell et al., *Sprawl Costs: Economic Impacts of Unchecked Development* (Washington, DC: Island Press, 2005); and Douglas E. Morris, *It's a Sprawl World After All: The Human Cost of Unplanned Growth – and Visions of a Better Future* (Gabriola Island, BC: New Society, 2005).

A number of advocacy movements and policy agendas have arisen since the mid-1970s to deal with the negative externalities of sprawl. Proposals from these groups vary greatly and include growth management techniques, land use, transportation, and design recommendations. Among these are Smart Growth organizations (see the online publication: *Getting to Smart Growth*, http://www.smartgrowth.org), the Congress for the New Urbanism (see the *Charter of the New Urbanism* in this *Reader*, and http://www.cnu.org), the California-based Local Government Commission (see the *Ahwahnee Principles* at http://www.lgc.org), the Urban Village Movement, see Peter Neal (ed.), *Urban Villages: The Making of Community* (London: E & FN Spon, 2003), and the Compact City Movement, see Mike Jenks, Elizabeth Burton, and Katie Williams (eds), *The Compact City: A Sustainable Urban Form?* (London: E & FN Spon, 1996).

Works on the history of suburbia and sprawl include: Leo Marx, *The Machine in the Garden: Technology and the Pastoral Idea in America* (New York: Oxford University Press, 1964); Robert Fishman, *Bourgeois Utopias: The Rise and Fall of Suburbia* (New York: Basic Books, 1987); Kenneth Jackson, *Crabgrass Frontier: The Suburbanization of the United States* (New York: Oxford University Press, 1985); Sam Bass Warner Jr., *Streetcar Suburbs: The Process of Growth in Boston 1870–1900* (Cambridge, MA: Harvard and MIT Presses, 1962); Herbert Gans, *The Levittowners: Ways of Life and Politics in a New Suburban Community* (New York: Pantheon, 1967); James Howard Kunstler, *The Geography of Nowhere: The Rise and Decline of America's Man-Made Landscape* (New York: Simon & Schuster, 1993); Andres Duany, Elizabeth Plater-Zyberk, and Jeff Speck, *Suburban Nation: The Rise of Sprawl and the Decline of the American Dream* (New York: North Point Press, 2000); Adam Rome, *The Bulldozer and the Countryside: Suburban Sprawl and the Rise of American Environmentalism* (Cambridge: Cambridge University Press, 2001); Dolores Hayden, *Building Suburbia: Green Fields and Urban Growth, 1820–2000* (New York: Vintage, 2004); Owen D. Gutfreund, *Twentieth-Century Sprawl: Highways and the Reshaping of the American Landscape* (New York: Oxford University Press, 2005); and Robert Bruegmann, *Sprawl: A Compact History* (Chicago: University of Chicago Press, 2005).

Other texts that address methods of combatting sprawl include: Dolores Hayden, *Redesigning the American Dream* (New York: W.W. Norton, 1984); Peter Calthorpe, *The Next American Metropolis: Ecology, Community and the American Dream* (New York: Princeton Architectural Press, 1993); Peter Calthorpe and William Fulton, *The Regional City* (Washington, DC: Island Press, 2001); Philip Langdon, *A Better Place to Live: Reshaping the American Suburb* (Amherst, MA: University of Massachusetts Press, 1994); David Bollier, *How Smart Growth Can Stop Sprawl* (Washington, DC: Sprawl Watch Clearinghouse, Essential Books, 1998); James Howard Kunstler, *Home from Nowhere: Remaking our Everyday World for the 21st Century* (New York: Simon & Schuster, 1996); Gregory D. Squires, *Urban Sprawl: Causes, Consequences, and Policy Responses* (Urban Institute Press, 2002); Howard Frumkin, Lawrence Frank, and Richard Jackson, *Urban Sprawl and Public Health: Designing, Planning and Building Healthy Communities* (Washington, DC: Island Press, 2004); Joel S. Hirschhorn, *Sprawl Kills: How Blandburbs Steal Your Time, Health and Money* (New York: Sterling & Ross, 2005); Andres Duany, Jeff Speck, and Mike Lydon, *The Smart Growth Manual* (New York: McGraw-Hill Professional, 2009); and Galina Tachieva, *Sprawl Repair Manual* (Washington, DC: Island Press, 2010).

Debates over the possible ills and benefits of sprawl continue. A number of researchers rely on isolated and reductionist demographic, economic, environmental, and transportation data to show that problems of sprawl may be highly mythologized and unsupported by fact-based realities. Others suggest that anti-sprawl efforts limit citizen choice and personal freedoms, are economically inefficient, and disregard improvements in technology in mitigating the impacts of sprawl. For additional material on the continuing sprawl debates see the following: Reid Ewing, "Is Los Angeles-Style Sprawl Desirable?," *Journal of the American Planning Association* (vol. 63, no. 1, pp. 107–126, 1997); Peter Gordon and Harry W. Richardson, "Are Compact Cities a Desirable Planning Goal?," *Journal of the American Planning Association* (vol. 63, no. 1, pp. 95–106, 1997) and *The Case for Suburban Development* (Los Angeles, CA: Lusk Center Research Institute, 1996); Jane S. Shaw and Ronald D. Utt (eds), *A Guide to Smart Growth: Shattering Myths, Providing Solutions* (Bozeman, MT: Property and Environment Research Center and Heritage Foundation, 2000); Randal O'Toole, *The Vanishing Automobile and Other Urban Myths: How Smart Growth Will Harm American Cities* (Brandon:

Thoreau Institute, 2001); Gregg Easterbrook, "Suburban Myth: The Case for Sprawl," *New Republic* (March 15, 1999); and importantly, the Lone Mountain Coalition, *The Lone Mountain Compact: Principles for Preserving Freedom and Livability in America's Cities and Suburbs* (Bozeman, MT: Property and Environment Research Center, 2000) – a Libertarian position statement supported by a number of academics and advocates.

More nuanced and recent debates over the costs of sprawl include: Anthony Flint, *This Land: The Battle over Sprawl and the Future of America* (Baltimore, MD: Johns Hopkins University Press, 2006); William T. Bogart, *Don't Call it Sprawl: Metropolitan Structure in the 21st Century* (Cambridge: Cambridge University Press, 2006); George A. Gonzales, *Urban Sprawl, Global Warming, and the Empire of Capital* (Albany, NY: State University of New York Press, 2009); and Thad Williamson, *Sprawl, Justice and Citizenship: The Civic Costs of the American Way of Life* (New York/Oxford: Oxford University Press, 2011).

Images of urban sprawl are familiar to almost everyone. Smart growth groups often flash images of the nation's great urban centers erupting across the countryside in a devastating flow of superhighways, shopping centers, baking asphalt, and twinkling cars. Our contemporary metropolitan areas have been widely described as a vast horizontal world of places and things that are accessible only through relentless driving.

These are the images that we read about in the work of James Howard Kunstler, Jane Holtz Kay, Andres Duany, and other well-known writers and urbanists vigorously protesting the ill effects of sprawl. Not everyone agrees, of course, that this suburban world is as negative as is often portrayed. And, as we shall see, it is a world that Americans have brought upon themselves willingly. Still, the rhetoric grows louder and more widespread each day, as more and more people decry the maze of crowded suburban expressways in which the nation has become lost. Even the supporters of the status quo no longer deny the existence of sprawl, but any consensus stops right there, because not everyone agrees about exactly what sprawl is.

CHARACTERISTICS AND INDICATORS OF SPRAWL

Despite powerful imagery and deepening national concern, there is no single, clear and succinct definition of sprawl that is shared by everyone. Moreover, the idea of what constitutes sprawl has been known to change over time. The definition from the *Merriam-Webster Online Dictionary* ("the spreading of urban developments . . . on undeveloped land near a city") actually dates from 1958.[1] The current *Encarta World English Dictionary* presents a subtly different, contemporary interpretation, stating that urban sprawl is "the expansion of an urban area into areas of countryside that surround it."[2] "Undeveloped" has become "countryside" (a word with more pastoral associations), while "city" has become "urban area" (a vaguer term that can include suburbs as well as city centers).[3] But the dictionaries aren't the last word on the subject. There are other definitions and descriptions offered by groups on both sides of the issue, and they vary from the subtle differences that can be found in dictionaries to much more extreme characterizations. The characterizations below provide a sampling of the different descriptions of what constitutes sprawl.

Sample characterizations of sprawl

The Heritage Foundation: " 'Sprawl' simply refers to the low-density, residential development beyond a city's limits."[4]

Reason Public Policy Institute: "Many people think sprawl is synonymous with suburbanization . . . Another way of characterizing this process is thinking of sprawl as the 'transitional period between rural and urban land use.' "[5]

Commonwealth of Massachusetts, Executive Office of Environmental Affairs: "What is sprawl? Planners define it as low-density, single-use development on the urban fringe that is almost totally dependent on private automobiles for transportation."[6]

National Trust for Historic Preservation, Rural Heritage Program: "Sprawl is dispersed, low-density development that is generally located at the fringe of an existing settlement and over large areas of previously rural landscape. It is characterized by segregated land uses and dominated by the automobile."[7]

U.S. Environmental Protection Agency: "[Sprawl is a] pattern of growth [that] has largely occurred in an unplanned, ad hoc fashion."[8]

The Sierra Club: "Sprawl – scattered development that increases traffic, saps local resources and destroys open space."[9]

Natural Resources Defense Council: "Sprawling development eats up farms, meadows, and forests, turning them into strip malls and subdivisions that serve cars better than people."[10]

As can be seen from these characterizations, descriptions of sprawl vary from simple portrayals of a transitional landscape to more suggestive characterizations of wholesale destruction of the nation's farms and forests. One thing that almost all of the definitions shown have in common is that they portray sprawl as essentially a suburban phenomenon – "beyond a city's limits," "transitional," or "on the urban fringe." It is also generally characterized as low density, favoring automobiles, and possibly "scattered," "unplanned," or "ad hoc" in its pattern.

One of the more widely accepted characterizations of sprawl (one that encompasses many of the attributes listed above) has been developed by Professor Reid Ewing of Florida International University, an architect of Florida's statewide growth management plan. His definition of sprawl is essentially a list of descriptors that has been used by groups working to curb sprawl (such as the Natural Resources Defense Council and the National Trust for Historic Preservation) as well as those defending the status quo (like the Reason Public Policy Institute). Ewing posits the following four forms of development as among the most widely cited characteristics of sprawl:

- Leapfrog or scattered development
- Commercial strip development
- Low density
- Large expanses of single-use development.[11]

Ewing goes on to note that one or more of these characteristics have been cited as descriptors of sprawl by a long list of widely regarded urban scholars dating back to 1957.[12] Still unsatisfied with this definition, Ewing names two additional "indicators" of sprawl, included in Florida's anti-sprawl rule, that he feels help to more accurately define the term:

- Poor accessibility
- Lack of functional (that is, public) open space.

Below, each of the characteristics and indicators cited by Ewing is explored in depth.

Leapfrog development

Leapfrog development means exactly that: subdivisions, shopping centers, and office parks that have "leapfrogged" over intervening tracts of farmland or forest or both. The result is a haphazard patchwork, widely spread apart and seeming to consume far more land than contiguous developments. Unless preserved or unbuildable, the remaining open tracts are usually filled in with new development as time progresses. Familiar to most people, this pattern characterizes many rapidly developing suburban and exurban fringe areas.

Commercial strip development

Commercial strip development is characterized by huge arterial roads lined with shopping centers, gas stations, fast-food restaurants, drive-thru banks, office complexes, parking lots, and many large signs. Retail is configured in long, low boxes or small pavilions surrounded by multiple acres of surface parking. Landscaping is usually minimal so as not to interfere with parking and signage. The office complexes differ little from the shopping centers, but usually are a little taller. Sidewalks and pedestrian crosswalks are rare, and trips between different centers on the strip are almost all by automobile. The concept of the strip is so famous that it has become an American icon, enshrined in Las Vegas and celebrated in the book *Learning from Las Vegas*, by architects Robert Venturi and Denise Scott Brown, as well as in such films as *American Graffiti*.

Low density

In terms of density, sprawl is neither a crowded urban core nor an open countryside. It lies between the two in varying gradations. Compared to older city and town centers, the density of sprawl is very low indeed. Suburban buildings are often single-story and widely spaced, with intervening parking lots and roadways. Sprawl is not a typical older city with solid blocks of eight- and ten-story buildings; nor is it a typical older Main Street of two- and three-story buildings. It isn't even a rural village of comfortably spaced single-family homes and stores. If present, tall buildings are often separated from one another by large areas of roadways and parking. Low-density and leapfrog patterns are both blamed for making sprawl both land consumptive and auto dependent.

Density can be defined several ways: by the number of people per acre or per square mile or by the number of dwelling units per acre or floor area ratio (FAR). FAR is the ratio of the number of square feet of built area to land area. Built area usually includes all floors of all buildings. Note that FAR takes account of built commercial space in an area while dwelling units and population do not. These different methods are appropriate to different scales of analysis. Population or employment per square mile is appropriate to the city and regional scale. Dwelling units and FAR are usually used for community and neighborhood scale. Table 1 provides a comparison of selected rural, suburban, and urban residential densities in dwelling units and FAR.

Single-use development

The low-density pattern of sprawl is often further characterized by the deliberate segregation of land uses. Housing consists predominantly of single-family homes on individual lots. While older downtowns may have a combination of stores, offices, and apartments all on one street – and sometimes on top of one another – such mixing of uses is rarely a feature of most post-World War II suburban areas. In these areas, different land uses are usually intentionally disconnected, sometimes by large distances. This separation is formalized through zoning and subdivision bylaws and the dictates of a compendium of widely used planning standards.

Table 1 Selected residential densities

	Building type	Dwelling units/acre	FAR
Rural	Single-family, 100 acres	0.01	0.0005
	Single-family, 25 acres	0.04	0.0018
Suburban	Single-family, acre	1	0.05
	Single-family, ¹/₂ acre	2	0.09
	Single-family, quarter-acre	4	0.18
Urban	Townhouse	24	0.88
	3-story apartment	50	1.38
	6-story apartment	75	1.72
	12-story apartment	125	2.87
High-density urban	Townhouse	36	1.16
	3-story apartment	75	2.07
	6-story apartment	110	2.53
	12-story apartment	220	5.05

Note: The above data is based on an analysis of characteristic development in the Boston metropolitan region. This data is given for illustrative purposes only. Typical developments may vary significantly from the examples given depending on age of project, target market, setting, local codes, and other factors.

Poor accessibility (or automobile dominance)

Low-density development combined with segregated land uses leads to what Ewing terms "poor accessibility." As he describes the situation:

> Residences may be far from out-of-home activities, a state of poor residential accessibility. Or out-of-home activities may be far from one another, a state of poor destination accessibility. Both types of accessibility affect the efficiency of household travel patterns.[13]

Ewing believes that this characteristic is a good indicator of sprawl because it is measurable in terms of typical trip lengths, average trip times, vehicle miles traveled (VMT), and vehicle hours traveled (VHT) – the idea being that the longer trips and trip times become (the higher the number of VMT or VHT or both), the worse the accessibility situation becomes.

"Poor accessibility" arguably may be a somewhat judgmental term. Essentially, this indicator shows that the distances between suburban origins and destinations are relatively far, a consequence of low-density development and large expanses of single-use development. Implicit within these distances is another widely used gauge of sprawl: automobile dominance or auto dependency.[14] The longer distances between activities means that the only way to get around easily is by car. For this reason, many people list auto dependency not only as an indicator but also as a main characteristic of sprawl.[15] Compared to denser downtown environments, suburban sprawl offers relatively little transit, and often walking or biking between home and different activities can be very difficult.

Lack of public open space

In ideal circumstances, the low-density residential pattern of sprawl can achieve the sought-after appearance of rustic cottages nestled in a leafy, parklike setting. It was this idyllic effect that the planners of some of the finest early suburbs tried to achieve. Yet, even in the best of situations, the parklike setting is rarely public. It belongs to individual homeowners as part of their yards and gardens. In other areas, much of the open space is taken over by paved parking areas that are also in private hands. The great malls may provide galleria-like "public" spaces, where crowds of shoppers gather, but again the malls are ultimately privately owned. Except around the school yard, public open space can be quite difficult to find in many suburban areas. This is another key indicator of sprawl: that it is, for the most part, an unbroken fabric of privately owned land divided only by public roads. The major civic open spaces, parks, and commons that grace many older urban-core areas can be few to nonexistent in much of the nation's post-war suburban world.

A DEFINITION OF SPRAWL

Having reviewed the principal characteristics and indicators of sprawl described by Ewing and accepted by many professionals in the field, it is now possible to propose a definition of sprawl that will be used throughout this book. It will be what a logician would call a connotative definition of sprawl – that is, an analytical definition by genus and difference, or by class and subclass.[16] In this kind of definition, sprawl is a type (or subclass) of urbanization (the broader class of urban development as a whole). As a subclass, sprawl has a set of distinct attributes that differentiate it from all other types of urbanization (for example, a city of crowded skyscrapers or a medieval hill town). Using the connotative method, we can translate Ewing's set of characteristics and indicators into a broad definition:

> *Sprawl (whether characterized as urban or suburban) is a form of urbanization distinguished by leapfrog patterns of development, commercial strips, low density, separated land uses, automobile dominance, and a minimum of public open space.*

This definition has no suggested connection with a nearby city center, which makes it a more accurate characterization of contemporary sprawl development patterns. (As we shall subsequently see, this form of urbanization can occur anywhere within or adjoining a metropolitan region, without any necessary connection to the core city.) The defining attributes of sprawl addressed earlier are also common to most types of late-twentieth-century suburban development. For this reason, we can add a secondary definition of sprawl:

> *Sprawl (whether characterized as urban or suburban) is the typical form of most types of late-twentieth-century suburban development.*

With this definition in hand, we can now explore the meaning of another very important term: *suburbanization*. The *Merriam-Webster Online Dictionary* defines suburbanization as "making suburban" or "giving a suburban character to."[17] Planners have sometimes used this term to describe the spreading of suburbs or suburban patterns across a region or a nation.[18] If we take this to mean specifically late-twentieth-century suburban development, then we can make the following definition:

> *Suburbanization is the spread of suburban development patterns across a region or a nation – that is, the proliferation of sprawl forms of urbanization across a region or a nation.*

The terms *sprawl* and *suburbanization* will be used interchangeably throughout this book.

WHAT MAKES SPRAWL?

The aforementioned definitions of sprawl and suburbanization still do not tell the whole story. While we now have an idea of what sprawl looks like and what its principal traits are, we still don't know why it is the way it is or exactly what goes into its construction. While sprawl development owes its existence to many factors, it is important to understand four essential ingredients of suburbanization:

- Land ownership and use
- Transportation patterns
- Telecommunications technology
- Regulations and standards.

The sections that follow deal with each factor in turn.

Land ownership and use

Most of the land in the United States – about 70 percent – is privately held.[19] Under American law, each parcel of land comes with a bundle of rights related to ownership, including water and air rights and the rights to sell the land, pass it along to heirs, use it, or develop it. These privately held entitlements give land value and marketability. As long as land remains privately owned – and its rights remain unencumbered – it is susceptible to being subdivided and built upon.

Land itself – along with the rights attendant to its ownership – can be bought and sold like any other commodity. Without a highly developed system of private land ownership and a viable market for land, sprawl as we know it would be virtually impossible. The concept of private land ownership is the foundation upon which the private home is built. It wasn't always that way, however. Native Americans viewed the land as something held in common. It was the early settlers from Europe who brought the concept of individual land ownership to the United States.

With the arrival of the Europeans, land ownership quickly achieved great importance in the New World. Since then, it has remained a basic tenet of the American ethos that being a landowner is the key to being a successful, fully vested member of society. In fact, during the decades following the ratification of the U.S. Constitution, many states limited voting rights to landowners. Thus, you not only had to be a white male over age twenty-one, but also had to own land to be counted as a real citizen. As Kenneth T. Jackson tells us in *Crabgrass Frontier*:

> The idea that land ownership was a mark of status, as well as a kind of sublime insurance against ill fortune, was brought to the New World as part of the baggage of the European settlers. They established a society on the basis of the private ownership of property, and every attempt to organize settlements along other lines ultimately failed. The principle of fee-simple tenure enabled families to buy, sell, rent, and bequeath land with great ease and a minimum of interference by Government. It became . . . "the freest land system anywhere in the world."[20]

Today, the American Dream is still to own one's own home on one's own piece of land. More than two-thirds of Americans own their own homes, and many have most of their money tied up in that very investment – which is also their shelter.[21] Purchasing a home is often the biggest investment Americans will make in their lifetimes.

Real estate markets

A colossal industry has been built around real estate, not only around simply buying and selling the land or its rights (or both) but also around deliberately increasing the value of the land by building on it. This is why most land gets developed: to increase its value and create wealth. Along with the basic bundle of entitlements, increasing land value is every landowner's right in America, just as making a profit is every individual's right whether that person owns land or not. The private ownership of land and the huge, almost liquid, market for it are vital to the very survival of suburban sprawl.

In 1997, the U.S. real estate industry produced revenues totaling over $240 billion.[22] That same year, related industry revenues for private construction totaled nearly $400 billion.[23] The size of the real estate and construction industries gives them significant influence in what gets built, where, and in what quantity. The real estate development industry delivers its products in response to demand – demand for houses, demand for offices, demand for shops, demand for hotel rooms, and so forth. Wheat fields in Kansas are wheat fields and not housing partly because of real estate markets. There is a smaller market for housing in the middle of rural Kansas than exists in a big metropolitan area, but there is a market for land on which to grow wheat. It is market demand that initially establishes what, where, and how much of everything gets built. The industry simply delivers the product.

But market demand is also determined to some degree by the product industry delivers. There was little demand for personal computers before the first one was invented and brought to market. Similarly, there was no recognizable market for indoor suburban shopping malls before the first one was built in Southdale, Minnesota, in 1956. When a successful formula like the indoor suburban shopping mall comes along, it can rapidly develop into a new market, exploding across the countryside. Financing feeds a growth industry, be it business or real estate. If a formula is successful and therefore profitable, it becomes easy to finance. The tendency is then to repeat the same formula many times, which partly explains the repetitiveness of suburban development. Single-family homes, shopping centers, and office parks in their current forms have been very successful models.

The cost of land

But sprawl would not have its current attributes if land were scarce and expensive. The existence of a large market for land development helps to explain U.S. patterns of urbanization overall, not just suburban sprawl. The unique pattern of sprawl can be partly attributed to the abundance and relatively low cost of land, which is necessary to allow dispersed, low-rise development to occur. Tall vertical cities like New York result, among other things, from the high cost of the land under the buildings. To justify the higher cost of the land, a developer has to build to a much higher density in Manhattan than in a typical suburban environment.

Why does land cost more in some center cities than it does in the suburbs? The higher cost can be traced to two factors: clustering and access. It is widely accepted that the monetary advantages of clustering (also known as the economies of agglomeration) are among the primary forces driving urbanization in general.[24] Businesses benefit economically by being able to shop for goods and services in a cluster. Furthermore, employees benefit from being able to shop for jobs in that same cluster and employers benefit from the large labor pool that results. The gathering of the labor pool in turn causes housing, stores, and other uses to be drawn into the resulting conurbation.

The second factor is access. Many cities originated by gathering around some major means of access to other, more distant markets in order to reduce transportation cost. Businesses originally needed to be as close as possible not only to one another, but also to a central import-export node, such as a harbor, river port, or rail station. This need reinforced clustering, which in turn drove up land cost and density. A typical result was the late-nineteenth or early-twentieth century U.S. manufacturing city with a high-density central business district gathered near port facilities and rail termini.

The equation changes when access becomes much more widespread, as happened with the introduction of cars, trucks, and pervasive high-speed roadway networks. Widespread access means that cheap land far from any city center becomes a usable commodity for businesses and homes alike. Without a compelling need to cluster, homes and businesses will naturally begin to spread out. As Terry Moore and Paul Thorsnes have written in *The Transportation/Land Use Connection:*

> Business firms ... respond to land prices by spacing themselves as widely as possible. Spacing reduces competition for land which reduces its price. No other reasons (such as proximity to a port) exist to cause competition for land, and businesses reduce cost by occupying lower-priced land.[25]

What is true for businesses is also true for home owners. Reduced land cost means that single-family homes on relatively generous individual plots of land within commuting distance of work suddenly become an affordable commodity for many Americans. This demonstrates the very close relationship between land and transportation in defining modern patterns of human settlement. To have any worth, land must be served by some means of transportation, whether a transit stop, a highway interchange, or even just a lane or an alleyway connecting to a larger roadway system. When land is both accessible and inexpensive, building at much lower densities can be profitable. This combination is fundamental to sprawl development.

Transportation patterns

Land and market forces alone could not establish the low-density membrane that characterizes sprawl. History and economics tell us that without a transportation system capable of serving this pattern, sprawl simply would not exist. Without automobiles and paved roadways, we would inhabit an entirely different world.

Mode choice

Two major transportation factors determine development patterns: mode (or modal) choice and the physical layout or pattern of the transportation system itself (sometimes known as the transportation network). Mode choice refers to the availability of different kinds of transportation. Transportation modes consist of everything from walking to automobiles, railroads, boats, and air travel. When you travel from your home to work, what choices do you have for making the trip? Can you, for example, choose between walking, biking, driving, and riding public transportation? Sometimes a trip may involve multiple modes – for instance, driving to the train from home or taking a bus from the train to work. The transfer between each mode is called a mode change.

In the suburbs and beyond, mode choices typically are few. In many instances, the car is the only choice. When trip origins and destinations are highly dispersed over a wide area (the result of a continuum of low-density development), the private automobile is often the only adequate mode of transportation. When alternative choices are available, a discouraging number of different mode changes may be required. A traveler may have to change from bus to bus to rail and back to bus again. All things being equal, the more mode changes that are required, the greater the disincentive will be to choosing an alternative to the automobile.

Travel time and cost also affect mode decisions. Travel time may be influenced by congestion on the roadways or the number of transit stops. Cost may be affected by the cost of passage as well as by the availability of reasonably priced parking. The automobile can sometimes seem to be the least expensive mode due to the tendency to ignore both the cost of the car and the overall cost of the auto/roadway transportation system – even though that cost is actually quite substantial in both dollars and externalities.

Modal choices can vary significantly, depending on the kind of trip taken. Trips generally can be categorized as either local or long distance. Local trips (also referred to as daily trips) are less than 100 miles one way. These trips basically fall into two categories: work trips or commuting (travel to and from work), and nonwork trips (errands, shopping, school, and so forth).

Local work trips

Commuting trips in contemporary suburbs are almost invariably beyond walking distance and mostly have been since the days of railroads and streetcars. In those cases where a major urban core or other high-density employment center is involved, bus or rail transit may be available for trip making, but a car may be needed to get to the train or bus. As suburban patterns develop farther and farther from major urban centers, the car becomes the only real mode choice for most commuter trips. More than 70 percent of all commuting trips in the nation have nothing to do with downtown; rather, they are to and from suburban and exurban destinations.[26] For this type of commuting trip, the automobile often is the only option.

Local nonwork trips

As with work trips, the car is usually the only choice for suburban nonwork trips because of the low density and horizontal separation of uses. This means that many basic errands are generally too far to walk, and the "trip-ends" – or origins and destinations – are too dispersed for any form of mass transit to make sense. These disparate origins and destinations do not usually lend themselves to any sort of fixed-route transit system. Bicycles might work, but because of lack of suitable roads, distance, weather, or other reasons, biking is often ruled out.

Furthermore, local trips may include a number of stops on each trip with varying numbers of people and bundles to be picked up or dropped off. This succession of stops is called trip chaining. A typical example might be a short journey where a parent takes a child to a music lesson and then drives on to drop off the dry cleaning, make a stop at a hardware outlet, and then do the grocery shopping. Interestingly, local nonwork trips are by far the largest segment of all travel. According to the U.S. Department of Transportation, nonwork trips make up more than 75 percent of total person miles traveled in the United States.[27]

Long-distance travel

In sheer numbers, the amount of local travel in the United States is overwhelming when compared to long-distance travel. More than 99 percent of all person trips made in the United States on all modes are local, accounting for more than 75 percent of all person miles traveled in the nation.[28] Thus, it is tempting to dismiss the contribution of long-distance travel in defining the pattern of sprawl as relatively trivial. This might be justified were it not for the issue of the central import-export node described earlier in this chapter.

In the early part of the twentieth century, long-distance passengers and freight accessed a typical city by means of one or more centrally located import-export nodes, such as a rail station or a port. This phenomenon reinforced the dense clustering of early-twentieth-century manufacturing cities. Roadways and airports have significantly changed that pattern. Clustering is still an urbanizing force, but highway interchanges and multiple regional airports have replaced rail terminals and harbors as primary import-export nodes, radically altering the geographic scale and pattern of clustering.

Today, about 83 percent of the value of all freight in the United States is shipped by truck and plane, while 97 percent of all passengers travel by air and by road when taking a long trip.[29] Ports and rail termini are still used for heavy bulk cargo, but almost all people and most valuable goods travel in planes, cars, and trucks. As suburbs have spread and air and roadway travel has increased, the center-city train depot has become increasingly less relevant. Long-distance trips are now more likely to be made from one suburban area to another, with the car being the only practical way to get to and from the airport at either end of the trip.

In the end, almost all contemporary transportation choices use the car somehow in the process. The car is often the choice for local trips, commuting, and long-distance travel. Because automobile travel accounts for 92 percent of the total person miles traveled in the United States, the roadway system is by far the nation's foremost transportation network.[30] This means that auto-dependent development is basically self-perpetuating. Any new land development that hopes to succeed has to hook into the transportation pattern that connects everything else, which means extending the pattern of automobile dominance and limited mode choice.

The transportation network

The nation's roadway network is one of the most powerful forces determining the shape of metropolitan regions across the United States. Railroad, water, and air transportation have never been able to match the access granted by roadways. Combine this omnipresent network with automobiles and trucks, and once-simple roadways are converted to a high-speed transportation system that often outmatches railroads in travel time and accessibility. Mode choice could never be so dramatically skewed toward the automobile if it were not for the universal presence of roadways. It is this vast network that has made decentralization possible on a truly gigantic scale. It also, to a very large extent, defines the look and feel of our suburban world. As James S. Russell recently observed in *Harvard Design Magazine:* "What unites suburbia is not shared public space, or a coherent architectural vision, but a vast civil-engineered network of roads."[31]

As noisy, congested, and chaotic as the nation's roadway system can appear, it actually possesses a very intricate hierarchical structure. Under ideal circumstances, all of its component roadways are designed to function together as a unified structure of greater and lesser arteries and veins – like the human circulatory system, only made to move vehicles instead of blood cells. As extensive as it is, the entire network ultimately comprises just a few distinct roadway types. Together, this system of expressways, arterial roads, collector roads, local streets, and cul-de-sacs makes up almost the entire public environment of our suburbs.

But roads alone don't describe all of the system. All of the automobiles need someplace to park, and these parking areas define suburban sprawl as much as, if not more than, the roadway system. Garages, carports, and driveways adorn every contemporary residential subdivision, and shopping centers, malls, and office parks offer great fields of surface parking. Sometimes, these areas are landscaped but often only minimally to avoid blocking clear views of commercial signs. These areas could be designed differently (the cars could be – and sometimes are – placed underground or in structures), but surface parking is the most economical way to build parking as long as land is inexpensive enough. And, as we have seen, it is the roadway and car transportation system that has helped to make the cost of accessible land inexpensive enough to decentralize clustering patterns while at

the same time leaving enough room to park most of the cars at grade.

Telecommunications technology

Electronic telecommunications are rapidly transforming the world around us. As William J. Mitchell recently wrote in his foreword to Thomas Horan's *Digital Places:*

> Digital telecommunications networks [will] transform urban form and function as radically as . . . mechanized transportation networks, telegraph and telephone networks and electrical grids [have] done in the past. These networks . . . loosen many of the spatial and temporal linkages that have traditionally bound human activities together in dense clusters, and they . . . allow new patterns to emerge.[32]

We cannot know for certain what kind of world will finally emerge from this new revolution. However, we can clearly see what electricity, telephones, and computers have already done.

Electricity

The electrical grid is as pervasive as the roadway system (in fact, it often follows it). This shared ubiquity has freed businesses and homes to locate just about anywhere and be assured of a power source to run the machinery necessary for modern living and commerce. Before the twentieth century, no such widespread infrastructure existed. The machinery that electricity runs includes much of the infrastructure of modern telecommunications, such as computers, remote telephones, modems, fax machines, printers, copiers, and the like. Without available electrical power everywhere, most of the machines of modern commerce would not exist, nor would the systems that run our homes.

Corporations could not do business in a low-density suburban environment without at least electricity and telephone. Initially, it was the telephone that greatly reduced the need for businesses to share a common location – such as a major city – in which communications are facilitated by proximity.

Telecommunications and computers

Although telephones have been in existence since the end of the nineteenth century, the truly exponential advances in telecommunications and information systems have occurred only in the past fifty years. This technology revolution has made suburban sprawl possible on a scale that could never have been envisioned in the early twentieth century. The development of mainframe computers connected by telephone lines in the 1950s and 1960s meant that information could be readily and simultaneously shared by a network of remote facilities. Until then, major corporations had struggled to keep all of their operations under one roof to realize what economists refer to as "economies of scale of production."

Businesses realize economies of scale when the average cost of a unit of output (anything from a camshaft to a bank statement) falls as the total volume or scale of output increases. To realize these economies, businesses typically massed people and machines together under one roof. This phenomenon, together with clustering, has historically been one of the primary forces shaping urbanization by centralizing urban development.[33] For example, many service industry businesses once realized economies of scale by having everyone in one building in a big city. This meant paying a single rent check while simplifying management, information sharing, and communications. At the same time, the businesses were clustered near their customers and vendors, giving them ready access to both.

Together with roadways, cars, and airports, advances in telecommunications and computer technology have substantially changed how these forces work, allowing many companies to abandon older models and to decentralize, relocating major portions of their businesses to suburban locations or even to other parts of the country or overseas – wherever land or labor or both cost less. Many major corporations also realized that they no longer needed to have even their headquarters downtown. Now, the head office could move closer to the suburban homes of the CEO and other corporate officers, while links with customers and vendors could be handled electronically. Combined with roadways, automobiles, and airports, the growth of electronic telecommunications helps explain why more than 80 percent of the employment growth in the United States between 1980 and 1990 was in suburban and exurban locations – not downtown.[34]

Wiring the home

Suburban housing owes much to telephone, radio, and television. The telephone allowed instant communication between worker and household, even if the worker was miles away, making it easier to manage business and domestic affairs in two locations. The spread of residential subdivisions far from any theater district or concert hall also has been helped considerably by radio and television. Countless channels of programming have brought entertainment right into the home. You no longer need to get in your car to go to the movies. By 2000, average daily household television viewing was approaching eight hours per day, the number of television sets was climbing toward an average of 2.5 per household, and more than 80 percent of American households owned a VCR. Between 1995 and 1998, the number of households connected to the Internet increased from less than 10 percent to more than 50 percent. Greater than 80 percent of the nation spends each evening watching television.[35] Thus, even suburban movie houses have had to transform themselves into huge multiplex entertainment centers to survive. The advent of home entertainment centers and digital TV and recording media may make further inroads into the cinema business.

The Internet and beyond

There is little question that modern information systems have vastly expanded the freedom of location in our society. Businesses and residences can now situate themselves practically anywhere. Employees don't even have to show up at the office to go to work anymore. The number of telecommuters (those who spend at least part of their days working from home via computer and telephone) quadrupled from 4 million to almost 16 million between 1990 and 1998.[36] By 2000, the number had jumped to nearly 24 million.[37] The fiscal 2001 appropriations bill for the U.S. Department of Transportation requires that every federal agency give at least 25 percent of its eligible work-force the option of working outside the office by fall 2001.[38]

The future of the retailing industry also may be changing as on-line retailing becomes more popular. Books, music, computers, and an ever expanding list of other items can now be ordered electronically on-line and sent via air express right to your door. The volume of "e-retailing," as it is called, increased at an annual rate of 67 percent from 1999 through the end of 2000.[39] Since then, there has been an industry shakeout, but people are still buying on-line. It is impossible to predict where all of this will ultimately lead, but these communications developments undeniably have given us more freedom than ever to choose where we live and work. It seems almost as certain that they have made decentralization increasingly easier.

Regulations and standards

Another key factor that helps determine the final pattern of suburbanization is the battery of regulations, codes, and standards that govern development in communities across the United States. The result of a century-long interdisciplinary effort, this vast compendium of rules forms the "genetic code" of sprawl. Various parts of the compendium can be found in the subdivision regulations and zoning codes of most U.S. municipalities. Other segments can be found in the roadway manuals and standards issued by state and federal governments. Still other sections appear in the myriad privately published standard planning and design reference works for engineers, surveyors, planners, architects, and land-scape architects.

These works set forth guidelines for minimum roadway widths, street patterns, parking layouts, lot grading, and many other items, right down to steps, curbing, and residential swimming pools. Although the patterns established by the genetic code can be very hard to make out from the monotony and chaos we see on the ground, they are very much a part of the suburban world around us. It is this genetic code that forms the pattern that we can see from the air, and it is this same compendium of rules, regulations, and standards that makes sprawl development in Georgia look just like sprawl development in California or New Jersey.

Zoning and building codes

As we have seen, the fact that land is private is fundamental to its development potential. How land gets developed – where and for what use – is largely determined by real estate markets. Even density and form are determined to some extent by market forces. But once the market for development has been established (or is on the way to becoming so), publicly regulated land use controls, or zoning, also can become a critical determinant in how land can be developed.

In most American communities where there is a market for new development, zoning controls land – and to some extent its value – by regulating both land use and density. Use districts are established together with height and bulk regulations, the number of units or square feet of building allowed per acre, and setbacks that buildings are required to observe from the street and from one another. Zoning can govern what landowners can build on their own land as well as clarify expectations about what can be built next door. For example, a home owner who decides to put an addition on a house may find that zoning controls the size and location of the new construction. The addition may be limited in height, square footage, how far it may extend toward the boundaries of the lot, and what its use may be. After market forces have been established, zoning can ultimately be a major factor in determining what any given development will consist of and what it will look like. Some early subdivisions were built in rural areas that had no zoning. As communities grew, zoning was often put in place with the endorsement of home owners for their own protection.

Without some sort of formal control over how land in a particular district is used, each landholder in the district is continually at risk from neighbors. If you invest in building a house, you don't know for sure that a tannery or a pulp mill won't get built next door someday. This is one reason for controls: to provide reasonable expectations for the continued value of a given piece of land and thereby create a relatively stable marketplace. Regulations also exist to protect the public. Building a tannery or a pulp mill in the middle of a residential neighborhood can endanger public health and welfare. Crowding wooden residential structures too close together without adequate ventilation or emergency access can be both a health hazard and a fire hazard. Thus, zoning bylaws, subdivision regulations, and related codes continue to be considered necessary and effective for protecting public health and welfare.

In suburban areas, separation of land uses can be far more extreme than in older, urban-core areas. In older cities, compatible land uses are often mixed together. But, as Reid Ewing notes in his definition of sprawl shown earlier in this chapter, classic suburban zoning partitions all land uses into distinctly separate districts, which often are defined by roadways. Large arterial roadways and highway corridors, for example, are often zoned commercial or light industrial. Typically, industrial uses will be buffered from any residential uses by roads, landscaping, and open spaces or by intervening commercial uses (or both). Commercial uses, in turn, are themselves buffered from adjoining residential uses, often by roadways and landscaped areas. While some contemporary planners may rue the extreme to which the separation of uses has been taken, it should be remembered that many people still prefer quiet residential streets with nothing but houses on them. To these people, dictating otherwise would disrupt the character of the neighborhood and threaten property values.

But the codes do not stop at simply separating uses. Frequently, they also distinguish between different varieties of the same kind of use. For example, housing is sometimes separated into multifamily and single-family detached housing or even into different kinds of single-family housing, usually based on lot size (for example, half an acre, one acre, or two acres per unit). It has been argued that such finer gradations may discriminate by segregating people by economic class, with the plots in large-lot zoning areas available only to wealthy people.

In many ways, horizontal zoning seems very rational, both from the private as well as the public perspective. Because it protects public health and welfare as well as property values, a lot of people support it. Yet, as we have seen, it is this very horizontal separation of uses – ruling out other possible outcomes – that helps to define sprawl. As Andres Duany, one of the founders of New Urbanism, writes in *Suburban Nation*:

The problem is that one cannot easily build Charleston any more, because it is against the law. Similarly, Boston's Beacon Hill, Nantucket, Santa Fe, Carmel – all of these well-known places, many of which have become tourist destinations, exist in direct violation of current zoning ordinances. Even the classic American Main Street, with its mixed-use buildings right up against the sidewalk, is now illegal in most municipalities.[40]

Many contemporary land use codes have ruled out older, walkable cities and downtowns in favor of horizontally separated zoning districts – in other words, sprawl zoning. This is why you can't walk to a corner store; it's usually too far away. It is true that not everyone wants to live over a store, but Duany's argument is that current codes don't allow any choice in the matter.

On the other hand, lest zoning be blamed for too much, it is useful to observe that places like Nantucket and Beacon Hill have zoning bylaws and other regulations that actually work to protect their historic character and require that new development fit the existing pattern. Also note that a sprawling city like Houston, Texas, has no zoning. In theory, Houston could have built itself like Manhattan or Colonial Williamsburg, or even a medieval Italian hill town, but it did not turn out that way. Even without zoning, Houston exhibits many of the sprawl characteristics of other metropolitan areas. It is spread out and generally low density, ranking fourth in degree of sprawl (ahead of Los Angeles and Miami) out of twenty-eight metropolitan areas ranked by the Surface Transportation Policy Project.[41]

The requirements of finance

To some degree, Houston makes up for its lack of zoning with other types of regulations, but market and financing factors have also helped fill the gap. As noted earlier, markets help define real estate product and most housing, offices, and shopping malls require financing to get built. In the case of housing, much of the financing takes the form of residential mortgages. Many home mortgages are guaranteed by government agencies who, over the years, have developed their own preferences and standards for what should be built. Those standards are reflected in many contemporary zoning codes and contribute to the genetic code of suburban development written into the manuals of many design and development professionals and sometimes even into covenants contained in the deeds of various projects.

The banks and insurance companies that finance many suburban commercial and residential projects have similar standards. Their requirements can dictate the size of the project, the uses that may be included, the number of parking spaces needed, and even the materials to be used in construction. To finance, build, and sell their real estate products, developers in places like Houston have had to follow many rules established elsewhere – just as if the missing suburban zoning were in place.

THE LIMITLESS CITY

The dictionary definition of urban sprawl presented earlier implies that sprawl emanates from a nearby city. Sprawl is fundamentally suburban in origin, and a suburb, as its name would suggest, is supposed to be subordinate to a city. That meaning is encapsulated in the *Webster's New World Dictionary* definition of a suburb: "a district, especially a residential district, on the outskirts of a city."[42] In 1966, when that definition was written, it was a fairly accurate characterization of the situation. From 1920 until the mid-1960s, big industrial cities were the nation's dominant centers of population and employment, the economic engines where most Americans lived and worked.[43] In that era, suburbs resembled the dictionary definition: generally less populated outlying residential areas that served as bedroom communities for the big cities. (Los Angeles, a polycentric city almost from the beginning, was a clear exception.)

Beyond suburbs

Since the 1960s, however, that situation has changed dramatically. At the dawn of the twenty-first century, more people live and work in suburbs than live and work in the nation's center cities. The statistics are revealing: slightly over 8 million people live within the city limits of New York City, but that is only 40 percent of the over 20 million people estimated to live in the total New York Consolidated Metropolitan Statistical Area (CMSA) defined by the U.S. Census Bureau.[44] The same is true of Boston, where almost 5.5 million people inhabit the CMSA but only 1.5 million live in the Boston urban-core area.[45]

What is true of New York and Boston is true of the nation. In 1950, nearly 60 percent of the nation's metropolitan population lived in the center city. By 1990, the balance had shifted markedly and more than 60 percent of the U.S. metropolitan population lived in suburban areas outside the center city.[46] By now, that figure has doubtless climbed higher.[47] Even though the year 2000 census shows population gains in cities like New York, Chicago, and Boston, it also shows that population has increased at a far more accelerated rate in suburban areas surrounding those same cities.[48] It is estimated that, if current trends continue, about four-fifths of the nation's growth in the decades ahead will be in the suburbs – and that means a growth in employment as well as in population.[49]

During the 1970s, 95 percent of the nation's population growth and 66 percent of job growth were in the suburbs. During the 1980s, all of the nation's population growth was in suburban and exurban areas along with more than 80 percent of employment growth. By 1990, 62 percent of the nation's jobs were in suburban and exurban locations.[50] Suburbs are also where the money is. By 1995, the median income in our older, urban-core areas was $29,000, while in what used to be the nation's suburbs, the median income was nearly $41,000 – more than 40 percent higher than in the cities.[51]

What is true of jobs, population, and income is also true of construction. As Joel Garreau has said in his book *Edge City: Life on the New Frontier*: "Americans are creating the biggest change in a hundred years in how we build cities. Every single American city . . . is growing in the fashion of Los Angeles."[52] In America today, single-family detached housing (that is, suburban housing) comprises more square feet of floor space than all other building types combined.[53] Between 1979 and 1999, new office space in the suburbs was constructed at triple the rate of that being built in U.S. central cities.[54] These simple facts demonstrate that, over the last few decades, far more construction has occurred in the nation's suburbs than in the cities.

These statistics and commentary highlight the fact that suburbia doesn't really seem to fit its dictionary definition anymore. As Michael Pollan wrote in the *New York Times Sunday Magazine*, suburbs are no longer "sub" to any "urb:"

> "Urban sprawl" might be a better term. Certainly sprawl hints at the centerlessness of it, "urban" at the fact that there's nothing in the city you can't find here. And maybe, as some have suggested, that is what [we're] looking at but can't quite see: a new kind of city, one we still don't have the words or name for.[55]

Metropolitan nation

Suburbia has so vastly outgrown our older cities that many urban planners and economists have come to recognize that the old distinctions are not as meaningful as they once were in determining what drives the nation's economy and defines society. Cities or suburbs no longer matter as much as do "metropolitan regions." To quote Robert Yaro, executive director of New York's Regional Plan Association:

> It is now widely recognized that the nation's metropolitan regions are its basic economic units. The largest of these places are incubators of new technologies and industries and centers of American culture, communications, and media. They are the crucibles in which the new American society of the early twenty-first century will be formed from the swelling ranks of immigrants and native-born Americans who live in them.[56]

Our once-great industrial cities have become subsumed into sprawling conurbations that cover hundreds and even thousands of square miles.[57] Metropolitan regions like Los Angeles-Riverside-Orange County don't even have a single dominant city center. They are polycentric. Predominantly suburban in geography, population, and employment, these urbanized areas are spread out like no metropolis has ever been before. Just as Manhattan is vertical, the new metropolitan region is flattened out beyond the horizon. Where the elevator made possible the skyscraper, so the automobile has enabled a new horizontal metropolis.

The nation's metropolitan regions have grown so quickly and spread so far that they have become multi-jurisdictional, overspreading city, town, county, and even state borders. When communities within a metropolitan region increasingly share more in common, the political boundaries created in earlier times can become quite transparent. As Bruce Katz and Jennifer Bradley of the Brookings Institution recently wrote in an article for the *Atlantic Monthly*:

> People work in one municipality, live in another, go to church or the doctor's office or the movies in yet another, and all these different places are somehow interdependent. Newspaper city desks have been replaced by the staffs of metro sections. Labor and housing markets are area-wide. Morning traffic reports describe pileups and traffic jams that stretch across a metropolitan area. Opera companies and baseball teams pull people from throughout a region. Air or water pollution affects an entire region, because pollutants, carbon monoxide, and run-off recognize no city or suburban or county boundaries.[58]

Most metropolitan regions are an elaborate mosaic of individual cities, towns, and villages, each with its own social, economic, and educational facilities. But, like a mosaic, each of these individual communities is part of the larger whole, set into a regional matrix of political, economic, infrastructure, and ecological systems. All regional communities share and depend upon this matrix for their well-being. Yet, even with these shared regional interests, only some cities have managed to keep up with this fact by continually annexing adjoining territory. For many older urban areas, annexation simply is not a viable option. This results in outdated jurisdictional boundaries in many areas, creating some of the allegedly more intractable problems of sprawl.

Local and regional tension

Older political boundaries persist in part because many localities still place great value on their independence, even though advancing suburbanization has made them an intimate part of a greater metropolitan region. Many people in the metropolitan United States still view themselves as residents of small, autonomous towns with little or no real connection to any larger region. Local determination is a proud American tradition dating back to the town meetings of colonial times, which are still the prevalent form of municipal government in places such as New England. Home rule invites local participation, offering many people a framework for a rich community life. Thus, home rule is widely perceived to be a good thing, even though it can sometimes result in haphazard municipal boundaries and fragmented political structures.

The tension between home rule and the regional nature of the nation's metropolitan areas is one of the most compelling characteristics of sprawl, as well as an engine that helps drive its continued spread. The self-perpetuating contest between different jurisdictions for commercial tax dollars to offset residential tax expenditures produces ever more shopping centers and office and industrial parks. New commercial development creates new employment, which in turn generates demand for more housing, which drives the need for more commercial tax dollars, and so on.

Because it is a regional phenomenon, sprawl development not only leapfrogs tracts of property but can also leapfrog entire municipalities, reacting to development controls in one community by sprouting up next door, in another town or county. While one town may turn down a major store or shopping mall on the grounds of community preservation, the town next door may roll out the carpet for the same project. Similarly, a new office park may generate new taxes for one locality but result in tax-draining, new residential subdivisions and schools in an adjacent community.

In the heat of this competition, local jurisdictions are sometimes unwilling or unable to accommodate such larger, areawide needs as affordable housing, infrastructure improvements, and regional land use controls within their boundaries, thus perpetuating the spread of sprawl while ensuring the continued existence of some of its main detractions. A related, familiar issue is dwindling urban resources in the face of suburban prosperity. Even though the city may remain a key part of the regional image and economy, suburban localities are not usually willing or eager to share their revenues with other jurisdictions. Furthermore, the endless quest for new suburban commercial development often draws still more resources out of the city.

Beyond metropolitan

In 1915, urban planner and regionalist Patrick Geddes predicted that America's northeastern cities would eventually flood over the landscape, depleting the urban cores, and that "the not very distant future will see practically one vast city-line along the Atlantic Coast for five hundred miles."[59] What may have seemed like science fiction eighty-five years ago seems a lot closer to becoming reality today.

Metropolitan areas are not necessarily composed entirely of urbanized area as defined by the U.S. Census Bureau (an area having a density of at least one thousand people per square mile). They are essentially functionally related regions containing large population nuclei and adjacent urbanized communities "having a high degree of economic and social integration."[60] In other words, some metropolitan areas can be a patchwork of urbanized areas and as yet undeveloped land. Others, such as New York, Chicago, and Philadelphia, contain more than one thousand people per square mile throughout the entire region.

Census Bureau maps depict America's northeastern cities as a chain of regional metropolitan areas, linked together along the Eastern Seaboard.[61] The Northeast is not alone. The same thing has happened to the nation's midwestern, southern, and West Coast cities. The Los Angeles-Riverside-Orange County metropolitan area flows south as far as Mexico and north to Santa Barbara and beyond. San Francisco-Oakland-San José spreads west to Sacramento-Yolo and south to Salinas. Chicago-Gary-Kenosha stretches east toward Detroit-Ann Arbor-Flint and north to Milwaukee-Racine. Seattle-Tacoma reaches out toward Salem-Portland, and so on. The nation's metropolitan regions are extending beyond their own limits to merge with other regions, perhaps to form even larger units in the future or maybe to redefine the meaning of the term *metropolitan area*, changing anew the scale in which we view urban sprawl. Perhaps it was a vision such as this that prompted Lewis Mumford to write in 1961 that "the whole coastal strip from Maine to

Florida might coalesce into an almost undifferentiated conurbation" composed of "undifferentiated urban tissue, without any relation either to an internally coherent nucleus or an external boundary of any sort."[62]

SPRAWL IN SUMMARY

Urban sprawl traditionally has been viewed as a suburban phenomenon, something that happens as an urbanized area spreads into undeveloped countryside. This spreading of development can be further characterized by leapfrog patterns, commercial strips, overall low density, large areas of single-use development, and a heavy reliance on automobiles for transportation. With these characteristics, sprawl can largely be equated with what the nation has called "suburbia" since at least the 1950s.

American attitudes toward the private ownership of land combined with market forces and a large industry in real estate and construction are preconditions to sprawl, just as they have been for much of the nation's urbanization. But it is inexpensive land – made so by the proliferation of automobiles and roads – that makes the low-density pattern of sprawl so widespread. Automobiles and roads have redefined the so-called economies of agglomeration or clustering, allowing businesses and residents alike to scatter widely. At the same time, reliance on the automobile reinforces low-density, single-use development patterns by ruling out many other transportation modes, basically compelling further expansion to be equally dependent on cars and roads.

Pervasive power and communications networks aided roadways and automobiles in redefining clustering. At the same time, these networks also changed the meaning of economies of scale, freeing businesses from the need to operate under one roof and freeing employees from the need to be in a central workplace. In these ways, both power and communications networks have helped foster low-density suburban patterns.

Although land, markets, automobiles, and communications networks form the framework of sprawl development, a regulatory environment of codes and standards act together with financial practices to create the finished product. These regulations, standards, and practices largely determine the shape, size, and configuration of the land subdivisions, houses, cul-de-sacs, parking lots, and strip commercial buildings that make up our sprawling suburbs.

But our suburbs are no longer suburbs in the strict sense of the word. Cities and suburbs together create the contemporary metropolitan regions that are now the fundamental economic units of our society. Within these metropolitan regions, our suburbs are bigger in geography, population, and employment than our cities. Our metropolitan regions are dominated by what we call sprawl, as we have now defined it: *a form of urbanization distinguished by leapfrog patterns, commercial strips, low density, separated land uses, automobile dominance, and a minimum of public open space*. We have defined the spread of this pattern throughout a region as suburbanization. Through suburbanization, sprawl can extend over thousands of square miles, encompassing many different political jurisdictions left over from an era before metropolitan regions became the dominant centers of our nation. Thus, sprawl is often politically fragmented, with different cities, towns, and even counties setting their interests before those of the broader region of which they are a part. This tension between home rule and regional interests has become a defining characteristic of our sprawling metropolitan regions.

Lastly, our metropolitan regions are getting bigger and more spread out everyday, merging into one another, forming areas of urbanization that now stretch across thousands of square miles. This is what urban sprawl has become: a city without limits.

NOTES

1 *Merriam-Webster Dictionary*, www.m-w.com.
2 *Encarta World English Dictionary*, www.encarta.msn.com.
3 The U.S. Census Bureau defines an "urbanized area" as basically an area with at least one thousand persons per square mile. That translated to somewhat less than two persons per acre – a fairly low residential density for many suburban areas. See the U.S. Census Bureau,

Urban and Rural Definitions, www.census.gov/population.census-data/urdef.txt.

4 Jane S. Shaw and Ronald D. Utt, eds, *A Guide to Smart Growth: Shattering Myths, Providing Solutions* (Washington, D.C.: The Heritage Foundation-Jane, 2000), 2.

5 Samuel R. Staley, *Policy Study No. 251 – The Sprawling of America: In Defense of the Dynamic City* (Los Angeles: Reason Public Policy Institute, 1999), 9.

6 Jay Wickrersham, *The State of Our Environment* (Boston: Commonwealth of Massachusetts, Executive Office of Environmental Affairs, 2000), 24.

7 National Trust for Historic Preservation, Rural Heritage Program Web site: www.ruralheritage.org/sprawl.html.

8 U.S. Environmental Protection Agency (EPA), New England, *The State of a New England Environment, 1998* (Boston: EPA, 1998), chapter on sprawl, as posted on their Web site: www.epa.gov/region01/ra/soe98.html.

9 Sierra Club Web site: www.sierraclub.org/sprawl.

10 Natural Resource Defense Council Web site: www.nrdc.org/cities/default.asp.

11 Reid Ewing, "Is Los Angeles-Style Sprawl Desirable?" *Journal of the American Planning Association*, vol. 63, no. 1 (Winter 1997): 2–4.

12 Ewing provides a table listing seventeen urban planners, theorists, and authors, starting with William Whyte and including Anthony Downs, Constance Beaumont, Richard Moe, and others. Ewing, "Is Los Angeles-Style Sprawl Desirable?," 3.

13 Ibid., 4.

14 For example, Anthony Downs as cited in Kenneth A. Small, "Urban Sprawl: A Non-Diagnosis of Real Problems," *Metropolitan Development Patterns 2000 Annual Roundtable* (Cambridge, MA: Lincoln Institute of Land Policy, 2000), 27.

15 For example, see the previous note and also Susan M. Wachter, "Cities and Regions: Findings from the 1990 State of the Cities Report", in *Metropolitan Development Patterns 2000 Annual Roundtable* (Cambridge, MA: Lincoln Institute of Land Policy, 2000), 22.

16 See Irving M. Copi, *Introduction to Logic* (New York: Macmillan, 1968), 89–114.

17 *Merriam-Webster Online Dictionary*, www.m-w.com.

18 See Kenneth T. Jackson, "Suburbanization," in *The Reader's Companion to American History*, ed. Eric Froner and John A. Garraty (Boston: Houghton Mifflin, 1991), 1040–43; see also Kenneth T. Jackson, *Crabgrass Frontier: The Suburbanization of the United States* (New York: Oxford University Press, 1985).

19 U.S. Department of Agriculture (USDA), Natural Resource Conservation Service (NRCS), *Land Ownership, 1992*, www.nhq.nrcs.usda.gov/cgibin/kmusser/mapgif.pl?mapid=2788. The figure excludes Alaska. Including Alaska and excluding nonland acreage, this figure falls to about 60 percent. See National Wilderness Institute, *State by State Government Land Ownership* (1995), www.nwi.org.

20 Jackson, *Crabgrass Frontier*, 53.

21 U.S. Census Bureau, *Housing Vacancy Survey: First Quarter 2001*, Table 5. *Homeownership Rates for the United States: 1965 to 2001*, www.census.gov/hhes/www/housing/hvs/q101tab5.html.

22 U.S. Census Bureau, *1997 Economic Census* (Washington, D.C.: U.S. Census Bureau, 2000), Table 1.

23 U.S. Department of Commerce, *U.S. Industry and Trade Outlook 2000* (Washington, D.C.: U.S. Department of Commerce, 2000), 6-2.

24 Terry Moore and Paul Thorsnes, *The Transportation / Land Use Connection: A Framework for Practical Policy* (Chicago: American Planning Association, 1994), 9.

25 Ibid., 20.

26 Alan E. Pisarski, *Commuting in America II: The Second National Report on Commuting Patterns and Trends* (Lansdowne, Va.: Eno Transportation Foundation, 1996), 72.

27 U.S. Department of Transportation (DOT), Bureau of Transportation Statistics (BTS), *1995 Nationwide Personal Transportation Survey* (Washington, D.C.: DOT, 1995), 11. See also Jane Holtz Kay, *Asphalt Nation: How the Automobile Took Over America and How We Can Take It Back* (New York: Crown, 1997), 21.

28 U.S. Department of Transportation (DOT), Bureau of Transportation Statistics *Transportation Statistics Annual Report, 1999* (Washington, D.C.: DOT, 1999), 36.

29 Ibid., 37, 46.

30 Ibid., 37.

31 James S. Russell, "Privatized Lives," *Harvard Design Magazine*, no. 12 (Fall 2000): 24.

32 William J. Mitchell, "The Electronic Agora," foreword in Thomas A. Horan, *Digital Places: Building Our City of Bits* (Washington, D.C.: Urban Land Institute, 2000), xi.

33 Moore and Thorsnes, *The Transportation / Land Use Connection*, 10 and following.

34 Pisarki, *Commuting in America II*, 25.

35 Robert Putnam, *Bowling Alone: The Collapse and Revival of American Community* (New York: Simon & Schuster, 2000), 222–23, 228.

36 Horan, *Digital Places*, 33.

37 Jonathan Glazer, "Telecommuting's Big Experiment," *New York Times*, May 9, 2001.

38 Glazer, "Telecommuting's Big Experiment."

39 U.S. Commerce Department, "Retail, E-Commerce Sales in First Quarter 2001," *U.S. Commerce Department News*, May 16, 2001, www.census.gov/mrts/www/current.html.

40 Andres Duany, Elizabeth Plater-Zyberk, and Jeff Speck, *Suburban Nation: The Rise of Sprawl and the Decline of the American Dream* (New York: North Point Press, 2000), xi.

41 See Barbara McCann *et al.*/Surface Transportation Policy Project/Centre for Neighborhood Technology, *Driven to Spend: The Impact of Sprawl on Household Transportation Expenses* (Washington, D.C.: 2001), chap. 3, fig. H, www.transact.org/reports/driven/.default.html. See also Haya El Nasser, "A Comprehensive Look at Sprawl in America," *USA Today*, February 22, 2001. *USA Today* used a different ranking methodology in which the Houston-Galveston-Brazoria region ranks number 234 in a range of scores from 26 to 536.

42 *Webster's New World Dictionary, College Edition* (New York: The World Publishing Co., 1966), 1455.

43 Sometime between 1960 and 1970, depending on source and definitions used, see U.S. Census Bureau/Campbell Gibson and Emily Lennon, *Historical Census Statistics on the Foreign Born Population of the United States, 1850–1990*, (Washington, D.C.: U.S. Census Bureau, 1999). See also U.S. Census Bureau, *Selected Historical Census Data: Urban and Rural Definitions and Data*, www.census.gov/population/www.censusdata/ur-def.html. See also Pisarski, *Commuting in America II*, 18–19.

44 The New York CMSA includes parts of New York, New Jersey, and Pennsylvania. CMSA data from U.S. Census Bureau, Census 2000 PHC-T-3 Tanking Tables for Metropolitan Areas, Table 1, www.census.gov/population/cen2000/phct3/tab01.pdf. Additional New York City data from U.S. Census Bureau, *Table 22: Population of the 100 Largest Urban Places: 1990*, www.census.gov/population/documentation/twps0027/tab22.txt. Released June 1998. New York City data for 2000 from Susan Sachs, "New York City Tops 8 Million for First Time," *New York Times*, March 16, 2000.

45 See previous note and the Boston Metropolitan Area Planning Council Area Web site (May 1999): www.mapc.org.

46 Pisarski, *Commuting in America II*, 18; and David Rusk, *Cities Without Suburbs* (Washington, D.C.: Woodrow Wilson Centre, 1995), 5 and following.

47 When this book was being written, the 2000 census data were only being made available. Where possible, the latest 2000 census data has been used. In many cases, only projections based on 1990 data have been available.

48 See for example David W. Chen, "Outer Suburbs Outpace City in Population Growth," *New York Times*, March 16, 2001; and Cindy Rodriguez, "City, State Take on New Cast," *Boston Globe*, March 22, 2001.

49 F. Kaid Benfield, Matthew D. Raimi, and Donald D.T. Chen, *Once There Were Greenfields: How Urban Sprawl Is Undermining America's Environment, Economy, and Social Fabric* (Washington, D.C.: Natural Resource Defense Council, 1999), 6.

50 Pisarski, *Commuting in America II*, 25–26.

51 U.S. Census Bureau, "March 1996 Current Population Survey: Income 1995 – Table A: Comparison of Summary Measures of Income by Selected Characteristics: 1994 and 1995," www.census.gov.hhes/income95/in95sum.html.

52 Joel Garreau, *Edge City: Life on the New Frontier* (New York: Doubleday, 1991), 3.

53 U.S. Department of Energy, Energy Information Administration, *Buildings and Energy in the 1980's* (Washington, D.C.: Department of Energy, 1995), 3.

54 Robert E. Lang, *Office Sprawl: The Evolving Geography of Business* (Washington, D.C.: The Brookings Institution, 2000), 3.

55 Michael Polland, "The Triumph of Burbopolis," *New York Times Magazine*, April 9, 2000, 54–55.

56 Robert D. Yaro, "Growing and Governing Smart: A Case Study of the New York Region" in Bruce Katz, ed., *Reflections on Regionalism* (Washington, D.C.: Brookings Institution Press, 2000), 43.

57 See also Robert Fishman's foreword in Peter Calthrope and William Fulton, *The Regional City* (Washington, D.C.: Island Press, 2001), xv.

58 Bruce Katz, and Jennifer Bradley, "Divided We Sprawl," *Atlantic Monthly*, December 1999, 26–42.

59 Patrick Geddes, *Cities in Evolution* (London: Williams & Norgate, 1915), 48–49. See also Richard Moe and Carter Wilkie, *Changing Places: Rebuilding Community in the Age of Sprawl* (New York: Henry Holt, 1997), 47.

60 U.S. Census Bureau, *Urban and Rural Definitions*, www.census.gov/population/censusdata/urdef.txt, and *About Metropolitan Areas*, www.census.gov/population/www/estimates/aboutmetro.html.

61 See U.S. Census Bureau map gallery, www.census.gov/geo/www/mapGallery/ma_1999.pdf.

62 Lewis Mumford, *The City in History: Its Origins, Its Transformations, Its Prospects* (New York: Harcourt, Brace and World, Inc., 1961), 540–41.

"Density in Communities, or the Most Important Factor in Building Urbanity"

from *Community Design and the Culture of Cities* (1990)

Eduardo Lozano

Editors' Introduction

Related to the sprawl debates of the past few decades, disagreements over the benefits and detriments of higher density development are just as heated. Proponents of denser and more compact cities suggest that greater densities have positive spillover effects in supporting transit, reducing car usage, enhancing local economic development, providing various environmental benefits, and promoting greater social interaction. Fear of higher density development is fostered in part by images of questionable mid-century new-town developments and poorly managed public housing. To many people, the term density itself frequently suggests ideas about various environmental and social problems. NIMBY (Not In My Backyard) responses to higher-density residential living are common, yet often unfounded and unsubstantiated. Opponents of higher density development are typically not opposed to higher densities elsewhere – just not next to their current low-density residences. Other fears are based on the effects of social and psychological overcrowding and its impacts on behavioral freedom.

Various studies have shown, however, that overcrowding (typically a function of economics and culture) need not be necessarily equated with density (a function of geography and urban form). Other empirical research has suggested that very high densities can be reached with urban forms that are quite acceptable to most people living in the city. Different studies have shown that negative perceptions of density can be mitigated through better design, for example, the use of vegetation to screen buildings, varied building heights, richer facade detailing, and careful design of transition spaces. Many desirable neighborhoods in pre-industrial walking cities maintain densities ten times higher than the typical low-density suburban forms in use today, but are generally perceived to be of much lower density. The use of classic high-density rowhouses and low- to mid-rise building forms provides the living space, private exterior space, mixed uses, and social amenities desirable in creating livable neighborhoods.

Measures of density used by urban designers are varied, but are typically a ratio of housing units, people, or floor space over a unit of land, such as acres, hectares, or square miles. Measures of gross density include all land uses and lands within a geographic area (including public rights-of-way), while net densities usually include only the parcel lands where residential uses are located. Gross density measures are inadequate predictors of urban form or the human experience of a place, as housing units may be clustered densely on a portion of the land, or distributed evenly across it in lower densities. Measures of density are important in understanding the thresholds necessary for various services and activities to function properly in the city, such as the number of people to support a bus system versus a light rail system, or the number required in the catchment area for a supermarket.

Eduardo Lozano's chapter on density from his book *Community Design and the Culture of Cities* discusses the uses of density in reinforcing communities and diminishing density fears and opposition. One of the key problems with perceptions of density, he discusses, has been the polarization of residential densities at either end of the scale; very low sub-urban living versus over-urban high-rise tower living in central city areas. He suggests restoring a range and balance of community-oriented densities, thereby minimizing the detrimental perceptions of both low- and higher-density places. Published in 1990, this reading presages later ideas about Smart Growth, Compact Cities, and Urban Villages that would emphasize densification, infill, and complete communities.

Born in Argentina, Eduardo Lozano is an architect and urban designer who holds a PhD in Planning from Harvard University. He taught at Princeton and Harvard Universities, and helped establish Princeton's Urban Studies program. His firm, Lozano, Baskin & Associates, is located in Watertown, Massachusetts.

Studies of population crowding and residential density have a long history in design and planning circles. Some of the best known works include: Rolf Jensen, *High Density Living* (London: L. Hill, 1966); Amos Rapopori, "Toward a Redefinition of Density," *Environment and Behavior* (vol. 7, no. 2, pp. 133–158, 1975); Andrew Baum, Glenn E. Davis, and John R. Aiello, "Crowding and Neighborhood Mediation of Urban Density," *Journal of Population* (vol. 1, Fall, pp. 266–279, 1978); Paul M. Insel and Henry Clay, *Too Close for Comfort: The Psychology of Crowding* (Englewood Cliffs, NJ: Prentice-Hill, 1978); and Mark Baldassare, *Residential Crowding in Urban America* (Berkeley, CA: University of California Press, 1979).

For contemporary literature on promoting density through design see the following: Richard Haughey, *Getting Density Right: Tools for Creating New Compact Development* (Washington, DC: ULI, 2008); Clare Cooper Marcus and Wendy Sarkissian, *Housing as if People Mattered: Guidelines* for *Medium-Density Family Housing* (Berkeley, CA: University of California Press, 1986); Steven Fader, *Density by Design: New Directions in Residential Development*, 2nd edn (Washington, DC: Urban Land Institute, 2000); Julie Campoli and Alex MacLean, *Visualizing Density: A Catalog Illustrating the Density of Residential Neighborhoods* (Washington, DC: Lincoln Institute of Land Policy – Working Paper, 2002); and Christian Schittich, *High-Density Housing: Concepts, Planning, Construction* (New York: Princeton Architectural Press and Birlhauser, 2004).

Material on achieving density through compact development and urban village concepts can be found in the following sources: Mike Jenks, Elizabeth Burton, and Katie Williams (eds), *Compact City: A Sustainable Urban Form?* (London: Spon Press, 1996); David Sucher, *City Comforts: How to Build an Urban Village*, revised edn (City Comforts Inc., 2003); Gert de Roo and Donald Miller (eds), *Compact Cities and Sustainable Urban Development* (London: Ashgate, 2000); Tony Aldous, *Urban Villages* (London: Urban Villages Group, 1992); Peter Neal (ed.), *Urban Villages: The Making of Community* (London: Spon Press, 2003); David Bell and Mark Jayne (eds), *City of Quarters: Urban Villages in the Contemporary City* (London: Ashgate, 2004); and Alberto Magnaghi, *The Urban Village: A Charter for Democracy and Sustainable Development in the City* (London: Zed Books, 2005).

DENSITY IN URBAN SETTLEMENTS

Urban settlements are characterized primarily by a high concentration of people and activities in space relative to the surrounding regions; that is, they are characterized by high-density. Density is basic to settlements because it generates urbanity, that elusive yet essential quality that is both cause and effect of dense clusters of human habitats. Urbanity can be defined as the potential capacity of the inhabitants of a town or city to interact with a sizable number of people and institutions concentrated in that town or city. This large potential for interaction is created by density and, in turn, encourages higher density.

Urbanity has also been defined in terms of sophisticated behavior – courtesy, refinement, politeness, and civility. Civility is related to a Latin word for city, *civitas*, to which other major concepts, such as civilization and citizenship, are related. The realm of the city, that is, the realm of dense human settlements, has always been identified with high levels of culture and linked with the most civilized expressions of social behavior. Clearly, because historical cities were not homogeneous, fairly uncivilized behavior coexisted with the most refined lifestyles; one need simply recall London in the writings of Dickens or the engravings of Hogarth. Today, especially in the United States, the identification of cities with civilization is rapidly losing validity, as shown by the association of social problems such as crime, vandalism, illiteracy, addiction, and morbidity with "urban problems," as if it were the nature of cities and not social factors that caused them.

Consistent with contemporary cultural values, no design variable has been so maligned as density. Most people associate density with crowded slums; and the complementary relationship between urbanity and density is ignored in favor of dispersed suburban environments. Myriad factors contribute to the reduction of density in U.S. metropolises. One factor is the private automobile, which enables people to live in scattered patterns. Another factor is a nostalgic desire to re-create the lifestyle of rural areas and small towns. A third, and seldom acknowledged, factor is the aim of excluding people of lower social strata from upper-class areas, where larger lots ensure higher land costs. Such government policies as federal housing and highway programs have provided critical support for low-density sub-urbanization – which has become, by default, practically the only choice for middle-class families.

The densities of U.S. cities today are the result, for the most part, of disjointed decisions by investors and developers pursuing financial objectives within the limitations of zoning regulations. Perceived market demand and the potential for profits are the guiding principles, quite often supported by incentives built into zoning regulations or the granting of special variances. The result is over-urban densities in downtown office centers and sub-urban densities in residential areas. In European cities, the influence of the public sector is far stronger than it is in the United States; decisions are, in general, affected by notions of the public interest and acceptance of higher residential densities. But the differences between urban areas in the world are rooted in more than political systems; they are rooted in the cultural values of each society, as is to be discussed later in this chapter.

Let us first make some comparisons of density within the so-called industrialized Western countries. To take well known European examples, the gross residential density of Paris is 84 people per acre, and that of London, 60 people per acre. In the United States, the gross residential density of New York is 47 people per acre, that of San Francisco is 24 people per acre, that of Chicago and Philadelphia, 23 per acre, and that of Boston, 21 people per acre.[1] Thus, the most dense U.S. metropolis, New York, has only between one-half and three-quarters the residential density of its European counterparts; the remaining major U.S. cities are in a completely different range, with residential densities that are barely one-fourth to one-third of the European values. And if we consider the almost three hundred urbanized areas in the United States, which include the gamut of smaller cities and towns, gross residential density decreases to a mere 6 people per acre, a value that raises serious doubts about the urbanity of U.S. cities and towns.

Localized density values also reveal differences between U.S. and European cities. In Paris, the central city residential density is 380 people per acre;[2] in Manhattan, residential density is around 100 people per acre. The lowest residential densities in Paris, in single-family-home neighborhoods, are around 12 to 15 people per acre, which correspond to fairly dense single-family-home areas in U.S. cities – less than one-quarter acre lots. But most Paris residential areas are composed of mid-rise apartment buildings, with values of around 60 to 75 people per acre.

New planned settlements show similar differences. To restrict the comparison to British new towns,[3] the net residential densities are 45 people per acre in Harlow, 48 in Peterborough, 62 in Runcorn, and 90 in Cumbernauld. In contrast, Reston, Virginia – heralded as the most urbane of the U.S. new towns – has a net residential density of 22 people per acre, while Columbia, Maryland – probably the most successful new town from a financial point of view – has only 15 people per acre. Indeed, the average net density of U.S. new towns is between 12 and 18 people per acre, which represents a gross density of 8 to 12 people per acre – that is, suburbs with single-family homes in quarter-and half-acre lots.

Clearly, the wide disparity between planning standards can be traced to radically different cultural expectations that translate into market acceptance. At the core of these cultural differences we will find the trade-off between the assumed negative sociopsychological effects of density – most of which have to do with crowding – and the positive effects of density – which have to do with urbanity, as will be discussed below.

A critical difference in the density structure of cities is found in the social allocation of density zones to population groups. In urban areas, there is a systematic organization of density values, with the highest values at the center and exponentially decreasing values toward the periphery. Within this general principle, there are complex relationships between density gradients, size of the settlement, level of economic development and technology, history and growth rate of the urban area, and other factors. Typically, in historical cities, the elite occupied central areas of high-density and perhaps some outlying sectors of summer residences in low-density patterns. Typically, the land use hetero-geneity of historical cities meant that there were congested poor areas near the center as well as poor suburbs at the periphery.

This has all changed in U.S. cities – and in other regions under their cultural influence – with the suburbanization of the upper and middle classes. As a result, most poor people live on expensive high-density, centrally located land, and most of the affluent groups live on cheaper low-density, suburban land. Some urban economists explain this apparent paradox as an efficient allocation of resources by allowing factor substitution of land and building inputs in the production function. Wealthy suburbia uses more land, the cheaper input, in relation to buildings, because its affluent population can afford long trips to work; central city housing uses less land, the expensive input, in relation to buildings, because its poor population cannot afford long trips to work and must be near the largest concentration of employment.[4]

The line of argument stemming from this explanation is that location is the result of social choices in a set of optimizing trade-offs. The wealthy select the cheaper suburban land because they can afford large tracts as well as the cost and time involved in long commuting trips. Correspondingly, the cheaper land is less dense than the expensive land closer to the centers.[5] This choice, which the middle class follows closely, can be explained by a cultural "hunger for land" typical of most of U.S. society, which willingly trades off propinquity for space. The resulting decline in density prevents the extension of mass-transit systems to most outlying residential areas, thus forcing residents to commute by private car at costs that are beyond the capacity of low-income groups to pay.

These cultural preferences are supported by local governments when, for example, they enact zoning limitations that block the development of greater density in suburbia, a major factor in the maintenance of suburban land values per acre at relatively low rates but land values per parcel at higher levels owing to the extensive area require-ments for minimum lots.

In central areas, the need to enlarge the supply of higher-density housing owing to the relatively limited capacity of these areas to expand, and the opposition of the inner suburbs – the old residential areas developed based on trolley car accessibility during the early decades of the twentieth century – results in higher land values for landlords,[6] and higher rents in the slums and ghettoes. In effect, the only option for expanding housing for the poor has been to accelerate deterioration, which results in social conflict with surrounding neigh-borhoods and increasing degradation of the urban environment.

A trend that has become apparent in the past decade or two, employment suburbanization, has increased social inequality and further eroded urbanity. Rather than having a major employment center in the downtown area, cities have begun to sprout suburban low-density employment belts dispersed along highways and, lately, major exurban employment centers. Only a fraction of urban employment today is located in central cities. The result is that the overwhelming majority of employees in suburban work places drive to work because public transportation is simply not eco-nomically feasible. The poor and minorities, locked in slums and ghettoes in central cities, have been particularly hard hit by this trend, since the only advantage of their location – easy access to down-town employment and urban transit systems – is becoming increasingly irrelevant as they, too, seek employment in the newer highway-oriented areas. The trend has been reinforced by the willingness of local governments to zone huge parcels of land for low-density business (e.g., the so-called office and industrial parks), guided by their own goal of expanding the local property tax base.

Indeed, local governments, which are responsible for the regulation of zoning, have been unanimous in adopting the objective of density reduction. Their purpose in establishing density ratios is not to encourage densities high enough to achieve urbanity, but rather to prevent densities from reaching certain maxima, supposedly for health and amenities reasons. Only rarely is a minimum density required for urban services, mass transportation, and social interaction.

Clearly, the emergence of segregated, low-density patterns in U.S. cities is, to a large degree, a self-fulfilling prophecy. By using zoning controls to limit densities, as well as by downgrading mass-transit systems to a "second rate option," cities have ensured a segregated pattern whereby the poor are crowded into expensive land near the center, the wealthy expand to cheaper land far away from the slums, and the image of success is a low-density estate. None of the social costs of this urban system are accounted for.

LOCATIONAL EFFECTS OF DENSITY, URBANITY, AND THRESHOLDS

Density is the critical variable in determining urbanity because of its locational effects. Density determines the accessibility of people to people, of people to work, of people to services and recreation; in short, it allows urban relationships to flourish.

Interaction among the elements of an urban system is a precondition for the system's existence. Interaction with a large number and variety of people and groups is at the core of the concept of communities, that is, organizations with sustained interpersonal relationships, because it not only fulfills the need for affiliation and belonging but offers an opportunity for a wide range of human behavior. Indeed, "interactions are the basis for the formation and continued existence of social organizations."[7] The presence of dense settlements maximizes the potential for such interactions.

The relationship between density and urbanity is based on the concept of viable thresholds: At certain densities (thresholds), the number of people within a given area is sufficient to generate the interactions needed to make certain urban functions or activities viable. Clearly, the greater the number and variety of urban activities, the richer the life of a community; thus, urbanity is based on density.

Urban interaction is ultimately equated with communication. Traditionally, the interactions of a population within an area were based on spatial propinquity, that is, on personal communication. Today instant communications have reduced our reliance on physical propinquity – and thus density – to generate interaction.

Public transportation and density are closely intertwined. High-density makes feasible various transportation modes, as well as pedestrian access to trains, subways, and buses, and thus is a crucial determinant of accessibility in an urban system. Capacity, technology, and the cost of transportation systems are intimately related to density; subways can move large amounts of people, for example, but because of their high cost they must run through high-density corridors to be efficient. Each mode of urban mass-transportation technology – with its respective cost and capacity – is associated with a density threshold.

The effect of density on transportation is visible in the process of daily commuting. The separation of workplaces from residential areas, forced by large-scale land use homogeneity and segregation means that very few people can walk to work. In addition, because of the low-density prevalent in many residential suburban areas, people have no way of getting to work except by automobile, since even buses are uneconomical to operate below certain thresholds. And to make the situation worse, the dispersion of employment in low-density outlying zones means that urban mass-transit service cannot be provided to those areas – forcing full reliance on the private automobile.

Many programs have been implemented in U.S. cities to remedy the shortcomings of a low-density urban pattern. Commuter rail and outlying subway stations have parking facilities to permit suburban residents to drive to the stations. This solution is limited by the capacity of parking lots – or the patience of driving spouses – except when costly parking garages arc provided, and is tailored mainly to commuting and other scheduled trips. Highway lanes are reserved for express buses and cars with more than two people. Given their constraints, some of these programs have succeeded in fulfilling their modest objectives. It is apparent that the largest of the U.S. metropolises could not function without mass-transportation systems, but the fact remains that those systems at best provide a second-rate service and at worst are poorly maintained and vandalized systems where crime is an everyday experience.

A comparison between the urban transportation systems of Boston and Paris illustrates the effects of density.[8] The city of Boston proper, with a population of more than 600,000 in 46 square miles, has a density of 21 people per acre, whereas Paris, with a population of more than 2,200,000 over 40 square miles, has 84 people per acre – a density four times higher than that of Boston. As a result, every Parisian is within four to five blocks of one of the 279 Metro stations, where silent and clean trains run every 60 to 90 seconds. For a Bostonian, this is a dream that could never be matched, simply because four very expensive miles of subway would be needed in Boston to serve the same population that can be served with only one mile in Paris.

The relationship between density and urbanity extends beyond transportation, reaching to the viability of, and accessibility to most urban services. In the retail sector, for example, there is an increase in the number of shops and stores as residential density increases. Population density and the available income of the population living within an accessible distance determine a series of thresholds. Below a certain density, no retail stores can exist; as density increases, feasibility thresholds are reached, allowing an increasing number and variety of stores. From the point of view of the merchant, commercial feasibility is an economic consideration; for residents, easy accessibility of commercial services is not only a convenience but a social amenity.

Recognizing density thresholds is thus critical to understanding the effects of density on urbanity. In the retail sector, for example, the effects of density on the number and variety of retail stores in a commercial center can be studied through the effects of distance on shopping trips, the size of the center as an attraction to shoppers, and balance with competing commercial centers. It is also possible to sketch a series of residential density ranges and suggest an initial set of thresholds; the relationships presented below, expressed in dwelling units per acre (du/acre), correspond to the ranges commonly found in the United States; other countries have different density thresholds.

A detached single-family house normally ranges from a net density of 1 to 5 du/acre. Tighter clustering would allow a density increase of up to 8 du/acre. A semidetached two-family house ranges from 5 to 12 du/acre. A town house with party walls could range from 10 to 16 du/acre. The net density of 12 du/acre is the first urbanity threshold, since below that level it is difficult to provide community facilities in close proximity to the dwellings.[9] The tight pattern of single- and two-family houses is commonly found in many inner metropolitan areas and in most small towns of Middle America. It is a small-scale, true urban environment, catalyst of many vital communities, immortalized by Frank Capra in his films of the 1930s and 1940s. The town house (or row house) has been the basic raw material for many cities, its density allowing the generation of an urban environment with community facilities nearby; the brownstones of New York and the townhouses of Boston are among the many examples found on the eastern seaboard.

Tighter clustering with perhaps some mix of two-story flats would allow density to increase to 20 du/acre. The net density of 20 du/acre is another threshold, since above it direct access to the ground cannot be provided from each unit, leading to a radical change in the nature of the outdoor open space, a reduction of unit identity, and a need for common parking areas.[10] Thus, the threshold of 20 du/acre is the watershed that divides the types of dwellings that can maintain a unit identity from those that are merged into larger combinations.

Low-rise apartment buildings, such as three-story walkups, have a net density that ranges from 35 to 50 du/acre. At the upper level of this range, 45 to 50 du/acre, visual intimacy can begin to be lost,[11] and a concentrated urban scale emerges. Midrise apartment buildings, six stories high, range from 65 to 75 du/acre. The upper range, 75 to 80 du/acre, is another threshold, since above this level there can be a wide variety of facilities and activities easily accessible to each dwelling, indicating that from two points of view – space and accessibility – we are already in the realm of the higher hierarchical levels of the urban environment. At the same time, the provision of parking and open space becomes an important design issue.[12]

At the top of the urban hierarchy, high-rise apartments can range from 50 to 100 du/acre. Above that range we enter the level of high-density central city buildings, with all the limitations and advantages that the core of urbanity can provide – maximum accessibility, but also limited open space, congested streets, and, in general, pressure for space. Clearly, cities that provide substitutes for the automobile in the form of good mass transit and some major open space – Central Park in New York, Luxembourg or Les Tuilleries in Paris, Hyde Park in London, Palermo in Buenos Aires – certainly offer attractive central locations.

SOCIAL AND PSYCHOLOGICAL EFFECTS OF DENSITY AND CROWDING

The pervasive aversion to urban density and the implementation of density control measures have been justified on the basis of the assumed negative effects of density on people. But how real are these effects?

It is important, first, to distinguish density from crowding. Although often confused, density and crowding are measures of different phenomena. Density is the ratio of people or dwelling units to land area. Differences in density have economic and physical implications but no clear social or psychological effects. Crowding is the ratio of people to dwelling units or rooms. Different degrees of crowding have clear social and psychological effects. Studies of urban patterns have shown that, at the neighborhood level, there is no correlation between density and crowding and that different densities have no systematic relationship to people's perception of crowding.[13] The difference between the two ratios can be shown by example: high-density and low crowding can exist in a high-rise, upper-class apartment building, where there are many dwelling units per acre but few persons per dwelling. In contrast, low-density and high crowding can be found in isolated rural shacks in a depressed region, where there are few dwellings per acre but many people per room.

The most important difference between the two concepts is that density reflects mainly physical and economic conditions, whereas crowding reflects social and psychological conditions. Thus, density is a measure of the physical (univariate) condition, involving limited use of space. In contrast, crowding is a perceived condition of limited space; it is a multivariate phenomenon due to the interaction of spatial, social, and personal factors and is characterized by stress.[14] As a result, density is a quantifiable index that is easy to apply universally and to measure physically and economically, whereas crowding is a subjective and highly personal experience translated into psychological stress, involving numerous factors, and impossible to apply universally. Clearly, many of the objections to density can be legitimately directed toward crowding.

The most general way to study the relationship among social variables is statistical correlation. This method will not prove that the relationship is one of cause and effect, but it will associate phenomena, highlighting areas for more conclusive research. In this respect, we must reiterate warnings about conceptualizing the relationship between the built environment and human behavior in a deterministic way, by mistakenly assuming that behavior is a direct response to environmental stimulus.[15] The effects of density have been statistically studied, and although on first impression density appears to be related to pathological behavior, more detailed analysis indicates otherwise. The small apparent effects of density on pathological behavior are reduced to insignificance when controls for social class and ethnicity are introduced.[16]

For example, a statistical analysis of census data, involving a number of public housing projects around the world,[17] correlates measures of population density with indices of social and medical pathology, as well as with the effects of intermediate variables such as income and education controlled through partial correlation. The results indicate that, although high population density is commonly associated with social disorganization, the positive correlation between density and pathology disappears when measures of social status are utilized as control variables.[18] In other words, such factors as poverty and low educational levels are at the root of social disorganization and pathological behavior. I should add that even this statistical interpretation must be qualified. There are many societies in which people with extremely low incomes and poor education lead a structured social life without such pathological behavior. The difference seems to lie in the existence of a traditional social order within the community pattern. This phenomenon is observed in the Third World, where rural migrants who lived a structured life in villages are traumatized by the breakup of traditional ties in cities, leading to social disorganization and environmental degradation, on top of economic poverty.

High density in U.S. slums is the result of the poor being forced to concentrate on expensive land around the city center in order to be near jobs and transportation, and being unable to move to other areas because of segregation barriers. Crowding is the result of the poor being forced to fit large families into small apartments because of high rents. Such concentration of poverty, with people living in crowded, deteriorating quarters, with limited access to jobs and education, is the cause of high incidences of disease, socially pathologic behavior, and the creation of a "lumpen" subculture.

Crowding, measured as the number of people per room, has been found to be highly correlated with such indices of social pathology as high mortality and juvenile delinquency since the earliest studies conducted in this field.[19] This conclusion has been supported by later studies, which strongly suggest that interpersonal pressure or crowding may be linked with pathological behavior.[20] It is important to note that studies conducted on different neighborhoods found no correlation between crowding and density and an inverse relationship between the level of crowding analysis and the importance of physical density measures at the city level.[21] But residential crowding has consistently been found to have negative consequences.[22]

Recall that crowding is a perceived condition. The perception of crowding is inversely related to one's ability to exercise behavioral freedom and to exert control over one's social and physical environment.[23] That is, crowding is experienced when the number of people in one's environment is large enough to reduce one's behavioral freedom and choice.[24] This gives rise to overmanned situations;[25] it imposes behavioral restrictions and creates social interference, leading to competition for scarce resources.[26]

Crowding is perceived when a person's demand for space exceeds the supply of space.[27] But this situation could originate in physical factors — restricted space, arrangement of space, light conditions — as much as it could originate in social factors, such as the presence of other persons felt to be competitors, since "an individual may feel crowded in the midst of strangers, but quite comfortable and secure in the presence of an equal number of friends."[28] In addition, laboratory research has shown that conditions that potentially cause crowding have no negative effects on the performance of human tasks if the physical consequences of spatial restrictions (high temperature, stuffiness, limited movement) and other environmental stresses (noise) are controlled.[29] Spatial restriction is a necessary precondition of, but is not sufficient by itself to cause, crowding stress. Thus, crowding is not objective and abstract, but subjective and personalized. The demand for space, however, originates in fairly universal needs for privacy and personal turf. Privacy does not mean withdrawal, but the ability to control visual and auditory interaction,[30] and can be defined at various levels: solitude, intimacy, anonymity in a crowd, and control of intrusion through psychological barriers.[31] But even privacy is not an absolute concept; it depends on the cultural milieu.

One of the most critical factors affecting the perception of crowding, as well as of density, is culture, which controls much of human behavior. In addition, expectations and past experiences affect one's perception of crowding. Correlation studies show that spatial restriction is not always associated with social pathology and that cultural traditions define different parameters for density and crowding. The fact that Hong Kong, with a residential density ten times higher than that of Manhattan, is a thriving city not particularly burdened with behavioral pathologies is one indication of the importance of a cultural framework. Indeed, the relationship between high neighborhood densities and social pathology is mediated by personal and cultural factors.[32]

The mediating effects of culture in spatial perception in general, and in the perception of crowding and density in particular, are probably the most important obstacle to the generalization of research findings outside of a specific environment. Different social groups have different perceptions of what constitutes trespassing in space and what constitutes permissible involvement in public and private areas, leading Hall to assert that "culture is possibly the most significant single variable in determining what constitutes stressful density," because "people brought up in different cultures live in different perceptual worlds . . . People perceive space quite differently."[33] Cultural norms mediate the perception and adjustment of interpersonal space and, thus, the sensory thresholds for residential crowding and urban density.

It has been suggested that crowding may be the result of perceived urban congestion and excessive social stimulation;[34] the inability to avoid or reduce social or visual contact[35] may cause a cognitive overload leading to stress and withdrawal.[36] Cultural norms radically change the thresholds of such perception.

However, cultural differences in the perception of crowding and density cannot be adjusted through an anthropological classification of cultures. It has been said, for example, that urban scale must be consistent with ethnic scale, since each ethnic group seems to have developed its own scale.[37] Does this mean that an Irish neighborhood must be planned in a different way than a Polish one? To what extent should subcultures be disaggregated in environments as rich as urban areas? A clue to understanding this issue, at least for planners and designers, is given by one of the oldest neighborhoods in Boston, the North End, which today is largely Italian; its tightly packed, mid-rise, relatively high-density pattern, its narrow streets and alleys seem to be ideally suited for an Italian neighborhood. However, the North End was built and settled by groups migrating from England in the eighteenth century (some of whose descendants now live in exclusive suburbs with quite different lifestyles). The explanation for this is that the original English settlers belonged to the same European urban culture from which the more recent Italians originated. Thus, a straightforward ethnic label may not account for the truly differential factors within urban subcultures, or the common elements they share.

The complexity of the relationships between built environment and human behavior has led to the formulation of various theories that go beyond the effects of crowding and density. Barker has proposed the concept of behavioral settings, in which the built environment is interpreted as affording (but not determining) behavioral opportunities;[38] in order to survive, an urban environment must be adaptable to different behaviors and to changing behaviors. One of the criticisms raised by Frampton to Modern and Postmodern architecture

is that they offer limited alternatives for patterns of behavior.[39] In addition, because of cultural variations in activity, family and gender, privacy and social intercourse,[40] the same environment would be perceived and used differently by different people, according to their values, experience, and motivation.[41] In the context of the postindustrial metropolis, where cosmopolitans share urban space with locals of various cultural extractions, these concepts are critical to community designers. Sommers developed the concept of personal space, in which territoriality is a way to attain privacy through physical or symbolic barriers, and space is personalized to satisfy one's needs for identity, security, self-fulfillment, and a frame of reference.[42] The personalization of the suburb of Levittown or Le Corbusier's project at Pessac is an indication of people's preference for diversity. Territoriality, like many other urban concepts, is culture specific; the hierarchy of private to public turfs varies with different cultural parameters.

In summary, crowding stress cannot be predicted on the basis of spatial considerations alone; it is determined by a combination of environmental and personal factors acting over time. The psychological stress of crowding involves not only realization that demands for space cannot be met by the supply, but also an emotional imbalance in which a person feels infringed upon, alienated, and deprived of privacy. The size of physical space – and thus the number of people per area – is only one of the variables of crowding. The noise and light levels in a space, the number of objects and their arrangement, the social situation, the activities taking place, and the personal psychology are all factors that, together, determine the perception of crowding and the level of stress. The close, personal proximity of urban life, when seen from the vantage point of suburban life, may seem threatening since the attraction (or focus) of urban activities may not be sufficiently perceived by suburban observers. A dense urban situation may be unappealing to a person not familiar with the activities taking place in that environment and unaccustomed to the urban rituals and routines that structure – and give meaning to – dense urban life.

Crowding has an opposite: undercrowding. Undercrowding is defined as an excessive abundance of space in which an individual suffers social isolation and needs enclosure and contact with others – sometimes manifesting as agoraphobia, or fear of large spaces. Too much space can be as undesirable as too little.

Thus, the limitation of density in a community does not address the problems caused by crowding. In the design of a community, crowding must be prevented through a sensitive handling of the various relationships between people and inhabited space. In contrast, density must be based on community-related considerations in order to reach desired thresholds of urban services.

TOWARD URBAN DENSITIES

As already mentioned, density planning has been used almost exclusively to establish maximum density limits, with a clear preference for low levels. Zoning is the typical mechanism for establishing density limits, using such criteria as ensuring adequate daylight, sunlight, air, usable open space, room for community facilities, a feeling of openness and privacy, and adequate relationship of building cost to land and improvement costs.[43] Except for the last one, an economic objective legitimately influenced by density, there are very few objective justifications for these requirements. Consequently, controls on density are frequently unwarranted, their real use being to prevent undesirable development.

Daylight and sunlight are, in fact, only very loosely related to density, since they begin to be restricted only at the highest values; they are influenced to a much greater degree by the type of building, landscaping, and fenestration. Usable open space has a tenuous connection with density; it is possible to obtain a large amount of open space in high-density areas (with high-rise buildings) and, vice versa, a small amount of open space in relatively low-density areas (with single-family unit subdivisions). Nor does privacy bear a consistent relation to density: some low-density areas have little privacy because windows open to surrounding yards facing neighboring windows without fences, and there is no transition between houses and the community.

There are better ways to fulfill these requirements than through the stringent application of density indices. If ensuring daylight and sunlight is the objective, then the establishment of a sky exposure plane would be more adequate. This control approach, tailored for central areas, limits the vertical height of buildings along the street line, but could allow setbacks determined by a sloping plane. If ensuring usable open space is the objective, then the use of an open-space ratio is recommended. This ratio states the percentage of a lot that must be kept undeveloped. If an adequate relationship to land in terms of future demands on municipal utilities and street capacity is the objective, then the establishment of a floor area ratio would be suitable. This ratio, equally valid in central or peripheral areas, limits the building gross floor area (i.e., the sum of all its floors) for given uses per lot area – which would ensure a balance between development and infrastructure capacity.

A more flexible use of various control approaches to suit the needs of a particular problem would be desirable: incentives could be introduced in order to foster additional community objectives. For example, if a setback at the sidewalk level were desired at a specific intersection, the sky exposure plane could be allowed at a steeper angle; or if more open space were desired, the incentive could be higher allowable density.

There are two distinct areas of concern. One is crowding on a residential scale; the other is density on an urban scale. Residential crowding, a cause of pathological behavior, is the result of the segregation of poor people in high-rent areas. Attempts to solve this complex problem must be an integral part of our efforts to eliminate discrimination in all its dimensions and to give everyone a share of the community wealth. Land use and housing integration, access to education and good employment, and provision of housing for all income groups must be high-priority public policies. Clearly, this amounts to a radical program, and in no way can one understate the seriousness of the obstacles likely to be encountered in trying to implement it. However, it is essential to recognize that the orthodox application of density limits in order to solve the problem of crowding has absolutely no effect on this problem.

On an urban scale, density can, and should, be handled through density regulation, among other planning and design tools. Yet regardless of the flexibility with which various control approaches can be used, the fact remains that the application of all of them is biased by cultural values. As already mentioned, the concern for over-dense areas has led to an almost complete disregard for the opposite problem – that of under-dense areas. Metropolitan densities are affected by two extremes, which we shall call areas of over-urban density and areas of sub-urban density. Over-urban density can create a perception of crowding. It reduces choice, privacy, and opportunities for personalization. The environment loses adaptability, flexibility, and opportunities for alternative human behavior. In short, people lose control of the environment. Sub-urban density can lead to isolation. It reduces the capacity for interaction and, thus, choice. The environment provides few options for human behavior. In another way, people also lose control of the environment.

The basic question is, How can we reestablish density as a building block of urban life and urban communities?

The pattern of density: balance and variety

The major obstacle to reestablishing a range of urban densities is that there has been a polarization of densities at both extremes of the spectrum. In addition, these density extremes are experienced daily by the metropolitan population, giving rise to a polarization that feeds on itself. The crowding of daily commuters in packed trains and buses or on congested highways, and the regimented anonymity of huge corporate workplaces, lead people to seek respite in quiet suburbia, with identifiable houses and patches of green. Millions of people experience daily the rather traumatic shift from a sub-urban environment to an over-urban one, and vice versa, in the belief that the first extreme is a cure for the ills of the other.

One design strategy is to ameliorate the crowding experienced during the trip to and from work and in the workplace itself, thereby reducing stress and thus the need for compensation in the form of low-density suburbs. This strategy assumes that, in order to restore a range of community densities, it is necessary to erode the two pathological extremes of over-urban and sub-urban densities. We could call this a strategy of balance.

This strategy faces serious obstacles. The improvement of the trip to and from work – making it shorter and more comfortable – is clearly linked to the existence of density corridors that make high-quality mass transit feasible. To paraphrase the chicken and the egg question: What comes first, urban densities or good mass transit? We will return to this issue later in this chapter.

Speculation in land values and gigantism in organizations and projects constitute another vicious circle that feeds on itself. As mentioned before, land values rise to astronomical levels in the expectation of huge profits reaped by giant developments; giant developments exist because land values are astronomically high and corporations demand ever larger built complexes. The reduction of over-urban densities; the elimination of huge anonymous lobbies, elevator banks, corridors, and office pools; the introduction of human scale in the workplace and of civilized urban scale in the community – these appear nothing short of impossible. For community designers to lead the charge against these corporate trends would seem folly . . . until one remembers David and Goliath. We shall return to this issue later as well.

A large proportion of the population in metropolitan areas is caught in the daily stressful swing either between over-urban and sub-urban areas or between suburban residential life and suburban employment. The balance strategy aims at restoring a wide range of urban densities. It must not be misunderstood, however, as leading toward a homogeneous environment. Far from it. Another design strategy is to open this wide range of urban density options to all population groups.

Optimal density is not one constant value but many different values. In the continuum between personal privacy and community-wide interaction, density is one of the key factors in increasing choice. The challenge for planners, designers, and civic leaders is to create neighborhoods of varying densities, with small semi-private community areas as well as large public spaces, so that both interaction and seclusion can be enjoyed. These are necessary conditions for a true community design. The optimal situation is to be able to choose, at different times, the thrill of urban life as well as the soothing quality of small-scale environments.

By "urban thrill" I do not mean Times Square, and by "small-scale environment" I do not mean an isolated suburb – not necessarily, at least. These two types of spaces, which could be near one another, need not evoke the stereotypical images of skyscrapers and single-family estates. London offers many urban-scale dense areas that do not oppress with crowding, anomie, or exhaustion, and yet constitute the highest level in the urban hierarchy – Regent Street is one of many examples – as well as intimate areas in close relation to the former – the famous Mews are delightful examples – plus many in between – Grosvenor Square, to mention one.

It is very important that the range of density options be kept open to all population groups. Today there is a wide range of options for only a very few – elite groups who could choose any space from a luxurious penthouse in the city center to a rural estate. As income decreases, choice narrows; the poor must accept subhuman conditions in marginal environments. The importance of the strategy proposed here lies in the opening of density choices – and thus lifestyles to some degree – to all.

The regulation of density

The implementation of the design strategy of balance demands a certain control of densities across the metropolitan area. A reduction of over-urban density and crowding in some central areas, a reconcentration of suburban workplaces in denser centers, and an increase in suburban densities require planning efforts on a metropolitan scale, with participation and consensus of the various municipalities forming the metro area. The most critical argument for metropolitan integration of efforts is the need to coordinate density and public transportation. One of the most ironic planning contradictions in the United States is that decisions on density and mass transportation not only are made independently but often are at odds with one another.

Although every transportation authority has responsibility over a metropolitan area, most planning of transit networks and services is undertaken without minimum coordination with the local municipal agencies responsible for density (and land use) zoning. Furthermore, every municipality has the right to veto improvements or extensions of mass transit to its residents, thus hampering the effective planning of urban transportation. In the past few years, for example, several Boston suburbs

have rejected a plan to extend the subway system to their communities: the probable reason was a fear of "undesirable people" gaining access to the community, as well as an aversion to converting low-density residential areas in the vicinity of the proposed transit corridor into higher-density multi-family residential and commercial uses.

Clearly, the selective coordination of zoning of key areas on the metropolitan scale would be a breakthrough of major proportions, because every municipality jealously guards its right to zone the land within its boundaries. There is a growing number of reasons to change this archaic political mosaic into a more responsive and integrated metropolitan organization. Among them are the need to develop a first-rate public transportation system, to protect water resources (including reserves and aquifers) and open space, to treat sewage properly, to isolate and clean contaminated waste dumps, as well as to open up location and housing choices to people of all races and social classes.

Meanwhile, planners and designers must explore a number of fronts in order to implement the design strategies of balance and variety in density. The reduction of overcrowding and anomie in corporate and bureaucratic workplaces demands a number of complementary controls and incentives, only the most important of which I will mention here. The scale and bulk of office buildings should be reduced through a combination of maximum floor area ratio (building floor area over land area), height, gross floor area served by one elevator core, and distance to windows. These controls aim at disaggregating the building bulk and providing less crowded, less anonymous, and more humane workplaces. This approach is part of the general decentralization and sub-optimization strategy for dealing with large organizations.

The introduction of giant office complexes, completely out of scale and character with the prevailing urban pattern, has resulted in over-urban densities and led to major environmental conflicts. Designing buildings in scale with the existing pattern is a first step toward regaining an urban community without overcrowding. Limiting the floor area that can be served by one elevator core and designating the maximum distance from a work station to the nearest window are controls that aim at providing a better environment while eliminating the disorientation, anonymity, and crowding of oversized buildings. The purpose of establishing realistic floor area ratios is to bring development in scale with, among other parameters, the traffic capacity of streets.

Central city zoning must support public transportation, offering incentives to developers and agencies that cooperate in improving it. Among other possibilities, buildings should provide access to underground subway stations, should give first priority to the upgrading of station entries with visibility and light from sidewalks, and should contribute additional amenities at the sidewalk level for pedestrians – for example, arcades to protect people from bad weather, waiting areas for bus and taxi stops, and restrooms. This type of public-oriented facility designed in coordination with the city and transit authorities – rather than the currently fashionable consumerist "atriums" – must be encouraged. A historical precedent are the galleries that flourished in the preceding century.

At the same time, incentives for the provision of small plazas in the front of every office building could well be eliminated. Most of these plazas are wind-swept barren spaces that break the continuity of streets and avenues. They are a clear example of an urban pattern being undermined by building types without community sense. Open space in central areas must be the result of a conscious planning decision within the urban pattern; Central Park in New York, the plazas of Savannah, the squares of London, and the tree-lined boulevards of Paris are examples of properly planned open spaces.

A strategy of reconcentration should be used to redirect the trend toward suburbanization of employment. Strategic nodes with actual or potential access to extensions of public transportation systems should be zoned for secondary or tertiary employment centers, with mixed uses and urban densities. Large dispersed employment areas along highways should ideally be phased out if serving them with public transportation proves to be unfeasible. Unfortunately, this is easier said than done because of a specific fiscal characteristic of many U.S. municipalities: the local property tax.

Most suburban towns, except the most affluent ones, compete strenuously to induce businesses to locate within their boundaries; they offer tax incentives, sometimes very generous ones, to tilt the balance in their favor. The major reason for this competition is that businesses pay more to towns in property taxes than what they consume in municipal services, thus providing substantial fiscal benefits. However, in the heat of the competition, towns offer incentives such as tax breaks to such a degree that they often end up losing the benefits.

Any strategy for reconcentrating suburban employment must face the fact that some municipalities would lose their property tax base. A solution to this problem is the already mentioned establishment of a metropolitan authority, which would be responsible for pooling the collection of property tax revenues and their distribution to each municipality based on some agreed-upon criteria. Currently, property taxes are used within the municipality that collects them, and tax revenues are raised on the basis of valuation and rate. A criterion for redistribution could be revenue allocation by population in general, and low-income groups in particular. This not only would assure each municipality of tax revenues regardless of the business uses within its boundaries, but also would improve the equality of distribution. If this approach were taken, land could be devoted to the best use – free of fiscal considerations – and densities could be more easily reconcentrated.

Finally, strategies for increasing suburban residential densities should combine a number of alternative approaches. Minimum lot sizes should be reduced; for areas with single-family units, quarter-acre lots satisfy the need for private open space while permitting some form of surface public transportation. Zero lot lines should be encouraged in more urban situations. Several communities have begun to experiment with cluster zoning, whereby the same number of dwelling units that can exist in a given area under normal zoning are concentrated in a much smaller area and the area remaining is devoted to open space. This approach, which is very valuable in low-density suburbs, could be improved by requiring that the remaining open space be planned as an integral part of the open-space system in the community and that the cluster of dwellings also be planned in relation to the existing built pattern.

Cluster zoning could be expanded into a full policy of channeling peripheral developments into "villages." In many suburban and exurban areas, new construction could replicate traditional settlement forms, such as villages and hamlets. If those villages were zoned at crossroads, certain thresholds would be reached: services and facilities within walking distance of the village inhabitants, as well as bus service, could be provided and rural areas and farmland preserved. The village approach is related to our previous proposal to redevelop obsolete shopping centers as mixed-use integrated local centers. Both approaches involve reconcentration and achievement of higher densities and urban thresholds.

Density and dwelling types

One of the problems of defining density in operational terms is the relatively weak relationship between density and building types. The same density can be obtained with radically different building types, and the same type can be used to obtain different densities. For example, the myth that high-density is equivalent to high-rise construction has been dispelled by the "rediscovery" of tightly packed, high-density, low-rise types. Since density is nothing more than a quantitative index with perhaps some clues to possible design solutions, it has few deterministic implications in terms of visual images and behavioral settings. Even environments with the same density and building type can be very different in character, depending on the design nuances – as the differences between old town house neighborhoods and newer versions in countless developments clearly show. Yet dwelling types offer some key opportunities for achieving certain density levels.

The Mediterranean cultures – Greek and Roman, Egyptian, Italian and Spanish, Moroccan, Portuguese, and French – all used a recurrent dwelling type in endless variations: the patio house or court house (which is also found across most of the American continent). The first known example is the so-called House of Abraham in Ur. Using this dwelling type, these cultures built urban communities that became the cradle of civilization. Their cultural values are reflected in the Arab proverb "Paradise without people should not be entered because it is hell." Middle Eastern culture treasures privacy, as shown in its architecture of walls and private gardens. And yet it allows itself the luxury – indeed, the basic requirement for human life – of a rich community life.

Another widespread dwelling type, originating in northern Europe and later transferred to North America, is the party-wall row house or town house, which has formed, with multiple variations, the majority of urban patterns in those countries. This type, like the preceding one, while preserving individual privacy within the house, combines into dense urban patterns that encourage community interaction.

At the level in which dwellings combine to form apartment buildings, there is a rich variety of types offering a trade-off between the advantages of higher densities and a lack of direct access to the ground. At the opposite end of the spectrum is the single-family dwelling on a lot with a range of options in terms of frontage, side yard requirements, and fences.

In all cases, a successful pattern should offer a proper gradation between the privacy of the house and the various levels of community. A proper sequence of intermediate levels must account for elements both on private turf – front yards, fences, entrances to buildings, balconies – and on public turf – residential and metropolitan streets, neighborhood and urban centers, quiet plazas and bustling squares. A successful density control system must consider those intermediate levels.

Ultimately, the repossessing of community densities, with all that this implies in terms of urbanity, will depend on the establishment of urban patterns in which suitable building types can be developed, a variety of conditions and environments can be achieved, a hierarchy of urban thresholds can be reached, and human beings can choose the level of community interaction at which they wish to participate.

NOTES

1 U.S. Bureau of Census, Statistical Abstract of the U.S.: 1970 Census of the Population.
2 Jean Bastié, "Paris: Baroque Elegance and Agglomeration," in H. Wentworth Eldredge (ed.), *World Capitals* (Garden City, N.Y.: Doubleday/Anchor Press, 1975), pp. 55–89.

3 David A. Crane and Associates, *A Comparative Study of New Towns* (New York Urban Development Corporation, 1970).

4 Edwin S. Mills, *Urban Economics* (Glenview, Ill.: Scott, Foresman, 1972).

5 William Alonso, *Location and Land Use* (Cambridge, Mass.: Harvard University Press, 1964).

6 Irving Hoch, "The Three-Dimensional City: Contained Urban Space" in Harvey S. Perloff (ed.), *The Quality of the Urban Environment* (Washington, D.C.: Resources for the Future, 1969), pp. 73–135.

7 Jon T. Lang, *Creating Architectural Theory: The Role of Behavioral Sciences in Environmental Design* (New York: Van Nostrand Reinhold, 1987).

8 Robert Campbell, "Romance of Paris is Fueled by its Density," *Boston Globe*, 14 August 1984.

9 Kevin Lynch, *Site Planning*, 2nd ed. (Cambridge, Mass.: MIT Press, 1971).

10 Ibid.

11 Ibid.

12 Ibid.

13 Donald E. Schmidt, "Crowding in the Urban Environment: An Integration of Theory and Research," in John R. Aiello and Andrew Baum (eds), *Residential Crowding and Design* (New York: Plenum Press, 1979), pp. 41–59.

14 Daniel Stokols, "A Social-Psychological Model of Human Crowding Phenomena," *Journal of the American Institute of Planners*, 38, No. 2 (1972): 72–83.

15 Lang, *Creating Architectural Theory*.

16 Omer R. Galle and Walter R. Grove, "Crowding and Behavior in Chicago, 1940–1970," in Aiello and Baum (eds), *Residential Crowding*, pp. 23–39.

17 R.S. Schmitt, "Density, Health, and Social Disorganization," *Journal of the American Institute of Planners*, 32, No. 1 (1996): 38–40; idem, "Implications of Density in Hong Kong," ibid., 29, No. 3 (1963): 210–17; idem, "Density, Delinquency, and Crime in Honolulu," *Sociology and Social Research*, 41 (1957): 247–6; Paul-Henry Chombart de Lauwe, *Famille et Habitation* (Paris: Edition du Centre National de la Recherche Scientific, 1967); H. Winsborough, "The Social Consequences of High Population Density," *Law and Contemporary Problems*, 30, No. 1 (1965): 120–6; R. Mitchell, "Some Social Implications of High Density Housing," *American Sociological Review*, 36 (1971): 18–29.

18 Stokols, "Social-Psychological Model."

19 Omer R. Galle, Walter R. Gove, and J. McPherson, "Population Density and Pathology," *Science*, 176 (1972): 23–30.

20 Galle and Grove, "Crowding and Behavior."

21 Schmidt, "Crowding in the Urban Environment."

22 Paul R. Hopstock, John R. Aiello, and Andrew Baum, "Residential Crowding Research," in Aiello and Baum (eds), *Residential Crowding*, pp. 9–21.

23 J. Brehm, *A Theory of Psychological Reactance* (New York: Academic Press, 1966).

24 H. Proshansky, W. Ittelson, and L. Rivkin, *Environmental Psychology* (New York: Holt, 1970).

25 A.W. Wickerm, "Undermanning Theory and Research: Implications for the Study of Psychological and Behavioral Effects of Excess Population," *Representative Research in Social Psychology*, 4 (1973): 185–206.

26 A. Sagert, "Crowding: Cognitive Overload and Behavioral Constraint," in W. Preiser (ed.), *Proceeding of the Environmental Research Association*, vol. 2 (Stoudsburg, Pa.: Dowden, Hutchinson & Ross, 1973), pp. 254–60; Daniel Stokols, "The Experience of Crowding in Primary and Secondary Environments," *Environment and Behavior*, 8 (1976): 49–86.

27 Stokols, "The Experience of Crowding."

28 Stokols, "Social-Psychological Model."

29 W. Griffitt and R. Veitch, "Hot and Crowded: Influences of Population Density and Temperature on Interpersonal Affective Behavior," *Journal of Personality and Social Psychology*, 17, No. 1 (1971): 92–8; D.C. Glass and J.E. Singer, *Urban Stress* (New York: Academic Press, 1972).

30 Lang, *Creating Architectural Theory*.

31 A. Westin, *Privacy and Freedom* (New York: Ballantine, 1970).

32 William H. Michaelson, *Man and His Urban Environment: A Sociological Approach* (Reading, Mass.: Addison-Wesley, 1970).

33 Edward T. Hall, *The Hidden Dimension* (Garden City, N.Y.: Doubleday, 1966).

34 J.A. Desor, "Towards a Psychological Theory of Crowding," *Journal of Personality and Social Psychology*, 21, No. 1 (1972): 79–83.

35 I. Altman, *The Environment and Social Behavior* (Monterey, Calif.: Brooks/Cole, 1975).

36 S. Milgram, "The Experience of Living in Cities," *Science*, 167 (1970).

37 Hall, *The Hidden Dimension*.

38 R.G. Barker, *Ecological Psychology* (Stanford, Calif.: Stanford University Press, 1968); idem, "Explorations in Ecological Psychology," *American Psychologist*, 20 (1965): 1–14.

39 Kenneth Frampton, *Modern Architecture: A Critical History* (New York: Oxford University Press, 1980).

40 Amos Rapoport, *House Form and Culture* (Englewood Cliffs, N.J.: Prentice Hall, 1969).

41 Lang, *Creating Architectural Theory*.

42 Robert Sommers, *Personal Space: The Behavioral Basis of Design* (Englewood Cliffs, N.J.: Prentice Hall, 1969).

43 American Public Health Association, *Planning the Neighborhood* (Chicago, 1960).

"Introduction," "Physical Activity and Public Health," and "Urban Design Characteristics"

from *Health and Community Design: The Impact of the Built Environment on Physical Activity* (2003)

Lawrence D. Frank, Peter O. Engelke, and Thomas L. Schmid

Editors' Introduction

Urban designers have long understood that built form influences human behavior, not by way of environmental determinism but rather through environmental possibilism. The design qualities of places make some activities possible and easy to undertake and other activities impossible or difficult. Spatial design can invite, welcome, and encourage certain behaviors and discourage others. In recent years, a growing interest in how built form relates to public health has emerged in the planning and public health fields, particularly the relationship with chronic diseases such as obesity and depression, which are becoming more prevalent in western societies. In the United States, childhood obesity affects so many young people that it has been identified as an epidemic, and there is also considerable alarm about adult obesity. In many individuals, obesity has been found to correlate with low levels of physical activity. Given the scale of the chronic obesity problem, might built form be a culprit, particularly the automobile-oriented cities and neighborhoods that dominate so much of the American landscape?

In the 1980s and 1990s, concerned public health researchers began focusing on moderate types of physical activity, such as walking and biking, because of the realization that these forms might be easier for most people to accomplish than intensively vigorous activity. They found that just 30 minutes of moderate physical activity a day is enough to generate substantial long-term health benefits. Building on this finding, many researchers are focusing on how built environments, particularly residential neighborhoods, support or don't support walking and biking. Larry Frank, Peter Engelke, and Thomas Schmid's work *Health and Community Design: The Impact of the Built Environment on Physical Activity* (2003) was one of the first books to present a comprehensive study of this issue. Drawing on their extensive research of neighborhoods in Atlanta and Seattle, and research done by others, they explore the dimensions of the problem, make cogent arguments for the importance of addressing it, and offer evidence-based assessments of the types of neighborhood environments that promote walking and biking. They identify transportation systems, land use patterns, and urban design characteristics of the built environment as key co-contributors to walkability and bikability, and identify American suburban sprawl environments as being largely unfriendly to these activities. In the end, admitting that the task will not be easy, they call for broad coordinated changes in public policy at national, regional and local levels directed at encouraging the creation of physical activity friendly environments. Essentially, they argue that a public policy paradigm shift must occur that would radically change street and neighborhood design standards, zoning requirements, development guidelines, and transportation funding initiatives, among other things.

In the chapter "Physical Activity and Public Health," they lay out the rationale for why moderate types of physical activity are the most important to focus on to combat the obesity problem. The chapter "Urban Design Characteristics" focuses on how the small-scale design characteristics of an environment influence how people perceive it – as friendly or threatening, interesting or dull, attractive or ugly – and hence the desirability of walking or biking there.

In many ways, contemporary city planning started with the public health movement of the late 1800s. At that time the focus was on diseases that seemed to be associated with terrible living conditions for the poor in cities. Peter Hall writes about these conditions and the public reaction that spawned city planning interventions in his book *Cities of Tomorrow* (Oxford/Malden, MA: Blackwell Publishers, 2002) within the chapter "The City of Dreadful Night."

Lawrence D. Frank holds the Bombardier Chair in Sustainable Urban Transportation Systems at the University of British Columbia and is a Senior Fellow of the Brookings Institution. He holds a PhD in Urban Design and Planning from the University of Washington, and has studied the effects of urban form on walkability, travel patterns, and sustainability for many years. His other works include *Urban Sprawl and Public Health: Designing, Planning, and Building for Healthy Communities* (Washington, DC: Island Press, 2004) co-authored with Howard Frumkin and Richard Jackson, and numerous journal articles and professional reports including "Many Pathways from Land use to Health: Associations between Neighborhood Walkability and Active Transportation, Body Mass Index, and Air Quality," *Journal of the American Planning Association* (vol. 72, no. 1, pp. 75–87, 2006), and "Multiple Impacts of the Built Environment on Public Health: Walkable Places and the Exposure to Air Pollution," *International Regional Science Review* (vol. 28, pp. 193–216, 2005), co-authored with Peter O. Engelke.

Peter O. Engelke is a Visiting Fellow at the Stimson Center in Washington, DC and also works as a research consultant on German energy policy. Subsequent to writing *Health and Community Design*, he earned his PhD in environmental history from Georgetown University. His current research focuses on placing global urbanization trends within environmental security and energy security contexts. A book on global environmental history since 1945 is forthcoming.

Thomas L. Schmid is Team Lead for the Research and Development Team, Division of Nutrition, Physical Activity and Obesity, Centers for Disease Control and Prevention in Atlanta, Georgia, where he conducts and evaluates research on effective strategies to promote physical activity and quality of life. He is also an Adjunct Professor in the School of Public Health at Emory University and a senior advisor to the Robert Wood Johnson Foundation's Active Living Research program. He earned a PhD in psychology, focusing on behavior analysis, from West Virginia University. He has published widely on issues related to community design and public health, evaluation and behavior change, with a particular focus on Latin America, including "A framework for physical activity policy research," *Journal of Physical Activity and Health*, (vol. 1, pp. S20–S29, 2006), co-authored with M. Pratt and M. Witmer.

A recent book that brings together and summarizes research investigating links between public health and the built environment is *Making Healthy Places: Designing and Building for Health, Well-being, and Sustainability* (Washington, DC: Island Press, 2011) edited by Andrew Dannenberg, Howard Frumkin, and Richard Jackson. A related book is Richard Jackson and Stacy Sinclair's *Designing Healthy Communities* (San Francisco, CA: Jossey-Bass, 2011), which is the companion book to a public television documentary that highlights how the design of the built environment can address or prevent childhood and adult health concerns. Another recent comprehensive study of public health and environmental design is Jason Corburn's *Toward the Healthy City: People, Places, and the Politics of Urban Planning* (Cambridge, MA: MIT Press, 2009). Going beyond concerns with how urban form can be changed to promote physical activity, this work argues for a broader conception of the healthy city that addresses health disparities arising from environmental inequities. James A. Kushner's *Healthy Cities: The Intersection of Urban Planning, Law, and Health* (Durham, NC: Carolina Academic Press, 2007) explores the legal mechanisms that can be used to better integrate health concerns into planning and urban design policy.

Recent years have seen a plethora of journal articles concerned with the impacts of urban form on public health. Those concerned with physical activity include Chanam Lee and Anne Vernez Moudon's "Neighbourhood

Design and Physical Activity," *Building Research & Information* (vol. 36, no. 5, pp. 395–411, 2008); Robert Cervero et al.'s "Influences of Built Environments on Walking and Cycling: Lessons from Bogota," *International Journal of Sustainable Transportation* (vol. 3, no. 4, pp. 203–226, 2009); and Brian Saelens and Susan Handy's "Built Environment Correlates of Walking: A Review," *Medicine and Science in Sports and Exercise* (vol. 40, no. 7, pp. S550–S556, 2008). Those concerned with environmental justice issues include B.B. Cutts et al.'s "City Structure, Obesity, and Environmental Justice: An Integrated analysis of physical and social barriers to walkable streets and park access," *Social Science & Medicine* (vol. 69, no. 9, pp. 1314–1322, 2009).

INTRODUCTION

Community design influences human behavior. The ways that cities, suburbs, and towns are designed and built impact the people who work, live, and play in them. The placement, layout, and design of transportation systems, of office complexes, of parks, and of the countless physical elements that make up communities result in real places that have real significance in terms of how we spend our time and what activities we engage in. Where people live, where they work, how they get around, how much pollution they produce, what kinds of environmental hazards they face, and what kinds of amenities they enjoy are a direct product of how communities are designed. This book is about how our communities influence one important type of "behavior," physical activity, and the health outcomes that are associated with it.

Unfortunately, the great majority of Americans do not get enough physical activity to maintain their health over the long run. Physical inactivity is an enormous health problem in this country, contributing to, among other things, premature death, chronic disease, osteoporosis, poor mental health, and obesity. The environments in which most people spend their time – the modern American city and the suburbs and exurbs that have been the dominant form of development in this country for over a half century – are an important contributor to this problem. The cities and suburbs that we inhabit are not now, and have not been for a long time, places that encourage some critically important forms of physical activity. In short, our physical environment inhibits many forms of activity, such as walking, and has become a significant barrier to more active lifestyles.

A century ago, American cities were highly walkable places. They were compact. Commercial, retail, and even industrial operations existed in close proximity to housing, allowing people to walk to work or school or the store. Out of necessity, buildings and streets were designed to the human scale. Streetcar and trolley systems provided a major form of transportation for millions of passengers every day, in every major city in the nation, which meant that people had the means to make longer journeys without the use of a car. When combined, all of this produced environments in which someone could satisfy their basic daily needs within a comfortable walking distance of their home or within a distance reachable through a combination of walking and trolley riding.

Unfortunately, the burgeoning cities of the industrial era also brought with them a host of serious problems. They were dirty and polluted. They were crowded. Most importantly, they produced health problems for their inhabitants. The worst of these were the communicable disease epidemics – typhus, yellow fever, and all manner of other infectious diseases – that swept through them with frightening regularity. The very conditions that made the industrial city a highly walkable place, including its concentration of people, its mixing of uses, and its high density of buildings, came to be blamed – not quite accurately, as research eventually showed – for creating the conditions in which epidemics could occur. So during the nineteenth and early twentieth centuries, critics tore away at the intellectual foundation of the compact industrial city. They sought to replace it with a new paradigm, a new way of thinking about how to build cities. In the old city's place they created the modern decentralized city, where housing was separated from workplaces and buildings placed far apart from one another, separated by expanses of grass and trees. America's new cities of big lawns and big distances would, they hoped and expected, produce more healthy living. What resulted was the city that we are so familiar with today – dominated by suburbs, spread out, with different uses separated one from another and almost everything reliant on automobile travel. This mass suburbanization also led directly to a decline, in terms of population, wealth, and public investment in the older, established central parts of most cities, resulting in the widespread abandonment of the fabric of the old walkable city.

Widespread criticism of this development model has appeared only during the last couple of decades. Much of it is a reaction to the omnipresent automobile congestion that is the hallmark of the decentralized city. Some of it is centered on the monstrous-yet-monotonous ugliness of the endless strip malls and parking lots that have proliferated from one end of the country to the other. Many people are concerned about the environmental consequences of the modern city. These concerns focus on the enormous amount of land consumed, the air quality problems produced by all of the cars needed to keep these cities running, the vast quantities of municipal water that is required to irrigate the lawns of the new suburban landscapes, or the rainwater that is wasted as polluted runoff from parking lots and streets. An even more recent source of criticism is from the field of public health, which is beginning to explore potentially uncomfortable linkages between the decentralized city and different indicators of health.

Physical activity, past and present

In the old cities, getting enough physical activity during one's day wasn't an issue because it was as much a part of life as eating or sleeping. Today, physical activity has been engineered out of most aspects of life. Work is no longer physically demanding for most people and daily living patterns, from mowing the grass to cooking dinner to washing clothes, require significantly less manual effort than they once did. The modern city has changed all of this, creating environments in which it is less and less common to work physical activity into the everyday patterns of life. The dominant forms of community design have contributed to this decline by making walking and cycling for transportation difficult if not impossible. Many of the reasons why are clear to even the casual observer. Long distances between places mean that most people cannot walk or bicycle from one place to another. The streets and roads that connect these far-flung places are designed for cars, often making them unsafe and extremely unattractive for pedestrians and bicyclists. To make matters worse, most developers and retailers have long given up on the profitability of designing places that are visually attractive to people who might want to walk from place to place, favoring instead designs that attract motorists. As a result, being physically active now requires planning for activities such as running, biking, aerobics, or weight lifting that can be done during leisure time.

Coincidentally, during the post-World War II period, public health research came to focus more and more on recreational and vigorous physical activity as the way to improve public health. For years, health experts recommended that each individual get at least twenty minutes of high-intensity exercise each day. The basic idea was that anything less would result in little or no improvement in long-term health. And, judging by the attention paid to such forms of exercise in the popular media, it would seem that vigorous physical activity has been a runaway success. Specialty magazines devoted to participatory sports and exercise programs ranging from running to weight lifting to climbing jam the racks at newsstands. An array of televised sports occupies much of the country's attention on weekends, bringing basketball, football, hockey, baseball, and a slew of other offerings into millions of homes. Advertisers in the print and electronic media perpetually barrage the country with images of the perfectly fit human figure, both male and female.

Yet this picture of a fit and healthy society is enormously misleading. The fact is that most Americans don't get enough physical activity to meet the health recommendations set by public health agencies. Despite the omnipresence of televised sports, the billions of dollars in exercise equipment and apparel sold every year, the millions of words published on fitness and exercise regimens, and the endless rhetoric springing from athletic shoe and apparel companies' advertising campaigns, only about 5 percent of the population – *one person in twenty* – gets enough physical activity through vigorous exercise to satisfy public health standards (CDC 2001b). Even worse, some studies have found that as much as 40 percent of the population is sedentary (being completely inactive) (Schoenborn and Barnes 2002); they report that they get no physical activity at all during their leisure hours. For all of the promotion and attention paid to sports- and gym-based exercise as the way to get people physically fit, the great majority of the population has not succeeded in becoming physically active through these means. While millions of people do get a great deal of health benefit as well as personal satisfaction from sports, from training for endurance and strength events, and from going to the gym for a workout, many more find that they don't have the will or the ability or the time or the resources to do any of these things.

These are some of the reasons why, beginning in the 1980s and continuing into the 1990s, public health agencies and researchers began to take a serious look at more moderate types of physical activity such as walking and bicycling. Mounting evidence from epidemiological studies began to reveal that moderate forms of physical activity could provide both short- and long-term health benefits, contributing to a reduction in the risk of premature mortality, chronic disease, and a host of other maladies. Moreover, public health researchers began to believe that a focus on more moderate forms of physical activity might enable a broader cross-section of the population to become physically active. Because moderate physical activity is lower in intensity, it is easier for a person who is sedentary to begin and to maintain their participation over the long term. Moderate physical activity can be purposive, meaning that it can be integrated into daily living habits, and as a result it should be more attractive to people who don't have the necessary free time to work out at a gym or go mountain biking in the woods.

What is old, then, is new: public health agencies now endorse those forms of moderate physical activity such as walking and bicycling that used to be very commonplace in American cities and towns. Public health officials recommend that people accumulate at least thirty minutes of moderate activity on most, preferably all days of the week. Adding any additional amount of moderate activity is good; in fact, while public health agencies recommend trying to get at least thirty minutes per day, there is a belief that even ten or twenty additional minutes per day might generate some benefits. Vigorous physical activity is still considered to be an important means of staying healthy, but public health experts now believe that adding a half hour or more of moderate physical activity per day on most days of the week is enough to generate long-term health benefits.

This consensus opinion carries enormous significance for addressing the problem of physical inactivity. It suggests – perhaps demands – that public health agencies not limit themselves to programs that rely solely on motivating individuals to take up vigorous exercise. Rather, the door has been opened for an examination of the environmental influences of moderate physical activity. If one needs a half hour or more of moderate physical activity per day, accumulated in numerous short bouts, it might be wise to focus on creating environments that allow these types of activities to occur as a matter of course, as incidental to doing other things. For many people, perhaps even the majority of the population, such an approach may be the only realistic way to increase physical activity (incidentally, increasing physical activity in this way may also be a way to reduce automobile use and lessen its attendant problems, such as air pollution and congestion). For different segments of the population who are disadvantaged – many elderly and physically handicapped people, for instance – vigorous activities may be out of the question completely. For physically capable people in the prime of life, other obstacles such as a lack of time may severely constrict their ability to work out on a regular basis. For the significant percentage of the population that is sedentary, the benefits of adding a half hour of moderate physical activity each day are enormous: physical activity follows a dose-response curve, wherein the marginal benefits to increased exercise accrue the most to those who are the least active to begin with.

Community design, physical activity, and health: a conceptual model

Figure 1 provides a simple model of the relationships between physical activity, health, and the environments in which people live and work. . . . Causality

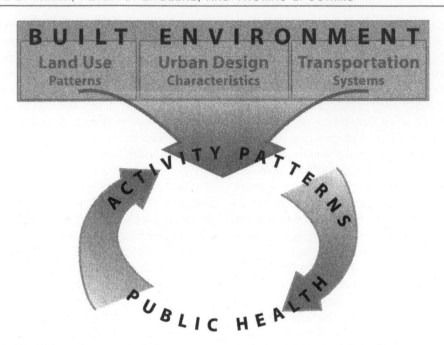

Figure 1 Model of linkages between the built environment, physical activity, and public health.

flows, roughly, from the built environment (the communities in which we live and environments in which we work) through physical activity patterns to public health outcomes. Physical activity is at the literal as well as conceptual center of the model, providing the linkage between the real, built environment and the health outcomes that are of such concern to public health officials.

The built environment denotes the form and character of communities. It is made up of the countless specific places – homes, streets, offices, parking lots, shopping malls, restaurants, parks, movie theaters – that constitute a city or town or suburb. Our model utilizes three broad categories – transportation systems, land use patterns, and urban design characteristics – to provide coherence to the built environment. Transportation systems connect places to each other, determining how feasible it is to use different types of transportation, including walking and bicycling, to get from one place to another. Local transportation systems are impacted by major investments in highways, airports, and other infrastructure decisions made by regional and state officials. Land use patterns consist of the arrangement of residences, offices, restaurants, grocery stores, and other places within the built environment. The

arrangement of these activities, or land uses, determine how close different places such as housing, work, and entertainment are to one another, thereby making journeys on foot or by bicycle practical or impractical. They also shape physical activity patterns through the distribution of open space and recreational facilities where sports and other activities can take place. Finally, urban design characteristics influence how people perceive the built environment. Design plays a large role in determining whether an environment is perceived as hostile or friendly, attractive or ugly, and vibrant or dull. Urban design denotes small-scale features of the built environment that impact how people feel about being in specific places.

The conceptual model provided in figure 1 illustrates the interactive nature between one's health and the environment in which one lives, works, and engages in other activities. The arrows that run in both directions between physical activity and health denote how physical activity is both a cause and an effect. The arrow extending from public health to physical activity reflects the likelihood that some health outcomes, such as high levels of obesity or chronic disease in the population, may make it harder for some people to engage in physical activity. Basically, the poorer the health of the population, the more difficult it becomes to increase physical activity levels. However, our central focus is on how the built environment influences physical activity levels.

This leads to a second observation on causality in the model: physical activity is only one contributor, albeit a very important one, to health outcomes. There are, of course, many other reasons why people suffer from ill health. To take one example, during the 1990s and into the new century, the high rates of obesity in the United States became the focus of much research within public health circles as well as a favorite subject of the press. Obesity has multiple causes, ranging from genetics to poor diet to environmental factors and personal behavior. While one's genetics are an important determinant of obesity, diet and physical activity are things that can be controlled. The built environment impacts both of these behaviors. (While we focus on physical activity in this book, the location of quality food outlets versus fast food venues is another way that the built environment impacts our health; in poorer parts of cities, for example, there tend to be fewer food establishments – restaurants and grocery stores – serving healthy foods.) As tempting as it is to point to the built environment as a main cause of problems such as obesity, it is not acceptable to draw a straight line between the two and imply that only environmental improvement will solve the problem; clearly there are other determinants of obesity.

Nonetheless, the intent . . . is to argue that most of the communities where Americans live are important contributors to current public health problems. Simultaneously, they can also be the source of important solutions to these problems. Communities can be designed to make physical activity in them possible and even desirable. Environments that encourage moderate physical activity may also have features that make them more livable in other ways, by improving one's quality of life – they may generate more social interaction, foster less dependence on the automobile, be safer for their inhabitants, and give people more choices with respect to how they get around and spend their time. In these pages we do not seek to condemn any particular form of community design. Rather, a central goal is to develop a better understanding of the ways in which the features of the built environment serve to encourage or discourage health-promoting behaviors, two of which are walking and bicycling. Public policies that influence how to build communities – which zoning and building codes to adopt, which transportation systems to build, and so on – can best be understood and assessed once the health benefits and costs of such choices are included in the calculus.

PHYSICAL ACTIVITY AND PUBLIC HEALTH

The prevention and cure of many infectious diseases, due in large part to advances in medical science as well as widespread improvements in sanitation, diet, and housing, was a contributing factor in the dramatic increase in longevity between the beginning and end of the twentieth century. In 1900, the average American could expect to live to age forty-nine; by 1997, this figure was around seventy-six years (Federal Interagency Forum on Aging-Related Statistics 2000). Obviously, the public health issues facing Americans and residents of other wealthy countries have changed in dramatic ways. Certainly, the suffering and premature deaths that used to accompany infectious disease epidemics are now rare. However, hundreds of thousands of Americans still die from *preventable* deaths each year. Deaths from chronic diseases, most notably heart disease and various cancers, have replaced deaths from infectious disease. Many deaths . . . can be traced to bad habits.

They are preventable in that they are mostly caused by behaviors that can be modified; smoking, for example, is a well-known cause of lung cancer. But premature mortality is not the only consequence of preventable medical problems. Chronic diseases and other preventable afflictions also subtract from one's quality of life. For instance, osteoporosis, a condition that tends to affect many older women, is characterized by a deterioration in one's bone mass and structure; the onset of osteoporosis may be delayed or prevented by modifiable behaviors, for example dietary and exercise patterns.

Unfortunately, Americans engage in many different behaviors that lead to such ill health. Physical inactivity is one of the most common and most preventable patterns of behavior. In this chapter we describe how this widespread inactivity is a major determinant of poor health in the general population, in terms of premature mortality, the onset of chronic diseases, and a poor quality of life. Physical activity can be a significant part of the solution to many of these health problems. Recent public health research has shown that moderate forms of physical activity can be helpful types of exercise. While more vigorous forms of activity such as running can generate health benefits for participants, from a public health perspective it may be better to focus on moderate types of physical activity because they are easier for inactive people to begin and maintain over time. Moderately intense activities can be built into the lives of many Americans by changing the way communities are designed and built. Two of the most common types, walking and bicycling, are easily incorporated into people's lives when the built environment is properly structured to encourage them. However, when our communities are structured so that they inhibit or prevent such activities, as is the case in most parts of the country, many people are unable to get the amount of physical activity needed for long-term health.

Physical activity and health: basic premises

While it has long been known that physical activity is an important component of a healthy lifestyle, a report issued by the Surgeon General in 1996 titled *Physical Activity and Health* represented a watershed moment in the history of the public health community's approach to physical activity and fitness (U.S. Department of Health and Human Services 1996, hereafter USDHHS 1996). Prior to this report, the general advice given by public health officials to the public was echoed in the phrase "no pain-no gain," whereby individuals were advised to try and get at least twenty minutes of high intensity aerobic exercise three or more days a week (Pate et al. 1995). Implicit in this advice was the idea that anything less than a sustained high-energy effort would be a waste of time, resulting in little or no health improvement over time. While the Surgeon General's report recognized the benefits of the increased fitness that vigorous exercise can provide, it took a much more inclusive view of physical activity and health. In a nutshell, it voiced the expert opinion, based upon an exhaustive reading of recent health research, that significant health benefits can be

obtained through moderate activities such as walking and bicycling. These new recommendations are for adults to accumulate at least thirty minutes of moderate physical activity on most, preferably each day of the week.

Since the publication of the Surgeon General's report, the body of scientific literature that supports this position has continued to grow. Regular, moderately intense physical activity helps to maintain the functional independence of older adults and enhances the quality of life for people of all ages. The literature also shows that such physical activity helps maintain normal muscle strength and joint structure and function, lower high blood pressure, relieve depression and anxiety, lower obesity levels, and is necessary for normal skeletal development during childhood. Physically inactive people are almost twice as likely to develop coronary heart disease as people who engage in regular physical activity. This risk is almost as high as several well-known risk factors such as cigarette smoking, high blood pressure and high cholesterol. Sadly, however, physical inactivity in the United States is more common than any of these other major risk factors, with different studies showing that the majority of Americans do not get enough physical activity to meet minimum standards set by the Surgeon General and other health organizations (USDHHS 1996). While a lifetime of regular physical activity is the goal, it is never too late to start. In fact when sedentary people become more active they gain immediate health benefits, often with a larger relative improvement than their more fit counterparts. . . . the marginal benefits that result from a unit increase in physical activity for the sedentary person is thought to be larger than the same increase would be for the person who is already a committed runner or soccer player.

While genetics provide an important contribution to longevity, daily habits may play an even more critical role in determining life expectancy. Epidemiological studies have consistently linked physical inactivity to mortality over the long run. Based upon statistical evidence, these studies generally show that individuals with higher physical activity levels experience lower mortality rates. One found, for example, that men who engaged in moderate physical activity had a risk of dying that was only 73 percent of that for the least active group of men in the study (Leon et al. 1987). Another study concluded that slight improvements in fitness can have a dramatic effect on long-term mortality risk (Blair et al. 1989).

Other studies have yielded similar findings, even after controlling for the influence of one's genetics (Paffenbarger and Lee 1996). In an effort to isolate the influence of physical activity patterns on mortality while taking genetics into account, Kujala et al. (1998) examined the relationship between exercise patterns and mortality in about 19,000 subjects who shared the same childhood environments and nearly identical genetic structure. The researchers tracked the health status of the subjects over a twenty-year period. The results showed that the risk of death declined with increasing physical activity in both men and women, even after genetic and other familial variables are taken into account.

Studies such as this one have contributed to an expanded interest, within public health circles, regarding how "behavioral risk factors" (e.g., smoking, poor diet, inadequate physical activity) influence health and mortality. Hundreds of thousands of premature deaths per year can be attributed to poor diet and inadequate levels of physical activity. One study estimated the number of deaths attributable to poor dietary and physical activity patterns in the United States in 1990 (McGinnis and Foege 1993). The authors' goal was to assess the role played by underlying behaviors (tobacco use, poor diet and activity patterns, alcohol abuse, etc.) instead of the immediate health conditions that caused death (lung disease, emphysema, diabetes, heart disease, etc.), which were seen as the result of risky behavior. The authors reviewed studies published between 1977 and 1993 of the causes of death in different study populations, allowing them to derive approximations of the number of deaths in the United States that could be assigned to underlying behavior. . . . Poor diet and sedentary living patterns, estimated to have caused some 300,000 deaths (14 percent of all deaths), ranked as the second leading cause, behind tobacco but ahead of such well-known causes as firearms and motor vehicle accidents.

Physical inactivity and chronic disease

Chronic diseases and mortality are, of course, intimately linked. National and international health organizations, for example the Centers for Disease Control and Prevention (CDC) in the United States, believe that long-term patterns of behaviors – in particular, tobacco use, poor nutrition, and lack of physical activity – play significant roles in the onset of four main chronic diseases (cardiovascular disease, cancer, diabetes, and chronic obstructive pulmonary disease) and, thus, in premature mortality (CDC 1999a). In a study of data from national health surveys, the CDC determined that a sedentary lifestyle was the most common modifiable risk factor for coronary heart disease (CHD, a form of cardiovascular disease), present in 58 percent of reported cases. In contrast, cigarette smoking was present 25 percent of the time, obesity 22 percent, and hypertension 17 percent (CDC 1990). Physical inactivity also has been linked to the other chronic diseases. The Surgeon General's 1996 report concluded that physical inactivity is associated with an increased risk of colon cancer and diabetes (USDHHS 1996). Other studies have addressed walking as a predictor of diabetes. One compared the activity patterns with the risk of becoming diabetic for women over a period of eight years; those who walked frequently had only 58 percent of the risk of becoming diabetic when compared with sedentary women, even after controlling for age, hypertension, and other variables (Hu et al. 1999).

There is enormous potential for physical activity to reduce the amount of chronic disease in the United States. One study (Powell and Blair 1994), found that between 32 percent and 35 percent of deaths attributable to CHD, colon cancer, and diabetes could have been prevented if every person in the United States were to become highly active. The authors of this study, realizing that it would be unlikely for all people in the country to be active at this level, also generated estimates based on smaller improvements in physical activity rates within the population. Modest improvements in physical activity levels, they estimated, would still result in substantial reductions in deaths attributable to the three diseases because of the huge numbers of people who fall into the inactive categories. For example, if half of the population classified as sedentary were to become irregularly active (meaning getting some activity but not enough to meet guidelines), the total number of deaths attributable to CHD, colon cancer, and diabetes would drop 3.9 percent, 2.5 percent, and 1.5 percent, respectively. If half of the people who are irregularly active were to become regularly active (thus meeting the guidelines), those figures would be 7.1 percent, 7.4 percent, and 5.2 percent. This study illustrates the public health principle of obtaining large population benefits from small average individual change. A few percentage points' improvement in the national average for blood pressure, or a few minutes added to the national average of daily exercise would result in a large number of saved lives.

Physical inactivity: overweight and obesity

In the United States, rising overweight and obesity is a serious public health problem. "Overweight" and "obesity" are clinical terms used by public health agencies that classify people according to their height and weight status; the overweight category is one category above normal (heavier than normal for one's height), while the obese category is yet another category above overweight.[1] Unfortunately, more than half of American adults are categorized as being overweight or obese. A national study of CDC data reported that in 1999–2000 nearly one-third (30.5 percent) of adults were obese and nearly two-thirds (64.5 percent) were overweight or obese (Flegal et al. 2002). To make matters worse, levels of overweight and obesity have been climbing for many years. Roughly speaking, the prevalence of obesity in the United States increased by 61 percent during the 1990s alone. This trend appears to be affecting all major demographic groups in society. Rising overweight and obesity is pervasive and widespread in the United States, affecting the young and old, black and white, rich and poor. Maps show both the rapid increase in obesity over time as well as the extent of the problem in the United States (Mokdad et al. 2001).

Levels of childhood obesity are similarly worrisome. In the 1960s and 1970s about 4 to 6 percent of children and adolescents (ages 6–19) were overweight; by 1999, this number had more than doubled to 13–14 percent (CDC 1999d). Overall, the rate of increase of obesity in the American population – about 50 percent during the 1990s – is considered so severe that many have compared its spread and dispersion characteristics to that of a communicable disease epidemic (Mokdad et al. 1999).[2]

Overweight and obesity have been linked in the public health literature to a variety of diseases and health problems. Overweight and obesity are associated with high blood pressure, gallbladder disease, osteoarthritis, and type 2 diabetes mellitus, relationships that get stronger as a person gets heavier. These findings are consistent for both men and women. Further, as a person's weight increases their chance of having two or more of these chronic conditions multiplies (Must et al. 1999).

While physical inactivity by itself does not generally cause overweight and obesity, the combination of sedentary lifestyles with other risk behaviors such as improper diet leads to these conditions. Only some of the increase in overweight and obesity rates can be explained by the increases in average caloric intake over time for the American population; low and declining levels of physical activity are also assumed to be a significant contributor (Koplan and Dietz 1999). The Surgeon General's report, for example, subscribes to the formulation that dietary patterns plus exercise are important determinants of overweight and obesity in the United States (USDHHS 1996; see also Must et al. 1999). Numerous cross-sectional studies reviewed by the Surgeon General reported lower weight among people with higher levels of physical activity.

The Surgeon General's report concluded that: physical activity promotes fat loss while preserving or increasing lean mass; the rate of weight loss is associated with the frequency and duration of physical activity; the combination of increased physical activity and dieting is more effective than dieting alone for long-term weight regulation; and the full extent that physical inactivity contributes to obesity levels in children is not yet determined.

Physical inactivity and quality of life

Regular physical activity has a large number of benefits beyond those of reducing the risk of chronic disease and premature mortality. Physical activity maintains muscle strength, bone mass, and proper joint function and may also play an important role in fostering and maintaining mental health. People may have a more positive self-evaluation of their physical and mental status if they are more active, a phenomenon that becomes more prevalent as they get older (Unger 1995).

A lifetime of physical activity may, in fact, generate its greatest benefits for the elderly. A recent analysis of elderly women, for example, reported that inactive, nonsmoking women at age sixty-five have 12.7 years of active life expectancy, compared to 18.4 years of active life expectancy for more highly active women (Ferucci et al. 2000). Because physical activity is believed to delay the onset of disability and chronic diseases, the functional limitations and subsequent loss of independence that are associated with aging are also delayed. Physical activity is believed to be able to help delay or prevent the onset of osteoporosis in the elderly, a condition characterized by decreased bone mass and increased bone fragility. This is a particularly severe problem in older women, contributing to the widespread and growing number of hip fractures from falls. Regular physical activity throughout one's life may prevent or delay the development of osteoporosis, particularly by helping to develop and maintain bone mass during adolescence and middle age (USDHHS 1996; Shephard 1997). Many studies also demonstrate that physical activity improves symptoms of depression in adults. One study found that exercise programs for adults produced improvements in depressive symptoms that were comparable to improvements from medication (Singh, Clemets, and Fiatarone 1997), while another reported that physical activity for adults reduces the amount of cognitive decline as an adult ages (Yaffe et al. 2001). The benefits of exercise are not limited to improvements in cognitive function. A Boston study of forty- to seventy-year-old men found that physical activity status was "significantly" associated with erectile dysfunction (impotence). The highest risk was for men who remained inactive, and the lowest was among those who remained active or became physically active, even if begun at middle age (Derby et al. 2000).

Economic cost of physical inactivity

Premature death and disability caused by coronary heart disease, diabetes mellitus, cancers, and other illnesses related to physical inactivity result in tremendous health care costs. According to the American Heart Association, cardiovascular disease costs the country more than $150 billion each year in direct and indirect costs, including hospital and nursing home services, prescription drugs, and lost productivity (Stone 1996). Studies that have examined the results of one of the most thorough national surveys of medical expenditures, the National Medical Expenditure Survey, report lower direct medical costs for people who are active versus those who are sedentary. Annual medical costs remained lower for the regularly active group (ranging from $330 to more than $1,000 per person), even after controlling for the independent influence of physical limitations, gender, and smoking status. These findings also applied to particular types of health care costs. For example, direct health care costs for treatment of people who had arthritis were found to be about $1,200 less for those who were physically active than those who were sedentary (Pratt, Macera, and Wang 2000; Wang et al. 2001).

Levels of physical inactivity

A minority of the American population engages in enough regular, sustained exercise to meet public health recommendations. Data released by the CDC in 2001 from the Behaviorial Risk Factor Surveillance System (BRFSS) showed that in 2000 only about one out of three adults reported enough moderate or vigorous activity to meet public health guidelines while a similar number (29 percent) were sedentary – reporting no leisure time physical activity. The remainder (about 46 percent) reported some activity but at a level insufficient to maintain personal health and wellness. . . . These patterns of leisure time activity have remained essentially stable since the 1980s (CDC 2001b).

Poor physical activity habits typically start at a young age. Among high school students more than one in three (35 percent) do not participate regularly in vigorous physical activity. Regular participation drops from 75 percent of ninth graders to 61 percent of twelfth graders. From 1991 to 2001 participation in daily physical education classes in high school dropped from 42 percent to 31 percent of students. Overall about one in three (31 percent) students do not meet minimum guidelines for physical activity (Grunbaum et al. 2002). Unfortunately, there is evidence that such bad habits persist into adulthood. Studies in the United States and Europe have found that there is a moderate to low correlation between activity levels in childhood and later as adults. Children who are inactive are more likely to be inactive when they are adults than their active peers (Malina 2001; Telama et al. 1997). Physical activity patterns also vary by other demographic and socioeconomic patterns. Rates of physical activity are lower for females than males, generally lower for minorities, the elderly, the less educated, and the poor, and declines with age.

Encouraging physical activity: adoption and adherence

One of the flaws in the "no pain–no gain" model of physical activity outlined at the beginning of this chapter is that people may have a difficult time beginning the types of exercise that this model prescribes and, further, an even more difficult time in sticking to such exercise routines over longer terms. Public health research often centers on these phenomena – called adoption (beginning a physical activity regimen) and adherence (sticking to one over time) – because they are important concepts in explaining why people have problems altering their physical activity patterns. Given the findings of the Surgeon General and others that significant health benefits for an individual can be achieved via thirty minutes or more of moderate physical activity, which can be accumulated throughout the course of the day in short bouts (i.e., in as little as ten minutes at a time), attention has been focused on the question of whether people can more readily adopt and adhere to these forms of physical activity. Sustained participation in structured activities (the gym-based model of exercise) has proven to be very difficult to achieve for many people. In contrast, there is some evidence to suggest that unstructured activities (where people do not have to join a gym or other structured, formal setting) of moderate intensity may be more effective. While structured exercise programs may have a slightly greater effect on health than unstructured activities *per unit of time*, the latter type may be better for many people because it is easier to get people to adopt and adhere to them (Dunn, Andersen, and Jakicic 1998).

Some health educators use the term "lifestyle" to denote that patterns of some behaviors are good predictors of other behaviors – that is, people who tend to be careful about what they eat also may be careful about getting enough physical activity (or, conversely, if people have some bad habits such as smoking or taking illegal drugs they may be less concerned about an unhealthy diet or abuse of alcohol).

While this approach has value for those in the field of public health who design health promotion programs, it is less salient for our purposes than a second meaning of the term. Within the context of physical activity research, lifestyle activities are those that can fit easily into one's daily routine. For instance, riding a bicycle to the store may be an easier habit to establish and maintain than finding the extra time to go to the gym and work out. This stands in contrast to traditional exercises that are, as the kinesiologist William Morgan has written, nonpurposeful and therefore have little meaning in and of themselves. (Morgan quotes the Roman poet Marcus Valerius Martialis [A.D. 38–103] in this context, who asked, "Why do strong arms fatigue themselves with frivolous dumbbells? To dig in a vineyard is worthier exercise for men." See Morgan 2001). The point is that if activities with more inherent meaning were emphasized, it would be easier for people to incorporate them into their routines. Gardening, walking to do an errand, and cycling to work have more inherent meaning than pedaling a stationary bike to nowhere.

This form of lifestyle intervention consists of public health programs that place their emphasis upon the environmental conditions that encourage or inhibit physical activity, and prescribe the creation of activity-supportive environments. For example, adding well-marked, extensive bike lanes throughout a small city would, according to this model, help to create an environment in which people find it safe and easy to bicycle to work or school. Similarly, educational programs that encourage taking the stairs at work instead of the elevator are designed to increase physical activity for people at work. In contrast are structured interventions, programs designed around structured exercise regimens. These latter interventions use guidelines of exercise frequency, intensity, and duration in order to set performance goals for participants – where intensity is the amount of exertion, duration is the amount of elapsed time spent exercising, and frequency is the number of exercise sessions engaged in over a period of time (Bouchard and Shephard 1994). In this type of intervention, public health researchers or practitioners take a direct role in getting people to participate in structured activities such as aerobics dance classes.

Lifestyle interventions have been shown to be as effective, and in some cases more effective, than structured interventions in overcoming the adoption and adherence hurdles. Lifestyle interventions can yield positive and long-term effects, in terms of increasing the levels of moderately intense physical activity and in reducing the levels of sedentariness within studied groups (Dunn et al. 1998). Those who are sedentary or mostly inactive are more likely to be more responsive to lifestyle interventions that encourage the adoption of moderately intense, inexpensive, and convenient forms of physical activity (Shephard 1997). Moderate activities of shorter duration may allow people to more readily fit physical activity into their daily schedule and habit patterns. Moreover, the lower intensity threshold allows sedentary people to start engaging in the activity without fear of the physical pain that accompanies vigorous exercise. Moderate physical activities also typically require less in the way of specialized equipment and/or access to specialized facilities, and may generate less apprehension for the beginner with respect to the social embarrassment that may accompany working out at a fitness facility. In contrast, vigorous activities in structured settings present a number of barriers: they simply may be too difficult, time-consuming, or embarrassing for many people, especially for people who are elderly, overweight/obese, or out of shape due to a prolonged sedentary lifestyle. In addition, people may be physically unable or mentally unprepared to participate in vigorous activities like jogging or aerobics over the long term.

An example of the effectiveness of lifestyle interventions is provided by a study published in the *Journal of the American Medical Association*. A group of researchers tracked how well two different interventions did at improving levels of physical activity, cardiorespiratory fitness, and cardiovascular disease risk factors amongst 235 adults. The study consisted of six months of direct interventions wherein the researchers monitored and encouraged participation; eighteen months of maintenance intervention (where the intervention was less frequent and intense) followed. One group was assigned to

a lifestyle intervention program wherein participants were simply encouraged to engage in moderate physical activities; the main components of this intervention focused on education. The other group was placed in a highly structured exercise program that consisted of enrolling participants in a health club. Results from the six months of direct intervention showed that the lifestyle physical activity intervention was as effective in increasing physical activity as the structured program. During the eighteen-month follow-up, the authors found that both groups continued to enjoy significant and comparable improvements in physical activity levels, cardiorespiratory fitness, blood pressure, and percentage of body fat (Dunn et al. 1999). Other studies have shown similar results, with lifestyle interventions performing as well as structured interventions in lowering weight, systolic blood pressure, and serum lipid and lipoprotein levels (Andersen et al. 1999). Once such activities are begun, participants are more likely to continue and to obtain long-term improvements in levels of physical activity (Dunn, Andersen, and Jakicic 1998). For these reasons, less strenuous forms of exercise may be more effective in inducing long-term changes in the behavior of sedentary adults (Owen and Bauman 1992).

Walking and bicycling are important in this context because they are two types of moderately intense physical activity that can be incorporated easily into daily routines in the built environment. Walking improves cardiovascular capacity, bodily endurance, lower body muscular strength and flexibility, posture, enhances metabolism of lipoproteins and insulin/glucose dynamics, and may increase bone strength (Morris and Hardman 1997). Walking may also help to manage arthritis – one study reported that regular walking reduces pain and improves function in people with knee arthritis (Kovar et al. 1992). In fact walking is a core component of many arthritis treatment programs. Walking is the most readily available form of physical activity in the world, as most people can and do engage in it every day, and thus is the easiest form of physical activity to undertake. As a result, walking is ideal as a start-up activity for the sedentary, the overweight/obese, and the elderly, because of its simplicity and low threshold of activity (Morris and Hardman 1997; Shephard 1997).

As with walking, cycling's independent effects on health continue to accumulate. In Europe, where cycling rates are much higher than in the U.S., there is a growing body of research suggesting that cycling for transportation or recreation can provide significant health benefits. For example, a number of studies have reported a lower risk of death for those who are active cyclists (for recreation or transportation) compared with those who are not (Andersen et al. 1999; Hillman 1992; Oja, Vuori, and Paronen 1998; Vuori, Oja, and Paronen 1994). It is also less stressful on joints and bones than is walking. Although cycling is slightly less accessible than walking (cycling requires some equipment, obviously, and also requires more balance and co-ordination than walking), it is an activity that most of the population can engage in if they so choose. The number of bicycles in the United States, at 100 million or more, alone testifies to the viability and affordability of this form of physical activity.

Conclusion

A consensus is developing within public health circles that lifestyles are key to understanding chronic disease patterns in the general population, leading to calls for more research into the underlying behavioral trends and patterns that produce chronic diseases and conditions. The dramatically increasing levels of overweight and obesity in the United States have also served to point many in the public health community toward understanding how poor dietary and physical activity patterns contribute to these problems. As this chapter has shown, there is increasing evidence suggesting that nonstructured forms of exercise can be a critical component in improving Americans' overall health. This perspective derives additional force from the fact that so many people get very little exercise, and even though most say they would like to be more active, they seem to have a hard time increasing the amount of activity they get. Because such a large percentage of the population is sedentary or only active occasionally, and because more health risks accrue to people within this category than to those who are more frequent exercisers, public health researchers repeatedly stress the need to activate sedentary individuals. The rationale is threefold: moderate forms of exercise such as walk-ing can actually be performed by beginning exercis-ers, whereas more strenuous forms of exercise such

as aerobic dance may be too difficult; moderate exercise can be more easily worked into a person's daily routines, becoming a part of one's lifestyle and thus requiring no long-term commitment to a structured exercise program at a facility; and adher-ence rates to exercise programs consisting of mod-erate and purposeful exercise may be higher than those involving more strenuous forms.

URBAN DESIGN CHARACTERISTICS

Urban design characteristics represent the third major category of the built environment. These characteristics influence an individual's percep-tions about the desirability of walking, bicycling, or engaging in recreational exercise at, on, or within a particular place. Most, if not all, features of the built environment constitute design elements. Un-like the motorist, a person who is walking, jogging, or bicycling is unsheltered from the elements, both human and natural. Furthermore, the distances that are typically covered while engaging in such activities are very short, at most a few miles or, frequently, only a few hundred yards. As a result, the individual is powerfully influenced by the design characteristics of their immediate surroundings: the streets, parks, squares, plazas, buildings, lawns, sidewalks, bus stop shelters, crosswalks, trash bins, curbs, fences, billboards, plantings, and the host of other elements that together define the world we inhabit.

Yet design for the purpose of encouraging phys-ical activity was not something that was given much emphasis during the last decades of the twentieth century. Perhaps this reflects a long-standing bias against aesthetic considerations within the dis-cipline of city planning, a position that has roots as far back as the reaction against the City Beautiful movement at the turn of the twentieth century. Many in the then-emerging field of city planning dismissed the emphasis on aesthetics that was an inherent part of the City Beautiful movement, calling instead for a discipline based on modern, rational principles and devoted to functional considerations such as the protection of public health, the free-flowing movement of people and goods throughout the city, and the efficiency of business operations. Some have called this change a shift from the City Beautiful to what is termed the "City Efficient." What transpired, in other words, was a shift in emphasis from urban *form* to urban *function*.

Similarly, too, changes were occurring in other fields that contributed to the idea that functional rather than aesthetic considerations ought to be given more prominence with respect to urban form. . . . during the course of the century, especially the middle part of the century, modern architectural thought about how to design important elements of the built environment underwent something of a major change, hastened by the automobile's increasing presence. A number of architects discarded principles that had ordered basic relationships between different design elements for millennia, as technological innovations such as the automobile demanded that cities be reorganized. Many of these ideas were, as it turned out, compatible with the goals established by the new subfield of transportation engineering. At mid-century, engineers were also wrestling with the problems and opportunities created by the automobile. The singular focus on the automobile that developed within transportation engineering resulted in a consensus about design that, among other things, downgraded streets from multifaceted instruments of urban design to cogs in a functional machine with a single purpose, to move automobile traffic as efficiently as possible.

By the final third of the century, such ideas had come to dominate the design and construction of basic elements of the built environment. Only in the very last decade of the twentieth century did challenges to these ideas begin to receive widespread attention. This chapter concentrates on how the design of two basic elements of the built environment – the street and the site – has evolved over time and how each contributes to physical activity. While modern approaches to design led to streets and sites that catered to the needs and interests of motorists, during the 1990s and into the new century there was a perceptible shift toward a more comprehensive view of the design of such spaces.

Street design

Of the two basic elements upon which this chapter focuses, streets are perhaps the most important,

for they are the places where much of the physical activity in the built environment occurs. Streets are the places where people walk, jog, and bicycle most often. They form the main component of the built environment connecting destinations to one another, including destinations such as parks that might themselves be locations for physical activity. Finally, they are places where social activities can and do occur, which contribute to the basic desirability of a place for certain forms of physical activity.

The term *street design* refers to the layout and design of individual streets and street segments. The influence of street design is independent of the basic structure of the street network, that is, whether the street network is highly connected or not. A street's design can discourage walking or bicycling, for example, even though it forms a part of a fine grid network (Antupit, Gray, and Woods 1996). Streets are important design elements and have a tremendous influence on the basic fabric of any place, whether urban or suburban. As Jane Jacobs once put it, "streets and their sidewalks, the main public places of a city, are its most vital organs. If a city's streets look interesting, the city looks interesting; if they look dull, the city looks dull" (Jacobs 1993, 37). Street design influences physical activity by shaping one's desires to engage in such activity within the built environment. Here, desirability can be defined in two ways: in terms of how the street's basic design influences one's perception of safety and in terms of how it influences one's perception of the physical and social attractiveness of the street and areas immediately adjacent to the street. Different design treatments can produce radically different settings for a person who wishes to engage in physical activity on or along the street. The street can be either dangerous and unpleasant, meaning that a person would be less likely to want to walk, jog, or bicycle along it, or safe and pleasant, which would encourage such activity.

. . . the definition of a "street" includes more than just the street surface itself. Not only does it include the carriageway (lanes dedicated to moving traffic) and special-purpose lanes on the street surface (for parking and/or bicycling), the definition also includes medians, tree planting strips immediately adjacent to the street surface, the sidewalk and objects on the sidewalk, and all spaces up to the private property lot line. The inclusiveness of this definition is fairly standard; urban designers tend to include these basic elements, or variations thereof, when defining the street. The mix of elements – the presence or absence of sidewalks, the number and width of street lanes, the presence of shade trees along the street – depends on the street's purpose. Among many, if not most, American traffic engineers as well as many transportation planners, street purpose is defined in functional terms having to do with moving the city's automobile traffic, measured by the number of vehicles that can be moved along the street over an hour or day. The nomenclature used to define streets within this hierarchy is itself illustrative. The streets with the heaviest traffic volumes are called arterials, while those that are slightly smaller but still carry a significant amount of traffic are called feeder streets. These names show that streets are designed with traffic flow uppermost in mind. This observation is well founded: typically, arterials and feeders have most of the street space devoted to the carriageway and very little, if any, space devoted to medians, sidewalks, and other elements.

Anyone who attempts to walk, jog, or bicycle on or alongside most nonresidential streets in the United States knows full well how difficult, unpleasant, and even dangerous such an experience can be. It is apparent to even the casual observer that streets are places where cars rule, in terms of the amount of street space devoted exclusively to the car, the sheer number of cars on the street, and the speed of the average car traveling along the street. This is no accident. Rather, it is the result of a few important assumptions about the purposes for which a street is designed.

Streets can be said to have at least two core purposes: first, to move people and goods between destinations and, second, to serve as a stage for social interaction in a public setting (Gutman 1986). In the twentieth century, many professionals involved in urban design questions designed streets to fulfill only the first purpose. They also did so for only one type of movement, that of the motorist. Over the course of the twentieth century, responsibility for the design and construction of the nation's roads and streets became the sole province of transportation engineering, which sought to standardize the construction of streets according to seemingly objective and technical engineering principles. These principles have focused on the needs of the motorist, to the exclusion of all other users of the street and also the wider interests of the community. Among the oldest and most influential engineering societies is the American Association of State and Highway Transportation Officials (AASHTO), whose members have had close links to road building, automotive, and trucking interest groups from its founding in 1914 forward (Ehrenhalt 1997). Since the 1950s, AASHTO has published the definitive set of design standards for the transportation engineering profession in a one-thousand-page manual titled *A Policy on Geometric Design of Highways and Streets*, but universally referred to as the "Green Book." These standards are central to understanding why most streets in the United States look and function the way that they do, for they have long been used by engineers in state or local transportation departments to design or redesign a very large percentage of the nation's roads and streets. Until 1991, federal law required Green Book standards to be used on any federally funded roadways. Basically, the Green Book's central imperative is to design streets around motorist safety and convenience, ignoring other design criteria for other users and purposes. The design standards contained in the Green Book have virtually eliminated certain types of streetscapes that enhance the experience of the nonmotorist on or along the street.

Guidelines contained in the Green Book result in two basic priorities for street design. First, the guidelines encourage the design of streets for the fast movement of traffic. Under the guidelines, engineers use the "eighty-fifth percentile" rule, wherein streets are designed or redesigned for the safety of the fifteenth fastest driver out of every one hundred on the street. In order for the fifteenth fastest motorist to be able to drive at high speeds in relative safety, inevitably the best type of street is one that is wide, straight, and level (with little elevation change). Width gives the driver enough room to safely operate the vehicle at a high speed, while straightness and a level surface provides the driver with a long and wide field of vision, necessary for safe braking distances at higher speeds (Burrington 1996). Second, the guidelines stress the importance of unimpeded traffic flow, defined in terms of the degree of traffic congestion on the street. Traffic congestion is addressed via "level of service" standards that rank stretches of roadway in terms of traffic flow performance. The level of service measure is based on a ratio, the number of vehicles distributed over a given stretch of roadway. A street segment where vehicles cannot move gets the worst grade, while the highest grade goes to a segment where cars are moving without obstruction. In many cases, streets are designed to ensure a high level of service to meet future demand, not just current demand. The level of service system is another way of formalizing street design criteria in favor of fast-moving automobile traffic. Vehicular movement trumps all other considerations, including the mobility of the auto passengers (level of service standards count the number of vehicles, not the number of passengers) as well as those outside the vehicle. Pedestrians tend to be seen as impeding the free flow of motorized traffic, for example through slowing traffic when crossing streets (Ewing 1997; Epperson 1994). American street design is, as a result, among the least pedestrian- and bicyclist-friendly in the world. In many other countries, streets are designed for slower vehicle speeds and to accommodate fewer vehicles – authorities create design guidelines that result in narrower streets, tighter curves, more sidewalks, and a much more intensive use of traffic calming devices.[3]

Modernist planners and architects of the early- and mid-twentieth century also shared many of the beliefs of engineers, in particular that street design parameters should be set by the needs of motorists. In their view, the street's central purpose was to move motorized traffic efficiently between the city's functional cells, between the far-flung districts (residential, industrial, and commercial) that single-use zoning had begun to impose upon the city's structure during the first decades of the twentieth century. The famed Swiss architect Le Corbusier, for example, considered the multiuse and multipurpose street to be a dangerous anachronism, out of touch with the requirements of the automobile. "Our streets no longer work," he wrote in *The Radiant City*, published in 1933. "Streets are an obsolete notion. There ought not to be such things as streets; we have to create something that will replace them." To protect pedestrians from the ravages of the automobile, he envisioned a city that not only completely separated pedestrians from vehicular traffic but also fundamentally changed the physical nature of the street in accordance with what he saw as its sole function, to move motorized

traffic rapidly from place to place. In his view, the perfect city was one in which pedestrians used an extensive system of ground-level walkways while automobiles and trucks whizzed around on massive elevated roads designed exclusively for long-distance and high-speed traffic (Le Corbusier 1964).

The modern, functional view of the street as a tool for the movement of motorized traffic contradicted centuries of thought on the purposes for which a street exists. This view seriously undermined the notion that streets are legitimate public spaces for multiple uses, including nonautomotive forms of movement along the street surface, which includes both utilitarian and recreational physical activity (walking, bicycling, jogging, rollerblading). This view, as referenced above, also completely discounted (or, perhaps more accurately, entirely ignored) the idea that the streetscape is a stage upon which social activity occurs. Social activity on the street includes planned and spontaneous activities – sitting on a bench, eating or drinking at an outdoor cafe table, window shopping, playing, conversing with others, dining outdoors, people watching, bumping into a neighbor for a chat, and so on. Socializing, both planned and spontaneous, tends to occur in environments that are place-specific, where people identify with a particular space and where they feel comfortable being around other people in that space; the presence of other people, in fact, is one of the key ingredients in making something – a park, square, or street – a desirable place to be (Selberg 1996; Gehl 1987). Socializing is important in its own right, contributing to social cohesion and community identity. However, it is also tremendously important with respect to physical activity. Streetscapes that encourage socializing also tend to be perfect environments for walking. The view of the street as a space for social interaction rejects the idea . . . that lots of people occupying the same space automatically translates into the perception that the space is crowded. In contrast, this view emphasizes the importance of having lots of people on the street in order to make the space appear lively and interesting. While there may be an absolute limit beyond which most people would define a place as uncomfortably crowded and therefore undesirable, this perspective emphasizes that having a healthy number of people in a space is a desirable feature for inducing activity.[4] A focus on the efficiency of movement completely misses this point.

Modernists did know that motorists have different needs with respect to street design than other users of the street. Unfortunately, they solved this design problem by reconfiguring the street for the use of motorists and to the detriment of all others. The design of streets for multiple uses and modes requires an understanding of how the different users of the street perceive, and behave upon, the streetscape, and what needs arise from these differences. At the most fundamental level, motorists, pedestrians, joggers, and bicyclists perceive street design features differently because of the divergence in speeds at which they move along the street. The rate of speed at which one is traveling will greatly determine the ability to process detail in the environment. In evolutionary terms, human senses are adapted to the speed at which humans move through space under their own power while walking. Our ability to distinguish detail in the environment is therefore ideally suited to movement at speeds of perhaps five miles per hour and under. The fastest users of the street, motorists, therefore have a much more limited ability to process details along the street – a motorist simply has little time or capacity to appreciate design subtleties. Conversely, pedestrian travel, being much slower, allows for the appreciation of environmental detail (Gehl 1987). Joggers and bicyclists fall somewhere in between these polar opposites; while they travel faster than pedestrians, their rate of speed is ordinarily much slower than that of the typical motorist.

These principles are easily translated into specific street design requirements for motorists versus nonmotorists. According to the architect Amos Rapoport, the ideal streetscape for pedestrians and bicyclists maintains the pedestrian's visual and sensory attention at the slow speeds at which they travel . . . Designing the best street for nonmotorists requires that the street and its immediate environs contain abrupt, irregular, complex, and detailed features, with these features being interspersed at short intervals (Rapoport 1987). Streets that have bland architecture and that are dominated by long featureless horizons will not only be less interesting to the nonmotorist but will also increase the perception of the distance that one needs to cover to reach a particular destination (Gehl 1987). The street designed primarily around the speeds at which the motorist travels will be radically different. To perform tasks at high speeds safely, motorists need streets that are wide, low in visual detail, and contain no abrupt corners. The street that is ideal for nonmotorists – narrow, with abrupt changes, and a high level of detail along its edges – will not allow for safe automobile travel at higher speeds. Large, boldly stated design elements (buildings, signage, etc.) that are spaced far apart from each other and that are set far back from the street surface itself are necessary for the fast-moving motorist to be able to drive quickly and safely yet still be able to process details in the environment. The typical arterial street in the United States provides ample evidence for this hypothesis. Here, all of the architectural cues of structures alongside these streets signal the influence of the street's design on everything that surrounds it. Huge billboards compete with the garish architecture of fast-food restaurants and strip malls in order to attract the motorist's attention as he or she zips past at forty miles per hour. Each design element is freestanding, with large surface parking lots separating them from each other in order to provide the necessary spacing to keep visual cues comprehensible to the motorist. It is very difficult, then, to integrate the need of motorists for fast movement with the needs of pedestrians and, to a somewhat lesser extent, of bicyclists. Only a few types of street designs can accomplish such a trick. Perhaps the most famous examples are Parisian boulevards such as the Champs-Elysées, where heavy traffic coexists alongside intense pedestrian activity. This is possible because of the enormous sidewalks on both sides of the street, the double rows of street trees, the extent and quality of street furniture on the sidewalks, and the highly detailed building facades containing pedestrian attractions (shops, cafes, etc.) that abut the sidewalk.

The design of the street surface itself – its width, the number of lanes for traffic, any provisions for on-street parking, the type of paving materials used, and so forth – is critical in determining the speed and volume of automobile traffic upon the street. This influences the nonmotorist's perceptions of the risk of danger from automobiles. For bicyclists, who must often share the carriageway with automobiles, these considerations are paramount. High-volume, fast-moving traffic represents perhaps the worst scenario for the bicyclist, especially as streets with this type of traffic tend to carry regular truck and bus traffic as well. These conditions also have negative consequences for spaces immediately adjacent to the street, as people who are not in vehicles tend to react negatively to the noise and stress that accompany high-traffic and high-speed streets (Appleyard 1981; Appleyard and Lintell 1982). To enhance the nonmotorist's sense of safety, the design of the carriageway and other elements must serve to slow traffic speeds and reduce volumes, for example by reducing the carriageway width and having shorter turning radii at intersections.

The design elements that parallel the carriageway surface also have an influence on the perception of the nonmotorist. Safety can be enhanced through the ways that nonmotorized facilities are designed. Some facilities, such as wide sidewalks and bike lanes, act as physical buffers to moving traffic on the carriageway. Others make crossing the street on foot safer, such as pedestrian-friendly medians and traffic signals and well-marked, raised cross-walks (Untermann 1987).[5] Design treatments such as appropriate street lighting can also enhance safety at nighttime by making pedestrians feel safer from crime (Painter 1996). Finally, amenities such as "street furniture" add aesthetic value to the streetscape, an important consideration for some-one who is not in a vehicle. Street furniture consists of interesting design touches that enhance the experience of the pedestrian, such as postal boxes, telephone booths, benches, street trees, bus stops, public art, and attractively designed street lamps (Project for Public Spaces 1993).

Fortunately, the long-standing dominance of the automobile in American street design may be eroding. There is growing pressure for acceptance of the basic premise that streets should serve a number of purposes, only one of which is the move-ment of vehicles. Some of this stems, of course, from complaints by pedestrian and bicycling advo-cates concerning road and street design. Some comes from ordinary citizens who have concerns about proposals to widen specific local roads and streets. Some comes from architects and urban designers who have reacted to modernist street design, recognizing that streets, when designed improperly, can destroy the urban fabric. Some, how-ever, also comes from quarters where one would least expect such pressure, from a few engineering professionals as well as a small number of state and local departments of transportation. With respect to the latter groups, in 1999 the Institute

of Transportation Engineers (ITE), a professional engineering society that is something of a com-petitor to AASHTO, released a publication containing street design guidelines for use in neo-traditional neighborhoods.[6] Design should be "specific for the particular street at hand," the document stated, meaning design for a broad set of purposes and for a streetscape defined by its architectural context. The ITE guidelines encouraged design with bicyc-lists and pedestrians uppermost in mind, including the provision of a full range of safety, mobility, and aesthetic design treatments for people engaging in these activities. The guidelines suggested replacing the current nomenclature for describing the street network that is used by nearly all transportation-planning agencies – arterials, collectors, and local streets. In their place, ITE proposed the use of terms such as boulevard, avenue, street, drive, and alley. The intent behind the reintroduction of these classic terms was to further the idea that streets contribute to the built environment through their design and are not just pipelines through which traffic is run (ITE 1999). Advocacy, citizen, and pro-fessional groups form a loose and diverse coalition that has organized around basic conceptual changes to street design standards. Unlike the premises behind the Green Book, "context sensitive design" – the general term given to this change in thinking regarding street design – does not elevate motorists' mobility to the highest goal. Rather, it seeks to supplement this goal with broader considerations, including design for multimodal transportation and for integrating the street into the built environment of which it is a part. In so doing, it explicitly acknowledges that engineers cannot continue to be the sole arbiters of street design. Rather, it proposes that a host of professional and nonprofessional stakeholders, including architects, environmental-ists, historians, landscape architects, and citizens' groups need to be incorporated into the design process from the outset (Stamatiadis 2001; Antupit, Gray, and Woods 1996).

In 1991, after the passage of ISTEA, states were allowed to set their own design guidelines for roads built with federal funds. A few states, such as Vermont, passed design standards of their own. Some also sought to protect transportation engineers from law-suits filed by accident victims where the accident occurred on street segments that weren't designed according to AASHTO guidelines. Vermont's law, implemented in 1997, gave engineers permission to deviate from the Green Book, including the right to design streets for lower speeds (Ehrenhalt 1997). A number of cities around the country have also begun to create guidelines oriented around design context and multimodality. In 1997, for example, Portland METRO, the metropolitan planning organization for the Portland region, issued street design guidelines consistent with these goals. Among other things, the guidelines stated that streets should accommodate multiple modes, ensure pedestrian and bicyclist safety, enhance sociability, contribute to a high quality built environment, and add to the identity of the neighborhoods in which streets are located. Further, as with the ITE guidelines, METRO outlined an alternative nomenclature for describing the street system, suggesting the use of terms such as throughway and boulevard to reflect the context-specific nature of streets (Metro Regional Services 1997). While METRO emphasized that these guidelines were not design standards, they nonetheless contributed to an erosion of confidence in the basic premises behind the Green Book standards.

There are other challenges to the dominance of autocentric street design that do not necessarily involve the rewriting of design standards. Traffic calming, for example, is an increasingly widespread practice in the United States. Traffic calming originated in Europe and it is there that it has been employed the most intensively. Starting in the late 1960s, Dutch towns began experimenting with the *woonerf* or "living yard" where neighborhood streets were transformed, through design interventions, into spaces wherein nonmotorists ruled the street and motorists had to move slowly and cautiously in order to avoid pedestrians and cyclists, rather than the other way around. Commonly, a *woonerf* scheme placed obstacles such as benches, play objects, and plantings on the street surface itself in order to require vehicles to weave in and out, at slow speeds, to negotiate the street.

Cobblestones and brick surfacing techniques were used to roughen the ride for vehicles. Roads were bent or narrowed, access points for vehicles were identified and their widths constricted, and strict rules for motorists were created. While *woonerven* proved to be enormously successful at slowing traffic, they were also very expensive. Nonetheless, they opened the way for a host of street design interventions between the 1970s and 1990s across northern Europe, inspiring public agencies to experiment with different types of traffic calming schemes. During the 1980s, for example, German state governments created, among other things, "Tempo 30" programs, wherein the goal was to reduce average vehicle speeds on neighborhood roads to thirty kilometers per hour (eighteen miles per hour). Measures taken included narrowing streets at critical points, creating pedestrian islands and crossings, introducing speed humps and on-street plantings, and, as in the Netherlands, introducing far stricter traffic rules (Clarke and Dornfeld 1994). Additionally, the Germans were among the first to recognize that traffic calming measures needed to be implemented across a larger area than just a single street, as such interventions tended to divert traffic to other local streets. As a result, German municipalities began creating Tempo 30 zones comprising an entire neighborhood or even larger area (Ewing 1999). Studies of areas where the Tempo 30 program was introduced have generally shown a successful reduction in average vehicle speeds as well as a decrease in accidents involving pedestrians and bicyclists.

In the United States, traffic calming was implemented later than in Europe and only within certain cities that were willing to implement it. Estimates of the number of communities that have implemented traffic calming schemes vary widely depending on the scope of the survey and the definition of "traffic calming," but it is generally accepted that a few hundred communities nationwide may have active traffic calming programs. In those areas in the United States where traffic calming has been tried, it has been implemented less intensively than in Europe, meaning that the multiple, overlapping design treatments found there are generally absent in the American context. Rather, frequently only one or two devices may be employed, often over a single street segment rather than over an entire area such as a neighborhood (Ewing 1999). To a significant degree, this is a function of the fact that Americans began traffic calming later than elsewhere. Studies from various American cities where traffic calming has been tried, most intensively perhaps in cities like Portland, Oregon, and Seattle, generally support the notion that traffic calming slows traffic speeds and reduces the number of accidents, although evidence for the latter is not as convincing. The bulk of studies from Europe, North America, and Japan show that traffic calming techniques can be very successful in achieving these goals. Like the disconnected network, traffic calming serves to discourage through traffic. Yet traffic calming offers a major advantage over the disconnected network in the fact that it leaves connections in place for nonmotorists, thereby serving to make driving more difficult and walking and bicycling less difficult in the areas in which traffic calming schemes are introduced.

Finally, the level of service concept has also been undergoing some scrutiny. Level of service measures for pedestrian and bicycle facilities were nonexistent until fairly recently. Transportation organizations, city governments, and individuals have, however, been working to develop such standards. It is generally recognized that these standards can be helpful tools in making streets more inviting to nonmotorists. Unlike motorists, nonmotorists probably do not make decisions about which route to choose based upon the flow of pedestrian or bicyclist travel. In fact, the opposite is probably true: nonmotorists may well seek out streetscapes that have characteristics that are opposite of those sought by the motorist. Relatively crowded pedestrian spaces, for example, including pedestrian malls, squares, markets, and parks, may be desirable for pedestrian and bicycle travel. Route choice for a nonmotorist is based on a myriad number of other variables, including safety, attractiveness, and distance (Highway Research Center 1994; Alexander et al. 1977). Professionals who specialize in nonmotorized transportation have been working to develop level of service measures for pedestrians and bicyclists that are based upon a more realistic understanding of how the street influences such behavior (Dixon 1995; Epperson 1994; Khisty 1994; Moe and Reavis 1997; Sarkar 1994). Aesthetic attractiveness, comfort, convenience, safety, security, and system coherence are all variables that can be included in these standards. Streets, then, are "graded" based upon performance measures for each variable: sidewalk width and continuity, the placement and design of crosswalks, the presence or absence of bike lanes, and the design of street intersections.

Site design

Site design is important for physical activity patterns in that sites contribute to the basic attractiveness of the street as a place for physical activity. This argument rests on the principle that the streetscape is not just a linear corridor that connects destinations. Rather, the streetscape is a multidimensional space that shapes, and is shaped by, objects on its periphery. There is, in other words, a direct interaction between the street and the environment adjacent to the street (Gutman 1986). While the street is an important instrument for placing the buildings, parks, squares, and other elements of urban form along it within a particular context, these same elements also define the basic qualities of the street. Buildings, squares, lawns, parking lots, trees, and other objects that border the street give it a frame of reference. Their placement and orientation to the street influences the types of behavior among street users, motorists and nonmotorists alike.

The basic elements of the site that are important include the size of the building (width and height), the design of the building's facade, the building's orientation to and setback (distance) from the street, the placement of parking spaces on the site, and the design of the spaces between the building facade and the street. As with the design of the streetscape itself, similar principles apply with respect to the relationship between site design and physical activity. Site design elements shape perceptions of how attractive and safe the street is, which in turn influences a person's decision to walk, jog, bicycle, or socialize on the street. Sites, in other words, are important for activity along the street: streets designed with the nonmotorist in mind need to have certain types of buildings and private spaces on their edges, otherwise the fullest potential of the street as a space for physical activity will not be realized. This holds true primarily for pedestrians and for people who are interested in socializing within the confines of the streetscape, for site design most directly shapes activities that are very slow or involve no movement at all. Once again, the relationship between site design and bicycling is less straightforward. Bicyclists move at higher speeds than pedestrians and, most frequently, ride along the street surface itself (in the carriageway or special-purpose bike lanes). Bicyclists thus should be, at least theoretically, less influenced by highly detailed site designs along the street edges.

There is a widespread belief that pedestrian travel is influenced by the characteristics of buildings and other site-level design attributes (Southworth 1997;

Pedestrian Federation of America 1995; Corbett and Velasquez 1994). For decades, urban designers have been pointing out the flaws inherent in buildings that are massive and featureless, designed with more regard for automobile than pedestrian access, or removed from the streetscape entirely. It is generally asserted that in order for a building to encourage pedestrian activity, it needs to sit close to the edge of the sidewalk, have an interesting facade with design treatments that encourage interaction between the interior and exterior of the structure (such as doors, windows, stoops, porches, etc.), and not be inordinately tall or wide. Related arguments extend to the interactive effects of multiple buildings along a street; there should be small gaps (or no gaps at all) between buildings and the architectural styles should be complementary but not uniform.

From the early twentieth century on, these principles were not heeded. Planners and architects placed structures far back from the road in an attempt to ensure that fresh air and sunshine reached the interior of the structure as well as to protect the building from the dirt and pollution of the motorized traffic that ran along the street. This divorced the private sphere from the public through the introduction of a large open space between the building facade and the streetscape, one that now tends to be occupied by either large amounts of parking or by expansive lawns fronting residential and corporate property (in the words of the architect Thomas Schumacher, lawns do not "function to enclose or define street space but only to isolate the street from the house" [Schumacher 1986, 141]). A contemporaneous development was the basic design of the house itself. During the course of the twentieth century, as neighborhoods became more auto-dependent, single family houses began to be designed with porches facing the rear of the house instead of the front, as in older architectural styles (Calthorpe 1993). Front porches encouraged social and physical activity in two ways: they facilitated interaction between the residents and passersby, and their elegant designs raised the detail level of the house's facade. At the same time as designers began to place porches on the back of the house, they began to replace the front porch with the garage door – a large, featureless vertical slab on the front of the house – as the dominant design feature on the house's facade. As a result, what had

been a quasi-public space (the front porch), deliberately designed to encourage social interaction, was replaced by a wholly private space (the garage) that had no relationship to the public sphere (the street).

These observations apply equally to commercial and retail site designs. Office and retail complexes have long been oriented toward the needs of the automobile user, containing linear design features, bland building exteriors, large building setbacks, significant distances between buildings, and enormous parking lots. Suburban office parks often sit behind huge lawns or are even hidden entirely from the street, buffered by large forested tracts. Retail developers site faceless, cheaply built structures behind massive surface parking lots, where the space between a development's sidewalks, if there are any, and the facade consists of an unappetizing combination of asphalt and cars. To make matters worse, these structures have few exterior features that make them interesting buildings in the first place – hence the term "big box" retail. It should therefore come as no surprise that most contemporary retail center and office complex designs inevitably generate less pedestrian activity than older designs that were built fronting a pedestrian-oriented street. This is not just because the newer designs have uninviting spaces. They also deconcentrate destinations. The huge parking lots and general orientation of the site's buildings to one another within such complexes often create significant distances between destinations even *within* the development itself (Cervero 1986). Smaller buildings with more intricate features that are placed close together attract pedestrians because they concentrate destinations and, as a result, pedestrian activity.

Unfortunately, retail, office, and residential site design has become uniform. Regulatory and financial mechanisms impede or outright prohibit the construction of buildings that might encourage more on-street, pedestrian activity. Real estate financing, for example, is systemically biased against projects that run counter to established design formulas for shopping centers and other developments. Banks and other real estate investors evaluate projects based upon the proven track record of standard development projects. Developers will obtain financing only if they conform to established design criteria, none of which encourage pedestrian activity; for example, lending institutions often require that a shopping center's parking lot be placed in front of the building so that it can be seen easily by motorists driving past (Leinberger 2001). Moreover, developments that have pedestrian-friendly design features are more complex and costlier to build. To lenders, this translates into higher project risk and, therefore, higher lending rates (Gyourko and Rybczynski 2000). The outcome is that builders often have trouble obtaining financing of any kind for novel projects that might include, for example, a mixture of uses or a pedestrian-oriented design.

Nonetheless, in recent years many groups have called for overhauling contemporary site design practices. Peter Calthorpe laid out a number of alternative criteria for site design, all of which are designed to encourage pedestrian travel. "Buildings should address the street and sidewalk with entries, balconies, porches, architectural features, and activities which help create safe, pleasant walking environments," he wrote. "Building intensities, orientation, and massing should promote more active commercial centers, support transit, and reinforce public spaces. Variation and human-scale detail in architecture is encouraged. Parking should be placed to the rear of the buildings" (Calthorpe 1993). Many of these principles have been integrated into the New Urbanist residential developments that have actually been developed, whether done by Calthorpe's firm itself or others (Southworth 1997). Moreover, these principles have been integrated into recommendations for the wholesale redesign of commercial and retail centers, including mainstream development and real estate organizations, and have even been incorporated into some "level of service" standards for pedestrians (see, e.g., Beyard and Pawlukiewicz 2001; Jaskiewicz 1996).

Empirical evidence

Because urban design is qualitative in nature, rigorous studies of the influence of design characteristics on behavior are rare. Much of the research into urban design, logically enough, is within the purview of architects, landscape architects, and urban designers. On-the-ground research in these fields emphasizes case studies and observational techniques. Therefore, many of the theories about design and behavior provided in this chapter are the result of insights provided from direct observation of how people react to specific surroundings.

There have been, however, a number of studies within the fields of planning and public health that have employed cross-sectional research designs that are focused on urban design variables. A public health study using Canadian data attempted to assess the relationship between environmental factors and walking to work (Craig et al. 2002). In this study, researchers created eighteen different measures of neighborhood characteristics and then rated twenty-seven different neighborhoods along each measure. Characteristics included such items as "complexity of stimulus" (amount and variety of visual and auditory stimulation, including building detail and architectural variety), "visual aesthetics" (color, composition, texture, and proportion of objects), and "social dynamics" (whether people could be seen moving about, sitting, and standing in the neighborhood). More people walked to work in the areas that had higher environmental scores. The relationships between social indicators (including income, education, and poverty status) and walking were not significant. A small number of other studies in the field of public health have also revealed that certain types of environments are associated with more physical activity (see, e.g., Ball et al. 2001).

Within planning circles, a few studies have also been conducted that have attempted to quantify micro-scale urban design features and to assess the relationship between these variables and physical activity. A well-known study conducted in Portland, Oregon, during the early 1990s (Parsons et al. 1993a, 1993b) offers a case in point. This study attempted to construct a composite variable of the pedestrian friendliness of some four hundred "traffic analysis zones" in and around Portland. The composite variable, termed the "Pedestrian Environment Factor" (PEF), assessed each zone using four environmental parameters: ease of street crossings, sidewalk continuity, street network characteristics, and topography. Points were assigned for each zone, with zones receiving a PEF ranking ranging from 4 (low) to 12 (high). Data from a household travel survey was then matched to the PEF rankings. The resulting data showed that zones with higher PEF's generated more transit, bicycle, and walk trips, and fewer auto trips, with persons in the highest four PEF categories making nearly four times as many walk and bike trips as households located in the bottom five categories. The study's authors also attempted to measure the effect of building setbacks on pedestrian travel in the Portland area. They gathered data for all commercial structures in three Portland-area counties in order to establish how many buildings in each of the region's traffic analysis zones were built before 1951. (The researchers believed that structures built during the decades before the 1950s were typically built to the front of the lot line, rather than set back to allow for automobile parking.) In areas with no buildings built before 1951, 1.9 percent of travelers walked or biked. In areas that were over four-fifths covered by older buildings, 5.3 percent did so.

Conclusion

A primary goal of this chapter was to show that design does matter. Although, as noted, this idea is denigrated by some in the planning and engineering disciplines, the built environment has been shaped by a paradigm that is centered on designing streetscapes for the motorists' convenience. Unfortunately, the street and site design guidelines and standards created and implemented over the last half century have served to create environments in which only drivers feel at home. Such regulatory and advisory devices form a large part of the explanation as to why the built environment seems to be so hostile to pedestrians and bicyclists. For example, the creation of level of service standards that are based upon vehicle-to-roadway capacity have served to downgrade alternative modes of travel, both within transportation planning and engineering circles as well in reality, on the ground. The level of service standard is an important tool driving transportation funding allocations. Because the methodology that has been erected in support of the level of service standard has emphasized the improvement of traffic flow along congested street segments, transportation dollars are prioritized for automobile travel at these locations. Until a new system for multiple modes of travel is devised, containing the same level of rigor and engendering the same amount of respect in engineering and planning circles, arguments for sufficient funding for nonmotorized investments will continue to be met with considerable resistance.

NOTES

1 The determination of one's weight status is defined by public health agencies using a measure called body mass index (BMI), which is a ratio of a person's weight to their height. The CDC defines a healthy BMI for an adult at 18–25 kilograms per square meter (kg/m^2). An overweight person is defined as having a BMI of 25–29.9 kg/m^2 while someone who is defined as obese has a BMI of 30 kg/m^2 and over.

2 This is also the position taken by the Centers for Disease Control. See "Obesity and Overweight: A Public Health Epidemic": Available online at http://cdc.gov/nccdphp/dnpa/obesity/epidemic.htm.

3 [See] Ewing 1994. Ewing compared American, British, and Australian residential street design guidelines, using standards contained in authoritative manuals in each country, and found that minimum road widths and turning radii were significantly larger in the American manual than in the British and Australian cases (turning radii are larger to extend sight distances for motorists, resulting in higher turning speeds). Along those streets where the British and Australian standards did not require sidewalks, both manuals mandated the use of intensive traffic calming methods and other design features to ensure that traffic could not safely move at speeds faster than twenty miles per hour.

4 Applying numbers to terms such as "uncomfortably crowded" or "over-crowded" would be exceedingly difficult, as crowding is an inherently subjective experience. Not only does the definition of overcrowding vary from person to person, each individual's assessment of overcrowding can vary from place to place. Also, different cultural settings likely produce different reactions with respect to what differentiates a comfortable experience from an uncomfortable one. For a fuller exposition see Churchman 1999.

5 Raised crosswalks have the potential to be safer than crosswalks that are placed on the same level as the carriageway. In A *Pattern Language*, Christopher Alexander and co-authors write, "No amount of painted white lines, crosswalks, traffic lights, button operated signals, ever quite manage to change the fact that a car weighs

a ton or more, and will run over any pedestrian, unless the driver brakes. . . . The people who cross a road will only *feel* comfortable and safe if the road crossing is a physical obstruction, which physically guarantees that the cars must slow down and give way to pedestrians." See Alexander et al. 1977, 281.

6 In a 1997 article in *Governing* magazine, Alan Ehrenhalt wrote that ITE is a more progressive rival to AASHTO because it has a broader constituency, consisting of planners and consultants as well as engineers. See Ehrenhalt 1997.

REFERENCES

Alexander, Christopher, Sara Ishikawa, and Murray Silverstein with Max Jacobson, Ingrid Fiksdahl-King, and Shlomo Angel. 1977. *A Pattern Language: Towns, Buildings, Construction.* New York: Oxford University Press.

Andersen, Ross, Thomas Wadden, Susan Bartlett, Babette Zemel, Tony Verde, and Shawn Franckowiak. 1999. Effects of lifestyle activity versus structured aerobic exercise in obese women. *Journal of the American Medical Association 281*: 335–40.

Antupit, Stephen, Barbara Gray, and Sandra Woods. 1996. Steps ahead: making streets that work in Seattle, Washington. *Landscape and Urban Planning 35*: 107–22.

Appleyard, Donald. 1981. *Livable Streets.* Berkeley: University of California Press.

Appleyard, Donald and Mark Lintell. 1982. The environmental quality of city streets: The residents; viewpoint. In *Humanscape: Environments for People*, eds. S. Kaplan and R. Kaplan. Ann Arbor, MI: Ulrich's Books, Inc.

Ball, Kylie, Adrian Bauman, Eva Leslie, and Neville Owen. 2001. Perceived environmental aesthetics and convenience and company are associated with walking for exercise among Australian adults. *Preventive Medicine 33*: 434–40.

Beyard, Michael and Michael Pawlukiewicz. 2001. *Ten Principles for Reinventing American's Suburban Strips.* Washington, D.C.: ULI – Urban Land Institute.

Blair, Steven, Harold Kohl, Ralph Paffenbarger, Diane Clark, K. Cooper, and L. Gibbons. 1989. Physical fitness and all-cause mortality: a prospective study of healthy men and women. *Journal of the American Medical Association 273*: 1093–8.

Bouchard, Claude, and Roy Shephard. 1994. *Physical activity, fitness, and health: International proceedings and consensus statement.* Conference Proceedings. Champaign, IL: Human Kinetic Publishers.

Burrington, Stephen. 1996. Restoring the rule of law and respect for communities in transportation. *New York University Environmental Law Journal 5*: 691–734.

Calthorpe, Peter. 1993. *The Next American Metropolis: Ecology, Community, and the American Dream.* New York: Princeton Architectural Press.

Centers for Disease Control and Prevention. 1990. Coronary heart disease attributable to sedentary lifestyle – selected states. 1988. *Morbidity and Mortality Weekly Report 39*: 541–4.

——. 1999a. *Chronic Diseases and Their Risk Factors: The Nation's Leading Cause of Death.* Atlanta: Centers for Disease Control and Prevention.

——. 1999d. Prevalence of overweight among children and adolescents: United States, 1999. Hyattsville, MD: National Center for Health Statistics. Available online at: http://www.cdc.gov/nchs/products/pubs/pubd/hstats/over99fig1.htm.

——. 2001b. Physical Activity Trends – United States, 1990–1998. *Morbidity and Mortality Weekly Report 50*, 9: 166–9.

Cervero, Robert. 1986. *Suburban Gridlock.* New Brunswick, NJ: Center for Urban Policy Research.

Clarke, Andrew and Michael Dornfeld. 1994. *National Bicycling and Walking Study, FHWA Case Study No. 19: Traffic Calming, Auto-Restricted Zones and Other Traffic Management Techniques – Their Effects on Bicycling and Pedestrians.* Washington, D.C.: Federal Highway Administration.

Corbett, Judith and Joe Velasquez. 1994. *The Ahwahnee Principle: Toward More Livable Communities.* Sacramento: Center for Livable Communities.

Craig, Cora, Ross Brownson, Sue Cragg, and Andrea Dunn. 2002. Exploring the effect of the environment on physical activity: a study examining walking to work. *American Journal of Preventive Medicine 23*, 2, Supplement 1: 36–43.

Derby, C., B. Mohr, I. Goldstein, H. Feldman, C. Johannes, and J. McKinlay. 2000. Modifiable risk factors and erectile dysfunction: can lifestyle changes modify risk? *Urology 56*, 2: 302–6.

Dixon, Linda. 1995. Bicycle and pedestrian level-of-service performance measures and standards for congestion management systems. *Transportation Research Record 1538*: 1–9.

Dunn, Andrea, Ross Andersen, and John Jakicic. 1998. Lifestyle physical activity interventions: history, short- and long-term effects, and recommendations. *American Journal of Preventive Medicine 15*, 4: 398–412.

Dunn, Andrea, Bess Marcus, James Kampert, Melissa Garcia, Harold Kohl, and Steven Blair. 1999. Comparison of lifestyle and structured interventions to increase physical activity and cardiorespiratory fitness. *Journal of the American Medical Association 281*, 4: 327–34.

Ehrenhalt, Alan. 1997. The asphalt rebellion. *Governing Magazine* (October). Available online at http://governing.com/archive/1997/oct/roads.txt.

Epperson, Bruce. 1994. Evaluating suitability of roadways for bicycle use: toward a cycling level-of-service standard. *Transportation Research Record 1438*: 9–16.

Ewing, Reid. 1997. *Transportation and Land Use Innovations: When You Can't Pave Your Way Out of Congestion.* Chicago: American Planning Association.

——. 1999. *Traffic Calming: State of the Practice.* Prepared for the U.S. Department of Transportation, Federal Highway Administration, Office of Safety Research and Development and Office of Human Environment; prepared by Institute of Transportation Engineers. Report number FHWA-RD-99-135.

Federal Interagency Forum on Aging-Related Statistics. August 2000. *Older Americans 2000: Key Indicators of Well-Being.* Federal Interagency Forum on Aging-Related Statistics. Washington D.C.: U.S. Government Printing Office.

Ferucci, Luigi, Brenda Penninx, Suzanne Leveille, Maria-Chiara Corti, Marco Pahor, Robert Wallace, Tamara Harris, Richard Havlik, and Jack Guralnik. 2000. Characteristics of nondisabled older persons who perform poorly in objective tests of lower extremity function. *Journal of the American Geriatrics Society 48*, 9: 1102–10.

Flegal, Katherine, Margaret Carroll, Cynthia Ogden, and Clifford Johnson. 2002. Prevalence and trends in obesity among U.S. adults, 1999–2000. *Journal of the American Medical Association 288*, 14: 1723–7.

Gehl, Jan. 1987. *Life Between Buildings: Using Public Space.* New York: Van Nostrand Reinhold Co.

Grunbaum, Jo Anne, Laura Kann, Steven Kinchen, Barbara Williams, James Ross, Richard Lowry, and Lloyd Kolbe. 2002. Youth risk behavior surveillance – United States, 2001. *Morbidity and Mortality Weekly Reports 51*, SS04: 1–64.

Gutman, Robert. 1986. The street generation. In *On Streets*, ed. S. Anderson. Cambridge, MA: MIT Press.

Gyourko, Joseph and Witold Rybczynski. 2000. Financing New Urbanism projects: obstacles and solutions. *Housing Policy Debates 11*, 3: 733–50.

Highway Research Center. 1994. *A Compendium of Available Bicycle and Pedestrian Trip Generation Data in the United States.* Prepared for the Federal Highway Administration. Chapel Hill, NC: University of North Carolina.

Hillman, Mayer. 1992. *Cycling: Towards Health and Safety.* Oxford: Oxford University Press, British Medical Association.

Hu, Patricia and Jennifer Young. 1999. *Summary of Travel Trends: 1995 Nationwide Personal Transportation Survey.* Prepared for U.S. Department of Transportation, Federal Highway Administration. Knoxville, TN: Oak Ridge National Laboratory.

Institute of Transportation Engineers. 1999. *Traditional Neighborhood Development: Street Design Guidelines.* Washington, D.C.: Institute of Transportation Engineers.

Jacobs, Jane. 1993. *The Death and Life of Great American Cities.* New York: The Modern Library.

Jaskiewicz, Frank. 1996. *Pedestrian Level of Service Based on Trip Quality.* Philadelphia, PA: Glatting Jackson Kercher Anglin Lopez Rinehart, Inc.

Khisty, C. Jotin. 1994. Evaluation of pedestrian facilities: beyond the level-of-service concept. *Transportation Research Record 1438*: 45–50.

Koplan, Jeffrey and William Dietz. 1999. Caloric imbalance and public health policy. *Journal of the American Medical Association 282*, 16: 1579–81.

Kujala, U., J. Kapiro, S. Sarna, and M. Koskenvuo. 1998. Relationship of leisure-time physical activity and mortality: the Finnish twin cohort. *Journal of the American Medical Association 279*, 6: 440–4.

Le Corbusier. 1964. *The Radiant City.* New York: Orion Press.

Leinberger, Christopher. 2001. Financing progressive development. *Capital Xchange*, May 2001. Washington, D.C.: Brookings Institute, Center of Urban and Metropolitan Policy; Boston, MA: Harvard University, Joint Center for Housing Studies. Available online at http://www.brook.edu/es/urban/capitalxchange/leinberger.pdf.

Leon, Arthur, J. Connett, D. Jacobs, and Rainer Rauramaa. 1987. Leisure-time physical activity levels and risk of coronary heart disease and death in the multiple risk factor intervention trial.

Journal of the American Medical Association 258: 2388–95.

Malina, Robert. 2001. Tracking of physical activity across the lifespan. *President's Council on Physical Fitness and Sports Research Digest 3*, 14 (September): 1–8.

McGinnis, J. Michael and William Foege. 1993. Actual causes of death in the U.S. *Journal of the American Medical Association 270*, 18: 2207–12.

Metro Regional Services. October 1997. *Creating Livable Streets: Street Design Guidelines for 2040*. Portland OR: Metro Regional Services.

Moe, Ray and Kathleen Reavis. 1997. *Pedestrian Level of Service*. Fort Collins, CO: Balloffet and Associates, Inc.

Mokdad, Ali, Mary Serdula, William Dietz, Barbara Bowman, James Marks, and Jeffrey Koplan. 1999. The spread of the obesity epidemic in the United States, 1991–1998. *Journal of the American Medical Association 282*, 16: 1519–22.

Mokdad, Ali, Barbara Bowman, Earl Ford, Frank Vinicor, James Marks, and Jeffrey Koplan. 2001. The continuing epidemics of obesity and diabetes in the United States. *Journal of the American Medical Association 286*, 10: 1195–1200.

Morgan, W. P. 2001. Prescription of physical activity: a paradigm shift. *Quest 53*, 3: 366–82.

Morris, Jeremy and Adrianne Hardman. 1997. Walking to health. *Sport Medicine 23*, 5: 307–31.

Must Aviva, Jennifer Spadano, Eugenie Coakley, Alison Field, Graham Colditz, and William Dietz. 1999. The disease burden associated with overweight and obesity. *Journal of the American Medical Association 282*, 16: 1523–9.

Oja, Pekka, Ilkka Vuori, and Olavi Paronen. 1998. Daily walking and cycling to work: their utility as health-enhancing physical activity. *Patient Education and Counseling 33*: S87–S94.

Owen, Neville and Adrian Bauman. 1992. The descriptive epidemiology of a sedentary lifestyle in adult Australians. *International Journal of Epidemiology 21*, 2: 305–10.

Paffenbarger, Ralph and I-Min Lee. 1996. Physical activity and fitness for health and longevity. *Research Quarterly for Exercise and Sport 67*, Supplement to number 3: 11–28.

Painter, Kate. 1996. The influence of street lighting improvements on crime, fear and pedestrian street use after dark. *Landscape and Urban Planning 35*: 193–201.

Parsons Brinckerhoff Quade & Douglas, Inc., Cambridge Systematics, Inc., and Calthorpe Associates. 1993a. *Building Orientation: A Supplement to The Pedestrian Environment: Volume 4B*. Portland, OR: 1000 Friends of Oregon.

———. 1993b. *The Pedestrian Environment: Volume 4A*. Portland, OR: 1000 Friends of Oregon.

Pate, Russell, Michael Pratt, Steven Blair, William Haskell, Caroline Macera, Claude Bouchard, David Buchner, Walter Ettinger, Gregory Heath, Abby King, Andrea Kriska, Arthur Leon, Bess Marcus, Jeremy Morris, Ralph Paffenbarger, Kevin Patrick, Michael Pollock, J.M. Rippe, James Sallis, and Jack Whitmore. 1995. Physical activity and public health: A recommendation from the Centers for Disease Control and Prevention and the American College of Sports Medicine. *Journal of the American Medical Association 273*: 402–7.

Pedestrian Federation of America. 1995. *Walk Tall: A Citizen's Guide to Walkable Communities*. Emmaus, PA: Rodale Press, Inc.

Powell, Kenneth and Steven Blair. 1994. The public health burdens of sedentary living habits: theoretical but realistic estimates. *Medicine and Science in Sports and Exercise 26*, 7: 851–6.

Pratt, Michael, Caroline Macera, and Guijing Wang. 2000. Higher direct medical costs associated with physical inactivity. *The Physician and Sports Medicine 28*, 10: 63–70.

Project for Public Spaces. 1993. *National Bicycling and Walking Study, FHWA Case Study No. 20: The Effects of Environmental Design on the Amount and Type of Bicycling and Walking*. Prepared for the U.S. Department of Transportation, Federal Highway Administration. Washington, D.C.

Rapoport, Amos. 1987. Pedestrian street use: Culture and perception. In *Public Streets for Public Use*, ed. A. Moudon. New York: Van Nostrand Reinhold Co., Inc.

Sarkar, Sheila. 1994. Determination of service levels for pedestrians, with European examples. *Transportation Research Record 1405*: 35–42.

Schoenborn, Charlotte and Patricia Barnes. 2002. Leisure-time physical activity among adults: United States, 1977–98. *Advanced Data from Vital and Health Statistics*, no. 325 (April 7, 2002). Hyattsville, MD: National Centers for Health Statistics, Centers for Disease Control and Prevention.

Schumacher, Thomas. 1986. Buildings and Streets: Notes on Configuration and Use. In *On Streets*, ed. S. Anderson. Cambridge, MA: MIT Press.

F
O
U
R

Selberg, Knut. 1996. Road and traffic environment. *Landscape and Urban Planning 35*: 153–72.

Shephard, Roy. 1997. What is the optimal type of physical activity to enhance health? *British Journal of Sports Medicine 31*, 4: 277–84.

Singh, N., K. Clemets, M. Fiatarone. 1997. A randomized controlled trial of progressive resistance training in depressed elders. *Journal of Gerontology 52A*: M27–M35.

Southworth, Michael. 1997. Walkable suburbs? An evaluation of neo-traditional communities at the urban edge. *Journal of the American Planning Association 63*, 1: 28–44.

Stamatiadis, Nikiforos. 2001. A European approach to Context Sensitive Design. *Transportation Quarterly 55*, 4: 41–8.

Stone, Neil. 1996. The clinical and economic significance of atherosclerosis. *The American Journal of Medicine 101*, 4A: 6S–9S.

Telama, R., X. Yang, L. Laakso, and J. Viikari. 1997. *American Journal of Preventive Medicine 13*, 4: 317–23.

Unger, Jennifer. 1995. Sedentary lifestyle as a risk factor of self-reported poor physical and mental health. *American Journal of Health Promotion 10*, 1: 15–17.

Untermann, Richard. 1987. Changing Design Standards for Street and Roads. In *Public Streets for Public Use*, ed. A. Moudon. New York: Van Nostrand Reinhold Co., Inc.

U.S. Department of Health and Human Services. 1996. *Physical Activity and Health: A Report of the Surgeon General*. Centers for Disease Control and Prevention, National Center for Chronic Disease Prevention and Health Promotion.

Wang, Guijing, Charles Helmick, Caroline Macera, Ping Zhang, and Michael Pratt. 2001. Inactivity-associated medical costs among US adults with arthritis. *Arthritis and Rheumatism 45*, 5: 439–45.

Yaffe, Kristine, Deborah Barnes, Michael Nevitt, Li-Ying Lui, and Kenneth Covinsky. 2001. A prospective study of physical activity and cognitive decline in elderly women: women who walk. *Archives of Internal Medicine 161*, 14: 1703–8.

"Introduction," "The Changing Nature of Public Space in City Centres," and "Whose Public Space?"

from *Whose Public Space?: International Case Studies in Urban Design and Development* (2010)

Ali Madanipour

Editors' Introduction

Public space has always played an important role in cities. Aside from housing, more urban land is devoted to public space – streets, squares, plazas, and parks – than any other use. In cities, public spaces provide the connective tissue between privately owned and occupied spaces. They give access to private property, and are places for congregation and exchange. Because the space is public, communities have both the opportunity and responsibility of saying how it should be designed and managed to meet community needs and aspirations. But is "public space" always public, in the sense of being available and accessible for use by everyone?

In America and Great Britain since the contraction of government in the 1970s, there has been a tendency to "privatize" public space. Many urban plazas and parks have commercial uses within them that cater to limited segments of society, such as relatively expensive cafés and restaurants. In central cities, there are many spaces that appear to be public but are not, such as shopping malls and some parks created in redevelopment areas, and many places that are public but appear not to be because of how they've been designed and are managed, such as plazas at the base of large office buildings provided to satisfy planning requirements that look like corporate spaces and are often overseen by private security guards. Many urban streets are largely effectively privatized because so much of their space is devoted to the use of privately owned vehicles.

The public realm is a primary focus of urban design theory and practice. How it should be provided and designed is a central issue for the field. The recent book, *Whose Public Space?: International Case Studies in Urban Design and Development*, edited by Ali Madanipour, adds an important contribution to the debate. The book presents case studies of public space development, management, and use in cities around the globe, illustrating the similarities and differences that exist in a range of urban and cultural contexts, and identifying inherent tensions and conflicts. Madanipour's introduction to the section of the book that focuses on public space in central cities, "The Changing Nature of Public Space in City Centres," excerpts of which are included here, highlights the particularly challenging issues involved where "demand for and tensions over public spaces' production and control are highest." In the book's concluding chapter "Whose Public Space?," Madanipour brings the case studies together and offers a critical analysis of how they "map out the changing nature of public space." He identifies the general themes that apply to public space across the global spectrum and ultimately concludes that public spaces should be designed and evaluated on the principle of access equality.

Ali Madanipour teaches architecture, urban design, and planning at the School of Architecture, Planning, and Landscape at the University of Newcastle in England, and is a founding member of the University's Global Urban Research Unit. Madanipour was born in Iran and practiced architecture before turning to an academic career. His interests include design, development, and management of cities, the social and psychological significance of urban space, processes that shape urban space, agencies of urban change, and implications of change for disadvantaged social groups and the environment. His writings have been widely translated.

Madanipour's other books include *Knowledge Economy and the City* (London: Routledge, 2011), *Designing the City of Reason* (London: Routledge, 2007), *Public and Private Spaces of the City* (London: Routledge, 2003), *Tehran: The Making of a Metropolis* (New York: John Wiley, 1998), *Social Exclusion in European Cities: Processes, Experiences, and Responses* (London: Jessica Kingsley, 1996), *Design of Urban Space: An Inquiry into a Socio-spatial Process* (New York: John Wiley, 1996), and three co-edited anthologies: *Social Exclusion in European Cities* (London: Routledge, 2003), co-edited with Judith Allen and Goran Cars; *Urban Governance, Institutional Capacity, and Social Milieux* (Aldershot: Ashgate, 2002), co-edited with Goran Cars and Patsy Healey; and *The Governance of Place* (Aldershot: Ashgate, 1996), co-edited with Angela Hull and Patsy Healey.

Recent anthologies on public space include *Common Ground?: Readings and Reflections on Public Space* (London: Routledge, 2010), edited by Anthony M. Orum and Zachary P. Neal; *Insurgent Public Space: Guerrilla Urbanism and the Remaking of Contemporary Cities* (New York: Routledge, 2010) edited by Jeffrey Hou; *The Politics of Public Space* (New York: Routledge, 2006), edited by Setha Low and Neil Smith; and the earlier *Variations on a Theme Park: The New American City and the End of Public Space* (New York: Hill and Wang, 1992), edited by Michael Sorkin.

Recent works that focus on planning and design issues related to public space include Anastasia Loukaitou-Sideris and Renia Ehren's *Sidewalks: Conflict and Negotiation over Public Space* (Cambridge, MA: MIT Press, 2009); Anastasia Loukaitou-Sideris and Trideb Banerjee's *Urban Design Downtown: Poetics and Politics of Form* (Berkeley: University of California Press, 1998); and Matthew Carmona et al.'s *Public Space: The Management Dimension* (London: Routledge, 2008).

Classic urban design texts on public space design include Allan Jacobs' *Great Streets* (Boston, MA: MIT Press, 1993); Jan Gehl's *Life Between Buildings: Using Public Space* (New York: Van Nostrand Reinhold, 1987); Randy Hester's *Planning Neighborhood Spaces with People* (New York: Van Nostrand Reinhold, 1984); and William H. Whyte's *The Social Life of Small Urban Spaces* (New York: Project for Public Spaces, 1980).

Stephen Carr et al.'s *Public Space* (Cambridge: Cambridge University Press, 1992) focuses on environment and behavior issues related to public space. Matthew Carmona, et al.'s *Public Places, Urban Spaces* (Oxford: Architectural Press, 2010) includes a chapter on the social dimension of urban design that summarizes urban design theory and practice related to public space.

Works that shed light on contemporary issues related to the production of public space include Nan Ellin's *Postmodern Urbanism* (Princeton, NJ: Princeton University Press, 1997) and Don Mitchell's *The Right to the City: Social Justice and the Fight for Public Space* (New York: Guilford Press, 2003).

Two of the major theorists of the public sphere in the twentieth century were Hannah Arendt and Jürgen Habermas. Hannah Arendt's *The Human Condition* (Chicago, IL: University of Chicago Press, 1998) analyzes the ancient public sphere, and Jürgen Habermas's *The Structural Transformation of the Public Sphere* (Cambridge: Polity Press, 1989) examines the bourgeois public sphere. Works of social theory which provide insight into the nature of public realm, including physical public space, include Richard Sennett's *The Fall of Public Man* (New York: Knopf, 1977) and *The Conscience of the Eye* (New York: Knopf, 1990); Mark Gottdiener's *The Social Production of Urban Space* (Austin, TX: University of Texas Press, 1994); and Fran Tonkiss's *Space, the City and Social Theory* (Cambridge: Polity Press, 2005).

INTRODUCTION

Public spaces mirror the complexities of urban societies: as historic social bonds between individuals have become weakened or transformed, and cities have increasingly become agglomerations of atomized individuals, public open spaces have also changed from being embedded in the social fabric of the city to being a part of more impersonal and fragmented urban environments. Can making public spaces help overcome this fragmentation, where accessible spaces are created through inclusive processes? Do the existing and new public spaces of the city serve the public at large, or are they contested and exclusive? Whose public spaces are they? This book offers some answers to these questions through case studies of making public space in different countries.

The book investigates the making of public space in contemporary cities, through analysing the process of urban design and development in international case studies, focusing on the changing nature of public space and the tensions that arise between different perspectives and groups. Two broad frameworks of *place* and *process* are used to study and analyse the urban public spaces in transition. Public spaces, it is argued in this book, should be *accessible places*, developed through *inclusive processes*. With these criteria, therefore, it would be possible to analyse and evaluate the spaces that are being developed in cities around the world.

The book's authors share a common concern about the quality and character of urban public spaces, a concern that has led us to investigate a series of major empirical case studies. Crossing the cultural divides, the book brings these investigations together to examine the similarities and differences of public space in different urban contexts, and engage in a critical analysis of the process of design, development, management and use of public space. While each case study investigates the specificities of particular cities, the book as a whole outlines some general themes in global urban processes. It shows how public spaces are a key theme in urban design and development everywhere, how they are appreciated and used by the people of these cities, but are also contested by and under pressure from different stakeholders.

The book builds on the theoretical foundations developed in earlier publications (Madanipour 1996,

1999, 2003a, 2007), and major research projects funded by the European Commission among others (Madanipour *et al.* 2003b; Madanipour 2004). The chapters, with the exception of Chapter 6, are written specifically for this book, reporting on major research projects funded by international organizations, national governments and research councils. All of these research projects, with the exception of Chapter 11, have recently been conducted at the School of Architecture, Planning and Landscape, Newcastle University. This book is the first attempt to bring together the results of these various research endeavours in a single volume. The book is written for scholars and practitioners in built environment and social sciences, including urban design and planning, architecture, urban geography and sociology, with an interest in the relationship between space and society, and the dynamics of change in contemporary cities around the world, as particularly manifested in urban public spaces.

The book's key argument is that, although the social and spatial composition of cities differ considerably across the world, there are a number of general trends that can be observed: that public spaces play a significant role in the life of cities everywhere, and that for cities to work, there is an undeniable need for public space; that the nature of this role, and therefore the nature of public space, in modern cities has radically changed; and that the development and use of these spaces mirror the way a society is organized, shaped by unequal distribution of power and resources, which creates tension and conflict as well as collaboration and compromise. Public spaces, it is argued here, should be produced on the basis of equality for all by being accessible places made and managed through inclusive processes.

Why has urban public space become a subject of interest?

Public space has been an integral part of cities throughout history, so much so that without it, human settlements would be unimaginable. How could people step out of their front doors if there were no public space to mediate between private territories? Like any other part of cities, such as houses, neighbourhoods, political and cultural institutions, it is part of an ever-present vocabulary of urbanism. It has been used in different forms and combinations in many different circumstances, with different degrees of accessibility and control, but they can all be seen as different variations on the same theme. This poses the question: if public spaces, in some form or other, have been a primary part of urban structure everywhere and at all times, why do we see a current wave of interest in public space as a subject of social concern, political action and academic research?

Recent attention to public space is rooted in the structural changes that societies around the world have experienced in the past thirty years whereby the provision of public goods, such as public space, has been under pressure through the ascendancy of the market-based paradigm. The aftermath of the Second World War was characterized by structural intervention by the state in the economy, resulting in large-scale public-sector schemes in urban development, particularly in western countries. Local authorities and their architects and planners were at the leading edge of urban renewal whereby cities were expanded and redeveloped with high-rise public housing schemes, motorways and new towns, implementing the ideas developed earlier by the garden city movement and the modern movement in architecture. As the prosperity of the 1960s was followed by economic decline in the 1970s, the post-war Keynesian accord between the state and the market came under pressure. Industrial decline deprived the public sector of its funds, and urban renewal projects and new town development schemes were abandoned. The solution that was introduced in the 1980s in the United Kingdom and the United States was to dismantle the age of consensus and stimulate economic growth through market revival and competition. Radical de-industrialization, reduction in the size of the state, privatization, individualization, globalization and liberalization of the economy were the new structural directions for the state and society, which spread around the world and lasted for three decades until coming to a halt with a global financial crisis. This paradigm shift had major implications for urban design, planning and development.

With reduction in the size and scope of the state, urban development was transferred to the private sector. The private sector, however, was interested in those aspects of urban development that would ensure a return on its investment. Private companies were answerable to their shareholders, and not to the urban community as a whole. Public goods, such as public space, therefore, were seen as a liability, as they could not be sold and had no direct profit for the private investor. Local authorities and their elected politicians, meanwhile, could not, or would not, invest in those public goods that did not have an immediate political or economic return. They also saw public space as a liability, as something that required higher maintenance costs and was a burden on their dwindling budgets. As a result, both public- and private-sector agencies abandoned public spaces as cities suffered from accelerated decline.

Large-scale schemes, however, could not be developed without some sort of mediating space, some public areas that would link different buildings and spaces. Private developers, therefore, preferred to control these spaces, so that the return on their investment could not be jeopardized by what they saw as potential threats to their operation. New public spaces that were developed after the 1980s, therefore, were controlled and restricted, in contrast to the more accessible and inclusive places of the past. This was a widespread phenomenon, and became known as the privatization of public space. It generated a fear that the city had become private territory in which people could not move easily and the democratic aspirations of liberty and equality would be undermined. This would be a fragmented city, in which some people would be free to go almost anywhere, whereas others would be trapped inside their ghettos or prevented from entering the exclusive spaces of the elite, facilitated through a process of gentrification. The loss of public space symbolized the loss of the idea of the city.

An associated trend was the change in disciplinary and professional division of labour, in which architects and planners both lost interest in public space, leaving it in an indeterminate state. Modernist architecture was interested in refashioning the entire built environment, from the scale of cities down to the level of individual pieces of furniture. Modernism was a relatively coherent, socially concerned movement that sought to solve social problems through physical transformation. With economic decline, which removed the possibility of large-scale urban development schemes, and the collapse of architecture's confidence in its ability to deal with social problems, it withdrew into an aesthetic sphere. The postmodern reaction to modernism was more interested in playfulness of appearance than in grappling with social concerns. It focused on the site, trying to respond to the needs of the client, and paid little attention to what lay outside, the urban context, of which public space was a major part. The architect's clients were private developers, and they were interested in rewards on their investment, which set the parameters for the architect's scope of action. Meanwhile, as a result of rapid economic decline and the heavily criticized consequences of post-Second World War planning schemes, urban planning became focused on social issues, which included large-scale unemployment and the decline of infrastructure. There was no scope for concentrating on public spaces, which would be considered as icing on the cake, a luxury rather than a necessity.

While public and private organizations and their associated professionals had lost interest in the public space, seeing it as irrelevant or expensive, or were encroaching upon it for private gains, the social need for public space in the city had not disappeared. There were increasing concerns about the rise of individualism and the decline of public goods, of which public space was a key manifestation in the urban environment. Individuals were encouraged to follow their own interests, expecting the market to deliver prosperity. But social goods could not be delivered by the market, which had little interest in non-monetary forms of benefit. Social goods could not be delivered by the public sector either, as its financial ability to develop and maintain public spaces was undermined. There was a crisis about public goods in general, and about public space in particular.

As the neoliberal market paradigm spread around the world, other countries adopted, or were encouraged to adopt, the path of economic regeneration through stimulating the market and reducing the state's size and scope. With the collapse of the Soviet bloc, the market paradigm grew in new countries, becoming the undisputed form of economic development. In these countries, therefore, the provision of public goods, which was already, or had become, less effective than in the rich western countries, faced similar issues and problems. Of course, the extent of marketization and the crisis of public space has not been the same everywhere, as is best evident in the differences between European

and American cities. However, the global neoliberal trend posed a major challenge to public goods everywhere, as partly evident in the threats facing public space, which has resulted from the restless process of globalization.

THE CHANGING NATURE OF PUBLIC SPACE IN CITY CENTRES

The nature and character of public spaces are closely related to the nature and character of cities. As cities have changed, so have their public spaces. In smaller towns and cities of agrarian societies, with their relatively cohesive and homogeneous populations, some public spaces were major focal points, where trade, politics, cultural performance and socialization all took place. As modern cities have grown larger, with heterogeneous populations spread across large areas, public spaces have multiplied and expanded, but have also become more impersonal, losing many of their layers of significance. In the city of strangers, the meaning of public space becomes less personal, more transient, and at best merely functional or symbolic.

There have been major changes in the nature of cities during their long existence throughout millennia (Southall 1998), despite some common features that they share across this time. According to Louis Wirth, cities are identified by size of population, density of settlement, and heterogeneity of inhabitants, and so are perceived as "relatively permanent, compact settlements of large numbers of heterogeneous individuals" (1964: 68). As these parameters of size, density and heterogeneity, and the relationship among urban inhabitants and with the outside world, have constantly taken new forms, the nature of cities and urban societies has changed considerably. These changes can be seen in the different analyses made of the city. For Aristotle (1992), the ancient city was an association, in which people participated by playing different roles to construct a political community. Max Weber (1966) wrote about medieval cities as a fusion of garrison and market, indicating the defensive and economic functions of cities, as well as their political and legal autonomy. In modern cities, however, the military function of the city has been lost, its political function weakened, its economic function integrated into a larger national and international system, and even its population spread out into the suburbs. This is why one observer decided to write, "The age of the city seems to be at an end" (Martindale 1966: 62). And yet we know that the age of the city has just begun, as the turn of the twenty-first century has been marked by a shift in the world's balance of population from a predominantly rural to a predominantly urban population.

The nature of public spaces has changed along-side the historic changes in the nature of cities. For most of urban history, the primary public spaces of the city were the core of the urban society, integrating the political, economic, social and cultural activities of a small and relatively coherent urban population. Examples of these primary spaces were the *agora* in Greek cities, the *forum* in Roman cities, and market squares in medieval cities. The other public open spaces of the city, such as streets, intersections, minor squares, etc., were also essential for everyday sociability and trade. In modern cities, however, the city has grown, with populations so large and heterogeneous that they could not rely on proximity and close encounters to engage in their complex range of activities. Its physical space has also grown to such an extent that co-presence is no longer possible, or even desirable. The role of public space in the close-knit community was fairly clear: facilitating a multiplicity of encounters that were essential for everyday life and helping consolidate the social order. In the modern city, a large number of anonymous individuals are engaged in non-converging networks, while the transport, information and communication technologies have changed the location and shape of these networks. These changes are reflected in the nature of public spaces, which have kept some of their historic functions but now primarily play residual roles.

The change in the nature of urban space can be traced in the relationship between "space" and "place" in the literature, whereby space is considered to be more abstract and impersonal, while place is interpreted as having meaning and value. One of the key criticisms of the urban development process in modern cities has been the transition from place to space, through a loss of meaning and personal association. The humanist critics of modernism, as well as others, have raised this criticism in response to the urban redevelopment programmes of the mid-twentieth century (Jacobs 1961). The same criticism was raised in the nineteenth century

against the modernization of cities with wide boulevards and soulless public spaces (Sitte 1986). While this criticism partly captures the changing condition of cities, it may also tend to misjudge the complexity of places and identities in cities, hence promoting place as a particular enclosed space with fixed identities, which is not what the spaces of modern cities can or should be (Massey 1994). This is part of a larger debate about the nature of modern cities, and of modernity itself.

The transition from an integrative community to the anonymity and alienation of large modern urban societies has been a key concern in the development of sociology (Engels 1993; Tönnies 1957; Simmel 1950). Behaviour in public spaces has been analysed as the reflection of this transition, from engaging with others to avoiding them, as the overload of encounters and emotional stimuli, and the wide gap between social classes, keep people apart and turn public spaces into residual places of avoidance rather than encounter. Two of the major theorists of the public sphere in the twentieth century, Hannah Arendt and Jurgen Habermas, mourned the passing of these integrative societies and complained about the rise of what was called a mass society. Arendt analysed the ancient polis (1958) and Habermas investigated the early modern bourgeois public sphere (1989), both as examples of situations in which interpersonal communication led to a rich public life. Both of them saw the rigid routines of the industrial city as alienating, and as tending to degrade the qualities of public life.

The result has been a degree of false romanticization of historic public spaces. The Greek *agora* has been portrayed as the material manifestation of this magnificent ancient civilization. This was a civilization, however, in which women, foreigners and slaves had no place in the public sphere. The medieval square has been portrayed as the picturesque heart of the city, in what are often little more than romantic and aesthetic notions of life in the medieval city, and yet at the time it was a place dominated by trade, and it displayed the hierarchies and harshness of life within the city walls. The eighteenth-century coffee houses in London or the salons in Paris are seen as the prototypes for the emergence of a public sphere, in which people were able to discuss matters of common interest and come to an informed opinion about their society, and yet these places were often accessible only to the elite among the emerging bourgeoisie. The early modern city squares and boulevards are portrayed as examples of the rise of a new age of reason and modernity, and yet they resulted from speculative development, monarchical power and suppression of the poor. What we often see is the architecture of the city, or at least a sanitized image of the history, on which we project our own expectations, aesthetic, political and social.

After the decline of industries and the collapse of the rigid routines of the industrial economy, the nature of public space has once again changed, now being integrated into the service economy. The quality of public space becomes an essential support mechanism for the flexible working practices of the service economy, and the consumption-driven basis on which this economy relies. Rather than treating public spaces as functional residues or breathing spaces of the city, which was the attitude of industrial modernism, service-based postmoderns embrace them for their aesthetic value, as well as their provision of spaces of consumption. Public spaces become an essential part of the regeneration of cities through promoting retail development. The association of public space creation and high-value consumption inevitably leads to gentrification, in which one group of people and activities are replaced by another.

The modern large city, which was once a western phenomenon, has now become a global one. The transition from integrative small communities to fragmented large societies, which was associated with the experiences of modernity in nineteenth-century Europe, has now been extended to most parts of the globe through a restless process of colonization, modernization and globalization. In this context, as cities grow everywhere and services form a major part of urban economies around the world, the condition of urban public spaces becomes ever more significant.

Accessible places

Public spaces play many different roles in urban societies and can be defined in a number of ways. The key feature of public space, however, is its accessibility. Without being accessible, a place cannot become public. If public open spaces are conceived as enclosed particular places with fixed identities, their flexibility and inclusiveness will be undermined, and so will their accessibility. They lie outside the boundaries of individual or small group control, providing spaces that mediate between, and give access to, private spaces, as well as performing a multiplicity of functional and symbolic roles in the life of an urban society. In the processes of urban change, the conditions of accessibility are subject to change, hence changing the nature of public spaces. In the controversies about privatization of public space, it is the access to public spaces that has been limited, narrowing the range of social groups who can use these spaces, and making these spaces accessible only to a smaller group of people, often judged by their ability to pay.

The word *public* originates from the Latin and refers to people, indicating a relationship to both society and the state. A public space may therefore be interpreted as open to people as a whole, and/or being controlled by the state on their behalf. Public has been defined as the opposite of private, which is the realm of individuals and their intimate relationships; and so public space is often defined in terms of its distinction from the private realm of the household. Public has also been seen as the opposite of the personal, hence equated with impersonal (Silver 1997: 43), the realm of the non-intimate others. What lies beyond personal, however, can also be inter-personal, where the boundaries between personal and impersonal, private and public, can be blurred.

The distinction between the public and the private is a key theme in liberal political theory, promoting the separation of private and public interests and roles in order to prevent private interests encroaching on and undermining public interests (Wacks 1993; Nolan 1995). The tension has been challenged by the critics of private property, who see this distinction as consolidating the power of the elite at the expense of the poor. It has also been challenged by women, who see it as consolidating the role of men in public affairs and associating the private sphere with women, hence keeping them locked in an inferior position in society (Fraser 1989). The subdivision of the social world into public and private spheres, and the establishment and maintenance of the boundaries between them, has therefore been challenged and criticized from a number of different perspectives.

Yet another challenge to the notion of public sphere and public space comes from social diversity. Public policy has often been justified as directed towards public interest. The idea of public interest has been used to explain and defend the actions of public authorities. Their critics, however, argue that the way this public interest has been defined is too narrow, and often privileges the elite. What is usually considered to be an average citizen, for whom the laws are written and who is the basis of public action, is argued to exclude women, the elderly, children, ethnic minorities and the poor. What is introduced as public interest, they argue, is not really public in an inclusive sense. This poses a challenge to the notion of public: either abandon the idea and replace it with a notion of society subdivided into tribes and interest groups, or try to expand the notion of public so as to include all citizens equally.

In spatial terms, public spaces are by definition public, and as such expected to be accessible to all. However, *public* is not a single entity, as it is composed of different social strata, each with a different set of characteristics, interests and powers. Furthermore, within those strata there are a large number of individual differences. There are strong centrifugal and fragmentary forces that create and separate social strata, which will then be reflected in the constitution of the public. The tension between the public and the private can be seen in the European medieval city, as well as in many cities around the world to this day, where the streets and open spaces of the city are gradually being threatened by the expanding houses and private spaces, to the extent that a minimum amount of space is left for passing through and for conducting trade and other essential functions (Saalman 1968). It is a tension that we can clearly see in our own time, in which private interests tend to claim the urban space, undermining the publicness of its public spaces, in what is termed the privatization of public space.

The nature and character of a public space depend on how it is distinguished from the private sphere. In other words, the way in which its boundaries are constructed determines the type of public space and its quality. If the boundary is rigidly guarded by walls, gates and guards, it is no longer considered a public space. In contrast, the more accessible and permeable a place becomes, the more public it will be. Its degree of publicness will also depend on the types of activities taking place, which can create symbolic boundaries around these activities, or be inviting to as many people as wish to join in. A degree of distinction between intimate and shared spaces, between private and public spaces, is essential for living in society. The controversy is usually about how these two areas are defined, distinguished from one another, and separated by what sort of boundary. Much of urban design has been interested in how this boundary is articulated, how a dividing line can be set up that is protective of the private sphere from the intrusion of others, while protecting the collective sphere from individual interest; in other words, how this boundary can enhance, rather than degrade, the quality of life in cities.

To determine the extent to which a place or activity is public or private, Benn and Gaus (1983) suggested three criteria as dimensions of social organization: access, interest and agency, with access divided further into access to spaces, activities, information and resources. A place is public, therefore, if it is controlled by public authorities, concerns people as a whole, is open or available to them, and is used or shared by all the members of a society. This provides a useful framework for assessing the publicness of a place. The criteria of interest, agency and access, however, approach space instrumentally, seeing it as an asset in exchange, using it as a resource, treating it as a commodity. This interpretation appears to draw on an analysis of social relations as exchange among strangers, rather than a set of emotional and meaningful ties (Madanipour 2003a). There must be additional dimensions at work, which should also be taken into account.

The symbolic dimensions of public spaces are as significant as their functional ones. In the small towns and cities of agrarian societies, public spaces were developed and used as integrative nodes for a variety of instrumental and expressive needs. Performing social rituals in public was as important as engaging in trade or deliberating on how to manage the town. Even before then, as can be observed in the remaining hunter-gatherer societies of today, the common spaces of a group, in which they sing and dance, tell stories and perform rituals, are a significant part of living together as a group. In modern urban societies, however, while humans have remained social beings, it is true that the nature and methods of expressiveness, and therefore the character of urban public spaces, have changed. Much of cultural reading of cities places a performative emphasis on public spaces, seeing them as places for performance and assertion of identity. On the other hand, the functionalist reading of the city appeared to ignore this symbolic dimension and focus entirely on the way cities functioned, hence seeing public spaces as essential for the health of the city, as its lungs. A key argument is that both these camps have failed to see the multidimensionality of public space. Access, therefore, has both instrumental and expressive dimensions. A public space is one that allows a range of necessary activities to take place, but also a place in which "unnecessary" social activities are performed. An example is the ritual of *passeggiata* in Italian cities, the evening walk in which the inhabitants of the city put on their best clothes and go out of their homes for a slow stroll in public spaces to see and be seen. This is a symbolic and expressive, as well as functional, exercise, a complex urban ritual that cannot be reduced to a single interpretation.

There are major tensions, however, inherent in the symbolic dimension of accessibility. On the one hand, the more accessible a place, the more impersonal it tends to become, particularly in large cities. If a place is reserved for a known group of individuals or a class of society on the basis of their economic or political resources, accessibility decreases and familiarity rises. While individuals may suffer from the anonymity of the large city (Simmel 1950) and prefer to establish a comfort realm of familiarity, they will have to come into contact with a large number of strangers in their everyday life in the city. However, if the city becomes subdivided into zones of comfort for social groups, it has been fragmented and tribalized. Much of the literature in urban design encourages designers and decision makers to subdivide the city into neighbourhoods and identifiable, defendable zones, hence knowingly or unknowingly limiting the accessibility of urban spaces. There is, therefore, a parallel between accessibility and anonymity: spaces that would deter strangers would not be accessible. They may have served local people well, but their accessibility would be controlled and limited.

Provision and free access to public spaces, therefore, are essential for any society. But we should not naively believe in physical determinism, thinking that spatial solutions are sufficient to address societal problems. As public space is a part of the public sphere, we can apply the logic of the public sphere in democratic societies to analysing public space. In these societies, the establishment of a political public sphere did not remove the social divide between rich and poor, but it did provide opportunities for expressing opinion and avenues for trying to influence action. In other words, the public sphere was an integral part of a democratic society. In the same sense, public space is a necessary part of an open society, a space that everyone is able to enter and participate in some collective experience. This may not amount to solving social and economic problems, but it does provide a forum for socialization and a counterweight to exclusionary and centrifugal forces that tend to tear apart the social fabric of polarized societies.

Inclusive processes

Different stages in design, planning, development and management of public spaces have a direct impact on their accessibility and identity. If public spaces are produced and managed by narrow interests, they are bound to become exclusive places. As the range of actors and interests in urban development varies widely, and places have different dimensions and functions, creating public spaces becomes a complex and multidimensional process. To understand places, and to promote the development of accessible public places, therefore, it is essential to study this process and to encourage its broadening, to make it inclusive.

Cities have historically grown and been developed by a large number of people over time. As new technologies have emerged, the size of companies has grown and the areas of expertise have multiplied through a process of specialization, constructing the built environment has become far more complex than hitherto. The process has also become faster than before, in line with the growth in the productive capacity of developers. An army of specialists and a mountain of resources can be employed to create new parts of cities in relatively short periods of time. While this complexity has multiplied the number of agencies involved in the process, it has allocated a specific task to each agency, as cogs in a large machine geared towards a particular mode of operation. As the number of agencies has grown, the organizational hierarchies and the division of labour have focused the process, ruled by technical and instrumental rationality. As technological know-how and the self-confidence of modern city builders have grown, city building has been consolidated in fewer hands, managing and coordinating complex hierarchies and networks of agencies and individuals.

The medieval city, and for that matter the nineteenth-century industrial city, were seen as the result of accidents rather than careful planning. The father of modern rationalist philosophy, René Descartes (1968), preferred cities to be designed by a single designer, who could devise and implement a single well-ordered system. The medieval city, as well as the laws and beliefs of the past, were the result of custom and example, rather than rational thinking. What he advocated was thinking everything anew, according to a rational order. This way of thinking was the basis of the modernist approach to design, aiming to create and impose a new order on the cities of the past, even at the cost of eradicating large parts of these cities. Rather than being conditioned by the past, modernist rationalists wanted a break with the past.

The considerable productive capacities of modern city builders have made this possible. Designers and planners are trained to think strategically and plan for strategic and large-scale transformation of cities. The changing nature of developers has a direct impact on what they build. A century ago, locally based developers could be engaged in single small developments, creating more diverse cities. Now, in contrast, large national or international developers are able to engage in large-scale projects. Developers can mobilize large amounts of capital and large teams of construction professionals, and can use new construction technologies and machinery, enabling them to develop cities at larger scales and faster speeds. A large part of a city, therefore, can be designed by a single organization within a relatively short period of time. As Descartes dreamed, a city can be designed by a single designer and developed by a single organization. The task is complex and will involve a large number of different teams. These are all, nevertheless, under the management of the main developer and the associated design team. However, while this increases efficiency and productivity in city building, it narrows the range of strategic actors and their considerations.

The logic of production, however, is only one among the logics with which cities are built and run (Madanipour 2007). In deciding the best course of action, the ability to make is certainly an important consideration, but not the only one. In deciding how to live our lives or how to manage our cities, we evaluate our options according to a wide range of issues and considerations. To narrow down the range of options to technical and instrumental ones, therefore, would lead to distorted decisions.

A key question in analysing the development process is: who is involved? An associated question is: who do the process and its outcome serve? An inclusive process would involve a larger number of people and agencies and would spread the benefits of the process to larger parts of society, while an exclusive process would limit the number and range of agencies and would reward a smaller number of people. The process of building cities involves complex regulatory frameworks and large financial resources, both of which are often closely entwined with political and financial elites. This tends to give these elites a powerful influence over the process and its outcome.

In market economies, financial resources are generated by the private sector, and it is taken for granted that private investors expect to maximize rewards on their investment. In democracies, the elected representatives are expected to act on behalf of their constituencies. However, the disadvantaged groups, who do not have access to financial resources and are frequently disconnected from the political process, end up having no control or stake in the city building process. The places that are created are not designed to serve them, as these groups are not often part of the decision-making formula. This tends to make city building dominated by powerful agencies and individuals, rather than involving a broad range of citizens. In the development process, development agencies work with resources, rules and ideas in response to the needs of society and demands of the market. However, if the needs and demands of the disadvantaged parts of society are not strongly represented, politically or financially, as is often the case, the process and its outcome may not serve them at all.

Another key question in the development process is the temporal dimension of change. Design as a goal-oriented problem-solving process tends to envisage the built environment as a finished product, working out its structure and details and leaving nothing to chance. Cities, however, are constantly changing, inhabited as they are by intelligent and dynamic people. At no point can there be a final shape for a city. The design and development of cities, therefore, will need to accommodate this change, embracing a dynamic conception of cities rather than a fixed and rigid one.

What is needed, therefore, in investigating, as well as making, the urban space is a multidimensional and multi-agency process involving as many individuals and agencies as possible, and a dynamic process that can accommodate time and change. The result will be a *dynamic multiplicity*, in which city building is envisaged and organized as an inclusive and responsive process. The public spaces that are created by this process will be more inclusive and accessible than the ones that serve narrow interests; will be driven by technical and instrumental concerns; or will be envisaged as fixed, exclusive and rigid places.

An interdependent world

Some readers may wonder why this book has brought together what appear to be disparate experiences from such a wide range of countries. What can African, European, Asian and Latin American cities have in common? Each city and each country has its own history and culture, with different social and economic conditions and prospects. What can we gain from bringing these cases together? On the surface, the differences between our case studies are large and wide, to the extent that the existence of any links or comparisons between their public spaces may seem improbable. Some of these cities are rapidly growing while others are shrinking. They belong to different cultures and economic conditions, each embedded in a completely different reality. What might we find, these readers may ask, in any attempt at placing them alongside one another?

A key answer is the universality of the existence of, and the need for, public space in cities. Everywhere and in any period of history, human settlements consist of a collection of different individuals and households, residing in their own private territories and connected to one another through semi-private, semi-public and public spaces. From the earliest traces of human settlements in Mesopotamia to the metropolises of our own time, this division of space into public and private has been a key feature of urban societies. While the character and use of these public spaces may differ, the universal existence of some form of public space and its social and economic significance for the city cannot be denied.

Another, related, similarity between the cities is in the converging methods of city building, in which the markets and new technologies are prominent. In our time, the spread of capitalism and the extent of global interdependency characterize cities everywhere. Before the arrival of the dramatic economic crisis of 2008, a global consensus seemed to have emerged in which markets were given free rein to come up with solutions to all the economic problems. All of the cities we have studied are part of the global market, albeit occupying different positions in the marketplace, from more central to more marginal. In all cities, the process of city building is subject to the logic of the market, in which land as a finite resource is the subject of competition. What connects these cities and their spaces, therefore, is the mechanism of the market. Even if it operates completely differently in each city, it is subject to the same general principle of risk and reward, and distinction between private and public interests. It also tends to generate, or accelerate, social stratification and division, creating tensions between the rich and poor, and social inequalities that become manifest in the making and use of public spaces.

Also, all cities are subject to the impact of technological change. Transport technologies have allowed them to spread, creating new social and spatial distinctions between the centre and periphery. Construction technologies have been embraced as the solution to city building problems, often applied by architects and planners with little consultation with the city's inhabitants. Cities' position with regard to manufacturing industries also creates overlaps and commonalities: while some are abandoning their industrial past, others are entering a period of industrialization, each with its own distinctive, but ultimately related, impact on the character of public space. Judging by their diverse character and trajectory, we cannot envisage these cities to be on a linear temporal path in which some are further along the line than the others, and the fate of some is going to be a model for the fate of the others. We can, however, see how their linkages, existing and potential, are forged through their current conditions and past histories. More than anything else, they are part of the same global urban process, different components of the same phenomenon and sharing many features of modern urban societies.

[. . .]

WHOSE PUBLIC SPACE?

After investigating these cases from around the world, through the theoretical frameworks of place and process, can we now answer the question that was posed as the title of this book, and identify to whom public spaces belong? The complexity of the urban design, development and management processes in these cases, and of the configuration of urban societies in which they are located, makes it impossible to find simple answers. But across the cases, we are able to identify a recurring theme whereby individuals, social groups and organizations make or withdraw claims over space, thereby implicitly or explicitly contesting the claim of others, instigating a process of inclusion and exclusion, creating spaces with overlapping meanings. We can see how public spaces are significant for all urban societies, no matter what the size of the city, its economic basis or its political and cultural configurations. Public spaces, as significant material and social components of cities, are therefore subject to intense processes of social interaction through which their quality and character are determined.

Claims could be made by powerful individuals and institutions, such as a supermarket chain or a shopping mall in England, a local authority in France, a local prince in Nigeria, or housing designers and developers in Saudi Arabia and Iran. Claims could also be made by individuals – or informal groups of people who try to shape the space, such as youth subcultures in the United Kingdom,

public housing residents in the Netherlands, street drinkers in Germany, low-income households in Mexico, local businessmen in Taiwan, or middle-class South Africans, each with widely different views and outcomes. Depending on their level of political, economic and cultural power and influence, these individuals and organizations can shape and determine some of the features of the urban space, creating the structural conditions within which others live and use the city. Their resources allow the more powerful individuals and institutions to make substantial physical and institutional changes in cities, while the claims by the less powerful groups may take softer, temporary forms. Each individual, group or organization may try to shape the city in their own image, creating spaces that would enable them to feel safe and in control, with or without consideration of what others may need. Public spaces, even in their most public forms, therefore, tend to find particular flavours, a different character associated with a particular combination of groups and interests, under pressure to find a fixed identity within a particular fragment of society.

Public spaces are shaped not only by claims, but also by the absence of claims, by withdrawal from the public sphere. Withdrawal from public space may be due to a fear of crime, mistrust of other social groups, and intensified social polarization. This withdrawal is reflected in neglect and decline, poor maintenance, accumulation of waste and refuse, or lack of care and attention. Neglect of public spaces may be a result of exaggerated preferences for vehicular movement, which was the dominant theme in shaping cities for much of the industrial era. Such neglect may also reflect the absence of local governance – that is, coordinating mechanisms to facilitate negotiation between different claims over space. Public spaces provide linkages between private spheres, and represent the character and quality of a city as a whole. The decline of public space reflects a breakdown in social and spatial linkages and a deterioration of the city as a whole.

The case studies presented in this book map out the changing nature of public space. Public open spaces are changing from being embedded in the social fabric of the city to being a part of more impersonal and fragmented urban environments. The various chapters *show* how public spaces are changing alongside the changing nature of cities and urban societies: from places embedded in particular communal traditions and routines to impersonal spaces produced by economic, political, technical and management considerations – in other words, they are undergoing a transition from an expressive to an instrumental character. Public spaces that once were meaningful places are becoming a mere part of a transportation network dominated by cars. They are also at risk of being taken over by minority interests, being privatized in the name of safety or exclusivity, further fragmenting the urban society and space.

The particular characters of public spaces may be instrumental or expressive. As instrumental spaces, they are used as a means to an end, such as the development of a public bus station, or the pedestrianization of a street for the purpose of gaining commercial profit for businesses, or the gating of streets for the perceived safety of resident groups. Instrumental use can also be made for an essential need, such as the public spaces in low-income neighbourhoods in Mexico or small towns in France, where the quality of urban life is closely connected with the process of urban development and the provision of public spaces. As expressive spaces, they may be used to project and explore identity, such as the gathering of youth subcultures or international migrants in a European city, or a festival space in a traditional African city. The inclusive and participatory development of a common good such as public spaces can help combine instrumental and expressive concerns, creating places that people use and can identify with, while reinvigorating society through collective action.

[. . .]

Urban spaces may physically change very slowly, but socially they may embody new beliefs and behaviours. Society's economic and social configuration may change from agrarian to industrial to services, and these changes may leave some spaces intact, but the pattern of their use and the nature of their meaning for the urban populations will have changed dramatically. The design and development processes may therefore result in substantial changes that introduce new beliefs and practices, undermining the established patterns, liberating some groups from their inferior positions, but also abandoning the built environment that reflected those traditions. Public spaces may retain some of the symbols and festivals, but these lose their original meanings, turning into aesthetic practices carrying only a fading trace of their economic and political content.

The city is often shaped at the intersection of these claims and characters. Each claim may shape one part of the city, or one aspect of a place, and the interaction among these claims and counterclaims shapes the complex city of people and places. Resistance, transgression and contest are as much a signifying character of these places as the claims to establish a fixed or abstract identity for them. The aims of designers to control the character of a housing scheme and its spaces may be met by a different use of the place, one that they did not envisage or approve. The intentions of local authorities to formalize development and promote a sanitized identity for the city may be met by the colonization of space by groups that threaten that image. The traditional authority and status of a place may be undermined by the growth of population around it and the expansion of places and activities. Actions may have more unintended consequences and challenges than there were intended outcomes.

City design and development becomes a continuous process of projection and contestation, in which some groups project an identity for a place and others accept or contest that identity, either by consciously transgressing the boundaries that this process sets, or by ignoring it – knowingly or unknowingly. Even those who admit the claims of the projected identity of places, and therefore appear to fall in with the planned character and routines, may undermine and transform these claims by performing new activities, or by forgetting or ignoring the intended routines and practices. The place takes on a life of its own, one that may be very different from what was intended, through conformity, accident or defiance.

How can the complex and fluid process of urban design and development be led so as to ensure the place is as public as possible, serving as many people as possible, rather than being at the service of a privileged few? If the design and development of cities lies at the intersection of different claims, how can these claims all be taken into account? There will be many occasions when the conflict is so powerful that no bridge can be built between different positions and interest groups. The choice appears to be between battling it out and trying to negotiate to find a solution. Such negotiation can only take place through an inclusive process of city design and development in which as many views as possible need to be involved. Desire for exclusivity goes hand in hand with social inequality, and so it is only through inclusive processes that the possibility of creating accessible and shared places increases.

There is a large degree of overlap between the book's chapters across its two parts. Overall, they show the gaps that exist between different perspectives and how the tension tends to be resolved in favour of more powerful groups. The power resides with the designer who shapes the place, the developer who initiates and coordinates the production of space, the investor who brings forward financial resources, the public-sector agencies that promote and regulate the transformation of the place, the homeowner who wishes to be in control of the neighbourhood, the male domination that prevents women from entering public arenas, the higher-income groups that demand exclusive places, the majority populations who keep minorities and subcultures out – and so on. Those who do not control resources and have no voice in political representation, those who remain silent in the process of spatial transformation, or those who are physically weak can be at the receiving end, and potentially lose out in a contest over the use and control of space. This is an interdependent process, with no one party in full control, although the degree of power and influence of agencies varies according to their economic and political capital or their relations with the others around them.

The ascendancy of the market paradigm in city building, which shifted the initiative for investment to the private sector, has had a clear impact on how the process of urban design and development may be influenced. By encouraging private investors, either through partnerships or through reducing regulatory pressures on them, the urban development process has been bent towards their expectations. This shift of power towards the market is perhaps the defining feature of many urban development schemes in recent decades, with the unavoidable outcome that the market determines the character of the outcome, which often means producing places that facilitate monetary exchange. The prevalence of economic justification for public spaces, therefore, becomes the norm rather than the exception. It becomes an integral part of the logic of place making; anybody who questions this logic may be accused of naivety or lack of economic awareness. As the aim of the urban development process is often economic regeneration, place finds an instrumental value, as a tool through which economic vibrancy can be delivered. Developers and local authorities may both look for quantity rather than quality.

Public space, urban regeneration and economic development, therefore, are closely entwined. In some cases, the only way that public spaces can be developed and maintained is through engaging private-sector resources. So, the solution is not to exclude private investment from the process, and thus argue for poorer places and more deprived cities. The argument is that individual interests should not be given free rein. The aim is to allow the character and quality of places to be established through a variety of criteria and at the intersection of different voices, giving ultimate primacy to the public and its different layers. Powerful groups inevitably try to exert a stronger influence in the process, and negotiations never become altruistic dialogues, which is why participation, inclusivity and transparency become essential.

Urban sprawl has put pressure on both urban centres and their peripheries. While urbanization in much of the developing world is still ongoing, suburbanization in the developed world is a primary feature, both trends leading to rapid and fragmented expansion of the city into the surrounding areas. In the outward growth of cities, city centres and their public spaces have lost much of their significance, even though the urban showcases are still in the centre, where the pressure of competition for space is still prevalent. Hollowing out of the centre, which is a feature of car-based urban growth, has been experienced in most of our case studies. Marginal areas, meanwhile, have suffered from the shortage of public spaces, both in rich suburbs and in poor inner-city or peripheral neighbourhoods, albeit at different levels. Public spaces are closely associated with the degree of urbanization in a city, and when urbanization suffers through suburbanization and individualization, public spaces also suffer from neglect and loss of meaning.

The key issue is to have a clear sense of what is gained and what is lost, as an inevitable component of any development process, and have some control over this balance in favour of a wider range of people than many plans may suggest. Images of busy and lively public spaces abound in the promotional material put out by city authorities, developers and designers to show the attractiveness of their cities, the success of their schemes or the desirable places that they aim to create. Inherent in these images is the notion of happy shoppers and joyous lifestyles, which would cause no problem if these developments did not exclude many people with limited financial means or people who were forced out of their places to make space for the new arrangement. A place, therefore, should not be seen as a cosy tool to facilitate the supply and demand of consumer goods and lifestyles. An urban place has many more layers, which should be taken into account in its design and development.

A primary concern in the production and use of a place is the intention by some agencies to narrow and control participation so as to ensure particular outcomes, namely creating places that ensure a return on investment, that support and facilitate commercial operations and consumerist lifestyles, and that can be used as brands and promotional vehicles to attract more investors and visitors. Another reductive pressure on public space is the assumptions made by the designers, developers and local decision makers concerning who people are and what they need. These assumptions may be biased in favour of particular social classes, cultural groups, individual tastes and aesthetic considerations, different concepts of order and disorder, and different historic periods, often reflective of those who make them. Designers and developers may decide to allocate the worst part of a scheme to public spaces, designating the leftover areas as public spaces. They may impose an abstract geometry without paying attention to the patterns of lived experience among the users, creating lines on the map rather than places defined by physical enclosures and supported by a range of activities.

How can these competing claims over space be assessed? Each group may be able to justify its claim on the basis of its needs and requirements. But if the impact on others is exclusionary, such justification may lose its legitimacy. The principle by which the claims are evaluated and the character of public spaces examined should be the principle of equality. If a place is equally accessible to everyone, irrespective of their physical abilities, age, gender, ethnicity, income level and social status, it can be called a public space. It is on this basis that

public spaces should be designed and developed, as places that embody the principles of equality, by being accessible places made through inclusive and democratic processes. Democratic and inclusive processes that create public space as a common good appear to be the best way of ensuring a better physical environment with social and psychological significance for the citizens. Where everyday needs for public spaces are met through participative processes, the result is both physical improvement and social development, laying the foundations for further enhancement of democratic practices.

REFERENCES

Arendt, Hannah. 1958. *The Human Condition*. Chicago: University of Chicago Press.

Aristotle. 1992. *The Politics*. London: Penguin Books.

Benn, Stanley I. and Gerald F. Gaus. 1983. The public and the private: concepts and action. In *Public and Private in Social Life*, eds S.I. Benn and G.F. Gaus. London: Croom Helm; New York: St Martin's Press.

Descartes, René. 1968. *Discourse on Method and The Meditations*. London: Penguin Books.

Engels, Friedrich. 1993. *The Conditions of the Working Class in England*, ed. D. McLellan. Oxford: Oxford University Press.

Fraser, Nancy. 1989. *Unruly Practices: Power, Discourse and Gender in Contemporary Social Theory*. Minneapolis, Minnesota: Minnesota University Press.

Habermas, Jurgen. 1989. *The Structural Transformation of the Public Sphere: An Inquiry into a Category of Bourgeois Society*. Cambridge: Polity Press.

Jacobs, Jane. 1961. *The Death and Life of Great American Cities*. New York: Vintage Books.

Madanipour, Ali. 1996. *Design of Urban Space*. Chicester: John Wiley.

——. 1999. Why are the design and development of public spaces significant for cities? *Environment and Planning B: Planning and Design:* 26: 879–91.

——. 2003a. *Public and Private Spaces in the City*. London: Routledge.

——. 2003b. *Cities' Actions against Social Exclusion*. Brussels: Eurocities.

——. 2003c. Why are the design and development of public spaces significant for cities? In *Designing Cities: Critical Readings on Urban Design*, ed. A.R. Cuthbert. Oxford: Blackwell.

——. 2004. Marginal public spaces in European cities. *Journal of Urban Design:* 9 (3): 267–86.

——. 2007. *Designing the City of Reason*. London: Routledge.

Martindale, D. 1966. Prefactory remarks: the theory of the city. In *The City*, M. Weber. New York: The Free Press.

Massey, Douglas. 1994. *Space, Place and Gender*. Cambridge: Polity Press.

Nolan, Lord. 1995. *Standards in Public Life: First Report on the Standards in Public Life*, vol. 1: Report (Cm 2850-I). London: HMSO.

Saalman, Howard. 1968. *Medieval Cities*. London: Studio Vista.

Silver, Allan. 1997. Two different sorts of commerce: friendship and strangership in civil society. In *Public and Private in Thought and Action*, eds J. Weintraub and K. Kumar. Chicago: University of Chicago Press.

Simmel, Georg. 1950. The metropolis and mental life. In *The Sociology of Georg Simmel*, ed. K. Wolff. New York: The Free Press.

Sitte, Camillo. [1889] 1986. City planning according to artistic principles. In *Camillo Sitte: The Birth of Modern City Planning*, eds G. Collins and C. Collins. New York: Rizzoli.

Southall, Aidan. 1998. *The City in Time and Space*. Cambridge: Cambridge University Press.

Tönnies, Ferdinand. 1957. *Community and Society (Gemeinschaft und Gesellschaft)*, trans. and ed. C. Loomis. New York: Harper & Row.

Wacks, Raymond, ed. 1993. *Privacy*. Aldershot, UK: Ashgate.

Weber, Max. 1966. *The City*. New York: The Free Press.

Wirth, Louis. 1964. Urbanism as a way of life. In *Louis Wirth on Cities and Social Life: Selected Papers*, ed. A. Reiss. Chicago: University of Chicago Press.

"Profit and Place"

from *Urban Transformations: Power, People and Urban Design* (1999)

Ian Bentley

Editors' Introduction

At some point in the professional career of every designer, there comes a moment when budgetary realities of projects cause great consternation and disappointment in their changes to design intentions. Whether this moment comes as a jolt to possibilities during schematic design – or a later whittling away of design details through value engineering – design outcomes get altered and incrementally change the visual and experiential quality of cities. In this chapter from *Urban Transformations: Power, People and Urban Design*, Professor Ian Bentley exposes the links between developer motivations for profit and the diminishment of design quality. Bentley frames the book around public disappointment with the evolution of city form over time as changes in development financing, land acquisition, and design practices have taken root. These cumulative changes create urban places that are different in scale, detail, materiality, and design quality – often producing places that are unloved. He suggests a different set of values might be in play between designers and developer clients, some of whom see profit as the primary intent of development. Much in the same line of thought as expressed by John Logan and Harvey Molotch in *Urban Fortunes: The Political Economy of Place*, 2nd edn. (Berkeley: University of California Press, 2007), the historic evolution of use value into exchange value creates a very different set of expectations for the design performance of cities.

Bentley educates the reader to some of the basic concepts of real estate development practice. He describes the capital accumulation process that occurs through three distinct transformation phases in the development process: 1. how development costs (wealth) are converted through those things bought in the marketplace for the production of projects, that is, land, materials, labor, services; 2. how these are converted into a product through the design process; and 3. how design products are transformed back into wealth again (as well as profit in the undertaking) through sales in the marketplace. The author illustrates how developers can utilize each of these phased wealth transformations into greater profits at the end of this process. The design outcomes of these transformations have often resulted in the following: projects sited on less expensive land further from desired locations; the increasing scale of development to maximize returns; a coarser grain development that encloses the most space for the least cost; less walkable places because of this scale transformation; specialized design firms who market more generic product expertise; deskilled construction labor that might scrimp on attention to detail and work quality; globalized design practices where designers aren't embedded within the cultures or locations of their projects – often producing homogenizing results; cost savings on material quality and innovative project components; the shortening of the construction calendar to save time and money; a reduced range of specialized building types; and importantly, reductions in contributions to public realm design and development. These are just a few of the many cost saving/quality reducing characteristics that Bentley discusses. This list is impressive and disheartening in both its scope and length. The cumulative impacts of these physical and wealth transformations change the experiential quality of urban living.

Declining urban design and architecture quality has provoked a series of "corrections" and a number of reactionary responses in practice – all of which raise a host of concerns and debates about the role of the public sector in managing private sector development. The public has grown distrustful of developers who master these cost cutting/profit maximization methods, as well as designers who are often deemed guilty by association. Planning agencies have imposed additional oversight practices to ensure higher quality products; sometimes resulting in design review boards as checks on shoddy design and development. Some cities impose developer agreements and community benefits agreements to ensure attention to public realm amenities, infrastructure, and service improvements – elements that developers might otherwise neglect. Other places have imposed supplemental design guidelines, regulations and form-based codes to manage design expectations and shape their cities in desired directions.

While Bentley is highly critical of the *modus operandi* of some developers for cost cutting and profit, we need to note that the associated decline in urban design quality is not a uniform outcome across all developer practices. Given that real estate development attracts different consumers and market niches, not all projects are targeted at increased profit margins through cost savings in design, materials, detailing, and location. Much to the contrary, development targeted at higher end consumers often elevates design characteristics to a marketing tactic. Most developers take great pride in the real estate projects they produce; many pioneering innovative, creative, and valued project and building types. For over a decade now, the City of Vancouver (through savvy collaboration between municipal urban designers and planners, the public, and developers) has suggested much the opposite – that improving urban design and project quality has beneficial effects on both short-term gain and long-term value.

Ian Bentley is Professor Emeritus in urban design at Oxford-Brookes University in the United Kingdom. For many years he coordinated the Oxford Urban Design Studio and the Joint Centre for Urban Design. His written works include: *Identity by Design*, with co-author Georgina Butina-Watson (London: Taylor & Francis/Architectural Press, 2007); *Responsive Environments*, with co-authors Sue McGlynn, Graham Smith, Alan Alcock, and Paul Murrain (London: Taylor & Francis/Architectural Press, 1985); and "Urban Design as an Anti-Profession," an article in which Bentley argues that urban design should remain a field of practice rather than becoming a full-fledged profession: http://www.rudi.net/books/11651.

Publication of literature on profit-inducing development practices that result in positive urban design outcomes is growing. Some of these publications include: Steve Tiesdell and David Adams, *Urban Design in the Real Estate Development Process* (New York: Wiley-Blackwell, 2011), and *Shaping Places: Urban Planning, Design and Development* (Abingdon: Routledge, 2012); Dennis Jerke, *Urban Design and the Bottom Line: Optimizing the Return on Perception* (Washington, DC: Urban Land Institute, 2008); Anne B. Frei and Richard B. Peiser, *Professional Real Estate Development: The ULI Guide to the Business*, 2nd edn. (Washington, DC: Urban Land Institute, 2003); and Rocky Mountain Institute et al., *Green Development: Integrating Ecology and Real Estate* (New York: Wiley, 1998).

INTRODUCTION

The form-production process takes place through a complex pattern of negotiation and struggle between various actors. The built outcome of this process depends on the internal and external economic, political and cultural resources available to each actor, and on the rules according to which the various actors deploy the resources they have. In capitalist situations, increasingly prevalent across the globe, private sector profit-oriented development agencies deploy very large resources in the form-production process. For example, the vast majority of developments are produced by private-sector developers specifically to be sold in the marketplace at a profit. Perhaps less obviously, the private sector produces a great deal of public space too. The streets within private sector housing estates, for example, are mostly produced as integral parts of profit oriented overall schemes, and then merely handed over to state agencies for management afterwards.

Once any private-sector project has been sold, profit-oriented economic considerations become as crucial to the buyers as they were to the original producers. This is perhaps most obvious in the case of commercial and industrial property, which is mostly bought specifically for investment, by large financial institutions such as pension funds and insurance companies, who then rent out their purchases for use by others. In turn, these end-users themselves see the properties they rent primarily in economic terms, as devices to help the cost-effective operation of their own businesses. Less obviously, but more pervasively, all real-estate properties have particular generic characteristics – not shared with other commodities – which make it very likely that all who buy them will have their future economic performance in mind, at least to some extent. First, they last for a very long time: in Britain, for example, it is estimated that only about 1 percent of the building stock is replaced each year, which implies that buildings are currently expected to last about a century, on average, before they are replaced. This means that there is a high probability that the original purchaser of any particular property will, at some stage, want to re-sell it. Second, real-estate properties are also far more expensive than almost all other commodities, so the eventual resale value is a very important matter. Everyone who buys a property has to be concerned about its likely economic performance over time.

In the private sector, then, producers and buyers alike are powerfully affected by economic rules. If they break these, then sanctions of bankruptcy await them. But what about State agencies? State agencies, after all, produce a certain amount of urban form themselves. And through town planning processes, they also affect what private-sector developers do. With the recent worldwide reduction in welfare state activities, the most important State involvement in producing urban form concerns the infrastructure, such as major roads, which are so important in the urban milieu. Infrastructure decisions, of course, are made partly on social grounds, but there is a powerful economic component here too. Indeed, with increasing global and regional economic competition, State decisions about the allocation of resources are increasingly driven by economic considerations of the most competitive kinds.

The same competitive constraints affect the practical operation of town planning controls. Here too, State agencies are often forced to accept that they need development more than the developers need them. Faced with the "OK, we'll invest in South Korea instead" line, from increasingly foot-loose capital, they too are gripped in the pincers of profit-oriented economic rules. And they are often backed in this by voters who become more and more worried about such issues as unemployment and falling property values, particularly in the de-industrializing rust-belt areas which form so prominent a feature of those countries which came early on to the industrial scene.

[. . .]

States, then, have commonly grown weaker in terms of their capacity to control local and national economies, and in practice we typically find some kind of alliance – if often an uneasy one – between the profit oriented private-sector developer, State agencies at the local and national level, and many voters too – that "alliance of classes, structures and social forces" which, for shorthand, Stuart Hall calls "the power bloc" [in much of the US literature, this equates with the "Growth Machine"]. The power bloc typically supports private-sector developers, and therefore helps them make a powerful impact on the vocabulary of types in good currency and on the wider production cultures through which these are defined as good design.

We must not, however, drift into economic determinism here: none of this means that either the typological vocabulary or the wider aspects of production culture are completely determined by the private-sector developer's economic requirements. The typification process is ultimately a process of negotiation and struggle, in which all the protagonists have at least some power, no matter how limited, to affect the outcome on the ground. As I know from my own experience, for example, well-organized community groups are often far from powerless, whilst design professionals always have at least some degree of autonomy in the form-production process, because they carry out complex work requiring personal judgment which it is difficult for others to control with any rigor. The power of those who might oppose the power-bloc, however, is limited; and the potential which it confers, in terms of working towards better-loved places, has to be carefully targeted if it is to make any significant impact. Attempts to use it in ways which run counter to developers' own profit-centered interests will be strongly resisted, so it is important to attempt this only where developers' interests really are inimical to getting better-loved places on the ground. If we are to avoid frittering away our limited resources in needless conflicts, we have to know as much as possible about which aspects of form-production culture support private-sector developers' interests, and so present likely barriers to change.

It is not too difficult to grasp the economic rules which private-sector developers have to follow, in capitalist situations, if they are to make enough profit to stay in business. There has been endless (often critical) discussion of these matters for more than a century, and the broad principles at least are widely known. But how do these economic rules relate to form-types and to the wider form-production culture within which these are situated? It is these far more difficult questions which are addressed herein.

The typological level of urban change can be viewed as a process through which new types develop near the surface of production culture, generated in relation to a matrix of relatively stable, long-lasting "deep" morphological elements, which are embedded in and guaranteed by legal institutions, and which constitute the basic "building blocks" which make typological changes possible within the social system concerned. To understand the typological changes of the capitalist era, therefore, we must first grasp the nature of the morphological elements which underpin them. Amongst the long-running morphological elements which the capitalist form-production process took over from earlier times, the most deeply institutionalized are those which underpin and constrain the making of profits. Profit-oriented developers themselves are concerned primarily with those elements of built form which can be bought and sold: plots of land, and the buildings and associated outdoor spaces which are developed on them to increase their market value. If the production of urban form were left entirely to the efforts of particular profit-oriented developers, however, there is every likelihood that their individual impacts would lead to an overall situation whose unplanned nature would have unprofitable disadvantages for them all. From the overall profit-generation point of view, therefore,

the attempts which central and local governments make to control developers' individual efforts, so as to maintain the competitiveness of the whole settlement in the global market place, are also crucial to keeping the capitalist development process going. Also of central importance, therefore, are the morphological elements around which government agencies focus their attempts to control development – the overall settlement which forms the area of jurisdiction itself, and the patterns of public space and land use within it. In the next section we shall focus on the ways in which this range of long-running morphological elements is called on to generate particular types of settlements, public space networks, patterns of land use, plots and building developments during the capitalist era.

[. . .]

PROFIT AND PLACE

If we want to understand how built form supports the current holders of economic power, in capitalist situations, we have to start by exploring how capital is put to work in the economic system. In as near to a politically "neutral" definition as we are likely to find, the *Oxford English Dictionary* defines capital as "wealth in any form used to help in producing more wealth." To understand how wealth itself can be employed to produce more wealth, we have to explore what is sometimes called a "capital accumulation process." In essence, this process can be thought of as a series of transformations. First wealth (in the form of money) is converted into supplies of raw materials and labor, bought as commodities in the marketplace. Second, these are then converted into some other saleable commodity. Third, this is then converted back into money by taking it to the market for sale.

For this process to be profitable, the final amount received from sales has to be greater than that with which the process began. When this happens, so that the process concerned is profitable enough to be worth setting up as an on-going enterprise, the original linear chain of transformations becomes a recurring cycle. This is the "capital accumulation cycle"; following the lead of Peter Ambrose. . . . This cyclical process has an important time dimension. The more often capital is cycled through the system the more it can grow. The quicker each cycle can

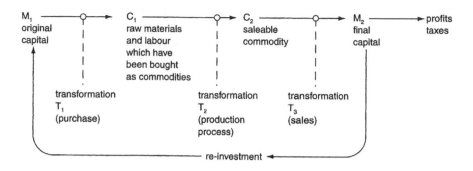

Figure 1 The capital accumulation cycle.

be completed, therefore, the faster the stock of capital will grow, giving the enterprise concerned an advantage over slower-cycling competitors.

Built form has direct effects on the speed and cost-effectiveness of the three key transformations in the capital accumulation process at two related levels. First, it forms the physical setting for the production and sale of all sorts of commodities, acting as what Henri Lefebvre calls "productive apparatus of a giant scale." This gives built form a potential economic value in the capital accumulation process, which in turn creates the opportunity, at a second level, for producing built form itself as a commodity which can be traded in the marketplace, and for developing the profit-oriented businesses of construction and property development through which so many urban places are produced.

When they make market decisions, those with capital to employ in these built form businesses will be drawn towards the particular working practices and the particular aggregate settlement patterns, public space networks, plot developments and interfaces which they see as offering the best opportunities for capital accumulation. It is these, therefore, which become abstracted to the level of "types" within development culture, and developers will defend them against less profitable proposals. To understand which types are likely to be abstracted and defended in this way, we have to explore the relationships between built form and the capital accumulation process in more depth.

The potential for capital accumulation in this process of property development arises from its three key transformations. The only potential for built form to affect profits, therefore, comes through any impact it may have on how these transformations are made. Of course, any given pattern of built form – or any working practice involved in producing it – might affect all the transformations in the capital accumulation process: the transformations themselves are not discrete "things," but merely significant moments in a continuous process. Proposals for forms or working practices which have a disadvantage in terms of the cost-effectiveness of any particular transformation (for example by costing more than their competitors, in materials or labor) may therefore still be implemented by developers, if they can eventually be sold for a disproportionately high price to offset these extra costs. It is the cost-effectiveness of the overall "package" of transformations, rather than that of any particular transformation in isolation, which is the key to understanding why profit-oriented developers choose one particular form or working practice rather than another.

In this chapter we shall explore how physical forms, considered as commodities to be traded in the marketplace are affected by the developer's search for the most competitive ways of making the three key transformations. As an analytical device for grappling with this highly complex process, we shall consider the three transformations one by one. First we shall explore the initial transformation from money into land, labor and building materials. Then we shall go on to investigate how these are transformed into saleable building complexes. Finally, we shall analyze the way these complexes are turned back into money in the marketplace.

TRANSFORMATION ONE: LAND, LABOR, MATERIAL COSTS

In the first of these transformations, the materials and workers needed for property development have to be brought to building sites which are geographically fixed. At the dawn of the capitalist era, pre-industrial transport limitations meant that labor and raw materials could only be purchased within a small geographical area near to the building site itself. Developers were therefore able to buy these prerequisites of production only in restricted markets, and in consequence there were only limited opportunities to shop around. All things being equal, any method of widening the area within which land, materials and labor could be purchased, for example through transport innovations, would be attractive to developers. This wider marketplace would increase competitive pressures on landowners, workers and the suppliers of raw materials alike, which in turn would lead to reduced unit costs for producers. Provided the cost of the transport innovation which created the opportunity for these savings was less than the savings themselves, then the innovation concerned would find a ready market.

Given the business opportunities this created in the transport field, it is hardly surprising that the last two centuries have been marked by an explosive proliferation of transport and communications innovations, from canals through railways, buses, automobiles and aircraft to the fax machine and the information super-highway. These increasing links between profitable production and processes of innovation in communications technology have had dramatic impacts on the repertoire of types through which urban form is generated.

Transport impacts on land availability

The first of these impacts is felt through the effects of transport innovations on the availability of the building land which, as the fundamental raw material of the property development process, gives real estate its unique character as distinct from other commodities. In order to survive in the capitalist marketplace, most landowners have to maximize their productivity in competition with one another. With the expansion of communications possibilities, markets for saleable buildings are created at ever-increasing distances from established centers. Each new communication innovation creates the potential for a further spread of development wherever demand exists, or new demand can be created. Landowners and land buyers alike are therefore attracted to ideas for settlements with ever-greater levels of dispersion. The pattern of land use at a smaller scale, within the settlement, has also been transformed through this market dynamic. In the competitive marketplace, landowners are only prepared to sell land to the highest bidder. Any developer wishing to acquire a particular site must therefore bid higher than the competition, whilst still ensuring that the development will generate an adequate profit overall.

Specialized as they are, however, not all developers can afford to bid to the same level. The price which can be paid, whilst still achieving an acceptable profit, depends on the particular developer's estimate of how much the finished project will fetch in the marketplace. In turn, this will depend on a forecast of the amount any likely purchaser might be willing to pay in the location concerned. For any particular location, different developers specialized in the production of space for different types of purchasers will make different forecasts. There is likely to be a considerable disparity between what (say) a well-to-do house buyer and a small manufacturer seek in terms of location, and this will be reflected in the different amounts they will be willing (or, perhaps able) to pay to locate in any particular place.

The price which purchasers are able to pay depends on their economic situation: typically, for example, profitable companies or rich individuals will be able to outbid their poorer counterparts for a given amount of space. All things being equal, therefore, only the richest of all the users who might want to locate in a particular area will in practice be able to do so. Over time, this has led to a marked change in the pattern of urban land use.

In pre-capitalist situations, this pattern was highly constrained by the reliance on feet and on animals for transport. Everything had to be near to everything else, which meant that there was no practical alternative to a fine grain of mixed land uses: housing near work, shops and cultural facilities. In contrast, the dynamic of the capitalist land market, set free by the increasing mobility made possible for those who could afford transport innovations, led over time to an ever-broader zoning of land uses, so that purchasers of space who had different levels of buying power become more and more segregated from one another within the overall settlement fabric.

The growing scale of development

The practical logistics of the way land is acquired for development also has important implications at the smaller scale of the individual development site. Developers seek economies of scale in land acquisition; they are drawn towards the largest suitable sites they can afford. As their available capital increases, through the successful operation of the capital accumulation cycle over time, there is therefore a tendency for the average size of development sites to grow. This has important effects on all the morphological elements with which we are concerned. First, it brings about changes in the walls of public space. In pre-capitalist cities plot widths were typically narrow, so that as many plots as possible could take advantage of the accessibility offered by the network of public space; and each plot was occupied by a different building. There were thus frequent entrances on to public space, and also a high level of visual complexity as each building differed, however slightly, from its neighbors.

With larger plots and buildings, these characteristics change. First, since most buildings have only one entrance each, any given length of wall now has fewer entrances, which reduce the liveliness of the public space edge. Second, any given building now has a wider frontage on to public space. Since the distinction between one building and another is usually very noticeable, this too changes the character of the walls of public space, which become simpler in their visual organization. . . . More generally, increases in plot size open the door for transformations in site layout. Small sites, hedged in by their neighbors, permit innovation only at the scale of the individual building; issues of how public access should be arranged, for example, are already fixed. As sites get larger, there are still fixes around their edges: any new development has to join up with the rest of the world, which is beyond the developer's own control. Larger sites, however, have a greater proportion of inner area which is under

the developer's control, as compared with edge which is not. This allows for innovations far beyond the scale of the individual building; for example to encompass new ways of structuring the public spaces which are required within large sites. Effectively, the practical constraints which bound cities for millennia to particular patterns of urban form become at least partially dissolved by the ability to seek for profit at this larger scale.

Labor costs, design specialization and deskilling

One of the most powerful factors governing the way these new opportunities have been taken up in practice is concerned with increasing the cost-effectiveness of labor. This is crucial for profitability, because labor costs are embedded in the costs of all the other commodities which are used for production: the costs of extracting and processing raw materials, and of making machinery and buildings to house production processes, in addition to the direct wages of those who carry out the processes themselves. If we add up all the cumulative labor costs involved, we shall find that they form an extremely large proportion of all the costs of production; some theoreticians of the left, indeed, would say that all these costs can ultimately be reduced to the costs of labor.

Labor costs, then, are crucial for individual companies; but it is important to realize that in these days of global competition they are also crucial at the level of the State, because of the great influence of labor costs on the market competitiveness of the products produced in any nation state. In this situation it is vital, for the market competitiveness of any State, or any enterprise within it, that labor operates as cost-effectively as possible.

Because labor costs are so important, developers constantly seek new working practices to gain competitive advantages. When labor innovations are offered in the marketplace, therefore, those which are most cost-effective in developers' terms are likely to be replicated, eventually to become typical. This encourages a continuous economic rationalization of the services on offer, through a process of ever-increasing specialization, in which broad and complex working tasks are split down into ever-narrower parts, enabling a greater degree of specialized expertise to be applied to each particular aspect of the development process. Developers themselves are not immune from this pull towards specialization. Increasingly, they produce space for particular specialized market sectors – particular types of housing, offices, shops or whatever. Within the complex division of labor which is generated through this process, the skills of innovation are particularly important to developers: faced with intense competition, they are always open to new ideas. This means that there are potential profits to be made from putting innovations on the market. This potential, in turn, sets the scene for working practices geared specifically towards innovation in the form-production process.

This is very different from the pattern of pre-capitalist working practices, in which the majority of run-of-the-mill proposals for built form were put forward by craft workers. The ability of craft workers to innovate was restricted by the fact that they made little distinction between what we would nowadays call "designing" and "making" in their work. Existing types of buildings, structural systems and constructional details were inextricably interlocked, and were embodied together in the worker's repertoire of practical skills. If major innovations were proposed, the whole package had to be relearned.

This did not mean that *no* innovation was possible. There was always the potential for innovation in small details, which therefore became the focus of aesthetic attention in this vernacular process. Innovation was needed at a larger scale too: since each particular building site must to some extent be different to all others, craft builders were constantly faced with new situations, and had to adapt their interlocking package of types from site to site. Overall, however, the potential for innovation in this process was limited by the fact that all the information used was tacitly embedded in the types of forms and working practices themselves – there were no abstract "principles," except the minimum needed for site-to-site adjustments. The prerequisite for more rapid innovation, with its inherent market appeal to developers seeking competitive advantage, was the abstraction of these principles from the tacit working practices of the craft approach, and their ever-wider extension, to develop a new working practice in which "design"

became conceptually separated from "making." Those who developed such a skill found a ready market amongst developers, so the history of capitalist property development is marked by the ascendance of "designers" to prominent positions in the form-production process as a whole.

The first designers, in this formalized sense, were architects; but they, of course, were not immune from pressures towards offering ever more specialized and rationalized working practices in the competitive marketplace. As each new service was offered, it had to be sold to potential buyers as something different from all the other services already on offer – it had to develop its own "unique selling point," emphasizing the factors distinguishing it from its competitors. Through this process, various architects found markets for more specialized expertise; giving rise to new types of engineering, surveying and so forth. To maintain differences between these new specialisms was easy enough, because they covered different areas of expertise. It was more difficult, however, to distinguish them from the more "generalist" approach of architecture, their original parent, since architecture had always included some degree of expertise in them all. The distinction here was made through emphasizing the new practitioners as "experts," as distinct from the generalist "artist" architect – a move with which architects had to concur, to preserve a unique selling point for themselves in this competitive situation.

For their own economic survival, experts and artists alike have to offer their products and services in as wide a marketplace as possible. Calling on the growing sophistication of communications technologies, as important here as in other sectors of capital accumulation, and taking advantage of opportunities offered first through imperialism and later through the development of a global economy integrated beyond the borders of former empires, those designers who have proved most successful in the marketplace – whether as experts or as artists – have progressively shifted their radii of action from a local through a regional to an increasingly global scale. This shift has led to important changes in the nature both of expertise and of art, as designers in all fields seek knowledge which can be used to underpin design practice anywhere around the world, creating a demand for increasingly general and abstract design cultures, uncoupled from particular local traditions of art or expertise, and from such considerations as local climates and building materials.

The disembedding of this global design culture from local particularities makes innovation easier in every local situation. Though profit-oriented developers need innovations for their own market survival, however, they do not want *everyone* in the development process to be innovative, because of the inherent difficulty of controlling creative workers who have complex skills. To make the process easier to control, developers are therefore drawn to new working practices which call for less creativity from those workers who are "makers" rather than "designers." This attraction is reinforced by the fact that less skilled workers are more easily replaced, and can therefore command only lower wages in the marketplace. The upshot of all this is that the creativity demanded from the designer is counterposed to a radical reduction in the creativity which is required from most other form-production workers.

Once under way, this deskilling process gains momentum by the way it interacts with the typification process. First, designers invent new forms which do not require craft skills. These forms are then bought in the marketplace. In this new context it becomes less and less rational, in economic terms, for workers to invest the time and effort required to acquire these skills in the first place. In turn, this makes it more difficult for any designers wanting to use craft skills in their buildings to find workers who can carry them out. By the 1920s, for example, the British architect Laurence Turner was bewailing the fact that:

> The average masons who frequent builders' yards in London are without experience and without knowledge of their craft, except in the performance of the simplest of their duties. To give them fine masonry to do would be to court disaster. It is not their fault, the work is not required from them. They lack experience.

The effects here were compounded by the fact that designers, themselves competing with one another in the labor market, were under constant pressure to reduce their fees. This made it more and more difficult for those designers who still wanted to use

a "crafts" vocabulary to take over, as part of their own work, the detailed design decisions which could no longer be made by skilled craft workers.

More and more designers, therefore, became attracted by typological innovations which did not require such skills; so the demand for them fell still further, in an accelerating spiral of deskilling. The effects of this process at the typological level were geared-up by the design media of magazines, museums and so forth. [. . .]

This interaction between economic pressures on the designer in particular, and the deskilling of the workforce in general, has led over time to a radical shift in aesthetic focus. In the vernacular process, where innovative creativity could only be focused on the small-scale details, it was these which received much of the craft worker's aesthetic attention, leading to a rich variety of detailed expression within relatively constant building types. With the shift from craft to design, however, innovation could be focused on the whole building, whose overall form now received the aesthetic attention which had formerly been restricted to the details. With cost-restrictions on the production of large-scale drawings, it became ever more difficult to focus aesthetic attention on the small details, which therefore became considered effectively as by-products of the whole, relevant largely to the technical rather than the aesthetic sphere. This dynamic fostered (and was, in turn, reinforced by) an ever-increasing simplification in the vocabulary of detail-types, [. . .] generating designs which require the production of the minimum number of drawings at the smallest feasible scale, within a rationalized, rectangular discipline – drawings which can readily be produced on the drawing board or through computer graphics systems, with the minimum of expensive hand work.

As we can see from all this, the developer's search for design innovations to improve the cost-effectiveness of the first transformation from money into labor, land and building materials clearly has radical implications for all types of labor. These implications feed through to affect not only built form itself, but also the relationship between all those involved in the form-production process on the one hand, and on the other hand those who will eventually use the results of their work on the ground. Before the rise of the speculative development process, during the period when most buildings were produced for particular known purchasers, there was a very direct, personal relationship between each purchaser and all those involved in the form-production process. With the onset of speculative markets, this link became increasingly indirect. Except for rich people building houses for their own occupation, for example, the process of innovation was now controlled primarily through considerations of market competition, and the acceptability of any particular innovation came to be judged almost entirely in terms of its capacity to help the developer survive in the competitive marketplace. What we see here, then, is the gradual opening-up of a "producer–consumer gap," with important consequences which we shall later explore in more depth.

Clearly, we can now see that the developer's drive to spend money on labor in the most profitable way has a wide range of important consequences for the form-production process. But what implications does it have for the other, inanimate commodities such as building materials which are also involved in this first transformation?

Cost impacts on material choice

When they (or their designers) choose materials in the marketplace, developers are attracted to those which they regard as having the best balance between on-site cost and sales impact. This does not necessarily mean that they will buy the cheapest materials, but it does mean that they will want to get any given material as cheaply as possible. The purchase price of materials at their point of production is crucially affected by two related factors. One is the labor cost of producing them. The other is the economies of scale which come from large-scale production. The developer is therefore likely to be attracted by materials which are produced by cheap labor in large quantities. As we have seen, however, this attraction is tempered by transport costs. Building sites are fixed in their geographical locations. The sites where building materials are produced, from factories to quarries, are also fixed; so materials have almost always to be transported from where they are produced to where they are used. Since even the lightest and most compact of building materials are heavy and bulky by comparison

with most other commodities, transport costs have important impacts on the cost-effectiveness of the materials concerned.

In the early years of capitalism, low-technology transport led to delivery delays and to transport costs which were necessarily high in relation to the cost of materials at their place of production. These factors usually limited developers and designers to locally produced materials, so the "zoning" of materials took place at a fine grain, often with much variation between one relatively small region and its neighbors. As innovations in transport technology came on-stream during the capitalist era, bringing the potential for reductions in transport costs, developers were enabled to draw materials from ever wider areas; to take advantage both of the availability of cheap materials-production labor in particular areas, and of increased economies of scale in production. This has led to a situation, fostered by the increasing globalization of design culture which we have already remarked, in which the materials produced in the largest quantities, with the greatest economies of scale in their production, are likely to be used over large geographical areas. At its extreme, this has fostered an internationalization of materials use, on the one hand concentrating the production of high added-value components in the so-called "first world," and on the other effectively buying cheap labor from the developing world for first-world building sites.

In rich countries, even the smallest of projects is nowadays affected by this global market. Whilst writing this chapter, I have been helping my son refurbish his house. In this tiny Oxford project, we have used rooflights from Denmark, plasterboard from Germany and Ireland, tiles from Thailand and Chile, and timber from Russia. In no case were these materials selected for exotic appeal – they were just the cheapest, reasonable quality items available. In larger projects, however, further economies of scale are possible if designers draw sparingly on this international palette of materials. Larger discounts can be achieved through buying large quantities from a small range of materials, rather than small quantities across a wide range; and this gives economic advantages to schemes which employ few materials.

Overall, then, the shift to a capitalist form-production process has carried with it radical changes in the way building materials are employed; with implications both at the largest and the smallest scales. At the scale of the overall settlement, we have seen a shift from locally produced to globally produced materials. At the scale of the individual building, however, materials are usually chosen from this wide range in restricted ways. This gives rise to a shift from a pre-capitalist situation in which, with rare exceptions, all buildings within a given settlement used the same materials palette, to one in which neighboring buildings can differ widely in the palette they employ. On the one hand, large-scale variations disappear; on the other, variations between particular buildings intensify. Everywhere becomes more and more varied, just like everywhere else.

To summarize, this analysis of the transformation from money into land, labor and materials – the first transformation in the capital accumulation cycle – has yielded a range of useful insights into the dynamics of profitable form. We have seen how this transformation entails a radical division of labor within the production workforce, associated with a separation between "designing" and "making"; entailing a polarization of creativity in work-patterns as designers – specialized as "experts" or "artists" – focus on innovation as a core skill, whilst a radical deskilling affects the tasks of others. We have noted how the materials used in construction have shifted from local to global in their geographical origins, but with only a restricted range being used in any particular building project. We have seen how settlement forms have become ever more dispersed, and how land use patterns have moved from a fine grain of mixed uses to a broader zoned pattern of segregation. And we have registered the ever-increasing scope for radical innovation which comes from the increasing size of development sites. All this is very revealing. Let us probe deeper, by analyzing the second key transformation in the form-production process: the transformation from labor, land and materials to the finished building complex.

TRANSFORMATION TWO: PRODUCTION PROCESSES

As long as capital is locked up in land, materials and labor, it is not circulating through the capital accumulation cycle, so it is not generating a profit.

It is therefore extremely important to the developer that the process of converting these commodities into a saleable product should take as short a time as possible. This requirement for rapid construction has important form implications.

First, it supports innovations which allow as much construction as possible to be carried out under efficient factory conditions, rather than on messy and inconvenient building sites, often at the mercy (at least in the countries where capitalism began) of the vagaries of the weather. In principle, this draws developers towards innovations which employ prefabricated, factory-made components. The attractiveness of such components, in developers' terms, is increased by the fact that they hasten the process of craft deskilling. From the mid-nineteenth century, for example, the possessors of craft skills found themselves competing with machine carving and pressing techniques, even in a period when developers and their designers still wanted to use the detailed vocabulary associated with a craft-based construction process. Clearly, this accelerated the relative decline in craftsmen's wages, and gave another twist to the deskilling spiral.

Factories producing prefabricated components, however, are inevitably limited in number, relative to the number of building projects which might potentially use their products. This disparity is increased when component-factories, themselves capitalist businesses seeking their own economies of scale, increase in size but decrease in number over time. Because both factories and building sites have fixed locations, prefabricated elements will often have to be transported long distances to the sites where they are eventually used. This transport process is disproportionately expensive in the case of large, heavy elements; so in practice small components such as tiles, bricks, lintels, doors, windows, staircases, cladding systems and the like, are far more common than large assemblies. Given this restriction on the scale of prefabrication, it becomes doubly important, in profitability terms, that the on-site constructional processes should be based as far as possible on simple, rationalized assembly techniques. Again, innovations which make this possible will have a double attraction to the developer, since simple assembly techniques can be implemented to an adequate standard by deskilled, easily disciplined workers.

The developer's desire to use workers in the most cost-effective way supports design innovations which involve repetitive building tasks, where identical construction procedures can be repeated many times in the course of a single building contract. This has a double impact on economic efficiency. First, the repetition of constructional tasks, which can never be completely deskilled, allows workers to speed up production and increase productivity, thereby reducing unit production costs, by spending more of their working time higher up the learning curve for the operations concerned. Second, it permits easier control of the whole production process. The storage and handling of materials, for example, is simplified as the variety of materials is reduced, whilst management is eased if design separates the work of the various trades so that no worker is delayed by waiting for another to finish. Attractions like these were already obvious to many actors in the development process by the beginning of the twentieth century: "Economical considerations require that as far as possible there should be a repetition of parts," as Cornes put it, in relation to housing development, as early as 1905.

If developers are attracted to innovations which generate these extra profit-potentials, architects have an equal motivation to propose them in the first place. This was already clear by the 1930s as the British architect H.S. Goodhart-Rendel saw:

> if we wished to build now in [an] informed and unhurried manner, we should find its cost prohibitive, not to the employer but to the architect. Just as in building itself, our methods have changed owing to the enormously increased cost of labor in relation to that of materials, so in practice we now must save all we can of the principal's time and that of his draftsman if any profit at all is to be got out of the six per cent fee.

Seventy years later, when the days of a 6 percent architect's fee seem like a far-off golden age, these pressures are intensified indeed.

Taken together, all these innovations allow a given size of building to be constructed with less design time, and less time spent in the production of construction information, than would be needed for a more varied repertoire of materials and constructional tasks. Not surprisingly, the capitalist era has seen an ever-widening range of such innovations, abstracted into the repertoire of detail-types

in good currency. Applied to ever-larger projects, as developers used the ever-growing availability of investment capital to gain economies of scale in production, this changed typological repertoire has further reinforced the reduction of close-up complexity endemic to the urban landscape in capitalist times.

To summarize, this analysis of the capital accumulation cycle's second transformation, from land, materials and labor into a saleable building complex, has given us further insights into the characteristics of modern urban form at an architectural level – an architecture of rationalized, deskilled construction techniques, using the minimum range of different details and materials in ever-larger projects. To complete this exploration of the form-production process, we have to consider the form implications of its final transformation – converting the completed project into money by selling it in the marketplace.

TRANSFORMATION THREE: SALES

The marketed product consists of a plot or plots of land, with built fabric on it. Only these can be sold as commodities; and it is only these, therefore, from which profits can potentially be made. Public space, in contrast, cannot be traded in the market. Cities, however, are deeply involved with processes of communication and exchange; and even in these days of the information super-highway, public space is still a key medium through which these processes take place. For the city to work in these terms, public space has to be freely available to all – free in the economic sense as much as (perhaps rather than) the political. If public space cannot directly be used to make profits, then it has no direct economic interest to developers. This means that it will be produced as a by-product of other commodities, such as buildings and cars, which *can* be used to generate profits. This "by-product quality" was already noticeable to the Austrian architect Camillo Sitte, for example, as early as 1889:

> In modern urban planning the relationship between built and open space has been reversed. In the past, open space – streets and squares – created a closed and expressive design. Today

the building plots are arranged as regular self-contained shapes, and *whatever is left* becomes street or square.

Given the increasing potential for very large schemes, however, there *is* scope to make profits through attempts to commodify the spaces which connect together the various buildings within them. This process involves a shift from the highly connected grid of streets, typical of the pre-capitalist city, towards introverted "enclave" spatial types such as culs-de-sac, malls, atria and the like, which can be given spectacular sales appeal . . . , and whose common characteristic is summed up in the word "exclusive" which is so often found in the real estate ads.

With all the building fronts facing inwards onto the enclave, this typological shift leaves only the backs of the development as a whole facing onto the outside world . . . , a transformation which sets the final seal on the "left over" quality of public space itself. Through the cumulative effects of this process, the public space network is transformed from a highly connected grid into a tree-like hierarchy, and the capitalist city as a whole is transformed into a series of islands, with spectacular interiors, set in a "left over" sea. Within these islands, developers are interested primarily in building plots and what is built on them, and they have to sell these to make as much profit as they can. This means that they are drawn to innovations which seem likely to improve sales appeal in the speculative market-place. Sales appeal must partly depend on prospective purchasers' individual preferences. Unlike bespoke producers, however, speculative developers cannot take these directly into account, since they cannot know the particular purchaser in advance. Speculative developers are therefore attracted to innovations which offer a wide and generalized market appeal, and are suspicious of idiosyncratic schemes. "Yes, *you* like it, and *I* like it, but will it appeal to anyone else?" is the kind of question which will have been heard many times by anyone who has worked in this field.

Building specialization and resale

The desire to avoid anything idiosyncratic leads to a homing-in on "market norms" through the typification process, guided by market signals, which we already explored. To understand more about market norms, and to grasp the economic value they have for those who buy them, we have to investigate the common factors which influence buyers when they make their market choices. As has been pointed out, buildings have particular characteristics which make them different from other commodities which are bought and sold in the market. First, by comparison with other commodities, they mostly last much longer. Second, they are much larger: large enough to influence the workings of the capital accumulation cycle by forming the settings for the production, distribution and sale of most other commodities. Third, they mostly cost more. All these characteristics have important implications for the market choices which building-buyers make.

In today's dynamic social systems, the longevity of built form means that any building is probably far more permanent than its users' social arrangements. For instance, British home-owners moved house on average about every six or seven years during the 1980s, and even now do so on average every twelve, whilst any particular house may well last a hundred years. This means that the house might be lived in by anywhere between eight and sixteen different households, and the members of each, when buying it, know perfectly well that they will be faced with the need to re-sell in due course. The purchasers of buildings for other, non-residential uses – buildings which often cost even more – will usually have to face this situation too. Given the high costs involved, and aware of this need to re-sell, purchasers of all sorts of buildings will be attracted to forms which seem likely to hold their value, at least until the next resale takes place. Like the building's original developer, therefore, each of its successive potential purchasers during its long life will take into account the extent to which it conforms to their own concept of a widely saleable "market norm."

These characteristics of market norms are themselves strongly affected by their perceived suitability for housing particular uses. Where buildings are bought to house processes of production, distribution and exchange, purchasers will clearly be attracted by those which seem to offer the best balance between purchase price and promises of economic efficiency. The first of these promises is offered by the building's location, which affects the economic efficiency both of bringing raw materials and labor into production processes, and of sending finished commodities to the point of sale. This reinforces the importance of all sorts of communication and transport systems, and underlies the well-known dictum in development industry folklore that "there are three key factors in profitable development: location, location and location."

In deciding whether to purchase a building in a given location, entrepreneurs will clearly be influenced by its capacity to promote the economic efficiency of the production or sales processes which they want to carry on within it. Its influence on the cost-effectiveness of labor has particular importance here: as we have seen, labor forms a major proportion of overall business costs. Physical design has an important effect in this regard. Building layouts or arrangements of equipment which are inconvenient for particular processes of production or sales can slow workers down, whilst more convenient arrangements make it possible for the same tasks to be done faster. Developers are therefore drawn to innovations which increase cost-effectiveness: layouts molded to support the particular processes concerned.

This has had a marked impact on the range of building types in good currency. Pre-capitalist settlements usually contained a relatively small number of highly adaptable types, in each of which a range of particular processes could, with some compromise, take place. This pattern has progressively been replaced with one which contains a far wider range of more specialized types, formed and named for particular uses. By the late nineteenth century, as the American architect Henry van Brunt noted in 1886: "The architect, in the course of his career, is called upon to erect buildings for every conceivable purpose, most of them adapted to requirements which have never before arisen in history."

As the speed of change affecting processes of production circulation and exchange increases, however, there is a limit to the proliferation of specialized building types. The problem here is that the processes housed in any building now often change quite radically within the economic lifespan of the building itself, with the ever-present danger that the building's form might begin to reduce

the efficiency of the processes within, rather than supporting them. Increasing dangers therefore arise when building interiors are tailored too tightly to any given pattern of activities. Adaptability and flexibility become watchwords now, and the vocabulary of building types in good currency represents the balance which is struck, at any particular time, between the specialized design which is needed to accommodate particular activities, and the flexibility required to allow for unpredictable change.

Purchasing or renting

The third characteristic which distinguishes buildings from other commodities – their higher purchase price – has further implications for purchasers' choices. Many purchasers, requiring space but faced with this expense, prefer (or are forced) to hire [rent] rather than to buy. This is particularly true for the most expensive types of property, such as commercial buildings in central locations, where demand for scarce space in the best locations has pushed prices highest. Most purchasers in such locations, therefore, buy buildings as investments for letting to others. Developers producing such buildings are therefore attracted to innovations which have particular investment advantages.

In deciding whether or not to buy a particular building investment, potential purchasers will take account of two main factors. The first is the financial return: how much money will end up in the investor's bank account each year, after all the costs of getting it have been allowed for? But this is not all that matters: a second key factor is the financial risk involved. How widely will the building appeal to likely purchasers or tenants? Will the location keep its appeal? These are the sorts of questions which prospective investors have to address. And in answering them, to choose between buildings which generate the same level of income, investors will be drawn towards those with the lowest management costs and widest market appeal, in locations which seem most likely to improve their letting prospects over time. Since investors will pay more for such buildings, developers will be attracted towards them too. What do these characteristics imply for physical form?

When buildings are let to tenants, some management costs are always present. These are likely to rise, all things being equal, as the number of tenants increases. This is partly because there is more effort involved in finding the tenants in the first place, in drawing up leases and in collecting the rents. But it is also because of the greater likelihood of disputes over the day-to-day running of the building, particularly if the tenants concerned are engaged in different kinds of activities: "how can you expect me to impress my clients when we get the smells from the restaurant kitchen all the time?"

Attracted by low management costs, potential investors are therefore drawn towards simple buildings with single tenants, rather than intricate ones with large numbers of small tenants involved in a wide range of different activities. If, through particular economic circumstances, no single tenant can be found to occupy all the space, it may in practice be necessary to let the building to a number of small occupiers. Even if this is known early in the development process, however, there is still an investment attraction in designing it so that it can eventually accommodate a single, larger tenant, should the opportunity arise in the future. The design, therefore, will be substantially the same as if it had been designed for letting as one unit in the first place. This creates further pressures towards the proliferation of single-use building types and towards market norms; but if all developers have the same market norms, why should any purchaser be attracted to one developer's product rather than another's? How can any developer steal a march on the competition?

The desire for positive appeal in the market, without falling into the trap of producing "idiosyncratic" schemes, attracts developers towards forms which have their own "unique selling point" – forms which stand out with a clear individual character, to be noticed by potential purchasers. To the extent that this can be achieved, to produce forms which are seen as "unique" by potential purchasers, there is always the potential of selling them for a monopoly price. There is a tension here, however. If the developer's product is too "individual," it may put off prospective purchasers, who fear it may have too narrow a resale appeal. If it is too "normal," then it runs the risk of not being noticed at all amongst its competitors. At one level, the profitability of development is about the balance between these poles.

Attracting attention

In almost all urban cultures, from all historical periods, there are two common ways in which all kinds of "important" buildings have been given forms which stand out from their neighbors. First, they are often physically separated from adjoining buildings, to take on a free-standing pavilion form. Second, they are often higher than the buildings around them. Developers seeking a unique selling proposition, with widely appealing connotations of importance and prestige, are therefore drawn to the tall free-standing pavilion type when other economic factors permit. [. . .]

Applied across a wide range of use-types, from family houses to office towers, this shift from connected building masses to the free-standing pavilion form has radical impacts on the character of public space. First, public spaces become less enclosed: not only are there gaps between the pavilions, but also they are often set back from the edge of the public space, separated from it by a band of private open space to set off their connotations of prestige. This makes it hard to perceive the public space itself as a positive "figure" in the urban scene. Now it is the buildings which stand out as figures, against a neutral "ground" of public space – that, of course, is the whole point of this shift, from the developer's perspective. At a typological level, the composition of the public space network changes from "streets" and "squares" towards a more generalized type of "space."

THE RESULTING FORM OF CITIES AND DEVELOPMENT

The story we have pieced together so far, through exploring the dynamics of the capital accumulation cycle, has proved a complex one. To get into sufficient depth to make our exploration useful, we have had to make all sorts of analytical distinctions between factors which, in the real world, are linked rather than separate. In conclusion, we have to pull together the overall patterns we have found.

In the course of our exploration, we have uncovered transformations in the types of forms and working practices in relation to every physical scale within the overall settlement. The overall settlement pattern, for example, has become ever more dispersed, whilst the typical pattern of land use has been transformed from a fine grain of mixed uses towards larger "zones" of single use, with increasing social segregation. The nature of public space has changed in two important ways: first from connected "grids" to introverted "enclaves," and second from "streets" and "squares" towards a more generalized type of "space." Building types have become more and more specialized in their intended uses, and the number of building types in good currency has consequently undergone a radical increase. In their physical massing, buildings have been transformed from constituent elements in a generalized, highly connected mass into separate, free-standing pavilions, whilst the typical size of building project has radically increased. The interfaces between buildings and the public spaces which adjoin them have increasingly shifted from "active" to "passive" in nature. Finally, at the smallest physical scale, the surfaces of buildings have also undergone radical transformations. They have shifted from a "local" to a "global" use of materials, and they have changed from complex to simple, in terms of the patterning of the various elements from which they are composed. And, in parallel with all these physical transformations, making sense of them and reinforcing them, we have seen the rise of designers as "experts" and as "artists" operating with an increasingly generalized and abstracted design culture in an increasingly global marketplace, in parallel with the gradual deskilling of most other workers in the form-production process.

These typological shifts support the operation of the capital accumulation cycle, so the current holders of economic power will want to defend them against profit-reducing changes of direction. But we must not drift into economic determinism here; these typological changes are produced not by "the economy" but by the very real people who are involved in the form-production process – a process which is shot through, in practice, with conflicts and contradictions. For anyone to make profits at all, the process which makes capital accumulation possible has to be reproduced through time, and this does not happen automatically. The current holders of power are constantly on the lookout for ways of helping this reproduction process to survive, in the face of the conflicts and contradictions which threaten it.

"Urban Dualities in the Arab World: From a Narrative of Loss to Neo-Liberal Urbanism" (2011)

Yasser Elsheshtawy

Editors' Introduction

Globalization is commonly explained as a series of international business linkages, a quickening time-space compression and shrinking of the planet, and worldwide economic restructuring that delinks manufacturing from decision-making. We should also remember that globalization is far from a new phenomenon, and can be seen in cross-continental empires throughout history: from Rome's reach across Europe, North Africa, and western Asia, to the global colonizing experiences of Britain, France, Spain, and Portugal. In contemporary practice, we see cities assuming different structural roles as the global economy restructures. Building from multiple global network theories that now exist (see various selections in *The City Reader, fifth edition*. Richard T. LeGates and Frederic Stout, eds, Abingdon, UK: Routledge, 2011; by the following selection authors: Saskia Sassen, Manuel Castells, Brenner/Keil, or Beaverstock/Smith/Taylor), some cities will retain their roles as command and control centers (e.g., Tokyo or New York) whereas others will become finance and banking centers (e.g., London or Hong Kong). At the other end of the economic ladder, cities will continue to supply affordable labor pools (e.g., Manila or Bangalore), continue as extraction and production centers (e.g., Johannesburg or Guangzhou), or struggle under the weight of their urban poor, who are often living in slum conditions (e.g., Lagos or Mumbai). To ensure increased accumulation and some degree of economic resiliency, it becomes a common urban strategy to compete for a more advantageous position in this global hierarchy and diversify one's economic base. Thus, beyond single function strategies, we see cities transforming themselves to keep up, speed up, and wise up. However, all this restructuring results in unexpected interurban contestations between classes – as people jostle for space, get displaced, seek political access, and colonize new areas within the city. A concern for urbanists, regardless of global location, is the increasing economic polarization (wealth gap) that descends upon urban areas everywhere with respect to the triumph of neo-liberal economic attitudes.

Dubai and Abu Dhabi are fascinating examples of global urbanization: how resource wealth, real estate development, tourism investment, and globalization can create cities in the blink of an eye. While Dubai has a longer history of urban establishment (as a small port and trading city) than Abu Dhabi (which was a mere palm thatched beach village at mid-century), both these cities have basically sprung up over the last few decades. The United Arab Emirates achieved independence from Britain in 1971 and was established as a country of semi-autonomous royal sheikdoms for defense purposes. In the years since the first export of oil in 1962, the advantages of vast resource wealth have enabled these so-called "insta-cities" (places that seemed to appear out of nowhere) to morph into legitimate metropoli. While the term "insta-city" is seen now as pejorative, the rapid development of these Gulf coast cities is impressive: Doha, Kuwait City, Manama, Muscat, Dubai, Abu Dhabi. Each used a different development strategy for achieving its goals – and the results vary widely.

Both Dubai and Abu Dhabi were largely developed by government parastatals directed by members of their royal families. Dubai is the great example of mega-projects colliding across the coast of the Arabian Gulf – the city is fragmented, confusing, and hard to fathom in scale. Abu Dhabi took a more integrated planning and infrastructure approach and is being studied by city planning students around the globe. Where Dubai has chosen to hop on the global "treadmill of superlatives," for example, the tallest building, mall-oriented ski resorts, seven star hotels, palm tree-shaped peninsulas, and new canals cutting through the desert; Abu-Dhabi is focused on becoming a place of global culture, education, government, and sustainability. Abu Dhabi's pace of physical development is also rapid – and its ambitions are just as impressive as Dubai's – but much more coordinated with respect to the overall structure and livability of the city. Both of them continue to capture the imagination – if not for their physical accomplishments, then, for the contrasts in wealth between minority Emirati citizens and the 80 percent + of the population who are disenfranchised guest workers living in far more Spartan conditions. These cities become perfect examples of both global spectacle and global polarization, but also examples of varied development strategy.

Yasser Elsheshtawy proposes that these global strategies are indicative of the ongoing modernization of Middle Eastern cities since the nineteenth century. In this new writing, he reinforces basic globalization themes, but also suggests these development strategies result in a narrative of loss – similar to the effects of gentrification in other boomtowns. He encourages critics to abandon orientalizing or "Arabian Nights" fantasies with respect to these new Gulf coast cities. Those exoticizing ideas are more aptly associated with tradition-based urbanisms found elsewhere in the Middle East. Instead, Elsheshtawy theorizes that Dubai and Abu Dhabi need to be seen within the evolving discourse on globalization: places of disenfranchised immigrant communities, the widening wealth gap, the expansion of slums, Darwinian winners and losers. Both cities also exhibit physical characteristics of the global city: neo-liberal urbanization, mega-projects, gated communities, and splintering of the city into places of rich and poor. Rather than illustrating this globalization with the well-published examples of spectacle, he opts instead to show what happens to a local residential community and a cherished market when they fall victim to global ambition. In the Dubai neighborhood case, the recent economic downturn saves a community of everyday life spaces, and forces reappreciation of modest urban qualities. In the Abu Dhabi case we see erasure of the market and its replacement with a souk-like high-end shopping mall that doesn't quite replicate the authentic experience of the original place. These cases offer lessons and cautions about over-generalizing these cities as mere global phenomena, when in fact they remain places of sentiment, local history, real people, and everyday reality.

Yasser Elsheshtawy is an Associate Professor of Architecture at United Arab Emirates University in Al Ain, Abu Dhabi-UAE. He teaches architectural history and design studios. He is the editor of two books on Middle Eastern urbanism and design: *Planning Middle Eastern Cities: An Urban Kaleidescope in a Globalizing World* (London: Routledge, 2004) and *The Evolving Arab City: Tradition, Modernity and Urban Development* (London: Routledge, 2008). The new writing in this selection further develops chapters in these books on Dubai and Abu Dhabi. His book on the growth and development of Dubai illustrates the dynamics of global urbanism in the Middle East more fully: *Dubai: Behind an Urban Spectacle* (London: Routledge, 2009).

The global spectacle of Dubai and the planning innovations of Abu Dhabi have received different amounts of attention. For material on Dubai's global ambitions and urban design see: Ahmed Kanna, *Dubai, the City as Corporation* (Minneapolis, MN: University of Minnesota Press, 2010; Stephen J. Ramos, *Dubai Amplified: Design and the Built Enviornment* (Farnham / London: Ashgate / Design and the Built Environment, 2010); Christopher M. Davidson, *Dubai: The Vulnerability of Success* (New York: Columbia University Press, 2009); and Syed Ali, *Dubai: Gilded Cage* (New Haven, CT: Yale University Press, 2010).

For readings on the development and design of Abu Dhabi, see the following: Christopher M. Davidson, *Abu Dhabi: Oil and Beyond* (New York: Columbia University Press, 2009); Mohammed Al Fahim, *From Rags to Riches: A Story of Abu Dhabi* (North Charleston, SC: Booksurge Publishing, 2008); Jo Tatchell, *A Diamond in the Desert: Behind the Scenes in Abu Dhabi, the World's Richest City* (New York: Grove Press, 2010); and Victoria Hockfield, *A History of Abu Dhabi and the United Arab Emirates* (Hockfield Press, 2010). To see the planning documents of Abu Dhabi's primary planning agency, the Urban Planning Council, please refer to: http://www.upc.gov.ae/?lang=en-US.

For general material on the Arab-Islamic city and modernism, see: Sandy Isenstadt and Kishwar Rizvi (eds), *Modernism and the Middle East: Architecture and Politics in the Twentieth Century* (Seattle, WA: University of Washington Press, 2008); Abdulazia Y. Saqqaf (ed.), *The Middle East City: Ancient Traditions Confront a Modern World* (St. Paul, MN: Paragon House, 1987); Khaled Ziadeh and Samah Selim (trans.), *Neighborhood and Boulevard: Reading through the Modern Arab City* (Basingstoke: Palgrave Macmillan, 2011); Besim Selim Hakim, *Arabic-Islamic Cities* (New York: Columbia University Press, 1986), and *Arabic-Islamic Cities: Building and Planning Principles* (EmergentCity Press, 2008); and Hisham Mortada, *Traditional Islamic Principles of Built Environment* (London: Routledge, 2003).

The word "Arab City" evokes a multitude of images, preconceptions and stereotypes. At its most elementary it is for many a place filled with mosques and minarets; settings characterized by chaotic, slum-like developments; a haven for terrorists; maze-like alleyways; crowded coffeehouses where people sit idling their time away smoking a *nerghile*; sensuality hidden behind veils and *mashrabiy'yas*. But it is also a place of unprecedented development, rising skyscrapers, modern shopping malls; unabashed consumerism. Most importantly it is a setting where one can observe the tensions of modernity and tradition; religiosity and secularism; exhibitionism and veiling; in short a place of contradictions and paradoxes. Each of these characterizations plays into clichés about what constitutes an Arab or Middle Eastern city. At the same time, arguments are made that there is a divide in this region between newly emerging cities (the Gulf) and the traditional centers – a form of "Gulfication" or "Dubaization" in which these new centers are influencing and shaping the urban form of "traditional" cities. Counter arguments are made that cities in the Middle East and North Africa are influenced by a variety of cities and regions throughout the world and that the relationship is far more complex than a one-way, linear directionality.

The Arab/Middle Eastern city is thus caught between a variety of worlds, ideologies and struggles. At its very essence it is a struggle for modernity and trying to ascertain one's place in the twenty-first century. Certainly colonialism did play a large role in defining the region's direction in the second half of last century, but that influence has largely faded. Traditional colonial powers have left, and new ones have taken their place, spurred in large part by globalization and neo-liberal economic policies.

Transnational institutions such as the World Bank and the International Monetary Fund (IMF), the increasing flow of labor in the form of low-income workers as well as highly paid consultants, are exerting a substantial influence – which could be felt at the level of architecture and urban development. Similar to what took place in the former colonial city, reserved for the colonizing power, cities are now configured to cater to the rich. Low-income inhabitants are excluded and relegated to the fringes – slums, labor camps and the like. High-end developments, luxurious shopping centers, gated communities have become defining features of the contemporary Arab city, much like what is taking place elsewhere in the world.

Many of these issues have been endlessly debated in global city theory. For example the notion of *exclusion* is being presented as a characteristic of world globalization (e.g., Friedman and Wolff, 1982; Marcuse and Van Kempen, 2000; Sassen, 2001). Furthermore, an essential component of world cities discourse is the construct of *networking*. Cities are conceived as lying on a network, and research is directed at ascertaining the level of connectivity – a *space of flows* opposed to the *space of places* as developed by Manuel Castells (1996). Along that same vein, the impact of network infrastructures on city form affirming the connectivity among cities and the fragmentary nature of contemporary urban structures was investigated as well (e.g., Sassen, 2002; Graham and Marvin, 2001). However, a number of critics have pointed out that the typical global city discourse has left out many cities – they are "off the map" – and increasingly have been calling for an examination of "marginalized" cities. A central construct underlying these developments is the notion of transnational urbanism in which urbanizing processes are examined from "below," looking at the lives of migrants, for example, and the extent to which they moderate globalizing processes, a form of low-end globalization (Robinson, 2002; Peter-Smith, 2001; Mathews, 2011). The global city discourse – whereby certain cities are offered as a model to which other cities must aspire to if they are to emerge from "off the map" – is essentially in dispute. Underlying all these critiques is the work of urban sociologist Janet Abu-Lughod (1995) who has written extensively on Middle Eastern cities and has reminded us that globalization needs to be placed in its proper historical context.

My aim in this writing is to discuss the development of Arab urbanization through this prism. Rather than engaging in a typical Orientalist discourse which has defined the discussion on Arab cities throughout the last two decades – essentially blaming the West, former colonialists, Israel and so on for all the ills that have befallen Arab societies – I would like to offer an alternative view: one that reframes the debate in a way that places more responsibility on Arab citizens, policy makers, planners and architects. Moreover, an underlying premise is that all that is taking place in our cities follows from, and is a response to, globalizing conditions occurring all over the world. I begin though with a brief historical overview, showing the rather limited, and limiting, margin within which this debate has been framed.

FRAMING ARAB CITIES

Starting from the 1970s, much of the typical architectural/urban narrative of the Middle Eastern city was a narrative of loss. This has been influenced by discourses concerning postmodernism and critical regionalism which centered on a revival of a historical dimension of the built environment, and moved away from modernizing discourses which had dominated much of the twentieth century, (e.g., Frampton, 1983). Within the Middle East this acquired another dimension due to colonization. Thus within this narrative arguments were made that a great, once flourishing civilization has through colonization been subjected to plundering and exploitation of resources – cities are therefore in a perpetual state of underdevelopment. Finding

theoretical backing through the work of Edward Said on Orientalism this became a rallying cry for urbanists and architects, strengthened by the emergence of the Arabian Gulf, and Saudi Arabia in particular, as a center for the debate concerning what came to be known as "Islamic Architecture" and the revival of terms such as "The Islamic City."

Accordingly such readings of the Middle Eastern city show it as an isolated entity somehow disconnected from developments occurring elsewhere in the "civilized" world. The city was always examined in relation to, and in association with, "heritage," "tradition" and "culture," as if it were divorced from any surrounding reality. Furthermore, the "Islamic" perspective became a framework through which every single decision was evaluated, judged and criticized. All developments taking place were framed within such an outlook, even in their interaction with "modern" counterparts. Examples are numerous but perhaps the work of Saudi scholars, Saleh Al-Hathloul and Jamil Akbar could be considered representative in this regard. They attempted to establish a legal framework through which the Moslem city emerged and developed. Various decisions pertaining to the built environment were thus always referred back to religious texts. Conferences in the 1980s and 1990s further legitimized these approaches, focusing on such constructs as the "Arab" city and the extent to which its "glory" could be revived by tying it to cultural/religious roots (e.g., Serageldin and El-Sadek, 1982). Attempts at modernization and development were constructed vis-à-vis such a framework.

These conceptualizations were based on a certain assumption, namely that the "Moslem" (Arab) has been unable to develop, grow and in turn modernize – in short go beyond the twelfth century, the pinnacle of Moslem civilization. S/he is thus condemned to remain within this historic perspective. This, of course, has been the Orientalist reading of the Moslem/Arab mind initially exposed by Edward Said (1978) from a literary perspective, but developed further by writers such as Zeynep Çelik dismantling the colonial French discourse in Algiers, and Timothy Mitchell exploring colonial policies in Egypt just to cite a few. Continuing this trend Nelida Fuccaro (2001) in reviewing urban studies in the Gulf region called for a comparative perspective both grounding urban settlements within their regional contexts and studying the "specificity" of each – thus moving away from the "static ideal type" of the "Islamic city." Her analysis showed that there is a body of research which examines Gulf cities from a sociopolitical perspective, showing that urban forms developed in response to unique contemporary conditions. She keenly noted, however, that grounding the city within the "Arab-Islamic cultural domain" serves among other things "processes of political legitimization."

Significantly these approaches show that Arab cities have been part of modernization efforts from the nineteenth century to the present. While being subjected to colonialism, they nevertheless were able to grow, develop and contribute to urbanization. Urban forms unique to each city were developed, responding to larger "global" issues. Even within the current discourse on globalization, the Arab city has responded in a unique manner which illustrates that it is not just an "Arabian nights" fantasy – but a real, vibrant, cosmopolitan entity which does not differ from anywhere else in the world – whether in the aspiration of its citizens or in their daily struggle to make a living, as exemplified by the events of the "Arab Spring" which took place in urban centers. These events have also shown that the exclusively "Islamic" reading of such cities is – to put it bluntly – outdated and counterproductive. Heritage and culture are vital issues, but they should not be the sole, or dominant, factors through which the Middle Eastern city is studied and analyzed.[1]

Instead there are much more relevant issues shaping the urbanization discourse in the Middle East. These pertain to neo-liberal urbanization policies, increased levels of migration, the proliferation of slums and informal settlements, an intensified gap between rich and poor, and higher levels of inequality. A particularly pressing question, which needs to be explored further, is the extent to which the Arab city has responded to, and engaged with, this shifting discourse concerning cities in the region. Moreover, should this shift away from the "narrative of loss" that has defined urbanization studies in the last century be viewed as a positive development and a catalyst for change? And what role does the rise of cities in the Arabian Peninsula play in all of this? I will explore this in more detail in the following section.

PROBLEMATIZING CITIES IN THE ARAB WORLD: NEO-LIBERAL URBANIZATION AND RISING INEQUALITY

One of the significant factors affecting urban development in the Middle East is what have come to be known as neo-liberal urbanization policies. These are based on the Washington Consensus originating in 1989, which constituted a set of policies liberating markets from state intervention and aimed for the most part at economies in developing nations (e.g. Newman and Thornley, 2005). Cities were particularly receptive to this, leading to what David Harvey (2006) has called "geographies of exclusion," that is, the creation of enclaves within the city. Others have dubbed this neo-liberal urbanization, whereby the city is being re-configured to cater to the rich and powerful at the cost of low-income city inhabitants, a development characterized as being inherently "evil" (e.g. Davis and Monk, 2008). Obviously this has taken on many forms and underwent changes as these policies were applied in different cities. If we examine the Arab city, this becomes even more problematic given varying geographical, political and financial contexts. Thus, the rich cities of the Arabian Peninsula cannot be compared to the declining traditional urban centers of the Middle East – yet given the interconnectedness in the region influences and exchanges do take place. In this section I will be examining this in more detail looking at the extent to which neo-liberal urbanization has impacted the Arab city in its varying manifestations. I will first show how the concept of the global city has been closely tied to neo-liberal transformations; my focus then shifts to an overall view of the Arab city and the degree to which it is tied to the global city discourse.[2]

The global city discourse in the Arab world

Within classical global theory the notion of a "Global City" indicates a city that concentrates financial services, acting as a command and control center for the rest of world. Three cities in particular are singled out: London, New York and Tokyo. While this concept can be attributed to many scholars, the work of social geographer Saskia Sassen is typically cited in this context. However the whole notion of *a* Global City is highly problematic and has undergone many transformations. Neil Brenner and Roger Keill in their introduction to the *Global City Reader* have argued for a contextualization of world city research and global city theory. This was largely supported by an emerging body of research at that time, focusing on marginalized cities, and a realization that local agents shape and interact with global processes. Herbert Marcuse and Robert van Kempen for instance noted that cities engage in globalizing processes in different ways and accordingly have introduced the more appropriate term *globalizing cities*.

Space is transformed in these cities to cater to a consumerist society; transnational migrants and so on. The most visible manifestation of the sizeable new consumer elite is the striking transformation of the city center to be found in virtually all our cities. Offices, hotels, luxury housing, and up-scale shops and restaurants have displaced low-income residents (Gugler, 2004; Zukin, 2010). Another aspect of this phenomenon is spectacularized urban space, and the steps cities have taken to attract foreign investment by engaging in image creation (e.g. Haila, 1997). As a result real estate investments have become important tools in this, which ties in with the work of geographer David Harvey (2006) in his examination of entrepreneurialism and urban governance favoring entrepreneurs at the expense of inhabitants. Peter Marcuse (2006) discusses spatial patterns in cities and the extent to which they have changed due to globalization (if at all). For example, one outcome is a variety of juxtaposed and sometimes overlapping residential cities and a city of unskilled work and the informal economy.

From the preceding it is clear that the concept of the global city is multi-layered, and more importantly has evolved significantly since it was introduced. For the purposes of this chapter it is useful however to highlight a few issues pertaining to this concept as it impacts urban space which would be of direct relevance for urban design in Arab cities, as I will discuss in the next sections. They are: enactment of neo-liberal urbanization policies; proliferation of megaprojects and gated communities; and the "splintering" role of infrastructure networks. The following is a brief elaboration on each of these:

Neo-liberal urbanization

One of the key changes occurring in cities due to globalizing processes is the relative decline of the nation-state and the increasing turn towards the private sector as a main actor in development. This can be seen through the proliferation of NGOs in various countries, and the emergence of powerful real estate companies who are increasingly shaping the skylines of globalizing cities. In that vein, governments are engaged in a process of selling public assets – such as land formerly occupied by the military – to foreign (and local) developers. Of course one drawback is that the role of the state in providing and ensuring welfare for its citizens is increasingly in decline – thus further exacerbating inequality. Another phenomenon related to this – prompted by the free flow of laborers, ideas and capital – is the increased reliance on foreign experts and consultants. Based for the most part in western societies, they bring their own expertise and background which influences and shapes many of the developments taking place in the region.

Megaprojects

Cities are assuming a powerful role, and as a result of such processes they are increasingly being viewed as a product that needs to be marketed. These marketing efforts involve attracting headquarters or regional branches of international companies and staging of "mega-events."[3] Other projects include luxury housing, dining establishments and entertainment amenities to attract the professional personnel required to operate these global activities. Urban projects are used to act as a catalyst in further encouraging investment and tourism such as trade centers, conference centers and hotels. Looking at the Arab world this is one of the most visible manifestations of change taking place in their respective urban centers.

Gated communities

This is perhaps one of the most significant issues impacting urban form in the region. Insecurity due to the increasing influx of migrants, for example, and economic disparity are resulting in the abandonment and stigmatization of certain neighborhoods, the development of an *architecture of fear*, and the gradual establishment of so-called "fortress cities" and "cities of walls" where response to crime has led to spatial transformation; thus changing parts of cities into protected enclaves and "no-go areas" separated by high walls, gates, electronic surveillance cameras and private security guards (UN-HABITAT, 2007; Caldeira, 2000). Another aspect of this relates to socio-cultural considerations, namely the desire of various groups to live in homogeneous areas. The wealthy thus assert their identity and status by living in clearly distinguishable neighborhoods and communities separated from the main city, or within enclaves in the city. These can be found in various cities in the region, ranging from the informal urban conglomerations of Cairo punctuated by exclusive hideaways, to the meticulous cityscape of Dubai more or less defined by its exclusionary urban form.

Splintering cities and the role of mobility

According to Graham and Marvin (2001), the contemporary city is characterized by a new "landscape infrastructure" containing embedded normative visions and social bias, which cause an "unbundling of infrastructure networks" which sustain the fragmentation of the social and physical fabric of the city. They have termed this phenomenon "splintering urbanism." Thus, the very tools of modernist planning become devices to further inequality: streets for the sole use of vehicular traffic; the absence of sidewalks; the "internalization" of shopping centers; and the prevalence of "spatial voids" isolating buildings by surrounding them with large parking lots. Examining the role of infrastructure within the Arab region would be particularly useful given that many cities are currently undergoing major transport initiatives.[4]

Having identified global factors affecting urban development in the region, ranging from enactment of neo-liberal urbanization policies, proliferation of megaprojects, prevalence of gated communities and the role played by infrastructure networks, I now turn to the extent to which these issues have directly influenced the region as a whole. In particular, the notion of inequality will be discussed in more detail.

THE CASE OF ARAB CITIES: UNEVEN URBANIZATION

The Arab city is not immune from these globalizing influences and their resultant patterns of inequality, which are observable not just within cities but also across cities in the region. Various economic statistics indicate that the pace of economic growth in the GCC (Gulf Cooperation Council) is stronger than the rest of the Arab world. Indeed, several indicators show an increasingly widening, and alarming, gap.

The total population of GCC countries was approximately 37 million in 2006, representing 12 percent of the Arab population of the Middle East and North Africa. However, the economy of GCC countries in 2006 accounted for more than 55 percent of the Arab world's $1.25 trillion economy. In 1995 the GCC countries had an average per capita income of $8500, which was 7.3 times larger than the remaining Arab countries. In 2006 the GCC per capita income rose to $19,300, which was 10.4 times larger than the average for other Arab countries. The per capita income in some GCC countries such as Qatar ($63,000) and the UAE ($38,000) was higher than many advanced industrial countries in 2006. By 2008 the average rose to $35,000. Moreover the economy is estimated to reach $2.3 trillion by 2020 according to McKinsey.[5] Latest figures indicate that the average GDP per capita in the Arab region is $8,200 USD whereas it has reached $75,000 USD in Qatar. This contrasts sharply with Yemen, standing at $2,090.[6]

The latest Human Development Index released by the UNDP in 2010 shows that there are only three countries from the region falling within the very high category: UAE (32), Qatar (38) and Bahrain (39). In the high category are: Kuwait (47), Saudi Arabia (55) and surprisingly Jordan (82). Medium includes: Egypt (101) and Syria (111). Egypt is ranked below African countries such as Botswana and Gabon. In the low category are Yemen (133) and Sudan (154). These numbers clearly indicate a growing gap between countries in the GCC – all of whom are ranked either very high or high, whereas the rest of the region is located in the lower groups. It is also interesting to observe that India is ranked at 119 – illustrating a very typical trend among newly emerging economies, whereby high economic indicators do not necessarily translate into improved lives and may even lead to greater inequalities.

Such divisions are of course based on oil wealth. As a result prior to 2008, estimates and studies projected a wildly optimistic picture. For instance the IMF noted that the bulk of the oil windfall would be invested in the region where more than $1,000 billion of projects were planned. A study by McKinsey at the time estimated that over the period 2005 to 2020 the Gulf is likely to have a $3,000 billion oil surplus, half of which will stay in the region, with another $750 billion or so of capital going into investments in the wider Middle East and North Africa.[7] These numbers have been largely modified, with many projects stalled or cancelled altogether. Moreover, the unfolding events of the Arab Spring are expected to change the proliferation and continuation of these projects.

Yet, it is clear that this "great divide" has and will remain, which will lead to many problems. Among them, an increased rate of migration from poor Arab countries and other regions as well to the richer ones in the GCC. This is particularly evident at the border between Yemen and Saudi Arabia. Every day, according to media reports, hundreds are sent back to Yemen, reaching hundreds of thousands annually. These include many who have come from Africa – countries such as Somalia or Ethiopia. They cross Yemen's deserts and mountains fleeing both war and hunger. Saudi authorities in an effort to curb this have embarked on a massive effort to secure their borders, using elaborate defense networks. Like the border between Mexico and the United States it has become symptomatic of barriers separating the rich and the poor.[8]

Looking at the rate of migration and labor mobility is another important factor. According to UN estimates the total number of migrants in the region has reached 28.6 million out of a total population of 352.2 million people. Income differences are the main drivers behind the movement of workers, as I indicated. The percentage of Arab workers in the GCC has significantly declined from 72 percent at the beginning of the 1970s to 56 percent in 1985, and 31 percent in 1996. Nowadays, according to data by the International Organization for Migration (IOM) the percentage is estimated to be around 25 percent. On the other hand the numbers of "economic" migrants from South Asia for example have increased. Additionally, there is also the issue of forced migrations – the region hosts 4.7 million refugees, including an estimated 2 million Iraqi refugees.[9]

The movement of these migrants across the region which is basically from those on the lower scale of human development to the GCC region has led to an intensification of spatial divisions in their respective cities. Accommodating such an influx – especially for those at the lower end of the scale – is done in specially designed labor camps or neighborhoods removed from the city center for example. At the same time the return of migrants to their respective countries has led to a boom in construction and real estate development that has adopted both the process and imagery associated with megaprojects and gated communities as they exist in the Gulf region. Significantly patterns of consumption acquired in the Gulf continue as evidenced in the construction of giant shopping malls for example, with many containing brands known in the Gulf. Thus these patterns of inequality have intensified as a result of the economic disparity that exists within the region, further adding to what one may describe as an "urban duality." I would argue that this is the single most significant factor affecting urban development in the region. Rather than being mired in past dreams of reviving past glories, what defines urban visions today is a market driven policy that aims at maximizing profit. Increased consumption and commodification of cultural traditions become one particular visible outcome of this. In the process, many are excluded or relegated to the fringes of respective cities. I will in the following sections discuss in greater details the extent to which this has manifested itself in two major cities in the region, focusing on the spatial impact of such policies.

CASE STUDIES: ABU DHABI AND DUBAI

This section looks at two important cities in the Gulf region: Dubai and Abu Dhabi. Both cities, while located within the same country, have adopted quite different urbanization policies and their degree of influence across the region has varied as well. Moreover, their enactment of globalization and neo-liberal policies is particularly poignant in relation to the discussion above. Dubai has of course been a beacon of sorts for all those aspiring to global city status in the Middle East, to the extent that the word *Dubaization* has become a term denoting the existence of a Dubai-based model of urbanization. The 2008 financial downturn has contributed to a slight dimming of this vision. Abu Dhabi, learning from its neighbor's mistakes, has taken a slightly more measured approach focusing on such catchy issues as environmental sustainability (Masdar City) or culture (the museum district in Saadiyat Island). The extent to which both cities have actually managed to effectively portray a modern mode of urbanism in the region is debatable and the following is an attempt at discussing this, looking at their historical development, urban vision, and a discussion of select projects.

DUBAI

Origins and urban development

In 1960, British architect John Harris was asked by the ruler to develop the city's first masterplan. The situation of Dubai at that time was quite primitive. The city had no paved roads, no utility networks and no modern port facilities. Water was only available from cans brought into town by donkeys. Traveling to Dubai from London took several days in unreliable piston-engine planes with overnight stops. Communication was also difficult. There were few telephones and cables were sent by radio. The masterplan developed by Harris aimed at rectifying this by addressing some fundamentals: a map, a road system and directions for growth. This initial plan would guide Dubai's development and be modified due to the discovery of oil in 1966.

Developments followed the Harris masterplan calling for the provision of a road system; zoning of the town into areas marked for industry, commerce and public buildings; areas for new residential quarters and the creation of a new town center. These rather modest goals were in line with the Emirate's limited financial resources (oil had not yet been discovered in sufficient quantities). In 1971, due to the city's expansion and increased

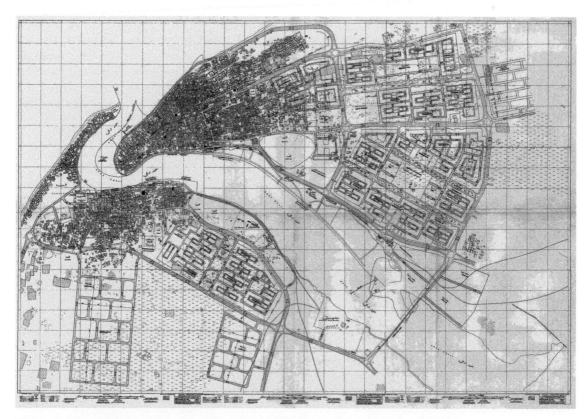

Figure 1 1962 Master Plan of Dubai prepared by John Harris (courtesy of Harris Architects).

economic resources a new masterplan by Harris was introduced. The plan called for the construction of a tunnel running beneath the Creek connecting Bur Dubai and Deira (the Shindagha Tunnel) and the construction of two bridges (Maktoum and Garhoud); in addition, the building of Port Rashid was also envisioned (Gabriel, 1987).

The late 1970s and early 1980s can be characterized as a period of rapid expansion (Al Shafieei, 1997). Of particular note was the emergence of the city's growth corridor along Sheikh Zayed Road towards Jebel Ali. Dubbed the "new Dubai," this area became the new commercial and financial center of the city. Numerous projects were constructed along this stretch of highway and the skyline of the city changed. These rapid developments are a result of increased resources and an attempt to provide alternative sources for revenue. Yet the main problem caused by these new axes of growth is fragmentation and the emergence of a city composed of disjointed archipelagos or islands. Furthermore, the speed with which some of these projects were constructed necessitated an approach that would not be based on a "rigid" masterplan – hence the development of the Dubai Structural Plan in 1995 whose main aim was to be flexible enough to accommodate any changes. Conceptually the Structural Plan is based on a series of nodes and growth axes, which, for the most part, account for the city's form as it appears today (also see Elsheshtawy, 2004b, 2010).

As a result of these various development plans with their primary focus on the efficiency of car movement, one of the first impressions of the city is its fragmentary nature. Dubai is composed of multiple, disconnected centers, which are separated by multi-lane highways. This precludes any meaningful pedestrian circulation or, for that matter, a conventional urban fabric which can only be found in the "traditional" areas of Bur Dubai/Shindagha and Deira. This *tabula rasa* type development has resulted in large gaps or patches between developments; vast expanses of sand which need to be filled. Thus the general feeling of the city in its present state is that of a construction site – it is still a work in progress – which no doubt has been further exacerbated by the financial crisis. Furthermore, lacking the high population density that would sustain such a momentous rate of building, many areas appear empty without a sign of life. Its

neighborhoods lack a sense of community – they have a transitory feeling.

Proliferation of megaprojects

Prior to the financial crisis, projects were announced on a daily basis, each attempting to upend the others in terms of size as well as architectural image. These include the waterfront development by Rem Koolhaas for the now infamous developer Nakheel. Here, a stylized version of Manhattan is planted on an artificial island next to Palm Jebel Ali. This particular project was portrayed in all seriousness by some observers as a model for a new urbanity in the Middle East.[10] Another project was Dubailand's Bawadi development – meant to evoke the Las Vegas strip and containing the world's largest hotel, Asia-Asia; or Palm Deira, 10 times larger than the original palm island; and the Universe, a series of islands resembling said universe located opposite the Jumeirah coast. The sheer folly of these projects – in some instances given legitimacy by the involvement of such architects as Rem Koolhaas – exposes the obsessive degree to which a flawed vision of urban development has been pursued. Ignoring social and cultural reality they never saw the light of day and have for all practical purposes been cancelled.[11] However, other projects and buildings came to define the city's rapid rise from obscurity and its appearance on the world stage and it is the focus on "tall" buildings that played a particularly important part in this.

One of the first architectural manifestations of modernization was the construction of the Dubai World Trade Centre, located at what was then the outskirts of the city, dating from 1979. For many years thereafter, indeed until the 1990s, the building was considered a major landmark in the city. The tower is even now known as Burj Rashid or Rashid's tower among locals, acknowledging the former ruler who initiated the project. The building itself addressed some regional concerns, its architecture responding to the harsh climate by the construction of a deep outer skin that moderates the intensity of light from the outside. In addition, the external features use triangular arches evoking "Islamic" or "Arab" elements.

The next building to emerge on the scene was the sail-shaped Burj Al-Arab. Another pair of buildings

Figure 2 Skyline of Sheikh Zayed Road in Dubai, dominated by super-tall buildings as seen from Dubai Metro.

using height to imply significance are the 51-storey twin Emirates Towers. Designed by Hong Kong based architect, Hazel Wong, who argues that the building is inspired by Islamic geometry and certain mythological constructs related to the sun, earth and moon, the towers' footprints consist of two triangles placed on a circular base. However, the buildings convey a high-tech, ultra-modern image, their sleek atria and speedy elevators visible from the main highway. This highway – Sheikh Zayed Road – also contains the World Trade Centre and passes close to the Burj Khalifa – the tallest building in the world (as of 2011). This particular project – designed by American based Adrian Smith, from SOM at the time – is interesting because a desert flower native to the region supposedly inspired it. Yet, statements attributed to the architect locate the tower's conceptual origins to the movie *The Wizard of Oz* and the emergence of a glass tower in the middle of a yellow field.[12]

Moreover, the tower has created its own context, spurring further developments around it such as a residential area called "Old Town" and a large mall.

All the buildings are located around an artificial lake. Advertisements for the project invariably draw comparisons with existing "famous downtowns" such as Manhattan, Paris and London. One could argue that this is a perfect example of a "Debordian" spectacle in a desert context – remote from any contextual relevance! Comparisons with existing record holders illustrate the sheer magnitude of the development and that the Burj has surpassed all of them.

The modernity discourse plays a prominent part in justifying the construction of such a gigantic building. Simply by placing this tower in Dubai, the city could proclaim itself to be truly modern, irrespective of the fact that it is designed by an American firm (SOM), built by a Korean construction company (Samsung), worked on by a plethora of Asian labourers, and that most of the apartments and hotels are purchased by an expatriate clientele. Regardless of this, the developers felt the need to contextualize the project and give it an "Arabian" touch, whether through some imaginary conceptual directions (a desert flower) or the creation of pseudo-Arabian districts, which are part of the overall development. Nevertheless it is important to point out that the tower is meant to show the emergence of Dubai as a regional powerhouse, enabling it to become a global city. Some local reactions do in fact suggest that the tower is a source of pride – both among Arab and local Emirati citizens – suggesting that "Arabs" do have the potential to develop such a project similar to others (the "West").

Satwa, and the failure of neo-liberal urbanization

Many of these megaprojects are envisioned in the desert or in the sea – away from any significant urban context – thus their impact on the city's social structure is somewhat limited. However, one particular interesting proposal concerns the city's district of Satwa – sandwiched between the ultra luxurious Sheikh Zayed Road, home of the above mentioned Burj Khalifa and Emirates Towers, and

the upscale residential district of Jumeirah. Initially home to locals who were given residences during the reign of the late Sheikh Rashid, founder of modern Dubai, it succumbed to migratory waves by its local population. As a result the residences were left to be occupied by South Asian and Filipino laborers, as well as a sizeable stateless (Bidoon) population – many of whom are Shiites. There are two parts to Satwa – divided by an active commercial thoroughfare. To the north of this dividing line is a middle class area, containing a mix of nationalities, and to the south, towards Sheikh Zayed Road, is the more run-down part. Composed of residences in various states of decay, it has a curious mix of outdoor seating areas, graffiti, informal gardens and Husseiniyas (Shiite religious buildings) – all in close proximity to the city's most visible landmarks. At night, according to popular perception, it becomes a haven for drug users and a place for illegal liquor consumption. Adding further to the tenuous status of the district is the presence of a large number of "illegals" – people who have overstayed their residency visa.

Figure 3 Skyline of Sheikh Zayed Road in Dubai, as it appears from the district of Satwa.

Given these conditions a decision was made by authorities in 2006 to raze the entire area to the ground and replace it with a luxurious mixed-use development. This wasn't merely about an island in the sea, but would have resulted in a massive relocation and exodus of its population, numbering about 100,000 – a huge number by Dubai standards. A model was unveiled during the 2008 Cityscape exhibition showing what was in store: canals weaving their way through the district, lined with indescribably shaped towers, surrounded by low-rise villas and gardens. The development – described as "utopian" by one of its architects, Gordon Gill – was named Jumeirah Gardens.[13] Prior to this unveiling residents had been issued with eviction notices and demolition work had seriously begun. Interestingly while all of this was going on filmmakers, artists and journalists lamented the district's destruction, portraying it as Dubai's version of Greenwich Village in Manhattan.

The Cityscape 2008 exhibition took place while the financial crisis was beginning to make its impact felt across the world. No sales were forthcoming and in the following months news about massive layoffs, collapse of financial markets and a halt to many projects heralded the end of the "Dubai dream." Jumeirah Gardens never left the ground – aside from a few demolished buildings, fences surrounding others and abandoned signage on the road. Residents began to return to their homes, and interestingly the partially demolished villas were for a while being used as shelter by an increasingly "homeless" population of construction workers.[14]

Satwa was viewed as a blight on the city's urban landscape that had to be wiped off. But, the financial crisis led to a paradigm shift with regard to viewing these spaces. A recent campaign advertisement by Emirates Airlines – a government-owned entity – shows a western tourist taking in the sights of Dubai moving between its various attractions. Among these is the district of Satwa. Our tourist walks among its modest houses, between teeming streets, and enjoys some ethnic eateries. During his walk he interacts with the district's residents. The advertisement seems to suggest a move away from merely focusing on its high-tech architecture and mega-projects. It aims to show that there is another, more humane, side to the city. It also shows that there is a return to appreciating and understanding the value of its everyday spaces – something that had been neglected in the city's feverish drive to establish some sort of relevance. There seems to

Figure 4 Scaled model of the Jumeirah Garden development during its unveiling at Cityscape Dubai, 2008.

be recognition that Dubai derives its uniqueness from precisely such settings. Or, some cynics may note, it is simply a marketing ploy meant to attract budget conscious travelers, as was suggested in a BBC Middle East business report.[15]

Dubai, in its overall development pattern – exemplified by the Satwa case – has become a byword for neo-liberal urbanization policies (e.g., Kanna, 2010; Vora, 2011). It has in effect become a guiding light, a frame of reference for the remainder of the region. Patterns of exclusion and an intensification of urban dualities are a by-product of this, which acquires more acute and serious dimensions in the region's traditional centers given the strong urban context and an absence of a *tabula rasa* type development. And while the vision of Dubai as a model has faded somewhat, new urban centers have engaged in similar approaches. Among these, Abu Dhabi is of importance given its proximity to Dubai and its adoption of urbanization policies that will apparently transcend anything Dubai ever envisioned, as I will discuss in the following section.

ABU DHABI

Overview of urban development

Abu Dhabi's urban trajectory took a slightly different path than Dubai. For one thing, it was considered a village of sorts, without any substantive urban structures, up until 1966 when its former ruler Sheikh Zayed initiated the city's urban development process. This entailed a complete eradication of the old city – mostly of mud huts and non-permanent structures. The city's road system of massive urban arterials was laid out along strict geometric lines following best practices at the time, forming incredibly large super blocks ringed by tower housing at their periphery; the center of these blocks left for low-rise housing for Emirati families and expatriate workers. Sheikh Zayed's vision of palm-lined boulevards and locally inspired villa architecture established a very different city than what was being developed in Dubai. The city grew exponentially, and in spite of these rapid changes, the extent of urbanization was measured compared to its neighbor Dubai. Indeed, up until 2004 – following the death of Sheikh Zayed – the notion of megaprojects was alien to the urbanization discourse.

Following the transfer of power, however, substantive changes took place aiming at transforming Abu Dhabi into a global player, which significantly impacted the city's growth and urban form. Chief among these was a change in the property ownership law, allowing the sale of government granted land by nationals, as well as introducing a form of ownership by foreigners.[16] Furthermore, even though Abu Dhabi had kept a low profile it invested its vast oil income through its main overseas financial arm – the Abu Dhabi Investment Authority (ADIA). Moreover, Abu Dhabi witnessed an increase in capital due to two factors: increasing oil prices and a changing political climate responsible for a move home of Arab money – a "repatriation of capital" – due to post 9/11 security measures in the West. Thus, according to reports at the time, "phenomenal amounts of liquidity produced by the current conditions have found a welcome home in real estate" (Oxford Business Group, 2006: 157). Projects ranged from entire new residential and tourist complexes to vast malls and town-sized commercial and industrial developments – as well as developing the vast number of islands surrounding the city.

In light of these massive developments the government of Abu Dhabi announced a modified masterplan – "Plan Abu Dhabi 2030: Urban Structure Framework Plan." The plan was developed by the Abu Dhabi Urban Planning Council (UPC); an institution created through the royal family to organize planning in the Emirate of Abu Dhabi, under the consultative advising of Larry Beasley, former Co-Director of City Planning for the City of Vancouver. Under the plan, the city is projected to grow to over three million people by 2030. A series of principles are outlined, emphasizing the city's focus on identity and sustainability. Thus the plan states that Abu Dhabi will be a "contemporary expression of an Arab city" and will continue its practice of measured growth, reflecting a sustainable economy. Furthermore it "pledges" to respect the natural environment of coastal and desert ecologies, and to manifest the role of Abu Dhabi as a capital city. The plan provides for large areas of new Emirati housing inspired by traditional family structures, and a diverse mix of affordable housing options for low-income (expatriate) residents. Land uses, building heights and transport plans for the city are specified as well.

Figure 5 Scaled model of Abu Dhabi according to its 2030 development framework, indicating all future projects.

This vision includes several megaprojects whose actual execution is in doubt given the general slow-down in the construction sector. Among the various projects proposed are: an expansion of the business district and the creation of new business and governmental centres; the Capital District, a massive 4,500 hectare development to be built 7km inland from Abu Dhabi; and Norman Foster's Masdar City, planned to be the world's first zero-carbon, zero-waste city relying entirely on renewable energy and recycling of waste. Its design has been initially envisioned as a walled city in the desert, where residents drive in, park at the periphery, and hop on personal-rapid-transit (PRT) to get to their destinations – all on a podium level below the city, which leaves the city's surface level primarily pedestrian. These utopian visions are currently undergoing revisions. Surrounding the development are solar panel fields, waste conversion and other sustainable infrastructure facilities. The project's location between the airport and one of the city's incredibly low-density villa suburbs undermines its

claim as a separate "city" and instead positions it as a well-intentioned urban experiment within the larger City of Abu Dhabi. Furthermore the city's islands are slated for massive development. Yas Island houses the Ferrari Theme Park and various sports and leisure attractions in addition to the futuristic Yas Hotel designed by avant-garde New York based architects, Asymptote. Saadiyat Island is being developed as a cultural island housing five international museums including the Frank Gehry designed branch of the Guggenheim Museum, and the Louvre Abu Dhabi designed by Jean Nouvel, among other museum designers such as Zaha Hadid, Norman Foster and Tadao Ando. Suwwah Island and Reem Island are emerging as main commercial and financial areas to supplement the existing Central Business District; while Lulu island – an artificial island facing the city's northern shores – will include a mix of residential, commercial and conservation areas. It should be noted however, that as of 2011, reports are suggesting that Abu Dhabi is shifting its focus away from real estate towards infrastructure projects such as the rail network, and the Emirates Surface Transport Masterplan (Oxford Business Group, 2011).

The notion of a paradigm shift in planning is no exaggeration. According to one report "the city as a whole, a mega project in itself, shall become gardens on the gulf shore adorned by bastions of glorious architecture."[17] However, such efforts raised a series of issues – among them whether there is a sufficient population to sustain these developments. Estimates in Abu Dhabi suggest that the population will increase to 800,000 and the number of visitors by 2012 will supposedly reach 3 million. Such estimates, based on pre-crisis studies, need to be revised, yet it is safe to say that within a span of 40 years the city has been transformed quite dramatically. However, this has also led to a series of problems, typical of rapidly urbanizing centers; among them an acute housing shortage and an increased cost of living. Furthermore, these projects have sparked a debate about what constitutes a proper Abu Dhabi identity and whether the city is only catering to tourists and transient residents – and perhaps most significantly the relevance of such developments within urban studies and in relation to the global cities discourse. To set this within a proper context, one project is representative of the changes taking place, to the extent that the past is constantly being re-invented and the city increasingly turning its back against low-income inhabitants. This project is the Central Market.

The Central Market and geographies of exclusion

Abu Dhabi seemingly lacks vibrant urban settings: its streets are lifeless, dominated by cars, and most public activities take place indoor in shopping malls. However, a particular episode in the city's march towards modernity illustrates the extent to which residents are able to reclaim some of its spaces and impose their own informal order; at the same time it also shows the degree to which authorities motivated by a desire for urban order as well as financial profit are willing to counteract these "informal" tendencies.

One of the memorable sights for anyone visiting Abu Dhabi in the 1990s was the Central Market nestled between high-rise buildings in its central business district. Entering it was like encountering a different world – a *Foucauldian Heterotopia* – composed of small, informal shops, low-income migrant workers – a sense of chaos contrasting sharply with the ordered appearance of its immediate context. It projected an air of provinciality and informality. The project was designed by Abd el Rahman Makhlouf in 1972, to replace an original market that was located nearby. Historic photographs of this original market show a ramshackle collection of huts and unpaved alleyways which in its primitive state was deemed unsuitable for a modern metropolis. Rather than engaging in a process of upgrading and conservation, it was decided to remove the original and build a new one, whose spirit evokes the traditional markets of Arabian cities. Addressing the city's primarily nomadic population, and in an attempt to settle them within an urban entity "each tribe was given a quota for shop space."[18] Even though references were made to Arab-Islamic principles the market was laid out along strictly geometric lines, following the general grid pattern of the city.

The project from its very outset – and in spite of its initial top-down design – was transformed by its users into a place that more closely resembled a bazaar, subjecting it to a certain level of informality. This informal character continued up until its demolition in 2005. Moreover the market was also a meeting point, a place of exchange and communication in a city where such open air spaces are a rarity. Yet, the very fact that within the ordered appearance of the surrounding business district and its gleaming towers, an informal, chaotic space like this could exist was disconcerting for city officials – hence the decision for removal.

Following a series of competitions Foster Architects was selected to design the market's replacement. The physical facts illustrate the sheer enormity of the project – standing in stark contrast to the original market, which was a humane, small-scale environment, fostering a sense of community and intimacy. This is exemplified by two high-rise towers clad in a shimmering, gleaming curtain wall dominating the Abu Dhabi skyline. The lower podium is covered in a lattice-like screen, evoking some sort of *mashrabiy'ya*, containing an upscale shopping mall called the "Emporium." In addition there is also a traditional market – replacing the original – which

Figure 6 The Central Market of Abu Dhabi prior to its demolition, 2004.

is basically an indoor, multi-storey, shopping mall, although its retail units replicate the old market's measurements. While the architects went out of their way to establish the project's historic credentials and that it will be the new heart of the city, a media director at Aldar, the developer, observed that everything possible was being done to keep the ambience and color of a traditional souq, but – and this is an important qualification – without the slightly chaotic qualities of a bazaar. Moreover, original owners will be compensated with shop space in the "new traditional market" – what is actually being sold though is subject to approval by the developer.[19]

Thus a significant transformation has occurred – from a small and dilapidated row of shops, which nevertheless catered to a very significant part of the population, to an ultra-luxurious shopping mall. What underlies all this, it seems, is a desire to exclude these elements which were in some way "spoiling" the modern metropolitan image that officials are trying to portray. There simply is no room for loitering Pakistani shoppers looking for a cheap bargain, or a gathering of Sri Lankan house maids exchanging news. As such this development by its very nature responds to the capital schemes depicted by David Harvey (2006) where he argues that capitalism favors a geography that caters to the rich and is based primarily on social exclusion – seen here in unmistakably clear terms. Moreover the project is symptomatic of the increased privatization of public space and the subsequent "sanitization" of urban settings (e.g. Elsheshtawy, 2008a).

The project was opened in 2010 and the open-air concept of the previous shopping area has been abandoned in favor of a conventional, indoor air-conditioned space. Significantly, the overall setting has the feel and character of a high-end shopping mall. Thus one finds a food court with the usual chain restaurants, souvenir shops and high-end retailers. Contributing to the sense of luxury is the high design quality of various construction details. Outside, some efforts have been made to connect to the street. A series of entrances from various roads lead to the ground floor and some store-fronts open to the outside as well. Benches in black granite are placed on sidewalks. Whether such a place could truly be the center of town as it used to be in the past is open for debate. Obviously for some segments in the population this has the potential to become a popular hangout, similar to many malls in the city. Yet for others it will never be the same again.[20]

In this discussion of Abu Dhabi I have chosen to focus on one project, the Central Market – given its historical origins, transformation and, perhaps

Figure 7 The newly designed Central Market project in Abu Dhabi, 2010.

more significantly, its actual completion and subsequent use. Its story is symptomatic of typical high-end developments taking place throughout the world – attributed to neo-liberal urbanization policies – showing both their success and their limitation. Yet clearly the city is engaging in many other ambitious projects – dwarfing the scale of the central market. While they are in various stages of planning and construction – some are on hold and others have been cancelled – the significance of Abu Dhabi's urban vision cannot be underestimated. If these projects are realized they are set to make the city one of the most important urban centers in the region.

CONCLUSION: THE RISE OF THE EAST

North and West and South up-breaking!
Thrones are shattering, Empires quaking;
Fly thou to the untroubled East,
There the patriarchs' air to taste!
> Johann Wolfgang von Goethe,
> *West-Eastern Divan*, 181

In the preceding sections I have attempted to narrate both Dubai's and Abu Dhabi's rise from obscurity to internationally recognized cities on their way to becoming major global centers. Their economic, cultural and urban initiatives have caught the imagination of writers, academics and urbanists. Yet their rise should not be seen as being merely an artificial and temporary growth fuelled by oil wealth – which is the common accusation directed at rapidly urbanizing cities, particularly those in the Arab Gulf. Rather, it is part of a much larger pattern witnessed within the last 25 years which has seen the rise of such cities as Mumbai and Bangalore in India, or Beijing and Shanghai in China, who have become major centers of trade and commerce; their cities are gleaming with newly built skyscrapers and shopping malls. As urbanist Joel Kotkin puts it "over the past 25 years, most of the biggest rail, road, airport and sanitation systems have been built not in Europe or America, but in East and South Asia, the Middle East and Brazil."[21]

Economists have been heralding the revival of a "new Silk Road" – the ancient trade route linking the Moslem world to China. In a forceful argument economist Ben Simpfendorfer (2009: 154) notes

that we are witnessing a "global historic rebalancing" which is due to three factors: the rise of the China growth model; the rise of Arab wealth funds; and the importance of geography – what he terms the rise of an "Islamic corridor." Cities will play a significant role in the revival of this new Silk Road. Iranian journalist Afshin Molavi argues that key "caravan posts" on the new Silk Road are regional economic "winners" or rising stars: Dubai, Beijing, Mumbai, Chennai, Tokyo, Doha, Kuala Lumpur, Singapore, Hong Kong, Riyadh, Shanghai, Abu Dhabi.[22]

Yet the rise of cities such as Dubai and Abu Dhabi has not been without its critics. Some arguments are made that these rapidly rising centers could never match the "flair" of global metropolises like Tokyo, London and New York which "have been able to hone the cultural amenities that make for a gracious urbanity."[23] Furthermore, according to architect Erich Kuhne (quoted in Kotkin) "these upstarts are often too busy building and trying to impress the rest of the world to focus on architecture or plan niceties to make the heroic routine of everyday life more pleasant." In much more severe language, leftist writer Mike Davis in a 2006 article on Dubai called "Fear and Money in Dubai" – an allusion to Hunter S. Thompson's novel *Fear and Loathing in Las Vegas* – argues, while using the writings of Marxist writer Baruch Knei-Paz,[24] that "backward societies" (and he is using both Dubai and China as examples) adapt products in their final stages of development without going through a necessary evolutionary process.[25] In his words "the arduous intermediate stages of commercial evolution have been telescoped or short-circuited to embrace the 'perfected' synthesis of shopping, entertainment and architectural spectacle, on the most pharaonic scale."

According to these readings Abu Dhabi and Dubai are "backward cities" whose entire urban development is based on oil wealth, and they are thus "artificial." They have no significance aside from being merely an amusing sideshow whose destiny is to be buried under the sand once the oil dries up. Aside from the rather pessimistic and extreme tone of such predictions they are prevalent to varying degrees of explicitness among many academics, journalists and observers of developments in the region. They hearken back to Orientalist conceptualizations, casting the Moslem/Arab region as an "other" that cannot seriously compete with the "advanced" West. However, it is critical to see the Arab Gulf in a different light to be able to develop a more balanced view and more significantly it is crucial to hear the voices of its citizens and residents who are familiar with its intricacies, daily life, and its aspirations and struggles. Cities such as Dubai and Abu Dhabi, unburdened by history, and given their unique cosmopolitan blend of cultures, are in a position to provide the blueprint for our urban future – and should thus command our attention. They are neither backward nor artificial but offer an urban vision for the twenty-first century. Significantly their urban discourse moves away from the "Islamic" perspective dominating in the past and instead suggests a course of modernity that uniquely blends the old and the new, adopts international practices and offers a (temporary) home for the world's nomads. They have the potential to become a model for our urban future – and may thus, finally, move us away from the shackles of Orientalism.

NOTES

1 This argument was further developed in Elsheshtawy, 2004a.
2 For further elaboration on this see my introductory chapter in Elsheshtawy, 2008b.
3 According to *The Economist* in a special report on cities, when wooing investors or companies ready to move their headquarters, rival cities will now flaunt their galleries, theaters and orchestras as much as their airline connections, modern hospitals and fiber optic networks. ("The World goes to Town: A special report on cities," May 5, 2007.)
4 For instance as Agnes Deboulet (2010) pointed out, the Malek Faysal project in Damascus or the Cairo ring road. Or as Sophia Shwayri (2008) noted with respect to the series of highways and underpasses linking the reconstructed central district to the "newly expanded Beirut International Airport which could be [reached] in seven minutes" (p. 91). As Deboulet puts it "such projects will dismantle once-unified neighbourhoods. Whatever justification they offer, they are destabilizing and often reinforcing or exaggerating inequalities."

5 http://www.ameinfo.com/146056.html. Accessed June 26, 2012.
6 UNDP, *Arab Human Development Report 2009: Challenges to Human Security in the Arab Countries*, Annex 1, Table 1, p. 229.
7 Khalaf, Roula (2007). "It's Boom Time," *Gulf News*, November 22, p. 22.
8 Worth, Robert F. (2010). "Saudi Border with Yemen is still inviting for Al Qaeda," *The New York Times*. October 26. http://www.nytimes.com/2010/10/27/world/middleeast/27saudi.html. Accessed June 26, 2012.
9 http://www.iom.int/jahia/jsp/index.jsp. Accessed June 26, 2012.
10 Ourossoff, Nicolai (2008). "City on the Gulf: Koolhaas Lays Out a Grand Urban Experiment in Dubai," *The New York Times*, March 3. http://www.nytimes.com/2008/03/03/arts/design/03kool.html. Accessed June 26, 2012.
11 According to the latest estimates some 842 projects valued at more than US$ 350 billion are currently on hold and a further 111 projects worth more than US$ 14 billion have been cancelled (http://www.alkhaleej.ae/portal/366a72a4-42ca-4544-897a-44e05af43b67.aspx. Accessed June 26, 2012).
12 Also see Elsheshtawy (2011b).
13 Architect Gordon Gill (from Smith + Gill Architects) during a symposium on Abu Dhabi's urban development at the Louvre Auditorium, Paris. December, 9, 2009.
14 Naylor, Hugh (2010). "Desperate lives of Dubai's car washers," *The National*, May 9. http://www.thenational.ae/apps/pbcs.dll/article?AID=/20100510/NATIONAL/705099940/0/rss. Accessed June 26, 2012.
15 Also see Elsheshtawy (2011b, c and d).
16 "According to article 3 in the new law, GCC citizens and legal personalities wholly owned by them may own properties, provided that the property should be located within the precinct of investment areas. However, they shall have the right to dispose and arrange any original or collateral right over any of those properties . . . According to Article (4)-Non-UAE nationals, natural or legal persons, shall have the right to own surface property in investment areas. Surface property refers to that property built on land. Thus, the non-nationals can own the property, but not the land on which it is built

... This shall be done through a long-term contract of 99 years or by virtue of long-term surface leasing contract of 50 years renewable by mutual consent." *Gulf News* (2007). "Foreigners get rights to own surface property," February 12, p. 37.

17 *The Economist*; Abu Dhabi report; 2009.

18 Howe, M. (1972). "Abu Dhabi adapting to modern world," *The New York Times*, January 14.

19 "Some of the original 286 owners will also be offered retail space in the new souk if their businesses are deemed suitable, Aldar said." Ligaya, Armina (2010). "New Souk to award original traders," *The National*, January 17, p. 2.

20 For a discussion on informal urbanism in Abu Dhabi see Elsheshtawy (2011a).

21 Kotkin, Joel (2009). "World Capitals of the Future," *Forbes*. September 2. http://www.forbes.com/2009/09/02/world-capitals-cities-century-opinions-columnists-21-century-cities-09-global-capitals.html. Accessed June 26, 2012.

22 Molavi, Afshin (2007). "The new Silk Road," *Washington Post*, April 10. http://www.newamerica.net/publications/articles/2007/the_new_silk_road_5133. Accessed June 26, 2012.

23 Kotkin, op. cit.

24 The reference in question is: Baruch Knei-Paz, *The Social and Political Thought of Leon Trotsky*, Oxford 1978, p. 91.

25 Davis, Mike (2006). "Fear and Money in Dubai," *New Left Review* (41, September–October). http://newleftreview.org/?page=article&view=2635. Accessed June 26, 2012.

REFERENCES

Abu-Lughod, Janet (1995). Comparing Chicago, New York and Los Angeles: testing some world city hypotheses, in Knox, P. and Taylor, P. (eds) *World Cities in a World System*. Cambridge: Cambridge University Press.

Akbar, Jamil (1988). *Crisis in the Built Environment: the case of the Muslim city*. Singapore: Mimar.

Al-Hathloul, Saleh (1996). *The Arab-Muslim City: Tradition, Continuity and Change in the Physical Environment*. Riyadh: Dar Al-Sahan.

Al Shafieei, Salem (1997). The Spatial Implications of Urban Land Policies in Dubai City. Unpublished Report, Dubai Municipality.

Brenner, Neil and Kiel, Roger (2006). Editors' introduction: global city theory in retrospect and prospect, in Brenner, Neil and Kiel, Roger (eds) *The Global Cities Reader*. London: Routledge.

Caldeira, Teresa (2000). *City of Walls: Crime, Segregation, and Citizenship in São Paulo*. Berkeley, CA: University of California Press.

Castells, Manuel (1996). *The Rise of the Network Society: The Information Age: Economy, Society and Culture Volume 1*. New York: Wiley-Blackwell.

Celik, Z. (1992). *Displaying the Orient: Architecture of Islam at nineteenth-century world's fairs*. Berkeley, CA: University of California Press.

Davis, Mike and Monk, Daniel (2008). *Evil Paradises: Dreamworlds of Neoliberalism*. New York: The New Press.

Deboulet, Agnes, et al. (2010). *La rénovation urbaine entre enjeux urbains et engagements citadins*. Rapport rendu au Puca, April 2010.

Dubai Municipality (1995). *Structure Plan for the Dubai Urban Area (1993–2012)*. Report prepared by Parsons Harland Bartholomew & Associates, Inc.

Elsheshtawy, Y. (2004a). Moving beyond the Narrative of Loss, in Elsheshtawy, Y. (ed.) *Planning the Middle East City: An Urban Kaleidoscope in a Globalizing World*. London: Routledge.

—— (2004b). Redrawing boundaries: Dubai, an emerging global city, in Elsheshtawy, Yasser (ed.) *Planning Middle Eastern Cities*. London: Routledge.

—— (2006). From Dubai to Cairo: competing global cities, models and shifting centers of influence, in Singerman, Diane and Amar, Paul (eds) *Cairo Cosmopolitan: Politics, Culture and Urban Space in the New Middle East*. Cairo: AUC Press.

—— (2008a). Cities of sand and fog: Abu Dhabi's global ambitions, in Elsheshtawy, Yasser (ed.) *The Evolving Arab City*. London: Routledge.

—— (2008b). The great divide: struggling and emerging cities in the Arab world, in Elsheshtawy, Yasser (ed.) *The Evolving Arab City*. London: Routledge.

—— (2008c). Transitory Sites: Mapping Dubai's "Forgotten" Urban Public Spaces. *The International Journal of Urban & Regional Research*. 32:4, pp. 968–988.

—— (2009). Arabian Tabula Rasa: Culture, Hegemony and the new Middle East. *New Geographies* 1, pp. 98–109.

—— (2010). *Dubai: Behind an Urban Spectacle*. London: Routledge.

—— (2011a). (In)formal Encounters: Mapping Abu Dhabi's Urban Public Spaces. *Built Environment.* 37:1, pp. 92–113.

—— (2011b). The Prophecy of Code 46: Afuera in Dubai or our Urban Future. *Traditional Dwellings and Settlement Review.* 22:11, Spring, pp. 19–32.

—— (2011c). Little Space/Big Space: Everyday Urbanism in Dubai. *Brown Journal of World Affairs.* 17:1, pp. 53–71.

—— (2011d). Urban (Im)mobility: Public Encounters in Dubai, in Edensor, Tim and Jayne, Mark (eds) *Urban Theory beyond the West.* London: Routledge.

Frampton, Kenneth (1983). Towards a Critical Regionalism: Six Points for an Architecture of Resistance, in Foster, Hal (ed.) *The Anti-Aesthetic: Essays on Postmodern Culture.* Seattle, WA: Bay Press.

Friedmann, Jon and Wolff, Gerald (1982). World city formation: an agenda for research and action. *International Journal of Urban and Regional Research,* 6:3, pp. 309–344.

Fuccaro, Nelida (2001). Urban studies of the Gulf: visions of the city. *Bulletin of the Middle East Studies Association of North America,* 35:2, pp. 175–188.

Gabriel, Erhard F. (1987). *The Dubai Handbook.* Ahrensburg: Institute for Applied Economic Geography.

Graham, Stephen and Marvin, Simon (2001). *Splintering Urbanism: Networked Infrastructures, Technological Mobilities and the Urban Condition.* London: Routledge.

Gugler, Josef (2004). *World Cities beyond the West: Globalization, Development and Inequality.* Cambridge: Cambridge University Press.

Haila, Anne (1997). The neglected builder of global cities, in Källtorp, O., Elander, I., Ericsson, O. and Franzén, M. (eds) *Cities in Transformation: Transformation in Cities.* Aldershot: Averbury.

Harvey, David (2006). *Spaces of Global Capitalism.* London: Verso.

Kanna, Ahmed (2010). *Dubai: The city as corporation.* Minneapolis: University of Minnesota Press.

Marcuse, Peter (2006). Space in the globalizing city, in Brenner, N. and Keil, R. (eds) *The Global City Reader.* London: Routledge.

Marcuse, Peter and van Kempen, Ronald (2000). *Globalizing Cities: A New Spatial Order.* Oxford: Blackwell.

Mathews, Gordon (2011). *Ghetto at the center of the world: Chungking Mansions, Hong Kong.* Chicago: University of Chicago Press.

Mitchell, Timothy (1988). *Colonizing Egypt.* Cambridge: Cambridge University Press.

Newman, Peter and Thornley, Andrew (2005). *Planning World Cities: Globalisation and Urban Politics.* Basingstoke: Palgrave Macmillan.

Oxford Business Group (2006). *Emerging Abu Dhabi 2006.* London, Oxford Business Group.

Oxford Business Group (2011). *The Report: Abu Dhabi 2011.* London: Oxford Business Group.

Peter-Smith, Michael (2001). *Transnational Urbanism: Locating Globalization.* Oxford: Blackwell.

Robinson, Jennifer (2002). Global and world cities. A view from off the map. *International Journal of Urban and Regional Research,* 26:3, pp. 531–554.

Said, Edward (1978). *Orientalism.* New York: Knopf.

Sassen, Saskia (2001). *The Global City. London, New York, Tokyo.* Princeton, NJ: Princeton University Press.

Sassen, Saskia (ed.). (2002). *Global Networks, Linked Cities.* London: Brunner-Routledge.

Serageldin, Ismail and El-Sadek, Samir (1982). *The Arab City: Its Character and Islamic Cultural Heritage.* Riyadh: Arab Urban Development Institute.

Shwayri, Sophi (2008). From Regional Node to Backwater and Back to Uncertainty: Beirut 1943–2006, in Elsheshtawy, Yasser (ed.) *The Evolving Arab City: Tradition, Modernity and Urban Development* (Abingdon, UK: Routledge, 2008).

Simpfendorfer, Ben (2009). *The New Silk Road: How a Rising Arab World is Turning Away from the West and Rediscovering China.* London: Palgrave Macmillan.

UN-HABITAT (2007). *The State of the World's Cities Report 2006/2007.* London: Earthscan.

Vora, Neha (2011). From Golden Frontier to Global City: Shifting Forms of Belonging, Freedom, and Governance among Indian Businessmen in Dubai. *American Anthropologist.* 113:2, pp. 306–318.

Zukin, Sharon (2010). *Naked City: the death and life of authentic urban places.* Oxford: Oxford University Press.

"The Urbanism of Ambition" and "China Reinvents the City"

from The Concrete Dragon: China's Urban Revolution and What it Means for the World (2008)

Thomas J. Campanella

Editors' Introduction

The breakneck pace and growth of China's cities over the last two decades is both numbing and worrisome. It provides example of how central government ambitions can shepherd vast resources into housing, infrastructure, services, and new consumer venues – and transform what was recently a developing country into a global player. A booming economy, rapid urbanization, and a massive construction industry (the size of California's population and barely keeping up with demand) are some of the key inputs to skylines that grow across the Chinese landscape. Although its urbanization rationales are extremely practical in function (providing places for a growing population to live, work, travel, and consume), its urban descriptors are largely targeted at achieving superlatives: the most housing, the biggest shopping mall, the longest freeway system, the fastest and most innovative train, and so on. This is the treadmill of global competition writ large. Sustaining and continuing this pace of growth will require huge resource demands. How this will impact the rest of the global population that will compete for these limited resources is unknown. In China's process of expansion, cities are also experiencing unexpected demolitions, rapid erasure of historic places, population displacement, immense sprawl, and environmental degradation. It becomes a living example of Joseph Schumpeter's concept of "creative destruction." While we look with awe at the scale and pace of this transformation, those in the west should be cautious with respect to the portability of China's urban lessons to other places.

These two chapters from *The Concrete Dragon: China's Urban Revolution and What it Means for the World* provide prologue and open-ended conclusion for understanding Chinese urbanization, urban design, environmental impacts, and scale of growth. In the book's first chapter, "The Urbanism of Ambition," Campanella illustrates the scale of the country's urbanization: construction, transportation, historical contrasts, and economic development. He compares China's ambitions with a younger USA that was once booming similarly but is now wising up to the negative externalities of unchecked growth. In the second chapter included here, "China Reinvents the City," the author selects six characteristics that define China's growing urbanism: speed, scale, spectacle, sprawl, segregation, and sustainability. Campanella problematizes all of these – posing questions about the impacts these will have both locally and globally.

Thomas J. Campanella is an urbanist, landscape architect, and urban historian, as well as Associate Professor of Urban Planning and Design at the University of North Carolina at Chapel Hill. He is a Fellow of the American Academy in Rome, and has won both Guggenheim and Fulbright Fellowships. Campanella teaches courses in planning, landscape history, and urban design. He has a PhD from MIT. His previous publication, *Republic of Shade: New England and the American Elm* (New Haven, CT: Yale University Press, 2003) won the Spiro Kostoff Award for 2005 from the Society of Architectural Historians. It was also named one of the ten best non-fiction books by the *Boston Globe* for 2003. Other Campanella publications include: *Cities from the Sky: An Aerial Portrait of America* (New York: Princeton Architectural Press, 2001); and *The Resilient*

City: How Modern Cities Recover from Disaster, co-authored with Lawrence Vale (New York: Oxford University Press, 2005). Important articles include: "The Roman Roots of Gotham's London Plane," *Wall Street Journal* (July 20, 2011, D5); and "Jane Jacobs and the Death and Life of American Planning," *Design Observer: Places* (April 2011). He has consulted on numerous urban design projects in Asia and the United States.

No shortage of material exists on the Chinese urban phenomenon. In a new selection for *The City Reader*, 5th edn. (London: Routledge 2011) Tingwei Zhang's "Chinese Cities in a Global Society" discusses China's recent urbanization and its worldwide impacts. Other key texts on Chinese urbanization include: Shahid Yusuf and Anthony Saich (eds), *China Urbanizes: Consequences, Strategies and Policies* (Washington, DC: World Bank Publications, 2008); Jieming Zhu, *The Transition of China's Urban Development: From Plan-Controlled to Market-Led* (Westport, CT: Praeger, 1999); John Friedman, *China's Urban Transition* (Minneapolis: University of Minnesota Press, 2005); and John Logan (ed.), *The New Chinese City: Globalization and Market Reform* (Oxford: Blackwell, 2002). For texts on Chinese urban form and design, see the following: Dieter Hassenpflug, *The Urban Code of China* (Cologne: Birkhäuser Architecture, 2010); and Duanfang Lu, *Remaking Chinese Urban Form: Modernity, Scarcity and Space 1945–2005* (London: Routledge, 2006).

THE URBANISM OF AMBITION

In the first few months of 2007, a remarkable story began spreading around China, largely via internet bulletin boards, bloggers, and cell phone instant messaging. It involved a plucky restaurateur named Wu Ping, whose Chongqing house had been condemned for a commercial mixed-use development. The woman refused all offers of compensation from the real estate developer and steadfastly defended her property even as the neighboring structures were pulled down one by one. By mid-March, her house stood alone at the center of a vast crater of mud and rubble. As the construction pit deepened, the structure slowly rose in prominence until it loomed defiantly over the entire site. Though forced to vacate the property, Wu Ping took her case to the media; dressed in a blazing red coat, she stood in front of news crews and cameramen waving her lease and demanding that the government make good on a groundbreaking new law, enacted only days before on March 16, 2007, that strengthened private property rights in China. Wu Ping's husband added to the drama by planting an oversized Chinese flag on the roof of the house and draping a banner across the front that read "A citizen's legal property is not to be encroached upon!"[1]

The case touched a national nerve, one rubbed raw by three decades of often cataclysmic development in China's major cities. Wu Ping's courageous act of defiance voiced the pent-up rage of millions of Chinese whose homes have been sacrificed in the nation's wholesale rush toward a gleaming urban future. The woman – and her house – became widely known as "the most stubborn nail in history" (*shi shang zui niu de ding zi hu*). The singular, unforgettable image of the "nail house" alone in the middle of an excavated pit is the very picture of resistance and immediately calls to mind that brave young man who stood down a tank on Chang'an Boulevard in June 1989. I relate this story because it touches on so many essential themes related to city making and urban redevelopment in China's post-Mao era – an age of unprecedented economic growth and societal transformation that has shaken both China and the world.

To write about China's urban revolution is to traffic in superlatives. Over the last twenty years, the People's Republic has undergone the greatest period of urban growth and transformation in history. Since the 1980s, China has built more skyscrapers; more office buildings; more shopping malls and hotels; more housing estates and gated communities; more highways, bridges, subways, and tunnels; more public parks, playgrounds, squares, and plazas; more golf courses and resorts and theme parks than any other nation on earth – indeed, than probably all other nations combined.

The number and size of cities alone is staggering. There were fewer than 200 cities in China in the late 1970s; today there are nearly 700. Many of these are simply reclassified towns and counties, but even the smallest among them are immense by American standards. Forty-six Chinese cities have passed the one million mark since 1992, making for a national total of 102 cities with more than a million residents. In the United States we have all of nine such cities. There are scores of Chinese cities most Americans have never heard of that rank with our largest. Guiyang and Jinan, for example, are roughly the same size as Phoenix and Philadelphia, and Hefei and Wuxi – middling cities in China – each exceed Los Angeles in population. What makes this all the more extraordinary is that only about 38 percent of the Chinese population is currently urban, as opposed to 80 percent in the United States. An equivalent urban population in China – 80 percent of the total – would mean more than one billion city dwellers.

In other words, China's urban revolution is just getting under way. Bigness and supersized sprawl may have once been American specialties, but that monopoly has been usurped. China is now home to the world's biggest airport and largest shopping mall, as well as some of the planet's tallest buildings and longest bridges; it boasts the world's largest automobile showrooms and the biggest gated community; it has built the most expansive golf course on earth and the biggest bowling alley, and even the world's largest skateboard park. The controversial Three Gorges Dam on the Yangtze River makes Boston's Big Dig look like child's play – a mega project that displaced more than one million people and destroyed nearly a dozen cities.[2]

China has indeed redefined the meaning of Joseph Schumpeter's much-quoted phrase "creative destruction," razing more urban fabric in its twenty-year building binge than any nation in peacetime – and easily surpassing the losses, human and physical, of urban renewal in America. In Shanghai alone, redevelopment projects in the 1990s displaced more people than thirty years of urban renewal in the United States.[3] Not even mountains can stand in the way of China's urban ambition. In 1997, a Lanzhou entrepreneur named Zhu Qihua launched a campaign to remove 900-foot Big Green Mountain, located on the outskirts of town, so that winds could flush clean the city's heavily polluted air. As one city resident, cheered by Zhu's bold scheme, put it, "If removing that mountain can do the trick, then get rid of the mountain. Get rid of them all." In the summit's stead would be built a 500-acre industrial park.[4]

Indeed, in terms of speed and scale and sheer audacity, China's urban revolution is off the charts of Western or even global experience. China is in the midst of a wholesale reinvention of the city as we know it, forcing urbanists worldwide to recalibrate their most basic tools and assumptions and develop a whole new vocabulary for describing and critiquing urban phenomena. In China precedents and practices may be borrowed willy-nilly from other cultures, but they undergo a process of transmutation that renders them both familiar and thoroughly Chinese at the same time. The only place remotely comparable to China today is Dubai, which, thanks to our addiction to oil, has been growing by leaps and bounds in recent years. But Dubai is a tiny city-state of just over a million people. China is a hundred Dubais, with a thousand times its ambition.

The numbers speak for themselves. In 2003 alone, China put up 28 billion square feet of new housing – one eighth of the housing stock of the United States.[5] In the year 2004 alone, some $400 billion was spent on construction projects in the People's Republic, nearly the total gross domestic product (GDP) of sub-Saharan Africa that year.[6] There were virtually no modern highrise office towers in Shanghai in 1980; today it has more than twice as many as New York City.[7] According to the Shanghai statistics bureau, some 925 million square feet of new building floor space was added to the city between 1990 and 2004, equivalent to 334 Empire State Buildings. By the end of the 1990s, Shanghai had more than 23,000 construction sites scattered across the city. Nationwide, China's construction industry employs a workforce equal to the population of California.[8] Nearly half the world's steel and cement is devoured by China, a level of demand that sends shock waves through the global building-supply chain.[9] Much of the world's heavy construction equipment is in China, and the tower crane is such a ubiquitous presence on the skyline that people call it China's national bird (a particular irony, given the esteemed place of cranes – the feathered sort – in classical Chinese painting).

China had a mere 180 miles of modern motorway in the 1980s; today its National Trunk Highway System spans nearly 30,000 miles and is second in length only to America's interstate system. By 2020, China will likely have 53,000 miles of national-level highway, surpassing the United States as the most freeway-laced nation on earth.[10] Even Mt. Everest is being scaled by the hydra of Chinese asphalt. In

June 2007, plans were announced for a 67 mile, $20 million highway winding up from the foot of the mountain to a base camp at 17,000 feet. The finished road will be part of the 2008 Olympic torch relay (itself the longest in Olympic history, encompassing five continents and 85,000 miles), but is also designed to make it easier for "tourists and mountaineers" to consume the once-remote peak.[11] Other roads have been hammered through some of the most dense and populous urban neighborhoods in the world, forcing the relocation of tens of thousands of families. Again, the American urban experience is quickly exceeded here. In Shanghai, the construction of a single section of the Inner Ring Road, through the Luwan and Huangpu districts – a mere two-mile run – displaced an estimated 12,000 people – many more than were displaced along the entire route of the much lamented Cross Bronx Expressway in New York, the first major American highway built through dense urban terrain.[12] How unsettling to see the most egregious, much-studied monuments of Western planning practice suddenly rendered insignificant! Robert Moses at his megalomaniacal max is tame in comparison to China. In his entire master-builder career, Moses constructed some 415 miles of highway in the New York metropolitan region; Shanghai officials built well over three times that amount in the 1990s alone.[13]

Given all these new roads, it's hardly surprising that China is the most rapidly motorizing society in the world today. The People's Republic was long a nation of bicycles, but now the two-wheelers are in decline: the number of bicyclists in China's cities dropped 26 percent between 2001 and 2006, and they are now even banned outright on many city streets. The domestic motor vehicle market, on the other hand, is booming, and second in size now only to that of the United States. Industry analysts forecast that China may well be the world's largest producer and consumer of cars by 2020, with total car ownership exceeding even that of the United States.[14] The number of cars in Shanghai jumped from a mere 212,000 to 1.2 million between 1990 and 2003; and Beijing swept past the million-car mark in the spring of 2002, when more than 1,000 new cars were being added to the city's streets and highways each day.[15] Today there are more automobile brands in China than in the United States, and while the total number of cars is still small in comparison, keep in mind that there were virtually

no private automobiles in the People's Republic as late as the 1970s.

The motorization trend has profound implications for the form and structure of China's cities. It is helping drive a complex process of land conversion on the urban fringe that yields a uniquely Chinese kind of urban sprawl. Sprawl in China is very different from its American cousin, but no less land hungry. Between about 1980 and 2004, nearly 44,000 square miles of agricultural land were lost to development in China – equivalent to the combined area of all of Massachusetts, Connecticut, Rhode Island, Vermont, New Hampshire, and half of Maine.[16] Due to such losses, the People's Republic is no longer self sufficient in agricultural production; for the first time in its history, China has become a net importer of food.[17] The situation is more than a little reminiscent of *The Good Earth*, in which the land Wang Lung worked all his life – that nurtured and enriched his family – is pawned off by his profligate sons. The extent of Chinese sprawl is readily evident from space, much the way the Great Wall was long rumored to be.

LANDSAT images of China's coastal cities from the early 1980s and today reveal an outward expansion of urban matter reminiscent of a colossal stellar explosion. While the Chinese suburban landscape is very different from that of the United States, it is no less catalytic in enabling a car-dependent lifestyle of commuting and big-box consumerism. Most housing on the urban fringe consists of mid- and high-rise condominium estates – much denser than anything in suburban America. Yet their outlying location and the lack of public transportation has encouraged high rates of automobile ownership among residents. Mixed among these housing estates are also tracts of single-family homes virtually identical in spirit – and often in architectural appointment – to "McMansion"-style gated communities in the United States. Other artifacts of American sprawl and "strip" culture have also appeared, albeit tailored to local (or at least Chinese) needs and tastes. These include drive-through fast-food restaurants like KFC and McDonald's; big-box retail giants such as Lotus and Wal-Mart, IKEA, Costco, and an Anglo-Chinese Home Depot knockoff called B&Q; shopping malls with expansive parking lots out front; colossal supermarkets; even budget motel chains and that vintage icon of American suburbia, the drive-in cinema.

What makes these and other facets of the new Chinese landscape so extraordinary is their sharp contrast with what came before. Scarcely a generation has passed between the Cultural Revolution and the present, yet what epochal change those three decades have wrought! The shopping malls and subdivisions, the cars and color TVs, the theme parks and golf courses – all unthinkable a short time ago. The dull blue-gray world of Mao suits and rationed goods is long gone; China today is a 24/7 frenzy of consumerism and construction. The birthplace of the Chinese Communist Party is now part of an exclusive shopping district in Shanghai, only steps from a Starbucks and upscale martini bars. Golf is a required course for business students at Xiamen University; and even the celebrated commune in Shanxi Province that cadres were implored to study in the 1960s – "In agriculture, learn from Dazhai!" – has struck out on the capitalist road, turning its famous name into a lucrative (and copyrighted) brand.

The saga of transition from Maoist scarcity to full-blown consumerism was driven home for me in 1999 by a television advertisement, of all things, for an upscale housing estate in the Pearl River Delta. I was at a restaurant in Zhongshan with Wallace Chang, as guests of a team of local planning officials for whom we were doing some consulting work. The television was playing silently in our private dining room, and a program came on that I took at first to be a historical drama about the hardships of life during the Cultural Revolution. The film was shot in black and white, and showed a young peasant working the fields and struggling to feed his family. The same man was then depicted as a foreman in a village factory, bicycling off now in the morning with an attaché case. Finally, the film turned full color, and the former peasant was now a well-groomed executive stepping confidently out of a suburban villa (at the advertised development, of course), waving goodbye to an adoring family before heading to the office in his late-model BMW. Here was, in effect, the creation story of post-Mao China, a rags-to-riches fable celebrating the economic miracle unleashed by Deng Xiaoping in the early 1980s.

The primary motive force behind China's urban revolution is, of course, the explosive growth of the Chinese economy over the last three decades. Not only did Deng Xiaoping's market reforms stimulate free enterprise at home – unleashing "a tidal wave of long suppressed entrepreneurial energy and ambition," as Li Conghua has written – but his "open-door" campaign brought a flood tide of money from foreign investors hungry for a piece of the Chinese pie.[18] Foreign direct investment flowed first to China via a series of special economic zones established for that purpose, initially from Hong Kong and the Chinese diaspora communities across Southeast Asia. But before long, investors from the United States, Japan, Canada, the United Kingdom, Australia, and Europe were also pouring millions into joint-venture projects in the People's Republic. China's economic engine stirred to life in the early 1980s, and then launched into the longest period of sustained economic growth in modern times. Between 1980 and 1990 the Chinese economy grew faster than even the vaunted "East Asian Tigers" (Hong Kong, Singapore, Taiwan, and South Korea) during their exuberant early years in the 1970s and 1980s. By 1994, the People's Republic accounted for fully 40 percent of the world's GDP growth; today its GDP represents 13 percent of global output, making it second in productivity only to the United States. China's economy has been expanding an average 9 percent per annum since the start of the reform era, a rate three times the growth of the American economy over the much-ballyhooed dot.com boom of the late 1990s.

Nor is it showing any signs of slowing: China overtook the United Kingdom in 2005 to become the third-largest economy in the world, and it may well soon eclipse Germany. In 2006, China's GDP increased by nearly 11 percent, the fastest growth rate in more than a decade. And as economist Pam Woodall has pointed out, China's growth is "real" – the result of real productivity growth rather than the funny-money gains of overvalued stock or inflated real estate. (As Woodall puts it, "rising house prices do not represent an increase in wealth for a country as a whole. They merely redistribute wealth to home-owners from non-home-owners who may hope to buy in the future.")[19] China is also now history's greatest exporter and churns out most of the world's televisions, stereos, DVD players, microwave ovens, vacuum cleaners, computer equipment, cameras, photocopiers, laser printers, telephones, tools, home furnishings, shoes, motors, and toys. Of course, just how long China can sustain this breakneck pace of growth is anyone's guess, and a subject of intense debate among economists. Unchecked environmental degradation, rising unemployment, a growing dependence on foreign oil and other resources, and a swollen property market are just some of the many issues that threaten to derail the growth locomotive. None, however, is more menacing to China's internal stability and continued growth than the widening gap between haves and have-nots, both within cities and between regions.

Capitalism in the People's Republic is in a brutally efficient early stage, largely unfettered by unions, workmen's compensation laws, well-enforced environmental regulations, and other inconveniences to capital accumulation. The economic juggernaut has crushed many a soul. While an estimated 300 million Chinese have been lifted out of poverty by economic growth in the last quarter century, such blessings have not been spread evenly throughout the nation. China's coastal cities and provinces have been the chief beneficiaries of the surging economy, a coastal swath not unlike the Boston-to-Washington, or "BosWash," corridor along the Atlantic seaboard. Official residents of Shenzhen, Guangzhou, Fuzhou, Shanghai, Beijing, Tianjin, Dalian, and other cities enjoy an average income significantly higher than the national average.

In their midst, however, is a vast "floating population" (*liudong renkou*) of migrant workers who receive few of the perks and privileges of full urban citizenship. The disequilibrium between booming coastal cities and poor inland provinces has prompted as many as 225 million peasants – roughly the population of the United States – to flock to China's cities in recent years in search of jobs and a better life. In 1998 alone, 27 million rural migrants made their way to China's major metropolitan centers. That equals the sum total of all European emigration to the United States between 1820 and 1920. Even the "Great Migration" of African Americans from the rural South to northern cities after the Second World War – a demographic shift that helped shape contemporary American culture – pales in comparison to internal Chinese migration in recent years. Migrant workers in Beijing alone outnumber all the African Americans who migrated to the urban north between 1940 and 1970.[20]

How ironic that China's urban revolution is so deeply indebted to the countryside. Chinese cities are built by farmers. Men from impoverished rural villages put up the posh malls and glittering skyscrapers and six-lane expressways, while their sisters and daughters work the mills and assembly lines that have made China the workshop of the world. But even though they turn the gears of China's economic engine, migrant workers are an unappreciated lot. They have little or no access to health care, educational opportunities, or good housing; they are blamed for nearly every social ill and literally live on the margins of society.

Far at the other end of fate's spectrum is the self-made millionaire, the folk hero of the new China. This one-time land of Red Guards and little red books is churning out more new millionaires than any country in the world. In a nation where a bicycle will set you back all of $15, a millionaire has the spending power of a billionaire in the United States. The legendary exhortation often attributed to Deng Xiaoping – "to get rich is glorious" – has rehabilitated wealth and affluence in China. Capitalists were once excoriated as "running dogs" of Western imperialism; now they are heaped with encomiums and can even join the Communist Party. On May Day 2005, several such self-made millionaires were feted as "model workers" by the Chinese Communist Party (so was Houston Rockets star Yao Ming, who first thought such awards were for "ordinary people who worked tirelessly . . . without asking for anything in return," but then allowed that perhaps he was "a special kind of migrant worker").[21]

Like the Hearsts, Vanderbilts, and Rockefellers before them, China's merchant elite has a penchant for arriviste extravagance. Beijing property mogul Zhang Yuchen, who made a fortune in the 1990s building single-family suburban homes, celebrated his arrival by replicating the Château de Maisons-Laffitte on a windswept site north of the Chinese capital. The nouveau chateau was crafted using François Mansart's original drawings from 1650 and constructed with the same Chantilly stone, this time shipped halfway across the globe. Unfortunately, some 800 peasants raising wheat on the land had to be forcibly evicted to make way for the trophy house – a particular irony given Zhang's membership in the Communist Party.[22]

Other magnates have built simulacra of Beverly Hills mansions or even the architectural landmarks of American democracy. On the outskirts of Hangzhou, Chinese tourism tycoon Huang Qiaoling built a $10 million full-scale replica of the White House, complete with a portrait gallery of American presidents, an Oval Office, and a Blue Room. Outside is a miniature Washington Monument, along with a one-third scale version of Mount Rushmore (quarters for his employees are neatly tucked behind). What inspired Huang's building spree was a glossy New Year calendar of American landmarks that his peasant parents received when he was a child.[23] In 2002 Huang was surprised with a visit from none other than George W. Bush, who was himself delighted to see a knockoff of the White House in China. Another tycoon, Li Qinfu, took the Washington trope a step further by erecting a mini U.S. Capitol in the Shanghai suburbs, the headquarters of his textile and manufacturing conglomerate. The building is topped with a three-ton statue of Li himself, a former Red Guard, and now one of China's richest men.[24]

China's roaring economy has also enriched professionals in the building, design, and development fields – from quantity surveyors and construction managers to real estate brokers, architects, engineers, and urban planners. Architects have been especially nimble in riding the zeitgeist of the building boom, and many have become fabulously rich in the process. Young architects still in their twenties often have several built projects in their portfolios, and not just a summer house for mom and dad. Architecture students in Shenzhen in the 1980s helped build that overnight city, working on real commissions alongside their studio assignments. By the 1990s Chinese architects had five times the volume of work of their American colleagues, who outnumbered them nonetheless by a factor of ten.[25] This relative scarcity has made Chinese architects the most influential in the world, if influence be measured by bricks and mortar. The great demand for skilled designers led to a surge in the number of architecture students in the last decade. Today, architecture ranks with computer science and economics as one of the most competitive fields of study in China; admission to a top-flight architecture program, say at Tsinghua or Nanjing universities, is statistically equivalent to getting into Harvard or Yale, and architects in China enjoy considerably higher occupational prestige than do their counterparts in the United States.

To architects overseas, China is nothing short of the Holy Grail. Foreign design and planning firms fall all over themselves for a piece of the action, and for good reason: the great Chinese building boom has made the skills and expertise of design professionals in demand as never before. There are architects and planners from Virginia to California whose previous contact with the Chinese world was limited to the local take-out, who now have half a dozen projects on the boards in Shenzhen, Beijing, and Shanghai. This is not the first time foreign professionals have helped shape China's future, of course; Americans and Europeans left a rich legacy of architecture and urban design in China in the first half of the twentieth century. But that early work was often related to missionary or philanthropic endeavors, or commissioned by foreign companies busily exploiting China. Today, foreign architects build in China at China's pleasure, and save for a handful of global superstars – Koolhaas, Foster, Herzog & de Meuron, and the like – they may well soon find themselves displaced by twenty-something Chinese kids.

There is a bewitching consonance between the American urban experience and the transfiguration of China's cities today. China's drive, energy, and ambition – its hunger to be powerful and prosperous, to be a player on the global stage – is more than a little reminiscent of America in its youth. Henry James's descriptions of lower Manhattan in 1904 – of the "multitudinous sky-scrapers standing up to the view, from the water, like extravagant pins in a cushion already overplanted" – could well describe Shanghai's Pudong District today.[26] We gazed in wonder at promise filled miniature metropoles like Norman Bel Geddes's Futurama exhibit at the 1939 New York World's Fair, just as Chinese today pore over spectacular models of the Shanghai- or Beijing-to-be. We were China once, and Europe was us. In spirit at least, China is like the United States of a century ago – punch-drunk with possibility, pumped and reckless and on the move. Americans invented the modern metropolis, and the world looked to us with wonder. It was on the blustery shores of Lake Michigan that the modern office tower was born, in the wake of the Great Chicago Fire, and in New York that the skyscraper city achieved its finest early form. We wrote poems once to our bridges and roads. We dreamed, like Moses King or Hugh Ferriss, of cities studded with impossible towers and airborne streets. Given wheels by Henry Ford, we scattered across the landscape and created a new kind of semicity in places like Los Angeles, Dallas, Atlanta, and Phoenix.

Of course, much of this ended badly. We got urban renewal and lost our past; we got the Cross Bronx Expressway and lost our homes. But the West End and the South Bronx did not die in vain. We are older and wiser now, more responsible, aware of the problems of building for automobiles rather than human beings – or of simply building too big. A new emphasis on sustainability impels us to rethink the way we make architecture and assemble cities. In short, our values have changed. But with wisdom has also come timidity. We are a suburban nation in tweedy middle age, cautious and conservative, no longer smitten with audacity. Our architecture and urbanism is retrospective, measured, and sane. We build new towns that look old, shop at Restoration Hardware and bury – like the Central Artery – the very icons of modernity we once celebrated. In America today, the notion of penning verse to a piece of infrastructure is a little laughable. Just as it once crossed the Atlantic, the urbanism of ambition has crossed the Pacific; Hart Crane has gone to China.

CHINA REINVENTS THE CITY

To summarize a revolution-in-progress is a fool's errand. Rather than attempt such a task, I have instead sketched out here six defining aspects or characteristics of contemporary Chinese urbanism and the evolving Chinese cityscape. These include speed, scale, spectacle, sprawl, segregation, and – on a final, hopeful note – sustainability. While, individually, many of these attributes are not wholly new in the annals of urban development, taken together they yield a pattern and process of city making that is largely without precedent. They are the hallmarks of an urban transformation unlike anything the world has seen before; a wholesale reinvention of the city as we know it.

Speed

China is the most rapidly urbanizing nation in the world, and perhaps in history. Never have so many urban settlements grown so fast, nor has more urban fabric been razed and reconstructed with such haste. In a single extraordinary generation, China has undergone a process of urban growth and transformation that took a century to unfold in the United States – itself a nation whose speed once awed the world. Chicago, after all, was the Shenzhen of the nineteenth century. Chicago's spectacular growth, especially after the Great Fire of 1871, made it the fastest-growing city in America, just as Shenzhen became the hasty pacesetter of post-Mao China. All through the 1980s and 1990s, Chinese cities strained to meet or beat "Shenzhen tempo" – a pace set by workers on the International Foreign Trade Center and defined as a finished building floor every three days. Appropriately enough, that mark was shattered a decade later by workers on another Shenzhen tower, who knocked a full half-day off the previous record.

Today, most of China moves at warp speed. In the hours it took to read this book, probably another thousand apartments units were readied for occupancy across the People's Republic; a dozen new shopping centers were likely opened; a score more office towers and housing estates topped off. Sinopec, the Chinese oil conglomerate, will likely open another 500 gas stations this year on China's roads and highways, as it has done for several years now. In 2007 alone, McDonald's opened 100 new restaurants in Chinese cities, many equipped for drive-through service.[27]

In China, whole new towns are conceived, planned, and constructed in the time it takes to get a small subdivision through the permitting process in the United States. China built its first Maglev rail system in Shanghai in just two years. It took a decade to build a similar line in Germany, and in the United States we still only dream of such space-age stuff. In England, once ruler of the seven seas, it took thirteen years for Heathrow Airport's new Terminal Five to see the light of day. The new terminal at Beijing Capital International Airport, the largest in the world, was built in thirty-six months.

Of course, speed is stunning, but it can also be stupid. Haste makes waste and tends to come at the cost of quality, longevity, and even safety. The frenetic pace with which Chinese cities are being built and rebuilt has struck many observers, foreign and Chinese, as reckless and chaotic. At least one critic, a geographer at the Chinese Academy of

Science, compared the present cyclone of creative destruction to the excesses of the Great Leap Forward, a period of political turmoil and misguided policy that led to, among other things, the worst famine in human history.[28] It is for good reason, usually, that it takes a month of Sundays to build anything in the United States. We have a vast system of checks and balances meant to slow things down, to rule out binge building and architectural excess. Colossal urban renewal and expressway projects in the 1960s pushed one too many citizens around and led to a backlash against "master plans" and the "physical planners" who concocted them. The planning profession in turn rejected urban design and snuggled closer to the social sciences. New theories of advocacy planning, community development, and public participation helped make developers and municipalities accountable for their actions.

This is just now beginning to make its way to China, where urban planning is mostly still about spiffy drawings and spectacular visions. There are few, if any, mechanisms to assure public participation in the development process. The Maoist dictum that the individual should be subordinate to the collective will has been handily exploited to excuse all sorts of abuses in the name of national progress. In mid-1990s Shanghai, residents who protested their eviction for the Inner Ring Road were excoriated for selfishly impeding China's development and modernization. But with the exception of occasional (and increasingly common) "stubborn nails" like Wu Ping, the refusenik of Chongqing, the development juggernaut faces little opposition. In the United States, democratic institutions at the state and local levels act like a giant sea-anchor on development. The resulting torpor can be frustrating, and the community input process is all too often hijacked by ignorance, fear, and not-in-my-backyard self-interest. But, just as often, going slow yields a better project. Unchecked, speed is costly and can even kill. Countless Chinese buildings, thrown up in haste, have already outlived their usefulness. The life span of architecture in China is measured in dog's years. In 2006 I counted half a dozen office towers in center-city Nanjing that were scheduled for demolition or in the process of being razed; all had been built in the late 1980s and early 1990s. In most places, a building of such recent vintage would still be considered new.

While there have been significant improvements in recent years, construction quality is still often abysmal, even on tony commercial projects. Binge building yields a high quotient of urban junk. A Beijing realtor to whom I was praising the spare, elegant architecture of a trendy housing estate in the central business district shook her head and advised me not to look too closely at how it was all put together. Up-market housing on the outskirts of Nanjing, built in late 2000, looks today as if it had been built in the 1960s: crumbling staircases, facades streaked and stained. Even Paul Andreu's signature Pudong International Airport, opened in 1999, was visibly aging when I was there in 2006. Shoddy construction, a lack of code enforcement, and poor building maintenance is not only wasteful, but has killed many people – such as the dozen shoppers who lost their lives when a Dongguan shopping mall collapsed in December 2000.

Scale

Bigness is another defining aspect of China's contemporary urban landscape – and of Chinese ambition generally. Like speed, scale too was once an American specialty. A century ago, visitors from England and the Continent were enraptured – or dismayed – by the sky-piercing loft of American commercial architecture, or by the vast power embodied in American industrial landscapes. Europeans were awed by the steel works of Pittsburgh, Gary, or, earlier, the sprawling textile mills of Lowell or Lawrence. The Chicago stockyards, a stygian merger of pastoralism and industry, held the greatest concentration of livestock on earth and was also as much a stop on the tourist circuit as Niagara Falls. From the Columbian Exposition to the Hoover Dam, the Empire State Building to the Interstate Highway System, the United States has long been the sultan of size. Its overreaching ambition was never more aptly summarized than by Daniel Burnham's famous dictum: "Make no little plans."

The pinnacle of American achievement in this regard – the Apollo Program and the first few moon landings – came, poetically enough, just before the fall. By the early 1970s, the cultural tide had turned against bigness and ambition – a turn greatly expedited by the American misadventure in Vietnam.

Suddenly, small was beautiful, and so were small plans; Burnham, purged by followers of Jane Jacobs, went down with Robert Moses and Edward J. Logue and the rest of the Great White planners. We still do things in a big way in the United States; we invented the internet, after all, and have hardly checked our global scale of military adventuring. But when it comes to large-scale urban projects, China has largely displaced the United States and the West in general.

There is hardly any category of building type, infrastructure, or amenity that China has not built in its largest incarnation. China is home to three of the five largest shopping malls on earth, two of the three longest bridges, five of the world's ten tallest buildings, and the world's new largest urban plaza (even Tiananmen Square has been displaced). It has built the largest dam and the biggest gated community and is well on its way to having the world's most extensive national highway network, greater in extent than even the American interstate system. China has the world's highest rail line and the world's longest, largest bus (half as wide as a football field, with room for 300 passengers). It has the biggest airport terminal and the largest bowling alley, the biggest tennis complex and the most expansive golf course, the largest skateboard park, and even the world's largest lamp. China has built the biggest Buddha on earth and, in Henan Province, even the world's largest dragon: a thirteen-mile tourist colossus meant also to protect the city of Zhengzhou from windblown sand. For a time, China even boasted the world's largest McDonald's restaurant. But, appropriately enough, the behemoth – which opened in 1990 just off Chang'an Avenue in Beijing – was itself rubbed out to make way for something bigger still: Oriental Plaza Shopping Center, also one of Asia's largest.

China has also built more housing in the last twenty-five years than any nation in history, indeed, more than most nations' total housing stock – more than 70 billion square feet nationwide between 1981 and 2001 (equivalent to some 30 million average-sized American houses).[29] Shanghai alone created 208 million square feet of new housing between 1990 and 2004. The human dimension of China's urban transformation is also immense in scale. Since 1992, some forty-six Chinese cities have joined the million-plus population club; there are but nine American members. Wholesale redevelopment of center-city neighborhoods in China has displaced more urban residents than anything else in the peacetime history of the world. The number of people who have migrated to China's cities in the last twenty-five years is greater than the entire population of the United States, and China's middle class alone could well be as big as the entire current population of Europe by 2020.

As Burnham understood, bigness has a life force and spirit all its own. Jovian architectural and urban interventions are deterministic by virtue of scale alone; they create their own weather, if you will. The enormous political and financial muscle necessary to get a big project rolling also gives it almost unstoppable forward momentum, while the simple act of clearing so vast a site fundamentally changes the context of a big project; "big schemes overrun the territory they require," writes Dana Cuff, "leaving no trace of the former land use."[30]

Such tabula rasa city making has particular appeal to an authoritarian regime, and to developers keen on turning a quick profit. Bigness is also seductive from a theoretical perspective. In an influential 1994 interview in *Artforum*, Rem Koolhaas claimed that urban-architectural bigness was an antidote to the chaos and disorder of the fin de siècle metropolis, and that only very large architectural works could sustain in a single urban container the "promiscuous proliferation of events" that make a city what it is. "In a landscape of disarray, disassembly, dissociation, disclamation," he argued, "the attraction of Bigness is its potential to reconstruct the Whole, resurrect the Real, reinvent the collective, reclaim maximum possibility." The big project might be destructive at the outset – the thousands of families dislodged for colossal projects in Beijing or Shanghai would wholeheartedly agree – but it also seems to promise greater things still; "it can reassemble," noted Koolhaas, "what it breaks."[31] Though it's unlikely that very many developers or government officials in the People's Republic have read Koolhaas, they might well be comforted to know their big plans could be so eloquently justified. And so, too, those from the West who come East to satisfy their inner Daniel Burnhams. For China is the last refuge of architectural audacity, the last place on earth (tiny Dubai aside) where ego, scale, and ambition can still be indulged in brick and mortar. In China the sky can still be pricked and poked far from the zoning officials and community activists and the picky planning boards that govern what gets built in America.

Spectacle

The issue of scale is closely linked to that of spectacle. The contemporary Chinese city is spectacular in the literal sense of the word; it is meant to dazzle and awe, and to do so both internally and to a larger world audience. Spectacle in city making is nothing new, and the use of architecture and urban design to create a sense of wonder or fear can be traced back to the earliest urban settlements. Doing so was often related to faith or politics or, in the case of colonial regimes, to make an indelible statement of power and control to a subject people. In modern capitalist societies, architectural spectacle is typically a function of the marketplace. The flashy corporate office tower is, of course, the most obvious example; the staggered skylines of Chicago or New York or Los Angeles are, in this sense, bar graphs of competing corporate ego. In China, urbanistic spectacle results from a more complex set of ego inputs, one that certainly involves private real estate developers, but is also driven by party cadres and local officials eager to make their mark on the skyline. Cities flush with money from land leasing, taxes, and development fees have embarked on a range of civic improvement projects, many of extraordinary scale, luxury, and extent. Many visitors to Chinese cities have been deeply impressed by all this – by airports and opera houses; museums and convention centers and exposition halls; public recreation facilities, extensive new parks, waterfront promenades, and vast urban plazas studded with fountains and public art.

At Xinghai, a booming part of Dalian just southwest of the city center, municipal officials have created the largest public plaza in the world; a spectacular oval-shaped space slashed by axes with a star at the center and embroidered all about with arabesque parterres that can only be fully appreciated from the air. The open space is at least two times larger than Tiananmen Square, and three Pentagons could easily fit within it with room to spare. Xinghai Square is enframed by luxury housing towers and anchored on one side by the sprawling Dalian World Expo and Convention Center, begun

in 2003 and designed by French architect Emmanuel Delarue.

In Xi'an, city officials built a spectacular new plaza to showcase the Tang Dynasty Big Goose Pagoda. But what really makes the scene is a vast fountain complex whose hundreds of shooting water jets, synchronized to music and illuminated at night by lasers and floodlights, is a sight not soon forgotten (nor is the incongruity, sharply noted by local residents, of such aqueous indulgence in an arid region and in a city challenged with perennial water shortages).

One of the most dazzling examples of grand public works in China is Dongguan's new administrative center, built about a 230-acre, mile-long terraced plaza anchored at one end by a monumental City Hall and at the other by a trapezoidal Youth and Children's Center – a relationship that says perhaps more about China's keen commitment to education than it does about its obsession with political order. Also on the axis, on the north side of the Children's Center, is a lake – nothing extraordinary, perhaps, until it is revealed to also be the roof of a vast parking garage. Deployed on either side of the axis is a remarkable ensemble of signature buildings – the kind of architectural trophy collection that every city mayor dreams about. Among the larger buildings is the Yulan Theater, Dongguan Science and Technology Museum, a conference center grand enough to serve as a national capitol, and the well-appointed Dongguan Public Library – the latter as much a bibliotechnic statement of arrival as was McKim, Mead & White's Boston Public Library more than a century ago. Dongguan is certainly not alone in building a glorious administrative headquarters for itself; equally spectacular districts have been built or are being developed by municipalities throughout the Pearl River Delta and coastal China.

There are also public works of relatively more modest scale in China's cities that are dazzling nonetheless as public improvements. Hangzhou officials, for example, transformed that city's once derelict, swampy lakefront into a splendid example of urban design, with miles of boardwalk promenades, teahouses, and gardens strung along the shore. Nanjing recently completed an extensive complex of new parks and pedestrian trails on Purple Mountain in the vicinity of Pipa Lake and the Sun Yat-sen Mausoleum.

All these public works spectacles appear to be the fruits of municipal largesse (not to say affluence) unlike anything seen in the United States since the New Deal. But caution is needed in assessing these projects, or at least the intentions of the responsible officials. Despite real and measurable benefits to the people, grand public works in China are often conceived with more self-serving interests in mind. They are typically undertaken by city and provincial officials to impress Party superiors and, especially, the leadership in Beijing. In China, officials have no democratic constituencies to please; they are rewarded and promoted based largely on what they do, and nothing brings rewards faster than having a spectacular new opera house or convention center to show a visiting VIP from the central government. For this reason, costly public works of the kind described above are commonly referred to in China as "face" or "image" projects (*xing xiang gong chen*).

This yearning for "face" plays out on a larger, global stage as well. China is a nation on the rise, keen on making its mark on the world and erasing the legacy of its past humiliation at the hands of the West and Japan. Like the self-made parvenu, China is striving to outbuild and outshine those who long kept her on her knees. This is, of course, the prime motive force behind China's fervent preparations for the 2008 Olympic Games. It is also clearly at work in the preparations for World Expo 2010 in Shanghai. The money and effort being poured into this event are more than a little reminiscent of the World's Columbian Exposition of 1893. The Columbian Expo, which nominally marked the 400th anniversary of Columbus's voyage to the New World, was really a coming-out party for the United States, thrown to celebrate the triumph of American industrialization, the closing of the frontier West, and the phoenix-like rebirth of Chicago after the Great Fire. In effect, it marked the start of the "American Century."

Shanghai's World Expo 2010 is just as ambitious, and it is expected to draw the largest number of visitors of any world's fair in history. Just as Pullman's coaches served the Chicago fair on their very own rail spur, Shanghai is building its second high-speed Maglev rail line to shuttle regional visitors to the Expo site. Even the theme of the Shanghai fair, "Better City – Better Life," is reminiscent of the Chicago event, whose "White City" set new standards for architecture and urban design that shaped American space for decades to come. That Shanghai should host this event is also poetically appropriate; Shanghai today is just as adrenaline-pumped as Chicago was a century ago – a harbinger of things to come that visitors will gaze upon with an unsettling mix of fear and wonder.

Sprawl

Cities in China are spreading out rapidly upon the landscape, undergoing a process of rapid centrifugal expansion. As explored in Chapter 7, "Suburbanization and the Mechanics of Sprawl," China-style sprawl differs in key ways from its American cousin. For one, Chinese suburbs are far more dense than anything in the suburban United States; even single-family "villa" developments are, on average, much more thickly laid upon the land than most American McMansion subdivisions. Chinese suburbs also lack the political and administrative autonomy that characterizes American suburban communities; they are, by and large, no more than outlying districts of a city whose administrative boundaries typically reach far into the hinterland (Chongqing, for example, encompasses 31,815 square miles – the largest city in the world in terms of land area).

While many affluent people are moving to the suburbs in China, they are accompanied on the urban fringe by those of lesser means – including workers whose places of employment have relocated to the edge of town and low-income urban residents displaced by wholesale redevelopment of the center city. Between 1990 and 2000 in Beijing, the city center lost 222,000 people while suburban districts gained some three million people, including many residents of *hutong* neighborhoods forced out by urban renewal.[32] Chinese suburbanization is also largely devoid of the underlying cultural ambivalence toward cities that helped drive urban flight in America, especially in the 1960s and 1970s. In China, cities are hot. But they are also increasingly expensive places to live, and this factor alone has driven millions of former city dwellers to seek less costly accommodations on the urban periphery. The homes they choose are also very different from those in the suburban United States. The single-family residence on a spacious lot is still only for the superrich in China. Much more common is the gated mid- to high-rise housing estate – the standard unit of Chinese suburban sprawl.

But there are also key commonalities between Chinese and American sprawl. As in the United States, sprawl in China has consumed an immense amount of productive agricultural land. Chinese sprawl is also a function of rising car ownership, for the People's Republic is going mobile with abandon. China is the fastest-growing automobile market in the world, and by 2020 may well be both the largest producer and consumer of cars in the world, with total ownership exceeding even that of the United States. This means a surfeit of highway asphalt, and it is also yielding a whole new exurban landscape oriented to motorists, one in which many of the forms and spaces of American-style suburban sprawl – from big-box retail stores and drive-through restaurants to motels and mega-malls – have been reproduced, now with Chinese characteristics.

Segregation

Chinese urban space is fast segregating along new lines of income, class, and social status. Maoism, for all its numerous shortcomings, did succeed in creating a society in which all people were equal, at least in theory. Today the tycoon has replaced the worker or soldier – or Chairman Mao – as the new cult hero in China. Chinese bookstores over-flow with "How I Earned My Fortune" titles by self-made millionaires like Pan Shiyi of SOHO China or Wang Shi, the former People's Liberation Army soldier who founded Vanke. China may still be nominally a socialist nation, a republic of the people still led by a communist regime, but in real-ity China has become one of the most stridently ambitious capitalistic societies on earth, a nation on the make, hungry to get rich. I often joke with my students that progressive cities like Chapel Hill or Cambridge are far more socialistic today than the People's Republic of China.

In the last thirty years economic reform and rising affluence in China have lifted hundreds of millions of people out of poverty, more perhaps than in any nation in history. Yet at the same time the ideals of social justice and equality that China has long purported to uphold have all but vaporized. Disparities between rich and poor, between the

haves and have-nots, are increasing rapidly and seem to promise that kind of bifurcated society that has long typified Latin America or India. China today is a brutally competitive, almost Darwinistic place; the weak, feeble, unintelligent, or unskilled are quickly crushed and cast aside. Migrant workers especially are ruthlessly exploited by the machinery of wealth production – the very men and women whose labors make the factories hum and the sky-scrapers rise. China's migrant workers, idled by an agricultural economy made more efficient by market reforms, come to the cities in search of a better life and to escape the crushing poverty of the rural countryside. This "floating population" has streamed into China's urban regions by the tens of millions in recent years, and may number as much as 140 million people nationwide. Migrant workers typically have no health care or insurance, let alone any sort of social-service net to fall back upon or unions to take up their case.

Expanding class and economic disparities are increasingly mirrored in the built environment. The city of the rising elite is one of bright lights and big ambition, of gated, guarded housing estates and glitzy shopping malls. But in the midst of such privilege is often another urban world, one inhabited by the poor and disenfranchised; the densely packed "urban villages" trapped in the middle of Shenzhen, Guangzhou, and other cities are only the most visible example.

Sustainability

In December 2006 it was widely reported in the global media that the Chinese river dolphin, the *baiji*, was extinct. The species, once abundant in the lower Yangtze River, had come under severe stress in recent years as a result of increasingly heavy ship traffic, dam construction, runoff, and pollution. Only a handful of the animals had been sighted in the previous decade, none since 2004. The dolphin, once known as "the goddess of the Yangtze," was the first large aquatic mammal to go extinct since the 1950s. The passing of this odd-looking creature, news of which barely caused a ripple in the People's Republic, is symbolic none-theless of China's looming environmental crisis – a problem of truly global proportions. China's environmental problems are legion. Nearly all of the most terribly polluted cities in the world are in China, and vital air and water resources are fast becoming toxic. Nanjing, renowned for its street trees, parks, and universities, is practically smothered most evenings by an acrid-smelling smog blown in by nocturnal winds from chemical plants on the outskirts of town. In Xi'an, a combination of Gobi Desert dust and smoke from farmers burning wheat fields in the surrounding countryside makes for near zero visibility at certain times of the year. Beijing on the best of days struggles with some of the highest levels of motor-vehicle-borne carbon emissions in Asia.

China is also consuming natural resources at a ferocious clip and scouring the planet in search of raw materials. It is now the second largest consumer of oil in the world and burns through more fossil fuel than Russia and India combined. As Thomas L. Friedman has pointed out, this hunger for oil has led China into making deals with some of the least savory regimes on earth, in Sudan, Zimbabwe, Angola, and elsewhere.[33] Although Chinese money pouring into sub-Saharan Africa has awakened the region's long-dormant economies and stimulated growth unseen in decades, China's Africa play is wholly absent of humanitarian impulse and is driven exclusively by rising demand for oil, coal, copper, iron, timber, and other natural resources.

From South America to Central Asia, China is literally consuming the world. All this comes at the very moment when the United States, Japan, and Western Europe – long the chief polluters of Spaceship Earth – have finally begun to end their decades of bad environmental behavior. Yet scientists have argued that even if all greenhouse gas emissions were to stop tomorrow, it would take centuries to reverse the damage already done. This daunting prospect is made more so by the likelihood, according to statistics from the Chinese government itself, that by 2008 China will eclipse the United States as the world's leading producer of greenhouse gases – an Olympian achievement indeed. "Today's global warming problem has been caused mainly by us in the West," observes David Fridley of the Lawrence Berkeley National Laboratory's China Energy Group, "but China is contributing to the global warming problem of tomorrow."[34]

When it comes to the environment, China and the West are moving in opposite directions, and at blinding speed. As recently as 2001, for example, China's total greenhouse gas emissions were only 42 percent of what the United States was producing at the time; just five years later that number was up to 97 percent.[35] China's usual response to such criticism is to claim exemption as a developing country, and to point out the hypocrisy of Western – and especially American – pots calling the Chinese kettle black. China's per capita energy consumption, after all, is a mere fraction of America's. Why should China hobble its growth, people ask, when the West got rich plundering the planet?

The answer, of course, is that China has no choice. Even if Beijing cares not a whit about the well-being of other peoples and nations, it cares greatly about keeping its own economy on an upward trend, and it has increasingly come to see that doing so will require taking positive steps to protect the environment and reduce its galloping pace of resource consumption. For China, "going green" is not the lifestyle option it is often construed to be in the United States. Spoiled by its enormous wealth, land, and resources, America has long been a wasteful and inefficient nation; only recently has it begun to take seriously the nexus between environmental health and future economic viability. For China, reducing resource consumption is an even more urgent matter. China is trying to run a marathon at a sprinter's pace. The nation's current course of fast growth and expanding resource use is utterly unsustainable. Moreover, its increasing dependence on foreign commodities exposes China to the uncertainties of global geopolitics and the whims of other countries. With the possible exception of social instability from the growing gap between rich and poor, nothing more fully threatens the future of the People's Republic than the prospect of catastrophic environmental collapse or the economic meltdown that would result from a sudden lack of oil. As George Perkins Marsh demonstrated in his book *Man and Nature* (1864), mighty civilizations have ground to a halt for less.

There are indeed encouraging signs that China has begun to take environmental matters seriously. And it need only look back to its own past for inspiration. China is a civilization with a long and rich history of harmonious and often sublime coexistence with the natural environment, perhaps best exemplified by the ancient gardens of Hangzhou or Suzhou. Vernacular architecture in nearly every region of China embodies centuries of environmental wisdom and includes some of the best examples of sustainable design and "green building" anywhere in the world.[36] One is the *yao dong* courtyard house of the loess plateau regions of Shaanxi, Henan, Shanxi, and Gansu provinces, among the oldest form of human habitation on earth. The cave-like hillside dwellings, landscape architecture in the truest sense, are set about excavated courtyards and provide a surprisingly comfortable living environment in all seasons; the houses are cool in summer and warm in winter. China's grassroots-level sustainability can also be seen on nearly every city street, in the old woman collecting empty water bottles or the rural migrants pedaling unbelievably overloaded tricycles full of recycled cardboard or Styrofoam. Every building demolition site in China is also a massive recycling operation. Anything that can be reused is set in neat piles to be carted off for new life – bricks, wiring, pipes, doors, window frames, scraps of structural timber, even mangled jumbles of reinforcement bar. Most such materials would end up in a landfill in the United States.

Of course, these and other examples of street-level sustainability in China are more a function of poverty than a strong ethic of environmental stewardship. As such, unfortunately, they are both stigmatized and bound to decline as China becomes increasingly affluent. Bicycle use has been falling in most cities for these very reasons; bikes are seen as a poor-person's transport option and are quickly thrown aside as families make their way up the socioeconomic ladder. In Henan and Shaanxi provinces, rural families who have lived in *yao dong* dwellings for generations yearn to move to fancy new high-rise flats with air conditioning and a modern kitchen. Architects in the region, such as Xia Yun and Liu Jia Ping of Xi'an University of Architecture and Technology, have been working to prevent this by developing a workable prototype of an updated, modern *yao dong* house.

In similar spirit, China's central government itself has launched a string of promising reforms in recent years aimed at reducing China's collective environmental impact. In a rare example of self-criticism in January 2007, the central government even admitted that China failed to meet its own goals for environmental protection, its "ecological modernization" lagging far behind economic and other achievements.[37] One of the most promising pieces of legislation is the Renewable Energy Promotion Law, passed in 2005 and implemented a year later. As conveyed by Article I, the law was intended "to promote the development and utilization of renewable energy . . . diversify energy supplies, safeguard energy security, protect the environment, and realize the sustainable development of the economy and society." Especially emphasized were renewable energy sources – wind, solar, tidal and hydroelectric, geothermal and biomass. The central government has further set itself a target of 12 percent of total power capacity from renewable energy sources by 2020.[38]

Indeed, despite the fact that a new coal-fired power plant opens every ten days in China, the nation may yet show the world how to go green. For all the automobiles crowding onto its city streets, China is also building more miles of subway and light-rail public transportation than any nation on earth. China already has the world's largest biofuels plant and the world's largest solar plant, a 100-megawatt facility in Dunhuang, Gansu Province, that dwarfs its closest rivals – a 12-megawatt plant in Germany and an 11-megawatt facility under construction in Portugal. In February 2007 China announced plans to earmark some 200 million acres of woodland for biomass production and to plant trees on more than 600,000 acres of land in Yunnan and Sichuan provinces for similar purposes. China's installed wind-power capacity has been growing exponentially, and the Global Wind Energy Council has predicted that by 2020 China could be drawing 150 million kilowatts of energy from the wind, surpassing Germany, Spain, and the United States to become the world's leading producer of wind power.[39]

China already boasts some 60 percent of the world's installed solar water heater capacity, and an estimated 30 million households nationwide use solar power in one form or another. Ready-to-install A-frame solar units come complete with a water tank and are sold at any major home-improvement store, displayed out front the way garden sheds are at American stores. Needless to say, no such ready-built solar equipment is available in the United States, where low-voltage garden lights are about the only solar-powered thing readily available at home-improvement stores. In September 2005, Shanghai officials approved a measure to install more than one million square feet of solar panels on rooftops across the city, in addition to several solar power plants.[40] In the early morning, from my twelfth-floor office window in Nanjing, I could see the sunlight glinting off hundreds of solar water-heating units on the rooftops of the city below – a comforting sight indeed.

The same economies of scale that have rockbottomed the cost of everything from air conditioners to Christmas ornaments may well also produce photovoltaic arrays affordable enough to make solar electricity a viable option for homeowners around the world. As architect William McDonough has put it, "When China comes on line with solar collectors that are cheaper than coal, it will be one of the greatest gifts to the United States" – and to the world. Making solar power more cost-effective than burning coal is, McDonough argues, "the assignment of our species at this moment in history. And China is the only place where this can happen."[41] It is a promising sign indeed that one of China's richest men, Shi Zhengrong of Suntech Power, a graduate of the School of Photovoltaic and Renewable Energy Engineering at the University of New South Wales, made a fortune manufacturing photovoltaic cells for solar panels.

China may well also show the world how to build a truly sustainable city. One of the most ambitious – and promising – urban development projects in the world today is planned for Chongming Island, a fifty-mile-long spit of land in the middle of the Yangtze River near Shanghai. Chongming is a largely rural landscape, but in coming decades it is to be transformed into a self-sufficient green city known as Dongtang. Powered by energy from wind turbines and biofuels derived from farm waste, Dongtang is meant to source 30 percent of its energy from renewables by 2020 and eventually achieve an overall carbon emission level of zero. No fossil-fueled cars or trucks will be permitted on the island, where transportation will be handled instead by solar-powered water taxis and buses running on hydrogen fuel cell technology. The urbanized portion of Dongtang will be compacted into three "villages" built with energy efficient green building technology. Large portions of the island will be forested or used for organic farming. The local economy will be sustained by ecotourism and low-polluting, high-tech industry. In its first phase, Dongtang will accommodate 25,000 people, but it is expected to eventually be home to as many as 500,000 by 2040.[42] The project is, of course, not without its critics and potential problems. It could well end up just a green theme park for eco-curious tourists from Shanghai. But the very fact that China has chosen to invest in such an ambitious experiment is much to its credit, and even if it fails to achieve every goal, Dongtang could well serve as a laboratory for green urbanism elsewhere.

Though environmental stewardship has a long and rich history in China, it is, as yet, surely not characteristic of contemporary Chinese urbanism. At present, sustainability in Chinese cities is no more than a faint spark against a vast, dark field. But again, the sheer scale of Chinese ambition potentially makes even this, a beacon for the world; "a glimmer in China," as McDonough put it to me recently, "is a bright light in the world indeed."[43] So I end this exploration of the new Chinese landscape on a somewhat hopeful note: that, whatever its motivations, China will reinvent the city as a more sustainable entity, and thus perhaps show the rest of this fast-urbanizing planet a new and greener approach to urban settlement and urban life. The continued growth of the Chinese economy – indeed the very viability of the People's Republic – surely depends upon it. And so do we all.

NOTES

1 See Howard W. French, "Homeowner Stares Down Wreckers, at Least for a While," *New York Times*, March 27, 2007; Joseph Kahn, "China Backs Property Law, Buoying Middle Class," *New York Times*, March 16, 2007. Eventually the building was pulled down, but not before its owner won generous compensation from the developers.

2 Photographer Edward Burtynsky captures the awesome scale of the Three Gorges project and the landscapes it doomed. See http://www.edwardburtynsky.com.

3 Piper Gaubatz, "China's Urban Transformation," *Urban Studies* 36, no. 9 (1999): 1515.

4 Ian Johnson, "Moving a Mountain to Clear the Bad Air in Lanzhou, China," *Wall Street Journal*, August 7, 1997.

5   The total housing stock in the United States in 2005 was 218,654,766,000 square feet; from U.S. Census Bureau, Current Housing Reports, Series H150/05, American Housing Survey for the United States, http://www.census.gov/hhes/www/housing/ahs/nationaldata.html. Also see Shruti Gupta, "China: Building a Strong Foundation," *Frost & Sullivan Market Insight*, September 16, 2004.

6   In 2004, GDP of sub-Saharan Africa at market prices was approximately $529 billion; see "Sub-Saharan Africa Data Profile," *World Development Indicators Database* (World Bank Group, April 2006), http://devdata.worldbank.org.

7   David Barboza, "China Builds its Dreams, and Some Fear a Bubble," *New York Times*, October 18, 2005.

8   In 2004 China's construction industry employed about 24 million people; *China Statistical Yearbook* (Beijing: China Statistics Press, 2004).

9   See Daniel B. Wood, "Cement Shortage Hits US Housing Boom," *Christian Science Monitor*, August 17, 2004; Sandra Fleishman, "China's Expansion Squeezes Cement Supply," *Washington Post*, September 18, 2004.

10 For an introduction to the subject of Chinese highways, see the three-volume compilation *Highways in China* (Beijing: Ministry of Communication, 1990, 1995, 2000). For an American perspective, see Rob Gifford, *China Road* (New York: Random House, 2007).

11 "China Plans Everest Highway for Olympics Event," *CNN News*, June 19, 2007.

12 Accurate data on urban-renewal displacement in China is difficult to find. I based this estimate on measurements of the actual road channel using aerial photographs, combined with population density data from the Wendell Cox Consultancy (http://www.demographia.com).

13 Chinese Academy of Engineering, National Research Council, et al., *Personal Cars and China* (Washington, DC: National Academies Press, 2003), 228.

14 "China Stands as World's 2nd Largest Auto Market," *People's Daily*, January 13, 2006; Eric Baculinao, "China's Auto Industry Takes Off," *NBC News*, January 12, 2007.

15 Chia-Liang Tai, "Transforming Shanghai: The Redevelopment Context of the Pudong New Area" (unpublished masters thesis, Columbia University, Faculty of Architecture and Planning, May 2005), 54; "Beijing's Private Autos Top One Million," *Xinhua News*, May 22, 2002.

16 Between 1978 and 1995, approximately 11 million acres (17,375 square miles) of cultivated land in China were lost to development; another 17 million acres (26,562 square miles) vanished between then and 2004. See Jonathan Watts, "China's Farmers Cannot Feed Hungry Cities," *Guardian Unlimited*, August 26, 2004. Also see Chengri Ding and Gerrit Knaap, "Urban Land Policy Reform in China," *Land Lines* (Lincoln Institute of Land Policy) 15, no. 2 (April 2003).

17 Watts, "China's Farmers Cannot Feed Hungry Cities," August 26, 2004.

18 Li Conghua, *China: The Consumer Revolution* (New York: Wiley, 1998), 5.

19 GDP measured at purchasing-power parity; Pam Woodall, "The Dragon and the Eagle," *Economist*, September 30, 2004. See also "The Real Great Leap Forward," *Economist*, September 30, 2004.

20 Approximately 29 million people emigrated from Europe to the United States between 1820 and 1920, while about five million African Americans moved out of the rural South between 1940 and 1970. Approximately 6.5 million Americans moved from farms and rural areas to cities between 1920 and 1930.

21 As the *Los Angeles Times* pointed out, Yao's NBA salary alone makes him "one of China's most profitable exports to the United States." ChingChing Ni, "Working-Class Hero? NBA Star Nets China's Proletarian Award," *Los Angeles Times*, April 28, 2005.

22 Joseph Kahn, "China's Elite Learn to Flaunt It While the New Landless Weep," *New York Times*, December 25, 2004.

23 Hannah Beech, "Wretched Excess," *TIME Asia Magazine* 160, no. 11 (September 23, 2002).

24 The bronze likeness shows Li gesturing toward the horizon with his palm facing down, as if hailing a far-off friend. As Li explained in a 2002 interview, to have cast himself with palm raised up and outward would have been politically provocative; it is still a gesture reserved for likenesses of Mao Zedong. Craig S. Smith, "For China's Wealthy, All but Fruited Plain," *New York Times*, May 15, 2002. See also Rupert Hoogewerf, "Li Qinfu, Size XL," *Forbes.com*, November 11, 2002.

25 Daniel Abramson, "'Marketization' and Institutions in Chinese Inner-city Redevelopment," *Cities* 14, no. 2 (1997): 71n; Nancy Lin cites similar statistics (1:30, 400 in China; 1:3, 120 in the United States) in "Architecture Shenzhen," in Chuihua Judy Chung, Jeffrey Inaba, Rem Koolhaas, Sze Tsung, et al., eds, *Great Leap Forward* (Kiiln: Taschen, 2001), 158–61.

26 James, who wrote *The American Scene* upon his return from a twenty-year hiatus in Europe, understood the ephemerality and impermanence of the skyscraper city: "They never begin to speak to you, in the manner of the builded majesties of the world as we have heretofore known such – towers or temples or fortresses or palaces – with the authority of things of permanence or even of things of long duration. One story is good ingenuity only till another is told, and sky-scrapers are the last word of economic ingenuity only till another word be written." Henry James, *The American Scene* (London: Chapman & Hall, 1907), 76–77.

27 "McDonald's Opens Drive-thru in Beijing," *International Business Times*, January 19, 2007.

28 This was reported in *Nan Feng*, July 13, 2006.

29 Yang Jianxiang, "Building Dreams in Bricks and Mortar," *China Daily*, September 14, 2004. The housing stock in the United States in 2005 was about 219 billion square feet; see U.S. Census Bureau, Current Housing Reports, Series H150/05, American Housing Survey for the United States, http://www.census.gov/hhes/www/housing/ahs/nationaldata.html.

30 Dana Cuff, *The Provisional City: Los Angeles Stories of Architecture and Urbanism* (Cambridge, MA: MIT Press, 2002), 4–5.

31 John Rajchman, "Thinking Big – Dutch Architect Rem Koolhaas – Interview," *Artforum*, December 1994.

32 Yixing Zhou and Laurence J.C. Ma, "Economic Restructuring and Suburbanization in China," *Urban Geography* 21, no. 3 (2000): 223.

33 Thomas L. Friedman, *The World Is Flat: A Brief History of the Twenty-First Century* (New York: Farrar, Straus & Giroux, 2005), 409.

34 Robert Collier, "A Warming World: China About to Pass U.S. as World's Top Generator of Greenhouse Gases," *San Francisco Chronicle*, March 5, 2007.

35 Ibid.

36 Ronald G. Knapp has written extensively on the subject of Chinese vernacular housing. See, for example, *China's Vernacular Architecture: House Form and Culture* (Honolulu: University of Hawaii Press, 1989) and Knapp and Kai-Yin Lo, eds, *House Home Family: Living and Being Chinese* (Honolulu: University of Hawaii Press, 2005).

37 "China Admits Failure to Make Environmental Progress," *Reuters*, January 29, 2007.

38 People's Republic of China, "Renewable Energy Law" (unofficial version) from the Renewable Energy and Energy Efficiency Partnership.

39 Alex Pasternack, "China Could Be World's Biggest Wind Power by 2020," *Treehugger: Science and Technology*, January 26, 2007, http://www.treehugger.com/files/2007/01/china_could_be.php.

40 "Shanghai to Install Solar Panels on Building Roofs," *Shanghai Daily News*, September 15, 2005.

41 "Q&A with William A. McDonough," *Urban Land*, January 2007, 119.

42 "Visions of Ecopolis," *Economist*, September 21, 2006.

43 William A. McDonough, phone interview by author, April 11, 2007.

PART FIVE

Addressing Environmental Challenges

Plate 6 The Southeast False Creek Development in Vancouver, British Columbia, Canada was consciously designed to become one of the greenest communities of the early twenty-first century. Initially designated as the Olympic Village for the 2010 Winter Olympic Games, the development is now a mixed-use community of residences, retail, and cultural amenities. This is one of a handful of megaprojects developed over the last two decades in downtown Vancouver that seeks to improve the quality of life and urban environment for city dwellers. Providing a continuous waterfront public realm allows residents access to recreation, biking, beaches, and open space. This is the compensatory exterior space for dense urban living that makes in-town living possible and attractive. The Southeast False Creek Development offers a scale of building, residential density, walkability, transit access, innovative utility infrastructure, and green building principles that help to conserve land, water, and energy resources that might have been spent on less sustainable projects. (Photo: E. Macdonald)

INTRODUCTION TO PART FIVE

The world is currently facing immense environmental challenges: global warming, climate change, sea level rise, lack of fresh water, over population, resource depletion, air and water pollution, loss of habitat, widespread species extinction – the list of problems and their mind-boggling complexity and scale goes on and on. These environmental problems loom large for the built environment professions as more and more voices around the world are calling for addressing them and moving toward greater sustainability.

This section of the *Reader* explores key environmental challenges being faced in cities around the world and the built environment professions' responses. We begin with two older writings that laid the ground work for a recent spate of ecologically driven design thought and practice. Ian McHarg's piece, "An Ecological Method for Landscape Architecture," describes the method of regional landscape analysis that he invented in the late 1960s, which instantly became standard practice in the landscape architecture and regional planning professions. His method, which involved overlay mapping on transparencies, sought to identify areas of sensitive ecological resources so that development could be appropriately sited to complement natural systems and do the least possible harm to them.

Two decades later, Michael Hough furthered McHarg's concerns by focusing on issues of regional identity in relation to natural factors. He argued that placelessness has become ubiquitous in part because designers lack awareness of and appreciation for regional environmental differences and thus do not design in ways to enhance and emphasize local place. In "Principles for Regional Design," a chapter taken from his book *Out of Place: Restoring Identity to the Regional Landscape*, he eloquently analyzes the forces influencing the degradation of regional environmental quality and advocates simple approaches that designers might take to gain more awareness and respect for regional difference and so better contribute to regional place-making.

The next two readings focus on Landscape Urbanism, a recently developed theoretical design approach for addressing ecological issues that has taken hold in university design programs and has begun to influence urban design practice, including some recent high-profile design and planning projects. Charles Waldheim's piece "Landscape as Urbanism," which comes from *The Landscape Urbanism Reader*, an anthology that he edited, is the classic articulation of the concerns of the Landscape Urbanism movement and its approach to design. Following this, several pieces from Alan Berger's book *Drosscape* look closely at one type of space identified by Landscape Urbanists as a key locus for design action, namely wasted landscapes and interstitial spaces left over from the processes of urban de-industrialization that have been going on around the world since the 1970s. Berger challenges urban designers to take on these often contaminated "brownfield" sites as places for design intervention and innovation, even in the face of no paying client and no design program.

The last two readings in this section focus on practical strategies that cities can take to address environmental problems and to strive for greater sustainability at the local level. Timothy Beatley's piece "Planning for Sustainability in European Cities: A Review of Practice in Leading Cities," first published in *The Sustainable Urban Development Reader* which is part of this reader series, reviews innovative sustainability approaches being taken by a number of European cities, including prioritization of low-energy-consuming forms of transportation, urban greening, and waste-fed district heating systems. The final piece, "Urban

Resilience: Cities of Fear and Hope," from Peter Newman, Timothy Beatley and Heather Boyer's recent book *Resilient Cities: Responding to Peak Oil and Climate Change*, identifies climate change and resource depletion as the most critical environmental problems that must be faced. It argues for the importance of creating resilient cities and urban forms, which can adapt to the changes that will inevitably come and recover from the shocks of all kinds that might need to be absorbed in the uncertain future. As well, strategies that cities can take to achieve greater resilience are discussed.

"An Ecological Method for Landscape Architecture"

from *Landscape Architecture Magazine* (1967)

Ian McHarg

Editors' Introduction

Conservation of natural areas has been a public concern since the turn of the twentieth century. In the United States, early efforts focused on the preservation of natural areas of great beauty, such as Yosemite Valley and Yellowstone, turning them into National Parks. Larger environmental concerns leapt to the forefront of public consciousness in the early 1960s spurred by a host of environmental ills, including air pollution, water pollution, pesticide poisoning, and dwindling energy sources. Books such as Rachel Carson's *Silent Spring* (New York: Fawcett Crest, 1962) and Barry Commoner's *The Closing Circle* (New York: Knopf, 1971) eloquently called attention to these matters. Members of the design professions responded by shifting their attention to environmental issues. Architects explored passive solar and energy efficient building designs, urban planners became environmental advocates and began focusing on regional-scale environmental planning, landscape architects dug deeper into the ecological issues of landscape design, and urban designers began exploring the dimensions of environmental perception. In practice, designers and the communities they worked for grappled with how to address environmental concerns in projects of large and small scale. The tool they turned to was the new "ecological method" articulated by landscape architect Ian McHarg (1920–2001) in his seminal book *Design with Nature* (Garden City, NY: Natural History Press, 1969), which became an instant classic. McHarg critiques the effects of urban sprawl and advocates plan-making based on natural processes. He calls for landscape architects to act within design processes as "interpreters" of the land and its resources by engaging in comprehensive analysis of the study area's geology, climate, slope, exposure, water regimens, soils, plants, animals, and land use. Such analysis, he argues, reveals appropriate sites for human land-using activities of various kinds as well as areas of particular environmental sensitivity or value that should be left untouched. Key to McHarg's method is the use of layered transparency mapping which creates a graphic matrix that identifies compatibilities and incompatibilities between various human uses and between those uses and the aggregated ecological contexts. Going beyond matters of functionality, McHarg argues that design inspiration should derive from the perception of natural form that comes from this analysis.

McHarg's ecological method was widely adopted in landscape architecture and regional planning practice, and remains standard practice today. Today, the method is generally applied using spatial mapping techniques conducted using Geographic Information Systems (GIS) technology. This new technology has the advantage of being able to link spatial maps with comprehensive databases covering not only ecological factors but also any number of physical, social, and economic factors.

In retrospect, McHarg can be criticized for being overly optimistic that ecological science could shape urban development in an ecologically responsible direction in the face of powerful social and economic forces promoting unsustainable development. As well, his emphasis on regional-scale ecological analysis and land use decision-making is at odds with how land use planning decisions are actually made in most places in America because few places have effective regional governance. Nonetheless, McHarg's exhortation that landscape architects and urban planners should take addressing environmental issues as a central charge still resonates across the design fields. His ecological method laid the groundwork for how designers and planners might begin the hard work of understanding complex environmental systems and learning to design from an ecological perspective.

The paper "An Ecological Method for Landscape Architecture" from *Landscape Architecture Magazine* (1967) is two years older than *Design with Nature*, but it provides a good summary of McHarg's seminal analytical method because it focuses on the actual processes illustrated in the more famous book.

Growing up in a small town near Glasgow, Scotland, McHarg was exposed to both the harshness of an industrial city and the beauty of natural countryside, and he attributed his lifelong concern with nature and development to that experience. After earning master's degrees in landscape architecture and city planning from Harvard, in 1954 he founded the department of landscape architecture at the University of Pennsylvania and taught there as a professor for many years, creating one of the most interdisciplinary programs in the United States. He was a founding member of the landscape architecture firm Wallace, McHarg, Roberts & Todd, through which he worked on many professional projects and garnered numerous awards. He was a Fellow of the American Society of Landscape Architects (ASLA) and the recipient of many honors including the ASLA Medal and the LaGasse Medal.

Design with Nature has been reprinted several times, most recently by John Wiley (1992). McHarg's two other books are *To Heal the Earth: Selected Writings of Ian L. McHarg* (Washington, DC: Island Press, 1998), co-edited with Frederick R. Steiner, and *A Quest for Life: An Autobiography* (New York: John Wiley, 1996). A book that stands alongside McHarg's *Design with Nature* in terms of influencing designers' early awareness of urban ecology issues is Anne Whiston Spirn's *The Granite Garden* (New York: Basic Books, 1984), which articulates the natural contexts and ecological processes to be found in cities. At the time of its publication, this book was radical in its insistence that cities are a part of nature and that nature is to be found everywhere within them. It continues to inspire today's designers with its simple ideas for how to design urban places in concert with natural systems rather than in opposition to them.

Classic works that anticipated the later twentieth-century concern with ecological systems are Patrick Geddes, *Cities in Evolution* (London: Williams & Norgate, 1915) and Benton MacKaye's *The New Exploration: A Philosophy of Regional Planning* (New York: Harcourt, Brace, 1928). A classic work that set the stage for the ecological consciousness that began in the 1960s is Aldo Leopold's *A Sand County Almanac* (1949), reprinted in many later editions including most recently by Oxford University Press (2001).

Recent works on ecological planning and design abound. A recently reprinted classic text on ecological design principles is Sim Van der Ryn and Stuart Cowan's *Ecological Design* (Washington, DC: Island Press, 2007), which encourages design across spatial scales and collaboration across design professions in the pursuit of low environmental impact development. More recent works include Robert G. Bailey's *Ecoregion-Based Design for Sustainability* (New York: Springer, 2002); Forster Ndubisi's *Ecological Planning: A Historical and Comparative Synthesis* (Baltimore, MD: Johns Hopkins University Press, 2002); and Wenche E. Dramstad et al.'s *Landscape Ecology Principles in Landscape Architecture and Landuse Planning* (Washington, DC: Island Press, 1996). Edited anthologies of essays include *Issues and Perspectives in Landscape Ecology* (Cambridge: Cambridge University Press, 2005), edited by John A. Wiens and Michael R. Moss, and *Ecological Design and Planning* (New York: John Wiley, 1997), edited by George F. Thompson and Frederick R. Steiner.

Randy Hester's *Design for Ecological Democracy* (Cambridge, MA: MIT Press, 2006) is a powerful book that outlines principles for urban design that allow communities to both connect with the natural environment and enhance a sense of community.

Recent architecturally oriented books that address ecological drivers for design include Douglas Farr's *Sustainable Urbanism: Urban Design with Nature* (Hoboken, NJ: John Wiley, 2008) and Ken Yeang's *Designing with Nature: The Ecological Basis for Architectural Design* (New York: McGraw Hill, 1995).

Works that address GIS applications in ecological analysis include Carol A. Johnston's *Geographic Information Systems in Ecology* (Oxford: Blackwell Science, 2001) and Mohammed A. Kalkhan's *Spatial Statistics: GeoSpatial Information Modeling and Thematic Mapping* (Boca Raton, FL: CRC Press, 2011).

In many cases a qualified statement is, if not the most propitious, at least the most prudent. In this case it would only be gratuitous. I believe that ecology provides the single indispensible basis for landscape architecture and regional planning. I would state in addition that it has now, and will increasingly have, a profound relevance for both city planning and architecture.

Where the landscape architect commands ecology he is the only bridge between the natural sciences and the planning and design professions, the proprietor of the most perceptive view of the natural world which science or art has provided. This can be at once his unique attribute, his passport to relevance and productive social utility. With the acquisition of this competence the sad image of ornamental horticulture, handmaiden to architecture after the fact, the caprice and arbitrariness of "clever" designs can be dismissed forever. In short, ecology offers emancipation to landscape architecture.

This is not the place for a scholarly article on ecology. We are interested in it selfishly, as those who can and must apply it. Our concern is for a method which has the power to reveal nature as process, containing intrinsic form.

Ecology is generally described as the study of the interactions of organisms and environment which includes other organisms. The particular interests of landscape architecture are focussed only upon a part of this great, synoptic concern. This might better be defined as the study of physical and biological processes, as dynamic and interacting, responsive to laws, having limiting factors and exhibiting certain opportunities and constraints, employed in planning and design for human use. At this juncture two possibilities present themselves. The first is to attempt to present a general theory of ecology and the planning processes. This is a venture which I long to undertake, but this is not the time nor place to attempt it. The other alternative is to present a method which has been tested empirically at many scales from a continent, a major region, a river basin, physiographic regions, sub-regional areas and a metropolitan region town to a single city. In every case, I submit, it has been triumphantly revelatory.[1]

First, it is necessary to submit a proposition to this effect: that the place, the plants, animals and men upon it are only comprehensible in terms of physical and biological evolution. Written on the place and upon its inhabitants lies mute all physical, biological and cultural history awaiting to be understood by those who can read it. It is thus necessary to begin at the beginning if we are to understand the place, the man, or his co-tenants of this phenomenal universe. This is the prerequisitie [sic] for intelligent intervention and adaptation. So let us begin at the beginning. We start with historical geology. The place, any place, can only be understood through its physical evolution. What history of mountain building and ancient seas, uplifting, folding, sinking, erosion and glaciation have passed here and left their marks? These explain its present form. Yet the effects of climate and later of plants and animals have interacted upon geological processes and these too lie mute in the record of the rocks. Both climate and geology can be invoked to interpret physiography, the current configuration of the place. Arctic differs from tropics, desert from delta, the Himalayas from the Gangetic Plain. The Appalachian Plateau differs from the Ridge and Valley Province and all of these from the Piedmont and the Coastal Plain. If one now knows historical geology, climate and physiography then the water regimen becomes comprehensible – the pattern of rivers and aquifers, their physical properties and relative abundance, oscillation between flood and drought. Rivers are young or old, they vary by orders; their pattern and distribution, as for aquifers, is directly consequential upon geology, climate and physiography.

Knowing the foregoing and the prior history of plant evolution, we can now comprehend the nature and pattern of soils. As plants are highly selective to environmental factors, by identifying physiographic, climatic zones and soils we can perceive order and predictability in the distribution of constituent plant communities. Indeed, the plant communities are more perceptive to environmental variables than we can be with available data, and we can thus infer environmental factors from the presence of plants. Animals are fundamentally plant-related so that given the preceding information, with the addition of the stage of succession of the plant communities and their age, it is possible both to understand and to predict the species, abundance or scarcity of wild animal populations. If there are no acorns there will be no squirrels; an old forest will have few deer; an early succession can support many. Resources also exist where they do for good and sufficient reasons – coal, iron, limestone, productive soils, water in relative abundance, transportation routes, fall lines and the termini of water transport. And so the land use map becomes comprehensible when viewed through this perspective.

The information so acquired is a gross ecological inventory and contains the data bank for all further investigations. The next task is the interpretation of these data to analyze existing and propose future human land use and management. The first objective is the inventory of unique or scarce phenomena, the technique for which Philip Lewis[2] is renowned. In this all sites of unique scenic, geological, ecological or historical importance are located. Enlarging this category we can interpret the geological data to locate economic minerals. Geology, climate and physiography will locate dependable water resources. Physiography will reveal slope and exposure which, with soil and water, can be used to locate areas suitable for agriculture by types; the foregoing, with the addition of plant communities will reveal intrinsic suitabilities for both forestry and recreation. The entire body of data can be examined to reveal sites for urbanization, industry, transportation routes, indeed any human land-using activity. This interpretive sequence would produce a body of analytical material but the end product for a region would include a map of unique sites, the location of economic minerals, the location of water resources, a slope and exposure map, a map of agricultural suitabilities by types, a similar map for forestry, one each for recreation and urbanization.

These maps of intrinsic suitability would indicate highest and best uses for the entire study area. But this is not enough. These are single uses ascribed to discrete areas. In the forest there are likely to be dominant or co-dominant trees and other subordinate species. We must seek to prescribe all coexistent, compatible uses which may occupy each area. To this end it is necessary to develop a matrix in which all possible land uses are shown on each coordinate. Each is then examined against all others to determine the degree of compatibility or incompatibility. As an example, a single area of forest may be managed for forestry, either hardwood or pulp; it may be utilized for water management objectives; it may fulfill an erosion control

function; it can be managed for wildlife and hunting, recreation, and for villages and hamlets. Here we have not land use in the normal sense but *communities* of land uses. The end product would be a map of present and prospective land uses, in communities of compatibilities, with dominants, co-dominants and subordinates derived from an understanding of nature as process responsive to laws, having limiting factors, constituting a value system and exhibiting opportunities and constraints to human use.

Now this is not a plan. It does not contain any information of demand. This last is the province of the regional scientist, the econometrician, the economic planner. The work is thus divided between the natural scientist, regional planner-landscape architect who interprets the land and its resources, and the economics-based planner who determines demand, locational preferences, investment and fiscal policies. If demand information is available, then the formulation of a plan is possible, and the demand components can be allocated for urban growth, for the nature and form of the metropolis, for the pattern of regional growth.

So what has our method revealed? First, it allows us to understand nature as process insofar as the natural sciences permit. Second, it reveals causality. The place is because. Next it permits us to interpret natural processes as resources, to prescribe and even to predict for prospective land uses, not singly but in compatible communities. Finally, given information on demand and investment, we are enabled to produce a plan for a continent or a few hundred acres based upon natural process. That is not a small accomplishment.

You might well agree that this is a valuable and perhaps even indispensible method for regional planning but is it as valuable for landscape architecture? I say that any project, save a small garden or the raddled heart of a city where nature has long gone, which is undertaken without a full comprehension and employment of natural process as form-giver is suspect at best and capriciously irrelevant at worst. I submit that the ecological method is the sine qua non for all landscape architecture.

Yet, I hear you say, those who doubt, that the method may be extremely valuable for regional rural problems, but can it enter the city and reveal a comparable utility? Yes, indeed it can but in crossing this threshold the method changes. When used to examine metropolitan growth the data remains the same but the interpretation is focused upon the overwhelming demand for urban land uses and it is oriented to the prohibitions and permissiveness exhibited by natural process to urbanization on the one hand and the presence of locational and resource factors which one would select for satisfactory urban environments on the other. But the litany remains the same: historical geology, climate, physiography, the water regimen, soils, plants, animals and land use. This is the source from which the interpretation is made although the grain becomes finer.

Yet you say, the method has not entered the city proper; you feel that it is still a device for protecting natural process against the blind despoliation of ignorance and Philistinism. But the method can enter the city and we can proceed with our now familiar body of information to examine the city in an ecological way. We have explained that the place was "because" and to explain "because," all of physical and biological evolution was invoked. So too with the city. But to explain "because" we invoke not only natural evolution but cultural evolution as well. To do this we make a distinction between the "given" and the "made" forms. The former is the natural landscape identity, the latter is the accumulation of the adaptations to the given form which constitute the present city. Rio is different from New Orleans, Kansas from Lima, Amsterdam from San Francisco, because. By employing the ecological method we can discern the reason for the location of the city, comprehend its natural form, discern those elements of identity which are critical and expressive both those of physiography and vegetation, and develop a program for the preservation and enhancement of that identity. The method is equally applicable when one confronts the made form. The successive stages of urbanization are examined as adaptations to the environment, some of which are successful, some not. Some enter the inventory of resources and contribute to the *genius loci*. As for the given form, this method allows us to perceive the elements of identity in a scale of values. One can then prepare a comprehensive landscape plan for a city and feed the elements of identity, natural process and the palette for formal expression into the comprehensive planning process.

You still demur. The method has not yet entered into the putrid parts of the city. It needs rivers and palisades, hill and valleys, woodlands and parkland. When will it confront slums and overcrowding, congestion and pollution, anarchy and ugliness? Indeed the method can enter into the very heart of the city and by so doing may save us from the melancholy criteria of economic determinism which have proven so disappointing to the orthodoxy of city planning or the alternative of unbridled "design" which haunts architecture. But here again we must be selective as we return to the source in ecology. We will find little that is applicable in energy system ecology, analysis of food pyramids, relations defined in terms of predator–prey, competition, or those other analytical devices so efficacious for plant and animal ecology. But we can well turn to an ecological model which contains multifaceted criteria for measuring ecosystems and we can select health as an encompassing criterion. The model is my own and as such it is suspect for I am not an ecologist, but each of the parts is the product of a distinguished ecologist.[3] Let us hope that the assembly of the constituents does not diminish their veracity, for they have compelling value.

The most obvious example is life and death. Life is the evolution of a single egg into the complexity of the organism. Death is the retrogression of a complex organism into a few simple elements. If this model is true, it allows us to examine a city, neighborhood, community institution, family, city plan, architectural or landscape design in these terms. This model suggests that any system moving towards simplicity, uniformity, instability with a low number of species and high entropy is retrogressing; any system moving in that direction is moving towards ill health.

Conversely, complexity, diversity, stability (steady state), with a high number of species and low entropy are indicators of health and systems moving in this direction are evolving. As a simple application let us map, in tones on transparencies, statistics of all physical disease, all mental disease and all social disease. If we also map income, age of population, density, ethnicity and quality of the physical environment we have on the one hand discerned the environment of health, the environment of pathology and we have accumulated the data which allow interpretation of the social and physical environmental components of health and pathology. Moreover, we have the other criteria of the model which permit examination from different directions.

F
I
V
E

If this model is true and the method good, it may be the greatest contribution of the ecological method to diagnosis and prescription for the city.

But, you say, all this may be very fine but landscape architects are finally designers – when will you speak to ecology and design? I will. Lou Kahn, the most perceptive of men, foresaw the ecological method even through these intractable, inert materials which he infuses with life when he spoke of "existence will," the will to be. The place is because. It is and is in the process of becoming. This we must be able to read, and ecology provides the language. By being, the place or the creature has form. Form and process are indivisible aspects of a single phenomenon. The ecological method allows one to understand form as an explicit point in evolutionary process. Again, Lou Kahn has made clear to us the distinction between form and design. Cup is form and begins from the cupped hand. Design is the creation of the cup, transmuted by the artist, but never denying its formal origins. As a profession, landscape architecture has exploited a pliant earth, tractable and docile plants to make much that is arbitrary, capricious and inconsequential. We could not see the cupped hand as giving form to the cup, the earth and its processes as giving form to our works. The ecological method is then also the perception of form, an insight to the given form, implication for the made form which is to say design, and this, for landscape architects, may be its greatest gift.

NOTES

1 Australia; Rhodesia; the United Kingdom; the Gangetic Plain; the Potomac River Basin; Allegheny Plateau; Ridge and Valley Province; Great Valley Province; Piedmont; Coastal Plain; the Green Spring and Worthington Valleys, Philadelphia Standard Metropolitan Statistical Area; and the City of Washington. [See "Plan for the Valleys vs. Spectre of Uncontrolled Growth," by Ian L. McHarg and David A. Wallace, *Landscape Architecture*, April, 1965. Ed.]

2 See "Quality Corridors for Wisconsin," by Philip H. Lewis Jr., *Landscape Architecture*, January, 1964.

3 "Simplicity, complexity; uniformity, diversity; independence, interdependence; instability, stability," thesis by Dr. Robert McArthur. "Stability, instability," thesis by Dr. Luna Leopold. "Low and high number of species," thesis by Dr. Ruth Patrick. "Low and high entropy," thesis by Dr. Harold F. Blum. "Ill-health, health," thesis by Dr. Ruth Patrick.

"Principles for Regional Design"

from *Out of Place: Restoring Identity to the Regional Landscape* (1990)

Michael Hough

Editors' Introduction

The idea that regional identity is a fundamental component of sense of place has gained prominence over the last several decades, hand in hand with the increasing advance of landscape homogenization. As the landscape architecture profession has steadily grown to encompass ecological concerns as well as aesthetic concerns, people concerned with issues of regional identity have come to understand that it is not only important for place-making, but also critical for sustainability because it is associated with biodiversity.

Michael Hough has been a leading voice in associating regional landscape identity with both sense of place and ecological responsibility. In *Out of Place: Restoring Identity to the Regional Landscape*, he asks why modern landscapes tend to look alike despite their different regional settings and determines that the causes include the rise of consumerism, the loss of rootedness and rise of transience that have come with the information society, and the rise of bureaucratic standardization. Having established the main contributing factors to placelessness, he outlines a regionally based approach to place-making in the final chapter of his book.

In "Principles for Regional Design," reprinted here, Hough, critical of most environmental design theory because of the emphasis on ideal forms and complete design, offers instead a design philosophy based on notions of restraint, minimal intervention, and respect for what is local. Instead of rigid design guidelines, he sets out principles for action, which include learning about places through direct experience of them, maintaining a sense of history, promoting environmental education, doing as little as possible, and starting where it's easiest. While all the principles are well articulated and useful, the latter two are particularly important for urban designers to pay attention to because they encourage modest design attitudes of a kind not generally prevalent within the design fields.

Hough's focus on regional eco-systems harkens back to ideas developed by Patrick Geddes over one hundred years ago. Geddes emphasized regional diversity and advocated extensive ecological surveys prior to undertaking any design or planning work. His innovative Valley Section, which cut a transect through a metropolitan region, identified the intricate ties between central cities and their rural hinterlands. A good discussion of Geddes' ideas can be found in Walter Stephen *et al.*'s *Think Global Act Local: The Life and Legacy of Patrick* Geddes (Edinburgh: Luath Press, 2004). Hough's ideas also relate to landscape architect Ian McHarg's work from the 1960s and 1970s (see p. 519). Concerned with ecological planning and representing an early attempt to integrate emerging green design concepts at the regional level, McHarg developed a method for analyzing landscapes through mapped overlays of soil, hydrology, slope, geology, viewshed, and vegetation. The idea was that this process would then indicate the best areas for development, and help designers avoid the least desirable locations.

Michael Hough trained as a landscape architect at the University of Pennsylvania in Philadelphia. In 1963, he founded the University of Toronto's undergraduate degree program in landscape architecture and later joined the Faculty of Environmental Sciences at York University, where he established the Environmental Landscape Design program, in 1971, and was a Professor for many years. He was a principal and founding partner in the Landscape Architecture firm of Hough Woodland Naylor Dance Leinster (HWNDL) in Toronto, and currently practices through Envision-The Hough Group. Both firms are widely recognized for their work in ecological design. In 2009, he received a Lifetime Achievement Award from the Canadian Society of Landscape Architects, that organization's highest honor.

Michael Hough's other writings include *City Form and Natural Processes: Towards an Urban Vernacular* (London: Croom Helm, 1984), which is considered a classic of the environmental design field. It has been published in updated versions under the titles *Cities and Natural Process* (London: Routledge, 1995) and *Cities and Natural Processes: A Basis for Sustainability* (London: Routledge, 2004).

Writings by others on regional landscapes include Paul Gobster's *Restoring Nature: Perspectives from the Social Sciences and Humanities* (Washington, DC: Island Press, 2000); Robert L. Thayer Jr.'s *LifePlace: Bioregional Thought and Practice* (Berkeley: University of California Press, 2003); Tony Hiss' *The Experience of Place: A New Way of Looking at and Dealing with Our Radically Changing Cities and Countryside* (New York: Random House, 1990); and *Regional Planning in America: Practice and Prospect* (Cambridge, MA: Lincoln Institute of Land Policy, 2011), edited by Ethan Seltzer and Armando Carbonell.

What role does design play in the development of a contemporary regional landscape? A historical perspective suggests that the differences between one place and another have arisen, not from efforts to create long-range visions and grand designs, but from vernacular responses to the practical problems of everyday life. Indeed, it can be argued that purposeful design has done more to generate placelessness than to promote a sense of place. The new forces shaping the landscape are no longer small and local in scope but are great in scale and consequence. The technological and economic impact of these forces on the environment has never before had such profound potential for the destruction of life systems. As a discipline dedicated to fitting man to the land and to giving it form, contemporary design is faced with solving problems that have traditionally not been a part of the agenda in the creation of vernacular places.

In the past, there were limits to what one was able to do and the extent to which one could modify the natural environment. The constraints of environment and society created an undisputed sense of being rooted to the place, but they were, nonetheless, limitations to be overcome, not inherent motivations to be at one with nature. In today's landscape the heterogeneity of the past is giving way to a more homogeneous, information-based society. In design terms, therefore, it becomes as much romantic nonsense to force the old regional differences upon this new landscape as it is to expect people to give up cars, washing machines, and television in the interest of a better environment. We are locked into our times and ways of doing things.

Yet, there is a dilemma for designers in the new and evolving landscape. The determinants that shaped the settlements and countryside of pre-industrial society and that gave rise to the physical forms which we now admire are now no longer those of environmental limitation but of choice. Creating a sense of place involves a conscious decision to do so. At the same time, the need to invest in the protection of nature has never been so urgent. The connections between regional identity and the sustainability of the land are essential and fundamental. A valid design philosophy, therefore, is tied to ecological values and principles; to the notions of environmental and social health; to the essential bond of people to nature, and to the biological sustainability of life itself. This is the new necessity that will counter-balance and bring some sanity to a world whose goals are focused on helping us "live in a society of abundance and leisure."[1] Yet values that espouse a truly sustainable future will only emerge when it is perceived that there are no alternatives. It is possible that over time the fragility of earth's life systems will create an imperative for survival on which a new ethic can flourish. The international agreement to protect the earth's ozone layer, signed in 1987, may be one indication of this trend. And it is only on this basis that regionalism can become an imperative – a fundamental platform for understanding and shaping the future landscape.

In the preceding chapters I examined the various factors affecting regional identity in order to establish a framework for a design philosophy for the contemporary landscape. This chapter suggests the principles that seem most appropriate to this objective.

KNOWING THE PLACE

Recognizing how people use different places to fulfill the practical needs of living is one of the building blocks on which a distinctive sense of place can be enhanced in the urban landscape. Regional identity is connected with the peculiar characteristics of a location that tell us something about its physical and social environment. It is what a place has when it somehow belongs to its location and nowhere else. It has to do, therefore, with two fundamental criteria: first, with the natural processes of the region or locality – what nature has put there; second, with social processes – what people have put there. It has to do with the way people adapt to their living environment; how they change it to suit their needs in the process of living; how they make it their own. In effect, regional identity is the collective reaction of people to the environment over time.

At the turn of the century Patrick Geddes taught that before attempting to change a place, one must seek out its essential character on foot in order to understand its patterns of movement, its social dynamics, history and traditions, its environmental possibilities. He commented on the way planners dictated form and solutions to problems with little reference to the reality. In his design studies for Madura in the Madras Presidency he wrote:

> One of the poor quarters is at present threatened with "relief from congestion" and we are shown a rough plan in which the usual gridiron of new thoroughfares is hacked through its old-world village life . . . the sanitary improvements begin by destroying an excellent house for the sole purpose of inclining the present lane from the position slightly oblique to the edge of the drawing board to one strictly parallel to it.[2]

In effect, he was saying that modifications to city plans, and for that matter modifications to any landscape, are based on thought processes that begin and end with paper, not the environmental and social realities of the place.

Underlying every urban or urbanizing environment that has developed an image of increasing sameness are unique natural or cultural attributes waiting to be revealed. A place's identity is rarely completely destroyed. There, are always elements of the original landscape that remain, sometimes deeply buried beneath the new. Landform, remnant native plant communities, an old hedge, a barn, old paving stones speak to natural and cultural origins and changing uses. The task is to build an identity based on these remnants.

The hidden elements of a place affect our senses, albeit unconsciously. Tony Hiss describes this in his analysis of experiencing places:

> Small, unnoticed changes in level play a larger organizing role in our activities than we suspect: in Manhattan, the right-angle street grid, which keeps people's eyes focused straight ahead, and the uniform paving of streets and sidewalks, together with the solid blocks of buildings on both sides, tend to keep New Yorkers from noticing the natural contours – or what's left of the natural contours – beneath their feet. The nineteenth-century Manhattan developers who covered midtown fields and meadows with brownstones did such a good job of lopping off the tops of hills and filling in valleys that a hundred years or so later . . . no one really knows what the original topography was . . . Nevertheless, almost every block has some rise or dip to it, and these hints of elevation do help people define certain districts.[3]

Several other examples of natural and cultural attributes will illustrate how these affect our sense of a place's identity.

Identity through the landscape

The deep, densely wooded ravines of Toronto that were cut from tableland by streams following the last ice age are part of a major system of rivers draining south to Lake Ontario. Twenty-one meters below the flat, urbanizing plateau of the growing city, they formed a unique system of remnant southern hardwood forest and streams, a habitat for animals and birds within an urban area, a place where the original forest and the natural history of the land could still be experienced. It was where sounds of traffic were no longer heard, where smells and tactile feelings were enhanced by the utter contrast of enclosing woods, suddenly experienced as one reached the valley floor from the level of the street. As the city expanded, many ravines were obliterated by encroaching development, and by the 1950s, 840 acres (340 hectares) of the 1,900 acres (770 hectares) of original ravine land in the city had been given over to houses, factories, and roads.[4] The unique character of Toronto's landscape – the city's structure and identity – rapidly gave way to featureless urban growth. Others were left alone, not as a consequence of planning but because they were simply a nuisance, or difficult, to fill in. Today they are recognized for their significance to the environmental and social well-being of the city. Within the urbanized environment they have become one of the key elements that make Toronto different from other places, both as identifiable landscape form and for the uniquely adapted recreational activity they have generated. Protected by dense woodland below the level of the city that eliminates winter winds and provides a markedly cool summer climate, they are ideal places for winter skiing, walking, birdwatching, and nature study. They have become Toronto's stamp of individuality.

Different places for different people

Many of our urban parks have developed as cookie-cutter patterns of grass and trees, models imposed on the city by a tradition of standard landscapes for standard people. These values have dominated design thinking and helped create a landscape that does little to reflect the inherent social diversity of neighborhoods. The quality of urban life today has to do, among other things, with the recognition that diverse social groups need diverse landscapes, that choices between one place and another must be available. A city that has places for foxes and urban woodland, regenerating fields and urban wilderness, is more interesting and pleasant to live in than those that lack such places. The identity of the urban

landscape is also based on "hard" urban spaces: busy plazas and markets; noisy and quiet places; cultivated landscapes and formal gardens; funfairs and cultural events. In multi-cultural cities, there are also many social needs that should be addressed by public spaces that reflect the cultural and physical identity of these groups. The elderly – an increasingly large group in North American cities – garden, cycle, bowl, take photographs, play cards and board games, watch the world go by. Ethnic groups, many of whom are moving out to the suburbs of large cities, take with them traditions of productive urban farming, festivals, family gatherings for picnics and intensive use of small spaces that are transforming hitherto conventionally landscaped suburban places. Over time, changing community structure in many suburban areas will create a new kind of environment, one that fits the people who live and work there. Thus by-laws and restrictions on what may or may not be done on private property, which have previously dominated the social and physical character of many suburbs, will need to be modified to reflect new communities' values.

The socially disadvantaged, the bag ladies, the homeless, and transients use parks and waste places in the city night and day and often year round. As a group, these people use the established parks more permanently and with more basic need than the people for whom the parks were actually intended. Yet these are the people who are not welcome in the parks system. The use of streets as community spaces by adults and children in healthy neighborhoods establishes an essential vitality, social character, and commitment to place that comes from common use. They are the spontaneous result of people using the street as a natural meeting place that the standard park cannot fulfill.

Randy Hester has shown how the daily ritual of people exchanging gossip, meeting friends, and negotiating business is place specific. The places that have significance for people, such as the local post office, corner store, community park, or parking lot, are those that "have become so essential to the lives of the residents through use or symbolism that the community collectively identifies with these places."[5] Most of these may have no appeal to the designer's eye as being "beautiful" or worthy of preservation, but they are nonetheless a basis for healthy communities.[6]

MAINTAINING A SENSE OF HISTORY

Rarely does the designer have the luxury, or more appropriately, the misfortune, to create a place from scratch. Something is always there before he begins: a history, a peculiar character, a meeting place. Design inevitably involves building on what's there in the process of change.

The protection of natural and cultural history – the reuse and integration of the old into the new without fanfare while avoiding the temptation to turn everything into a museum because it is old – lies at the heart of maintaining a continuing link with the past and with a place's identity. Our overwhelming desire to eliminate our past is nowhere more evident than in the destruction of nature that we find in every corner of the globe in large or small measure. Similarly, the tendency for the new in urban development to destroy the old in the interests of economics is one of the major reasons for placelessness in the changing urban landscape. There are no longer any historical reference points by which one understands where one has come from in the process of building the new. The remnant native plant communities that still survive in protected parts of the city – in cemeteries, valley lands, older residential areas – also link us with the past, with the pre-development landscape, and with the historic interactions of man and environment. Evolving and fortuitous naturalizing plant communities in the city's forgotten places – railway corridors, abandoned lands, industrial properties, the corner spaces found in every city lot tell us more about the dynamics of natural processes and the sustainability of nature in urban areas than those that have been imposed, in aesthetic, or horticultural terms, on the environment.

The same is true of new urban developments that have ignored cultural history. The absence of fine or significant architecture has often been a red herring in arguments about the worthiness of preserving and reusing old buildings. The basic purpose of maintaining old parts of town is to link us with the past – to enhance one's knowledge of a place's cultural roots. An example is the redevelopment of urban waterfronts that since the 1970's has become one of the most important development trends in North America.

The way in which cities have developed and have been modified by their waterways has varied considerably from place to place. This is particularly apparent in countries of intense regional differences such as Canada. In the western prairies, for instance, the flatness of the land and great distances from the mountains to the sea have produced shallow, winding, erosion, and flood-prone river landscapes that were unsuitable as major modes of transportation. Patterns of urban development evolved in response to these environments. The rivers, essential as a water supply, have nonetheless been historically neglected, or used as convenient dumping grounds or for water-dependent industry. They were not integrated with the cities that grew around them until their potential for recreational use was realized. One exception is the city of Saskatoon, Saskatchewan, which has had a long tradition of preserving open space. The temperance colonizers who settled this prairie city in 1884 dedicated the river banks as public land and set the pattern of connected linear open spaces along the river for the future.[7] Today, western rivers project the distinct and immediate image of a prairie link between city and farmland. Their identity as places lies in their intrinsic "naturalness" in the way they have evolved into "green valleys" that wind through urban environments seemingly keeping the fabric of streets and buildings at bay. In contrast, the industrial cities of eastern Canada, such as Montreal or Toronto, which grew on the shores of the deep, wide-flowing rivers and waterways of the Great Lakes system, have provided the essential water transportation from which has grown the commercial and industrial base of Canada.

It is the environment of work – the vast scale and drama of large cargo boats and cranes, quays, railways, and storage sheds – that makes these waterfronts so exciting and gives them a special presence. They symbolize the oceans, travel to strange and exotic lands, and international trade. All great waterfronts have this quality; Istanbul, Halifax, and Stockholm are among them. For many cities, however, the old functions of the working port have given way to recreational ones. Redevelopment, too, frequently leads to the total destruction of the previous landscape of industry, grain silos, and railways that used to provide their economic base and their reason for being. The observer of many new developments may be excused the temptation of wondering why the previous landscape of industry, often carefully preserved in old photographs, looks so much more interesting than the new commercial developments that have replaced it. In 1987 the city of Toronto rejected a proposal to retain the old grain silos on its waterfront as historic landmarks. A letter to the local newspaper on this issue made the following point:

> These silos are a vital part of the history of Canada in the same way as the brooding castles of Europe reflect the past. Both structures were born out of the needs of their time and have become symbols of an era and a country . . . we would today take a rather dim view of a council in Europe that had condemned their castles to demolition because they had become useless. The silos are not useless in the memory of a collective Canadian consciousness.[8]

The making of memorable places is linked to history.

ENVIRONMENTAL LEARNING AND DIRECT EXPERIENCE

Environmental literacy lies at the heart of understanding the places with which we are familiar, and thus at the heart of the issue of identity. It is necessary for people who live in and use urban places, indeed places of any kind, to know the environment around them. An awareness of place can only be enhanced when it becomes a part of people's everyday lives. Formal school programs, like the once-a-year visit to the country to "educate" urban children in nature lore, do little to engender or deepen knowledge of the environment, or more importantly, to encourage environmental values. These are more likely to come from understanding the places that are close to home. The same principle applies to the interpretive programs provided for the enlightenment of adult campers in provincial parks, that explain the workings of unspoiled nature out in the woods, but totally ignore the problems of water pollution, deterioration of vegetation, garbage dumps, and disruption to wildlife from human presence that occurs in the campgrounds themselves.

An urban waterfront on the Great Lakes, for example, can speak to its place within the system.

Through its entertainment and cultural facilities, it can capitalize on key subjects and issues of the region, such as the international implications of pollution that begin here, its history of sailing vessels, trade, and discovery, the aquatic ecosystem, local plant and animal communities, and the interrelationships between people and environment. But the marine aquaria, tropical fish tanks, captive porpoises, and killer whales that leap through hoops and kiss the girl in the bikini for our entertainment that have become the prime attractions of many waterfronts tell us nothing about the place and are environmentally and ethically bankrupt. They contribute instead to environmental ignorance, to a lack of context and identity. It is possible, though, to reinforce a sense of place through educational exhibits that are at once instructive and fun. An example was the headquarters building of the now-defunct Greater London Council. Two large fish tanks lined the entrance foyer to the building. One showed what the Thames used to be like in the days of the river's worst pollution – a lifeless murky underwater environment. The other showed the rehabilitated Thames as it is today with the dozens of species of fish that now live in its much improved waters. It told one a great deal about the river on which London depends and about some of the environmental concerns of government at the time.

Knowledge through education of a place's environmental or cultural significance changes our attitudes and the way we experience it. Public reaction to a highway "no-mow" experimental program in North Dakota, for instance, was initially negative. In a survey of motorists about the program along the right-of-way, 82 percent of those interviewed said that if they had to make a choice, they preferred the mown plots to those that had been left unmown. However, when they were informed that the unmown plots provided waterfowl nesting habitats, many wished to change their answer.[9]

Giving meaning and significance to ordinary and largely unnoticed places, whether this happens to be a suburban street, a few square feet of prairie, or a representative forest landscape is the basis of regional identity. The task of design is to encourage an understanding and enjoyment of the landscape that comes from both emotional experience and scientific knowledge. In this way, normally overlooked landscapes can become memorable.

DOING AS LITTLE AS POSSIBLE

Kevin Lynch remarks, "A hunger for the control of large-scale form is all the more dangerous because it coincides with strong contemporary trends towards large-scale investment."[10] The pressures (that come from educational conditioning) to do as much as possible in making changes to places often appears endemic to the land design disciplines. In the absence of a basic ecological foundation on which design can rest, this is to be expected. Doing as little as possible, or economy of means, involves the idea that from minimum resources and energy, maximum environmental and social benefits are available. The greatest diversity and identity in a place, whether a regenerating field or urban wetland, or a cohesive neighborhood community, often comes from minimum, not maximum interference. This does not mean that planning and design are irrelevant or unnecessary to a world that if left alone would take care of itself. It implies, rather, that change can be brought about by giving direction, by capitalizing on the opportunities that site or social trends reveal, or by setting a framework from which people can create their own social and physical environments and where landscapes can flourish with health, diversity, and beauty.

Urban street systems, for instance, provide the overall physical framework within which neighborhoods flourish and diversify. Local by-laws and design requirements may enhance or inhibit the social and physical complexity of a community. In [a previous chapter] I discussed those situations where political power seeks to impose control on nature or humanity, thereby obliterating the inherent diversity of places. The over-regulation of what can be done to private property has an inherent potential to generate tedium. Compare the planned shopping arcades of many new developments, where regulations and design dictate the style and positioning of signs and setbacks, with the shopping streets that have grown up in response to the needs of individual store owners. The former somehow lack the vitality, life, and interest of the latter. Similarly, the formal landscaped avenues, parks, and gardens that grace the institutional centers of many cities and speak to their sense of civic pride lose their special identity as places when they become universal expressions of the city's landscape.

At another scale, it has long been an article of faith that the designers of public landscapes should be able to predict human behavior, on the basis, first, that behavior is indeed predictable and controllable; second, that it will not change; and third, that it is a necessary measure of a designer's competence. The isolated benches that no one sits on, the playgrounds that children avoid, the pathways and pedestrian routes that no one follows, and the gathering places without people bear witness to the emptiness of that claim. William Whyte's careful observations about what people in New York actually do in city spaces has demonstrated the key elements of design: understanding the psychology of behavior (how people actually behave, what they actually do) and how to bring in those elements that enhance the diverse use of public space.[11]

People need to control how they use the environment around them, and in the process of doing so the designed landscape becomes a vernacular one, responding to practical needs. As Whyte has shown, dynamic and interesting places can be created simply by locating a food-vending stand in a place where passersby can see it from the sidewalk, or by providing seats that can be moved around at will.[12] Similarly, the experience of a natural place can be enhanced beyond measure by uncovering a clogged stream so that its sound can be heard, or by removing trash from a pond so that its natural beauty is revealed.

In *City Form and Natural Process* I argued that the horticultural tradition has long been the basis for getting the least results for the most effort in money, energy, and manpower.[13] Yet it is not horticulture per se that is at the root of the problem. It is the lack of an ecological perspective that permits doctrine, or expediency, or both to impose similar environments on differing places. The desire for universal solutions is strong and lends credence to the adage that design style – those characteristics of a designer's work that identify him – is in fact a series of never questioned mistakes repeated over and over again. For instance, there is no doubt that the move toward natural landscapes is based on a genuine concern for greater variety and sustainability in our cities. Yet from the point of view of regional identity, the inspiration for naturalization can be tarred with the same brush as that which inspired our current "pedigree" urban landscape. It becomes another doctrine. The designer, determined to create alternative landscapes, finds himself tied to "wildflower seed mixes" that are, for the most part, drawn from plants found from the prairies to the east coast. The result is an international naturalized meadow replacing the international green carpet. Inspired by the native flora and roadside wildflower program in Texas, commercial seed mixes are often selected for the color and spectacle of their flowers. But they are often alien to the local region and are, consequently, taken over by native flora after a couple of years, which defeats the original, sustainable, low-cost objective. Only the local setting can create the kind of regional landscape that we are concerned with, and it is from here that one must draw inspiration. The natural communities that are indigenous or adapted to the place are those that occur with the least effort and with the greatest sustainability and variety.

As a design principle, doing as little as possible implies, first, an understanding of the processes that make things work; second, providing the structure that will encourage the development of diverse and relevant natural or social environments; third, knowing where to intervene to create the conditions for them to occur; and fourth, having the humility to let natural diversity evolve on its own where it will.

SUSTAINABILITY

Sustainable landscapes are central to the regional imperative. Sustainability involves, among other things, the notion that human activity and technological systems can contribute to the health of the environments and natural systems from which they draw benefit. This involves a fundamental acceptance of investment in the productivity and diversity of natural systems. Conflicting points of view over the priorities of development versus the preservation of natural wealth have been the focus of discussion and argument for a very long time, particularly as it affects the Third World. The World Commission on Environment and Development, established by the United Nations in 1983, and whose report appeared in 1987, has examined and proposed ways in which economic development initiatives and environmental conservation might be reconciled. For this to be workable would require the development of an environmental ethic far different from current attitudes and perceptions that see nature as "resources for the benefit of

mankind." Such a notion would seem practically to be unattainable. However, Maurice Strong, the Canadian member of the commission, has commented on the need for countries to shed their narrow concepts of self interest, parochialism and, in the economic field, protectionism.[14] Although he recognizes the odds against the emergence of such a world view, he sees no alternative: "The principle basis for optimism that the kind of changes I foresee as necessary will occur is, very simply, that they are necessary and therefore must occur."[15]

Irrespective of such a world view, however, the principle of investment in nature, where change and technological development are seen as positive forces to sustain and enhance the environment, must be the basis for an environmental design philosophy. Its principles of energy and nutrient flows, common to all ecosystems when applied to the design of the human environment, provide the only ethical and pragmatic alternative to the future health of the emerging regional landscape. And this leads naturally to the last principle.

STARTING WHERE IT'S EASIEST

This principle, borrowed from Jane Jacobs,[16] is fundamental to achieving anything in a world where the statistics of global environmental disaster are at once horrifying and numbing. Through the media, the visibility of environmental issues everywhere in the world is immediate, vivid, and emotionally involving. At the same time, these media reports have two things in common. First, they are almost inevitably out of town. They are somewhere else: in the diminishing rain forests of Brazil; in the burgeoning population and desperate poverty of Africa; in the dying northern lakes of Canada and Sweden that are succumbing to acid rain generated by polluting industries a thousand miles away. We have the paradox that in a world increasingly concerned with deteriorating environments and explosive urban growth, there is a marked propensity to ignore the very places where most people live. Second, the issues are so enormously complicated and of such magnitude that most concerned people feel helpless to do much about them.

Beginning where it's easiest, therefore, has to do with where most people are and where one can be reasonably certain of a measure of success from efforts made, no matter how small. Successes in small things can be used to make connections to other larger and more significant ones. This is, consequently, an encouraging environmental principle to follow in bringing about change. It is, in fact, the only practical basis for doing so. In design terms, the regional imperative is about the need for environmental ideals that are firmly rooted in pragmatic reality. It is about focusing on things that work and that are achievable at any one point in time. It is about a concerned and environmentally literate community prepared to insure that the health and quality of the places where they live are made a reality; where the role of technology is integrated with people, urbanism, and nature in ways that are biologically and socially self-sustaining and mutually supportive of life systems. These are the goals for shaping a new landscape based on fundamental environmental values.

[. . .]

SOME FINAL REFLECTIONS

Armed with a broad environmental perspective on the nature of the regional imperative, design can begin to make a contribution to establishing a viable contemporary landscape. It is a perspective that is rooted in ecological and cultural diversity. If we look for it, the inherent potential for diversity shines like a beacon through the placeless dreariness of much contemporary urbanization. The making of memorable places involves principles of evolving natural process and change over time. It involves economy of means where often the less one does to make purposeful change the better. It involves variety and choice that evolve naturally through countless interactions between people and nature, providing a secure basis for ecological and social health. It also has to do with understanding the nature of places as a precursor to making purposeful change, which is a far more significant act of creativity than imposing pre-packaged solutions on the land. The familiar and overworked analogy of the Eskimo carver who, staring at the stone in his hand, wonders what it is within that wants to come out, serves to encapsulate the underlying philosophy of what place is about. When the carver recognizes what it is, he simply carves the stone to release it. Where the processes of nature are

allowed to become part of an organic as opposed to a fixed view of the planning process, the opportunities for regional identity are enhanced. Both human and nonhuman nature are fueled by similar underlying processes and motivating forces. The true nature of the regional imperative has little to do with mega-projects or utopian dreams. It has to do with what is, with understanding the forces that make change and making the most of opportunities wherever and in whatever form they may arise. Eutopia (*good place*) not Utopia (*no place*) is the goal toward which we must strive.

NOTES

1 Cordell, Arthur J. "The Uneasy Eighties: The Transition to an Information Society," *Alternatives* 14, no. 3–4 (1987): 4–7.

2 Boardman, Philip. *The Worlds of Patrick Geddes*. London: Routledge and Kegan Paul, 1978.

3 Hiss, Tony. "Experiencing Places I," *New Yorker*, June 22, 1987: 45–68.

4 City of Toronto Planning Board. *Natural Parklands*. Toronto: City of Toronto Planning Board, June 1960.

5 Hester, Randolph T. Jr. "Subconscious Landscapes of the Heart," *Places* 2, no. 3 (1985): 10–22.

6 Ibid.

7 Kerr, Don and Hanson, Stan. *Saskatoon: The First Half-Century*. Edmonton: NeWest Press, 1982.

8 Zeidler, E.H. *Toronto Globe and Mail*, Sept. 5, 1987.

9 Scott, Richard. "Ecological and Cultural Process as a Basis for Rural Freeway Right-of-Way Management." Toronto: Major Paper in Environmental Studies. York University (Dec. 1987).

10 Lynch, Kevin. *Managing the Sense of a Region*. Cambridge, Mass.: MIT Press, 1976.

11 Whyte, William H. *The Social Life of Small Urban Spaces*. Washington, D.C.: The Conservation Foundation, 1980.

12 Ibid.

13 Hough, Michael. *City Form and Natural Process*. New York: Van Nostrand Reinhold, 1984.

14 *Toronto Globe and Mail*, April 18, 1987.

15 Ibid.

16 Jacobs, Jane. "Guiding Principles for Streets that Work." Energy Probe Symposium. *The Streetscape: Planning and Retrofitting as if People Mattered*. Toronto (June 1986).

"Landscape as Urbanism"
from *The Landscape Urbanism Reader* (2006)

Charles Waldheim

Editors' Introduction

Our current times are fraught with realities of large-scale crises occurring or looming in many environmental realms – global warming, climate change, sea level rise, loss of animal and plant habitat, species extinction, water scarcity, air and water pollution, waste accumulation, desertification, loss of agricultural lands, massive human population increases. The list seems endless and the consequences of allowing these trends to continue into even the near future are predicted by many to be dire. Identifying solutions and putting them into practice is incredibly complicated given the interconnected global scope of environmental problems and the growth-oriented human socio-economic systems in which most people today live, which are the root cause of the problems.

In the face of the enormous environmental crisis, the late twentieth and early twenty-first centuries have been rife with debate about how the design and physical planning fields can best address the ecological issues that attend urbanization. A central debate concerns what built forms most contribute to environmental health: compact, densely built cities or more dispersed settlement. Another debate concerns what designers' roles can and should be in addressing environmental problems, given that their role in development processes is somewhat limited and circumscribed because other actors in those processes, particularly developers and investors, hold the purse strings and wield much greater decision-making power.

These debates, and others like them, have spurred the emergence of a new design approach called Landscape Urbanism, which first crystalized into a distinct intellectual and disciplinary strategy at the 1997 Landscape Urbanism symposium and exhibition held in Chicago that was organized by Charles Waldheim, who coined the term. *The Landscape Urbanism Reader* (2006), which is edited by Charles Waldheim and grew out of the symposium, is a collection of essays by the movement's leading theorists and practitioners. Waldheim's seminal essay "Landscape as Urbanism," reprinted here, defines the rationales, interests, purposes, methods, and scope of the Landscape Urbanism movement.

Landscape Urbanism identifies the contemporary city as decentralized, horizontal urbanism (meaning low scale and low density), characterized by rapid change and successive abandonment of developed land, in other words urban sprawl. Adherents view the urbanization processes that are creating such cities as embedded in natural processes, and so focus on identifying opportunities for ecologically responsive design within the urbanized places that result rather than seeking to shape a different kind of urbanization. The first premise is that landscape, often vast in scale, rather than densely built architectural form is the new organizing element of the contemporary city, hence the joining of the seemingly opposite terms "landscape" and "urbanism." Whereas for many, "landscape" conjures images of bucolic, natural or natural-looking open spaces and "urban" evokes images of tightly built places and bustling human activity, Landscape Urbanists use the term "landscape" to mean places shaped by human occupation. The focus of interest is on abandoned "brownfield" sites in inner cities and city peripheries, often former industrial areas, on interstitial spaces between buildings, and on pieces of infrastructure, such as freeways, highways and rail corridors. The method for design begins with a McHargian regional-scale ecological analysis (p. 519) combined with an analysis of human interventions, such as infrastructure and habitation. This layered analysis then forms the basis for re-design and re-use proposals aimed at transforming despoiled and fragmented spaces into something new. Citing ecological theory, design responses stress open-endedness, indeterminacy, and flexibility. Rather than creating master plans where design and use is fixed Landscape Urbanists create structuring framework plans that set key public realm and development criteria but allow the fleshing out of design specifics over time by multiple development actors responding to changing economic conditions.

Critics of Landscape Urbanism argue that it shies away from addressing the most difficult environmental issues, such as whether or not urbanization should happen in particular places. As well, the emphasis on built landscape infrastructure is faulted because of its reliance on technological rather than natural fixes for environmental problems.

A new idea called Ecological Urbanism is currently coalescing as both an extension of Landscape Urbanism and a critique of it. The key principles of Ecological Urbanism were framed at the 2009 Ecological Urbanism conference at Harvard's Graduate School of Design. It is postulated as a broader conceptual design approach that sheds the dependence on landscape and the disciplinary baggage that goes with the term, and focuses on the city as an ecological construct whose sustainability can be addressed through design and architectural proposals at a range of scales.

Charles Waldheim is Professor and Chair of the Department of Landscape Architecture at the Graduate School of Design (GSD) at Harvard University. He was formerly Associate Dean and Director of the Landscape Architecture program at the University of Toronto, and prior to that taught at the University of Illinois at Chicago and the University of Michigan. He earned a Master of Architecture (1989) from the University of Pennsylvania and he has practiced architecture and landscape architecture for over 25 years, most recently as a principal of the firm Urban Agency.

Waldheim's other books include three edited anthologies: *Chicago Architecture and Urbanism: Histories, Revisions, Alternatives* (Chicago: University of Chicago Press, 2005), co-edited with Katerina Rüedi Ray; *Lafayette Park Detroit* (Cambridge/Munich: Harvard University/Prestel, 2004) and *Stalking Detroit* (Barcelona: ACTR, 2001) co-edited with Georgia Daskalakis and Jason Young; and two monographs: *Post-Fordist Public Works: Landscape Urbanism Strategies for Milwaukee's Tower Automotive Site* (Cambridge, MA: Harvard University Graduate School of Design, 2006) and *Constructed Ground: The Millennium Garden Design Competition* (Urbana and Chicago: University of Illinois Press/Chicago Cultural Center, 2001). Waldheim has also authored several chapters in books, including "Motor City" in *Shaping the City: Case Studies in Urban History, Theory and Design*, ed. Rodolphe el-Khoury and Edward Robbins (London: Routledge, 2003) and "Aerial Representation and the Recovery of Landscape" in *Recovering Landscape*, ed. James Corner (New York: Princeton Architectural Press, 1999).

Waldheim credits the work of Ian McHarg, James Corner, Kenneth Frampton, Peter Rowe, and Rem Koolhaas as providing inspiration for Landscape Urbanism. The most relevant writings of these theorists are Ian McHarg (p. 544); Rem Koolhaas' *Delirious New York* (New York: Oxford University Press, 1978); James Corner's *Recovering Landscape: Essays in Contemporary Landscape Architecture* (New York: Princeton Architectural Press, 1999); Kenneth Frampton's "Towards a Critical Regionalism: Six Points for an Architecture of Resistance," in *The Anti-Aesthetic* (Seattle, WA: Bay Press, 1983) edited by Hal Foster, and "Toward an Urban Landscape" in *Columbia Documents* (New York: Columbia University, 1995); and Peter Rowe, *Making a Middle Landscape* (Cambridge, MA: MIT Press, 1991).

The other essays contained in *The Landscape Urbanism Reader* flesh out the initial thinking about the movement's concerns, scope, and practice applications. Key essays include James Corner's "Terra Fluxus," which describes the intellectual and practice underpinnings of Landscape Urbanism, and Alan Berger's "Drosscape" which conceptualizes strategies for addressing the abandoned landscapes that result from de-industrialization processes (see pp. 544–557). Other contemporaneous books that address emerging Landscape Urbanism ideas include David Grahame Shane's *Recombinant Urbanism* (London: John Wiley, 2005) and

Mohsen Mostafavi and Najle Ciro's *Landscape Urbanism: A Manual for the Machinic Landscape* (London: Architectural Association, 2003).

The recently published text *Ecological Urbanism* (Baden, Switzerland: Lars Müller, 2010), edited by Mohsen Mostafavi with Gareth Doherty, contains a series of essays developed from the 2009 Ecological Urbanism conference that describe the dimensions of this new school of thought.

■ ■ ■ ■ ■ ■

Over the past decade landscape has emerged as a model for contemporary urbanism, one uniquely capable of describing the conditions for radically decentralized urbanization, especially in the context of complex natural environments. Over that same decade the landscape discipline has enjoyed a period of intellectual and cultural renewal. While much of the landscape discipline's renewed relevance to discussions of the city may be attributed to this renewal or to increased environmental awareness more generally, landscape has improbably emerged as the most relevant disciplinary locus for discussions historically housed in architecture, urban design, or planning.

Many of the conceptual categories and projective practices embodied in landscape urbanism and documented in this publication arise from outside those disciplines traditionally responsible for describing the city. As such, landscape urbanism offers an implicit critique of architecture and urban design's inability to offer coherent, competent, and convincing explanations of contemporary urban conditions. In this context, the discourse surrounding landscape urbanism can be read as a disciplinary realignment in which landscape supplants architecture's historical role as the basic building block of urban design. Across a range of disciplines, many authors have articulated this newfound relevance of landscape in describing the temporal mutability and horizontal extensivity of the contemporary city. Among the authors making claims for the potential of landscape in this regard is architect and educator Stan Allen, Dean of the School of Architecture at Princeton University:

> Increasingly, landscape is emerging as a model for urbanism. Landscape has traditionally been defined as the art of organizing horizontal surfaces ... By paying close attention to these surface conditions – not only configuration, but also materiality and performance – designers can

activate space and produce urban effects without the weighty apparatus of traditional space making.[1]

This efficiency – the ability to produce urban effects traditionally achieved through the construction of buildings simply through the organization of horizontal surfaces – recommends the landscape medium for use in contemporary urban conditions increasingly characterized by horizontal sprawl and rapid change. In the context of decentralization and decreasing density, the "weighty apparatus" of traditional urban design proves costly, slow, and inflexible in relation to the rapidly transforming conditions of contemporary urban culture.

The idea of landscape as a model for urbanism has also been articulated by landscape architect James Corner, who argues that only through a synthetic and imaginative reordering of categories in the built environment might we escape our present predicament in the cul-de-sac of post-industrial modernity, and "the bureaucratic and uninspired failings" of the planning profession.[2] His work critiques much of what landscape architecture has become as a professional concern in recent years – especially its tendency to provide scenographic screening for environments engineered and instrumentalized by other disciplines.[3] For Corner, the narrow agenda of ecological advocacy that many landscape architects profess to is nothing more than a rear-guard defense of a supposedly autonomous "nature" conceived to exist *a priori*, outside of human agency or cultural construction. In this context, current-day environmentalism and pastoral ideas of landscape appear to Corner, and many others, as naïve or irrelevant in the face of global urbanization.[4]

Landscape urbanism benefits from the canonical texts of regional environmental planning, from the work of Patrick Geddes and Benton MacKaye to Lewis Mumford to Ian McHarg, yet it also remains distinct from that tradition.[5] Corner acknowledges the historical importance of McHarg's influential *Design with Nature* yet, himself a student and faculty colleague of McHarg's at the University of Pennsylvania, rejects the opposition of nature and city implied in McHarg's regionally scaled environmental planning practice.[6]

The origins of landscape urbanism can be traced to postmodern critiques of modernist architecture and planning.[7] These critiques, put forth by Charles Jencks and other proponents of postmodern architectural culture, indicted modernism for its inability to produce a "meaningful" or "livable" public realm,[8] for its failure to come to terms with the city as an historical construction of collective consciousness,[9] and for its inability to communicate with multiple audiences.[10] In fact, the "death of modern architecture," as proclaimed by Jencks in 1977, coincided with a crisis of industrial economy in the United States, marking a shift toward the diversification of consumer markets.[11] What postmodern architecture's scenographic approach did not, in fact could not, address were the structural conditions of industrialized modernity that tended toward the decentralization of urban form. This decentralization continues apace today in North America, remarkably indifferent to the superficial stylistic oscillations of architectural culture.

In the wake of the social and environmental disasters of industrialization, postmodern architecture retreated to the comforting forms of nostalgia and seemingly stable, secure, and more permanent forms of urban arrangement. Citing European precedents for traditional city form, postmodern architects practiced a kind of preemptive cultural regression, designing individual buildings to invoke an absent context, as if neighborly architectural character could contravene a century of industrial economy. The rise of the urban design discipline in the 1970s and '80s extended interest in the aggregation of architectural elements into ensembles of nostalgic urban consumption. During this same time, the discipline of city planning abdicated altogether, seeking refuge in the relatively ineffectual enclaves of policy, procedure, and public therapy.[12]

The postmodern *rappelle a l'ordre* indicted modernism for devaluing the traditional urban values of pedestrian scale, street grid continuity, and contextual architectural character. As has been well documented, the post modern impulse can be equally understood as a desire to communicate with multiple audiences or to commodify architectural images for diversifying consumer markets. But this dependence upon sympathetically styled and spatially sequenced architectural objects could not be sustained, given the rise of mobile capital, automobile culture, and decentralization. And yet the very indeterminacy and flux of the contemporary city, the bane of traditional European citymaking, are precisely those qualities explored in emergent works of landscape urbanism. This point is perhaps best exemplified in Barcelona's program of public space and building projects in the 1980s and early '90s, which focused primarily on the traditional center of the Catalan capital. Today the push in Barcelona to redevelop the airport, logistical zone, industrial waterfront, metropolitan riverways, and water-treatment facilities has less to do with buildings and plazas than with large-scale infrastructural landscapes. These examples, along with recent work in the Netherlands, reveal the role of large-scale landscape as an element of urban infrastructure. Of course many traditional examples of nineteenth century urban landscape architecture integrate landscape with infrastructure – Olmsted's Central Park in New York and Back Bay Fens in Boston serve as canonical examples. Contrasting this tradition, contemporary practices of landscape urbanism reject the camouflaging of ecological systems within pastoral images of "nature." Rather, contemporary landscape urbanism practices recommend the use of infrastructural systems and the public landscapes they engender as the very ordering mechanisms of the urban field itself, shaping and shifting the organization of urban settlement and its inevitably indeterminate economic, political, and social futures.

Landscape is a medium, it has been recalled by Corner, Allen, and others, uniquely capable of responding to temporal change, transformation, adaptation, and succession. These qualities recommend landscape as an analog to contemporary processes of urbanization and as a medium uniquely suited to the open-endedness, indeterminacy, and change demanded by contemporary urban conditions. As Allen puts it, "landscape is not only a formal model for urbanism today, but perhaps more importantly, a model for process."[13]

Tellingly, the first projects to reveal this potential for landscape to operate as a model for urban process were produced not in North America but rather in Europe. Among the first projects to orchestrate urban program as a landscape process was the 1982 Competition for Parc de la Villette. In 1982, la Villette invited submissions for an "Urban Park for the 21st Century" over a 125-acre site, once the site of Paris's largest slaughterhouse. The demolition of the Parisian *abattoir* and its replacement with intensively programmed public activities is precisely the kind of project increasingly undertaken in post-industrial cities across the globe. Just as more recent design competitions in North America such as Downsview and Fresh Kills, la Villette proposed landscape as the basic framework for an urban transformation of what had been a part of the working city, left derelict by shifts in economies of production and consumption. The competition for la Villette began a trajectory of postmodern urban park, in which landscape was itself conceived as a complex medium capable of articulating relations between urban infrastructure, public events, and indeterminate urban futures for large post-industrial sites, rather than simply as healthful exceptions to the unhealthy city that surrounded them.[14]

Four hundred and seventy entries from over 70 countries were submitted for la Villette, the vast majority of which retraced familiar profiles for public parks and typologies for the recovery of the traditional city, while two submissions clearly signaled a paradigm shift still underway in the reconception of contemporary urbanism. The winning scheme, by the office of Bernard Tschumi, represented a conceptual leap in the development of landscape urbanism; it formulated landscape as the most suitable medium through which to order programmatic and social change over time, especially complex evolving arrangements of urban activities. This continued Tschumi's longstanding interest in reconstituting event and program as a legitimate architectural concern in lieu of the stylistic issues dominating architectural discourse in the postmodern era, as he stated in his competition entry:

The '70s witnessed a period of renewed interest in the formal constitution of the city, its typologies and its morphologies. While developing analyses focused on the history of the city, this attention was largely devoid of programmatic justification. No analysis addressed the issue of the activities that were to occur in the city. Nor

did any properly address the fact that the organization of functions and events was as much an architectural concern as the elaboration of forms or styles.[15]

Equally significant was the influence of the second-prize entry submitted by the Office at Metropolitan Architecture and Rem Koolhaas. The unbuilt scheme explored the juxtaposition of unplanned relationships between various park programs. Koolhaas's organizational conceit of parallel strips of landscape, itself having become something of a canonical cliché, radically juxtaposed irreconcilable contents, invoking the vertical juxtaposition of various programs on adjacent floors of Manhattan skyscrapers as described in Koolhaas's *Delirious New York*.[16] As conceived by Koolhaas/OMA, the infrastructure of the park would be strategically organized to support an indeterminate and unknowable range of future uses over time:

[I]t is safe to predict that during the life of the park, the program will undergo constant change and adjustment. The more the park works, the more it will be in a perpetual state of revision. . . . The underlying principle of programmatic indeterminacy as a basis of the formal concept allows any shift, modification, replacement, or substitutions to occur without damaging the initial hypothesis.[17]

Through their deployment of postmodern ideas of open-endedness and indeterminacy, Tschumi's and Koolhaas's projects for Parc de la Villette signaled the role that landscape would come to play as a medium through which to articulate a postmodern urbanism: layered, non-hierarchical, flexible, and strategic. Both schemes offered a nascent form of landscape urbanism, constructing a horizontal field of infrastructure that might accommodate all sorts of urban activities, planned and unplanned, imagined and unimagined, over time.

In the wake of la Villette's influence, architectural culture has become increasingly aware of landscape's role as a viable framework for the contemporary city. Across a diverse spectrum of cultural positions landscape has emerged as the most relevant medium through which to construct a meaningful and viable public realm in North American cities. Consider how the thinking of architectural historian and theorist Kenneth Frampton has shifted in recent years. In the 1980s, Frampton lamented the impediments to making meaningful urban form given the power of speculative capital and the rise of automobile culture:

> Modern building is now so universally conditioned by optimized technology that the possibility of creating significant urban form has become extremely limited. The restrictions jointly imposed by automotive distribution and the volatile play of land speculation serve to limit the scope of urban design to such a degree that any intervention tends to be reduced either to the manipulation of elements predetermined by the imperatives of production, or to a kind of superficial masking which modern development requires for the facilitation of marketing and the maintenance of social control.[18]

Against the forces of "optimized technology," Frampton argued for an architecture of "resistance." During the following decade, however, Frampton's call for architecture as an instrument of local resistance to global culture gave way to a more subtly shaded position that concedes the unique role of landscape in providing a modicum of market-based urban order. In this later formulation, landscape rather than object formalism affords the greater (albeit still slim) prospect of constructing meaningful relations within the detritus of market production:

> The dystopia of the megalopolis is already an irreversible historical fact: it has long since installed a new way of life, not to say a new nature . . . I would submit that instead we need to conceive of a remedial landscape that is capable of playing a critical and compensatory role in relation to the ongoing, destructive commodification of the man-made world.[19]

To invoke Frampton and Koolhaas together is perhaps curious, for Frampton's interest in local cultural resistance to globalization could not be further afield from Koolhaas's project of engagement with the very mechanisms of global capital. Indeed Koolhaas's practice of spinning a neo-avant gardist position from the working of global brands is by now familiar. Despite their divergent cultural politics, by the mid '90s, Koolhaas and Frampton had

come to occupy curiously convergent positions, concurring on the fact that landscape had supplanted architecture's role as the medium most capable of ordering contemporary urbanism. As Koolhaas put it in 1998: "Architecture is no longer the primary element of urban order, increasingly urban order is given by a thin horizontal vegetal plane, increasingly landscape is the primary element of urban order."[20]

Arguably a third significant cultural position, a *realpolitik* of laissez faire economic development and public-private partnerships in planning processes, is articulated by Peter Rowe in *Making a Middle Landscape*.[21] Interestingly, Rowe's conclusions are not dissimilar; he advocates a critical role for the design disciplines in the making of a meaningful public realm in the exurban "middle" between traditional city center and greenfield suburb beyond. Rowe's position is summarized by Frampton, who identifies two salient points: "first, that priority should now be accorded to landscape, rather than to freestanding built form and second, that there is a pressing need to transform certain megalopolitan types such as shopping malls, parking lots, and office parks into landscaped built forms."[22]

If landscape urbanism offers strategies for design, it also provides a cultural category – a lens through which to see and describe the contemporary city, many of which, absent intervention by designers and without the benefit of planning, have been found to emulate natural systems. Again, the work of Koolhaas is notable, but not exceptional.[23] The clearest example of this tendency can be found in Koolhaas's essay on Atlanta:

> Atlanta does not have the classical symptoms of the city; it is not dense; it is a sparse, thin carpet of habitation, a kind of suprematist composition of little fields. Its strongest contextual givens are vegetal and infrastructural: forests and roads. Atlanta is not a city; it is a *landscape*.[24]

The tendency to view the contemporary city through the lens of landscape is most evident in projects and texts which appropriate the terms, conceptual categories, and operating methodologies of field ecology: that is, the study of species as they relate to their natural environments.[25] This reveals one of the implicit advantages of landscape urbanism: the conflation, integration, and fluid exchange between (natural) environmental and (engineered) infrastructural systems.

While this newfound relevance for landscape in conceptions of urbanism first manifested itself in the work of architects, it has been quickly corroborated from within the profession of landscape architecture itself. Though still largely marginalized by the dominant culture of mainstream landscape architecture, it is increasingly seen as a viable aspect of the profession's future in much of the academy and for a variety of progressive professional practices. This is possible in part given the critical reassessment that landscape architecture is presently enjoying, in many ways analogous to the transformations within architectural culture with the rise of postmodernism. In fact, it is perfectly reasonable to understand the recent renaissance of landscape discourse as the impact of postmodern thought on the field.

As the discipline of landscape architecture is examining its own historical and theoretical underpinnings, the general public is increasingly conscious of environmental issues, and thus more aware of landscape as a cultural category. Simultaneously many landscape architecture practices in North America have become proficient in professional activities that were once the domain of urban planners. This has allowed landscape architects to fill a professional void, as planning has largely opted out of responsibility for proposing physical designs. Landscape architects have also been increasingly involved in work for both post-industrial sites and the easements of various infrastructural systems such as electrical, water, and highway systems. As Australian landscape architect Richard Weller describes the landscape profession's newfound relevance:

> Postmodern landscape architecture has done a boom trade in cleaning up after modern infrastructure as societies – in the first world at least – shift from primary industry to post industrial, information societies. In common landscape practice, work is more often than not conducted in the shadow of the infrastructural object, which is given priority over the field into which it is to be inserted. However, as any landscape architect knows, the landscape itself is a medium through which all ecological transactions must pass: it is *the* infrastructure of the future.[26]

The efficacy of landscape as a remediating practice – a salve for the wounds of the industrial age – is evident in the work of many contemporary landscape architects. Projects by Peter Latz at Duisburg Nord Steelworks Park in Germany and Richard Haag at Gas Works Park in Seattle, are useful illustrations of this tendency. Many landscape architects have taken up this work for brownfield sites in North America as the body of technical knowledge, modes of practice, and availability of funding have increased in recent years. Projects by Hargreaves Associates, Corner/Field Operations, and Julie Bargmann's DIRT Studio are representative here, among others. Another key strategy of landscape urbanism is the integration of transportation infrastructure into public space. This is exemplified by Barcelona's program of public space and peripheral road improvements, including projects such as Trinitat Cloverleaf Park by Enric Batlle and Joan Roig, among others. While this genre of work – the use of landscape in the stitching of infrastructure into urban fabrics – has well-established precedents, the Barcelona peripheral roadwork is distinct. It offers public parks conceived and constructed simultaneously with the public conveyance of the highway, subtly inflecting its design away from an optimized artifact of civil engineering toward a more complex synthesis of requirements, in which neither civil engineering nor landscape dominate.

One of the more outspoken proponents of landscape as urbanism is Adriaan Geuze, principal of West 8 Landscape Architects, based in Rotterdam. West 8 has worked on projects at various scales, articulating multiple roles for landscape in the shaping of contemporary urbanism.[27] Several of these have imaginatively reordered relationships between ecology and infrastructure, deemphasizing the middle scale of decorative or architectural work and favoring instead the large-scale infrastructural diagram and the small-scale material condition.

West 8's Shell Project, for instance, organizes dark and light mussel shells and the corresponding flocks of similarly shaded dark and light birds naturally adapted to feed from them. These surfaces form parallel strips of shoulders along the highway connecting the constructed islands of the East Scheldt stormtide barrier. This project organizes an ecology of natural selection and renders it for public perception via the automobile. By contrast, historical precedents for urban parkways typically reproduce a pastoral image of "nature" without intervening in their ecological surroundings in any substantial way. Likewise, West 8's ambitious scheme for the Schiphol Amsterdam Airport Landscape abandons the professional tradition of specifically detailed planting plans, deploying instead a general botanical strategy of sunflowers, clover, and beehives. This work, by avoiding intricate compositional designs and precise planting arrangements, allows the project to respond to future programmatic and political changes in Schiphol's planning, positioning landscape as a strategic partner in the complex process of airport planning rather than (as is usually the case) simply an unfortunate victim of it. Another example of landscape urbanism as a professional framework is West 8's redevelopment plan for Borneo and Sporenburg in Amsterdam Harbor. The planning and design of this large-scale redevelopment is conceived as an enormous landscape urbanism project, orchestrated by West 8, into which the work of numerous other architects and designers is inserted. The project suggests the potential diversity of landscape urbanist strategies through the insertion of numerous small landscaped courts and yards, and the commissioning of numerous designers for individual housing units. Taken together, the range of West 8's recent production illustrates the potential for landscape architecture to supplant architecture, urban design, and urban planning as design disciplines responsible for reordering post-industrial urban sites.

Several recent international design competitions for the reuse of enormously scaled industrial sites in North American cities have used landscape as their primary medium. Downsview Park, located on the site of an underutilized military airbase in Toronto, and Fresh Kills, on the site of the world's largest landfill on Staten Island, New York, are representative of these trends and offer the most fully formed examples of landscape urbanism practices to date applied to the detritus of the industrial city.[28] While significant distinctions exist between these two commissions, as do questions regarding their eventual realization, the body of work produced for Downsview and Fresh Kills represents an emerging consensus that designers of the built environment, across disciplines, would do well to examine landscape as the medium through which to conceive the renovation of the post-industrial city. James Corner's projects for Downsview (with Stan

Allen) and Fresh Kills are exemplary in this regard, illustrating mature works of landscape urbanism through their accumulation and orchestration of absolutely diverse and potentially incongruous contents. Typical of this work, and by now standard fare for projects of this type, are detailed diagrams of phasing, animal habitats, succession planting, and hydrological systems, as well as programmatic and planning regimes. While these diagrams initially overwhelm with information, they present an understanding of the enormous complexities confronting any work at this scale. Particularly compelling is the complex interweaving of natural ecologies with the social, cultural, and infrastructural layers of the contemporary city.

While both Koolhaas/OMA (in partnership with designer Bruce Mau) and Tschumi submitted entries as finalists at Downsview, they found their historical fortunes reversed, more or less precisely. The imageable and media friendly Mau and Koolhaas/OMA scheme "Tree City" was awarded first prize and the commission; while the more sublime, layered, and intellectually challenging scheme of the office of Bernard Tschumi will doubtless enjoy greater influence within architectural culture, particularly as the information age transforms our understandings and limits of the "natural." Tschumi's "The Digital and the Coyote" project for Downsview presented an electronic analog to his longstanding interest in urban event, with richly detailed diagrams of succession planting and the seeding of ambient urbanity in the midst of seemingly desolate prairies. Tschumi's position at Downsview is symmetrical with his original thesis for la Villette. Both projects were based on a fundamental indictment of the nineteenth-century Olmstedian model, offering in its place an understanding of landscape conflated with a pervasive and ubiquitous urbanism. As Tschumi put it in his project statement for Downsview:

> Neither theme park or wildlife preserve, Downsview does not seek to renew using the conventions of traditional park compositions such as those of Vaux or Olmsted. The combination of advanced military technologies with water courses and flows and downstreams suggests another fluid, liquid, digital sensibility. Airstrips, information centers, public performance spaces, internet and worldwide web access all point to a redefinition

of received ideas about parks, nature, and recreation, in a 21st century setting where everything is "urban," even in the middle of the wilderness.[29]

The Downsview and Fresh Kills projects are notable for the presence of landscape architects on interdisciplinary teams of consultants, whereas the la Villette competition named a single lead architect to orchestrate the entire project. Striking and consistent in this regard are the central involvement of ecologists as well as information or communication designers on virtually all teams. This is clearly distinct from the overarching role of architects in previous regimes of urban design and planning, where these concerns were either absent altogether (ecology) or simply subsumed within the professional practice of the architect (information design).

While it remains unclear if either of the winning schemes by Mau and Koolhaas/OMA for Downsview and Corner and Allen/Field Operations for Fresh Kills will be fully realized, we must see this as a challenge of political imagination and cultural leadership rather than as a failure of the competition processes or the projects they premiated. These projects and the work of their competitors, taken collectively, point to transformations currently underway which are profoundly changing the disciplinary and professional assumptions behind the design of the built environment. Particularly evident is the fact that projects of this scale and significance demand professional expertise at the intersections of ecology and engineering, social policy and political process. The synthesis of this range of knowledge and its embodiment in public design processes recommend landscape urbanism as a disciplinary framework for reconceiving the contemporary urban field.

NOTES

1 Stan Allen, "Mat Urbanism: The Thick 2-D," in Hashim Sarkis, ed., *CASE: Le Corbusier's Venice Hospital* (Munich: Prestel, 2001), 124.

2 See James Corner, "Terra Fluxus," in Charles Waldheim, ed., *The Landscape Urbanism Reader*, (New York: Princeton Architectural Press, 2006). See also James Corner, ed., *Recovering Landscape* (New York: Princeton Architectural Press, 1999).

3 Corner, *Recovering Landscape*, 1–26.

4 One marker of a generational divide between advocacy and instrumentalization has been the recent emergence of complex and culturally derived understanding of natural systems. An example of this can be found in the shift from pictorial to operational in landscape discourse that has been the subject of much recent work. See for example James Corner, "Eidetic Operations and New Landscapes," in *Recovering Landscape*, 153–69. Also useful on this topic is Julia Czerniak, "Challenging the Pictorial: Recent Landscape Practice," in *Assemblage* 34 (December 1997): 110–20.

5 Ian McHarg, *Design with Nature* (Garden City, N.Y.: Natural History Press, 1969). For an overview of Mumford's work, see Mark Luccarelli, *Lewis Mumford and the Ecological Region: The Politics of Planning* (New York: Guilford Press, 1997).

6 See Corner, "Terra Fluxus," in Charles Waldheim, ed., *The Landscape Urbanism Reader* (New York: Princeton Architectural Press, 2006).

7 Early critiques of modernist architecture and urban planning ranged from the populist Jane Jacobs, *Death and Life of Great American Cities* (New York: Vintage Books, 1961), to the professional Robert Venturi, *Complexity and Contradiction in Architecture* (New York: Museum of Modern Art, 1966).

8 Kevin Lynch, *A Theory of Good City Form* (Cambridge, Mass.: MIT Press, 1981). Also see Lynch's earlier empirical research in *Image of the City* (Cambridge, Mass.: MIT Press, 1960).

9 The most significant of these critiques was Aldo Rossi. See Rossi, *The Architecture of the City* (Cambridge, Mass.: MIT Press, 1982).

10 Robert Venturi and Denise Scott-Brown's work is indicative of these interests. See Venturi, Scott-Brown, and Steven Izenour, *Learning From Las Vegas: The Forgotten Symbolism of Architectural Form* (Cambridge, Mass.: MIT Press, 1977).

11 Charles Jencks, *The Language of Post-Modern Architecture* (New York: Rizzoli, 1977). On Fordism and its relation to postmodern architecture: see Patrik Schumacher and Christian Rogner, "After Ford," in Georgia Daskalakis, Charles Waldheim, and Jason Young, eds., *Stalking Detroit* (Barcelona: ACTAR, 2001), 48–56.

12 Harvard University's Urban Design Program began in 1960, and the discipline grew in

popularity with increased enrollments, increased numbers of degrees conferred and the addition of new degree programs during the 1970s and '80s.

13 Allen, "Mat Urbanism: The Thick 2-D," 125.

14 For contemporaneous critical commentary on la Villette, see Anthony Vidler, "Trick-Track," *La Case Vide: La Villette* (London: Architectural Association, 1985), and Jacques Derrida, "Point de Folie-Maintenant l'architecture," *AA Files* 12 (Summer 1986): 65–75.

15 Bernard Tschumi, La Villette Competition Entry, "The La Villette Competition," *Princeton Journal* vol. 2, "On Landscape" (1985): 200–10.

16 Rem Koolhaas, *Delirious New York: A Retroactive Manifesto for Manhattan* (New York: Oxford University Press, 1978).

17 Rem Koolhaas, "Congestion without Matter," *S, M, L, XL* (New York: Monacelli, 1999), 921.

18 Kenneth Frampton, "Towards a Critical Regionalism: Six Points for an Architecture of Resistance," in Hal Foster, ed., *The Anti-Aesthetic* (Seattle: Bay Press, 1983), 17.

19 Kenneth Frampton, "Toward an Urban Landscape," *Columbia Documents* (New York: Columbia University, 1995), 89, 92.

20 Rem Koolhaas, "IIT Student Center Competition Address," Illinois Institute of Technology, College of Architecture, Chicago, March 5, 1998.

21 Peter Rowe, *Making a Middle Landscape* (Cambridge, Mass.: MIT Press, 1991).

22 Kenneth Frampton, "Toward an Urban Landscape," 83–93.

23 Among these see, for example, Lars Lerup, "Stim and Dross: Rethinking the Metropolis," *After the City* (Cambridge, Mass.: MIT Press, 2000), 47–61.

24 Rem Koolhaas, "Atlanta," *S, M, L, XL* (New York: Monacelli, 1999), 835.

25 Among the sources of this material of interest to architects and landscape architects is field ecologist Richard T.T. Forman. See Wenche E. Dramstad, James D. Olson, and Richard T.T. Forman, *Landscape Ecology Principles in Landscape Architecture and Land-use Planning* (Cambridge, Mass. and Washington, D.C.: Harvard University and Island Press, 1996).

26 Richard Weller, "Landscape Architecture and the City Now," unpublished manuscript based on "Toward an Art of Infrastructure in the Theory and Practice of Contemporary Landscape Architecture," keynote address, *MESH* Conference, Royal Melbourne Institute of Technology, Melbourne, Australia, July 9, 2001.

27 On the work of Adriaan Geuze/West 8 see, "West 8 Landscape Architects," in *Het Landschap/The Landscape: Four International Landscape Designers* (Antwerpen: deSingel, 1995), 215–53, and Luca Molinari, ed., *West 8* (Milan: Skira, 2000).

28 Downsview and Fresh Kills have been the subject of extensive documentation, including essays in *Praxis*, no. 4, *Landscapes* (2002). For additional information see Julia Czerniak, ed., *CASE: Downsview Park Toronto* (Cambridge, Mass./Munich: Harvard/Prestel, 2001), and Charles Waldheim, "Park=City? The Downsview Park Competition," in *Landscape Architecture Magazine* vol. 91, no. 3 (March 2001): 80–85, 98–99.

29 Bernard Tschumi, "Downsview Park: The Digital and the Coyote," in Czerniak, ed., *CASE: Downsview Park Toronto*, 82–89.

"Discourses for Landscape and Urbanization," "The Production of Waste Landscape," and "Drosscape Explained"

from Drosscape: Wasting Land in Urban America (2006)

Alan Berger

Editors' Introduction

As global restructuring continues, what gets left behind are deindustrialized wastelands: brownfields, unpurposed interstitial spaces, demographic contraction, detritus/pollution/contamination, and by-passed places. In his manifesto-like book *Drosscape*, Alan Berger suggests these wasted places accumulate as once-thriving industrial areas begin to hollow out with the evolution of manufacturing processes and the changing locations of production. In some instances "dross" is the result of companies and institutions that leave behind their obsolete facilities; or perhaps they undertook cost-cutting/profit-maximization by abandoning the country, their sites, and employees for less expensive labor and resources overseas. At other times, dross can be caused by leapfrogged interstitial space as a result of horizontal urbanization and sprawl. The scale of these wastelands is immense, becoming a norm in some regions by-passed by the global or local economy – or conversely as a result of poor physical planning oversight. They can be found both within the inner-core of deindustrializing cities and on the periphery of sprawling megapolitan areas. One need think only of the vast expanses of decline in rustbelt places like Detroit, Philadelphia, or Cleveland to understand what Berger is onto here (not to mention the industrial wastelands of Europe, or the post-colonial traces of industry in the global south). Photographs of abandoned military facilities and decaying factories in the book help us to understand the huge scale and "common" condition of these wastelands we pass on an everyday basis – but rarely see.

Early in the writing, Berger problematizes the term "post-industrial" by suggesting that sites of production are never static in urban areas, but always changing. Abandoning use of the term might be a first step in appreciating the realities of constant economic dynamism; but might also help in reconceptualizing dross sites and valuing them differently. As such, dross becomes a naturally occurring phenomenon of most industrial evolution and a signpost of capitalist creative destruction, as suggested by Schumpeter. Waste becomes an expected by-product of industrial process – waste sites happen. The question becomes: what to do with them?

Drosscape helps to identify the problematics of wasteland reclamation and proposes a way forward for planners and designers to begin repurposing, reusing, and infilling these waste landscapes – or conversely "landscraping" that might help in speeding up their return to what might be perceived as nature. The term "drosscape" (coined by Berger himself) becomes an attitude about redesign and repurposing – which requires a physical resurfacing (a "scaping") of the waste site. At the end of the book he begins to define the term as "a design pedagogy that emphasizes the productive integration and reuse of waste landscapes throughout the urban world." Methodological and operational implications that might convert "dross" into "drosscape" are offered by Berger as new theory and practice in landscape analysis and design. What becomes difficult for the reader is the open-endedness and scale of undertaking in these wasteland conversions. What become the challenge in practice for planners and designers are the lack of paying clients, lack of strategic design program, and snail's pace of the evolutionary time frame. In "drosscape" production then, planners and designers take on new roles as facilitators, collaborators, spokespersons, and mid-wives. Interestingly, this open-ended lack of program is the *modus operandi* of many design studios in academia – forcing young designers into hypothetical propositions that at times can be infuriating for their lack of real-world application – and at other times can provide the opportunity for design innovation beyond pragmatic expectation. Matching real-world solutions and innovation to these wastelands is the next challenge for a task that seems so unbelievably overwhelming.

This text was published contemporaneously as a shorter essay of the same name that appeared in the *The Landscape Urbanism Reader* edited by Charles Waldheim and published by Princeton Architectural Press in 2006. Many tendencies of the Landscape Urbanism movement can be found in *Drosscape*, including: the temporal nature of landscape and ecological processes, new methods of practice, the possibility of imagined futures, and design as resistance. What becomes refreshing about this piece is its understanding of the role of land and economy in urbanization and ecology. However at the same time, it avoids any substantive prescription about how landscape urbanism (or the "big four" – architecture, landscape architecture, planning, urban design) might begin reconciling their shortcomings in dross response. In his shorter essay version of *Drosscape*, Berger begins to suggest ways of doing this: by designers shifting attention from small-scale site design projects to larger regional landscape concerns; by de-prioritizing traditional place-making because of its inability to address big picture challenges; and by finding new ground for landscape urbanism that is not already claimed by the "big four." While few would disagree with these recommendations (there are plenty of challenges for everyone, after all), some traditionalists find them to be a direct attack on their values and priorities.

Alan Berger is an Associate Professor of Landscape Architecture and Urban Design at the Massachusetts Institute of Technology and Director of P-REX (the Project for Reclamation Excellence), a multi-disciplinary research effort focusing on the design and reuse of waste landscapes worldwide. His work emphasizes the link between our consumption of natural resources and the waste and destruction of landscape, to help instruct people in reusing waste landscapes for productive use. His other books include: *Reclaiming the American West* (New York: Princeton Architectural Press, 2002); *Nansha Coastal City: Landscape and Urbanism in the Pearl River Delta* (Cambridge, MA: Harvard University GSD, 2006); *Designing the Reclaimed Landscape* (Abingdon: Taylor & Francis, 2008); and *Systemic Design Can Change the World* (Amsterdam/San Francisco: Sun Architecture, 2009). Prior to teaching at MIT, he taught at the University of Colorado and Harvard's GSD. He has lectured and taught studios around the world.

For further reading on landscapes of deindustrialization and wasteland reclamation see: Jefferson Cowie and Joseph Heathcott, eds., *Beyond the Ruins: The Meanings of Deindustrialization* (Ithaca, NY: Cornell University Press, 2003); Ann O'M. Bowman and Michael A. Pagano. *Terra Incognita: Vacant Land and Urban Strategies* (Washington, DC: Georgetown University Press, 2001); Niall Kirkwood, ed., *Manufactured Sites: Rethinking the Post-Industrial Landscape* (Abingdon: Taylor & Francis, 2001); and Steven High and David W. Lewis, *Corporate Wasteland: The Landscape and Memory of Deindustrialization* (Ithaca, NY: ILR Press, 2007). For literature on the destructive impacts of urbanism on the landscape, see the following: William Cronon, *Nature's Metropolis* (New York: Norton, 1992) and Mark Reisner, *Cadillac Desert* (New York: Penguin, 1993).

DISCOURSES FOR LANDSCAPE AND URBANIZATION

What is place in this new "in-between" world?
                Nigel Thrift – *Writing the Rural*

Home was BAMA, the Sprawl, the Boston-Atlanta Metropolitan Axis.

                William Gibson – *Neuromancer*

The horizontal city and the in-between

At the beginning of the twenty-first century, as well as in Gibson's prognosticated future, the American city is characterized by rapid horizontal growth, having a dispersed and sparsely populated surface of activities.[1] The resultant landscape is difficult to describe in words. Everyone who dwelled in or traveled through and around urbanized areas in America, however, is familiar with this landscape. It may be vacant strips alongside roadways, seas of parking lots, unused land, surfaces awaiting development, dumping grounds, warehouse districts, a seemingly endless stretch of setbacks and perimeters framing housing communities. Seen at the *local* scale, (e.g. walking or driving through one's neighborhood or shopping district) the landscape of the horizontal city may appear diminished and wasteful. It appears poorly planned, designed, and unmaintained and as irregular and indiscreet leftovers from other, more dominant forms of development like buildings or highways. Viewed at the metropolitan, or *regional*, scale (e.g. from the top of a tall building or airplane) the landscape of the horizontal city often appears as extensive and plentiful – open space and vegetation – such as large agricultural tracts surrounded by new development or forests with office parks nestled in their interior.

The "building out" of the horizontal city has formed a new frontier across the American landscape. This frontier embodies characteristics both internal (within the built-out zone) and external (beyond the leading edge of development) to the horizontal city. The *internal* frontier emerges from the composite of many landscape fragments within the local urbanized area: strips, lots, and unbuilt or unbuildable properties. With the exception of large public parks and protected open space, the unbuilt portions of the urbanized landscape have become

smaller in aggregate size, increasingly marginalized *in-between* architectural objects in the urban fabric.[2] This reduction may be attributed to many factors, such as the planning and zoning codes that restrict the ways landscape can be incorporated into development. It may also be the result of the new transportation or manufacturing trends (such as agglomerations), or land's economic value.[3] In general, urban land with income-generating structures is worth more to taxing authorities and private developers than vacant lands. At the same time, public or private entities speculate and may leave land strategically vacant until market conditions warrant sale or development. The outcome then is another kind of aggregated patchwork.

The *external* frontier of the American landscape was once collectively considered the vast continental stretch of open land outside the largest centralized cities – the city's other. This frontier evolved into what we experience today as a fragmented entity, best described as the landscape existing between nodes of urbanization. Today's external frontier exhibits a closer proximity of each urbanized area to its neighboring one, or what geographers Stephen Graham and Simon Marvin describe as the more totally urbanized world.[4] The external frontier is neither here nor there. Some three decades ago, realizing that urban growth and land use changes are much more than visual problems, geographer Pierce Lewis identified the disappearance of clear boundaries between city and country. Lewis writes, "The boundary that has separated city from country throughout American history is now almost gone, and that is true whether one talks about physical boundaries or about more subtle forms of intellectual or psychological boundaries. To some degree, in most parts of America's inhabited domain the metropolis is almost everywhere."[5] Lewis's contention is that today's city is so diffuse that it has become a "galactic metropolis," a cityform resembling a galaxy of stars and planets, with large empty areas in-between, held together with something akin to gravitational attraction.[6] These "large empty areas" are what he terms new metropolitan tissue, or areas that do not lay directly adjacent to existing nucleated cities but often lie great distances from city centers. Lewis asks the reader to accept the fact that this tissue is here to stay as the result of the horizontal urbanization, and he provokes readers to rethink its use. Lewis's "tissue" of course, hauntingly fits the description of the external frontier.

Internal and external frontiers should not all be salvaged by society. Landscape attributes of these frontiers are indistinct: they are regarded as either too small and fragmented at the local scale or aggregated into isolation at the regional scale. It is difficult for society to identify and value them. The traditional way to value urban landscapes is by using landscape as a place-making medium (such as a small-scale public park or plaza). Today, this idea is blurred. The landscape of the contemporary horizontal city is no longer a place-making or condensing medium. Instead it is fragmented and chaotically spread throughout the city in small bits and pieces. Because it is so difficult to see in its entirety, the contemporary city's landscape escapes wholeness and public consciousness, once poignantly referred to as "terra incognita."[7]

But since it plays a necessary role in urban evolution, why is the in-between undervalued? Because it is the exact opposite of a vertical sight for sore eyes (such as a deteriorating building), the in-between landscape lies flat around such objects and is thus likely to dissuade close inspection. Publicity campaigns for cities always depict institutional buildings, cultural centers, airports, even sports stadia as the most valuable cultural attractions. A city's landscape assets – public parks, golf courses, water bodies, tree-lined promenades, pedestrian malls, and conservation greenways – typically serve as the stage supporting these attractions. Missing are the unsightly but crucial transitional landscapes such as railroad yards, vacant lots, derelict buildings, contaminated fields, smokestacks, industrial manufacturing, and parking lots. Or, as stated above, these transitional landscapes are simply ignored.

A liminal landscape

Liminality is frequently likened to death, to being in the womb, to invisibility, to darkness, to bisexuality, to the wilderness, and to an eclipse of the sun or moon.

Victor W. Turner – *The Ritual Process*

Much of the landscape surface left in the wake of rapid horizontal urbanization is not a clearly defined, stable, and fixed entity. It is between occupancies

and uses, successional phases, and (dis)investment cycles. The term *in-between* describes a state of liminality, something that lives in transition and eludes classification, something that resists new stability and reincorporation. The in-between landscapes of the horizontal city are liminal because they remain at the margins (or *limen*, which means "threshold" in Latin), awaiting a societal desire to inscribe them with value and status.[8]

[. . .]

The homogenizing effects of the horizontal city (cookie-cutter planning and zoning codes, standardized engineering practices, master planning, etc.) and new communication technologies have led to novel forms of social activities because people do not want to spend twenty-four hours a day in the same type of designed environment. It is easy to understand how these activities take advantage of a city's landscape leftovers because urban open space is increasingly becoming privatized. In the urbanized world, the in-between landscape should be valued because it provides a threshold, or platform, for liminal cultural phenomena to play out. Thus *communitas* is cultivated.

[. . .]

From in-between to freedom and waste

The problem that is usually being visualized is how capitalism administers existing structures, whereas the relevant problem is how it creates and destroys them.

Joseph Schumpeter – *Capitalism, Socialism and Democracy*

Future urban infill and growth depend on salvaging and re-imagining the collective body of in-between landscapes. For many American cities, as landscape surfaces accumulate through horizontal urbanization, it becomes paramount to locate waste and identify potential problems and opportunities for reusing it.

As revealed in recent history, public perception can be manipulated and manufactured (to create and pass referenda and balloting measures) to fund public and private urban infill projects like sporting-event facilities, libraries, museums, etc., with public tax revenues.[9] Voters consistently approve new funding mechanisms for infrastructural improvements such as buildings, roadway widening, school construction, and flood-control/sewer projects. Conversely, they often disapprove of tax increases earmarked for urban landscape improvements.[10] These are typically left to the workings of the private-sector or existing city department budgets (such as Parks and Recreation) or piggybacked on engineering projects.

This points to the fact that there is resistance surrounding the legitimacy of publicly funded improvements to the in-between landscape. Pro- and anti-sprawl, as well as conservation advocates, may serve as examples of this phenomenon. Both constituencies try to extinguish the existence of the in-between landscape. The mission of pro-sprawl constituencies is to develop as much land as possible (or as much as the market demands). Conversely, the mission of anti-sprawl constituencies is to conserve as much land and open space as possible. Both groups use private funding to achieve their landscape missions.

In terms of the urban landscape a consensus on what one considers in-between is improbable. This is because the definition of waste is at issue. Americans consciously choose the types of waste landscape they value. This decision is highly personal. The issue evokes arguments of individual freedom and liberty. The International Society for Individual Liberty (ISL), for example, developed the world's largest libertarian portal to the Internet to discuss, in part, environmental topics. One of the ISL's services is Free-Market.net, which contains free-market analyses and literature on urban sprawl.

It is largely produced by independent, conservative research institutes and other think tanks. One can find a variety of libertarian arguments that link issues of waste, landscape, city form, and individual liberties. These groups support market-oriented alternatives to conventional urban-development and planning policy in contrast to traditional forms of government intervention and controls. Any legislation controlling urban growth, in the libertarian view, compromises individual freedom as well as the values that formed and galvanized America's founding principles.

Waste was long regarded as part of urbanization. For example, cities as diverse as ancient Rome and Manhattan dumped garbage, bones, and all matter of debris from daily life into the streets as a means of disposing trash while physically elevating the city. In older cities, people live on top of their waste.[11]

Today, of course, there are requirements for appropriate fill materials and most solid municipal wastes are dumped in landfills outside populated areas. Water is treated in specialized sewage-treatment plants. After World War II, the production of waste became associated with social processes of freedom, power, and convenience.[12] According to historian Susan Strasser, "Disposable products, food packaging, and the convenience, cleanliness, and labor savings they represented were understood to distinguish the freedom of modernity from the drudgery of old-fashioned life."[13]

Travel to any American urbanized area, and you will find "wastefulness" in many forms. Might this reveal the values of the people who live and govern there? Just like physical waste, what is considered "wasteful" is deeply embedded in a culture's value system. Americans carefully choose the ways they weave wastefulness, inefficiencies, and excesses – or the opposites – into their lives. As a result, cultural preferences and environmental ethics play larger and larger roles in the structuring of cities.[14] The recent ascension of the politically correct slogan "sustainability," or more precisely, "sustainable development" is an example. How one determines that a condition is sustainable has everything to do with local values and context. Someone living in a developing country, for example, would not define sustainability on the same ethical grounds as someone living in a highly industrialized nation. Moreover, it has been argued that sustainable development is nothing more than an excuse created by rich, developed countries to further impoverish poorer nations.[15] Regardless of one's moral or ethical position on sustainability, it is clear that issues of consumption and waste are not based on homogeneous value systems, but rather on local, contextual doxa, and praxis. The result is that multitudes of "waste" spread unevenly in numerous ways throughout the landscape.

With regards to "waste," it is impossible to isolate re-characterizations of the city from its socioeconomic milieu. Horizontal urbanization results in part from what, in 1942, Harvard University economist Joseph Schumpeter called "The Process of Creative Destruction."[16] Schumpeter believed that innovations made by entrepreneurs began with this process, which relegated old inventories, technologies, equipment, and even craftsmen's skills to obsolescence.[17] From this one can derive a contemporary reading of the horizontal city's in-between landscape, Lars Lerup's *dross*, as a palimpsest of waste leftover from creative destruction. Lerup's *stim* and *dross* is the physical cognate for creative destruction.[18] These terms acknowledge the totality of the consumption-waste cycle and the organic integration of waste into the urban world as the result of socioeconomic processes.

Other theories have been posited over the past century concerning relationships between waste and economic production. The key to economic achievement is to spend and consume.[19] So stated J. George Frederick, president of the Business Bourse publishing house, and his wife, Christine Frederick, a prominent home economist and advertising consultant more than a decade prior to Schumpeter's "creative destruction" thesis. They coined the phrases "progressive obsolescence" and "creative waste." Progressive obsolescence essentially means that the new business of industrialization is founded on the principle of wasting things before they are completely used or worn out. A similar idea was promoted by President George W. Bush, after the 9/11 terrorist attacks under the guise of creating economic stimulus: "We need to stimulate the economy through boosting consumer confidence with some kind of money in the hands of consumers."[20] Strasser notes that economically driven accumulation creates waste whether through consumer goods (raw consumption) or by the ways we choose to live (freedom): "Trash and trash-making became integral to the economy in a wholly new way: the growth of markets for new products came to depend in part on the continuous disposal of old things."[21] Today an entire field of study is devoted to understanding the social and environmental implications of waste and the industrial past. Two such organizations are the Society for Industrial Archeology, with some 1,800 members worldwide, and the University of Arizona's Garbage Project, which, over the past several decades, has been studying the archaeology of garbage by using data, digging through landfills, and analyzing solid-waste streams.[22]

Coda: urban landscape is a natural thing to waste

Films such as *Koyaanisqatsi* and *Baraka* image the city from aerial overviews and via time-lapse photo-graphy in such a way as to reveal their strikingly organism-like aspects. The city is ultimately a natural process whose unperceived complexity cannot be completely controlled and planned.[23]

The situation is not unlike that of living organisms, whose hard parts, from the bones and shells of terrestrial vertebrates and marine invertebrates, to the iron and other elements and compounds precipitated by cells, originated in the expelling and/or managing of wastes. Calcium, for example, used for that living infrastructure of the human body, the skeleton, is routinely extruded by cells in the marine environment; this striking example is not an analogy, but arguably a homology for how waste becomes incorporated into landscape structure and function. The economies that provide the energy and materials for the growth of cities, such as manufacturing output and housing starts, are not so much things as processes. And, as is true for organisms, the faster they grow the more (potentially hazardous) waste they produce. This is a natural process that can be ignored, maligned, or embraced, but never stopped. "What is now emerging is an 'intermediate' description (of reality) that lies somewhere between the two alienating images of a deterministic world and an arbitrary world of pure chance," wrote Nobel Laureate Ilya Prigogine.[24] These words, regarding the unpredictability of complex systems, apply perfectly to the realm of landscapes in urbanization. Cities are not static structures, but active arenas marked by continuous energy flows and transformations of which landscapes and physical buildings and other parts are not permanent but transitional structures. Like a biological organism, the urbanized landscape is an open system, whose planned complexity always entails unplanned dross. To expect a planned city to function without waste (such as in a cradle to cradle approach), which represents the *in situ* or exported excess not only of its growth but of its maintenance, is as naïve as expecting an animal to thrive in a sensory deprivation tank. The challenge for designers is thus not to achieve drossless urbanization, but to integrate inevitable dross into more flexible aesthetic and design strategies.

With these ideas in the conceptual background, my goal is to link together the practical and theoretical issues concerning urbanization and dross to make associations among industrial, economic, and consumption activity and the landscapes created as a result of these processes. Contemporary modes of industrial production, driven by economical and consumerist influences, contribute to urbanization and the formation of "waste landscapes" – meaning actual *waste* (such as municipal solid waste, sewage, scrap metal, etc.), *wasted* places (such as abandoned and/or contaminated sites), or *wasteful* places (such as huge parking lots, retail malls, etc.). The term *urban sprawl* and the rhetorics of pro- and anti-urban sprawl advocates all but obsolesce under the realization that there is no growth without waste and that urban growth and dross go hand in hand, and always have, not because of anything human, or indeed even pertaining to life, but due to physics itself. Complex processes must export waste to their boundaries in order to maintain and grow. This is the lesson that designers of the built environment should learn from non-equilibrium thermodynamics; and it is one we need to belabor, but which must be incorporated as an assumption into our understanding of landscape in urbanization.

THE PRODUCTION OF WASTE LANDSCAPE

We are shifting not out of industry into services, but from one kind of industrial economy to another.

Stephen Cohen and John Zysman – *Manufacturing Matters*

Deindustrialization: waste landscape through attrition

America is deindustrializing. Since 1990 more than 600,000 abandoned and contaminated waste sites have been identified within American cities.[25] How did this waste landscape come to be? What will we do with it? How will it affect urbanizing areas in the future? Who is best qualified to deal with the abundance of waste landscape? Controversial questions like these are difficult to answer. This subject has produced some of the late twentieth century's most debated bodies of scholarship.[26] A book such as this cannot definitively answer these questions. It can and does, however, address the topic of deindustrialization in the context of the relationships between landscape and urbanization. As America rapidly deindustrializes, it is simultaneously urbanizing

faster than at any other time in modern history. What then are the links between urbanization, deindustrialization and the production of waste landscape in American cities?

Designers often paint a black-and-white picture of complex industrial processes. The most commonly used term, *postindustrial*, has been used both spatially and formalistically to describe everything from polluted industrial landscapes to former factory buildings, usually found in older, declining sections of a city.[27] The term itself, *postindustrial*, arguably creates as many (or more) problems than solutions in rethinking landscapes leftover from previous industrial eras. The reason for this may be that the concept of the postindustrial narrowly isolates and objectifies the landscape as being the result of very specific processes that no longer operate upon a given site (residual pollution aside). This outlook reifies the site as essentially static and in isolation and defines it in terms of a pre-industrial past rather than as an ongoing industrial process that forms other parts of the city. There are many examples of this outlook that manifest in the redesigning of industrial production sites for reuse.[28] I suggest that it would be strategically helpful in the short term to suspend the term postindustrial and its value system when discussing the city.

[…]

For much of the late-eighteenth and nineteenth centuries the American city landscape was designed and built to represent a view opposite to those developed by industrialization. The professions of landscape architecture and urban planning were influenced by anti-industrialization offerings. Three seminal designers of the late-nineteenth and twentieth centuries promoted the use of landscape as a means to counter the environmentally and socially destructive impact of the industrialized city. Their landscapes were designed and invested in as a respite from urban congestion and the pollution created by industrialization. Ebenezer Howard's "garden cities" of the late nineteenth century were planned with integrated road and railway networks. They were intended to promote and sustain decentralization of older cities and the creation of garden cities on the perimeter of congested production zones. Frank Lloyd Wright's plan for Broadacre City, designed in the 1920s, envisioned universal car ownership as inevitable. The plan, therefore, provided for an ever-extending grid of public highways to support a shift toward decentralization, sustainability, and progressive abandonment of the big, "obsolete" industrial city. Le Corbusier's plan for the Radiant City proposed to replace the old, chaotic industrial city with a "rationalized urban landscape." It was to be composed of clean, modern interconnections and land-use separations. The quintessential example of this line of thinking evolved during the City Beautiful movement (1900–10), as middle class citizens attempted to transform their cities into beautiful, functional places after the Industrial Revolution.

Arguably, the result of such approaches is a net increase in the amount of waste landscape in cities. Many of the landscapes found throughout older urbanized areas are manifestations of previous anti-urban attitudes associated with industrialization. Urban populations continue to decentralize and the dense city is no longer the hub of industrial activity. As the result of fewer constituents, "respite" landscapes in many inner cities are now in severe decline and disinvestment. Thirty states in 2004 operated with frozen or reduced Parks and Recreation budgets. Currently hundreds of state parks are closed or operate for fewer hours with reduced services, such as maintenance, in order to remain fiscally solvent.[29] In 2003 California's Department of Parks and Recreation, the Nation's largest with 274 parks, raised entrance fees to compensate for a $35 million budget cut. Roughly $600 million is still needed for deferred maintenance projects.[30] The U.S. National Park Service also seeks private-sector support for park maintenance in the face of staffing shortages and budget cutbacks of billions of dollars.[31]

For the past four decades American industrial production has been undergoing an imperceptible relocation from traditional downtown cores to the urban periphery, and even to other countries. This mass exodus from older urban, industrialized areas changes the physical appearance of cities. It creates a serious economic impact for cities now forced to compete with newer urbanizing areas for the public funding needed to maintain deteriorating inner-city landscapes and infrastructures. Together deindustrialization, decentralization, and horizontal urbanization are the largest factor for land vacancy in large American cities during the 1990s.[32]

Deindustrialization is not homogeneous: it has affected every major city in the U.S. in varying ways, some of which are positive. Deindustrialization creates new employment opportunities; the plight of industrial workers has been an economic boon to other businesses. Mike Davis describes the deindustrialization of Los Angeles in *Dead Cities*:

Unlike Detroit or Youngstown, LA's derelict industrial core was not simply abandoned. Almost as fast as Fortune 500 corporations shut down their LA branch plants, local capitalists rushed in to take advantage of the Southeast's cheap leases, tax incentives, and burgeoning supply of immigrant Mexican labor. . . . Within the dead shell of heavy manufacturing, a new sweatshop economy emerged.

The old Firestone Rubber and American Can plants, for instance, have been converted into nonunion furniture factories, while the great Bethlehem Steel Works on Slauson Avenue has been replaced by a hot-dog distributor, a Chinese food-products company, and a maker of rattan patio furniture. Chrysler Maywood is now a bank "back office," while US Steel has metamorphosed into a warehouse complex, and the "Assyrian" wall of Uniroyal Tire has become a facade for a designer-label outlet center.[33]

All deindustrialized sites are not equal. Some find new life immediately by filling an economic niche, such as the immigrant labor force in Los Angeles, or by filling a cultural niche, such as the California Speedway in Fontana. Others are immediately cordoned off due to severe contamination. Many others are left abandoned for decades until market forces or technological innovation produce resources for their rehabilitation. Imperatively, deindustrialized sites are all transitional places. They await some form of reclamation prior to reprogramming and reuse. Another characteristic they have in common is their pedigree: they were previously active industrial sites, located in close proximity to densely populated urban areas. Optimistically, it could be argued that as deindustrialization proliferates and as industry relocates from central cities to peripheral areas, America's cities will enjoy a net gain in the total landscapes (and buildings) available for other uses.[34] Changes in manufacturing and production and modes of communication and transportation have resulted in the dispersal and relocation of industrial production to outlying areas and beyond. Deindustrialization creates waste landscape through the attrition of industrial landscapes and buildings in the older parts of the traditional central city. Adaptively reusing this waste landscape figures to be one of the twenty-first century's great infrastructural design challenges as these sites are potentially transformable into new productive uses such as permanent open landscapes or infill developments.

[...]

DROSSCAPE EXPLAINED

All world's glory is but dross unclean.

Edmund Spenser (1595)

Drosscape defined

Thus far, we have focused on the waste landscapes of urban America, along with the processes that are contributing to their formation. This last section introduces *drosscape*, a term created to describe a design pedagogy that emphasizes the productive integration and reuse of waste landscapes throughout the urban world.

Planning and design cannot solve all problems associated with the vast amount of urban waste landscape. However, the alarm has sounded to those who cope with the increased pessimism and cynicism spawned by the inefficacy of the "big four" design disciplines (landscape architecture, urban design, planning, and architecture) in the face of unfettered, market-driven development. The recent emergence of landscape urbanism may be a reaction to the frustration shared by many people in the landscape, planning, and architectural design arenas.[35] The polarizing rhetorical arguments of the pro- and anti-urbanization contingencies, as well as dynamic economic processes make traditional master planning approaches for future cities seem absurd. But advocating a revolutionary form of urban landscape study and practice, such as landscape urbanism, is *not* exclusive of the big four design disciplines. There is no need to develop an entirely new design discipline in order to rethink landscape's relationship to urbanization. Drosscape has the potential to coexist with the big four design disciplines. By working within current educational and professional practices, designers can still promote a radically different outcome.

The term *drosscape* implies that dross, or waste, is scaped, or resurfaced, and reprogrammed by human intentions. Moreover, the ideas of dross and scape have individual attributes.[36] The use of the term *dross* in this chapter builds on Lars Lerup's use of the term, but departs from Lerupian origin in scope and value. The suggestive etymology of the word includes shared origins with the words *waste* and *vast*, two terms frequently used to describe the contemporary nature of horizontal urbanization, as well as connections to the words *vanity*, *vain*, *vanish*, and *vacant*, all of which relate to waste through the form of empty gestures.[37]

Both dross and scape are created and destroyed by processes and values derived from, or because of cultural tastes and actions. Drosscape is the creation of a new condition in which vast, wasted, or wasteful land surfaces are modeled in accordance with new programs or new sets of values that remove or replace real or perceived wasteful aspects of geographical space (i.e., redevelopment, toxic waste removal, tax revenues, etc.). Drosscaping, as a verb, is the placement upon the landscape of new social programs that transform waste (real or perceived) into more productive urbanized landscapes to some degree.

Drosscape demands a strategically phased implementation of design that other "clean" or "green" types of urbanization lack because they are not immediately wholly occupiable.[38] Sites formerly containing industrial or manufacturing facilities, for instance, have soil, water, and building contamination problems left over from chemicals and hazardous materials. This condition, and all of the others described herein, presents a novel set of challenges for the landscape, infrastructure, and building design professions, which must face the spatio-temporary dimensions of redevelopment as a site is decontaminated, re-regulated, or otherwise transformed for reuse over time.

Drosscape proposed

Drosscapes are dependent on the production of waste landscapes from other types of development in order to survive. In this rubric one may describe drosscaping as a sort of scavenging on the urbanized surface for interstitial landscape remains. The designer, presumably before finding his or her client(s), works in a bottom-up manner conducting fieldwork while collecting and interpreting large-scale trends, data, and other phenomena in search of underutilized, or wasted, urban land.[39] Once these landscapes are identified, the designer proposes a strategy to productively integrate them. As degraded and interstitial entities, drosscapes have few stakeholders, caretakers, guardians, or spokespersons. This requires the designer to search for, identify, and educate the stakeholder or group most likely to realize the need for change.

The future of any given drosscape, or any entity that is undervalued, lies profoundly in the interaction of human agency and the sharing of explicit knowledge. The designer, as the strategist conducting this advocacy process, understands the future as being under perpetual construction. Drosscapes require design to be implemented as an activity that is capable of adapting to changing circumstances while at the same time avoiding being so open-ended as to succumb to future schemes that are better organized.[40]

Processes of deindustrialization, post-Fordism, and technological innovation will continue in the foreseeable future to saturate urbanized regions with waste landscape. Subsequent to these processes, designers will need to rethink their roles in creating built environments. Urbanization will no doubt be controlled by a wider array of factors in the future. As post-Fordism illustrates, analyzing cities can no longer be done by one source, nor by one body of knowledge, nor by one bureaucracy. Designers must identify opportunities within the production modes of their time to enable new ways of thinking about the city and its landscape (whatever form it may take). Landscape architects, architects, and urban planners often follow too far behind these processes, scavenging commissions from their jetsam as they change course. It is time for designers to find opportunities *within* these processes by advocating more culturally ambitious ways of challenging urbanization.

As a strategy, drosscape provides an avenue for rethinking the role of the designer in the urban world. Given a constriction of natural and other resources, politicians and developers will shift attention to infill and reuse development.[41] None of the work will require a single disciplinary design approach nor will the sites operate under univalent environmental conditions. All, however, will be affected by countless unconventional adjacencies and unforeseen complex reclamations.

With drosscape, a new paradigm is cast. It asks designers to consider working in the margins rather than at the center and to shift the paradigm of what is considered urban design and what landscape means to urbanism and urbanization processes. It requires designers to think strategically of themselves as charged with identifying the undervalued and overlooked potentials of the urban region within which they live and work. It further suggests a move away from the heroic, modernist master planner toward the advocacy designer who engenders inventiveness, entrepreneurialism, and visioning. These qualities are neither taught sufficiently in design school nor represented on professional registration examinations.

Strategies for designing with drosscapes

ONE: Dross is understood as a natural component of every dynamically evolving city. As such it is an indicator of healthy urban growth.

TWO: Drosscapes accumulate in the wake of socio- and spatio-economic processes of deindustrialization, post-Fordism, and technological innovation.

THREE: Drosscapes require the designer to shift thinking from tacit and explicit knowledge (designer as sole expert and authority) to complex interactive and responsive processing (designer as collaborator and negotiator).

FOUR: The designer does not rely on the client–consultant relationship or the contractual agreement to begin work. In many cases a client may not even exist but will need to be searched out and custom-fit in order to match the designer's research discoveries. In this way the designer is the consummate spokesperson for the productive integration of waste landscape in the urban world.[42]

FIVE: Drosscapes are interstitial. The designer integrates waste landscapes left over from any form or type of development.

SIX: The adaptability and occupation of drosscapes depend upon qualities associated with decontamination, health, safety, and reprogramming. The designer must act, at times, as the conductor and at times the agent of these effects in order to slow down or speed them up.[43]

SEVEN: Drosscapes may be unsightly.[44] There is little concern for contextual precedence, and resources are scarce for the complete scenic amelioration of drosscapes that are located in the declining, neglected, and deindustrializing areas of cities.

EIGHT: Drosscapes may be visually pleasing. Wasteful landscapes are purposefully built within all types of new development located on the leading, peripheral edges of urbanization. The designer must discern which types of "waste" may be productively reintegrated for higher social, cultural, and environmental benefits.

In his criticism of the scientific world Bruno Latour states that "soon nothing, absolutely nothing, will be left of [a] top-down model of scientific influence. The matter of fact of science becomes matters of concern of politics. As a result, contemporary scientific controversies are emerging in what have been called hybrid forums. We used to have two types of representations and two types of forums: one, science . . . and another politics . . . A simple way to characterize our times is to say that the two meanings of representation have now merged into one, around the key figure of the spokesperson."[45] Latour's brilliant elucidation leads one out of the lab to discover the city anew. Its composition is part economics, part science, part politics, and part speculation. This new city is reconceptualized from drosscape. As such, it will serve as the stage for the performance of Latour's hybrid forum.

Such ripe conscious design attention mirrors the unconscious refashioning of natural environments that are inescapably marked by waste. The continuous material transformation of the environment produces dross and this waste is most profound in the areas of the highly successful growing civilizations. Thus dross will always accompany growth, and responsible design protocols will always flag such dross as the expanding margin of the designed environment. The energy that goes into rapid growth, after populations and civilization reach temporary limits, can then be used to refashion and organize the stagnant in-between realm, thus going back like an artist to touch up the rough parts of an otherwise elegant production. Humanity's fantastic growth has inevitably confronted us with commensurate wastelands. Drosscape, far from marking failure, testifies to previous urban successes and establishes a design challenge for its continuance. Analyzing how urbanization elegantly co-opts dross and reincorporates it in the service of efficiency, aesthetics, and functionality should shift the evaluation of wastes from the repressed edges of landscape architecture more toward the center, which is, one need hardly emphasize, increasingly where we find drosscape in the real urban world.

NOTES

1 One of the earliest examples of this characterization was published in 1958 by the editors of *Fortune* magazine. Originally appearing as a series of articles in 1957, *The Exploding Metropolis* is one of the early post-World War II volumes to document urban growth as chaotic, disorderly, unnatural, and problematic. See *The Exploding Metropolis* (New York: Doubleday, 1958). See especially William H. Whyte's essay "Urban Sprawl," 133–56.

2 This does not mean that urbanization is good or bad, but that it could be a more sustainable endeavor if landscape were incorporated in a more substantial way. See Chris Berdik, "Give me Land, Lots of Land . . ." *Boston Globe*, June 12, 2005, H1, 4. And Richard T. T. Forman, *Land Mosaics: The Ecology of Landscapes and Regions* (Cambridge: Cambridge University Press, 1995). This book views landscapes left over from urban development practices as having potential ecological benefits. I argue that his type of landscape sustainability is a form of reclamation, since it appears after development and market capitalism run their course.

3 For an understanding of manufacturing trends see: Sukkoo Kim, "Expansion of Markets and the Geographic Distribution of Economic Activities: The Trends in U.S. Regional Manufacturing Structure, 1860–1987," *The Quarterly Journal of Economics*, 110, no. 4 (Cambridge: MIT Press, 1995), 881–908; Glaeser and Kohlhase, "Cities, Regions and the Decline of Transport Costs," 2003.

4 Graham and Marvin, *Telecommunications and the City* (New York: Routledge, 1996), 378.

5 Pierce Lewis, "The Galactic Metropolis," *Beyond the Urban Fringe: Land Use Issues of Nonmetropolitan America*, ed. Rutherford Platt and George Macinko (Minneapolis: University of Minnesota Press, 1983), 23.

6 Ibid., 34.

7 Ann O'M. Bowman and Michael A. Pagano, *Terra Incognita: Vacant Land and Urban Strategies* (Washington, DC: Georgetown University Press, 2004).

8 Victor W. Turner, *The Ritual Process* (New York: Aldine De Gruyter, 1969), 94.

9 Raymond Keating, "Sports Pork: The Costly Relationship between Major League Sports and Government," *Cato Policy Analysis*, no. 339 (Washington, DC: Cato Institute, 1999). Since the early 1990s, fourteen new Major League Baseball stadia have been built with at least three more under construction. Upon completion, seventeen of the thirty Major League Baseball teams will be playing in stadia built since 1992. The National Football League has seventeen of thirty-two teams playing in stadia built since 1992, once those currently under construction are completed. It is estimated that approximately $10 billion of public money has gone to thirty-eight all new sports stadia since the mid 1980s. Also see Kevin J. Delaney and Rick Eckstein, *Public Dollars, Private Stadiums: The Battle over Building Sports Stadiums* (Piscataway, NJ: Rutgers University Press, 2003).

10 Valerie Alvord, "State Parks Squeezed, Shut by Budget Woes," *USA Today*, July 24, 2002; Kristen Mack, "Police, Fire Departments New Budget's Bid Winners," *Houston Chronicle*, May 21, 2004; Ralph Ranalli, "Funding Urged to Preserve Ecology," *Boston Globe*, March 31, 2005, B1, B6; Stephan Lovgren, "U.S. National Parks Told to Quietly Cut Services," *National Geographic News*, March 19, 2004, http://news.national geographic.com/news/2004/03/0319_040319_parks.html (accessed May 10, 2005).

11 William Rathje and Cullen Murphy, *Rubbish: The Archeology of Garbage* (Tuscon, AZ: University of Arizona Press, 2001), 34–35.

12 Susan Strasser, *Waste and Want: A Social History of Trash* (New York: Henry Holt and Company, 1999), 9, 266–68.

13 Ibid., 268.

14 Georges Bataille, *The Accursed Share, Volume 1: Consumption*, trans. Robert Hurley (reprint ed., New York: Zone Books, 1991). Bataille develops the idea of a "general economy" based on waste and excess energy from the sun rather than having and hoarding. Also see Mira Engler, *Designing America's Waste Landscapes* (Baltimore, MD: Johns Hopkins University Press, 2004).

15 Wilfred Beckerman, *A Poverty of Reason: Sustainable Development and Economic Growth* (Oakland, CA: The Independent Institute, 2003), 64–66.

16 Joseph A. Schumpeter, *Capitalism, Socialism and Democracy*, 3rd ed. (New York: Harper & Row Publishers, 1950), 81–110. See also Sharon Zukin, *Landscapes of Power* (Berkeley, CA: University of California Press, 1991), 41. Zukin describes Schumpeter's "creative destruction" as a "liminal" landscape, thus bringing my discussion of a liminal landscape full circle.

17 Schumpeter, *Capitalism, Socialism and Democracy*, 84.

18 Lars Lerup, "Stim & Dross: Rethinking the Metropolis," *Assemblage 25* (Cambridge: MIT Press, 1995). To Lerup, *stim* refers to the buildings, objects, programs, and events people identify as being developed for human use, while *dross* refers to the landscape leftovers or waste landscapes, typically found in-between the *stims*.

19 George Frederick, *A Philosophy of Production* (New York: The Business Bourse, 1930), 227. See Also Roland Marchand, *Advertising the American Dream* (Berkeley, CA: University of California Press, 1986), 156; Susan Strasser, *Waste and Want: A Social History of Trash* (New York: Henry Holt and Company, 1999), 198.

20 White House Office of the Press Secretary, "President Works on Economic Recovery During NY Trip," press release, October 3, 2001 at http://www.whitehouse.gov/news/releases/2001/10/20011003-4.html (accessed December 9, 2004).

21 Strasser, *Waste and Want*, 15.

22 Rathje and Murphy, *Rubbish*.

23 *Koyaanisqatsi: Life Out of Balance*, is an independent film by Francis Ford Coppola, Godfrey Reggio, and The Institute for Regional Education. Created between 1975 and 1982, the film

is an apocalyptic vision of the collision of urban life and technology with the natural environment. *Baraka* (1992) directed by Ron Fricke, uses breathtaking shots from around the world to show the beauty and destruction of nature and humans.

24 Ilya Prigogine, *The End of Certainty* (New York: The Free Press, 1996), 189.

25 "$76.7 Million in Brownfield Grants Announced," May 10, 2005, and "EPA Announces $73.1 Million in National Brownfields Grants in 37 States and Seven Tribal Communities," June 20, 2003, U.S. EPA Brownfield official web site http://www. epa.gov/brownfields/archive/pilot_arch.htm (accessed May 21, 2005); Niall Kirkwood, "Why is There So Little Residential Redevelopment on Brownfields? Framing Issues for Discussion," paper WO1-3, *Joint Center for Housing Studies* (Cambridge, MA: Harvard University, January 2001), 3–4.

26 Daniel Bell, *The Coming of Post-Industrial Society* (New York: Basic Books, 1999); Barry Bluestone and Bennett Harrison, *The Deindustrialization of America* (New York: Basic Books, 1982); Stephen Cohen and John Zysman, *Manufacturing Matters: The Myth of the Post-Industrial Economy* (New York: Basic Books, 1987); Michael J. Piore and Charles F. Sabel, *The Second Industrial Divide* (New York: Basic Books, 1984).

27 My use of this term *postindustrial* here and in other publications, does not imply that industrial production and/or industrial-induced land alteration has stopped. I suggest that a new condition exists, which shifts industrial production toward technology and away from mechanics, leaving vacant and contaminated mechanical-industrial sites in its wake. There is no break from "industrial" to "post-industrial" landscape formation, only a shift in industrial-landscape types.

28 See various contemporary examples of this approach and outlook in Kirkwood, *Manufactured Sites*.

29 Alvord, *USA Today*; Ralph Ranalli, *Boston Globe*. Also see "2004 Chicago Park District Budget Crisis, Park Advocates Requests" at Chicago's Hyde Park-Kenwood Community Conference Parks Committee (HPKCC) web site, http://www.hydepark.org/parks/04budcrisisreqs.htm (accessed June 14, 2005); Mike Tobin and Angela Townsend, "Budget Assumes Flat Economy," *The Plain Dealer*, January 28, 2004, http://www.cleveland.com/budgetcrisis/index. ssf?/budgetcrisis/more/1075285840190290. html (accessed June 14, 2005).

30 Ibid. Also see Joy Lanzendorfer, "Parks and Wreck," *North Bay Bohemian*, July 3–9, 2003. The Project for Public Spaces is an organization that campaigns against landscape budget, http://www.pps.org. A much different picture of open space funding is depicted by the Trust for Public Land. See their LandVote Database, http://www.tpl.org/tier2_kad.cfm?content_ item_id=0&folder_id=2607 (accessed June 14, 2005), which reveals that the majority of the ballot measures for the "conservation" of open space have passed over the last decade.

31 For national parks, see Stephan Lovgren, *National Geographic News*; Geoffrey Cantrell, "Critics Fear Park Service Headed Down Wrong Path," *Boston Globe*, March 10, 2005.

32 Bowman and Pagano, *Terra Incognita*, 12.

33 Davis, *Dead Cities*, 193.

34 For example, see Philadelphia Neighborhood Transformation Initiative (NTI), http://www. phila.gov/nti/pressrelease05.htm (accessed June 14, 2005). Philadelphia reports: "In April 2001, The City of Philadelphia officially launched the Neighborhood Transformation Initiative (NTI), a multi-faceted, $300 million+ effort to improve the quality of life in all neighborhoods. Since then, under NTI the City has amassed a wide array of successes: more than 224,000 abandoned cars removed from its streets and 44,000 tons of debris cleared from 31,000 vacant lots; 23,000 dead trees cut down; 6,000 dangerous buildings demolished; and, at last count, more than 21,000 units of new housing, (either completed, planned or underway), to serve buyers or renters at all income levels – at affordable, low income and market rates."

35 Charles Waldheim, ed., *Landscape Urbanism: A Reference Manifesto* (New York: Princeton Architectural Press, 2006); Dean J. Almy III and Michael Benedikt, eds., *CENTER 14: Landscape Urbanism* (Austin, TX: Center for American Architecture and Design, 2006).

36 I discuss a similar position for the term *reclaiming landscape*, of "land" and "scape" in *Reclaiming the American West*.

37 *American Heritage Dictionary.*

38 Sandra Alker, Victoria Joy, Peter Roberts, Nathan Smith, "The Definition of Brownfield," *Journal of Environmental Planning and Management*, 43, no. 11, (London: Routledge, January 2000), 49–69. Note the temporal aspects of the definition of a brownfield by this academic journal: "A Brownfield site is any land or premises which has previously been used or developed and is not currently fully in use, although it may be partially occupied or utilized. It may also be vacant, derelict or contaminated. Therefore a Brownfield site is not necessarily available for immediate use without intervention." Also see Niall Kirkwood, "Here Come the Hyperaccumulators!" *Harvard Design Magazine* 17, Fall 2002/Winter 2003, 52–56.

39 Jared Diamond, *Collapse* (New York: Viking Press, 2005), 277–88. Diamond suggests that different societies of the world use a bottom-up approach to deal with environmental problemsolving. The successful bottom-up approaches tend to be in small societies with small amounts of land (such as local neighborhoods) because more people can see the benefit of working together in managing the environment.

40 See James Corner, "Not Unlike Life Itself: Landscape Strategy Now," *Harvard Design Magazine* 21, Fall 2003/Winter 2004, 32–34. Also see Ralph D. Stacy, *Complex Responsive Processes in Organizations* (London: Routledge, 2001).

41 This is already underway. A recent search of the *Avery Index to Architecture Periodicals* turned up more than 6,100 entries for the words *adaptive* reuse.

42 A "design studio" education is an ideal laboratory to begin this process. See Alan Berger, Linda Corkery, and Kathryn Moore, "Researching the Studio," *Landscape Review*, 8, no. 1, (Canterbury, New Zealand: Lincoln University Press, 2002), 1–2.

43 Ibid.

44 One usage of the term ugliness related to the topics presented in this book can be read "Seventy-five Percent: The Next Big Architectural Project," Ellen Dunham Jones, *Harvard Design Magazine* 12, Fall 2000, 5.

45 Bruno Latour, "The World Wide Lab," *Wired*, June 2003, 147.

"Planning for Sustainability in European Cities: A Review of Practice in Leading Cities"

from *The Sustainable Urban Development Reader* (2008)

Timothy Beatley

Editors' Introduction

The vast scope of the environmental challenges the world is currently facing is daunting. Global warming, energy depletion, waste accumulation, and a host of related problems loom large around the world. The interconnected global scale of environmental problems can make them seem intractable. How can designers and communities respond and make a difference? In the face of the current challenge, the popular 1960s adage "think globally, act locally" seems all the more apt.

Many European cities, mindful that the ecological footprint of western societies has been unsustainably large for too long and spurred by governmental incentives, have recently embraced urban design strategies aimed at reducing carbon emissions. New "zero-carbon" neighborhoods are being built and low-carbon transportation systems are being inserted into old and new areas of cities alike. Sprawl is being limited, regional green networks are being preserved and enhanced, and nature is being brought into the city. There are lessons to be learned from the efforts of European cities, both in terms of understanding what policies have enabled and encouraged the development of low-carbon-producing urban areas, and gaining knowledge of the practical on-the-ground design approaches that are being used and which seem to be successful.

In his essay "Planning for Sustainability in European Cities: A Review of Practice in Leading Cities" from *The Sustainable Urban Development Reader*, Timothy Beatley surveys and brings together the key sustainability ideas, policies, and urban design strategies found in 30 European cities that he has studied. The practices reviewed in this selection are discussed in greater detail in Beatley, *Green Urbanism: Learning from European Cities* (Washington, DC: Island Press, 2000). The overall goal common to these cities is the maintenance of the compact city forms that they were originally built with, which means urban limits, high density, infill development, and strategically planned areas, all of which is undertaken with an eye to maintaining urban livability and quality design. Another goal is urban greening, which means the creation of ecological corridors and the enhancement of urban forests. A major design strategy involves the prioritization of low-carbon forms of transportation, including public transit, walking, and biking. As well, many cities are experimenting with creating local renewable energy sources, focusing particularly on solar panel and wind farm installations. Most ambitiously, some cities are putting in place neighborhood-scale designs directed at creating closed-loop energy systems, where human and industrial wastes are recycled to provide the energy source for district heating systems.

Timothy Beatley is the Theresa Heinz Professor of Urban and Environmental Planning at the University of Virginia, Charlottesville. He does research in the areas of environmental planning and policy, with special emphasis on coastal and natural hazards planning, environmental values and ethics, and biodiversity conservation. Professor

Beatley's other books include *Native to Nowhere: Sustaining Home and Community in a Global Age* (Washington, DC: Island Press, 2005); *Natural Hazard Mitigation* with David Godschalk and others (Washington, DC: Island Press, 1998); *The Ecology of Place* with Kristy Manning (Washington, DC: Island Press, 1997); *After the Hurricane: Linking Recovery To Sustainable Development in the Caribbean* with Philip Berke (Baltimore, MD: Johns Hopkins University Press, 1997); *An Introduction to Coastal Zone Management*, 2nd edn. (Washington, DC: Island Press, 1994); *Ethical Land Use: Principles of Policy and Planning* (Baltimore, MD: Johns Hopkins University Press, 1994); *Habitat Conservation Planning: Endangered Species and Urban Growth* (Austin: University of Texas Press, 1994).

Key classic and contemporary writings on sustainable urban development and green urbanism are contained in *The Sustainable Urban Development Reader*, 2nd edn. (London: Routledge, 2008), which Beatley co-edited with Stephen Wheeler. Stephen Wheeler's *Planning for Sustainability: Creating Livable, Equitable and Ecological Communities* (London: Routledge, 2004) presents a systematic analysis of how more sustainable cities can be achieved and illustrates how sustainability initiatives at different scales of planning – international, national, regional, municipal, neighborhood, site, and building – are interrelated.

Important writings on sustainable urban development include *Sustainable and Resilient Communities: A Comprehensive Action Plan for Towns, Cities, and Regions* (Hoboken, NJ: Wiley, 2011) edited by Stephen Coyle, Peter Newman, and Isabella Jennings; *Cities as Sustainable Ecosystems: Principles and Practices* (Washington, DC: Island Press, 2008); Douglas Farr, *Sustainable Urbanism: Urban Design With Nature* (Hoboken, NJ: Wiley, 2007); Richard Register, *EcoCities: Rebuilding Cities in Balance with Nature Revised edition* (Gabriola Island, BC: New Society Publishers, 2006); Mike Jencks and Nicola Dempsey, *Future Forms and Design for Sustainable Cities* (Oxford: Architectural Press, 2005).

Jeffrey Tumlin's *Sustainable Transportation Planning: Tools for Creating Vibrant, Healthy, and Resilient Communities* (Hoboken, NJ: John Wiley & Sons, 2011) offers a comprehensive look at fresh ways of thinking about transportation systems and real-world strategies for creating more sustainable transportation options in cities.

For more on green politics in Europe see Michael Dobson, *Green Political Thoughts*, 4th edn. (London: Routledge, 2007); Andrew Dobson and Robyn Eckersley (eds) *Political Theory and the Ecological Challenge* (Cambridge: Cambridge University Press, 2006); John S. Dryzek (ed.), *Green States and Social Movements: Environmentalism in the United States, United Kingdom, Germany and Norway* (London: Oxford University Press, 2002); and Michael O'Neill, *Green Parties and Political Change in Contemporary Europe: New Politics, Old Predicaments* (Aldershot: Ashgate, 1997). For green politics in America, see John Rensenbrink, *Against All Odds: The Green Transformation of American Politics* (Raymond: Leopold Press, 1999).

A number of websites devoted to issues of sustainable cities maintain repositories of resources on sustainable urban design practices around the world. Notable sites include: http://www.sustainablecities.net, http://www.sustainablecitiesinstitute.org, and http://www.sustainable-cities.eu.

INTRODUCTION: LEARNING FROM EUROPEAN CITIES

In few other parts of the world is there as much interest in sustainability as in Europe, especially northern and northwestern Europe, and as much tangible evidence of applying this concept to cities and urban development. For approximately the last six years this author has been researching innovative urban sustainability practice in European cities. The findings from the first phase of this work are presented in the book *Green Urbanism: Learning from European Cities* (Island Press, 2000). What follows is a summary of some of the key themes and most promising ideas and strategies found in the 30 or so cities, in 11 countries, described in this book, as well as more recent case studies and field work.

An initial observation from this work is just how important sustainability is at the municipal level in Europe, especially evident in the cities chosen. "Sustainable cities" resonates well and has important political meaning and significance in these cities, and on the European urban scene generally. One measure of this is the success of the Sustainable Cities and Towns campaign, an EU-funded informal network of communities pursuing sustainability begun in 1994. Participating cities have signed the so-called Aalborg Charter (from Aalborg, Denmark, the site of the first campaign conference), and more than 1800 cities and towns have done so. Among the activities of this organization are the publication of a newsletter, networking between cities, and initiation of conferences and workshops. The organization has also created the annual European Sustainable City award (with the first of these awards issued in 1996), and it is clear that they have been coveted and highly valued by politicians and city officials.

Many European cities have also gone through, or are currently going through, some form of local Agenda 21 process (including many of the same cities that have signed the Aalborg charter), and this is another important indicator of the relevance of local sustainability. Indeed, in the countries studied, high percentages of municipal governments are participating (for instance, in Sweden 100 percent of all local governments are at some stage in the local Agenda 21 process). Often these programs represent tremendous local efforts to engage the community in a dialogue about sustainability, and typically involve the creation of a local sustainability forum, sustainability indicators, local state-of-the-environment reports, and the preparation of comprehensive local sustainability action plans. European cities and towns demonstrate serious commitment to environmental and sustainability values and what follows are a few of the more important ways in which these concerns are being addressed.

COMPACT CITIES AND REGIONS

Urban form and land use patterns are primary determinants of urban sustainability. While European cities have been experiencing considerable decentralization pressures, they are typically much more compact and dense than American cities. Peter Newman and Jeffrey Kenworthy have monitored and tracked average density in a number of cities throughout the world. Western European cities like

Amsterdam and Paris have substantially higher densities, as measured in persons per hectare, than typical American cities. Overall or whole-city densities for European cities are typically in the 40–60 persons per hectare range; American cities are much lower, commonly under 20 persons per hectare (Newman and Kenworthy 2000). Even American cities that we tend to think of as particularly dense, for example New York, are comparatively less dense when the entire metropolitan wide pattern is considered. Density and compactness directly translate into much lower energy use, per capita, and lower carbon emissions, air and water pollution, and other resource demands compared with less dense, less compact cities.

Many of these European examples, moreover, show that compactness and density need not translate to skyscrapers and excessive high-rise. Density and compactness in cities like Amsterdam happens through a building pattern of predominately low-rise structures. While many sustainability proponents advocate the need for the green high-rise development (e.g. see Ken Yeang's designs for bio-climatic skyscrapers), these European cities demonstrate convincingly that tremendous compactness and density can be accomplished at a clearly human scale. The European model is appealing to many precisely because of its more traditional form of density and compactness, and many believe its more human scale.

These characteristics of urban form make many other dimensions of local sustainability more feasible, of course (e.g. public transit, walkable places, energy efficiency). There are many factors that explain this urban form, including an historic pattern of compact villages and cities, a limited land base in many countries, and different cultural attitudes about land. Nevertheless in the cities studied there are conscious policies aimed at strengthening a tight urban core. Indeed, the major new growth areas in almost every city studied are situated in locations within or adjacent to existing developed areas, and are designed generally at relatively high densities.

Exemplary and for the most part effective efforts at maintaining the traditional tight urban form can be seen in many cities. Cities like Amsterdam are actively promoting urban redevelopment and industrial reuse (e.g. through its eastern docklands redevelopment). Berlin's plan calls for most future growth to be accommodated with its urbanized area through a variety of infill and re-urbanization strategies. Freiburg, Germany, has been able to effectively steer relatively compact, high-density new growth along the main corridors of its tram system, as well as to protect existing housing supply in the center (there is now a prohibition on the conversion of housing to offices and other uses).

European cities are utilizing a variety of planning strategies to promote compactness and to maintain a tight urban form. These include strict limits on building outside of designated development areas, a strong role for municipal governments in designing and developing new growth areas, extensive public acquisition and ownership of land (especially in Scandinavian cities like Stockholm), and a willingness to make significant transportation and other infrastructure investments that facilitate and support compactness.

GREEN URBANISM: COMPACT AND ECOLOGICAL URBAN FORM

Growth areas and redevelopment districts in these European cities are incorporating a wide range of ecological design and planning concepts, from solar energy to natural drainage to community gardens, and effectively demonstrate that *ecological* and *urban* can go together. Good examples of this compact green growth can be seen in the new development districts planned for or recently completed in Utrecht (Leidsche Rijn), Frieburg (Rieselfeld), Amsterdam (e.g. IJburg), Copenhagen (Orestad), Helsinki (Viikki), and Stockholm (Hammerby Sjostad).

Leidsche Rijn, for example, is an innovative new growth district in the Dutch city of Utrecht. In addition to incorporating a mixed-use design, and a balance of jobs and housing (30,000 dwelling units and 30,000 new jobs), it will include a number of ecological design features. Much of the area will be heated through district heating supplied from the waste energy of a nearby power plant, a double-water system which will provide recycled water for non-potable uses, and storm water management through a system of natural swales (what the Dutch call "wadies"). Higher-density uses will be clustered around several new train stations and bicycle-only and bicycle/pedestrian only bridges will provide fast, direct connections to the city center. Homes and buildings will meet a low-energy standard and only certified sustainably harvested wood will be allowed.

European cities also provide excellent and generally successful examples of redevelopment and adaptive reuse of older, deteriorated areas within the center-city. Good examples include Amsterdam's eastern docklands, where 8000 new homes have been accommodated on recycled land. In *Java-eiland*, one major piece of this project, an overall plan (prepared by urban designer Sjoerd Soeters) lays out broad density, massing, and circulation for the district. Diversity and distinctiveness in actual design of the buildings, however, was encouraged through a restriction on the number of buildings that could be designed by a single architect. The result is a stimulating community where buildings have been created by scores of different designers. This island district successfully balances connection to the past (a series of canals and building scale reminiscent of historic Amsterdam) with unique modern design (each of the pedestrian bridges crossing the canals offers a distinctive look and design). *Java-eiland* demonstrates that city building can occur in ways that create interesting and organically evolved places, and which also acknowledge and respect history and context, overcoming sameness.

European cities on the whole (and especially the cities examined in this study) have been able to maintain and strengthen their center cities and urban cores. In no small part this is a function of historic density and compactness, they are also the result of numerous efforts to maintain and enhance the quality and attractiveness of the city-center. In the cities studied, the center has remained a mixed-use zone, with a significant residential population. *Groningen*, for instance, has undertaken a host of actions to improve its center including the creation of new pedestrian-only shopping areas (creating a system of two linked circles of pedestrian areas), and installation of (yellow) brick surfaces and new street furniture in walking areas, among other actions. Committed to a policy of compact urban form, Groningen has also made strong effort to keep all major new public buildings and public attractions close-in. As one example, a new modern art museum has been sited and designed to provide an important pedestrian link between the city's main train station and the town center.

SUSTAINABLE MOBILITY

Achieving a more sustainable mix of mobility options is a major challenge, and in almost all of the cities studied in *Green Urbanism* a very high level of priority is given to building and maintaining a relatively fast, comfortable, and reliable system of public transport.

There are impressive examples of cities that have been working hard to expand and enhance transit, in the face of rising auto use in many areas. Zurich implements an aggressive set of measures to give priority to its transit on streets. Trams and buses travel on protected, dedicated lanes. A traffic control system gives trams and buses green lights at intersections and numerous changes and improvements have been made to reduce the interference of autos with transit movement (e.g. bans on left turns on tram line roads; prohibiting stopping or parking in certain areas; building pedestrian islands; etc.). A single ticket is good for all modes of transit in the city (including buses, trams, and a new underground regional metro system). The frequency of service is high and there are few areas in the canton that are not within a few hundred meters of a station or stop. Cities like Freiburg and Copenhagen have made similar strides.

In these European cities transit modes are integrated to an impressive degree. This means coordination of investments and routes so that transit modes complement each other. In most of the cities studied, for instance, regional and national trains systems are fully integrated with local routes. It is easy, as well, to shift from one mode to another. Local transit centers are viewed in these cities as multi-modal, mixed-use centers of activity. Arnhem's new central train station in the Netherlands is a case in point. It integrates in a single location high-speed and conventional train service, local transit, bicycle parking, rental, and repair, as well as shops, offices, and housing. These uses are all within a few hundred meters of the city center.

The ease of traveling throughout Europe is aided tremendously by the commitment on this continent to high-speed rail. Cross-national movement by high-speed train is increasingly comfortable and easy, and investments in dedicated tracks and infrastructure reflect impressive forward thinking on this issue. And increasingly it is not just the northern and northwestern European nations leading the way. Major new high-speed rail systems are under construction in Italy and Spain for instance. Overall,

plans are on the books to double the length of dedicated high-speed rail track in Europe over the next eight years. And, the newest generation of trains will travel faster – on average 300 kph or higher.

Importantly, investments in transit complement, and are coordinated with, important land use decisions. Virtually all the major new growth areas identified in this study have good public transit service as a basic, underlying design assumption. The cities studied here do not wait until after the housing is built, but rather the lines and investments occur contemporaneously with the projects. The new community growth area *Rieselfeld* in Freiburg, for instance, has a new tram line even before the project has been fully built. In Amsterdam, as a further example, at the new neighborhood of *Nieuw Sloten*, tram service began when the first homes were built. In the new ecological housing district *Kronsberg*, in Hannover, three new tram stops ensure that no resident is further than 600 meters away from a station. There is a recognition in these cities of the importance of providing new residents with options, and establishing mobility patterns early.

Car sharing has become a viable and increasingly popular option in Europe cities. Here, by joining a car sharing company or organization residents have access to neighborhood-based cars, on an hourly or per-kilometer cost. There are now some 100,000 members served by car sharing companies or organizations in 500 European cities. Some of the newest car sharing companies, such as *GreenWheels* in the Netherlands, are also pursuing creative strategies for enticing new customers. This company has been developing strategic alliances, for example with the national train company, to provide packages of benefits at reduced prices. One of the key issues for the success of car sharing is the availability of convenient spaces, and a number of cities, including Amsterdam and Utrecht, have been setting aside spaces for this purpose. In cities such as Hannover, Germany, the car sharing organization there (a non-profit called Okostadt) has strategically placed cars at the stations of the Stadtbahn, or city tram, furthering enhancing their accessibility.

THINKING BEYOND THE AUTOMOBILE

Many of these cities are in the vanguard of new mobility ideas and concepts and are working hard to incorporate them into new development areas. Amsterdam, for example, has taken an important strategy in developing *Jjburg*. It is working to develop a comprehensive mobility package that all new residents will be offered and which includes, among other things, a free transit pass (for certain specified period) and discounted membership in local car sharing companies. Minimizing from the beginning the reliance on automobiles, and giving residents more mobility options, are the goals. Eventually this new area will be served both by an extension of the city's underground metro and fast tram.

An increasing number of carfree housing estates are also being developed in these cities, as a further reflection of the commitment to minimizing auto-dependence. The *GWL-Terrein* project, also in Amsterdam, built on the city's old waterworks site, incorporates only very limited peripheral parking. An on-site car sharing company, in combination with good tram service, are part of what makes this concept work there. The interior of the project incorporates extensive gardens (and 120 community gardens available to residents) and pedestrian environment, with key-lock access for fire and emergency vehicles.

Another carfree experiment is the new ecological district *Vauban*, in Freiburg. Built on the former site of an army barracks, this project is unique because it gives new residents the opportunity to declare their intentions to be carfree, and rewards them financially for doing so. Specifically, if residents choose to have a car, they must pay approximately $13,000 for the cost of a space in the nearby parking garage (a bit less than one-tenth the cost of the housing units). In this way there is a strong financial incentive to choose to be carfree and so far about half the residents have taken the carfree path. Projects like *Vauban* challenge new residents to think and act more sustainably and reward them for doing so.

Bicycles are an impressive mobility option in almost all of the cities studied in *Green Urbanism*, and many of these cities have taken tremendous efforts to expand bicycle facilities and to promote bicycle use. Berlin has 800 km of bike lanes, and Vienna has more than doubled its bicycle network since the late 1980s. Copenhagen now has a policy of installing bike lanes along all major streets, and bicycle use in that city has risen substantially. Few have gone as far, of course, as the Dutch cities, with cities like Groningen, where more than half of the daily trips are made on bicycles. In virtually all new growth areas in the Dutch cities, as well as many Scandinavian and German cities, bicycle mobility is an essential design feature, including providing important connections to existing city bicycle networks.

A number of actions have been taken by these cities to promote bicycle use. These include separated bike lanes with separate signaling, separate signaling and priority at intersections, signage and provision of extensive bicycle parking facilities (e.g. especially at train stations, public buildings), and minimum bicycle storage and parking standards for new development. Many cities are gradually converting spaces for auto parking to spaces for bicycles. Utrecht has discovered that it can fit 6–10 bicycles in the same space it takes to park one automobile. Tilburg, in the Netherlands, has recently built an underground valet bicycle parking facility in the heart of that city's shopping district. Freiburg's mobility center combines two levels of bicycle parking, with car-sharing cars on the ground level, a café, travel agency, and office of the Deutsche Bahn (and the structure has a green roof and a photovoltaic array generating electricity!).

These cities are also innovating in the area of public bikes. The most impressive program is Copenhagen's "City Bikes," which now makes available more than 2000 public bicycles throughout the center of the city. The bikes are brightly painted (companies sponsor and purchase the bikes in exchange for the chance to advertise on their wheels and frames), and can be used by simply inserting a coin as a deposit. The bikes are geared in such a way that the pedaling is difficult enough to discourage their theft. The program has been a success, and the number of bikes has been expanding. These sustainable European cities have discovered that bicycles are an important and legitimate alternative mode of transport to the car and with modest planning and investments substantial ridership can be achieved.

BUILDING PEDESTRIAN CITIES; EXPANDING THE PUBLIC REALM

European cities represent, as well, exemplary efforts at creating walkable, pedestrian urban environments.

Relatively compact, dense, and mixed-use urban environments make cities much more walkable, of course. And most European cities and regions benefit from having a compact historic core, designed and evolved around walking and face-to-face commerce. The vitality, beauty, and attraction of European cities is in no small part a function of the impressive public and pedestrian spaces. Cities like Barcelona and Venice remain positive and compelling models of pedestrian urban society. The uses of these spaces are varied and many: they are outdoor stages, the "living rooms" in which citizens socialize, interact, and come together, places where political events occur and democracy plays itself out. These areas are now the social heart of these communities – places where children play, casual conversations and unexpected meetings take place, and people come to watch and be seen.

The overall land use pattern in these cities, and the priority given to maintaining their compact form, certainly make a walking culture more feasible. What is especially impressive, however, is the continued attention given to this issue and the continued expanding of pedestrian areas and the strengthening of the public and pedestrian realm. Cities like Copenhagen have set the stage, beginning in the early 1960s, gradually taking back their urban centers from cars. That city pedestrianized the Stroget, one of its main downtown streets, in 1962. Copenhagen continues this pedestrianizing in a gradual way each year. The city has adopted the policy of converting 2–3 percent of its downtown parking to pedestrian space each year, to dramatic effect over a 20–40 year period. Today the amount of pedestrian space is tremendous. Eighteen pedestrian squares have been created in Copenhagen where there was once auto parking – some 100,000 square meters in all. Had proponents of public space in Copenhagen attempted to convert this amount of space all at once it would have been very politically difficult to do so.

Many other cities have followed suit, especially Dutch and German cities, but examples can be found throughout Europe. Cities like Vienna and Groningen have pedestrianized much of their centers, creating delightful, highly functional public spaces. Groningen's compact city policy ensures that major new public buildings and facilities are kept in the center, and accessible through walking – it is a compact city of "short distances." In cities like Leiden, emphasis has been given to installing new pedestrian bridges over canals connecting major streets, and every new residential area is designed to include a grocery, post office, and other shops within an easy walk. The greater mixing of uses means that residents of these cities typically have many shops, services, cafés within a walkable range.

The experience of these European cities in pedestrianizing much of their urban centers has been a positive one, both economically and in terms of quality of life. The spaces created commonly contain fountains, sculptures and public art, extensive seating and, of course, many reasons for being there – restaurants, cafés, shops. Each city has its own unique history and features that can be used to strengthen the unique character of its pedestrian environment. Freiburg's "backle," or urban streams that run through the streets of its old center, as well as its pebble mosaics are delightful and special and this city has done an excellent job expanding and adding on to these unique qualities of place.

Good public transit appears a major factor strengthening the pedestrian realm in these cities, as well as commitments to bicycles, as in the case of Copenhagen (Hass-Klau, et al. 1999). Extensive efforts to calm urban traffic, to restrict auto access, and to raise the cost of parking and auto mobility are also important elements. A number of European cities have experimented with or are anticipating some form of road pricing. The City of London is the most recent notable example, now charging a fee of five pounds for cars wishing to enter central London (and already resulting in a significant reduction in car traffic there). These European experiences support that a pedestrian culture and community life is indeed possible, even where the climate may be harsh, and that these spaces serve an incredible range of social, cultural, and economic functions.

GREENING THE URBAN ENVIRONMENT

Ensuring that compact cities are also green cities is a major challenge, and there are a number of impressive greening initiatives among the study cities. First, in many of these cities there is an extensive greenbelt and regional open space structure, with a considerable amount of natural land actually owned by the cities. Extensive tracts of forest and open lands are owned by cities such as

Vienna, Berlin, and Graz, among others. Cities such as Helsinki and Copenhagen are spatially structured so that large wedges of green nearly penetrate the center for these cities. Helsinki's large *Keskuspuisto* central park extends in an almost unbroken wedge from the center to an area of old growth forest to the north of the city. It is 1000 hectares in size and 11 km long.

In Hannover an extensive system of protected greenspaces exists, including the *Eilenriede*, a 650 hectare dense forest located in the center of the city. Hannover has also recently completed a 80-kilometre long *green ring* (*der grune ring*) which circles the city, providing a continuous hiking and biking route, and exposing residents to a variety of landscape types, from hilly Borde to the river valleys of the Leineaue river.

There is a trend in the direction of creating and strengthening ecological networks within and between urban centers. This is perhaps most clearly evident in Dutch cities, where extensive attention to ecological networks has occurred at the national and provincial levels. Under the national government's innovative Nature Policy Plan, a national ecological network has been established consisting of core areas, nature development areas, and corridors, which must be more specifically elaborated and delineated at the provincial level. Cities in turn are attempting to tie into this network and build upon it. At a municipal level, such networks can consist of ecological waterways (e.g. canals), tree corridors, and green connections between parks and open space systems. Dutch cities like Groningen, Amsterdam, and Utrecht have full time urban ecology staff, and are working to create and restore these important ecological connections and corridors.

Many examples exist of efforts to mandate or subsidize the greening of existing urban areas. There is a continuing trend, for instance, towards installation of ecological or green rooftops, especially in German, Austrian, and Dutch cities. Linz, Austria, for instance, has one of the most extensive green roof programs in Europe. Under this program, the city frequently requires building plans to compensate for the loss of green space taken by a building. Creation of green roofs has frequently been the response. Also since the late 1980s the city has subsidized the installation of green roofs – specifically, it will pay up to 35 percent of the costs. The program has been quite successful and there are

now some 300 green roofs scattered around the city. They have been incorporated into many different types of buildings including a hospital, a kindergarten, a hotel, a school, a concert hall, and even the roof of a gas station. Green roofs have been shown to provide a number of important environmental benefits, and to accommodate a surprising amount of biological diversity. Many other innovative urban greening strategies can be found in these cities from green streets, to green bridges, to urban stream daylighting.

RENEWABLE ENERGY AND CLOSED-LOOP CITIES

A number of the cities have taken action to promote more closed-loop urban metabolism, in which, as in nature, wastes represent inputs or "food," for other urban processes (e.g. Girardet, 1999). The city of Stockholm has made some of the most impressive progress in this area, and has even administratively reorganized its governmental structure so that the departments of waste, water, and energy are grouped within an eco-cycles division. A number of actions in support of ecocycle balancing have already occurred. These include, for instance: the conversion of sewage sludge to fertilizer and its use in food production, and the generation of biogas from sludge. The biogas is used to fuel public vehicles in the city, and to fuel a combined heat and power plant. In this way, wastes are returned to residents in the form of district heating. Another powerful example of the closed-loop concept can be seen in Rotterdam, in the Roca3 power plant, which supplies district heating and carbon dioxide to 120 greenhouses in the area. A waste product becomes a useful input, and in this case prevents some 130,000 metric tonnes of carbon emissions annually.

Energy is very much on the planning agenda, and these exemplary cities are taking a host of serious measures to conserve energy and to promote renewable sources. The heavy use of combined heat and power (CHP) generation, and district heating, especially in northern European cities, is one reason for typically lower per capita levels of CO_2 production here. Helsinki, for instance, has one of the most extensive district heating systems: more than 91 percent of the city's buildings are connected to it. The result is a substantial increase in fuel efficiency, and significant reductions in pollution emissions. District heating and decentralized combined heat and power plants are now commonly integrated into new housing districts in these cities. In *Kronsberg*, in Hannover, for instance, heat is provided by two CHP plants, one of which, serving about 600 housing units and a small school, is actually located in the basement of a building of flats.

Many cities, including Heidelberg and Freiburg, have set ambitious maximum energy consumption standards for new construction projects. Heidelberg has recently sponsored a low-energy social housing project, to demonstrate the feasibility of very low-energy designs (specifically a standard of 47 kwh/m^2 per year). The Dutch are promoting the concept of energy-balanced housing – housing that will over the course of a year produce as much energy as it uses – and the first two of these units have been completed in the *Nieuwland* district in Amersfoort.

Many cities such as Heidelberg have undertaken programs to evaluate and reduce energy consumption in schools and other public buildings. Incentive programs have been established which allow schools to keep a certain percentage of the savings from energy conservation and retrofitting investments. Heidelberg has engaged in an innovative system of performance contracts, in which private retrofitting companies get to keep a certain share of the conservation benefits.

There is an explosion of interest in solar and other renewable energy sources in these cities (and countries). Cities like Freiburg and Berlin have been competing for the label "solar city," with each providing significant subsidies for solar installations. In the Netherlands, major new development areas, such as *Nieuwland* in Amersfoort and *Nieuw Sloten* in Amsterdam, are incorporating solar energy, both passive and active, into their designs. In Nieuwland, described as a "solar suburb," there are more than 900 homes with rooftop photovoltaics, 1100 homes with thermal solar units, and a number of major public buildings producing power from solar (including several schools, a major sports hall, and a childcare facility). What is particularly exciting is to see the effective integration of solar into the architectural design of homes, schools, and other buildings.

The degree of public and governmental support in these European cities, financial and technical, for renewable energy developments is truly impressive. Reflecting a generally overall level of concern for global warming issues and energy self-sufficiency, significant production subsidies and consumer subsidies have both been given. The degree of creativity in incorporating renewable energy ideas and technologies in many of these cities is also quite impressive. Oslo's new international airport, for example, provides heating through a bark/wood bio-energy district heating system. This system provides heat for buildings through 8 km of pipes, as well as the airport's de-icing system. The moist bark fuel is a local product, and costs only one-third as much as fuel oil. In Sundsvall, Sweden, snow is collected, stored, and used as a major cooling source for the city's main hospital. In Copenhagen, twenty 2 MW wind turbines have been installed offshore which will together generate enough energy for about 30,000 homes.

GREEN CITIES, GREEN GOVERNANCE

Many of these cities are taking a hard look at ways their own operations and management can become more environmentally responsible. As a first step, many local governments have undertaken some form of internal environmental audit. Variously called green audits or environmental audits, they represent attempts to study comprehensively the environmental implications of a city's policies and governance structure. A number of local governments are now going through the process of becoming certified (the London borough of Sutton being the first) under the EU's Eco-Management and Audit Scheme (EMAS), an environmental management system more commonly applied to private companies. Several German cities are preparing environmental budgets, under a pilot program. The cities of Den Haag and London have calculated their ecological footprints and are using these measures as policy guideposts (e.g. see Best Foot Forward Ltd, 2002). Albertslund, Denmark, has developed an innovative system of "green accounts," used to track and evaluate key environmental trends at city and district levels, and many of the study cities have developed sustainability indicators (e.g. Leicester, London, and Den Haag). Cities like Lahti, Helsinki, and Bologna have gone through extensive in-house education and involvement of city personnel, often as part of the local Agenda 21 process, in examining environmental impacts and in identifying ways that personnel and city departments can reduce waste, energy, and environmental impacts.

Municipal governments have taken a variety of measures to reduce the environmental impacts of their actions. A number of communities have adopted environmental purchasing and procurement policies. Cities like Alberstlund have adopted policies mandating that only organic food can be served in schools and child care facilities, and restricting use of pesticides in public parks and grounds. Other cities are aggressively promoting the development of environmental vehicles. Stockholm's environmental vehicles program is one of the largest (a pilot program under the EU-funded initiative ZEUS), with over 300 vehicles. A number of cities have sought to modify the mobility patterns of employees, for instance by creating financial incentives for the use of transit or bicycles. Cities like Saarbrucken, Germany, have made great strides in reducing energy, waste, and resource consumption in public buildings.

Communities have also engaged in extensive public involvement and outreach on sustainability matters. A variety of creative approaches have been taken. Leicester [UK], for instance, has developed alliances with the local media and has sponsored a series of educational campaigns on particular community issues. As a further example, it has established (with its NGO partner Environ) an environmental center and cyber-café called the Ark, as well as a demonstration ecological home. Officials in these exemplary cities often express the belief that it is essential to set a positive example for the community and that before they could ask citizens to change their behaviors and lifestyles, the municipal government must have its environmental house in order.

UNDERSTANDING EUROPEAN CITIES: SOME CONCLUDING THOUGHTS

To be sure, many European cities are facing some serious problems and trends working against sustainability, in particular a dramatic rise in automobile ownership and use, and a continuing pattern of de-concentration of people and commerce. And, with their relatively affluent populations consuming substantial amounts of resources, European cities exert a tremendous ecological footprint on the world. Yet, these most exemplary cities provide both tangible examples of sustainable practice, and inspiration that progress can be made in the face of these difficult pressures.

The lessons are several. These cities demonstrate the critical role that municipalities can and must play in addressing serious global environment problems, including reliance on fossil-fuels and global climate change. Innovations in the urban environment offer tremendous potential for dramatically reducing our ecological impacts (European cities produce about half the per-capita carbon emissions of American cities), while at the same time enhancing our quality of life (e.g. by expanding personal mobility options with bicycles and transit).

Many, indeed most, of the ideas, initiatives, strategies undertaken in these innovative cities serve, in addition to reducing ecological footprints, to enhance livability and quality of life. Taking back space from the auto and converting it to pedestrian and public space does much to enhance the desirability of these cities. Investments in public transit reduce dramatically energy consumption, CO_2 emissions, and urban air quality problems, but at the same time provide tremendous levels of independence and mobility to the youngest and oldest members of society. Making bicycle riding safer and easier helps the environment, but also provides a badly needed form of physical exercise.

These experiences demonstrate clearly that it is possible to apply virtually every green or ecological strategy or technique, from solar and wind energy to greywater recycling, in very urban, very compact settings. Green Urbanism is not an oxymoron. Moreover, the lesson of these European cities is that municipal governments can do much to help bring these ideas about, from making parking spaces available for car sharing companies to providing density bonuses for green rooftops, to producing or purchasing green power.

There are also process lessons here. Key among them is an understanding of the great power of partnerships and collaboration between different parties with an interest in sustainability. While not always easy, success at achieving sustainability will depend on them. This means getting different departments to talk to each other and to work together (as in Stockholm), and getting different public and private actors to join together in common initiatives that demonstrate that green urban ideas are possible and desirable.

It is important to recognize, to be sure, the differences in governmental structure. The economic and planning frameworks in place in these countries (compared with, say, the United States) often facilitate many of the exemplary urban sustainability projects described here. The role of economic incentives and the economic incentive structures is critical and undeniable. High prices at the gas pump (typically $4–5 per gallon in Western Europe) have been a conscious policy decision in European countries, and in countries like Germany, have provided essential funding for public transit. Such high prices, relative to countries like the United States, undoubtedly help to encourage more compact land use and personal choices in favor of more sustainable modes of mobility. Also, carbon taxes in countries like Denmark help to substantially level the economic playing field between conventional fossil-fuel energy and more sustainable, renewable forms of energy. Higher energy prices generally help to promote greater conservation and energy efficiency improvements. The important role of adjusting incentives and economic signals is itself a key lesson from the European scene. Rather than seen as a pre-existing background condition, raising gasoline and energy taxes can be seen as an example of an important strategic societal and political choice.

There are other political, social, and cultural conditions, to be sure, that favor many of the exemplary ideas discussed here. Parliamentary governmental structures that give relative voice and power to green party and other social and environmental views (with local representation of these views as well) have been important. Historically stronger planning and land use control systems are helpful also, as well as generally stronger and more proactive roles afforded to government. Many of the important (more activist) urban sustainability activities undertaken in these European cities – as market stimulators, promoters of innovation, and financial underwriters for innovative urban sustainability practices and projects – are common and accepted roles for local governments to play.

But there are also certainly many underlying value differences (compared with the US) that further explain good practice. Prevailing European views of land are less imbued with a sense of personal use and freedom, and there is little expectation, for instance, on the part of a rural landowner or farmer that his or her land will eventually be convertible to urban development.

There are also a number of more regionally unique cultural values and differences, each with significant planning and land use shaping implications. A stronger desire to live within a city or town center clearly exists throughout much of Europe, borne undoubtedly from an older, more developed urban culture. Importance given to strolling, spending time in public places, and to the values of the public realm more generally, in countries like Spain and Italy, certainly help explain the success of pedestrian spaces in these countries. Pace of life, cultural organization of the day, and the number of hours in the work week are also clearly important. In Italy, public and pedestrian spaces are used in part because there is time to use them – the culture organizes its day so as to support the early evening stroll, after the shops close but before the evening meal. To many observers of the European scene there are also lessons to emulate – suggestions and ideas for humanizing cities and strengthening their livability and sociability, as well as their sustainability. The lessons are many and profound on many levels.

REFERENCES

Beatley, Timothy. (2000) *Green Urbanism: Learning from European Cities*, Washington, DC: Island Press.

Best Foot Forward, Ltd. (2002) *City Limits*, London: Best Foot Forward Ltd.

Gehl, Jan and Lars Gemzoe. (2000) *New City Spaces*, Copenhagen: The Danish Architectural Press.

Girardet, Herbert. (1999) *Creating Sustainable Cities*, Devon, UK: Green Books.

Hass-Klau, Carmen, Graham Crampton, Clare Dowland, and Inge Nold. (1999) *Streets as Living Space: Helping Public Places Play Their Proper Role*, London: Lander Publishing Ltd.

Newman, Peter and Jeffrey Kenworthy. (1999) *Sustainable Cities: Overcoming Automobile Dependence*, Washington, DC: Island Press.

"Urban Resilience: Cities of Fear and Hope"

from *Resilient Cities: Responding to Peak Oil and Climate Change* (2009)

Peter Newman, Timothy Beatley, and Heather Boyer

Editors' Introduction

Two of the greatest challenges to our collective future are the negative impacts of resource depletion and the uncertainties of climate change. Each of these threats is addressed in the following selection by Newman, Beatley and Boyer. The Hubbert Peak (Oil) Theory hypothesizes that global petroleum extraction will peak and begin a period of decline, causing major negative economic, social, and transportation shocks that will stress global relations and force societies to change their way of life. The model was first created by M. King Hubbert in 1956 to predict US oil production declines beginning in the late-1960s. On the world stage, many Peak Oil adherents suggest this production decline will begin sometime after 2020 (this estimate having been adjusted many times previously). Though continuing price shocks, scientific research, and production crises provide evidence for Peak Oil proponents, new fossil fuel discoveries, innovative extraction technologies, and alternative energy possibilities diminish these concerns for Peak Oil opponents. On whichever side of the debate one falls, oil price instability is already awakening some cities to the need for urban form, development, and infrastructure evolution; with the smarter places already beginning to make fundamental changes (many of these places are in Europe, Latin America, the Gulf States, and Asia).

Compounding these energy challenges are the impacts of impending climate change. Al Gore's 2006 documentary film (and companion book) *An Inconvenient Truth* helped to advance the climate change position by educating the public about the risks of global warming. Gore's exhaustive slide presentation linked aggregate human activity and population growth with negative global climate warming impacts. While a small minority questions the global warming thesis, growing weather unpredictability and increasing natural disaster frequency suggest to most observers that a longer-term climate change is coalescing. A number of authors are now addressing how the design professions can respond.

While a call-to-action has picked up speed over the last half century through the sustainability movement, many advocates suggest the bandwagon of policy and design response is too slow moving. Where progressives in many places are able to invest in long-term resilience, other places facing economic difficulty continue to focus on short-term concerns. This is becoming a classic socio-political differentiation between those who champion the long view of resiliency, versus those who champion the consumer/job needs of continuing everyday life as currently lived, albeit with blinders. In contrast, most design schools now accept the sustainability imperative to change status quo development patterns – and are actively drinking the "koolaid" through innovative studio topics, research seminars, and community-based engagement. Professional design and development practice on the other hand has been much slower on the uptake. Focusing primarily on oil depletion, this selection provides a set of arguments for urban resilience and how we might evolve our cities to reduce the economic and resource shocks of the potential crisis. Resilience here is defined as the ability to absorb disturbances and weather crises; to bounce back after disaster, to dispel fear in the face of challenge, and to strengthen both built environment and infrastructure systems. Through the writing, the authors suggest how cities might change, what resilient cities might look like, and how we might move our cities toward resiliency. They outline several strategies for achieving urban resiliency: renewable energy, carbon neutrality, more localized infrastructure, place-making, transit advocacy, green infrastructure, and eco-efficiency. In presenting this palette of change, they offer a vision of hope for cities and their citizens.

Peter Newman is widely known for his expertise in automobile dependence, transit-oriented development, urban transport, and sustainability advocacy. He is an environmental scientist and Professor at Curtin University in Perth, Australia; and continues to consult for a number of international sustainability organizations and governments. His works include: *Sustainability and Cities: Overcoming Automobile Dependence*, with Jeffrey Kenworthy (Washington, DC: Island Press, 1999); *An International Sourcebook on Automobile Dependence in Cities 1960–1990*, with J. Kenworthy and F. Laube (Boulder, CO: University of Colorado Press, 1999); and *Cities as Sustainable Ecosystems: Principles and Practices*, with Isabella Jennings (Washington, DC: Island Press, 2008).

Timothy Beatley is an environmental planner and the Teresa Heinz Professor of Sustainable Communities at the University of Virginia. He coined the term Green Urbanism, and is a widely published researcher in natural hazard planning, environmental ethics, and environmental conservation. His most recent texts include: *The Principles of Green Urbanism* (London: Earthscan, 2010); *Biophilic Cities: Integrating Nature into Urban Design and Planning* (2010); *Planning for Coastal Resilience: Best Practices for Calamitous Times* (2009); *Native to Nowhere: Sustaining Home and Community in a Global Age* (2004); *Green Urbanism: Learning from European Cities* (2000); and *The Ecology of Place: Planning for Environment, Economy, and Community*, with Kristy Manning (1997) (all published by Island Press in Washington DC). With Professor Stephen Wheeler of UC Davis, he is the co-editor of *The Sustainable Urban Development Reader* (London: Routledge, 2nd edn. 2008).

Heather Boyer is a senior editor at Island Press in Washington DC. She was a 2005 Loeb Fellow at the Harvard Graduate School of Design. Island Press has become one of the leading environmental policy and sustainability publishers.

The topic of urban resilience has become a key aspect of sustainability theory. Jared Diamond's book *Collapse: How Societies Choose to Fail or Succeed* (New York: Viking, 2005) is notable for its historical analysis of civilization demise as a result of resource depletion. Other books on the impacts of resilience and resource depletion include: Brian Walker, David Salt, and Walter Reid, *Resilience Thinking: Sustaining Ecosystems and People in a Changing World* (Washington, DC: Island Press, 2006); J. Howard Kunstler, *The Long Emergency: Surviving the End of the Oil Age, Climate Change, and Other Converging Catastrophes of the Twenty-first Century* (New York: Atlantic Monthly Press, 2005); and Douglass Farr, *Sustainable Urbanism: Urban Design with Nature* (New York: Wiley, 2007).

For more on the challenges of climate change and urban design response, see: Peter Calthorpe, *Urbanism in the Age of Climate Change* (Washington, DC: Island Press, 2010); Stephen M. Wheeler, *Climate Change and Social Ecology: A New Perspective on the Climate Challenge* (London: Routledge, 2012); and Peter Droege, *Climate Design: Design and Planning for the Age of Climate Change* (Novato, CA: ORO Editions, 2010). For primers in the science of climate change see: David Archer and Stefan Rahmstorf, *The Climate Crisis: An Introductory Guide to Climate Change* (Cambridge: Cambridge University Press, 2010); Michael Mann and Lee Kump, *Dire Predictions: Understanding Global Warming – The Illustrated Guide to the Findings of the International Panel on Climate Change* (London: DK Publishing, 2008); and not surprisingly, Al Gore, *An Inconvenient Truth: the Planetary Emergency of Global Warming and What We Can Do About It* (Emmaus, PA: Rodale Books, 2006).

Acknowledging that both the peak oil crisis and climate change are highly debated topics, see: Andrew Dessler and Edward A. Parson, *The Science and Politics of Global Climate Change: A Guide to the Debate* (Cambridge: Cambridge University Press, 2010); and Stephen M. Gorelick, *Oil Panic and the Global Crisis: Predictions and Myths* (New York: Wiley-Blackwell, 2009).

Look at the world around you. It may seem like an immovable, implacable place. It is not. With the slightest push – in just the right place – it can be tipped.

Malcolm Gladwell, *The Tipping Point*

Resilience in our personal lives is about lasting, about making it through crisis, about inner strength and strong physical constitution. Resilience is destroyed by fear, which causes us to panic, reduces our inner resolve, and eventually debilitates our bodies. Resilience is built on hope, which gives us confidence and strength. Hope is not blind to the possibility of everything getting worse, but it is a choice we make when faced with challenges. Hope brings health to our souls and bodies.

Resilience can be applied to cities. They too need to last, to respond to crises and adapt in a way that may cause them to change and grow differently; cities require an inner strength, a resolve, as well as a strong physical infrastructure and built environment.

Fear undermines the resilience of cities. The near or total collapse of many cities has been rooted in fear: health threats like the plague or yellow fever have struck cities and emptied them of those with the resources to escape, leaving only the poor behind. Invading armies have destroyed cities by sowing fear before an arrow or shot was fired. The racial fears of a generation in American cities decanted millions to the suburbs and beyond. Perhaps the biggest fear today in many cities is terrorism. In New York after 9/11, fear stopped people from congregating on streets or using the subway and sent many urban dwellers scurrying for the suburbs, but the city proved to be resilient and resisted collapse. After the terrorist bombings in London, the city immediately steeled itself to be normal, to resolve to go to work and to use the subway; signs appeared everywhere "7 million Londoners, 1 London."

A danger that few think about with such immediacy is the threat of the collapse of our metropolitan regions in the face of resource depletion – namely, the reduction in the availability of oil and the necessary reduction in all fossil fuel use to reduce human impact on climate change. This book is not about introducing a new fear, but of understanding the implications of our actions and finding hope in the steps that can be taken to create resilient cities in the face of peak oil and climate change.

Some cities exude hope as they grow and confront the future, others reek of fear as the processes of decline set in and the pain of change causes distrust and despair. Most cities have a combination of the two. For example, Atlanta is a city with some of the nation's worst traffic congestion (sixty hours of delay annually per traveler in 2005) and rapidly growing urban sprawl. While it is experiencing areas of abandonment as a result of the subprime mortgage meltdown, its inner city continues to grow, reclaiming old areas once abandoned and reversing the decline of generations.[1]

Atlanta has been dubbed a little Los Angeles for its similar sprawling highways and automobile dependence, but Los Angeles was ranked second lowest in carbon emissions (from transportation and residential buildings) per capita, while Atlanta ranks sixty-seventh.[2] However, cities of hope will use considerably less fuel and produce much less carbon than both of these in an age of carbon constraint. Cities of fear make decisions based on short-term, even panicked, responses; cities of hope plan for the long term, with each decision building toward that vision, hopeful that some of the steps will be tipping points that lead to fundamental change. Cities of fear engage in competition as their only driving force, while cities of hope build consensus around cooperation and partnership. Cities of fear see threats everywhere while cities of hope see opportunities to improve in every crisis.

This book focuses on the challenges our metropolitan areas face in responding to their increasing carbon footprint, dependence on fossil fuels, and impact on our irreplaceable natural resources. Jared Diamond's book *Collapse* looks at how some settlements and regions have collapsed due to the inability to adapt, leading to an undermining of the natural resource base on which they depend. A characteristic of those societies appears to be that they became fixated by their fear of the future and were unable to adapt. On the other hand, Diamond outlines examples of societies facing the same pressures that were able to adapt – they turned their hope into resilience.[3]

Diamond speculates that climate change and resource degradation are threatening our cities and regions today. These are slow-moving phenomena that can undermine the continued growth of cities. Our book takes this potential of urban collapse seriously but is focused on how we *can* adapt to our present crises, how we *can* make our cities more resilient to the future in ways that are socially and economically acceptable and feasible.

The book takes the dual issues of peak oil and climate change as the key focus and rationale for our need to change. It describes how the production peak in global oil may already have occurred, or is very close at hand due to a combination of physical shortages and political control in vulnerable regions. For all practical purposes we must adapt our cities to lessen our dependence on petroleum. This is no small task as oil use in every city in the world has grown each year for most of the twentieth century; yet turning this trend around is within our reach. Global governance is recognizing the implications of climate change and the impact of cities, and there is a movement to require all cities to use less and less fossil fuels each year. This is no longer a speculative plea to cities, but is becoming a political and legal necessity.

Few would suggest that creating resilient cities is possible with technological advances alone, and agree that it must involve change in our cultures, our economies, and our lifestyles. It is the human capacity of our cities that is ultimately being tested by these challenges.

While understanding the implications of our current lifestyle is important, the response should not be driven by fear of collapse, but by the hopeful vision of the livable, equitable, resilient places our cities can become. We want to show that there is hope in our cities.

WHY CONCENTRATE ON CITIES?

Cities have grown rapidly in the age of cheap oil and now consume 75 percent of the world's energy and emit 80 percent of the world's greenhouse gases.[4] Cities are presently growing globally at 2 percent per year (over 3 percent in less developed regions and 0.7 percent in more developed regions), while rural areas have leveled out and are in many places declining. For the first time, half of humanity lives in cities, and it is estimated that by 2030 the number of city dwellers will reach five billion, or 60 percent, of the world's population.[5]

Urbanization has been happening since the Neolithic revolution when agriculture enabled food surpluses to create a division of labor in settlements. The unlocking of human ingenuity to work on technology, trade, and urban culture has created ever-expanding opportunities in cities. However, while some cities took advantage of these new opportunities, many remained a little more than rural trading posts. Urban opportunities accelerated with the Industrial Revolution and more recently with the globalization of the economy. But again not every city has taken advantage of these opportunities. Some cities, such as Liverpool, Philadelphia, and Pittsburgh, have struggled to adapt to the new opportunities and have relied for too long on outmoded methods of industrial production as the basis for their cities. Yet other cities, such as Manchester and New York, have made the transition and are thriving.

Peter Hall, who has examined why some cities adapt more rapidly than others, suggests that the desire to experiment and innovate is found in the heart of the city's culture. Robert Friedel calls it the "culture of improvement," Lewis Mumford refers to this instinct in a city as a "collective work of art," and Tim Gorringe as "creative spirituality."[6] Whatever it is called, the ability to experiment and innovate is the tissue of hope and the core of resilience.

Overcoming the fear of change today must involve new experiments in green urbanism, as cities seek to improve themselves in ways that fit their culture. Which cities will respond to the new set of opportunities opening up around this global sustainability issue? Rethinking how we create our built environment is critical in lessening our dependence on oil and minimizing our carbon footprint. Buildings produce 43 percent of the world's carbon dioxide emissions and consume 48 percent of the energy produced. It is projected that by shifting 60 percent of new growth to compact patterns the United States will save 85 million metric tons of carbon dioxide annually by 2030.[7] We believe that the change when dealing with global issues like peak oil and climate change, needs to come from the cities. Nations can do a lot to help or hinder these efforts, but the really important initiatives have to begin at the city level because there is great variation in how cities cope with issues within any nation. Great leadership and innovation can be found in cities. For example, while the United States has yet to ratify the Kyoto Protocol, over 825 mayors of U.S. cities signed onto the U.S. Mayors Climate Protection Agreement to commit their city to reaching the goals of the Protocol. The initiative, which was spearheaded by Seattle Mayor Greg Nickels, strives to meet these goals through leadership and action advanced by a network of forward-thinking cities large and small. Similarly, the Clinton Foundation has coordinated an approach to reducing greenhouse gases for the big cities in the world through its C40 Large Cities Climate Leadership Group, an association of large global cities dedicated to tackling climate change.[8]

Our book tells many of these stories of hope in cities across the globe, which show there is leadership coming from government, industry, universities, and community groups. Although the focus is on American cities where so much more is needed, many of the examples will come from elsewhere in the world.

WHAT ARE RESILIENT CITIES?

Since the devastation of many Gulf Coast cities from Hurricane Katrina in 2005, the Indian Ocean tsunami of 2004 that impacted eleven countries, and the Burmese Cyclone of 2008, resilient cities have most often been discussed in relation to the city's ability to respond to a natural disaster. Here we use an expanded definition to include a city's ability to respond to a natural resource shortage and respond to the recognition of the human impact on climate change. There is debate about the link between climate change and natural disasters, which has been renewed as scientists try to understand the increasing incidence of devastating natural disasters, such as the super cyclones that devastated New Orleans and Myanmar.[9]

We have focused on the idea of resilient cities as those that can substantially reduce their dependence on petroleum fuels in ways that are socially and economically acceptable and feasible. But whether the impetus for pursuing resiliency is to respond to natural or to human made disasters, the outcome is similar. Resilient cities have built-in systems that can adapt to change, such as a diversity of transport and land-use systems and multiple sources of renewable power that will allow a city to survive shortages in fuel supplies.[10]

Brian Walker, David Salt, and Walter Reid have summarized the academic area of "resilience thinking," which has emerged as a way of managing ecosystems like coral reefs or farming systems and other complex social-economic-ecological systems. Their principles of resilience are applicable to cities. They write, "Resilience is the capacity of a system to absorb disturbance and still retain its basic function and structure." Tabitha Wallington, Richard Hobbes, and Sue Moore say that ecological resilience "may be measured by the magnitude of disturbance the system can tolerate and still persist." This book attempts to apply this concept to the complex social-economic-ecological systems of cities.[11]

In New Orleans the resilience of the city to withstand winds and waves from Katrina was reduced by the loss of wetlands and mangroves around the Gulf shores, and by the inadequate infrastructure provided by the levees. But the main human disaster came about because the transit system was so inadequate that people who did not own a car (around a third of the population) could not evacuate, and the freeways were at capacity due to the number of individuals in cars. No plan for using school buses and other transit vehicles was in place, so those resources were all washed away with the first floods. The transport system was not resilient and it undermined the rest of the urban system, which turned rapidly into social chaos.

In a resilient city every step of development and redevelopment of the city will make it more sustainable: it will reduce its ecological footprint (consumption of land, water, materials, and energy, especially the oil so critical to their economies and the output of waste and emissions) while simultaneously improving its quality of life (environment, health, housing, employment, community) so that it can better fit within the capacities of local, regional, and global ecosystems. Resilience needs to be applied to all the natural resources on which cities rely.[12]

In resilience thinking, the more sustainable a city, the more it will be able to cope with reduction in the resources that are used to make the city work. Sustainability recognizes there are limits in the local, regional, and global systems within which cities fit, and that when those limits are breached the city can rapidly decline. The more a city can minimize its dependence on resources such as fossil fuels in a period when there are global constraints on supply and global demand is increasing, the more resilient it will be. Atlanta needs 782 gallons of gasoline per person each year for its urban system to work, but in Barcelona it is just 64 gallons. With oil supply cuts and carbon taxes the decline in availability of oil will seriously confront Atlanta, yet Barcelona is likely to cope with ease. Both cities will still need to have plans in place that help their citizenry cope with such a disturbance.[13]

WHY SHOULD CITIES MOVE TOWARD RESILIENCY?

Resilience in cities can be rationalized by simply understanding why we need to reduce oil dependence in urban regions.

- *Reducing oil use is a political necessity.* The waning of petroleum resources and the global climate change imperatives discussed in this book require all cities to act; if they don't their citizenry will suffer from the inevitable increase in prices as we are seeing in the U.S. right now. The $100-a-barrel oil has been broken and some analysts are saying that it could go over $300 within five years.[14]
- *Reducing oil use will reduce impacts on the environment.* Oil use is responsible for approximately one-third of greenhouse gases. Transport greenhouse is seen as the most worrying part of the climate change agenda as it continues to grow during a period when more renewable or efficient options are available.
- *Reducing oil use and investing in green building will reduce impacts on human health.* Improvements in urban air quality from technological advances are being washed out by the growing use of vehicles. Thirty-nine different air quality districts are over the required standards (this is 40 percent of the United States). Developing cities desperately need to lower air emissions as they are often well above WHO recommended health limits.[15] Other health issues, such as obesity due to lack of activity, as well as stress and depression could be reduced by minimizing auto dependence.

  In the United States buildings account for 36 percent of energy use and 30 percent of greenhouse gas emissions. The immediate benefits of natural sunlight, however, go beyond energy savings and reducing our impact on climate change. Studies show that people in proximity to natural daylight are more productive and healthier. Workers in green buildings report fewer sick days and are more productive. When schools have gone green, test scores have improved.[16] Green buildings are attracting developers now not just because they can reduce their ongoing costs but because their tenants and purchasers want a more healthy and productive building in which to live, learn, and work. The urban heat island effect from the waste heat generated has also been problematic. For example, this has been a motivation for Mayor Daley in Chicago to green his city after an extreme summer heat wave proved to be fatal.

- *Reducing oil use will result in greater equity and economic gain.* The inequities of heavily car dependent cities for the elderly, the young, and the poor, will be reduced by greater walkability and transit access; the social issues such as noise, neighborhood severance, road rage, and loss of public safety will be reduced; the economic costs from loss of productive agricultural land to sprawl and bitumen, the cost of accidents, pollution, and congestion, all will be reduced.[17]
- *Reducing our dependence on petroleum fuels will make us less economically vulnerable.* The next agenda for the global economy, sometimes called the Sixth Wave [. . .], is about responding with technology and services for a new and more clever kind of resource use. Cities will compete within this economic framework, and those cities that get in first will likely do best. But the same economic competition is facing households, depending on which city they live in and where they live in those cities. In U.S. cities the proportion of household expenditure on transportation increased from 10 percent in the 1960s to 19 percent in 2005, before the 2006 oil price increase (which only reduced the percentage to 18 percent), with very car dependent cities like Houston and Detroit having even higher percentages. A more detailed study by the Center for Housing Policy shows working families with household incomes between $20,000 and $50,000 spend almost 30 percent of their income on transportation. In Atlanta within this income range the percentage is 32 and for families who have found cheap housing on the fringe, transportation can account for over 40 percent of

their expenses. In Australia surveys show that 40 percent of household income goes to transportation in some urban fringe areas. Almost all of this is for car travel. Households on the fringes of car-dependent cities are more vulnerable as the cost of transport escalates, especially after oil reached one hundred dollars a barrel in late 2007 (at one hundred and thirty-nine dollars a barrel as we go to press). This increase in oil prices coincides with the sub-prime mortgage crisis, hitting many with a double whammy of increased transportation costs and a ballooning mortgage payment. Cities, and parts of cities, are now economically vulnerable to oil as it increases in cost.[18]

■ *Reducing dependence on foreign oil is likely to result in more resilient, peaceful cities.* Cities that are able to successfully reduce their dependence on imported oil, especially from politically sensitive areas, will have greater energy security. Terrorism and war have many causes, but one deep and underlying issue is the need by high-oil-consuming countries to secure access to oil in foreign areas, whether they are friendly or not. As oil becomes more and more valuable, the security of supply will become a more and more central part of geopolitics. Fear can drive us to make security decisions that are not going to help create resilient cities. Thus underneath all these arguments is the fact that reducing our oil dependence – *could result in less war.*

Most importantly we are convinced that resilient cities will be better places to live. The many benefits of a resilient city include greater overall physical and emotional health; ease of movement in higher density, mixed-use communities that are walkable and have accessible transit options; better food that is produced locally and is therefore fresher; efficiency of energy resources, greater affordability, healthier indoor environments; easier access to natural environment; and more awareness of the local urban area and bioregion enabling us to have a greater sense of place and identity. Some of these factors are challenging to quantify – but are nevertheless real opportunities that will emerge from this book.[19]

No models are readily available to illustrate this positive approach to cities in the age of reduced oil availability. Most cities have strategic plans based on coping with anticipated growth in population,

and a growing number of cities have sustainability plans to handle this growth in an environmentally sound manner. All Australian cities, for example, have recently had strategic planning studies done for the next thirty years of development. Although the studies have recognized that there is a need to reduce automobile dependence and save on oil, the government has not intervened in any radical way to curb oil-consumption behavior, even with the recognition that urbanization is likely to continue and tax already strained resources. New York City is a similar example. On Earth Day 2007 Mayor Bloomberg released an ambitious twenty-five-year plan for a greener city, which goes as far as committing to a 30 percent reduction in greenhouse gases by 2030. But it is not clear how the city plans to achieve this reduction, though there is pressure from urban design groups to require developers to analyze and disclose their impacts on climate change before having their projects approved (79 percent of New York City's greenhouse gas emissions are produced by buildings).[20]

Few cities anywhere have focused on the transportation implications of reducing their oil dependence. San Francisco passed a resolution recognizing peak oil in April 2006 and fourteen other U.S. cities have followed suit, but none of these cities have a detailed plan for reducing their oil use. Austin, Texas, approved a Climate Protection Plan in 2008, which has many innovative features but almost no reference to transportation. Many cities do have plans for reducing their dependence on oil for energy use. For example, the city of Hamilton in Ontario, Canada has developed an energy strategy, which includes the promotion of clean, renewable electricity such as wind, solar, and water power, but energy rarely is taken to mean gasoline.[21]

Cities of course cannot be separated from their hinterlands or bioregions. Although rural regions have generally been declining or are at least static (apart from the movement of people to the coasts in wealthy countries), they also have increased in their oil dependence. Rural economic productivity based on agriculture, tourism, and mining has been growing based on cheap oil. These activities have a large component of oil for travel in the case of tourism, and both agriculture and mining use diesel for transport, machinery, and processing, and also depend on chemicals (especially fertilizer in agriculture's case) made from oil. Food is now transported huge distances, with an average U.S. meal taking between 1,300 and 2,000 "food miles" to reach the plate.[22]

While the focus of this book is on cities, it will also look at questions facing rural regions around cities as they relate to resiliency. What will happen to this rural productivity in the age of declining oil availability? How will cities and their associated rural regions cope? Where do you start in responding to this issue?

While environmentalists are quite able to point out the limitations of current resource consumption trends, they are often criticized for their inability to set forth a positive and compelling alternative vision. Michael Shellenberger and Ted Norhaus have called this the "death of environmentalism." There is a certain amount of truth to this claim as it is always easier to criticize than to suggest the next step. And when it comes to these global issues it can become hard to focus constructively. But this book will show us how we can respond to these twin crises.[23]

WHAT DO RESILIENT CITIES LOOK LIKE?

What could happen to the world's cities if we ignore the need to reduce oil? What will our cities actually look like if we do seriously reduce our dependence on oil? Not much can be projected from recent experience as it is described as a point of "singularity" (a term from science fiction about what is beyond black holes). Trends cannot just be extended to see the future when we are dealing with discontinuities. Nor can we just turn history back to cities as they were. Few people could see what industrialization would do to cities; few could anticipate the global knowledge economy and what cheap oil would do to cities. But there are lessons to be learned from history and the fate of cities that have not been able or willing to adapt. So we have some speculation about collapse and how some cities are adapting and others are not adapting. We are more interested in what we can do to *change* our cities so they start to become more resilient.

According to urban critic Jane Jacobs, cities throughout history have competed by examining innovations in other cities and building upon them. This, she believed, is the basis of wealth creation. We see the response to climate change and peak oil as the impetus for the next burst of innovation. This book looks at those innovative cities that are beginning

to grasp this new agenda and have moved (often timidly) down the track toward change. There are only a few cities around the world showing such leadership, as most are watching tentatively. It is our belief that those cities that begin this transition first will manage better socially and economically in a world where the constraints on petroleum fuels will be pressing.[24]

Although no one can predict the future of cities, we are able to visualize where we use gasoline, diesel, heating oil, and natural gas, and then try to imagine home, neighborhood, and region without them. How might they look and feel if these resources were not available, or at least were in decline, so that each next step in development or redevelopment had to show how it would help to wean us off these resources? Can we imagine a city where we radically reduce the amount of driving we do? This is not simply a set of abstract arguments about the fate of the planet, but something that has relevance and is potentially understandable to everyone in terms of the places in which we all live. A future can then be imagined that involves alternative energy sources as well as funding for the design of transit and bicycling systems and the creation or redevelopment of buildings, communities, cities, and regions around the need for less petroleum fuel.

[. . .]

A VISION FOR RESILIENT CITIES: THE BUILT ENVIRONMENT

What does a resilient city look like? Bike paths and virtually car-free streets that lead from solar homes to grocery stores, recreation areas, parks, or a free tram to reach places too far to walk or bike. A solar office block filled with new Sixth Wave businesses. Schools with parents lined up on bikes to pick up kids instead of waiting in idling cars. A local farmers' market for buying bioregional produce.

This is a common scene in Vauban, a development of five thousand households on a former military base in Freiburg, Germany. Vauban is considered a model ecological community that is being studied with increasing interest as the economic, health, and environmental costs of car dependence come into focus.[25] Residents are offered numerous incentives (such as free tram passes and options for carpooling) and disincentives (extremely pricey parking only available on the edge of town) to live car free. (There is already a strong disincentive to driving with gas over U.S. eight dollars per gallon.) The car ownership rate in Vauban is 150 vehicles per 1,000 inhabitants, compared to the U.S. average of 640 vehicles per 1,000 residents.[26]

How does a city achieve resiliency? The positive examples that illuminate the steps toward resiliency have been achieved by a mixture of visionary grassroots initiatives demanding more options for sustainable living and transport, innovative business, and strong political leadership offering incentives or regulating for more livable, sustainable environments from the regional to the building level.

[. . .]

Below we specify the seven key elements of a resilient city in the built environment that flow from these themes.

1 *Renewable Energy City*. Urban areas will be powered by renewable energy technologies from the region to the building level.
2 *Carbon Neutral City*. Every home, neighborhood, and business will be carbon neutral.
3 *Distributed City*. Cities will shift from large centralized power, water, and waste systems to small-scale and neighborhood-based systems.
4 *Photosynthetic City*. The potential to harness renewable energy and provide food and fiber locally will become part of urban green infrastructure.
5 *Eco-Efficient City*. Cities and regions will move from linear to circular or closed-loop systems, where substantial amounts of their energy and material needs are provided from waste streams.
6 *Place-Based City*. Cities and regions will understand renewable energy more generally as a way to build the local economy and nurture a unique and special sense of place.
7 *Sustainable Transport City*. Cities, neighborhoods, and regions will be designed to use energy sparingly by offering walkable, transit-oriented options for all supplemented by electric vehicles.

[. . .]

CONCLUSIONS: CITIES OF FEAR OR CITIES OF HOPE?

Most advanced countries have developed highly complex scenarios for dealing with terrorism in the past five years. There are few such scenarios for dealing with oil and carbon vulnerability (or even for responding to natural disasters, in spite of recent extreme weather catastrophes).

The scenario we envision is that some cities will respond to the peak oil crisis in time and will adapt to avoid collapse. These cities will respond by cutting back substantially in demand for oil and any other transport fuel through a combination of city form and lifestyle change. This will be facilitated by sustainable transport modes, higher density, walkable, mixed-use communities, and community-based localism, together with new technologies for buildings including renewable energy, which will also be integrated into electric vehicles for transit through a Smart Grid. Other alternative fuels will fill some of the gap left by conventional oil decline. And some unconventional oil will be developed in deeper and remote areas. It will be inside our cities that the most change will happen as we respond to the new demands of peak oil and climate change.

This is only a sketch of the kind of future we could make. But it is a city of hope as it is imaginable with a series of steps we can take to get us underway, though none will be easy.

The first step is to create a clear plan. We need all our strategic analysts to take oil depletion and climate change seriously, to see what must be done in short-, medium-, and long-term scenarios for reductions in oil supplies. We need to see how we can reach the future of resiliency in a series of steps. If we cannot take the next steps we never reach the goal, fear takes over, and the paralysis begins to set in.

Some cities will not make the transition. They will be left waiting for the magic technology or the mystical market to sweep in with the solutions. As they push on with their present consumption patterns they will be hit by a series of shocks that are not hard to predict as the fuel begins to dry up. Those cities that are prepared with short-term contingencies, alternative transport availability, alternative fuel programs, household awareness programs, will be resilient. Those cities that are not ready will begin to crumble and fall apart, looking for someone to blame without looking in the mirror. People will leave and the problems of decline will set in. Finances to deal with the change will be limited and options will become less and less available as the processes of fear take hold of the financial institutions and the personal creativity of its citizens. The cities of fear can be scoffed at now by those who sit in comfort in the dying days of cheap oil. But they will not be good places in which to live when the lights of hope begin to go out.

NOTES

1 Atlanta was ranked eleventh in the nation in percentage of foreclosures. RealtyTrac.com, February 13, 2008; data on growth of inner city from William Lucy, University of Virginia, unpublished data.

2 Andrea Sarzynski, Marilyn A. Brown, Frank Southworth, "Shrinking the Carbon Footprint of Metropolitan America," Brookings Institution, May 29, 2008.

3 Jared Diamond, *Collapse: How Societies Choose to Fail or Succeed* (New York: Viking Books, 2005).

4 Caroline Ash, Barbara R. Jasny, Leslie Roberts, Richard Stone, and Andrew M. Sugden, "Reimagining Cities" *Science* special issue 319(5864): 739 (February 8, 2008).

5 Worldwatch Institute, *State of the World 2007: Our Urban Future* (New York: W.W. Norton, 2007), www.citymayors.com/society/urban-population.html.

6 Peter Hall, *Cities in Civilization: Culture, Innovation and the Urban Order* (London: Wiedenfeld and Nicolson, 1998); Robert Friedel, *A Culture of Improvement: Technology and the Western Millennium* (Cambridge, MA: MIT Press, 2007); Lewis Mumford, *The City in History* (Harmondsworth: Penguin Press, 1991); T.J. Gorringe, *A Theology of the Built Environment: Justice, Empowerment, Redemption* (Cambridge: Cambridge University Press, 2002), 140.

7 Ed Mazria, *Urban Land*, November/December 2007, 35.

8 Office of the Mayor, City of Seattle, seattle. gov/mayor/climate (February 15, 2008); www. clintonfoundation.org

9 "Climate Link with Killer Cyclones Spurs Fierce Scientific Debate," Agence France-Presse (AFP), May 6, 2008.

10 On resilience to natural disasters see Mark Felling, *The Vulnerability of Cities: Natural Disasters and Social Resilience* (London: Earthscan Publications, 2003); Larry Vale and Tom Campanella, *The Resilient City: How Modern Cities Recover from Disaster* (Oxford: Oxford University Press, 2005).

11 Brian Walker, David Salt, and Walter Reid, *Resilience Thinking: Sustaining Ecosystems and People in a Changing World* (Washington, D.C.: Island Press, 2006), 13; T. Wallington, R. Hobbes, and S. Moore, "Implications of Current Thinking for Biodiversity Conservation: A Review of Salient Issues," *Ecology and Society* 10(1): 15 (2005).

12 This definition of sustainability for cities is from Peter Newman and Jeffery Kenworthy, *Sustainability and Cities* (Washington, D.C.: Island Press, 1999); in other books we have looked at the ecosystems and biodiversity that are part of city functions – see Peter Newman and Isabella Jennings, *Cities as Sustainable Ecosystems* (Washington, D.C.: Island Press, 2008); Timothy Beatley and Kristy Manning, *The Ecology of Place* (Washington, D.C.: Island Press, 1997).

13 Data on fuel use in cities are from J. Kenworthy, F. Laube, P. Newman, P. Barter, T. Raad, C. Poboon, and B. Guia, *An International Sourcebook of Automobile Dependence in Cities, 1960–1990* (Boulder: University Press of Colorado, 1999); Peter Newman and Jeff Kenworthy, "Greening Urban Transport," *State of the World 2007: Our Urban Future*, Worldwatch Institute (New York: W.W. Norton, 2007); Reid Ewing, *Growing Cooler: The Evidence on Urban Development and Climate Change* (Washington, D.C.: Urban Land Institute, 2007).

14 M. Simmons in www.ArabianBusiness.com, February 28, 2008.

15 World Health Organizations fact sheet, "Use of the Air Quality Guidelines in Protecting Public Health: A Global Update." See www.who.int/mediacentre/factsheets/fs313/en/index.html.

16 Gregory Kats, "Greening America's Schools: Costs and Benefits," A Capital E Report, October, 2006.

17 See Peter Newman and Jeff Kenworthy, *Sustainability and Cities* (Washington, D.C.: Island Press, 1999); Howard Frumkin et al., *Urban Sprawl and Public Health* (Washington, D.C.: Island Press, 2002).

18 Mayer Hillman, *The Impact of Transport Policy on Children's Development* (London: Policy Studies Institute, 1999); G. C. Gee and D. T. Takeuchi, "Traffic Stress, Vehicular Burden and Well-Being: A Multi-Level Analysis," *Social Science and Medicine* 59(2): 404–414 (2004); www.usgbc.org (Green Building Research) accessed February 2008. Surface Transportation Policy Project, "Driven to Spend: The Impact of Sprawl on Household Transportation Expenses," 2005. Barbara Lipman, *A Heavy Load: The Combined Housing and Transportation Burdens on Working Families* (Washington, D.C.: Center for Housing Policy, 2006).

19 On issues of place see Tim Beatley, *Native to Nowhere* (Washington, D.C.: Island Press, 2005) and Peter Newman and Isabella Jennings, *Cities as Sustainable Ecosystems* (Washington, D.C.: Island Press, 2008).

20 Municipal Arts Society, www.mas.org/climate change, accessed February 2008.

21 Press release, The New Democratic Party (NDP) September 30, 2007. See www.ontariondp.com/hampton-proposes-clean-green-energy-plan

22 Timothy Beatley, "Envisioning Solar Cities: Urban Futures Powered By Sustainable Energy," *Journal of Urban Technology* 14(2): 31–46 (2006).

23 Michael Shellenberger and Ted Norhaus, "The Death of Environmentalism," 2004, available at www.changethis.com

24 Jane Jacobs, *Cities and the Wealth of Nations* (Harmondsworth: Penguin Press, 1984).

25 Jan Scheurer, *Car Free Housing*, PhD Thesis ISTP, Murdoch University, www.sustainability.murdoch.edu.au; Jan Scheurer and Peter Newman, "Vauban: Integrating the Green and Brown Agenda," UN Global Review of Human Settlements, 2008, www.unep.org

26 Isabelle de Pommereau, "New German Community Models Car-Free Living," *Christian Science Monitor*, December 20, 2006.

PART SIX

Urban Design Practice Now and Tomorrow

Plate 7 The Jay Pritzker Pavilion at Millennium Park in Chicago, Illinois invites concert-goers to relax on the lawn before the performance. As one of the most successful park projects in recent history, Millennium Park is the result of a multi-stakeholder and collaborative design process that brought together city officials, numerous designers, corporate sponsors, and innovative implementation techniques. It is an example of finding "lost space" in the city, by building over railroad tracks and an immense parking garage that helps pay for the park's development and management. The recently expanded High Line Park in New York City is another example of this trend in finding lost space. The Jay Pritzker Pavilion, designed by Frank Gehry, is an outdoor performance space that allows concert-goers choice in seating (in fixed theater seating or spreading out on the lawn). It is but one element in a park that has several areas created by different designers, including: the Crown Fountain, the Cloud-Gate interactive sculpture (aka the "bean"), the Lurie Garden, Wrigley Square, the McDonald's Cycle Center, and the BP Pedestrian Bridge. The park is the result of creative project implementation and new urban design practices that broaden the base of funding, ownership, design, and use. The resulting park is one of the most popular and loved spaces in the City of Chicago. (Photo: M. Larice)

INTRODUCTION TO PART SIX

In the final part of this reader, we turn to professional practice. The world of urban design practice is complex. Professional work encompasses a wide range of project types and the whole array of urban scales. As well, urban designers practice within widely varying urban contexts and may operate from either public or private sector places of employment, and so have different design mandates. It is not possible here to present examples of all the many scales and types of urban design projects regularly undertaken on behalf of both public agencies and private clients: city-wide urban design plans, neighborhood design plans, large or small project area designs, street designs, urban system designs, and even regional development strategies. There are many practice-oriented publications and manuals that offer guidance on the best practices/approaches associated with each of these project types. As well, detailed substantive information about recent innovative urban design projects can be found in the documentation of actual plans and projects, which can often be accessed from project websites or the websites of city planning or regional planning agencies.

Presented in Part Six is a group of writings that speak to over-arching issues related to urban design practice, including the scopes and types of practice, the teaching of urban design, public sector design guidance, and seminal critiques and opportunities for the field. We start by delving into the multiple conceptualizations of the urban design discipline that inform urban designers' action in practice. Alex Krieger's piece "Where and How Does Urban Design Happen?" reviews the definitions of the nascent urban design discipline that were advanced in the mid-1950s and identifies the many spheres of "urbanistic action" that urban designers have since assumed as their professional domain. The discussion both traces the historical progression of thought about the discipline and articulates how urban design thinking has differed among practitioners depending upon whether they approach it from urban planning, architecture, or landscape architecture perspectives. The narrative helps make sense of the often disparate ways that the urban design enterprise is conceptualized and offers the optimistic view that given the complexities of urbanism, vastly different responses are needed for different issues and spatial environments, and so the many different ways urban designers approach practice is appropriate.

We turn next to urban design education. Elizabeth Macdonald's piece "Designing the Urban Design Studio," written for this edition of *The Urban Design Reader*, argues for the importance of studio-based learning for urban design students. Drawing on a wealth of experience teaching design studios, she offers insights about the opportunities presented by studio learning and about how to structure a studio so that students will learn the methods and tools used in urban design practice, how to work in teams as they will have to do in real world practice, and how to communicate effectively. Following this, we consider the topic of public sector design guidance, one of the main products of planning-based urban design practice. In the conclusion to his book, *Design Guidelines in American Cities: A Review of Design Policies and Guidance in Five West Coast Cities*, John Punter lays out a framework for how urban design guidance and design review processes should best be structured to be legally valid, effective, well-received by developers, and encompassing of community goals and aspirations.

The final two selections in this chapter present opposing views of contemporary urban design practice and its future opportunities. Michael Sorkin's piece "The End(s) of Urban Design," first printed in

Harvard Design Magazine, provocatively asserts that the field of urban design has not only reached a dead-end in terms of its ability to meet today's pressing environmental and social challenges but also fails to inspire because it has become boring. An architecture professor and the creator of many un-built "paper" projects, Sorkin laments the limits on creativity that he feels have come with the mainstreaming of urban design practice, and is particularly critical of design approaches that in any way look to the past, such as neo-traditional design and other approaches that are informed by typological or morphological study. Kenneth Greenberg's piece "A Third Way for Urban Design," which was published as a chapter in a recent edited anthology of current perspectives on the field, offers a much more optimistic view of where urban design practice currently stands and the possibilities for how it may transform in the future. A practicing professional with many, many built projects under his belt, Greenberg has also taught in urban design programs in prestigious universities in the United States and Canada. His positive view of practice springs from his own experience of the rich creativity that creative professionals bring to their projects. In particular, he highlights how most practitioners are unbounded by the confines of any single academic discourse, melding the best ideas to suit particular contexts and projects, and calls for new creative collaborations and alliances between urban designers and other professionals, particularly environmental scientists.

"Where and How Does Urban Design Happen?"

from *Urban Design* (2008)

Alex Krieger

Editors' Introduction

Practice in urban design takes many forms. Because it is a hybrid field drawing the expertise of disciplines across the built environment professions, we find urban designers practicing in the private, public, and institutional sectors. From the foundation of the field in the late 1950s, tension has existed within the field between the disciplines that consider urban design its particular territory. While architecture and planning both have legitimate historic claims to the field, we increasingly see landscape architects, real estate developers, civil engineers, and politicians assuming larger roles in urban design practice. As such, practice in the field is increasingly collaborative: teams of professionals work together on large contracted projects that no single firm could possibly staff itself – design professionals by default are forced to work with developers, communities, public works departments, and government officials to get projects implemented. Despite the various antipathies and pre-dispositions found in design schools (where the disciplines often find difficulty working together), those in practice are finding ways to work together.

This message is implicit in this comprehensive chapter from *Urban Design*, edited by Alex Krieger and William S. Saunders (Minneapolis, MN: University of Minnesota Press, 2008). In the selection, Harvard Professor Alex Krieger maps the territory of urban design into ten "spheres of urbanistic action" where urban designers most naturally find their professional roles. These ten roles describe a rough chronology of the field's development and evolution over time, in addition to the field's key substantive interests in response to specific urban challenges. Starting with the intention of collaboration between planners and architects, who were deemed to be partners in a joint project – the field has devolved into professionals whose differing values are not always in sync. Planners champion some notion of the public interest through regulatory form-making policy – formulating plans and guidelines for others to follow. Designers, on the other hand, often see architecture and landscape architecture as some type of urban salvation. Having to translate the work of planners into built form, the values of designers are often at odds with their planning brethren. Other generations of urban designers instead focus on specific urban/suburban/exurban challenges: stemming suburban sprawl, restoring urbanism after decline, imageability and place reinforcement, or remaking urban infrastructure. At the end of the essay, Krieger suggests a variety of roles that offer hope for the future of cities, and perhaps new foundations for a more collaborative urban design. These include visionary urbanism, community advocacy, and an urban mindset, similar to the call for an urban attitude suggested by Rem Koolhaas in his earlier selection. Overcoming the territorial infighting of the disciplines will require a true joint project which is bigger than the professions themselves – an agreed challenge, a renewed focus on the future, and finding common purpose in improving livability, making urban places, and ensuring sustainability. Krieger's mapping of these territories is a necessary start in understanding contemporary urban design practice.

This chapter appeared previously as an essay and lecture by Alex Krieger titled: "The Territories of Urban Design." Alex Krieger is a professor of urban design at Harvard University's Graduate School of Design, as well as previous Director of the Urban Design Program and Chair of the Department of Urban Planning and Design. He continues to teach an urban design proseminar and a number of studios, most recently focusing on Vienna and the Danube. He is an architect, urban designer, and founding principal of Chan Krieger Sieniewicz in Cambridge, Massachusetts, which has won numerous urban design awards for the following projects: the Anacostia Waterfront Framework Plan; A Balanced Vision Plan for the Trinity River Corridor in Dallas, Texas; Reinventing the Riverfront Crescent, New Orleans, Louisiana; and the Shanghai Bund Waterfront Urban Design Concept. Chan Krieger recently merged with NBBJ, a multi-office design firm headquartered in Seattle, Washington. Krieger continues to consult for a number of organizations and municipalities.

He has edited two editions of the *Harvard Design Magazine*, and, as well as *Urban Design,* the books *Mapping Boston*, co-edited with David Cobb (Cambridge, MA: MIT Press, 2001); and *Past Futures: Two Centuries of Imagining Boston*, with Lisa J. Green (Cambridge, MA: Harvard University GSD, 1985). His essays and chapters have appeared in a number of journals and books, including: "Reinventing Public Space," *Architectural Record* (June 1995); "The Virtues of Cities," *Places* (September 1995); "Whose Urbanism?" *Architecture* (November 1998); "Beyond the Rhetoric of Smart Growth," *Architecture* (May 1999); "Chapter Two: The Unique Characteristics of Urban Waterfront Development," *Remaking the Urban Waterfront* (Washington DC: Urban Land Institute Press, 2003); and *Towns and Town Making Principles* (New York: Rizzoli, 2006), which he co-authored.

Apart from a significant literature on theory and advocacy already existing from the early days of the field (and represented elsewhere in this volume), the literature on urban design practice has steadily grown over the last decade. Since the last edition of *The Urban Design Reader*, a significant amount of material has been written that describes the practice of urban designers. For general texts on urban design and its chronology see the following: Paul Knox and Peter Ozolins (eds), *Design Professionals and the Built Environment: An Introduction* (Fletcher, NC: Academy Press, 2001); Lance Jay Brown, David Dixon, and Oliver Gillham, *Urban Design for an Urban Century: Placemaking for People* (New York: Wiley, 2009); Matthew Carmona, Steve Tiesdell, Tim Heath, and Taner Oc, *Public Places – Urban Spaces*, 2nd edn. (Oxford: Elsevier/Architectural Press, 2010); David Grahame Shane, *Urban Design Since 1945: A Global Perspective* (New York: Wiley, 2011); Ron Kasprisin, *Urban Design: The Composition of Complexity* (London: Routledge, 2011); and Paul L. Knox, *Cities and Design* (London: Routledge, 2011).

Critical works in the practice of urban design include: Ian Bentley, "What is Urban Design? Towards a Definition," *Urban Design Forum* (vol. 1: 1976); R. Dagenhart and D. Sawicki, "If Urban Design is Everything, Maybe It's Nothing," *Journal of Planning Education and Research* (vol. 13, no. 2, 1994); Ian Bentley, "Urban Design as an Anti-Profession," *Urban Design Quarterly* (vol. 65, no. 15, 1998); and Malcolm Moor and Jon Rowland (eds), *Urban Design Futures* (London: Routledge, 2006).

For compilation readers and references see: Donald Watson (ed.), *Time-Saver Standards for Urban Design* (New York: McGraw-Hill Professional, 2003); and Tridib Banerjee and Anastasia Loukaitou-Sideris (eds), *Companion to Urban Design* (London: Routledge, 2011).

A separate literature on urban design process and method has also burgeoned over the past few years: Hamid Shirvani, *Urban Design Process* (New York: Von Nostrand Reinhold, 1997); Mike Biddulph and John Punter (eds), "Urban Design Strategies in Practice," *Built Environment* (vol. 25, no. 4, 1999); Urban Design Associates and Ray Gindroz, *The Urban Design Handbook: Techniques and Working Methods* (New York: W.W. Norton, 2003); Jon Lang, *Urban Design – A Typology of Procedures and Products* (Oxford: Elsevier/Architectural Press, 2005); Cliff Moughtin, Rafael Cuesta, Christine Sarris, and Paola Signoretta (eds), *Urban Design: Method and Techniques*, 2nd edn. (Oxford: Elsevier/Architectural Press, 2005); and Alexander Cuthbert, *Understanding Cities: Method in Urban Design* (London: Routledge, 2011).

A few authors have tackled urban design from an American perspective, including ideas on what makes American urban design process different from other places in the world: Jon Lang, *Urban Design: The American Experience* (New York: Von Nostrand Reinhold, 1994); John Punter, *Design Guidelines in American Cities* (Liverpool: Liverpool University Press, 1999); and David Gosling, *The Evolution of American Urban Design: A Chronological Anthology* (Fletcher, NC: Academy Press, 2002).

For disciplinary perspective on urban design practice, see the following texts: **(Landscape Architecture and Environmental Planning):** Charles Waldheim (ed.), *The Landscape Urbanism Reader* (New York:

Princeton Architectural Press, 2006); Tim Waterman and Ed Wall, *Basics Landscape Architecture: Urban Design* (Brighton: Ava Publishing, 2009); Timothy Beatley, *Biophilic Cities: Integrating Nature into Urban Design and Planning* (Washington, DC: Island Press, 2010); and Mohsen Mostafavi and Gareth Doherty (eds), *Ecological Urbanism* (Zurich: Lars Müller Publishers, 2010). **(City Planning):** Jonathan Barnett, *Urban Design as Public Policy* (New York: Architectural Record, 1974); Daniel G. Parolek, Karen Parolek, and Paul C. Crawford, *Form-Based Codes: A Guide for Planners, Urban Designers, Municipalities, and Developers* (Hoboken, NJ: Wiley, 2008); Antti Ahlava and Harry Edelman (eds) *Urban Design Management: A Guide to Good Practice* (London: Taylor & Francis, 2009); and Stephen Marshall (ed.), *Urban Coding and Planning* (London: Routledge, 2011). **(Real Estate Development):** Steve Tiesdell and David Adams, *Urban Design in the Real Estate Development Process* (New York/Oxford: Wiley-Blackwell, 2011); and *Shaping Places: Urban Planning, Design and Development* (London: Routledge, 2012).

■ ■ ■ ■ ■ ■

In 1956, José Luis Sert convened an international conference at the Harvard University Graduate School of Design with a determination to assemble evidence on behalf of a desired discipline he called *urban design*. An impressive number of people then engaged in thinking about the future of cities participated. Among them were a not-yet-famous Jane Jacobs, an already prominent Edmund Bacon, the Olympian figure of Lewis Mumford, several leaders of the soon-to-be formed Team 10, prominent landscape architects such as Hideo Sasaki and Garrett Eckbo, urban renewal-empowered mayors such as David Lawrence of Pittsburgh, and innovators such as Victor Gruen, "the creator of the shopping mall."

The participants seemed to concur that the widening midcentury intellectual split between the "art of building" and the "systemic nature of planning" was not helpful to city building or the rebuilding that the post-World War II era still demanded. Hopes and ideas for a new discipline dedicated to city design were in the air, both in the United States and in Europe, with CIAM (Congrès Internationaux d'Architecture Moderne), since the early 1940s, focusing more attention on urbanization. Conference participants were determined to share and further such thinking, hopeful that a new discipline could stem this perceived split between design and planning. Indeed, within several years Harvard would begin one of the first formal degree-granting curricula focused on urban design, and, through that institution's prestige, lend weight to the idea that educating a design professional to become an urban designer was essential for a rapidly urbanizing world.

The proceedings of the 1956 conference reveal two working definitions for urban design, both articulated by Sert, who organized and presided over the conference. Urban design, he stated at one point, "is that part of city planning which deals with the physical form of the city." Here is the idea of urban design as a subset of planning, a specialization that he described as "the most creative phase of city planning, in which imagination and artistic capacities play the important part." At the beginning of the conference he identified a yet more ambitious goal: "to find the common basis for the joint work of the Architect, the Landscape Architect, and the City Planner . . . Urban Design [being] wider than the scope of these three professions." Here is the notion of a new overarching design discipline to be practiced by all those who were, in Sert's phrase, "urban-minded."

Half a century later, these two conceptualizations are still very much in play, and a precise definition for *urban design* has not been broadly accepted. Whether urban design has become a distinct professional specialization or a general outlook that can be embodied in the work of several of the design disciplines dedicated to city making remains unsettled. Nevertheless, few argue about the need for something called urban design.

In a world producing unprecedented kinds, numbers, and sizes of settlements, urban design is an increasingly sought-after (though not always well-recognized) expertise. Expectations are many and myriad for those presuming to know how to design cities, yet there is skepticism about how much such know-how exists. At the same time, it seems presumptuous for any one person to claim overarching knowledge of something as immensely complex as urbanism. It therefore seems prudent to track several territories – spatial and conceptual – in and through which urban designers operate. Indeed, scanning the definitions of the word *territory* in a dictionary eventually gets you past geography to "sphere of action." This I find a particularly useful way of thinking about urban design – as *spheres of urbanistic action* to promote the vitality, livability, and physical character of cities. There are several such spheres of action rather than a singular, overarching way to describe what constitutes the urban design enterprise.

While *urban design* is a phrase first popularized during the twentieth century, cities have, of course, been the subject of design theory and action for centuries. It is the notion of urban design as an activity distinct from architecture, planning, or even military and civil engineering that is relatively new – as is the label *urban designer*.

Though Pope Sixtus V's impact on the physicality of sixteenth century Rome was profound, contemporaries would not have thought of him as an urban designer. Spain's Philip II, who promulgated one of the most precise codes for laying out cities – the Laws of the Indies – was, well, king. Baron Haussmann was Napoleon Ill's Prefect of the Seine, an administrator, closer in point of view and responsibilities to Robert Moses, an engineer and civil servant, than to Raymond Unwin or Daniel Burnham, both architects acting as city planners. Ebenezer Howard, who truly had a new theory for urbanism, was an economist. Camillo Sitte was an art historian. Frederick Law Olmsted, who influenced American cities more than anyone in the nineteenth century, was a landscape architect and earlier still a social activist. Lewis Mumford was an urban historian and social critic. The foremost Renaissance urban theorists were architects and artists, as was Le Corbusier. During much of the history of city making, an architect's expertise was assumed to extend to matters of town layout, and popes, prefects, and Utopian economists quite naturally turned to architects to realize their urban visions. Many of the 1956 conference participants were also architects, and an architectural point of view has tended to prevail in most efforts to describe what urban design is – prevail but not encapsulate.

So I will describe ten spheres of *urbanistic action* that people calling themselves "urban designers" have assumed to be their professional domain, though obviously not all at once nor even with

unanimity about the list overall. The list begins with a foundational idea of urban design, at least as identified at the 1956 Harvard conference: urban design occupies a hypothetical intersection between planning and architecture and thus fills any perceived gaps between them. Urban design, many continue to believe, is necessarily and unavoidably:

THE BRIDGE CONNECTING PLANNING AND ARCHITECTURE

The most frequent answer to "What do urban designers do?" is that they mediate between plans and projects. Their role is to somehow translate the objectives of planning for space, settlement patterns, and even the allocation of resources into (mostly) physical strategies to guide the work of architects, developers, and other implementers. For example, many public planning agencies now incorporate one or more staffers titled urban designers, whose role is to establish design criteria for development projects beyond basic zoning and then help review, evaluate, and approve the work of project proponents as they advance their projects through design and into construction. Such a design review process is an increasingly common component of regulatory frameworks especially in larger cities and facilitates discussion of traditionally controversial issues like aesthetics. It is the urban designer's presumed insights about good or appropriate urban form that are seen as crucial to translate public policy or programmatic objectives into architectural concepts, or to recognize the urban potential in an emerging architectural design and advocate for its realization.

However, a subtlety within this process is often misunderstood. The translation of general or framework plans into designs is not meant to be a sequential process – always emanating from planning to affect design – but instead an interactive one. The urban designer's own expertise in architectural thinking should inform the formulation of planning concepts so that these are not fixed prior to consideration of physical implications. This design version of shuttle diplomacy between planner-formulators and design-translators is important, to be sure, but it cannot rely only on mediation or persuasion to be effective. Urban designers must help others see the desired effects of planning. This requires various visualization and programmatic narrative techniques by which goals and policies are converted into useful design guidelines and sometimes specific design ideas. It leads to the idea of urban design as a special category of public policy, an improvement on traditional land-use regulations that shy away from qualitative assessments of form. So urban design should then be considered:

A FORM-BASED CATEGORY OF PUBLIC POLICY

Jonathan Barnett's 1974 *Urban Design as Public Policy* argued this very point and became highly influential. If one could agree on specific attributes of good urbanism (at least in a particular setting, as Barnett tried to with New York City), then one should be able to mandate or encourage these through regulatory requirements. The radicalism embedded in this self-described pragmatic approach was to incorporate many more formal and aesthetic judgments – indeed *much* more judgment, period – into a standard zoning ordinance, and especially into the permitting and evaluative process. Restrictions on height or massing that in pioneering zoning codes (such as New York's own landmark 1916 code) were ostensibly determined through measurable criteria, such as access to sunlight, could now be introduced as commonly held good form-based values. The mandating of continuous block-length cornice heights, for example, gained the status of a lot-coverage restriction, though the former could not as easily be considered a matter of "health, safety and public welfare" as the latter.

But why shouldn't public policy as it pertains to the settled environment not aspire to quality and even beauty? More recently, a New York disciple of Barnett, Michael Kwartler, expressed this via the poetic notion of "regulating the good that you can't think of," or, one may infer, seeking to achieve through regulation *what is not* normally provided by conventional real estate practices. Since American planning is often accused of being reactive to real estate interests, interests that do not always prioritize public benefit, here would be a way to push developer-initiated projects to higher qualitative standards. So again, given the presumption that what constitutes good urban form (or desirable uses, or amenities such as ground-level retail, or

open space) can be agreed upon by a community, these should be legislated. And the natural champions for this are those individuals identified as urban designers. The appeal behind this interpretation of urban design is twofold. It maintains lofty ideals by arguing on behalf of codifiable design qualities, while operating at the pragmatic level of the real estate industry, facilitating better development. New York's Battery Park project is generally acknowledged as a successful example.

This may all be well and good, but such mediating and regulating are not sufficiently rewarding for those who believe that less creativity is involved in establishing guidelines for others to interpret then to design oneself. It seems too administrative and passive a role for urban design. Is not urban design about giving shape to urbanism? Is it not about:

THE ARCHITECTURE OF THE CITY

This conception of urban design is at once more ambitious yet narrower than the idea of urban design as public policy. The roots of this view may be traced earlier in the twentieth century to the American City Beautiful movement, and further into the nineteenth century to the European Beaux Arts tradition. Its proponents seek above all to control the shaping of those areas of the city that are public and, therefore, of common concern. It is a sphere populated by mainly architect-urbanists, but it makes kindred spirits of diverse figures such as Colin Rowe, Camillo Sitte, and William H. Whyte.

Shaping public space is considered the first order of urbanism by the architect/urbanist. Thus, the primary role of urban design is to develop methods and mechanisms for doing this. Done with authority and artistry (and proper programming and furnishings – Whyte's contribution), it allows the rest of the city, all that is private, to distribute itself logically and properly in relationship to this public realm. During the 1970s and 1980s, particularly in Europe, a related theory of the "Urban Project" emerged. This entailed the programming, financing, and design of a catalytic development, often a joint public/private venture, that would stimulate or revive an urban district. This notion of urban design is best embodied by a stable and stabilizing form, one that anchors its part of the city with unique characteristics that are expected to endure and influence future neighbors. The 1980s "Grand Projects" of Paris are generally regarded as such valuable catalysts for urban reinvestment.

The idea of urban design as the architecture of the city is often conceptualized in terms of the ideality of Rome as portrayed in the Nolli map, or in Piranesi's more fantastical description of imperial Rome in his *Compo Marzio* engraving. Or it is simply absorbed via our touristic encounters with the preindustrial portions of the European city in which the emphasis on the public realm – at least in the places we regularly visit – seems so clear. It is a small conceptual leap from this formulation of urban design to the idea of:

URBAN DESIGN AS RESTORATIVE URBANISM

The form of the preindustrial western city – compact, dense, layered, and slow-changing – holds immense power over city dreaming among both urbanists and the public. The traditional city seems at once clearly organized, humanely sized, manageable, and beautiful. Such virtues seem absent in the modern metropolis. Why not mobilize to regain these? At present the New Urbanists are most closely associated with this effort but are part of a long tradition of those guarding or extolling the advantages of traditional urban typologies. As did the polemicists of the City Beautiful movement in America a century earlier and Christopher Alexander in his 1977 *A Pattern Language*, the New Urbanists advocate a return to what they consider time tested principles of urbanism, now as appealing to a disillusioned suburban culture as to those still facing the onslaught of urban modernization.

Americans today seem particularly sympathetic to restorative urbanism for two reasons. They hunger for a "taste" of urbanity, preassembled and sanitized perhaps – "lite urbanism" in Rem Koolhaas's wry phrase – having for several generations disengaged from (and still unsure about) the real thing. Assaulted by the new, they seek comfort in the familiar. Traditionally, homes and neighborhoods have offered respite from the anxieties of change. Thus, it is understandable how an era of seemingly unending innovation in business, technology, and lifestyle marketing engenders sentimental nostalgia for the places we used to (or think we used to) live in.

Though we may demand the conveniences of modern kitchens and attached garages, many prefer to package these in shapes and facades reminiscent of earlier (assumed to be) slower and pleasanter paces of life. Many a New Urbanist endeavor from Seaside to Kentlands to Crocker Park, Ohio, exhibits such a hybridization of modern lifestyles in traditional building forms.

The walkable city, the city of public streets and public squares, the low-rise, high-density city, the city of defined neighborhoods gathered around valued institutions, the city of intricate layers of uses free of auto-induced congestion – of course these remain appealing. Americans are not alone in pining for such qualities. In today's Berlin, to refer to one European example, the city planning administration's highly conservative architectural design guidelines for the reunified center are but another manifestation of this instinct to slow the pace of change – at least as it pertains to the physical, if not the social or political, environment. Many urban designers believe that it is their discipline's responsibility to slow excess change, resist unwarranted newness, or at least advocate for such old-fashioned notions as "human scale" and "place-making." Then we should think of:

URBAN DESIGN AS AN ART OF "PLACE-MAKING"

A corollary to restorative urbanism is an increasing commitment to "place-making," the provision of distinctive, lively, appealing centers for congregation to alleviate the perceived homogeneity of many and large contemporary urban areas. There are architecture and urban design firms in the United States that advertise themselves as "placemakers," as the ads in any issue of the *Urban Land* illustrate. It is easy to succumb to cynicism. So many ordinary developments advertise their placeless character with catchy names ending in "place" (among the most common of these being "Center Place," a moniker promising precisely what is missing in new subdivisions).

Yet, creating exceptional places to serve human purposes has always been central to the design professions. We have just never called ourselves place-makers before or have been so self-conscious about the task. Economists often remind society that it is the *rare* commodity that gains value over time. As more contemporary urban development acquires generic qualities or is merely repetitive, the distinctive urban place, old or new, is harder to find. This alone will continue to fuel preservation movements across the urban world. But in a world that adds sixty million people to urban populations each year, preservation and restoration cannot be the answers to place-making. More urban designers should devote their attention to making new places as worthy as those made by their time-honored predecessors. Again, it is the American New Urbanists who have articulated this goal most clearly but with mixed results. Their rhetoric extols intimate scale, texture, the mixing of uses, connectivity, continuity, the privileging of what is shared, and other such characteristics of great urban places, but their designs tend to employ familiar old forms and traditional aesthetic detailing that usually seem forced and phony, out of key with how we now live.

The obvious merits of preserving venerable old urban places or the wisdom of treading lightly in the midst of historic districts aside, doubts remain about how successfully we might organize and clothe the complexities of modern life in traditional iconography. What if we place less faith in dressing up new development with emblems of urbanity and devote more effort to wiser distribution of resources or better land management? We then call for:

URBAN DESIGN AS SMART GROWTH

While there has been a strong association of urban design with "downtowns," demand for suburban growth management and reinvestment strategies for the older rings around city centers has gathered many advocates. Indeed, to protect urbanism, not to mention minimize environmental harm and needless land consumption, it is imperative, many argue, to control sprawl and make environmental stewardship a more overt part of urban thinking. Expressed opportunistically, it is also where the action is. Since 90 percent of development takes place at the periphery of existing urbanization, the urban designer should be operating there and, if present, advocating "smarter" planning and design. Conversely, ignoring the metropolitan periphery as if it were unworthy of a true urbanist or limiting one's efforts to urban "infill" may simply be forms of problem avoidance.

As social observers have long pointed out, suburban and exurban areas, where most Americans live, are not nonurban, merely providing different, certainly less traditional degrees of urban experience or intensity.

That the twenty-first century will be more conservation-minded is not in doubt. That the world overall must be smarter about managing resources and land is also clear. Therefore, the traditional close allegiance of urban design to an architectural and development perspective must be broadened. Exposure to the natural sciences, to ecology, to energy management, to systems analysis, to the economics of land development, to land-use law, and to issues of public health has not been but should become fundamental to an urbanist's training. Urban designers advocating a "smart growth" agenda today generally do so out of an ideological conviction that sprawl abatement or open-space conservation are necessary. But as they enter this territory, they quickly realize that acquiring additional skills and partners in planning is equally necessary.

To actually manage metropolitan growth requires dealing with needs – like land conservation, water management, and transportation – that cut across jurisdictional boundaries. Therefore, and increasingly for many, urban design must be about:

THE INFRASTRUCTURE OF THE CITY

The arrangement of streets and blocks, the distribution of open and public spaces, the alignment of transit and highway corridors, and the provision of municipal services certainly constitute essential components of city design. Indeed, to focus on just one category of urban infrastructure, few things are more important to cities or virtually any form of contemporary settlement than well-functioning transportation systems. Yet, the optimization of mobility pursued as an independent variable, separate from the complex and overlapping web of other urban systems, ultimately works against healthy communities. Engineering criteria, we have learned, are not by themselves sufficient city-producing tools.

Apart from the occasional efforts to "architecturalize" infrastructure, as in the various megastructure proposals of the 1960s (a source of fascination today), neither planners nor designers have played a significant role in transportation or other urban infrastructure planning. Thus, it has become another sphere for an urban designer to attempt to address at both the pragmatic level of calibrating demands for mobility with other social needs and in advancing new (or reviving old) ways in which city form and transportation systems may be integrated. At a fairly mundane yet significant level, this is what fuels the current fascination with Transit-Oriented Development in newer areas of urbanization, and with dense mixed-use, often joint public-private development adjacent to multimodal transportation centers in larger cities.

The twentieth-century love affair with the car – still considered the ideal personal mobility system – has diminished the range of conceptualizing about urban form and transportation. We were too mesmerized by the magic of Sant'Elia's Italian Futurist renderings and those of Le Corbusier's *Ville Radieuse*. An entire century later we are rediscovering that integrating urban form and mobility depends on more sophisticated umbilical cords than open roads. This is especially so since the engineering world is shifting emphasis from hardware to systems design, from adding lanes, for example, to traffic management technology. It is their acknowledgment that factors such as livability, sustainability, and economic and cultural growth – in other words good urban design – are the real goals of infrastructure optimization.

Agreeing with such a sensibility, some leaders of landscape architecture, a field that has generally pursued a humanistic perspective on planning, have recently advanced another perspective on urbanistic action that they are calling:

URBAN DESIGN AS "LANDSCAPE URBANISM"

In the past few years a new school of thought about cities has emerged: "landscape urbanism." Its proponents seek to incorporate ecology, landscape architecture, and infrastructure into the discourse of urbanism. The movement's intellectual lineage includes Ian McHarg, Patrick Geddes, and even Frederick Law Olmsted, though its polemical point of departure seems to be that landscape space, not architecture any longer, is the generative force in the modern metropolis.

To return to the 1956 conference for a moment: it produced a good deal of rhetoric about how landscape architecture was to be an integral part of urban design. But this aspect was quickly subsumed under the architecture/planning spectrum in which urban design would occupy the mediating middle. Momentarily there was no conceptual space left for landscape architecture. Ironically, more areas of settlement in North America have been designed by landscape architects than any other professionals. However, an accusation (sometimes accurate) has persisted that landscape architect-directed urban design favors low densities, exhibits little formal sensibility, and contains too much open space – in other words, it produces sub- or non-urban environments.

Proponents of landscape urbanism, such as James Corner, challenge such a cliché, instead insisting that the conception of the solid, "man-made" city of historic imagination perpetuates the no longer pertinent view that nature and human artifice are opposites. Landscape urbanism projects purport to overcome this opposition, holding neither a narrow ecological agenda nor mainstream (read architectural) city-making techniques as primary. Valuable urban design, landscape urbanists insist, is to be found at the intersection of ecology, engineering, design, careful programming, and social policy. Largely a set of values rather than a mature practice to date, landscape urbanism may prove its utility as endeavors such as the Fresh Kills landfill reuse project on Staten Island proceed.

In one regard the movement may be a reaction to the Nolli map view of urbanism, the binary conception of cities as made up of buildings and the absence of buildings, where the white of the map – the voids – is the result of built form, the black of the map. Maybe this was a useful interpretation of the preindustrial city – of the Italian piazza as space carved out of the solidity of built fabric. Outside the preindustrial walled city were certainly landscapes and undesignated space, but within the city, space resulted from built form. But any careful perusal of a preindustrial-era city map proves this assertion false: surely the "white" of the Nolli plan comes in many hues and nuances of meaning. Besides, the landscape urbanist asks, isn't the landscape the glue that now holds the contemporary, low-density, sprawling metropolis together?

The radicalism inherent in thinking of the landscape as determining or organizing urban patterns, a radicalism in which Nolli's white, today colored green, becomes the central component of urban design, brings us at last to the territory of:

URBAN DESIGN AS VISIONARY URBANISM

I have saved, nearly for the end, this long-standing expectation of urban design: that its practitioners – or rather, in this instance, its theorists – provide insight and models about the way we *ought to* organize spatially in communities and not simply accept the ways we do. The prospect of hypothesizing about the future of urbanism surely attracts more students to urban design programs than any other lure. Being engaged in transforming urbanism is a sphere of action associated with the great figures of modern urban change, from Baron Haussmann to Daniel Burnham, Ebenezer Howard, Raymond Unwin, Le Corbusier, and maybe even Rem Koolhaas and Andres Duany. But such deliverers of bold saber strokes (to borrow a phrase from Giedion) are rarer today than they were at the turn of the twentieth century, or we act on their visions less often. A new generation of visionary designers may emerge out of China or other parts of the world rapidly urbanizing today, but they have yet to do so.

In the relative absence of contemporary visionaries, others have stepped forward to explore the nature of urban culture today. The urban sociologist/theorist – from Louis Wirth earlier in the twentieth century to Henri Lefebvre, Richard Sennett, Edward Soja, and David Harvey – is not normally considered an urban designer but in a sense has become so, having supplanted in our own time the great urban transformers of the past, not in deeds but in understandings of urban culture.

The heroic form-giving tradition may be in decline. After all, the twentieth century witnessed immense urban harm caused by those who offered a singular or universal idea of what a city is, or what urbanization should produce. But our cultural observers remind us that pragmatism and technique cannot be a sufficient substitute, nor can design professionals be mere *absorbers* of public opinion waiting for consensus to build. One must offer new ideas as well. Still, there is the perennial conundrum about how directly engaged urban design must be

with the "real world." Maybe, after all, urban design is about direct community engagement:

URBAN DESIGN AS COMMUNITY ADVOCACY (OR DOING NO HARM)

Mostly since 1956 and in academia largely still, "urban design" connotes large-scale thinking – either the consideration of substantial areas of settlement or theorizing at a grand scale about the nature of urbanism. But among contemporary dwellers of urban neighborhoods – the ostensive beneficiaries of this broad thinking – "urban design" is increasingly coming to be associated with local, immediate concerns such as improving neighborhoods, calming traffic, minimizing negative impacts of new development, expanding housing choices while keeping housing affordable, maintaining open space, improving streetscapes, and creating more humane environments in general.

In this newer, almost colloquial use of the term, urban design approximates what used to be called "community planning." A young Jane Jacobs's prescient comment during the 1956 conference comes to mind. "A store is also a storekeeper," she said then, with the implication that her designer colleagues at the conference better remember that a storekeeper is also a citizen, and that citizens have a stake in decisions being made about their environment. Not much follow-up of her point was recorded in the proceedings. It would take another generation to bring this view to the foreground.

The association of urban design and citizen participation was finally the result of the gradual bureaucratization of the planning profession itself. Sometime following the social unrest of the 1960s and a growing consensus about the failures of urban renewal, the focus of planning began to shift dramatically from physical planning to process and policy formulation. If the architect and urban designer were hell-bent on producing visions of a better tomorrow, the theory went, then the role of the planner must be to determine need and rational process, not to pursue (the often illusive and sometimes dubious) vision. Indeed, a fear of producing more top-down, failed plans before an increasingly demanding, less patient public led the planning profession to embrace broad participatory techniques and community advocacy. But ironically the concurrent disengagement from spatial concerns on the part of the planner began to distance the activities of planning from the stuff the beneficiaries of planning wish for most: nicer neighborhoods, access to better places of work and commerce, and special environments to periodically escape everyday pressures.

As the planning profession continues to operate in the broader spheres of policy formulation, the focus of planning increasingly appears to the public as abstract, even indifferent to immediate concerns or daily needs. The urban design-minded planner who addresses immediate, often spatially related concerns has come to be seen as the professional most attuned to tangible urban problem-solving, not as the agent of bold urban transformation. In citizens' minds, those who practice urban design are not the "shapers of cities" – in large part because such shapers, if they exist, are mistrusted. They are instead custodians of the qualities valued by a community, qualities that the urban designer is asked to protect and foster. Today, it is the urban designer, not the planner, who has emerged as the place-centered professional, with "urban design" often assuming a friendlier, more accessible popular connotation than "planning."

URBAN DESIGN AS A FRAME OF MIND

The above list is not intended to be exhaustive; other urban design activities could surely be added. In rapidly modernizing parts of the world, urban design has emerged as an important component of managing this modernization. An example is the BOT (Build, Operate, Transfer) transportation and related mixed-use projects common in both South American and Asian countries. (BOT is a form of project financing in which a private entity receives a franchise from the public sector to finance, design, construct, and operate a facility for a specified period, after which ownership is transferred back to the public sector.) Nor is

the point of identifying – even caricaturing – the above spheres of urban design to lay claim to vast jurisdictional territory for the discipline. On the contrary, it is to strongly suggest that instead of moving toward professional specificity, urban design has come to represent – and its varied practitioners have come to be aligned with – distinct avenues for engaging and facilitating urbanity. Rodolfo Machado, my colleague at Harvard, offers an appealing (if somewhat rhetorical) definition for urban design: the process of design (or planning, I would add) that produces or enhances urbanity. Is this but an "amiable generality"?

Perhaps Sert would be disappointed that half a century after his first conference no more precise definition for urban design has emerged. Around the third or fourth of the near-annual urban design conferences that he hosted at Harvard throughout the 1960s and early 1970s, he expressed concern about the "fog of amiable generalities" that the conversations had so far produced. He hoped to move past them, but they have persisted.

Following a quarter of a century of practicing and teaching urban design, my own conclusion is the following. Urban design is less a technical discipline than a mind-set among those of varying disciplinary foundations seeking, sharing, and advocating insights about forms of community. What binds urban designers is their commitment to improving the livability of cities, to facilitating urban reinvestment and maintenance, and indeed to enhancing urbanity. The need for a narrow definition for such a constellation of interests is not self-evident. Because of this commitment to cities, urban designers distinguish among mandates: they realize that to renew the centers of cities, build new cities, restore the parts of old cities worthy of preservation, and construct equitable growth management programs on the periphery requires vastly different strategies, theories, and design actions. Indeed, one may rejoice that there are many spheres of urbanistic action for those who are passionate lovers of cities.

"Designing the Urban Design Studio"

Elizabeth Macdonald

Editors' Introduction

Urban design is a professionally oriented field and it is the norm for most students who study urban design to have the goal of becoming professional practitioners. Within urban design study programs, they learn by gaining new knowledge and by applying that knowledge to problem-solving; by self-criticism and that of their teachers and colleagues; by trying out their creative ideas and getting responses to them from professors, professionals, community activists, and others. Anticipating graduation, they want to know what might be expected of them as professionals and they want to have the skills necessary to get a job in either public agencies or private consulting firms. Studios have long been a part of urban design education because they incorporate these types of learning. In studio, students bring together all they are learning in their other courses and grapple with how to make use of that knowledge as a professional. The best studios take qualitative and quantitative learning and direct it to the activity of making urban design proposals for specific places, responding to complex existing conditions and community needs, with the goal of creating good urban environments as defined through the considered weighing of competing values. As well, they encourage both collaborative and individual creative work. This experience approximates best urban design practice. Studios let students know what might be expected of them as professionals and gives them some experience of professional work.

Elizabeth Macdonald's piece "Designing the Urban Design Studio" explores how an introductory studio for an urban design concentration within a city planning program can be structured for multiple learning objectives: knowledge-building about good urbanism, team work skills, methods of visual thinking, design creativity, expertise about urban physical form, an introduction to the urban design tools and techniques, and effective communication. She speaks to the importance of selecting studio study areas and subject matters as well as the appropriate scale of possible undertakings. Field research and first-hand data gathering are advocated, as is the relevance of researching precedents. The importance of knowing citizen concerns and at the same time understanding the inherent limits of community participation in a studio project are discussed, as is the importance of teaching students how to create clear graphic and verbal presentations. Effective communication between urban designers and others involved in building cities − the public, local officials, developers, and other professionals − is no small issue. The complex world of urban design includes many participants and decision-makers with different perspectives, and often takes place over extended time periods. Beyond listening to and understanding the perspectives of their many clients, urban designers must be able to communicate their own understandings of places and urbanism, and clearly articulate design ideas in ways that are comprehensible to non-designers. The studio is an effective place for students to develop these skills.

The issue of studio-based education for urban design education is of critical importance to the future of professional practice. The studio teaching method has long been at the heart of planning education, but in recent years studio courses have become less and less emphasized in many curricula, giving way to planning policy subjects taught, often with some abstraction, in seminar classes. Macdonald's writing reaffirms the importance of studios for urban design education planning programs and offers a roadmap for how such studios might be designed.

Elizabeth Macdonald is Associate Professor of Urban Design at the University of California's College of Environmental Design, where she holds appointments in both the Department of City and Regional Planning and the Department of Landscape Architecture and Environmental Planning. She is also a faculty member of the Urban Design Graduate Group which sponsors a Masters of Urban Design program. She practices urban design through her firm Cityworks.

Macdonald's research and design practice focuses on streets. Her works include *The Boulevard Book: History, Evolution, Design of Multiway Boulevards* (Boston, MA: MIT Press, 2003), co-authored with Allan B. Jacobs and Yodan Rofé; and *Pleasure Drives and Promenades: A History of Olmsted's Brooklyn Parkways* (Chicago, IL: Center for American Places, forthcoming). As well, she has written numerous book chapters and journal articles including "Streets and the Public Realm: Growing Opportunities/Emerging Designs," in *Urban Design: Roots, Influences, and Trends: The Routledge Companion to Urban Design* (London: Routledge, 2011); "The Efficacy of Long-Range Physical Planning: The Case of Vancouver," *Journal of Planning History* (vol. 7, no. 3, 175–213, 2008); "Urban Waterfront Promenades and Physical Activity by Older Adults: The Case of Vancouver," *Journal of Architecture and Planning Research* (vol. 24, no. 3, 181–198, 2007); "Wasted Space/Potential Place: Reconsidering Urban Streets," *Places: Forum of Design for the Public Realm* (vol. 19, no. 1, 22–27, 2007); "Suburban Vision to Urban Reality: The Evolution of Olmsted and Vaux's Brooklyn Parkway Neighborhoods," *Journal of Planning History* (vol. 4, no. 4, 295–321, 2005); "Street-Facing Dwelling Units and Livability: The Impacts of Emerging Building Types in Vancouver's New High-Density Residential Neighborhoods," *Journal of Urban Design* (vol. 10, no. 1, 13–38, 2005); and "Structuring a Landscape/Structuring a Sense of Place: The Enduring Complexity of Olmsted and Vaux's Brooklyn Parkways," *Journal of Urban Design* (vol. 7, no. 2, 117–143, 2002).

An early comprehensive assessment of urban design education in the United States is found in *Education for Urban Design: Proceedings of the Urban Design Educators' Retreat* (Purchase, NY: Institute for Urban Designers, 1982). This compilation includes several writings that address the importance of studio education including Jon Lang's piece "For the Studio Method," and Allan B. Jacobs' piece "Education for Successful Practice." More recently, Kathryn H. Anthony's piece "Design Studios," contained in the anthology *Companion to Urban Design* (Oxford: Routledge, 2011), edited by Tridib Banerjee and Anastasia Loukaitou-Sideris, explores the evolution of design studio culture, highlighting its usefulness as a vehicle for teaching urban design but also the pitfalls that can happen if the studio experience is not well planned and executed.

Several recent books provide excellent overviews of the urban design field and touch on issues related to urban design communication. These include Jon Lang's *Urban Design: A Typology of Procedures and Products* (Oxford: Elsevier, Architectural Press, 2005) and Matthew Carmona, Tim Heath, Taner Oc, and Steve Tiesdell's *Public Places – Urban Spaces: The Dimensions of Urban Design* (Oxford: Architectural Press, 2010). In particular, the chapter "The Communication Process" in *Public Places – Urban Spaces*, contains perhaps the best description of the types of typical communication problems urban designers may encounter and offers approaches to dealing with them. The problems include "communication gaps," between professionals and laypeople, designers and non-designers, the powerful and the powerless, and designers and users, as well as between reality and representations of reality. Issues related to communication problems that occur because of the limitations of graphic representation methods used by urban designers are analyzed at length in Peter Bosselmann's well-illustrated book *Representation of Places: Reality and Realism in City Design* (Berkeley, CA: University of California Press, 1998).

In universities today, urban design may be taught within city planning programs, architecture programs, or landscape architecture programs. Sometimes, different programs within the same university offer students different paths to achieve an urban design education. Design pedagogy and theoretical ideas underlying advocated design approaches may vary widely depending on what program the teaching is situated in. However, for most programs that teach urban design, whatever discipline they might be situated in, studio courses are central to the curriculum.

Studios are the venue where teachers and students collaborate on learning about places and exploring their possibilities, and create and articulate planning and design proposals that draw on the discovered knowledge, usually through engaged teamwork. Studio projects are collaborative endeavors that explore urban physical areas with the objective of arriving at a proposal or set of proposals about how that area might be transformed, in large or small ways, to meet community needs and aspirations and take best advantage of development opportunities. The studio environment, where a group works together for extended periods in a dedicated work space, fosters joint learning at the same time that it allows and encourages individual creative development and expression. Students learn from each other as well as from their professors, especially if there is room for creative efforts to be pinned up on studio walls so that everyone can learn from them, respond to them, and be inspired in their own creative efforts by them.

I have taught graduate urban design studios for twelve years, mostly at the University of California at Berkeley's College of Environmental Design but also at the University of Toronto and the University of British Columbia. The students I teach are mostly pursuing Master of City Planning, Master of Landscape Architecture or Master of Urban Design degrees, and some are in Master of Architecture programs. Those pursuing city planning degrees have a wide range of backgrounds and many have no previous design experience. Some are focusing on urban design, while others are concentrating in transportation planning, land use planning, environmental planning, or community development.

The paper specifically addresses studio teaching for urban design concentrations situated within city planning programs, but the ideas discussed are also relevant for urban design teaching in other types of programs. For planning-based programs, studio projects and processes can be designed to mirror a significant part of what the staff of urban design groups within city planning departments or the staff of private urban design firms working for local government agencies, actually do, helping students learn to be professionals.

A MIX OF STUDENTS AND TEAMWORK

Having a mix of students from many backgrounds and with diverse interests is important to a planning-based urban design studio. It means many different perspectives, skills, and ways of thinking about urbanism are brought to the "drawing board." This mix is very fruitful and creates an environment similar to that found on the best real-world professional urban design projects, where design efforts are conducted via multi-disciplinary teams.

Teamwork is an important part of the urban design studio. The studio experience is not about fostering individual, stand alone "star-architect" work. Rather, it provides an environment where burgeoning young urban designers experience the complex and rich creativity that can come from working as a part of a multi-disciplinary team. At the same time, they develop their individual abilities, knowing that these relate to the larger effort. To be sure, there is no guarantee that a studio class will draw a mix of students with the whole range of interests one might wish. No matter. In such cases students can be asked to take on whatever "discipline" or subject analysis studies that are deemed necessary. And so they do, for a period, learning along the way, and then returning to their central interests.

STUDIO SUBJECT MATTERS

Ready access and topicality are the two most important criteria for selecting the place the studio will focus on. Places that can be easily accessed are best because that allows students to immerse themselves in the study area and encourages them to use their own senses for direct knowledge-building rather than an over-reliance on second-hand data collected by others. Students tend to get most engaged with a place if there are real, urgent issues related to it because this helps focus where their attention might be directed and also offers the possibility that their work can play a role in real world planning and design processes. With this in mind, it is good to choose places facing strong development pressures, where major public infrastructure projects are being contemplated, or where a pressing ecological concern, such as sea-level rise, can be addressed.

For introductory studios, focusing on one area for the whole semester allows deep exploration and consideration of the place. It also gives time for students to develop graphic presentation skills, because many enter the class not knowing how to draw or use any of the digital graphics programs. I typically select either a neighborhood scale area or a major corridor that cuts across or lies between multiple neighborhoods. In the real world, these are two of the main types of projects for which urban design plans are typically prepared. I like to pick areas where community activists are working, so that community voices and concerns can be easily connected with.

The issue of community participation in university urban design studio classes can be a tricky one. Aside from the reality that teaching objectives and studio schedules may not always coincide with immediate neighborhood concerns or real world planning process schedules, it is important to remember not to promise the community anything that can't be delivered upon. Usually, when the studio is over, the work is over, except, perhaps, if there is a center at the university, or a group of locally engaged professors, dedicated to fostering on-going relationships with local communities and keeping connections going from year to year, bridging different student cohorts. Students may present their work to community groups or local decision-makers after the studio is finished, and some may follow-through on a studio project through individual efforts taken on as a capstone thesis or professional report project. Certainly, studio products can be made available to communities and planning departments for use in real world planning processes.

KNOWLEDGE-BUILDING

Knowledge-building about a place precedes design. The first thing students should do is to explore the study area on their own, on foot, without a camera but with a sketchbook, for at least half a day. Being without companions or a camera is conducive to a deeper kind of observation than otherwise, a closer looking. They may be given guidance on the kinds of things they might want to pay attention to, but mostly it should be left up to them to explore as they will. A good first assignment involves the preparation of a reconnaissance map that articulates their

first impressions of the study area in graphic form. When these are pinned up together in the studio and discussed it leads to an understanding of the many different lenses through which people view urban places and their experience of them. Some common observations always emerge and so do unique ones. These initial gleanings form a starting point for more systematic knowledge-building.

Discovering contexts and opportunities

One of the key opportunities afforded by the University studio environment is that there is time to explore in some depth all the many contexts in which the neighborhood or corridor being studied is situated. Students divide into two or three person teams focused on gaining knowledge about particular contexts: the area's history, physical form, natural factors, social and economic factors, and how movement and access work. As a class, we brainstorm the questions we want each group to address, and possible data gathering approaches. At least some of the data gathering must come from the students' own fieldwork – observations, measurements, counts, surveys, and interviews – because spending time in a place leads to different insights than simply analyzing abstract datasets prepared by others. Each team of students prepares a graphic presentation of their findings. Rather than presenting a "data dump" of everything they have discovered, they are asked to thoughtfully sift through the knowledge they have gathered to determine what the key "stories" are that they have uncovered.

As students begin working on knowledge-gathering, they are taught how to communicate their ideas, to their team mates and faculty, through visual thinking. Early on, students are asked to develop thumbnail sketches of the presentation boards they will create to articulate their findings. The thumbnail sketches help make the analysis process concrete and grounded, and keep students from getting stuck in an abstract realm of endless "analysis paralysis." Talking over these thumbnail sketches, we work together to identify key finds and clear ways to show them and their relationships with other findings via clear graphics and succinct text. Students are asked to keep refining their thumbnail sketches at the same time that they are preparing individual presentation boards so that they keep the whole picture in mind.

While doing research on the study area, students should be encouraged to think about design possibilities. Design ideas can help inform the type of research that should be done. Students can be asked to keep a sketchbook and some studio time can be spent on quick design charettes where students can explore emerging design ideas in graphic form. The products of these exploratory design exercises can be pinned up on the wall for others to contemplate.

Learning from precedents

While existing contexts certainly should form the foundation upon which urban design ideas are based, for beginning students, inspiration and innovation are often best unlocked by looking at precedents. Even at the graduate level, many students have limited personal experience of cities and may be lacking in knowledge of innovative approaches to city-building. As a class, it is helpful to spend an intensive period of time, a week or so, gathering visual images and supporting data about a whole range of precedents that have something to teach that is relevant for our study area. The class can first collectively brainstorm issues relevant to the studio subject matter that it wants to know more about and also identify specific places or projects where these issues have been addressed, both in tried and true ways and with the latest innovations. By casting a wide net and pooling collective knowledge and creative resources, the class ends up with many design ideas to contemplate and, hopefully, be inspired by.

FORMULATING AND ARTICULATING URBAN DESIGN PROPOSALS

The design proposal phase of studio work is where students learn key methods used in real-world urban design practice.

Guiding vision and principles

The best urban design plans articulate a clear design vision supported by a handful of key goals. These function as the high-order criteria from which the planning and design proposals should derive. Succinctly articulating main concepts and gaining team agreement on them replicates, in abbreviated form, how successful decision-making processes work in real world planning processes. Once the high-level criteria are set, students have a benchmark to strive for and to test ideas against. Every design decision should form and reinforce the guiding vision and goals.

Visions for changes become most imageable and memorable when they are articulated with a clear graphic, or set of graphics, that encapsulates the idea. For instance, the vision developed for the *Saint Paul on the Mississippi Downtown Revitalization Plan* was "Downtown Saint Paul will be a system of interconnected urban villages nestled in a reforested river valley." This compelling idea was illustrated with a freehand drawn, watercolor, aerial view of the Mississippi River flowing through the center of the city, with tree-lined banks and neighborhoods spilling down to the water. This is an image meant to capture the community's aspirations for its future, aspirations that were worked out during a highly participatory planning process, and to inspire a long term commitment to realizing those aspirations.

Urban design framework plans

In the past, urban design plans were often conceived as masterplans. Today, recognizing that economic and other circumstances might change over the course of implementing an urban design development, which can take many years or even decades, the key element of urban design plans are urban structure framework plans. These framework plans set the basic built form and use parameters for an area. For most projects, a series of framework plans are prepared. The focus of each framework plan and how many of them there are is determined by the specifics of the urban design project. Typically, each framework plan describes a single system or pattern. They address things like the patterns of street types, the spatial locations of different movement flows, open space patterns, hydrological systems, land use patterns, locations of activity nodes and special landmarks, built form intensity, and so on. They are typically plan drawings, all covering the same area and drawn to the same scale so that the ways various frameworks fitted together can be easily understood.

Re-envisioning the public realm

A key focus of creative effort in urban design studios, as in urban design practice, is on the urban public realm. Contemporary urban design projects often involve strategies for enhanced public realm systems and networks. Such strategies might focus on sustainable infrastructure, such as green streets or district heating and cooling systems, or on creating more pedestrian-oriented or multi-modal-oriented streets. The studio provides the opportunity to encourage students to explore innovative street designs that meet other purposes than those promulgated by traffic engineers, such as maximizing vehicle capacity. All too often in the real world, street standards are allowed to dictate urban street design. And very often, these standards result in wider than necessary roadways, narrower than necessary sidewalks, little in the way of bicycle facilities, and, quite often, few trees or permeable surfaces.

Shaping private development without designing buildings

The urban structure framework plans set an area's overall form and use patterns and may also set criteria for building height and bulk. In the real world, most urban design plans go further in shaping built form through the use of design guidelines. The studio provides the opportunity to explore how design guidance should be articulated to shape development that will contribute to the community vision. Particular attention is paid to the interface zone between the private realm and the public realm.

URBAN DESIGN COMMUNICATION

Graphic presentations

The point of urban design graphic presentations is to communicate clearly with a wide range of people: other planners and designers, engineers, public decision-makers such as mayors and members of city councils, and, most important, community members. As such, graphics should be designed to be easily to read and comprehended. They should not be designed to dazzle through mystification.

Ideally, visual graphics should "speak for themselves," conveying key findings and proposals even if the author is not present to explain them. A clear visual display of information depends upon organization. Rarely can urban design analyses or design proposals be presented on a single drawing. A basic strategy for creating easily accessible visual presentations is to establish coordinated graphic formats that link across multiple sheets. In other words, a visual language should be created and used consistently throughout a presentation. Viewers should not be asked to learn multiple visual languages, because they may become lost or frustrated. If this happens, attention will deteriorate and communication will become ineffective.

Verbal presentations

The urban design studio offers an opportunity for students to learn good verbal presentation techniques, a very important skill for professional practice. They learn basic things, like the importance of facing the audience and not the graphics. As might be expected, students become immersed in their group processes, but for presentations they must focus on findings and proposals rather than a rehash of the group deliberations that went before. Students might very well not accomplish all they had hoped they might, but it does no good to tell the audience the things they didn't do. Presentation time constraints help students understand the importance of succinct verbal presentations, an important skill for professionals. Interruptions from someone in the audience to ask a question always seem to happen. It is important to learn how to gracefully let the questioner know that the answer will be forthcoming, or to answer the question quickly and then continue with the presentation, not giving the questioner time to keep his or her personal concern going. Reviews of the students' work by a group of professionals and lay people is important because it exposes students to the reality that professional work elicits many responses, some of which conflict with each other. Professionals must learn to both listen to and weigh multiple responses.

Practice, practice, practice. Presentation of research and planning and design proposals in verbal and graphic form is different than the type of work students do in other classes. Presenting before a live, sometimes critical audience is a road to professional practice that studios offer budding professionals. More than one such presentation over the course of a studio is important.

"Design Guidelines in American Cities: Conclusions"

from *Design Guidelines in American Cities: A Review of Design Policies and Guidance in Five West Coast Cities* (1999)

John Punter

Editors' Introduction

What constitutes best practice urban design policy? What are ways of doing urban design and making it effective within different political and regulatory contexts? Substantively and process-wise, what has worked over periods of time and what hasn't? What can urban designers in one city or country learn from those practicing elsewhere? On the one hand, each city is different from every other one, particularly in regards to governance, bureaucratic structure, economic bases, physical, climatic, social, and cultural contexts, and the roles of citizens in decision-making, so it seems difficult to gain meaningful lessons from how one city does things that apply to another. On the other hand, detailed knowledge about how urban design initiatives are practically accomplished in different cities, particularly when their physical, social, economic, and governmental contexts are well explained, can inspire practitioners to transcend entrenched ways of doing things and explore new possibilities.

In this regard, John Punter's extensive comparative research on design policy is very important, not least because he is very thorough at explaining how things work in different cities in relation to their contexts. Here, in the conclusion to his book *Design Guidelines in American Cities: A Review of Design Policies and Guidance in Five West Coast Cities*, Punter summarizes and synthesizes the findings that come from analyzing the urban design public policy of five cities on the west coast of the United States – Seattle, Portland, San Francisco, Irvine, and San Diego – cities that he posits are generally understood to have put in place best practice urban design guidance. From the analysis, which includes a review of legal issues related to planning regulatory controls, Punter distills a framework for how design guidance should be structured that he argues is applicable to cities elsewhere, including in different countries. He finds that design policies should be based on careful study of the locality and full consultation with the community. Design review should be part of a comprehensive coordinated effort at design regulation and integrated into the planning process. The design review process should be efficient, fair, and effective, and design guidelines should be precise but not overly prescriptive, underpinned by design principles, and backed by implementation advice.

John Punter's other writings on design policy include the edited anthology *Urban Design and the British Urban Renaissance* (London: Routledge, 2010); *The Design Dimension of Practice: Theory, Content, and Best Practice for Design Policies*, co-authored with Matthew Carmona (London: E & FN Spon, 1997), which describes and analyzes British design policy; *From Design Policy to Design Quality: The Treatment of Design in Community Strategies, Local Development Frameworks and Action Plans*, co-authored with Matthew Carmona and David Chapman (London: Thomas Telford, 2002); and *The Vancouver Achievement: Urban Planning and Design* (Vancouver, BC: UBC Press, 2003). This last is a detailed look at Vancouver's unique discretionary zoning system and approach to design regulation, including the use of urban design framework plans that shape building types and set the form and character of public spaces, resulting in what some consider one of the best examples of recent city-building. Vancouver has built new high-density residential neighborhoods on former industrial lands in and around its downtown core while at the same time building a vibrant, pedestrian-oriented public realm and whole communities. The unique building type that has emerged from Vancouver's design guidance is what has come to be known as a "point-tower-over-podium-base," where the base contains townhouses with individual entries facing onto streets and pedestrian walkways. Elizabeth Macdonald's article "Street-Facing Dwelling Units and Livability: The Impacts of Emerging Building Types in Vancouver's New High-Density Residential Neighborhoods," *Journal of Urban Design* (vol 10, no. 1, pp. 13–38, 2005) provides a look at on-the-ground impacts of these new buildings.

One of the best ways for students and practitioners to learn how to be effective design regulators and to write well-articulated guidelines is to look directly at examples of design guidelines and design review systems. This is becoming easier and easier to do because many cities are starting to post their urban design and planning policies on websites in easily downloadable form. The cities of Portland, Oregon (http://www.portlandonline.com/planning/) and Vancouver, British Columbia (http://www.vancouver.ca/commsvcs/planning/) both have highly sophisticated design guidance systems and their planning departments have well-structured websites that make their design guidance documents easily accessible.

AUTHOR'S INTRODUCTION

The task of this monograph was to illustrate and explain 'best practice' American design review to an international audience, providing as many illustrations, plan excerpts, and samples of guidance as possible in the belief that this would stimulate thought and encourage innovation in design guidelines and review processes in countries beyond the USA. West coast cities of the USA were selected to illustrate this 'best practice', four of them major metropolitan areas and two of them suburban municipalities. Collectively these were considered to display a long-standing commitment to design quality; a full range of design visions, strategies, goals, objectives and policies at different scales from city-wide to the neighbourhood; a sophisticated review process; a high degree of public consultation and public ownership of policies; and a wide range of implementation devices and investment programmes.

The evolution of the respective planning and design policies has been discussed and their strengths and weaknesses assessed. Their outcomes have been assessed to a much lesser extent, and it has rarely been possible to assess the effectiveness of policies in any depth. In the opening chapter design review was carefully located in the planning and permit-granting process in the largest cities, and comparisons were made with Canadian, British and French planning systems to illustrate where commonalities exist. It was seen that there are more similarities between American planning and continental European systems than there are between American and British systems; the latter have no zoning controls and no clear development entitlements. Instead, the latter's design controls on all planning applications operated with a very large measure of professional and political discretion (notwithstanding Central Government's strong policy constraints). For the British reader the key observation is that while many of the American design documents look familiar in terms of their goals, objectives, principles, policies and guidelines, it must never be forgotten that these are backed by detailed control on bulk and use that in themselves exert a major impact on built form. For the continental European, the zoning controls will be familiar, as will the issues about how to make such controls more flexible, more responsive to development interests, and more qualitatively sophisticated. However, the question as to how new guidelines, documents or review processes might be built into a more plan-led system will loom large for the British reader.

Some time was spent explaining the key criticisms of design review in the USA in a bid to provide a conceptual framework with which to review each city's endeavours. It was seen that there were problems with the process, its efficiency and effectiveness; with the competence of planners, politicians and review boards; with the abuse of power, going beyond legal powers to impose additional constraints and obligations on developers; with issues of freedom in terms of rights to self-expression and cultural identity, and of justice in terms of treating all applicants fairly and reasonably; and finally of aesthetics in terms of the subjectivity of design judgment (Scheer and Preiser 1994, pp. 1–10). Legal observers focused their criticisms on the process of control and the rules/principles/policies that are applied. Blaesser, in particular, focused on the legality of design review within state planning law; the need to derive policy from analysis of area character, the need to ensure that guidelines remain non-mandatory and non-prescriptive, but detailed and precise rather than vague or visionary; the need to underpin guidelines with both design principles and implementation advice, and to explain the weight to be attached to each (Blaesser 1994, pp. 49–50). Lai took a broader and more general view, on the one hand looking at general weaknesses of American planning and zoning, and on the other arguing that design review must be part of a 'comprehensive coordinated effort' to promote design quality in which other public and private agencies participate (Lai 1988).

A FRAMEWORK FOR SYNTHESIS

These criticisms provided the framework for drawing together the findings of the study in terms of the comprehensiveness of the pursuit of design quality; how policies were derived (particularly the analytical studies and consultation that underpin them); their level of precision; their basis in design theory; the extent to which they prescribe solutions; and finally the efficiency and effectiveness of the review process. Particular attention was devoted to the policy hierarchy, to the relationship between urban design at the citywide scale and the level of the individual plot, and to the relationship between goals, objectives, principles, policies and guidelines.

In these conclusions the findings of the study will be assembled around six issues which can help to organise the key arguments that have arisen in the analysis. The key issues may be encapsulated as politics; public participation; the review process; policy hierarchy, policy generation and the levels of prescription; implementation; and comprehensive co-ordination. These are not mutually exclusive issues – politics, participation and policy generation are particularly closely related – and some aspects could be explored under several of these categories, but these issues can help structure the general conclusions of the study.

THE POLITICS OF URBAN DESIGN

The west coast cities clearly demonstrate that urban design in its broadest sense is a politically contested arena. This is most evident in the citizen revolts against the 1984 Downtown Seattle Plan and the 1985 Downtown San Francisco Plan where there was strong opposition to further large-scale, high-rise commercial development on the basis of its impact on the character of downtown, and its broader effects on congestion, transportation and housing. In San Diego the concern was suburban sprawl and the spread of new communities up the coast and into the arid interior; a balanced growth strategy soon disintegrated when existing suburban communities began to experience intensification, congestion and higher demands on existing services.

Portland provides the most positive example of how urban design goals and strategies have won powerful political support that has ensured their continuous implementation over 25 years. Carl Abbott has detailed the connection between *what* the city has accomplished in design terms and *how* it has accomplished this through its politics. He emphasises Portland's traditions of conservatism, conservation, and consensus politics (non-partisan government) developed through extensive public-private partnerships and thoroughgoing community planning as the platform for a long-term urban growth management and downtown development strategy (Abbott 1997). Others see support for these strategies being built through economic self-interest in higher property values and more stable neighbourhoods, in more profitable development opportunities and more affordable housing, and through widely shared interests in the commercial and cultural vitality of the compact city, and the protection of valuable agricultural land and natural landscapes (Richmond 1997).

SIX

The same kind of political consensus building was evident in Seattle with the 1994 Comprehensive Plan and its urban villages strategy, which tried to accommodate growth and maintain housing affordability at the same time as improving neighbourhood amenities, increasing accessibility and reducing congestion, and increasing neighbourhood design control while nonetheless allowing intensification. It remains to be seen if Seattle will succeed where San Diego failed, but certainly the Comprehensive Plan provides the basis for accommodating the growth that San Diego's mature suburbs have resisted.

Another example of the importance of politics is provided by San Diego's failure to build a political consensus for design-led planning downtown, in the face of powerful development interests and a powerful City Center Development Corporation driven by the tax increments provided through redevelopment. A further problem was a political leadership that, at least until recently, regarded design control as arbitrary, expensive and off-putting to developers.

The political complexion of the city, the extent to which it can pick and choose between developers and developments (particularly the level of economic competition between developers), the mutuality of interest between developers and residents, between business and environmental groups are all critical to the effective implementation of long-term design strategies and enhancement programmes. It is remarkably easy for policy to get out of step with public aspirations, particularly in periods of rapid growth (as in Seattle and San Francisco). One of the best ways of preventing this is to develop a very high level of public participation and neighborhood/community input into plan making and design development/regulation, but even this is not an absolute guarantee of harmony.

PUBLIC PARTICIPATION IN FORMULATING DESIGN POLICY

Issues of the politics of urban design are inseparable from issues of public participation in planning and design regulation. However, the level and extent of this participation constitutes, at one extreme, mere publicity for a plan or guidelines, and at the other extreme genuine empowerment of the community (Arnstein 1969). A wider range of different levels of participation is evident in west coast cities, from extremely limited public involvement in subdivision development and planning in Irvine (land owner planning through market research) to an extremely high level of involvement and devolved resources in Portland.

Portland is the exemplar in terms of its neighbourhood participation programme which funds neighbourhood associations, trains activists, gives associations early notification of impending development, and allows them to participate in development briefing. The 1988 Center City Plan was led by a voluntary citizen steering committee, and both this and the 1993 Albina plan had huge budgets to ensure high levels of public participation. It is noticeable that there were no citizen revolts over the 1988 Downtown Plan in Portland as there were in Seattle and San Francisco, although there was some modification of its content (a refocus on land-use issues) when the Planning Bureau took over from the citizens' committee to complete it.

Other cities have been much less ambitious with their participation initiatives, but there are some interesting experiments in the devolution of both guidance production and design control to the local level in both San Francisco and Seattle. In San Francisco, at least in part, this has been a product of financial exigencies constraining planning department initiatives, so that communities wishing to undertake closer control have had to write their own guidance or finance its production themselves. In Seattle, it is part of a pact that will allow the city to intensify development in a series of urban villages, while allowing the neighbourhoods to control the detailed design of new development, and to participate in pre-development discussions with prospective developers with a firm prospect of having their views incorporated into the final design.

There is a clear trend not just towards public consultation in design matters, but towards the public defining the principles of control and contributing to the administration of the control process itself. Such ventures provide a mechanism for managing disputes between the community and development interests, and for giving the community far greater 'ownership' of the control mechanism. The Seattle experiment in empowering neighbourhood groups will be especially interesting as the intensification process generated by zoning changes in the 1994 plan gathers pace. It will provide an interesting comparison with San Diego's experiences.

The management or neighbourhood change through elected neighbourhood associations and codes, covenants and restrictions [CC&Rs] is another form of empowerment, often dismissed as a purely negative and exclusionary process by those who see design control as a purely public activity. Baab argues that these can be devices for subordinating individual property rights to community values, and is very positive about both their effectiveness in maintaining environmental quality and their ability to translate community goals into action (Baab 1994). Taking the example of Woodbridge in Irvine, it is difficult to see anything but enforced conformity and claustrophobia, but a more positive role is evidenced in Westwood Park, San Francisco, where a less rigid set of CC&Rs has been supplemented by tailored guidelines to ensure the retention of neighbourhood qualities.

With the obvious exception of Irvine, west coast cities have made an especial effort to consult the public on design matters, and a number are now going a stage further to devolve both the production of guidance and first stage design controls to the local community. However, these efforts are at odds with the general trend identified by Southworth (1989, p. 345) to allow less participation, and to concentrate upon elite business and professional interests to capture key decision-makers and to save money. They are also at odds with Habe's research findings which found that only one-quarter of the communities surveyed promoted 'active' participation in design matters (Habe 1989, pp. 204–6). This is one of the reasons why these west coast cities continue to be exemplars of enlightened design control.

THE PROCESS OF DESIGN REVIEW

Opponents of design review, particularly developers and architects, focus upon the nature of the processes of design review and the extent to which they are subject to professional and political discretion. Lawyers are especially concerned about the abuse of discretionary power (see Blaesser 1994) and the tendency of applicants to succumb to its requirements rather than to challenge it. They have made a variety of suggestions about how the process might be made efficient, fair and effective (Lai 1988). A number of these relate to the way guidelines are developed, their basis in the nature of the locality and public values, their relationship to established principles of design, and their level of prescription, all of which will be discussed in subsequent sections. Some of their suggestions relate specifically to the administrative procedures and the need for written opinions, principles derived from precedents, tests of the reasonableness of the decision and the right of appeal.

Abbott noted how in Portland the city routinised and depoliticised design review early on by establishing clear guidelines, trained officers, treating each case on its merits, and appointing design and landmark commissions to give decisions (Abbott 1997). The review process itself has written reports, hearings (on more complex developments) and appeal procedures all with strict timetables that will yield a decision in 11 or 17 weeks depending on the size and complexity of the proposal, even after appeal. A key aspect of Portland's system is that state legislation demands that decisions be based on demonstrable findings, hence the emphasis on clear and precise guidelines and checklists against which an application can be assessed and can be seen to be systematically evaluated. This same approach is evident in Seattle's neighbourhood design review where it is extended to emphasize pre-application negotiations and community agreement on what the decisive issues are, so that these can be used in a broader evaluation of the eventual planning application. Due process was seen to be lacking in San Francisco where discretionary review could be initiated even where a developer had met all the requirements of the zoning ordinance, and where politicians used the review mechanism to respond to citizen pressures against particular developments.

The evidence from Seattle, Bellevue, Portland and San Francisco is that design review has been fully integrated into the planning process, and it has been systematised, made transparent, democratised and professionalised, the latter by virtue of planning officers' advice and expert design or landmarks commissions' judgments. In San Diego design review has yet to be fully established, but communities have set out their design requirements in their zoning ordinances and community plans. Meanwhile Irvine demonstrates the power of landowner control that can be exercised on developers when there is a high demand for development, and how these controls can be perpetuated through the imposition of CC&Rs on the title deeds.

THE POLICY HIERARCHY AND THE WRITING OF GUIDELINES

At the heart of the examination of the design guidelines used in west coast cities has been the question of how to write policies or guidelines that are clear, meaningful and easy for lay people to understand, and easily applicable to the control of development. Throughout the case studies the relationship between community goals, design objectives and design guidelines has been repeatedly discussed, compared and contrasted one to another in the search for well-articulated, concise and comprehensive policy frameworks. To re-emphasise the importance of the task, a recent court case in Washington State overturned permit refusals which stated that development proposals were 'incompatible' and 'non-harmonious', because such judgments were not based on properly researched and explained policies and guidelines. The court in the case of Anderson v. Issaquah ruled that the use of such adjectives in zoning ordinances was not acceptable, that property owners must know what they are expected to do in advance, and that decision-making cannot just be turned over to a board or committee without clear guidelines being established to support their decisions (Hinshaw 1994, p. 288).

[. . .]

The value of design appraisal

One of the key characteristics of the best American urban design planning is that they are based upon thoroughgoing analysis of the character of the locality. The best example anywhere is provided by San Francisco where the 1968–70 design studies undertaken by the City Planning Department established the character of the city, the key qualities that needed to be protected, and the principles and policies that could help achieve this. Other cities undertook similar appraisals, but not on the same scale – the Lynch and Appleyard study of San Diego being one of the most interesting and comprehensible (Lynch and Appleyard 1974). The Portland studies were among the most participative – involving various architectural and conservation groups, using Kevin Lynch methodologies in the former and identifying all potential landmark buildings in the latter. Portland has been proceeding area by area with detailed analyses of design character through all downtown, inner city and historic districts, developing detailed guidelines from each appraisal (City of Portland 1993). The analyses make particular use of axonometrics and maps at the large scale to distil and communicate ideas, moving on to detailed analysis of architectural and street character at the micro-scale.

Southworth's research reveals that such thoroughgoing appraisals are now much less common than they used to be in the period 1960–73, and further reveals that 20 percent of the newer design plans surveyed have no such analytical base (Southworth 1989). Furthermore, he is critical of many professional field surveys which he regards as vague and unstructured. His prescription for a good survey is that it sets 'clear goals and categories of analysis, and establishes a system for covering the survey area so that all areas receive equal attention [and] provides for multiple opinions in subjective analyses to reduce personal biases' (Southworth 1989, p. 376). His research reveals a rich array of analytical techniques that provide a good basis for area appraisals anywhere, but emphasises that significant public consultation remains a vital component in order to establish public, as opposed to professional, values.

Residents' views were an important component of the San Francisco Urban Design Study in 1970. In Portland since 1974 the Office of Downtown Neighborhood Associations has ensured major public inputs into all planning, zoning and guideline reviews, including most notably the 1988 Center City Plan which was largely prepared under the auspices of a citizen steering committee with its own budget. Current initiatives in Seattle attempt to kill two birds with one stone by encouraging communities to conduct their own area appraisals, and thereafter to develop their own objectives and guidelines, thereby ensuring that it is *their* values which are expressed in the controls rather than those of the professionals or specialised amenity or development interests. It has already been seen that quite ordinary communities are capable of writing their own design guidelines, and that these can be quite original, unprescriptive and refreshingly neutral about matters of elevational treatment and architectural style (e.g. Bernal Heights in San Francisco). Certainly Seattle's manual, *Preparing Your Own Design Guidelines*, will be of value to many small communities worldwide as they contemplate the task of expressing what it is about the physical character of their settlement or neighbourhood they wish to maintain.

Objectives and principles

The appropriate development of goals, objectives, principles, policies and guidelines is problematic in the sense that many of these terms are used interchangeably, and loosely, by different designers and indeed different critics and planners. In the west coast cities the three best examples seem to rely on a few key objectives each split into a number of design principles. The 1972 San Francisco Master Plan relies on four design objectives, each with nine to twelve policies (design principles); the 1985 Downtown Plan is similar but with nine objectives each split into two to five policies (also essentially principles). In the latter, further guidance is offered in a couple of paragraphs on each, with much more detailed guidelines and standards for open space and for pedestrian improvement standards.

Portland's 1988 Downtown Plan has three objectives and 26 principles (called guidelines). They are very broad and general – reinforce the pedestrian system, protect the pedestrian, bridge pedestrian obstacles, provide pedestrian stopping places, make open spaces successful – and are barely elaborated in the four sentences which accompany each guideline. They are brought together in a checklist so that planners can determine whether or not the guideline is applicable to the proposed development or not, and whether it complies or not. A very similar approach has been adopted in Seattle with 27 principles (also called guidelines) for site planning, bulk, architectural treatment, pedestrian relationship and landscaping. These are described as guidelines and the checklist is used to establish which are the priority considerations from the neighbourhood's viewpoint. Both checklists provide valuable ways of briefing developers, or articulating community wishes, or of evaluating proposals, because they can identify which broad but widely supported principles, collectively, will be critical to design quality.

Urbanistic principles

One of the features of the best design principles is the emphasis they place upon the proposed building's relationship to the public realm and the pedestrian experience. In the most progressive authorities these urbanistic criteria receive more attention than architectural or townscape factors. Payton, relating an experience in Virginia, draws a clear line between these two kinds of factors and makes an important recommendation:

> Urbanistic criteria relate to the relationship of buildings to other buildings (vis-à-vis height relative to street width and other buildings), to set back lines, to parks etc. In essence all of those characteristics that determine the walls of the urban room. Architectural criteria are those that relate to the buildings themselves, or objects within the urban milieu. In an ideal world buildings would be successful urbanistically and architecturally. However, if only one were possible, the greatest effort should be applied to the former, consistently throughout the entire locale.
>
> Payton 1992, p. 238

Portland's design guidelines clearly illustrate some resolution of these architectural (townscape) and urbanistic (public realm) criteria, seeking to ensure first that a project is consistent with the city's character, and the broad urban design framework; secondly that it makes a contribution to the pedestrian environment; and finally that the detailed design is sensitive to the character of the locality and creates appropriate amenities. All these examples illustrate the important broadening of the concept of design beyond visual-architectural considerations. They emphasise the importance, stressed by Buchanan, Habe, and other design critics, of employing definitions of context that embrace patterns of use, activity and movement in an area. However, as recent American research demonstrates, such perspectives tend to be more exceptions than the general rule (Southworth 1989).

Guidelines and their elaboration: appropriate levels of prescription

How then should guidelines elaborate these basic principles? Guidelines can be divided into two kinds – those that are prescriptive in terms of prescribing the form of the development scheme; and those that are performance related, which seek to ensure that the development 'performs' in a certain way by responding to a particular issue. A good example of the two approaches is provided by the San Francisco Zoning Code, which is very prescriptive, and the San Francisco Residential Guidelines (1989) which try hard to be performance related. The Zoning Code specifies the provision of bay windows, their angles and overhangs, the maximum spacing of pedestrian entrances, the maximum proportion of garage doors vis-a-vis the facade, and detailed setback and landscaping provisions. The Residential Design Guidelines (1989) articulate a series of detailed design principles and how these might be applied, with key questions that the controller/applicant can ask themselves, and analytical devices to establish appropriate responses. There is no doubt that the application of these principles places significant constraints on the client and designer; it is obviously the intention of the guide to ensure that new development responds to the quality of townscape that it is placed in, and the less uniform the context the less binding the principles. These guidelines do not prescribe solutions, rather they encourage full consideration of the design issues at stake and demonstrate clearly to applicants what their designs are expected to achieve. Compatibility, not conformity, is the watchword.

The same is true of Seattle's multi-family housing guidelines (1993). Here, compatibility was defined more broadly to embrace aspects of landscape as well as architecture and urban form. The guidelines directly embrace the relationship to the public realm and seek to retain existing qualities of visibility, surveillance and private/public space, promoting both pedestrian safety and a rich pedestrian experience. In Seattle a concept like human scale is not just interpreted as an aspect of elevational treatment or building size. It embraces the social and functional aspects of the relationship between buildings and space, and in this sense it operates more like a performance standard against which the proposal can be evaluated. Most of the guidelines are similarly sophisticated. The Albina plan in Portland offers developers the alternatives of meeting a set of prescriptive supplemental compatibility standards or of submitting the project to a design review process in which the community will play an important role.

The level of prescription in design policies remains a fundamental issue that greatly exercises architects, designers and often clients. Most commentators favour policies and guidelines which do not prescribe solutions or particular built forms, but which set out principles or performance criteria leaving the designer to be free to use his or her creativity to resolve the design problem. They recognise that without full use of the designer's skills there will be no quality, and even those who wish to write detailed codes to control the form of development still try not to propose architectural solutions.

In the United States it is still quite common for both local government and landowners/developers to become obsessed with matters of style and design detail, rather like the community of Golden Hill in San Diego. Habe's research reveals that architectural considerations are the key focus of control in 98 per cent of all authorities surveyed (Habe 1989, p. 202), while nearly a third of all authorities specify certain architectural styles; others are preoccupied with architectural details often without reference to specific contexts. The west coast cities illustrate a much broader and less prescriptive approach in which architectural issues are integrated with urbanistic and landscape isssues to achieve a holistic approach to urban environmental quality. Careful study of the context (broadly interpreted) is required of every applicant, but design principles rather than design solutions still allow the developer and designer the opportunity to respond creatively to the carefully defined constraints.

Legal experts concerned with the potential and actual abuse of discretionary powers have particularly emphasised the need for a clear division between mandatory controls (which are limited to judicially accepted parameters like height, bulk, density, building line, setback) and design guidelines (Blaesser 1994). Portland and Seattle provide two good examples where this has been achieved successfully.

Visions and strategies – conveying the desired future form

One of the most striking features of the American experience is the way that design thinking has recently come back to permeate planning at the metropolitan, district and neighbourhood levels. Mark Hinshaw (1994, pp. 287–8) has argued that through most of the 1970s and 1980s urban design fell into severe disfavour as planners moved into policy planning. Other relevant factors are likely to have been the deep economic recessions of the 1970s and 1980s, public disenchantment with the results of urban renewal and redevelopment, while increasing competition between cities in the 1990s has tended to revive design concerns. Hinshaw notes that urban design is now making a strong comeback in the United States as community image, community design and environmental quality become more widely discussed, and as its potential to express desired qualities in built form and environmental regulation is realised. He considers urban design to be particularly relevant as growth management is developed in the United States and the reshaping of suburban development becomes an urgent necessity.

In the west coast cities, most notably perhaps in Portland and most recently in Seattle, the importance of thinking strategically in urban design terms is palpable in the attempts to convey city wide future urban form. This embraces the areas for major intensification and concentration of commercial development; the patterns of infrastructure investment especially transportation; the accessible areas for residential intensification; the townscapes to be conserved and the agricultural and natural areas to be protected. Seattle's new urban villages strategy set out in the 1994 Comprehensive Plan is a fine example of how a generalised urban design concept can express a city-wide vision of the future that is comprehensible to the public and the development industry. Developed through two years of debate with broadly-based discussion groups and community forums, the vision expresses with great simplicity what Seattleites want for their city in terms of reduced congestion and improved transit, protection of the environment and neighbourhood quality, living compactly but ensuring housing affordability, improving suburban services and ensuring economic vitality and employment growth.

One might criticise Seattle for not clearly presenting this vision with the kinds of maps, diagrams, sketches and axonometrics that make such ideas accessible to a wide constituency, but no such criticism can be made of Portland's design strategy for its downtown. Established in 1972 and refined in 1988, this design strategy is expressed largely through maps and axonometric line drawings, starting with a concept plan emphasising the areas of intensive development and infrastructure investment. Then it expresses each planning policy in a spatial way on a map – economic development, riverfront, historic preservation and, finally, urban design. The latter then attempts to integrate these different aspects into an overall design framework. The key concepts employed, and the notation for the strategy have been the subject of much thought and refinement, but they are still not entirely satisfactory in the way that they integrate aspects of built form, public space, and activities, both current and projected. They are, however, more complete and more sophisticated than other known examples.

These detailed spatial strategies are backed up by a set of action proposals, and supplemented by a set of programmes with timings and relevant implementation agencies identified. The whole provides a clear framework for private development decisions and acts as a corporate document to guide public investment and initiative. Like the Seattle plan, it sets out a vision for the future of the central city developed in conjunction with business and resident groups. What is striking about the strategy is that the 1988 version, while extended, elaborated and more detailed than its 1972 forebear, is still essentially promulgating the same vision and approach, and it is this continuity which is a testament to the robustness of the original concept and a key to the sustained positive impacts upon downtown itself.

Of course, design strategies necessarily precede the writing of design policies and guidelines, and should emerge from the whole process of visioning and goal setting citywide, at the district or neighbourhood levels. They are a key element in ensuring that urban design thought plays a much more prominent role in the coordination, integration and modification of systematic planning policies. They provide a spatial framework for developing enhancement programmes and other forms of direct public action to ensure that the various initiatives are mutually reinforcing. While, inevitably, many strategies will be developed to aid regeneration initiatives or major urban restructurings from time to time, the revision of a comprehensive or neighbourhood plan provides the ideal opportunity to inject strategic thinking into the design review process.

Presenting policies and guidelines in accessible ways

Finally, there is the question of how policy is presented to make it attractive to the designers and public and easy to absorb and use. Many plans, zoning codes and guideline documents are notable for their impenetrability, inaccessibility and lack of appeal to all but the most dedicated professional. Portland has done most work on this issue, with concise, highly illustrated and imaginatively presented plans that do not get bogged down in detail, but allow the reader to grasp the essentials and keep in mind both the 'vision' and the overall policy framework. The presentational quality of Portland's City Center Plan has already been mentioned, but this is now supplemented by a *Developer's Handbook* (1992), very much a state-of-the-art document which assembles the various plans, policies, legal requirements and review processes which control development. The presentation is outstanding, with a minimal use of text and maximum use of maps, checklists, matrices, and flow diagrams that help make the various regulatory procedures comprehensible, and which encourage an imaginative approach to project development. The same kind of innovative thinking went into the presentation of the 1993 Albina Community Plan.

These and other plans will impress any planner or designer with the sheer wealth of technical material for establishing uses and densities, massing and site coverage, building heights, landscape and parking, and even some aspects of architecture and 'pedestrian standards'. They are supplemented by a bonus system for residential, retail, theatres, rooftop gardens, day-care facilities and public art/fountains, all of which are now evident in Portland's city centre. Regrettably, the city would not have the resources to produce such a document again, and few other cities would be able to finance the production of guidance of such comprehensiveness, clarity and imagination. The document is a testament to the sophistication of the control system, and to the city planners' determination to make it comprehensible and accessible to the development industry, the community and business interests. Among the other documents that are exemplary in terms of accessibility and presentational quality are Seattle's *Design Review: Guidelines for Multi-family Residential and Commercial Buildings* with its excellent line drawings, explanations and examples of how to apply the principles, its *Preparing Your Own Design Guidelines Manual for Neighbourhoods*, and San Francisco's *Residential Design Guidelines* (1989) where line drawings and minimal, but very carefully selected, text sets out the key considerations.

IMPLEMENTATION

Much has been written about visions, goals, objectives, principles and guidelines, but very little has been said about implementation. In the opening chapter the nature of development control in west coast cities was explored in outline, and comparisons were drawn with more discretionary systems of control and systems with less overt design review. It is important to remember that design review operates selectively, not universally, as it is by definition focused upon proposals which are likely to have a major impact upon the local environment, by virtue of their size, the activities they generate or the sensitivity of the site and location. It also operates alongside zoning controls which help to fix issues such as floor space, car parking, open space, land-use mix and the like. Design review may have been designed to overcome a number of the shortcomings of zoning, but it still relies on it to provide strong controls on the amount of development. The zoning system itself has been made more flexible and more effective (and more complex) in a variety of ways. In some instances it has been closely specified and detailed to extend its dimensional controls into the details of architectural form (e.g. San Francisco in 1979), but perhaps the most important innovation from a design perspective was the introduction of bonus systems which reward the provision of amenities, facilities, affordable housing and the like. Bonus systems were invented to improve the urban design of cities and to create more public amenities in the form of plazas, pocket parks, accessible atria, retail and catering facilities, as well as more mixed uses. However, they seem to cause as many problems as they solve, as exemplified by the Washington Mutual Building in Seattle, which produced extremes of overdevelopment in the pursuit, if not the achievement, of design quality. Public disaffection with such overdevelopment was very clearly expressed in Seattle, as it was in New York (Whyte 1988). Nonetheless, bonus systems remain an important feature of downtown planning in Seattle and Portland, and an important determinant of design outcomes.

Alongside bonus systems there are sometimes linkage requirements. San Francisco's linkage requirements include contributions to affordable housing, child care, education, parks and transportation, but they also prescribe the required amounts of open space in the commercial development at a floor space ratio of 1:50. This requirement produces pedestrian amenities downtown and gives the necessary impetus to the extensive guidelines and standards for pedestrian improvement and open space provision. Mention should also be made of Transferred Development Rights to ensure landmark preservation which can be critical to quality townscape and mixed-use in a project.

Design review works with all these 'incentives' are powerful forces for over-development, as well as positive encouragements to the provision of amenities. This tension creates interesting design challenges in terms of creating pedestrian-friendly and permeable ground floor frontages, a building bulk that can be accommodated in the streetscene, and a three-dimensional form that will not detract from the city's skyline or overshadow open spaces. These incentives give planners something to offer in their design negotiations, ways of encouraging improved design and the provision of facilities and amenities, in exchange for the allowance of extra floorspace. A well-designed bonus system remains an asset to design quality, but its impacts need to be carefully and regularly reviewed. Seattle's bonus system, revised downwards in 1989, was revised again in 1994 to reduce the level of bonuses. In Portland the bonus system has been limited to a maximum of 3.1 FAR, and is mainly directed at housing provision.

Finally, as was seen in Irvine, land ownership controls through development agreements and subsequently through the imposition of CC&Rs provide the ultimate in design control. Their increasing popularity in affluent suburbia is a testament to the public desire to protect property values and to maintain the environmental quality of their neighbourhood. CC&Rs are of course relatively unproblematic in the short term, but in the longer term they pose major questions about the ability of the neighbourhood to change and respond to new patterns of life and accessibility, and thus the ability to reshape urban form at large to new social and economic realities.

A COMPREHENSIVE CO-ORDINATED EFFORT

There is a general agreement amongst cities that design review needs to be part of a 'comprehensive coordinated effort' to raise design standards and promote environmental quality. This phrase used in Supreme Court Justice Brennan's judgment in two cases in San Diego in the early 1980s (Lai 1994, pp. 39–41) emphasizes the need for local government to demonstrate a comprehensive plan and programme to provide a framework for design review.

> it is only reasonable that a prerequisite for design regulation and review be adoption of a public policy and plan that specify in advance the precise urban design objectives and the standards that the community is committed to enforce and against which the design of private development can be gauged without prejudice or arbitrariness.
>
> Lai 1988, p. 319

These notions might be extended to the observation that cities need to be advancing the cause of urban design and sustainable environmental quality in all spheres of regulation and intervention, so that higher quality design is a clear corporate objective.

One of the key lessons of west coast American experience is the need for good design to be a long-term corporate goal permeating all aspects of municipal enterprise, and capturing the support of both the community and business / development interests. The best example of this in the United States is again provided by Portland, where a coincidence of factors has placed good design high on the political agenda since 1970 – some would argue long before. These factors include a century of positive planning initiatives, a non-partisan form of government, a stable and thriving local business community, a less cyclical pattern of urban development, a tradition of public-private partnerships, a strong community/participative planning emphasis since the 1960s, the retention of strong middle-class neighbourhoods in the inner city, and a succession of design-enlightened city officials in a variety of roles including estates, planning and transport.

It is the coming together of all these factors and related initiatives that makes downtown Portland such an attractive and civilised city. While the design guidelines provide the framework for all new development, and ensure that it is visually and functionally consistent with the form of the city, it is the municipal investment in the public realm (sometimes greatly supplemented by development contributions), which sets the standards for the private sector, and raises the tone and quality of the neighbourhood. It is this that provides both the confidence for investment and the standard for design quality.

The decisions a city takes – about the architect and budget for its City Hall, about the design team for its LRT system, about the landscape architect for its parks, about whether to put a multi-storey car park underground and create public space, about the design, location and facilities of its performing arts centres, about the design and landscaping of its transit mall – are critical to set the standards of development which it expects the private sector to achieve. Portland, of course, has turned each of these instances into a design triumph and given developers a clear signal about the standards required. Elsewhere there are many examples of corporate decisions which have produced the bland, mediocre or just plain cheap and ugly solutions.

In other cities the experience is not so clearcut, and corporate commitment to design quality is more intermittent. In San Diego, for example, design was downgraded in importance for years under a previous mayor, partly as a result of the lobbying of the development industry, which undermined any interventionist role by city planners. In San Francisco, where much innovative design thinking occurred in the late 1960s, there is evidence of both the impoverishment of planning as a result of the city's budgetary crisis, and a change in its

agenda to address the city's problems of homelessness, unemployment and economic activity. Design initiatives are no longer a high priority. In Seattle the urban villages strategy in the Comprehensive Plan with its associated experiments in transit provision, rezoning and devolved neighbourhood design control, sets an ambitious corporate agenda for all manner of public investments to create a more sustainable city. Finally, it is important to record that the Irvine Company as large-scale private developers are only too aware of design quality and its relationship to economic attractiveness and long-term development profitability. Would that all developers took a similar view.

THE LESSONS FROM WEST COAST CITIES

The general lessons for design control from the experience of west coast cities of the USA lie in a set of interconnected propositions/recommendations that can provide a framework for design control in a wide range of different planning systems. These recommendations are predicated upon a set of assumptions about the importance of thinking about design as a process rather than a product, building a hierarchy of guidance that works in two ways: from goals through objectives, principles, guidelines and on to quantitative standards on the one hand and from the sub-regional to the city-wide, district and neighbourhood levels to the individual site. They are also predicated upon the assumption that those wishing to practise design control are obliged to set out clearly what broad forms and qualities of development they wish to see in different localities, and what the criteria are by which applications for building permits or planning permission will be assessed. This latter 'assumption' is, of course, firmly insisted upon by the courts and the legal profession who represent development interests. They argue that losses of development rights, or even the loss of the right to freedom of expression in architecture or landscaping or to deal with property as the individual sees fit, must be based upon clear rules that have been democratically and reasonably established, and whose application can be challenged in the event of policy contravention or inadequacies in decision-making processes.

The recommendations require:

- design policies (see below) to be a direct expression of publicly surveyed or expressed goals and objectives for the community;
- design policies to be derived from a careful analysis of character of the locality that embraces visual, social, functional and environmental aspects, all interpolated through public values;
- design policies to consist essentially of a set of design principles that are directly linked to key design objectives, and which do not unnecessarily prescribe design solutions, leaving as much scope as possible for the skilled designer;
- such principles to have more emphasis on urbanistic qualities than on visual architectural factors;
- such principles to be clearly communicated to citizens and the development industry;
- such principles to be applied in as systematic and transparent a system of review as is feasible in terms of development efficiency, with adequate public hearings and appeal procedures, including appeals against the grant of a permit on the grounds of infringement of principles or lack of due process;
- design policies to be developed at the sub-regional scale down to the level of the site scale through a variety of plans and advice documents, but particularly to be expressed in a city-wide design strategy that can be subsequently elaborated in a series of design frameworks to guide policy, direct environmental action, and initiatives in other policy areas;
- design policies to embrace clearly principles of environmental sustainability as an urgent necessity for growth management, large-scale suburban design, retrofitting suburbs and subcentres, and urban regeneration.

Portland's experience with the compact city, flexible rezoning and a commitment to affordable housing, Seattle's attempt to create a polynucleated urban structure with its villages and hub centres, and San Diego's progress with nature conservation as a guiding consideration in suburban expansion all contribute parts of the sustainability agendas for urban design. They do not constitute a coherent model for wider application.

Lessons for other countries

In the latter respect particularly, European experience probably has a great deal to teach American towns and cities in terms of transit-oriented development, sustainable densities and mixed uses, the conservation of critical environmental capital, the maintenance of biodiversity, and the minimisation of energy expenditure and pollution. However, looking at continental Europe, there are a variety of ways in which they might learn from the west coast cities. For example, Sweden seeks to inject more design advice and guidelines into its comprehensive plans to take advantage of its traditions of consensus decision-making, but also to make sure that developers are fully aware of what is expected of them when they develop in a community (Nyström 1994, pp. 122–6). In the Netherlands the existence of design control committees to provide advice on design control might similarly benefit from the experience of the west coast cities through developing appropriate review processes and guidelines to assist such committees and limiting their freedom of judgment to key design issues (Nelissen and de Vocht 1994, pp. 147–51). In France there is much debate about zoning controls and the accompanying regulations which can closely govern the building envelope and associated car parking, open space and landscaping. There is a major trend to conduct much more rigorous area appraisals, morphological and historic analyses in order to derive new rules and regulations that are more responsive to place and locality (Samuels 1993; Kropf 1996). There are also interesting developments in the formulation of design strategies that follow in the footsteps of the *grands projets*, and which attempt to provide direction for the largescale restructuring of provincial cities. While these have a stronger public sector lead than American cities the comparative development of design ideas and notations can be revealing.

Beyond European examples any zoning-based system is likely to find the American experience valuable. For example, *Urban Design in Australia* (Government of Australia 1994), the report by the Prime Minister's Urban Design Task Force, considered the whole issue of the hierarchy of policy from visions through strategies, through briefs, performance codes, prescriptive codes and guidelines, and the value of 'future character statements' (pp. 46–52). Similarly the intention was to provide constructive guidance to numerous local authorities across the country struggling to come to grips with the problems of effectively managing urban change and ensuring environmental quality. Meanwhile in cities in Asia, there are concerted attempts to inject design guidelines into zoning systems which have hitherto largely failed to deliver an acceptable level of environmental quality and activity (Cheng Wu forthcoming).

The relevance to British practice

To conclude, however, the author feels duty bound to consider how these 'best practice' ideas might be translated into the British system. Since this issue has been very much the sub-text of the research undertaken, and indeed was in many senses its *raison d'être*, it would be remiss to ignore the opportunity to comment (see Punter 1996). As has been stressed at numerous points in the foregoing, the British system, based as it is upon a discretionary system of decision-making, at both the technical advice and political decision-making stages, is the exception rather than rule in the world system, so the applicability of British experience to other countries is severely limited. Nonetheless, looking at the issue the other way round, it is clear that the American system of design review has much to teach the British system of design control.

Many of these lessons are embedded in the critiques of and responses to design control, that have already been reviewed. They embrace the need for clear principles, the need for guidelines to be based on study of the locality, the problems of high levels of subjectivity, lack of appropriate review skills and discrimination against the new, different and minority taste. The British system has attempted to respond to these issues over the last twenty years. Many local planning authorities, especially some of the London Boroughs, larger provincial cities as well as a number of historic cities, have developed a sophisticated range of policies and guidance, other advisory agencies and design initiatives to respond to these difficulties. Since 1994 Central Government has taken a much more positive attitude to design, and the personal interests of the then Secretary of State, the Rt. Hon. John Gummer, led to the sponsorship of a number

of valuable research projects and experiments which have raised the level of debate and knowledge.

This is not the point at which to explain in any detail recent developments in British practice, though it is important to know that urban design has undergone a major revival in the 1990s, just as it has in the USA, due to a complex of changes in environmental consciousness (sustainability), European competitiveness, a desire to counter standardization / globalization in urban forms and retain local distinctiveness in town and country.

Having miraculously survived the deregulatory tide of the 1980s, design control and urban design were revived by the campaigns of the Prince of Wales and the previous Secretary of State, and eagerly exploited by local planning authorities, design consultants and the Urban Design Group, and now enjoy a position of considerable prominence in the planning agenda. Whether they can retain that prominence, particularly under a new Labour Government, is a moot point, and it depends in no little measure upon the ability of the profession to articulate the kinds of visions, strategies, clear objectives and principles that we have discussed in this book, and to win public support for them. These visions embrace quite different scales of planning from the national questions of where new housing should be located (4.4 m new houses in England by 2015), to the sub-regional questions of suburban expansion and new settlements, down to the local level in terms of intensification, inner-city regeneration and revitalisation.

Unlike most other developed planning systems, Central Government maintains tight control on local initiative in British planning, especially in the area of design where, interestingly, it has maintained a critical eye on 'overprescriptive policies', rooting them out of plans and dismissing them when they have led to an appeal by a developer. Until very recently it has discouraged local authorities from preventing all but the very worst designs ('outrages'), and told them to concentrate upon basic issues of height, bulk, massing, scale, layout, access and landscape. In 1997, however, three new ideas were added to Government advice, at least partly in response to studies of US experience (Delafons 1990; Punter 1996):

■ the importance of urbanistic criteria;
■ the importance of design appraisal;
■ the public's role in guidance preparation.

In his 'Quality in Town and Country' initiative the previous Secretary of State provoked a national debate about how design quality might be promoted through the planning system. The main outcome was an urban design campaign which has led to a wide range of design brief/framework/strategy experiments in towns and cities across the country, and which has particularly encouraged others to think more ambitiously about city-wide design strategies and frameworks as additional documents to the development plan (Cowan 1997).

Whether these initiatives are going to continue depends essentially, as we have seen, on whether local government is prepared, and has the resources, to undertake a sustained effort to put design at the heart of its planning efforts, and to take it beyond into other spheres of corporate activity. That in turn depends on establishing a constituency for good design, political will and a process by which local authorities can continually involve significant numbers of people in the planning process, and win the confidence of local business and the development industry. Local government continues to struggle with minimal resources and often absurd boundaries, factors which work against the kind of initiatives that are necessary to take forward large-scale sustainable urban design initiatives. (Perhaps this is a task for the new integrated Government Regional Offices.)

The lessons from America about resources indicate that major design policy initiatives, thorough analysis, plan and guideline preparation, are very expensive activities. The breadth and depth of Portland's consultation was explained in large part by the huge proportion of the planning budget allocated to plan preparation, neighbourhood group support and the like. Seattle's recent planning efforts have been underwritten by a grant of $500,000 from the Federal Government, while San Francisco's urban design plan was paid for by the Federal Government out of the urban renewal budget. Limited planning budgets mean limited initiatives. Neighbourhood groups can be encouraged to undertake appraisals and develop and operate guidelines, but design initiatives demand money, whether they be staff resources, consultants' expertise, or budgets for environmental enhancement. It is a sign of the times that Portland can no longer afford to produce its *Developer's Handbook* or to update it. As a recent symposium on *The New Agenda for Urban Design*

has recognised, resources and funding, and Central Government support for the lead role of the local authority, lie at the heart of more innovative and more strategic design interventions in British cities (Cowan 1997, p. 23).

To return to the relevance of American models to British practice design guidelines, or design objectives and principles as we have come to perceive them, is to enter the complex debate about the nature of British development plans and development control (Booth 1996). In 1990 the Government introduced a new system of district-wide development plans which would be given greater weight than hitherto in the determination of planning applications. References to a plan-led system are somewhat misleading because the plan remains only one, albeit important, consideration in development control decisions in the British discretionary system. Comprehensive plan coverage has yet to emerge – after seven years only half the English local authorities have completed the long and cumbersome process of analysis, drafting, government review, consultation, redrafting, objection, public inquiry, (Government) inspector's report, redrafting and adoption. There are plenty of opportunities for public involvement in this process, but limited resources for focus groups, 'planning for real' and other activities that might generate a true sense of plan ownership.

The design policies in British development plans have two major difficulties from an American perspective. First of all they have to respond to all developments, not just the major schemes – 80 percent of planning applications are house extensions, minor residential developments, and small alterations and extensions to commercial premises. Second the policies are the only controls available to a planning authority, and there are no zoning maps, use or dimensional controls to reinforce the design dimension. Density and plot ratio controls have largely disappeared from plans, driven out by deregulatory tendencies to give more freedom to house builders and developers, and by dissatisfaction with their design outcomes which often frustrate sensitive design. (By 1998 density policies were being readvocated by Central Government to support more sustainable forms of development.)

Both these 'difficulties' place serious constraints on design policies and invest them with a much weightier and more comprehensive role. This must embrace aspects of density, use, open space, and car parking, etc., as well as issues of site and context, architectural character and relationships with the public realm. Perhaps inevitably it makes the policies more cautious, negative, contested and legalistic, and much more difficult to absorb as a whole.

Neither of these factors should prevent policies from being clearly related to vision statements, design objectives and plan strategy, and from being very well structured and organised with checklists of criteria and considerations against which applications can be evaluated. Nor should it prevent these policies being supplemented by valuable design guidance on common problems such as the design of residential layout, shop fronts or car parking. Some plans particularly those of the London Boroughs which have had twenty years to perfect them, are models of a well-organised and disciplined approach to policy making, but many others, prepared for the first time, are quite the opposite. Almost all the policies suffer from the problems of being inaccessible and unassimilable by the lay person; being too long, too complex, and too poorly presented, so that it becomes better not to contemplate whether anyone (including the control officer) actually reads and uses them (Punter and Carmona 1997).

One of the major questions American practice raises for British planning is whether it should persist with its attempts to offer detailed design control on the minutiae of development. Lewis Keeble once remarked that British planning 'often swallowed the camels and strained at the gnats', by which he meant that it was preoccupied with minor development issues at the expense of major, and often strategic, decisions. Could planners devise 'supplemental compatibility rules' (Portland) to allow minor development to be largely self-regulating? Could they go a stage further and abandon householder control to neighbourhood agreements? Would the more selective and strategic approach to design intervention and control practised in America be more successful and more effective? Or is design control at this level a vital part of the public expectations of planning as a neighbourhood protection service, and would the myriad of less regulated developments seriously erode the quality of the British built environment?

Thinking the unthinkable is one of the benefits of cross-comparative work, but the new system of development plans with comprehensive, district-wide coverage should not be abandoned without a proper trial and evaluation of its effectiveness. Perhaps new design documents are already emerging alongside statutory plans to achieve some of those things achieved by American guidelines-quarters studies, design frameworks, city-wide strategy documents, character assessments (for conservation areas) and landscape character assessments on the urban fringes, urban nature conservation strategies, and legibility studies. In the meantime design appraisal, thoroughgoing public consultation, clear goals, objectives and design principles, supported by a wide range of design guidance that is accessible and comprehensible to the average applicant, all consolidated into a clear policy hierarchy, will offer important advances to many local planning authorities. However, the experience of the most design-progressive American and European cities (Portland, Seattle, Barcelona, Berlin, etc.), also demonstrates that the public sector has to lead by example in investing in design quality whenever it builds facilities or infrastructure, and whenever it modifies streets and public spaces.

REFERENCES

Abbott, C., "The Portland Region: Where City and Suburbs Talk to Each Other – and Often Agree", *Housing Policy Debate*, 8(1), 1997, pp. 11–52.

Arnstein, S., "A Ladder of Citizen Participation", *American Institute of Planners Journal*, July, 1969, pp. 216–24.

Baab, D.G., "Private Design Review in Edge City" in B.C. Scheer and W. Preiser, eds, *op. cit.*, 1994, pp. 187–96.

Banerjee, T. and Southworth, M., eds, *City Sense and City Design: Writing and Projects of Kevin Lynch*, Cambridge Mass, MIT Press, 1990.

Blaesser, B.W., "The Abuse of Discretionary Power" in B.C. Scheer and W. Preiser, eds, *op. cit.*, 1994, pp. 42–55.

Booth, P., *Controlling Development, Certainty and Discretion in Europe, the USA and Hong Kong*, London, UCL Press, 1996.

City of Portland, *Adopted Albina Community Plan*, Portland, OR, Bureau of Planning, 1993.

Cowan, R., "The New Urban Design Agenda", *Urban Design Quarterly*, 63, 1997, pp. 18–37.

Delafons, J., *Aesthetic Control: A Report on Methods used in the USA to Control the Design of Buildings*, Berkeley, University of California, Institute of Urban and Regional Development, Monograph 41, 1990.

Government of Australia, *Urban Design in Australia*, Report by the Prime Minister's Urban Design Task Force, Canberra, Government of Australia, 1994.

Habe, R., "Public Design Control in American Communities", *Town Planning Review*, 60(3), 1989, pp. 195–219.

Hinshaw, M., "The New Legal Dimensions of Urban Design" in A.V. Moudon, ed., *op. cit.*, 1994, pp. 287–9.

Kropf, K., "An Alternative Approach to Zoning in France: Typology, Historical Character and Development Control", *European Planning Studies*, 4(6), 1996, pp. 717–38.

Lai, R.T-Y., *Law in Urban Design and Planning: The Invisible Web*, New York, Van Nostrand Reinhold, 1988.

Lai, R.T-Y., "Can the Process of Architecture Review Withstand Legal Scrutiny?" in B.C. Scheer and W. Preiser, eds, *op. cit.*, 1994, pp. 31–40.

Lightner, B.C. and Preiser, W., eds, *Proceedings of the International Symposium on Design Review*, Cincinnati, University of Cincinnati, 1992.

Lynch, K. and Appleyard, D. "Temporary Paradise? A Look at the Special Landscape of the San Diego Region" in T. Banerjee and M. Southworth, eds, *op. cit.*, 1974, pp. 720–63.

Moudon, A.V., ed., *Urban Design: Reshaping our City*, Seattle, University of Washington (Conference Proceedings), 1994.

Nelissen, N. and de Vocht, C.L.F.M., "Design Control in the Netherlands", *Built Environment*, 20(2), 1994, pp. 142–57.

Nyström, L., "Design Control in Planning: The Swedish Case", *Built Environment*, 20(2), 1994, pp. 113–26.

Payton, N.I., "Corrupting the Masses with Good Taste" in B.C. Lightner and W. Preiser, eds, *op. cit.*, 1992, pp. 235–42.

Punter, J.V., "Developments in the Urban Design Review: The Lessons of West Coast Cities of the United States for British Practice", *Journal of Urban Design*, 1(1), 1996, pp. 23–45.

Punter, J.V. and Carmona, M., *The Design Dimension of Local Plans: Theory, Content and Best Practice*, London, Chapman & Hall, 1997.

Richmond, H.R., "Comment . . . on the Portland Region . . .", *Housing Policy Debate*, 8(1), 1997, pp. 53–64.

Samuels, I., "The Plan d'Occupation des Sol for Asnièressur Oise: a Morphological Design Guide" in R. Hayward and S. McGlynn, eds, *Making Better Places: Urban Design Now*, Oxford, Butterworth, 1993, pp. 113–21.

Scheer, B.C. and Preiser, W., eds, *Design Review: Challenging Urban Aesthetic Control*, New York, Chapman & Hall, 1994.

Southworth, M., "Theory and Practice of Contemporary Urban Design – a Review of Urban Design Plans in the United States", *Town Planning Review*, 60(4), 1989, pp. 369–402.

Whyte, W.H., *City: Rediscovering the Center*, New York, Doubleday, 1988.

SIX

"The End(s) of Urban Design"

from *Harvard Design Magazine* (2006)

Michael Sorkin

Editors' Introduction

In "The End(s) of Urban Design," Michael Sorkin provides an unrelenting and much debated critique of the urban design field and its associated "mainstream" practice. He contends that the field has reached a "dead end" with respect to its ability to either inspire passion or answer the deep challenges of sustainability, population, equity, and diversity. Positioned somewhere in the theoretical middle between the nostalgic traditionalism of the New Urbanism and the fragmented, self-aggrandizing dystopia of Post Urbanism, urban design has failed to produce the type of city that Sorkin desires: an urbanism and architecture of creative disruption that responds to social equity challenges; the open urbanism of the rock concert; the science-fiction polemic of paper architect provocateurs, who present visions with little hope of implementation (a claim leveled by some against Sorkin himself). More to the point, he thinks contemporary urban design is too "restrictive" and "boring"; perhaps the greatest critique of all. Sorkin suggests urban design needs to confront a new reality that helps in retrofitting and reconfiguring the planet to address exponential population growth, resource limits, and environmental demands. The task of reconceptualizing the field is made more difficult by growing complexity (stakeholder, economic, environmental, legal, resource, infrastructural) and an impending sense of urgency that we may be running out of time. Sorkin's critique can be divided into three parts: 1. failure of field consolidation and collaboration in the design academies; 2. the mainstreaming of the field through regulation and backward-looking methods; and 3. the rise of neo-traditional urbanism, primarily through the Congress for the New Urbanism (CNU).

The critique begins with an examination of the birth of the urban design field at the Harvard Urban Design Conference of 1956, which set for its task the definition of the field and a strategic direction for practice. Sorkin identifies the contradictions and conflicts of this urban design task, including: opposition to City Beautiful-oriented formalism (without acknowledging a similar formalism within modernist circles); the problematic turn of the planning field to "scientific" methods, thus abandoning its physical planning and artistic origins; differential values and disrespect between the built environment professions; and importantly, the desire for any prescriptive scheme that would recommend a singular best urbanism. Not surprisingly the Harvard "urban design project" met with some degree of failure and the eventual relegation/banishment of the planning field (both voluntarily and forcefully to the policy domain of the Kennedy School). For Sorkin, the troubled birth of the field plays into his current critique.

A second phase of critique begins in 1961 with the contributions of Jane Jacobs, Lewis Mumford, Jean Gottman, and Kevin Lynch; and later environmental amendments by Rachel Carson and Ian McHarg. While much of this is lauded, Sorkin regrets the failure of Kevin Lynch to transform urban design into a collaborative multi-disciplinary practice that recognizes the city's ecological complexity – beyond the reductive nature of architecture projects. The implied result is the mainstreaming of the field by urban design advocates, the development community, powerful urban interests, business improvement districts, and the growing influence of design regulators. Sorkin's critique begins to be understood here: limits on creativity that reinforce status quo design politics are unacceptable.

The last part of the critique is leveled directly at neo-traditional design practice, the CNU, and at backward-looking design methods (typology, pattern, archetypes, precedents, etc.). Sorkin disdains both the imagery and content of postmodern traditionalism found both at Disneyland and in the greenfield new towns championed by the New Urbanists. The arguments he uses in this critique range from claims of neo-liberalism, romantic nostalgia, "family values," and "Starbucks urbanism." Few are left unscathed in these paragraphs, including: architecture sellouts, the cities of Seattle/Portland/Vancouver, quality of life advocates, suburbanites, and the Clinton-Era Hope VI program.

It's this last section of Sorkin's essay that's received the most pushback from the defenders of the New Urbanism, including Professor Emily Talen of Arizona State University, whose retort essay in the same volume, "Bad Parenting," takes on Sorkin's critiques directly. She begins with the statement: "It is time to wrestle urban design away from the bad parenting of architects." Architectural thinking, Talen suggests, is focused more on the cliché of originality than allowing consumer friendly design values (which, not surprisingly, have been vetted through market popularity of the New Urbanism). Talen may be onto something here. Although Sorkin is not uncritical of architectural collusion with neo-traditional design (even suggesting it may be a means of regaining "lost credibility and continu[ing] its own traditional role as an instrument of power"), he is not happy with it.

Missing in this essay is a fundamental critique of architectural practice and values, which might be a more powerful argument for the failure of the larger "urban design project" *in toto*. From the incessant need for design authorship, professional arrogance, the lust for innovation and "edge" (at the expense of familiarity and comfort), language obfuscation, and the belief of universal design knowledge – architecture might settle down to the agreed-upon challenges facing cities. Thankfully Sorkin gets to this at the end of his essay. To his credit, a certain degree of critical balance is provided in the writing, with various appreciations dropped at points to Jacobs, Mumford, advocacy planning, Everyday Urbanism, and even the CNU Charter itself. Much like Rem Koolhaas' writing in this volume, Michael Sorkin's writing is lively, colorful, and thought provoking. The essay remains one of the more compelling challenges to the urban design field and its component professions.

Michael Sorkin is a Professor of Architecture and Director of the Graduate Program in Urban Design at City College of New York. He is a practicing architect and founder of the Michael Sorkin Studio, and chairs the New York-based Institute for Urban Design. He is widely published and has written many pieces on New York urbanism and the design of cities in general: *Exquisite Corpse: Writing on Building* (New York: Verso, 1991); *Local Code: The Constitution of a City at 42 Degrees North Latitude* (New York: Princeton Architectural Press, 1996); *Michael Sorkin Studio: Wiggle* (New York: Springer, 1998); *Some Assembly Required* (Minneapolis: University of Minnesota Press, 2001); *Starting from Zero: Reconstructing Downtown New York* (London: Routledge, 2003); and *All Over the Map: Writing on Buildings and Cities* (New York: Verso, 2011).

Other critiques of the urban design field can be found in the following compilation texts: Alex Krieger and William S. Saunders (eds), *Urban Design* (Minneapolis: University of Minnesota Press, 2006) (in particular see the selections therein by Richard Marshall and Jonathan Barnett); Malcolm Moor and Jon Rowland (eds), *Urban Design Futures* (London: Routledge, 2008) (within this edited volume Mardie Townsend provides a gendered critique of the field and advocates for increased contributions by women; and Adriaan Geuze provides commentary on street design).

Urban design has reached a dead end. Estranged both from substantial theoretical debate and from the living reality of the exponential and transformative growth of the world's cities, it finds itself pinioned between nostalgia and inevitabilism, increasingly unable to inventively confront the morphological, functional, and human needs of cities and citizens. While the task grows in urgency and complexity, the disciplinary mainstreaming of urban design has transformed it from a potentially broad and hopeful conceptual category into an increasingly rigid, restrictive, and boring set of orthodoxies.

In many ways, the enterprise was misbegotten from the get-go. The much marked conference at Harvard's Graduate School of Design (GSD) in April 1956 both is a useful origin point for the discipline and reveals the embedded conflicts and contradictions that have brought urban design to its current state of intellectual and imaginative inertia. For José Luis Sert – Dean of the GSD, convener of the gathering, and president of CIAM (Congrès Internationaux d'Architecture Moderne) since 1947 – the conference was surely part of a last gasp at recuperating the increasingly schismatic CIAM project, which finally collapsed at the CIAM 10 meeting in Dubrovnik the following year, largely because of the growing dissent of the younger Team 10 group, one of whose mainstays, Aldo van Eyck, had groused that since CIAM 8 in 1951 the organization had been "virtually 'governed' from Harvard."

Sert's project was both a strategy for including U.S. cities in the expat ambit of the Euro-Modernist urban fantasies of the Charter of Athens and a bid to recover the lost influence of architecture – erstwhile mother of the arts – from its dissolution in an urban field dominated by planners. In his introductory remarks, Sert observed, "Our American cities, after a period of rapid growth and suburban sprawl, have come of age and acquired responsibilities that the boom towns of the past never knew." This trope of maturity, suggesting that American cities were reaching a point where their undisciplined native morphologies needed to be brought under the umbrella of some greater idea of order, has proved durable (as has the repeated appropriation of the Harvard imprimatur for the personal ideological projects of imported celebrities from Sert to Gropius to Koolhaas).

Sert identified two hostile forces at which urban design was to be directed. The first was the "superficial" City Beautiful approach, which, he argued, ignored the "roots of the problems and attempted only window-dressing effects," presumably both by failing to observe the "functional city" strictures of the Athens Charter and through its nostalgic forms of expression. The second hemming discourse was that of city planning itself, which, Sert suggested, had evolved to a point where the "scientific phase has been more emphasized than the artistic one." Urban design, by contrast, was to be "that part of city planning which deals with the physical part of the city . . . the most creative phase of city planning and that in which imagination and artistic capacities can play a more important part."

The delicacy of this criticism surely reflected the dilemma of Modernist urbanism, with its growing conflict between a proclaimed social mission and a dogmatic formalism less and less able to make the connection. Nonetheless, Sert's contention that academic planning had become preoccupied with economic, social, policy, and other "non-architectural" issues was certainly true, and fifty years of subsequent experience – marked by intramural indifference and open hostility – only reinforced the conceptual estrangement. The other pole, the assault on the Beaux Arts formalism of the City Beautiful movement – a weirdly anachronistic straw man in 1956 – was to prove more contradictory, if unexpectedly prescient. Sert, after all, was arguing that it was necessary to create a discipline that would restore an artistic sense to urban architecture, but he clearly had issues of taste with the City Beautiful, whatever his affinities might have been for its scale of operation, its protofunctionalist zoning, and its foregrounded formalism. The charge of superficiality, however, was not simply an orthodox Modernist riposte to historicist architecture; it was meant to resonate with the social problem embedded in CIAM's discourse on the sputtering effort to globalize European styles of rationality in its putative project of amelioration – and to concretely realize insights shared with planners who lacked the inclination and the means to produce architectural responses.

This constellation of arguments – that cities were important to civilization, that abandoning centers for sprawling suburbs was no answer, that design could reify, for better or worse, social arrangements, and that "correct" and deep architectural projects that commanded all the physical components of city building could solve their problems – has dominated the field of urbanism from the early nineteenth century to the present. And the critique of this discourse has also had a consistent focus: we must be wary of all totalizing schemes, especially those that propose universal formal solutions to complex social and environmental problems, that obliterate human, cultural, and natural differences, and that usurp individual rights through top-down, command application.

Many of those gathered at the conference clearly felt some disquiet not simply at the 1950s America of conspicuous consumption and sprawl but also at the America of urban renewal, then in the years of its raging glory. Strikingly, the nondesigners in attendance – including Charles Abrams, Jane Jacobs, Lewis Mumford, and Lloyd Rodwin – were those to voice the claims of the intricate social city, to decry the racist agendas of urban renewal, to argue for the importance of small-scale commerce, and to denounce the "tyranny" of large-scale, market-driven solutions. Indeed, the presence of this group – none of whom was a member of either the architect-dominated CIAM or Team 10 – represented the seeds of doom for the constricted urbanism promoted by CIAM, the inescapably contaminating *other* that continues to haunt the narrow project of urban design.

This critique of the CIAM project was scarcely news. In his indispensable volume on CIAM, Eric Mumford quotes a letter from Lewis Mumford that sets out his reasons for declining Sert's invitation in 1940 to write an introduction to what was eventually published as the remarkably flakey *Can Our Cities Survive?* in 1942. As with the demurral of the nonarchitect conferees of 1956, Mumford's disagreement was with a reading of the city that seemed to exclude politics and culture, to reduce the urban function to the schema of housing, recreation, transportation, and industry. "The organs of political and cultural association," wrote Mumford about an especially conspicuous lacuna in Sert's polemic, "are the *distinguishing* marks of the city; without them, there is only an urban mass."

In 1961 – a year after Harvard formally established its degree program in urban design – Jane Jacobs published *The Death and Life of Great American Cities*, still the definitive critique of functionalist urbanism. As the 1960s progressed, this attack on the forms and assumptions that comprised the pedigree of virtually every aspect of contemporary urbanism came hot and heavy from various quarters. The civil rights movement exposed the racist agenda behind much urban renewal and highway construction. The women's movement revealed the sexist assumptions underlying the organization of suburban and other forms of domestic space. The environmental and consumer movements showed the toxic inefficiencies of the automotive system and the selfish, world-dooming wastefulness of U.S. hyper-consumption. The counterculture protested the anemic expressive styles of Modernist architecture and the homogeneous spatial pattern of American conformity. Preservationism celebrated the value of historic urban textures, structures, and relationships. Advocacy planning and the close investigation of indigenous "self-help" solutions to building for the poor espoused user empowerment, democratic decision making, low-tech, and private expressive variety. And the assault on functionalist orthodoxy fomented by both rebellious visionaries and liberated historicists within the architectural profession made the CIAM writ seem both sinister and ridiculous.

All of this called into question the form the new urban design would take as well as what urban ideology it would defend – its response to the complex of social, political, and environmental crises everywhere exposed and exploding. New York City was to be the most visible battleground, and 1961 opened the decade with a clarifying statement of thesis and antithesis: the simultaneous publication of *Death and Life* and the passage of a revised bulk-zoning law that overturned the pioneering regulations of 1916 – with their codification of street walls and setbacks – in favor of the paradigm of the slab in the plaza, the official enshrinement, at last, of the *Ville Radieuse*. This was controversial from the outset – such planning had already dominated public housing construction and urban renewal for years – and the atmosphere in the city was roiling. The tide was turning against Robert Moses – Le Corbusier's most idiomatic legatee – who, thanks to Jacobs among others, was soon to suffer his Waterloo downtown with the defeat of a planned urban renewal massacre for Greenwich Village and of the outrageous Lower Manhattan Expressway, intended to wipe out what is now SoHo to speed traffic across the island.

SIX

This triumphant resistance – galvanized too by the contemporaneous loss of Penn Station – helped both to create an enduring culture of opposition and to revalue the fine grain of the city's historic textures and mores, asserting the rights of citizens to remain in their homes and neighborhoods. Jacobs's nuanced conflation of neighborhood form and human ecology was – and continues to be – precisely the right theoretical construct to animate the practice of urban design. Unfortunately, although her example continues to be tonic for neighborhood organization and defense, her legacy has been deracinated by its selective uptake by the far narrower, formally fixated concerns of preservationism, by an ongoing strain of behaviorist crime fighters (from Oscar Newman to the Giuliani "zero tolerance" crowd), and by the spreading mine field of institutionalized urban design, narrowly attached to its Disney version of urbanity and its fierce suppression of accident and mess, the wellsprings of public participation and the core of Jacobs's argument about urban vitality. And Jacobs's focus on a circumscribed set of U.S. environments and disdain for the idea of new towns unfortunately helped retard the investigation of how her unarguable ideas about the good city might inform other realizations.

Nineteen sixty-one was an urbanistic *annus mirabilis*, bringing publication not only of Jacobs's text but also of Jean Gottman's *Megalopolis* and Lewis Mumford's *The City in History*. This astonishing trifecta – to which I would add Rachel Carson's *Silent Spring* of 1963 and Ian McHarg's *Design with Nature* of 1969 – are the headwaters of a critique that urban design shares with virtually all thoughtful students of the city. Together they reinstated the conceptual centrality of ecology – first systematically introduced by the Chicago School decades earlier – in the production of urban models. But ecology is not a fixed construct and is comprehensible only in its specific inflections. On the one hand, an ecological understanding of urban dynamics can promote stewardship, community, and responsibility. On the other, it can support a fish-gotta-swim determinism that implies that the urban pattern is as genetic as male pattern baldness and that urban design is equivalent to intelligent design, revealing only the inevitable.

In this debate, Mumford retains special importance (although his reputation is often submerged as the result of his boorish and myopic treatment of Jacobs). Mumford was an unparalleled reader of the forms and meanings of the historic city, direct heir of the regionalist ecology descending from Patrick Geddes, and an unabashed fan of the Garden City so reviled by Jacobs: the omega point of Mumford's urban teleology was the movement for new towns, incarnate in a history spanning Letchworth, Radburn, and Vallingby. Mumford was utopian in the received Modernist sense, a believer both in the therapeutic value of thoughtful order and in the importance of formal principles, qualities he actually shared with Jacobs. But Mumford also understood the depth of his oppositional role and saw with clarity the way that the "pentagon of power" inscribed itself in the tissue of the city. For Mumford, the city was infused with the political, and he understood its future as a field of struggle for an equitable and just society. Alas, this principled insight only seemed to reinforce his unyielding formal partisanship.

Within the academy, skepticism about urban design's narrowness as a discipline paralleled its consolidation and growth. In 1966, Kevin Lynch published the first of an increasingly critical series of articles in which he sought to distinguish urban design from a more expansive idea of "city design." Lynch's critique was – and is – fundamental. Objecting to urban design's fixation on essentially architectural projects and its reliance on a limited set of formal typologies, Lynch argued throughout his work for an urban discipline more attuned to the city's complex ecologies, its contending interests and actors, its elusive and layered sites, and for complex readings, unavailable within the discipline of architecture, that would allow the city to achieve its primary social objective as the setting for variegated and often unpredictable human activities, behaviors that had to be understood from the mingled perspectives of many individuals, not simply from the enduring Modernist search for a universal subjectivity, however "egalitarian."

But Lynch's was clearly a minority view, and urban design as practice rapidly developed along the lines he feared. In 1966 – the year of Lynch's initial sally (and of Robert Venturi's *Complexity and Contradiction in Architecture*) – John Lindsay set up his Mayor's Task Force on Urban Design, which soon morphed into the Urban Design Group (UDG), inserted as a special, semiautonomous branch within the City Planning Department and intended to make an end run around its lumbering bureaucracy. The Planning Department was itself then in the throes of producing a new master plan for the city, the last such to be attempted. Despite the inherent dangers of giant, single-sourced plans, this ongoing willed incapacity to think comprehensively now haunts the city with a counterproductive imaginative boundary, a suspicion of big plans that refuses, however provisionally, to sum up its parts.

The department's plan – ambitious, outdated, and strangely reticent about formal specifics – was ignominiously turned down by the City Council in 1969, victim both of its own unpersuasive vision and of a then-boiling suspicion of master planning in general. Urban design represented a clear alternative to the overweening command style of such big, infrastructure-fixated, one-size-fits-all, urban renewal-tainted plans. Reflecting the reborn interest in neighborhood character and the relevance of historic urban forms, the UDG's main m.o. [*modus operandi*] was to designate special districts, each subject to customized regulatory controls intended to preserve and enhance (and sometimes invent) their singular character. This districting – and its zoning and coding strategies – was later extended politically by the devolution of a degree of planning authority to local community boards, part of a larger wave of administrative decentralization that included, catastrophically, the school system. The move to neighborhood planning, however, has proved a generally positive development, if seriously undercut in practice by the restricted budgets and limited statutory authority of the boards themselves and by a continuing failure to balance local initiative with a more comprehensive vision.

The work of the UDG was very much the product of its time, weighted toward the reestablishment of traditional streetscapes threatened by Modernist zoning formulations and visual sensibilities; the group's recommendations were an amalgam of prescribed setbacks, materials, arcades, signage, view corridors, and other formal devices for consolidating visual character. These prescriptions defined, at a stroke, the formal repertoire of American urban design and fixed its more limited social agenda on supporting the centrality of the street (whose life was the focus of Jacobs's urbanism) and efforts to reinforce the "character" of local identities in areas like the Theater District, the Financial District, and

Lincoln Center, where it sought to create hospitable, reinforcing environments for already concentrated but weakened economic uses.

The operational conundrum in the approach lay in finding the means for finessing and financing the formal improvements intended to engender the turnaround, and the search for implementation strategies produced two problematic offspring that remain central to the city's planning efforts: the bonus and the Business Improvement District (BID). The importance of these instruments has only grown as government has become increasingly enthralled by the model of the "public-private partnership," the ongoing re-description of the public interest as the facilitation of private economic activity-government intervention to prime the pump of trickle-down. The bonus system, which exchanges some specified form of urban good behavior for additional bulk or for direct subsidy in the form of tax relief or low-rate financing, is founded on a fundamental contradiction: one public benefit must be surrendered to obtain another. In the case of increased bulk, access to light and air and limitations of scale are traded for an "amenity," for a plaza, an arcade, or simply a shift in location to some putatively underdeveloped area. With financial subsidy, the city sacrifices its own income stream – with whatever consequences for the hiring of teachers or police – in favor of the allegedly greater good of business "retention" or a projected rise in property "values" and downstream taxation. Of course, both systems are rife with opportunities for blackmail and corruption, and these continue to be exploited fulsomely.

While BIDs do not involve the same levels of public subsidy, they collude in creating a culture of exception in which the benefits of urban design (and maintenance) are directed to commercially driven players operating outside normal public frameworks, disproportionately benefiting the rich neighborhoods able to pony up for the improvements. This nexus of special districts and overlays, bulk bonuses, tax subsidies, BIDs, preservation, and gentrification has now coalesced to form the primary apparatus for planning in New York and most other cities in the United States. This outcome is yet another triumph for neoliberal economics, the now virtually unquestioned idea that the role of government is to assure prosperity at the top, an idea that has produced both the most obscene national income gap in history as well as the unabated froth of development that is rapidly turning Manhattan – where the average apartment price now exceeds one million dollars – into the world's largest gated community.

Urban design has acted as enabler in this precisely because of its ostensible divorce from the social engineering of planning, nominally expressed in its circumspect scales of intervention and resensitized approach to the physical aspects of urbanism. In New York – a city where our municipal leadership evaluates all development by the single metric of real estate prices – the Planning Department has largely refashioned itself as the Bureau of Urban Design, executor of policies emanating from the Deputy Mayor for Economic Development, the city's actual director of planning, the man who would be Moses. While attention to the quality and texture of the city's architecture and spaces – both new and historic – is of vital importance, the role of design as the expression of privilege has never been clearer. Whether in the wave of celebrity architects designing condos for the superrich, the preservation of historic buildings and districts at the ultimate expense of their inhabitants, the sacrifice of industrial space in favor of more remunerative residential developments, or the everyday cruelties of the exodus driven by the exponential rise in real estate prices, the city seems to everywhere sacrifice its rich ecology of social possibilities for simply looking good.

The most important physical legacy of the UDG approach is the 1979 plan for Battery Park City by Alexander Cooper (a former member of the UDG) and Stanton Eckstut, which – because of its successful execution and succinct embodiment of the new traditionalist lexicon of urban design – has achieved a conceptual potency unmatched since the *Plan Voisin.* This project, created ex nihilo on a spectacular landfill site, was controlled by a specially created state authority with a raft of special condemnation, bonding, and other powers, including relief from virtually all local codes and reviews (another Moses legacy and an ever-increasing element in the collusive style of large-scale development in the city), and attempted to channel the spirit and character of the historic city in a completely invented environment. It was surely also heavily influenced by the seminal *Collage City* of Colin Rowe and Fred Koetter, published in 1978, an argument

for looking at the city as a series of interacting fragments, a promising strategy dissipated – like so much subsequent urban design – by inattention to the contemporary capacity for assuming meanings derived from the formal arrangements of imperial or seventeenth-century Rome. Battery Park City, by translating the UDG's historicist ethos of urban design as a contextual operator into an agent for something entirely new and literally disengaged from the existing city, was the crucial bridge to the emerging New Urbanism and its universalizing polemics of "tradition."

Like many subsequent New Urbanist formulations – not to mention the original cities from which its forms were derived – Battery Park City has its virtues. Its scale is reasonable, and its look conventionally orderly. Its waterfront promenade is comfortably dimensioned, beautifully maintained, and blessed with one of the most spectacular prospects on the planet. Vehicular traffic is a negligible obstacle to circulation on foot (although there is almost no life on the street to get in its way). The deficit is the unrelieved dullness of its bone-dry architecture, the homogeneity of its population and use, the repression of alternatives under the banner of urban correctness, the weird isolation, the sense of generic simulacrum, and the political failure to leverage its economic success to help citizens whose incomes are inadequate to live there.

By the time of the construction of Battery Park City, the assault on Modernist urbanism and the spirited defense of the fabric and culture of the historic city had long been paralleled by a withering interrogation of life in the suburbs. These were not simply the most rapidly growing component of the metropolis but were – largely under the analytical radar – increasingly taking over center-city roles en route to becoming the dominating edge city of today. The difficult reciprocities of city and suburb were longstanding as both facts and tropes. Indeed, the city itself was first recognized as a "problem" at the moment its boundaries exploded to produce the idea of the suburban during its industrialization-driven expansion in the nineteenth century. At that moment were realized the political, economic, social, technical, and imaginative forces that created the repertoire of forms of the modern city – the factory zone, the slum, and the suburb – as well as the array of formal antidotes that constitute the lineage of urban design. More, the invention of the city as the primal scene of class struggle, of self-invention, of a great efflorescence of new ways of pleasure and deviance, of habit and ritual, and of possibility and foreclosure, had immediate and deep implications for the creation and valuation of fresh form.

The mainstreaming of urban design in the 1960s and 1970s was, in part, a product of the diminished appeal of the suburbs, contingent on a parallel revaluing of the city as the site of desirable middle-class lifestyles, the happinesses that a previous generation had understood itself obliged to flee the city to achieve. The widespread critical revisiting of suburbia – which was showing strong signs of dysfunction and fatigue – gave urban design's project both relevance and register by establishing it as an instrument of a broader critique of the sprawling spatiality of the postwar city. Like the threat to city life posed by the obliteration of neighborhood character, the attack on suburbanism was both formal and social. Strip development was reviled for its chaotic visuality and its licentious consumption of the natural environment. Highways were defended from obtrusive billboards and honky-tonk businesses via "beautification." Suburban living was criticized for its alienating, "conformist" lifestyles. Racist and sexist underpinnings were assailed. Tract houses were denigrated for being made out of ticky-tacky and looking all just the same. Cars were unsafe at any speed. Even the nuclear family was becoming fissile, chafing at life in its split-level castle.

However, like Modernist urbanism, suburbia was not simply the automatic outcome of market forces and its hidden persuaders but had a strong utopian tinge. Heavily ideological realizations of the American dream of freestanding property, new frontiers, and unlimited consumption, the suburbs felt, to millions, like manifest destiny. However, as they leapfrogged one another farther and farther into the "virgin" landscape, their destruction of the very qualities that had defined them became an increasingly untenable contradiction. The critique of the one-dimensionality of suburban sprawl that arose as a result was both social and environmental, and it reciprocated on both levels with the development of more deeply ecological views of city and region. This was advanced by such observers of the meta-scale as Jean Gottman, by a series of mordant observers – from Peter Blake

to Pete Seeger – of suburban forms, and by social commentators – like Vance Packard, Herbert Gans, and Betty Friedan – who analyzed their patterns of consumption, conformity, and exclusion. And the boomer generation – invigorated by rebellion and fresh from its intensive introduction to the newly accessible cities of Europe – confronted its own oedipal crisis and increasingly drew the conclusion that it could never go home again to the pat certainties of its parents' uptight lifestyles. As it had for centuries, the city represented an alternative.

But comfort and consumption had been too thoroughly embedded, and the vision of the city that emerged as the model for urban design was highly suburbanized – suburban conformities reformatted for urban densities and habits. The incrementalism of urban design, although conceptually indebted to the generation of activists that had risen in defense of the fragile balance of neighborhood ecologies, had none of their rebellious edge: urban design became urban renewal with a human face. While it took a little longer for the "this will kill that" antinomies of suburb and city to become theoretically reconsolidated in the neither here nor there formats of New Urbanism, a consistent disciplinary discourse was quickly consolidated under the rubric of "traditional urbanism." This formulation provided – at least initially – what seemed a very big tent, capacious enough to shelter neighborhood and preservation activists, Modernists looking for a reinvigorated schema for total design, defenders of the natural environment, critics of suburban profligacy, and cultural warriors in pursuit of transformative lifestyles of various stripes.

Collisions were inevitable, and urban design's prejudice for the formulaic, for a reductive "as of right" approach to planning based on the translation of general principles (formal variety, mixed use, etc.) into legal constraints, was necessarily imperfect. And each of the positions that urban design sought to amalgamate into its increasingly homogeneous practice came with its own evolving history and arguments about the bases of correct urban form, replete with potential incompatibilities and often driven – like the city itself – by a refusal to be fixed. Questions of the relationship of city and country, of the rights of citizens to space and access, of the limits on their power to transform their environments, of zoning and mix, of the role of the street, of the meaning of density, of the appropriateness of various architectures, of the nature of neighborhoods, of the relations of cities and health, and of the epistemological and practical limits of the very knowability of the city, have formed the matrix of urban theory from its origins, and its constant evolution is not easily repressed.

This continuous remodeling of paradigms for the form and elements of the modern good city is also – and necessarily – an architectural enterprise. Models of the city – from those of Pierre L'Enfant to those of Joseph Fourier, Ebenezer Howard, Arturo Soria y Mata, Le Corbusier, Victor Gruen, and Paolo Soleri – remain indispensable conceptual drivers for urban progress, for making urban life better by refreshing choice and by holding up one pole of the indispensable dialectic of permanence and provisionality that describes the city. Unfortunately, such concrete visions have become thoroughly suspect – victims of the failed experiences of Modernist urbanism – tarred with the brush of authoritarian totalization, by the willful insistence that every utopia is a dystopia, that certain scales of imagining can only come to bad ends. The theoretical underpinnings of urban design seek to deflect – and correct – this problem by claiming to find principles situationally, via the sympathetic understanding and extension of styles and habits already indigenous to the sites of its operations. The imputation is not simply that urban design is respectful in some general sense but that its formal preferences – because they are "traditional" – embody consent.

In staking this claim, urban design operates as a kind of prospective preservationism. As a result, it becomes radically anticontextual by assuming that the meaning of space, once produced, is fixed, that an arcade is an arcade is an arcade is an arcade. By extension, it remains an item of faith for urban design that – however far removed from its originating contexts of meaning – an architectural object retains the power to re-create the values and relationships that first gave it form. This is a remarkably utopian position in the very worst way. Urban design's project to reconfigure America's towns and cities along largely imaginary eighteenth- and nineteenth-century lines, enabled and buttressed by rigorously restrictive codes, is chilling not simply for its blinkered and fantasmatic sense of history but

also for its reductive and oppressive universalism and staggering degree of constraint.

But what exactly – beyond its stylistic peccadilloes – does urban design presume to preserve, and how does it know it when it sees it? In the already existing city, the recognition of living social systems and accumulated compacts about the value of place are necessary points of departure for any intervention. The formal medium for generalizing from such situations is the identification and analysis of pattern, the translation of some specific observation about the experience of people in space into a broader assertion about the desirable. This mode of inquiry – whether practiced by Aristotle, Baudelaire, Walter Benjamin, William H. Whyte, or Christopher Alexander – mediates between the limits and capacities of the body, a rich sense of individual psychology, and a set of assumptions about the social and cultural relations immanent to a specific place and time. Each of these is susceptible to great variation, and as a result, any pattern produced by their conjunction will inevitably shift, however slowly.

Architecture can respond to the dynamism of social patterns by closely accommodating well-observed particulars, by creating spaces of usefully loose fit, or by proposing arrangements that attempt to conduce or facilitate specific behaviors outside the conventions of the present and familiar. The last of these possibilities – which can include both amusement parks and prison camps – always understands architecture as an agent of transformation because, by being inventive, it brings something experientially new to a situation. And because it changes the situation, it begs the question of the terms of participation, of the means by which a user or inhabitant is persuaded to take part, of the difference between coercion and consent. Here is the central dilemma for utopia, for master planning, for any architecture that proposes to make things better: what exactly is meant by "better"? and better for *whom?*

The language of pattern seeks to deal with this problem either by the quasi-statistical suggestion that the durability, "timelessness," and cross-cultural reproduction of certain forms are markers of agreement or by more direct psychological or ethnographic observations and measurements of contentment and utility. Urban design borrows the aura of such techniques of corroboration to validate the grafting of a particular system of taste onto a limited set of organizational ideas. This entails a giant – and absurd – conceptual leap. As framed by the Congress for the New Urbanism (CNU) – the Opus Dei of urban design – pattern is not understood in the manner of Levi Strauss's *Tristes Tropiques* but rather that of *The American Builder's Companion*. These patterns do not emerge from the patient parsing of the networks of social behavior in some specific community but from pure millenarianism – from the idea of the utter singularity of the "truth" – that produces tools not for analyzing patterns but for imposing them. The validity of these patterns – promulgated in insane specificity – is established tautologically. Because obedience produces a *distinct* uniformity, one to which particular values have already been imputed, urban design argues that its codes are merely heuristic devices for recovering traditional values and meanings *already* encoded in the heart of every real American, faith-based design.

Urban design has successfully dominated physical planning both because of this resonant fundamentalism and because it has, from its inception, been able to appropriate a number of well-established reconfigurings of "traditional" architecture. Urban design's remarkable timing allowed it both to claim to embody the meanings of the historic city and to fit into a space already replete with a range of tractable and demanding prototypes – or patterns – produced by the market without direct benefit of academic theory and prejudice. The current urban design default is, for the most part, a recombinant form of various developer-driven formats for sub-urban building that themselves became prominent in the 1960s and 1970s. The extensive emergence of greenfield "town house" developments (often as a means of realizing the appreciated value of inner-ring suburban land), the transformation of shopping centers to "street"-based malls, the proliferation of "autonomous" gated communities, the rehabilitation of exclusionary zoning to restore traditional styles of segregation, and the uninterrupted semiotic refinement of the appliquéd historicity of virtually all the architecture involved, had, by the 1960s, already become ubiquitous. And behind it all loomed the synthesizing figure of America's preeminent twentieth-century utopia: Disneyland. The theme

park is the critical and synthetic pivot on which both the ideological and formal character of urban design continues to turn.

Disneyland – fascinating not just to a broad public but also to a gamut of professional observers including Reyner Banham, Charles Moore, Louis Marin (who memorably described it in a 1990 book as a "degenerate" utopia), and even Kevin Lynch – is urban design's archetype, sharing its successes and failures and grounded in a common methodology of paring experience to its outline. Disneyland favors pedestrianism and "public" transport. It is physically delimited. It is designed to the last detail. It is segmented into "neighborhoods" of evocative historical character. It is scrupulously maintained. Its pleasures are all G-rated. It is safe. Grounded in the sanctification of an imaginary idea of the historic American town, each park enrolls its visitors in its animating fantasy with an initiating stroll down a Hollywoodized "Main Street" that acculturates its diversity of guests to a globally uniform architectural inflection of good city form.

But what is most relevant about Disneyland – like all simulacra – is the power of its displacement. Disneyland is a concentration camp for pleasure, the project of an ideologue of great power and imagination, the entertainment industry's version of Robert Moses. Disneyland is not a city, but it selectively extracts many of the media of urbanity to create a city-like construct that radically circumscribes choice, that heavily polices behavior, that commercializes every aspect of participation, that understands subjectivity entirely in terms of consumption and spectatorship, and that sees architecture and space as a territory of fixed and inflexible meanings. Like shopping malls or New Urbanist town centers, Disneyland provides evanescent moments of street-style sociability within a larger system entirely dependent on cars. And, of course, no one lives in Disneyland, and employment there is limited to "cast members" working to produce the scene of someone else's enjoyment. Girded against all accident, Disneyland produces no new experiences, only the opportunity for the compulsive repetition in its rigorously programmed repertoire of magic moments.

America's greatest export is entertainment: hedonism has become our national project. But our cultural mullahs – from Michael Eisner to Pat

SIX

Robertson – want to tell people exactly how to have fun, to force our product on them, just as we force democracy on Iraq or "Love Boat" reruns on Indonesia. Urban design, with its single, inflexible formula, is also produced for customers – or worshippers rather than citizens. This fetish for the correct betrays to the core the urbanity evoked by Jane Jacobs, the vital links between sociability, self-determination, and pleasure. The 1960s – which Jacobs did so much to help found – were constantly engaged in sorting through the meanings and relationships of pleasure and justice. Crystallizing slogans – like "Tune In, Turn On, Drop Out" and "Beneath the Pavement, the Beach" – were post-Freudian assaults on an enduringly Puritan style of repression and saw free expression and the pursuit of pleasure as instruments of cooperation and equity, a way of making a connection between the personal and the political, insubordinate fun. One of the singularities of postwar American culture was surely the degree to which the terms and proprietorship of enjoyment became both central to the character of the national economy and the object of struggle and critique. The movements for racial, gender, and sexual equality, the spread of environmentalism, the revaluing of urban life, and the assault on colonialism and its wars were all filtered through the perquisites of prosperity, which insistently argued that the fight was never simply for bread but always also for roses.

Urban design, from its origins, was a way into the system, a means for architecture to recover its lost credibility and continue its own traditional role as an instrument of power. The perfect storm of urban design's invention was a miraculous convergence of the overthrow of the old Modernist formal and social model, a broad reappreciation of urban life, a freshly legitimated historicism with a new sophistication in the formal reading of the structure and conventions of urban environments, an expanded system of consumption that particularly glamorized European lifestyles (we were suddenly eating yogurt), and the scary emptiness of available late-Modern alternatives like the megastructure. Its success was also immeasurably aided by the defection of many architects from the field, a desertion that continues to mark a political split in the profession, reinforced by the inexorable drift to the right of the CNU and its fellow travelers.

Indeed, the social and political priorities of a large cadre of baby boomer architectural graduates led, for quite a few, to a suspicion of architecture itself, which – seen as an inevitable coalescence of power and established regimes of authority – became an impossible instrument. The focus on "alternative" architectures, on small-scale, self-help solutions, and on repair rather than reconstruction – all foregrounded notions of service and consent, disdaining grand visions of any sort as incapable of embodying the shifting, diverse, and plural character of a democratic polity. Such arguments were only reinforced as the decade wore on by the easy connection between DDT and urban renewal at home with Agent Orange and carpet bombing in Vietnam. The consequences were both inspiring and crippling, discouraging a large cohort of fresh-minted architects and planners from establishing themselves in mainstream practice either permanently or temporarily, turning many to communalism, self-reliance, lifestyle experiment, and various modes of righteous exile. Seeking gentler solutions and warmed by a soft, Thoreauvian glow, youth culture created a profusion of alternative communities in the form of urban communes squatting abandoned tenements, rural settlements under karmic domes, or nomadic enclaves cruising in psychedelic school buses, even if such places were more envied than engaged by the majority, who, for their part, pursued altered consciousness through other means.

Because of their anti-authoritarian foundation, these styles of settlement never received – never could receive – a formal manifesto that strategically summed them up, despite a profuse, if diffuse, literature ranging from *The Whole Earth Catalog* to *Eros and Civilization* to *Ecotopia*. Nevertheless, this collection of forms and actions was clearly a cogent urbanism, one that continues to inform contemporary debates, if only because the boomers who were their authors are now in their years of peak social authority, dragging their lingering consciences behind them. Without doubt, the environmental ethos of a light lie on the land and of self-sufficient styles of consumption, the fascinations of the nomad as an urban subject, the ideal of a democratic architecture expressively yoked to new and co-operative lifestyles, the antipathy to big plans, the prejudice for the participatory, and the fetishization of the natural are the direct progenitors of today's green architecture and urbanism.

The debilitating paradox of these positions lay in seeing the meaning of assembly – and citizenship – as increasingly displaced from fixed sites and patterns. The ideas of the "instant" city and global village were seductive constructs for a generation for which the authority of permanence seemed both suspect and dangerous. The ephemeral utopia of the rock festival was, perhaps, the most coherent expression of an urbanism that sought to operate as a perfect outlaw and suggested an architecture of pure and invisible distribution, a stingless infrastructural rhizome that established a planetary operational parity, a ubiquitous set of potentials accessible anywhere as a successor to the city. The idea of the oak tree with an electrical outlet and a world grid of caravan hookups was the ultimate fantasy of a post-consumption nomadology, resistant to The Man's styles of order, a "place" in which possessions were to be minimal, nature at once wired and undisturbed, and money no longer an issue. The vision was warm, silly, and prescient, virtuality before the fact. Like the rock festival, this was a clear proposition for organizing a world in which location has been radically destabilized, and it anticipated one of the great drivers of urban morphology today with its Web-enabled anything-anywhere orders.

One group – Archigram – was particularly successful in formalizing all of this, tapping, with insight and wit, into the tensions between the contesting technological and Arcadian visions of the era. Operating on the level of pure but architecturally precise polemic, Archigram was a master of *détournement*, of playing with goaded migrations of meaning and at embedding critique in the carnivalesque. From their initial fascinations with the high-tech transformation of nineteenth-century mechanics into the "degenerate" utopias of the megastructuralists, Metabolists, and other megalomaniac schemers, they moved quickly to describe a range of nomadic structures: moving cities, aerial circuses floating from place to place by balloon, self-sufficient wanderers wearing their collapsible "Suitaloons." They proposed the infiltration of small towns and suburbs by a variety of subversive pleasure-parasites and sought, during the productively unsettled post-McLuhan, pre-Internet interregnum, to reconfigure the landscape as a new kind of commons, a global fun fair. Operating within the bounds of the physically possible and producing

a stream of intoxicating forms, their project was at once hugely influential formally and almost completely ineffectual politically. Not exactly an unusual fate for countercultural product.

However, the most important attempt to create an alternative style of formal urban practice at the point of emergence of urban design was advocacy planning, which – given the nature of the times – arose as explicitly oppositional, dedicated to stopping community destruction by highways, urban renewal, and gentrification. In its specifically physical operations, the focus was on restoration and self-defense, on the delivery of municipal services to disadvantaged communities, on the repair of the frayed fabric of poor neighborhoods, on tenement renovations, community gardens, and playgrounds in abandoned lots. The redistributive logic of advocacy work looked on architecture and planning with suspicion as an instrument of destruction or privilege. The problem – an analysis descending from Engels – was not a lack of architecture, but the fact that too much of it was in the wrong hands.

While this was both a logical and a consistent position, its morphological modesty was a hard sell for anyone eager to build and offered no clear proposition for greenfield sites, certainly no strong insights for transforming the suburbs, which were also viewed with suspicion as enemies of diversity and as economic threats, sucking the inner city dry of resources. Advocacy's visual culture, such as it was, was very much fixed on community expression, on self-built parks, inner-city murals, and the improvisational workings of the favela, its own over-romanced utopia. These preferences were infused by an old dream of a political aesthetic, but advocacy's taste was reductive, looking for the artistic reproduction of social content only when it was presumed direct, when it was authored (not simply authorized) by "the people." This position, which looks to produce design as midwifery, continues to enjoy substantial currency in a range of community-based design practices and has found coherent ideological backing both from the school of "Everyday Urbanism" as well as from the progressive wing of planners and geographers – for whom equity and social justice are the gold standard – which is still the most lucid voice on urban issues in the academy.

These multiple strains remain the dialectical substrate of urban design today. A matrix of traditionalism, environmentalism, Modernism, and self-help configures the practices – and ideological accountancy – for virtually all contemporary design that purports to build the city. Although every current tendency embodies some degree of conceptual hybridity, the basic terms of the argument about urbanism have remained remarkably consistent from the nineteenth century to the present. What has shifted – and continues to shift – are the political and ideological valences associated not simply with each formation but also their rapid pace of conceptual and ideological reconfiguration, and the promiscuity of meaning and representation that attach and slip away from each. These migrations of meaning are crucial: the way we make cities marks our politics and possibilities, and the struggle over their form is, as it has ever been, deeply enmeshed with the future of our polity.

Today, U.S.-style urban design – global exemplar from Ho Chi Minh City to Dubai – has arrived at a set of concerns and strategies, as well as a formal repertoire, that is as limited as those of CIAM, though with an ultimately even more chilling social message. The current default is essentially a splicing of Modernist universalist dogmatism, City Beautiful taste, and the cultural presumptions of neoliberalism, producing its urbanist double spawn: gentrification and the neotraditional suburb. Not since the Modernism of the 1920s has a visual system so successfully (and spuriously) identified itself with a particular set of social values: the elision of an architecture of stripped traditionalism (a pediment on every Shell station and 7-Eleven) with the imagined happinesses of a bygone golden age has been breathtaking.

It was surely no coincidence that this specificity grew out of a more general turn to the right, the new Republican majority that took to historicist expression as a means of instant authentication and prestige, all with a redemptive gloss derived from a thin idea of the social authority of convention that culminated in the mendacity, indifference, and sumptuary Hollywood taste of Reaganism. New Urbanism was the perfect theory of settlement for the Age of Reagan, the urbanistic embodiment of "family values," forcefully enshrined at the very moment that American culture was moving in the direction of transformative diversity. The New Urbanists' success is surely the result of making common cause with a right-tinged social theory,

the Puritan-inspired vision of a "shining city on a hill" that ascendant neocon intellectuals and the burgeoning religious Right thought to so embody the values of a "traditional" America, and the New Urbanist idea of a single set of correct urban principles is surely balm to those upset with the dissipation of real Americanism under the assault of an excess of difference, the threatening pluralism of an America no longer dominated by WASP culture, a place of too many languages, too many suspect lifestyles, too much uncontrollable choice. As Paul Weyrich, founding president of the reactionary Heritage Foundation, recently remarked, "New Urbanism needs to be part of the next conservatism."

Of course, this oversimplifies both origins and outcomes. The broad acquiescence to the neo-traditional approach that characterizes American urban design is also the result of its proclaimed embodiment – sometimes tenuous and occlusive, sometimes genuine and persuasive – of many of the elements of more progressive approaches to the environment that provided much of the amniotic fluid for its gestation. Indeed, the powerful attraction of neotraditional urbanism must be seen not only in its neoliberal, end-of-history arguments, in which historicism stands in for capitalism and "Modernism" for the various forms of vanquished collectivism, but also in its claims on the inescapably relevant politics and practices of environmentalism, a genuine universalism with a very broad consensus. Self-proclaimed as the nemeses of sprawl, as friends to the idea of neighborhood, as advocates for public transportation, and as priests of participation, the New Urbanism and much of the current urban design default would seem to be a logical outgrowth of many of the progressive tendencies so lively at their origins. A number of the tendency's nominal proponents – Peter Calthorpe, Doug Kelbaugh, Jonathan Barnett (a UDG stalwart), and others – tilt to these positions as priorities, designing with greater tolerance, modesty, and depth. More, the CNU cannot be faulted for seeking solutions consonant with the scale of the problem: the idea of the creation of new towns and cities is crucial not simply to the control of sprawl but also to housing the exponential growth of the planet, urbanizing at the rate of a million people a week.

In fact, nothing in the charter of the Congress for New Urbanism, with its spirited defense of both urban and natural environments and its call for reinvigorating both local and regional perspectives, is likely to be opposed by any sensible urbanist. The controversy, rather, is over the dreary and uniform translation of principles to practice, the weirdly religious insistence on "traditional" architectural form, the dubious bedfellows, and, most especially, the weakness of most New Urbanist product, almost invariably car-focused, class-uniform, exclusively residential, and without environmental innovation. At this point the clarion principles seem so much cover, much as the CNU's vaunted instrument of community participation – the charrette (one of advocacy planning's more successful tools) – seems most often used not to produce new ideas or to give citizens entrée to the process of design, but to manufacture consent for New Urbanist predilections. No matter what the input, the outcome always seems the same.

Such remorseless formal orthodoxy is what killed Modernism, and it is not exactly surprising that the New Urbanist charter and congress are structural vamps of the Charter of Athens and its organizational vanguard, CIAM, nor that New Urbanism relies on charismatic, evangelizing leadership, the star power that is such a uniform object of CNU derision. This is the very definition of old-fashioned utopianism. The net effect is a vision that reproduces the self-certain, universalizing mood of CIAM both formally and ideologically, but that offers a new, if equally restricted, lexicon of formal behaviors. The ideological convergence of Modernist and "New" Urbanism is striking. Both are invested in an idea of a universal, "correct" architecture. Both are hostile to anomaly and deviance. Both have an extremely constrained relationship to human subjectivity and little patience for the exercise of difference. Both claim to have solutions for the urban crisis, which is identified largely with formal issues. Both purport to have an agenda that embraces an idea of social justice, but neither has a theory adequate to the issues involved. Finally, both are persuaded that architecture can independently leverage social transformation, become the conduit for good behavior, the factory grinding out happy workers or consumers.

It is not surprising that the two most celebrated formal accomplishments of the New Urbanism – Seaside and Celebration – are both figuratively and literally Disneyesque. That is, both are programmed and designed to produce a specific visual character

held to conduce a fixed set of urban pleasures. Such pleasures are encoded in stylistic expression and heavily protected against deviancy, in a privileged typology in which the single-family house is the invariable alpha form, in highly static and ritualized physical infrastructures of sociability – the porch, the main street, the band shell – in compaction and the careful disposition of cars, and in an idea of sociability rooted in homogeneity and discipline. These are model environments for a leisured class, and they do produce both a dull serenity and a set of spaces for "public" activity with clear advantages over the thoughtlessly cul-de-saced McMansions whose pattern they interrupt.

Seaside is the Battery Park City of the New Urbanism, its first comprehensive codification and expression, and a clear expression of its possibilities and limits. A small, upper-middle-class holiday community, it is modeled on the indisputable charms of Martha's Vineyard, Fire Island, and Portmeirion, environments whose beautiful settings, consistent architectures, and common programs of relaxation support that special amiable subjectivity of people on holiday. These atmospheres are both delightful and artificial, and their viability as precedents for more general town making is limited precisely by the inevitability of their exclusions, the things that one takes a vacation to escape: work, mess, encounters with the nonvacationing other, unavoidable inequalities, demanding formal variety, schools, mass transit, unsightly infrastructure, nonconforming behaviors, and so on.

Celebration, an actual project of the Disney Corporation, is slightly closer to the idea of a town. It is larger, its residents work, it has a bit more social and economic infrastructure and a slightly wider spread of price points for the buy-in, but – like most New Urbanist work – is mainly a repatterning of the suburbs. Celebration's sole economic sector is consumption, and its residents are no less dependent on the automobile to get to work than suburbanites anyplace else. Like Seaside, its orderliness is assured by strict covenants that conspire to produce both hygienic conformity and the vaguely classical architecture that is of such bizarre importance to the New Urbanist leadership. The homeowners' associations that provide the necessary instruments of governance and constraint are, as organizations, something between co-op boards and BIDs, with similar agendas to maintain property

S
I
X

values, to police levels of otherness, to secure the physical character of the place, and to supplement and evade normal democratic legality.

Although New Urbanists' work has been primarily suburban, their rhetoric derives much of its authority from the example of the city, and there has been much reciprocation between the New Urbanist project and the broader workings of American urban design in the richer and more resistant environment of actual cities. Both tendencies understand their performative tasks as the provision of "urban" amenity, and the good city is primarily associated with the ability of its physical spaces to support a rich and intricate visuality that promotes what is, in practice, the pleasures of the yuppie lifestyle and its program of shopping and dining, of fitness, of stylishness and mobility, and of a certain level of associative urban connoisseurship, based on the recognizability of their programs and architectures. To the degree that they embody a social or political affect, it revolves around old-fashioned forms of bourgeois decorum and the deployment of a limited set of signifiers of sustainability. Over the past twenty-five years many American cities have seen dramatic – if restricted – transformations in form and habit, and virtually no town of any size now seems to lack zones replete with sidewalk cafes, street trees and furnishings, contextually scaled architectures, artistic shop fronts, loft living, bike paths, and other attractive elements from the urban design pattern book. This collusion of pleasant infrastructures has, in fact, emerged as the salient professional measure of urban quality.

I had the opportunity, not long ago, to look over plans for a major extension to the core of Calgary, a succinct encapsulation of the progress of urban design since Battery Park City. The plan had many fine features, including light-rail, mixed-use buildings, variegated scale, attention to solar orientation, a well-manicured streetscape with a wealth of prescribed detail and a strong rhetoric of urbanity. But the net effect was formidably dull, and its gridiron plan and fastidious coding insufficiently responsive to the possibility of exception, a foreclosure visible in the plan's unnuanced response to the very divergent conditions around it (river, park, rail yard, and downtown core), in its limited ability to accommodate architectures (such as a proposed university complex) that might be sources of creative

disruption, and in its standard-issue pattern book of formal moves, from its little plazas to its proscriptions on nonconforming signage. The image of the plan conveyed in a series of winsome renderings was a perfect rendition of urban design's certifying palette of amenities – the wee shops and artistic signage, the Georgian squares, the bowered streets – all depicted in an apparently perpetual summer.

The Calgary plan was Starbucks urbanism, a suitable home for forms and traditions already translated into generic versions of themselves. With its derivation from the idea of the isolated district in its descent from the tabula rasa of urban renewal though the special districting and BIDs that succeeded it, the plan was more inflected by ideology than by place, by urban design's Platonic city increasingly identified with the Seattle/Portland/ Vancouver prototype. Of course, these are cities that have achieved many successes, and as a default for urbanism, one could surely choose a lot worse. The issue is not the many good formal ideas embodied in the urban design – or the New Urbanist – paradigm but rather in their roles in dumbing urbanism down to create a culture of generic urban "niceness" intolerant of disorder or exception, in stifling the continued transformation and elaboration of urban morphologies under the influence of new technical, social, conceptual, and formal developments, and in disallowing the influence of communities of difference. Urban design and the New Urbanism are the house styles of gentrification, urban renewal with a human face.

The problem with this is not with the pursuit of the subtle visualities and comfortable infrastructures of humanely dimensioned neighborhoods, it is rather with gentrification's parasitic economy, feeding on the homes of the poor, on precisely the order of mix central to the arguments of Jane Jacobs. Today's dominant urban design is all lifestyle and no heart, and has nothing to say to the planet's immiserated majority, whether Americans victimized by our obscenely widening income gap or the billion and half people housed in the part of the world's cities undergoing the most explosive growth: slums. Modernist urbanism, for all its ultimate failings, was the extension of social movements for the reform of the squalid inequalities of the urbanism of the nineteenth century, and the clear subject of its address was slum dwellers, men and women victimized by oppressive economic arrangements and by the urban environments that grew out of them, the workers' houses of Manchester, the *Mietkasernen* of Berlin, and the tenements of New York. If the sun, space, and greenery of the Radiant City and its identical architectures appear alienating and vapid today, it is crucial to think about what they were meant to replace: the dark, disease-ridden, dangerous hypercrowding of the industrial city.

The New Urbanism substitutes sprawl for slum as its polemical target and its ideal subjects are members of the suburban upper-middle class whose problem is a mismatch between existing economic privilege and inappropriate spatial organization. The difficulty here is of having too much, rather than too little, and if this is a rational observation from the perspective of the environment, it is a radically different issue from the perspective of what is to be done. What is missing is an idea of justice, a theory that addresses not simply the reconfiguration of space but also the redistribution of wealth. The reduction of urbanism to a battle of styles is a formula for ignoring its most crucial issues. For example, there is no doubt that the neotraditionalist row houses that have replaced the penitential public housing towers being demolished in so many American cities represent a far more livable alternative. But it is equally clear that the net effect of the Hope VI program behind this transformation is the cruel displacement of 90 percent of the former population and that arguments about architecture obscure the larger political agendas at work. Likewise the continued, virtually unquestioned association of Modernist architecture with progressive politics has long since been insupportable, given the lie by the real meaning of urban renewal, by its expressive congeniality for multinational corporatism, by the ease with which it becomes the ready emblem of the Chinese ministry of propaganda, by the abandonment of politics by most of the leading lights of the architectural avant-garde.

At a conference in New York last year convened by the Cities Programme at the London School of Economics, Rem Koolhaas began his presentation with a slide of Jane Jacobs, whom he snidely denounced as an anachronism and an ideological drag. As a leading advocate of a robust, top-down idea of bigness and as one of globalization's most sophisticated and visible model citizens, Koolhaas was surely consistent in recognizing Jacobs's position as an affront to his own ethical ambivalence and corporatist cultural proclivities. And it was surely an enjoyably naughty performance to stage in front of New Yorkers for whom Jacobs is widely thought a saint. Koolhaas has a fine aptitude for irony, for blurring the line between critique and apology, accepting the market-knows-best inevitability of what he appears to disdain, and then, self-inoculated, designing it. For him, critical interrogations of the megascale and its received formats are simply doomed, and any attempt to redirect the forms of the generic global city is hopeless naïveté.

"New" Urbanism and Koolhaasian "Post"-Urbanism represent a Hobson's choice, a Manichean dystopianism that leaves us trapped between *The Truman Show* and *Blade Runner*. There is something both infuriating and tragic in the division of the urban imaginary into faux and fab, and the tenacious identification of the project of coming to grips with what is genuinely a crisis with the cookie-cutter conformities of the former and the solipsistic, retro avant-gardism of the latter. Cities are becoming inhuman in both old and new ways, in the prodigious growth of slums, in the endlessness of megalopolitan sprawl, in the homogenizing routines of globalization, and in the alienating effects of disempowerment. But the scale has so shifted that the future of cities is now implicated with an inescapable immediacy in the fate of the earth itself.

Urban design needs to grow beyond its narrowly described fixation on the "quality" of life to include its very possibility. This will require a dramatically broadened discourse of effects that does not establish its authority simply analogically or artistically but that is inculcated with the project of enhancing equity and diversity and of making a genuine contribution to the survival of the planet. Our cities must undergo continuous retrofit and reconfiguration, their growth rigorously managed, and we must build hundreds of new towns and cities along radically sustainable lines as a matter of utmost urgency. It also means that Sert's call for an urban discipline that narrows the field of its intelligence to formal matters has become a dangerous anachronism, that the aesthetics of the urban must recapture the idea of their inseparability from the social and the environmental: as an academic matter, this will entail more than another repositioning of urban practices within the trivium of architecture, planning, and landscape. Finally, urban theory must renounce, for once and for all, the teleological fantasy of a convergence on a singular form for the good city.

The thwarting configuration of the traditionally isolated disciplines must now yield to the broader relational understandings of environmentalism and take up the challenges of finitude and equity. This refreshment of design's epistemology is a necessary and inevitable outcome of our ability to read both global and local ecologies as complex, comprehensive, and contingent, and to see our own instrumental and haphazard roles in their workings and meanings. It is simply no longer possible to understand the city and its morphology as isolated from the life and welfare of the planet as a whole or to shirk the necessary investigation of dramatically new paradigms at every scale to secure happy and fair futures. Cities – bounded and responsible – must help rebalance a world of growing polarities between overdevelopment and underdevelopment, offer hospitality to styles of difference that globalizing culture does not require, and rigorously account for and provide the means of their own respiration without prejudice to the survival of others'. This calls for the recovery of the "utopian" idea of heroic measures *and* a rigorous defense of the most widely empowered ideas of consent.

Which brings us back to those two model New Yorkers, Jane Jacobs and Lewis Mumford. Both loved cities passionately, and both dedicated their lives to understanding their character and possibilities. Both fought tirelessly to help give shape to the inevitability of urban transformation based on the desire for social justice and a deep connection to an urban history that inhered in intersecting forms, habits, and rights. Neither argued for the stifling imaginary fixities of a golden age, but each saw the good city as an evolving project, informed by the unfolding possibilities of new knowledge and experience. Jacobs celebrated her centuries-old neighborhood but happily rode the subway that ran beneath it. Mumford lived in the suburban fringes but never learned to drive. Each found happiness in a different relationship to the city, and both based their advocacy on preferences they actually lived. A future for urban designing must not dictate the good life but instead endlessly explore the ethics and expression of consent and diversity.

"A Third Way for Urban Design"

from Alex Krieger and William S. Saunders (eds), *Urban Design* (2009)

Kenneth Greenberg

Editors' Introduction

Today's urban design field has an abundance of theory to draw on, both seminal theories that helped establish the field and more recent theories directed at establishing new directions. Key theoretical ideas and debates have been presented throughout *The Urban Design Reader*. The older theories helped shape the evolution of the field, but it is important to recognize that successive ideas did not completely supplant earlier ones. Late nineteenth and early twentieth century ideas about urban form – the parks movement, the garden city movement, neighborhood units, modernism – continue to inspire urban designers today. It is likewise with mid-twentieth-century theories: ideas about the importance of place-making, imageability, and regional ecological analyses remain central to the field. In recent times, there has been a proliferation of theories claiming to be the important new approach to urbanism – New Urbanism, Post Urbanism, Everyday Urbanism, Landscape Urbanism, Ecological Urbanism. Within academia, proponents of each theory claim its intellectual and practical basis to be the most compelling. What is an urban design practitioner to do?

In practice, many urban designers don't align themselves solely with a single academic theory of urban design. Rather, when crafting design solutions for given projects, they draw on the relevant ideas from whatever theoretical ideas seem to resonate most strongly for the project at hand. The real world of practice is, in many ways, more flexible and adaptive than academic theory allows for, and the results can be very interesting. As Kenneth Greenberg states in his important recent essay "A Third Way for Urban Design," in practice "a great deal is happening" that lies between the extremes of theory. Addressing particularly the seemingly polar opposite positions taken by New Urbanism and Post Urbanism, he argues that a "third way" is emerging in real world practice that is not limited by the strictures of academic discourse. This "unbounded" way is propelled by environmental imperatives, the demands of communities for real participation in city-building decision-making which has spawned more creative participation approaches, and a better understanding of how cities evolve and adapt over time.

Greenberg references a number of recent development projects that have in common the overarching goal of creating more sustainable places, different design aspects of which can be seen as being informed by different theories. Common to many of the projects is the approach of creating flexible design frameworks, an idea associated with Landscape Urbanism, rather than fixed masterplans, an idea associated with modernism, or form-based codes, an idea associated with New Urbanism. By creating as design products flexible framework plans that can be fleshed out by multiple development actors over time as economic and social conditions change and evolve, Greenberg argues that "urban design becomes more like improvisational jazz."

Along with highlighting the creative theoretical merging that characterizes urban design practice, Greenberg's seminal contribution in this selection is his call for a new collaboration between the various environmental design professions and new alliances with those working in other allied applied fields, such as the environmental sciences and engineering. Cities are complex evolving organisms, and a truly interdisciplinary design approach, he argues, better reflects this understanding and results in more adaptive city-building.

Kenneth Greenberg is an architect and urban designer based in Toronto. A former Director of Urban Design and Architecture for the City of Toronto, and interim Chief Planner for the Boston Redevelopment Agency, he currently practices through his firm Greenberg Consultants. His projects throughout North America and Europe, many of them award winning, have involved a range of scales and design issues including downtown rejuvenation, waterfront revitalization, campus master planning, and regional growth management. A vision he brings to his design and planning work is to restore "the vitality, relevance and sustainability of the public realm in urban life." His approach involves strategic consensus-building, often using innovative processes that encourage active and diverse public participation. Design projects he has collaborated on include the Crossroads Initiative for the Big Dig, Brooklyn Bridge Park, and the Saint Paul on the Mississippi Development Framework Plan.

Kenneth Greenberg's recent book *Walking Home: The Life and Lessons of a City Builder* (Toronto: Random House, 2011) argues for the importance and possibilities of rejuvenating neglected cities and offers accessibly written guidance on how to achieve transformative city-building. Books that have inspired Greenberg's thinking include James Surowiecki's *The Wisdom of Crowds* (New York: Random House, 2004), which is helpful for understanding how creative change can occur in democratic settings; and Chris Turner's *The Leap: How to Survive and Thrive in the Sustainable Economy* (Toronto: Random House Canada, 2011), which speaks to how the paradigm shift away from unsustainable ways of life to sustainable ones can be made, a "leap" critically necessary for our survival in cities.

Other writings on adaptive urbanism include Andrew Scott and Eran Ben-Joseph's *ReNew Town* (London: Routledge, 2011); Peter Calthorpe's *Urbanism in the Age of Climate Change* (Washington, DC: Island Press, 2011); and Stephen J. Coyle's *Sustainable and Resilient Communities* (Hoboken, NJ: John Wiley & Sons, 2011).

Jon Lang's *Urban Design: The American Experience* (New York: Van Nostrand Reinhold, 1994) discusses the evolution of the urban design field, its knowledge, and the practical roles played by urban designers in the public and private sectors. He highlights in particular emerging roles in the field involved with place-making, ecological responsibility, community activism, participatory design, and creative leadership. Like Greenberg, he suggests that the future of the field requires a more integrative profession where designers act more as midwives and collaborators, utilizing a broader base of knowledge than is used in the narrow traditional roles of practice.

▪ ▪ ▪ ▪ ▪ ▪

Michael Sorkin asserts in "The End(s) of Urban Design" that we have reached a dead end where "'New' Urbanism and Koohaasian 'Post'-Urbanism represent a Hobson's choice, a Manichean dystopianism that leaves us trapped between *The Truman Show* and *Blade Runner*, . . . [a] division of the urban imaginary into faux and fab . . . with the cookie-cutter conformities of the former and solipsistic, retro avant-gardism of the latter."

The pinpointing of this no-win dichotomy between New Urbanism and posturbanism has surfaced over and over in different forms in recent years in talks, articles, and symposia. It permeates this book, arising in the discussion, "Urban Design Now," as well as the wide-ranging and provocative

pieces by Edward W. Soja, Richard Sommer, and Timothy Love, and is conclusively nailed by Michelle Provoost and Wouter Vanstiphout in "Facts on the Ground": "The post-Katrina urban design experiences present us with a tragic divide between the self-conscious heirs to Modernist and experimental urban design and the apostates of Modernism who have the ear of policy makers, business people, and the general populace. The first group rightly accuses the second of being conservative and opportunistic; the second rightly accuses the first of being irrelevant, elitist, and naive."

The critique of these bifurcated positions is valid and the frustration palpable. Yet between the extremes represented by this dichotomy a great deal is happening, as the real and unbridled world of urban design continues to evolve in myriad positive ways. It can be argued in fact that a "third way" has begun to emerge, one not bounded by the strictures of this double dead end. The new way is increasingly propelled by the environmental imperative, informed by the need to integrate this perspective with competing social, economic, and cultural forces and by closer observation of how cities actually behave and evolve.

Numerous examples, including some cited in this book, have been built or are in planning stages around the world in which urban districts and neighborhoods explore new more self-sustaining models, making advances in generating their own energy, processing their own waste, and reducing auto dependence with a greater mix of uses and more mobility alternatives. With support from national and local governments, these new communities that showcase the design and integration of new technologies and approaches are being monitored with an eye to changing standards and norms and developing knowledge-based industries that can export these innovations.

In Freiburg, Germany, Vauban, a derelict military zone, has become a Sustainable Model City District. After an intensive planning process and awareness campaign in the mid-1990s, implementation targeted the issues of mobility, energy, housing, and social life. The outcome was presented as a German model of urban development to the HABITAT II conference in 1996 because of its inclusion of environmentally supportive elements and the close cooperation it fostered between the municipality, public utilities, project management, and local residents.

In Finland, a few kilometers from downtown Helsinki in a university district, the Vikki residential and work zone has been developed as a living laboratory for green design that integrates gardens and pathways, composting, recycling, solar panels, a 30 percent reduction in water consumption, and 25 percent less fossil fuel.

In the live-work Hammarby Sjostad area in Stockholm, Sweden, tough environmental requirements were imposed on buildings, municipal infrastructure, and the traffic environment. The Stockholm Water Company, Fortum, and the Stockholm Waste Management Administration jointly developed a common ecocycle model designed to ensure recycling of organic material.

Malmo, Sweden, designated its docklands "Bo01" site as an ecological quarter with strict environmental codes for developers on formerly industrial land with significant contamination challenges. For education, research, housing, culture, and recreation, an ecological approach to planning was key in the creation of this district. Oriented to the sea, canals, and parks, this community has maximized biodiversity by building up a range of biotopes.

In British Columbia residents have begun moving into Dockside Green in Victoria, a former industrial wasteland that will house twenty-five hundred people and includes provisions for income mix, LEED platinum certification, and employment and local businesses. In Vancouver, Southeast False Creek will be a model sustainable community built on the last remaining large tract of undeveloped waterfront land near downtown. When Vancouver was awarded the 2010 Olympic and Paralympic Winter Games, this development site of eighty acres was chosen as the future site of the Olympic Village. It is being planned as a model sustainable development based on environmental, social, and economic principles with a focus on mixed-use and housing for families. This complete community of up to sixteen thousand people will ensure goods and services within walking distance and housing that is linked by transit and close to local jobs.

In Toronto, WATERFRONToronto (a joint federal, provincial, and city revitalization corporation) has selected the winner of the Lower Don Lands Design Competition (a team led by Michael Van Valkenburgh of which I am a member). The winning design proposes an innovative approach to naturalizing the mouth of the Don River, transforming a long neglected area into sustainable new parks and communities through an integrated approach to urban design, transportation, naturalization of the river edges by expanding habitats, sustainability, and other ecological focuses. The area will become a "green" city district where city, lake, and river interact in a dynamic and balanced relationship.

So, perhaps more rapidly than we realize, we are witnessing a major dissolution of the false professional and conceptual dichotomy that divided the city from the natural world. Like many powerful and timely impulses, this reconciliation has had many sources, scientific, cultural, and aesthetic. It is a striking example of simultaneous discovery motivated by a sense of crisis, as the scientific community calls attention to appalling degradation, dangerous consequences, and the undeniable fragility of human life on the planet.

This change in consciousness was anticipated and fostered by inspired practitioners and writers including Ian McHarg in *Design with Nature* (1971), Ann Spirn in *The Granite Garden* (1984), and Michael Hough in *City Form and Natural Process* (1984). Their ideas opened possibilities for a new way of thinking beyond conventional mitigation of impacts on nature to one based on new possibilities for creative synthesis working *with* natural process and on the acknowledgment that humans are part of nature and that to some extent nature everywhere on the planet has become a built environment deeply altered by human interaction with it.

As the imperative to modify our self-destructive practices begins to suggest forms of development inherently more environmentally sustainable, cities (now our dominant place of living) are the crucibles where solutions are found to problems that are otherwise intractable. The environmental thrust is gaining traction and broad popular appeal as a common ground that cuts across class, cultural, and political lines and is rapidly pushing urban design into new areas of investigation. In ways both superficial and profound, this desire for greener solutions is giving birth to lower-impact lifestyles and new design approaches for city districts as well as individual buildings and landscapes. It augurs a greater mix and proximity of daily life activities – living, working, shopping, culture, recreation, and leisure – increased walkability, cycling, and transit and less car dependency; lower energy consumption and alternative energy sources; improved waste management and treatment; and new approaches to storm- and wastewater management.

This seismic shift in goals and priorities is also producing a cultural predisposition to a new form of coexistence, the intertwining of city and nature in a new sense of place. Renewed places reflecting these approaches will be more rooted and specific, with the underlying layers of natural setting revealed and better appreciated. In the words of Betsy Barlow Rogers, the former executive director of the Central Park Conservancy, "As the city becomes more park-like, the park becomes more city-like."

A number of extremely powerful corollaries to this increased environmental and ecological consciousness exist. A better understanding of the complexities of succession and interdependence in nature can be linked directly to a greater awareness of the dynamic and evolving character of sustainable cities and to diverse and evolving environments with greater mix and complexity of land use and a broader demographic of people served by full life-cycle housing options. A second and related corollary is that the need to cope with this increased complexity clearly demands new and expanded professional alliances.

Once we accept cities as complex, multigenerational and never-finished artifacts, we are forced to confront our limitations as urban designers. Experience is teaching that prescriptive templates do not hold up well when market forces, changing programs, and new needs come into play. What are needed instead are flexible frameworks that allow for innovation, hybridization, organic growth, change, and surprise. While this shift is challenging to planning that aspires to an illusionary end-state predictability, its inherent pragmatism has the potential to liberate design and harness many kinds of creativity coming from others. Urban design becomes more like improvisational jazz. In Stuart Brand's terminology, we are learning "how cities learn." Rather than producing finite products, urban design is increasingly about the anticipation and guidance of long-term transformations without fixed destinations, mediating between values, goals, and actual outcomes.

The true test for urban design then becomes to achieve coherence and build relationships but at the same time leave ample room for the emergence of new ideas, market and social innovations, and an expanded creative space for the handoff to the whole array of design disciplines (including architecture, landscape, industrial design, graphic design, and lighting design) that will help materialize the plan.

By its very nature, successful urban design for complex and evolving environments cannot be the hegemony of a single profession. The preoccupation of the Harvard University Graduate School of Design's (GSD's) First Urban Design Conference with the integration of the work of architects, planners, and landscape architects has effectively been subsumed within a much larger dynamic enterprise with fluid boundaries and the sharing of leadership. Necessity has created new alliances with colleagues in engineering, economics, environmental sciences, and the arts, among others. This broad fusion of expertise and knowledge is not compromising – it enables richer and better outcomes.

The nature of such teamwork demands an extended dialogue in real time. Methodologies and working styles are emerging that are much less hierarchical, supported by an explosion in communications technology that permits and facilitates rapid information sharing and the layering in of many complex variables. And in a North American and European context this work must increasingly be done in a highly public and contested environment with an acknowledged right and need for affected communities to be at the table.

It is now clear that shared and overlapping leadership needs to extend well beyond the creation of a design into its implementation and the stewardship of the evolving places created. This stewardship occurs over periods that extend over several administrations and project leaders. Credit for urban design must now be spread broadly, and this frustrates the media's desire to fixate on design "stars." It will now be *teams* that earn the glory.

Coinciding with these new ways of approaching urban design is the opening up of remarkable new opportunities to forge relationships of cities to nature. Waterfronts of oceans, lakes, and rivers have become a new frontier for many cities with the potential for reuse of vast tracts of obsolescent port, industrial, railway, and warehousing lands. Another related systemic opportunity arises as the aging mid-20th century highway infrastructure nears the end of its useful life and demands repair and renewal.

A critical issue raised by the nondesigners like Jane Jacobs and Lewis Mumford at the 1956 GSD Conference was insufficient acknowledgment of politics. There can no longer be any doubt that the practice of urban design is inextricably bound by the political environment in which it operates. The shift to the right in recent years and the corresponding withdrawal of traditional funding have created a crisis for cities and profoundly challenged the capacity of the public sector to deliver services and undertake major initiatives. This has meant a shift in the locus of urban design leadership to the private and nonprofit sectors.

The need to chart a responsible course under these circumstances has forced another breaching of traditional adversarial dichotomies – left/right, community/developer, haves/have-nots – to seek a third way in more explicitly political terms. Urban design in this context requires a continual balancing of the roles and expectations of the private sector, drawing on its entrepreneurial talent and enterprise while defending the public realm, public interests, and a broader set of social goals. One of the contributions of urban design to the working out of now inevitable public-private partnerships is to seek and articulate opportunities for mutually reinforcing wins that straddle this divide.

All this reinforces some of the definitions of urban design offered in this book, in particular Richard Marshall's in "The Elusiveness of Urban Design": "Urban design . . . is a 'way of thinking.' It is not about separation and simplification but rather about synthesis. It attempts . . . to deal with the full reality of the urban situation, not the narrow slices seen through disciplinary lenses." This open-ended, non-hierarchical stance should make urban design a leading part of impending environmental work.

EPILOGUE

The urban design field has grown substantially over the last two decades and the pace of growth seems poised to keep accelerating. Many university-based urban design programs and concentrations have been created or are expanding. A growing number of practitioners call themselves urban designers and more and more professional firms – large and small; planning-based, architecture-based, or landscape architecture-based – advertise that they provide urban design services. The many forces and pressures that are compelling the expansion of the urban design field, which have been explored in the readings contained in this *Reader* and the editors' introductions to them, are at the same time contributing to its splintering. It remains to be seen whether the many strains of the contemporary field of urban design that have been introduced in the *Reader* will continue to diverge or if they will coalesce under some new definition of urban design.

The strongest over-arching force driving both the growth of the urban design field and its stratification is the pervasive sense of urgency that accompanies three central realities of our times: the escalation of wide-scale environmental crises that are already with us but which loom catastrophically larger in the near future; the accelerating pace of change in every dimension of life, propelled by the constant proliferation of new technologies, which requires constant adaptation; and the constantly increasing interconnectedness of the world – resulting from new communications and social-networking technologies, the worldwide flow of resources, goods, services, and capital, and the border-crossing impacts of environmental degradation – which, among other things, heightens competition and again requires constant adaptation. The ever-changing and often intensifying opportunities and problems that these realities have unleashed, and will continue to unleash, means that we live in an age of extreme uncertainty. The urban design field is increasingly perceived as having an important role to play in addressing the accelerating pace of change and the uncertainties that accompany it.

On the environmental uncertainty front, we know that in the not too distant future cities around the world and the people that live in them will have to face problems stemming from climate change, which we know will take different forms in different areas but we don't know exactly what forms. The experts tell us, however, that along with general warming and sea-level rise we are likely to witness an increase in extreme weather events. We know that cities and people will have to adapt but there is little consensus on what to do to prepare for this need to adapt. On the socio-economic front, the economic downturn that began in western countries five years ago and shows little sign of ending soon has made real estate development markets very uncertain, which means that many urban design projects have been put on hold, private and public sector projects alike. Boom conditions still prevail in parts of Asia and the Middle East, but there is considerable nervousness about what the future may hold. Meanwhile, the human population keeps expanding exponentially and many people around the world are scrambling to find good places to live and raise their families, often being challenged by difficult environmental circumstances. It is clear that more sustainable forms of development must be created across the globe.

Individuals and communities face uncertainties related to their abilities to survive and prosper. The world is trending in the direction of greater wealth inequality, more widely divergent spatial concentrations of poverty and affluence, a growing underclass facing little opportunity for improving their lot, and increasing racial, ethnic, class, and religious hostilities. Achieving long-term sustainable development is only possible if these difficult human conditions are addressed. Otherwise, along with the inhumanity of not addressing these issues, the best sustainability approaches will be over-run by sheer human need.

There is growing consensus that today's and tomorrow's challenges must be met with innovative ideas and strong responses – to do nothing is not an option – but accomplishing everything that needs to be done, including the urban form and human behavior paradigms that are required, is a daunting task. The growth of the urban design field in recent years has been driven by increasing awareness that the design of cities has enormous impacts on both environmental quality and the quality of people's everyday lives, and growing understanding that an urbanistic approach to city-building is necessary because of the complexity involved.

Accompanying the growth of the urban design field has been a proliferation of divergent theories about how urban design practice should respond to current and projected future conditions. People now talk in terms of multiple urbanisms: new urbanism, everyday urbanism, landscape urbanism, ecological urbanism, to name just the most dominant. Within the academy, this outpouring of theory has led to the emergence of radically different ideological camps, wars over rights to academic territory, and a hardening of divisions between planning, architecture, and landscape architecture approaches to urban design. Within professional practice, however, something very different seems to be going on, as Ken Greenberg so eloquently articulates in the last piece in this *Reader*. Because practitioners are on the front line of actually confronting pressing environmental and socio-economic issues on a project-by-project basis, they must make practical choices about how best to proceed, and this usually means flexibility. Rather than adopting a singular theoretical ideology, many practitioners take what is helpful from multiple theories and meld it together into an approach that is tailored to the circumstances of a particular project. In general, urban design practice is becoming more collaborative, participatory, and open-ended. Urban design products reflect this new flexibility: instead of pre-determined and fixed masterplans the emphasis is now on urban structure framework plans that identify and encapsulate over-arching design and planning goals for nurture over the long term, but whose specifics can be adapted to changing socio-economic conditions as necessary. This is an approach that makes infinite sense for the current times and will help maintain the relevance of the urban design field.

From the wealth of readings assembled here, it is clear that there is a copious and diverse literature relating to the urban design field. This book has focused on the most salient of what is considered the best and most thought-provoking literature. Rather than assembling readings that bolster a particular approach to urban design, we have sought to present a wide range of ideas, some of which complement or build upon each other and some of which are at distinct odds with each other. The dissonance reflects the nature of the contemporary urban design field. The reader should remember that each of the readings comes from larger contexts, discourses, and debates that bear further exploration. The selections in this *Reader* are just samples. Serious students will want to engage with the wider literature; to read the whole of Jane Jacobs and Kevin Lynch, and, if for nothing else than to realize how wrongly focused design fields can become, the whole of Le Corbusier. We hope that the further readings suggested with each selection provide a good roadmap for how to engage with the larger literature. As well, there is a wealth of information about what urban design practitioners around the world are actually designing – projects, plans, design guidance, and visually based design decision-making processes – that is available in print and on-line.

As we observed in the first edition of *The Urban Design Reader* and still firmly believe, for urban designers, learning from observed reality is just as important as being grounded in the literature. Directly looking at and experiencing cities is perhaps the best way to learn about the relationship between urban form and human activity in all of its beautiful complexity. Experience of cities, their elements, and their peoples allows an urban designer to build up a repertoire of precedents and urban form possibilities that are not abstract but directly known. Immersed in the experience of the city, the urban connoisseur more deeply understands the success and limitations of what has come before and what is possible. As well, valuable knowledge about form dimensions and relationships comes from experiencing spatial forms in relation to one's own bodily capacities and one's own perceptions. In other words, it is important to get out there and experience cities—the more the better.

ILLUSTRATION CREDITS

Every effort has been made to contact copyright holders for their permission to reprint illustrations in this book. The publishers would be grateful to hear from any copyright holder who is not here acknowledged and will undertake to rectify any errors or omissions in future editions of this book. Following is copyright information for the plates and illustrations that appear in this book.

PART ONE: HISTORICAL PRECEDENTS IN URBAN DESIGN

BACON. Figure 1: Florence. Illustration by Alois K. Strobl, from *Design of Cities* by Edmund Bacon. Copyright © 1967, 1974 by Edmund N. Bacon. Used by permission of Penguin, a division of Penguin Group (USA) Inc. Figure 2: The Capitoline Hill before reconstruction by Michelangelo; and Figure 3: The Campidoglio by Michelangelo. Illustrations by Joseph Aronson, from *Design of Cities* by Edmund Bacon. Copyright © 1967, 1974 by Edmund N. Bacon. Used by permission of Penguin, a division of Penguin Group (USA) Inc.

HOWARD. All images from *Garden Cities of To-morrow* by Ebenezer Howard (1902). Public domain.

PERRY. All images from "The Neighborhood Unit," from *Neighborhood and Community Planning: Regional Survey Volume VII – Regional Plan of New York and Its Environs*, by Clarence A. Perry (New York: Russell Sage Foundation, 1929). Reprinted by permission of the Russell Sage Foundation.

PART TWO: FOUNDATIONS OF THE FIELD

CULLEN. Serial Vision from *The Concise Townscape*, by Gordon Cullen (London: Van Nostrand Reinhold, 1961). Copyright © 1961 by Elsevier. Reprinted by permission of Taylor & Francis.

LYNCH. All images from *Image of the City*, by Kevin Lynch (Cambridge, MA: MIT Press, 1960, pp. 1–13, 46–49, 83–90). Copyright © 1960 by Massachusetts Institute of Technology, by permission of the MIT Press.

ALEXANDER. All images from "A City Is Not a Tree," *Architectural Forum* (vol. 122, no. 1, pp. 58–61, April 1965). *Architectural Forum* ceased publication in 1974. Every effort was made to get reprint permission through subsequent copyright holders of *Architectural Forum* and Christopher Alexander. Unfortunately we were unsuccessful in locating either copyright holder.

ROWE and KOETTER. All images from *Collage City*, by Colin Rowe and Fred Koetter (1978). Public domain.

WHYTE. Typical Sighting Map. From *The Social Life of Small Urban Spaces*, by William H. Whyte (New York: Project for Public Spaces, 2001; original 1980). Copyright © 1980 by William H. Whyte. Reprinted by permission of the estate of William H. Whyte and The Project for Public Spaces.

PART THREE: GROWTH OF A PLACE AGENDA

KELBAUGH. Illustration from "Critical Regionalism: An Architecture of Place," from *Repairing the American Metropolis: Common Place Revisited*, by Douglas Kelbaugh (Seattle, WA: University of Washington Press, 2002). Copyright © 2002 by the University of Washington Press. Reprinted by permission of the University of Washington Press.

SCHEER. All images from *The Evolution of Urban Form: Typology for Planners and Architects*, by Brenda Case Scheer (Chicago: Planners Press, 2010). Copyright © 2010 by The American Planning Association and Brenda Case Scheer. Reprinted by permission of Brenda Case Scheer.

ELLIN. The Axes of Postmodern Urbanism, from *Postmodern Urbanism*, by Nan Ellin (New York: Princeton Architectural Press, 1999). Copyright © 1999 by Princeton Architectural Press Inc. Reprinted by permission of Princeton Architectural Press through the Copyright Clearance Center.

PART FOUR: DESIGN ISSUES IN URBAN DEVELOPMENT

FRANK, ENGELKE, SCHMID: Image from *Health and Community Design: The Impact of the Built Environment on Physical Activity*, by Lawrence Frank, Peter Engelke, and Thomas Schmid (Washington, D.C.: Island Press, 2003). Copyright © 2003 by Lawrence D. Frank and Peter O. Engelke. Reprinted by permission of Island Press.

BENTLEY. The Capital Accumulation Cycle, from "Profit and Place," from *Urban Transformations – Power, People and Urban Design*, by Ian Bentley (London: Routledge, 1999). Copyright © 1999 Routledge. Reprinted by permission of Routledge, an imprint of the Taylor & Francis Group.

ELSHESHTAWY. Figure 1: 1962 Master Plan of Dubai. Copyright © Harris Architects. Reprinted by permission of the author Yasser Elsheshtawy. Figures 2–7 reprinted by permission of the author/photographer Yasser Elsheshtawy.

EDITORIAL CREDITS

MICHAEL LARICE was responsible for writing the following sections of the *Urban Design Reader, Second Edition*: Prologue; Introductions to Parts Two, Three and Four; Selection Introductions for the following authors: (Part One) Bacon, Abu-Lughod; (Part Two) Marshall, Lynch-Image of the City, Alexander, Venturi and Scott Brown, Rowe and Koetter, Whyte, Lynch-Dimensions of Performance; (Part Three) Norberg-Schulz, Oldenburg, Kelbaugh, Ellin, Koolhaas; (Part Four) Gillham, Lozano, Bentley, Elsheshtawy, Campanella; (Part Five) Berger, Newman et al.; and (Part Six) Kreiger, Sorkin.

ELIZABETH MACDONALD was responsible for writing the following sections of the *Urban Design Reader, Second Edition*: Epilogue; Introductions to Parts One, Five, and Six; Selection Introductions for the following authors: (Part One) Berman, Olmsted, Sitte, Howard, Wilson, Perry, Le Corbusier; (Part Two) Cullen, J. Jacobs, A. Jacobs, Jacobs and Appleyard, Vernez Moudon; (Part Three) Relph, Case Scheer, CNU, Crawford; (Part Four) Frank et al., Madanipour; (Part Five) McHarg, Hough, Waldheim, Beatley; and (Part Six) Macdonald, Punter, Greenburg.

COPYRIGHT INFORMATION

PART ONE: HISTORICAL PRECEDENTS IN URBAN DESIGN

PART FOUR: DESIGN ISSUES IN URBAN DEVELOPMENT

PART FIVE: ADDRESSING ENVIRONMENTAL CHALLENGES

PART SIX: URBAN DESIGN PRACTICE NOW AND TOMORROW

INDEX

Page numbers in **BOLD** represent Figures.